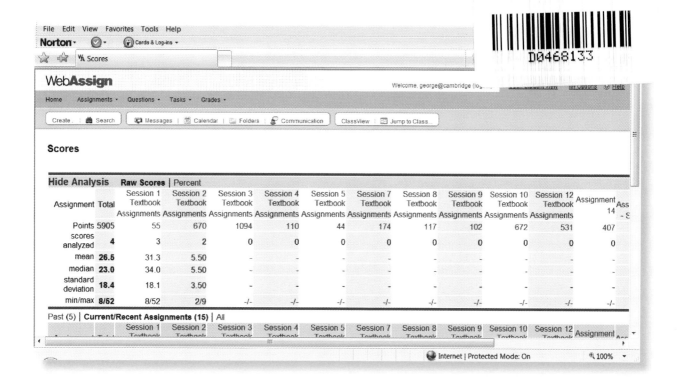

Make Instruction Needs-Based

◆ Identify where your students are struggling and customize your instruction to address their needs.

◆ Gauge how your entire class or individual students are doing by viewing the easy to use grade book.

◆ Ensure your MBAs are getting the additional reinforcement and direction they need between class meetings.

Provide Instruction and Practice When You Are Not Available

◆ With our eLectures, your students can revisit accounting topics as many times as they like or until they master the topic.

◆ You can create a set of practice problems that students can attempt and receive feedback on outside your class.

Want to learn more about WebAssign.?

Contact your sales representative or email customerservice@cambridgepub.com

Cambridge Business Publishers
Series in Accounting

Financial Accounting

- **Financial Accounting, 2e** by Dyckman & Pfeiffer
- **Financial Accounting for MBAs, 4e** by Easton, Wild, Halsey, and McAnally
- **Financial Accounting for Executives, 1e** by Ferris & Wallace
- **Cases in Financial Reporting and Analysis, 6e** by Engel, Hirst, and McAnally

Managerial Accounting

- **Managerial Accounting, 5e** by Hartgraves, Morse, and Davis
- **Cases in Managerial and Cost Accounting, 1e** by Allen, Brownlee, Haskins, and Lynch

Combined Financial & Managerial Accounting

- **Financial & Managerial Accounting for MBAs, 2e** by Easton, Halsey, McAnally, Hartgraves, and Morse

Intermediate Accounting

- **Cases in Financial Reporting and Analysis, 6e** by Engel, Hirst, and McAnally

Cost Accounting

- **Cases in Managerial and Cost Accounting, 1e** by Allen, Brownlee, Haskins, and Lynch

Financial Statement Analysis & Valuation

- **Financial Statement Analysis & Valuation, 2e** by Easton, McAnally, Fairfield, Zhang, and Halsey
- **Cases in Financial Reporting and Analysis, 6e** by Engel, Hirst, and McAnally

Advanced Accounting

- **Advanced Accounting, 1e** by Hamlen, Huefner, and Largay
- **Advanced Accounting, 1e** by Halsey & Hopkins

Fourth Edition

Financial Accounting for MBAs

PETER D. EASTON

JOHN J. WILD

ROBERT F. HALSEY

MARY LEA McANALLY

Cambridge
BUSINESS PUBLISHERS

To my daughters, Joanne and Stacey
—PDE

To my wife Gail and children, Kimberly, Jonathan, Stephanie, and Trevor;
and my parents, Leonard and Mary
—JJW

To my wife Ellie and children, Grace and Christian
—RFH

To my husband Brittan and my children Loic, Maclean, Quinn and Kay.
—MLM

Cambridge Business Publishers

FINANCIAL ACCOUNTING FOR MBAs, Fourth Edition, by Peter D. Easton,
John J. Wild, Robert F. Halsey, and Mary Lea McAnally.

ISBN 978-1-934319-34-5

Bookstores & Faculty: to order this book, call **800-619-6473** or email
customerservice@cambridgepub.com.

Students: to order this book, please visit the book's Website and order directly online.

Printed in Canada.
10 9 8 7 6 5 4 3 2

The combined skills and expertise of Easton, Wild, Halsey, and McAnally create the ideal team to author the first new financial accounting textbook for MBAs in more than a generation. Their collective experience in award-winning teaching, consulting, and research in the area of financial accounting and analysis provides a powerful foundation for this innovative textbook.

PETER D. EASTON is an expert in accounting and valuation and holds the Notre Dame Alumni Chair in Accountancy in the Mendoza College of Business. Professor Easton's expertise is widely recognized by the academic research community and by the legal community. Professor Easton is a Principal in Chicago Partners LLC, where he serves as a consultant on accounting and valuation issues.

Professor Easton holds undergraduate degrees from the University of Adelaide and the University of South Australia. He holds a graduate degree from the University of New England and a PhD in Business Administration (majoring in accounting and finance) from the University of California, Berkeley.

Professor Easton's research on corporate valuation has been published in the *Journal of Accounting and Economics, Journal of Accounting Research, The Accounting Review, Contemporary Accounting Research, Review of Accounting Studies,* and *Journal of Business Finance and Accounting.* Professor Easton has served as an associate editor for 11 leading accounting journals and he is currently an associate editor for the *Journal of Accounting Research, Journal of Business Finance and Accounting,* and *Journal of Accounting, Auditing, and Finance.* He is an editor of the *Review of Accounting Studies.*

Professor Easton has held appointments at the University of Chicago, the University of California at Berkeley, Ohio State University, Macquarie University, the Australian Graduate School of Management, the University of Melbourne, Tilburg University, National University of Singapore, Seoul National University, and Nyenrode University. He is the recipient of numerous awards for excellence in teaching and in research. Professor Easton regularly teaches accounting analysis and security valuation to MBAs. In addition, Professor Easton has taught managerial accounting at the graduate level.

JOHN J. WILD is a distinguished professor of accounting and business at the University of Wisconsin at Madison. He previously held appointments at Michigan State University and the University of Manchester in England. He received his BBA, MS, and PhD from the University of Wisconsin.

Professor Wild teaches courses in accounting and analysis at both the undergraduate and graduate levels. He has received the Mabel W. Chipman Excellence-in-Teaching Award, the departmental Excellence-in-Teaching Award, and the MBA Teaching Excellence Award from the 2003 and 2005 graduation class at the University of Wisconsin. He also received the Beta Alpha Psi and Salmonson Excellence-in-Teaching Award from Michigan State University. Professor Wild is a past KPMG Peat Marwick National Fellow and is a prior recipient of fellowships from the American Accounting Association and the Ernst & Young Foundation.

Professor Wild is an active member of the American Accounting Association and its sections. He has served on several committees of these organizations, including the Outstanding Accounting Educator Award, Wildman Award, National Program Advisory, Publications, and Research Committees. Professor Wild is author of several best-selling books. His research articles on financial accounting and analysis appear in *The Accounting Review, Journal of Accounting Research, Journal of Accounting and Economics, Contemporary Accounting Research, Journal of Accounting, Auditing & Finance, Journal of Accounting and Public Policy, Journal of Business Finance and Accounting, Auditing: A Journal of Theory and Practice,* and other accounting and business journals. He is past associate editor of *Contemporary Accounting Research* and has served on editorial boards of several respected journals, including *The Accounting Review* and the *Journal of Accounting and Public Policy.*

ROBERT F. HALSEY is an associate professor at Babson College. He received his MBA and PhD from the University of Wisconsin. Prior to obtaining his PhD he worked as the chief financial officer (CFO) of a privately held retailing and manufacturing company and as the vice president and manager of the commercial lending division of a large bank.

Professor Halsey teaches courses in financial and managerial accounting at both the graduate and undergraduate levels, including a popular course in financial statement analysis for second year MBA students. He has also taught numerous executive education courses for large multinational companies through Babson's school of Executive Education as well as for a number of stock brokerage firms in the Boston area. He is regarded as an innovative teacher and has been recognized for outstanding teaching at both the University of Wisconsin and Babson College.

Professor Halsey co-authors *Advanced Accounting* and *Financial Statement Analysis & Valuation*, both published by Cambridge Business Publishers. Professor Halsey's research interests are in the area of financial reporting, including firm valuation, financial statement analysis, and disclosure issues. He has publications in *Advances in Quantitative Analysis of Finance and Accounting, The Journal of the American Taxation Association, Issues in Accounting Education, The Portable MBA in Finance and Accounting,* the *CPA Journal, AICPA Professor/Practitioner Case Development Program,* and in other accounting and analysis journals. He has also developed exam preparation materials for the CFA examination and administers numerous CFA review courses in the Northeast.

Professor Halsey is an active member of the American Accounting Association and other accounting, analysis, and business organizations. He is widely recognized as an expert in the areas of financial reporting, financial analysis, and business valuation.

MARY LEA McANALLY is an associate professor and Mays Research Fellow at Texas A&M University. Professor McAnally teaches financial accounting and reporting in the MBA and Executive programs. Her casebook (co-authored with D. Eric Hirst and Ellen Engel), *Cases in Financial Reporting* is published by Cambridge Business Publishers. She has received several faculty-determined teaching awards including the Beazley Award and the Trammell/CBA Foundation Award. She has also received numerous student-initiated awards including the MBA Teaching Award at UT (1995, 2000, 2001, 2002), the MBA Association Distinguished Faculty Award at A&M (2003, 2004, and 2007) and the Class of 1997 Award for Outstanding and Memorable Faculty Member (2002). In 2006, the A&M Association of Former Students granted Professor McAnally the Distinguished Achievement Award.

Professor McAnally's research interests include accounting and disclosure of stock options, and accounting for risk. She has published articles in the leading academic journals including *Journal of Accounting and Economics, Journal of Accounting Research, The Accounting Review, Contemporary Accounting Research,* and *Journal of Accounting Auditing and Finance.* In 2005, Professor McAnally received the Mays Business School Research Achievement Award. She works closely with doctoral students and has served on numerous doctoral committees. She was the director of A&M's doctoral program until 2007.

Professor McAnally is active in the American Accounting Association and its FARS section and has been involved with the New Faculty Consortium, the FASB conference, several doctoral consortia and the KPMG PhD project.

Professor McAnally holds an undergraduate degree from the University of Alberta and a PhD from Stanford University. She is a Chartered Accountant (Canada) and Certified Internal Auditor. Prior to arriving at A&M in 2002, Professor McAnally held positions at University of Texas at Austin, University of Calgary, University of Alberta, Canadian National Railways, and Dunwoody and Company Chartered Accountants.

Welcome to the Fourth Edition of *Financial Accounting for MBAs*. Our main goal in writing this book was to satisfy the needs of today's business manager by providing the most contemporary, relevant, engaging, and user-oriented textbook available. This book is the product of extensive market research including focus groups, market surveys, class tests, manuscript reviews, and interviews with faculty from across the country. We are grateful to students and faculty who used the First, Second, and Third Editions and whose feedback greatly benefited this Fourth Edition.

TARGET AUDIENCE

Financial Accounting for MBAs is intended for use in full-time, part-time, executive, and evening MBA programs that include a financial accounting course as part of the curriculum, and one in which managerial decision making and analysis are emphasized. This book easily accommodates mini-courses lasting several days as well as extended courses lasting a full semester.

INNOVATIVE APPROACH

Financial Accounting for MBAs is managerially oriented and focuses on the most salient aspects of accounting. It teaches MBA students how to read, analyze, and interpret financial accounting data to make informed business decisions. This textbook makes financial accounting **engaging, relevant,** and **contemporary.** To that end, it consistently incorporates **real company data,** both in the body of each module and throughout assignment material.

FLEXIBLE STRUCTURE

The MBA curricula, instructor preferences, and course lengths vary across colleges. Accordingly and to the extent possible, the 12 modules that make up *Financial Accounting for MBAs* were designed independently of one another. This modular presentation enables each college and instructor to "customize" the book to best fit the needs of their students. Our introduction and discussion of financial statements constitute Modules 1, 2, and 3. Module 4 presents the analysis of financial statements with an emphasis on analysis of operating profitability. Modules 5 through 10 highlight major financial accounting topics including assets, liabilities, equity, and off-balance-sheet financing. Module 11 explains forecasting financial statements and Module 12 introduces simple valuation models.

Transaction Analysis and Statement Preparation

Instructors differ in their coverage of accounting mechanics. Some focus on the effects of transactions on financial statements using the balance sheet equation format. Others include coverage of journal entries and T-accounts. We accommodate both teaching styles in this Fourth Edition. Specifically, Module 2 provides an expanded discussion of the effects of transactions using our innovative financial statement effects template. Emphasis is on the analysis of Apple's summary transactions, which concludes with the preparation of its financial statements. Module 3, which is entirely optional, allows an instructor to drill down and focus on accounting mechanics: journal entries and T-accounts. It illustrates accounting for numerous transactions, including those involving accounting adjustments. It concludes with the preparation of a trial balance and the four financial statements. This detailed transaction analysis uses the same financial statement effects template, with journal entries and T-accounts highlighted in the margin. Thus, these two modules accommodate the spectrum of teaching styles—instructors can elect to use either or both modules to suit their preferences, and their students are not deprived of any information as a result of that selection.

Flexibility for Courses of Varying Lengths

Many instructors have approached us to ask about suggested class structures based on courses of varying length. To that end, we provide the following table of possible course designs:

	15 Week Semester-Course	10 Week Quarter-Course	6 Week Mini-Course	1 Week Intensive-Course
MODULE 1 Financial Accounting for MBAs	Week 1	Week 1	Week 1	Day 1 (Module 1 and either Module 2 or Module 3)
MODULE 2 Introducing Financial Statements and Transaction Analysis	Week 2	Week 2	Week 2	
MODULE 3 Accounting Adjustments and Constructing Financial Statements	Week 2 (optional)	Week 2 (optional)	Week 2 (optional)	
MODULE 4 Analyzing and Interpreting Financial Statements	Weeks 3 and 4	Week 3	Week 3	Day 2
MODULE 5 Reporting and Analyzing Operating Income	Week 5	Week 4	Skim	Skim
MODULE 6 Reporting and Analyzing Operating Assets	Week 6	Week 5	Week 4	Day 3
MODULE 7 Reporting and Analyzing Intercorporate Investments	Week 7	Optional	Optional	Optional
MODULE 8 Reporting and Analyzing Nonowner Financing	Week 8	Week 6	Week 5	Day 4
MODULE 9 Reporting and Analyzing Owner Financing	Week 9	Week 7	Week 6	Day 5
MODULE 10 Reporting and Analyzing Off-Balance-Sheet Financing	Weeks 10 and 11	Week 8	Optional	Optional
MODULE 11 Forecasting Financial Statements	Weeks 12 and 13	Week 9	Optional	Optional
MODULE 12 Analyzing and Valuing Equity Securities	Weeks 13 and 14	Week 10	Optional	Optional

MANAGERIAL EMPHASIS

Tomorrow's MBA graduates must be skilled in using financial statements to make business decisions. These skills often require application of ratio analyses, benchmarking, forecasting, valuation, and other aspects of financial statement analysis for decision making. Further, tomorrow's MBA graduates must have the skills to go beyond basic financial statements and to interpret and apply nonfinancial statement disclosures, such as footnotes and supplementary reports. This book, therefore, emphasizes real company data, including detailed footnote and other management disclosures, and shows how to use this information to make managerial inferences and decisions. This approach makes financial accounting interesting and relevant for all MBA students.

As MBA instructors, we recognize that the core MBA financial accounting course is not directed toward accounting majors. *Financial Accounting for MBAs* embraces this reality. This book highlights **financial reporting, analysis, interpretation,** and **decision making.** We incorporate the following **financial statement effects template** to train MBA students in understanding the economic ramifications of transactions and their impacts on all key financial statements. This analytical tool is a great resource for MBA students in learning accounting and applying it to their future courses and careers. Each transaction is identified in the "Transaction" column. Then, the dollar amounts (positive or negative) of the financial statement effects are recorded in the appropriate balance sheet or income statement columns. The template also reflects the statement of cash flow effects (via the cash column) and the statement of stockholders' equity effects (via the contributed capital and earned capital columns). The earned capital account is immediately updated to reflect any income or loss arising from each transaction (denoted by the arrow line from net income to earned capital). This template is instructive as it reveals the financial impacts of transactions, and it provides insights into the effects of accounting choices.

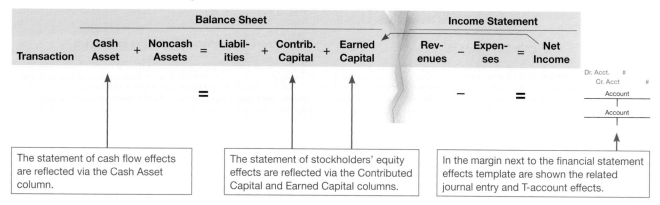

The statement of cash flow effects are reflected via the Cash Asset column.

The statement of stockholders' equity effects are reflected via the Contributed Capital and Earned Capital columns.

In the margin next to the financial statement effects template are shown the related journal entry and T-account effects.

INNOVATIVE PEDAGOGY

Financial Accounting for MBAs includes special features specifically designed for the MBA student.

Focus Companies for Each Module

Each module's content is explained through the accounting and reporting activities of real companies. Each module incorporates a "focus company" for special emphasis and demonstration. The enhanced instructional value of focus companies comes from the way they engage MBA students in real analysis and interpretation. Focus companies were selected based on the industries that MBA students typically enter upon graduation.

MODULE 1	Berkshire Hathaway	MODULE 8	Verizon
MODULE 2	Apple	MODULE 9	Hewitt Associates
MODULE 3	Apple	MODULE 10	American Airlines
MODULE 4	General Mills	MODULE 11	Procter & Gamble
MODULE 5	Pfizer	MODULE 12	Johnson & Johnson
MODULE 6	Cisco	APPENDIX B	Starbucks
MODULE 7	Google		

Real Company Data Throughout

Market research and reviewer feedback tell us that one of instructors' greatest frustrations with other MBA textbooks is their lack of real company data. We have gone to great lengths to incorporate real company data throughout each module to reinforce important concepts and engage MBA students. We engage nonaccounting MBA students specializing in finance, marketing, management, real estate, operations, and so forth, with companies and scenarios that are relevant to them. For representative examples, **SEE PAGES 4-7, 5-5, 6-11.**

Footnotes and Other Management Disclosures

Analyzed on their own, financial statements reveal only part of a corporation's economic story. Information essential for a complete analysis of a company's financial position must be gleaned from the footnotes and other disclosures provided by the company. Consequently, we incorporate footnotes and other disclosures generously throughout the text and assignments. For representative examples, **SEE PAGES 6-7, 8-9, 9-11.**

Decision Making Orientation

One primary goal of a MBA financial accounting course is to teach students the skills needed to apply their accounting knowledge to solving real business problems and making informed business decisions. With that goal in mind, Managerial Decision boxes in each module encourage students to apply the material presented to solving actual business scenarios. For representative examples, **SEE PAGES 5-16, 6-12, 8-23.**

Mid-Module and Module-End Reviews

Financial accounting can be challenging—especially for MBA students lacking business experience or previous exposure to business courses. To reinforce concepts presented in each module and to ensure student comprehension, we include mid-module and module-end reviews that require students to recall and apply the financial accounting techniques and concepts described in each module. For representative examples, **SEE PAGES 4-14, 5-17, 8-6.**

Excellent, Class-Tested Assignment Materials

Excellent assignment material is a must-have component of any successful textbook (and class). We went to great lengths to create the best assignments possible from contemporary financial statements. In keeping with the rest of the book, we used real company data extensively. We also ensured that assignments reflect our belief that MBA students should be trained in analyzing accounting information to make business decisions, as opposed to working on mechanical bookkeeping tasks. There are five categories of assignments: **Discussion Questions**, **Mini Exercises**, **Exercises**, **Problems**, and **Management Applications**. For representative examples, **SEE PAGES 4-35, 6-45, 9-41.**

FOURTH EDITION CHANGES

Based on classroom use and reviewer feedback, a number of substantive changes have been made in the fourth edition to further enhance the MBA students' experiences:

■ **Updated Financial Data**: We have updated all Focus Company financial statements and disclosures to reflect each company's latest available filings. We also explain the SEC's new IDEA financial statement retrieval software.

■ **Updated Assignments**: We have updated all assignments using real data to reflect each company's latest available filings and have added many new assignments that also utilize real financial data and footnotes.

■ **International Financial Reporting Standards (IFRS)**: We have added new IFRS Insight boxes and IFRS Alert boxes throughout the text to introduce students to the similarities and differences between U.S. GAAP and IFRS. In addition, we include expanded coverage of IFRS by module and topic in a new appendix to the book (Appendix D).

■ **Fair Value:** We have added discussion of the Fair Value option throughout the text as appropriate.

■ **New Focus Companies**: We now utilize General Mills instead of Home Depot as the focus company of Module 4, Hewitt Associates instead of Accenture as the focus company of Module 9, and American Airlines instead of Southwest Airlines as the focus company of Module 10.

■ **ROA Coverage:** We introduce students to profitability analysis in Module 1 with a very basic introduction to ROA and ROE, and defer the introduction of RNOA with operating and nonoperating components to Module 4.

■ **Simplified Operating Tax Coverage:** We have simplified the method for calculating the tax on operating and nonoperating profit in Module 4.

■ **DuPont Model**: We include a new appendix to Module 4 that explains and illustrates the traditional DuPont Model using financial information for General Mills.

■ **Focus on Classification issues related to R&D Expense**: We have rewritten the R&D expense section of Module 5 to focus on classification issues relating to R&D costs.

■ **Simplified discussion of income taxes:** We have rewritten the presentation of income taxes in Module 5 in a much more intuitive manner to focus on the accrual aspects of the tax entry instead of book-tax reversing differences.

■ **Intercorporate Investments:** Consistent with recent changes in accounting standards, we have revised Module 7 to emphasize investors' control of securities and deemphasize the percentage of ownership as the determining factor in selecting the method used for financial reporting.

■ **Credit Ratings:** We have expanded the section on Credit Ratings in Module 8 to add a discussion on trends in credit ratings. We have also updated the credit rating statistics to reflect the latest publication of Moody's Financial Metrics.

■ **Restricted Stock:** We have updated the stock compensation section of Module 9 to include an expanded discussion of restricted stock units and employee stock options.

■ **Lease Capitalization:** We illustrate the lease capitalization process in Module 10 using Excel (and HP and TI financial calculators along with the traditional present value tables).

- **Updated Pension Coverage:** Our discussion of pensions in Module 10 continues to reflect the recent changes in pension accounting. We have also expanded our analysis of pensions to focus on profitability and cash flow effects.
- **Special Purpose Entities.** We have moved the SPE discussion into the appendix to Module 10 and have revised that discussion to reflect the pending standard revision for QSPEs.
- **Revised Forecasting Module**: We have completely rewritten Module 11 on forecasting financial statements to help students understand the forecasting process. The revised module is built around Procter & Gamble and introduces a 4-step process that simplifies and codifies the forecasting process for students. We provide a detailed discussion of each item forecasted, together with references to items P&G highlights in recent analyst meetings. We provide a real-world forecasting example by analysts from Oppenheimer & Co. in the appendix.

COMPANION CASEBOOK

Cases in Financial Reporting, 6th edition by Ellen Engel (University of Chicago), D. Eric Hirst (University of Texas – Austin), and Mary Lea McAnally (Texas A&M University). This book comprises 28 cases and is a perfect companion book for faculty interested in exposing students to a wide range of real financial statements. The cases are current and cover companies from Canada, France, Austria, the Netherlands, the UK, India, as well as from the U.S. Many of the U.S. companies are major multinationals. Each case deals with a specific financial accounting topic within the context of one (or more) company's financial statements. Each case contains financial statement information and a set of directed questions pertaining to one or two specific financial accounting issues. This is a separate, saleable casebook (**ISBN 978-1-934319-19-2**). Contact your sales representative to receive a desk copy or email customerservice@cambridgepub.com.

ONLINE INSTRUCTION AND HOMEWORK MANAGEMENT SYSTEM

This supplement is ideal for distance/online/hybrid instruction, faculty responsible for large sections, and/or courses requiring independent learning. Available for an additional fee, WebAssign is a Web-based instruction and homework management system that enables students to solve select assignments in each module and receive instant feedback. Assignments with the Web**Assign**. logo in the margin next to them are available in WebAssign. For more information, contact your sales representative or try the WebAssign demo at www.webassign.com/textbooks/accounting_textbooks.html.

Web**Assign**.

SUPPLEMENT PACKAGE
For Instructors

Solutions Manual: Created by the authors, the *Solutions Manual* contains complete solutions to all the assignments in the textbook.

PowerPoint: Created by the authors, the PowerPoint slides outline key elements of each module.

Test Bank: Written by the authors, the test bank includes multiple-choice items, matching questions, short essay questions, and problems.

Computerized Test Bank: This computerized version of the test bank enables you to add and edit questions; create up to 99 versions of each test; attach graphic files to questions; import and export ASCII files; and select questions based on type or learning objective. It provides password protection for saved tests and question databases and is able to run on a network.

Website: All instructor materials are accessible via the book's Website (password protected) along with other useful links and information. www.cambridgepub.com

For Students

Student Solutions Manual: Created by the authors, the student solutions manual contains all solutions to the even-numbered assignment materials in the textbook. This is a **restricted** item that is only available to students after their instructor has authorized its purchase. ISBN 978-1-934319-45-1

Website: Useful links are available to students free of charge on the book's Website.

ACKNOWLEDGMENTS

All four editions of this book benefited greatly from the valuable feedback of focus group attendees, reviewers, students, and colleagues. We are extremely grateful to them for their help in making this project a success.

Ashiq Ali, *University of Texas—Dallas*
Steve Baginski, *University of Georgia*
Eli Bartov, *New York University*
Dan Bens, *University of Arizona*
Denny Beresford, *University of Georgia*
Mark Bradshaw, *Boston College*
Dennis Bline, *Bryant University*
James Boatsman, *Arizona State University*
John Briginshaw, *Pepperdine University*
Thomas Buchman, *University of Colorado—Boulder*
Mary Ellen Carter, *Boston College*
Judson Caskey, *University of California—Los Angeles*
Agnes Cheng, *Louisiana State University*
Ellen Cook, *University of Louisiana—Lafayette*
Roger Debreceny, *University of Hawaii—Manoa*
Carol Dee, *University of Colorado—Denver*
Elizabeth Demers, *INSEAD*
Vicki Dickinson, *University of Florida*
Jeffrey Doyle, *University of Utah*
Thomas Dyckman, *Cornell University*
James Edwards, *University of South Carolina*
John Eichenseher, *University of Wisconsin*
Gerard Engeholm, *Pace University*
Mark Finn, *Northwestern University*
Richard Frankel, *Washington University*
Dan Givoly, *Pennsylvania State University*
Julia Grant, *Case Western Reserve University*
Karl Hackenbrack, *Vanderbilt University*
Michelle Hanlon, *University of Michigan*
Al Hartgraves, *Emory University*
David Harvey, *University of Georgia*
Carla Hayn, *University of California—Los Angeles*
Frank Heflin, *Florida State University*
Clayton Hock, *Miami University*
Judith Hora, *University of San Diego*
Richard Hurley, *University of Connecticut*
Ross Jennings, *University of Texas—Austin*
Sanjay Kallapur, *Indian School of Business*
Greg Kane, *University of Delaware*
Saleha Khumawala, *University of Houston*
Marinilka Kimbro, *University of Washington—Tacoma*
Ron King, *Washington University*
Michael Kirschenheiter, *University of Illinois—Chicago*
Krishna Kumar, *George Washington University*
Lisa Kutcher, *University of Oregon*
Brian Leventhal, *University of Illinois—Chicago*
Joshua Livnat, *New York University*
Barbara Lougee, *University of San Diego*
Luann Lynch, *University of Virginia—Darden*

James McKinney, *University of Maryland*
Greg Miller, *University of Michigan*
Melanie Mogg, *University of Minnesota*
Steve Monahan, *INSEAD*
Dennis Murray, *University of Colorado—Denver*
Sandeep Nabar, *Oklahoma State University*
Siva Nathan, *Georgia State University*
Doron Nissim, *Columbia University*
Susan Parker, *Santa Clara University*
William Pasewark, *Texas Tech*
Stephen Penman, *Columbia University*
Mark Penno, *University of Iowa*
Kathy Petroni, *Michigan State University*
Christine Petrovits, *New York University*
Kirk Philipich, *University of Michigan—Dearborn*
Morton Pincus, *University of California—Irvine*
Grace Pownall, *Emory University*
Ram Ramanan, *University of Notre Dame*
Susan Riffe, *Southern Methodist University*
Bruce Samuelson, *Pepperdine University*
Andrew Schmidt, *Columbia University*
Chandra Seethamraju, *Washington University*
Stephen Sefcik, *University of Washington*
Kenneth Shaw, *University of Missouri*
Evan Shough, *University of North Carolina - Greensboro*
Paul Simko, *University of Virginia—Darden*
Pam Smith, *Northern Illinois University*
Sri Sridharan, *Northwestern University*
Charles Stanley, *Baylor University*
Jens Stephan, *University of Cincinnati*
Phillip Stocken, *Dartmouth College*
K.R. Subramanyam, *University of Southern California*
Gary Taylor, *University of Alabama*
Suzanne Traylor, *State University of New York Albany*
Sam Tiras, *Louisiana State University*
Brett Trueman, *University of California—Los Angeles*
Jerry Van Os, *Westminster College*
Mark Vargus, *University of Texas—Dallas*
Robert Vigeland, *Texas Christian University*
James Wallace, *Claremont Graduate School*
Charles Wasley, *University of Rochester*
Greg Waymire, *Emory University*
Edward Werner, *Drexel University*
Jeffrey Williams, *University of Michigan*
David Wright, *University of Michigan*
Michelle Yetman, *University of California—Davis*
Tzachi Zack, *Ohio State University*
Xiao-Jun Zhang, *University of California—Berkeley*

In addition, we are extremely grateful to George Werthman, Jill Fischer, Keith Chasse, Debbie Golden, Terry McQuade, and the entire team at Cambridge Business Publishers for their encouragement, enthusiasm, and guidance. Their market research, editorial development, and promotional efforts have made this book the best-selling MBA text in the market. We have had a very positive textbook authoring experience with each edition of this book thanks, in large part, to our publisher.

Peter   *John*   *Bob*   *Mary Lea*
                                                April 2009

BRIEF CONTENTS

CONTENTS

MODULE **Three**

Accounting Adjustments and Constructing Financial Statements 3-1

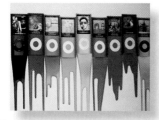

MODULE **Four**

Analyzing and Interpreting Financial Statements 4-1

MODULE **Five**

Reporting and Analyzing Operating Income 5-1

MODULE **Twelve**

Analyzing and Valuing Equity Securities 12-1

APPENDIX **B**

Constructing the Statement of Cash Flows B-1

Module One

Financial Accounting for MBAs

LEARNING OBJECTIVES

LO1 Identify and discuss the users and suppliers of financial statement information. (p. 1-5)

LO2 Identify and explain the four financial statements, and define the accounting equation. (p. 1-9)

LO3 Explain and apply the basics of profitability analysis. (p. 1-19)

LO4 Describe business analysis within the context of a competitive environment. (p. 1-20)

LO5 Describe the accounting principles and regulations that frame financial statements. (p. 1-25)

BERKSHIRE HATHAWAY

Berkshire Hathaway owns numerous businesses that pursue diverse activities. The legendary Warren Buffett, the "Sage of Omaha," manages the company. Buffett's investment philosophy is to acquire and hold companies over the long run. His acquisition criteria, taken from Berkshire Hathaway's annual report, follow:

1. Large purchases.
2. Demonstrated consistent earning power (future projections are of *no* interest to us, nor are 'turnaround' situations).
3. Businesses earning good returns on equity while employing little or no debt.
4. Management in place (we can't supply it).
5. Simple businesses (if there's lots of technology, we won't understand it).
6. An offering price (we don't want to waste our time or that of the seller by talking, even preliminarily, about a transaction when price is unknown).

At least three of Buffett's six criteria relate to financial performance. First, he seeks businesses with large and consistent earning power. Buffett is not only looking for consistent earnings, but earnings that are measured according to accounting policies that closely mirror the underlying economic performance of the business.

Second, Buffett focuses on "businesses earning good returns on equity," defined as income divided by average stockholders' equity: "Our preference would be to reach our goal by directly owning a diversified group of businesses that generate cash and consistently earn above-average returns" (Berkshire Hathaway annual report). For management to earn a good return on equity, it must focus on both income (financial performance) and equity (financial condition).

Third, Buffett values companies based on their ability to generate consistent earnings and cash. He focuses on *intrinsic value,* which he defines in each annual report as follows:

Intrinsic value is an all-important concept that offers the only logical approach to evaluating the relative attractiveness of investments and businesses. Intrinsic value can be defined

simply: It is the discounted value of the cash that can be taken out of a business during its remaining life.

The discounted value Buffett describes is the present (today's) value of the cash flows the company expects to generate in the future. Cash is generated when companies are well managed and operate profitably and efficiently.

Warren Buffett provides some especially useful investment guidance in his Chairman's letter from the Berkshire Hathaway annual report:

> Three suggestions for investors: First, beware of companies displaying weak accounting. If a company still does not expense options, or if its pension assumptions are fanciful, watch out. When managements take the low road in aspects that are visible, it is likely they are following a similar path behind the scenes. There is seldom just one cockroach in the kitchen.
>
> Second, unintelligible footnotes usually indicate untrustworthy management. If you can't understand a footnote or other managerial explanation, it's usually because the CEO doesn't want you to. Enron's descriptions of certain transactions still baffle me.
>
> Finally, be suspicious of companies that trumpet earnings projections and growth expectations. Businesses seldom operate in a tranquil, no-surprise environment, and earnings simply don't advance smoothly (except, of course, in the offering books of investment bankers).

This book will explain Buffett's references to stock option accounting and pension assumptions as well as a host of other accounting issues that affect interpretation and valuation of companies' financial performance. We will analyze and interpret the footnotes, which Buffett views as crucial to quality financial reporting and analysis. Our philosophy is simple: we must understand the intricacies and nuances of financial reporting to become critical readers and users of financial reports for company analysis and valuation.

Sources: Berkshire Hathaway *10-K Reports,* Berkshire Hathaway *Annual Reports; The Wall Street Journal,* January 2009.

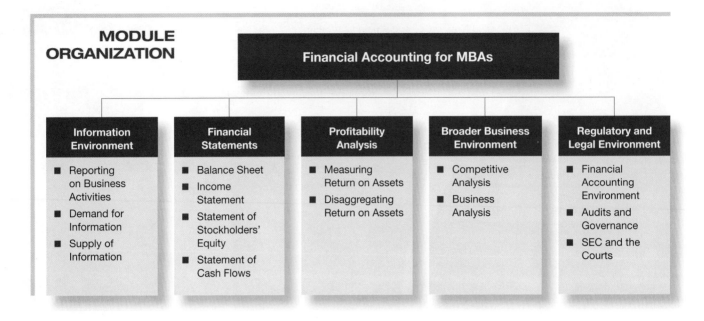

Financial accounting information serves many purposes. To understand this, imagine that we are a specific user of accounting information. For example, imagine we are a stock investor—how might we use accounting information to identify a stock to buy? Imagine we are a bond trader—how might we use accounting information to assess whether a company is able to repay its debt? Imagine we are a manager—how might we use accounting information to decide whether to acquire another company or divest of a current division? Imagine we are an equity or credit analyst—how might we use accounting to assess and communicate an investment appraisal or credit report?

This book explains the concepts, preparation, and application of financial accounting information and, importantly, how decision makers use such information. Accounting information informs many decisions beyond the few listed above. In general, managers use financial accounting information to make operating, investing, and financing decisions. Investors and analysts use financial accounting information to help decide whether to buy or sell stock. Lenders and rating agencies use accounting information to help decide on a company's creditworthiness and lending terms. Regulators use accounting information to enact social and economic policies and to monitor compliance with laws. Legal institutions use accounting information to assess fines and reparations in litigation. Other decision makers rely on accounting information for purposes ranging from determining demands in labor union negotiations to levying damages for environmental abuses.

This module begins with an overview of the information environment that companies face and it discusses the demand for and supply of financial information. We then review financial statements and explain what they convey about a company. Profitability is described next and is used as a focus of much of our application of accounting information. We conclude the module with an introduction to business analysis, which is an important part of drawing inferences from financial statements. We include (in the appendix) a discussion of the regulatory environment that defines current financial reporting for companies.

The remainder of the book can be broken into four parts–see figure at top of next page. Part 1 consists of Modules 1, 2 and 3 and offers an introduction of accounting fundamentals and the business environment. Part 2 consists of Module 4, which introduces analysis of financial statements. Although an aim of this book is to help us understand the application of financial statements, it is important that we understand their preparation. Thus, Part 3, which consists of Modules 5 through 10, describes the accounting for assets, liabilities, and equity. Part 4 consists of Modules 11 and 12, which explain the forecasting of accounting numbers and the valuation of common stock.

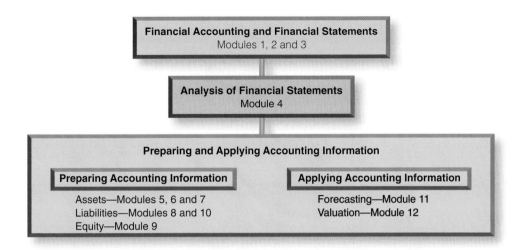

REPORTING ON BUSINESS ACTIVITIES

To effectively manage a company or infer whether it is well managed, we must understand the company's business activities. Financial statements help us understand these business activities. These statements report on a company's performance and financial condition, and reveal executive management's privileged information and insights.

Financial statements satisfy the needs of different users. The functioning of the accounting information system involves application of accounting standards to produce financial statements. Effectively using this information system involves making judgments, assumptions, and estimates based on data contained in the financial reports. The greatest value we derive from this information system as users of financial reports is the insight we gain into the business activities of the company under analysis.

To effectively analyze and use accounting information, we must consider the business context in which the information is created—see Exhibit 1.1. Without exception, all companies *plan* business activities, *finance* those activities, *invest* in those activities, and then engage in *operating* activities. Companies conduct all these activities while confronting *business forces*, including market constraints and competitive pressures. Financial statements provides crucial input for strategic planning. They also provide information about the relative success of those plans, which can be used to take corrective action or make new operating, investing, and financing decisions.

Exhibit 1.1 depicts the business activities for a typical company. The outer (green) ring is the planning process that reflects the overarching goals and objectives of the company within which strategic decisions are made. Those strategic decisions involve company financing, asset management, and daily operations. Apple, Inc., the focus company in Modules 2 and 3, provides the following description of its business strategy in its annual report:

Business Strategy The Company is committed to bringing the best personal computing, portable digital music and mobile communication experience to students, educators, creative professionals, businesses, government agencies, and consumers through its innovative hardware, software, peripherals, services, and Internet offerings. The Company's business strategy leverages its unique ability to design and develop its own operating system, hardware, application software, and services to provide its customers new products and solutions with superior ease-of-use, seamless integration, and innovative industrial design. The Company believes continual investment in research and development is critical to the development and enhancement of innovative products and technologies. In addition to evolving its personal computers and related solutions, the Company continues to capitalize on the convergence of the personal computer, digital consumer electronics and mobile communications by creating and refining innovations, such as the iPod, iPhone, iTunes Store and Apple TV. The Company's strategy also includes expanding its distribution network to effectively reach more of its targeted customers and provide them a high-quality sales and post-sales support experience.

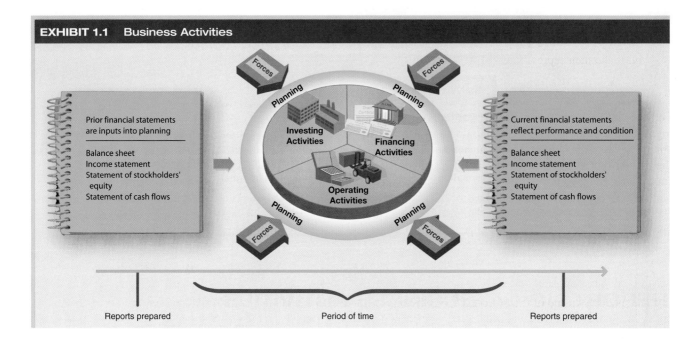

EXHIBIT 1.1   Business Activities

A company's *strategic* (or *business*) *plan* reflects how it plans to achieve its goals and objectives. A plan's success depends on an effective analysis of market demand and supply. Specifically, a company must assess demand for its products and services, and assess the supply of its inputs (both labor and capital). The plan must also include competitive analyses, opportunity assessments, and consideration of business threats.

Historical financial statements provide insight into the success of a company's strategic plan, and are an important input to the planning process. These statements highlight portions of the strategic plan that proved profitable and, thus, warrant additional capital investment. They also reveal areas that are less effective, and provide information to help managers develop remedial action.

Once strategic adjustments are planned and implemented, the resulting financial statements provide input into the planning process for the following year; and this process begins again. Understanding a company's strategic plan helps focus our analysis of financial statements by placing them in proper context.

FINANCIAL STATEMENTS: DEMAND AND SUPPLY

LO1 Identify and discuss the users and suppliers of financial statement information.

Demand for financial statements has existed for centuries as a means to facilitate efficient contracting and risk-sharing. Decision makers and other stakeholders demand information on a company's past and prospective returns and risks. Supply of financial statements is driven by companies that wish to lower their costs of financing and less obvious costs such as political, contracting, and labor. Managers decide how much financial information to supply by weighing the costs of disclosure against the benefits of disclosure. Regulatory agencies intervene in this process with various disclosure requirements that establish a minimum supply of information.

Demand for Information

The following broad classes of users possess a demand for financial accounting information:

- Managers and employees
- Investment analysts and information intermediaries
- Creditors and suppliers
- Shareholders and directors

- Customers and strategic partners
- Regulators and tax agencies
- Voters and their representatives

Managers and Employees

For their own well-being and future earnings potential, managers and employees demand accounting information on the financial condition, profitability, and prospects of their companies as well as comparative financial information on competing companies and business opportunities. This permits them to benchmark their company's performance and condition. Managers and employees also demand financial accounting information for use in compensation and bonus contracts that are tied to such numbers. The popularity of employee profit sharing and stock ownership plans has further increased demand for financial information. Other sources of demand include union contracts that link wage negotiations to accounting numbers and pension and benefit plans whose solvency depends on company performance.

Investment Analysts and Information Intermediaries

Investment analysts and other information intermediaries, such as financial press writers and business commentators, are interested in predicting companies' future performance. Expectations about future profitability and the ability to generate cash impact the price of securities and a company's ability to borrow money at favorable terms. Financial reports reflect information about past performance and current resources available to companies. These reports also provide information about claims on those resources, including claims by suppliers, creditors, lenders, and shareholders. This information allows analysts to make informed assessments about future financial performance and condition so they can provide stock recommendations or write commentaries.

Creditors and Suppliers

Banks and other lenders demand financial accounting information to help determine loan terms, loan amounts, interest rates, and required collateral. Loan agreements often include contractual requirements, called **covenants**, that restrict the borrower's behavior in some fashion. For example, loan covenants might require the loan recipient to maintain minimum levels of working capital, retained earnings, interest coverage, and so forth to safeguard lenders. Covenant violations can yield technical default, enabling the creditor to demand early payment or other compensation. Suppliers demand financial information to establish credit terms and to determine their long-term commitment to supply-chain relations. Both creditors and suppliers use financial information to monitor and adjust their contracts and commitments with a company.

Shareholders and Directors

Shareholders and directors demand financial accounting information to assess the profitability and risks of companies. Shareholders and others (such as investment analysts, brokers and potential investors) search for information useful in their investment decisions. **Fundamental analysis** uses financial information to estimate company value and to form buy-sell stock strategies. Both directors and shareholders use accounting information to evaluate managerial performance. Managers similarly use such information to request an increase in compensation and managerial power from directors. Outside directors are crucial to determining who runs the company, and these directors use accounting information to help make leadership decisions.

Customers and Strategic Partners

Customers (both current and potential) demand accounting information to assess a company's ability to provide products or services as agreed and to assess the company's staying power and reliability. Strategic partners wish to estimate the company's profitability to assess the fairness of returns on mutual transactions and strategic alliances.

Regulators and Tax Agencies

Regulators (such as the SEC, the Federal Trade Commission, and the Federal Reserve Bank) and tax agencies demand accounting information for antitrust assessments, public protection, price setting, import-export analyses, and setting tax policies. Timely and reliable information is crucial to effective regulatory policy, and accounting information is often central to social and economic policy. For example, governments often grant monopoly rights to electric and gas companies serving specific areas in exchange for regulation over prices charged to consumers. These prices are mainly determined from accounting measures.

Voters and their Representatives

Voters and their representatives to national, state, and local governments demand accounting information for policy decisions. The decisions can involve economic, social, taxation, and other initiatives. Voters and their representatives also use accounting information to monitor government spending. We have all heard of the $1,000 hammer type stories that government watchdog groups uncover while sifting through accounting data. Contributors to nonprofit organizations also demand accounting information to assess the impact of their donations.

IFRS INSIGHT   **Development of International Standards**

The accounting standards explained in this book are consistent with generally accepted accounting principles (GAAP) accepted by the Financial Accounting Standards Board (FASB). A similar organization, known as the International Accounting Standards Board (IASB), develops a global set of International Financial Reporting Standards (IFRS) for preparation of financial statements. To increase comparability of financial statements and reduce reporting complexity, the Securities Exchange Commission (SEC), the FASB, and the IASB are committed to a process of convergence to one set of world accounting standards. As we progress through the book, we will provide IFRS Insight boxes like this to identify differences between GAAP and IFRS.

Supply of Information

In general, the quantity and quality of accounting information that companies supply are determined by managers' assessment of the benefits and costs of disclosure. Managers release information provided the benefits of disclosing that information outweigh the costs of doing so. Both *regulation* and *bargaining power* affect disclosure costs and benefits and thus play roles in determining the supply of accounting information. Most areas of the world regulate the minimum levels of accounting disclosures. In the U.S., publicly traded firms must file financial accounting information with the Securities Exchange Commission (SEC). The two main compulsory SEC filings are:

- Form **10-K**: the audited annual report that includes the four financial statements, discussed below, with explanatory notes and the management's discussion and analysis of financial results.

- Form **10-Q**: the unaudited quarterly report that includes summary versions of the four financial statements and limited additional disclosures.

Forms 10-K and 10-Q are available electronically from the SEC Website (see Appendix 1A). The minimum, regulated level of information is not the standard. Both the quantity and quality of information differ across companies and over time. We need only look at several annual reports to see considerable variance in the amount and type of accounting information supplied. For example, differences abound on disclosures for segment operations, product performance reports, and financing activities. Further, some stakeholders possess ample bargaining power to obtain accounting information for themselves. These typically include private lenders and major suppliers and customers.

Benefits of Disclosure

The benefits of supplying accounting information extend to a company's capital, labor, input, and output markets. Companies must compete in these markets. For example, capital markets provide debt and equity financing; the better a company's prospects, the lower is its cost of capital (as reflected in lower interest rates or higher stock prices). The same holds for a company's recruiting efforts in labor markets and its ability to establish superior supplier-customer relations in the input and output markets.

A company's performance in these markets depends on success with its business activities *and* the market's awareness of that success. Companies reap the benefits of disclosure with good news about their products, processes, management, and so forth. That is, there are real economic incentives for companies to disclose reliable (audited) accounting information enabling them to better compete in capital, labor, input, and output markets.

What inhibits companies from providing false or misleading good news? There are several constraints. An important constraint imposed by stakeholders is that of audit requirements and legal repercussions associated with inaccurate accounting information. Another relates to reputation effects from disclosures as subsequent events either support or refute earlier news.

Costs of Disclosure

The costs of supplying accounting information include its preparation and dissemination, competitive disadvantages, litigation potential, and political costs. Preparation and dissemination costs can be substantial, but companies have often already incurred those costs because managers need similar information for their own business decisions. The potential for information to yield competitive disadvantages is high. Companies are concerned that disclosures of their activities such as product or segment successes, strategic alliances or pursuits, technological or system innovations, and product or process quality improvements will harm their competitive advantages. Also, companies are frequently sued when disclosures create expectations that are not met. Highly visible companies often face political and public pressure, which creates "political costs." These companies often try to appear as if they do not generate excess profits. For example, government defense contractors, large software conglomerates, and oil companies are favorite targets of public scrutiny. Disclosure costs are higher for companies facing political costs.

The SEC adopted Regulation FD, or Reg FD for short, to curb the practice of selective disclosure by public companies (called *issuers* by the SEC) to certain shareholders and financial analysts. In the past, many companies disclosed important information in meetings and conference calls that excluded individual shareholders. The goal of this rule is to even the playing field for all investors. Reg FD reads as follows: "Whenever an issuer discloses any material nonpublic information regarding that issuer, the issuer shall make public disclosure of that information . . . simultaneously, in the case of an intentional disclosure; and . . . promptly, in the case of a non-intentional disclosure." Reg FD increased the cost of voluntary financial disclosure and led some companies to curtail the supply of financial information to all users.

International Accounting Standards and Convergence

The International Accounting Standards Board (IASB) oversees the development of accounting standards for a vast number of countries outside the U.S. More than 100 countries, including those in the European Union, require use of International Financial Reporting Standards (IFRS) developed by the IASB. For many years, IASB and the FASB operated as independent standard-setting bodies. In the early 2000s, pressure mounted for these two standard-setting organizations to collaborate and create one set of internationally acceptable standards. At a joint meeting in September 2002, the FASB and the IASB each acknowledged their commitment to the development of high-quality, compatible accounting standards that could be used for both domestic and cross-border financial reporting. At that meeting, both the FASB and IASB pledged to use their best efforts to (a) make their existing financial reporting standards fully compatible as soon as practicable and (b) to coordinate their future work programs to ensure that once achieved, compatibility is maintained.

In 2008, the SEC issued a road map for the use of IFRS by U.S. companies. The SEC envisions that all companies will report under IFRS by 2014. Larger companies have begun to issue IFRS compliant financial statements, and foreign private issuers on U.S. stock exchanges are currently permitted to file financial statements in accordance with IFRS without reconciliation to U.S. GAAP as was previously required. As remaining differences are eliminated, the convergence of accounting standards is becoming a reality.

Are financial statements issued under IFRS substantially different from those issued under U.S. GAAP? At a broad level, the answer is no. Both are prepared using accrual accounting and utilize similar conceptual frameworks. Both require the same set of financial statements: a balance sheet, income statement, a statement of cash flows, a statement of stockholders' equity, and a set of explanatory footnotes. That does not mean that no differences remain. However, the remaining differences are typically technical in nature, and do not differ on broad principles discussed in this book. Indeed, recent accounting standards issued by the FASB and the IASB, such as the accounting for acquisitions of companies, were developed jointly and issued simultaneously to minimize differences as the two standard-setting bodies work toward harmonization of international standards.

Appendix D, near the end of this book, summarizes differences between U.S. GAAP and the IFRS. Also, there are a variety of sources that provide more detailed and technical analysis of similarities and differences between U.S. GAAP and IFRS. The FASB, the IASB, and each of the "Big 4" accounting firms also maintain Websites devoted to this issue. (Search under IFRS and PwC, KPMG, EY and Deloitte; the two standard-setting bodies also provide useful information, see: FASB (**www.fasb.org/intl/**) and IASB (**www.iasb.org/Home.htm**).

BUSINESS INSIGHT Accounting Quality

In the bear market that followed the bursting of the **dot.com** bubble, and amid a series of corporate scandals such as Enron, Tyco, and WorldCom, Congress passed the ***Sarbanes-Oxley Act,*** often referred to as *SOX*. SOX sought to rectify perceived problems in accounting, including weak audit committees and deficient internal controls. Increased scrutiny of financial reporting and internal controls has had some success. A report by Glass, Lewis and Co., a corporate-governance research firm, shows that the number of financial restatements by publicly traded companies surged to a record 1,295 in 2005—which is one restatement for each 12 public companies, and more than triple the 2002 total, the year SOX passed. The Glass, Lewis and Co. report concluded that "when so many companies produce inaccurate financial statements, it seriously calls into question the quality of information that investors relied upon to make capital-allocation decisions" (**CFO.Com**). Bottom line: we must be critical readers of financial reports.

FINANCIAL STATEMENTS

LO2 Identify and explain the four financial statements, and define the accounting equation.

Companies use four financial statements to periodically report on business activities. These statements are the: balance sheet, income statement, statement of stockholders' equity, and statement of cash flows. Exhibit 1.2 shows how these statements are linked across time. A balance sheet reports on a company's financial position at a *point in time*. The income statement, statement of stockholders' equity, and the statement of cash flows report on performance over a *period of time*. The three statements in the middle of Exhibit 1.2 (period-of-time statements) link the balance sheet from the beginning to the end of a period.

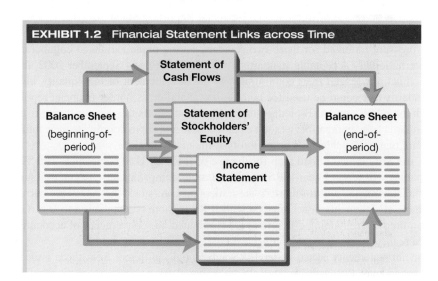

EXHIBIT 1.2 Financial Statement Links across Time

A one-year, or annual, reporting period is common and is called the *accounting,* or *fiscal, year.* Of course, firms prepare financial statements more frequently; semiannual, quarterly, and monthly financial statements are common. *Calendar-year* companies have reporting periods beginning on January 1 and ending on December 31. Berkshire Hathaway is a calendar-year company. Some companies choose a fiscal year ending on a date other than December 31, such as when sales and inventory are low. For example, Best Buy's fiscal year-end is always near February 1, after the busy holiday season.

Balance Sheet

A balance sheet reports a company's financial position at a point in time. The balance sheet reports the company's *resources* (*assets*), namely, what the company owns. The balance sheet also reports the *sources* of asset financing. There are two ways a company can finance its assets. It can raise money from shareholders; this is *owner financing.* It can also raise money from banks or other creditors and suppliers; this is *nonowner financing.* This means that both owners and nonowners hold claims on company assets. Owner claims on assets are referred to as *equity* and nonowner claims are referred to as *liabilities* (or debt). Since all financing must be invested in something, we obtain the following basic relation: *investing equals financing.* This equality is called the **accounting equation,** which follows:

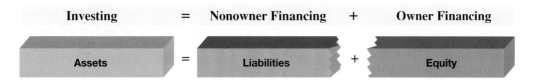

The accounting equation works for all companies at all points in time.

The balance sheet for Berkshire Hathaway is in Exhibit 1.3 (condensed). Refer to this balance sheet to verify the following amounts: assets = $273,160 million; liabilities = $149,759 million; and equity = $123,401 million. Assets equal liabilities plus equity, which reflects the accounting equation: investing equals financing.

Investing Activities

Balance sheets are organized like the accounting equation. Investing activities are represented by the company's assets. These assets are financed by a combination of nonowner financing (liabilities) and owner financing (equity).

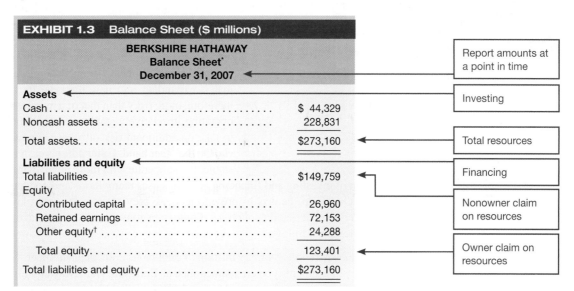

EXHIBIT 1.3	Balance Sheet ($ millions)	
BERKSHIRE HATHAWAY		
Balance Sheet*		
December 31, 2007		Report amounts at a point in time
Assets		Investing
Cash	$ 44,329	
Noncash assets	228,831	
Total assets	$273,160	Total resources
Liabilities and equity		Financing
Total liabilities	$149,759	
Equity		Nonowner claim on resources
Contributed capital	26,960	
Retained earnings	72,153	
Other equity†	24,288	
Total equity	123,401	Owner claim on resources
Total liabilities and equity	$273,160	

* Financial statement titles often begin with the word *consolidated.* This means that the financial statement includes a parent company and one or more subsidiaries, companies that the parent company owns.

† For Berkshire Hathaway, other equity includes accumulated other comprehensive income and minority interests.

For simplicity, Berkshire Hathaway's balance sheet in Exhibit 1.3 categorizes assets into cash and noncash assets. Noncash assets consist of several asset categories (Module 2 explains the composition of noncash assets). These categories are listed in order of their nearness to cash. For example, companies own a category of assets called inventories. These are goods that the company intends to sell to its customers. Inventories are converted into cash when they are sold within a short period of time. Hence, they are classified as short-term assets. Companies also report a category of assets called property, plant and equipment. This category includes a company's office buildings or manufacturing facilities. Property, plant and equipment assets will be held for an extended period of time and are, therefore, generally classified as long-term assets.

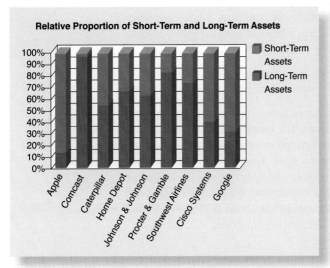

The relative proportion of short-term and long-term assets is largely determined by a company's business model. This is evident in the graph to the side that depicts the relative proportion of short and long-term assets for several companies that we feature in this book. Companies such as Apple and Google require little investment in long-term assets. On the other hand, Comcast and Procter & Gamble require a large investment in long-term assets. Although managers can influence the relative amounts and proportion of assets, their flexibility is somewhat limited by the nature of their industries.

Financing Activities

Assets must be paid for, and funding is provided by, a combination of owner and nonowner financing. Owner (or equity) financing includes resources contributed to the company by its owners along with any profit retained by the company. Nonowner (creditor or debt) financing is borrowed money. We distinguish between these two financing sources for a reason: borrowed money entails a legal obligation to repay amounts owed, and failure to do so can result in severe consequences for the borrower. Equity financing entails no such legal obligation for repayment.

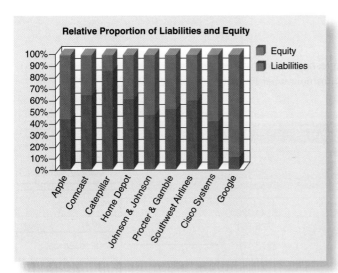

The relative proportion of nonowner (liabilities) and owner (equity) financing is largely determined by a company's business model. This is evident in the graph to the side, again citing many of the companies we feature as focus companies in this book. Google is a relatively new company that is expanding into new markets. Its business model is, therefore, more risky than that of a more established company operating in relatively stable markets. Google cannot afford to take on additional risk of higher nonowner financing levels. On the other hand, Caterpillar's cash flows are relatively stable. It can operate with more nonowner financing.

Our discussion of investing and financing activities uses many terms and concepts that we explain later in the book. Our desire here is to provide a sneak preview into the interplay among financial statements, manager behavior, and economics. Some questions that we might have at this early stage regarding the balance sheet follow:

■ Berkshire Hathaway reports $44,329 million of cash on its 2007 balance sheet, which is 16% of total assets. Many investment-type companies such as Berkshire Hathaway and high-tech companies such as Cisco Systems carry high levels of cash. Why is that? Is there a cost to holding too much cash? Is it costly to carry too little cash?

■ The relative proportion of short-term and long-term assets is largely dictated by companies' business models. Why is this the case? Why is the composition of assets on balance sheets for companies in the same industry similar? By what degree can a company's asset composition safely deviate from industry norms?

■ What are the trade-offs in financing a company by owner versus nonowner financing? If nonowner financing is less costly, why don't we see companies financed entirely with borrowed money?

■ How do shareholders influence the strategic direction of a company? How can long-term creditors influence strategic direction?

■ Most assets and liabilities are reported on the balance sheet at their acquisition price, called *historical cost*. Would reporting assets and liabilities at fair values be more informative? What problems might fair-value reporting cause?

Review the Berkshire Hathaway balance sheet summarized in Exhibit 1.3 and think about these questions. We provide answers for each of these questions as we progress through the book.

IFRS INSIGHT **Balance Sheet Presentation and IFRS**

Balance sheets prepared under IFRS tend to classify accounts in reverse order of liquidity (lack of nearness to cash). For example, intangible assets are typically listed first and cash is listed last among assets. Also, equity is typically listed before liabilities, where liabilities are again listed in order of decreasing liquidity.

Income Statement

An **income statement** reports on a company's performance over a period of time and lists amounts for revenues (also called sales) and expenses. Revenues less expenses yield the bottom-line net income amount. Berkshire Hathaway's income statement is in Exhibit 1.4. Refer to its income statement to verify the following: revenues = $118,245 million; expenses = $105,032 million; and net income = $13,213 million. Net income reflects the profit (also called earnings) to owners for that specific period.

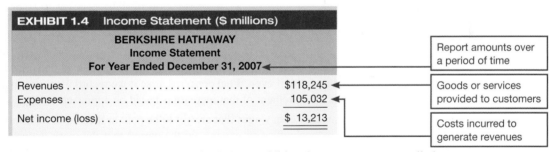

EXHIBIT 1.4 Income Statement ($ millions)

BERKSHIRE HATHAWAY Income Statement For Year Ended December 31, 2007	
Revenues	$118,245
Expenses	105,032
Net income (loss)	$ 13,213

Report amounts over a period of time

Goods or services provided to customers

Costs incurred to generate revenues

Manufacturing and merchandising companies typically include an additional expense account, called cost of goods sold (or cost of sales), in the income statement following revenues. It is also common to report a subtotal called gross profit (or gross margin), which is revenues less cost of goods sold. The company's remaining expenses are then reported below gross profit. This income statement layout follows:

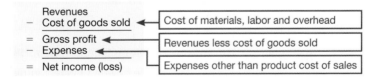

Revenues
− Cost of goods sold ◄— Cost of materials, labor and overhead
= Gross profit ◄— Revenues less cost of goods sold
− Expenses
= Net income (loss) — Expenses other than product cost of sales

Operating Activities

Operating activities use company resources to produce, promote, and sell its products and services. These activities extend from input markets involving suppliers of materials and labor to a company's output markets involving customers of products and services. Input markets generate most *expenses*

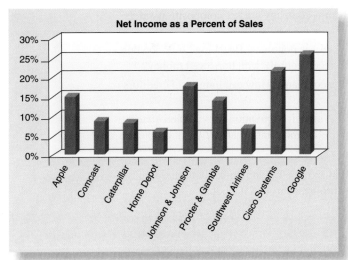

Net Income as a Percent of Sales

(or *costs*) such as inventory, salaries, materials, and logistics. Output markets generate *revenues* (or *sales*) to customers. Output markets also generate some expenses such as marketing and distributing products and services to customers. Net income arises when revenues exceed expenses. A loss occurs when expenses exceed revenues.

Differences exist in the relative profitability of companies across industries. Although effective management can increase the profitability of a company, business models play a large part in determining company profitability. These differences are illustrated in the graph (to the side) of net income as a percentage of sales for several companies.

Home Depot operates in a mature industry with little ability to differentiate its products from those of its competitors. Hence, its net income as a percentage of sales is low. Southwest Airlines faces a different kind of problem: having competitors that are desperate and trying to survive. Profitability will not return to the transportation industry until weaker competitors are no longer protected by bankruptcy courts. At the other end of the spectrum are Cisco Systems and Google. Both are dominant in their industries with products protected by patent laws. Their profitability levels are more akin to that of monopolists.

As a sneak preview, we might consider the following questions regarding the income statement:

■ Assume that a company sells a product to a customer who promises to pay in 30 days. Should the seller recognize the sale when it is made or when cash is collected?

■ When a company purchases a long-term asset such as a building, its cost is reported on the balance sheet as an asset. Should a company, instead, record the cost of that building as an expense when it is acquired? If not, how should a company report the cost of that asset over the course of its useful life?

■ Manufacturers and merchandisers report the cost of a product as an expense when the product sale is recorded. How might we measure the costs of a product that is sold by a merchandiser? By a manufacturer?

■ If an asset, such as a building, increases in value, that increase in value is not reported as income until the building is sold, if ever. What concerns arise if we record increases in asset values as part of income, when measurement of that increase is based on appraised values?

■ Employees commonly earn wages that are yet to be paid at the end of a particular period. Should their wages be recognized as an expense in the period that the work is performed, or when the wages are paid?

■ Companies are not allowed to report profit on transactions relating to their own stock. That is, they don't report income when stock is sold, nor do they report an expense when dividends are paid to shareholders. Why is this the case?

Review the Berkshire Hathaway income statement summarized in Exhibit 1.4 and think about these questions. We provide answers for each of these questions as we progress through the book.

BUSINESS INSIGHT **Warren Buffett on Financial Reports**

"When Charlie and I read reports, we have no interest in pictures of personnel, plants or products. References to EBITDA [earnings before interest, taxes, depreciation and amortization] make us shudder—does management think the tooth fairy pays for capital expenditures? We're very suspicious of accounting methodology that is vague or unclear, since too often that means management wishes to hide something. And we don't want to read messages that a public relations department or consultant has turned out. Instead, we expect a company's CEO to explain in his or her own words what's happening." —Berkshire Hathaway annual report

Statement of Stockholders' Equity

The **statement of stockholders' equity** reports on changes in key types of equity over a period of time. For each type of equity, the statement reports the beginning balance, a summary of the activity in the account during the year, and the ending balance. Berkshire Hathaway's statement of stockholders' equity is in Exhibit 1.5. During the recent period, its equity changed due to share issuances and income reinvestment. Berkshire Hathaway classifies these changes into three categories:

■ *Contributed capital*, the stockholders' net contributions to the company

■ *Retained earnings*, net income over the life of the company minus all dividends ever paid

■ *Other*, consists of amounts that we explain later in the book

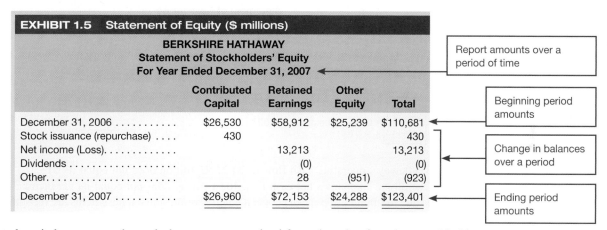

EXHIBIT 1.5   Statement of Equity ($ millions)

BERKSHIRE HATHAWAY
Statement of Stockholders' Equity
For Year Ended December 31, 2007

	Contributed Capital	Retained Earnings	Other Equity	Total
December 31, 2006	$26,530	$58,912	$25,239	$110,681
Stock issuance (repurchase)	430			430
Net income (Loss).		13,213		13,213
Dividends		(0)		(0)
Other.		28	(951)	(923)
December 31, 2007	$26,960	$72,153	$24,288	$123,401

Report amounts over a period of time

Beginning period amounts

Change in balances over a period

Ending period amounts

Contributed capital represents the cash the company received from the sale of stock to stockholders (also called shareholders), less any funds expended for the repurchase of stock. Retained earnings (also called *earned capital* or *reinvested capital*) represent the cumulative total amount of income that the company has earned and that has been retained in the business and not distributed to shareholders in the form of dividends. The change in retained earnings links consecutive balance sheets via the income statement: Ending retained earnings = Beginning retained earnings + Net income − Dividends. For Berkshire Hathaway, its recent year's retained earnings increases from $58,912 million to $72,153 million. This increase of $13,241 million is explained by net income of $13,213 million, no payment of dividends, and $28 million related to a mandated accounting change.

RESEARCH INSIGHT   Are Earnings Important?

A recent study asked top finance executives of publicly traded companies to *rank the three most important measures to report to outsiders.* The study reports that:

> "[More than 50% of] CFOs state that earnings are the most important financial metric to external constituents . . . this finding could reflect superior informational content in earnings over the other metrics. Alternatively, it could reflect myopic managerial concern about earnings. The emphasis on earnings is noteworthy because cash flows continue to be the measure emphasized in the academic finance literature."

The study also reports that CFOs view year-over-year change in earnings to be of critical importance to outsiders. Why is that? The study provides the following insights.

> "CFOs note that the first item in a press release is often a comparison of current quarter earnings with four quarters lagged quarterly earnings . . . CFOs also mention that while analysts' forecasts can be guided by management, last year's quarterly earnings number is a benchmark that is harder, if not impossible, to manage after the 10-Q has been filed with the SEC . . . Several executives mention that comparison to seasonally lagged earnings numbers provides a measure of earnings momentum and growth, and therefore is a useful gauge of corporate performance."

Thus, are earnings important? To the majority of finance chiefs surveyed, the answer is a resounding yes. (Source: Graham, et al., *Journal of Accounting and Economics,* 2005)

Statement of Cash Flows

The **statement of cash flows** reports the change (either an increase or a decrease) in a company's cash balance over a period of time. The statement reports on cash inflows and outflows from operating, investing, and financing activities over a period of time. Berkshire Hathaway's statement of cash flows is in Exhibit 1.6. Its cash balance increased by $586 million in the recent period: operating activities generated a $12,550 million cash inflow, investing activities reduced cash by $13,428 million, and financing activities yielded a cash inflow of $1,464 million.

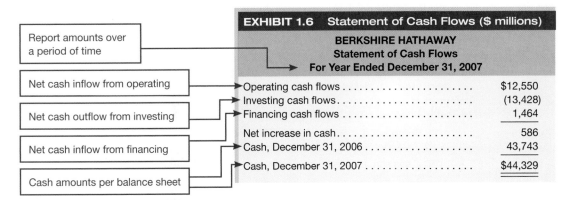

EXHIBIT 1.6	Statement of Cash Flows ($ millions)
	BERKSHIRE HATHAWAY
	Statement of Cash Flows
	For Year Ended December 31, 2007

Operating cash flows	$12,550
Investing cash flows	(13,428)
Financing cash flows	1,464
Net increase in cash	586
Cash, December 31, 2006	43,743
Cash, December 31, 2007	$44,329

Report amounts over a period of time

Net cash inflow from operating

Net cash outflow from investing

Net cash inflow from financing

Cash amounts per balance sheet

Berkshire Hathaway's operating cash flow of $12,550 million does not equal its $13,213 million net income. Generally, a company's net cash flow for a period does *not* equal its net income for the period. This is due to timing differences between when revenue and expense items are recognized on the income statement and when cash is received and paid. (We discuss this concept further in subsequent modules.)

Both cash flow and net income numbers are important for business decisions. Each is used in security valuation models, and both help users of accounting reports understand and assess a company's past, present, and future business activities. As a sneak preview, we might consider the following questions regarding the statement of cash flows:

■ What is the usefulness of the statement of cash flows? Do the balance sheet and income statement provide sufficient cash flow information?

■ What types of information are disclosed in the statement of cash flows and why are they important?

■ What kinds of activities are reported in each of the operating, investing and financing sections of the statement of cash flows? How is this information useful?

■ Is it important for a company to report net cash inflows (positive amounts) relating to operating activities over the longer term? What are the implications if operating cash flows are negative for an extended period of time?

■ Why is it important to know the composition of a company's investment activities? What kind of information might we look for? Are positive investing cash flows favorable?

■ Is it important to know the sources of a company's financing activities? What questions might that information help us answer?

■ How might the composition of operating, investing and financing cash flows change over a company's life cycle?

■ Is the bottom line increase in cash flow the key number? Why or why not?

Review the Berkshire Hathaway statement of cash flows summarized in Exhibit 1.6 and think about these questions. We provide answers for each of these questions as we progress through the book.

Financial Statement Linkages

The four financial statements are linked within and across periods—consider the following:

■ The income statement and the balance sheet are linked via retained earnings. For Berkshire Hathaway, the $13,213 million increase in retained earnings (reported on the balance sheet) equals its net income (reported on the income statement) plus a $28 million adjustment relating to adoption of a new accounting standard (see Exhibit 1.5). Berkshire Hathaway did not pay dividends in 2007.

■ Retained earnings, contributed capital, and other equity balances appear both on the statement of stockholders' equity and the balance sheet.

■ The statement of cash flows is linked to the income statement as net income is a component of operating cash flow. The statement of cash flows is also linked to the balance sheet as the change in the balance sheet cash account reflects the net cash inflows and outflows for the period.

Items that impact one financial statement ripple through the others. Linkages among the four financial statements are an important feature of the accounting system.

Information Beyond Financial Statements

Important financial information about a company is communicated to various decision makers through means other than the four financial statements. These include the following:

■ Management Discussion and Analysis (MD&A)
■ Independent Auditor Report
■ Financial statement footnotes
■ Regulatory filings, including proxy statements and other SEC filings

We describe and explain the usefulness of these additional information sources throughout the book.

Choices in Financial Accounting

Some people mistakenly assume that financial accounting is an exact discipline—that is, companies select the one proper accounting method to account for a transaction, and then follow the rules. The reality is that GAAP allows companies choices in preparing financial statements. The choice of methods often yields financial statements that are markedly different from one another in terms of reported income, assets, liabilities, and equity amounts.

People often are surprised that financial statements comprise numerous estimates. For example, companies must estimate the amounts that will eventually be collected from customers, the length of time that buildings and equipment will be productive, the value impairments of assets, the future costs of warranty claims, and the eventual payouts on pension plans. Following are examples of how some managers are alleged to have abused the latitude available in reporting financial results.

Company	Allegations
Adelphia Communications (ADELQ)	Founding Rigas family collected $3.1 billion in off-balance-sheet loans backed by Adelphia; it overstated results by inflating capital expenses and hiding debt.
TWX Time Warner (TWX)	As the ad market faltered and AOL's purchase of Time Warner loomed, AOL inflated sales by booking revenue for barter deals and ads it sold for third parties. These questionable revenues boosted growth rates and sealed the deal. AOL also boosted sales via "round-trip" deals with advertisers and suppliers.
Bristol-Myers Squibb (BMY)	Inflated its 2001 revenue by $1.5 billion by "channel stuffing," or forcing wholesalers to accept more inventory than they could sell to get inventory off Bristol-Myers' books.
Enron	Created profits and hid debt totaling over $1 billion by improperly using off-the-books partnerships; manipulated the Texas power market; bribed foreign governments to win contracts abroad; manipulated California energy market.
Global Crossing	Engaged in network capacity "swaps" with other carriers to inflate revenue; shredded documents related to accounting practices.

continued

continued from prior page

Company	Allegations
Halliburton (HAL)	Improperly booked $100 million in annual construction cost overruns before customers agreed to pay for them.
Qwest Communications International (Q)	Inflated revenue using network capacity "swaps" and improper accounting for long-term deals.
Tyco (TYC)	Ex-CEO L. Dennis Kozlowski indicted for tax evasion; Kozlowski and former CFO Mark H. Swartz, convicted of taking unauthorized loans from the company.
WorldCom	Overstated cash flow by booking $11 billion in operating expenses as capital costs; loaned founder Bernard Ebbers $400 million off-the-books.
Xerox (XRX)	Falsified financial results for five years, over-reported income by $1.5 billion.

Accounting standard setters walk a fine line regarding choice in accounting. On one hand, they are concerned that choice in preparing financial statements will lead to abuse by those seeking to gain by influencing decisions of financial statement users. On the other hand, standard setters are concerned that companies are too diverse for a "one size fits all" financial accounting system.

Enron exemplifies the problems that accompany rigid accounting standards. A set of accounting standards relating to special purpose entities (SPEs) provided preparers with guidelines under which those entities were or were not to be consolidated. Unfortunately, once the SPE guidelines were set, some people worked diligently to structure SPE transactions so as to narrowly avoid the consolidation requirements and achieve *off-balance-sheet* financing. This is just one example of how, with rigid standards, companies can adhere to the letter of the rule, but not its intent. In such situations, the financial statements are not fairly presented.

For most of its existence, the FASB has promulgated standards that were quite complicated and replete with guidelines. This invited abuse of the type embodied by the Enron scandal. In recent years, the pendulum has begun to swing away from such rigidity. Now, once financial statements are prepared, company management is required to step back from the details and make a judgment on whether the statements taken as a whole "fairly present" the financial condition of the company as is asserted in the company's audit report (see below).

Moreover, since the enactment of the **Sarbanes-Oxley Act,** the SEC requires the chief executive officer (CEO) of the company and its chief financial officer (CFO) to personally sign a statement attesting to the accuracy and completeness of the financial statements. This requirement is an important step in restoring confidence in the integrity of financial accounting. The statements signed by both the CEO and CFO contain the following declarations:

■ Both the CEO and CFO have personally reviewed the annual report.

■ There are no untrue statements of a material fact that would make the statements misleading.

■ Financial statements fairly present in all material respects the financial condition of the company.

■ All material facts are disclosed to the company's auditors and board of directors.

■ No changes to its system of internal controls are made unless properly communicated.

The Sarbanes-Oxley Act also imposed fines and potential jail time for executives. Presumably, the prospect of personal losses is designed to make these executives more vigilant in monitoring the financial accounting system.

MANAGERIAL DECISION | **You Are the Product Manager**

There is often friction between investors' need for information and a company's desire to safeguard competitive advantages. Assume that you are a key-product manager at your company. Your department has test-marketed a potentially lucrative new product, which it plans to further finance. You are asked for advice on the extent of information to disclose about the new product in the MD&A section of the company's upcoming annual report. What advice do you provide and why? [Answer, p. 1-30]

MID-MODULE REVIEW

The following financial information is from Allstate Corporation, a competitor of Berkshire Hathaway's GEICO Insurance, for the year ended December 31, 2007 ($ millions).

Cash, ending year	$ 422
Cash flows from operations	5,433
Revenues	36,769
Stockholders' equity	21,851
Cash flows from financing	(5,339)
Total liabilities	134,557
Expenses	32,133
Noncash assets	155,986
Cash flows from investing	(115)
Net income	4,636
Cash, beginning year	443

Required

1. Prepare an income statement, balance sheet, and statement of cash flows for Allstate at December 31, 2007.
2. Compare the balance sheet and income statement of Allstate to those of Berkshire Hathaway in Exhibits 1.3 and 1.4. What differences do we observe?

Solution

1.

ALLSTATE CORPORATION
Income Statement
For Year Ended December 31, 2007

Revenues	$36,769
Expenses	32,133
Net income	$ 4,636

ALLSTATE CORPORATION
Balance Sheet
December 31, 2007

Cash	$ 422	Total liabilities	$134,557
Noncash assets	155,986	Stockholders' equity	21,851
Total assets	$156,408	Total liabilities and equity	$156,408

ALLSTATE CORPORATION
Statement of Cash Flows
For Year Ended December 31, 2007

Cash flows from operations	$5,433
Cash flows from investing	(115)
Cash flows from financing	(5,339)
Net increase (decrease) in cash	(21)
Cash, beginning year	443
Cash, ending year	$ 422

2. Berkshire Hathaway is a larger company; its total assets are $273,160 million compared to Allstate's assets of $156,408 million. The income statements of the two companies are markedly different. Berkshire Hathaway reports more than three times as much revenue ($118,245 million compared to $36,769 million). The difference in net income is also large; Berkshire Hathaway earned $13,213 million whereas Allstate reported net income of only $4,636 million.

ANALYSIS OF FINANCIAL STATEMENTS

LO3 Explain and apply the basics of profitability analysis.

This section previews the analysis framework of this book. This framework is used extensively by market professionals who analyze financial reports to evaluate company management and value the company's debt and equity securities. Analysis of financial performance is crucial in assessing prior strategic decisions and evaluating strategic alternatives.

Return on Assets

Suppose we learn that a company reports a profit of $10 million. Does the $10 million profit indicate that the company is performing well? Knowing that a company reports a profit is certainly positive as it indicates that customers value its goods or services and that its revenues exceed expenses. However, we cannot assess how well it is performing without considering the context. To explain, suppose we learn that this company has $500 million in assets. We now assess the $10 million profit as low because relative to the size of its asset investment, the company earned a paltry 2% return, computed as $10 million divided by $500 million. A 2% return on assets is what a much lower-risk savings account might yield. The important point is that a company's profitability must be assessed with respect to the size of its investment. One common metric is the *return on assets* (ROA)—defined as net income for that period divided by the average assets for that period.

Components of Return on Assets

We can separate return on assets into two components: profitability and productivity. Profitability relates profit to sales. This ratio is called the *profit margin* (PM), and it reflects the net income (profit after tax) earned on each sales dollar. Management wants to earn as much profit as possible from sales.

Productivity relates sales to assets. This component, called *asset turnover* (AT), reflects sales generated by each dollar of assets. Management wants to maximize asset productivity, that is, to achieve the highest possible sales level for a given level of assets (or to achieve a given level of sales with the smallest level of assets).

Exhibit 1.7 depicts the disaggregation of return on assets into these two components. Profitability (PM) and productivity (AT) are multiplied to yield the return on assets (ROA). Average assets are commonly defined as (beginning-year assets + ending-year assets)/2.

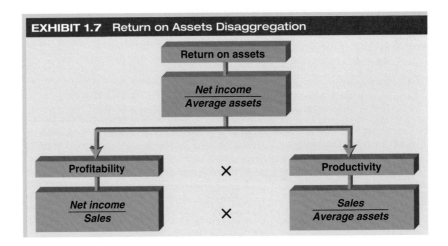

EXHIBIT 1.7 Return on Assets Disaggregation

There are an infinite number of combinations of profit margin and asset turnover that yield the same return on assets. To illustrate, Exhibit 1.8 graphs actual combinations of these two components for companies that we highlight in this book (each is identified by their ticker symbol). Retailers, like Costco (COST), Best Buy (BBY) and TJX Companies (TJX) are characterized by relatively low profit margins and a high turnover of their assets. The business models for other companies such as the pharmaceuticals [Johnson & Johnson (JNJ) and Pfizer (PFE)] require a larger investment in assets. These companies must earn a higher profit margin to yield an acceptable ROA. We might be surprised to see technology companies in the group with high asset investments. Technology companies typically maintain a high level of cash and short-term investments on their balance sheets, which allows them to respond quickly to opportunities. The solid line represents those profitability and productivity combinations that yield about a 10% return on assets.

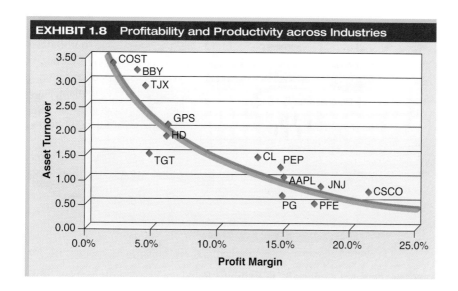

EXHIBIT 1.8 Profitability and Productivity across Industries

Return on Equity

Another important analysis measure is return on equity (ROE), which is defined as net income divided by average stockholders' equity, where average equity is commonly defined as (beginning-year equity + ending-year equity)/2. In this case, company earnings are compared to the level of stockholder (not total) investment. ROE reflects the return to stockholders, which is different from the return for the entire company (ROA).

MANAGERIAL DECISION **You Are the Chief Financial Officer**

You are reviewing your company's financial performance for the first six months of the year and are unsatisfied with the results. How can you disaggregate return on assets to identify areas for improvement? [Answer, p. 1-30]

FINANCIAL STATEMENTS AND BUSINESS ANALYSIS

Analysis and interpretation of financial statements must consider the broader business context in which a company operates. This section describes how to systematically consider those broader business forces to enhance our analysis and interpretation. This business analysis can sharpen our insights and help us better estimate future performance and company value.

LO4 Describe business analysis within the context of a competitive environment.

Analyzing the Competitive Environment

Financial statements are influenced by five important forces that confront the company and determine its competitive intensity: (A) industry competition, (B) buyer power, (C) supplier power, (D) product substitutes, and (E) threat of entry (for further discussion, see Porter, *Competitive Strategy: Techniques for Analyzing Industries and Competitors,* 1980 and 1998).

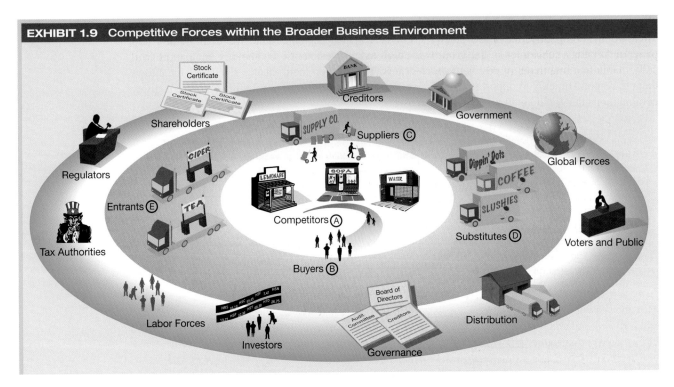

EXHIBIT 1.9 Competitive Forces within the Broader Business Environment

These five forces are depicted graphically in Exhibit 1.9 and are key determinants of profitability.

(A) **Industry competition** Competition and rivalry raise the cost of doing business as companies must hire and train competitive workers, advertise products, research and develop products, and engage in other related activities.

(B) **Bargaining power of buyers** Buyers with strong bargaining power can extract price concessions and demand a higher level of service and delayed payment terms; this force reduces both profits from sales and the operating cash flows to sellers.

(C) **Bargaining power of suppliers** Suppliers with strong bargaining power can demand higher prices and earlier payments, yielding adverse effects on profits and cash flows to buyers.

(D) **Threat of substitution** As the number of product substitutes increases, sellers have less power to raise prices and/or pass on costs to buyers; accordingly, threat of substitution places downward pressure on profits of sellers.

(E) **Threat of entry** New market entrants increase competition; to mitigate that threat, companies expend monies on activities such as new technologies, promotion, and human development to erect *barriers to entry* and to create *economies of scale*.

The broader business environment affects the level of profitability that a company can expect to achieve. Global economic forces and the quality and cost of labor affect the macroeconomy in which the company operates. Government regulation, borrowing agreements exacted by creditors, and internal governance procedures also affect the range of operating activities in which a company can engage. In addition, strategic plans are influenced by the oversight of equity markets, and investors are loathe to allow companies the freedom to manage for the longer term. Each of these external forces affects a company's strategic planning and expected level of profitability.

The relative strength of companies within their industries, and vis-à-vis suppliers and customers, is an important determinant of both their profitability and the structure of their balance sheets. As competition intensifies, profitability likely declines, and the amount of assets companies need to carry on their balance sheet likely increases in an effort to generate more profit. Such changes are revealed in the income statement and the balance sheet.

Applying Competitive Analysis

We apply the competitive analysis framework to help interpret the financial results of McLane Company. McLane is a subsidiary of Berkshire Hathaway and was acquired several years ago as explained in the following note to the Berkshire Hathaway annual report:

> On May 23, 2003, Berkshire acquired McLane Company, Inc., ("McLane") a distributor of grocery and food products to retailers, convenience stores and restaurants. Results of McLane's business operations are included in Berkshire's consolidated results beginning on that date. McLane's revenues in 2005 totaled $24.1 billion compared to $23.4 billion in 2004 and approximately $22.0 billion for the full year of 2003. Sales of grocery products increased about 5% in 2005 and were partially offset by lower sales to foodservice customers. McLane's business is marked by high sales volume and very low profit margins. Pretax earnings in 2005 of $217 million declined $11 million versus 2004. The gross margin percentage was relatively unchanged between years. However, the resulting increased gross profit was more than offset by higher payroll, fuel and insurance expenses. Approximately 33% of McLane's annual revenues currently derive from sales to Wal-Mart. Loss or curtailment of purchasing by Wal-Mart could have a material adverse impact on revenues and pre-tax earnings of McLane.

McLane is a wholesaler of food products; it purchases food products in finished and semifinished form from agricultural and food-related businesses and resells them to grocery and convenience food stores. The extensive distribution network required in this business entails considerable investment. Our business analysis of McLane's financial results includes the following observations:

- **Industry competitors** McLane has many competitors with food products that are difficult to differentiate.

- **Bargaining power of buyers** The note above reveals that 33% of McLane's sales are to Wal-Mart, which has considerable buying power that limits seller profits; also, the food industry is characterized by high turnover and low profit margins, which implies that cost control is key to success.

- **Bargaining power of suppliers** McLane is large ($24 billion in annual sales), which implies its suppliers are unlikely to exert forces to increase its cost of sales.

- **Threat of substitution** Grocery items are usually not well differentiated; this means the threat of substitution is high, which inhibits its ability to raise selling prices.

- **Threat of entry** High investment costs, such as warehousing and logistics, are a barrier to entry in McLane's business; this means the threat of entry is relatively low.

Our analysis reveals that McLane is a high-volume, low-margin company. Its ability to control costs is crucial to its financial performance, including its ability to fully utilize its assets. Evaluation of McLane's financial statements should focus on that dimension.

Analyzing the Broader Business Environment

Quality analysis depends on an effective business analysis. Before we analyze a single accounting number, we must ask questions about a company's business environment such as the following:

- *Life cycle* At what stage in its life is this company? Is it a startup, experiencing growing pains? Is it strong and mature, reaping the benefits of competitive advantages? Is it nearing the end of its life, trying to milk what it can from stagnant product lines?

- *Outputs* What products does it sell? Are its products new, established, or dated? Do its products have substitutes? How complicated are its products to produce?

- *Buyers* Who are its buyers? Are buyers in good financial condition? Do buyers have substantial purchasing power? Can the seller dictate sales terms to buyers?

- *Inputs* Who are its suppliers? Are there many supply sources? Does the company depend on a few supply sources with potential for high input costs?

- *Competition* In what kind of markets does it operate? Are markets open? Is the market competitive? Does the company have competitive advantages? Can it protect itself from new entrants? At what cost? How must it compete to survive?

- *Financing* Must it seek financing from public markets? Is it going public? Is it seeking to use its stock to acquire another company? Is it in danger of defaulting on debt covenants? Are there incentives to tell an overly optimistic story to attract lower cost financing or to avoid default on debt?

- *Labor* Who are its managers? What are their backgrounds? Can they be trusted? Are they competent? What is the state of employee relations? Is labor unionized?

- *Governance* How effective is its corporate governance? Does it have a strong and independent board of directors? Does a strong audit committee of the board exist, and is it populated with outsiders? Does management have a large portion of its wealth tied to the company's stock?

- *Risk* Is it subject to lawsuits from competitors or shareholders? Is it under investigation by regulators? Has it changed auditors? If so, why? Are its auditors independent? Does it face environmental and/or political risks?

We must assess the broader business context in which a company operates as we read and interpret its financial statements. A review of financial statements, which reflect business activities, cannot be undertaken in a vacuum. It is contextual and can only be effectively undertaken within the framework of a thorough understanding of the broader forces that impact company performance. We should view the above questions as a sneak preview of the types we will ask and answer throughout this book when we read and interpret financial statements.

MODULE-END REVIEW

Following are selected data from Progressive Corporation's 2007 10-K.

$ millions	2007
Sales	$14,687
Net income	1,183
Average assets	19,163
Average stockholders' equity	5,892

Required
a. Compute Progressive's return on assets. Disaggregate the ROA into its profitability and productivity components.
b. Compute Progressive's return on equity (ROE).

Solution
a. ROA = Net profit/Average assets = $1,183/$19,163 = 6.2%. The profitability component is Net profit/Sales = $1,183/$14,687 = 8.1%, and the productivity component is Sales/Average assets = $14,687/$19,163 = 0.77. Notice that 8.1% × 0.77 = 6.2%. Thus, the two components, when multiplied yield ROA.
b. ROE = Net income/Average stockholders' equity = $1,183/$5,892 = 20.1%.

APPENDIX 1A: Accessing SEC Filings using IDEA

All publicly traded companies are required to file various reports with the SEC, two of which are the 10-Q (quarterly financial statements) and the 10-K (annual financial statements). The SEC archives these reports in a system called IDEA, an acronym for interactive data electronic applications. Following is a brief tutorial to access these electronic filings. The SEC's Website is **http://www.sec.gov**.

1. Following is the opening screen. Click on IDEA (highlighted below)

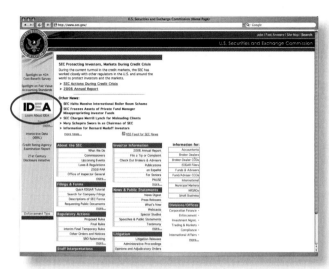

2. Click on company or fund name, ticker symbol, CIK (Central Index Key), file number, state, country, or SIC (Standard Industrial Classification)

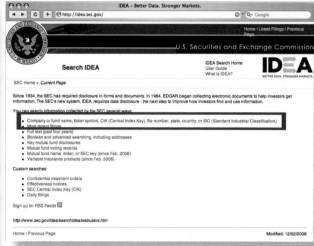

3. In Company name, type in the name of the company we are looking for. In this case, we are searching for Berkshire Hathaway. Then click enter.

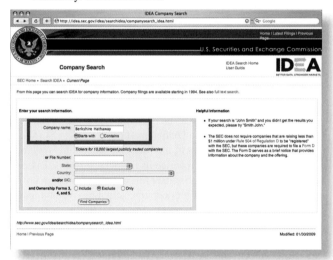

4. Several references to Berkshire appear. Click on the CIK (the SEC's numbering system) next to Berkshire Hathaway, Inc.

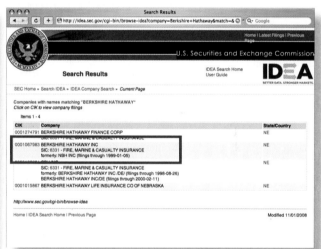

5. Enter the form number under "filing type" that we want to access. In this case we are looking for the 10-K.

6. Click on the document link for the year that we want to access.

7. Exhibits relating to Berkshire Hathaway's 10-K filing appear; click on the 10-K document.

8. The Berkshire Hathaway 10-K will open up; the file is searchable.

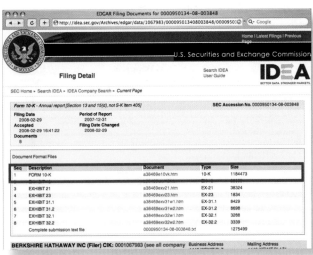

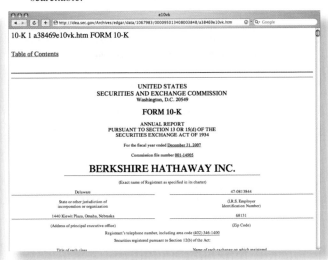

APPENDIX 1B: Accounting Principles and Governance

Financial Accounting Environment

LO5 Describe the accounting principles and regulations that frame financial statements.

Information in financial statements is crucial to valuing a company's debt and equity securities. Financial statement information can affect the price the market is willing to pay for the company's equity securities and interest rates attached to its debt securities.

The importance of financial statements means that their reliability is paramount. This includes the crucial role of ethics. To the extent that financial performance and condition are accurately communicated to business decision makers, debt and equity securities are more accurately priced. When securities are mis-priced, resources can be inefficiently allocated both within and across economies. Accurate, reliable financial statements are also important for the effective functioning of many other markets such as labor, input, and output markets.

To illustrate, recall the consequences of a breakdown in the integrity of the financial accounting system at Enron. Once it became clear that Enron had not faithfully and accurately reported its financial condition and performance, the market became unwilling to purchase Enron's securities. The value of its debt and equity securities dropped precipitously and the company was unable to obtain cash needed for operating activities. Within months of the disclosure of its financial accounting irregularities, Enron, with revenues of over $100 billion and total company value of over $60 billion, the fifth largest U.S. company, was bankrupt!

Further historical evidence of the importance of financial accounting is provided by the Great Depression of the 20th century. This depression was caused, in part, by the failure of companies to faithfully report their financial condition and performance.

Oversight of Financial Accounting

The stock market crash of 1929 and the ensuing Great Depression led Congress to pass the 1933 Securities Act. This act had two main objectives: (1) to require disclosure of financial and other information about securities being offered for public sale; and (2) to prohibit deceit, misrepresentations, and other fraud in the sale of securities. This act also required that companies register all securities proposed for public sale and disclose information about the securities being offered, including information about company financial condition and performance. This act became and remains a foundation for contemporary financial reporting.

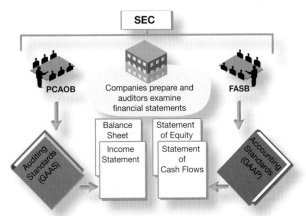

Congress also passed the 1934 Securities Exchange Act, which created the **Securities and Exchange Commission** (SEC) and gave it broad powers to regulate the issuance and trading of securities. The act also provides that companies with more than $10 million in assets and whose securities are held by more than 500 owners must file annual and other periodic reports, including financial statements that are available for download from the SEC's **IDEA** database (**www.sec.gov**).

The SEC has ultimate authority over U.S. financial reporting, including setting accounting standards for preparing financial statements. Since 1939, however, the SEC has looked primarily to the private sector to set accounting standards. One such private sector organization is the American Institute of Certified Public Accountants (AICPA), whose two committees, the Committee on Accounting Procedure (1939–59) and the Accounting Principles Board (1959–73), authored the initial body of accounting standards.

Currently, the **Financial Accounting Standards Board (FASB)** sets U.S. financial accounting standards. The FASB is an independent body overseen by a foundation, whose members include public accounting firms, investment managers, academics, and corporate managers. The FASB has published over 150 accounting standards governing the preparation of financial reports. This is in addition to over 40 standards that were written by predecessor organizations to the FASB, numerous bulletins and interpretations, Emerging Issues Task Force (EITF) statements, AICPA statements of position (SOP), and direct SEC guidance, along with speeches made by high-ranking SEC personnel, all of which form the body of accounting standards governing financial statements. Collectively, these pronouncements, rules and guidance create what is called **Generally Accepted Accounting Principles (GAAP).**

The standard-setting process is arduous, often lasting up to a decade and involving extensive comment by the public, public officials, accountants, academics, investors, analysts, and corporate preparers of financial reports. The reason for this involved process is that amendments to existing standards or the creation of new standards affect the reported financial performance and condition of companies. Consequently, given the widespread impact of financial accounting, there are considerable economic consequences as a result of accounting changes. To influence the standard-setting process, special interest groups often lobby members of Congress to pressure the SEC and, ultimately, the FASB, on issues about which constituents feel strongly.

Audits and Corporate Governance

Even though key executives must personally attest to the completeness and accuracy of company financial statements, markets demand further assurances from outside parties to achieve the level of confidence necessary to warrant investment, credit, and other business decisions. To that end, companies engage external auditors to provide an opinion about financial statements. Further, companies implement a system of checks and balances that monitor managers' actions, which is called *corporate governance*.

Audit Report

Financial statements for each publicly traded company must be audited by an independent audit firm. There are a number of large auditing firms that are authorized by the SEC to provide auditing services for companies that issue securities to the public: PriceWaterhouseCoopers, KPMG, Ernst & Young, Deloitte, RSM McGladrey, Grant Thornton, and BDO Seidman, to name a few. These firms provide opinions about financial statements for the large majority of publicly traded U.S. companies. A company's Board of Directors hires the auditors to review and express an opinion on its financial statements. The audit opinion expressed by Deloitte & Touche, LLP, on the financial statements of **Berkshire Hathaway** is reproduced in Exhibit 1.10.

The basic 'clean' audit report is consistent across companies and includes these assertions:

- Financial statements are management's responsibility. Auditor responsibility is to express an *opinion* on those statements.
- Auditing involves a sampling of transactions, not investigation of each transaction.
- Audit opinion provides *reasonable assurance* that the statements are free of *material* misstatements, not a guarantee.
- Auditors review accounting policies used by management and the estimates used in preparing the statements.
- Financial statements *present fairly, in all material respects* a company's financial condition, in conformity with GAAP.

If the auditor cannot make all of these assertions, the auditor cannot issue a clean opinion. Instead, the auditor issues a "qualified" opinion and states the reasons a clean opinion cannot be issued. Financial report readers should scrutinize with care both the qualified audit opinion and the financial statements themselves.

The audit opinion is not based on a test of each transaction. Instead, auditors usually develop statistical samples to make inferences about the larger set of transactions. The audit report is not a guarantee that no misstatements exist. Auditors only provide reasonable assurance that the statements are free of material misstatements. Their use of the word "reasonable" is deliberate, as they do not want to be held to an absolute standard should problems be subsequently uncovered. The word *material* is used in the sense that an item must be of sufficient magnitude to change the perceptions or decisions of the financial statement user (such as a decision to purchase stock or extend credit).

EXHIBIT 1.10 Audit Report for Berkshire Hathaway

To the Board of Directors and Shareholders, Berkshire Hathaway Inc.

We have audited the accompanying consolidated balance sheets of Berkshire Hathaway Inc. and subsidiaries (the "Company") as of December 31, 2007 and 2006, and the related consolidated statements of earnings, cash flows and changes in shareholders equity and comprehensive income for each of the three years in the period ended December 31, 2007. We also have audited the Company's internal control over financial reporting as of December 31, 2007, based on criteria established in *Internal Control— Integrated Framework* issued by the Committee of Sponsoring Organizations of the Treadway Commission. The Company's management is responsible for these financial statements, for maintaining effective internal control over financial reporting, and for its assessment of the effectiveness of internal control over financial reporting, included in the accompanying Management's Report on Internal Control over Financial Reporting. Our responsibility is to express an opinion on these financial statements and an opinion on the effectiveness of the Company's internal control over financial reporting based on our audits.

We conducted our audits in accordance with the standards of the Public Company Accounting Oversight Board (United States). Those standards require that we plan and perform the audit to obtain reasonable assurance about whether the financial statements are free of material misstatement and whether effective internal control over financial reporting was maintained in all material respects. Our audits of the financial statements included examining on a test basis, evidence supporting the amounts and disclosures in the financial statements. assessing the accounting principles used and significant estimates made by management, and evaluating the overall financial statement presentation. Our audit of internal control over financial reporting included obtaining an understanding of internal control over financial reporting, assessing the risk that a material weakness exists. and testing and evaluating the design and operating effectiveness of internal control based on the assessed risk. Our audits also included performing such other procedures as we considered necessary in the circumstances. We believe that our audits provide a reasonable basis for our opinions.

A company's internal control over financial reporting is a process designed by, or under the supervision of, the company's principal executive and principal financial officers, or persons performing similar functions, and effected by the company's board of directors, management, and other personnel to provide reasonable assurance regarding the reliability of financial reporting and the preparation of financial statements for external purposes in accordance with generally accepted accounting principles. A company's internal control over financial reporting includes those policies and procedures that (1) pertain to the maintenance of records that, in reasonable detail, accurately and fairly reflect the transactions and dispositions of the assets of the company: (2) provide reasonable assurance that transactions are recorded as necessary to permit preparation of financial statements in accordance with generally accepted accounting principles, and that receipts and expenditures of the company are being made only in accordance with authorizations of management and directors of the company. and (3) provide reasonable assurance regarding prevention or timely detection of unauthorized acquisition, use, or disposition of the company's assets that could have a material effect on the financial statements.

Because of the inherent limitations of internal control over financial reporting, including the possibility of collusion or improper management override of controls, material misstatements due to error or fraud may not be prevented or detected on a timely basis. Also, projections of any evaluation of the effectiveness of the internal control over financial reporting to future periods are subject to the risk that the controls may become inadequate because of changes in conditions, or that the degree of compliance with the policies or procedures may deteriorate.

In our opinion, the consolidated financial statements referred to above present fairly. in all material respects, the financial position of Berkshire Hathaway Inc. and subsidiaries as of December 31, 2007 and 2006, and the results of their operations and their cash flows for each of the three years in the period ended December 31, 2007, in conformity with accounting principles generally accepted in the United States of America. Also, in our opinion, the Company maintained, in all material respects, effective internal control over financial reporting as of December 31, 2007, based on the criteria established in *Internal Control—Integrated Framework* issued by the Committee of Sponsoring Organizations of the Treadway Commission.

As discussed in Note 1(r) to the consolidated financial statements, the Company changed its method of accounting for uncertainty in income taxes in 2007 and pension and other postretirement benefit plans in 2006.

DELOITTE & TOUCHE LLP

Omaha, Nebraska
February 29, 2008

The requirement of auditor independence is the cornerstone of effective auditing and is subject to debate because the company pays the auditor's fees. Regulators have questioned the perceived lack of independence of auditing firms and the degree to which declining independence compromises the ability of auditing firms to challenge a client's dubious accounting.

The Sarbanes-Oxley Act contained several provisions designed to encourage auditor independence:

1. It established the **Public Company Accounting Oversight Board** (PCAOB) to oversee the development of audit standards and to monitor the effectiveness of auditors,
2. It prohibits auditors from offering certain types of consulting services, and requires audit partners to rotate clients every five years, and
3. It requires audit committees to consist of independent members.

Audit Committee

Law requires each publicly traded company to have a board of directors, where stockholders elect each director. This board represents the company owners and oversees management. The board also hires the company's executive management and regularly reviews company operations.

The board of directors usually establishes several subcommittees to focus on particular governance tasks such as compensation, strategic plans, and financial management. Governance committees are commonplace. One of these, the audit committee, oversees the financial accounting system. Exhibit 1.11 illustrates a typical organization of a company's governance structure.

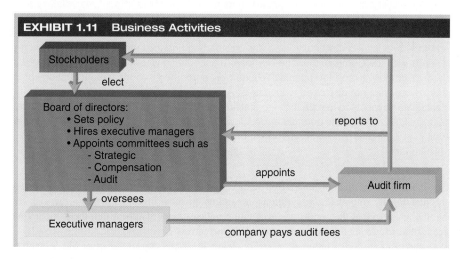

EXHIBIT 1.11 Business Activities

The audit committee must consist solely of outside directors, and cannot include the CEO. As part of its oversight of the financial accounting system, the audit committee focuses on **internal controls**, which are the policies and procedures used to protect assets, ensure reliable accounting, promote efficient operations, and urge adherence to company policies.

BUSINESS INSIGHT   Warren Buffett on Audit Committees

"Audit committees can't audit. Only a company's outside auditor can determine whether the earnings that a management purports to have made are suspect. Reforms that ignore this reality and that instead focus on the structure and charter of the audit committee will accomplish little. As we've discussed, far too many managers have fudged their company's numbers in recent years, using both accounting and operational techniques that are typically legal but that nevertheless materially mislead investors. Frequently, auditors knew about these deceptions. Too often, however, they remained silent. The key job of the audit committee is simply to get the auditors to divulge what they know. To do this job, the committee must make sure that the auditors worry more about misleading its members than about offending management. In recent years auditors have not felt that way. They have instead generally viewed the CEO, rather than the shareholders or directors, as their client. That has been a natural result of day-to-day working relationships and also of the auditors' understanding that, no matter what the board says, the CEO and CFO pay their fees and determine whether they are retained for both auditing and other work. The rules that have been recently instituted won't materially change this reality. What will break this cozy relationship is audit committees unequivocally putting auditors on the spot, making them understand they will become liable for major monetary penalties if they don't come forth with what they know or suspect."

—Warren Buffett, Berkshire Hathaway annual report

Regulatory and Legal Environment

The regulatory and legal environment provides further assurance that financial statements are complete and accurate.

SEC Enforcement Actions

Companies whose securities are issued to the public must file reports with the SEC (see **www.sec.gov**). One of these reports is the 10-K, which includes the annual financial statements (quarterly statements are filed on report 10-Q). The 10-K report provides more information than the company's glossy annual report, which is partly a marketing document (although the basic financial statements are identical). We prefer to use the 10-K because of its additional information.

The SEC has ultimate authority to accept or reject financial statements that companies submit. Should the SEC reject a company's financial statements, the company must restate and refile them. Restatements are time-consuming and publicly known, and restating companies typically see their stock market value slide. For example, in 2006, the SEC required Fannie Mae to restate its financial statements. The SEC commenced litigation, and the following excerpts are from the criminal complaint:

> The Federal National Mortgage Association engaged in a financial fraud involving multiple violations of Generally Accepted Accounting Principles ("GAAP") in connection with the preparation of its annual and quarterly financial statements. These violations had the effect, among other things, of falsely portraying stable earnings growth and reduced income statement volatility and, for year-ended 1998, of maximizing bonuses and achieving forecasted earnings. Between 1998 and 2004, Fannie Mae, a shareholder-owned government sponsored enterprise, misstated its results of operations and issued materially false and misleading financial statements in various reports and in filings with the Commission. The Company's accounting was inconsistent with GAAP. Additionally, the Company's reported financial results were smoothed through misapplications of GAAP. These practices were not disclosed to investors. As a direct result of these violations, and other errors, Fannie Mae expects to restate its historical financial statements for the years ended December 31, 2003 and 2002, and for the quarters ended June 30, 2004 and March 31, 2004. This restatement will result in at least a $1.1 billion reduction of previously reported net income.

The Commission's investigation uncovered numerous transactions over several years where Fannie Mae management intentionally smoothed out gyrations in earnings to show investors it was a low-risk company. In addition, the SEC charged that the company's accounting policies made it appear that the company had reached earnings targets, thus triggering the maximum possible bonus payout for executives.

Following this legal complaint, Fannie Mae's board of directors fired its senior management team, including its CEO and CFO. It also agreed to pay a $400 million penalty, restate its previously issued financial reports, reform its accounting policies, and institute stricter internal controls over its accounting procedures. Fannie Mae's stock (FNM) lost a third of its market value during the proceedings—see margin graph. The SEC's power to require restatement, with its consequent damage to company reputation and company stock price, is a major deterrent to those desiring to bias their financial accounts to achieve a particular goal.

Courts

Courts provide remedies to individuals and companies that suffer damages as a result of material misstatements in financial statements. Typical court actions involve shareholders who sue the company and its auditors, alleging that the company disclosed, and the auditors attested to, false and misleading financial statements. Shareholder lawsuits are chronically in the news; although, the number of such suits has declined in recent years. Stanford Law School's Securities Class Action Clearinghouse commented that "Two factors are likely responsible for the decline. First, lawsuits arising from the dramatic boom and bust of U.S. equities in the late 1990s and early 2000s are now largely behind us. Second, improved corporate governance in the wake of the Enron and WorldCom frauds likely reduced the actual incidence of fraud." Nevertheless, courts continue to wield considerable power. For example, the SEC and the New York District Attorney successfully brought suit against Adelphia Communications Corporation and its owners on behalf of the U.S. Government and numerous investors, creditors, employees and others affiliated with the company. The press release announcing the settlement read, in part:

Washington, D.C., April 25, 2005—The Securities and Exchange Commission today announced that it and the United States Attorney's Office for the Southern District of New York (USAO) reached an agreement to settle a civil enforcement action and resolve criminal charges against Adelphia Communications Corporation, its founder John J. Rigas, and his three sons, Timothy J. Rigas, Michael J. Rigas and James P. Rigas, in one of the most extensive financial frauds ever to take place at a public company.

In its complaint, the Commission charged that Adelphia, at the direction of the individual defendants: (1) fraudulently excluded billions of dollars in liabilities from its consolidated financial statements by hiding them on the books of off-balance sheet affiliates; (2) falsified operating statistics and inflated earnings to meet Wall Street estimates; and (3) concealed rampant self-dealing by the Rigas family, including the undisclosed use of corporate funds for purchases of Adelphia stock and luxury condominiums.

Mark K. Schonfeld, Director of the SEC's Northeast Regional Office, said, "This settlement agreement presents a strong, coordinated approach by the SEC and the U.S. Attorney's Office to resolving one of the most complicated and egregious financial frauds committed at a public company. The settlement provides an expedient and effective way to provide victims of Adelphia's fraud with a substantial recovery while at the same time enabling Adelphia to emerge from Chapter 11 bankruptcy."

The settlement terms of this action, and related criminal actions against the Rigas family, resulted in the following:

- Rigas family members forfeited in excess of $1.5 billion in assets derived from the fraud; the funds were used, in part, to establish a fund for the fraud victims.
- Rigas family members were barred from acting as officers or directors of a public company.
- John Rigas, the 80-year-old founder of Adelphia Communications, was sentenced to 15 years in prison; he applied for a Presidential pardon in January 2009 but was denied.
- Timothy Rigas, the ex-finance chief, was sentenced to 20 years and is currently serving time at a federal correctional complex in North Carolina.

GUIDANCE ANSWERS

MANAGERIAL DECISION **You Are the Product Manager**

As a manager, you must balance two conflicting objectives—namely, mandatory disclosure requirements and your company's need to protect its competitive advantages. You must comply with all minimum required disclosure rules. The extent to which you offer additional disclosures depends on the sensitivity of the information; that is, how beneficial it is to your existing and potential competitors. Another consideration is how the information disclosed will impact your existing and potential investors. Disclosures such as this can be beneficial in that they inform investors and others about your company's successful investments. Still, there are many stakeholders impacted by your disclosure decision and each must be given due consideration.

MANAGERIAL DECISION **You Are the Chief Financial Officer**

Financial performance is often measured by return on assets, which can be disaggregated into the profit margin (profit after tax/sales) and the asset turnover (sales/average assets). This disaggregation might lead you to review factors affecting profitability (gross margins and expense control) and to assess how effectively your company is utilizing its assets (the turnover rates). Finding ways to increase profitability for a given level of investment or to reduce the amount of invested capital while not adversely impacting profitability contributes to improved financial performance.

Superscript ^A(B) denotes assignments based on Appendix 1A (1B).

DISCUSSION QUESTIONS

Q1-1. A firm's planning activities motivate and shape three types of business activities. List the three activities. Describe how financial statements can provide useful information for each activity. How can subsequent financial statements be used to evaluate the success of each of the activities?

Q1-2. The accounting equation (Assets = Liabilities + Equity) is a fundamental business concept. Explain what this equation reveals about a company's sources and uses of funds and the claims on company resources.

Q1-3. Companies prepare four primary financial statements. What are those financial statements and what information is typically conveyed in each?

Q1-4. Does a balance sheet report on a period of time or at a point in time? Explain the information conveyed in the balance sheet.

Q1-5. Does an income statement report on a period of time or at a point in time? Explain the information conveyed in the income statement.

Q1-6. Does a statement of cash flows report on a period of time or at a point in time? Explain the information and activities conveyed in the statement of cash flows.

Q1-7. Explain how a company's four primary financial statements are linked.

Q1-8. Financial statements are used by several interested stakeholders. List three or more potential external users of financial statements. Explain how each constituent on your list might use financial statement information in their decision making process.

Q1-9. What ethical issues might managers face in dealing with confidential information?

Procter & Gamble (PG)   **Q1-10.**^{A} Access the 2008 10-K for Procter & Gamble at the SEC's IDEA database of financial reports (**www.sec.gov**). Who is P&G's auditor? What specific language does the auditor use in expressing its opinion and what responsibilities does it assume?

Q1-11.^{B} Business decision makers external to the company increasingly demand more financial information from companies. Discuss the reasons why companies have traditionally opposed the efforts of regulatory agencies like the SEC to require more disclosure.

Q1-12.^{B} What are generally accepted accounting principles and what organizations presently establish them?

Enron   **Q1-13.**^{B} Corporate governance has received considerable attention since the collapse of Enron and other accounting-related scandals. What is meant by corporate governance? What are the primary means by which sound corporate governance is achieved?

Q1-14.^{B} What is the primary function of the auditor? In your own words, describe what an audit opinion says.

Q1-15. Describe a decision that requires financial statement information, other than a stock investment decision. How is financial statement information useful in making this decision?

Q1-16. Users of financial statement information are vitally concerned with the company's strategic direction. Despite their understanding of this need for information, companies are reluctant to supply it. Why? In particular, what costs are companies concerned about?

Q1-17. One of Warren Buffett's acquisition criteria is to invest in businesses "earning good return on equity." The return on equity (ROE) formula uses both net income and stockholders' equity. Why is it important to relate net income to stockholders' equity? Why isn't it sufficient to merely concentrate on companies with the highest net income?

Q1-18. One of Warren Buffett's acquisition criteria is to invest in businesses "earning good return on equity, while employing little or no debt." Why is Buffett concerned about debt?

Assignments with the WebAssign logo in the margin are available in WebAssign.
See the Preface of the book for details.

MINI EXERCISES

Dell, Inc. (DELL)   **M1-19. Relating Financing and Investing Activities (LO2)**
In a recent year, the total assets of Dell, Inc. equal $27,561 million and its equity is $3,735 million. What is the amount of its liabilities? Does Dell receive more financing from its owners or nonowners? What percentage of financing is provided by Dell's owners?

Best Buy (BBY)   **M1-20. Relating Financing and Investing Activities (LO2)**
In a recent year, the total assets of Best Buy equal $8,652 million and its liabilities equal $5,230 million. What is the amount of Best Buy's equity? Does Best Buy receive more financing from its owners or nonowners? What percentage of financing is provided by its owners?

M1-21. **Applying the Accounting Equation and Computing Financing Proportions** **(LO2)**

WebAssign.

Use the accounting equation to compute the missing financial amounts (a), (b), and (c). Which of these companies is more owner-financed? Which of these companies is more nonowner-financed? Discuss why the proportion of owner financing might differ across these three businesses.

($ millions)	Assets	=	Liabilities	+	Equity	
Hewlett-Packard.............	$113,331	=	$74,389	+	$ (a)	Hewlett-Packard (HPQ)
General Mills................	$ 19,110	=	$ (b)	+	$ 5,295	General Mills (GIS)
Target.....................	$ (c)	=	$33,461	+	$13,580	Target (TGT)

M1-22.[A] **Identifying Key Numbers from Financial Statements** **(LO2)**

Access the September 28, 2008, 10-K for Starbucks Corporation at the SEC's IDEA database for financial reports (**www.sec.gov**). What did Starbucks report for total assets, liabilities, and equity at September 28, 2008? Confirm that the accounting equation holds. What percent of Starbucks' assets is financed by nonowners?

Starbucks (SBUX)

M1-23.[A] **Verifying Linkages Between Financial Statements** **(LO2)**

Access the 2007 10-K for DuPont at the SEC's IDEA database of financial reports (**www.sec.gov**). Using its December 31, 2007, consolidated statement of stockholders' equity, prepare a table to reconcile the opening and ending balances of its retained (reinvested) earnings for 2007 by showing the activity in the account during the year.

E. I. DuPont de Nemours (DD)

M1-24. **Identifying Financial Statement Line Items and Accounts** **(LO2)**

WebAssign.

Several line items and account titles are listed below. For each, indicate in which of the following financial statement(s) we would likely find the item or account: income statement (IS), balance sheet (BS), statement of stockholders' equity (SE), or statement of cash flows (SCF).

a.	Cash asset	d.	Contributed capital	g.	Cash inflow for stock issued
b.	Expenses	e.	Cash outflow for capital expenditures	h.	Cash outflow for dividends
c.	Noncash assets	f.	Retained earnings	i.	Net income

M1-25. **Identifying Ethical Issues and Accounting Choices** **(LO5)**

Assume that you are a technology services provider and you must decide on whether to record revenue from the installation of computer software for one of your clients. Your contract calls for acceptance of the software by the client within six months of installation. According to the contract, you will be paid only when the client "accepts" the installation. Although you have not yet received your client's formal acceptance, you are confident that it is forthcoming. Failure to record these revenues will cause your company to miss Wall Street's earnings estimates. What stakeholders will be affected by your decision and how might they be affected?

M1-26.[B] **Understanding Internal Controls and Their Importance** **(LO5)**

The **Sarbanes-Oxley Act** legislation requires companies to report on the effectiveness of their internal controls. The SEC administers the Sarbanes-Oxley Act, and defines internal controls as follows:

> "A process designed by, or under the supervision of, the registrant's principal executive and principal financial officers . . . to provide reasonable assurance regarding the reliability of financial reporting and the preparation of financial statements for external purposes in accordance with generally accepted accounting principles."

Why would Congress believe that internal controls are such an important area to monitor and report on?

EXERCISES

E1-27. **Composition of Accounts on the Balance Sheet** **(LO2)**

Answer the following questions about the Target balance sheet.

Target (TGT)

a. Accounts Receivable comprises a large proportion of its total assets. Why would a retailer such as Target report accounts receivable on its balance sheet?

b. Briefly describe the types of assets that Target is likely to include in its inventory.

c. What kinds of assets would Target likely include in its Property, Plant and Equipment?

d. Target reports about two-thirds of its total assets as long-term. Given Target's business model, why do we see it report a relatively high proportion of long-term assets?

WebAssign. ♪ E1-28. Applying the Accounting Equation and Assessing Financial Statement Linkages (LO2)

Answer the following questions. (*Hint*: Apply the accounting equation.)

Intel (INTC)

a. Intel had assets equal to $50,715 million and liabilities equal to $11,627 million for a recent year-end. What was Intel's total equity at year-end? Why would we expect a company like Intel to report a relatively high proportion of equity vis-á-vis liabilities?

JetBlue (JBLU)

b. At the beginning of a recent year, JetBlue's assets were $5,598 million and its equity was $1,036 million. During the year, assets increased $486 million and liabilities increased $241 million. What was JetBlue's equity at the end of the year?

c. What balance sheet account provides the link between the balance sheet and the income statement? Briefly describe how this linkage works.

E1-29. Specifying Financial Information Users and Uses (LO1)

Financial statements have a wide audience of interested stakeholders. Identify two or more financial statement users that are external to the company. For each user on your list, specify two questions that could be addressed with financial statement information.

౩ E1-30. Applying Financial Statement Relations to Compute Dividends (LO2)

Colgate-Palmolive (CL)

Colgate-Palmolive reports the following dollar balances in its retained earnings account.

($ millions)	2007	2006
Retained earnings	$10,627.5	$9,643.7

During 2007, Colgate-Palmolive reported net income of $1,737.4 million. What amount of dividends, if any, did Colgate-Palmolive pay to its shareholders in 2007? What percent of its net income did Colgate-Palmolive pay out in 2007?

E1-31. Computing and Interpreting Financial Statement Ratios (LO3)

Colgate-Palmolive (CL)

Following are selected ratios of Colgate-Palmolive for 2007 and 2006.

Return on Assets (ROA) Component	2007	2006
Profitability (Net income/Sales)	13%	11%
Productivity (Sales/Average net assets).	1.43	1.39

a. Was the company profitable in 2007? What evidence do you have of this?

b. Is the change in productivity (asset turnover) a positive development? Explain.

c. Compute the company's return on assets (ROA) for 2007 (show computations).

౩ E1-32. Computing Return on Assets and Applying the Accounting Equation (LO3)

Nordstrom, Inc. (JWN)

Nordstrom, Inc., reports net income of $715 million for its fiscal year ended January 2008. At the beginning of that fiscal year, Nordstrom had $4,822 million in total assets. By fiscal year-end 2008, total assets had grown to $5,600 million. What is Nordstrom's return on assets (ROA)?

E1-33. Assessing the Role of Financial Statements in Society (LO1)

Financial statement information plays an important role in modern society and business.

a. Identify two or more external stakeholders that are interested in a company's financial statements and what their particular interests are.

b. What are *generally accepted accounting principles*? What organizations have primary responsibility for the formulation of GAAP?

c. What role does financial statement information play in the allocation of society's financial resources?

d. What are three aspects of the accounting environment that can create ethical pressure on management?

E1-34. Computing Return on Equity (L03)

Starbucks reports net income for 2008 of $315.5 million. Its stockholders' equity is $2,490.9 million and $2,284.1 million for 2008 and 2007, respectively.

Starbucks (SBUX)

a. Compute its return on equity for 2008.

b. Starbucks repurchased over $311 million of its common stock in 2008. How did this repurchase affect Starbucks' ROE?

c. Why do you think a company like Starbucks repurchases its own stock?

PROBLEMS

P1-35. Computing Return on Equity and Return on Assets (L03)

The following table contains financial statement information for IBM Corporation.

WebAssign.

IBM Corp. (IBM)

($ millions)	Total Assets	Net Income	Sales	Equity
2005	$105,748	$ 7,934	$91,134	$33,098
2006	103,234	9,492	91,424	28,506
2007	120,431	10,418	98,786	28,470

Required

a. Compute the return on equity (ROE) for 2006 and 2007. What trend, if any, is evident? How does IBM's ROE compare with the approximately 19% median ROE for companies in the Dow Jones Industrial average for 2007?

b. Compute the return on assets (ROA) for 2006 through 2007. What trends, if any, are evident? How does IBM's ROA compare with the approximate 7.5% median ROA for companies in the Dow Jones Industrial average for 2007?

c. What factors might allow a company like IBM to reap above-average returns?

P1-36. Formulating Financial Statements from Raw Data (L02)

Following is selected financial information from General Mills, Inc., for its fiscal year ended May 25, 2008 ($ millions).

WebAssign.

General Mills, Inc. (GIS)

Revenue	$13,652.1
Cash from operating activities	1,729.9
Cash, beginning year	417.1
Total equity	6,215.8
Noncash assets	18,380.6
Cash from financing activities	(1,043.6)
Cost of goods sold	8,778.3
Total expenses (other than cost of goods sold)	3,579.1
Cash, end of year	661.0
Total liabilities	12,825.8
Cash from investing activities	(442.4)

Required

a. Prepare the income statement, the balance sheet, and the statement of cash flows for General Mills for the fiscal year ended May 2008.

b. Do the negative amounts for cash from investing activities and cash from financing activities concern us? Explain.

c. Using the statements prepared for part *a*, compute the following ratios (for this part only, use the year-end balance instead of the average for assets and stockholders' equity):
  i. Profit margin
  ii. Turnover of total assets
  iii. Return on assets
  iv. Return on equity

P1-37. Formulating Financial Statements from Raw Data (L02)

Following is selected financial information from Abercrombie & Fitch for its fiscal year ended February 2, 2008 ($ millions).

Abercrombie & Fitch (ANF)

Noncash assets	$2,449.6
Total expenses (other than cost of goods sold)	2,035.6
Cash from investing activities.	(500.2)
Cash, ending year	118.0
Revenue	3,749.8
Total liabilities	949.3
Cash from operating activities	817.8
Cash from financing activities	(281.6)
Cost of goods sold.	1,238.5
Cash, beginning year	82.0
Total equity	1,618.3

Required

a. Prepare the income statement, the balance sheet, and the statement of cash flows for Abercrombie & Fitch for the fiscal year ended February 2008.

b. Do the negative amounts for cash from investing activities and cash from financing activities concern us? Explain.

c. Using the statements prepared for part *a*, compute the following ratios (for this part only, use the year-end balance instead of the average for assets and stockholders' equity):
    i. Profit margin
    ii. Turnover of total assets
    iii. Return on assets
    iv. Return on equity

P1-38. Formulating Financial Statements from Raw Data (LO2)

Cisco Systems, Inc. (CSCO)

Following is selected financial information from Cisco Systems, Inc., for the year ended July 30, 2008 ($ millions).

Cash, ending year	$ 5,191
Cash from operating activities	12,089
Sales.	39,540
Stockholders' equity	34,402
Cost of goods sold.	14,056
Cash used in financing activities	(6,433)
Total liabilities	24,332
Total expense (other than cost of goods sold)	17,432
Noncash assets	53,543
Cash used in investing activities	(4,193)
Net income.	8,052
Cash, beginning year	3,728

Required

a. Prepare the income statement, the balance sheet, and the statement of cash flows for Cisco Systems for the fiscal year ended July 30, 2008.

b. Do the negative amounts for cash from investing activities and cash from financing activities concern us? Explain.

c. Using the statements prepared for part *a*, compute the following ratios (for this part only, use the year-end balance instead of the average for assets and stockholders' equity):
    i. Profit margin
    ii. Asset turnover
    iii. Return on assets
    iv. Return on equity

P1-39. Formulating a Statement of Stockholders' Equity from Raw Data (LO2)

Crocker Corporation began calendar-year 2009 with stockholders' equity of $100,000, consisting of contributed capital of $70,000 and retained earnings of $30,000. During 2009, it issued additional stock for total cash proceeds of $30,000. It also reported $50,000 of net income, and paid $25,000 as a cash dividend to shareholders.

Required

Prepare the 2009 statement of stockholders' equity for Crocker Corporation.

P1-40. **Formulating a Statement of Stockholders' Equity from Raw Data** **(LO2)**

EA Systems, Inc., reports the following selected information at December 31, 2009 ($ millions).

Contributed capital, December 31, 2008 and 2009	$ 550
Retained earnings, December 31, 2008	2,437
Cash dividends, 2009	281
Net income, 2009	859

Required

Use this information to prepare the statement of stockholders' equity for EA Systems, Inc., for 2009.

P1-41. **Computing, Analyzing, and Interpreting Return on Equity** **(LO3)**

Following are summary financial statement data for Kimberly-Clark for 2003 through 2007.

Kimberly-Clark (KMB)

KIMBERLY-CLARK CORPORATION (KMB)				
($ millions)	Total Assets	Net Income	Sales	Equity
2003	$16,779.9	$1,694.2	$14,026.3	$6,766.3
2004	17,018.0	1,800.2	15,083.2	6,629.5
2005	16,303.2	1,568.3	15,902.6	5,558.2
2006	17,067.0	1,499.5	16,746.9	6,097.4
2007	18,439.7	1,822.9	18,266.0	5,223.7

Required

a. Compute the return on assets and return on equity for 2003–2007, together with the components of ROA (profit margin and asset turnover). What trends do we observe? Which component appears to be driving the change in ROA over this time period?

b. KMB repurchased a large amount of its common shares over the past three years at a cost of over $5 billion. How did this repurchase affect its return on equity?

P1-42. **Computing, Analyzing, and Interpreting Return on Equity** **(LO3)**

Following are summary financial statement data for Procter & Gamble for 2004 through 2008.

Procter & Gamble (PG)

($ millions)	Total Assets	Net Income	Sales	Equity
2004	$ 57,048	$ 6,156	$51,407	$17,278
2005	61,527	6,923	56,741	18,475
2006	135,695	8,684	68,222	62,908
2007	138,014	10,340	76,476	66,760
2008	143,992	12,075	83,503	69,494

Required

a. Compute return on assets and return on equity for each year 2005 through 2008, together with the components of ROA (profit margin and asset turnover). What trends, if any, do we observe? Which component, if any, appears to be driving the change in ROA over this time period?

b. Procter & Gamble acquired Gillette Company in fiscal 2006 for $53 billion. How did this acquisition affect the ratios we computed in part *a*?

c. Procter & Gamble repurchased a large amount of its common shares during 2006 through 2008 at a cost of over $32 billion. How did this repurchase affect its return on equity?

P1-43. **Computing, Analyzing, and Interpreting Return on Equity** **(LO3)**

Nokia manufactures, markets, and sells phones and other electronics. Total stockholders' equity for Nokia is €17,338 in 2007 and €12,060 in 2006. In 2007, Nokia reported net income of €7,205 on sales of €51,058.

Nokia (NOK)

Required

a. What is Nokia's return on equity for 2007?

b. What are total expenses for Nokia in 2007?

c. Nokia used cash to repurchase a large amount of its common stock during the period 2005 through 2007. What motivations might Nokia have for repurchasing its common stock?

P1-44.   Comparing Abercrombie & Fitch and TJX Companies   (LO3)

Following are selected financial statement data from Abercrombie & Fitch (ANF—upscale clothing retailer) and TJX Companies (TJX—value priced clothing retailer including TJ Maxx)—both dated the end of January 2008.

($ millions)	Company	Total Assets	Net Income	Sales
2007	TJX Companies Inc...........	$6,086	$738	$17,405
2008	TJX Companies Inc...........	6,600	772	18,647
2007	Abercombie & Fitch	2,248	422	3,318
2008	Abercombie & Fitch	2,568	476	3,750

Required

a.   Compute the return on assets for both companies for the year ended January 2008.
b.   Disaggregate the ROAs for both companies into the profit margin and asset turnover.
c.   What differences are observed? Evaluate these differences in light of the two companies' business models. Which company has better financial performance?

P1-45.   Computing and Interpreting Return on Assets and Its Components   (LO3)

McDonald's Corporation (MCD) reported the following balance sheet and income statement data for 2005 through 2007.

($ millions)	Total Assets	Net Income	Sales
2005	$29,989	$2,602	$19,117
2006	28,975	3,544	20,895
2007	29,392	2,395	22,787

Required

a.   What is MCD's return on assets? Decompose MCD's ROA into its net profit margin and its asset turnover.
b.   What factor is mainly responsible for the decrease in MCD's ROA over this two-year period?

P1-46.   Disaggregating Return on Assets over Multiple Periods   (LO3)

Following are selected financial statement data from 3M Company for 2003 through 2007.

($ millions)	Total Assets	Net Income	Sales
2003	$17,600	$2,403	$18,232
2004	20,708	2,841	20,011
2005	20,541	3,111	21,167
2006	21,294	3,851	22,923
2007	24,694	4,096	24,462

Required

a.   Compute 3M Company's return on assets for 2004 through 2007. Disaggregate 3M's ROA into the profit margin and asset turnover for 2004 through 2007. What trends do we observe?
b.   Which ROA component appears to be driving the trend observed in part a? Explain.

P1-47.ᴬ   Reading and Interpreting Audit Opinions   (LO5)

Apple, Inc.'s 2008 financial statements include the following audit report from KPMG LLP.

REPORT OF INDEPENDENT REGISTERED PUBLIC ACCOUNTING FIRM

To the Board of Directors and Shareholders, Apple, Inc.:

We have audited the accompanying consolidated balance sheets of Apple Inc. and subsidiaries (the Company) as of September 27, 1008, and September 29, 2007, and the related consolidated statements of operations, shareholders' equity, and cash flows for each the years in the three-year period ended September 27, 2008. These consolidated financial statements are the responsibility of the Company's management. Our responsibility is to express an opinion on these consolidated financial statements based on our audits.

We conducted our audits in accordance with the standards of the Public Company Accounting Oversight Board (United States). Those standards require that we plan and perform the audit

continued

continued from prior page

to obtain reasonable assurance about whether the financial statements are free of material misstatement. An audit includes examining, on a test basis, evidence supporting the amounts and disclosures in the financial statements. An audit also includes assessing the accounting principles used and significant estimates made by management, as well as evaluating the overall financial statement presentation. We believe that our audits provide a reasonable basis for our opinion.

In our opinion, the consolidated finical statements referred to above present fairly, in all material respects, the financial position of Apple Inc. and subsidiaries as of September 27, 2008, and September 29, 2007, and the results of their operations and their cash flows for each of the years in the three-year period ended September 27, 2008, in conformity with U.S. generally accepted accounting principles.

As discussed in note 1 to the Consolidated Financial Statements, effective September 30, 2007, the Company adopted Financial Accounting Standards Board Interpretation No. 48, *Accounting for Uncertainty in Income Taxes—an interpretation of FASB Statement No. 109.*

We also have audited, in accordance with the standards of the Public Company Accounting Oversight Board (United States), Apple Inc.'s internal control over financial reporting as of September 27, 2008, based on criteria established in *Internal Control—Integrated Framework* issued by the Committee of Sponsoring Organizations of the Teadway Commission (COSO), and our report dated November 4, 2008, expressed and unqualified opinion on the effectiveness of the Company's internal control over financial reporting.

/s/ KPMG LLP
Mountain View, California
November 4, 2008

Required

a.   To whom is the report addressed? Why?

b.   In your own words, briefly describe the audit process. What steps do auditors take to determine whether a company's financial statements are free from material misstatement?

c.   What is the nature of KPMG's opinion? What do you believe the word *fairly* means? Is KPMG providing a guarantee to Apple's financial statement users?

d.   What other opinion is KPMG rendering? Why is this opinion important?

P1-48.   Reading and Interpreting CEO Certifications   (LO5)

Following is the CEO Certification required by the Sarbanes-Oxley Act and signed by Apple CEO Steve Jobs. Apple's Chief Financial Officer signed a similar form.   Apple, Inc. (AAPL)

CERTIFICATIONS

I, Steven P. Jobs, certify that:

1.   I have reviewed this annual report on Form 10-K of Apple, Inc.;

2.   Based on my knowledge, this report does not contain any untrue statement of a material fact or omit to state a material fact necessary to make the statements made, in light of the circumstances under which such statements were made, not misleading with respect to the period covered by this report;

3.   Based on my knowledge, the financial statements, and other financial information included in this report, fairly present in all material respects the financial condition, results of operations and cash flows of the registrant as of, and for, the periods presented in this report;

4.   The registrant's other certifying officer(s) and I are responsible for establishing and maintaining disclosure controls and procedures (as defined in Exchange Act Rules l3a-l5(e) and 15d-l5(e)) and internal control over financial reporting (as defined in Exchange Act Rules 13a-15(f) and 15d-15(f) for the registrant) and have:

(a) Designed such disclosure controls and procedures, or caused such disclosure controls and procedures to be designed under our supervision, to ensure that material information relating to the registrant, including its consolidated subsidiaries, is made known to us by others within those entities, particularly during the period in which this report is being prepared;

continued

continued from prior page

(b) Designed such internal control over financial reporting, or caused such internal control over financial reporting to be designed under our supervision, to provide reasonable assurance regarding the reliability of financial reporting and the preparation of financial statements for external purposes in accordance with generally accepted accounting principles;

(c) Evaluated the effectiveness of the registrant's disclosure controls and procedures and presented in this report our conclusions about the effectiveness of the disclosure controls and procedures, as of the end of the period covered by this report based on such evaluation; and

(d) Disclosed in this report any change in the registrant's internal control over financial reporting that occurred during the registrant's most recent fiscal quarter (the registrant's fourth fiscal quarter in the case of an annual report) that has materially affected, or is reasonably likely to materially affect, the registrant's internal control over financial reporting; and

5. The registrant's other certifying officer(s) and I have disclosed, based on our most recent evaluation of internal control over financial reporting, to the registrant's auditors and the audit committee of the registrant's board of directors (or persons performing the equivalent functions):

(a) All significant deficiencies and material weaknesses in the design or operation of internal control over financial reporting which are reasonably likely to adversely affect the registrant's ability to record, process, summarize, and report financial information; and

(b) Any fraud, whether or not material, that involves management or other employees who have a significant role in the registrant's internal control over financial reporting.

Date: November 4, 2008

By: /s/ STEVEN P. JOBS
Steven P. Jobs
Chief Executive Officer

Required

a. Summarize the assertions that Steve Jobs made in this certification.

b. Why did Congress feel it important that CEOs and CFOs sign such certifications?

c. What potential liability do you believe the CEO and CFO are assuming by signing such certifications?

P1-49. **Assessing Corporate Governance and Its Effects** **(LO5)**

General Electric (GE)

Review the corporate governance section of General Electric's Website (find and click on: "Our Company"; then, find and click on: "Governance").

Required

a. In your words, briefly describe GE's governance structure.

b. What is the main purpose of its governance structure?

MANAGEMENT APPLICATIONS

MA1-50. **Strategic Financing** **(LO2)**

You and your management team are working to develop the strategic direction of your company for the next three years. One issue you are discussing is how to finance the projected increases in operating assets. Your options are to rely more heavily on operating creditors, borrow the funds, or to sell additional stock in your company. Discuss the pros and cons of each source of financing.

MA1-51. **Statement Analysis** **(LO3)**

You are evaluating your company's recent operating performance and are trying to decide on the relative weights you should put on the income statement, the balance sheet, and the statement of cash flows. Discuss the information each of these statements provides and its role in evaluating operating performance.

MA1-52. **Analyst Relations** **(LO2)**

Your investor relations department reports to you that stockholders and financial analysts evaluate the quality of a company's financial reports based on their "transparency," namely the clarity and completeness of the company's financial disclosures. Discuss the trade-offs of providing more or less transparent financial reports.

3 **MA1-53.** **Ethics and Governance: Management Communications** **(LO5)**

The Business Insight box on page 1-13 quotes Warren Buffett on the use of accounting jargon. Many companies publicly describe their performance using terms such as "EBITDA" or "earnings purged of various expenses" because they believe these terms more effectively reflect their companies' performance than GAAP-defined terms such as net income. What ethical issues might arise from the use of such terms and what challenges does their use present for the governance of the company by shareholders and directors?

MA1-54.[B] **Ethics and Governance: Auditor Independence** **(LO5)**

The SEC has been concerned with the "independence" of external auditing firms. It is especially concerned about how large non-audit (such as consulting) fees might impact how aggressively auditing firms pursue accounting issues they uncover in their audits. Congress recently passed legislation that prohibits accounting firms from providing both consulting and auditing services to the same client. How might consulting fees affect auditor independence? What other conflicts of interest might exist for auditors? How do these conflicts impact the governance process?

Module Two

Introducing Financial Statements and Transaction Analysis

LEARNING OBJECTIVES

LO1 Describe information conveyed by the financial statements. (p. 2-3)

LO2 Explain and illustrate linkages among the four financial statements. (p. 2-20)

LO3 Illustrate use of the financial statement effects template to summarize accounting transactions. (p. 2-22)

APPLE

In 1985, the board of directors of Apple along with the new CEO John Sculley, dismissed Steve Jobs, Apple's co-founder. Fast forward 12 years—Apple is struggling to survive. After a series of crippling financial losses, the company's stock price is at an all-time low. In a complete about-face, the board asks Steve Jobs to return as interim CEO to begin a critical restructuring of the company's product line. True to form, Jobs shows up at his first meeting with Apple senior executives wearing shorts, sneakers, and a few days' beard growth. Sitting in a swivel chair and spinning slowly, Jobs begins quizzing the executives. "O.K., tell me what's wrong with this place," asks Jobs. Mumbled replies and embarrassed looks ensue. Jobs cuts them short and jumps up: "It's the products! So what's wrong with the products?" Again, more weak answers and again Jobs cut them off. "The products SUCK!" he roars. "There's no sex in them anymore!"

Jobs was right—Apple was mired in a sea of problems, many stemming from a weak product line. The company's decision to design proprietary software that was often incompatible with Windows had relegated Apple to a niche player in the highly competitive, low-margin PC business. Years before, Microsoft had replicated the Mac operating system and licensed the software to PC manufacturers such as Dell. Apple's cumulative profit from 2001-2003 was an anemic $109 million and its prospects were dim.

That was then. This is now. Apple's iPod sales now surpass $8 billion annually, one-third of the company's total sales. Accompanying the meteoric rise of its music player, Apple's iTunes now accounts for over 10% of total sales.

Apple's shares (ticker: AAPL) traded around $100 in late 2008, a staggering 25 times the $4 they fetched ten years earlier when Jobs rejoined the team. Indeed, Apple's stock has doubled in price in the past two years, as the following price chart illustrates. The total stock market value of Apple stock (called the market capitalization or market cap) exceeded $130 billion in late 2008.

This module defines and explains the components of each financial statement: the balance sheet, the income statement, the statement of cash flows, and the statement of stockholders' equity. Let's begin with a sneak preview of Apple's financial statements.

Apple's balance sheet is very liquid as many of its assets can be readily converted to cash. Indeed, Apple holds over 60% of its assets in cash and marketable securities. Liquidity is important for companies like Apple that must react quickly to opportunities and changing market conditions. Like other technology companies, much of Apple's production is subcontracted. Consequently, Apple's property, plant and equipment make up only 7% of its assets.

The funnest iPod ever

On the financing side of its balance sheet, over one-half of Apple's resources come from owner financing: from common stock sold to shareholders and from past profits that have been reinvested in the business. Technology companies such as Apple, which have uncertain product life-cycles and highly volatile cash flows, strive to avoid high debt levels that might cause financial problems in a business downturn. Apple's nonowner financing consists of low-cost credit from suppliers (accounts payable) and unpaid overhead expenses (accrued liabilities).

Consider Apple's income statement: driven by the popularity and high profit margins of iPods, Apple recently reported over $4.4 billion of operating income. This is impressive given that Apple spends three cents of every sales dollar on research and development and runs expensive advertising campaigns.

Yet, companies cannot live by profits alone. It is cash that pays bills. Profits and cash flow reflect two different concepts, each providing a different perspective on company performance. Apple generated over $5.4 billion of cash flow from operating activities, over 1.5 times its profit level. This is due to noncash expenses included on Apple's income statement and effective management of its balance sheet. We review Apple's cash flows in this module.

Apple pays no dividends and its newly issued common stock relates primarily to executive stock options. These capital transactions are reported in the statement of stockholders' equity.

While it is important to understand what is reported in each of the four financial statements, it is also impor-tant to know what is *not* reported. To illustrate, *Fortune* reported that "Jobs cut a deal with the Big Five record companies . . . to sell songs on iTunes, but they were afraid of Internet piracy. So Jobs promised to wrap their songs in Apple's *FairPlay*—the only copy-protection soft-ware that is iPod-compatible. Other digital music services such as Yahoo Music Unlimited and Napster reached similar deals with the big record labels. But Apple refused to license *FairPlay* to them. So those companies turned to Microsoft for copy protection. That means none of the songs sold by those services can be played on the wildly popular iPod. Instead, users of the services had to rely on inferior devices made by companies like Samsung and SanDisk that supported Microsoft's Windows Media format."

Apple's copy-protection software described above cre-ates a barrier to competition that allows iPod to earn above-average profits. This represents a valuable resource to Apple, but it is not reported as an asset on Apple's bal-ance sheet. Consider another example. Apple's software engineers write code and create software that will generate profits for Apple in the future. While this represents a valu-able resource to Apple, it is not reported on the balance sheet because Apple expenses the software engineers' salaries when the code is written. We discuss these and other issues relating to asset recognition and measurement in this module.

Sources: Apple 2008 10-K; Apple 2008 Annual Report; *BusinessWeek*, 2006; *Fortune*, 2006 and 2009.

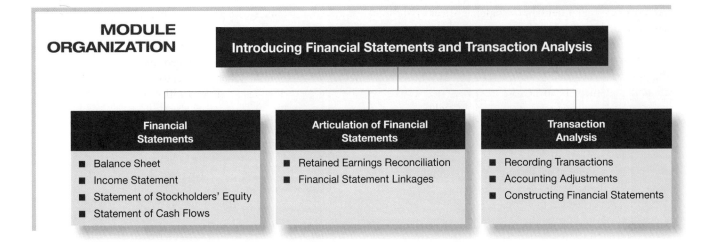

MODULE ORGANIZATION

Introducing Financial Statements and Transaction Analysis

Financial Statements	**Articulation of Financial Statements**	**Transaction Analysis**
■ Balance Sheet ■ Income Statement ■ Statement of Stockholders' Equity ■ Statement of Cash Flows	■ Retained Earnings Reconciliation ■ Financial Statement Linkages	■ Recording Transactions ■ Accounting Adjustments ■ Constructing Financial Statements

This module explains further the details of financial statements and how those statements articulate (relate to each other). Transaction analysis and accounting adjustments conclude the module.

BALANCE SHEET

LO1 Describe information conveyed by the financial statements.

The balance sheet is divided into three sections: assets, liabilities, and stockholders' equity. It provides information about the resources available to management and the claims against those resources by creditors and shareholders. The balance sheet reports the assets, liabilities and equity at a *point* in time. Balance sheet accounts are called "permanent accounts" in that they carry over from period to period; that is, the ending balance from one period becomes the beginning balance for the next.

Balance Sheet and the Flow of Costs

Companies incur costs to acquire resources that will be used in operations. Every cost creates either an immediate or a future economic benefit. Determining when the company will realize the benefit from a cost is paramount. When a cost creates an immediate benefit, such as gasoline used in delivery vehicles, the company records the cost in the income statement as an expense. When a cost creates a future economic benefit, such as inventory to be resold or equipment to be later used for manufacturing, the company records the cost on the balance sheet as an asset. The definition of an asset is "a future economic benefit." An asset remains on the company's balance sheet until it is used up. When an asset is used up, the company realizes the economic benefit from the asset; that is, there is no future economic benefit left so there is no asset left. Then, the asset's cost is transferred from the balance sheet to the income statement where it is labeled an expense. This is why purchased assets are sometimes referred to as future expenses.

Companies expense certain costs, such as advertising, as they are incurred because even though the costs will likely bring future economic benefits, the related asset cannot be reliably measured. Exhibit 2.1 illustrates how costs flow from the balance sheet to the income statement.

EXHIBIT 2.1 Flow of Costs

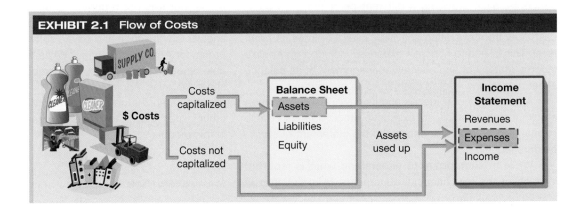

All costs are either held on the balance sheet or are transferred to the income statement. When costs are recorded on the balance sheet (referred to as *capitalized*), assets are reported and expenses are deferred to a later period. Once the company receives benefits from the assets, the related costs are transferred from the balance sheet to the income statement. At that point, assets are reduced and expenses are recorded in the current period. Tracking the flow of costs from the balance sheet to the income statement is an important part of accounting. GAAP allows companies some flexibility in transferring costs. As such, there is potential for abuse, especially when managers confront pressures to achieve income targets.

Corporate scandals involving WorldCom and Enron regrettably illustrate improper cost transfers designed to achieve higher profit levels. Neither company transferred costs from the balance sheet to the income statement as quickly as they should have. This had the effect of overstating assets on the balance sheet and net income on the income statement. In subsequent litigation, the SEC and the Justice Department contended that these companies intentionally overstated net income to boost stock prices. A number of senior executives from both Enron and WorldCom were sentenced to lengthy jail terms as a result of their criminal actions.

What does GAAP advise about the transfer of costs? Asset costs should transfer to the income statement when the asset no longer has any future economic benefit (which is when it no longer meets the definition of an asset). For example, when inventories are purchased or manufactured, their cost is recorded on the balance sheet as an asset called *inventories*. When inventories are sold, they no longer have an economic benefit to the company and their cost is transferred to the income statement in an expense called *cost of goods sold*. Cost of goods sold represents the cost of inventories sold during that period. This expense is recognized in the same period as the revenue generated from the sale. As another example, consider equipment costs. When a company acquires equipment, the cost of the equipment is recorded on the balance sheet in an asset called *equipment* (often included in the general category of property, plant, and equipment, or PPE). When equipment is used in operations, a portion of the acquisition cost is transferred to the income statement to match against the sales the equipment helped generate. To illustrate, if an asset costs $100,000, and 10% of it is used up this period in operating activities, then $10,000 of the asset's cost is transferred from the balance sheet to the income statement. This process is called *depreciation* and the expense related to this transfer of costs is called depreciation expense.

Assets

Companies acquire assets to yield a return for their shareholders. Assets are expected to produce economic benefits in the form of revenues, either directly such as with inventory or indirectly such as with a manufacturing plant that produces inventories for sale. To create shareholder value, assets must yield income that is in excess of the cost of the funds used to acquire the assets.

The asset section of the Apple balance sheet is shown in Exhibit 2.2. Apple reports $25,347 million of total assets as of September 29, 2007, its year-end (this report was made public on November 15, 2007). Amounts reported on the balance sheet are at a *point in time*—that is, the close of business on the day of the report. An asset must possess two characteristics to be reported on the balance sheet:

1. It must be owned (or controlled) by the company.
2. It must possess expected future economic benefits.

The first requirement, owning or controlling an asset, implies that a company has legal title to the asset, such as the title to property, or has the unrestricted right to use the asset, such as a lease on the property. The second requirement implies that a company expects to realize a benefit from the asset. Benefits can be cash inflows from the sale of an asset or from sales of products produced by the asset. Benefits also can refer to the receipt of other assets such as an account receivable from a credit sale. Or, benefits can arise from future services the company will receive, such as prepaying for a year-long insurance policy.

Current Assets

The balance sheet lists assets in order of decreasing **liquidity**, which refers to the ease of converting noncash assets into cash. The most liquid assets are called **current assets** and they are listed first. A

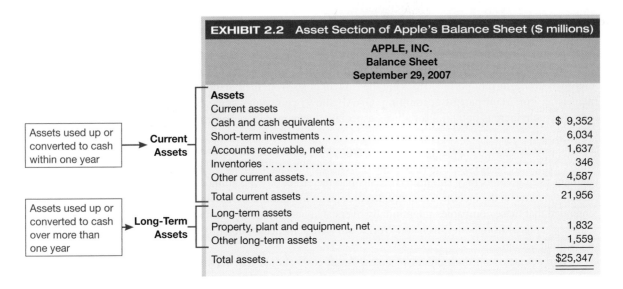

EXHIBIT 2.2 Asset Section of Apple's Balance Sheet ($ millions)

APPLE, INC.
Balance Sheet
September 29, 2007

Assets	
Current assets	
Cash and cash equivalents	$ 9,352
Short-term investments	6,034
Accounts receivable, net	1,637
Inventories	346
Other current assets	4,587
Total current assets	21,956
Long-term assets	
Property, plant and equipment, net	1,832
Other long-term assets	1,559
Total assets	$25,347

(left side annotations:) Assets used up or converted to cash within one year → **Current Assets**

Assets used up or converted to cash over more than one year → **Long-Term Assets**

company expects to convert its current assets into cash or use those assets in operations within the coming fiscal year.[1] Typical examples of current assets follow:

Cash—currency, bank deposits, and investments with an original maturity of 90 days or less (called *cash equivalents*);

Short-term investments—marketable securities and other investments that the company expects to dispose of in the short run;

Accounts receivable, net—amounts due to the company from customers arising from the sale of products and services on credit ("net" refers to the subtraction of uncollectible accounts);

Inventories—goods purchased or produced for sale to customers;

Prepaid expenses—costs paid in advance for rent, insurance, advertising and other services.

Apple reports current assets of $21,956 million in 2007, which is 87% of its total assets. The amount of current assets is an important measure of liquidity, which relates to a company's ability to make short-term payments. Companies require a degree of liquidity to operate effectively, as they must be able to respond to changing market conditions and take advantage of opportunities. However, current assets are expensive to hold (they must be stored, insured, monitored, financed, and so forth)—and they typically generate relatively low returns. As a result, companies seek to maintain only just enough current assets to cover liquidity needs, but not so much to unnecessarily reduce income.

Long-Term Assets

The second section of the balance sheet reports long-term (noncurrent) assets. Long-term assets include the following:

Property, plant and equipment (PPE), net—land, factory buildings, warehouses, office buildings, machinery, motor vehicles, office equipment and other items used in operating activities ("net" refers to subtraction of accumulated depreciation, the portion of the assets' cost that has been expensed);

Long-term investments—investments that the company does not intend to sell in the near future;

Intangible and other assets—assets without physical substance, including patents, trademarks, franchise rights, goodwill and other costs the company incurred that provide future benefits.

---

[1] Technically, current assets include those assets expected to be converted into cash within the upcoming fiscal year or the company's operating cycle (the cash-to-cash cycle), whichever is longer. Fortune Brands (manufacturer of Jim Beam Whiskey) provides an example of a current asset with a cash conversion cycle of longer than one year. Its inventory footnote reports: "In accordance with generally recognized trade practices, bulk whiskey inventories are classified as current assets, although the majority of such inventories, due to the duration of aging processes, ordinarily will not be sold within one year."

Long-term assets are not expected to be converted into cash for some time and are, therefore, listed after current assets.

Measuring Assets

Most assets are reported at their original acquisition costs, or **historical costs**, and not at their current market values. The concept of historical costs is not without controversy. The controversy arises because of the trade-off between the **relevance** of current market values for many business decisions and the **reliability** of historical cost measures.

To illustrate, imagine we are financial analysts and want to determine the value of a company. The company's value equals the value of its assets less the value of its liabilities. Current market values of company assets (and liabilities) are more informative and relevant to our analysis than are historical costs. But how can we determine market values? For some assets, like marketable securities, values are readily obtained from online quotes or from *The Wall Street Journal*. For other assets like property, plant, and equipment, their market values are far more subjective and difficult to estimate. It would be easier for us, as analysts, if companies reported credible market values on their balance sheet. However, allowing companies to report estimates of asset market values would introduce potential *bias* into financial reporting. Consequently, companies continue to report historical costs because the loss in reliability from using subjective market values on the balance sheet is considered to be greater than the loss in relevance from using historical costs.

It is important to realize that balance sheets only include items that can be reliably measured. If a company cannot assign a monetary amount to an asset with relative certainty, it does not recognize an asset on the balance sheet. This means that there are, typically, considerable "assets" that are not reflected on a balance sheet. For example, the well-known apple image is absent from Apple's balance sheet. This image is called an "unrecognized intangible asset." Both requirements for an asset are met: Apple owns the brand and it expects to realize future benefits from the logo. The problem is reliably measuring the expected future benefits to be derived from the image. Intangible assets such as the Coke bottle silhouette, the iPod brandname, and the Nike swoosh also are not on their respective balance sheets. Companies only report intangible assets on the balance sheet when the assets are purchased. Any internally created intangible assets are not reported on a balance sheet. A sizable amount of resources is, therefore, potentially omitted from companies' balance sheets.

Excluded intangible assets often relate to *knowledge-based* (intellectual) assets, such as a strong management team, a well-designed supply chain, or superior technology. Although these intangible assets confer a competitive advantage to the company, and yield above-normal income (and clear economic benefits to those companies), they cannot be reliably measured. This is one reason why companies in knowledge-based industries are so difficult to analyze and value.

Presumably, however, companies' market values reflect these excluded intangible assets. This can yield a large difference between the market value and the book (reported) value of a company's equity. This is illustrated in the following ratios of market value to book value (averages from 2007): Apple is 8.7; Cisco is 5.9; IBM is 6.7; and Target is 3.3. These market-to-book values (ratios) are greater for companies with large knowledge-based assets that are not reported on the balance sheet, but are reflected in company market value. Companies such as Target have fewer of these assets. Hence, their balance sheets usually reflect a greater portion of company value.

Liabilities and Equity

Liabilities and stockholders' equity represent the sources of capital the company uses to finance the acquisition of assets. In general, liabilities represent a company's future economic sacrifices. Liabilities are borrowed funds such as accounts payable and obligations to lenders. They can be interest-bearing or non-interest-bearing.

Equity represents capital that has been invested by the shareholders, either directly via the purchase of stock or indirectly in the form of *retained earnings* that reflect earnings that are reinvested in the business and not paid out as dividends.

The liabilities and stockholders' equity sections of the Apple balance sheet are reproduced in Exhibit 2.3. Apple reports $10,815 million of total liabilities and $14,532 million of stockholders' equity as of its 2007 year-end.

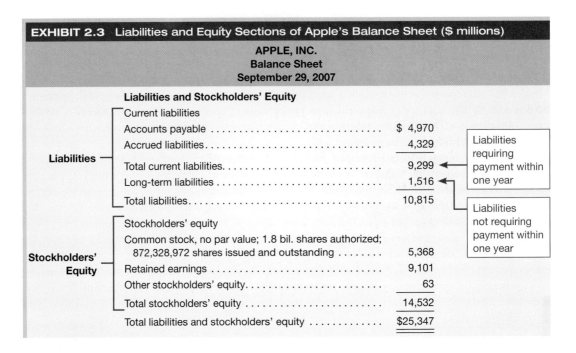

EXHIBIT 2.3   Liabilities and Equity Sections of Apple's Balance Sheet ($ millions)

APPLE, INC.
Balance Sheet
September 29, 2007

Liabilities and Stockholders' Equity

Liabilities	Current liabilities	
	Accounts payable	$ 4,970
	Accrued liabilities.	4,329
	Total current liabilities.	9,299
	Long-term liabilities	1,516
	Total liabilities.	10,815
Stockholders' Equity	Stockholders' equity	
	Common stock, no par value; 1.8 bil. shares authorized; 872,328,972 shares issued and outstanding	5,368
	Retained earnings	9,101
	Other stockholders' equity.	63
	Total stockholders' equity	14,532
	Total liabilities and stockholders' equity	$25,347

Liabilities requiring payment within one year

Liabilities not requiring payment within one year

Why would Apple obtain capital from both borrowed funds and shareholders? Why not just one or the other? The answer lies in their relative costs and the contractual agreements that Apple has with each.

Creditors have the first claim on the assets of the company. As a result, their position is not as risky and, accordingly, their expected return on investment is less than that required by shareholders. Also, interest is tax deductible whereas dividends are not. This makes debt a less expensive source of capital than equity. So, then, why should a company not finance itself entirely with borrowed funds? The reason is that borrowed funds entail contractual obligations to repay the principal and interest on the debt. If a company cannot make these payments when they come due, creditors can force the company into bankruptcy and potentially put the company out of business. Shareholders, in contrast, cannot require repurchase of their stock, or even the payment of dividends. Thus, companies take on a level of debt that they can comfortably repay at reasonable interest costs. The remaining balance required to fund business activities is financed with more costly equity capital.

Current Liabilities

The balance sheet lists liabilities in order of maturity. Obligations that must be settled within one year are called **current liabilities.** Examples of common current liabilities follow:

Accounts payable—amounts owed to suppliers for goods and services purchased on credit.

Accrued liabilities—obligations for expenses that have been incurred but not yet paid; examples are accrued wages payable (wages earned by employees but not yet paid), accrued interest payable (interest that is owing but has not been paid), and accrued income taxes (taxes due).

Unearned revenues—obligations created when the company accepts payment in advance for goods or services it will deliver in the future; also called advances from customers, customer deposits, or deferred revenues.

Short-term notes payable—short-term debt payable to banks or other creditors.

Current maturities of long-term debt—principal portion of long-term debt that is due to be paid within one year.

Apple reports current liabilities of $9,299 million on its 2007 balance sheet.

Accounts payable arise when one company purchases goods or services from another company. Typically, sellers offer credit terms when selling to other companies, rather than expecting cash on delivery. The seller records an account receivable and the buyer records an account payable. Apple reports accounts payable of $4,970 million as of the balance sheet date. Accounts payable are relatively uncomplicated liabilities. A transaction occurs (inventory purchase), a bill is sent, and the amount owed is reported on the balance sheet as a liability.

Apple's accrued liabilities total $4,329 million. Accrued liabilities refer to incomplete transactions. For example, employees work and earn wages, but usually are not paid until later such as several days after the period-end. Wages must be reported as expense in the period that employees earn them because those wages payable are obligations of the company and a liability (wages payable) must be set up on the balance sheet. This is an *accrual*. Other common accruals include the recording of liabilities such as rent and utilities payable, taxes payable, and interest payable on borrowings. All of these accruals involve recognition of expense in the income statement and a liability on the balance sheet.

Net working capital, or simply working capital, reflects the difference between current assets and current liabilities and is defined as follows:

$$\text{Net working capital} = \text{Current assets} - \text{Current liabilities}$$

We usually prefer to see more current assets than current liabilities to ensure that companies are liquid. That is, companies should have sufficient funds to pay their short-term debts as they mature. The net working capital required to conduct business depends on the company's **operating (or cash) cycle**, which is the time between paying cash for goods or employee services and receiving cash from customers—see Exhibit 2.4.

Companies, for example, use cash to purchase or manufacture inventories held for resale. Inventories are usually purchased on credit from suppliers (accounts payable). This financing is called **trade credit**. Inventories are sold, either for cash or on credit (accounts receivable). When receivables are ultimately collected, a portion of the cash received is used to repay accounts payable and the remainder goes to the cash account for the next operating cycle.

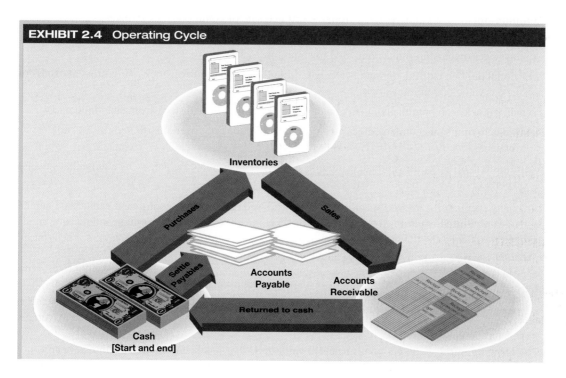

EXHIBIT 2.4 Operating Cycle

When cash is invested in inventory, the inventory can remain with the company for 30 to 90 days or more. Once inventory is sold, the resulting accounts receivable can remain with the company for another 30 to 90 days. Assets such as inventories and accounts receivable are costly to hold and, as such, companies strive to reduce operating cycles with various initiatives that aim to:

- Decrease accounts receivable by better collection procedures
- Reduce inventory levels by improved production systems and management
- Increase trade credit to minimize the cash invested in inventories

Analysts often use the "cash conversion cycle" to evaluate company liquidity. The cash conversion cycle is the number of days the company has its cash tied up in receivables and inventories, less the number of days of trade credit provided by company suppliers.

Noncurrent Liabilities

Noncurrent liabilities are obligations due after one year. Examples of noncurrent liabilities follow:

Long-term debt—amounts borrowed from creditors that are scheduled to be repaid more than one year in the future; any portion of long-term debt that is due within one year is reclassified as a current liability called *current maturities of long-term debt*. Long-term debt includes bonds, mortgages, and other long-term loans.

Other long-term liabilities—various obligations, such as pension liabilities and long-term tax liabilities, that will be settled a year or more into the future.

Apple reports $1,516 million of noncurrent liabilities. As is typical of high-tech companies, Apple has no long-term debt. Instead, all of its noncurrent liabilities relate to deferred revenue and deferred taxes. Deferred (unearned) revenue arises when a company receives cash in advance of providing a good or service.

Stockholders' Equity

Stockholders' equity reflects financing provided from company owners. Equity is often referred to as *residual interest*. That is, stockholders have a claim on any assets in excess of what is needed to meet company obligations to creditors. The following are examples of items typically included in equity:

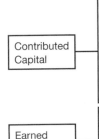

Common stock—par value received from the original sale of common stock to investors.

Preferred stock—value received from the original sale of preferred stock to investors; preferred stock has fewer ownership rights compared to common stock.

Additional paid-in capital—amounts received from the original sale of stock to investors in excess of the par value of common stock.

Treasury stock—amount the company paid to reacquire its common stock from shareholders.

Retained earnings—accumulated net income (profit) that has not been distributed to stockholders as dividends.

Accumulated other comprehensive income or loss—accumulated changes in equity that are not reported in the income statement.

The equity section of a balance sheet consists of two basic components: contributed capital and earned capital. **Contributed capital** is the net funding that a company received from issuing and reacquiring its equity shares; that is, the funds received from issuing shares less any funds paid to repurchase such shares. Apple reports $14,532 million in total stockholders' equity. Its contributed capital is $5,368 million.

Apple's common stock is "no par" (see Exhibit 2.3). This means that Apple records all of its contributed capital in the common stock account and records no additional paid-in capital. Apple's stockholders (via its board of directors) have authorized it to issue up to 1.8 billion shares of common stock. To date, it has sold (issued) 872,328,972 shares for total proceeds of $5,368 million, or $6.15 per share, on average. Apple has repurchased no shares of stock to date.

Earned capital is the cumulative net income (loss) that has been retained by the company (not paid out to shareholders as dividends). Apple's earned capital (titled Retained Earnings) totals $9,101 million as of its 2007 year-end. Its other equity accounts total $63 million.

Retained Earnings

There is an important relation for retained earnings that reconciles its beginning balance and its ending balance as follows:

	Beginning retained earnings
+	Net income (or − net loss)
−	Dividends
=	Ending retained earnings

This is a useful relation to remember. Apple's retained earnings increases (or decreases) each year by the amount of its reported net income (loss). If Apple paid dividends, it would decrease retained earnings, but Apple currently pays no dividends. (There are other items that can impact retained earnings that we discuss in later modules.) After we explain the income statement, we will revisit this relation and show how retained earnings link the balance sheet and income statement.

BUSINESS INSIGHT **How Much Debt Is Reasonable?**

Apple reports total assets of $25,347 million, liabilities of $10,815 million, and stockholders' equity of $14,532 million. This reveals that it finances 43% of its assets with borrowed funds and 57% with shareholder investment. This is a lower percentage of nonowner financing than other companies such as The Gap, Target, and Procter & Gamble (P&G), but about the same as Cisco Systems. Companies must monitor their financing sources and amounts. Too much borrowing is risky as borrowed amounts must be repaid with interest. The level of debt that a company can effectively manage depends on the stability and reliability of its operating cash flows. Companies such as P&G, Target, and The Gap can manage relatively high debt levels because their cash flows are relatively stable. Apple and Cisco, on the other hand, operate in industries that change rapidly. They cannot afford to take on too much borrowing risk.

($ millions)	Assets	Liabilities	Liabilities to Assets ratio	Equity	Equity to Assets ratio
Apple, Inc.	$ 25,347	$10,815	42.7%	$14,532	57.3%
Target Corporation	44,560	29,253	65.6%	15,307	34.4%
Gap, Inc.	7,838	3,564	45.5%	4,274	54.5%
Procter & Gamble Co.	143,992	74,498	51.7%	69,494	48.3%
Cisco Systems, Inc.	58,734	24,332	41.4%	34,402	58.6%

Book Value vs Market Value Stockholders' equity is the "value" of the company determined by GAAP and is commonly referred to as the company's **book value**. This value is different from a company's **market value** (market capitalization or *market cap*), which is computed by multiplying the number of outstanding common shares by the per share market value. We can compute Apple's market cap by multiplying its outstanding shares at September 29, 2007, (872,328,972 shares) by its stock price on that date ($153.47), which equals $133,876 million. This is considerably larger than its book value of equity on that date of $14,532 million. Book value and market value can differ for several reasons, mostly related to the recognition of transactions and events in financial statements such as the following:

■ GAAP generally reports assets and liabilities at historical costs, whereas the market attempts to estimate fair market values.

■ GAAP excludes resources that cannot be reliably measured such as talented management, employee morale, recent innovations and successful marketing, whereas the market attempts to value these.

■ GAAP does not consider market differences in which companies operate such as competitive conditions and expected changes, whereas the market attempts to factor in these differences in determining value.

■ GAAP does not usually report expected future performance, whereas the market attempts to predict and value future performance.

Presently for U.S. companies, book value is, on average, about two-thirds of market value. This means that the market has drawn on information in addition to that provided in the balance sheet and income statement in valuing equity shares. A major part of this information is in financial statement notes, but not all. It is important to understand that, eventually, all factors determining company market value are reflected in financial statements and book value. Assets are eventually sold and liabilities are settled. Moreover, talented management, employee morale, technological innovations, and successful marketing are eventually recognized in reported profit. The difference between book value and market value is one of timing.

BUSINESS INSIGHT **Apple's Market and Book Values**

Apple's market value has historically exceeded its book value of equity (see graph below). Much of Apple's market value derives from intangible assets such as brand equity that are not fully reflected on its balance sheet, and from favorable expectations of future financial performance (particularly in recent years). Apple has incurred many costs such as R&D, advertising, and promotion that will probably yield future economic benefits. However, Apple expensed these costs (did not capitalize them as assets) because their future benefits were uncertain and therefore could not be reliably measured. Companies capitalize intangible assets only when those assets are purchased, and not when they are internally developed. Consequently, Apple's balance sheet and the balance sheets of many knowledge-based companies are, arguably, less informative about company value.

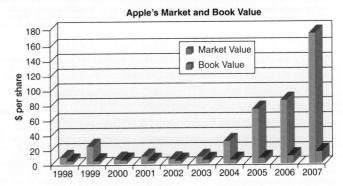

INCOME STATEMENT

The income statement reports revenues earned during a period, the expenses incurred to produce those revenues, and the resulting net income or loss. The general structure of the income statement follows:

	Revenues
−	Cost of goods sold
	Gross profit
−	Operating expenses
	Operating profit
−	Nonoperating expenses (+ Nonoperating revenues)
−	Tax expense
	Income from continuing operations
+/−	Nonrecurring items, net of tax
=	Net income

Apple's income statement from its 2007 10-K is shown in Exhibit 2.5. Apple reports net income of $3,496 million on sales of $24,006 million. This means that about $0.15 of each dollar of sales is brought down to the bottom line, computed as $3,496 million divided by $24,006 million. Apple's net income margin is higher than that of the average publicly-traded company, which reports about $0.06 cents in profit for each sales dollar. The remaining $0.85 of each sales dollar for Apple (computed as $1 minus $0.15) is consumed by costs incurred to generate sales. These costs include production costs (cost of sales), wages, advertising, research and development, equipment costs (such as depreciation), and taxes.

EXHIBIT 2.5 Apple's Income Statement ($ millions)	
APPLE, INC. **Income Statement** **For Year Ended September 29, 2007**	
Net sales.	$24,006
Cost of sales.	15,852
Gross margin	8,154
Operating expenses	
Research and development	782
Selling, general, and administrative	2,963
Total operating expenses	3,745
Operating profit	4,409
Other revenue and expense	
Interest and other income, net	599
Income before provision for income taxes.	5,008
Provision for income taxes.	1,512
Net income.	$ 3,496

To analyze an income statement we must understand some terminology. **Revenues** (Sales) are increases in net assets (assets less liabilities) as a result of ordinary operating activities. **Expenses** are decreases in net assets used to generate revenues, including costs of sales, operating costs like wages and advertising (usually titled selling, general, and administrative expenses or SG&A), and nonoperating costs like interest on debt. The difference between revenues and expenses is **net income** when revenues exceed expenses, or **net loss** when expenses exceed revenues. The terms income, profit, and earnings are used interchangeably (as are revenues and sales, and so are expenses and costs).

    Operating expenses are the usual and customary costs that a company incurs to support its operating activities. Those include cost of goods sold, selling expenses, depreciation expense, and research and development expense. Not all of these expenses require a cash outlay; for example, depreciation expense is a noncash expense, as are many liabilities such as wages payable, that recognize the expense in advance of cash payment. **Nonoperating expenses** relate to the company's financing and investing activities, and include interest expense, interest or dividend income, and gains and losses from the sale of securities. Business decision makers and analysts usually segregate operating and nonoperating activities as they offer different insights into company performance and condition.

> **Alert** The FASB has released a preliminary draft of a proposal to restructure financial statements to, among other things, better distinguish operating and nonoperating activities.

MANAGERIAL DECISION	You Are the Securities Analyst

You are analyzing the performance of a company that hired a new CEO during the current year. The current year's income statement includes an expense labeled "asset write-offs." Write-offs represent the accelerated transfer of costs from the balance sheet to the income statement. Are you concerned about the legitimacy of these expenses? Why or why not? [Answer, p. 2-34]

Recognition of Revenues and Expenses

An important consideration in preparing the income statement is *when* to recognize revenues and expenses. For many revenues and expenses, the decision is easy. When a customer purchases groceries, pays with a check, and walks out of the store with the groceries, we know that the sale is made and revenue should be recognized. Or, when companies receive and pay an electric bill with a check, they have clearly incurred an expense that should be recognized.

    However, should Apple recognize revenue when it sells iPods to a retailer that does not have to pay Apple for 60 days? Should Apple recognize an expense for employees who work this week but will not be paid until the first of next month? The answer to both of these questions is yes.

    Two fundamental principles guide recognition of revenues and expenses:

Revenue Recognition Principle—recognize revenues when *earned*

Matching Principle—recognize expenses when *incurred*.

These two principles are the foundation of **accrual accounting**, which is the accounting system used to prepare all GAAP-based financial statements. The general approach is this: first, recognize revenues in the time period they are earned; then, record all expenses *incurred* to generate those revenues during that same time period (this is called matching expenses to revenues). Net income is then correctly reported for that period.

Recognizing revenues when earned does not necessarily imply the receipt of cash. Revenue is *earned* when the company has done everything that it is supposed to do. This means that a sale of goods on credit would qualify for recognition as long as the revenues are earned. Likewise, companies recognize an expense when it is *incurred*, even if no cash is paid. For example, companies recognize as expenses the wages earned by employees, even though they will not be paid until the next pay period. The company records an expense but pays no cash; instead, it records an accrued liability for the wages payable.

Accrual accounting requires estimates and assumptions. Examples include estimating how much revenue has been earned on a long-term contract, the amount of accounts receivable that will not be collected, the degree to which equipment has been "used up," the cleanup costs that a company must eventually pay for environmental liabilities, and numerous other estimates. All of these estimates and assumptions affect both reported net income and the balance sheet. Judgments affect all financial statements. This is an important by-product of accrual accounting. We discuss these estimates and assumptions, and their effects on financial statements, throughout the book.

MANAGERIAL DECISION **You Are the Operations Manager**

You are the operations manager on a new consumer product that was launched this period with very successful sales. The Chief Financial Officer (CFO) asks you to prepare an estimate of warranty costs to charge against those sales. Why does the CFO desire a warranty cost estimate? What hurdles must you address in arriving at such an estimate? [Answer, p. 2-34]

Reporting of Transitory Items

To this point, we have only considered income from continuing operations and its components. A more complete income statement format is in Exhibit 2.6. The most noticeable difference involves two additional components of net income located at the bottom of the statement. These two components are specifically segregated from the "income from continuing operations" and are defined as follows:

1. **Discontinued operations** Gains or losses (and net income or loss) from business segments that are being sold or have been sold in the current period.
2. **Extraordinary items** Gains or losses from events that are both *unusual* and *infrequent* and are, therefore, excluded from income from continuing operations.

These two components are segregated because they represent **transitory items**, which reflect transactions or events that are unlikely to recur. Many readers of financial statements are interested in *future* company performance. They analyze current year financial statements to gain clues to better *predict* future performance. (Stock prices, for example, are based on a company's expected profits and cash flows.)

Transitory items, by definition, are unlikely to arise in future periods. Although transitory items can help us analyze past performance, they are largely irrelevant to predicting future performance. This means that investors and other users tend to focus on income from continuing operations because that

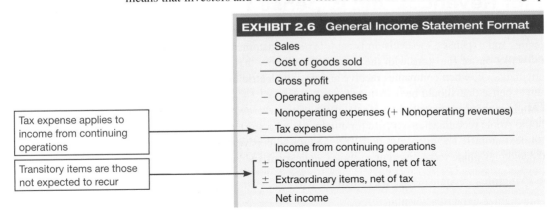

EXHIBIT 2.6 General Income Statement Format

Sales
− Cost of goods sold
Gross profit
− Operating expenses
− Nonoperating expenses (+ Nonoperating revenues)
− Tax expense
Income from continuing operations
± Discontinued operations, net of tax
± Extraordinary items, net of tax
Net income

Tax expense applies to income from continuing operations

Transitory items are those not expected to recur

is the level of profitability that is likely to **persist** (continue) into the future. Likewise, the financial press tends to focus on income from continuing operations when it discloses corporate earnings (often described as *earnings before one-time charges*).

IFRS INSIGHT Balance Sheet and Income Statement under IFRS

U.S. GAAP and IFRS require a similar set of financial statements with similar formats. Both standards require current and long-term classifications for assets and liabilities, and both recognize revenues when earned and match expenses to those revenues in the same period. Although differences between U.S. GAAP and IFRS do exist at the "detailed level," there are at least three broader differences worth mention:

- GAAP makes no formal prescription for the balance sheet and the income statement, however, the SEC does prescribe the types of accounts and number of years that should be disclosed per Reg. S-X. This listing of required accounts is more detailed: Reg. S-X requires three years of comparative income statements whereas IFRS requires only two.

- GAAP requires the reporting of extraordinary items as a separate category of the income statement if they are unusual and infrequent; IFRS has no extraordinary item category.

- For items that are either unusual or infrequent, but not both, GAAP requires separate presentation in the income statement as a component of earnings from continuing operations; IFRS also requires disclosure of these items, but allows for such disclosure in footnotes to financial statements as an alternative to the income statement.

STATEMENT OF STOCKHOLDERS' EQUITY

The statement of stockholders' equity reconciles the beginning and ending balances of stockholders' equity accounts. The statement of stockholders' equity for Apple is shown in Exhibit 2.7.

EXHIBIT 2.7 Apple's Statement of Stockholders' Equity

APPLE, INC.
Statement of Stockholders' Equity
For Year Ended September 29, 2007

($ millions)	Common Stock	Retained Earnings	Other Stockholders' Equity	Total Stockholders' Equity
Balance at September 30, 2006......	$4,355	$5,607	$22	$ 9,984
Common stock issued..............	1,013			1,013
Net income......................		3,496		3,496
Dividends.......................		(0)		(0)
Other...........................		(2)	41	39
Balance at September 29, 2007......	$5,368	$9,101	$63	$14,532

Apple's first equity component is common stock. The balance in common stock at the beginning of the year is $4,355 million. During 2007, Apple issued $1,013 million worth of common stock to employees who exercised stock options. At the end of 2007, the common stock account reports a balance of $5,368 million.

Apple's second stockholders' equity component is retained earnings. It totals $5,607 million at the start of fiscal 2007. During the year, it increased by $3,496 million from net income. Apple's retained earnings do not decrease for dividends because Apple pays no dividends; it also reports $(2) million of miscellaneous adjustments. The balance of retained earnings at year-end is $9,101 million.

In sum, total stockholders' equity begins the year at $9,984 million (including $22 million relating to miscellaneous accounts that increase total stockholders' equity) and ends fiscal 2007 with a balance of $14,532 million (including $63 million relating to miscellaneous accounts that increase total stockholders' equity) for a net increase of $4,548 million.

STATEMENT OF CASH FLOWS

The balance sheet and income statement are prepared using accrual accounting, in which revenues are recognized when earned and expenses when incurred. This means that companies can report income even though no cash is received. Cash shortages—due to unexpected cash outlays or when customers refuse to or cannot pay—can create economic hardships for companies and even cause their demise.

To assess cash flows, we must assess a company's cash management. Obligations to employees, creditors, and others are usually settled with cash. Illiquid companies (those lacking cash) are at risk of failure. Given the importance of cash management, companies must report a statement of cash flows in addition to the balance sheet, income statement, and statement of equity.

The income statement provides information about the economic viability of the company's products and services. It tells us whether the company can sell its products and services at prices that cover its costs and provide a reasonable return to lenders and stockholders. On the other hand, the statement of cash flows provides information about the company's ability to generate cash from those same transactions. It tells us from what sources the company has generated its cash (so we can evaluate whether those sources are persistent or transitory) and what it has done with the cash it generated.

Statement Format and Data Sources

The statement of cash flows is formatted to report cash inflows and cash outflows by the three primary business activities:

- *Cash flows from operating activities* Cash flows from the company's transactions and events that relate to its operations.
- *Cash flows from investing activities* Cash flows from acquisitions and divestitures of investments and long-term assets.
- *Cash flows from financing activities* Cash flows from issuances of and payments toward borrowings and equity.

The combined cash flows from these three sections yield the net change in cash for the period. The three sections of the statement of cash flows relate to the income statement and to different parts of the balance sheet. These relations are highlighted in the table below:

Cash flow section	Information from income statement	Information from balance sheet	
Net cash flows from operating activities....	Revenues − Expenses = Net income	**Current assets** Long-term assets	**Current liabilities** Long-term liabilities Equity
Net cash flows from investing activities....	Revenues − Expenses = Net income	Current assets **Long-term assets**	Current liabilities Long-term liabilities Equity
Net cash flows from financing activities....	Revenues − Expenses = Net income	Current assets Long-term assets	Current liabilities **Long-term liabilities Equity**

Specifically, the three sections draw generally on the following information:

- **Net cash flows from operating activities** relate to the income statement and to the current asset and current liabilities sections of the balance sheet.
- **Net cash flows from investing activities** relate to the long-term assets section of the balance sheet.
- **Net cash flows from financing activities** relate to the long-term liabilities and stockholders' equity sections of the balance sheet.

These relations do not hold exactly, but they provide us a useful way to visualize the construction of the statement of cash flows.

In analyzing the statement of cash flows, we should not necessarily conclude that the company is better off if cash increases and worse off if cash decreases. It is not the change in cash that is most important, but the reasons behind the change. For example, what are the sources of cash inflows? Are these sources transitory? Are these sources mainly from operating activities? To what uses have cash inflows been put? Such questions and answers are key to properly using the statement of cash flows.

Exhibit 2.8 shows Apple's statement of cash flows. Apple reported $5,470 million in net cash inflows from operating activities in 2007. This is substantially greater than its net income of $3,496 million. The operating activities section of the statement of cash flows reconciles the difference between net income and operating cash flow. The difference is due to the add-back of depreciation, a noncash expense in the income statement, and other noncash expenses, together with year-over-year changes in operating assets and liabilities.

Apple reports a net cash outflow of $3,249 million for investing activities, mainly for investments in marketable securities. Apple also generated $739 million from financing activities, mainly cash received when employees exercised their options to purchase common stock.

Overall, Apple's cash flow picture is strong. It is generating cash from operating activities and the sale of stock to employees, and is investing excess cash in marketable securities to ensure future liquidity.

EXHIBIT 2.8 Apple's Statement of Cash Flows ($ millions)	
APPLE, INC. **Statement of Cash Flows** **For Year Ended September 29, 2007**	
Operating Activities	
Net income...	$3,496
Depreciation and amortization...............................	317
Other noncash expenses, net	332
Increase in accounts receivable	(385)
Increase in inventories	(76)
Increases in other current assets, net	(1,459)
Increases in accounts payable..............................	1,494
Increases in other liabilities	1,751
Cash generated by operating activities	5,470
Investing Activities	
Increase in short-term investments, net......................	(2,312)
Purchases of property, plant and equipment...................	(735)
Increase in other long-term assets, net	(202)
Cash used for investing activities...........................	(3,249)
Financing Activities	
Proceeds from issuance of common stock, net.................	362
Other financing activities	377
Cash generated by financing activities	739
Increase in cash and cash equivalents.......................	$2,960
Cash and cash equivalents, beginning of year	6,392
Cash and cash equivalents, end of year	$9,352

Cash Flow Computations

It is sometimes difficult to understand why certain accounts are added to and subtracted from net income to yield net cash flows from operating activities. It often takes more than one pass through this section to grasp how this part of the cash flow statement is constructed.

A key to understanding these computations is to remember that under accrual accounting, revenues are recognized when earned and expenses when incurred. This recognition policy does not necessarily coincide with the receipt or payment of cash. The top line (net income) of the operating section of the statement of cash flows represents net (accrual) income under GAAP. The bottom line (net cash flows from operating activities) is the *cash profit* the company would have reported had it constructed its income statement on a cash basis rather than an accrual basis. Computing net cash flows from operating activities begins with GAAP profit and adjusts it to compute cash profit using the following general approach:

	Add (+) or Subtract (−) from Net Income
Net income.	$ #
Add: depreciation expense	+
Adjust for changes in current assets	
Subtract increases in current assets	−
Add decreases in current assets	+
Adjust for changes in current liabilities	
Add increases in current liabilities	+
Subtract decreases in current liabilities . .	−
Cash from operating activities	$ #

BUSINESS INSIGHT | Insights into Apple's Statement of Cash Flows

The following provides insights into the computation of some amounts in the operating section of Apple's statement of cash flows in Exhibit 2.8 ($ millions).

Statement amount	Explanation of computation
Depreciation and amortization, $317	When buildings and equipment are acquired, their cost is recorded on the balance sheet as assets. Subsequently, as the assets are used up to generate revenues, a portion of their cost is transferred from the balance sheet to the income statement as an expense, called *depreciation*. Depreciation expense does not involve the payment of cash (that occurs when the asset is purchased). If we want to compute *cash profit*, we must add back depreciation expense to zero it out from income. The $317 in the second line of the statement of cash flows merely zeros out (undoes) the depreciation expense that was subtracted when Apple computed GAAP net income. Likewise, the third line (other noncash expenditures of $332) uses the same concept.
Increase in accounts receivable, $(385)	When a company sells goods *on credit*, it records revenue because it is earned, even though cash is not yet received. When Apple sold $385 of goods on credit, its revenues and net income increased by that amount, but no cash was received. Apple's cash profit is, thus, $385 less than net income. The $385 is subtracted from net income in computing net cash inflows from operations.
Increase in inventories, $(76)	When Apple purchases inventories, the purchase cost is reported on its balance sheet as a current asset. When inventories are sold, their cost is removed from the balance sheet and transferred to the income statement as an expense called cost of goods sold. If some inventories acquired are not yet sold, their cost is not yet reported in cost of goods sold and net income. The subtraction of $76 relates to the increase in inventories; it reflects the fact that cost of goods sold does not include all of the cash that was spent on inventories. That is, $76 cash was spent that is not yet reflected in cost of goods sold. Thus, the $76 is deducted from net income to compute *cash profit* for the period.
Increases in accounts payable, $1,494	Apple purchases much of its inventories on credit. The $1,494 increase in accounts payable reflects inventories that have been purchased, but have not yet been paid for in cash. The add-back of this $1,494 to net income reflects the fact that *cash profit* is $1,494 higher because $1,494 of accounts payable are not yet paid.

Typically, net income is first adjusted for noncash expenses such as depreciation, and is then adjusted for changes during the year in current assets and current liabilities to yield cash flow from operating activities, or *cash profit*. The depreciation adjustment merely zeros out (undoes the effect of) depreciation expense, a noncash expense, which is deducted in computing net income. The following table provides brief explanations of adjustments for receivables, inventories, and payables and accruals, which are frequent sources of adjustments in this section:

	Change in account balance...	Means that...	Which requires this adjustment to net income to yield cash profit...
Receivables	Increase	Sales and net income increase, but cash is not yet received	Deduct increase in receivables from net income
	Decrease	More cash is received than is reported in sales and net income	Add decrease in receivables to net income
Inventories	Increase	Cash is paid for inventories that are not yet reflected in cost of goods sold	Deduct increase in inventories from net income
	Decrease	Cost of goods sold includes inventory costs that were paid for in a prior period	Add decrease in inventories to net income
Payables and accruals	Increase	More goods and services are acquired on credit, delaying cash payment	Add increase in payables and accruals to net income
	Decrease	More cash is paid than is reflected in cost of goods sold or operating expenses	Deduct decrease in payables and accruals from net income

It is also helpful to use the following decision guide, involving changes in assets, liabilities, and equity, to understand increases and decreases in cash flows.

	Cash flow increases from	Cash flow decreases from
Assets..................	Account decreases	Account increases
Liabilities and equity.......	Account increases	Account decreases

The table above applies to all sections of the statement of cash flows. To determine if a change in each asset and liability account creates a cash inflow or outflow, examine the change and apply the decision rules from the table. For example, in the investing section, cash decreases when PPE assets increase. In the financing section, borrowing from a bank increases cash. Module 3 and Appendix B near the end of the book describe the preparation of the statement of cash flows in detail.

Sometimes the cash flow effect of an item reported in the statement of cash flows does not agree with the difference in the balance sheet accounts that we observe. This can be due to several factors. One common factor is when a company uses its own stock to acquire another entity. There is no cash effect from a stock acquisition and, hence, it is not reported in the statement of cash flows. Yet, the company does increase its assets and liabilities when it adds the acquired company's assets and liabilities to its balance sheet.

Knowledge of how companies record cash inflows and outflows helps us better understand the statement of cash flows. Determining how changes in asset and liability accounts affect cash provides an analytic tool *and* offers greater insight into managing a business. For instance, reducing the levels of receivables and inventories increases cash. Similarly, increasing the levels of accounts payable and accrued liabilities increases cash. Managing cash balances by managing other accounts is called *working capital management*, which is important for all companies.

MID-MODULE REVIEW 1

Following are account balances ($ millions) for Dell, Inc. Using these data, prepare Dell's income statement and statement of cash flows for the fiscal year ended February 1, 2008. Prepare its balance sheet dated February 1, 2008.

Cash and cash equivalents, ending year	$ 7,764	Inventories	$ 1,180
Net cash used in financing activities and other	(3,968)	Accounts payable	11,492
Long-term debt	362	Other stockholders' equity	(24,959)
Property, plant and equipment, net	2,668	Long-term Investments	1,560
Other noncurrent assets	3,453	Other current assets	3,035
Accrued and other liabilities	7,034	Retained earnings	18,199
Other noncurrent liabilities	4,844	Receivables	7,693
Short-term investments	208	Selling, general and administrative expenses	7,538
Income tax expense	880	Research and development expenses	693
Net cash provided by operating activities	3,949	Cost of revenue	49,462
Paid-in capital	10,589	Net cash provided by investing activities	(1,763)
Cash and cash equivalents, beginning year	9,546	Investment and other income, net	387
Net revenue	61,133		

Solution

DELL, INC.
Income Statement
For Fiscal Year Ended February 1, 2008

Net revenue	$61,133
Cost of revenue	49,462
Gross margin	11,671
Operating expenses	
Selling, general, and administrative expenses	7,538
Research and development expenses	693
Total operating expenses	8,231
Operating income	3,440
Investment and other income, net	387
Income before income taxes	3,827
Income tax provision	880
Net income	$ 2,947

DELL, INC.
Statement of Cash Flows
For Fiscal Year Ended February 1, 2008

Net cash provided by operating activities	$ 3,949
Net cash provided by investing activities	(1,763)
Net cash used in financing activities and other	(3,968)
Net increase in cash and cash equivalents	$(1,782)
Cash and cash equivalents, beginning year	9,546
Cash and cash equivalents, ending year	$ 7,764

DELL, INC.
Balance Sheet
February 1, 2008

Assets		Liabilities and Equity	
Current assets		Current liabilities	
Cash and cash equivalents	$ 7,764	Accounts payable	$11,492
Short-term investments	208	Accrued and other liabilities	7,034
Receivables	7,693	Total current liabilities	18,526
Inventories	1,180	Long-term debt	362
Other current assets	3,035	Other noncurrent liabilities	4,844
Total current assets	19,880	Total liabilities	23,732
Property, plant, and equipment, net	2,668	Stockholders' equity	
Long-term Investments	1,560	Paid-in capital	10,589
Other noncurrent assets	3,453	Retained earnings	18,199
		Other stockholders' equity	(24,959)
		Total stockholders' equity	3,829
Total assets	$27,561	Total liabilities and stockholders' equity	$27,561

ARTICULATION OF FINANCIAL STATEMENTS

The four financial statements are linked with each other and linked across time. This linkage is called **articulation**. This section demonstrates the articulation of financial statements using Apple.

LO2 Explain and illustrate linkages among the four financial statements.

Retained Earnings Reconciliation

The balance sheet and income statement are linked via retained earnings. Recall that retained earnings is updated each period as follows:

Beginning retained earnings
± Net income (loss)
− Dividends
= Ending retained earnings

Retained earnings reflect cumulative income that has not yet been distributed to shareholders. Exhibit 2.9 shows Apple's retained earnings reconciliation for 2007.

EXHIBIT 2.9 Apple's Retained Earnings Reconciliation
APPLE, INC. **Retained Earnings Reconciliation ($ millions)** **For Year Ended September 29, 2007**

Retained earnings, September 30, 2006	$5,607
Add: Net income	3,496
Less: Dividends	(0)
Other adjustments	(2)
Retained earnings, September 29, 2007	$9,101

This reconciliation of retained earnings links the balance sheet and income statement.

In the absence of transactions with stockholders—such as stock issuances and repurchases, and dividend payments—the change in stockholders' equity equals income or loss for the period. The income statement, thus, measures the change in company value as measured by *GAAP*. This is not necessarily company value as measured by the *market*. Of course, all value-relevant items eventually find their way into the income statement. So, from a long-term perspective, the income statement does measure change in company value. This is why stock prices react to reported income and to analysts' expectations about future income.

Financial Statement Linkages

Articulation of the four financial statements is shown in Exhibit 2.10. Apple begins fiscal 2007 with assets of $17,205 million, consisting of cash for $6,392 million and noncash assets for $10,813 million. These investments are financed with $7,221 million from nonowners and $9,984 million from shareholders. The owner financing consists of contributed capital of $4,355 million, retained earnings of $5,607 million, and other stockholders' equity of $22 million.

Exhibit 2.10 shows balance sheets at the beginning and end of Apple's fiscal year on the left and right columns, respectively. The middle column reflects operating activities for 2007. The statement of cash flows explains how operating, investing, and financing activities increase the cash balance by $2,960 million from $6,392 million at the beginning of the year to $9,352 million at year-end. The ending balance in cash is reported in the year-end balance sheet on the right.

Apple's $3,496 million net income reported on the income statement is also carried over to the statement of shareholders' equity. The net income explains nearly all of the change in retained earnings reported in the statement of shareholders' equity because Apple paid no dividends in that year (other adjustments reduce retained earnings by $2 million).

EXHIBIT 2.10   Articulation of Apple Financial Statements ($ millions)

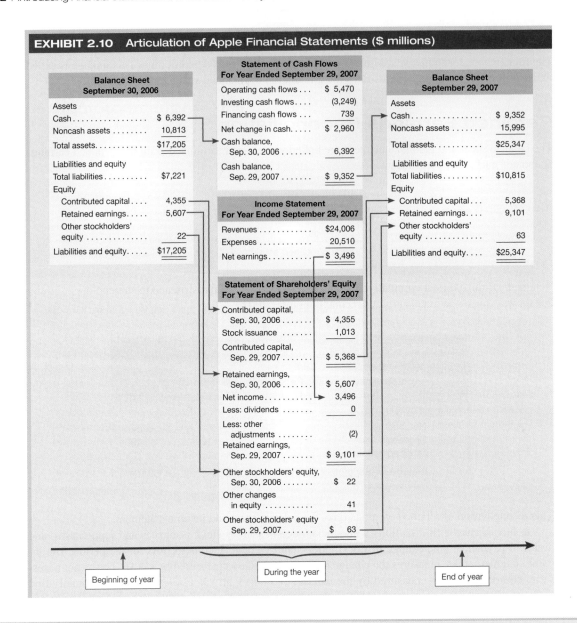

MID-MODULE REVIEW 2

Refer to information in Mid-Module Review 1; assume that Dell reports the following balances for the prior year balance sheet and current year income statement. Prepare the articulation of Dell's financial statements from fiscal years 2007 to 2008 following the format of Exhibit 2.10.

Balance Sheet, February 2, 2007	
Assets	
Cash	$ 9,546
Noncash assets	16,089
Total assets.................	$25,635
Liabilities and Equity	
Total liabilities	$21,196
Equity	
Contributed capital............	10,107
Retained earnings.............	15,282
Other stockholders' equity	(20,950)
Liabilities and equity...........	$25,635

Income Statement, For Year Ended February 1, 2008	
Revenues	$61,133
Expenses	58,186
Net earnings..................	$ 2,947

Solution

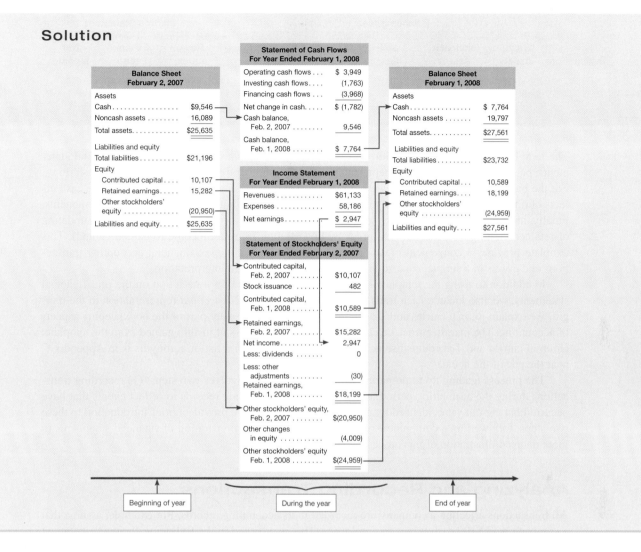

| Beginning of year | During the year | End of year |

TRANSACTION ANALYSIS AND ACCOUNTING

This section introduces our financial statement effects template, which we use throughout the book to reflect the effects of transactions on financial statements. A more detailed explanation is in Module 3, but that module is not required to understand and apply the template.

LO3 Illustrate use of the financial statement effects template to summarize accounting transactions.

Apple reports total assets of $25,347 million, total liabilities of $10,815 million, and equity of $14,532 million. The accounting equation for Apple follows ($ million):

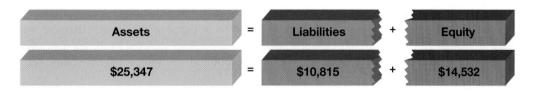

Assets	=	Liabilities	+	Equity
$25,347	=	$10,815	+	$14,532

We often draw on this relation to assess the effects of transactions and events, different accounting methods, and choices that managers make in preparing financial statements. For example, we are interested in knowing the effects of an asset acquisition or sale on the balance sheet, income statement, and cash flow statement. Or, we might want to understand how the failure to recognize a liability would understate liabilities and overstate profits and equity. To perform these sorts of analyses, we employ the following **financial statement effects template**:

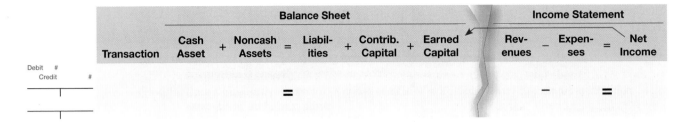

The template captures the transaction and its financial statement effects on the four financial statements: balance sheet, income statement, statement of stockholders' equity, and statement of cash flows. For the balance sheet, we differentiate between cash and noncash assets so as to identify the cash effects of transactions. Likewise, equity is separated into the contributed and earned capital components. Finally, income statement effects are separated into revenues, expenses, and net income (the updating of retained earnings is denoted with an arrow line running from net income to earned capital). This template provides a convenient means to represent relatively complex financial accounting transactions and events in a simple, concise manner for both analysis and interpretation.

In addition to using the template to show the dollar effects of a transaction on the four financial statements, we also include each transaction's *journal entry* and *T-account* representation in the margin. We explain journal entries and T-accounts in Module 3; these are part of the bookkeeping aspects of accounting. The margin entries can be ignored without any loss of insight gained from the template. (Journal entries and T-accounts use acronyms for account titles; a list of acronyms is in Appendix C near the end of the book.)

The process leading up to preparing financial statements involves two steps: (1) recording transactions during the accounting period, and (2) adjusting accounting records to reflect events that have occurred but are not yet evidenced by an external transaction. We provide a brief introduction to these two steps, followed by a comprehensive example that includes preparation of financial statements (a more detailed illustration of this process is in Module 3).

Analyzing and Recording Transactions

All transactions affecting a company are recorded in its accounting records. For example, assume that a company paid $100 cash wages to employees. This is reflected in the following financial statement effects template.

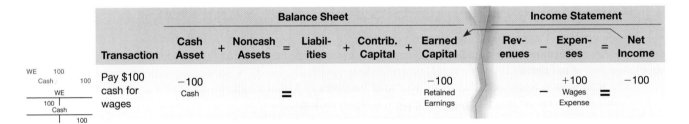

Cash assets are reduced by $100, and wage expense of $100 is reflected in the income statement, which reduces income and retained earnings by that amount. All transactions incurred by the company during the accounting period are recorded similarly. We show several further examples in our comprehensive illustration later in this section.

Adjusting Accounts

We must understand accounting adjustments (commonly called *accruals*) to fully analyze and interpret financial statements. In the transaction above, we record wage expense that has been earned by (and paid to) employees during the period. What if the employees were not paid for wages earned at period-end?

Should the expense still be recorded? The answer is yes. All expenses incurred to generate, directly or indirectly, the revenues reported in the period must be recorded. This is the case even if those expenses are still unpaid at period-end. Failure to recognize wages expense would overstate net income for the period because wages have been earned and should be reported as expense in this period. Also, failure to record those wages at period-end would understate liabilities. Thus, neither the income statement nor the balance sheet would be accurate. Adjustments are, therefore, necessary to accurately portray financial condition and performance of a company.

There are four types of adjustments, which are illustrated in the following graphic. The two adjustments on the left relate to the receipt or payment of cash before revenue or expense is recognized. The two on the right relate to the receipt or payment of cash after revenue or expense is recognized.

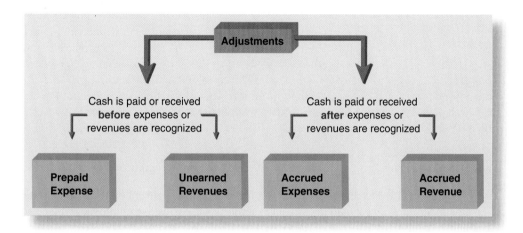

One of two types of accounts arise when cash is received or paid *before* recognition of revenue or expense.

Prepaid expenses Prepaid expenses reflect advance cash payments that will ultimately become expenses; an example is the payment of radio advertising that will not be aired until sometime in the future.

Unearned revenues Unearned revenues reflect cash received from customers before any services or goods are provided; an example is cash received from patrons for tickets to an upcoming concert.

To illustrate the adjustment required with prepaid expenses, assume that Apple pays $3,000 cash at the beginning of this year to rent office space, and that this allows Apple to use the space for the current year and two additional years. When paid, the prepaid rent is an asset for Apple (it now controls the space, which is expected to provide future benefits for its business). At the end of the first year, one-third of the Prepaid Rent asset is used up. Apple, therefore, removes that portion from its balance sheet and recognizes it as an expense in the income statement. The beginning-year payment and year-end expensing of the rental asset are recorded as follows:

	Balance Sheet						Income Statement		
Transaction	Cash Asset	+ Noncash Assets	= Liabilities	+ Contrib. Capital	+ Earned Capital		Revenues	− Expenses	= Net Income
a. Beginning-year $3,000 cash payment in advance of 3-year rent	−3,000 Cash	+3,000 Prepaid Rent	=					−	=
b. Recognition of 1-year rent expense of $1,000		−1,000 Prepaid Rent	=		−1,000 Retained Earnings			+1,000 Rent Expense	−1,000 =

PPRNT 3,000
   Cash 3,000

PPRNT	
3,000	
Cash	
	3,000

RNTE 1,000
   PPRNT 1,000

RNTE	
1,000	
PPRNT	
	1,000

To illustrate unearned revenues, assume that Apple receives $5,000 cash in advance of providing ser-vices to a client. That amount is initially recorded as a liability for services owed the client. Later, when Apple provides the services, it can recognize that revenue since it is now earned. The receipt of cash and subsequent recognition of revenue are recorded as follows:

	Balance Sheet							Income Statement		
Transaction	Cash Asset	+	Noncash Assets	=	Liabil-ities	+	Contrib. Capital	+	Earned Capital	
a. Receive $5,000 cash in advance for future services	+5,000 Cash			=	+5,000 Unearned Revenue					
b. Rec-ognition of $5,000 services revenue earned				=	−5,000 Unearned Revenue			+5,000 Retained Earnings		

	Income Statement			
	Rev-enues	−	Expen-ses	=	Net Income
a.	−		=	
b.	+5,000 Revenue	−	=	+5,000

Cash   5,000
  UR   5,000

  Cash
5,000 |
  UR
      | 5,000

UR   5,000
  REV   5,000

  UR
5,000 |
  REV
      | 5,000

One of two types of accounts arise when cash is received or paid *after* recognition of revenue or expense.

Accrued expenses Accrued expenses are expenses incurred and recognized on the income statement, even though they are not yet paid in cash; an example is wages owed to employees who performed work but who have not yet been paid.

Accrued revenues Accrued revenues are revenues earned and recognized on the income statement, even though cash is not yet received; examples include accounts receivable and revenue earned under a long-term contract.

To illustrate accrued expenses, assume that $100 of wages earned by Apple employees this period is paid the following period. The period-end adjustment, and subsequent payment the following period, are both reflected in the following template.

	Balance Sheet									
Transaction	Cash Asset	+	Noncash Assets	=	Liabil-ities	+	Contrib. Capital	+	Earned Capital	
Period 1: Accrue $100 wages expense and liability				=	+100 Wages Payable			−100 Retained Earnings		
Period 2: Pay $100 cash for wages	−100 Cash			=	−100 Wages Payable					

	Income Statement			
	Rev-enues	−	Expen-ses	=	Net Income
Period 1:	−		+100 Wages Expense	=	−100
Period 2:	−		=	

WE   100
  WP   100

  WE
100 |
  WP
      | 100

WP   100
  Cash   100

  WP
100 |
  Cash
      | 100

Wages expense is recorded in period 1's income statement because it is incurred by the company and earned by employees in that period. Also, a liability is recorded in period 1 reflecting the company's obligation to make payment to employees. In period 2, the wages are paid, which means that both cash and the liability are reduced.

To illustrate the accrual of revenues, assume that Apple is performing work under a long-term contract that allows it to bill the customer periodically as work is performed. At the end of the current period, it determines that it has earned $100,000 per contact. The accrual of this revenue and its subsequent collection are recorded as follows ($ 000s):

Transaction	Balance Sheet						Income Statement					
	Cash Asset	+	Noncash Assets	=	Liabil- ities	+	Contrib. Capital	+	Earned Capital	Rev- enues	−	Expen- ses	=	Net Income
a. Accrual of $100 of earned revenue			+100 Accounts Receivable	=					+100 Retained Earnings	+100 Revenue	−		=	+100
b. Collection of account receivable	+100 Cash		−100 Accounts Receivable	=							−		=	

Companies make these sort of adjustments to more accurately and completely report their financial performance and condition. Each of these adjustments is made by company managers and accountants based on the review of financial statements and information suggesting that adjustments are necessary to properly reflect financial condition and performance.

Constructing Financial Statements

We can prepare each of the four financial statements directly from our financial statement effects template. The balance sheet and income statement accounts, and their respective balances, can be read off the bottom row that totals the transactions and adjustments recorded during the period. The statement of cash flows and statement of stockholders' equity are represented by the cash column and the contributed and earned capital columns, respectively.

Illustration: Recording Transactions, Adjusting Accounts, and Preparing Statements

This section provides a comprehensive illustration that uses the financial statement effects template with a number of transactions related to Apple's 2007 financial statements shown earlier. These summary transactions are described in the far left column of the following template. Each column is summed to arrive at the balance sheet and income statement totals which tie to Apple's statements. Detailed explanations for each transaction are provided after the template. Then, we use the information in the template to construct Apple's financial statements.

		Balance Sheet						Income Statement		
Transaction	Cash Asset	+ Noncash Assets	= Liabil- ities	+ Contrib. Capital	+ Earned Capital		Rev- enues	− Expen- ses	= Net Income
Bal., Sept. 30, 2006	6,392	10,813 =	7,221	4,355	5,629		−	=
1. Issue common stock for $1,013 cash	+1,013 Cash	=		+1,013 Common stock			−	=
2. Purchase $738 of PPE, financed by $738 of long-term debt		+738 PPE, net =	+738 Long-Term Debt				−	=
3. Purchase $15,928 of inventories on credit		+15,928 Inventories =	+15,928 Accounts Payable				−	=
4. Sell inventories for $24,006 on credit; the cost of inventories is $15,852		+24,006 Accounts Receivable =			+24,006 Retained Earnings		+24,006 Sales −	= +24,006
		−15,852 Inventory =			−15,852 Retained Earnings		− +15,852 Cost of Goods Sold =	−15,852
5. Receive $23,621 cash for accounts receivable;	+23,621 Cash	−23,621 Accounts Receivable =					−	=
Pay $14,348 cash for accounts payable	−14,348 Cash	=	−14,348 Accounts Payable				−	=
6. Pay $3,664 cash for R&D, SGA (excluding depreciation), interest, and taxes	−3,664 Cash	=			−3,664 Retained Earnings		− +3,664 Operating Expenses =	−3,664
7. Accrue expenses of $1,276		=	+1,276 Accrued Liabilities		−1,276 Retained Earnings		− +1,276 Operating Expenses =	−1,276
8. Purchase securities for $4,261 cash	−4,261 Cash	+4,261 Marketable Securities =					−	=
9. Record depreciation of $317		−317 PPE, net =			−317 Retained Earnings		− +317 Depreciation Expense =	−317
10. Record net investment income of $599	+599 Cash	=			+599 Retained Earnings		+599 Investment Income −	= +599
11. Miscellaneous		+39 Other Assets =			+39 Accumulated Other Comp. Income		−	=
Bal., Sept. 29, 2007	9,352	+ 15,995 =	10,815	+ 5,368	+ 9,164		24,605 −	21,109 = 3,496

Left margin T-accounts:

```
Cash   1,013
   CS        1,013
       Cash
1,013 |
     CS
       | 1,013

PPE   738
   LTD       738
       PPE
738 |
     LTD
       | 738

INV   15,928
   AP        15,928
       INV
15,928 |
      AP
       | 15,928

AR   24,006
   Sales     24,006
       AR
24,006 |
     Sales
       | 24,006

COGS  15,852
   INV       15,852
      COGS
15,852 |
      INV
       | 15,852

Cash  23,621
   AR        23,621
      Cash
23,621 |
      AR
       | 23,621

AP   14,348
   Cash      14,348
      AP
14,348 |
     Cash
       | 14,348

OE   3,664
   Cash      3,664
       OE
3,664 |
     Cash
       | 3,664

OE   1,276
   ACC       1,276
       OE
1,276 |
     ACC
       | 1,276

MS   4,261
   Cash      4,261
       MS
4,261 |
     Cash
       | 4,261

DE   317
   PPE       317
       DE
317 |
     PPE
       | 317

Cash  599
   OI        599
      Cash
599 |
      OI
       | 599

OA   39
   AOCI      39
       OA
39 |
     AOCI
       | 39
```

Transaction Explanation Apple begins fiscal year 2007 with $17,205 million in total assets, consisting of $6,392 million of cash and $10,813 million of noncash assets. It also reports $7,221 million of liabilities and $9,984 million of stockholders' equity ($4,355 million of contributed capital and $5,629 million of earned capital, which includes other equity for this exhibit). During the year, eleven summary transactions occur that are described below.

1. **Owner Financing.** Companies raise funds from two sources: investing from shareholders and borrowing from creditors. Transaction 1 reflects issuance of common stock for $1,013 million. Cash is increased by that amount, as is contributed capital. Stock issuance (as well as its repurchase and any dividends paid to shareholders) does not impact income. Companies cannot record profit by trading in their own stock.

2. **Purchase PPE financed by debt.** Apple acquires $738 million of property, plant and equipment (PPE), and it finances this acquisition with a $738 million loan. Noncash assets increase by the $738 million of PPE, and liabilities increase by $738 million of long-term debt. PPE is initially reported on the balance sheet at the cost Apple paid to acquire it. When plant and equipment are used, a portion of the purchase cost is transferred from the balance sheet to the income statement as an expense called depreciation. Accounting for depreciation is shown in Transaction 9. The borrowing of money does not yield income, and repaying the principal amount borrowed is not an expense. Paying interest *on* liabilities, however, is an expense.

3. **Purchase inventories on credit.** Companies commonly acquire inventories from suppliers *on credit* (also called *on account*). The phrase "on credit" means that the purchase has not yet been paid for. A purchaser is typically allowed 30 days or more during which to make payment. When acquired in this manner, noncash assets (inventories) increase by the $15,928 million cost of the acquired inventory, and a liability (accounts payable) increases to reflect the amount owed to the supplier. Although inventories (iPods, for example) normally carry a retail selling price that is higher than cost, this eventual profit is not recognized until inventories are sold.

4. **Sell inventories on credit.** Apple subsequently sells inventories that cost $15,852 million for a retail selling price of $24,006 million *on credit*. The phrase "on credit" means that Apple has not yet received cash for the selling price; cash receipt is expected in the future. The sale of inventories is recorded in two parts: the revenue part and the expense part. First, the sale is recorded by an increase in both revenues and noncash assets (accounts receivable). Revenues increase net income which, in turn, increases earned capital (via retained earnings). Second, the cost of inventories sold is removed from the balance sheet (Apple no longer owns those assets), and is transferred to the income statement as an expense, called *cost of goods sold,* which decreases both net income and earned capital by $15,852 (again, via retained earnings).

5. **Collect receivables and settle payables.** Apple receives $23,621 million cash from the collection of its accounts receivable, thus reducing noncash assets (accounts receivable) by that amount. Apple uses these proceeds to pay off $14,348 of its liabilities (accounts payable and other liabilities). Collecting accounts receivable does not yield revenue; instead, revenue is recognized when *earned* (see Transaction 4). Thus, recognizing revenue when earned does not necessarily yield an immediate cash increase.

6. **Pay cash for expenses.** Apple pays $3,664 million cash for expenses. This payment increases expenses, and reduces net income (and earned capital). Expenses are recognized when incurred, regardless of when they are paid. Expenses are both incurred and paid in this transaction. Transaction 7 is a case where expenses are recognized *before* being paid.

7. **Accrue expenses.** Accrued expenses relate to expenses that are incurred but not yet paid. For example, employees often work near the end of a period but are not paid until the next period. The company must record wages expense even though employees have not yet been paid in cash. The rationale is that expenses must be *matched* against current period revenues to report the correct income for the period. In this transaction, Apple accrues $1,276 million of expenses, which reduces net income (and earned capital). Apple simultaneously records a $1,276 million increase in liabilities for its obligation to make future payment. This transaction is an accounting adjustment, or accrual.

8. **Purchase noncash assets.** Apple uses $4,261 million of its excess cash to purchase marketable securities as an investment. Thus, noncash assets increase. This is a common use of excess cash,

especially for high-tech companies that desire added liquidity to take advantage of opportunities in a rapidly changing industry.

9. **Record depreciation.** Transaction 9 is another accounting adjustment. In this case, Apple recognizes that a portion of its plant and equipment is "used up" while generating revenues. Thus, it matches a portion of the PPE cost as an expense against the revenues recognized during the period. In this case, $317 million of PPE cost is removed from the balance sheet and transferred to the income statement as depreciation expense. Net income (and earned capital) are reduced by $317 million.

10. **Record investment income.** Apple recognizes $599 of investment income in transaction 10. Profit increases by this same amount, resulting in an increase in Retained Earnings.

11. **Miscellaneous.** The final transaction is a miscellaneous adjustment to noncash assets and an earned capital account called accumulated other comprehensive income, which is distinct from retained earnings. We discuss this account in Module 9.

We can use the column totals from the financial statement effects template to prepare Apple's financial statements (in condensed form). We derive Apple's 2007 balance sheet and income statement from the template as follows ($ millions).

APPLE, INC. Condensed Balance Sheet September 29, 2007	
Cash asset	$ 9,352
Noncash assets	15,995
Total assets	$25,347
Liabilities	$10,815
Contributed capital	5,368
Earned capital	9,164
Total liabilities and equity	$25,347

APPLE, INC. Condensed Income Statement For the Year Ended September 29, 2007	
Revenues	$24,605
Expenses	21,109
Net income	$ 3,496

We can summarize Apple's cash transactions from the cash column of the template. The cash column of the financial effects template reveals that cash increases by $2,960 million during the year from $6,392 million to $9,352 million, see the following statement. Items that contribute to this net increase are identified by the cash entries in that column (the subtotals for operating, investing, and financing sections are slightly different from actual results because of simplifying assumptions we make for our transactions example).

APPLE, INC. Statement of Cash Flows ($ millions) For the Year Ended September 29, 2007	
Operating cash flows (+ $23,621 − $14,348 − $3,664 + $599)	$6,208
Investing cash flows	(4,261)
Financing cash flows	1,013
Net change in cash	$2,960
Cash balance, Sep. 30, 2006	6,392
Cash balance, Sep. 29, 2007	$9,352

Apple's statement of stockholders' equity summarizes the transactions relating to its equity accounts. This statement follows and is organized into its contributed capital and earned capital categories of equity.

($ millions)	Contributed Capital	Earned Capital	Total
APPLE, INC. Condensed Statement of Stockholders' Equity September 29, 2007			
Balance, September 30, 2006	$4,355	$5,629	$ 9,984
Issuance of common stock	1,013		1,013
Net income.		3,496	3,496
Miscellaneous.		39	39
Balance, September 29, 2007	$5,368	$9,164	$14,532

Apple's financial statements are abbreviated versions of those reproduced earlier in the module. We describe the preparation of financial statements and other accounting details at greater length in Module 3.

MODULE-END REVIEW

At December 31, 2008, assume that the condensed balance sheet of Gateway shows the following.

Cash.	$ 80,000	Liabilities.	$200,000
Noncash assets	270,000	Contributed capital.	50,000
		Earned capital	100,000
Total assets.	$350,000	Total liabilities and equity	$350,000

Assume the following summary transactions occur during 2009.

1. Purchase inventory of $80,000 on credit.
2. Pay employees $10,000 cash for wages earned this year.
3. Sell inventory costing $40,000 for $70,000 on credit.
4. Collect $15,000 cash from the account receivables in transaction 3.
5. Pay $35,000 cash toward the account payables in transaction 1.
6. Purchase advertising for $25,000 cash that will air next year.
7. Employees earn $5,000 in wages that will not be paid until next year.
8. Record $3,000 depreciation on its equipment.

Required

a. Record transactions 1 through 8 using the financial statement effects template.
b. Prepare the income statement and balance sheet for 2009.
c. Show linkage(s) between the income statement and the balance sheet.

Solution

a.

	Balance Sheet					Income Statement		
Transaction	Cash Asset	+ Noncash Assets	= Liabil- ities	+ Contrib. Capital	+ Earned Capital	Rev- enues	− Expen- ses	= Net Income
Beginning balance	+80,000	+270,000	= +200,000	+50,000	+100,000		−	=
1. Purchase inventory of $80,000 on credit		+80,000 Inventory	= +80,000 Account Payable				−	=

continued

continued from prior page

	Balance Sheet					Income Statement		
Transaction	Cash Asset	+ Noncash Assets	= Liabil- ities	+ Contrib. Capital	+ Earned Capital	Rev- enues	− Expen- ses	= Net Income
2. Pay employees $10,000 cash for wages earned this year	−10,000 Cash		=		−10,000 Retained Earnings		− +10,000 Wages Expense	= −10,000
3. Sell inventory costing $40,000 for $70,000 on credit		+70,000 Accounts Receivable −40,000 Inventory	=		+70,000 Retained Earnings −40,000 Retained Earning	+70,000 Sales	− +40,000 Cost of Goods Sold	= +70,000 = −40,000
4. Collect $15,000 cash from the account receivables in transaction 3	+15,000 Cash	−15,000 Accounts Receivable	=				−	=
5. Pay $35,000 cash toward the account payables in transaction 1	−35,000 Cash		= −35,000 Account Payable				−	=
6. Purchase advertising for $25,000 cash that will air next year	−25,000 Cash	+25,000 Prepaid Advertising	=				−	=
7. Employees earn $5,000 in wages that will not be paid until next year			= +5,000 Wages Payable		−5,000 Retained Earnings		− +5,000 Wages Expense	= −5,000
8. Record $3,000 depreciation on its equipment		−3,000 PPE, net	=		−3,000 Retained Earnings		− +3,000 Depreciation Expense	= −3,000
Ending balance	+25,000	+387,000	= +250,000	+50,000	+112,000	+70,000	− +58,000	= +12,000

b.

GATEWAY Income Statement For Year Ended December 31, 2009	
Revenues	$70,000
Expenses	58,000
Net income.	$12,000

GATEWAY Balance Sheet December 31, 2009			
Cash.................	$ 25,000	Liabilities.................	$250,000
Noncash assets........	387,000	Contributed capital..........	50,000
		Earned income............	112,000
Total assets...........	$412,000	Total liabilities and equity.....	$412,000

c. The linkage between the income statement and the balance sheet is Retained Earnings. Each period, the Retained Earnings account is updated for the profit earned less dividends paid. For this period, that updating follows.

GATEWAY Retained Earnings Reconciliation For Year Ended December 31, 2009	
Retained earnings, Dec. 31, 2008.....	$100,000
Add: Net income..................	12,000
Less: Dividends...................	(0)
Retained earnings, Dec. 31, 2009.....	$112,000

APPENDIX 2A: Additional Information Sources

The four financial statements are only a part of the information available to financial statement users. Additional information, from a variety of sources, provides useful insight into company operating activities and future prospects. This section highlights additional information sources.

Form 10-K

Companies with publicly traded securities must file a detailed annual report and discussion of their business activities in their Form 10-K with the SEC (quarterly reports are filed on form 10-Q). Many of the disclosures in the 10-K are mandated by law and include the following general categories: Item 1, *Business;* Item 1A. *Risk Factors;* Item 2, *Properties;* Item 3, *Legal Proceedings;* Item 4, *Submission of Matters to a Vote of Security Holders;* Item 5, *Market for Registrant's Common Equity and Related Stockholder Matters;* Item 6, *Selected Financial Data;* Item 7, *Management's Discussion and Analysis of Financial Condition and Results of Operations;* Item 7A, *Quantitative and Qualitative Disclosures About Market Risk;* Item 8, *Financial Statements and Supplementary Data;* Item 9, *Changes in and Disagreements With Accountants on Accounting and Financial Disclosure;* Item 9A, *Controls and Procedures.*

Description of the Business (Item 1)

Companies must provide a general description of their business, including their principal products and services, the source and availability of required raw materials, all patents, trademarks, licenses, and important related agreements, seasonality of the business, any dependence upon a single customer, competitive conditions, including particular markets in which the company competes, the product offerings in those markets, and the status of its competitive environment. Companies must also provide a description of their overall strategy. Apple's partial disclosure follows:

> The Company is committed to bringing the best personal computing, portable digital music and mobile communication experience to students, educators, creative professionals, businesses, government agencies, and consumers through its innovative hardware, software, peripherals, services, and Internet offerings. The Company's business strategy leverages its unique ability to design and develop its own operating system, hardware, application software, and services to provide its customers new products and solutions with superior ease-of-use, seamless integration, and innovative industrial design. The Company believes continual investment in research and development is critical to the development and enhancement of innovative products and technologies. In addition to evolving its personal computers and related solutions, the Company continues to capitalize on the convergence of the personal computer, digital consumer electronics and mobile communications by creating and refining innovations, such as the iPod, iPhone, iTunes Store, and Apple TV. The Company's strategy also includes expanding its distribution network to effectively reach more of its targeted customers and provide them with a high-quality sales and post-sales support experience.

Management's Discussion and Analysis of Financial Condition and Results of Operations (Item 7)

The management discussion and analysis (MD&A) section of the 10-K contains valuable insight into the company's results of operations. In addition to an executive overview of company status and its recent operating results, the MD&A section includes information relating to its critical accounting policies and estimates used in preparing its financial statements, a detailed discussion of its sales activity, year-over-year comparisons of operating activities, analysis of gross margin, operating expenses, taxes, and off-balance-sheet and contractual obligations, assessment of factors that affect future results and financial condition. Item 7A reports quantitative and qualitative disclosures about market risk. For example, Apple makes the following disclosure relating to its Mac operating system and its iPods.

> The Company is currently the only maker of hardware using the Mac OS. The Mac OS has a minority market share in the personal computer market, which is dominated by makers of computers using competing operating systems, most notably Windows. The Company's financial condition and operating results substantially depend on its ability to continually develop improvements to the Mac platform to maintain perceived design and functional advantages. Use of unauthorized copies of the Mac OS on other companies' hardware products may result in decreased demand for the Company's hardware products, and materially adversely affect its financial condition and operating results.

Form 8-K

Another useful report that is required by the SEC and is publicly available is the Form 8-K. This form must be filed within four business days of any of the following events:

- Entry into or termination of a material definitive agreement (including petition for bankruptcy)
- Exit from a line of business or impairment of assets
- Change in the company's certified public accounting firm
- Change in control of the company
- Departure of the company's executive officers
- Changes in the company's articles of incorporation or bylaws

Outsiders typically use Form 8-K to monitor for material adverse changes in the company.

Analyst Reports

Sell-side analysts provide their clients with objective analyses of company operating activities. Frequently, these reports include a discussion of the competitive environment for each of the company's principal product lines, strengths and weaknesses of the company, and an investment recommendation, including financial analysis and a stock price target. For example, Deutsche Bank provides the following in its June 2008 report to clients on Apple:

Credit Services

Several firms including Standard & Poor's (**StandardAndPoors.com**), Moody's Investors Service (**Moodys. com**), and Fitch Ratings (**FitchRatings.com**) provide credit analysis that assists potential lenders, investors, employees, and other users in evaluating a company's creditworthiness and future financial viability. Credit analysis is a specialized field of analysis, quite different from the equity analysis illustrated here. These firms issue credit ratings on publicly issued bonds as well as on firms' commercial paper.

Data Services

A number of companies supply financial statement data in easy-to-download spreadsheet formats. Thomson Corporation (**Thomson.com**) provides a wealth of information to its database subscribers, including the widely quoted *First Call* summary of analysts' earnings forecasts. Standard & Poor's provides financial data for all publicly traded companies in its *Compustat* database. This database reports a plethora of individual data items for all publicly traded companies or for any specified subset of companies. These data are useful for performing statistical analysis and making comparisons across companies or within industries. Finally, Capital IQ (www.CapitalIQ. com), a division of Standard & Poors, provides "as presented" financial data that conform to published financial statements as well as additional statistical data and analysis.

GUIDANCE ANSWERS

MANAGERIAL DECISION You are the Securities Analyst

Of special concern is the possibility that the new CEO is shifting costs to the current period in lieu of recording them in future periods. Evidence suggests that such behavior occurs when a new management team takes control. The reasoning is that the new management can blame poor current period performance on prior management and, at the same time, rid the balance sheet (and the new management team) of costs that would normally be expensed in future periods.

MANAGERIAL DECISION You are the Operations Manager

The CFO desires a warranty cost estimate that matches the sales generated from the new product. To arrive at such an estimate, you must estimate the expected number and types of deficiencies in your product and the costs to repair each deficiency per the warranty provisions. This is often a difficult task for product engineers because it forces them to focus on product failures and associated costs.

Superscript [A] denotes assignments based on Appendix 2A.

DISCUSSION QUESTIONS

Q2-1. The balance sheet consists of assets, liabilities, and equity. Define each category and provide two examples of accounts reported within each category.

Q2-2. Two important concepts that guide income statement reporting are the revenue recognition principle and the matching principle. Define and explain each of these two guiding principles.

Q2-3. GAAP is based on the concept of accrual accounting. Define and describe accrual accounting.

Q2-4. Analysts attempt to identify transitory items in an income statement. Define transitory items. What is the purpose of identifying transitory items?

Q2-5. What is the statement of stockholders' equity? What useful information does it contain?

Q2-6. What is the statement of cash flows? What useful information does it contain?

Q2-7. Define and explain the concept of financial statement articulation. What insight comes from understanding articulation?

Q2-8. Describe the flow of costs for the purchase of a machine. At what point do such costs become expenses? Why is it necessary to record the expenses related to the machine in the same period as the revenues it produces?

Q2-9. What are the two essential characteristics of an asset?

Q2-10. What does the concept of liquidity refer to? Explain.

Q2-11. What does the term *current* denote when referring to assets?

3 **Q2-12.** Assets are recorded at historical costs even though current market values might, arguably, be more relevant to financial statement readers. Describe the reasoning behind historical cost usage.

3 **Q2-13.** Identify three intangible assets that are likely to be *excluded* from the balance sheet because they cannot be reliably measured.

Q2-14. Identify three intangible assets that are recorded on the balance sheet.

Q2-15. What are accrued liabilities? Provide an example.

Q2-16. Define net working capital. Explain how increasing the amount of trade credit can reduce the net working capital for a company.

3 **Q2-17.** What is the difference between company *book value* and *market value*? Explain why these two amounts differ.

Q2-18. The financial statement effects template includes an arrow line running from net income to earned capital. What does this arrow line denote?

Assignments with the WebAssign. logo in the margin are available in WebAssign. See the Preface of the book for details.

MINI EXERCISES

M2-19. Identifying and Classifying Financial Statement Items (LO1)
For each of the following items, indicate whether they would be reported in the balance sheet (B) or income statement (I).

a.	Net income	*d.*	Accumulated depreciation	*g.*	Interest expense
b.	Retained earnings	*e.*	Wages expense	*h.*	Interest payable
c.	Depreciation expense	*f.*	Wages payable	*i.*	Sales

WebAssign. *3* **M2-20. Identifying and Classifying Financial Statement Items (LO1)**
For each of the following items, indicate whether they would be reported in the balance sheet (B) or income statement (I).

a.	Machinery	*e.*	Common stock	*i.*	Taxes expense
b.	Supplies expense	*f.*	Factory buildings	*j.*	Cost of goods sold
c.	Inventories	*g.*	Receivables	*k.*	Long-term debt
d.	Sales	*h.*	Taxes payable	*l.*	Treasury stock

M2-21. Computing and Comparing Income and Cash Flow Measures (LO1)
Penno Corporation recorded service revenues of $100,000 in 2009, of which $70,000 were on credit and $30,000 were for cash. Moreover, of the $70,000 credit sales for 2009, Penno collected $20,000 cash on those receivables before year-end 2009. The company also paid $25,000 cash for 2009 wages. Its employees also earned another $15,000 in wages for 2009, which were not yet paid at year-end 2009. (a) Compute the company's net income for 2009. (b) How much net cash inflow or outflow did the company generate in 2009? Explain why Penno's net income and net cash flow differ.

M2-22. Assigning Accounts to Sections of the Balance Sheet (LO1)
Identify each of the following accounts as a component of assets (A), liabilities (L), or equity (E).

a.	Cash and cash equivalents	_____	*e.*	Long-term debt	_____
b.	Wages payable	_____	*f.*	Retained earnings	_____
c.	Common stock	_____	*g.*	Additional paid-in capital	_____
d.	Equipment	_____	*h.*	Taxes payable	_____

WebAssign. **M2-23. Determining Missing Information Using the Accounting Equation (LO1)**
Use your knowledge of accounting relations to complete the following table for Boatsman Company.

	2008	2009
Beginning retained earnings.....	$89,089	$?
Net income (loss).............	?	48,192
Dividends..................	0	15,060
Ending retained earnings.......	69,634	?

M2-24. **Reconciling Retained Earnings** **(LO1)**

Following is financial information from Johnson & Johnson for 2007. Prepare the 2007 retained earnings reconciliation for Johnson & Johnson ($ millions).

Johnson & Johnson (JNJ)

Retained earnings, Dec. 31, 2006	$49,290	Dividends......................	$4,670
Net earnings.....................	10,576	Retained earnings, Dec. 31, 2007....	?
Other retained earnings changes.....	84		

M2-25. **Analyzing Transactions to Compute Net Income** **(LO1)**

Wasley Corp., a start-up company, provided services that were acceptable to its customers and billed those customers for $350,000 in 2009. However, Wasley collected only $280,000 cash in 2009, and the remaining $70,000 was collected in 2010. Wasley employees earned $200,000 in 2009 wages that were not paid until the first week of 2010. How much net income does Wasley report for 2009? For 2010 (assuming no additional transactions)?

M2-26. **Analyzing Transactions Using the Financial Statement Effects Template** **(LO3)**

Report the effects for each of the following transactions using the financial statement effects template.

a. Issue stock for $1,000 cash.
b. Purchase inventory for $500 cash.
c. Sell inventory in transaction *b* for $2,000 on credit.
d. Receive $2,000 cash toward transaction *c* receivable.

EXERCISES

E2-27. **Constructing Financial Statements from Account Data** **(LO1)**

WebAssign.

Barth Company reports the following year-end account balances at December 31, 2009. Prepare the 2009 income statement and the balance sheet as of December 31, 2009.

Accounts payable.............	$ 16,000	Inventory	$ 36,000
Accounts receivable...........	30,000	Land........................	80,000
Bonds payable, long-term	200,000	Goodwill....................	8,000
Buildings....................	151,000	Retained earnings	60,000
Cash.......................	48,000	Sales revenue...............	400,000
Common stock...............	150,000	Supplies inventory	3,000
Cost of goods sold...........	180,000	Supplies expense............	6,000
Equipment	70,000	Wages expense	40,000

E2-28. **Constructing Financial Statements from Transaction Data** **(LO1)**

Baiman Corporation commences operations at the beginning of January. It provides its services on credit and bills its customers $30,000 for January sales. Its employees also earn January wages of $12,000 that are not paid until the first of February. Complete the following statements for the month-end of January.

Income Statement	
Sales...................	$
Wages expense	
Net income (loss)	$

Balance Sheet	
Cash...................	$
Accounts receivable.......	
Total assets.............	$
Wages payable...........	$
Retained earnings	
Total liabilities and equity ...	$

E2-29. **Analyzing and Reporting Financial Statement Effects of Transactions** **(LO3)**

M.E. Carter launched a professional services firm on March 1. The firm will prepare financial statements at each month-end. In March (its first month), Carter executed the following transactions. Prepare an income statement for Carter Company for the month of March.

    a. Carter (owner) invested in the company, $100,000 cash and $20,000 in property and equipment. The company issued common stock to Carter.

    b. The company paid $3,200 cash for rent of office furnishings and facilities for March.

    c. The company performed services for clients and immediately received $4,000 cash earned.

    d. The company performed services for clients and sent a bill for $14,000 with payment due within 60 days.

    e. The company compensated an office employee with $4,800 cash as salary for March.

    f. The company received $10,000 cash as partial payment on the amount owed from clients in transaction *d.*

    g. The company paid $935 cash in dividends to Carter (owner).

2 E2-30. Analyzing Transactions Using the Financial Statement Effects Template (LO3)
Enter the effects of each of the transactions *a* through *g* from Exercise 2-29 using the financial statement effects template shown in the module.

E2-31. Identifying and Classifying Balance Sheet and Income Statement Accounts (LO1)
Following are selected accounts for Procter & Gamble. (*a*) Indicate whether each account appears on the balance sheet (B) or income statement (I). (*b*) Using the following data, compute total assets and total expenses. (*c*) Compute net profit margin (net income/sales) and total liabilities-to-equity ratio (total liabilities/stockholders' equity).

($ millions)	Amount	Classification
Sales.	$83,503	
Accumulated depreciation	17,446	
Depreciation expense.	3,166	
Retained earnings	48,986	
Net income.	12,075	
Property, plant & equipment, net	20,640	
Selling, general & administrative expense	25,725	
Accounts receivable.	6,761	
Total liabilities.	74,498	
Stockholders' equity	69,494	

2 E2-32. Identifying and Classifying Balance Sheet and Income Statement Accounts (LO1)
Following are selected accounts for Target Corporation. (*a*) Indicate whether each account appears on the balance sheet (B) or income statement (I). (*b*) Using the following data, compute total assets and total expenses. (*c*) Compute net profit margin (net income/sales) and total liability-to-equity ratio (total liabilities/stockholders' equity).

($ millions)	Amount	Classification
Sales.	$61,471	
Accumulated depreciation	7,887	
Depreciation expense.	1,659	
Retained earnings	12,761	
Net income.	2,849	
Property, plant & equipment, net	24,095	
Selling, general & administrative expense	13,704	
Accounts receivable.	8,054	
Total liabilities.	29,253	
Stockholders' equity	15,307	

E2-33. Comparing Income Statements and Balance Sheets of Competitors (LO1)
Following are selected income statement and balance sheet data from two retailers: Abercrombie & Fitch (clothing retailer in the high-end market) and TJX Companies (clothing retailer in the value-priced market).

Income Statement ($ millions)	ANF	TJX
Sales.	$3,750	$18,647
Cost of goods sold.	1,239	14,082
Gross profit.	2,511	4,565
Total expenses	2,035	3,793
Net income.	$ 476	$ 772

Balance Sheet ($ millions)	ANF	TJX
Current assets	$1,140	$3,992
Long-term assets	1,427	2,608
Total assets.	$2,567	$6,600
Current liabilities.	$ 543	$2,761
Long-term liabilities	406	1,708
Total liabilities	949	4,469
Stockholders' equity	1,618	2,131
Total liabilities and equity	$2,567	$6,600

a. Express each income statement amount as a percentage of sales. Comment on any differences observed between these two companies, especially as they relate to their respective business models.

b. Express each balance sheet amount as a percentage of total assets. Comment on any differences observed between these two companies, especially as they relate to their respective business models.

c. Which company has a higher proportion of stockholders' equity (and a lower proportion of debt)? What do the ratios tell us about relative riskiness of the two companies?

E2-34. Comparing Income Statements and Balance Sheets of Competitors (LO1)
Following are selected income statement and balance sheet data from two computer competitors: Apple and Dell.

Apple (AAPL)
Dell (DELL)

Income Statement ($ millions)	Apple	Dell
Sales.	$24,006	$61,133
Cost of goods sold.	15,852	49,462
Gross profit.	8,154	11,671
Total expenses	4,658	8,724
Net income.	$ 3,496	$ 2,947

Balance Sheet ($ millions)	Apple	Dell
Current assets	$21,956	$19,880
Long-term assets	3,391	7,681
Total assets.	$25,347	$27,561
Current liabilities.	$ 9,299	$18,526
Long-term liabilities	1,516	5,206
Total liabilities	10,815	23,732
Stockholders' equity	14,532	3,829
Total liabilities and equity	$25,347	$27,561

a. Express each income statement amount as a percentage of sales. Comment on any differences observed between the two companies, especially as they relate to their respective business models. (*Hint:* Apple's gross profit as a percentage of sales is considerably higher than Dell's. What aspect of Apple's business do we believe is driving its profitability?)

b. Apple has chosen to structure itself with a higher proportion of equity (and a lower proportion of debt) than Dell. How does this capital structure decision affect our evaluation of the relative riskiness of these two companies?

E2-35.   **Comparing Income Statements and Balance Sheets of Competitors   (LO1)**

Comcast (CMCSA)

Verizon (VZ)

Following are selected income statement and balance sheet data for two communications companies: Comcast and Verizon.

Income Statement ($ millions)	Comcast	Verizon
Sales.	$30,895	$93,469
Operating costs	25,317	77,891
Operating profit	5,578	15,578
Nonoperating expenses	2,991	10,057
Net income.	$ 2,587	$ 5,521

Balance Sheet ($ millions)	Comcast	Verizon
Current assets	$ 3,667	$ 18,698
Long-term assets	109,750	168,261
Total assets.	$113,417	$186,959
Current liabilities.	$ 7,952	$ 24,741
Long-term liabilities	63,875	79,349
Total liabilities	71,827	104,090
Stockholders' equity	41,590	82,869
Total liabilities and equity	$113,417	$186,959

a. Express each income statement amount as a percentage of sales. Comment on any differences observed between the two companies.

b. Express each balance sheet amount as a percentage of total assets. Comment on any differences observed between the two companies, especially as they relate to their respective business models.

c. Both Verizon and Comcast have chosen a capital structure with a higher proportion of liabilities than equity. How does this capital structure decision affect our evaluation of the riskiness of these two companies? Take into consideration the large level of capital expenditures that each must make to remain competitive.

E2-36.   **Comparing Financial Information Across Industries   (LO1)**

TJX Companies (TJX)

Apple, Inc (AAPL)

Use the data and computations required in parts *a* and *b* of exercises E2-33 and E2-34 to compare TJX Companies and Apple, Inc.

a. Compare gross profit and net income as a percentage of sales for these two companies. How might differences in their respective business models explain the differences observed?

b. Compare sales versus total assets. What do observed differences indicate about the relative capital intensity of these two industries?

c. Which company has the higher percentage of total liabilities to stockholders' equity? What do these ratios imply about the relative riskiness of these two companies?

d. Compare the ratio of net income to stockholders' equity for these two companies. Which business model appears to yield higher returns on shareholder investment? Using answers to parts *a* through *c* above, identify the factors that appear to drive the ratio of net income to stockholders' equity.

E2-37. **Analyzing Transactions Using the Financial Statement Effects Template** **(LO3)**
Record the effect of each of the following transactions for Hora Company using the financial statement effects template.

    a.   Wages of $500 are earned by employees but not yet paid.
    b. $2,000 of inventory is purchased on credit.
    c.   Inventory purchased in transaction *b* is sold for $3,000 on credit.
    d.   Collected $3,000 cash from transaction *c*.
    e.   Equipment is acquired for $5,000 cash.
    f.   Recorded $1,000 depreciation expense on equipment from transaction *e*.
    g.   Paid $10,000 cash toward a note payable that came due.
    h.   Paid $2,000 cash for interest on borrowings.

PROBLEMS

P2-38. **Constructing and Analyzing Balance Sheet Amounts from Incomplete Data** **(LO1)**
Selected balance sheet amounts for 3M Company, a manufacturer of consumer and business products, for three recent years follow.

3M Company (MMM)

$ millions	Current Assets	Long-Term Assets	Total Assets	Current Liabilities	Long-Term Liabilities	Total Liabilities	Stockholders' Equity*
2005.....	$7,115	$?	$20,541	$?	$4,908	$10,146	$10,395
2006.....	8,946	12,348	?	7,323	4,012	?	9,959
2007.....	?	14,856	24,694	5,362	7,585	12,947	?

* includes minority interest

Required
    a.   Compute the missing balance sheet amounts for each of the three years shown.
    b.   What types of accounts would we expect to be included in current assets? In long-term assets?

P2-39. **Analyzing Transactions Using the Financial Statement Effects Template** **(LO3)**
Sefcik Company began operations on the first of October. Following are the transactions for its first month of business.

    1.   S. Sefcik launched Sefcik Company and invested $50,000 into the business in exchange for common stock. The company also borrowed $100,000 from a local bank.
    2.   Sefcik Co. purchased equipment for $95,000 cash and purchased inventory of $40,000 on credit (the company stills owes its suppliers for the inventory at month-end).
    3.   Sefcik Co. sold inventory costing $30,000 for $50,000 cash.
    4.   Sefcik Co. paid $10,000 cash for wages owed employees for October work.
    5.   Sefcik Co. paid interest on the bank loan of $1,000 cash.
    6.   Sefcik Co. recorded $500 of depreciation expense related to its equipment.
    7.   Sefcik Co. paid a dividend of $2,000 cash.

Required
    a.   Record the effects of each transaction using the financial statement effects template.
    b.   Prepare the income statement and balance sheet at the end of October.

P2-40. **Analyzing Transactions Using the Financial Statement Effects Template** **(LO3)**
Following are selected transactions of Mogg Company. Record the effects of each using the financial statement effects template.

    1.   Shareholders contribute $10,000 cash to the business in exchange for common stock.
    2.   Employees earn $500 in wages that have not been paid at period-end.
    3.   Inventory of $3,000 is purchased on credit.
    4.   The inventory purchased in transaction 3 is sold for $4,500 on credit.
    5.   The company collected the $4,500 owed to it per transaction 4.
    6.   Equipment is purchased for $5,000 cash.
    7.   Depreciation of $1,000 is recorded on the equipment from transaction 6.

continued

8. The Supplies account had a $3,800 balance at the beginning of this period; a physical count at period-end shows that $800 of supplies are still available. No supplies were purchased during this period.

9. The company paid $10,000 cash toward the principal on a note payable; also, $500 cash is paid to cover this note's interest expense for the period.

10. The company receive $8,000 cash in advance for services to be delivered next period.

WebAssign. **P2-41. Comparing Operating Characteristics Across Industries (LO1)**

Following are selected income statement and balance sheet data for companies in different industries.

$ millions	Sales	Cost of Goods Sold	Gross Profit	Net income	Assets	Liabilities	Stockholders' Equity
Target Corp.	$63,367	$41,895	$21,472	$2,849	$44,560	$29,253	$15,307
Nike, Inc.	18,627	10,240	8,387	1,883	12,443	4,617	7,826
Harley-Davidson. . . .	5,727	3,613	2,114	934	5,657	3,282	2,375
Cisco Systems	39,540	14,056	25,484	8,052	58,734	24,332	34,402

Target (TGT)
Nike (NKE)
Harley-Davidson (HOG)
Cisco Systems (CSCO)

Required

a. Compute the following ratios for each company.
   1. Gross profit/Sales
   2. Net income/Sales
   3. Net income/Stockholders' equity
   4. Liabilities/Stockholders' equity

b. Comment on any differences among the companies' gross profit to sales ratios and net income as a percentage of sales. Do differences in the companies' business models explain the differences observed?

c. Which company reports the highest ratio of net income to equity? Suggest one or more reasons for this result.

d. Which company has financed itself with the highest percentage of liabilities to equity? Suggest one or more reasons why this company can take on such debt levels.

P2-42. Comparing Cash Flows Across Retailers (LO1)

Following are selected accounts from the income statement and the statement of cash flows for several retailers.

$ millions	Sales	Net Income	Cash Flows from Operating	Cash Flows from Investing	Cash Flows from Financing
Macy's	$ 26,313	$ 893	$ 2,231	$ (789)	$ (2,069)
Home Depot, Inc.	77,349	4,395	5,727	4,758	(10,639)
Staples, Inc.	19,373	996	1,361	(218)	(966)
Target Corp.	63,367	2,849	4,125	(6,195)	3,707
Wal-Mart Stores	378,799	12,731	20,354	(15,670)	(7,134)

Macy's (M)
Home Depot (HD)
Staples (SPLS)
Target (TGT)
Wal-Mart (WMT)

Required

a. Compute the ratio of net income to sales for each company. Rank the companies on the basis of this ratio. Do their respective business models give insight into these differences?

b. Compute net cash flows from operating activities as a percentage of sales. Rank the companies on the basis of this ratio. Does this ranking coincide with the ratio rankings from part *a*? Suggest one or more reasons for any differences you observe.

c. Compute net cash flows from investing activities as a percentage of sales. Rank the companies on the basis of this ratio. Does this ranking coincide with the ratio rankings from part *a*? Suggest one or more reasons for any differences you observe.

d. All of these companies, except Target, report negative cash flows from financing activities. What does it mean for a company to have net cash *outflow* from financing?

P2-43. Interpreting the Statement of Cash Flows (LO1)

Wal-Mart (WMT)

Following is the statement of cash flows for Wal-Mart Stores, Inc.

WAL-MART STORES, INC
Statement of Cash Flows
For Year Ended January 31, 2008 ($ millions)

Cash flows from operating activities	
Net income	$ 12,731
Loss from discontinued operations, net of tax	153
Income from continuing operations	12,884
Adjustments to reconcile income from continuing operations	
to net cash provided by operating activities:	
Depreciation and amortizations	6,317
Deferred income taxes	(8)
Other operating activities	601
Changes in certain assets and liabilities, net of effects of acquisitions:	
Increase in accounts receivable	(564)
Increase in inventories	(775)
Increase in accounts payable	865
Increase in accrued liabilities	1,034
Net cash provided by operating activities of continuing operations	20,354
Net cash provided by operating activities	20,354
Cash flows from investing activities	
Payments for property and equipment	$(14,937)
Proceeds from disposal of property and equipment	957
(Payments for) proceeds from disposal of certain international operations, net	(257)
Investment in international operations, net of cash acquired	(1,338)
Other investing activities	(95)
Net cash used in investing activities of continuing operations	(15,670)
Net cash used in investing activities	(15,670)
Cash flows from financing activities	
Increase (decrease) in commercial paper	2,376
Proceeds from issuance of long-term debt	11,167
Payment of long-term debt	(8,723)
Dividends paid	(3,586)
Purchase of company stock	(7,691)
Payment of capital lease obligations	(343)
Other financing activities	(334)
Net cash used in financing activities	(7,134)
Effect of exchange rate changes on cash	252
Net (decrease) increase in cash	$ (2,198)
Cash at beginning of year	7,767
Cash at end of year	$ 5,569

Required

a. Why does Wal-Mart add back depreciation to compute net cash flows from operating activities?

b. Explain why the increase in receivables and inventories is reported as a cash outflow. Why do accounts payable provide a source of cash? Explain why the increase in accrued liabilities is reported as a cash inflow.

c. Wal-Mart reports that it invested $14,937 million in property and equipment. Is this an appropriate type of expenditure for Wal-Mart to make? What relation should expenditures for PPE assets have with depreciation expense?

d. Wal-Mart indicates that it paid $7,691 million to repurchase its common stock in fiscal 2007 and, in addition, paid dividends of $3,586 million. Thus, Wal-Mart paid $11,277 million of cash to its shareholders during the year. How do we evaluate that use of cash relative to other possible uses for Wal-Mart's cash?

e. Provide an overall assessment of Wal-Mart's cash flows for 2007. In the analysis, consider the sources and uses of cash.

Verizon (VZ)

P2-44. **Interpreting the Statement of Cash Flows** **(LO1)**

Following is the statement of cash flows for Verizon.

VERIZON Statement of Cash Flows For Year Ended December 31, 2007 ($ millions)	
Cash Flows from Operating Activities	
Net income.	$ 5,521
Adjustments to reconcile net income to net cash provided by operating activities—continuing operations:	
Depreciation and amortization expense.	14,377
Employee retirement benefits.	1,720
Deferred income taxes	408
Provision for uncollectible accounts.	1,047
Equity in earnings of unconsolidated businesses, net of dividends received	1,986
Extraordinary item, net of tax	131
Changes in current assets and liabilities, net of effects from acquisition or disposition of businesses:	
Accounts receivabe.	(1,931)
Inventories.	(255)
Other assets	$ (140)
Accounts payable and accrued liabilities	(567)
Other, net	4,012
Net cash provided by operating activities—continuing operations	26,309
Net cash provided by operating activities—discontinued operations	(570)
Net cash provided by operating activities	25,739
Cash Flows from Investing Activities	
Capital expenditures (including capitalized software)	(17,538)
Acquisitions, net of cash acquired, and investments.	(763)
Net change in short-term and other current investments	169
Other, net	1,267
Net cash used in investing activities—continuing operations	(16,865)
Net cash provided by (used in) investing activities—discontinued operations	757
Net cash used in investing activities	(16,108)
Cash Flows from Financing Activities	
Proceeds from long-term borrowings	3,402
Repayments of long-term borrowings and capital lease obligations.	(5,503)
Increase (decrease) in short-term obligations, excluding current maturities	(3,252)
Dividends paid	(4,773)
Proceeds from sale of common stock	1,274
Purchase of common stock for treasury	(2,843)
Other, net	(2)
Net cash used in financing activities—continuing operations	(11,697)
Increase (decrease) in cash and cash equivalents.	$ (2,066)
Cash and cash equivalents, beginning of year	3,219
Cash and cash equivalents, end of year	$ 1,153

Required

a. Why does Verizon add back depreciation to compute net cash flows from operating activities? What does the size of the depreciation add-back indicate about the relative capital intensity of this industry?

b. Verizon reports that it invested $17,538 million in property and equipment. These expenditures are necessitated by market pressures as the company faces stiff competition from other communications companies, such as Comcast. Where in the 10-K might we find additional information about these capital expenditures to ascertain whether Verizon is addressing the company's most pressing needs? What relation might we expect between the size of these capital expenditures and the amount of depreciation expense reported?

continued

c. Verizon's statement of cash flows indicates that the company paid $8,755 million in debt payments, financed, in part, by the additional borrowing of $3,402 million on short-term notes. What problem does Verizon's high debt load pose for its ability to maintain the level of capital expenditures necessary to remain competitive in its industry?

d. During the year, Verizon paid dividends of $4,773 million but did not repay a sizeable portion of its debt. How do dividend payments differ from debt payments? Why would Verizon continue to pay dividends in light of cash demands for needed capital expenditures and debt repayments?

e. Provide an overall assessment of Verizon's cash flows for 2007. In the analysis, consider the sources and uses of cash.

P2-45. Analyzing Transactions Using the Financial Statement Effects Template (LO3)

On March 1, S. Penman (owner) launched AniFoods, Inc., an organic foods retailing company. Following are the transactions for its first month of business.

1. S. Penman (owner) contributed $100,000 cash to the company in return for common stock. Penman also lent the company $55,000. This $55,000 note is due one year hence.
2. The company purchased equipment in the amount of $50,000, paying $10,000 cash and signing a note payable to the equipment manufacturer for the remaining balance.
3. The company purchased inventory for $80,000 cash in March.
4. The company had March sales of $100,000 of which $60,000 was for cash and $40,000 on credit. Total cost of goods sold for its March sales was $70,000.
5. The company purchased future advertising time from a local radio station for $10,000 cash.
6. During March, $7,500 worth of radio spots purchased in transaction 5 are aired. The remaining spots will be aired in April.
7. Employee wages earned and paid during March total $15,000 cash.
8. Prior to disclosing the financial statements, the company recognized that employees had earned an additional $1,000 in wages that will be paid in the next period.
9. The company recorded $2,000 of depreciation for March relating to its equipment.

Required

a. Record the effect of each transaction using the financial statement effects template.

b. Prepare a March income statement and a balance sheet as of the end of March for AniFoods, Inc

P2-46. Analyzing Transactions Using the Financial Statement Effects Template (LO3)

Hanlon Advertising Company began the current month with the following balance sheet.

Cash	$ 80,000	Liabilities	$ 70,000
Noncash assets	135,000	Contributed capital	110,000
		Earned capital	35,000
Total assets	$215,000	Total liabilities and equity	$215,000

Following are summary transactions that occurred during the current month.

1. The company purchased supplies for $5,000 cash; none were used this month.
2. Services of $2,500 were performed this month on credit.
3. Services were performed for $10,000 cash this month.
4. The company purchased advertising for $8,000 cash; the ads will run next month.
5. The company received $1,200 cash as partial payment on accounts receivable from transaction 2.
6. The company paid $3,400 cash toward the accounts payable balance reported at the beginning of the month.
7. Paid $3,100 cash toward this month's wages expenses.
8. The company declared and paid dividends of $500 cash.

Required

a. Record the effects of each transaction using the financial statement effects template.

b. Prepare the income statement for this month and the balance sheet as of month-end.

P2-47. Reconciling and Computing Operating Cash Flows from Net Income (LO1)

Petroni Company reports the following selected results for its calendar year 2009.

Net income...................	$130,000
Depreciation expense..........	25,000
Accounts receivable increase....	10,000
Accounts payable increase	6,000
Prepaid expenses decrease.....	3,000
Wages payable decrease.......	4,000

Required

a. Prepare the operating section only of Petroni Company's statement of cash flows for 2009.
b. Does the positive sign on depreciation expense indicate that the company is generating cash by recording depreciation? Explain.
c. Explain why the increase in accounts receivable is a use of cash in the statement of cash flows.
d. Explain why the decrease in prepaid expense is a source of cash in the statement of cash flows.

P2-48. **Analyzing Transactions Using the Financial Statement Effects Template** (LO3)

Werner Realty Company began the month with the following balance sheet.

Cash.......................	$ 30,000	Liabilities.....................	$ 90,000
Noncash assets	225,000	Contributed capital.............	45,000
		Earned capital	120,000
Total assets..................	$255,000	Total liabilities and equity........	$255,000

Following are summary transactions that occurred during the current month.

1. The company purchased $6,000 of supplies on credit.
2. The company received $8,000 cash from a new customer for services to be performed next month.
3. The company paid $6,000 cash to cover office rent for two months (the current month and the next).
4. The company billed clients for $25,000 of work performed.
5. The company paid employees $6,000 cash for work performed.
6. The company collected $25,000 cash from accounts receivable in transaction 4.
7. The company recorded $3,000 depreciation on its equipment.
8. At month-end, $2,000 of supplies purchased in transaction 1 are still available; no supplies were available when the month began.

Required

a. Record the effects of each transaction using the financial statement effects template.
b. Prepare the income statement for this month and the balance sheet as of month-end.

MANAGEMENT APPLICATIONS

MA2-49. **Understanding the Company Operating Cycle and Management Strategy** (LO1)

Consider the operating cycle as depicted in Exhibit 2.4, to answer the following questions.

a. Why might a company want to reduce its cash conversion cycle? (*Hint*: Consider the financial statement implications of reducing the cash conversion cycle.)
b. How might a company reduce its cash conversion cycle?
c. Examine and discuss the potential impacts on *customers* and *suppliers* of taking the actions identified in part *b*.

MA2-50. **Ethics and Governance: Understanding Revenue Recognition and Expense Matching** **(LO1)**
Revenue should be recognized when it is earned and expense when incurred. Given some lack of specificity in these terms, companies have some latitude when applying GAAP to determine the timing and amount of revenues and expenses. A few companies use this latitude to manage reported earnings. Some have argued that it is not necessarily bad for companies to manage earnings in that, by doing so, management (1) can better provide investors and creditors with reported earnings that are closer to "core" earnings (that is, management purges earnings of components deemed irrelevant or distracting so that share prices better reflect company performance); and (2) can present the company in the best light, which benefits both shareholders and employees—a Machiavellian argument that "the end justifies the means."

a. Is it good that GAAP is written as broadly as it is? Explain. What are the pros and cons of defining accounting terms more strictly?

b. Assess (both pro and con) the Machiavellian argument above that defends managing earnings.

Module Three

Accounting Adjustments and Constructing Financial Statements

LEARNING OBJECTIVES

LO1 Analyze and record transactions using the financial statement effects template. (p. 3-4)

LO2 Prepare and explain accounting adjustments and their financial statement effects. (p. 3-8)

LO3 Explain and construct the trial balance. (p. 3-12)

LO4 Construct financial statements from the trial balance. (p. 3-16)

LO5 Describe the closing process. (p. 3-20)

APPLE

Apple Computer launched the iPod in late 2001, arguably the most important product in the company's history. A basic hard-drive-based player, the iPod was not a new concept. Yet, Apple created a durable, slim, and sexy package, paired it with ear buds, and made the iPod a fashion statement as well as a great music player. Marrying the hardware with the intuitive Apple-like software for navigation, the company had a winning combination. By the end of 2001, nearly 125,000 iPods had flown off the shelves.

The following March, Apple launched a 10 GB version of the iPod followed by a 20 GB version in July. Apple soon introduced its scroll wheel, similar to a touch pad with no moving parts. Apple sold 700,000 iPods in 2002.

The company announced even more innovations in early 2003: a 30 GB version, an improved connector that could use both FireWire and USB ports, and, the biggest coup: the iTunes music store. With that innovation, consumers could play songs on a PC, burn songs to a CD, or download them to their iPod. 2003 also witnessed the advent of the now-famous marketing campaign showcasing black silhouettes holding the blazing white iPod while dancing to its tunes. By mid-2003, Apple announced a new 40 GB version and unit sales soared to 939,000.

Apple soon introduced a smaller model, the iPod mini in five colors, and boasted more sophisticated ear buds to reduce background noise. But the major innovation was the advent of iPod video. The iPod was now a complete audio-visual phenomenon and well positioned to compete in the growing handheld communications market. 2004 unit sales were 4.4 million, a 370% increase over the prior year! But the story wasn't over: in 2008, Apple sold over 55 million iPods for a total of over $9 billion.

To bring each iPod to market, Apple must purchase component parts, manufacture the iPods, hire sales personnel, pay advertisers, and distribute finished iPods. Each of these activities involves a transaction that Apple's accounting records must capture. The resulting financial statements tell the story of Apple's manufacturing and sales process in financial language.

This module explains how the accounting system captures business transactions, creates financial records, and aggregates the individual records to produce the financial reports that we read and interpret in company 10-Ks. The resulting financial statements tell the story of Apple's business activities.

Sources: Apple 2007 10-K and 2008 3Q 10-Q; *Fortune*, January 2007 and 2009.

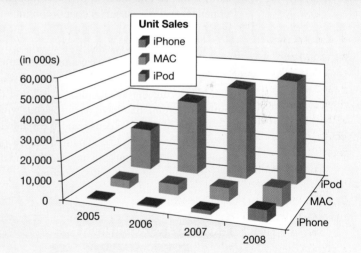

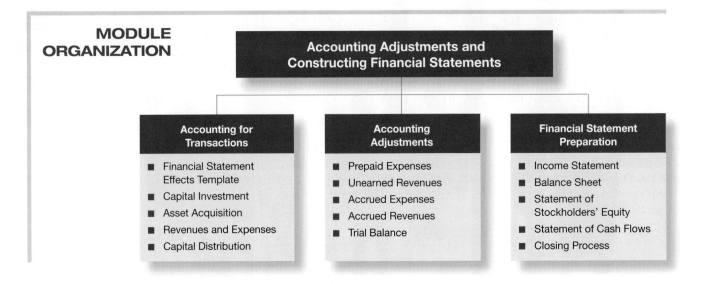

Financial statements report on the financial performance of a business using the language of accounting. To prepare these statements, companies translate day-to-day transactions into accounting records (called journals), and then record (post) them to individual accounts. At the end of an accounting period, each of these accounts is totaled, and the resulting balances are used to prepare financial statements. After the financial statements are prepared, the temporary (income statement) accounts are "zeroed out" so that the next period can begin anew—akin to clearing a scoreboard for the next game. Permanent (balance sheet) accounts continue to reflect financial position and carry over from period to period—akin to keeping track of wins and losses even when a particular scoreboard is cleared.

The *accounting cycle* is illustrated in Exhibit 3.1. Transactions are first recorded in the accounting records. Each of these transactions is, generally, the result of an external transaction, such as recording a sale to a customer or the payment of wages to employees. Once all of the transactions have been recorded during the accounting period, the company adjusts the accounting records to recognize a number of events that have occurred, but which have not yet been recorded. These might include the recognition of wage expense and the related wages payable for those employees who have earned wages, but have not yet been paid, or the recognition of depreciation expense for buildings and equipment. These adjustments are made at the end of the accounting period to properly adjust the accounting records before the financial statements are prepared. Once all adjustments are made, financial statements are prepared.

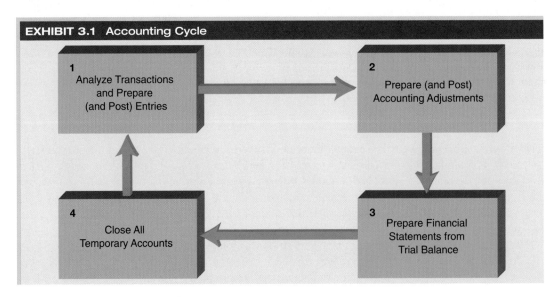

EXHIBIT 3.1 Accounting Cycle

The purpose of Module 3 is to explain further details of the accounting cycle. Our illustration includes journalizing transactions, posting entries to accounts, adjusting those accounts, preparing unadjusted and adjusted trial balances, constructing financial statements, and closing out temporary accounts before beginning the next accounting period. We also show how to construct the statement of cash flows under both the direct and indirect methods. Some topics from Module 2 are repeated here for completeness (the template, accounting adjustments, and basic financial statement preparation, for example). This module provides a more detailed introduction to the accounting recordkeeping process. However, understanding topics in the other modules does not require knowledge of the details in this Module.

Understanding the financial statement preparation process requires an understanding of the language used to record business transactions in accounting records. The recording and statement preparation processes are readily understood once we learn that language (of financial effects) and its mechanics (entries and posting). Even if we never journalize a transaction or prepare a financial statement, understanding the accounting process aids us in analyzing and interpreting accounting reports. Understanding the accounting language also facilitates our communication with business professionals within a company and with members of the business community outside of a company.

ACCOUNTING FOR TRANSACTIONS

This section explains how we account for and assess business transactions. We describe the financial statement effects template that we use throughout the book. We then illustrate its application to four main categories of business transactions.

LO1 Analyze and record transactions using the financial statement effects template.

Financial Statement Effects Template

Transaction analysis refers to the process of identifying, analyzing, and recording the financial statement effects of transactions. For this purpose, we use the following **financial statement effects template**.

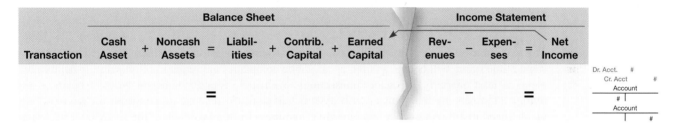

Each transaction is identified in the "Transaction" column. Then, the dollar amounts (positive or negative) of the financial statement effects are recorded in the appropriate balance sheet or income statement columns. The template also reflects the statement of cash flow effects (via the cash column) and the statement of stockholders' equity effects (via the contributed capital and earned capital columns). The retained earnings account, one of the accounts in earned capital, is immediately updated to reflect any income or loss arising from each transaction (denoted by the arrow line from net income to earned capital). This template is instructive as it reveals the financial impacts of transactions, and it provides insights into the effects of accounting choices.

T-Accounts and Journal Entries

The related journal entry and T-account effects are displayed in the margin next to the financial statement effects template. The **T-Accounts,** named for their likeness to a large 'T', are used to reflect increases and decreases to individual accounts. When a transaction occurs, it is recorded (*journalized*); once recorded, the specific accounts affected are updated in the accounting books (*general ledger*) of the company, and the affected accounts are increased or decreased. This process of continuously updating individual account balances is referred to as *posting* transactions to accounts. A T-account provides a simple illustration of the financial effects of each transaction.

Specifically, one side of the T-account is used for increases and the other for decreases. A convenient way to remember which side records increases is to recall the accounting equation: **Assets =**

Liabilities + Equity. Assets are on the left side of the equation. So, the left side of an asset T-account records increases in the asset and the right side records decreases. Liabilities and equity are on the right side of the accounting equation. So, the right side of a liability and an equity T-account records increases and the left side records decreases. This relation is represented graphically as follows:

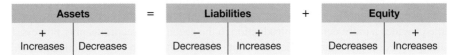

Assets		=	Liabilities		+	Equity	
+	−		−	+		−	+
Increases	Decreases		Decreases	Increases		Decreases	Increases

Journal entries also capture the effects of transactions. Journal entries reflect increases and decreases to accounts using the language of debits and credits. Debits and credits simply refer to the left or right side of a T-account, respectively. We can superimpose the descriptors of debit and credit on a T-account as follows.

Account Title	
Debit	Credit
(Left side)	(Right side)

The left side of the T-account is the "debit" side and the right side is the "credit" side. This holds for all T-accounts. Thus, to record an increase in an asset, we enter an amount on the left or debit side of the T-account—that is, we *debit the account*. Decreases in assets are recorded with an entry on the opposite (credit) side. To record an increase in a liability or equity account, we enter an amount on the right or credit side of the T-account—we *credit the account*. Decreases in liability or equity accounts are recorded on the left (debit) side.

In the margin of our financial statement effects template, we show the journal entry first, followed by the related T-accounts. In accounting jargon, this sequence relates to *journalizing* the entry and *posting* it to the affected accounts. The T-accounts represent the financial impact of each transaction on the respective asset, liability or equity accounts.

Transaction Analysis

This section uses Apple, Inc., to illustrate the accounting for selected business transactions. The assumed time frame will be one quarter, as all public companies are required to prepare financial statements at least quarterly. We select transactions to illustrate four fundamental types of business activities: (1) financing the company, (2) asset acquisition, (3) revenue and expense recognition, and (4) dividend distribution. Next, we record accounting adjustments, prepare the financial statements, and close the books.

Capital Investment
Assume that Apple investors contribute $300 cash to the company in exchange for common stock. Apple's cash and common stock both increase. Recall that common stock is a component of contributed capital. The following financial statement effects template reflects this transaction. If cash financing was obtained from a bank instead of shareholders, the only change would be to increase liabilities by $300, not contributed capital.

	Balance Sheet								Income Statement				
Transaction	Cash Asset	+	Noncash Assets	=	Liabil- ities	+	Contrib. Capital	+	Earned Capital	Rev- enues	−	Expen- ses	=	Net Income
Issue stock for $300 cash	+300 Cash			=			+300 Common Stock				−		=

Cash 300
CS 300

Cash
300 |
CS
| 300

Journal Entry and T-Account
Although we will not repeatedly refer to journal entries and T-accounts, we will describe them for this first transaction. Specifically, the $300 debit equals the $300 credit in the journal entry: assets ($300 cash) = liabilities ($0) + equity ($300 common stock). This balance in transactions is the basis of

double-entry accounting. For simplicity, we use acronyms (such as CS for common stock) in journal entries and T-accounts. (A listing of accounts and acronyms is located in Appendix C near the end of the book.) The journal entry for this transaction is

```
Cash..............................................    300
    CS (Common Stock) ................................        300
```

Convention dictates that debits are listed first, followed by credits—the latter are indented.[1] The total debit(s) must always equal the total credit(s) for each transaction. The T-account representation for this transaction follows:

Cash		CS	
300			300

Cash is an asset; thus, a cash increase is recorded on the left or debit side of the T-account. Common stock is an equity account; thus, a common stock increase is recorded on the right or credit side.

Asset Acquisition

Assume that Apple purchases $2,000 worth of iPods from its supplier (we keep this illustration simple by ignoring Apple's manufacturing activities). When one company buys from another, it is normal to give a period of time in which to pay the obligation due, usually 30 to 60 days, or more. This purchase "on credit" (also called *on account*) means that Apple owes its supplier $2,000 for the purchase. Apple records the cost of the purchased iPods as an asset called inventories, which are goods held for resale. This acquisition of iPods on credit is recorded as follows.

	Balance Sheet					Income Statement		
Transaction	Cash Asset	+ Noncash Assets	= Liabil- ities	+ Contrib. Capital	+ Earned Capital	Rev- enues	− Expen- ses	= Net Income
Purchase iPods for $2,000 on credit		+2,000 Inventory	+2,000 Accounts Payable			−	=	

INV   2,000
    AP   2,000
    INV
2,000 |
    AP
    | 2,000

Revenue and Expense Recognition

Assume that Apple sells iPods that cost $600 to a retailer for $700 on credit. The sale *on credit* means that the customer has not yet paid and Apple has a $700 account receivable. Can Apple record the $700 sale as revenue even though it has not collected any cash? The answer is yes. This decision reflects an important concept in accounting, called the **revenue recognition principle.** The revenue recognition principle prescribes that a company can recognize revenues provided that two conditions are met:

1. Revenues are *earned*, and
2. Revenues are *realized* or *realizable.*

Earned means that the company has done whatever it is required to do. In this case, it means that Apple has delivered the iPods to its retail customer. **Realized** or **realizable** means that the seller has either received cash or will receive cash at some point in the future. That is, Apple can recognize revenue if it expects to collect the $700 account receivable in the future.

Recording the $700 sale is only half the transaction. Apple must also record the decrease in iPod inventory of $600. When a company purchases inventory, it records the cost on the balance sheet as an asset. When inventory is sold, the "asset" is used up and its cost must be transferred from the balance sheet to the income statement as an expense. In particular, the expense associated with inventory is

---

[1] There can be more than one debit and one credit for a transaction. To illustrate, assume that Apple raises $300 cash, with $200 from investors and $100 borrowed from a bank. The resulting journal entry is:

```
Cash............................................    300
    CS (common stock) .................................        200
    NP (note payable)..................................        100
```

called cost of goods sold. Thus, the second part of Apple's revenue transaction is to remove the cost of the iPods from the balance sheet and recognize the cost of goods sold (an expense) in its income statement. This will match the cost of the inventory to the related revenue.

Matching of expenses with revenues in this manner is evidence of the **matching principle.** Once revenues are recognized (using the revenue recognition principle), we then match all related expenses incurred to generate those revenues *in the same period* that we recognize the revenue. This yields the proper measure of income for the period and is an application of accrual accounting.

The $700 sale of Apple iPods that cost $600 is recorded as follows.

	Balance Sheet						Income Statement		
Transaction	Cash Asset	+ Noncash Assets	= Liabil- ities	+ Contrib. Capital	+ Earned Capital		Rev- enues	− Expen- ses	= Net Income
Sell $700 of iPods on credit		+700 Accounts Receivable =			+700 Retained Earnings		+700 Sales	−	= +700
Record $600 cost of iPod sale		−600 Inventory =			−600 Retained Earnings			− +600 Cost of Goods Sold	= −600

Margin: AR 700 / Sales 700 / AR 700 | Sales | 700 / COGS 600 / INV 600 / COGS 600 | INV | 600

The first part of this sales transaction records the $700 sale and the $700 increase in accounts receivable. Revenues are earned and therefore recognized even though no cash was received. The sale is reflected in the account receivable that will later be converted to cash. The increase in revenues increases income, which increases retained earnings.[2]

The second part of this sale transaction transfers the $600 in inventory on the balance sheet to the income statement as the cost of iPods sold. This entry increases expenses, and decreases both income and retained earnings. The transaction also reduces assets because Apple no longer owns the inventory; it is "used up."

Capital Distributions

Assume that Apple decides to pay $50 to its shareholders in the form of a cash dividend. Dividends are treated as a return of shareholders' investment. All transactions between the company and its shareholders are considered financing transactions. This includes payment of dividends, the issuance of stock, and any subsequent stock repurchase. Financing transactions affect only the balance sheet; they do not affect the income statement. Dividends are distributions of income. They represent the portion of income that the company chooses to distribute to shareholders—the portion that will no longer be retained. Thus, dividends reduce retained earnings. It is important to distinguish dividends from expenses—dividends are NOT an expense, they do not reduce net income. They are a distribution of net income; they reduce retained earnings. Apple's $50 dividend payment is reflected in the following template. (Companies typically record dividends in a separate dividends account and then later, in the closing process, this account is transferred to retained earnings. The template depicts dividends as a reduction of earned capital; more precisely, it is a reduction of retained earnings, which is part of earned capital. Alternatively, one could record dividends as an immediate reduction to retained earnings; the end result of both approaches is identical.)

	Balance Sheet						Income Statement		
Transaction	Cash Asset	+ Noncash Assets	= Liabil- ities	+ Contrib. Capital	+ Earned Capital		Rev- enues	− Expen- ses	= Net Income
Pay $50 cash for dividends	−50 Cash		=		−50 Dividends			−	=

Margin: DIV 50 / Cash 50 / DIV 50 | Cash | 50

[2] The retained earnings account is not automatically updated in most accounting software programs as our financial effects template illustrates. Instead, accountants transfer income to retained earnings using a journal entry as part of the closing process. We briefly explain the closing process near the end of this module and more fully in Appendix 3A.

MID-MODULE REVIEW 1

Assume that Symantec Corporation experienced the following six transactions relating to a capital investment, the purchase and sale of inventory, the collection of an account receivable, and the payment of an account payable.

1. Shareholders contribute $3,000 cash to Symantec in exchange for its common shares.
2. Symantec purchases $1,000 of inventory on credit.
3. Symantec sells $300 of inventory for $500 on credit.
4. Symantec collects $300 cash owed by customers.
5. Symantec pays $400 cash toward its accounts payable to suppliers.
6. Symantec pays $20 cash for dividends to its stockholders.

Required

Record each transaction in the financial statement effects template. Include journal entries for each account in the margin and post those entries to T-accounts.

Solution

	Balance Sheet					Income Statement				
Transaction	Cash Asset	+ Noncash Assets	= Liabil- ities	+ Contrib. Capital	+ Earned Capital	Rev- enues	− Expen- ses	= Net Income		
1. Issue stock for $3,000 cash	+3,000 Cash		=	+3,000 Common Stock			−	=		Cash 3,000 / CS 3,000 / Cash: 3,000 / CS: 3,000
2. Purchase $1,000 of inventory on credit		+1,000 Inventory	= +1,000 Accounts Payable				−	=		INV 1,000 / AP 1,000 / INV 1,000 / AP 1,000
3a. Sell inventory for $500 on credit		+500 Accounts Receivable	=		+500 Retained Earnings	+500 Sales	−	= +500		AR 500 / Sales 500 / AR 500 / Sales 500
3b. Record $300 cost of inventory sold		−300 Inventory	=		−300 Retained Earnings		+300 Cost of Goods Sold	= −300		COGS 300 / INV 300 / COGS 300 / INV 300
4. Collect $300 cash owed by customers	+300 Cash	−300 Accounts Receivable	=				−	=		Cash 300 / AR 300 / Cash 300 / AR 300
5. Pay $400 cash toward accounts payable	−400 Cash		= −400 Accounts Payable				−	=		AP 400 / Cash 400 / AP 400 / Cash 400
6. Pay $20 cash for dividends	−20 Cash		=		−20 Dividends		−	=		DIV 20 / Cash 20 / DIV 20 / Cash 20

ACCOUNTING ADJUSTMENTS (ACCRUALS)

Recognizing revenue when earned (even if not received in cash), and recording expenses when incurred (even if not paid in cash), are cornerstones of **accrual accounting,** which is required under GAAP.[3] Understanding accounting adjustments, commonly called *accruals*, is crucial to effectively

L02 Prepare and explain accounting adjustments and their financial statement effects.

---

[3] **Cash accounting** recognizes revenues when cash is received and expenses when cash is paid. This is not acceptable accounting under GAAP. However, small businesses that do not prepare financial reports for public investors and creditors, sometimes use cash accounting.

analyzing and interpreting financial statements. In this module's Apple illustration, we recorded inventory as a purchase even though no cash was paid, and we recognized the sale as revenue even though no cash was received. Both of these transactions reflect accrual accounting. Some accounting adjustments affect the balance sheet alone (as with purchasing inventory on account). Other adjustments affect the balance sheet *and* the income statement (as with selling inventory on account). Accounting adjustments can affect asset, liability or equity accounts, and can either increase or decrease net income.

Companies make adjustments to more accurately report their financial performance and condition. For example, employees might not have been paid for wages earned at the end of an accounting period. Failure to recognize this labor cost would understate the company's total liabilities (because wages payable would be too low), and would overstate net income for the period (because wages expense would be too low). Thus, neither the balance sheet nor the income statement would be accurate.

Accounting adjustments yield a more accurate presentation of the economic results of a company for a period. Despite their generally beneficial effects, adjustments can be misused. Managers can use adjustments to bias reported income, rendering it higher or lower than it really is. Adjustments, if misused, can adversely affect business and investment decisions. Many recent accounting scandals have resulted from improper use of adjustments. Although outsiders cannot directly observe companies' specific accounting entries, their impact can be detected as changes in balance sheet and income statement accounts. Those changes provide signals for financial statement analysis. Consequently, understanding the accrual process will help us know what to look for as we analyze companies' financial reports. Exhibit 3.2 identifies four general types of accounting adjustments which are briefly described below.

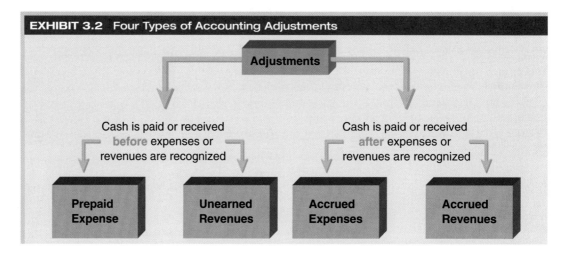

EXHIBIT 3.2 Four Types of Accounting Adjustments

Prepaid expenses Prepaid expenses reflect advance cash payments that will ultimately become expenses. An example is the payment for radio advertising that will not be aired until sometime in the future.

Unearned revenues Unearned revenues reflect cash received from customers before any services or goods are provided. An example is cash received from patrons for tickets to an upcoming concert.

Accrued expenses Accrued expenses are expenses incurred and recognized on the income statement, even though they are not yet paid in cash. An example is wages owed to employees who performed work but who have not yet been paid.

Accrued revenues Accrued revenues are revenues earned and recognized on the income statement, even though cash is not yet received. Examples include sales on credit and revenue earned under a long-term contract.

The remainder of this section illustrates how Apple's financial statements would reflect each of these four types of adjustments.

Prepaid Expenses (Assets)

Assume that Apple pays $200 to purchase time on MTV for future iPod ads. Apple's cash account decreases by $200. Should the $200 advertising cost be recorded as an expense when Apple pays

MTV, when MTV airs the ads, or at some other point? Under accrual accounting, Apple must record an expense when it is incurred. That means Apple should expense the cost of the ads when MTV airs them. When Apple pays for the advertisement, it records an asset; Apple "owns" TV time that will presumably provide future benefits when the ads air. In the interim, the cost of the ads is an asset on the balance sheet. Apple's financial statement effects template follows for this transaction. There is a decrease in cash and an increase in the advertising asset, titled prepaid advertising, when the ad time is paid for. At period end, $50 of advertisements had aired. At that point, Apple must record an accounting adjustment to reduce the prepaid advertising account by $50 and transfer the cost to the income statement as advertising expense.

	Balance Sheet							Income Statement			
Transaction	Cash Asset	+	Noncash Assets	=	Liabil- ities	+	Contrib. Capital	+	Earned Capital		
Pay $200 cash in advance for ad time	−200 Cash		+200 Prepaid Advertising	=							
Record $50 cost of ad air time			−50 Prepaid Advertising	=					−50 Retained Earnings		

Rev- enues	−	Expen- ses	=	Net Income
	−		=	
	−	+50 Advertising Expense	=	−50

PPDA 200 / Cash 200
PPDA 200 | / Cash | 200
AE 50 / PPDA 50
AE 50 | / PPDA | 50

Unearned Revenues (Liabilities)

Assume that Apple receives $400 cash from a customer as advance payment on a multi-unit iPod sale to be delivered next month. Apple must record cash received on its balance sheet, but cannot recognize revenue from the order until earned, which is generally when iPods are delivered to the customer. Until then, Apple must recognize a liability called unearned or deferred revenue that represents Apple's obligation to fulfill the order at some future point. The financial statement effects template for this transaction follows.

Transaction	Cash Asset	+	Noncash Assets	=	Liabil- ities	+	Contrib. Capital	+	Earned Capital	Rev- enues	−	Expen- ses	=	Net Income
Receive $400 cash in advance for iPod sale	+400 Cash			=	+400 Unearned Revenue						−		=	

Cash 400 / UR 400
Cash 400 | / UR | 400

Assume that Apple delivers the iPods a month later (but still within the fiscal quarter). Apple must recognize the $400 as revenue at delivery because it is now earned. Thus, net income increases by $400. The second part of this transaction is to record the cost of the iPods sold. Assuming the cost is $150, Apple reduces iPod inventory by $150 and records cost of goods sold by the same amount. These effects are reflected in the following template.

Transaction	Cash Asset	+	Noncash Assets	=	Liabil- ities	+	Contrib. Capital	+	Earned Capital	Rev- enues	−	Expen- ses	=	Net Income
Deliver $400 of iPods paid in advance				=	−400 Unearned Revenues				+400 Retained Earnings	+400 Sales	−		=	+400
Record $150 cost of $400 iPod sale			−150 Inventory	=					−150 Retained Earnings		−	+150 Cost of Goods Sold	=	−150

UR 400 / Sales 400
UR 400 | / Sales | 400
COGS 150 / INV 150
COGS 150 | / INV | 150

Accrued Expenses (Liabilities)

Assume that Apple's sales staff earns $100 of sales commissions this period that will not be paid until next period. The sales staff earned the wages as they made the sales. However, because Apple pays its employees twice a month, the related cash payment will not occur until the next pay period. Should Apple record the wages earned by its employees as an expense even though payment has not yet been made? The answer is yes. The matching principle requires Apple to recognize wages expense when it is *incurred*, even if not paid in cash. It must record wages expense incurred as a liability (wages payable). In the next period, when Apple pays the wages, it reduces both cash and wages payable. Net income is not affected by the cash payment; instead, net income decreased in the previous period when Apple accrued the wage expense.

WE 100
 WP 100
 WE
100 |
 WP
 | 100
WP 100
 Cash 100
 WP
100 |
 Cash
 | 100

	Balance Sheet						Income Statement		
Transaction	Cash Asset	+ Noncash Assets	= Liabil- ities	+ Contrib. Capital	+ Earned Capital		Rev- enues	− Expen- ses	= Net Income
Current period: Incur $100 of wages not yet paid		=	+100 Wages Payable		−100 Retained Earnings			− +100 Wages Expense	= −100
Next period: Pay $100 cash for accrued wages	−100 Cash	=	−100 Wages Payable					−	=

As another example of accrued expenses, assume that Apple rents office space and that it owes $25 in rent at period-end. Apple has incurred rent expense in the current period and that expense must be recorded this period. Failing to make this adjustment would mean that Apple's liabilities (rent payable) would be understated and its income would be overstated. The entry to record the accrual of rent expense for office space follows.

RNTE 25
 RNTP 25
 RNTE
25 |
 RNTP
 | 25

	Balance Sheet						Income Statement		
Transaction	Cash Asset	+ Noncash Assets	= Liabil- ities	+ Contrib. Capital	+ Earned Capital		Rev- enues	− Expen- ses	= Net Income
Incur $25 of rent not yet paid		=	+25 Rent Payable		−25 Retained Earnings			− +25 Rent Expense	= −25

Accrued Revenues (Assets)

Assume that Apple delivers iPods to a customer in Boston who will pay next quarter. The sales price for those units is $500 and the cost is $400. Apple has completed its revenue earning process with this sale and must accrue revenue from the Boston customer even though Apple received no cash. Like all sales transactions, Apple must record two parts, the sales revenue and the cost of sales. The financial effects template for this two-part transaction follows.

AR 500
 Sales 500
 AR
500 |
 Sales
 | 500
COGS 400
 INV 400
 COGS
400 |
 INV
 | 400

	Balance Sheet						Income Statement		
Transaction	Cash Asset	+ Noncash Assets	= Liabil- ities	+ Contrib. Capital	+ Earned Capital		Rev- enues	− Expen- ses	= Net Income
Sell $500 of iPods on credit		+500 Accounts Receivable =			+500 Retained Earnings		+500 Sales	−	= +500
Record $400 cost of $500 iPod sale		−400 Inventory =			−400 Retained Earnings			− +400 Cost of Goods Sold	= −400

Summary of Accounting Adjustments

Adjustments are an important part of the accounting process and are crucial to accurate and informative financial accounting. It is through the accruals process that managers communicate information about future cash flows. For example, from accrual information, we know that Apple paid for a resource (inventories) that it has not yet sold. We know that suppliers have money owed to them (accounts payable) but Apple won't pay them until a future period. We know that revenues have been earned but cash is not yet received (accounts receivable). Those accruals tell us about Apple's past performance and, perhaps more importantly, about Apple's future cash flows. When used properly, accruals convey information about the past and the future that is useful in our evaluation of company financial performance and condition. Thus, we can use accrual information to more precisely value companies' equity and debt securities.

Not all managers are honest; some misuse accounting accruals to improperly recognize revenues and expenses. Abuses include accruing revenue before it is earned; and accruing expenses in the wrong period or in the wrong amount. These actions are fraudulent as they deliberately overstate or understate revenues and expenses and, thus, reported net income is incorrect. Safeguards against this type of managerial behavior include corporate governance systems (internal controls, accounting policies and procedures, routine scrutiny of accounting reports, and audit committees) and external checks and balances (independent auditors, regulatory bodies, and the court system). Collectively, these safeguards aim to protect interests of companies' internal and external stakeholders. When managers abuse accounting systems, tough and swift sanctions remind others that corporate malfeasance is unacceptable. Videos of police officers leading corporate executives to jail in handcuffs (the infamous "perp walk") sends that message.

RESEARCH INSIGHT | **Accruals: Good or Bad?**

Researchers use accounting accruals to study the effects of earnings management on financial accounting. Earnings management is broadly defined as the use of accounting discretion to distort reported earnings. Managers have incentives to manage earnings in many situations. For example, managers have tendencies to accelerate revenue recognition to increase stock prices prior to equity offerings. In contrast, other research shows that managers decelerate revenue recognition to depress stock prices prior to a management buyout (where management repurchases common stock and takes the company "private"). Research also shows that managers use discretion when reporting special items to either meet or beat analysts' forecasts of earnings and/or to avoid reporting a loss. Not all earnings management occurs for opportunistic reasons. Research shows that managers use accruals to communicate private information about future profitability to outsiders. For example, management might signal future profitability through use of income-decreasing accruals to show investors that it can afford to apply conservative accounting. This "signaling" through accruals is found to precede stock splits and dividend increases. In sum, we must look at reported earnings in conjunction with other earnings quality signals (such as levels of disclosure, degree of corporate governance, and industry performance) to interpret information in accruals.

Trial Balance Preparation and Use

After Apple records all of its transactions, it must prepare financial statements so it can assess its financial performance and condition for the quarter. The following template shows a summary of Apple's transactions thus far.

The first step in preparing financial statements is to prepare a **trial balance,** which is a listing of all accounts and their balances at a point in time. Its purpose is to prove the mathematical equality of debits and credits, provide a useful tool to uncover any accounting errors, and help prepare the financial statements. To prepare a trial balance we compile a listing of accounts and their balances, we determine whether that balance is a debit or credit, and then we check to ensure that the total of all debit balances equals the total of all credit balances. (If those totals do not agree, then an accounting error has occurred that must be identified and corrected.) The accounting adjustments at period-end, discussed earlier in this module, are set in dark green font.

LO3 Explain and construct the trial balance.

	Balance Sheet									Income Statement				
Transaction	Cash Asset	+	Noncash Assets	=	Liabil-ities	+	Contrib. Capital	+	Earned Capital		Rev-enues	−	Expen-ses	= Net Income
Issue stock for $300 cash	+300 Cash			=			+300 Common Stock					−		=
Purchase $2,000 of iPods on credit			+2,000 Inventory	=	+2,000 Accounts Payable							−		=
Sell $700 of iPods on credit			+700 Accounts Receivable	=					+700 Retained Earnings		+700 Sales	−		= +700
Record $600 cost of $700 iPod sale			−600 Inventory	=					−600 Retained Earnings			−	+600 Cost of Goods Sold	= −600
Pay $50 cash for dividends	−50 Cash			=					−50 Dividends			−		=
Pay $200 cash in advance for ad time	−200 Cash		+200 Prepaid Advertising	=								−		=
Record $50 cost of ad air time			−50 Prepaid Advertising	=					−50 Retained Earnings			−	+50 Advertising Expense	= −50
Receive $400 cash in advance for iPod sale	+400 Cash			=	+400 Unearned Revenue							−		=
Deliver $400 of iPods paid in advance				=	−400 Unearned Revenues				+400 Retained Earnings		+400 Sales	−		= +400
Record $150 cost of $400 iPod sale			−150 Inventory	=					−150 Retained Earnings			−	+150 Cost of Goods Sold	= −150
Incur $100 of wages not yet paid				=	+100 Wages Payable				−100 Retained Earnings			−	+100 Wages Expense	= −100
Incur $25 of rent not yet paid				=	+25 Rent Payable				−25 Retained Earnings			−	+25 Rent Expense	= −25
Sell $500 of iPods on credit			+500 Accounts Receivable	=					+500 Retained Earnings		+500 Sales	−		= +500
Record $400 cost of $500 iPod sale			−400 Inventory	=					−400 Retained Earnings			−	+400 Cost of Goods Sold	= −400
Total	450	+	2,200	=	2,125	+	300	+	225		1,600	−	1,325	= 275

Left margin T-accounts:

```
Cash    300
    CS      300
------------------
   Cash
   300 |
      CS
         | 300

INV    2,000
    AP      2,000
------------------
   INV
   2,000 |
      AP
         | 2,000

AR     700
    Sales   700
------------------
   AR
   700 |
      Sales
         | 700

COGS   600
    INV     600
------------------
   COGS
   600 |
      INV
         | 600

DIV    50
    Cash    50
------------------
   DIV
   50 |
      Cash
         | 50

PPDA   200
    Cash    200
------------------
   PPDA
   200 |
      Cash
         | 200

AE     50
    PPDA    50
------------------
   AE
   50 |
      PPDA
         | 50

Cash   400
    UR      400
------------------
   Cash
   400 |
      UR
         | 400

UR     400
    Sales   400
------------------
   UR
   400 |
      Sales
         | 400

COGS   150
    INV     150
------------------
   COGS
   150 |
      INV
         | 150

WE     100
    WP      100
------------------
   WE
   100 |
      WP
         | 100

RNTE   25
    RNTP    25
------------------
   RNTE
   25 |
      RNTP
         | 25

AR     500
    Sales   500
------------------
   AR
   500 |
      Sales
         | 500

COGS   400
    INV     400
------------------
   COGS
   400 |
      INV
         | 400
```

The trial balance for Apple, which we assume to be as of December 31, 2009, follows.

APPLE Trial Balance December 31, 2009		
	Debit	**Credit**
Cash	$ 450	
Accounts receivable	1,200	
Inventory	850	
Prepaid advertising	150	
Accounts payable		$2,000
Wages payable		100
Rent payable		25
Unearned revenues		0
Common stock		300
Dividends	50	
Sales		1,600
Cost of goods sold	1,150	
Wages expense	100	
Advertising expense	50	
Rent expense	25	
Totals	$4,025	$4,025

The trial balance amounts consist of the ending balance for each of the accounts. For the Apple illustration, we total all transactions for each account listed in the template. To illustrate, cash has an ending balance of $450 ($300 − $50 − $200 + $400). Also, because cash is an asset (which is on the left-hand side of the balance sheet), it normally has a debit balance (which is on the left-hand side of the T-accounts). We can confirm the ending cash debit balance by totalling each of the cash T-account entries. Liabilities and equity accounts normally have credit balances (because they are on the right-hand side of the balance sheet), and we can confirm these ending credit balances by referring to individual account balances in the template. (See that Apple's trial balance includes all of the income statement accounts as well as the dividend account, but it does not include the retained earnings account from the financial statement effects template. This is because the template updates retained earnings immediately for each transaction. If we did include both the income statement accounts *and* retained earnings, we would double count all income statement transactions. Most companies' accounting systems do not update retained earnings immediately, which means the retained earnings balance [on the trial balance] is the beginning balance, which for our Apple example is zero.)

The trial balance shows total debits equal $4,025, which equals total credits. Accordingly, we know that all of the template transactions balance. We do not know, however, that all required journal entries have been properly included, or if Apple recorded entries that it should not have.

Precisely speaking, the trial balance above is an **adjusted trial balance**, prepared after all accounting adjustments have been recorded. In practice, we will also encounter an **unadjusted trial balance**, which is a trial balance prepared *before* the accounting adjustments are recorded. For the Apple example here, we show the following spreadsheet that contains the unadjusted and adjusted trial balances, along with middle columns containing the accounting adjustments. Remember that *financial statements are prepared from the adjusted trial balance.*

	APPLE Trial Balances December 31, 2009					
	Unadjusted		Adjustments		Adjusted	
	Debit	Credit	Debit	Credit	Debit	Credit
Cash.....................................	$ 450				$ 450	
Accounts receivable......................	700		$ 500		1,200	
Inventory................................	1,250			$ 400	850	
Prepaid advertising......................	200			50	150	
Accounts payable........................		$2,000				$2,000
Wages payable..........................		0		100		100
Rent payable		0		25		25
Unearned revenues		0				0
Common stock..........................		300				300
Dividends	50				50	
Sales..................................		1,100		500		1,600
Cost of goods sold......................	750		400		1,150	
Wages expense	0		100		100	
Advertising expense.....................	0		50		50	
Rent expense...........................	0		25		25	
Totals	$3,400	$3,400	$1,075	$1,075	$4,025	$4,025

MID-MODULE REVIEW 2

Refer to the transactions in Mid-Module Review 1. Assume that Symantec Corporation has the following two additional transactions (*a* and *b*) and four accounting adjustments (1 through 4).

a. Symantec pays $100 cash for current and future periods rent of VoIP software.
b. Symantec receives $500 cash in advance from a client for consulting services.

1. As of period-end, Symantec had incurred rent expense of $30; $70 of the prepayment remains for future periods.
2. As of period-end, Symantec had earned $80 of the $500 paid in advance for consulting services.
3. Symantec employees earn $40 in wages that will not be paid until the next period.
4. Symantec provides $150 of services revenue but has not yet billed the client.

Required

Record each of the two accounting transactions and four adjustments using the financial statement effects template. Also record the journal entry for each in the margin and post each entry to T-accounts. Prepare a trial balance spreadsheet that contains columns for the unadjusted and adjusted trial balances and for the accounting adjustments. The unadjusted trial balance should reflect those transactions for Symantec from Mid-Module Review 1 and the two transactions *a* and *b* above.

Solution

	Balance Sheet					Income Statement		
Transaction	Cash Asset	+ Noncash Assets	= Liabil- ities	+ Contrib. Capital	+ Earned Capital	Rev- enues	− Expen- ses	= Net Income
a. Pay $100 cash for next period rent	−100 Cash	+100 Prepaid Rent	=				−	=
b. Receive $500 cash advance for future services	+500 Cash		= +500 Unearned Revenues				−	=
1. Record $30 of rental fees incurred		−30 Prepaid Rent	=		−30 Retained Earnings		+30 Rent Expense −	= −30

Margin journal entries:

PPRNT 100
Cash   100
    PPRNT
100
    Cash
        100

Cash   500
  UR   500
    Cash
500
    UR
      500

RE   30
  PPRNT   30
    RE
30
    PPRNT
      30

continued

continued from prior page

	Balance Sheet						Income Statement		
Transaction	**Cash Asset**	**+ Noncash Assets**	**= Liabil- ities**	**+ Contrib. Capital**	**+ Earned Capital**		**Rev- enues**	**– Expen- ses**	**= Net Income**
2. Record $80 of services earned			= −80 Unearned Revenues		+80 Retained Earnings		+80 Sales	–	= +80
3. Incur $40 in wages to be paid next period			= +40 Wages Payable		−40 Retained Earnings			– +40 Wages Expense	= −40
4. Provide $150 of services and bills client		+150 Accounts Receivable	=		+150 Retained Earnings		+150 Sales	–	= +150

SYMANTEC Trial Balances						
	Unadjusted		**Adjustments**		**Adjusted**	
	Debit	**Credit**	**Debit**	**Credit**	**Debit**	**Credit**
Cash.	$3,280				$3,280	
Accounts receivable.	200		$150		350	
Inventory.	700				700	
Prepaid rent	100			$ 30	70	
Accounts payable.		$ 600				$ 600
Wages payable.		0		40		40
Unearned revenues		500	80			420
Common stock.		3,000				3,000
Dividends	20				20	
Sales.		500		230*		730
Cost of goods sold.	300				300	
Wages expense	0		40		40	
Rent expense	0		30		30	
Totals	$4,600	$4,600	$300	$300	$4,790	$4,790

*The $230 adjustment is a combination of the $150 and $80 adjustments.

FINANCIAL STATEMENT PREPARATION

Financial statement preparation involves working with the accounts in the adjusted trial balance to properly report them in financial statements. There is an order to financial statement preparation. First, a company prepares its income statement using the income statement accounts. It then uses the net income number and dividend information to update the retained earnings account. Second, it prepares the balance sheet using the updated retained earnings account along with the remaining balance sheet accounts from the trial balance. Third, it prepares the statement of stockholders' equity. Fourth, it prepares the statement of cash flows using information from the cash account (and other sources).

LO4 Construct financial statements from the trial balance.

Income Statement

Apple's income statement follows. Apple's trial balance reveals four income statement accounts. Those income statement accounts are called *temporary accounts* because they begin each accounting period with a zero balance. Apple's income statement also includes a line for gross profit because that subtotal is important to evaluate manufacturers' performance and profitability. Income for this quarterly period is $275 (we ignore taxes in this illustration).

APPLE Income Statement For Quarter Ended December 31, 2009	
Sales.	$1,600
Cost of goods sold.	1,150
Gross profit.	450
Wages expense	100
Advertising expense.	50
Rent expense.	25
Net income.	$ 275

Retained Earnings Computation

Apple updates its retained earnings balance at period-end using income from the income statement and the dividend information from its trial balance. (For simplicity, we assume retained earnings is zero at the beginning of this period). This computation follows.

APPLE Retained Earnings Computation For Quarter Ended December 31, 2009		
Retained earnings, beginning of period.		$ 0
Add:	Net income (loss).	275
Deduct:	Dividends.	50
Retained earnings, end of period.		$225

Balance Sheet

Once Apple computes the ending balance in retained earnings, it can prepare its balance sheet, which follows. Balance sheet accounts are called *permanent accounts* because their respective balances carry over from one period to the next. For example, the cash balance at the end of the current accounting period (ended December 31, 2009) is $450, which will be the balance at the beginning of the next accounting period (beginning January 1, 2010).

APPLE Balance Sheet December 31, 2009	
Assets	
Cash.	$ 450
Accounts receivable.	1,200
Inventory.	850
Prepaid advertising.	150
Total assets.	$2,650
Liabilities and Stockholders' Equity	
Liabilities	
Accounts payable.	$2,000
Wages payable.	100
Rent payable	25
Total liabilities.	2,125
Stockholders' equity	
Common stock.	300
Retained earnings	225
Total stockholders' equity	525
Total liabilities and stockholders' equity.	$2,650

Statement of Stockholders' Equity

Apple uses the information pertaining to its contributed capital and earned capital categories to prepare the statement of stockholders' equity, as follows.

APPLE Statement of Stockholders' Equity For Quarter Ended December 31, 2009	Contributed Capital	Earned Capital	Total Stockholders' Equity
Beginning balance	$ 0	$ 0	$ 0
Stock issuance.	300		300
Net income (loss)		275	275
Dividends		(50)	(50)
Ending balance.	$300	$225	$525

Statement of Cash Flows

The statement of cash flows summarizes the cash-based transactions for the period and reports the sources and uses of cash. Each cash transaction represents an operating, investing, or financing activity.

Direct Method Presentation

To prepare the statement, Apple uses the Cash column of the financial statement effects template, see above. The following cash flow statement for Apple is based on the **direct method** for reporting operating cash flows. During the current period, Apple's cash increased by $450. Its increase in cash consists of a $200 net cash inflow from operating activities plus a $250 net cash inflow from financing activities. There were no investing activities during this period.

APPLE Statement of Cash Flows (Direct Method) For Quarter Ended December 31, 2009	
Operating activities	
Receipts from sales contracts	$400
Payments for advertising	(200)
Net cash flows from operating activities	200
Investing activities	
Net cash flows from investing activities.	0
Financing activities	
Issuance of common stock	300
Payment of cash dividends	(50)
Net cash flows from financing activities.	250
Net change in cash	$450
Cash, beginning of period	0
Cash, end of period	$450

In practice, preparing a statement of cash flows is more complicated. Companies can have millions of transactions in the cash account and the task of classifying each transaction as operating, investing or financing would be costly and time consuming. Instead, companies prepare the statement of cash flows using the current income statement and the balance sheets for the current and prior periods. The basic approach is to adjust net income to arrive at net cash flows from operating activities (the so-called *indirect method*) and then review changes in balance sheet accounts (by comparing the opening and ending balances) to arrive at net cash flows from investing and financing activities.

Indirect Method Presentation

There are two methods to display net cash flows from operating activities: the direct method and the indirect method. Both methods report the same net operating cash flow, the only difference is in presentation. Companies can choose which method to follow. Apple's simplified statement of cash flows above, is an example of the direct method. However, the **indirect method** is, by far, the most widely used method in practice today (over 98% of public companies use it). The indirect method computes operating cash flows *indirectly* by adjusting net income using the following format.

	Add (+) or Subtract (−) from Net Income
Net income............................	$ #
Add: depreciation expense	+
Adjust for changes in current assets	
Subtract increases in current assets	−
Add decreases in current assets	+
Adjust for changes in current liabilities	
Add increases in current liabilities	+
Subtract decreases in current liabilities	−
Net cash flow from operating activities	$ #

Adjustments for noncash revenues, expenses, gains and losses (bracketing "Add: depreciation expense" and "Adjust for changes in current assets")

Adjustments for changes in noncash current assets and current liabilities (bracketing the current assets and current liabilities adjustment rows)

Net income is first adjusted for noncash expenses such as depreciation and amortization, and is then adjusted for changes during the year in current assets and current liabilities to yield cash flow from operating activities, or *cash profit*. The depreciation adjustment merely zeros out (undoes the effect of) depreciation expense, a noncash expense, which is deducted in computing net income. The following table provides brief explanations of adjustments for receivables, inventories, and payables and accruals.

	Change in account balance ...	Means that ...	Which requires this adjustment to net income to yield cash profit ...
Receivables	Increase	Sales and net income increase, but cash is not yet received	Deduct increase in receivables from net income
	Decrease	More cash is received than is reported in sales and net income	Add decrease in receivables to net income
Inventories	Increase	Cash is paid for inventories that are not yet reflected in cost of goods sold	Deduct increase in inventories from net income
	Decrease	Cost of goods sold includes inventory costs that were paid for in a prior period	Add decrease in inventories to net income
Payables and accruals	Increase	More goods and services are acquired on credit, delaying cash payment	Add increase in payables and accruals to net income
	Decrease	More cash is paid than that reflected in cost of goods sold or operating expenses	Deduct decrease in payables and accruals from net income

It is also helpful to use the following decision guide, involving changes in assets, liabilities, and equity, to understand increases and decreases in cash flows.

	Cash flow increases from	Cash flow decreases from
Assets......................	Account decreases	Account increases
Liabilities and equity............	Account increases	Account decreases

Using this decision guide we can determine the cash flow effects of the income statement and balance sheet information and categorize them into the following table for our Apple illustration.

Financial Element	Change	Source or Use	Cash Flow Effect	Classification on SCF
Current assets				
Accounts receivable	+ $1,200	Use	$(1,200)	Operating
Increase in inventories	+ 850	Use	(850)	Operating
Prepaid advertising.........	+ 150	Use	(150)	Operating
Noncurrent assets				
PPE....................	0		0	Investing
Accumulated depreciation ...		Neither	0*	Operating
Current liabilities				
Accounts payable..........	+ 2,000	Source	2,000	Operating
Wages payable............	+ 100	Source	100	Operating
Rent payable.............	+ 25	Source	25	Operating
Long-term liabilities	0		0	Financing

continued

continued from prior page

Financial Element	Change		Source or Use	Cash Flow Effect	Classification on SCF
Stockholders' equity					
Common stock	+	300	Source	300	Financing
Retained earnings					
Net income	+	275	Source	275	Operating
Dividends	+	50	Use	(50)	Financing
Total (net cash flow)				$ 450	

*Depreciation expense for the period, if present, is added to net income in computing cash flows from operating activities.

Increases in the three current assets reflect a use of cash, and are subtracted in the operating section of the statement of cash flows. Increases in noncurrent PPE assets also reflect a use of cash, which are classified as an investing activity. An increase in accumulated depreciation reflects the recording of depreciation expense in the income statement, which is a noncash expense that must be zeroed out (with an addition to net income) to yield cash profit. Increases in the three current liabilities reflect sources of cash, and are recorded as positive amounts in the statement of cash flows.

APPLE Statement of Cash Flows (Indirect Method) For Quarter Ended December 31, 2009	
Operating activities	
Net income	$ 275
Depreciation and other noncash expenses	0
Increase in accounts receivable	(1,200)
Increase in inventories	(850)
Increase in prepaid advertising.	(150)
Increase in accounts payable	2,000
Increase in wages payable	100
Increase in rent payable	25
Net cash flows from operating activities	200
Investing activities	
Net cash flows from investing activities.	0
Financing activities	
Issuance of common stock	300
Payment of cash dividends	(50)
Net cash flows from financing activities.	250
Net change in cash.	$ 450
Cash, beginning of period	0
Cash, end of period	$ 450

Issuance of common stock is a source of cash, and the payment of dividends to shareholders is a use of cash. Both of these are reflected in the financing section of the statement of cash flows. The financing section also reflects any increases or decreases in borrowings as sources or uses, respectively. The increase in retained earnings, resulting from net income, is a source of cash, but it is reported as an operating activity. (Components of the change in retained earnings, net income less dividends, are reflected in the statement of cash flows and, consequently, the change in retained earnings is already recognized.)

The sum of these elements yields a net increase in cash of $450. This is the same result we obtained earlier using the direct method. To reiterate, the indirect method represents a different presentation of the operating section only of the statement of cash flows. The investing and financing sections are identical under the direct and indirect approaches. Reporting these elements by operating, investing and financing activities yields the familiar form of the statement of cash flows previously shown.

Closing Process

The **closing process** refers to "zeroing out" the temporary accounts by transferring their ending balances to retained earnings. Recall, income statement accounts—revenues and expenses—and the dividend account

LO5 Describe the closing process.

are temporary accounts because their balances are zero at the end of each accounting period; balance sheet accounts carry over from period to period and are called permanent accounts. The closing process is typically carried out via a series of journal entries that successively zero out each revenue and expense account, and the dividend account, transferring those balances to retained earnings. The result is that all income statement accounts and the dividend account begin the next period with zero balances. The balance sheet accounts do not need to be similarly adjusted because their balances carry over from period to period. Recall the scoreboard analogy.

Our financial statement effects template makes the closing process unnecessary because the template updates retained earnings with each revenue and expense entry. The arrow that runs from net income to retained earnings (part of earned capital) highlights the continual updating. To illustrate, recall the following entries that reflect Apple's initial sale of iPods on credit.

		Balance Sheet							Income Statement		
Transaction	Cash Asset	+	Noncash Assets	=	Liabil- ities	+	Contrib. Capital	+	Earned Capital	Rev- enues	−	Expen- ses	=	Net Income
Sell $700 of iPods on credit			+700 Accounts Receivable =						+700 Retained Earnings	+700 Sales	−		= +700
Record $600 cost of $700 iPod sale			−600 Inventory =						−600 Retained Earnings		−	+600 Cost of Goods Sold	= −600

(Margin T-accounts:)

AR 700
Sales 700
AR 700 |
Sales | 700

COGS 600
INV 600
COGS 600 |
INV | 600

Sales of $700 increase net income by $700, which the template immediately transfers to retained earnings. Likewise, cost of goods sold reduces net income by $600, and this reduction is immediately carried to retained earnings. Consequently, the financial statement effects template always reports an updated retained earnings, making the closing process unnecessary.

It is important to distinguish our financial statement effects template from companies' accounting systems. The financial statement effects template and T-accounts are pedagogical tools that represent transactions' effects on the four financial statements. The template is highly stylized but its simplicity is instructive. In practice, managers use journal entries to record transactions and adjustments. The template captures these in summarized fashion. However, in practice, income statement transactions are not automatically transferred to retained earnings and retained earnings is not continuously updated. All companies perform the closing process—someone or some program must transfer the temporary account balances to retained earnings. Thus, it is important to understand the closing process and why companies "close" the books each period. We describe the mechanical details of the closing process in Appendix 3A.

The entire accounting process, from analysis of basic transactions to financial statement preparation to the closing process, is called the **accounting cycle.** As we discuss at the outset of this module and portray graphically in Exhibit 3.1, there are four basic processes in the accounting cycle. First, companies analyze transactions and prepare (and post) entries. Second, companies prepare (and post) accounting adjustments. Third, financial statements are prepared from an adjusted trial balance. Fourth, companies perform the closing process. The analysis and posting of transactions is done regularly during each accounting period. However, the preparation of accounting adjustments and financial statements is only done at the end of an accounting period. At this point, we have explained and illustrated all aspects of the accounting cycle.

MANAGERIAL DECISION **You Are the CFO**

Assume that you learn of the leakage of hazardous waste from your company's factory. It is estimated that cleanup will cost $10 million. Part 1: What effect will recording this cost have on your company's balance sheet and its income statement? Part 2: Accounting rules require you to record this cost if it is both probable and can be reliably estimated. Although the cleanup is relatively certain, the cost is a guess at this point. Consequently, you have some discretion whether to record it. Discuss the parties that are likely affected by your decision on whether or not to record the liability and related expense, and the ethical issues involved. [Answer 3-25]

MODULE-END REVIEW

Refer to the transactions in Mid-Module Reviews 1 and 2. From those transactions, assume that Symantec Corporation prepares the following adjusted trial balance. Also assume its transactions are for the quarter ended December 31, 2009.

SYMANTEC Adjusted Trial Balance December 31, 2009		
	Debit	Credit
Cash........................	$3,280	
Accounts receivable...........	350	
Inventory....................	700	
Prepaid rent	70	
Accounts payable.............		$ 600
Wages payable...............		40
Unearned revenues		420
Common stock...............		3,000
Dividends	20	
Sales.......................		730
Cost of goods sold............	300	
Wages expense	40	
Rent expense	30	
Totals	$4,790	$4,790

Required

Prepare Symantec's income statement (including a separate retained earnings computation), statement of stockholders' equity, balance sheet, and statement of cash flows.

Solution

SYMANTEC Income Statement For Quarter Ended December 31, 2009	
Sales......................................	$730
Cost of goods sold..........................	300
Gross profit................................	430
Wage expense	40
Rent expense	30
Net income................................	$360

SYMANTEC Retained Earnings Computation For Quarter Ended December 31, 2009	
Retained earnings, beginning of period............	$ 0
Add: Net income (loss)	360
Deduct: Dividends	(20)
Retained earnings, end of period................	$340

SYMANTEC Balance Sheet December 31, 2009	
Assets	
Cash	$3,280
Accounts receivable.	350
Inventory.	700
Prepaid rent	70
Total assets.	$4,400
Liabilities and Stockholders' Equity	
Liabilities	
Accounts payable.	$ 600
Wages payable.	40
Unearned revenues	420
Total liabilities	1,060
Stockholders' equity	
Common stock.	3,000
Retained earnings	340
Total stockholders' equity	$3,340
Total liabilities and stockholders' equity.	$4,400

SYMANTEC Statement of Stockholders' Equity For Quarter Ended December 31, 2009			
	Contributed Capital	Earned Capital	Total Stockholders' Equity
Beginning balance	$ 0	$ 0	$ 0
Stock issuance.	3,000		3,000
Net income (loss)		360	360
Dividends		(20)	(20)
Ending balance.	**$3,000**	**$340**	**$3,340**

SYMANTEC Statement of Cash Flows For Quarter Ended December 31, 2009	
Operating activities	
Net income	$ 360
Depreciation and other noncash expenses	0
Increase in accounts receivable	(350)
Increase in inventories	(700)
Increase in prepaid rent	(70)
Increase in accounts payable.	600
Increase in wages payable	40
Increase in unearned revenues.	420
Net cash flows from operating activities	300
Investing activities	
Net cash flows from investing activities.	0
Financing activities	
Issuance of common stock	3,000
Payment of cash dividends	(20)
Net cash flows from financing activities.	2,980
Net change in cash.	$3,280
Cash, beginning of period	0
Cash, end of period	$3,280

APPENDIX 3A: Closing Process Using Journal Entries

The idea of the closing process is to zero-out all temporary accounts—all the income statement accounts and any dividend account. The balance in each temporary account is transferred to retained earnings leaving the temporary accounts with zero balances. That way, the temporary accounts are ready to capture transaction data for the next period. The closing process brings the retained earnings account up to date so that it accurately reflects the current period's income statement activity and dividends so that the balance sheet can be prepared. To illustrate, let's return to Apple's income statement.

APPLE Income Statement For Quarter Ended December 31, 2009	
Sales.	$1,600
Cost of goods sold.	1,150
Gross profit.	450
Wages expense	100
Advertising expense.	50
Rent expense	25
Net income.	$ 275

The closing process transfers the ending balances for each of these income statement accounts, to retained earnings. The dividend account is a temporary account and therefore, it also must be closed to retained earnings. The journal entries, and the related T-accounts, follow for this three-step process.

1. Close all revenue accounts.

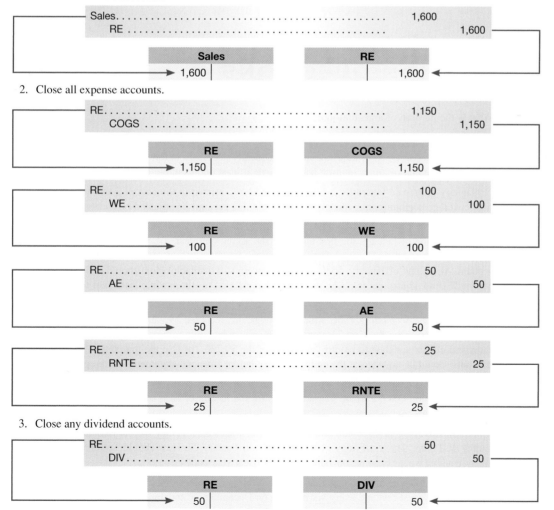

2. Close all expense accounts.

3. Close any dividend accounts.

Apple must close one revenue account, three expense accounts, and a dividend account to retained earnings at the end of the period. The first closing entry transfers the $1,600 balance in the sales account to retained earnings. The closing entry debits sales for $1,600 (because the sales account has a $1,600 credit balance at period-end) and credits retained earnings. The second closing entry closes cost of good sold ($1,150), wages expense ($100), advertising expense ($50), and rent expense ($25). The entry credits each of the expense accounts because their ending balances are debit balances. Third, the $50 dividend account balance is transferred to retained earnings. All the temporary accounts are now *closed*.

Retained earnings, which began the period with a zero balance, now reports a balance of $225, which equals net income for the period less the dividends paid to shareholders. This is the balance Apple reports in the stockholders' equity section of its balance sheet. Further, all of the income statement accounts (sales, cost of goods sold, wages expense, and rent expense) and the dividend account now show zero balances to begin the next period.

GUIDANCE ANSWERS

MANAGERIAL DECISION **You Are the CFO**

Part 1: Liabilities will increase by $10 million for the estimated amount of the cleanup, and an expense in that amount will be recognized in the income statement, thus reducing both income and retained earnings (equity) by $10 million. Part 2: Stakeholders affected by recognition decisions of this type are often much broader than first realized. Management is directly involved in the decision. Recording this cost can affect the market value of the company, its relations with lenders and suppliers, its auditors, and many other stakeholders. Further, if recording this cost is the right accounting decision, failure to do so can foster unethical behavior throughout the company, thus affecting additional company employees.

Superscript ᴬ denotes assignments based on Appendix 3A.

DISCUSSION QUESTIONS

Q3-1. What does the term *fiscal year* mean?

Q3-2. What is the purpose of a general journal?

Q3-3. Explain the process of posting.

Q3-4. What four different types of adjustments are frequently necessary before financial statements are prepared at the end of an accounting period? Give at least one example of each type.

Q3-5. On January 1, Prepaid Insurance was debited for $1,872 related to the cost of a two-year premium, with coverage beginning immediately. How should this account be adjusted on January 31 before financial statements are prepared for the current month?

Q3-6. At the beginning of January, the first month of the accounting year, the Supplies account (asset) had a debit balance of $825. During January, purchases of $260 worth of supplies were debited to the account. At the end of January, $630 of supplies were still available. How should this account be adjusted? If no adjustment is made, describe the impact on (a) the income statement for January, and (b) the balance sheet prepared at January 31.

Q3-7. The publisher of *Accounting View*, a monthly magazine, received $9,720 cash on January 1 for new subscriptions covering the next 24 months, with service beginning immediately. (a) Use the financial statement effects template to record the receipt of the $9,720. (b) Use the template to show how the accounts should be adjusted at the end of January before financial statements are prepared for the current month.

Q3-8. Refer to Question Q3-7. Prepare journal entries for the receipt of cash and the delivery of the magazines.

Q3-9. Trombley Travel Agency pays an employee $475 in wages each Friday for the five-day work week ending on Friday. The last Friday of January falls on January 27. How should Trombley Travel Agency adjust wages expense on January 31, its fiscal year-end?

Q3-10. The Basu Company earns interest amounting to $360 per month on its investments. The company receives the interest revenue every six months, on December 31 and June 30. Monthly financial statements are prepared. Which accounts should Basu adjust on January 31?

Q3-11. ^A^ What types of accounts are closed at the end of the accounting year? What are the three major steps in the closing process?

Assignments with the Web Assign. logo in the margin are available in WebAssign.
See the Preface of the book for details.

MINI EXERCISES

M3-12. **Assessing Financial Statement Effects of Transactions   (LO1)**

WebAssign.

DeFond Services, a firm providing art services for advertisers, began business on June 1, 2009. The following accounts are needed to record the transactions for June: Cash; Accounts Receivable; Supplies; Office Equipment; Accounts Payable; Common Stock; Retained Earnings; Service Fees Earned; Rent Expense; Utilities Expense; and Wages Expense. Record the following transactions for June using the financial statement effects template.

June	1	M. DeFond invested $12,000 cash to begin the business in exchange for common stock.
	2	Paid $950 cash for June rent.
	3	Purchased $6,400 of office equipment on credit.
	6	Purchased $3,800 of art materials and other supplies; the company paid $1,800 cash with the remainder due within 30 days.
	11	Billed clients $4,700 for services rendered.
	17	Collected $3,250 cash from clients on their accounts billed on June 11.
	19	Paid $3,000 cash toward the account for office equipment (see June 3).
	25	Paid $900 cash for dividends.
	30	Paid $350 cash for June utilities.
	30	Paid $2,500 cash for June wages.

M3-13. **Preparing Journal Entries and Posting   (LO1)**

WebAssign.

Refer to the information in M3-12. Prepare a journal entry for each transaction. Create a T-account for each account, and then post the journal entries to the T-accounts (use dates to reference each entry).

M3-14. **Assessing Financial Statement Effects of Transactions   (LO1)**

Verrecchia Company, a cleaning services firm, began business on April 1, 2009. The company created the following accounts to record the transactions for April: Cash; Accounts Receivable; Supplies; Prepaid Van Lease; Equipment; Notes Payable; Accounts Payable; Common Stock; Retained Earnings; Cleaning Fees Earned; Wages Expense; Advertising Expense; and Van Fuel Expense. Record the following transactions for April using the financial statement effects template.

April	1	R. Verrecchia invested $9,000 cash to begin the business in exchange for common stock.
	2	Paid $2,850 cash for six months' lease on van for the business.
	3	Borrowed $10,000 cash from bank and signed note payable agreeing to repay it in one year plus 10% interest.
	4	Purchased $5,500 of cleaning equipment; the company paid $2,500 cash with the remainder due within 30 days.
	5	Paid $4,300 cash for cleaning supplies.
	7	Paid $350 cash for advertisements to run in the area newspaper during April.
	21	Billed customers $3,500 for services performed.
	23	Paid $3,000 cash toward the account for cleaning equipment (see April 4).
	28	Collected $2,300 cash from customers on their accounts billed on April 21.
	29	Paid $1,000 cash for dividends.
	30	Paid $1,750 cash for April wages.
	30	Paid $995 cash for gasoline used during April.

M3-15. **Preparing Journal Entries and Posting   (LO1)**

Refer to the information in M3-14. Prepare a journal entry for each transaction. Create a T-account for each account, and then post the journal entries to the T-accounts (use dates to reference each entry).

M3-16. **Assessing Financial Statement Effects of Transactions and Adjustments   (LO1, 2)**

Schrand Services offers janitorial services on both a contract basis and an hourly basis. On January 1, 2008, Schrand collected $20,100 cash in advance on a six-month contract for work to be performed evenly during the next six months.

a. Prepare the entry on January 1 to reflect the receipt of $20,100 cash for contract work; use the financial statements effect template.

b. Adjust the appropriate accounts on January 31, 2008, for the contract work done during January; use the financial statements effect template.

c. At January 31, a total of 30 hours of hourly rate janitor work was unbilled. The billing rate is $19 per hour. Prepare the accounting adjustment needed on January 31, 2008, using the financial statements effect template. (The firm uses the account Fees Receivable to reflect amounts due but not yet billed.)

M3-17. Preparing Accounting Adjustments (LO1, 2)
Refer to the information in M3-16. Prepare a journal entry for each of parts a, b, and c.

WebAssign.

M3-18. Assessing Financial Statement Effects of Transactions and Adjustments (LO2)
Selected accounts of Piotroski Properties, a real estate management firm, are shown below as of January 31, 2010, before any accounts have been adjusted.

	Debits	Credits
Prepaid Insurance	$6,660	
Supplies	1,930	
Office Equipment	5,952	
Unearned Rent Revenue		$ 5,250
Salaries Expense	3,100	
Rent Revenue......................		15,000

Piotroski Properties prepares monthly financial statements. Using the following information, adjust the accounts as necessary on January 31 using the financial statements effect template.

a. Prepaid insurance represents a three-year premium paid on January 1, 2010.

b. Supplies of $850 were still available on January 31.

c. Office equipment is expected to last eight years (or 96 months).

d. On January 1, 2010, Piotroski collected $5,250 for six months' rent in advance from a tenant renting space for $875 per month.

e. Salaries of $490 have been earned by employees but yet not recorded as of January 31.

M3-19. Preparing Accounting Adjustments (LO2)
Refer to the information in M3-18. Prepare journal entries for each of parts a through e.

M3-20. Inferring Transactions from Financial Statements (LO1, 2)

Foot Locker, Inc. (FL)

Foot Locker, Inc., a retailer of athletic footwear and apparel, operates 3,785 stores in the United States, Canada, Europe and Asia Pacific. During its fiscal year ended in 2008, Foot Locker purchased merchandise inventory costing $4,017 ($ millions). Assume that Foot Locker makes all purchases on credit, and that its accounts payable is only used for inventory purchases. The following T-accounts reflect information contained in the company's fiscal 2007 and 2008 balance sheets ($ millions).

Inventories			Accounts Payable		
2007 Bal.	1,303			256	2007 Bal.
2008 Bal.	1,281			233	2008 Bal.

a. Use the financial statement effects template to record Foot Locker's 2008 purchases.

b. What amount did Foot Locker pay in cash to its suppliers during fiscal year 2008? Explain.

c. Use the financial statement effects template to record cost of goods sold for its fiscal year 2008.

M3-21. Preparing Journal Entries (LO1, 2)
Refer to the information in M3-20. Prepare journal entries for each of parts a, b and c.

M3-22. Preparing a Statement of Stockholders' Equity (LO4)
On December 31, 2007, the accounts of Leuz Architect Services showed credit balances in its Common Stock and Retained Earnings accounts of $30,000 and $18,000, respectively. The company's stock issuances for 2008 totaled $6,000, and it paid $9,700 in cash dividends. During 2008, the company had net income of $29,900. Prepare a 2008 statement of stockholders' equity for Leuz Architect Services.

M3-23.^A Preparing Closing Journal Entries (LO5)

Procter & Gamble (PG)

The adjusted trial balance at June 30, 2008, for Procter & Gamble includes the following selected accounts.

($ millions)	Debits	Credits
Net sales.		$83,503
Cost of goods sold.	$40,695	
Selling, general and administrative expense	25,725	
Interest expense, net	1,005	
Income tax expense.	4,003	
Retained earnings		36,911

Assume that the company has not yet closed any accounts to retained earnings. Prepare journal entries to close the temporary accounts above. Set up the needed T-accounts and post the closing entries. After these entries are posted, what is the balance of the Retained Earnings account?

M3-24. Inferring Transactions from Financial Statements **(LO1, 2)**

Lowe's is the second-largest home improvement retailer in the world with 1,534 stores. During its fiscal year ended in 2008, Lowe's purchased merchandise inventory at a cost of $32,023 ($ millions). Assume that all purchases were made on account and that accounts payable is only used for inventory purchases. The following T-accounts reflect information contained in the company's 2008 and 2007 balance sheets.

Lowe's Companies (LOW)

Merchandise Inventories	
2007 Bal. 7,144	
2008 Bal. 7,611	

Accounts Payable	
	3,524 2007 Bal.
	3,713 2008 Bal.

  a. Use the financial statement effects template to record Lowe's purchases during fiscal 2008.
  b. What amount did Lowe's pay in cash to its suppliers during fiscal-year 2008? Explain.
  c. Use the financial statement effects template to record cost of goods sold for its fiscal year ended in 2008.

M3-25.[A] **Closing Journal Entries** **(LO5)**

The adjusted trial balance as of December 31, 2009, for Hanlon Consulting contains the following selected accounts.

	Debits	Credits
Service Fees Earned		$80,300
Rent Expense.	$20,800	
Salaries Expense	45,700	
Supplies Expense.	5,600	
Depreciation Expense	10,200	
Retained Earnings		67,000

Prepare entries to close these accounts in journal entry form. Set up T-accounts for each account and record the adjusted trial balance amount in each account. Then, post the closing entries to the T-accounts. After these entries are posted, what is the balance of the Retained Earnings account?

EXERCISES

E3-26. Assessing Financial Statement Effects of Adjustments **(LO2)**

WebAssign.

For each of the following separate situations, prepare the necessary accounting adjustments using the financial statement effects template.

  a. Unrecorded depreciation on equipment is $610.
  b. The Supplies account has an unadjusted balance of $2,990. Supplies still available at the end of the period total $1,100.
  c. On the date for preparing financial statements, an estimated utilities expense of $390 has been incurred, but no utility bill has yet been received or paid.
  d. On the first day of the current period, rent for four periods was paid and recorded as a $2,800 debit to Prepaid Rent and a $2,800 credit to Cash.
  e. Nine months ago, The Allstate Corporation sold a one-year policy to a customer and recorded the receipt of the premium by crediting Unearned Revenue for $624. No accounting adjustments have been prepared during the nine-month period. Allstate's annual financial statements are now being prepared.

Allstate Corp. (ALL)

continued

f.   At the end of the period, employee wages of $965 have been incurred but not paid or recorded.

g.   At the end of the period, $300 of interest has been earned but not yet received or recorded.

E3-27.   Preparing Accounting Adjustments   (LO2)
Refer to the information in E3-26. Prepare journal entries for each accounting adjustment.

E3-28.   Assessing Financial Statement Effects of Adjustments Across Two Periods   (LO1, 2)
Engel Company closes its accounts on December 31 each year. The company works a five-day work week and pays its employees every two weeks. On December 31, 2008, Engel accrued $4,700 of salaries payable. On January 9, 2009, the company paid salaries of $12,000 cash to employees. Prepare entries using the financial statement effects template to (a) accrue the salaries payable on December 31; and (b) record the salary payment on January 9.

E3-29.[A]   **Preparing Accounting Adjustments   (LO1, 2)**
Refer to the information in E3-28. Prepare journal entries to accrue the salaries in December; close salaries expense for the year; and pay the salaries in January. Assume that there is no change in the pay rate during the year, and no change in the company's work force.

E3-30.   Financial Analysis Using Adjusted Account Data   (LO2)
Selected T-account balances for Bloomfield Company are shown below as of January 31, 2010; accounting adjustments have already been posted. The firm uses a calendar-year accounting period but prepares *monthly* accounting adjustments.

Supplies		Supplies Expense	
Jan. 31 Bal. 800		Jan. 31 Bal. 960	

Prepaid Insurance		Insurance Expense	
Jan. 31 Bal. 574		Jan. 31 Bal. 82	

Wages Payable		Wages Expense	
	Jan. 31 Bal. 500	Jan. 31 Bal. 3,200	

Truck		Accumulated Depreciation-Truck	
Jan. 31 Bal. 8,700			Jan. 31 Bal. 2,610

a.   If the amount in Supplies Expense represents the January 31 adjustment for the supplies used in January, and $620 worth of supplies were purchased during January, what was the January 1 beginning balance of Supplies?

b.   The amount in the Insurance Expense account represents the adjustment made at January 31 for January insurance expense. If the original insurance premium was for one year, what was the amount of the premium and on what date did the insurance policy start?

c.   If we assume that no beginning balance existed in either Wages Payable or Wages Expense on January 1, how much cash was paid as wages during January?

d.   If the truck has a useful life of five years (or 60 months), what is the monthly amount of depreciation expense and how many months has Bloomfield owned the truck?

E3-31.   Assessing Financial Statement Effects of Adjustments   (LO2)
T. Lys began Thomas Refinishing Service on July 1, 2009. Selected accounts are shown below as of July 31, before any accounting adjustments have been made.

	Debits	Credits
Prepaid Rent	$5,700	
Prepaid Advertising	630	
Supplies	3,000	
Unearned Refinishing Fees		$ 600
Refinishing Fees Revenue		2,500

Using the following information, prepare the accounting adjustments necessary on July 31 using the financial statement effects template.

    a.   On July 1, the firm paid one year's rent of $5,700 in cash.

    b.   On July 1, $630 cash was paid to the local newspaper for an advertisement to run daily for the months of July, August, and September.

    c.   Supplies still available at July 31 total $1,100.

    d.   At July 31, refinishing services of $800 have been performed but not yet recorded or billed to customers. The firm uses the account Fees Receivable to reflect amounts due but not yet billed.

    e.   In early July, a customer paid $600 in advance for a refinishing project. At July 31, the project is one-half complete.

E3-32.   **Preparing Accounting Adjustments and Posting**   **(LO2)**

Refer to the information in E3-31. Prepare adjusting journal entries for each transaction. Set up T-accounts for each of the ledger accounts and post the journal entries to them.

E3-33.   **Inferring Transactions from Financial Statements**   **(LO1)**

Harley-Davidson manufactures and sells motorcycles as well as retail parts and accessories throughout the world. The following information is taken from Harley-Davidson's fiscal 2007 annual report.

Harley-Davidson, Inc. (HOG)

Selected Balance Sheet Data	2007	2006
Inventories	$349,697	$287,798
Accounts Receivable	181,217	143,049

    a.   Harley-Davidson spent $3,674,647 to purchase and manufacture inventories during its 2007 fiscal year. Use the financial statement effects template to record cost of goods sold for Harley-Davidson's fiscal year ended 2007.

    b.   Assume that Harley-Davidson had $5,726,848 sales on credit during fiscal year 2007. What amount did the company collect from credit customers during the year? Record this with the financial statement effects template.

E3-34.   **Inferring Transactions and Preparing Journal Entries**   **(LO1)**

Refer to the information in E3-33. Prepare journal entries for each transaction.

Harley-Davidson, Inc. (HOG)

E3-35.[A]   **Preparing Closing Journal Entries**   **(LO5)**

The adjusted trial balance of The GAP, Inc., dated February 2, 2008, contains the following selected accounts.

The GAP, Inc. (GPS)

($ millions)	Debit	Credit
Net Sales		$15,763
Cost of Goods Sold	$10,071	
Operating Expenses	4,377	
Interest Income, net		91
Loss from Discontinued Operation	34	
Income Tax Expense	539	
Retained Earnings		8,390

Prepare entries to close these accounts in journal entry form. Set up T-accounts for each of the ledger accounts and post the entries to them. After these entries are posted, what is the balance of the Retained Earnings account?

E3-36.   **Inferring Transactions from Financial Statements**   **(LO1, 2)**

Costco Wholesale Corporation operates membership warehouses selling food, appliances, consumer electronics, apparel and other household goods at 488 locations across the U.S. as well as in Canada, Mexico and Puerto Rico. As of its fiscal year-end 2007, Costco had approximately 50 million members. Selected fiscal-year information from the company's balance sheets follows ($ thousands).

WebAssign.

Costco Wholesale Corporation (COST)

Selected Balance Sheet Data	2007	2006
Merchandise inventories	$4,879,465	$4,561,232
Deferred membership income (liability)	692,176	583,946

    a.   During fiscal 2007, Costco collected $1,204,324 cash for membership fees. Use the financial statement effects template to record the cash collected for membership fees.

b. Calculate the membership fee revenue that Costco recognized during the year. Use the financial statement effects template to record this revenue.

c. Costco recorded merchandise costs (that is, cost of goods sold) of $56,449,702 in 2007. Record this transaction in the financial statements effects template.

d. Determine the value of merchandise that Costco purchased during fiscal-year 2007. Use the financial statement effects template to record these merchandise purchases. Assume all of Costco's purchases are on credit.

E3-37. Inferring Transactions and Preparing Journal Entries (LO1, 2)

Costco Wholesale
Corporation (COST)

WebAssign.

Refer to the information in E3-36. Prepare journal entries for transactions in parts *a* through *d*.

E3-38.[A] **Preparing Financial Statements and Closing Entries (LO4, 5)**

The adjusted trial balance for Beneish Corporation is as follows.

BENEISH CORPORATION Adjusted Trial Balance December 31, 2010		
	Debit	**Credit**
Cash..........................	$ 4,000	
Accounts receivable..............	6,500	
Equipment	78,000	
Accumulated depreciation...........		$ 14,000
Notes payable		10,000
Common stock...................		43,000
Retained earnings		20,600
Dividends	8,000	
Service fees earned		71,000
Rent expense....................	18,000	
Salaries expense	37,100	
Depreciation expense.............	7,000	
Totals	$158,600	$158,600

a. Prepare Beneish Corporation's income statement and statement of stockholders' equity for year-end December 31, 2010, and its balance sheet as of December 31, 2010. The company paid cash dividends of $8,000 and there were no stock issuances or repurchases during 2010.

b. Prepare journal entries to close Beneish's temporary accounts.

c. Set up T-accounts for each account and post the closing entries.

PROBLEMS

P3-39. Assessing Financial Statement Effects of Transactions and Adjustments (LO2)

The following information relates to December 31 accounting adjustments for Koonce Kwik Print Company. The firm's fiscal year ends on December 31.

1. Weekly salaries for a five-day week total $1,800, payable on Fridays. December 31 of the current year is a Tuesday.

2. Koonce Kwik Print has $20,000 of notes payable outstanding at December 31. Interest of $200 has accrued on these notes by December 31, but will not be paid until the notes mature next year.

3. During December, Koonce Kwik Print provided $900 of printing services to clients who will be billed on January 2. The firm uses the account Fees Receivable to reflect amounts earned but not yet billed.

4. Starting December 1, all maintenance work on Koonce Kwik Print's equipment is handled by Richardson Repair Company under an agreement whereby Koonce Kwik Print pays a fixed monthly charge of $400. Koonce Kwik Print paid six months' service charge of $2,400 cash in advance on December 1, and increased its Prepaid Maintenance account by $2,400.

5. The firm paid $900 cash on December 15 for a series of radio commercials to run during December and January. One-third of the commercials have aired by December 31. The $900 payment was recorded in its Prepaid Advertising account.

6. Starting December 16, Koonce Kwik Print rented 400 square feet of storage space from a neighboring business. The monthly rent of $0.80 per square foot is due in advance on the first of each month. Nothing was paid in December, however, because the neighbor agreed to add the rent for one-half of December to the January 1 payment.

7. Koonce Kwik Print invested $5,000 cash in securities on December 1 and earned interest of $38 on these securities by December 31. No interest will be received until January.

8. Annual depreciation on the firm's equipment is $2,175. No depreciation has been recorded during the year.

Required

Prepare Koonce Kwik Print Company's accounting adjustments required at December 31 using the financial statement effects template.

P3-40. Preparing Accounting Adjustments (LO2)

Refer to the information in P3-39. Prepare adjustments required at December 31 using journal entries.

P3-41. Assessing Financial Statement Effects of Adjustments Across Two Periods (LO1, 2)

The following selected accounts appear in Sloan Company's unadjusted trial balance at December 31, 2010, the end of its fiscal year (all accounts have normal balances).

Prepaid Advertising	$ 1,200	Unearned Service Fees	$ 5,400
Wages Expense	43,800	Service Fees Earned	87,000
Prepaid Insurance	3,420	Rental Income	4,900

Required

a. Prepare Sloan Company's accounting adjustments at December 31, 2010, using the financial statement effects template and the following additional information.
1. Prepaid advertising at December 31 is $800.
2. Unpaid wages earned by employees in December are $1,300.
3. Prepaid insurance at December 31 is $2,280.
4. Unearned service fees at December 31 are $3,000.
5. Rent revenue of $1,000 owed by a tenant is not recorded at December 31.

b. Prepare entries on January 4, 2011, using the financial statement effects template to record (1) payment of $2,400 cash in wages and (2) cash receipt from the tenant of the $1,000 rent revenue.

P3-42. Preparing Accounting Adjustments (LO1, 2)

Refer to the information in P3-41. Prepare journal entries for parts a and b.

P3-43. Journalizing and Posting Transactions, and Preparing a Trial Balance and Adjustments (LO1, 2, 3)

WebAssign.

D. Roulstone opened Roulstone Roofing Service on April 1, 2010. Transactions for April follow.

Apr. 1 Roulstone contributed $11,500 cash to the business in exchange for common stock.
2 Paid $6,100 cash for the purchase of a used truck.
2 Purchased $3,100 of ladders and other equipment; the company paid $1,000 cash, with the balance due in 30 days.
3 Paid $2,880 cash for two-year (or 24-month) premium toward liability insurance.
5 Purchased $1,200 of supplies on credit.
5 Received an advance of $1,800 cash from a customer for roof repairs to be done during April and May.
12 Billed customers $5,500 for roofing services performed.
18 Collected $4,900 cash from customers toward their accounts billed on April 12.
29 Paid $675 cash for truck fuel used in April.
30 Paid $100 cash for April newspaper advertising.
30 Paid $2,500 cash for assistants' wages earned.
30 Billed customers $4,000 for roofing services performed.

Required

a. Set up T-accounts for the following accounts: Cash; Accounts Receivable; Supplies; Prepaid Insurance; Trucks; Accumulated Depreciation–Trucks; Equipment; Accumulated Depreciation–Equipment; Accounts Payable; Unearned Roofing Fees; Common Stock; Roofing Fees Earned; Fuel Expense; Advertising Expense; Wages Expense; Insurance Expense; Supplies Expense; Depreciation Expense–Trucks; and Depreciation Expense–Equipment.

b. Record these transactions for April using journal entries.
c. Post these entries to their T-accounts (reference transactions in T-accounts by date).
d. Prepare an unadjusted trial balance at April 30, 2010.
e. Prepare entries to adjust the following accounts: Insurance Expense, Supplies Expense, Depreciation Expense—Trucks, Depreciation Expense—Equipment, and Roofing Fees Earned in journal entry form. Supplies still available on April 30 amount to $400. Depreciation for April was $125 on the truck and $35 on equipment. One-fourth of the roofing fee received on April 5, was earned by April 30.
f. Post adjusting entries to their T-accounts.

P3-44. Assessing Financial Statement Effects of Transactions and Adjustments   (LO1, 2)
Refer to the information in P3-43.

Required
a. Use the financial statement effects template to record the transactions for April.
b. Use the financial statement effects template to record the adjustments at the end of April (described in part *e* of P3-43).

P3-45. Preparing an Unadjusted Trial Balance and Accounting Adjustments   (LO2, 3)
Pownall Photomake Company, a commercial photography studio, completed its first year of operations on December 31, 2010. General ledger account balances before year-end adjustments follow; no adjustments have been made to the accounts at any time during the year. Assume that all balances are normal.

Cash	$ 2,150	Accounts Payable	$ 1,910
Accounts Receivable	3,800	Unearned Photography Fees	2,600
Prepaid Rent	12,600	Common Stock	24,000
Prepaid Insurance	2,970	Photography Fees Earned	34,480
Supplies	4,250	Wages Expense	11,000
Equipment	22,800	Utilities Expense	3,420

An analysis of the firm's records discloses the following (business began on January 1, 2010).

1. Photography services of $925 have been rendered, but customers have not yet paid or been billed. The company uses the account Fees Receivable to reflect amounts due but not yet billed.
2. Equipment, purchased January 1, 2010, has an estimated life of 10 years.
3. Utilities expense for December is estimated to be $400, but the bill will not arrive or be paid until January of next year. (All prior months' utilities bills have been received and paid.)
4. The balance in Prepaid Rent represents the amount paid on January 1, 2010, for a 2-year lease on the studio it operates from.
5. In November, customers paid $2,600 cash in advance for photos to be taken for the holiday season. When received, these fees were credited to Unearned Photography Fees. By December 31, all of these fees are earned.
6. A 3-year insurance premium paid on January 1, 2010, was debited to Prepaid Insurance.
7. Supplies still available at December 31 are $1,520.
8. At December 31, wages expense of $375 has been incurred but not yet paid or recorded.

Required
a. Prepare Pownall Photomake's unadjusted trial balance at December 31, 2010.
b. Prepare its adjusting entries using the financial statement effects template.

P3-46. Recording Adjustments with Journal Entries and T-Accounts   (LO2, 3)
Refer to the information in P3-45.

Required
a. Prepare journal entries to record the accounting adjustments.
b. Set up T-accounts for each account and post the journal entries to them.

P3-47. Preparing an Unadjusted Trial Balance and Accounting Adjustments   (LO2, 3)
BensEx, a mailing service, has just completed its first year of operations on December 31, 2010. Its general ledger account balances before year-end adjustments follow; no adjusting entries have been made to the accounts at any time during the year. Assume that all balances are normal.

Cash............................	$ 2,300	Accounts Payable................	$ 2,700
Accounts Receivable	5,120	Common Stock..................	9,530
Prepaid Advertising	1,680	Mailing Fees Earned...............	86,000
Supplies	6,270	Wages Expense	38,800
Equipment	42,240	Rent Expense	6,300
Notes Payable	7,500	Utilities Expense................	3,020

An analysis of the firm's records reveals the following (business began on January 1, 2010).

1. The balance in Prepaid Advertising represents the amount paid for newspaper advertising for one year. The agreement, which calls for the same amount of space each month, covers the period from February 1, 2010, to January 31, 2011. BensEx did not advertise during its first month of operations.
2. Equipment, purchased January 1, has an estimated life of eight years.
3. Utilities expense does not include expense for December, estimated at $325. The bill will not arrive until January 2011.
4. At year-end, employees have earned $1,200 in wages that will not be paid until January.
5. Supplies available at year-end amount to $1,520.
6. At year-end, unpaid interest of $450 has accrued on the notes payable.
7. The firm's lease calls for rent of $525 per month payable on the first of each month, plus an amount equal to 0.5% of annual mailing fees earned. The rental percentage is payable within 15 days after the end of the year.

Required
a. Prepare its unadjusted trial balance at December 31, 2010.
b. Prepare its adjusting entries using the financial statement effects template.

P3-48. Recording Accounting Adjustments with Journal Entries and T-Accounts (LO2, 3)
Refer to information in P3-47.

Required
a. Prepare journal entries to record the accounting adjustments.
b. Set up T-accounts for each account and post the journal entries to them.

P3-49.ᴬ Preparing Accounting Adjustments (LO2, 4, 5)
Wysocki Wheels began operations on March 1, 2010, to provide automotive wheel alignment and balancing services. On March 31, 2010, the unadjusted trial balance follows.

WYSOCKI WHEELS Unadjusted Trial Balance March 31, 2010		
	Debit	**Credit**
Cash............................	$ 1,900	
Accounts receivable................	3,820	
Prepaid rent	4,770	
Supplies	3,700	
Equipment	36,180	
Accounts payable..................		$ 2,510
Unearned service revenue		1,000
Common stock....................		38,400
Service revenue		12,360
Wages expense	3,900	
	$54,270	$54,270

The following information is also available.

1. The balance in Prepaid Rent was the amount paid on March 1 to cover the first 6 months' rent.
2. Supplies available on March 31 amounted to $1,720.
3. Equipment has an estimated life of nine years (or 108 months).
4. Unpaid and unrecorded wages at March 31 were $560.
5. Utility services used during March were estimated at $390; a bill is expected early in April.

6.   The balance in Unearned Service Revenue was the amount received on March 1 from a car dealer to cover alignment and balancing services on cars sold by the dealer in March and April. Wysocki Wheels agreed to provide the services at a fixed fee of $500 each month.

Required

a.   Prepare its accounting adjustments at March 31, 2010 in journal entry form.

b.   Set up T-accounts and post the accounting adjustments to them.

c.   Prepare its income statement for March and its balance sheet at March 31, 2010.

d.   Prepare entries to close its temporary accounts in journal entry form. Post the closing entries to the T-accounts.

MANAGEMENT APPLICATIONS

MA3-50.   Preparing Accounting Adjustments and Financial Statements   (LO1, 2, 4)

Stocken Surf Shop began operations on July 1, 2010, with an initial investment of $50,000. During the first three months of operations, the following cash transactions were recorded in the firm's checking account.

Deposits	
Initial investment by owner	$ 50,000
Collected from customers	81,000
Borrowings from bank	10,000
	$141,000
Checks drawn	
Rent	$ 24,000
Fixtures and equipment	25,000
Merchandise inventory.	62,000
Salaries	6,000
Other expenses	13,000
	$130,000

Additional information:

1. Most sales were for cash, however, the store accepted a limited amount of credit sales; at September 30, 2010, customers owed the store $9,000.

2. Rent was paid on July 1 for six months.

3. Salaries of $3,000 per month were paid on the 1st of each month for salaries earned in the month prior.

4. Inventories were purchased for cash; at September 30, 2010, inventory of $21,000 was still available.

5. Fixtures and equipment were expected to last five years (or 60 months) with zero salvage value.

6. The bank charges 12% annual interest (1% per month) on the $10,000 bank loan. Stocken took the loan out July 1.

Required

a. Record all of Stocken's cash transactions and prepare any necessary adjusting entries at September 30, 2010. You may either use the financial statement effects template or journal entries combined with T-accounts.

b. Prepare the income statement for the three months ended September 30, 2010, and the balance sheet at September 30, 2010.

c. Analyze the statements from part b and assess the company's performance over its initial three months.

MA3-51.   Analyzing Transactions, Impacts on Financial Ratios, and Loan Covenants   (LO2)

Kadous Consulting, a firm started three years ago by K. Kadous, offers consulting services for material handling and plant layout. Its balance sheet at the close of 2010 follows.

KADOUS CONSULTING				
Balance Sheet				
December 31, 2010				
Assets			**Liabilities**	
Cash..................		$ 3,400	Notes payable	$30,000
Accounts receivable......		22,875	Accounts payable...............	4,200
Supplies		13,200	Unearned consulting fees	11,300
Prepaid insurance........		4,500	Wages payable.................	400
Equipment	$68,500		Total liabilities..................	45,900
Less: Accumulated			**Equity**	
depreciation	23,975	44,525	Common stock.................	8,000
			Retained earnings	34,600
Total assets............		$88,500	Total liabilities and equity.........	$88,500

Earlier in the year Kadous obtained a bank loan of $30,000 cash for the firm. A provision of the loan is that the year-end debt-to-equity ratio (total liabilities to total equity) cannot exceed 1.0. Based on the above balance sheet, the ratio at the end of 2010 is 1.08. Kadous is concerned about being in violation of the loan agreement and requests assistance in reviewing the situation. Kadous believes that she might have overlooked some items at year-end. Discussions with Kadous reveal the following.

1. On January 1, 2010, the firm paid a $4,500 insurance premium for two years of coverage; the amount in Prepaid Insurance has not yet been adjusted.
2. Depreciation on equipment should be 10% of cost per year; it inadvertently recorded 15% for 2010.
3. Interest on the bank loan has been paid through the end of 2010.
4. The firm concluded a major consulting engagement in December, doing a plant layout analysis for a new factory. The $6,000 fee has not been billed or recorded in the accounts.
5. On December 1, 2010, the firm received an $11,300 cash advance payment from Dichev Corp. for consulting services to be rendered over a two-month period. This payment was credited to the Unearned Consulting Fees account. One-half of this fee was earned but unrecorded by December 31, 2010.
6. Supplies costing $4,800 were available on December 31; the company has made no adjustment of its Supplies account.

Required
a. What is the correct debt-to-equity ratio at December 31, 2010?
b. Is the firm in violation of its loan agreement? Prepare computations to support the correct total liabilities and total equity figures at December 31, 2010.

MA3-52. Ethics, Accounting Adjustments, and Auditors (LO1, 2)
It is the end of the accounting year for Anne Beatty, controller of a medium-sized, publicly held corporation specializing in toxic waste cleanup. Within the corporation, only Beatty and the president know that the firm has been negotiating for several months to land a large contract for waste cleanup in Western Europe. The president has hired another firm with excellent contacts in Western Europe to help with negotiations. The outside firm will charge an hourly fee plus expenses, but has agreed not to submit a bill until the negotiations are in their final stages (expected to occur in another 3 to 4 months). Even if the contract falls through, the outside firm is entitled to receive payment for its services. Based upon her discussion with a member of the outside firm, Beatty knows that its charge for services provided to date will be $150,000. This is a material amount for the company.

Beatty knows that the president wants negotiations to remain as secret as possible so that competitors will not learn of the contract the company is pursuing in Europe. In fact, the president recently stated to her, "This is not the time to reveal our actions in Western Europe to other staff members, our auditors, or the readers of our financial statements; securing this contract is crucial to our future growth." No entry has been made in the accounting records for the cost of contract negotiations. Beatty now faces an uncomfortable situation. The company's outside auditor has just asked her if she knows of any year-end adjustments that have not yet been recorded.

Required
a. What are the ethical considerations that Beatty faces in answering the auditor's question?
b. How should Beatty respond to the auditor's question?

Analyzing and Interpreting Financial Statements

LEARNING OBJECTIVES

LO1 Compute return on equity (ROE) and disaggregate it into components of operating and nonoperating returns. (p. 4-4)

LO2 Disaggregate operating return (RNOA) into components of profitability and asset turnover. (p. 4-11)

LO3 Explain nonoperating return and compute it from return on equity and the operating return. (p. 4-20)

LO4 Compute and interpret measures of liquidity and solvency. (p. 4-26)

LO5 Describe and illustrate traditional DuPont disaggregation of ROE. (p. 4-29)

GENERAL MILLS

General Mills employs a number of financial measures to assess its overall performance and financial condition. These measures include ratios related to profitability and asset turnover as well as the return on invested capital. Analysts, too, use a variety of measures to capture different aspects of company performance to answer questions such as: Is it managed efficiently and profitably? Does it use assets effectively? Is performance achieved with a minimum of debt?

One fundamental measure is return on capital, which Warren Buffett, CEO of the investment firm Berkshire Hathaway, lists in his acquisition criteria cited in Module 1: "Our preference would be to reach our goal by directly owning a diversified group of businesses that generate cash and consistently earn above-average returns on capital." All return metrics follow the same basic formula—they divide some measure of profit by some measure of investment. A company's performance is commonly judged by its profitability. Although analysis of profit is important, it is only part of the story. A more meaningful analysis is to compare level of profitability with the amount of capital than has been invested in the business. The most common return measure is return on equity (ROE), which focuses on shareholder investment as its measure of invested capital. By focusing on the *equity* investment, ROE measures return from the perspective of the common shareholder rather than the company overall. General Mills' ROE for 2008 was 20.0%, up from 15.9% three years ago.

This module focuses on analysis of return metrics. Beyond ROE, we put special emphasis on the return on net operating assets (RNOA), computed as net operating profit after tax (NOPAT) divided by average net operating assets (NOA). RNOA focuses on operating activities—operating profit relative to investment in net operating assets. It is important to distinguish operating activities from nonoperating activities because the capital markets value each component differently, placing much greater emphasis on operations. General Mills' RNOA has improved from 10.3% to 11.9% in the past three years.

RNOA consists of two components: profitability and asset productivity. Increasing either component increases

RNOA. These components reflect on the first two questions we posed above: Is the company managed efficiently and profitably? Does it use assets effectively?

The profitability component of RNOA measures net operating profit after tax for each sales dollar (NOPAT/Sales), and is called the net operating profit margin (NOPM). General Mills' NOPM has fluctuated little from 11.3% to 11.4% in the past three years.

Asset productivity, the second component of RNOA, is reflected in net operating asset turnover (NOAT). NOAT is measured as sales divided by average net operating assets—it captures the notion of how many sales dollars are generated by each dollar of invested assets. General Mills has increased its NOAT from 0.90 to 1.05 in the past five years. Increasing the turnover for large asset bases is difficult, and NOAT measures tend to fluctuate in a narrow band. When companies are able to make a meaningful improvement in NOAT, however, it usually has a large impact on RNOA.

RNOA is an important metric in assessing the performance of company management. We can use the RNOA components, NOPM and NOAT, to assess how effectively

and efficiently management uses the company's operating assets to produce a return.

The difference between ROE and RNOA is important for our analysis. Specifically, ROE consists of a return on operating activities (RNOA) *plus* a return on nonoperating activities, where the latter reflects how well the company uses borrowed funds. Companies can increase ROE by borrowing money and effectively using those borrowed funds. However, debt can increase the company's risk—where severe consequences can result if debt is not repaid when due. This is why Warren Buffett focuses on "businesses earning good returns on equity while employing little or no debt." For those companies that do employ debt, our analysis seeks to evaluate their ability to repay the amounts owed when due.

Over the years, analysts, creditors and others have developed hundreds of ratios to measure specific aspects of financial performance. Most of these seek answers to the root question: Can the company achieve a high return on its invested capital and, if so, is that return sustainable?

Sources: *General Mills 10-K, 2008*; Berkshire Hathaway 10-K, 2006; *The Wall Street Journal*, January 2009.

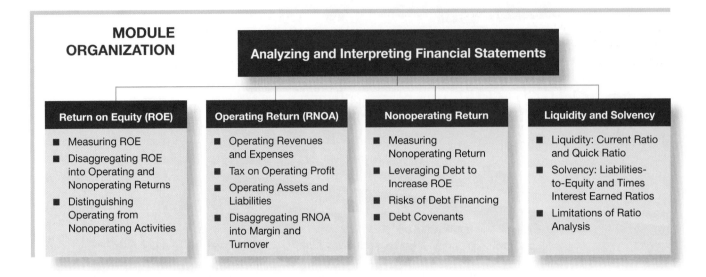

MODULE ORGANIZATION

Analyzing and Interpreting Financial Statements

Return on Equity (ROE)
- Measuring ROE
- Disaggregating ROE into Operating and Nonoperating Returns
- Distinguishing Operating from Nonoperating Activities

Operating Return (RNOA)
- Operating Revenues and Expenses
- Tax on Operating Profit
- Operating Assets and Liabilities
- Disaggregating RNOA into Margin and Turnover

Nonoperating Return
- Measuring Nonoperating Return
- Leveraging Debt to Increase ROE
- Risks of Debt Financing
- Debt Covenants

Liquidity and Solvency
- Liquidity: Current Ratio and Quick Ratio
- Solvency: Liabilities-to-Equity and Times Interest Earned Ratios
- Limitations of Ratio Analysis

A key aspect of any analysis is identifying the business activities that drive company success. We pursue an answer to the question: Is the company earning an acceptable rate of return on its invested capital? We also want to know the extent to which the company's return on invested capital results from its operating versus its nonoperating activities. The distinction between returns from operating and nonoperating activities is important and plays a key role in our analysis.

Operating activities are the core activities of a company. They consist of those activities required to deliver a company's products or services to its customers. A company engages in operating activities when it conducts research and development, establishes supply chains, assembles administrative support, produces and markets its products, and follows up with after-sale customer services.

The asset side of a company's balance sheet reflects resources devoted to operating activities with accounts such as cash, receivables, inventories, and property, plant and equipment (PPE). Operating activities are reflected in liabilities with accounts such as accounts payable, accrued expenses, and long-term operating liabilities such as pension and health care obligations. The income statement reflects operating activities through accounts such as revenues, costs of goods sold, and operating expenses such as selling, general, and administrative expenses that include wages, advertising, depreciation, occupancy, insurance, and research and development. Operating activities create the most long-lasting (persistent) effects on future profitability and cash flows of the company. Operations provide the primary value drivers for company stakeholders. It is for this reason that operating activities play such a prominent role in assessing profitability.

Nonoperating activities relate to the investing of excess cash in marketable securities and in other nonoperating investments. Nonoperating activities also relate to borrowings through accounts such as short- and long-term debt. These nonoperating assets and liabilities expand and contract to buffer fluctuations in operating asset and liability levels. When operating assets grow faster than operating liabilities, companies typically increase their nonoperating liabilities to fund the deficit. Later, these liabilities decline when operating assets decline. When companies have cash in excess of what is needed for operating activities, they often invest the cash temporarily in marketable securities or other investments to provide some return until those funds are needed for operations.

The income statement reflects nonoperating activities through accounts such as interest and dividend revenue, capital gains or losses relating to investments, and interest expense on borrowed funds. Nonoperating expenses, net of any nonoperating revenues, provide a nonoperating return for a company. Although nonoperating activities are important and must be managed well, they are not the main value drivers for company stakeholders.

We begin this module by explaining the return on equity (ROE). We then discuss in more detail how ROE consists of both an operating return (RNOA) and a nonoperating return. Next, we discuss the two RNOA components that measure profitability and asset turnover. We conclude this module with a discussion of nonoperating return, focusing on the notion that companies can increase ROE through judicious use of debt.

Appendixes 4A and 4B expand our explanation of nonoperating return by exploring how much debt a company can reasonably manage. For this purpose, we examine a number of liquidity and solvency metrics in Appendix 4B. As part of that analysis, we identify ratios that credit analysts typically use to develop credit ratings, which are key determinants of bond prices and the cost of debt financing for public companies.

RETURN ON EQUITY (ROE)

Return on equity (ROE) is the principal summary measure of company performance and is defined as follows:

$$\text{ROE} = \frac{\text{Net income}}{\text{Average stockholders' equity}}$$

ROE relates net income to the average investment by shareholders as measured by total stockholders' equity from the balance sheet. Warren Buffett highlights this return as part of his acquisition criteria: "Businesses earning good returns on equity while employing little or no debt." The ROE formula can be rewritten in a way to better see the point Buffett is making (derivation of this ROE formula is in Appendix 4A):

$$\text{ROE} = \text{Operating return} + \text{Nonoperating return}$$

The equation above shows that ROE consists of two returns: (1) the return from the company's operating activities, linked to revenues and expenses from the company's products or services, and (2) the return from the company's use of debt, net of any return from nonoperating investments. Companies can use debt to increase their return on equity, but this increases risk as the failure to make required debt payments can yield many legal consequences, including bankruptcy. This is one reason why Warren Buffett focuses on companies whose return on equity is derived primarily from operating activities.

> **BUSINESS INSIGHT**   General Mills' ROE and RNOA
>
> The following graph shows that General Mills' ROE and RNOA have increased steadily in the past 3 years. ROE exceeds RNOA in all years, widening more in the most recent year as the company increased its net debt and the nonoperating return component of its ROE.

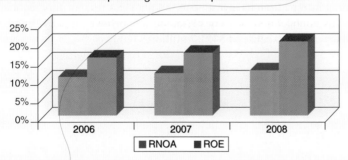

OPERATING RETURN (RNOA)

Operating returns are reflected in the **return on net operating assets (RNOA),** defined as follows:

$$\text{RNOA} = \frac{\text{Net operating profit after tax (NOPAT)}}{\text{Average net operating assets (NOA)}}$$

To implement this formula, we must first classify the income statement and balance sheet into operating and nonoperating components so that we can assess each separately. We first consider operating activities on the income statement and explain how to compute NOPAT. Second, we consider operating activities on the balance sheet and explain how to compute NOA.

LO1 Compute return on equity (ROE) and disaggregate it into components of operating and nonoperating returns.

ALERT The FASB recently released a preliminary draft of proposed new financial statements to, among other things, better distinguish operating and nonoperating activities. It appears that the FASB is beginning to recognize the crucial importance of distinguishing between operating and nonoperating activities for analysis purposes.

Operating Items in the Income Statement —NOPAT

The income statement reports both operating and nonoperating activities. Exhibit 4.1 shows a typical income statement with the operating activities highlighted.

EXHIBIT 4.1 Operating and Nonoperating Items in the Income Statement
Typical Income Statement   **Operating Items Highlighted**
Revenues
Cost of sales
Gross profit
Operating expenses
Selling, general and administrative
Asset impairment expense
Gains and losses on asset disposal
Total operating expenses
Operating income
Interest expense
Interest and dividend revenue
Investment gains and losses
Total nonoperating expenses
Income before tax, minority interest and discontinued operations
Tax expense
Income before minority interest and discontinued operations
Minority (noncontrolling) interest (see Appendix 4A)
Discontinued operations (see Appendix 4A)
Net income

Operating activities are those that relate to bringing a company's products or services to market and any after-sales support. The income statement in Exhibit 4.1 reflects operating activities through revenues, costs of goods sold (COGS), and other expenses. Selling, general, and administrative expense (SG&A) includes wages, advertising, occupancy, insurance, research and development, depreciation, and many other operating expenses the company incurs in the ordinary course of business (some of these are often reported as separate line items in the income statement). Companies also dispose of operating assets, and can realize gains or losses from their disposal, or write them off partially or completely when they become impaired. These, too, are operating activities. Finally, the reported tax expense on the income statement reflects both operating and nonoperating activities. Later in this section we use General Mills' income statement to explain how to separately compute tax expense related to operating activities only.

Nonoperating activities relate to borrowed money that creates interest expense. Nonoperating activities also relate to investments such as marketable securities and other investments that yield interest or dividend revenue and capital gains or losses from any sales of nonoperating investments during the period.

Following is General Mills' 2008 income statement with the operating items highlighted. General Mills' operating items include sales, cost of sales, SG&A, and depreciation expense. General Mills' pretax operating income is $2,227.8 million (it also earns pretax operating income from its investments in joint ventures, but only reports its after-tax profit of $110.8 million). Its nonoperating activities relate to its borrowed money (interest expense) which yield pretax net nonoperating expense of $421.7 million.

GENERAL MILLS Income Statement ($ millions) For Year Ended May 25, 2008	
Revenues	$13,652.1
Cost of sales.	8,778.3
Gross profit.	4,873.8
Operating expenses	
Selling, general and administrative.	2,625.0
Restructuring and other costs	21.0
Total operating expenses	2,646.0
Operating income.	2,227.8
Interest expense, net	421.7
Earnings before taxes and joint venture earnings	1,806.1
Tax expense	622.2
After-tax earnings from joint ventures	110.8
Net income.	$ 1,294.7

Computing Tax on Operating Profit

General Mills' income statement reports net operating profit *before* tax (NOPBT) of $2,227.8 million. But, the numerator of the RNOA formula, defined previously, uses net operating profit *after tax* (NOPAT). Thus, we need to subtract taxes to determine NOPAT.

$$\textbf{NOPAT = NOPBT − Tax on operating profit}$$

The tax expense of $622.2 million that General Mills reports on its income statement pertains to both operating *and* nonoperating activities. To compute NOPAT, we need to compute the tax expense relating solely to operating profit as follows:

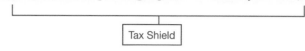

Tax on operating profit = Tax expense + (Pretax net nonoperating expense × Statutory tax rate)

Tax Shield

The amount in parentheses is called the *tax shield*, which are the taxes that General Mills saved by having tax-deductible nonoperating expenses (see Tax Shield box on the next page for details). By definition, the taxes saved (by the tax shield) do not relate to operating profits; thus, we must add back the tax shield to total tax expense to compute tax on operating profit. (For companies with nonoperating revenue greater than nonoperating expense, so-called *net nonoperating revenue*, the tax on operating profit is computed as: Tax expense − [Pretax net nonoperating revenue × Statutory tax rate]).

Applying this method, we see that General Mills had a tax shield of $162.4 million (computed as pretax net nonoperating expense of $421.7 million times its statutory tax rate of 38.5%) and tax on operating profit of $784.6 million (computed as $622.2 million + $162.4 million).[1] We then subtract the tax on operating profit from the net operating profit before tax to obtain NOPAT. Thus, General Mills' net operating profit after tax is computed as follows ($ millions):[2]

Net operating profit before tax (NOPBT)		$2,227.8
Less tax on operating profit		
Tax expense (from income statement)	$622.2	
Tax shield ($421.7 × 38.5%)	+162.4	(784.6)
After-tax earnings from joint ventures		110.8*
Net operating profit after tax (NOPAT)		$ 1,554

* Its joint ventures are accounted for using the equity method (see Module 7); these earnings are part of operations because the joint ventures manufacture and market products outside the U.S. that are similar to those it manufactures and markets in the U.S. The income statement reports this joint-venture profit on an after-tax basis; thus, it is not part of tax computations for operating profit.

---

[1] The statutory federal tax rate for corporations is 35% (per U.S. tax code). Also, most states and some local jurisdictions tax corporate income, and those state taxes are deductible for federal tax purposes. The *net* state tax rate is the statutory rate less the federal tax deduction. Most companies provide both the federal and net state tax percentages in the income tax footnote (although, some report dollar amounts for taxes that must be converted to percentages for use in the formula). The tax rate on operating profit is the sum of the two. General Mills reports the following as part of its income tax footnote in its 2008 10-K:

United States statutory rate	35.0%
State and local income taxes, net of federal tax benefits	3.5

[2] Alternatively, by rearranging terms, we can compute NOPAT using the following two-step method. First, we compute the tax rate on operating profit as follows:

$$\textbf{Tax rate on operating profit} = \frac{\textbf{Tax expense + (Pretax net nonoperating expense × Statutory tax rate)}}{\textbf{Net operating profit before taxes}}$$

Next, we compute NOPAT (before the after-tax earnings from joint ventures) as follows:

$$\textbf{NOPAT = Net operating profit before tax × (1 − Tax rate on operating profit)}$$

BUSINESS INSIGHT **Tax Shield**

Persons with home mortgages understand well the beneficial effects of the "interest tax shield." To see how the interest tax shield works, consider two individuals, each with income of $50,000 and each with only one expense: a home. Assume that one person pays $10,000 per year in rent; the other pays $10,000 in interest on a home mortgage. Rent is not deductible for tax purposes, whereas mortgage interest (but not principal) is deductible. Assume that each person pays taxes at 25%, the personal tax rate for this income level. Their tax payments follow.

	Renter	Home owner
Income before interest and taxes..............	$50,000	$50,000
Less interest deduction	0	(10,000)
Taxable income	$50,000	$40,000
Taxes paid (25% rate).......................	$12,500	$10,000

The renter reports $50,000 in taxable income and pays $12,500 in taxes. The home owner deducts $10,000 in interest, which lowers taxable income to $40,000 and reduces taxes to $10,000. By deducting mortgage interest, the home owner's tax bill is $2,500 lower. The $2,500 is the *interest tax shield*, and we can compute it directly as the $10,000 interest deduction multiplied by the 25% tax rate.

BUSINESS INSIGHT **Tax Rates for Computing NOPAT**

Computing NOPAT requires the tax rate on operating profit, which in turn requires the statutory tax rate (sum of federal and state tax rates). These are disclosed in the required income tax footnote to the 10-K. Following is this footnote from General Mills' 10-K.

Fiscal Year	2008
United States statutory rate..................................	35.0%
State and local income taxes, net of federal tax benefits	3.5
Foreign rate differences	(1.2)
U.S. Federal District Court decision, including related interest	(1.7)
Other, net	(1.2)
Effective income tax rate	34.4%

The federal statutory rate is 35.0%, and General Mills pays state and local taxes amounting to an additional 3.5%. It also reports reductions of 1.2% relating to lower foreign taxes and 1.7% relating to a favorable tax court ruling. Thus, General Mills effective tax rate for *ALL* its income is the sum of all its taxes paid less benefits received, or 34.4%. However, the tax shield that we add back in computing NOPAT only uses *federal and state tax rates*. For General Mills, the tax rate used to compute the tax shield is 38.5% (35.0% + 3.5%). It would be incorrect to use General Mills' 34.4% effective tax rate to compute NOPAT, which is the average tax rate during 2008 (computed as tax expense of $622.2 million divided by earnings before taxes of $1,806.1 million) and includes operating and nonoperating items. Footnote 2, above, explained that its tax rate on operating income is 35.2%, computed as ($622.2 million + $162.4 million)/$2,227.8 million. Thus, operating income is taxed at 35.2% and nonoperating expenses shield the company from the 38.5% statutory rate, which yields an average (effective) tax rate of 34.4%.

MID-MODULE REVIEW 1

Following is the income statement and the income tax footnote of Kellogg Company.

KELLOGG COMPANY Income Statement ($ millions) For Fiscal Year Ended December 29, 2007	
Net sales...	$11,776
Cost of sales.......................................	6,597
Gross margin	5,179
Selling, general and administrative expense	3,311
Interest expense....................................	321
Pretax earnings	1,547
Income tax provision	444
Net earnings.......................................	$ 1,103

Difference between Statutory Rate and Effective Rate	2007
U.S. statutory income tax rate	35.0%
Foreign rates varying from 35%	(4.0)
State income taxes, net of federal benefit	1.1
Foreign earnings repatriation	2.3
Net change in valuation allowances	(0.5)
Statutory rate changes, deferred tax impact	(0.6)
International restructuring	(2.6)
Other	(2.0)
Effective income tax rate	28.7%

Required

Compute Kellogg's net operating profit after tax (NOPAT).

Solution

Drawing on Kellogg's tax footnote we compute its total statutory state and federal tax rate as 36.1% (35.0% federal rate + 1.1% state rate net of federal benefits). Next, we identify the operating and nonoperating items comprising income. Specifically, all expenses reported in its income statement pertain to operating activities except for interest expense. Therefore, Kellogg's net operating profit after tax (NOPAT) equals $1,308 million, computed as ($ millions): $11,776 − $6,597 − $3,311 − ($444 + [$321 × 36.1%]) = $1,308.

Operating Items in the Balance Sheet —NOA

RNOA relates NOPAT to the average net operating assets (NOA) of the company. We compute NOA as follows:

$$\text{Net operating assets} = \text{Operating assets} - \text{Operating liabilities}$$

To compute NOA we must partition the balance sheet into operating and nonoperating items. Exhibit 4.2 shows a typical balance sheet and highlights the operating items.

EXHIBIT 4.2 Operating and Nonoperating Items in the Balance Sheet

Typical Balance Sheet — Operating Items Highlighted

Current assets	Current liabilities
Cash and cash equivalents	Short-term notes and interest payable
Short-term investments	Current maturities of long-term debt
Accounts receivable	Accounts payable
Inventories	Accrued liabilities
Prepaid expenses	Unearned revenue
Deferred income tax assets	Deferred income tax liabilities
Other current assets	
	Long-term liabilities
Long-term assets	Bonds and notes payable
Long-term investments in securities	Capitalized lease obligations
Property, plant and equipment, net	Pension and other post-employment liabilities
Capitalized lease assets	Deferred income tax liabilities
Natural resources	
Equity method investments	**Stockholders' equity**
Goodwill and Intangible assets	All equity accounts
Deferred income tax assets	
Other long-term assets	Minority (noncontrolling) interest

Operating assets are those assets directly linked to operating activities, the company's ongoing business operations. They typically include cash, receivables, inventories, prepaid expenses, property, plant and equipment (PPE), and capitalized lease assets, and exclude short-term and long-term investments in marketable securities. Equity investments in affiliated companies and goodwill are considered operating assets if they pertain to the ownership of stock in other firms linked to the company's operating activities (see Module 7). Deferred tax assets (and liabilities) are operating items because they relate to future tax deductions (or payments) arising from operating activities (see Module 5). We assume that "other" assets and liabilities, and "other" revenues and expenses, are operating unless information suggests otherwise. Contrary information can involve footnotes that suggest a nonoperating classification or separate statement classification such as when a company reports "other" as nonoperating, for example, by reporting "other" *after* a subtotal for income from operations.

Operating liabilities are liabilities that arise from operating revenues and expenses and commonly relate to operating assets. For example, accounts payable and accrued expenses help fund inventories, wages, utilities, and other operating expenses; also, unearned revenue (an operating liability) relates to operating revenue. Similarly, pension and other post-employment obligations relate to long-term obligations for employee retirement and health care, which by definition are operating activities (see Module 10). Operating liabilities exclude bank loans, mortgages or other debt, which are nonoperating. Further, companies often use capitalized leases to finance long-term operating assets, and these capitalized lease liabilities are also nonoperating (see Module 10).

The following is General Mills' balance sheets for 2008 and 2007. Its operating assets and operating liabilities are highlighted.

GENERAL MILLS Balance Sheet		
(In millions)	May 25, 2008	May 27, 2007
Assets		
Cash and cash equivalents	$ 661.0	$ 417.1
Receivables, net	1,081.6	952.9
Inventories	1,366.8	1,173.4
Prepaid expenses and other current assets	510.6	443.1
Deferred income taxes	—	67.2
Total current assets	3,620.0	3,053.7
Land, buildings, and equipment	3,108.1	3,013.9
Goodwill	6,786.1	6,835.4
Other intangible assets	3,777.2	3,694.0
Other assets	1,750.2	1,586.7
Total assets	$19,041.6	$18,183.7
Liabilities and Equity		
Accounts payable	$ 937.3	$ 777.9
Current portion of long-term debt	442.0	1,734.0
Notes payable	2,208.8	1,254.4
Other current liabilities	1,239.8	2,078.8
Deferred income taxes	28.4	—
Total current liabilities	4,856.3	5,845.1
Long-term debt	4,348.7	3,217.7
Deferred income taxes	1,454.6	1,433.1
Other liabilities	1,923.9	1,229.9
Total liabilities	12,583.5	11,725.8
Stockholders' equity		
Common stock, 377.3 and 502.3 shares issued, $0.10 par value	37.7	50.2
Additional paid-in capital	1,149.1	5,841.3
Retained earnings	6,510.7	5,745.3
Common stock in treasury, at cost, shares of 39.8 and 161.7	(1,658.4)	(6,198.0)
Other equity*	419.0	1,019.1
Total stockholders' equity	6,458.1	6,457.9
Total liabilities and equity	$19,041.6	$18,183.7

* For simplification, minority interest is included with other equity; this amounts to $242.3 million and $1,138.8 million in 2008 and 2007, respectively. The final section of Appendix 4A explains minority interest and how it affects ROE computations.

We assume that General Mills' "other" assets and liabilities are operating. We can sometimes make a finer distinction if footnotes to financial statements provide additional information. For now, assume that these "other" items reported in balance sheets pertain to operations.

Using the highlighted balance sheet above, we compute net operating assets for General Mills in 2008 and 2007 as follows (recall that Net operating assets (NOA) = Total operating assets − Total operating liabilities).

General Mills ($ millions)	May 25, 2008	May 27, 2007
Operating assets		
Cash and cash equivalents	$ 661.0	$ 417.1
Receivables, net	1,081.6	952.9
Inventories	1,366.8	1,173.4
Prepaid expenses and other current assets	510.6	443.1
Deferred income taxes	—	67.2
Land, buildings, and equipment	3,108.1	3,013.9
Goodwill	6,786.1	6,835.4
Other intangible assets	3,777.2	3,694.0
Other assets	1,750.2	1,586.7
Total operating assets	19,041.6	18,183.7
Operating liabilities		
Accounts payable	937.3	777.9
Other current liabilities	1,239.8	2,078.8
Deferred income taxes (current)	28.4	—
Deferred income taxes (noncurrent)	1,454.6	1,433.1
Other liabilities	1,923.9	1,229.9
Total operating liabilities	5,584.0	5,519.7
Net operating assets (NOA)	$13,457.6	$12,664.0

To determine average NOA, we take a simple average of two consecutive years' numbers. Thus, return on net operating assets (RNOA) for General Mills for 2008 is computed as follows ($ millions).

$$\text{RNOA} = \frac{\text{NOPAT}}{\text{Average NOA}} = \frac{\$1,554}{(\$13,457.6 + \$12,664.0)/2} = 11.9\%$$

General Mills' 2008 RNOA is 11.9%. By comparison, Kellogg's (its main competitor) RNOA is 17.6% (this computation is shown in Mid-Module Review 2), and the average for all publicly traded companies is about 12% for the past decade.

Recall that RNOA is related to ROE as follows: ROE = Operating return + Nonoperating return, where RNOA is the operating return. Thus, we can ask how do General Mills' RNOA and ROE compare? To answer this we need General Mills' 2008 ROE, which is computed as follows ($ millions).

$$\text{ROE} = \frac{\text{Net income}}{\text{Average stockholders' equity}} = \frac{\$1,294.7}{(\$6,458.1 + \$6,457.9)/2} = 20.0\%$$

In relative terms, General Mills' operating return is 59% (11.9%/20.0%) of its total ROE, which is less than the average publicly traded company's percent of near 80%. Its nonoperating return of 8.1% (20.0% − 11.9%) makes up the remaining 41% of ROE.

ALERT Financial statements for reporting periods beginning after December 15, 2008, must identify the interests of both controlling (parent) and noncontrolling (minority) parties. This affects the balance sheet presentation but not ROE computations. ROE components are as follows: Net income = Net income excluding income attributable to noncontrolling interests; and, Stockholders' equity = Total equity excluding noncontrolling interests.

Exhibit 4.3 provides a summary of key terms introduced to this point and their definitions.

EXHIBIT 4.3 Key Ratio and Acronym Definitions

Ratio	Definition
ROE: Return on equity	Net income/Average stockholders' equity
NOPAT: Net operating profit after tax	Operating revenues less operating expenses such as cost of sales, selling, general and administrative expense, and taxes; it excludes nonoperating revenues and expenses such as interest revenue, dividend revenue, interest expense, gains and losses on investments, and minority interest.
NOA: Net operating assets	Operating assets less operating liabilities; it excludes investments in marketable securities and interest-bearing debt.
RNOA: Return on net operating assets . . .	NOPAT/Average NOA
NNE: Net nonoperating expense	NOPAT − Net income; NNE consists of nonoperating expenses and revenues, net of tax

RNOA DISAGGREGATION INTO MARGIN AND TURNOVER

LO2 Disaggregate operating return (RNOA) into components of profitability and asset turnover.

Disaggregating RNOA into its two components, profit margin and asset turnover, yields further insights into a company's performance. This disaggregation follows.

$$\text{RNOA} = \frac{\text{NOPAT}}{\text{Average NOA}} = \frac{\text{NOPAT}}{\text{Sales}} \times \frac{\text{Sales}}{\text{Average NOA}}$$

Net operating profit margin (NOPM)   Net operating asset turnover (NOAT)

Net Operating Profit Margin

Net operating profit margin (NOPM) reveals how much operating profit the company earns from each sales dollar. All things equal, a higher NOPM is preferable. NOPM is affected by the level of gross profit the company earns on its products (revenue minus cost of goods sold), which depends on product prices and manufacturing or purchase costs. NOPM is also affected by the level of operating expenses the company requires to support its products or services. This includes overhead costs such as wages, marketing, occupancy, and research and development. Finally, NOPM is affected by the level of competition (which affects product pricing) and the company's willingness and ability to control costs.

General Mills' net operating profit margin is computed as follows ($ millions).

$$\text{NOPM} = \frac{\text{NOPAT}}{\text{Revenues}} = \frac{\$1,554}{\$13,652.1} = 11.4\%$$

This result means that for each dollar of sales at General Mills, the company earns roughly 11.4¢ profit after all operating expenses and taxes. As a reference, the median NOPM for publicly traded companies is about 7 to 7.5¢.

Net Operating Asset Turnover

Net operating asset turnover (NOAT) measures the productivity of the company's net operating assets. This metric reveals the level of sales the company realizes from each dollar invested in net operating assets. All things equal, a higher NOAT is preferable. General Mills' net operating asset turnover ratio follows ($ millions).

$$\text{NOAT} = \frac{\text{Revenues}}{\text{Average NOA}} = \frac{\$13,652.1}{(\$13,457.6 + \$12,664.0)/2} = 1.05$$

BUSINESS INSIGHT General Mills' NOPM

The following chart shows that General Mills' net operating profit margin has fluctuated between 11.3% and 11.4% of revenues, which is fairly stable.

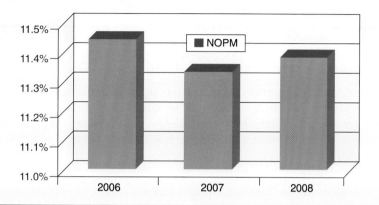

This result means that for each dollar of net operating assets, General Mills realizes $1.05 in sales. As a reference, the median for publicly traded companies is about $2.10.

NOAT can be increased by either increasing sales for a given level of investment in operating assets, or by reducing the amount of operating assets necessary to generate a dollar of sales, or both. Reducing operating working capital (current operating assets less current operating liabilities) is usually easier than reducing long-term net operating assets. For example, companies can implement strategies to collect their receivables faster, reduce their inventories, and delay payments to their suppliers. All of these actions reduce operating working capital and, thereby, increase NOAT. These strategies must be managed, however, so as not to negatively impact sales or supplier relations. Working capital management is an important part of managing the company effectively.

It is usually more difficult to reduce the level of long-term net operating assets. The level of PPE required by the company is determined more by the nature of the company's products or services than by management action. For example, telecommunications companies require more capital investment than do retail stores. Still, there are several actions that managers can take to reduce capital investment. Some companies pursue novel approaches, such as corporate alliances, outsourcing, and use of special purpose entities; we discuss some of these approaches in Module 10.

BUSINESS INSIGHT General Mills' NOAT

The following chart shows General Mills' net operating asset turnover from 2006 to 2008. General Mills' operating asset turnover has increased from about 0.90 to about 1.05 during this period, but remains only about one-half that of publicly traded companies.

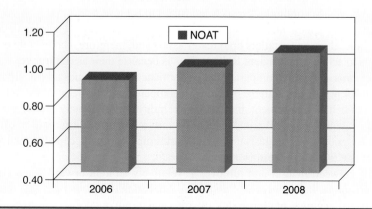

MANAGERIAL DECISION   You Are the CEO

You are analyzing the performance of your company. Your analysis of RNOA reveals the following (industry benchmarks in parenthesis): RNOA is 16% (10%), NOPM is 18% (17%), and NOAT is 0.89 (0.59). What interpretations do you draw that are useful for managing your company? [Answer, p. 4-32]

Trade-Off between Margin and Turnover

Operating profit margin and turnover of operating assets are largely affected by a company's business model. This is an important concept. Specifically, an infinite number of combinations of net operating profit margin and net operating asset turnover will yield a given RNOA. This relation is depicted in Exhibit 4.4 (where the curved line reflects the median RNOA for all publicly traded companies during the most recent decade).

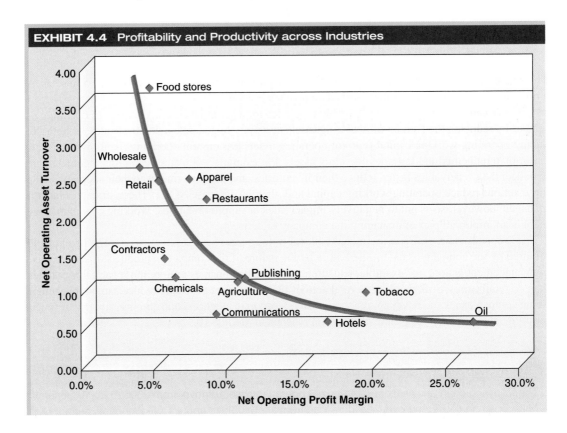

EXHIBIT 4.4   Profitability and Productivity across Industries

This exhibit reveals that some industries, like oil and hotels, are capital intensive with relatively low operating asset turnover. Accordingly, for such industries to achieve a required RNOA (to be competitive in the overall market), they must obtain a higher profit margin. On the other hand, companies such as food stores, wholesalers, and retailers hold fewer assets and, therefore, can operate on lower operating profit margins to achieve a sufficient RNOA. This is because their asset turnover is far greater.

This exhibit warns of blindly comparing the performance of companies across different industries. For instance, a higher profit margin in the oil industry compared with the food stores industry is not necessarily the result of better management. Instead, the oil industry is extremely capital intensive and thus, to achieve an equivalent RNOA, oil companies must earn a higher profit margin to offset their lower asset turnover. Basic economics suggests that all industries must earn an acceptable return on investment if they are to continue to attract investors and survive.

The trade-off between margin and turnover is relatively straightforward when comparing companies that operate in one industry (*pure-play* firms). Analyzing conglomerates that operate in several industries is more challenging. Conglomerates' margins and turnover rates are a weighted average of the margins and turnover rates for the various industries in which they operate. For example, Caterpillar,

Inc., is a blend of a manufacturing company and a financial institution (Caterpillar Financial Services Corp.); thus, the margin and turnover benchmarks for Caterpillar on a consolidated basis are a weighted average of those two industries.

To summarize, ROE is the sum of the returns from operating (RNOA) and nonoperating activities. Further, RNOA is the product of NOPM and NOAT.

RESEARCH INSIGHT | **NOPM and NOAT Explain Stock Prices**

Research shows that stock returns are positively associated with earnings—when companies report higher than expected earnings, stock returns rise. Research also reports that the RNOA components (NOPM and NOAT) are more strongly associated with stock returns and future profitability than earnings (or return on assets) alone. This applies to the short-term market response to earnings announcements and long-term stock price changes. Thus, disaggregating earnings and the balance sheet into operating and nonoperating components is a useful analysis tool.

Source: Soliman, Mark T., *Use of DuPont Analysis by Market Participants* (October 2007), SSRN: ssrn.com/abstract=1101981.

MID-MODULE REVIEW 2

Following is the balance sheet of Kellogg Company.

KELLOGG COMPANY Balance Sheet		
(millions, except share data)	December 29, 2007	December 30, 2006
Cash and cash equivalents	$ 524	$ 411
Accounts receivable, net	1,026	945
Inventories	924	824
Other current assets	243	247
Total current assets	2,717	2,427
Property, net	2,990	2,816
Goodwill	3,515	3,448
Other intangibles, net	1,450	1,420
Other assets	725	603
Total assets	$11,397	$10,714
Current maturities of long-term debt	$ 466	$ 723
Notes payable	1,489	1,268
Accounts payable	1,081	910
Other current liabilities	1,008	1,119
Total current liabilities	4,044	4,020
Long-term debt	3,270	3,053
Other liabilities	1,557	1,572
Shareholders' equity		
Common stock, $.25 par value, 1,000,000,000 shares authorized Issued: 418,669,193 shares in 2007 and 418,515,339 shares in 2006	105	105
Capital in excess of par value	388	292
Retained earnings	4,217	3,630
Treasury stock at cost: 28,618,052 shares in 2007 and 20,817,930 shares in 2006	(1,357)	(912)
Accumulated other comprehensive income (loss)	(827)	(1,046)
Total shareholders' equity	2,526	2,069
Total liabilities and shareholders' equity	$11,397	$10,714

Required

1. Compute Kellogg's net operating assets for 2007 and 2006.

2. Refer to Kellogg's income statement and NOPAT from Mid-Module Review 1. Compute Kellogg's return on net operating assets (RNOA) for 2007.
3. Compute Kellogg's 2007 ROE. What percentage of Kellogg's ROE comes from operations?
4. Disaggregate Kellogg's 2007 RNOA into net operating profit margin (NOPM) and net operating asset turnover (NOAT).
5. Compare and contrast Kellogg's ROE, RNOA, NOPM, and NOAT with those same measures computed in this module for General Mills. Interpret the results.

Solution ($ millions)

1.

Net Operating Assets ($ millions)	December 29, 2007	December 30, 2006
Operating assets		
Cash and cash equivalents	$ 524	$ 411
Accounts receivable, net	1,026	945
Inventories	924	824
Other current assets	243	247
Property, net	2,990	2,816
Goodwill	3,515	3,448
Other intangibles, net	1,450	1,420
Other assets	725	603
Total operating assets	11,397	10,714
Operating liabilities		
Accounts payable	1,081	910
Other current liabilities	1,008	1,119
Other long-term liabilities	1,557	1,572
Total operating liabilities	3,646	3,601
Net operating assets (NOA)	$ 7,751	$ 7,113

2. $\text{RNOA} = \dfrac{\$1,308}{(\$7,751 + \$7,113)/2} = 17.6\%$

3. $\text{ROE} = \dfrac{\$1,103}{(\$2,526 + \$2,069)/2} = 48.0\%$

Kellogg's RNOA makes up 37% of its ROE, computed as 17.6%/48%.

4. $\text{NOPM} = \dfrac{\$1,308}{\$11,776} = 11.1\%$

$\text{NOAT} = \dfrac{\$11,776}{(\$7,751 + \$7,113)/2} = 1.58$

5. Despite similar business models, Kellogg is superior on the profitability measures of ROE, RNOA, and NOAT.

	ROE	RNOA	NOPM	NOAT
General Mills	20.0%	11.9%	11.4%	1.05
Kellogg	48.0%	17.6%	11.1%	1.58

The NOPM for the two companies are nearly identical. Kellogg is able to turn its net operating assets 50% faster than General Mills. As a result, Kellogg's RNOA is 48% higher than General Mills'. General Mills' RNOA makes up 59% (11.9%/20.0%) of its ROE, while Kelloggs' is only 37% (17.6%/48.0%). This reveals that Kellogg is relying on nonoperating return in addition to its higher net operating asset turnover rate to achieve its higher ROE.

Further RNOA Disaggregation

While disaggregation of RNOA into net operating profit margin (NOPM) and net operating asset turnover (NOAT) yields valuable insight into factors driving company performance, analysts and creditors usually disaggregate those components even further. The purpose is to better identify the specific drivers of both profitability and turnover.

To disaggregate NOPM, we examine the gross profit on products sold and the individual expense accounts that affect operating profit as a percentage of sales (such as Gross profit/Sales and SG&A/ Sales). These margin ratios aid comparisons across companies of differing sizes and across different time periods for the same company. We further discuss profit margin disaggregation in other modules that focus on operating results.

To disaggregate NOAT, we examine the individual balance sheet accounts that comprise NOA and compare them to the related income statement activity. Specifically, we compute accounts receivable turnover (ART), inventory turnover (INVT), property, plant and equipment turnover (PPET), as well as turnovers for liability accounts such as accounts payable (APT). Analysts and creditors often compute the net operating working capital turnover (NOWCT) to assess a company's working capital management compared to its competitors and recent trends. These turnover rates are further discussed in other modules that focus on operating assets and liabilities. Exhibit 4.5 provides a broad overview of ratios commonly used for component disaggregation and analysis.

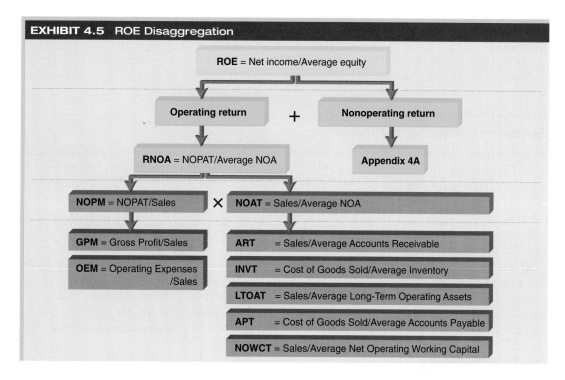

EXHIBIT 4.5 ROE Disaggregation

NONOPERATING RETURN

This section discusses a company's nonoperating return. In simplest form, the return on nonoperating activities measures the extent to which a company is using debt to increase its return on equity.

Equity Only Financing

The following example provides the intuition for this return. Assume that a company has $1,000 in average assets for the current year in which it earns a 20% RNOA. It finances those assets entirely with equity investment (no debt). To simplify this example, we assume that taxes are 0%; later, we explain the impact of taxes. Its ROE is computed as follows:

$$
\begin{aligned}
\text{ROE} &= \text{Operating return} + \text{Nonoperating return} \\
&= \quad\quad 20\% \quad\quad + \quad\quad 0\% \\
&= \quad\quad\quad\quad\quad 20\%
\end{aligned}
$$

Equity and Debt Financing

Next, assume that this company borrows $500 at 7% interest and uses those funds to acquire additional assets yielding the same 20% operating return as above. Its average assets for the year now total $1,500, and its profit is $265, computed as follows:

Profit from assets financed with equity ($1,000 × 20%)		$200
Profit from assets financed with debt ($500 × 20%).	$100	
Less interest expense from debt ($500 × 7%)	(35)	65
Net profit.		$265

We see that this company has increased its profit to $265 (up from $200) with the addition of debt, and its ROE is now 26.5% ($265/$1,000). The reason for the increased ROE is that the company borrowed $500 at 7% (and paid $35 of interest expense) and invested those funds in assets earning 20% (which generated $100 of profits). That difference of 13% ($65 profit, computed as [20% − 7%] × $500) accrues to shareholders. Stated differently, the company's ROE now consists of the following.

$$\textbf{ROE} = \textbf{Operating return} + \textbf{Nonoperating return}$$
$$= \quad 20\% \quad + \quad 6.5\%$$
$$= \quad 26.5\%$$

The company has made effective use of debt to increase its ROE. Here, we infer the nonoperating return as the difference between ROE and RNOA. This return can be computed directly, and we provide an expanded discussion of this computation in Appendix 4A.

Advantages and Disadvantages of Equity versus Debt Financing

We might further ask: If a higher ROE is desirable, why don't companies use the maximum possible debt? The answer is that creditors, such as banks and bondholders, charge successively higher interest rates for increasing levels of debt (see Module 8). At some point, the cost of the additional debt exceeds the return on the additional assets that a company can acquire from the debt financing. Thereafter, further debt financing does not make economic sense. The market, in essence, places a limit on the level of debt that a company can effectively acquire. In sum, shareholders benefit from increased use of debt provided that the assets financed with the debt earn a return that exceeds the cost of the debt.

Creditors usually require a company to execute a loan agreement that places varying restrictions on the company's operating activities. These restrictions, called *covenants*, help safeguard debtholders in the face of increased risk. Covenants exist because debtholders do not have a voice on the board of directors like stockholders do. These debt covenants impose a "cost" on the company beyond that of the interest rate, and these covenants are more stringent as a company increases its reliance on debt financing.

RESEARCH INSIGHT Ratio Behavior over Time

How do RNOA and ROE behave over time? Following is a graph of these ratios (on average for a large set of firms) over the past decade. We see there is considerable variability in these ratios over time. The proportion of RNOA to ROE is greater for some periods of time than for others. Yet, in all periods, ROE exceeds RNOA. This is evidence of a positive effect, on average, for ROE from financial leverage.

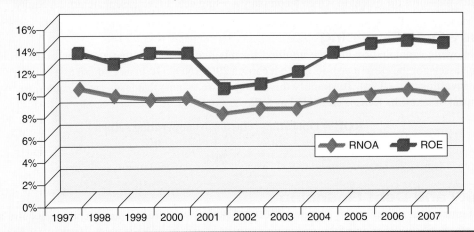

LIQUIDITY AND SOLVENCY

As we have seen, companies can effectively use debt to increase ROE with returns from nonoperating activities. The advantage of debt is that it typically is a less costly source of financing; currently the cost of debt is about 4% versus a cost of equity of about 12%, on average. Although it reduces financing costs, debt does carry default risk: the risk that the company will be unable to repay debt when it comes due. Creditors have several legal remedies when companies default, including forcing a company into bankruptcy and possibly liquidating its assets.

The median ratio of total liabilities to stockholders' equity, which measures the relative use of debt versus equity in a company's capital structure, is about 1.0 for all publicly traded companies. This means that the average company is financed with about half debt and half equity. However, the relative use of debt varies considerably across industries as illustrated in Exhibit 4.6.

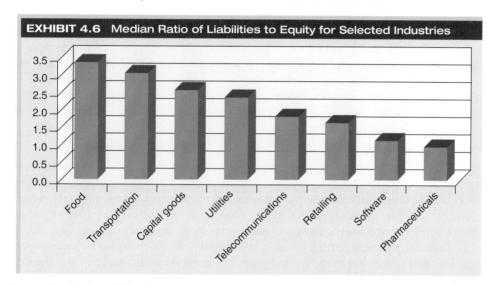

EXHIBIT 4.6 Median Ratio of Liabilities to Equity for Selected Industries

Companies in the utilities industry have a large proportion of debt. Because the utilities industry is regulated, profits and cash flows are relatively certain and stable and, as a result, utility companies can support a higher debt level. The transportation industry also utilizes a relatively high proportion of debt. However, this industry is not regulated, its market is more competitive and volatile and, consequently, its use of debt carries more risk. At the lower end of debt financing are pharmaceuticals and software companies. Historically, these industries have been characterized by relatively uncertain profits and cash flows. Consequently, they use less debt in their capital structures.

The core of our analysis relating to debt is the examination of a company's ability to generate cash to *service* its debt (that is, to make required debt payments of both interest and principal). Analysts, investors and creditors are primarily concerned about whether the company either has sufficient cash available or whether it is able to generate the required cash in the future to cover its debt obligations. The analysis of available cash and a company's ability to service its debt in the short run is called *liquidity analysis*. The analysis of the company's ability to generate sufficient cash in the long run is called *solvency analysis* (so named because a bankrupt company is said to be "insolvent").

Limitations of Ratio Analysis

The quality of financial statement analysis depends on the quality of financial information. We ought not blindly analyze numbers; doing so can lead to faulty conclusions and suboptimal decisions. Instead, we need to acknowledge that current accounting rules (GAAP) have limitations, and be fully aware of the company's environment, its competitive pressures, and any structural and strategic changes. This section discusses some of the factors that limit the usefulness of financial accounting information for ratio analysis.

GAAP Limitations   Several limitations in GAAP can distort financial ratios. Limitations include:

1. **Measurability.** Financial statements reflect what can be reliably measured. This results in nonrecognition of certain assets, often internally developed assets, the very assets that are most likely to

confer a competitive advantage and create value. Examples are brand name, a superior management team, employee skills, and a reliable supply chain.

2. **Non-capitalized costs.** Related to the concept of measurability is the expensing of costs relating to "assets" that cannot be identified with enough precision to warrant capitalization. Examples are brand equity costs from advertising and other promotional activities, and research and development costs relating to future products.

3. **Historical costs.** Assets and liabilities are usually recorded at original acquisition or issuance costs. Subsequent increases in value are not recorded until realized, and declines in value are only recognized if deemed permanent.

Thus, GAAP balance sheets omit important and valuable assets. Our analysis of ROE and our assessment of liquidity and solvency, must consider that assets can be underreported and that ratios can be distorted. We discuss many of these limitations in more detail in later modules.

Company Changes Many companies regularly undertake mergers, acquire new companies and divest subsidiaries. Such major operational changes can impair the comparability of company ratios across time. Companies also change strategies, such as product pricing, R&D, and financing. We must understand the effects of such changes on ratios and exercise caution when we compare ratios from one period to the next. Companies also behave differently at different points in their life cycles. For instance, growth companies possess a different profile than do mature companies. Seasonal effects also markedly impact analysis of financial statements at different times of the year. Thus, we must consider life cycle and seasonality when we compare ratios across companies and over time.

Conglomerate Effects Few companies are pure-play; instead, most companies operate in several businesses or industries. Most publicly traded companies consist of a parent company and multiple subsidiaries, often pursuing different lines of business. Most heavy equipment manufacturers, for example, have finance subsidiaries (Ford Credit Corporation and Cat Financial are subsidiaries of Ford and Caterpillar respectively). Financial statements of such conglomerates are consolidated and include the financial statements of the parent and its subsidiaries. Consequently, such consolidated statements are challenging to analyze. Typically, analysts break the financials apart into their component businesses and separately analyze each component. Fortunately, companies must report financial information (albeit limited) for major business segments in their 10-Ks.

Means to an End Ratios reduce, to a single number, the myriad complexities of a company's operations. No scalar can accurately capture all qualitative aspects of a company. Ratios cannot meaningfully convey a company's marketing and management philosophies, its human resource activities, its financing activities, its strategic initiatives, and its product management. In our analysis we must learn to look through the numbers and ratios to better understand the operational factors that drive financial results. Successful analysis seeks to gain insight into what a company is really about and what the future portends. Our overriding purpose in analysis is to understand the past and present to better predict the future. Computing and examining ratios is one step in that process.

MODULE-END REVIEW

Refer to the income statement and balance sheet of Kellogg Company, from Mid-Module Reviews 1 and 2 earlier in this module.

Required
1. Compute Kellogg's nonoperating return on equity for 2007.
2. Compute General Mills' nonoperating return on assets for 2008 (fiscal 2007) from the return information reported in this module. Compare and contrast the nonoperating return for Kellogg and General Mills. Interpret the results.
3. Compute Kellogg's liabilities-to-equity ratio for 2007.
4. Compute General Mills' liabilities-to-equity ratio for 2008 from the balance sheet in this module. Compare and contrast the ratio to Kellogg's liabilities-to-equity ratio. Interpret the results.

Solution ($ millions)

1. Kellogg ROE = Operating return (RNOA) + Nonoperating return
    Using solutions from Mid-Module Review 2, and substituting, we get:
    48.0% = 17.6% + Nonoperating return
    30.4% = Nonoperating return
2. General Mills' ROE = Operating return (RNOA) + Nonoperating return
    20.0% = 11.9% + Nonoperating return
    8.1% = Nonoperating return
    Kellogg's 30.4% nonoperating return is considerably higher than General Mills' 8.1% nonoperating return. The nonoperating return is a function of both the relative amount of debt in their capital structures and the spread of the return on net operating assets over the cost of that debt. Both companies are increasing their ROE by the use of financial leverage. Further analysis is warranted to investigate whether either company is taking on too much default risk by their use of debt.
3. Kellogg's liabilities-to-equity ratio = Total liabilities/Total equity
    ($4,044 + $3,270 + $1,557)/$2,526 = 3.51
4. General Mills' liabilities-to-equity ratio = Total liabilities/Total equity
    $12,583.5/$6,458.1 = 1.95

Kellogg's 3.51 liabilities-to-equity ratio is much higher than the 1.95 for General Mills. Further, both ratios are higher that the average 1.0 level of all companies as reported in the module. Thus, both seem overly exposed for debt obligations, and further analysis is necessary to evaluate if that debt exposure is excessive. That additional analysis will examine the amount of projected debt payments (found in the long-term debt footnote) with projected net cash from operating activities.

APPENDIX 4A: Nonoperating Return Component of ROE

In this appendix, we consider the nonoperating return component of ROE in more detail. We also provide a derivation of that nonoperating return and discuss several special topics pertaining to it. We begin by considering three special cases of capital structure financing.

L03 Explain nonoperating return and compute it from return on equity and the operating return.

Nonoperating Return Framework

In the module, we infer the nonoperating return as the difference between ROE and RNOA. The nonoperating return can also be computed directly as FLEV × Spread, where FLEV is the degree of financial leverage and Spread is the difference between the assets' after-tax operating return (RNOA) and the after-tax cost of debt.

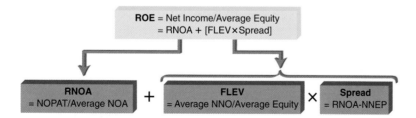

Exhibit 4A.1 provides definitions for each of the terms required in this computation.

EXHIBIT 4A.1 Nonoperating Return Definitions	
NNO: Net nonoperating obligations	Nonoperating liabilities less nonoperating assets
FLEV: Financial leverage	Average NNO/Average equity
NNE: Net nonoperating expense	NOPAT – Net income; NNE consists of nonoperating expenses and revenues, net of tax
NNEP: Net nonoperating expense percent	NNE/Average NNO
Spread	RNOA – NNEP

Nonoperating Return—With Debt Financing, but Without Nonoperating Assets

To illustrate computation of the nonoperating return when the company has debt and equity financing (without nonoperating assets), let's refer to our example in this module of the company that increases its ROE through use of debt. (For this first illustration, view FLEV as the relative use of debt in the capital structure, and Spread as the difference between RNOA and the net nonoperating expense percent). Again, assume that this company has $1,000 of equity, $500 of 7% debt, total assets of $1,500 that earn a 20% return, and a tax rate of 0%. The net income of this firm is $265, computed as follows:

Profit from assets financed with equity ($1,000 × 20%)		$200
Profit from assets financed with debt ($500 × 20%).	$100	
Less interest expense from debt ($500 × 7%)	(35)	65
Net profit.		$265

This company's ROE is 26.5%, computed as $265/$1,000 (assuming income received at year-end for simplicity and average equity is $1,000). Its RNOA is 20%, FLEV is 0.50 (computed as $500 of average net nonoperating obligations divided by $1,000 average equity), and its Spread is 13% (computed as 20% less 7%). This company's ROE, shown with the nonoperating return being directly computed, is as follows:

$$
\begin{aligned}
\text{ROE} &= \text{RNOA} + [\, \text{FLEV} \times \text{Spread} \,] \\
&= 20\% + [\, 0.50 \times 13\% \,] \\
&= 26.5\%
\end{aligned}
$$

We see that when a company's nonoperating activities relate solely to the borrowing of money (without nonoperating assets), FLEV collapses to the debt-to-equity ratio.

Nonoperating Return—Without Debt Financing, but With Nonoperating Assets

Some companies, such as many high-tech firms, have no debt, and maintain large portfolios of marketable securities. They hold these highly liquid assets so that they can respond quickly to new opportunities or react to competitive pressures. With high levels of nonoperating assets and no nonoperating liabilities, then net nonoperating obligations (NNO) has a negative sign (NNO = Nonoperating liabilities − Nonoperating assets). Likewise, FLEV is negative: Average NNO (−) / Average Equity (+). Further, net nonoperating expense (NNE = NOPAT − Net income) is negative because investment *income* is a negative nonoperating expense. However, the net nonoperating expense percent (NNEP) is positive because the negative NNE is divided by the negative NNO. *This causes ROE to be less than RNOA* (see computations below). We use the 2008 10-K of Cisco Systems to illustrate this curious result (all numbers exclude minority, or noncontrolling, interests).

Cisco Systems ($ millions, except percents)	2008	2007
NOA	$ 20,251	$ 19,360
NNO	$(14,102)	$(12,120)
Stockholders' equity	$ 34,353	$ 31,480
Net income.	$ 8,052	
NOPAT	$ 7,524	
NNE	$ (528)	
FLEV.	−0.3983	
RNOA	37.99%	
NNEP	4.03%	
Spread	33.96%	

Cisco's NNO is negative because its investment in marketable securities exceeds its debt. Cisco's ROE is 24.46%, and it consists of the following:

$$
\begin{aligned}
\text{ROE} &= \text{RNOA} + [\, \text{FLEV} \times \text{Spread} \,] \\
&= 37.99\% + [\, -0.3983 \times 33.96\% \,] \\
&= 37.99\% + [\, -13.53\% \,] \\
&= 24.46\%
\end{aligned}
$$

Cisco's ROE is lower than its RNOA because of its large investment in marketable securities. That is, its excessive liquidity is penalizing its return on equity. The rationale for this seemingly incongruous result is this: Cisco's ROE derives from operating and nonoperating assets. Cisco's operating assets are providing an outstanding return (38.05%), much higher than the return on its marketable securities (4.02%). Holding liquid assets that are less productive means that Cisco's shareholders are funding a sizeable level of liquidity, and sacrificing returns in the process. Why? Many companies in high-tech industries feel the need to maintain excessive liquidity to gain flexibility—the flexibility to take advantage of opportunities and to react quickly to competitor maneuvers. Cisco's management, evidently, feels that the investment of costly equity capital in this manner will reap future rewards for its shareholders. Its 24.46% ROE provides some evidence that this strategy is not necessarily misguided.

Nonoperating Return—With Debt Financing and Nonoperating Assets

Many companies report both debt and investments on their balance sheets. If that debt markedly exceeds the investment balance, their ROE will look more like our first example (with debt only). Instead, if investments predominate, their ROE will look more like Cisco's. It is important to remember that both the average NNO (and FLEV) and NNE can be either positive (debt) or negative (investments), and it is not always the case that ROE exceeds RNOA. We now compute nonoperating return for General Mills, a company with both debt and investments.

Nonoperating Return for General Mills

In Exhibit 4A.1, we define net nonoperating expense (NNE) as NOPAT − Net income. For General Mills, we can compute NNE as NOPAT of $1,554.0 million less net income of $1,294.7 million, which yields $259.3 million. More generally, NNE can include a number of nonoperating items such as interest expense, interest revenue, dividend income, investment gains and losses, and the income (loss) on discontinued operations; all net of tax. (Recall that the simple illustration at the beginning of this appendix *ignored taxes*, which meant NNE was equal to the $35 interest paid.)

To compute operating return (RNOA) we divided NOPAT from the income statement, by NOA from the balance sheet. Similarly, to compute the net nonoperating expense percent (NNEP), we divide NNE from the income statement by net nonoperating obligations from the balance sheet (NNO). Exhibit 4A.2 shows how a balance sheet can be reorganized into operating and nonoperating items.

EXHIBIT 4A.2 Simplified Balance Sheet		
	Assets	**Liabilities**
Net operating assets (NOA) . . . . (assets – liabilities)	Current Operating Assets + Long-Term Operating Assets = Total Operating Assets	Current Operating Liabilities + Long-Term Operating Liabilities = Total Operating Liabilities
Net nonoperating obligations (NNO). . . . . . . (liabilities – assets)	Current Nonoperating Assets + Long-Term Nonoperating Assets = Total Nonoperating Assets	Current Nonoperating Liabilities + Long-Term Nonoperating Liabilities = Total Nonoperating Liabilities
		Equity
Equity (NOA – NNO)		Stockholders' Equity
	Total Assets	Total Liabilities and Equity

Net nonoperating obligations are total nonoperating liabilities less total nonoperating assets. The accounting equation stipulates that Assets = Liabilities + Equity, so we can adjust it to yield the following key identity:

Net operating assets (NOA) = Net nonoperating obligations (NNO) + Stockholders' equity

For General Mills, we compute NNO as follows:

General Mills ($ millions)	2008	2007
Nonoperating liabilities		
Short-term borrowings and current maturities of long-term debt	$2,650.8	$2,988.4
Long-term debt	4,348.7	3,217.7
Total nonoperating liabilities.....................................	6,999.5	6,206.1
Nonoperating assets		
Short-term investments	0	0
Long-term investments	0	0
Total nonoperating assets	0	0
Net nonoperating obligations (NNO)	$6,999.5	$6,206.1

Accordingly (drawing on NNE from the income statement and NNO from the balance sheet), we compute the net nonoperating expense percent (NNEP) as follows:

$$\text{Net nonoperating expense percent (NNEP)} = \frac{\text{Net nonoperating expense (NNE)}}{\text{Average net nonoperating obligations (NNO)}}$$

The net nonoperating expense percent (NNEP) measures the average cost of net nonoperating obligations. The denominator uses the average NNO similar to the return calculations (such as ROE and RNOA).

In the simple illustration from earlier in this appendix, the company's net nonoperating expense percent is 7%, computed as $35/$500, which is exactly equal to the interest rate on the loan. With real financial statements, NNEP is more complicated because NNE often includes both interest on borrowed money and nonoperating income, and NNO is the net of operating liabilities less nonoperating assets. Thus NNEP often reflects an average return on nonoperating activities. For General Mills, its 2008 NNEP is 3.9%, computed as $259.3 million/ [($6,999.5 million + $6,206.1 million)/2].

General Mills' 2008 RNOA is 11.9%, which means that net operating assets generate more return than the 3.9% cost of net nonoperating obligations. That is, General Mills earns a Spread of 8%, the difference between RNOA (11.9%) and NNEP (3.9%), on each asset financed with borrowed funds. By borrowing funds, General Mills creates leverage, which can be measured relative to shareholder's equity; that ratio is called financial leverage (FLEV). In sum, total nonoperating return is computed by the following formula:

$$\text{Nonoperating return} = \underbrace{\frac{\text{Average net nonoperating obligations (NNO)}}{\text{Average stockholders' equity}}}_{\text{FLEV}} \times \underbrace{(\text{RNOA} - \text{NNEP})}_{\text{Spread}}$$

Two points are immediately clear from this equation. First, ROE increases with the spread between RNOA and NNEP. The more profitable the return on operating assets, the higher the return to shareholders. Second, the higher the debt relative to equity, the higher the ROE (assuming, of course, a positive spread).

General Mills' 2008 spread between RNOA and NNEP is 8%. It has average NNO of $6,602.8 million [($6,999.5 million + $6,206.1 million)/2] and average equity of $6,458.0 million [($6,458.1 million + $6,457.9 million)/2]. Thus, General Mills' ROE is as follows:

$$
\begin{aligned}
\text{ROE} &= \text{Operating return} + \quad \text{Nonoperating return} \\
&= \quad 11.9\% \quad + (\$6,602.8/\$6,458.0) \times (11.9\% - 3.9\%) \\
&= \quad 11.9\% \quad + \quad (1.0224) \times (8.0\%) \\
&= \quad 20\% \text{ (rounded)}
\end{aligned}
$$

Most companies report both debt and investments on their balance sheets. If that debt markedly exceeds the investment balance, their ROE will look more like our General Mills' example (with debt only). Instead, if investments predominate, their ROE will look more like Cisco's (with investments only). It is important to remember that both the average NNO (and FLEV) and NNE can be either positive (debt) or negative (investments), and it is not always the case that ROE exceeds RNOA.

Derivation of Nonoperating Return Formula

Following is the algebraic derivation of the nonoperating return formula, where NI is net income, SE is average stockholders' equity, and all other terms are as defined in Exhibits 4.3 and 4A.1.

$$
\begin{aligned}
\text{ROE} &= \frac{\text{NI}}{\text{SE}} \\[4pt]
&= \frac{\text{NOPAT} - \text{NNE}}{\text{SE}} \\[4pt]
&= \frac{\text{NOPAT}}{\text{SE}} - \frac{\text{NNE}}{\text{SE}} \\[4pt]
&= \left(\frac{\text{NOA}}{\text{SE}} \times \text{RNOA}\right) - \left(\frac{\text{NNO}}{\text{SE}} \times \text{NNEP}\right) \\[4pt]
&= \left(\frac{(\text{SE} + \text{NNO})}{\text{SE}} \times \text{RNOA}\right) - \left(\frac{\text{NNO}}{\text{SE}} \times \text{NNEP}\right) \\[4pt]
&= \left[\text{RNOA} \times \left(1 + \frac{\text{NNO}}{\text{SE}}\right)\right] - \left(\frac{\text{NNO}}{\text{SE}} \times \text{NNEP}\right) \\[4pt]
&= \text{RNOA} + \left(\frac{\text{NNO}}{\text{SE}} \times \text{RNOA}\right) - \left(\frac{\text{NNO}}{\text{SE}} \times \text{NNEP}\right) \\[4pt]
&= \text{RNOA} + \left(\frac{\text{NNO}}{\text{SE}}\right)(\text{RNOA} - \text{NNEP}) \\[4pt]
&= \text{RNOA} + (\text{FLEV} \times \text{Spread})
\end{aligned}
$$

Special Topics

The return on equity (ROE) computation becomes a bit more complicated in the presence of discontinued operations, preferred stock, and minority (or noncontrolling) equity interest. The first of these apportions ROE between operating and nonoperating returns, and the other two affect the dollar amount included in the denominator (average equity) of the ROE computation. Recall that ROE measures the return on investment for common shareholders. The ROE numerator should include only the income available to pay common dividends and the denominator should include common equity only, not the equity of preferred or minority shareholders.

Discontinued Operations Discontinued operations are subsidiaries or business segments that the board of directors has formally decided to divest. Companies must report discontinued operations on a separate line, below income from continuing operations. The separate line item includes the net income or loss from discontinued operations along with any gains or losses on the disposal of discontinued net assets (see Module 5 for details). Although not required, many companies disclose the net assets of discontinued operations on the balance sheet to distinguish them from continuing net assets. If the net assets are not separated on the balance sheet, the footnotes provide details to facilitate a disaggregated analysis. These net assets of discontinued operations should be treated as nonoperating (they represent a nonoperating "investment" once they have been classified as discontinued) and their after-tax profit (loss) should be treated as nonoperating as well. Although the ROE computation is unaffected, the nonoperating portion of the ROE for the year will include the contribution of discontinued operations.

Preferred Stock The ROE formula takes the perspective of the common shareholder in that it relates the income available to pay common dividends to the average common shareholder. As such, preferred stock should not be included in average stockholders' equity in the denominator of the ROE formula. Similarly, any dividends paid on preferred stock should be subtracted from net income to yield the profit available to pay common dividends. (Dividends are not an expense in computing net income; thus, net income is available to both preferred and common shareholders. To determine net income available to common shareholders, we must subtract preferred dividends.) Thus, the presence of preferred stock requires two adjustments to the ROE formula.

1. Preferred dividends must be subtracted from net income in the numerator.
2. Preferred stock must be subtracted from stockholders' equity in the denominator.

This modified return on equity formula is more accurately labeled return on common equity (ROCE).

$$
\text{ROCE} = \frac{\text{Net income} - \text{Preferred dividends}}{\text{Average stockholders' equity} - \text{Average preferred equity}}
$$

Minority (or Noncontrolling) Interest When a company acquires controlling interest of the outstanding voting stock of another company, the parent company must consolidate the new subsidiary in its balance sheet and income statement (see Module 7). This means that the parent company must include 100% of the subsidiary's assets, liabilities, revenues and expenses. Beginning in 2009, if the parent acquires less than 100% of the subsidiary's voting stock, the remaining claim of minority shareholders is reported on the balance sheet as a component of stockholders' equity called noncontrolling interest, and net income is separated into income attributable to company shareholders and that attributable to noncontrolling interests. The ROE computation, then, should use the net income attributable to company shareholders divided by the average stockholders' equity where equity excludes minority (noncontrolling) interest. This ratio is more aptly labelled, ROCE, return on common equity.

For firms with noncontrolling interest, we compute RNOA as usual because NOPAT is operating income before any noncontrolling interest on the income statement, and NOA excludes noncontrolling interest on the balance sheet. Similarly, we compute Spread as usual. However, we must make two modifications because a company's operating and nonoperating activities generate returns to both the controlling interest (the common shareholders' equity, labeled CSE) and minority shareholders (labeled MI). First, we adjust FLEV as follows: FLEV = NNO/(CSE + MI). Second, a ratio that captures the relative income statement and balance sheet effects of the noncontrolling (minority) interest, called the *minority interest sharing ratio*, is computed as follows:

$$\text{Minority interest sharing ratio} = \left[\frac{\left(\dfrac{\text{Net income}}{\text{Net income + Minority interest expense}}\right)}{\left(\dfrac{\text{Common equity}}{\text{Common equity + Minority interest equity}}\right)}\right]$$

Further, with a noncontrolling (minority) interest, the disaggregated return on common equity is expressed as:

$$\textbf{ROCE} = \textbf{[RNOA} + \{\textbf{[NNO/(CSE + MI)]} \times \textbf{Spread}\}] \times \textbf{Minority interest sharing ratio}$$

To illustrate this disaggregation, consider the following selected balance sheet and income statement items from Verizon for fiscal 2007 ($ millions).

Balance sheet items	
Net operating assets (NOA)	$111,782
Net nonoperating obligations (NNO)	$ 28,913
Minority (noncontrolling) interest	32,288
Stockholders' equity	50,581
Total (NNO + MI + Equity)	$111,782
Income statement items	
Net operating profit after tax (NOPAT)	$ 11,559
Net nonoperating expense (NNE)	(985)
Net income	10,574
Less: Net income attributable to noncontrolling interest	5,053
Net income attributable to Verizon shareholders	$ 5,521

We then compute the following key ratios; we use year-end balances rather than averages for mathematical simplification ($ millions):

RNOA	10.34%	($11,559/$111,782)
ROE	10.92%	($5,521/$50,581)
Adjusted FLEV	0.3489	($28,913/[$32,288 + $50,581])
NNEP	3.41%	($985/$28,913)
Spread	6.93%	(10.34% − 3.41%)
MI sharing ratio	0.8554	[$5,521/$10,574]/($50,581/[$50,581 + $32,288])
ROCE	10.92%	[10.34% + (0.3489 × 6.93%)] × 0.8554

APPENDIX 4B: Tools of Liquidity and Solvency Analysis

Liquidity Analysis

Liquidity refers to cash availability: how much cash a company has, and how much it can raise on short notice. Two of the most common ratios used to assess the degree of liquidity are the current ratio and the quick ratio. Both of these ratios link required near-term payments to cash available in the near-term.

LO4 Compute and interpret measures of liquidity and solvency.

Current Ratio

Current assets are assets that a company expects to convert into cash within the next operating cycle, which is typically a year. *Current liabilities* are liabilities that come due within the next year. An excess of current assets over current liabilities (Current assets − Current liabilities), is known as *net working capital* or simply *working capital*.[3] Positive working capital implies that cash generated by "liquidating" current assets would be sufficient to pay current liabilities. The current ratio expresses working capital as a ratio and is computed as follows:

$$\text{Current ratio} = \frac{\text{Current assets}}{\text{Current liabilities}}$$

A current ratio greater than 1.0 implies positive working capital. Both working capital and the current ratio consider existing balance sheet data only and ignore cash inflows from future sales or other sources. The current ratio is more commonly used than working capital because ratios allow comparisons across companies of different size. Generally, companies prefer a higher current ratio; however, an excessively high current ratio indicates inefficient asset use. Furthermore, a current ratio less than 1.0 is not always bad for at least two reasons:

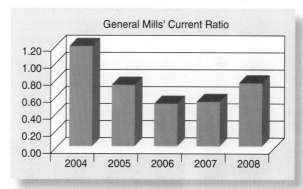

General Mills' Current Ratio

1. A cash-and-carry company (like a grocery store) can have potentially few current assets (and a low current ratio), but consistently large operating cash inflows ensure the company will be sufficiently liquid.
2. A company can efficiently manage its working capital by minimizing receivables and inventories and maximizing payables. Dell and Wal-Mart, for example, use their buying power to exact extended credit terms from suppliers. Consequently, because both companies are essentially cash-and-carry companies, their current ratios are less than 1.0 and both are sufficiently liquid.

The aim of current ratio analysis is to discern if a company is having, or is likely to have, difficulty meeting its short-term obligations. General Mills' current ratio for 2008 is 0.75 ($3,620.0 million/$4,856.3 million). Its current ratio has rebounded somewhat after three years of decline.

Quick Ratio

The quick ratio is a variant of the current ratio. It focuses on quick assets, which are assets likely to be converted to cash within a relatively short period of time. Specifically, quick assets include cash, marketable securities, and accounts receivable; they exclude inventories, prepaid assets, and other current assets. The quick ratio is defined as follows:

$$\text{Quick ratio} = \frac{\text{Cash + Marketable securities + Accounts receivables}}{\text{Current liabilities}}$$

The quick ratio reflects on a company's ability to meet its current liabilities without liquidating inventories. It is a more stringent test of liquidity than the current ratio.

---

[3] Both operating assets and operating liabilities can be either current or long-term. "Current" means that the asset is expected to be used, or the liability paid, within the next operating cycle or one year, whichever is longer, which for most companies means a year. Using the current versus long-term nature of operating assets and liabilities we derive two types of net operating assets: net operating working capital (NOWC), and net long-term operating assets. Net operating working capital is defined as:

Net operating working capital (NOWC) = Current operating assets − Current operating liabilities

For General Mills, NOWC is $1,414.5 million for 2008 ($3,620.0 − $2,205.5).

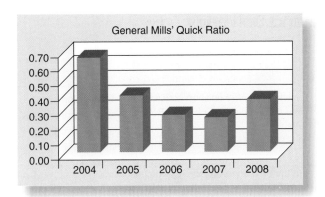

General Mills' 2008 quick ratio is 0.36 $\left(\frac{\$661.0 + \$1,081.6}{\$4,856.3}\right)$. Like the current ratio, General Mills' quick ratio has rebounded in the past two years following three years of decline—see margin graph. It is not uncommon for a company's quick ratio to be less than 1.0. Although liquidity is not a major concern for General Mills, the relatively low level for the current and quick ratios and their modest rebound is something financial statement users would want to monitor.

Solvency Analysis

Solvency refers to a company's ability to meet its debt obligations, including both periodic interest payments and the repayment of the principal amount borrowed. Solvency is crucial because an insolvent company is a failed company. There are two general approaches to measuring solvency. The first approach uses balance sheet data and assesses the proportion of capital raised from creditors. The second approach uses income statement data and assesses the profit generated relative to debt payment obligations. We discuss each approach in turn.

Liabilities-to-Equity

The liabilities-to-equity ratio is a useful tool for the first type of solvency analysis. It is defined as follows:

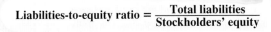

$$\text{Liabilities-to-equity ratio} = \frac{\text{Total liabilities}}{\text{Stockholders' equity}}$$

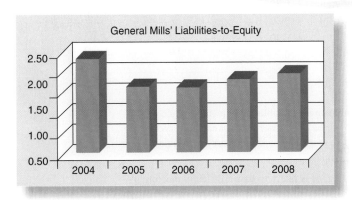

This ratio conveys how reliant a company is on creditor financing compared with equity financing. A higher ratio indicates less solvency, and more risk. General Mills' 2008 liabilities-to-equity ratio is 1.95 $\left(\frac{\$12,583.5 \text{ million}}{\$6,458.1 \text{ million}}\right)$, which includes minority interest in stockholders' equity. This ratio has increased over the past three years—see margin graph. Also, its ratio is greater than 1.0, the average for publicly traded companies.

A variant of this ratio considers a company's long-term debt divided by equity. This approach assumes that current liabilities are repaid from current assets (so-called self-liquidating). Thus, it assumes that creditors and stockholders need only focus on the relative proportion of long-term capital.

Times Interest Earned

The second type of solvency analysis compares profits to liabilities. This approach assesses how much operating profit is available to cover debt obligations. A common measure for this type of solvency analysis is the times interest earned ratio, defined as follows:

$$\text{Times interest earned} = \frac{\text{Earnings before interest and taxes}}{\text{Interest expense}}$$

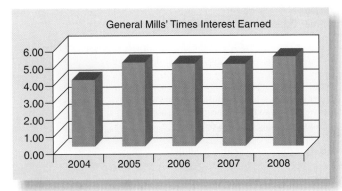

The times interest earned ratio reflects the operating income available to pay interest expense. The underlying assumption is that only interest needs to be paid because the principal will be refinanced. This ratio is sometimes abbreviated as EBIT/I. The numerator is similar to net operating profits after tax (NOPAT), but it is *pretax* instead of after tax.

Management wants this ratio to be sufficiently high so that there is little risk of default. General Mills' 2008 times interest earned is a healthy 5.28, computed as $\frac{\$1,806.1 \text{ million} + \$421.7 \text{ million}}{\$421.7 \text{ million}}$. This ratio has increased over the past five years—see margin graph. This result implies that General Mills could suffer a large decline in profitability and still be able to service its interest payments when due. Any solvency concerns we might have had relating to General Mills' lack of liquidity and relatively high debt load are mitigated by its earning power.

There are many variations of solvency and liquidity analysis and the ratios used. The basic idea is to construct measures that reflect a company's credit risk exposure. There is not one "best" financial leverage ratio. Instead, as financial statement users, we want to use measures that capture the risk we are most concerned with. It is also important to compute the ratios ourselves to ensure we know what is included and excluded from each ratio.

Vertical and Horizontal Analysis

Companies come in all sizes, which presents difficulties when making comparisons among firms or over time. There are several methods that attempt to overcome this obstacle.

Vertical analysis expresses financial statements in ratio form. Specifically, it is routine to express income statement items as a percent of net sales, and balance sheet items as a percent of total assets. Such *common-size financial statements* facilitate comparisons *across companies* of different sizes and comparisons of accounts within a set of financial statements.

Horizontal analysis is the scrutiny of financial data *across time*. Comparing data across two or more consecutive periods assists in analyzing trends in company performance and in predicting future performance.

Exhibits 4B.1 and 4B.2 present General Mills' common-size balance sheet and common-size income statement. We also present data for horizontal analysis by showing three years of common-size statements.

EXHIBIT 4B.1 Common-Size Comparative Balance Sheets

GENERAL MILLS
Common-Size Comparative Balance Sheets

	Amounts ($ millions)			Percentages*		
	2008	2007	2006	2008	2007	2006
Assets						
Cash and cash equivalents	$ 661.0	$ 417.1	$ 647.0	3.5%	2.3%	3.6%
Receivables	1,081.6	952.9	912.0	5.7	5.2	5.0
Inventories	1,366.8	1,173.4	1,055.0	7.2	6.5	5.8
Prepaid expenses and other current assets	510.6	443.1	377.0	2.7	2.4	2.1
Deferred income taxes	—	67.2	50.0	—	0.4	0.3
Total current assets	3,620.0	3,053.7	3,041.0	19.1	16.8	16.8
Noncurrent assets						
Land, buildings, and equipment, net	3,108.1	3,013.9	2,997.0	16.3	16.6	16.6
Goodwill	6,786.1	6,835.4	6,652.0	35.6	37.6	36.8
Other intangible assets	3,777.2	3,694.0	3,607.0	19.8	20.3	20.0
Other assets	1,750.2	1,586.7	1,778.0	9.2	8.7	9.8
Total assets	$19,041.6	$18,183.7	$18,075.0	100.0%	100.0%	100.0%
Liabilities and Equity						
Accounts payable	$ 937.3	$ 777.9	$ 673.0	4.9%	4.3%	3.7%
Current portion of long-term debt	442.0	1,734.0	2,131.0	2.3	9.5	11.8
Notes payable	2,208.8	1,254.4	1,503.0	11.6	6.9	8.3
Other current liabilities	1,239.8	2,078.8	1,831.0	6.5	11.4	10.1
Deferred income taxes	28.4	—	—	0.1	—	—
Total current liabilities	4,856.3	5,845.1	6,138.0	25.5	32.1	34.0
Noncurrent liabilities						
Long-term debt	4,348.7	3,217.7	2,415.0	22.8	17.7	13.4
Deferred income taxes	1,454.6	1,433.1	1,690.0	7.6	7.9	9.3
Other liabilities	1,923.9	1,229.9	924.0	10.1	6.8	5.1
Total liabilities	12,583.5	11,725.8	11,167.0	66.1	64.5	61.8
Shareholders' equity						
Common stock—par value	37.7	50.2	50.0	0.2	0.3	0.3
Additional paid-in capital	1,149.1	5,841.3	5,737.0	6.0	32.1	31.7
Retained earnings	6,510.7	5,745.3	5,107.0	34.2	31.6	28.3
Treasury stock—common	(1,658.4)	(6,198.0)	(5,163.0)	(8.7)	(34.1)	(28.6)
Other equity	419.0	1,019.1	1,177.0	2.2	5.6	6.5
Total shareholders' equity	6,458.1	6,457.9	6,908.0	33.9	35.5	38.2
Total liabilities and shareholders' equity	$19,041.6	$18,183.7	$18,075.0	100.0%	100.0%	100.0%

*Percentages are rounded to one decimal and, thus, might not exactly sum to totals and subtotals.

EXHIBIT 4B.2 Common-Size Comparative Income Statements

GENERAL MILLS
Common-Size Comparative Income Statements

	Amounts ($ millions)			Percentages*		
	2008	2007	2006	2008	2007	2006
Net sales.	$13,652.1	$12,441.5	$11,711.3	100.0%	100.0%	100.0%
Expenses						
Cost of sales.	8,778.3	7,955.1	7,544.8	(64.3)	(63.9)	(64.4)
Selling, general and administrative.	2,625.0	2,389.3	2,177.7	(19.2)	(19.2)	(18.6)
Restructuring, impairment, and other exit costs	21.0	39.3	29.8	(0.2)	(0.3)	(0.3)
Interest, net.	421.7	426.5	399.6	(3.1)	(3.4)	(3.4)
Earnings before taxes and joint venture earnings . . .	1,806.1	1,631.3	1,559.4	13.2	13.1	13.3
Provision for income tax.	(622.2)	(560.1)	(538.3)	(4.6)	(4.5)	(4.6)
After-tax earnings from joint ventures.	110.8	72.7	69.2	0.8	0.6	0.6
Net income	$ 1,294.7	$ 1,143.9	$ 1,090.3	9.5%	9.2%	9.3%

*Percentages are rounded to one decimal and, thus, might not exactly sum to totals and subtotals.

General Mills' total assets in dollars have increased by 5% since 2006. However, we are primarily interested in the *composition* of the balance sheet, or the proportion invested in each asset category. Specifically, liquidity has generally increased in the most recent year as cash and cash equivalents represent 3.5% of total assets in 2008, up from 2.3% in 2007. Receivables and inventories have also increased as a percentage of total assets. Long-term assets have not changed markedly over the three years shown in this table.

General Mills' short-term liabilities have decreased as a percentage of total financing. Current maturities of long-term debt have largely been replaced by notes payable. There is usually not substantive difference between these two forms of debt as both are interest-bearing and are evidenced by loan agreements. Other current liabilities have decreased as a percentage of the total. In general, General Mills has substituted long-term financing for short-term financing over this three-year period. This is generally regarded as positive as short-term liabilities usually present a greater current demand on operating cash flow. The proportion of equity in its capital structure has remained fairly constant over this three-year period at 29% to 33% of total financing.

APPENDIX 4C: DuPont Disaggregation Analysis

LO5 Describe and illustrate traditional DuPont disaggregation of ROE.

Disaggregation of return on equity (ROE) into three components (profitability, turnover, and financial leverage) was initially introduced by the E.I. DuPont de Nemours and Company to aid its managers in performance evaluation. DuPont realized that management's focus on profit alone was insufficient because profit can be simply increased by additional investment in low-yielding, but safe, assets. Further, DuPont wanted managers to think like investors and to manage their portfolio of activities using investment principles that allocate scarce investment capital to competing projects in descending order of return on investment (the *capital budgeting approach*). The DuPont model incorporates this investment perspective into performance measurement by disaggregating ROE into the following three components:

1. Profitability
2. Turnover (asset utilization)
3. Financial leverage

Each of these measures is generally positive, in which case an increase in any one would increase ROE. A focus on these measures encourages managers to focus on *both* the balance sheet and the income statement. Such an analysis typically examines each of these components over time. Managers then seek to reverse adverse trends and to sustain positive trends.

Basic DuPont Model

The basic DuPont model disaggregates ROE as follows:

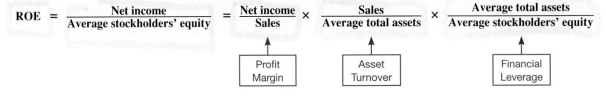

$$\text{ROE} = \frac{\text{Net income}}{\text{Average stockholders' equity}} = \underbrace{\frac{\text{Net income}}{\text{Sales}}}_{\substack{\text{Profit} \\ \text{Margin}}} \times \underbrace{\frac{\text{Sales}}{\text{Average total assets}}}_{\substack{\text{Asset} \\ \text{Turnover}}} \times \underbrace{\frac{\text{Average total assets}}{\text{Average stockholders' equity}}}_{\substack{\text{Financial} \\ \text{Leverage}}}$$

These three components are described as follows:

- **Profit margin** is the amount of profit that the company earns from each dollar of sales. A company can increase its profit margin by increasing its gross profit margin (Gross profit/Sales) and/or by reducing its expenses (other than cost of sales) as a percentage of sales.

- **Asset turnover** is a productivity measure that reflects the volume of sales that a company generates from each dollar invested in assets. A company can increase its asset turnover by increasing sales volume with no increase in assets and/or by reducing asset investment without reducing sales.

- **Financial leverage** measures the degree to which the company finances its assets with debt rather than equity. Increasing the percentage of debt relative to equity increases the financial leverage. Although financial leverage increases ROE (when performance is positive), debt must be used with care as it increases the company's relative riskiness (see our following discussion of financial leverage).

Return on Assets

The first two terms in the DuPont model, profit margin and asset turnover, relate to company operations and combine to yield return on assets (ROA) as follows:

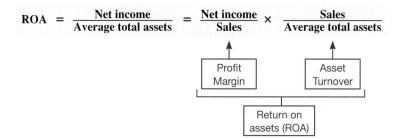

Return on assets combines the first two terms in the ROE disaggregation, profit margin and turnover. It measures the return on investment for the company without regard to how it is financed (the relative proportion of debt and equity in its capital structure). Operating managers of a company typically grasp the income statement. They readily understand the pricing of products, the management of production costs, and the importance of controlling overhead costs. However, many managers do not appreciate the importance of managing the balance sheet. The ROA approach to performance measurement encourages managers to also focus on the returns that they achieve from the invested capital under their control. Those returns are maximized by a joint focus on both profitability and productivity.

Profitability

Profitability is measured by the profit margin (Net income/Sales). Analysis of profitability typically examines performance over time relative to benchmarks (such as competitors' or industry performance), which highlight trends and abnormalities. When abnormal performance is discovered, managers either correct suboptimal performance or protect superior performance. There are two general areas of profitability analysis: gross profit margin analysis and expense management.

Gross profit margin   The gross profit margin (Gross profit/Sales) is crucial. It measures the gross profit (sales less cost of goods sold) for each sales dollar. Gross profit margin is affected by both the selling prices of products and their manufacturing cost. When markets are more competitive (or when products lose their competitive advantage), a company must reduce product prices to maintain market share and any increases in manufacturing costs cannot be directly passed on to customers; suggesting managers must focus on reducing costs. This might result in outsourcing of activities to lower labor costs and/or finding lower-cost raw materials. Such measures can yield a loss of product quality if not managed properly, which could further deteriorate the product's market position. Another strategy is to reduce product features not valued by the market. Focus groups of consumers can often identify these non-value-added product features that can be eliminated to save costs without affecting the product's value to consumers.

Expense Management   Managers can focus on reducing manufacturing and/or administrative (*overhead*) expenses to increase profitability. *Manufacturing overhead* refers to all production expenses other than labor and materials. These expenses include utilities, depreciation, and administrative costs. *Administrative overhead* refers to all expenses not in cost of goods sold such as administrative salaries and benefits, marketing, legal, accounting, research and development. These overhead costs must be managed carefully as they represent investments. Reductions in spending on advertising and research yield short-run, positive impacts on profitability, but usually yield long-run deterioration in the company's market position. Likewise, requiring employees to work harder and longer can delay increases in wage-related costs, but the likely decline in employee morale can create long-run negative consequences.

Productivity

Productivity in the DuPont model refers to the volume of dollar sales resulting from each dollar invested in assets. When a decline in productivity is observed, managers have two avenues of attack:

1. Increase sales volume from the existing asset base, and/or
2. Decrease the investment in assets without reducing sales volume.

The first approach focuses on capacity utilization. Increasing throughput lowers per unit manufacturing costs as fixed costs are spread over a larger sales base. The second approach focuses on elimination of excess assets. That reduction increases cash and also reduces carrying costs associated with the eliminated assets.

Manager efforts to reduce assets often initially focus on working capital (current assets and liabilities). Receivables can be reduced by better credit-granting policies and better monitoring of outstanding receivables. Inventories can be reduced through just-in-time delivery of raw materials, elimination of bottlenecks in production to reduce work-in-process inventories, and producing to order rather than to estimated demand to reduce finished goods inventories. Companies can also delay payment of accounts payable to generate needed cash. Payables management is more art than science, and reductions must be managed with care so as not to threaten valuable supply channels.

Manager efforts to reduce long-term assets are more difficult. Recent years have witnessed an increase in use of corporate alliances, joint ventures, and activities that seek joint ownership of assets such as manufacturing, distribution, service facilities, and information technology (IT). Another strategy is to outsource production to reduce manufacturing assets. Outsourcing is effective provided the benefits from eliminating manufacturing assets more than offset the increased costs of purchasing goods from outsourced producers.

Financial Leverage

The third term in the basic DuPont model is financial leverage, the relative proportion of debt versus equity in the company's capital structure. Financial leverage in the DuPont model is measured by the ratio of average total assets to average stockholders' equity. An increase in this ratio implies an increase in the relative use of debt. This is evident from the accounting equation: assets = liabilities + equity. For example, assume that assets are financed equally with debt and equity. The accounting equation, expressed in percentage terms, follows: 100% = 50% + 50%, and the financial leverage of the company is 2.0 (100%/50%). If we increase the proportion of debt to 75% (decrease the proportion of equity to 25%), the financial leverage increases to 4.0 (100%/25%). The measure of financial leverage is important because debt is a contractual obligation (dividends are not), and a company's failure to make required debt payments can result in legal repercussions and even bankruptcy. As financial leverage increases, so do the required debt payments along with the probability that the company is unable to meet its debt obligations in a business downturn.

Adjustments in the Basic DuPont Model

The basic DuPont model disaggregates ROE into three components in a multiplicative process. This formulation makes it easy to see that increasing any of the components will increase ROE (as each term is typically positive). This basic model, however, is not entirely accurate, and further modifications are typically made to address these inaccuracies. These variations include adjusting the return on assets and the return on equity.

Return on Assets Adjustment

Return on assets typically focuses on the operating side of the business (profit margin and asset turnover). Further, ROA is typically under the control of operating managers while the capital structure decision (the relative proportion of debt and equity) is not. Accordingly, an adjustment is often made to the numerator of ROA, and sometimes to the denominator. The numerator adjustment adds back the after-tax expense related to interest on borrowed funds and is computed as follows:

$$\text{ROA} = \frac{\text{Net income} + [\text{Interest expense } (1 - \text{Statutory tax rate})]}{\text{Average total assets}}$$

This adjusted numerator better reflects the company's operating profit as it measures return on assets exclusive of financing costs (independent of the capital structure decision). This adjusted ROA is typically reported by data collection services such as Compustat and Capital IQ, while the unadjusted is not.[4]

---

[4] "Statutory tax rate" in the ROA formula is the tax rate from the jurisdictions in which the company obtained its debt; this includes the federal statutory tax rate *plus* the state tax rate net of any federal tax benefits *plus* the rate on taxable income in foreign tax jurisdictions. Form 10-K footnotes often do not disclose the foreign tax rate and, thus, in these cases we use the 38.5% federal and state tax rates as we explained in the NOPAT computation.

The denominator adjustment is less common. That adjustment removes non-interest-bearing short-term liabilities (accounts payable and accrued liabilities) from total assets. The adjusted assets in the denominator are considered to better approximate the net assets that must be financed by long-term creditors and stockholders. In sum, adjustments to ROA move the numerator closer to net operating profit after-tax (NOPAT) and move the denominator closer to net operating assets (NOA). The resulting ROA ratio is then closer to the return on net operating assets (RNOA).

Return on Common Equity Adjustment

The typical return on equity reported by the data collection services is the return on common equity (ROCE) which is computed as follows:

$$\text{ROCE} = \frac{\text{Net income} - \text{Preferred dividends}}{\text{Average common equity} - \text{Average preferred equity}}$$

This ratio focuses on the common shareholder. Namely, the numerator seeks to compute earnings available to pay common dividends, and the denominator is the equity investment from common shareholders. This reflects the reality that common shareholders have a junior claim on earnings (they are paid after interest is paid to creditors and after dividends are paid to preferred shareholders). Net income is already net of after-tax interest expense paid to creditors, but dividends are not an expense in computing net income. Accordingly, preferred dividends are subtracted in the numerator leaving profits from which common dividends can be paid. This ROE measure then divides this income available for common dividends by the average investment from common shareholders.

Illustration of DuPont Disaggregation

To illustrate DuPont disaggregation analysis, we use General Mills' income statement and balance sheet reported earlier in this module. Exhibit 4C.1 shows the computation for each component of the DuPont disaggregation analysis applied to General Mills.

EXHIBIT 4C.1	Computation of DuPont Disaggregation Analysis for General Mills	
Ratio Component	**Definition**	**Computation**
Profit margin (PM).................	$\dfrac{\text{Net income}}{\text{Sales}}$	$\dfrac{\$1,294.7}{\$13,652.1} = 9.484\%$
Asset turnover (AT)................	$\dfrac{\text{Sales}}{\text{Average total assets}}$	$\dfrac{\$13,652.1}{(\$19,041.6 + \$18,183.7)/2} = 0.733$
Financial leverage (FL)	$\dfrac{\text{Average total assets}}{\text{Average total equity}}$	$\dfrac{(\$19,041.6 + \$18,183.7)/2}{(\$6,458.1 + \$6,457.9)/2} = 2.882$
Return on equity (ROE).............	$\dfrac{\text{Net income}}{\text{Average total equity}}$	$\dfrac{\$1,294.7}{(\$6,458.1 + \$6,457.9)/2} = 20.0\%$
	or PM × AT × FL	or 9.484% × 0.733 × 2.882 = 20.0%
Adjusted components		
Return on assets (Adjusted)	$\dfrac{\text{Net income} + \text{Interest expense} \times (1 - \text{Statutory Tax rate})}{\text{Average total assets}}$	$\dfrac{\{\$1,294.7 + [\$421.7 \times (1 - 38.5\%)]\}}{(\$19,041.6 + \$18,183.7)/2} = 8.35\%$
Return on common equity (ROCE)...	$\dfrac{\text{Net income} - \text{Preferred dividends}}{\text{Average total equity}}$	$\dfrac{\$1,294.7 - \$0}{(\$6,458.6 + \$6,457.9)/2} = 20.0\%$

GUIDANCE ANSWERS

MANAGERIAL DECISION   **You Are the CEO**

Your company is performing substantially better than its competitors. Namely, your RNOA of 16% is markedly superior to competitors' RNOA of 10%. However, RNOA disaggregation shows that this is mainly attributed to your NOAT of 0.89 versus competitors' NOAT of 0.59. Your NOPM of 18% is essentially identical to competitors' NOPM of 17%. Accordingly, you will want to maintain your NOAT as further improvements are probably difficult to achieve. Importantly, you are likely to achieve the greatest benefit with efforts at improving your NOPM of 18%, which is only marginally better than the industry norm of 17%.

Superscript $^{A(B, C)}$ denotes assignments based on Appendix 4A (4B, 4C).

DISCUSSION QUESTIONS

Q4-1. Explain in general terms the concept of return on investment. Why is this concept important in the analysis of financial performance?

Q4-2.^{A} (a) Explain how an increase in financial leverage can increase a company's ROE. (b) Given the potentially positive relation between financial leverage and ROE, why don't we see companies with 100% financial leverage (entirely nonowner financed)?

Q4-3. Gross profit margin (Gross profit/Sales) is an important determinant of NOPAT. Identify two factors that can cause gross profit margin to decline. Is a reduction in the gross profit margin always bad news? Explain.

Q4-4. When might a reduction in operating expenses as a percentage of sales denote a short-term gain at the cost of long-term performance?

Q4-5. Describe the concept of asset turnover. What does the concept mean and why it is so important to understanding and interpreting financial performance?

Q4-6. Explain what it means when a company's ROE exceeds its RNOA.

Q4-7.^{A} Discontinued operations are typically viewed as a nonoperating activity in the analysis of the balance sheet and the income statement. What is the rationale for this treatment?

Q4-8. Describe what is meant by the "tax shield."

Q4-9. What is meant by the term "net" in net operating assets (NOA).

Q4-10. Why is it important to disaggregate RNOA into operating profit margin (NOPM) and net operating assets turnover (NOAT)?

Q4-11. What insights do we gain from the graphical relation between profit margin and asset turnover?

Q4-12. Explain the concept of liquidity and why it is crucial to company survival.

Q4-13. Identify at least two factors that limit the usefulness of ratio analysis.

Q4-14.^{A} Define (1) net nonoperating obligations and (2) the net nonoperating expense percent.

Assignments with the Web**Assign** logo in the margin are available in WebAssign.
See the Preface of the book for details.

MINI EXERCISES

M4-15. Identify and Compute Net Operating Assets (LO2)

Target Corporation
(TGT)

Following is the balance sheet for Target Corporation. Identify and compute fiscal year-end 2008 net operating assets.

($ millions)	February 2, 2008	February 3, 2007
Assets		
Cash and cash equivalents	$ 2,450	$ 813
Accounts receivable, net	8,054	6,194
Inventory	6,780	6,254
Other curret assets	1,622	1,445
Total current assets	18,906	14,706
Property and equipment		
Land	5,522	4,934
Buildings and improvements	18,329	16,110
Fixtures and equipment	3,858	3,553
Computer hardware and software	2,421	2,188
Construction-in-progress	1,852	1,596
Accumulated depreciation	(7,887)	(6,950)
Property and equipment, net	24,095	21,431
Other noncurrent assets	1,559	1,212
Total assets	$44,560	$37,349

continued

continued from prior page

($ millions)	February 2, 2008	February 3, 2007
Liabilities and shareholders' investment		
Accounts payable.	$ 6,721	$ 6,575
Accrued liabilities	3,097	3,180
Current portion of long-term debt and notes payable	1,964	1,362
Total current liabilities.	11,782	11,117
Long-term debt	15,126	8,675
Deferred income taxes.	470	577
Other noncurrent liabilities	1,875	1,347
Shareholders' investment		
Common stock	68	72
Additional paid-in-capital	2,656	2,387
Retained earnings.	12,761	13,417
Accumulated other comprehensive loss	(178)	(243)
Total shareholders' investment.	15,307	15,633
Total liabilities and shareholders' investment	$44,560	$37,349

M4-16. Identify and Compute NOPAT (LO2)

Following is the income statement for Target Corporation. (*a*) Compute Target's NOPBT—net operating profit *before* tax. (*Hint:* Treat Target's credit card revenues and related expenses as operating.) (*b*) Assume that the combined federal and state statutory tax rate is 39%. Compute NOPAT for Target for 2008.

Target Corporation (TGT)

($ millions)	2008
Sales.	$61,471
Net credit card revenues	1,896
Total revenues.	63,367
Cost of sales.	41,895
Selling, general and administrative expenses	13,704
Credit card expenses	837
Depreciation and amortization	1,659
Earnings from continuing operations before interest expense and income taxes.	5,272
Net interest expense	647
Earnings from continuing operations before income taxes	4,625
Provision for income taxes.	1,776
Net earnings.	$ 2,849

M4-17. Compute RNOA, Net Operating Profit Margin, and NOA Turnover (LO2)

Selected balance sheet and income statement information for Target Corporation, a department store retailer, follows.

Target Corporation (TGT)

Company ($ millions)	Ticker	2008 Revenues	2008 NOPAT	2008 Net Operating Assets	2007 Net Operating Assets
Target Corp.	TGT	$63,367	$3,244	$32,397	$25,670

a. Compute its 2008 return on net operating assets (RNOA).

b. Disaggregate RNOA into net operating profit margin (NOPM) and net operating asset turnover (NOAT). Confirm that RNOA = NOPM × NOAT.

M4-18. Identify and Compute Net Operating Assets (LO2)

FedEx Corp. (FDX)

Following is the balance sheet for FedEx. Identify and compute its 2008 net operating assets (NOA).

FEDEX CORPORATION		
May 31 ($ millions, except per share amount)	**2008**	**2007**
Assets		
Cash and cash equivalents	$ 1,539	$ 1,569
Receivables, less allowances of $158 and $136	4,359	3,942
Spare parts, supplies and fuel, less allowances of $163 and $156	435	338
Deferred income taxes	544	536
Prepaid expenses and other	367	244
Total current assets	7,244	6,629
Property and equipment, at cost		
Aircraft and related equipment	10,165	9,593
Package handling and ground support equipment	4,817	3,889
Computer and electronic equipment	5,040	4,685
Vehicles.	2,754	2,561
Facilities and other	6,529	6,362
	29,305	27,090
Less accumulated depreciation and amortization	15,827	14,454
Net property and equipment	13,478	12,636
Other long-term assets		
Goodwill	3,165	3,497
Pension assets	827	—
Intangible and other assets	919	1,238
Total other long-term assets	4,911	4,735
Total assets.	$25,633	$24,000
Liabilities and stockholders' investment		
Current portion of long-term debt	$ 502	$ 639
Accrued salaries and employee benefits	1,118	1,354
Accounts payable.	2,195	2,016
Accrued expenses	1,553	1,419
Total current liabilities	5,368	5,428
Long-term debt, less current portion	1,506	2,007
Other long-term liabilities		
Deferred income taxes	1,264	897
Pension, postretirement healthcare and other benefit obligations	989	1,164
Self-insurance accruals	804	759
Deferred lease obligations	671	655
Deferred gains, principally related to aircraft transactions	315	343
Other liabilities	190	91
Total other long-term liabilities	4,233	3,909
Common stockholders' investment		
Common stock, $0.10 par value; 800 million shares authorized;		
311 million shares issued for 2008 and 308 million shares		
issued for 2007	31	31
Additional paid-in capital	1,922	1,689
Retained earnings.	13,002	11,970
Accumulated other comprehensive loss	(425)	(1,030)
Treasury stock.	(4)	(4)
Total common stockholders' investment	14,526	12,656
Total liabilities and equity	$25,633	$24,000

M4-19. Identify and Compute NOPAT (LO2)

FedEx Corp. (FDX)

Following is the income statement for FedEx. Compute its 2008 net operating profit after tax (NOPAT) assuming a 37.1% total statutory tax rate and that "Other, net" reported under other income (expense) is nonoperating.

FEDEX CORPORATION			
Year ended May 31 ($ millions)	2008	2007	2006
Revenues	$37,953	$35,214	$32,294
Operating Expenses			
Salaries and employee benefits	14,202	13,740	12,571
Purchased transportation	4,447	3,873	3,251
Rentals and landing fees	2,441	2,343	2,390
Depreciation and amortization	1,946	1,742	1,550
Fuel	4,596	3,533	3,256
Maintenance and repairs	2,068	1,952	1,777
Impairment charges	882	—	—
Other	5,296	4,755	4,485
	35,878	31,938	29,280
Operating income	2,075	3,276	3,014
Other income (expense)			
Interest expense	(98)	(136)	(142)
Interest income	44	83	38
Other, net	(5)	(8)	(11)
	(59)	(61)	(115)
Income before income taxes	2,016	3,215	2,899
Provision for income taxes	891	1,199	1,093
Net income	$ 1,125	$ 2,016	$ 1,806

M4-20. Compute RNOA, NOPAT Margin, and NOA Turnover (LO2)

Selected balance sheet and income statement information for FedEx, a service company, follows.   FedEx Corp. (FDX)

Company ($ millions)	Ticker	2008 Sales	2008 NOPAT	2008 Net Operating Assets	2007 Net Operating Assets
FedEx	FDX	$37,953	$1,162	$17,205	$15,957

a. Compute FedEx's 2008 return on net operating assets (RNOA).
b. Disaggregate RNOA into net operating profit margin (NOPM) and net operating asset turnover (NOAT). Confirm that RNOA = NOPM × NOAT.

M4-21. Compute RNOA, Net Operating Profit Margin and NOA Turnover for Competitors (LO2)

Selected balance sheet and income statement information from Abercrombie & Fitch and TJX Companies, clothing retailers in the high-end and value-priced segments, respectively, follows.   Abercrombie & Fitch (ANF) and TJX Companies (TJX)

Company ($ millions)	Ticker	2008 Sales	2008 NOPAT	2008 Net Operating Assets	2007 Net Operating Assets
Abercrombie & Fitch	ANF	$ 3,750	$464	$1,340	$1,197
TJX Companies	TJX	18,647	771	2,987	3,100

a. Compute the 2008 return on net operating assets (RNOA) for both companies.
b. Disaggregate RNOA into net operating profit margin (NOPM) and net operating asset turnover (NOAT) for each company. Confirm that RNOA = NOPM × NOAT.
c. Discuss differences observed with respect to NOPM and NOAT and interpret these differences in light of each company's business model.

M4-22.[B] Compute and Interpret Liquidity and Solvency Ratios (LO4)

Selected balance sheet and income statement information from Verizon follows.   Verizon (VZ)

($ millions)	2007	2006
Current assets	$ 18,698	$ 22,538
Current liabilities.	24,741	32,280
Total liabilities	104,090	111,932
Equity	82,869	76,872
Earnings before interest and taxes.	11,321	10,503
Interest expense.	1,829	2,349
Net cash flow from operating activities	25,739	24,106

    a. Compute the current ratio for each year and discuss any trend in liquidity. What additional information about the numbers used to calculate this ratio might be useful in helping us assess liquidity? Explain.

    b. Compute times interest earned, the liabilities-to-equity, and the net cash from operating activities to total liabilities ratios for each year and discuss any noticeable change. (The average liabilities-to-equity ratio for the telecommunications industry is 1.70.) Do you have any concerns about the extent of Verizon's financial leverage and the company's ability to meet interest obligations? Explain.

    c. Verizon's capital expenditures are expected to increase substantially as it seeks to respond to competitive pressures to upgrade the quality of its communication infrastructure. Assess Verizon's liquidity and solvency in light of this strategic direction.

M4-23. **Compute Tax Rate on Operating Profit and NOPAT** **(LO2)**

Proctor & Gamble
(PG)
Abercrombie & Fitch
(ANF)

Selected income statement information is presented below for Proctor & Gamble and Abercrombie & Fitch.

Company ($ millions)	Ticker	Net Operating Profit Before Tax	Pretax Net Nonoperating Expense (Revenue)	Tax Expense	Statutory Tax Rate
Procter & Gamble.	PG	$17,083	$1,005	$4,003	37.5%
Abercrombie & Fitch.	ANF	740	(19)	$284	38.1%

    a. Compute the tax shield for each company: Net nonoperating expense (revenue) × Statutory rate.

    b. Use the following equation to compute the tax rate on net operating profit for each company.

$$\text{Tax rate on operating profit} = \frac{\text{Tax expense} + (\text{Pretax net nonoperating expense} \times \text{Statutory tax rate})}{\text{Net operating profit before tax}}$$

    c. Compute NOPAT using the tax rate from part *b*.

M4-24.[c] **Compute and Interpret Measures for DuPont Disaggregation Analysis** **(LO5)**

3M Company (MMM)

Refer to the 2007 fiscal year financial data of 3M Company from P4-36 to answer the following requirements.

    a. Compute the DuPont Model component measures for profit margin, asset turnover, and financial leverage.

    b. Compute ROE. Confirm that ROE equals ROE computed using the component measures from part a (ROE = PM × AT × FL).

    c. Compute adjusted ROA (assume a tax rate of 35.9% and pretax net interest expense of $78).

EXERCISES

E4-25. **Compute and Interpret RNOA, Profit Margin, and Asset Turnover of Competitors** **(LO2)**

Target Corporation
(TGT)
Wal-Mart Stores
(WMT)

Selected balance sheet and income statement information for department store retailers Target Corporation and Wal-Mart Stores follows.

Company ($ millions)	Ticker	2008 Sales	2008 NOPAT	2008 Net Operating Assets	2007 Net Operating Assets
Target	TGT	$ 63,367	$ 3,244	$32,397	$25,670
Wal-Mart.	WMT	378,799	14,428	111,218	102,751

a. Compute the 2008 return on net operating assets (RNOA) for each company.

b. Disaggregate RNOA into net operating profit margin (NOPM) and net operating asset turnover (NOAT) for each company.

c. Discuss any differences in these ratios for each company. Your interpretation should reflect the distinct business strategy of each company.

E4-26. Compute, Disaggregate, and Interpret RNOA of Competitors (LO2)

Selected balance sheet and income statement information for the clothing retailers, Abercrombie & Fitch and The GAP, Inc., follows.

WebAssign.

Abercrombie & Fitch (ANF)

The GAP, Inc. (GPS)

Company ($ millions)	Ticker	2008 Sales	2008 NOPAT	2008 Net Operating Assets	2007 Net Operating Assets
Abercrombie & Fitch...	ANF	$ 3,750	$464	$1,340	$1,197
The GAP.............	GPS	15,763	845	5,366	6,027

a. Compute the 2008 return on net operating assets (RNOA) for each company.

b. Disaggregate RNOA into net operating profit margin (NOPM) and net operating asset turnover (NOAT) for each company.

c. Discuss any differences in these ratios for each company. Your interpretation should reflect the distinct business strategy of each company.

E4-27. Compute, Disaggregate, and Interpret RNOA of Competitors (LO2)

Selected balance sheet and income statement information for the drug retailers CVS Corporation and Walgreen Company follows.

CVS Corporation (CVS)

Walgreen Company (WAG)

Company ($ millions)	Ticker	2007 Sales	2007 NOPAT	2007 Net Operating Assets	2006 Net Operating Assets
CVS Corporation*.....	CVS	$76,330	$2,901	$41,776	$14,975
Walgreen Company ...	WAG	53,762	2,017	11,983	9,701

* In 2007, CVS acquired Caremark Rx, Inc.

a. Compute the 2007 return on net operating assets (RNOA) for each company.

b. Disaggregate RNOA into net operating profit margin (NOPM) and net operating asset turnover (NOAT) for each company.

c. Discuss any differences in these ratios for each company. Identify the factor(s) that drives the differences in RNOA observed from your analyses in parts a and b.

E4-28. Compute, Disaggregate, and Interpret ROE and RNOA (LO1, 2)

Selected fiscal year balance sheet and income statement information for the computer chip maker, Intel, follows ($ millions).

Intel (INTC)

Company	Ticker	2007 Sales	2007 Net Income	2007 Net Operating Profit After Tax	2007 Net Operating Assets	2006 Net Operating Assets	2007 Stockholders' Equity	2006 Stockholders' Equity
Intel.......	INTC	$38,334	$6,976	$6,364	$31,443	$30,955	$42,762	$36,752

a. Compute the 2007 return on equity (ROE) and the 2007 return on net operating assets (RNOA).

b. Disaggregate RNOA into net operating profit margin (NOPM) and net operating asset turnover (NOAT). What observations can we make about the company's NOPM and NOAT?

c. Compute the percentage of RNOA to ROE, and compute the company's nonoperating return for 2008.

E4-29. Compute, Disaggregate and Interpret ROE and RNOA (LO1, 2)

Selected balance sheet and income statement information from Macy's follows ($ millions).

Macy's (M)

Company	Ticker	2008 Sales	2008 Net Income	2008 Net Operating Profit After Tax	2008 Net Operating Assets	2007 Net Operating Assets	2008 Stockholders' Equity	2007 Stockholders' Equity
Macy's	M	$26,313	$893	$1,231	$19,660	$20,673	$9,907	$12,254

a.   Compute the 2008 return on equity (ROE) and 2008 return on net operating assets (RNOA)
b.   Disaggregate RNOA into net operating profit margin (NOPM) and net operating asset turnover (NOAT). What observations can we make about Macy's NOPM and NOAT?
c.   Compute the percentage of RNOA to ROE, and compute Macy's nonoperating return for 2008.

E4-30.   Compute, Disaggregate and Interpret ROE and RNOA   (LO1, 2)

Cisco Systems
(CSCO)

Selected balance sheet and income statement information from the software company, Cisco Systems, Inc., follows ($ millions).

Company	Ticker	2008 Sales	2008 Net Income	2008 Net Operating Profit After Tax	2008 Net Operating Assets	2007 Net Operating Assets	2008 Stockholders' Equity	2007 Stockholders' Equity
Cisco Systems	CSCO	$39,540	$8,052	$7,524	$20,202	$19,350	$34,353	$31,480

a.   Compute the 2008 return on equity (ROE) and 2008 return on net operating assets (RNOA)
b.   Disaggregate the RNOA from part *a* into net operating profit margin (NOPM) and net operating asset turnover (NOAT).
c.   Compute the percentage of RNOA to ROE. Explain the relation we observe between ROE and RNOA, and Intuit's use of equity capital.

E4-31.[B]   Compute and Interpret Liquidity and Solvency Ratios   (LO4)

Comcast Corporation
(CMCSA)

Selected balance sheet and income statement information from Comcast Corporation for 2005 through 2007 follows ($ millions).

	Total Current Assets	Total Current Liabilities	Pretax Income	Interest Expense	Total Liabilities	Stockholders' Equity
2005	$2,594	$6,269	$1,880	$1,796	$62,524	$40,876
2006	5,202	7,191	3,594	2,064	68,997	41,408
2007	3,667	7,952	4,349	2,289	71,827	41,590

a.   Compute the current ratio for each year and discuss any trend in liquidity. Do you believe the company is sufficiently liquid? Explain. What additional information about the accounting numbers comprising this ratio might be useful in helping you assess liquidity? Explain.
b.   Compute times interest earned and the liabilities-to-equity ratio for each year and discuss any noticeable change.
c.   What is your overall assessment of the company's liquidity and solvency from the analyses in (*a*) and (*b*)? Explain.

E4-32.[B]   Compute and Interpret Liquidity and Solvency Ratios   (LO4)

Verizon
Communications, Inc.
(VZ)

Selected balance sheet and income statement information from Verizon Communications, Inc., for 2005 through 2007 follows ($ millions).

	Total Current Assets	Total Current Liabilities	Pretax Income	Interest Expense	Total Liabilities	Stockholders' Equity
2005	$19,320	$26,700	$8,448	$2,129	$102,017	$66,113
2006	22,538	32,280	8,154	2,349	111,932	76,872
2007	18,698	24,741	9,492	1,829	104,090	82,869

a.   Compute the current ratio for each year and discuss any trend in liquidity. Do you believe the company is sufficiently liquid? Explain. What additional information about the accounting numbers comprising this ratio might be useful in helping you assess liquidity? Explain.
b.   Compute times interest earned and the liabilities-to-equity ratio for each year and discuss any noticeable change.
c.   What is your overall assessment of the company's liquidity and solvency from the analyses in (*a*) and (*b*)? Explain.

E4-33.[B] **Compute and Interpret Solvency Ratios for Business Segments** **(LO2, 4)**

Selected balance sheet and income statement information from General Electric Company and its two principal business segments (Industrial and Financial) for 2007 follows.

General Electric (GE)

($ millions)	Pretax Income	Interest Expense	Total Liabilities	Stockholders' Equity
Industrial segment	$25,262	$ 1,993	$ 92,724	$115,559
Financial segment	13,764	22,731	586,962	57,676
Other.	(12,428)[1]	(937)[2]	(7,912)[2]	0
General Electric Consolidated	$26,598	$23,787	$671,774	$115,559[3]

[1] Includes unallocated corporate operating activities.

[2] Includes intercompany loans and related interest expense; these are deducted (eliminated) in preparing consolidated financial statements.

[3] The consolidated equity equals the equity of the parent (industrial); this is explained in Module 7.

a. Compute times interest earned and the liabilities-to-equity ratio for 2007 for the two business segments (Industrial and Financial) and the company as a whole

b. What is your overall assessment of the company's solvency? Explain. What differences do you observe between the two business segments? Do these differences correspond to your prior expectations given each company's business model?

c. Discuss the implications of the analysis of consolidated financial statements and the additional insight that can be gained from a more in-depth analysis of primary business segments.

E4-34.[A] **Direct Computation of Nonoperating Return** **(LO1, 3)**

Refer to the income statement and balance sheet of Kellogg Company, from Mid-Module Reviews 1 and 2.

Kellogg Company (K)

a. Compute the FLEV and SPREAD for Kellogg's for 2007.

b. Use RNOA from Mid-Module review 2, and the FLEV and SPREAD from part *a,* to compute ROE. Compare the ROE calculated in this exercise with the ROE from the Mid-Module Review 2.

E4-35. **Compute Tax Rates on Operating Profit and NOPAT** **(LO1)**

The income statement for The TJX Companies, Inc., follows.

Web**Assign**.

The TJX Companies, Inc. (TJX)

THE TJX COMPANIES, INC. Consolidated Statements of Income			
Fiscal Year Ended ($ thousands)	January 26, 2008	January 27, 2007	January 28, 2006
Net sales.	$18,647,126	$17,404,637	$15,955,943
Cost of sales, including buying and occupancy costs. . . .	14,082,448	13,213,703	12,214,671
Selling, general and administrative expenses	3,126,565	2,923,560	2,703,271
Provision for computer intrusion related costs	197,022	4,960	0
Interest expense (revenue), net*.	(1,598)	15,566	29,632
Income before provision for income taxes.	1,242,689	1,246,848	1,008,369
Provision for income taxes.	470,939	470,092	318,535
Discontinued operations	0	(38,717)	589
Net income.	$ 771,750	$ 738,039	$ 690,423

* Interest expense and revenue are both nonoperating for TJX.

a. Compute the tax shield for 2008. Assume that the combined statutory tax rate is 39.1%.

b. Use the following equation to compute TJX's tax rate on operating profit for 2008.

$$\frac{\text{Tax rate on}}{\text{operating profit}} = \frac{\text{Tax expense} + (\text{Pretax net nonoperating expense} \times \text{Statutory tax rate})}{\text{Net operating profit before taxes}}$$

c. Compute NOPAT using the tax rate from part *b,* for 2008.

PROBLEMS

P4-36. **Analysis and Interpretation of Profitability** **(LO1, 2)**

Balance sheets and income statements for 3M Company follow.

Income Statement			
Year ended December 31 ($ millions)	2007	2006	2005
Net sales..	$24,462	$22,923	$21,167
Operating expenses			
Cost of sales...................................	12,735	11,713	10,408
Selling, general and administrative expenses	5,015	5,066	4,631
Research, development and related expenses	1,368	1,522	1,274
Gain on sale of businesses.......................	(849)	(1,074)	—
Total	18,269	17,227	16,313
Operating income...............................	6,193	5,696	4,854
Interest expense and income			
Interest expense	210	122	82
Interest income...............................	(132)	(51)	(56)
Total	78	71	26
Income before income taxes, minority interest and cumulative effect of accounting change.............	6,115	5,625	4,828
Provision for income taxes........................	1,964	1,723	1,627
Minority interest	55	51	55
Income before cumulative effect of accounting change ...	4,096	3,851	3,146
Cumulative effect of accounting change	—	—	(35)
Net income.....................................	$ 4,096	$ 3,851	$ 3,111

Balance Sheet		
($ millions)	December 31, 2007	December 31, 2006
Assets		
Cash and cash equivalents	$ 1,896	$ 1,447
Marketable securities—current	579	471
Accounts receivable—net of allowances of $75 and $71	3,362	3,102
Inventories		
Finished goods......................................	1,349	1,235
Work in process	880	795
Raw materials and supplies	623	571
Total inventories	2,852	2,601
Other current assets....................................	1,149	1,325
Total current assets.................................	9,838	8,946
Marketable securities—noncurrent	480	166
Investments	298	314
Property, plant and equipment............................	18,390	17,017
Less: Accumulated depreciation	(11,808)	(11,110)
Property, plant and equipment—net	6,582	5,907
Goodwill..	4,589	4,082
Intangible assets—net	801	708
Prepaid pension and postretirement benefits	1,378	395
Other assets...	728	776
Total assets...	$24,694	$21,294

continued

continued from prior page

($ millions)	December 31, 2007	December 31, 2006
Liabilities and stockholders' equity		
Short-term borrowings and current portion of long-term debt	$ 901	$ 2,506
Accounts payable.	1,505	1,402
Accrued payroll	580	520
Accrued income taxes	543	1,134
Other current liabilities	1,833	1,761
Total current liabilities	5,362	7,323
Long-term debt	4,019	1,047
Other liabilities	3,566	2,965
Total liabilities	12,947	11,335
Stockholders' equity		
Common stock, par value $.01 per share (Shares outstanding—		
2007: 709,156,031 Shares outstanding—2006: 734,362,802)	9	9
Additional paid-in capital	2,785	2,484
Retained earnings	20,316	17,933
Treasury stock	(10,520)	(8,456)
Unearned compensation	(96)	(138)
Accumulated other comprehensive income (loss)	(747)	(1,873)
Stockholders' equity—net	11,747	9,959
Total liabilities and stockholders' equity.	$24,694	$21,294

Required

a. Compute net operating profit after tax (NOPAT) for 2007 and 2006. Assume that combined federal and state statutory tax rates are 35.9% for 2007 and 36.0% for 2006.

b. Compute net operating assets (NOA) for 2007 and 2006.

c. Compute and disaggregate 3M's RNOA into net operating profit margin (NOPM) and net operating asset turnover (NOAT) for 2007 and 2006; the 2005 NOA is $12,776 million. Has its RNOA improved or worsened? Explain why.

d. Compute net nonoperating obligations (NNO) for 2007 and 2006. Confirm the relation: NOA = NNO + Stockholders' equity.

e. Compute return on equity (ROE) for 2007 and 2006. (Stockholders' equity in 2005 is $10,395 million.)

f. What is the nonoperating return component of ROE for 2007 and 2006?

g. Comment on the difference between ROE and RNOA. What inference can we draw from this comparison?

P4-37.[B] **Analysis and Interpretation of Liquidity and Solvency (LO4)**

Refer to the financial information of 3M Company in P4-36 to answer the following requirements.

3M Company (MMM)

Required

a. Compute the current ratio and quick ratio for 2007 and 2006. Comment on any observed trends.

b. Compute times interest earned and liabilities-to-equity ratios for 2007 and 2006. Comment on any noticeable changes.

c. Summarize your findings about the company's liquidity and solvency. Do you have any concerns about its ability to meet its debt obligations?

P4-38.[A] **Direct Computation of Nonoperating Return (LO1, 2, 3)**

Refer to the financial information of 3M Company in P4-36 to answer the following requirements.

3M Company (MMM)

Required

a. Compute its financial leverage (FLEV) and Spread for 2007. Recall that NNE = NOPAT − Net income.

b. Assume that its return on equity (ROE) for 2007 is 37.74% and its return on net operating assets (RNOA) is 30.15%. Confirm computations to yield the relation: ROE = RNOA + (FLEV × Spread).

c. What do your computations of the nonoperating return imply about the company's use of borrowed funds?

P4-39. **Analysis and Interpretation of Profitability (LO1, 2)**

Balance sheets and income statements for Target Corporation follow.

WebAssign.

Target Corporation (TGT)

Income Statement			
For Fiscal Years Ended ($ millions)	**2008**	**2007**	**2006**
Sales..	**$61,471**	$57,878	$51,271
Credit card revenues	**1,896**	1,612	1,349
Total revenues	**63,367**	59,490	52,620
Cost of sales..	**41,895**	39,399	34,927
Selling, general and administrative expenses	**13,704**	12,819	11,185
Credit card expenses.......................................	**837**	707	776
Depreciation and amortization...............................	**1,659**	1,496	1,409
Earnings before interest expense and income taxes.............	**5,272**	5,069	4,323
Net interest expense	**647**	572	463
Earnings before income taxes	**4,625**	4,497	3,860
Provision for income taxes................................	**1,776**	1,710	1,452
Net earnings...	**$ 2,849**	$ 2,787	$ 2,408

Balance Sheet		
($ millions, except footnotes)	**February 2, 2008**	**February 3, 2007**
Assets		
Cash and cash equivalents	**$ 2,450**	$ 813
Accountings receivable, net...........................	**8,054**	6,194
Inventory...	**6,780**	6,254
Other current assets................................	**1,622**	1,445
Total current assets................................	**18,906**	14,706
Property and equipment		
Land	**5,522**	4,934
Buildings and improvements	**18,329**	16,110
Fixtures and equipment	**3,858**	3,553
Computer hardware and software	**2,421**	2,188
Construction-in-progress	**1,852**	1,596
Accumulated depreciation	**(7,887)**	(6,950)
Property and equipment, net	**24,095**	21,431
Other noncurrent assets.............................	**1,559**	1,212
Total assets.......................................	**$44,560**	$37,349
Liabilities and shareholders' investment		
Accounts payable...................................	**$ 6,721**	$ 6,575
Accrued and other current liabilities....................	**3,097**	3,180
Current portion of long-term debt and notes payable	**1,964**	1,362
Total current liabilities.............................	**11,782**	11,117
Long-term debt	**15,126**	8,675
Deferred income taxes...............................	**470**	577
Other noncurrent liabilities	**1,875**	1,347
Shareholders' investment		
Common stock..................................	**68**	72
Additional paid-in-capital	**2,656**	2,387
Retained earnings................................	**12,761**	13,417
Accumulated other comprehensive income.............	**(178)**	(243)
Total shareholders' investment......................	**15,307**	15,633
Total liabilities and shareholders' investment.............	**$44,560**	$37,349

Required

a. Compute net operating profit after tax (NOPAT) for 2008 and 2007. Assume that the combined federal and state statutory tax rates for both 2008 and 2007 are 39%.

b. Compute net operating assets (NOA) for 2008 and 2007.

continued

c. Compute and disaggregate Target's RNOA into net operating profit margin (NOPM) and net operating asset turnover (NOAT) for 2008 and 2007; the 2006 NOA is $24,451 million. Comment on the drivers of the change in Target's RNOA.
d. Compute net nonoperating obligations (NNO) for 2008 and 2007. Confirm the relation: NOA = NNO + Stockholders' equity.
e. Compute return on equity (ROE) for 2008 and 2007; the 2006 stockholders' equity is $14,205 million.
f. Infer the nonoperating return component of ROE for both 2008 and 2007.
g. Comment on the difference between ROE and RNOA. What does this relation suggest about Target's use of equity capital?

P4-40.ᴮ Analysis and Interpretation of Liquidity and Solvency (LO4)

Refer to the financial information of Target Corporation (TGT) in P4-39 to answer the following requirements.

Required

a. Compute Target's current ratio and quick ratio for 2008 and 2007. Comment on any observed trends.
b. Compute Target's times interest earned and its liabilities-to-equity ratios for 2008 and 2007. Comment on any noticeable change.
c. Summarize your findings about the company's liquidity and solvency. Do you have any concerns about Target's ability to meet its debt obligations?

P4-41.ᴬ Direct Computation of Nonoperating Return (LO1, 3)

Refer to the financial information of Target Corporation (TGT) in P4-39 to answer the following requirements.

Required

a. Compute Target's financial leverage (FLEV) and Spread for 2008; recall, NNE = NOPAT − Net income.
b. Assume that Target's return on equity (ROE) for 2008 is 18.42% and its return on net operating assets (RNOA) is 11.17%. Confirm computations to yield the relation: ROE = RNOA + (FLEV × Spread).
c. What do your computations of the nonoperating return in parts a and b imply about the company's use of borrowed funds?

P4-42. Analysis and Interpretation of Profitability (LO1, 2)

Balance sheets and income statements for Intel Corporation follow. Refer to these financial statements to answer the requirements.

INTEL CORPORATION Consolidated Statements of Income			
Year Ended December 31 (In Millions)	2007	2006	2005
Net revenue	$38,334	$35,382	$38,826
Cost of sales	18,430	17,164	15,777
Gross margin	19,904	18,218	23,049
Research and development	5,755	5,873	5,145
Marketing, general and administrative	5,401	6,096	5,688
Restructuring and asset impairment charges	516	555	—
Amortization of acquisition-related intangibles and costs	16	42	126
Operating expenses	11,688	12,566	10,959
Operating income	8,216	5,652	12,090
Gains (losses) on equity investments, net	157	214	(45)
Interest and other, net	793	1,202	565
Income before taxes	9,166	7,068	12,610
Provision for taxes	2,190	2,024	3,946
Net income	$ 6,976	$ 5,044	$ 8,664

INTEL CORPORATION Consolidated Balance Sheets December 31 (In millions, except par value)	2007	2006
Assets		
Cash and cash equivalents	$ 7,307	$ 6,598
Short-term investments	5,490	2,270
Trading assets	2,566	1,134
Accounts receivable, net of allowance for doubtful accounts of $27 ($32 in 2006)	2,576	2,709
Inventories	3,370	4,314
Deferred tax assets	1,186	997
Other current assets.	1,390	258
Total current assets.	23,885	18,280
Property, plant and equipment, net	16,918	17,602
Marketable equity securities	987	398
Other long-term investments	4,398	4,023
Goodwill.	3,916	3,861
Other long-term assets	5,547	4,204
Total assets.	$55,651	$48,368
Liabilities and stockholders' equity		
Short-term debt	$ 142	$ 180
Accounts payable.	2,361	2,256
Accrued compensation and benefits	2,417	1,644
Accrued advertising	749	846
Deferred income on shipments to distributors.	625	599
Other accrued liabilities	1,938	1,192
Income taxes payable	339	1,797
Total current liabilities	8,571	8,514
Long-term income taxes payable.	785	—
Deferred tax liabilities.	411	265
Long-term debt	1,980	1,848
Other long-term liabilities.	1,142	989
Stockholders' equity		
Common stock, $0.001 par value, 10,000 shares authorized; 5,818 issued and outstanding (5,766 in 2006) and capital in excess of par value.	11,653	7,825
Accumulated other comprehensive income.	261	(57)
Retained earnings.	30,848	28,984
Total stockholders' equity	42,762	36,752
Total liabilities and stockholders' equity.	$55,651	$48,368

Required

a. Compute net operating profit after tax (NOPAT) for 2007 and 2006. Assume that the combined federal and state statutory tax rates are 35.6% for 2007 and 35.8% for 2006.

b. Compute net operating assets (NOA) for 2007 and 2006. (*Hint:* Assume that trading assets, long-term marketable equity securities, and other long-term investments are investments in marketable securities and are therefore, nonoperating assets.)

c. Compute RNOA and disaggregate it into net operating profit margin (NOPM) and net operating asset turnover (NOAT) for 2007 and 2006; the 2005 NOA is $28,481 million. Comment on the drivers of RNOA.

d. Compute net nonoperating obligations (NNO) for 2007 and 2006. Confirm the relation: NOA = NNO + Stockholders' equity.

e. Compute return on equity (ROE) for 2007 and 2006; the 2005 stockholders' equity is $36,182 million.

f. Infer the nonoperating return component of ROE for both 2007 and 2006.

g. Comment on the difference between ROE and RNOA. What does this relation suggest about Intel's use of equity capital?

P4-43. **Analysis and Interpretation of Profitability** **(LO1, 2)**
Balance sheets and income statements for Johnson & Johnson follow. Refer to these financial statements to answer the requirements.

WebAssign.
Johnson & Johnson
(JNJ)

JOHNSON & JOHNSON AND SUBSIDIARIES Consolidated Statement of Earnings			
Years Ended ($ millions)	2007	2006	2005
Sales to customers.	$61,095	$53,324	$50,514
Costs of products sold.	17,751	15,057	14,010
Gross profit.	43,344	38,267	36,504
Selling, marketing and administrative expenses	20,451	17,433	17,211
Research expense	7,680	7,125	6,462
Purchased in-process research and development.	807	559	362
Restructuring	745	—	—
Interest income.	(452)	(829)	(487)
Interest expense, net of portion capitalized.	296	63	54
Other (income) expense, net	534	(671)	(214)
	30,061	23,680	23,388
Earnings before provision for taxes on income	13,283	14,587	13,116
Provision for taxes on income	2,707	3,534	3,056
Net earnings.	$10,576	$11,053	$10,060

JOHNSON & JOHNSON AND SUBSIDIARIES Consolidated Balance Sheets		
($ millions)	December 30, 2007	December 31, 2006
Assets		
Cash and cash equivalents	$ 7,770	$ 4,083
Marketable securities.	1,545	1
Accounts receivable trade, less allowances for doubtful accounts $193 (2006, $160). . .	9,444	8,712
Inventories	5,110	4,889
Deferred taxes on income	2,609	2,094
Prepaid expenses and other receivables	3,467	3,196
Total current assets	29,945	22,975
Marketable securities, noncurrent	2	16
Property, plant and equipment, net	14,185	13,044
Intangible assets, net	14,640	15,348
Goodwill, net	14,123	13,340
Deferred taxes on income	4,889	3,210
Other assets.	3,170	2,623
Total assets.	$80,954	$70,556
Liabilities and Shareholders' Equity		
Loans and notes payable.	$ 2,463	$ 4,579
Accounts payable.	6,909	5,691
Accrued liabilities	6,412	4,587
Accrued rebates, returns and promotions	2,318	2,189
Accrued salaries, wages and commissions.	1,512	1,391
Accrued taxes on income.	223	724
Total current liabilities.	19,837	19,161
Long-term debt	7,074	2,014
Deferred taxes on income	1,493	1,319
Employee related obligations.	5,402	5,584
Other liabilities	3,829	3,160
Total liabilities.	37,635	31,238

continued

continued from prior page

Shareholders' equity		
Preferred stock—without par value (authorized and unissued 2,000,000 shares).	—	—
Common stock—par value $1.00 per share (authorized 4,320,000,000 shares;		
issued 3,119,843,000 shares).	3,120	3,120
Accumulated other comprehensive income.	(693)	(2,118)
Retained earnings	55,280	49,290
	57,707	50,292
Less: common stock held in treasury, at cost (279,620,000 shares and	14,388	10,974
226,612,000 shares)		
Total shareholders' equity	43,319	39,318
Total liabilities and shareholders' equity.	$80,954	$70,556

Required

a. Compute net operating profit after tax (NOPAT) for 2007 and 2006. Assume that other income or expense are operating items, and that the combined federal and state statutory tax rates are 37.1% for 2007 and 36.6% for 2006.

b. Compute net operating assets (NOA) for 2007 and 2006.

c. Compute RNOA and disaggregate it into net operating profit margin (NOPM) and net operating asset turnover (NOAT) for 2007 and 2006; the 2005 NOA is $41,292 million. Comment on the drivers of RNOA.

d. Compute net nonoperating obligations (NNO) for 2007 and 2006. Confirm the relation: NOA = NNO + Stockholders' equity.

e. Compute return on equity (ROE) for 2007 and 2006; the 2005 stockholders' equity is $38,710 million.

f. Infer the nonoperating return component of ROE for both 2007 and 2006.

g. Comment on the difference between ROE and RNOA. What does this relation suggest about JNJ's use of equity capital?

P4-44. Analysis and Interpretation of Profitability (LO1, 2)

Amgen, Inc. (AMGN)

Balance sheets and income statements for Amgen, Inc. follow. Refer to these financial statements to answer the following requirements.

AMGEN, INC. Income Statements			
Years Ended December 31 (In millions)	**2007**	**2006**	**2005**
Revenues:			
Product sales	$14,311	$13,858	$12,022
Other revenues	460	410	408
Total revenues	14,771	14,268	12,430
Operating expenses:			
Cost of sales (excludes amortization of acquired			
intangible assets presented below).	2,548	2,095	2,082
Research and development	3,266	3,366	2,314
Selling, general and administrative.	3,361	3,366	2,790
Amortization of acquired intangible assets.	298	370	347
Write-off of acquired in-process research and development	590	1,231	—
Other items (primarily certain restructuring costs in 2007).	728	—	49
Total operating expenses	10,791	10,428	7,582
Operating income.	3,980	3,840	4,848
Other income (expense):			
Interest and other income, net	309	309	119
Interest expense, net	(328)	(129)	(99)
Total other income (expense)	(19)	180	20
Income before income taxes	3,961	4,020	4,868
Provision for income taxes.	795	1,070	1,194
Net income.	$ 3,166	$ 2,950	$ 3,674

AMGEN, INC. Balance Sheets		
December 31 (In millions, except per share amounts)	2007	2006
Assets		
Cash and cash equivalents	$ 2,024	$ 1,283
Marketable securities	5,127	4,994
Trade receivables, net	2,101	2,124
Inventories	2,091	1,903
Other current assets	1,698	1,408
Total current assets	13,041	11,712
Property, plant and equipment, net	5,941	5,921
Intangible assets, net	3,332	3,747
Goodwill	11,240	11,302
Other assets	1,085	1,106
Total assets	$34,639	$33,788
Liabilities and stockholders' equity		
Accounts payable	378	555
Accrued liabilities	3,801	4,589
Convertible notes	—	1,698
Current portion of other long-term debt	2,000	100
Total current liabilities	6,179	6,942
Deferred tax liabilities	480	367
Convertible notes	5,080	5,080
Other long-term debt	4,097	2,134
Other noncurrent liabilities	934	301
Commitments and contingencies		
Stockholders' equity:		
Common stock and additional paid-in capital; $0.0001 par value; 2,750 shares authorized; outstanding—1,087 shares in 2007 and 1,166 shares in 2006	24,976	24,155
Accumulated deficit	(7,160)	(5,203)
Accumulated other comprehensive income	53	12
Total stockholders' equity	17,869	18,964
Total liabilities and equity	$34,639	$33,788

Required
a. Compute net operating profit after tax (NOPAT) for 2007 and 2006. Assume that the combined federal and state statutory tax rates are 36.1% for 2007 and 36.6% for 2006.
b. Compute net operating assets (NOA) for 2007 and 2006.
c. Compute RNOA and disaggregate it into net operating profit margin (NOPM) and net operating asset turnover (NOAT) for 2007 and 2006; the 2005 NOA is $20,993 million. Comment on the drivers of the improvement in RNOA.
d. Compute net nonoperating obligations (NNO) for 2007 and 2006. Confirm the relation: NOA = NNO + Stockholders' equity.
e. Compute return on equity (ROE) for 2007 and 2006; the 2005 stockholders' equity is $20,451 million.
f. Infer the nonoperating return component of ROE for both 2007 and 2006.
g. Comment on the difference between ROE and RNOA. What does this relation suggest about its use of debt?

P4-45.B **Analysis and Interpretation of Liquidity and Solvency (LO4)**
Refer to the financial information of Amgen, Inc. in P4-44 to answer the following requirements. Amgen, Inc. (AMGN)

Required
a. Compute current ratio and quick ratio for 2007 and 2006. Comment on any observed trends.
b. Compute times interest earned and its liabilities-to-equity ratios for 2007 and 2006. Comment on any noticeable change.
c. Summarize your findings about the company's liquidity and solvency. Do you have any concerns about its ability to meet its debt obligations?

Amgen, Inc. (AMGN)

P4-46.[A]   **Direct Computation of Nonoperating Return   (LO1, 3)**

Refer to the financial information of Amgen, Inc. in P4-44 to answer the following requirements.

Required

a.   Assume that 2007 net nonoperating expenses (NNE) are $12 million and that 2007 RNOA is 13.55%. Compute financial leverage (FLEV) and Spread for 2007.

b.   Assume that 2007 return on equity (ROE) is 17.14%. Confirm computations to yield the relation: ROE = RNOA + (FLEV × Spread).

c.   What do your computations of the nonoperating return in parts a and b imply about the company's use of borrowed funds?

P4-47.   **Analysis and Interpretation of Profit Margin, Asset Turnover, and RNOA for Several Companies   (LO2)**

Net operating profit margin (NOPM) and net operating asset turnover (NOAT) for several selected companies for 2007 follow.

Johnson & Johnson (JNJ)

Intel (INTC)

CVS (CVS)

Kraft (KFT)

Walgreen's (WAG)

P&G (PG)

Target (TGT)

TJX (TJX)

	NOPM	NOAT
Johnson & Johnson	17.15%	1.26
Intel	16.60%	1.23
CVS	3.80%	2.69
Kraft	7.96%	0.85
Walgreen's	3.75%	4.96
P&G	15.01%	0.75
Target	5.12%	2.18
TJX	4.14%	6.13

Required

a.   Graph NOPM and NOAT for each of these companies. Do you see a pattern that is similar to that shown in this module? Explain. (The graph in the module is based on medians for selected industries; the graph for this problem uses fewer companies than in the module and, thus, will not be as smooth.)

b.   Consider the trade-off between profit margin and asset turnover. How can we evaluate companies on the profit margin and asset turnover trade-off? Explain.

WebAssign

Target Corp. (TGT)

P4-48.[C]   **Compute and Analyze Measures for DuPont Disaggregation Analysis   (LO5)**

Refer to the fiscal 2008 financial data of Target Corporation in P4-39 to answer the following requirements.

Required

a.   Apply the basic DuPont Model and compute the component measures for profit margin, asset turnover, and financial leverage.

b.   Compute ROE. Confirm that ROE equals ROE computed using the component measures from part a (ROE = PM × AT × FL).

c.   Compute adjusted ROA (assume a tax rate of 39.0%).

d.   Interpret the component measures computed in part a using Exhibit 4.4 as a rough gauge of market measures.

Intel (INTC)

P4-49.[C]   **Compute and Analyze Measures for DuPont Disaggregation Analysis   (LO5)**

Refer to the fiscal 2008 financial data of Intel Corporation in P4-42 to answer the following requirements.

Required

a.   Apply the basic DuPont Model and compute its component measures for profit margin, asset turnover, and financial leverage.

b.   Compute ROE. Confirm that ROE equals ROE computed using the component measures from part a (ROE = PM × AT × FL).

c.   Compute adjusted ROA (assume a tax rate of 35.6%).

MANAGEMENT APPLICATIONS

MA4-50. **Gross Profit and Strategic Management** (LO2)

One way to increase overall profitability is to increase gross profit. This can be accomplished by raising prices and/or by reducing manufacturing costs.

Required

a. Will raising prices and/or reducing manufacturing costs unambiguously increase gross profit? Explain.

b. What strategy might you develop as a manager to (i) increase product prices, or (ii) reduce product manufacturing cost?

MA4-51. **Asset Turnover and Strategic Management** (LO2)

Increasing net operating asset turnover requires some combination of increasing sales and/or decreasing net operating assets. For the latter, many companies consider ways to reduce their investment in working capital (current assets less current liabilities). This can be accomplished by reducing the level of accounts receivable and inventories, or by increasing the level of accounts payable.

Required

a. Develop a list of suggested actions that you, as a manager, could undertake to achieve these three objectives.

b. Describe the marketing implications of reducing receivables and inventories, and the supplier implications of delaying payment. How can a company reduce working capital without negatively impacting its performance?

MA4-52. **Ethics and Governance: Earnings Management** (LO1)

Companies are aware that analysts focus on profitability in evaluating financial performance. Managers have historically utilized a number of methods to improve reported profitability that are cosmetic in nature and do not affect "real" operating performance. These methods are subsumed under the general heading of "earnings management." Justification for such actions typically includes the following arguments:

- Increasing stock price by managing earnings benefits shareholders; thus, no one is hurt by these actions.
- Earnings management is a temporary fix; such actions will be curtailed once "real" profitability improves, as managers expect.

Required

a. Identify the affected parties in any scheme to manage profits to prop up stock price.

b. Do the ends (of earnings management) justify the means? Explain.

c. To what extent are the objectives of managers different from those of shareholders?

d. What governance structure can you envision that might inhibit earnings management?

Module Five

Reporting and Analyzing Operating Income

LEARNING OBJECTIVES

LO1 Explain revenue recognition criteria and identify transactions of special concern. (p. 5-5)

LO2 Describe accounting for operating expenses, including research and development, and restructuring. (p. 5-11)

LO3 Explain and analyze accounting for income taxes. (p. 5-17)

LO4 Explain how foreign currency fluctuations affect the income statement. (p. 5-24)

LO5 Compute earnings per share and explain the effect of dilutive securities. (p. 5-27)

PFIZER

Pfizer's business is to discover, develop, manufacture and market leading prescription medicines. These endeavors define the company's operating activities and include research and development, manufacturing, advertising, sales, after-sale customer support, and all administrative functions necessary to support Pfizer's various activities.

Accounting for operating activities involves numerous estimates and choices, and GAAP often grants considerable latitude. To illustrate, consider the choice of when to recognize sales revenue. Should Pfizer recognize revenue when it receives a customer order? When it ships the drug order? Or, when the customer pays? GAAP requires that revenues be recognized when *earned*. It is up to the company to decide when that condition is met. This module identifies several revenue-recognition scenarios that are especially troublesome for companies, their auditors, regulators, and outside stakeholders.

Pfizer's key operating activity is its research and development (R&D). To protect its discoveries, Pfizer holds thousands of patents and applies for hundreds more each year. However, patents don't protect Pfizer indefinitely—patents expire or fail legal challenges and, then, Pfizer's drugs face competition from other drug manufacturers. In 2007, for example, Pfizer's sales of Zoloft and Norvasc declined by about $3.5 billion because patent protection expired on both drugs. Even the company's blockbuster drug, Lipitor, with sales exceeding $12 billion in 2007 (26% of Pfizer's

total revenues), is not a panacea for what ails Pfizer—the Lipitor patent expires in 2010.

Wall Street is not optimistic about Pfizer's ability to replace patents that will lapse over the next decade. While Pfizer's revenues have increased by over 60% in the past five years, its profits have decreased by about 10%, and Pfizer's stock price has fallen 60 percent—see stock price chart below.

Although R&D activities generally yield future benefits and, thus, meet the criteria to be recorded as an asset, GAAP requires that companies expense most R&D costs. This creates balance sheets with significant "missing" assets. For example, the only asset that Pfizer has on its books specifically related to Lipitor is the legal cost of filing the patent with the U.S. Patent Office. Clearly this does not capture Lipitor's full value to Pfizer. This module explains

R&D accounting and the resulting financial statement implications.

Pfizer has restructured its activities several times in an attempt to maintain operating profit in light of declining sales. Restructurings typically involve two types of costs: severance costs relating to employee terminations and asset write-offs. GAAP grants leeway in how to account for restructuring activities. Should Pfizer expense the severance costs when the board of directors approves the layoffs? Or when the employees are actually paid? Or at some other point? This module discusses accounting for restructurings, including footnote disclosures that can help financial statement readers interpret restructuring activities.

A necessary part of operations is paying income taxes on profits earned. The IRS has its own rules for computing taxes owed. These rules, called the Internal Revenue Code, are different from GAAP. Thus, it is legal (and necessary) for companies to prepare two sets of financial reports, one for shareholders and one for tax authorities. In this module, we will see that tax expense reported on the income statement is not computed as a simple percentage of pretax income. The module also discusses the valuation allowance that is related to deferred tax assets, and explains how the allowance can markedly affect net income.

Earnings per share (EPS) is the most frequently quoted operating number in the financial press. It represents earnings that are available to pay dividends to common shareholders. Companies report two EPS numbers: basic and diluted. The latter represents the lower bound on that year's EPS. It is important that we understand the difference between the two, and this module describes the two EPS computations.

Pfizer does business around the world, transacting in many currencies. Indeed, many of Pfizer's subsidiaries maintain their entire financial records in currencies other than the U.S. dollar. Consequently, to prepare its financial statements in $US, Pfizer must translate each transaction from foreign currencies into $US. This module describes the effects of foreign currency translation. When the dollar strengthens and weakens against other world currencies, a company's foreign revenues and expenses increase or decrease even if unit volumes remain unchanged. Pfizer's 2007 sales, for example, were unchanged from 2006, but they occurred during a period of a weakening $US. Had exchange rates been unchanged, Pfizer's 2007 sales would have declined by 3%. It is important to understand the mechanical relation between foreign exchange rates and income statement items if we are to properly analyze companies with global operations. This module considers these issues.

Sources: Pfizer 2007 10-K, Pfizer 2007 Annual Report; *Fortune*, January 2009; *BusinessWeek*, January 2009.

Operating activities refer to a company's primary transactions. These include the purchase of goods from suppliers, the conversion of goods into finished products, the promotion and distribution of goods, the sale of goods to customers, and post-sale customer support. For manufacturing companies, operating activities include the conversion of goods into finished products. The income statement reports on these operating activities such as sales, cost of goods sold, and selling, general, and administrative expenses. Because they are the lifeblood of any company, operating activities must be executed successfully for a company to consistently succeed.

Nonoperating activities relate to the borrowing of money and the ancillary investment activities of a company. They are not a company's primary activities.[1] These activities are typically reported in the income statement as interest revenues and expenses, dividend revenues, and gains and losses on sales of securities.

Proper identification of operating and nonoperating components is important for valuation of companies' equity (stock) and debt (notes and bonds). It is important, for example, to know whether company profitability results from operating activities, or whether poor operating performance is being masked by income from nonoperating activities. (We know that income from nonoperating activities usually depends on a favorable investment climate, which can be short-lived.)

Exhibit 5.1 classifies several common income components as operating or nonoperating.

EXHIBIT 5.1 Distinguishing Operating and Nonoperating Income Components	
Operating Activities	**Nonoperating Activities**
• Sales	• Interest revenues and expenses
• Cost of goods sold	• Dividend revenues
• Selling, general and administrative expenses	• Gains and losses on sales of investments
• Depreciation expense	• Gains and losses on debt retirement
• Research and development expenses	• Gains and losses on discontinued operations
• Restructuring expenses	• Allocation of profit to noncontrolling interests (previously titled "minority interest expense")
• Income tax expenses	• Investment write-downs
• Extraordinary gains and losses	
• Gains and losses on sales of operating assets	
• Foreign currency translation effects	
• Operating asset write-downs	
• Other income or expenses	

---

[1] Exceptions exist; for example, income derived from investments is operating income for financial-services firms such as banks and insurance companies. As another example, the income derived from financing subsidiaries of manufacturing companies, such as Ford Motor Credit and Caterpillar Financial, is part of operating income because these activities can be viewed as extensions of the sales process.

The list of operating activities above includes all the familiar operating items, as well as gains and losses on transactions relating to operating assets and the write-down of operating assets.[2] The list also includes "other" income statement items. We treat these as operating unless the income statement designates them as nonoperating or footnote information indicates that some or all of these "other" items are nonoperating. Footnotes are usually uninformative about "other" income statement items and "other" balance sheet items, and GAAP does not require specific disclosure of such items unless they are deemed *material*.[3]

We build our discussion of operating income around Pfizer's income statement (see Exhibit 5.2), which includes all of the typical operating accounts. We highlight the following topics in this module:

- Revenues
- Research and development expenses
- Restructuring expenses
- Income tax expenses

- Extraordinary gains and losses
- Earnings per share (EPS)
- Foreign currency translation effects

BUSINESS INSIGHT | **Ratios Across Industries**

Over time, industries evolve and reach equilibrium levels for operating activities. For example, some industries require a high level of selling, general and administrative (SG&A) expenses, perhaps due to high advertising demands or high occupancy costs. Other industries require intense research and development (R&D) expenditures to remain competitive. To a large extent, these cost structures dictate the prices that firms in the industry charge—each industry prices its product or service to yield a sufficient level of gross profit (sales less cost of sales) to cover the operating expenses and allow the industry to remain viable. Review the following table of selected operating margins for companies in various industries (NOPM is net operating profit margin as defined in Module 4).

	Gross profit/Sales	SG&A/Sales	R&D/Sales	NOPM
Pfizer	76.8%	32.3%	16.7%	14.9%
Cisco Systems	64.5	21.2	13.0	19.0
Intel	51.9	14.1	15.0	16.6
Procter & Gamble	51.3	30.8	0.0	15.0
Target	33.9	20.7	0.0	5.1
Home Depot	33.6	22.0	0.0	5.9
Dell	19.1	12.3	1.0	4.4

We see that Cisco, Intel, Pfizer, and Proctor & Gamble report high gross profit margins. This does not necessarily suggest they are better managed than Dell. Instead, their industries require higher levels of gross profit to cover their high levels of SG&A and R&D. Dell, on the other hand, is in a highly price-competitive segment of the computer industry. To maintain its competitive advantage, Dell must control costs. Indeed, Dell reports the lowest SG&A-to-sales ratio of any of the companies listed.

---

[2] To explain, a loss on the sale of equipment implies that the company did not depreciate the equipment quickly enough. Had the company recorded the "right" amount of depreciation over the years (that is, the amount of depreciation that perfectly matched the equipment's economic devaluation over time), the equipment's book value would have been exactly the same as its market value and no loss would have been recorded. Thus, we treat the loss on disposal in the same manner as depreciation expense—as operating. The same logic applies to write-downs of operating assets, which occur when the fair value of assets such as property and intangibles has declined below their book value.

[3] *Material* is an accounting term that means the item in question is important enough to make a difference to someone relying on the financial statements when making a business decision. Investors, for example, might find an item material if it is large enough to change their investment decision (whether to buy or sell the stock). This *materiality* judgment is in the eye of the beholder and this subjectivity makes materiality an elusive concept.

OPERATING INCOME COMPONENTS

Pfizer's 2007 income statement in Exhibit 5.2 highlights the operating income components discussed in this module. We defer discussion of cost of goods sold (cost of sales) to Module 6, which focuses on inventories and other operating assets. Modules 2 and 4 discuss items typically included in selling, general and administrative (SG&A) expenses, and Module 7 addresses the accounts related to acquisitions of other companies (such as amortization of intangible assets, merger-related in-process research and development charges, minority interest, and discontinued operations).

EXHIBIT 5.2 Pfizer Income Statement	
(Millions, Except per share data)	**2007**
Revenues.	$48,418
Costs and expenses	
Cost of sales.	11,239
Selling, informational and administative expenses.	15,626
Research and development expenses	8,089
Amortization of intangible assets	3,128
Acquisition-related in-process research and development charges	283
Restructuring charges and acquisition-related costs.	2,534
Other income—net	(1,759)
Income from continuing operations before provision for taxes on income, minority interests and cumulative effect of a change in accounting principles	9,278
Provision for taxes on income.	1,023
Minority interest	42
Income from continuing operations	8,213
Discontinued operations	
Loss from discontinued operations—net of tax	(3)
Loss on sales of discontinued operations—net of tax	(66)
Discontinued operations—net of tax	(69)
Net income	$ 8,144
Earnings per common share—basic	
Income from continuing operations	$ 1.19
Discontinued operations.	(0.01)
Net income	$ 1.18
Earnings per common share—diluted	
Income from continuing operations	$ 1.18
Discontinued operations.	(0.01)
Net income	$ 1.17
Weighted-average shares—basic	6,917
Weighted-average shares—diluted	6,939

We begin by discussing revenue, including the revenue recognition criteria that companies must employ and improper revenue recognition that the SEC has recently challenged. Next, we discuss Pfizer's research and development expenses, restructuring charges, provision for taxes, effects of foreign currency fluctuations, extraordinary items, and earnings per share (EPS).

Revenue and its Recognition

LO1 Explain revenue recognition criteria and identify transactions of special concern.

Pfizer reports $48,418 million in revenue. This revenue represents the culmination of a process that includes the manufacture of the drugs, their promotion, the receipt of orders, delivery to the customer, billing for the sale amount, and collection of the amounts owed. At what point in this process should Pfizer recognize its revenue and the related profit? When the drugs are delivered to the customer? When payment is received? And, how should Pfizer treat sales discounts or rights of return?

GAAP specifies two **revenue recognition criteria** that must both be met for revenue to be recognized on the income statement. Revenue must be (1) **realized or realizable**, and (2) **earned**.[4] *Realized or realizable* means that the seller's net assets (assets less liabilities) increase. That is, the seller receives an asset, such as cash or accounts receivable, or satisfies a liability, such as deferred revenue, as a result of a transaction. The company does not have to wait to recognize revenue until after it collects the accounts receivable; the increase in the account receivable (asset) means that the revenue is realizable. *Earned* means that the seller has performed its duties under the terms of the sales agreement and that title to the product sold has passed to the buyer with no right of return or other contingencies. As long as Pfizer has delivered the drugs ordered by its customers, and its customers are obligated to make payment, Pfizer can recognize revenue. The following conditions would each argue *against* revenue recognition:

- *Rights of return exist,* other than due to routine product defects covered under product warranty.
- *Consignment sales,* where products are held on consignment until ultimately sold by the consignee.
- *Continuing involvement by seller in product resale,* such as where the seller retains possession of the product until it's resold.
- *Contingency sales,* such as when product sales are contingent on product performance or further approvals by the customer.

Revenue is not recognized in these cases until the factors inhibiting revenue recognition are resolved.

Companies are required to report their revenue recognition policies in footnotes to their 10-K reports. Pfizer recognizes its revenues as follows:

> Revenue Recognition—We record revenue from product sales when the goods are shipped and title passes to the customer. At the time of sale, we also record estimates for a variety of sales deductions, such as sales rebates, discounts and incentives, and product returns.

Pfizer adopts the position that its revenues are *earned* when its products are shipped and the title to the merchandise passes to its customers. At that point, Pfizer has done everything required and, thus, recognizes the sale in the income statement. Most companies recognize revenues using these same criteria. Pfizer does *not* recognize revenues for the gross selling price. Instead, Pfizer deducts that portion of gross sales that is likely to be refunded to customers through sales rebates, discounts and incentives (including volume purchases). Pfizer estimates the likely cost of those price reductions and deducts that amount from gross sales. Similarly, Pfizer does not recognize revenues for those products that it estimates will be returned, possibly because the drugs hit their expiration date before they are sold by Pfizer's customers. In sum, Pfizer recognizes revenues for products delivered to customers, and for only the sales price *net* of anticipated discounts and returns. This is why we often see "Revenues, net" on companies' income statements.

IFRS INSIGHT   Revenue Recognition and IFRS

Revenue is generally recognized under both U.S. GAAP and IFRS when the earning process is complete (when the seller has performed all obligations under the sales arrangement and no contingencies remain) and benefits are realized or realizable. Further, there is extensive guidance under U.S. GAAP for specific industry transactions. That guidance is not present in IFRS. Moreover, public companies in the U.S. must follow additional guidance set by the SEC. In many cases, companies will recognize revenue earlier under IFRS than under GAAP.

---

[4] SEC provides guidance for revenue recognition in *Staff Accounting Bulletin (SAB) 101* (http://www.sec.gov/interps/account/sab101.htm) that states that revenue is realized, or realizable, and earned when *each* of the following criteria are met: (1) there is persuasive evidence that a sales agreement exists; (2) delivery has occurred or services have been rendered; (3) the seller's price to the buyer is fixed or determinable; and (4) collectibility is reasonably assured.

BUSINESS INSIGHT Cisco's Revenue Recognition

Following is an excerpt from Cisco Systems' policies on revenue recognition as reported in footnotes to its recent annual report.

> The Company recognizes revenue when persuasive evidence of an arrangement exists, delivery has occurred, the fee is fixed or determinable, and collectability is reasonably assured. In instances where final acceptance of the product, system, or solution is specified by the customer, revenue is deferred until all acceptance criteria have been met. Technical support services revenue is deferred and recognized ratably over the period during which the services are to be performed . . . When a sale involves multiple elements, such as sales of products that include services, the entire fee from the arrangement is allocated to each respective element based on its relative fair value and recognized when revenue recognition criteria for each element are met . . . The Company accrues for warranty costs, sales returns, and other allowances based on its historical experience.

Cisco's criteria for revenue recognition mirror SEC guidance. The key components are that revenue is *earned* and that proceeds are *realized or realizable*. For Cisco, earned means that delivery to and acceptance by the customer occurs, or that Cisco is available to perform service commitments, even if not called upon.

Risks of Revenue Recognition

More than 70% of SEC accounting and auditing enforcement actions involve misstated revenues (see Dechow, P., and C. Schrand. "Earnings quality," The Research Foundation of CFA Institute. Charlottesville, VA 2004). The SEC's concern about aggressive (premature) revenue recognition prompted the issuance of a special *Staff Accounting Bulletin (SAB) 101* on the matter. The SEC provides the following examples of problem areas to assist companies in properly recognizing revenue:

■ *Case 1: Channel stuffing.* Some sellers use their market power over customers to induce (or even require) them to purchase more goods than they actually need. This practice, called *channel stuffing*, increases period-end sales and net income. If no side agreements exist for product returns, the practice does not violate GAAP revenue recognition guidelines, but the SEC contends that revenues are misrepresented and that the practice is a violation of securities laws.

■ *Case 2: Barter transactions.* Some barter transactions are concocted to create the illusion of revenue. Examples include the advertising swaps that dot-com companies have sometimes engaged in, and the excess capacity swaps of fiber optic communications businesses. The advertising swap relates to the simultaneous sale and purchase of advertising. The excess capacity swap relates to a company selling excess capacity to a competitor and, simultaneously, purchasing excess capacity from that competitor. Both types of swaps are exchanges of nearly identical services; they do not provide income or create an expense for either party. Further, these transactions do not represent a culmination of the normal earning process and, thus, the "earned" revenue recognition criterion is not met.

■ *Case 3: Mischaracterizing transactions as arm's-length.* Transfers of inventories or other assets to related entities are typically not recognized as revenue until arm's-length sales occur. Sometimes, companies disguise non-arm's-length transactions as sales to unrelated entities. This practice is improper when the buyer is related to the seller, or the buyer is unable to pay for the merchandise other than from its resale. Revenue should not be recognized unless the sales process is complete, that is, goods have been transferred and an asset has been created (future payment from a solvent, independent party).

■ *Case 4: Pending execution of sales agreements.* Sometimes companies boost current period profits by recording revenue for goods delivered for which formal customer approval has yet to be received. The SEC's position is that if the company's practice is to obtain sales authorization, then revenue is *not* earned until such approval is obtained, even though product delivery is made and customer approval is anticipated.

■ *Case 5: Gross versus net revenues.* Some companies use their distribution network to sell other companies' goods for a commission. There are increasing reports of companies that inflate revenues by reporting such transactions on a gross basis (separately reporting both sales and cost of goods sold) instead of reporting only the commission (typically a percentage of sales price). The incentives for such reporting are high for some dot.com companies and start-ups that believe the market prices of their stocks are based on revenue growth and not on profitability. Reporting revenues at gross rather than net could have enormous impact on the valuations of those companies. The SEC prescribes that such sales be reported on a net basis.

■ *Case 6: Sales on consignment.* Some companies deliver goods to other companies with the understanding that these goods will be ultimately sold to third parties. At the time of delivery, title does not pass to the second company, and the second company has no obligation to make payment to the seller until the product is sold. This type of transaction is called a *consignment sale.* The SEC's position is that a sale has not occurred, and revenue is *not* to be recognized by the original company, until the product is sold to a third party. Further, the middleman (consignee) cannot report the gross sale, and can only report its commission revenue.

■ *Case 7: Failure to take delivery.* Some customers may not take delivery of the product by period-end. In this case, revenue is *not* yet earned. The earning process is only complete once the product is delivered and accepted. An example is a layaway sale. Even though the product is ordered, and even partially paid for, revenue is not recognized until the product is delivered and final payment is made or agreed to be made.

■ *Case 8: Nonrefundable fees.* Sellers sometimes receive fees that are nonrefundable to the customer. An example is a health club initiation fee or a cellular phone activation fee. Some sellers wish to record these cash receipts as revenue to boost current sales and income. However, even though cash is received and nonrefundable, revenue is not recognized until the product is delivered or the service performed. Until that time, the company reports the cash received as a liability (deferred revenue). Once the obligation is settled, the liability is removed and revenue is reported.

In sum, revenue is only recognized when it is earned and when it is realized or realizable. This demands that the seller has performed its obligations (no contingencies exist) and the buyer is an independent party with the financial capacity to pay the amounts owed.

Percentage-of-Completion Revenue Recognition

Challenges arise in determining the point at which revenue is earned for companies with long-term sales contracts (spanning more than one period), such as construction companies, consultants, and defense contractors. For these companies, revenue is often recognized using the percentage-of-completion method, which recognizes revenue by determining the costs incurred under the contract relative to its total expected costs.

To illustrate, assume that Bayer Construction signs a $10 million contract to construct a building. Bayer estimates construction will take two years and will cost $7,500,000. This means the contract yields an expected gross profit of $2,500,000 over two years. The following table summarizes construction costs incurred each year and the revenue Bayer recognizes.

	Construction costs incurred	Percentage complete	Revenue recognized
Year 1	$4,500,000	$\frac{\$4,500,000}{\$7,500,000} = 60\%$	$10,000,000 × 60% = $6,000,000
Year 2	$3,000,000	$\frac{\$3,000,000}{\$7,500,000} = 40\%$	$10,000,000 × 40% = $4,000,000

This table reveals that Bayer would report $6 million in revenue and $1.5 million ($6 million − $4.5 million) in gross profit on the construction project in the first year; it would report $4 million in revenue and $1 million ($4 million − $3 million) in gross profit in the second year.

Next, assume that Bayer's client makes a $1 million deposit at the signing of the contract and that Bayer submits bills to the client based on the percentage of completion. The following table reflects the bills sent to, and the cash received from, the client.

	Revenue recognized	Client billed	Cash received
At signing	$ 0	$ 0	$1,000,000
Year 1	6,000,000	5,000,000	3,000,000
Year 2	4,000,000	4,000,000	6,000,000

At the signing of the contract, Bayer recognizes no revenue because construction has not begun and thus, Bayer has not earned any revenue. By the end of the second year, Bayer has recognized all of the contract revenue and the client has paid all monies owed per the accounts receivable. The following template captures Bayer Construction's transactions over this two-year period (M indicates millions).

	Balance Sheet										Income Statement				
Transaction	Cash Asset	+	Noncash Assets	=	Liabilities	+	Contrib. Capital	+	Earned Capital		Revenues	−	Expenses	=	Net Income
Start of year 1: Record $1M deposit received at contract signing	+1M Cash			=	+1M Unearned Revenue							−		=	
Year 1: Record $4.5M construction costs	−4.5M Cash			=					−4.5M Retained Earnings			−	+4.5M Cost of Sales	=	−4.5M
Year 1: Recognize $6M revenue on partly completed contract			+5M Accounts Receivable	=	−1M Unearned Revenue				+6M Retained Earnings		+6M Revenue	−		=	+6M
Year 1: Record $3M cash received from client	+3M Cash		−3M Accounts Receivable	=								−		=	
Year 2: Record $3M construction costs	−3M Cash			=					−3M Retained Earnings			−	+3M Cost of Sales	=	−3M
Year 2: Recognize $4M revenue for completed contract			+4M Accounts Receivable	=					+4M Retained Earnings		+4M Revenue	−		=	+4M
Year 2: Record $6M cash received from client	+6M Cash		−6M Accounts Receivable	=								−		=	

Journal entries (left margin):

- Cash 1M / UR 1M; Cash 1M / UR 1M
- COGS 4.5M / Cash 4.5M; COGS 4.5M / Cash 4.5M
- AR 5M, UR 1M / REV 6M; AR 5M, UR 1M / REV 6M
- Cash 3M / AR 3M; Cash 3M / AR 3M
- COGS 3M / Cash 3M; COGS 3M / Cash 3M
- AR 4M / Rev 4M; AR 4M / Rev 4M
- Cash 6M / AR 6M; Cash 6M / AR 6M

Revenue recognition policies for these types of contracts are disclosed in a manner typical to the following from the 2007 10-K report footnotes of Raytheon Company.

Revenue Recognition We account for our contracts . . . using the percentage-of-completion accounting method. Under this method, revenue is recognized based on the extent of progress towards completion of the long-term contract . . . We generally use the cost-to-cost measure of

continued

continued from prior page

> progress for all of our long-term contracts . . . Under the cost-to-cost measure of progress, the extent of progress towards completion is measured based on the ratio of costs incurred-to-date to the total estimated costs at completion of the contract.

The percentage-of-completion method of revenue recognition requires an estimate of total costs. This estimate is made at the beginning of the contract and is typically the one used to initially bid the contract. However, estimates are inherently inaccurate. If the estimate changes during the construction period, the percentage-of-completion is computed as the total costs incurred to date divided by the *current* estimate of total anticipated costs (costs incurred to date plus total estimated costs to complete).

If total construction costs are underestimated, the percentage-of-completion is overestimated (the denominator is too low) and revenue and gross profit to date are overstated. The estimation process inherent in this method has the potential for inaccurate or, even, improper revenue recognition. In addition, estimates of remaining costs to complete projects are difficult for the auditors to verify. This uncertainty adds additional risk to financial statement analysis.

BUSINESS INSIGHT | Disney's Revenue Recognition

The Walt Disney Company uses a method similar to percentage-of-completion to determine the amount of production cost to match against film and television revenues. Following is an excerpt from its 10-K.

> Film and television production and participation costs are expensed based on the ratio of the current period's gross revenues to estimated remaining total gross revenues from all sources on an individual production basis. Ultimate Revenues for film productions includes revenue that will be earned within ten years of the date of the initial theatrical release.

As Disney pays production costs, it records those costs on the balance sheet as inventory. Then, as film and television revenues are recognized, the company matches a portion of production costs (from inventory) against revenues in computing income. Each period, the costs recognized are equal to the proportion of total revenues recognized in the period to the total revenues expected over the life of the film or television show. Thus, estimates of both costs and income depend on the quality of Disney's revenue estimates, which are, likely, imprecise.

Recognition of Unearned Revenue

In some industries it is common to receive cash before recording revenue. Customers might pay in advance for special orders, make deposits for future services, or buy concert tickets, subscriptions, or gift cards. In those cases, companies must record unearned revenues, a liability, and only record revenue when those products and services are provided. Specifically, deposits or advance payments are not recorded as revenue until the company performs the services owed or delivers the goods. Until then, the company's balance sheet shows the advance payment as a liability (called unearned revenue or deferred revenue) because the company is obligated to deliver those products and services.

To illustrate, assume that on January 1 a client pays Pfizer $360,000 for a guaranteed one-year supply of a rare medicine. Pfizer initially records $360,000 cash and a $360,000 liability (unearned revenue). Pfizer will earn that revenue by delivering the medicine during the coming year. Revenue is computed as a proportion of medicine delivered to the total amount purchased under the contract. For example, if Pfizer prepares quarterly financial statements and it has provided one-fourth of the contracted medicine by first quarter-end, it will record one-fourth of that revenue as earned. As revenue is earned, the unearned revenue account on the balance sheet is reduced and revenue is recorded in the income statement. The following template reflects the cash received for the medicine contract and the subsequent first quarter accounting adjustment.

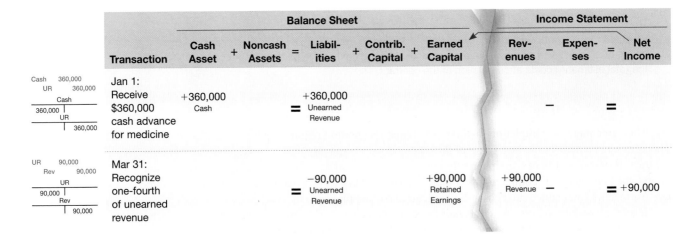

	Balance Sheet						Income Statement		
Transaction	Cash Asset	+ Noncash Assets	= Liabil-ities	+ Contrib. Capital	+ Earned Capital		Rev-enues	− Expen-ses	= Net Income
Jan 1: Receive $360,000 cash advance for medicine	+360,000 Cash		+360,000 Unearned Revenue				−		=
Mar 31: Recognize one-fourth of unearned revenue			−90,000 Unearned Revenue		+90,000 Retained Earnings		+90,000 Revenue	−	= +90,000

Cash 360,000
UR 360,000
Cash
360,000 |
UR
| 360,000

UR 90,000
Rev 90,000
UR
90,000 |
Rev
| 90,000

Research and Development (R&D) Expenses

LO2 Describe accounting for operating expenses, including research and development, and restructuring.

R&D activities are a major expenditure for many companies, especially for those in technology and pharmaceutical industries. Pfizer's R&D costs, for example, make up 16.7% of revenues ($8,089 million/$48,418 million). These expenses include employment costs for R&D personnel, R&D materials and supplies, R&D related contract services, and R&D fixed-asset costs.

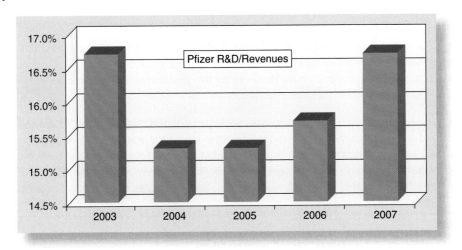

Accounting for R&D

Accounting for R&D is straightforward: R&D costs are expensed as incurred. The key issue is how to classify the expenses for financial reporting purposes. Salaries paid to researchers, and the depreciation and other expenses related to general purpose research facilities, are accounted for in the usual manner (which is to expense salaries when paid and to capitalize and depreciate general-purpose research facilities). However, these expenses are totaled separately and are classified as R&D in the income statement rather than as SG&A. An exception to this general rule relates to the purchase of R&D assets that are only used for a specific project and then retired when that project is complete. These project-specific assets are expensed when purchased. Consequently, income is reduced in the year of acquisition (but higher in subsequent years) relative to what the company would have reported had the asset been capitalized and depreciated. (Project-specific assets are said to have no "alternate use." One alternate use could be reselling the asset. In that case, the asset is *not* considered project-specific and is accounted for like other long-term assets.)

Following is a footnote excerpt from Pfizer's 2007 annual report related to its research and development expenditures:

> Research and development (R&D) costs are expensed as incurred. These expenses include the costs of our proprietary R&D efforts, as well as costs incurred in connection with our third-party collaboration efforts.

Pfizer capitalizes and depreciates general research facilities (those with alternate uses). All other R&D costs are expensed as incurred.

IFRS INSIGHT Research and Development Expenses and IFRS

IFRS accounts for research costs and development costs separately. Research costs are always expensed. Development costs must be capitalized if all of the following conditions are affirmed:

- Technical feasibility of completing the intangible asset.

- Intention to complete the intangible asset.

- Ability to use or sell the intangible asset.

- Intangible asset will generate future economic benefits (the company must demonstrate the existence of a market or, if for internal use, the usefulness of the intangible asset).

- Availability of adequate resources to complete development.

- Ability to measure reliably the expenditure attributable to the intangible asset during its development.

U.S. GAAP allows for capitalization of costs related to the development of software for sale to third parties once the software achieves "commercial feasibility," but is silent on the capitalization of other intangible assets—thus, implicitly prescribing expensing of these assets.

Analysis of R&D

When R&D expenses are large, such as that for technology-based and pharmaceutical companies, a question arises as to how we should treat those expenses in our company analysis. If R&D outlays are expected to yield future benefits, companies would (conceptually) understate assets and income because GAAP requires expensing of R&D outlays. One approach is to capitalize and amortize the reported R&D expenses. To illustrate, assume that a company reports the following income statement:

Sales...................	$500
Expenses other than R&D ...	350
R&D expenses	**100**
Net income (per GAAP)	$ 50

Next, assume that R&D expenses create economic benefits over the next five years. Accordingly, the method would treat the $100 R&D expenditures as an asset and amortize it over its useful life. Specifically, the adjusted balance sheet would reflect the $80 of unamortized R&D assets remaining, computed as $100 in R&D asset less $20 in R&D amortization (current-year equity is also $80 greater from the $80 of expenses postponed to future years). The adjusted income statement would reflect the $20 amortization of the $100 R&D asset as follows (computed as $100/5 years):

Sales...................	$500
Expenses other than R&D ...	350
R&D amortization	**20**
Net income (per GAAP)	$130

This adjusted income makes the company look more profitable than suggested using GAAP income. (However, if the company is not experiencing abnormal growth and the $100 annual R&D expenditures continue as usual, then after the five-year initial amortization period the R&D amortization in the adjusted income statement will approximate the R&D expenses in the GAAP income statement.)

While this approach might be conceptually appealing, it has problems. First, determining the proportion of R&D expenses that create future economic benefits is extremely subjective. GAAP income statements do not distinguish between research and that of development and, instead, report them as one combined item. (Under IFRS, research outlays are expensed while development outlays are capitalized when they meet defined criteria.) As users of financial reports, we have little basis to make such an allocation, let alone decide if outlays meet certain criteria. Second, there is considerable judgment in determining the period over which future economic benefits will occur. Some intangible assets such as patents are protected for specific lengths of time, but most other intangibles have no such defined period of potential benefit. Third, the manner in which future benefits will be realized is uncertain, so amortization of an R&D asset would be arbitrary. A straight-line method (as in our example above) would be easy, but would it reflect the asset's pattern of use?

For these reasons, we do not advise routinely creating pro forma net income and balance sheet numbers by capitalizing and amortizing R&D expenses. (An exception might be for growth companies that have yet to reach a steady level of R&D outlays, for companies with product breakthroughs, and for companies that require financial comparisons to IFRS-compliant reports.) Further, for companies that spend about the same amount each year on R&D, the income statement adjustment would be small. To see this, recall our example above: if the company spends $100 on R&D each year, then after five years, the amortization of previously capitalized amounts will be $100 (5 × $20) which is exactly the same as the R&D expense itself. However, the balance sheet adjustment can be more substantial as the R&D asset is "missing" entirely from the GAAP balance sheet (in the same way that benefits from the payment of wages or advertising are missing). Hence, when we compute ratios that involve income and assets (such as ROA or RNOA) or income and equity (such as ROE), the effects of expensing R&D are likely to overstate such ratios (from the absence of R&D assets in balance sheets).

A similar conclusion is reached in a recent study (Danielson and Press, "When Does R&D Expense Distort Profitability Estimates?" *Journal of Applied Finance*, 2005):

> . . . the accounting and finance literatures provide no guidance as to when potential distortion in accounting-based return measures makes an adjustment necessary. The expensing of R&D costs affects both the income statement and balance sheet, and therefore has an uncertain impact on a firm's accounting rate of return. It is possible for the income statement and balance sheet errors to cancel out—resulting in a small difference between adjusted and unadjusted accounting rates of return—even for a firm with high R&D costs. Thus, it is not obvious when complex and time-consuming adjustments for historical R&D costs are an essential step in a profitability analysis.

The study concludes that: "unadjusted ROA and adjusted (for R&D costs) ROA typically rank firm profitability in a similar order. Thus, unadjusted ROA is a reasonable proxy for firms' underlying economic profitability in many research applications, and complex adjustment procedures are often unnecessary."

Consequently, what analysis and/or adjustment for R&D expenses should we implement? Unfortunately, there is no simple computational adjustment. Instead, we begin our quantitative analysis by comparing common-sized R&D expenditures over time and across companies in the same industry (see Business Insight below). Differences in R&D outlays and marked departures from industry benchmarks call for further analysis. For our qualitative analysis, we look to the MD&A section of the 10-K, along with external sources of information, to gauge the effectiveness of the company's R&D efforts. Pharmaceutical companies typically disclose the drugs under development ("pipeline") as well as newly patented drugs. We can also evaluate new product introductions resulting from R&D expenditures. However, the disclosures for technology companies (and most other companies) are typically not as detailed. For those companies, we must seek information about new product introductions and other successes that management highlights in the MD&A.

BUSINESS INSIGHT   R&D at Pfizer and its Peers

Pfizer spent $8.1 billion in 2007 for R&D compared with its revenues of $48.4 billion, or about 16.7%. This reflects a high percent of revenues devoted to R&D for the pharmaceutical industry. Following is the R&D-expense-to-sales ratio for Pfizer and some of its competitors.

	2007	2006	2005
Bristol-Meyers Squibb	17.0%	17.3%	14.4%
Eli Lilly	18.7	19.9	20.7
Merck.	20.2	21.1	17.5
Pfizer	16.7	15.7	15.3

Restructuring Expenses and Incentives

Restructuring expenses are substantial in many income statements. Because of their magnitude, GAAP requires enhanced disclosure, either as a separate line item in the income statement or as a footnote. Restructuring costs typically include three components:

1. Employee severance or relocation costs
2. Asset write-downs
3. Other restructuring costs

The first part, **employee severance or relocation costs**, represents accrued (estimated) costs to terminate or relocate employees as part of a restructuring program. To accrue those expenses, the company must:

■ Estimate total costs of terminating or relocating selected employees; these costs might include severance pay (typically a number of weeks of pay based on the employee's tenure with the company), outplacement costs, and relocation or retraining costs for remaining employees.

■ Report *total* estimated costs as an expense (and a liability) in the period the restructuring program is announced. Subsequent payments to employees reduce the restructuring accrual (the liability).

The second part of restructuring costs is **asset write-downs**, also called *write-offs* or *charge-offs*. Restructuring activities usually involve closure or relocation of manufacturing or administrative facilities. This can require the write-down of assets whose fair value is less than book value. For example, restructurings can necessitate the write-down of long-term assets (such as plant assets or goodwill) and of inventories. Recall that asset cost is first recorded on the balance sheet and is subsequently transferred from the balance sheet to the income statement as expense when the asset is used. The write-down of an asset accelerates this process for a portion, or all, of the asset cost. Write-downs have no cash flow effects unless the write-down has some potential tax consequences.

The third part of restructuring costs is typically labeled "Other" and includes costs of vacating duplicative facilities, fees to terminate contracts (such as lease agreements and service contracts), and other exit costs (such as legal and asset-appraisal fees). Companies estimate and accrue these costs and reduce the restructuring liability as those costs are paid in cash.

The financial statement effects of restructuring charges can be large and frequent. We must remember that management determines the

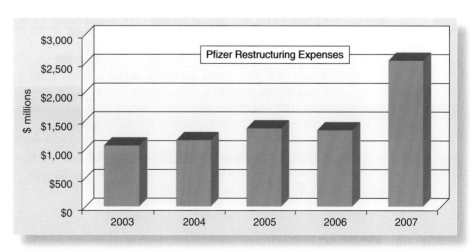

amount of restructuring costs and when to recognize them. As such, it is not uncommon for a company to time recognition of restructuring costs in a period when its income is already depressed. This behavior is referred to as a **big bath**.

BUSINESS INSIGHT | **Pfizer's Restructuring**

Pfizer explains its restructuring efforts as follows in its 2007 10-K:

> In the first quarter of 2005, we launched cost-reduction initiatives to increase efficiency and stream-line decision-making across the company . . . From the beginning of the cost-reduction initiatives in 2005, through December 31, 2007, the restructuring charges primarily relate to our plant network optimization efforts and the restructuring of our worldwide sales, marketing and research and development operations, while the implementation costs primarily relate to accelerated depreciation of certain assets, as well as system and process standardization and the expansion of shared services. The components of restructuring charges associated with our cost-reduction initiatives follow:

(Millions of Dollars)	Costs Incurred 2007	Costs Incurred 2006	Costs Incurred 2005	Total	Activity through Dec. 31, 2007	Acrual as of Dec. 31, 2007
Employee termination costs....	$2,034	$809	$303	$3,146	$1,957	$1,189
Asset impairments	260	368	122	750	750	—
Other.....................	229	119	13	361	261	100
Total	$2,523	$1,296	$438	$4,257	$2,968	$1,289

Financial statement effects of Pfizer's accounting for restructuring costs are illustrated in the following template ($ millions).

RSE   4,257
  RSL   3,507
  AD   750
      RSE
4,257 |
      RSL
     | 3,507
      AD
     | 750
RSL 2,218
  Cash   2,218
      RSL
2,218 |
      Cash
     | 2,218

Transaction	Balance Sheet					Income Statement		
	Cash Asset	+ Noncash Assets	= Liabil-ities	+ Contrib. Capital	+ Earned Capital	Rev-enues	− Expen-ses	= Net Income
2005-2007: Record restructuring expense and liability		−750 Accumulated Depreciation	+3,507 = Restructuring Liability		−4,257 Retained Earnings		+4,257 − Restructuring Expense	= −4,257
2005-2007: Paid $2,218 cash toward liability	−2,218 Cash		−2,218 = Restructuring Liability				−	=

The template reflects three years' restructuring transactions. From 2005 to 2007, Pfizer estimated total restructuring costs of $4,257 million and discloses the three usual types of restructuring costs of employee termination, asset impairment, and other. Asset impairments ($750 million) do not involve cash. Pfizer shifts the asset cost from the balance sheet to the income statement (by increasing the assets' accumulated depreciation by $750 million). Employee termination and other costs will eventually be settled in cash and so Pfizer accrues $3,507 million on its balance sheet as a restructuring liability for those estimated costs (employee termination costs of $3,146 million plus other costs of $361 million). Over the three years, Pfizer pays $2,218 to settle the restructuring liability ($1,957 million + $261 million). GAAP requires disclosure of the initial liability, along with subsequent reductions or reversals of amounts not ultimately used. Pfizer includes the remaining $1,289 million in *Other current liabilities* ($1.1 billion) and *Other noncurrent liabilities* ($189 million) on its 2007 balance sheet.

The FASB has tightened rules relating to restructuring costs in an effort to mitigate abuses. For example, a company is required to have a formal restructuring plan that is approved by its board of directors before any restructuring charges are accrued. Also, a company must identify the relevant employees and notify them of its plan. In each subsequent year, the company must disclose in its footnotes the original amount of the liability (accrual), how much of that liability is settled in the current period (such as employee payments), how much of the original liability has been reversed because of original cost overestimation, any new accruals for unforeseen costs, and the current balance of the liability. This creates more transparent financial statements, which presumably deters earnings management.

RESEARCH INSIGHT   Restructuring Costs and Managerial Incentives

Research has investigated the circumstances and effects of restructuring costs. Some research finds that stock prices increase when a company announces a restructuring as if the market appreciates the company's candor. Research also finds that many companies that reduce income through restructuring costs later reverse a portion of those costs, resulting in a substantial income boost for the period of reversal. These reversals often occur when the company would have otherwise reported an earnings decline. Whether or not the market responds favorably to trimming the fat or simply disregards restructuring costs as transitory and, thus, as uninformative, managers have incentives to classify such income-decreasing items as "nonoperating" on the income statement. These incentives often derive from contracts such as debt covenants and managerial bonus plans.

Restructuring costs are typically large and, as such, greatly affect reported profits. Our analysis must consider whether these costs are properly chargeable to the accounting period in which they are recognized. Following are some guidelines relating to the components of restructuring costs:

1. **Employee severance or relocation costs *and* Other costs** GAAP permits recognition of costs relating to employee separation or relocation that are *incremental* and that do not benefit future periods. Similarly, other accrued costs must be related to the restructuring and not to expenses that would otherwise have been incurred in the future. Thus, accrual of these costs is treated like other liability accruals. We must, however, be aware of over- or understated costs and their effect on current and future profitability. GAAP requires a reconciliation of this restructuring accrual in future years (see Business Insight on Pfizer's restructuring). A reconciliation reveals overstatements or understatements: overstatements are followed by a reversal of the restructuring liability, and understatements are followed by further accruals. Should a company develop a reputation for recurring reversals or understatements, its management loses credibility.

2. **Asset write-downs** Asset write-downs accelerate (or catch up) the depreciation process to reflect asset impairment. Impairment implies the loss of cash-generating capability and, likely, occurs over several years. Thus, prior periods' profits are arguably not as high as reported, and the current period's profit is not as low. This measurement error is difficult to estimate and, thus, many analysts do not adjust balance sheets and income statements for write-downs. At a minimum, however, we must recognize the qualitative implications of restructuring costs for the profitability of recent prior periods and the current period.

MANAGERIAL DECISION   You Are the Financial Analyst

You are analyzing the 10-K of a company that reports a large restructuring expense, involving employee severance and asset write-downs. How do you interpret and treat this cost in your analysis of the company's current and future profitability? [Answer, p. 5-31]

MID-MODULE REVIEW 1

Merck & Co., Inc., reports the following income statements for 2005 through 2007.

($ in millions)	2007	2006	2005
Sales.	$24,197.7	$22,636.0	$22,011.9
Costs, expenses and other			
Materials and production	6,140.7	6,001.1	5,149.6
Marketing and administrative	7,556.7	8,165.4	7,155.5
Research and development	4,882.8	4,782.9	3,848.0
Restructuring costs.	327.1	142.3	322.2
Equity income from affiliates.	(2,976.5)	(2,294.4)	(1,717.1)
U.S. Vioxx Settlement Agreement charge	4,850.0	—	—
Other (income) expense, net.	46.2	(382.7)	(110.2)
	20,827.0	16,414.6	14,648.0
Income before taxes.	3,370.7	6,221.4	7,363.9
Taxes on income	95.3	1,787.6	2,732.6
Net income.	$ 3,275.4	$ 4,433.8	$ 4,631.3

Required

1. Merck's revenue recognition policy, as outlined in footnotes to its 10-K, includes the following: "Revenues from sales of products are recognized when title and risk of loss passes to the customer." Evaluate Merck's revenue recognition policy.
2. Merck's research and development (R&D) efforts often require specialized equipment and facilities that cannot be used for any other purpose. How does Merck account for costs related to this specialized equipment and facilities? Would Merck account for these costs differently if they had alternate uses? Explain.
3. Merck reports restructuring expense each year. What are the general categories of restructuring expenses? How do accrual accounting and disclosure requirements prevent companies from intentionally overstating restructuring expenses in one year (referred to as taking a "big bath") and reversing the unused expenses in a future year?

Solution

1. Revenues are only recognized when the earning process is complete. Merck delivers its product before the customer is obligated to make payment. Passage of title typically constitutes delivery. Merck's policy appears to be reasonable given its product and GAAP requirements.
2. All R&D related equipment and/or facilities that have no alternative use must be expensed under GAAP. Assets that have other uses are capitalized and depreciated like other plant assets. R&D costs are aggregated into one line item (research and development expense) on Merck's income statement. Other costs are reported under materials and production and/or marketing and administrative expenses.
3. Restructuring expenses generally fall into three categories: severance costs, asset write-offs, and other costs. Restructuring programs must be approved by the board of directors before they are recognized in financial statements. Further, companies are required to disclose the initial liability accrual together with the portion that was subsequently utilized or reversed, if any. Because the restructuring accrual is an estimate, overestimates and subsequent reversals are possible. Should the company develop a reputation for recurring reversals, it will lose credibility with analysts and other stakeholders.

Income Tax Expenses and Allowances

LO3 Explain and analyze accounting for income taxes.

Companies prepare financial statements for shareholders using GAAP. When these companies file their income tax returns, they prepare financial statements using the *Internal Revenue Code (IRC)*. These two different sets of accounting rules recognize revenues and expenses differently in many cases and, as a result, can yield markedly different levels of income. In general, companies desire to report lower income to taxing authorities than they do to their shareholders so that they can reduce their tax liability and increase after-tax cash flow. This practice is acceptable so long as the financial statements are prepared in conformity with GAAP and tax returns are filed in accordance with the IRC.

As an example, consider the depreciation of long-term assets. For shareholder reports, companies typically depreciate long-term assets using straight-line depreciation (meaning the same amount of depreciation expense is reported each year over the useful life of the asset). However, for reports sent to tax authorities, companies use an *accelerated* method of depreciation (meaning more depreciation is taken in the early years of the asset's life and less depreciation in later years). When a company depreciates assets at an accelerated rate for tax purposes, the depreciation deduction for tax purposes is higher and taxable income is lower in the early years of the assets' lives. As a result, tax payments are reduced and after-tax cash flow is increased. That excess cash can then be reinvested in the business to increase its returns to shareholders.

To illustrate, assume that Pfizer purchases an asset with a five-year life. It depreciates that asset using the straight-line method (equal expense per year) when reporting to shareholders and depreciates the asset at a faster rate (accelerated depreciation) for tax purposes. Depreciation expense per year under these two methods is depicted in Exhibit 5.3.

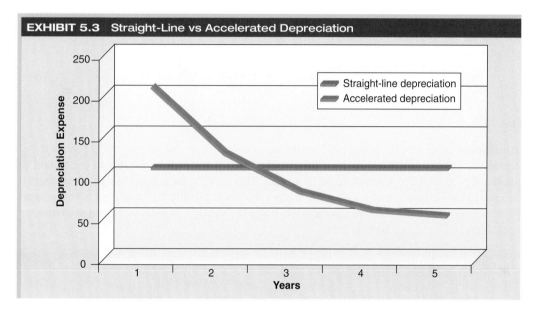

EXHIBIT 5.3   Straight-Line vs Accelerated Depreciation

During the first 2.5 years in this example, depreciation is higher in the company's tax returns than it is in its report to shareholders. In the last 2.5 years, this is reversed, with lower depreciation expense for tax purposes. Taxable income and tax payments are, therefore, higher during the last 2.5 years. The same total amount of depreciation is recognized under both methods over the five-year life of the asset. Only the timing of the recognition of the expense differs.[5]

We use this timing concept to illustrate the accounting for a **deferred tax liability**. Assume that a company purchases a depreciable asset with a cost of $100 and a two-year useful life. For financial reporting purposes (for GAAP-based reports for shareholders), it depreciates the asset using the straight-line method, which yields depreciation expense of $50 per year. For tax reporting (when filing income tax returns), it depreciates the asset on an accelerated basis, which yields depreciation deduction of $75 in the first year and $25 in the second year (the same total amount of depreciation is reported under the two depreciation methods; only the amount of depreciation reported per year differs). Assume that this company reports income before depreciation and taxes of $200 and that its tax rate is 40%. Its income statements, for both financial reporting and tax reporting, for the asset's first year are in Exhibit 5.4A.

---

[5] The Modified Accelerated Cost Recovery System (MACRS) is the current method of accelerated asset depreciation required by the United States income tax code. Under MACRS, all assets are divided into classes that dictate the number of years over which an asset's cost is "recovered" and the percentage of the asset cost that can be depreciated per year is fixed by regulation. For a five-year asset, such as in our example, the depreciation percentages per year are 20%, 32%, 19.2%, 11.52%, 11.52%, and 5.76%. This assumes that assets are acquired in the middle of the year, hence a half-year depreciation in Year 1 and a half-year depreciation in Year 6. The point at which straight-line depreciation exceeds MACRS depreciation is after about 2.5 years as assumed in the example.

EXHIBIT 5.4A	Year 1 Income Statements: Financial Reporting vs Tax Reporting	
Year 1	**Financial Reporting**	**Tax Reporting**
Income before depreciation	$200	$200
Depreciation	50	75
Income before tax	150	125
Income tax (40%)	60 [expense]	50 [cash paid]
Net income	$ 90	$ 75

This company records income tax expense and a related deferred tax liability for the first year as re-flected in the following financial statement effects template:

Year 1	Balance Sheet						Income Statement		
Transaction	Cash Asset	+	Noncash Assets	=	Liabil-ities	+	Contrib. Capital	+	Earned Capital
Record tax expense: expense exceeds cash because of deferral of tax	−50 Cash				+10 Deferred Tax Liability				−60 Retained Earnings

Income Statement: Rev-enues − Expen-ses = Net Income

Record tax expense: +60 Tax Expense, −60 Net Income

TE 60
DTL 10
Cash 50

TE
60 |
DTL
| 10
Cash
| 50

The reduction in cash reflects the payment of taxes owed to the taxing authority. The increase in deferred tax liability represents an estimate of additional tax that will be payable in the second year (which is the tax liability deferred in the first year). This liability for a future tax payment arises be-cause second-year depreciation expense for tax purposes will be only $25, resulting in taxes payable of $70, which is $10 more than the income tax expense the company reports in its income statement to shareholders in Year 2 (see Exhibit 5.4B).

EXHIBIT 5.4B	Year 2 Income Statements: Financial Reporting vs Tax Reporting	
Year 2	**Financial Reporting**	**Tax Reporting**
Income before depreciation	$200	$200
Depreciation	50	25
Income before tax	150	175
Income tax (40%)	60 [expense]	70 [cash paid]
Net income	$ 90	$105

At the end of Year 1, the company knows that this additional tax must be paid in Year 2 because the financial reporting and tax reporting depreciation schedules are set when the asset is placed in service. Given these known amounts, the company accrues the deferred tax liability in Year 1 in the same manner as it would accrue any estimated future liability, say for wages payable, by recognizing a liability and the related expense.

At the end of Year 2, the additional income tax is paid and the company's deferred tax liability is now satisfied. Financial statement effects related to the tax payment and expense in Year 2 are reflected in the following template:

Year 2	Balance Sheet						Income Statement		
Transaction	Cash Asset	+	Noncash Assets	=	Liabil-ities	+	Contrib. Capital	+	Earned Capital
Record tax expense: cash exceeds expense because deferred taxes are reversed	−70 Cash				−10 Deferred Tax Liability				−60 Retained Earnings

Income Statement: Rev-enues − Expen-ses = Net Income

Record tax expense: +60 Tax Expense, −60 Net Income

TE 60
DTL 10
Cash 70

TE
60 |
DTL
10 |
Cash
| 70

The income tax expense for financial reporting purposes is $60 each year. However, the cash payment for taxes is $70 in Year 2; the $10 excess reduces the deferred tax liability accrued in Year 1.

This example demonstrates how accelerated depreciation for tax reporting and straight-line for financial reporting creates deferred tax liabilities. Other differences between tax reporting and financial reporting create other types of deferred tax accounts. **Deferred tax assets** arise when the tax payment is *greater* than the tax expense for financial reporting purposes (opposite of the illustration above).

Restructuring accruals are one source of deferred tax assets. In the year in which a company approves a reorganization plan, it will accrue a restructuring liability for estimated employee severance payments and other costs and it will write down assets to their market values (this reduces the net book value of those assets on the balance sheet). However, tax authorities do not recognize these accrual accounting transactions until they are realized. In particular, for tax purposes, restructuring costs are not deductible until paid in the future, and asset write-downs are not deductible until the loss is realized when the asset is sold. As a result, the restructuring accrual is not a liability for tax reporting until the company makes the payment, and the write-down of assets is not a deductible expense for tax purposes until the assets are sold. Both of these differences (the liability and the assets) give rise to a deferred tax asset. The deferred tax asset cost will be transferred to the income statement in the future as an expense when the company pays the restructuring costs and sells the impaired assets for a loss.

Another common deferred tax asset relates to **tax loss carryforwards**. Specifically, when a company reports a loss for tax purposes, it can carry back that loss for up to two years to recoup previous taxes paid. Any unused losses can be carried forward for up to twenty years to reduce future taxes. This creates a benefit (an "asset") for tax reporting for which there is no corresponding financial reporting asset. Thus, the company records a deferred tax asset but only if the company is "more likely than not" to be able to recoup past taxes. This depends on the company's assessment of whether it will have sufficient profits in the future.

Companies are required to establish a *deferred tax asset valuation allowance* for deferred tax assets when the future realization of their benefits is uncertain. The effect on financial statements of such an allowance is to reduce reported assets, increase tax expense, and reduce equity (this is similar to accounting for the write-down of any asset). These effects are reversed if the allowance is reversed in the future when, and if, realization of such tax benefits becomes more likely. To illustrate, Pfizer reported an allowance of $194 million in 2006, of which $36 million was reversed in 2007 when it determined that the realization of the tax benefits was more certain. Increases and decreases in the deferred tax valuation allowance have a dollar-for-dollar effect on net income. Thus, Pfizer's net income increased by $36 million in 2007 from the reversal in its allowance account.

Disclosures Relating to Income Taxes

Pfizer's tax footnote to its income statement is shown in Exhibit 5.5. Pfizer's $1,023 million tax expense reported in its income statement (called the provision) consists of the following two components:

1. *Current tax expense.* Current tax expense is determined from the company's tax returns; it is the amount payable (in cash) to tax authorities (some of these taxes have been paid during the year as the company makes installments). Pfizer labels this "Taxes currently payable" and reports separate amounts for taxes to federal, state, local, and international tax authorities.

2. *Deferred tax expense.* Deferred tax expense is the effect on tax expense from changes in deferred tax liabilities and deferred tax assets. Pfizer labels this "Deferred income taxes" and reports separate amounts for deferrals related to U.S. and international tax rules.

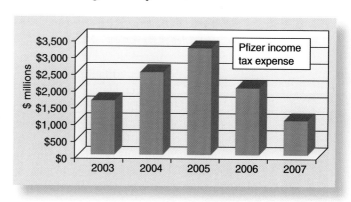

In financial statement footnotes, companies must disclose the components of deferred tax liabilities and assets. Pfizer's deferred tax footnote to its balance sheet (shown in Exhibit 5.6) reports total deferred tax assets of $8,842 million and total deferred tax liabilities of $12,463 million. On the balance

EXHIBIT 5.5   Income Tax Expense Footnote for Pfizer

Year Ended Dec. 31 (Millions of dollars)	2007	2006
United States		
Taxes currently payable		
Federal	$1,393	$1,399
State and local	243	205
Deferred income taxes	(1,986)	(1,371)
Total U.S. tax (benefit) provision	(350)	233
International		
Taxes currently payable	2,175	1,913
Deferred income taxes	(802)	(154)
Total international tax provision	1,373	1,759
Total provision for taxes on income	$1,023	$1,992

sheet companies report deferred tax assets and liabilities as either current or noncurrent based on when the benefit (payment) is expected to be received (made). Companies are permitted to net some deferred tax assets and liabilities, and Pfizer reports a net deferred tax liability of $3,621 million on its 2007 balance sheet. Many of Pfizer's deferred tax assets relate to accrued liabilities or asset write-downs arising from expenses included in financial reporting income, but not yet recognized for tax reporting (such as employee benefits and restructuring accruals). Pfizer also has a deferred tax asset from a net operating loss carryforward and has recorded a small valuation allowance. These various items all yield future reductions of the company's tax payments and are, therefore, classified as assets.

EXHIBIT 5.6   Deferred Taxes Footnote for Pfizer

(Millions of Dollars)	2007 Deferred Tax Assets	(Liabilities)	2006 Deferred Tax Assets	(Liabilities)
Prepaid (deferred) items	$1,315	$ (431)	$1,164	$ (312)
Intangibles	897	(6,737)	841	(7,704)
Property, plant and equipment	300	(957)	104	(1,105)
Employee benefits	2,552	(740)	3,141	(804)
Restructurings and other charges	717	(11)	573	(19)
Net operating loss/credit carryforwards	1,842	—	1,061	—
Unremitted earnings	—	(3,550)	—	(3,567)
State and local tax adjustments	529	—	—	—
All other	848	(37)	912	(392)
Subtotal	9,000	(12,463)	7,796	(13,903)
Valuation allowance	(158)	—	(194)	—
Total deferred taxes	$8,842	$(12,463)	$7,602	$(13,903)
Net deferred tax liability		$ (3,621)		$ (6,301)

Pfizer's deferred tax liabilities relate to a varied assortment of items. As we illustrate above, Pfizer uses accelerated depreciation in its tax return, which results in a deferred tax liability. The deferred tax liability relating to employee benefits arises from pension contributions and other cash payments that are deductible for tax purposes but that Pfizer has not yet accrued for financial reporting purposes (thus there is no GAAP pension liability). The deferred tax liability relating to unremitted earnings results from investments that Pfizer has in affiliated companies. Pfizer reports income related to those investments, but the income is not taxable until the companies actually pay dividends to Pfizer. Thus, reported profit is greater than taxable income and a deferred tax liability is recognized (we discuss accounting for intercompany investments in Module 7). Pfizer will pay taxes on the subsidiaries' profits when the subsidiaries pay dividends in the future and then the deferred tax liability will be reduced.

Pfizer's 2007 income before tax is $9,278 million. Its tax expense of $1,023 million represents an effective tax rate of 11.0%. The *effective tax rate* is defined as tax expense divided by pretax income ($1,023 million/$9,278 million $= 11.0\%$).[6] By comparison, the federal *statutory tax rate* for corporations (the rate prescribed in tax regulations) is 35%. Companies must provide a schedule that reconciles the effective tax rate (11.0% for Pfizer) with the Federal statutory rate of 35%. Following is the schedule that Pfizer reports in its 10-K.

Reconciliation of the U.S. statutory income tax rate to our effective tax rate for continuing operations before the cumulative effect of a change in accounting principles follows:

Year Ended Dec. 31	2007	2006	2005
U.S. statutory income tax rate	35.0%	35.0%	35.0%
Earnings taxed at other than U.S. statutory rate	(21.6)	(15.7)	(20.6)
Resolution of certain tax positions	—	(3.4)	(5.4)
Tax legislation impact	—	(1.7)	—
U.S. research tax credit and manufacturing deduction	(1.5)	(0.5)	(0.8)
Repatriation of foreign earnings	—	(1.0)	15.4
Acquired IPR&D	1.1	2.2	5.4
All other—net	(2.0)	0.4	0.4
Effective tax rate for income from continuing operations before cumulative effect of a change in accounting principles	11.0%	15.3%	29.4%

In addition to federal taxes (paid to the IRS), companies also pay taxes to state, local, and foreign jurisdictions where they operate. These tax rates are typically lower than the statutory rate of 35%. In 2007, for example, these taxes reduced Pfizer's effective tax rate by 21.6%. In addition, Pfizer received tax credits for research (reducing the effective tax rate by another 1.5%). Two other miscellaneous differences amounted to a net reduction of 0.9%.

In sum, Pfizer's effective tax rate for 2007 is 11.0%, which is 24 percentage points below the 35% statutory rate. In 2006, however, the effective tax rate was 15.3% and in 2005 it was 29.4% as a result of tax legislation that encouraged the repatriation of foreign profits at lower tax rates (companies paid tax at lower rates in 2005 to avoid paying tax at predicted higher rates on repatriated profits in future years). Fluctuations, such as these, in the effective tax rate are not uncommon and highlight the difference between income reported under GAAP and that computed using multiple tax codes under which companies operate. Appendix 5A explains accounting for deferred taxes in more detail.

Analysis of Income Tax Disclosures

Analysis of deferred taxes can yield useful insights. Some revenue accruals (such as accounts receivable for longer-term contracts) increase deferred tax liabilities as GAAP income exceeds tax income (similar to the effect of using straight-line depreciation for financial reporting purposes and accelerated depreciation for tax returns).

An increase in deferred tax liabilities indicates that a company is reporting higher GAAP income relative to taxable income and can indicate the company is managing earnings upwards. The difference between reported corporate profits and taxable income increased substantially in the late 1990s, just prior to huge asset write-offs. *CFO Magazine* (November 2002) implied that such differences are important for analysis and should be monitored:

Fueling the sense that something [was] amiss [was] the growing gap between the two sets of numbers. In 1992, there was no significant difference between pretax book income and taxable net income . . . By 1996, according to IRS data, a $92.5 billion gap had appeared. By 1998 [prior to the market decline], the gap was $159 billion—a fourth of the total taxable income reported . . . If people had seen numbers showing very significant differences between book numbers for trading and tax numbers, they would have wondered if those [income] numbers were completely real.

---

[6] This is the effective tax rate for *all* of Pfizer's income. In the previous module we compute the tax rate on operating profit by first deducting the taxes related to nonoperating income (or adding back the tax shield related to nonoperating expenses). The effective tax rate on total income, is a weighted average of the two (operating and nonoperating).

Although an increase in deferred tax liabilities can legitimately result, for example, from an increase in depreciable assets and the use of accelerated depreciation for tax purposes, we must be aware of the possibility that such an increase is the result of improper revenue recognition in that the company might not be reporting those revenues to tax authorities.

Adequacy of Deferred Tax Asset Valuation

Analysis of the deferred tax asset valuation account provides us with additional insight. This analysis involves (1) assessing the adequacy of the valuation allowance and (2) determining how and why the valuation account changed during the period and how that change affects net income.

When a company reports a deferred tax asset, the company implies that it will, more likely than not, receive a future tax benefit equal to the deferred tax asset. If the company is uncertain about the future tax benefit, it records an allowance to reduce the asset. How can we gauge the adequacy of a valuation allowance account? We might assess the reasons for the valuation account (typically reported in the tax footnote). We might examine other companies in the industry for similar allowances. We might also review the MD&A for any doubt on company prospects for future profitability.

We can quantify our analysis in at least three ways. First, we can examine the allowance as a percentage of the deferred tax assets (most valuation allowances relate to tax loss carryforwards). For Pfizer, this 2007 percentage is 8.6%; see below. We also want to gather data from other pharmaceutical companies and compare the sizes of their allowance accounts relative to their related deferred tax assets. The important point is that we must be comfortable with the size of the valuation account and remember that management has control over the adequacy and reporting of the allowance account (with audit assurances).

Pfizer ($ millions)	2007	2006	2005
Deferred tax asset from net operating loss carryforward................	$1,842	$1,061	$403
Valuation allowance	$158	$194	$142
Valuation allowance as a percent of net operating loss carryforward	8.6%	18.3%	35.2%

Second, we can examine changes in the allowance account. During a year, circumstances change and the company might be more or less assured of receiving the tax benefit. In that case, the company might decrease or increase its allowance account. For Pfizer, its 2007 allowance markedly declined from prior years (from 35.2% in 2005 and 18.3% in 2006). What does such a decline denote? Perhaps Pfizer's overall economic environment has improved, rendering it more likely that it will be profitable for tax purposes. We want to determine why it reduced the allowance and assess the validity of its claims in light of industry and economy-wide factors.

Third, we can quantify how a change in the valuation allowance affects net income and its effective tax rate (see Exhibit 5.7). To see this, recall that changes in the valuation allowance affect tax expense in the same direction, dollar for dollar. This in turn, affects net income (in the opposite direction) again, dollar for dollar. For Pfizer, its 2007 valuation allowance decreased by $36 million ($194 million to $158 million), which decreased tax expense and increased net income by $36 million. This is not a large effect on income for Pfizer, or on its effective tax rate (11.03% after the valuation allowance change versus 11.41% before). However, changes in valuation allowances can have (and have had) marked effects on net income for numerous companies. (Further, reductions in the deferred tax asset valuation account can occur as a result of unused loss carryforwards; in that

EXHIBIT 5.7 Effect of Deferred Tax Asset Valuation Account on Tax Expense			
Pfizer ($ millions)	2007	2006	2005
Change in valuation allowance.............................	$ (36)	$ 52	$ (35)
Impact of valuation allowance change on net income............	$ 36	$ (52)	$ 35
Income before tax	$ 9,278	$13,028	$10,800
Tax expense...	$ 1,023	$ 1,992	$ 3,178
Effective tax rate (Tax expense/Income before tax)..............	11.0%	15.3%	29.4%
Tax expense before change in valuation account	$ 1,059	$ 1,940	$3,213
Effective tax rate before change in valuation account...........	11.4%	14.9%	29.8%

case, a company reduces the deferred tax asset and the related valuation account, which is similar in concept to the write-off of an account receivable discussed in Module 6.) For our analysis, we must remember, however, that a company can increase current period income by deliberately decreasing the valuation allowance. Knowing that such decreases can boost net income, companies might deliberately create too large a valuation allowance in one or more prior years and use it as a *cookie jar reserve* to boost income in future periods. We want to assess the details of the valuation account and changes therein from company footnotes and from the MD&A.

MID-MODULE REVIEW 2

Refer to the Merck & Co., Inc., 2007 income statement in the Mid-Module Review 1. Merck provides the following additional information in footnotes to its 10-K.

Taxes on income from continuing operations consisted of:

Years Ended December 31 ($ in millions)	2007	2006	2005
Current provision			
Federal	$ 988.1	$1,618.4	$1,688.1
Foreign	687.0	458.3	739.6
State	202.2	241.1	295.9
	1,877.3	2,317.8	2,723.6
Deferred provision			
Federal	(1,671.5)	(374.1)	97.0
Foreign	157.2	(130.3)	(134.0)
State	(267.7)	(25.8)	46.0
	(1,782.0)	(530.2)	9.0
	$ 95.3	$1,787.6	$2,732.6

Required
1. What is the total income tax expense that Merck reports in its 2007 income statement?
2. What amount of its total tax expense did (or will) Merck pay in cash (that is, what amount is currently payable)?
3. Explain how Merck calculates its income tax expense.

Solution
1. Total income tax expense is $95.3 million.
2. Of the $95.3 million total, $1,877.3 million is currently payable or has already been paid during 2007.
3. Income tax expense is the sum of current taxes (that is, currently payable as determined from the company's tax returns) plus the change in deferred tax assets and liabilities. It is a calculated figure, not a percentage that is applied to pretax income. For 2007, reported tax expense was *reduced* by the increase in deferred tax liabilities of $1,782 million.

Foreign Currency Translation Effects

Many companies conduct international operations and transact business in currencies other than $US. It is common for companies to purchase assets in foreign currencies, borrow money in foreign currencies, and transact business with their customers in foreign currencies. Increasingly many companies have subsidiaries whose balance sheets and income statements are prepared in foreign currencies.

Financial statements prepared according to U.S. GAAP must be reported in $US. This means that the financial statements of any foreign subsidiaries must be translated into $US before consolidation with the U.S. parent company. This translation process can markedly alter both the balance sheet and income statement. We discuss income statement effects of foreign currency translation in this module; we discuss the effects on stockholders' equity in Module 9.

L04 Explain how foreign currency fluctuations affect the income statement.

Effects of Foreign Currency Transactions on Income

A change in the strength of the $US vis-à-vis foreign currencies has a direct effect on the $US equivalent for revenues, expenses, and income of the foreign subsidiary because revenues and expenses are translated at the average exchange rate for the period. Exhibit 5.8 shows those financial effects.

EXHIBIT 5.8	**Income Statement Effects from Foreign Currency Movements**			
	Revenues	**– Expenses**	**=**	**Profit**
$US Weakens.........	Increase	Increase		Increase
$US Strengthens	Decrease	Decrease		Decrease

Specifically, when the foreign currency strengthens (implying $US weakens), the subsidiary's revenues and expenses translate into more $US and, thus, reported income is higher than if the currencies had not fluctuated. On the other hand, when the $US strengthens, the subsidiary's revenues, expenses, and income decrease in $US terms. (The profit effect assumes that revenues exceed expenses; if expenses exceed revenues, a loss occurs, which increases if the $US weakens and decreases if the $US strengthens.)

Pfizer discusses how currency fluctuations affect its income statement in the following excerpt from footnotes to the company's 2007 10-K.

> 52.2% of our total 2007 revenues were derived from international operations, including 32.9% from the Europe/Canada region and 13.4% from the Japan/Asia region. These international-based revenues as well as our substantial international net assets expose our revenues and earnings to foreign currency exchange rate changes.

The $US weakened against many foreign currencies for several years preceding and including 2007. Thus, each unit of foreign currency purchased more $US. Therefore, revenues and expenses denominated in foreign currencies were translated to higher $US equivalents, yielding increased revenues and profits even when unit volumes remained unchanged. Pfizer also discloses that it attempts to dampen the effect that these fluctuations have on reported profit:

> Depending on the direction of change relative to the U.S. dollar, foreign currency values can increase or decrease the reported dollar value of our net assets and results of operations. In 2007, both revenues and net income were favorably impacted by foreign exchange, as foreign currency movements relative to the U.S. dollar increased our revenues and net income in many countries. While we cannot predict with certainty future changes in foreign exchange rates or the effect they will have on us, we attempt to mitigate their impact through operational means and by using various financial instruments.

The phrase "operational means" includes attempts to structure transactions in $US rather than a foreign currency. Foreign currency financial instruments are common and include forward and futures contracts, which lock in future currency values. We explain how these instruments (called derivatives) work in Appendix 7C. In sum, we must be cognizant of the effects of currency fluctuations on reported revenues, expenses, and profits for companies with substantial foreign-currency transactions.

OPERATING COMPONENTS BELOW-THE-LINE

Pfizer's income statement includes a subtotal labeled "income from continuing operations." Historically, this presentation highlighted the nonrecurring (*transitory*) portions of the income statement so that they could be eliminated to facilitate the projection of future profitability. The word "continuing" was meant to imply that income was purged of one-time items, as these were presented "below-the-line," that is, below income from continuing operations. Two categories of items are presented below-the-line:[7]

1. **Discontinued operations**   Net income (loss) from business segments that have been or will be sold, and any gains (losses) on net assets related to those segments sold in the current period.
2. **Extraordinary items**   Gains or losses from events that are both *unusual* and *infrequent*.

Discontinued operations are generally viewed as nonoperating, and we discuss their accounting treatment in Module 7. Explanation of the accounting for extraordinary items follows.

Extraordinary Items

Extraordinary items refer to events that are both unusual *and* infrequent. Their effects are reported following income from continuing operations. Management determines whether an event is unusual and infrequent (with auditor approval) for financial reporting purposes. Further, management often has incentives to classify unfavorable items as extraordinary because they will be reported separately, after income from continuing operations (*below-the-line*). These incentives derive from managers' beliefs that investors tend to focus more on items included in income from continuing operations and less on nonrecurring items that are not included in continuing operations.

GAAP provides the following guidance in determining whether or not an item is extraordinary:

- *Unusual nature.* The underlying event or transaction must possess a high degree of abnormality and be clearly unrelated to, or only incidentally related to, the ordinary activities of the entity.

- *Infrequency of occurrence.* The underlying event or transaction must be of a type that would not reasonably be expected to recur in the foreseeable future.

The following items are generally **not** reported as extraordinary items:

- Gains and losses on retirement of debt[8]
- Write-down or write-off of operating or nonoperating assets
- Foreign currency gains and losses
- Gains and losses from disposal of specific assets or business segment
- Effects of a strike
- Accrual adjustments related to long-term contracts
- Costs of a takeover defense

Extraordinary items are reported separately (net of tax) and below income from continuing operations on the income statement.

---

[7] Prior accounting standards included a third category, **changes in accounting principles.** This category included voluntary and mandated changes in accounting policies utilized by a company, such as a change in the depreciation method. Under current GAAP, changes in accounting principles are no longer reported below-the-line. Instead, they are applied retrospectively (unless it is impractical to do so, in which case they are applied at the earliest practical date). No cumulative effect adjustment is made to income as was the case in prior standards. Instead, changes in depreciation methods are now accounted for as changes in estimates, which are applied prospectively.

[8] Until recently, gains and losses on debt retirement were treated as extraordinary items. To explain, understand that debt is accounted for at historical cost, just like the accounting for equipment. The *market price* of debt, however, is determined by fluctuations in interest rates. As a result, if a company retires (pays off) its debt before maturity, the cash paid to settle the debt often differs from the debt amount reported on the balance sheet, resulting in gains and losses on retirement. These gains and losses were formerly treated as extraordinary. Following passage of SFAS 145, these gains and losses are no longer automatically treated as extraordinary, but instead must be unusual and infrequent to be designated as extraordinary.

IFRS INSIGHT   Extraordinary Items and IFRS

IFRS does not permit the reporting of income and expense items as "extraordinary." The IASB justified its position in IAS1 as follows: "The Board decided that items treated as extraordinary result from the normal business risks faced by an entity and do not warrant presentation in a separate component of the income statement. The nature or function of a transaction or other event, rather than its frequency, should determine its presentation within the income statement. Items currently classified as 'extraordinary' are only a subset of the items of income and expense that may warrant disclosure to assist users in predicting an entity's future performance" (IAS1, ¶BC63).

Earnings Per Share

LO5 Compute earnings per share and explain the effect of dilutive securities.

The income statement reports earnings per share (EPS) numbers. Most firms report two EPS numbers: basic and diluted. The difference between the two measures is shown in Exhibit 5.9.

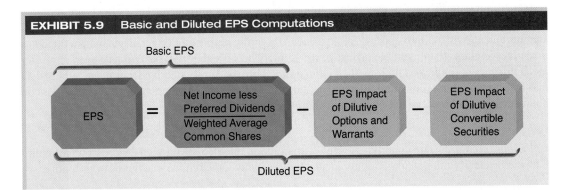

EXHIBIT 5.9   Basic and Diluted EPS Computations

Basic EPS is computed as: (Net income − Dividends on preferred stock)/Weighted average number of common shares outstanding during the year. Subtracting preferred stock dividends yields the income available for dividend payments to common shareholders. Computation of **diluted EPS** reflects the additional shares that would be issued if all stock options, warrants, and convertible securities had been converted into common shares at the beginning of the year or when issued, if issued during the year. Diluted EPS never exceeds basic EPS.

Pfizer reports Basic EPS of $1.18 in 2007 and Diluted EPS of $1.17. Given the near identical results for basic and diluted EPS, we know that Pfizer has few dilutive securities. Autodesk, Inc., however, reports a dilution of 5% in its EPS that is related to outstanding employee stock options as evident from its following disclosure:

Fiscal year ended January 31 (in millions, except per share)	2008	2007	2006
Net income	$356.2	$289.7	$333.6
Basic net inome per share	$ 1.55	$ 1.26	$ 1.46
Diluted net income per share	$ 1.47	$ 1.19	$ 1.35

While the numerator (Net income) is unaffected by the potential exercise of its stock options, the denominator will increase as reported in the following table that Autodesk reports in footnotes to its 10-K:

Fiscal year ended January 31 (in millions, except per share)	2008	2007	2006
Numerator:			
Numerator for basic and diluted net income per share—net income	$356.2	$289.7	$333.6
Denominator:			
Denominator for basic net income per share—weighted average shares . . .	230.3	230.7	229.0
Effect of dilutive common stock options	11.7	12.5	18.5
Denominator for dilutive net income per share	242.0	243.2	247.5

The diluted earnings per share calculation presumes a worst case scenario that all employees holding options exercise their right to purchase additional shares as of the beginning of the year. In that event, Autodesk will issue an additional 11.7 million shares, thus increasing the denominator by that amount and reducing earnings per share from $1.55 to $1.47.[9]

Employee stock options typically explain most of the difference between basic and diluted earnings per share. Other dilutive securities include convertible preferred stock and convertible debt. Each of these convertible securities carries an option that allows the holder of the security to exchange that security for a specified number of common shares under certain circumstances. Pfizer has convertible preferred stock outstanding, and provides the following description of its conversion feature in its footnotes:

Preferred Stock   The Series A convertible perpetual preferred stock is held by an Employee Stock Ownership Plan ("Preferred ESOP") Trust and provides dividends at the rate of 6.25%, which are accumulated and paid quarterly. The per-share stated value is $40,300 and the preferred stock ranks senior to our common stock as to dividends and liquidation rights. Each share is convertible, at the holder's option, into 2,574.87 shares of our common stock with equal voting rights. The conversion option is indexed to our common stock and requires share settlement, and therefore, is reported at the fair value at the date of issuance. We may redeem the preferred stock at any time or upon termination of the Preferred ESOP, at our option, in cash, in shares of common stock or a combination of both at a price of $40,300 per share.

Analysts and investors often use EPS figures to compare operating results for companies of different sizes under the assumption that the number of shares outstanding is proportional to the income level (that is, a company twice the size of another will report double the income and will have double the common shares outstanding, leaving EPS approximately equal for the two companies). This assumption is erroneous. Management controls the number of common shares outstanding and there is no relation between firm size and number of shares outstanding. Different companies also have different philosophies regarding share issuance and repurchase. For example, consider that most companies report annual EPS of less than $5, while Berkshire Hathaway reported EPS of $8,548 for 2007! This is because Berkshire Hathaway has so few common shares outstanding, not necessarily because it has stellar profits.

RESEARCH INSIGHT   **"Pro Forma" Income**

Transitory items such as discontinued operations, restructuring charges, and extraordinary items make it difficult for investors to predict future income. The past decade has seen more companies reporting pro forma income, which excludes nonrecurring or noncash items that companies feel are unimportant for valuation purposes. Research, however, provides no evidence that pro forma income is a better predictor of future cash flows. More important, investors appear to be misled when firms report pro forma income. Research also finds that companies reporting pro forma income tend to be young companies concentrated in technology and business services. Too often, these companies have below-average sales and income, which might explain why they choose to report pro forma income.

---

[9] The effects of dilutive securities are only included if they are, in fact, dilutive. Securities that are *antidilutive* would actually increase EPS, and are, thus, excluded from the computation. An example of an antidilutive security is employee stock options whose exercise price is greater than the stock's current market price. These *underwater* (or out-of-the-money) options are antidilutive and are, therefore, excluded from the EPS computation. Autodesk, for example, excludes 6.8 million shares from its 2008 diluted EPS calculation, and provides the following explanation for this exclusion in its footnotes:

"computation of diluted net income per share does not include 6.8 million share for fiscal 2008, 8.3 million shares for fiscal 2007 and 0.2 million shares for fiscal 2006 of common stock underlying stock options whose exercise price was above the closing market price of Autodesk's common stock on the last day of the period. These shares were excluded in the computation of basic and diluted net income per share because they were anti-dilutive under the treasury stock method"

BUSINESS INSIGHT | **Pro Forma Income and Managerial Motives**

Income from continuing operations per GAAP, once a key measure of company performance, is often supplemented or even supplanted by pro forma income in company financial statements and press releases. **Pro forma income** begins with the GAAP income from continuing operations (that excludes discontinued operations and extraordinary items), and then excludes other one-time items (most notably, restructuring charges), and some additional items such as acquisition expenses (goodwill amortization and other acquisition costs), stock-option compensation expense, and research and development expenditures.

The purported motive for reporting pro forma income is to eliminate transitory (one-time) items to enhance year-to-year comparability. Although this might be justified on the basis that pro forma income has greater predictive ability, important information is lost in the process. One role for accounting is to report how effective management has been in its stewardship of invested capital. Asset write-downs, liability accruals, and other charges that are eliminated in calculating pro forma income often reflect outcomes of poor management decisions. Our analysis must not blindly eliminate information contained in nonrecurring items by focusing solely on pro forma income. Critics of pro forma income also argue that the items excluded by managers from GAAP income are inconsistent across companies and time. They contend that a major motive for pro forma income is to mislead stakeholders. Legendary investor Warren Buffet puts pro forma in context: "When companies or investment professionals use terms such as 'EBITDA' and 'pro forma,' they want you to unthinkingly accept concepts that are dangerously flawed." (Berkshire Hathaway, Annual Report)

MODULE-END REVIEW

Refer to the Merck & Co., Inc., 2007 income statement in the Mid-Module Review.

Required

1. Assume that during 2007 the $US weakened with respect to the currencies in which Merck conducts its business. How would that weakening affect Merck's income statement?
2. What is the difference between basic and diluted earnings per share?

Solution

1. Income statement accounts that are denominated in foreign currencies must be translated into $US before the financial statements are publicly disclosed. When the $US weakens, each foreign currency unit is worth more $US. Consequently, each account in Merck's income statement is larger because the dollar weakened. Because Merck reported *positive* earnings (a profit) for 2007, net income also would be larger.
2. Basic earnings per share is equal to net income (less preferred dividends) divided by the weighted average number of common shares outstanding during the period. Diluted EPS considers the effects of dilutive securities. In diluted EPS, the denominator increases by the additional shares that would have been issued assuming exercise of all options and conversion of all convertible securities. The numerator is also adjusted for any preferred dividends and/or interest that would not have been paid upon conversion.

APPENDIX 5A: Expanded Explanation of Deferred Taxes

The module provided an example of how different depreciation methods for tax and financial reporting create a deferred tax liability. That example showed that total depreciation over the life of the asset is the same under both tax and financial reporting, and that the only difference is the timing of the expense or tax deduction. Because depreciation differs each year, the amount at which the equipment is reported will differ as well for book and tax purposes (cost less accumulated depreciation is called *net book value* for financial reporting purposes and *tax basis* for tax purposes). These book vs tax differences are eliminated at the end of the asset's useful life.

To understand this concept more completely, we modify the example from the module to include a third year. Assume that the company purchases PPE assets at the start of Year 1 for $120. For financial reporting purposes, the company uses straight-line depreciation and records depreciation of $40 each year (with zero salvage). For tax purposes, assume that the company takes tax depreciation deductions of $60, $50, and $10. Exhibit 5A.1 reports the annual depreciation along with the asset's net book value and its tax basis, for each year end.

EXHIBIT 5A.1					
	Financial Reporting (Net Book Value)	Tax Reporting (Tax Basis)	Book vs Tax Difference	Deferred Tax Liability (Book vs Tax Difference × Tax Rate)	Deferred Tax Expense (Increase or Decrease in Deferred Tax Liability)
At purchase: PPE carrying value	$120	$120	$ 0	$ 0	
Year 1: Depreciation	(40)	(60)			
End of Year 1: PPE carrying value . . .	80	60	$20	$ 8	$ 8
			($80 − $60)	($20 × 40%)	($8 − $0)
Year 2: Depreciation	(40)	(50)			
End of Year 2: PPE carrying value . . .	40	10	$30	$12	$ 4
			($40 − $10)	($30 × 40%)	($12 − $8)
Year 3: Depreciation	(40)	(10)			
End of Year 3: PPE carrying value . . .	0	0	$ 0	$ 0	$(12)
			($0 − $0)		($0 − $12)

The third column in Exhibit 5A.1 shows the "book-tax" difference, which is the difference between GAAP net book value and the tax basis at the end of each year. The fourth column shows the deferred tax liability at the end of each period, computed as the book-tax differences times the tax rate. We see from the fourth column that when the financial reporting net book value is greater than the tax basis, the company has a deferred tax liability on its balance sheet (as in Years 1 and 2). Companies' footnotes provide information about deferred taxes. For example, Pfizer's footnote reports a deferred tax liability (net) of $657 for its property, plant and equipment, which indicates that tax basis for PPE is less than GAAP net book value, on average, for Pfizer's PPE.

Accounting standards require a company to first compute the taxes it owes (per its tax return), then to compute any changes in deferred tax liabilities and assets, and finally to compute tax expense reported in the income statement (as a residual amount). Thus, tax expense is not computed as pretax income multiplied by the company's tax rate as we might initially expect. Instead, tax expense is computed as follows:

Tax Expense = Taxes Paid − Increase (or + Decrease) in Deferred Tax Assets + Increase (or − Decrease) in Deferred Liabilities

The far-right column in Exhibit 5A.1 shows the deferred tax expense per year, which is the amount added to, or subtracted from, taxes paid, to arrive at tax expense. If we assume this company had $100 of pre-depreciation income, its taxable income and tax expense (assuming a 40% rate) follows:

	Taxes Paid	Deferred Tax Expense	Total Tax Expense
Year 1	$16	$ 8	$24
	($100 − $60) × 40%		
Year 2	$20	$ 4	$24
	($100 − $50) × 40%		
Year 3	$36	$(12)	$24
	($100 − $10) × 40%		

In this example, the timing difference between the financial reporting and tax reporting derives from PPE and creates a deferred tax liability. Other differences between the two sets of books create other types of deferred tax accounts. Exhibit 5A.2 shows the relation between the financial reporting and tax reporting net book values, and the resulting deferred taxes (liability or asset) on the balance sheet.

EXHIBIT 5A.2 Sources of Deferred Tax Assets and Liabilities		
For Assets...		
Financial reporting net book value	> Tax reporting net book value	→ Deferred tax liability on balance sheet
Financial reporting net book value	< Tax reporting net book value	→ Deferred tax asset on balance sheet
For Liabilities...		
Financial reporting net book value	< Tax reporting net book value	→ Deferred tax liability on balance sheet
Financial reporting net book value	> Tax reporting net book value	→ Deferred tax asset on balance sheet

A common deferred tax asset relates to accrued restructuring costs (a liability for financial reporting purposes). Restructuring costs are not deductible for tax purposes until paid in the future and, thus, there is no accrual restructuring liability for tax reporting, which means it has a tax basis of $0. To explain how this timing difference affects tax expense, assume that a company accrues $300 of restructuring costs in Year 1 and settles the liability in Year 2 as follows:

	Financial Reporting (Net Book Value)	Tax Reporting (Tax Basis)	Book vs Tax Difference	Deferred Tax Asset (Book vs Tax Difference × Tax Rate)	Deferred Tax Expense (Decrease (or Increase) in Deferred Tax Asset)
Year 1: Accrue restructuring costs...	$(300)	$ 0			
End of Year 1: Liability book value...	$ 300	$ 0	$300	$120	$(120)
			($300 − $0)	($300 × 40%)	($120 − $0)
Year 2: Pay restructuring costs		$(300)			
End of Year 2: Liability book value...	$ 0	0	$ 0	$ 0	$120
			($0 − $0)	($0 × 40%)	($120 − $0)

Timing differences created by the restructuring liability yield a deferred tax asset in Year 1. Timing differences disappear in Year 2 when the company pays cash for restructuring costs. To see how tax expense is determined, assume that this company has $500 of pre-restructuring income; computations follow:

	Taxes Paid	Deferred Tax Expense	Total Tax Expense
Year 1	$200	$(120)	$ 80
	($500 − $0) × 40%		
Year 2	$ 80	$ 120	$200
	($500 − $300) × 40%		

Deferred tax accounts derive from timing differences between GAAP expenses and tax deductions. This creates differences between the net book value and the tax basis for many assets and liabilities. Pfizer's footnote (see Exhibit 5.6) reports several deferred tax assets and liabilities that explain its book-tax difference and the tax basis. For example, in 2007, its deferred tax liability associated with PPE is $657 million ($957 million liability less $300 million asset). This reflects the cumulative tax savings to Pfizer from accelerated depreciation for its PPE. If we assume a tax rate of 35%, we can compute the book-tax difference for Pfizer's PPE as $1,877 million ($657 million/0.35). Its balance sheet reveals total PPE of $15,734, which implies that the tax basis for these assets is $13,857 million ($15,734 − $1,877).

GUIDANCE ANSWERS

MANAGERIAL DECISION **You Are the Financial Analyst**

Typically, restructuring charges have three components: asset write-downs (such as inventories, property, plant, and goodwill), severance costs, and other restructuring-related expenses. Write-downs occur when the cash-flow-generating ability of an asset declines, thus reducing its current market value below its book value reported on the balance sheet. Arguably, this decline in cash-flow-generating ability did not occur solely in the current year and, most likely, has developed over several periods. It is not uncommon for companies to delay loss recognition, such as write-downs of assets. Thus, prior period income is, arguably, not as high as reported, and the current period loss is not as great as reported. Turning to severance and other costs, GAAP permits restructuring expense to include only those costs that are *incremental* and will *not* benefit future periods. The accrual of restructuring-related expenses can be viewed like other accruals; that is, it might be over- or understated. In future periods, the required reconciliation of the restructuring accrual will provide insight into the adequacy of the accrual in that earlier period.

DISCUSSION QUESTIONS

Abercrombie & Fitch
(ANF)

Q5-1. What are the criteria that guide firms in recognition of revenue? What does each of the criteria mean? How are the criteria met for a company like Abercrombie & Fitch, a clothing retailer? How are the criteria met for a construction company that builds offices under long-term contracts with developers?

Q5-2. Why are extraordinary items reported separately from continuing operations in the income statement?

Q5-3. What are the criteria for categorizing an event as an extraordinary item? Provide an example of an event that would properly be categorized as an extraordinary item and one that would not.

⅜ Q5-4. What is the difference between basic earnings per share and diluted earnings per share? Are potentially dilutive securities always included in the EPS computation?

Q5-5. What effect, if any, does a weakening $US have on reported sales and net income for companies operating outside the United States?

⅜ Q5-6. Identify the three typical categories of restructuring costs and their effects on the balance sheet and the income statement. Explain the concept of a big bath and why restructuring costs are often identified with this event.

Q5-7. What is the current accounting treatment for research and development costs? Why are R&D costs normally not capitalized under GAAP?

Q5-8. Under what circumstances will deferred taxes likely result in a cash outflow?

Q5-9. What is the concept of pro forma income and why has this income measure been criticized?

Q5-10. What is unearned revenue? Provide three examples of unearned revenue.

Assignments with the Web**Assign.** logo in the margin are available in WebAssign.
See the Preface of the book for details.

MINI EXERCISES

M5-11. Computing Percentage-of-Completion Revenues (LO1)
Bartov Corporation agreed to build a warehouse for a client at an agreed contract price of $2,500,000. Expected (and actual) costs for the warehouse follow: 2007, $400,000; 2008, $1,000,000; and 2009, $500,000. The company completed the warehouse in 2009. Compute revenues, expenses, and income for each year 2007 through 2009 using the percentage-of-completion method.

M5-12. Applying the Financial Statement Effects Template. (LO1)
Refer to the information for Bartov Corporation in M5-11.

a. Use the financial statement effects template to record contract revenues and expenses for each year 2007 through 2009 using the percentage-of-completion method.
b. Prepare journal entries and T-accounts to record contract revenues and expenses for each year 2007 through 2009 using the percentage-of-completion method.

M5-13. Assessing Revenue Recognition of Companies (LO1)
Identify and explain when each of the following companies should recognize revenue.

a. The GAP: The GAP is a retailer of clothing items for all ages.
The GAP (GPS)

b. Merck & Company: Merck engages in developing, manufacturing, and marketing pharmaceutical products. It sells its drugs to retailers like CVS and Walgreen.
Merck & Company (MRK)

c. Deere & Company: Deere manufactures heavy equipment. It sells equipment to a network of independent distributors, who in turn sell the equipment to customers. Deere provides financing and insurance services both to distributors and customers.
Deere & Company (DE)

d. Bank of America: Bank of America is a banking institution. It lends money to individuals and corporations and invests excess funds in marketable securities.
Bank of America (BAC)

e. Johnson Controls: Johnson Controls manufactures products for the government under long-term contracts.
Johnson Controls (JCI)

M5-14. Assessing Risk Exposure to Revenue Recognition (LO1)
BannerAD Corporation manages a Website that sells products on consignment from sellers. It pays these sellers a portion of the sales price, and charges a commission. Identify two potential revenue recognition problems relating to such sales.

M5-15. Estimating Revenue Recognition with Right of Return (LO1)
The GAP offers an unconditional return policy. It normally expects 2% of sales at retail selling prices to be returned before the return period expires. Assuming that The GAP records total sales of $5 million for the current period, what amount of *net* sales should it record for this period?
The GAP (GPS)

M5-16. Assessing Research and Development Expenses (LO2)
Abbott Laboratories reports the following (summary) income statement.
Abbott Laboratories (ABT)

Year Ended December 31 ($ millions)	2007
Net sales.	$25,914
Cost of products sold.	(11,422)
Research and development	(2,506)
Selling, general and administrative	(7,408)
Pretax operating earnings	$ 4,578

a. Compute the percent of net sales that Abbott Laboratories spends on research and development (R&D). Compare this level of expenditure with the percentages for other companies that are discussed in the Business Insight box on page 5-4. How would you assess the appropriateness of its R&D expense level?

b. Describe how accounting for R&D expenditures affects Abbott Laboratories' balance sheet and income statement.

M5-17. Interpreting Foreign Currency Translation Disclosure   (LO4)

Bristol-Myers Squibb (BMY) reports the following table in its 10-K report relating to the year-over-year change in sales.

		Analysis of % Change		
	Total Change	Volume	Price	Foreign Exchange
2007 vs. 2006.	12%	7%	2%	3%
2006 vs. 2005.	(7)%	(9)%	2%	—

a. Did sales increase or decrease in 2006 and 2007? By what percentage? What amount of this change was attributable to fluctuations in the value of foreign currencies vis-a-vis the $US?

b. What can we infer from the table about the relative strength of the $US compared with the currencies in the countries in which BMY does business?

Cisco Systems
(CSCO)

M5-18. Analyzing Income Tax Disclosure   (LO3)

Cisco Systems reports the following footnote disclosure to its 10-K report ($ millions).

Year Ended	July 26, 2008
Federal	
Current	$2,384
Deferred	(693)
	1,691
State	
Current	173
Deferred	(62)
	111
Foreign	
Current	418
Deferred	(17)
	401
Total	$2,203

a. What amount of income tax expense does Cisco report in its income statement for 2008?

b. How much of Cisco's income tax expense is current (as opposed to deferred)?

c. Why do deferred tax assets and liabilities arise? How do they impact the tax expense that Cisco reports in its 2008 income statement?

Goodyear Tire and
Rubber Company (GT)

♂ M5-19. Defining and Computing Earnings per Share   (LO5)

Goodyear Tire and Rubber Company reports the following basic and diluted earnings per share information in its 2007 10-K report. (a) Describe the accounting definitions for basic and diluted earnings per share. (b) Identify the Goodyear numbers that make up both EPS computations. (c) Why does Goodyear add back $13 million for interest expense on the convertible debt securities in the diluted EPS calculation?

Year Ended December 31 (in millions, except per share amounts)	2007
Net Income (Loss)	$602
Net Income (Loss) Per Share—Basic	
Income (Loss) from Continuing Operations	$0.70
Discontinued Operations	2.30
Income (Loss) before Cumulative Effect of Accounting Change	3.00
Cumulative Effect of Accounting Change	—
Net Income (Loss) Per Share—Basic	$3.00
Weighted Average Shares Outstanding (Note 4)	201
Net Income (Loss) Per Share—Diluted	
Income (Loss) from Continuing Operations	$0.65
Discontinued Operations	2.00
Income (Loss) before Cumulative Effect of Accounting Change	2.65
Cumulative Effect of Accounting Change	—
Net Income (Loss) Per Share—Diluted	$2.65
Weighted Average Shares Outstanding (Note 4)	232
Note 4: Per Share of Common Stock	
Income (Loss) from Continuing Operations	$139
After-tax impact of 4% Convertible Senior Notes due 2034	13
Adjusted Income (Loss) from Continuing Operations	152
Discontinued Operations	463
Cumulative Effect of Accounting Change	—
Adjusted Net Income (Loss)	$615
Weighted average shares outstanding	
Weighted average shares outstanding—basic	200,933,767
4% convertible senior notes due 2034	26,673,721
Stock options and other dilutive securities	4,110,442
Weighted average shares outstanding—diluted	231,717,930

M5-20. **Assessing Revenue Recognition for Advance Payments   (LO1)**

Koonce Company operates a performing arts center. The company sells tickets for its upcoming season of six Broadway musicals and receives $420,000 cash. The performances occur monthly over the next six months.

  a.   When should Koonce record revenue for the Broadway musical series?

  b.   Use the financial statement effects template to show the $420,000 cash receipt and recognition of the first month's revenue.

M5-21. **Reporting Unearned Revenue   (LO1)**

Target Corporation sells gift cards that can be used at any of the company's Target or Greatland stores. Target encodes information on the card's magnetic strip about the card's value, the date it expires (typically two years after issuance), and the store where it was purchased.

  a.   How will Target's balance sheet reflect the gift card?

  b.   When does Target record revenue from the gift card?

Target Corporation (TGT)

EXERCISES

E5-22. **Assessing Revenue Recognition Timing   (LO1)**

Explain when each of the following businesses should recognize revenues:

  a.   A clothing retailer like The Limited.

  b.   A contractor like Boeing Company that performs work under long-term government contracts.

  c.   A grocery store like Supervalu.

  d.   A producer of television shows like MTV that syndicates its content to television stations.

  e.   A residential real estate developer that constructs only speculative houses and later sells these houses to buyers.

Limited (LTD)

Boeing Co. (BA)

Supervalu, Inc. (SVU)

MTV

continued

f. A banking institution like Bank of America that lends money for home mortgages.

g. A manufacturer like Harley-Davidson.

h. A publisher of magazines such as Time-Warner.

E5-23. Assessing Revenue Recognition Timing and Income Measurement (LO1)

Explain when each of the following businesses should recognize revenue and identify any income measurement issues that could arise.

TheStreet.Com (TSCM)

a. RealMoney.Com, a division of TheStreet.Com, provides investment advice to customers for an up-front fee. It provides these customers with password-protected access to its Website where customers can download investment reports. RealMoney has an obligation to provide updates on its Website.

Oracle (ORCL)

b. Oracle develops general ledger and other business application software that it sells to its customers. The customer pays an up-front fee for the right to use the software and a monthly fee for support services.

Intuit (INTU)

c. Intuit develops tax preparation software that it sells to its customers for a flat fee. No further payment is required and the software cannot be returned, only exchanged if defective.

d. A developer of computer games sells its software with a 10-day right of return period during which the software can be returned for a full refund. After the 10-day period has expired, the software cannot be returned.

E5-24. Constructing and Assessing Income Statements Using Percentage-of-Completion (LO1)

General Electric Company (GE)

Assume that General Electric Company agreed in May 2008 to construct a nuclear generator for NSTAR, a utility company serving the Boston area. The contract price of $500 million is to be paid as follows: $200 million at the time of signing; $100 million on December 31, 2008; and $200 million at completion in May 2009. General Electric incurred the following costs in constructing the generator: $100 million in 2008, and $300 million in 2009.

a. Compute the amount of General Electric's revenue, expense, and income for both 2008 and 2009 under the percentage-of-completion revenue recognition method.

b. Discuss whether or not you believe the percentage-of-completion method provides a good measure of General Electric's performance under the contract.

E5-25. Constructing and Assessing Income Statements Using Percentage-of-Completion (LO1)

On March 15, 2007, Frankel Construction contracted to build a shopping center at a contract price of $120 million. The schedule of expected (which equals actual) cash collections and contract costs follows:

Year	Cash Collections	Cost Incurred
2007	$ 30 million	$15 million
2008	50 million	40 million
2009	40 million	30 million
Total	$120 million	$85 million

a. Calculate the amount of revenue, expense, and net income for each of the three years 2007 through 2009 using the percentage-of-completion revenue recognition method.

b. Discuss whether or not the percentage-of-completion method provides a good measure of this construction company's performance under the contract.

E5-26. Interpreting the Income Tax Expense Footnote (LO3)

FedEx Corp (FDX)

The income tax footnote to the financial statements of FedEx Corporation follows.

The components of the provision for income taxes for the years ended May 31 were as follows:

($ millions)	2007	2006	2005
Current provision			
Domestic			
Federal	$ 829	$ 719	$634
State and local	72	79	65
Foreign	174	132	103
	1,075	930	802

continued

continued from prior page

($ millions)	2007	2006	2005
Deferred provision (benefit)			
Domestic			
Federal	90	151	67
State and local	27	13	(4)
Foreign	7	(1)	(1)
	124	163	62
Provision for income taxes	$1,199	$1,093	$864

a. What is the amount of income tax expense reported in FedEx's 2007, 2006 and 2005 income statements?
b. What percentage of total tax expense is currently payable in each of 2005, 2006, and 2007? Explain why the percentages are different each year.
c. One possible reason for the $90 million federal deferred tax expense in 2007 is that deferred tax liabilities increased during that year. Provide an example that gives rise to an increase in the deferred tax liability.

E5-27. Identifying Operating Income Components (LO2)
Following is the Bristol-Myers Squibb income statement. Identify the components that we would consider operating.

Bristol-Myers Squibb (BMY)

(Dollars in millions)	2007
Net sales	$19,348
Cost of products sold	6,218
Marketing, selling and administrative	4,855
Advertising and product promotion	1,465
Research and development	3,282
Acquired in-process research and development	230
Provision for restructuring, net	183
Litigation expense, net	14
Gain on sale of product assets and businesses	(273)
Equity in net income of affiliates	(524)
Other expense, net	364
Total expenses, net	15,814
Earnings from continuing operations	$ 3,534

Note: Equity in net income of affiliates refers to income BMY earned on investments in affiliated (but unconsolidated) companies.

E5-28. Identifying Operating Income Components (LO2)
Following is the Deere & Company income statement for 2007.

Deere & Company (DE)

($ millions)	2007
Net Sales and Revenues	
Net sales	$21,489.1
Finance and interest income	2,054.8
Other income	538.3
Total	24,082.2

continued

continued from prior page

($ millions)	2007
Costs and Expenses	
Cost of sales.	16,252.8
Research and development expenses.	816.8
Selling, administrative and general expenses	2,620.8
Interest expense.	1,151.2
Other operating expenses	565.1
Total	21,406.7
Income of Consolidated Group before Income Taxes	2,675.5
Provision for income taxes.	883.0
Income of Consolidated Group.	1,792.5
Equity in income of Unconsolidated Affiliates	29.2
Income from Continuing Operations	1,821.7
Income from Discontinued Operations	—
Net Income	$ 1,821.7

Notes:

- Income statement includes John Deere commercial and consumer tractor segment, a finance subsidiary that provides loan and lease financing relating to the sales of those tractors, and a health care segment that provides managed health care services for the company and certain outside customers.

- **Equity in income of unconsolidated affiliates** refers to income John Deere has earned on investments in affiliated (but unconsolidated) companies. These are generally investments made for strategic purposes.

a. Identify the components in its income statement that you would consider operating.

b. Discuss your treatment of the company's finance and interest income that relates to financing of its John Deere lawn and garden, and commercial tractors.

E5-29. Assessing the Income Tax Footnote (LO3)

Colgate-Palmolive
(CL)

Colgate-Palmolive reports the following income tax footnote disclosure in its 10-K report.

Deferred Tax Balances at December 31 (In millions)	2007	2006
Deferred tax liabilities		
Intangible assets	$(432.3)	$(380.9)
Property, plant and equipment.	(226.8)	(233.4)
Other.	(101.0)	(150.5)
	(760.1)	(764.8)
Deferred tax assets		
Pension and other retiree benefits	178.4	259.2
Tax loss and tax credit carryforwards	210.8	189.4
Accrued liabilities	97.8	77.3
Stock-based compensation.	63.5	57.1
Other.	81.3	94.2
Valuation allowance	(10.8)	(125.4)
	621.0	551.8
Net deferred income taxes.	$(139.1)	$(213.0)

a. Colgate reports $226.8 million of deferred tax liabilities in 2007 relating to "Property." Explain how such liabilities arise.

b. Describe how a deferred tax asset can arise from pension and other retiree benefit obligations.

c. Colgate reports $210.8 million in deferred tax assets for 2007 relating to tax loss and credit carryforwards. Describe how tax loss carryforwards arise and under what conditions the resulting deferred tax assets will be realized.

d. Colgate has established a deferred tax asset valuation allowance of $10.8 million for 2007. What is the purpose of this allowance? How did the decrease in this allowance of $114.6 million from 2006 to 2007 affect net income?

e. Colgate's income statement reports income tax expense of $759.1 million. Assume that cash paid for income tax is $731.8 million and that taxes payable increased by $101.2 million. Use the financial statement effects template to record tax expense for 2007. (*Hint*: Show the effects of changes in deferred taxes.)

E5-30. **Analyzing and Assessing Research and Development Expenses** (LO2)

Advanced Micro Devices (AMD) and Intel (INTC) are competitors in the computer processor industry. Following is a table ($ millions) of sales and R&D expenses for both companies.

AMD	R&D Expense	Sales	INTC	R&D Expense	Sales
2005	$1,144	$4,972	2005	$5,145	$38,826
2006	1,205	5,649	2006	5,873	35,382
2007	1,847	6,013	2007	5,755	38,334

a. What percentage of sales are AMD and INTC spending on research and development?

b. How are AMD and INTC's balance sheets and income statements affected by the accounting for R&D costs?

c. How can one evaluate the effectiveness of R&D spending? Does the difference in R&D as a percentage of sales necessarily imply that one company is more heavily invested in R&D? Why might this not be the case?

E5-31. **Analyzing and Interpreting Foreign Currency Translation Effects** (LO4)

Kellogg Co. reports the following table and discussion in its 2007 10-K.

The following tables provide an analysis of net sales and operating profit performance for 2007 versus 2006:

(Dollars in millions)	North America	Europe	Latin America	Asia Pacific	Corporate	Consolidated
2007 net sales	$7,786	$2,357	$984	$649	$—	$11,776
2006 net sales	$7,349	$2,057	$891	$610	$—	$10,907
% change—2007 vs. 2006:						
Volume (tonnage)	1.7%	2.2%	6.5%	−.9%	—	2.1%
Pricing/mix	3.8%	3.1%	2.3%	.6%	—	3.3%
Subtotal—internal business	5.5%	5.3%	8.8%	−.3%	—	5.4%
Foreign currency impact. . .	.5%	9.3%	1.6%	6.7%	—	2.6%
Total change	6.0%	14.6%	10.4%	6.4%	—	8.0%

(Dollars in millions)	North America	Europe	Latin America	Asia Pacific	Corporate	Consolidated
2007 operating profit	$1,345	$397	$213	$88	$(175)	$1,868
2006 operating profit	$1,341	$321	$220	$90	$(206)	$1,766
% change—2007 vs. 2006:						
Internal business.	−.1%	14.2%	−4.7%	−9.5%	14.4%	3.1%
Foreign currency impact. . .	.5%	9.7%	1.5%	7.2%	—	2.7%
Total change	.4%	23.9%	−3.2%	−2.3%	14.4%	5.8%

Foreign exchange risk Our Company is exposed to fluctuations in foreign currency cash flows related to third-party purchases, intercompany loans and product shipments. Our Company is also exposed to fluctuations in the value of foreign currency investments in subsidiaries and cash flows related to repatriation of these investments. Additionally, our Company is exposed to volatility in the translation of foreign currency earnings to U.S. Dollars. Primary exposures include the U.S. Dollar versus the British Pound, Euro, Australian Dollar, Canadian Dollar, and Mexican Peso, and in the case of inter-subsidiary transactions, the British Pound versus the Euro. We assess foreign currency risk based on transactional cash flows and translational volatility and enter into forward contracts, options, and currency swaps to reduce fluctuations in net long or short currency positions. Forward contracts and options are generally less than 18 months duration. Currency swap agreements are established in conjunction with the term of underlying debt issuances.

> a. How did foreign currency exchange rates affect sales and operating profit for Kellogg Co. in 2007?
> b. Describe how the accounting for foreign exchange translation affects reported sales and profits.
> c. How does Kellogg Co. manage the risk related to its foreign exchange exposure? Describe the financial statement effects of this risk management activity.

E5-32.   Interpreting Revenue Recognition for Gift Cards   (LO1)

Barnes & Noble (BKS)

Footnotes to the 2007 annual report of Barnes & Noble disclose the following:

> The Barnes & Noble Member program entitles the Member to receive a 10% discount on all purchases made (20% discount for adult hardcover books) during the twelve-month period. The annual fee of $25.00 is nonrefundable after the first 30 days. Revenue is being recognized over the twelve-month period based upon historical spending patterns for Barnes & Noble Members. Refunds of fees due to cancellations within the first 30 days are minimal.

> a. Explain in layman terms how Barnes & Noble accounts for the cash received for its membership program. When does Barnes & Noble record revenue from this program?
> b. How does Barnes & Noble's balance sheet reflect those membership fees?
> c. Does the 10% discount affect Barnes & Noble's income statement when memberships fees are received?

PROBLEMS

P5-33.   Analyzing and Interpreting Revenue Recognition Policies and Risks   (LO1)

Amazon.com (AMZN)

Amazon.com, Inc., provides the following explanation of its revenue recognition policies in its 10-K report.

> We offer Earth's Biggest Selection and seek to be Earth's most customer-centric company for three primary customer sets: consumer customers, seller customers and developer customers. In addition, we generate revenue through co-branded credit card agreements and other marketing and promotional services, such as online advertising.
>
> We recognize revenue from product sales or services rendered when the following four revenue recognition criteria are met: persuasive evidence of an arrangement exists, delivery has occurred or services have been rendered, the selling price is fixed or determinable, and collectibility is reasonably assured. Additionally, revenue arrangements with multiple deliverables are divided into separate units of accounting if the deliverables in the arrangement meet the following criteria: the delivered item has value to the customer on a standalone basis; there is objective and reliable evidence of the fair value of undelivered items; and delivery of any undelivered item is probable.
>
> We evaluate the criteria of Emerging Issues Task Force (EITF) Issue No. 99-19, *Reporting Revenue Gross as a Principal Versus Net as an Agent*, in determining whether it is appropriate to record the gross amount of product sales and related costs or the net amount earned as commissions. Generally, when we are the primary party obligated in a transaction, are subject to inventory risk, have latitude in establishing prices and selecting suppliers, or have several but not all of these indicators, revenue is recorded gross. If we are not primarily obligated and amounts earned are determined using a percentage, a fixed-payment schedule, or a combination of the two, we generally record the net amounts as commissions earned.
>
> Product sales and shipping revenues, net of promotional discounts, rebates, and return allowances, are recorded when the products are shipped and title passes to customers. Retail items sold to customers are made pursuant to sales contracts that generally provide for transfer of both title and risk of loss upon our delivery to the carrier. Return allowances, which reduce product revenue by our best estimate of expected product returns, are estimated using historical experience. Revenue from product sales and services rendered is recorded net of sales taxes. Amounts paid in advance for subscription services, including amounts received for Amazon Prime and other membership programs, are deferred and recognized as revenue over the subscription term. For our products with multiple elements, where a standalone value for each element cannot be established, we recognize the revenue and related cost over the estimated economic life of the product.
>
> We periodically provide incentive offers to our customers to encourage purchases. Such offers include current discount offers, such as percentage discounts off current purchases, inducement offers, such as offers for future discounts subject to a minimum current purchase,

continued

continued from prior page

and other similar offers. Current discount offers, when accepted by our customers, are treated as a reduction to the purchase price of the related transaction, while inducement offers, when accepted by our customers, are treated as a reduction to purchase price based on estimated future redemption rates. Redemption rates are estimated using our historical experience for similar inducement offers. Current discount offers and inducement offers are classified as an offsetting amount in "Net sales."

Commissions and per-unit fees received from sellers and similar amounts earned through Amazon Enterprise Solutions are recognized when the item is sold by the seller and our collectibility is reasonably assured. When we are responsible for fulfillment-related services, commissions are recognized when risk of loss and title transfer to the customer. We record an allowance for estimated refunds on such commissions using historical experience.

Required

a. Identify and discuss the main revenue recognition policies for its two primary sources of business revenues.

b. Identify and describe at least three revenue recognition issues in a business such as Amazon.

P5-34. Analyzing and Interpreting Income Tax Disclosures (LO3)

The 2007 income statement for **Pfizer** is reproduced in this module. Pfizer also reports the following footnote relating to its income taxes in its 2007 10-K report.   Pfizer (PFE)

Deferred Taxes Deferred taxes arise because of different treatment between financial statement accounting and tax accounting, known as "temporary differences." We record the tax effect of these temporary differences as "deferred tax assets" (generally items that can be used as a tax deduction or credit in future periods) or "deferred tax liabilities" (generally items for which we received a tax deduction, but that have not yet been recorded in the consolidated statement of income). The tax effect of the major items recorded as deferred tax assets and liabilities . . . as of December 31 is as follows:

(Millions of dollars)	2007 Deferred Tax Assets	2007 Deferred Tax (Liabilities)	2006 Deferred Tax Assets	2006 Deferred Tax (Liabilities)
Prepaid/deferred items.	$1,315	$ (431)	$1,164	$ (312)
Intangibles	897	(6,737)	841	(7,704)
Property, plant and equipment.	300	(957)	104	(1,105)
Employee benefits	2,552	(740)	3,141	(804)
Restructurings and other charges	717	(11)	573	(19)
Net operating loss/credit carryforwards.	1,842	—	1,061	—
Unremitted earnings.	—	(3,550)	—	(3,567)
State and local tax adjustments.	529	—	—	—
All other	848	(37)	912	(392)
Subtotal	9,000	(12,463)	7,796	(13,903)
Valuation allowance	(158)	—	(194)	—
Total deferred taxes	$8,842	$(12,463)	$7,602	$(13,903)
Net deferred tax liability		$ (3,621)		$ (6,301)

The reduction in the net deferred tax liability position in 2007 compared to 2006 is primarily due to amortization of deferred tax liabilities related to identifiable intangibles in connection with our acquisition of Pharmacia in 2003, partially offset by an increase in noncurrent deferred tax assets related to the impairment of Exubera.

We have carryforwards primarily related to foreign tax credit carryovers and net operating losses, which are available to reduce future U.S. federal and state, as well as international, income with either an indefinite life or expiring at various times between 2008 and 2026. Certain of our U.S. net operating losses are subject to limitations under Internal Revenue Code Section 382.

Valuation allowances are provided when we believe that our deferred tax assets are not recoverable, based on an assessment of estimated future taxable income that incorporates ongoing, prudent, feasible tax planning strategies.

Required

a. Describe the terms "deferred tax liabilities" and "deferred tax assets." Provide an example of how these accounts can arise.

b. Intangible assets (other than goodwill) acquired in the purchase of a company are depreciated (amortized) similar to buildings and equipment (see Module 7 for a discussion). Describe how the deferred tax liability of $6,737 million relating to intangibles arose.

c. Pfizer has many employee benefit plans, such as a long-term health plan and a pension plan. Some of these are generating deferred tax assets and others are generating deferred tax liabilities. Explain the timing of the recognition of expenses under these plans that would give rise to these different outcomes.

d. Pfizer reports a deferred tax liability labelled "unremitted earnings." This relates to an investment in an affiliated company for which Pfizer is recording income, but has not yet received dividends. Generally, investment income is taxed when received. Explain what information the deferred tax liability for unremitted earnings conveys.

e. Pfizer reports a deferred tax asset relating to net operating loss carryforwards. Explain what loss carryforwards are.

f. Pfizer reports a valuation allowance of $158 million in 2007. Explain why Pfizer has established this allowance and its effect on reported profit. Pfizer's valuation allowance was $194 million in 2006. Compute the change in its allowance during 2007 and explain how that change affected 2007 tax expense and net income.

Xerox Corporation
(XRX)

P5-35.   Analyzing and Interpreting Income Components and Disclosures   (LO2, 3)
The income statement for Xerox Corporation follows.

Year ended December 31 (in millions)	2007	2006	2005
Revenues			
Sales.	$ 8,192	$ 7,464	$ 7,400
Service, outsourcing and rentals	8,214	7,591	7,426
Finance income	822	840	875
Total Revenues	17,228	15,895	15,701
Costs and Expenses			
Cost of sales.	5,254	4,803	4,695
Cost of service, outsourcing and rentals	4,707	4,328	4,207
Equipment financing interest	316	305	326
Research, development and engineering expenses	912	922	943
Selling, administrative and general expenses	4,312	4,008	4,110
Restructuring and asset impairment charges	(6)	385	366
Other expenses, net.	295	336	224
Total Costs and Expenses	15,790	15,087	14,871
Income from Continuing Operations before Income Taxes, Equity Income, Discontinued Operations and Cumulative Effect of Change in Accounting Principle.	1,438	808	830
Income tax expenses (benefits)	400	(288)	(5)
Equity in net income of unconsolidated affiliates.	97	114	98
Income from Continuing Operations before Discontinued Operations and Cumulative Effect of Change in Accounting Principle.	1,135	1,210	933
Income from Discontinued Operations, net of tax	—	—	53
Cumulative Effect of Change in Accounting Principle, net of tax	—	—	(8)
Net income	$ 1,135	$ 1,210	$ 978

Notes:

• The income statement includes sales of Xerox copiers and revenue earned by a finance subsidiary that provides loan and lease financing relating to the sales of those copiers.

• **Equity in net income of unconsolidated affiliates** refers to income Xerox has earned on investments in affiliated (but unconsolidated) companies.

• Xerox tax expense was reduced in 2005 as a result of an audit. The company makes the following disclosure in its footnotes: "In June 2005, the 1996–1998 IRS audit was finalized. As a result, we recorded an aggregate second quarter 2005 net income benefit of $343."

Required

a. Xerox reports three main sources of income: sales, service, and finance income. How should revenue be recognized for each of these business activities? Explain.

b. Xerox reports research and development (R&D) expenses of $912 million in 2007, which is 5.3% of its total revenues. How are R&D expenses accounted for under GAAP?

c. Xerox reports restructuring costs of $(6) million in 2007, $385 million in 2006, and $366 million in 2006. (1) Describe the three typical categories of restructuring costs and the accounting for each. (2) How do you recommend treating these costs for analysis purposes? (3) Should regular recurring restructuring costs be treated differently than isolated occurrences of such costs for analysis purposes? (4) What does the $(6) expense in 2007 imply about one or more previous year's accruals?

d. Xerox's tax expense was reduced as a result of a $343 million favorable IRS ruling in 2005. How should this benefit be treated in your analysis of the company?

e. Xerox reports $295 million in expenses in 2007 labeled as 'Other expenses, net.' How can a company use such an account to potentially obscure its actual financial performance?

P5-36. **Analyzing and Interpreting Income Tax Footnote** **(LO3)**

FedEx reports the following footnote for income taxes in its 2007 10-K report.   FedEx (FDX)

The components of the provision for income taxes for the years ended May 31 were as follows.

($ millions)	2007	2006	2005
Current provision			
Domestic			
Federal	$ 829	$ 719	$634
State and local	72	79	65
Foreign	174	132	103
	1,075	930	802
Deferred provision (benefit)			
Domestic			
Federal	90	151	67
State and local	27	13	(4)
Foreign	7	(1)	(1)
	124	163	62
Provision for income taxes	$1,199	$1,093	$864

The significant components of deferred tax assets and liabilities as of May 31 were as follows.

(in millions)	2007 Deferred Tax Assets	2007 Deferred Tax Liabilities	2006 Deferred Tax Assets	2006 Deferred Tax Liabilities
Property, equipment, leases and intangibles ..	$ 328	$1,655	$ 329	$1,559
Employee benefits	406	53	413	648
Self-insurance accruals	350	—	339	—
Other.	346	95	360	78
Net operating loss/credit carryforwards	61	—	64	—
Valuation allowance	(49)	—	(48)	—
Totals	$1,442	$1,803	$1,457	$2,285

Required

a. What income tax expense does FedEx report in its 2007 income statement? How much of this expense is currently payable?

b. FedEx reports deferred tax liabilities relating to property, equipment, leases and intangibles. Describe how these liabilities arise. How likely is it that these liabilities will be paid? Specifically, describe a scenario that will (i) defer these taxes indefinitely, and (ii) will result in these liabilities requiring payment within the near future.

c. FedEx reports a deferred tax asset relating to self-insurance accruals. When a company self-insures, it does not purchase insurance from a third-party insurance company. Instead, it records an expense and related liability to reflect the probable payment of losses that can occur in the future. Explain why this accrual results in a deferred tax asset.

d. FedEx reports net loss carryforwards. Explain how these arise and how they will result in a future benefit.

e. FedEx reports a valuation allowance related to its deferred tax assets. Why did FedEx set up such an allowance? How did the increase in the allowance from 2006 to 2007 affect net income? How can a company use this allowance to meet its income targets in a particular year?

WebAssign.

Benihana Inc. (BNHN)

P5-37.[A] **Analyzing and Interpreting Tax Footnote (Financial Statement Effects Template)** **(LO3)**

Benihana, Inc. (BNHN), reports total tax expense of $5,065 (in thousands) on its income statement for year ended March 30, 2008. The tax footnote in the company's 10-K filing, reports the following deferred tax information.

Income Taxes Deferred tax assets and liabilities reflect the tax effect of temporary differences between amounts of assets and liabilities for financial reporting purposes and the amounts of such assets and liabilities as measured by income tax law. A valuation allowance is recognized to reduce deferred tax assets to the amounts that are more likely than not to be realized. The income tax effects of temporary differences that give rise to deferred tax assets and liabilities are as follows (in thousands):

($ thousands)	March 30, 2008	April 1, 2007
Deferred tax assets		
Straight-line rent expense......	$3,771	$2,046
Gift certificate liability.........	1,427	1,258
Amortization of gain..........	705	744
Employee benefit accruals.....	742	807
Workers' compensation.......	283	—
Other.....................	272	30
	7,200	4,885
Deferred tax liabilities		
Property and equipment.......	2,970	1,085
Inventories	997	910
Goodwill	2,140	1,790
	6,107	3,785
Net deferred tax assets	$1,093	$1,100

Accounting for Leases—*Operating Leases* Rent expense for the Company's operating leases, which generally have escalating rentals over the term of the lease, is recorded on a straight-line basis over the lease term. Generally, the lease term commences on the date when the Company becomes legally obligated for the rent payments or as specified in the lease agreement. Recognition of rent expense begins when the Company has the right to control the use of the leased property, which is typically before rent payments are due under the terms of most of the Company's leases. The difference between rent expense and rent paid is recorded as deferred rent obligation and is included in the consolidated balance sheets.

Required

a. Did Benihana's deferred tax assets increase or decrease during the most recent fiscal year? Interpret the change. (*Hint:* Consider Benihana's accounting for leases.)

b. Did Benihana's deferred tax liabilities increase or decrease during the most recent fiscal year? Explain how the change arose (*Hint:* Look at the individual deferred tax liabilities and the most significant change during the year.)

continued

c. Use the financial statement effects template to record Benihana's income tax expense for the fiscal year 2008 along with the changes in both deferred tax assets and liabilities. Assume that the amount needed to balance the tax transaction represents the cash paid or payable to tax authorities.

P5-38. **Analyzing and Interpreting Restructuring Costs and Effects   (LO2)**

Web**Assign**.
Kraft Foods, Inc. (KFT)

Kraft Foods, Inc., reports the following footnote disclosure in its 2007 10-K relating to its restructuring programs.

Asset Impairment, Exit and Implementation Costs

Restructuring Program

In January 2004, we announced a three-year restructuring program (the "Restructuring Program") and, in January 2006, extended it through 2008. The objectives of this program are to leverage our global scale, realign and lower our cost structure, and optimize capacity. As part of the Restructuring Program we anticipate:

- incurring approximately $2.8 billion in pre-tax charges reflecting asset disposals, severance and implementation costs;
- closing up to 35 facilities and eliminating approximately 13,500 positions; and
- using cash to pay for approximately $1.7 billion of the $2.8 billion in charges.

We incurred charges under the Restructuring Program of $459 million in 2007, $673 million in 2006 and $297 million in 2005. Since the inception of the Restructuring Program we have incurred $2.1 billion in charges and paid cash for $1.1 billion.

Restructuring liability activity for the years ended December 31, 2007 and 2006 was:

(in millions)	Severance	Asset Write-Downs	Other	Total
Liability balance, January 1, 2006	$114	$ —	$ 1	$115
Charges.	272	252	54	578
Cash (spent)/received.	(204)	16	(21)	(209)
Charges against assets	(25)	(268)	—	(293)
Currency/other	8	—	(2)	6
Liability balance, December 31, 2006 . . .	165	—	32	197
Charges.	156	99	77	332
Cash (spent)/received.	(155)	6	(94)	(243)
Charges against assets	(25)	(109)	1	(133)
Currency	13	4	—	17
Liability balance, December 31, 2007 . . .	$154	$ —	$16	$170

Severance costs include the costs of benefits received by terminated employees. In connection with our severance initiatives, we have eliminated approximately 11,000 positions as of December 31, 2007; at that time we had announced the elimination of an additional 400 positions. Severance charges against assets primarily relate to incremental pension costs, which reduce prepaid pension assets. Asset write-downs relate to the impairment of assets caused by plant closings and related activity. Cash received on asset write-downs relates to proceeds received from the sale of assets that had previously been written-off under the Restructuring Program. We incurred other costs related primarily to the renegotiation of supplier contract costs, workforce reductions associated with the plant closings and the termination of leasing agreements.

Asset Impairment Charges

In 2007, we sold our flavored water and juice brand assets and related trademarks, including *Veryfine* and *Fruit2O*. In recognition of the sale, we recorded a $120 million asset impairment charge for these assets. The charge included the write-off of the associated goodwill of $3 million, intangible assets of $70 million and property, plant and equipment of $47 million, and was recorded as asset impairment and exit costs on the consolidated statement of earnings.

Required

a. Briefly describe the general cost categories associated with this company's restructuring program.
b. Using the financial statement effects template, show the effects on financial statements of the (1) 2007 severance expense of $156 million, and (2) 2007 cash payment of $155 million.

continued

    c. Assume that instead of accurately estimating the anticipated severance costs in 2007, the company overestimated them by $30 million. How would this overestimation affect financial statements in (1) 2007, and (2) 2008 when severance costs are paid in cash?

    d. Describe how the sale of its flavored water and juice brand assets affected Kraft's financial statements.

P5-39. **Analyzing and Interpreting Income Tax Footnote**   **(LO3)**

DuPont (DD)

Consider the following income tax footnote information for the E. I. du Pont de Nemours and Company.

Provision for Income Taxes

($ millions)	2007	2006	2005
Current tax expense (benefit)			
U.S. federal.	$357	$505	$ 699
U.S. state and local.	13	(1)	13
International	379	307	649
	749	811	1,361
Deferred tax expense (benefit)			
U.S. federal.	63	(297)	204
U.S. state and local.	(24)	(18)	(13)
International	(40)	(300)	(82)
	(1)	(615)	109
Provision for income taxes.	$748	$196	$1,470

The significant components of deferred tax assets and liabilities at December 31, 2007 and 2006, are as follows:

	2007		2006	
($ millions)	Asset	Liability	Asset	Liability
Depreciation.	$ —	$1,392	$ —	$1,380
Accrued employee benefits	1,469	196	2,302	137
Other accrued expenses	1,225	656	934	489
Inventories	238	121	169	49
Unrealized exchange gains	81	—	43	—
Tax loss/tax credit carryforwards/backs	2,830	—	2,602	—
Investment in subsidiaries and affiliates.	38	338	31	337
Amortization of intangibles.	92	643	75	661
Other.	201	128	348	206
	$6,174	$3,474	$6,504	$3,259
Valuation allowance	(1,424)		(1,467)	
	$4,750		$5,037	

An analysis of the company's effective income tax rate (EITR) follows:

	2007	2006	2005
Statutory U.S. federal income tax rate.	35.0%	35.0%	35.0%
Exchange gains/losses[1]	(0.9)	0.6	9.4
Domestic operations	(3.2)	0.1	(1.4)
Lower effective tax rates on international operations-net	(7.5)	(12.4)	(6.8)
Tax settlements	(3.4)	(10.4)	(1.4)
Lower effective tax rate on export sales	—	(0.8)	(1.0)
The American Jobs Creation Act of 2004 (AJCA)[2].	—	(0.6)	8.2
Valuation allowance release.	—	(5.6)	(0.7)
	20.0%	5.9%	41.3%

[1] Principally reflects the benefit of non-taxable exchange gains resulting from remeasurement of foreign currency denominated monetary assets and liabilities. Further information about the company's foreign currency hedging program is included in Note 23 under the heading Currency Risk.

[2] Reflects the tax impact associated with the repatriation of $9.1 billion under the AJCA.

Required

a. What is the total amount of income tax expense that DuPont reports in its 2007 income statement? What portion of this expense does DuPont expect to pay in 2008?

b. Explain how the deferred tax liability called "depreciation" arises? Under what circumstances will the company settle this liability? Under what circumstances might this liability be deferred indefinitely?

c. Explain how the deferred tax asset called "accrued employee benefits" arises? Why is it recognized as an asset?

d. Explain how the deferred tax asset called "tax loss/tax credit carryforwards/backs" arises. Under what circumstances will DuPont realize the benefits of this asset?

e. DuPont reports a 2007 valuation allowance of $1,424 million. How does this valuation allowance arise? How did the change in valuation allowance for 2007 affect net income? Valuation allowances typically relate to questions about the realizability of tax loss carryforwards. Under what circumstances might DuPont not realize the benefits if its tax loss carryforwards?

f. DuPont reports an effective tax rate of 20%, 5.9%, and 41.3% in 2007, 2006, and 2005, respectively. What factors caused the marked change in the effective tax rate from 2005 to 2006? From 2006 to 2007? What tax rate would seem reasonable to use when projecting DuPont's income statement for 2008? Explain.

P5-40. **Assessing Revenue Recognition, R&D Expense, EPS, and Income Taxes**   (LO1, 2, 3, 5)

Following are the income statement and relevant footnotes from the 10-K of Intuit, Inc.   Intuit, Inc. (INTU)

INTUIT INC. CONSOLIDATED STATEMENTS OF OPERATIONS Twelve Months Ended July 31 (In thousands, except per share amounts)	2008	2007	2006
Net revenue			
Product.	$1,496,655	$1,447,392	$1,335,430
Service and other	1,574,319	1,225,555	957,580
Total net revenue.	3,070,974	2,672,947	2,293,010
Costs and expenses			
Cost of revenue			
Cost of product revenue	154,147	169,101	165,949
Cost of service and other revenue	414,100	309,419	232,588
Amortization of purchased intangible assets	56,011	30,926	8,785
Selling and marketing.	859,647	742,368	657,588
Research and development	605,818	472,516	385,795
General and administrative.	294,966	291,083	267,233
Acquisition-related charges	35,518	19,964	9,478
Total costs and expenses	2,420,207	2,035,377	1,727,416
Operating income from continuing operations	650,767	637,570	565,594
Interest expense.	(52,290)	(27,091)	—
Interest and other income	46,520	52,689	43,023
Gains and marketable equity securities and other investments, net . . .	1,417	1,568	7,629
Gain on sale of outsourced payroll assets	51,571	31,676	—
Income from continuing operations before income taxes	697,985	696,412	616,246
Income tax provision	245,579	251,607	234,592
Minority interest expense, net of tax	1,656	1,337	691
Net income from continuing operations.	450,750	443,468	380,963
Net income (loss) from discontinued operations	26,012	(3,465)	36,000
Net income.	$ 476,762	$ 440,003	$ 416,963
Basic net income per share from continuing operations	$ 1.37	$ 1.29	$ 1.10
Basic net income (loss) per share from discontinued operations	0.08	(0.01)	0.10
Basic net income per share	$ 1.45	$ 1.28	$ 1.20
Shares used in basic per share amounts	328,545	342,637	347,854
Diluted net income per share from continuing operations	$ 1.33	$ 1.25	$ 1.06
Diluted net income (loss) per share from discontinued operations	$ 0.08	$ (0.01)	$ 0.10
Diluted net income per share	$ 1.41	$ 1.24	$ 1.16
Shares used in diluted per share amounts.	339,268	355,815	360,471

The following table presents the composition of shares used in the computation of basic and diluted net income per share for the periods indicated.

Twelve Months Ended July 31 **(In thousands, except per share amounts)**	**2008**	**2007**	**2006**
Denominator:			
Shares used in basic per share amounts:			
Weighted average common shares outstanding	328,545	342,637	347,854
Shares used in basic per share amounts:			
Weighted average common shares outstanding	328,545	342,637	347,854
Dilutive common equivalent shares from stock			
options and restricted stock awards.	10,723	13,178	12,617
Dilutive weighted average common shares outstanding . . .	339,268	355,815	360,471

Revenue Recognition

We derive revenue from the sale of packaged software products, license fees, software subscriptions, product support, hosting services, payroll services, merchant services, professional services, transaction fees and multiple element arrangements that may include any combination of these items.

Sale of Outsourced Payroll Assets

In March 2007 we sold certain assets related to our Complete Payroll and Premium Payroll Service businesses to Automatic Data Processing, Inc. (ADP) for a price of up to approximately $135 million in cash. The final purchase price was contingent upon the number of customers that transitioned to ADP pursuant to the purchase agreement over a period of approximately one year from the date of sale. In the twelve months ended July 31, 2008 and 2007 we recorded pre-tax gains of $51.6 million and $31.7 million on our statement of operations for customers who transitioned to ADP during those periods. We received a total purchase price of $93.6 million and recorded a total pre-tax gain of $83.2 million from the inception of this transaction through its completion in the third quarter of fiscal 2008. The assets were part of our Payroll and Payments segment.

In accordance with the provisions of SFAS 144, *"Accounting for the Impairment or Disposal of Long-lived Assets,"* we have not accounted for this transaction as a discontinued operation because the operations and cash flows of the assets could not be clearly distinguished, operationally or for financial reporting purposes, from the rest of our outsourced payroll business. We held deposits received from ADP of $30.3 million in other current liabilities on our balance sheet at July 31, 2007. Assets held for sale at July 31, 2007 consisted of $5.1 million in customer lists and were included in purchased intangible assets on our balance sheet. There were no deposits received from ADP or assets held for sale on our balance sheet at July 31, 2008.

Intuit Information Technology Solutions Discontinued Operations

In December 2005 we sold our Intuit Information Technology Solutions (ITS) business for approximately $200 million in cash and recorded a net gain on disposal of $34.3 million. The decision to sell ITS was a result of our desire to focus resources on our core products and services. ITS was part of our Other Businesses segment. In accordnce with the provisions of SFAS 144, *"Accounting for the Impairment or Disposal of Long-lived Assets,"* we accounted for the sale of ITS as discontinued operations. We have therefore separated the operating results and cash flows of ITS from continuing operations in our statements of operations and statements of cash flows for all periods prior to the sale. See the table later in this Note 7 for the components of revenue and net income or loss from discontinued operations.

Income Taxes

Differences between income taxes calculated using the federal statutory income tax rate of 35% and the provision for income taxes from continuing operations were as follows for the periods indicated:

continued

continued from prior page

Twelve Months Ended July 31 (In thousands)	2008	2007	2006
Income from continuing operations before income taxes	$697,985	$696,412	$616,246
Statutory federal income tax	$244,294	$243,744	$215,686
State income tax, net of federal benefit	28,878	30,404	24,658
Federal research and experimental credits	(7,842)	(13,341)	(3,464)
Domestic production activities deduction	(11,816)	(4,985)	(4,375)
Share-based compensation	311	5,048	1,929
Tax exempt interest	(11,641)	(15,940)	(11,771)
Federal tax related to divestiture	—	—	8,748
Other, net	3,395	6,677	3,181
Total provision for income taxes from continuing operations	$245,579	$251,607	$234,592

Significant deferred tax assets and liabilities were as follows at the dates indicated:

July 31 (In thousands)	2008	2007
Deferred tax assets		
Accruals and reserves not currently deductible	$28,178	$34,095
Deferred rent	13,859	21,363
Accrued and deferred compensation	33,954	30,397
Loss and tax credit carryforwards	38,782	19,448
Property and equipment	12,130	30,385
Share-based compensation	77,336	46,021
Other, net	21,002	22,740
Total deferred tax assets	225,241	204,449
Deferred tax liabilities		
Intangible assets	65,925	41,152
Other, net	5,095	4,022
Total deferred tax liabilities	71,020	45,174
Total net deferred tax assets	154,221	159,275
Valuation allowance	—	(2,527)
Total net deferred tax assets, net of valuation allowance	$154,221	$156,748

We had provided a valuation allowance related to the benefits of certain state capital loss carryforwards and state net operating losses that we believed were unlikely to be realized. The valuation allowance decreased by $2.5 million during the twelve months ended July 31, 2008 as a result of the elimination of the deferred tax asset in connection with the sale of certain outsourced payroll assets. See Note 7. The valuation allowance decreased by $1.9 million during the twelve months ended July 31, 2007 due to utilization of $1.0 million and expired losses of $0.9 million.

Required

a. Describe the differences in revenue recognition between product sales and after-sale services.

b. Intuit reports $605,818 thousand of Research and Development expense, up from $472,516 thousand in the prior year.
   i. What kind of research activities would we expect for a company like Intuit?
   ii. Given the kind of research activities described in part i, how does the accounting for Inuit's R&D costs differ from the way that those costs would have been accounted for had they not been categorized as R&D?

c. Intuit's earnings per share (EPS) is $1.41 on a diluted basis, compared with its basic EPS of $1.45. What factor(s) accounts for this dilution?

d. Intuit accounts for the sale of its Information Technology Solutions segment as a discontinued operation but does not give that designation for its Sale of Outsourced Payroll Assets. Why is Intuit not treating the Sale of Outsourced Payroll Assets as a discontinued operation?

e. Drawing on Intuit's income tax footnote, prepare a table in percentages showing computation of its effective tax rate for each fiscal year 2008, 2007 and 2006. What tax-related items, if any, would we not expect to continue into fiscal year 2009?

continued

f. Intuit reports deferred tax assets of $225,241 thousand.
   i. Describe how deferred tax assets relating to accruals and share-based compensation arise.
   ii. Explain how deferred tax assets relating to loss carryforwards arise.
   iii. Intuit reports a reduction of its deferred tax asset valuation allowance from $2,527 thousand in fiscal 2007 to $0 in fiscal 2008. How does this reduction in its valuation allowance affect Intuit's income? (*Hint:* See its footnote for the deferred tax assets table.)

WebAssign

Costco Wholesale
(COST)

P5-41. **Analyzing Unearned Revenue Disclosures** **(LO1)**

The following disclosures are from the August 31, 2008, annual report of Costco Wholesale Corporation.

> **Revenue Recognition** Membership fee revenue represents annual membership fees paid by substantially all of the Company's members. The Company accounts for membership fee revenue on a deferred basis, whereby revenue is recognized ratably over the one-year term of the membership period.

Revenue ($ thousands)	52 weeks ended August 31, 2008	52 weeks ended September 2, 2007	52 weeks ended September 3, 2006
Net sales	$70,977,484	$63,087,601	$58,963,180
Membership fees	1,505,536	1,312,554	1,188,047
Total revenue	$72,483,020	$64,400,155	$60,151,227

Current Liabilities ($ thousands)	August 31, 2008	September 2, 2007
Short-term borrowings	$134,409	$53,832
Accounts payable	5,224,753	5,124,990
Accrued salaries and benefits	1,320,715	1,226,666
Accrued sales and other taxes	283,048	267,920
Deferred membership fees	748,438	692,176
Current portion long-term debt	6,003	59,905
Other current liabilities	1,156,799	1,156,264
Total current liabilities	$8,874,165	$8,581,753

Required

a. Explain in layman terms how Costco accounts for the cash received for its membership fees.
b. Use the balance sheet information on Costco's Deferred Membership Fees liability account and its income statement revenues related to Membership Fees earned during 2008 to compute the cash that Costco received during 2008 for membership fees.
c. Use the financial statement effects template to show the effect of the cash Costco received during 2008 for membership fees and the recognition of membership fees revenue for 2008.

P5-42. **Analyzing Unearned Revenue Transactions** **(LO1)**

Apple, Inc. (AAPL)
AT&T (T)

Apple, Inc., sells its iPhones through an exclusive arrangement with AT&T that requires a two-year contract upon purchase of the iPhone. Analysts estimate that AT&T is paying Apple over $300 per iPhone for the exclusive right to service contacts bundled with the iPhone. Apple describes its accounting for iPhones in its 2007 10-K as follows:

> In January 2007, the Company announced iPhone, a handheld device that combines in a single product a mobile phone, a widescreen iPod with touch controls, and an Internet communications device. AT&T Mobility LLC ("AT&T") is the exclusive U.S. cellular network carrier for iPhone . . . The Company indicated it may provide future unspecified features and additional software products free of charge to customers. Therefore, sales of iPhone handsets are recognized under subscription accounting in accordance with SOP No. 97-2. The Company recognizes the associated revenue and cost of goods sold on a straight-line basis over the currently estimated 24-month economic lives of these products with any loss recognized at the time of sale.

Apple provides the following schedule of unit and dollar sales by product in its 2008 10-K:

(in millions, except unit sales in thousands)	2008	Change	2007	Change	2006
Net sales by product					
Desktops.	$ 5,603	39%	$ 4,020	21%	$ 3,319
Portables.	8,673	38%	6,294	55%	4,056
Total Mac net sales.	14,276	38%	10,314	40%	7,375
iPod	9,153	10%	8,305	8%	7,676
Other music related products and services	3,340	34%	2,496	32%	1,885
iPhone and related products and services.	1,844	NM	123	NM	—
Peripherals and other hardware	1,659	32%	1,260	15%	1,100
Software, service, and other sales.	2,207	46%	1,508	18%	1,279
Total net sales.	$32,479	35%	$24,006	24%	$19,315
Unit Sales by Product					
Desktops.	3,712	37%	2,714	12%	2,434
Portables.	6,003	38%	4,337	51%	2,869
Total Mac unit sales	9,715	38%	7,051	33%	5,303
Net sales per Mac unit sold	$ 1,469	0%	$ 1,463	5%	$ 1,391
iPod unit sales	54,828	6%	51,630	31%	39,409
Net sales per iPod unit sold.	$ 167	4%	$ 161	(17)%	$ 195
iPhone unit sales	11,627	NM	1,389	NM	—

Apple discloses the following schedules of short-term accrued expenses and noncurrent liabilities (other than debt) in its 2008 10-K.

Accrued Expenses (in millions)	2008	2007
Deferred revenue—current.	$4,853	$1,391
Deferred margin on component sales	681	545
Accrued marketing and distribution.	329	288
Accrued compensation and employee benefits.	320	254
Accrued warranty and related costs	267	230
Other accrued tax liabilities	100	488
Other current liabilities.	2,022	1,114
Total accrued expenses.	$8,572	$4,310

Noncurrent Liabilities (in millions)	2008	2007
Deferred revenue—noncurrent.	$3,029	$ 849
Deferred tax liabilities.	675	619
Other noncurrent liabilities	746	67
Total noncurrent liabilities.	$4,450	$1,535

Required

a. What amount does Apple report for unit and dollar sales of iPhones in 2008 and in 2007? Compute the average per-unit revenue that Apple is reporting on iPhone sales for each year.

b. Apple's cash and short-term investments grew by 59% from 2007 to 2008, while revenues grew by 35%. Given the magnitude of iPhone sales to Apple's product line, describe how the accounting for iPhone sales can impact the relations between revenue recognized, cash generated, and the growth of deferred revenues.

c. Compute Apple's adjusted revenues and EPS for 2008 assuming that iPhone sales are accounted for like iPod sales (full value recognized at the point of sale). (*Hint:* Start with reported 2008 revenues; then, subtract one-half of the 2007 deferred revenue, both current and noncurrent, under the assumption that deferred revenue of iPhones were recognized over the two-year service contract;

and then, add the total 2008 deferred revenue, both current and noncurrent, under the assumption that these amounts related to 2008 iPhone sales.) Next, multiply Apple's income-to-sales percentage (computed from its income statement as 14.9% [$4,834/$32,479]) by the adjusted revenues to get its adjusted 2008 income. Then, divide that adjusted income by 888 million shares outstanding (from the end of 2007) to get adjusted EPS.

d. Apple's PE ratio at the end of 2008 was 32. Assume that the adjusted EPS from part *c* is $6.58. Estimate Apple's 2008 market price per share. Compare this estimate with the reported market price of $128.24 at fiscal year-end and comment on the potential for accounting to affect the use of PE ratios for stock price estimation.

MANAGEMENT APPLICATIONS

MA5-43. Managing Foreign Currency Risk (LO4)
Fluctuations in foreign currency exchange rates can result in increased volatility of revenues, expenses, and profits. Companies generally attempt to reduce this volatility.

a. Identify two possible solutions to reduce the volatility effect of foreign exchange rate fluctuations. (*Hint*: Examine the risk management discussion for Kellogg Company in Exercise E5-31.)

Kellogg Co. (K)

b. What costs would arise if you implemented each of your solutions?

MA5-44. Ethics and Governance: Revenue Recognition   (LO1)
GAAP offers latitude in determining when revenue is earned. Assume that a company that normally required acceptance by its customers prior to recording revenue as earned, delivers a product to a customer near the end of the quarter. The company believes that customer acceptance is assured, but cannot obtain it prior to quarter-end. Recording the revenue would assure "making its numbers" for the quarter. Although formal acceptance is not obtained, the sales person records the sale, fully intending to obtain written acceptance as soon as possible.

a. What are the revenue recognition requirements in this case?
b. What are the ethical issues relating to this sale?
c. Assume you are on the board of directors of this company. What safeguards can you put in place to provide assurance that the company's revenue recognition policy is followed?

MA5-45. Ethics and Governance: Earnings Management   (LO2)
Assume that you are CEO of a company. Your company has reported a loss for the current year. Since it cannot carry back the entire loss to recoup taxes paid in prior years, it records a loss carryforward as a deferred tax asset. Your expectation is that future profitability will be sufficient to realize the tax benefits of the carryforward. Your chief financial officer approaches you with an idea to create a deferred tax valuation allowance that will reduce the deferred tax asset, increase tax expense for the year, and increase your reported loss. He reasons that the company's stock price will not be reduced markedly by the additional reported loss since a loss year has already been factored into the current price. Further, this deferred tax valuation allowance will create a reserve that can be used in future years to increase profit (via reversal of the allowance) if needed to meet analyst expectations.

a. What stakeholders are potentially affected by the CFO's proposal?
b. How do you respond to the proposal? Justify your response.

Module Six

Reporting and Analyzing Operating Assets

LEARNING OBJECTIVES

LO1 Describe accounting for accounts receivable and the importance of the allowance for uncollectible accounts in determining profit. (p. 6-3)

LO2 Explain accounting for inventories and assess the effects on the balance sheet and income statement from different inventory costing methods. (p. 6-13)

LO3 Describe accounting for property, plant and equipment and explain the impacts on profit and cash flows from depreciation methods, disposals and impairments. (p. 6-26)

CISCO SYSTEMS

Cisco Systems, Inc., manufactures and sells networking and communications products for transporting data, voice, and video within buildings, across town and around the world. Cisco's products are everywhere; here are a few applications:

- Schoolchildren can view a virtual science experiment from a neighborhood center's Cisco-outfitted computer room.

- Airline passengers can check flight information and print boarding passes at convenient Cisco kiosks.

- Hospital nurses check medication levels at patients' bedsides using Cisco handheld devices and wireless networks.

- Auto designers in Japan, assembly technicians in the U.S., and component makers worldwide trade manufacturing data over a Cisco network in real time.

- Police rely on citywide Cisco wireless networks to deliver fingerprint files, mug shots, and voicemail to mobile units.

- Customers call their banks' Cisco Internet Protocol (IP) based center, where account profiles appear to call agents.

- Companies shore up their databases with Cisco network security.

Cisco reported 2008 net income of $8.1 billion on $39.5 billion in sales, and a return on net operating assets (RNOA) of 38%. Six years earlier, Cisco reported a *loss* of $1 billion after recording $2.25 billion of restructuring costs, including costs related to the severance of 6,000 employees and the write-off of obsolete inventory and other assets.

Cisco's turnaround is remarkable. Sales have increased by 39% in the past two years, and its return on net operating assets has remained at a lofty 38%, which reflects Cisco's effective asset (balance sheet) management. Recall that RNOA comprises both a profitability component and a productivity component (see Module 4). The productivity component (reflected in net operating asset turnover, NOAT) is measured as sales divided by average net operating assets. Effective management of operating assets is crucial to achieving a high RNOA. We focus on three important operating assets in this module: accounts receivable, inventories, and property, plant and equipment (PPE).

As part of their overall marketing efforts, companies extend credit to customers. At Cisco, for example, accounts receivable are an important asset because nearly all sales are on account. While favorable credit terms stimulate sales, the resulting accounts receivable are costly. First, accounts receivable are generally non-interest bearing and tie up a company's working capital in non-earning assets.

Courtesy of Cisco Systems

Second, receivables expose the company to collectibility risk—the risk that some customers won't pay. Third, companies incur the administrative costs associated with billing and collection. These costs must be weighed against the costs of other marketing tools, like advertising, sales incentives, and price discounts. Management of receivables is critical to financial success.

Inventories are significant assets at many companies, particularly for manufacturers such as Cisco, where inventories consist of raw materials (the basic product inputs), work in process (the cost of partially completed products), and finished goods (completed products awaiting sale). Inventories are also costly to maintain. The cost of buying and manufacturing the goods must be financed and inventories must be stored, moved, and insured. Consequently, companies prefer lower inventory levels whenever possible. However, companies must be careful to hold enough inventory. If they reduce inventory quantities too far, they risk inventory stock-outs, that is, not having enough inventory to meet demand. Management of inventories is also a critical activity.

Property, plant and equipment (PPE) is often the largest, and usually the most important, asset on the balance sheet. Companies need administrative offices, IT

and R&D facilities, regional sales and customer service offices, manufacturing and distribution facilities, vehicles, computers, and a host of other fixed assets. Fixed asset costs are substantial and are indirectly linked to sales and profits. Consequently, fixed-asset investments are often difficult to justify and, once acquired, fixed assets are often difficult to divest. Effective management of PPE assets usually requires management review of the entire value chain.

John Chambers, CEO of Cisco, recalls a conversation he once had with the legendary Jack Welch, former Chairman of GE. Following Cisco's announced restructuring program in 2001, Welch commented, "John, you'll never have a great company until you go through the really tough times. What builds a company is not just how you handle the successes, but it's the way you handle the real challenges." Cisco survived the tech bubble burst and is now reporting impressive financial results. To ensure future financial performance, however, Cisco must effectively manage both its income statement and its operating assets.

Sources: *BusinessWeek,* 2006 and 2003; Cisco Systems 10-K, 2008; Cisco Systems Annual Report, 2008; *Fortune,* April 2009.

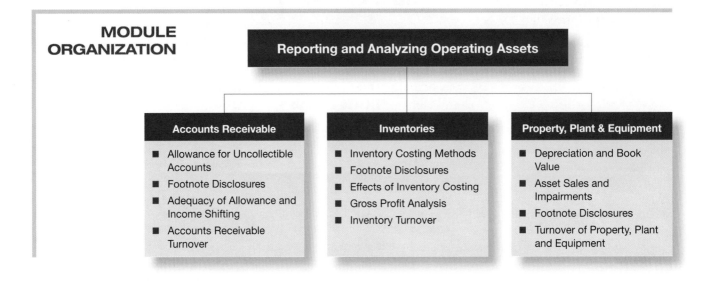

Managing net operating assets is crucial to creating shareholder value. To manage and assess net operating assets, we need to understand how they are measured and reported. This module describes the reporting and measuring of operating working capital, mainly receivables and inventories, and of long-term operating assets such as property, plant, and equipment. We do not discuss other long-term operating assets, such as equity investments in affiliated companies, investment in intangible assets, and nonoperating investments in marketable securities, as they are covered in other modules.

Receivables are usually a major part of operating working capital. They must be carefully managed as they represent a substantial asset for most companies and are an important marketing tool. GAAP requires companies to report receivables at the amount they expect to collect. This requires estimation of uncollectible accounts. The receivables reported on the balance sheet, and the expenses reported on the income statement, reflect management's estimate of uncollectible amounts. Accordingly, it is important that companies accurately assess uncollectible accounts and timely report them. It is also necessary that readers of financial reports understand management's accounting choices and their effects on reported balance sheets and income statements.

Inventory is another major component of operating working capital. Inventories usually constitute one of the three largest assets (along with receivables and long-term operating assets). Also, cost of goods sold, which flows from inventory, is the largest expense category for retailing and manufacturing companies. GAAP allows several methods for inventory accounting, and inventory-costing choices can markedly impact balance sheets and income statements, especially for companies experiencing relatively high inflation, coupled with slowly turning inventories.

Long-term plant assets are often the largest component of operating assets. Indeed, long-term operating assets are typically the largest asset for manufacturing companies, and their related depreciation expense is typically second only in amount to cost of goods sold in the income statement. GAAP allows different accounting methods for computing depreciation, which can significantly impact the income statement and the balance sheet. When companies dispose of fixed assets, a gain or loss may result. Understanding these gains and losses on asset sales is important as we assess performance. Further, asset write-downs (impairments) not only affect companies' current financial performance, but also future profitability. We must understand these effects when we forecast future income statements. This module considers all of these fixed asset accounting choices and consequences.

LO1 Describe accounting for accounts receivable and the importance of the allowance for uncollectible accounts in determining profit.

ACCOUNTS RECEIVABLE

Our focus on operating assets begins with accounts receivable. To help frame our discussion, we refer to the following graphic as we proceed through the module:

Income Statement	Balance Sheet	
Sales	Cash	Current liabilities
Cost of goods sold	**Accounts receivable, net**	Long-term liabilities
Selling, general & administrative	Inventory	
Income taxes	Property, plant, and equipment, net	Shareholders' equity
Net income	Investments	

The graphic highlights the balance sheet and income statement effects of accounts receivable. This section explains the accounting, reporting, and analysis of these highlighted items.

Retail companies transact mostly in cash. But other companies, including those that sell to other firms, usually do not expect cash upon delivery. Instead, they offer credit terms and have *credit sales* or *sales on account*.[1] An account receivable on the seller's balance sheet is always matched by a corresponding account payable on the buyer's balance sheet. Accounts receivable are reported on the seller's balance sheet at *net realizable value*, which is the net amount the seller expects to collect.

Sellers do not expect to collect all accounts receivable; they anticipate that some buyers will be unable to pay their accounts when they come due. For example, buyers can suffer business downturns that limit the cash available to meet liabilities. Then, buyers must decide which liabilities to pay. Typically, financially distressed companies decide to pay off liabilities to the IRS, to banks, and to bondholders because those creditors have enforcement powers and can quickly seize assets and disrupt operations, leading to bankruptcy and eventual liquidation. Buyers also try to cover their payroll, as they cannot exist without employees. Then, if there is cash remaining, buyers will pay suppliers to ensure continued flow of goods.

Accounts payable are *unsecured liabilities,* meaning that buyers have not pledged collateral to guarantee payment of amounts owed. As a result, when a company declares bankruptcy, accounts payable are comingled with other unsecured creditors (after the IRS and the secured creditors), and are typically not paid in full. Consequently, there is risk in the collectibility of accounts receivable. This *collectibility risk* is crucial to analysis of accounts receivable.

Cisco reports $3,821 million of accounts receivable in the current asset section of its fiscal year-end 2008 balance sheet.

$ millions	July 26, 2008
Cash and cash equivalents	$ 5,191
Investments	21,044
Accounts receivable, net of allowance for doubtful accounts of $177	3,821
Inventories	1,235
Deferred tax assets	2,075
Prepaid expenses and other current assets	2,333
Total current assets	$35,699

Cisco reports its receivables net of allowances for doubtful (uncollectible) accounts of $177 million. This means the total amount owed to Cisco is $3,998 million ($3,821 million + $177 million), but Cisco *estimates* that $177 million are uncollectible and reports on its balance sheet only the amount it expects to collect.

We might ask why buyers would sell to companies from whom they do not expect to collect. The answer is they would not have extended credit *if* they knew beforehand which companies would eventually not pay. For example, Cisco probably cannot identify precisely those companies that constitute the $177 million in uncollectible accounts. Yet, it knows from past experience that a certain portion of its

---

[1] An example of common credit terms are 2/10, net 30. These terms indicate that the seller offers the buyer an early-pay incentive, in this case a 2% discount off the cost if the buyer pays within 10 days of billing. If the buyer does not take advantage of the discount, it must pay 100% of the invoice cost within 30 days of billing. From the seller's standpoint, offering the discount is often warranted because it speeds up cash collections and then the seller can invest the cash to yield a return greater than the early-payment discount. The buyer often wishes to avail itself of attractive discounts even if it has to borrow money to do so. If the discount is not taken, however, the buyer should withhold payment as long as possible (at least for the full net period) so as to maximize its available cash. Meanwhile, the seller will exert whatever pressure it can to collect the amount due as quickly as possible. Thus, it is normal for there to be some tension between sellers and buyers.

receivables will prove uncollectible. GAAP requires companies to estimate the dollar amount of uncollectible accounts (even if managers cannot identify specific accounts that are uncollectible), and to report accounts receivable at the resulting *net realizable value* (total receivables less an allowance for uncollectible accounts).

Allowance for Uncollectible Accounts

Companies typically use an *aging analysis* to estimate the amount of uncollectible accounts. This requires an analysis of receivables as of the balance sheet date. Specifically, customer accounts are categorized by the number of days that the related invoices have been unpaid (outstanding). Based on prior experience, or on other available statistics, uncollectible percentages are applied to each category, with larger percentages applied to older accounts. The result of this analysis is a dollar amount for the allowance for uncollectible accounts (also called allowance for doubtful accounts) at the balance sheet date.

Aging Analysis

To illustrate, Exhibit 6.1 shows an aging analysis for a seller with $100,000 of gross accounts receivable at period-end. The current accounts are those that are still within their original credit period. As an example, if a seller's credit terms are 2/10, net 30, all invoices that have been outstanding for 30 days or fewer are current. Accounts listed as 1–60 days past due are those 1 to 60 days past their due date. This would include an account that is 45 days outstanding for a net 30-day invoice. This same logic applies to all categories.

EXHIBIT 6.1 Aging of Accounts Receivable

Age of Accounts	Receivable Balance	Estimated Percent Uncollectible	Estimated Uncollectible Accounts
Current	$ 50,000	2%	$1,000
1-60 days past due	30,000	3	900
61-90 days past due	15,000	4	600
Over 90 days past due	5,000	8	400
Total	$100,000		$2,900

Exhibit 6.1 also reflects the seller's experience with uncollectible accounts, which manifests itself in the uncollectible percentages for each aged category. For example, on average, 3% of buyers' accounts that are 1-60 days past due prove uncollectible for this seller. Hence, the company estimates a potential loss of $900 for the $30,000 in receivables 1 to 60 days past due.

Reporting Receivables

The seller represented in Exhibit 6.1 reports its accounts receivable on the balance sheet as follows:

Accounts receivable, net of $2,900 in allowances $97,100

Assume that, as of the end of the *previous* accounting period, the company had estimated total uncollectible accounts of $2,200 based on an aging analysis of the receivables at that time. Also assume that the company did not write off any accounts receivable during the period. The *reconciliation* of its allowance account for the period follows:

Beginning allowance for uncollectible accounts . . . . $ 2,200
Add: Provision for uncollectible accounts (bad debts expense)   700
Less: Write-offs of accounts receivable   0
Ending allowance for uncollectible accounts . . . . $ 2,900

The aging analysis revealed that the allowance for uncollectible accounts is $700 too low and therefore, the company increased the allowance accordingly. This adjustment affects the financial statements as follows:

1. Accounts receivable are reduced by an additional $700 on the balance sheet (receivables are reported *net* of the allowance account).

2. A $700 expense, called bad debts expense, is reported in the income statement (usually part of SG&A expense). This reduces pretax profit by the same amount.[2]

The allowance for uncollectible accounts, a contra-asset account, increases with new provisions (additional bad debts expense) and decreases as accounts are written off. Individual accounts are written off when the seller identifies them as uncollectible. (A write-off reduces both accounts receivable and the allowance for uncollectible accounts as described below.) As with all permanent accounts on the balance sheet, the ending balance of the allowance account is the beginning balance for next period.

Writing Off Accounts

To illustrate the write-off of an account receivable, assume that subsequent to the period-end shown above, the seller receives notice that one of its customers, owing $500 at the time, has declared bankruptcy. The seller's attorneys believe that legal costs in attempting to collect this receivable would likely exceed the amount owed. So, the seller decides not to pursue collection and to write off this account. The write-off has the following effects:

1. Gross accounts receivable are reduced from $100,000 to $99,500.
2. Allowance for uncollectible accounts is reduced from $2,900 to $2,400.

After the write-off, the seller's balance sheet appears as follows:

Accounts receivable, net of $2,400 in allowances. $97,100

Exhibit 6.2 shows the effects of this write-off on the individual accounts.

EXHIBIT 6.2 Effects of an Accounts Receivable Write-Off			
Account	Before Write-Off	Effects of Write-Off	After Write-Off
Accounts receivable.	$100,000	$(500)	$99,500
Less: Allowance for uncollectible accounts.	2,900	(500)	2,400
Accounts receivable, net of allowance.	$ 97,100		$97,100

The balance of net accounts receivable is the same before and after the write-off. This is always the case. The write-off of an account is a non-event from an accounting point of view. That is, total assets do not change, liabilities stay the same, and equity is unaffected as there is no net income effect. The write-off affects individual asset accounts, but not total assets.

Let's next consider what happens when additional information arrives that alters management's expectations of uncollectible accounts. To illustrate, assume that sometime after the write-off above, the seller realizes that it has underestimated uncollectible accounts and that $3,000 (not $2,400) of the remaining $99,500 accounts receivable are uncollectible. The company must increase the allowance for uncollectible accounts by $600. The additional $600 provision has the following financial statement effects:

1. Allowance for uncollectible accounts increases by $600 to the revised estimated balance of $3,000; and accounts receivable (net of the allowance for uncollectible accounts) declines by $600 from $97,100 to $96,500 (or $99,500 − $3,000).
2. A $600 bad debts expense is added to the income statement, which reduces pretax income. Recall that in the prior period, the seller reported $700 of bad debts expense when the allowance account was increased from $2,200 to $2,900.

---

[2] Companies can also estimate uncollectible accounts using the *percentage of sales* method. The percentage of sales method computes bad debts expense directly, as a percentage of sales and the allowance for uncollectible accounts is estimated indirectly. In contrast, the aging method computes the allowance balance directly and the bad debts expense is the amount required to bring the allowance account up to (or down to) the amount determined by the aging analysis. To illustrate, if the company in Exhibit 6.1 reports sales of $100,000 and estimates the provision at 1% of sales, it would report a bad debts expense of $1,000 and an allowance balance of $3,200 instead of the $700 bad debts expense and the $2,900 allowance as determined using the aging analysis. The two methods nearly always report different values for the allowance, net accounts receivable, and bad debts expense.

Analyzing Receivable Transactions

To summarize, recording bad debts expense increases the allowance for uncollectible accounts, which affects both the *balance sheet* and *income statement*. Importantly, the financial statement effects occur when the allowance is estimated, and not when accounts are written off. In this way, bad debts expense is matched with sales on the income statement, and accounts receivable are reported net of uncollectible accounts on the balance sheet. Exhibit 6.3 illustrates each of the transactions discussed in this section using the financial statement effects template:

EXHIBIT 6.3 Financial Statement Effects of Key Accounts Receivable Transactions

	Balance Sheet						Income Statement		
Transaction	Cash Asset	+ Noncash Assets	= Liabil- ities	+ Contrib. Capital	+ Earned Capital		Rev- enues	− Expen- ses	= Net Income
a. Credit sales of $100,000		+100,000 Accounts Receivable =			+100,000 Retained Earnings		+100,000 Sales −		= +100,000
b. Increase allowance for uncol- lectible accounts by $700		−700 Allowance for Uncollectible Accounts =			−700 Retained Earnings		−	+700 Bad Debts Expense	= −700
c. Write off $500 in accounts receivable		−500 Accounts Receivable +500 Allowance for Uncollectible Accounts =					−		=
d. Increase allowance for uncol- lectible accounts by $600		−600 Allowance for Uncollectible Accounts =			−600 Retained Earnings		−	+600 Bad Debts Expense	= −600

T-account notations in left margin:

a. AR 100,000 / Sales 100,000; AR 100,000 | ; Sales | 100,000

b. BDE 700 / AU 700; BDE 700 | ; AU | 700

c. AU 500 / AR 500; AU 500 | ; AR | 500

d. BDE 600 / AU 600; BDE 600 | ; AU | 600

Footnote Disclosures

To illustrate the typical accounts receivable footnote disclosure, consider Cisco's discussion of its allowance for uncollectible accounts:

> **Allowance for Doubtful Accounts and Sales Returns** Our accounts receivable balance, net of allowance for doubtful accounts, was $3.8 billion and $4.0 billion as of July 26, 2008 and July 28, 2007, respectively. The allowance for doubtful accounts was $177 million, or 4.4% of the gross accounts receivable balance, as of July 26, 2008, and $166 million, or 4.0% of the gross accounts receivable balance, as of July 28, 2007. The allowance is based on our assessment of the collectability of customer accounts. We regularly review the allowance by considering factors such as historical experience, credit quality, age of the accounts receivable balances, and current economic conditions that may affect a customer's ability to pay. Our provision for doubtful accounts was $34 million, $6 million, and $24 million for fiscal 2008, 2007, and 2006, respectively. If a major customer's creditworthiness deteriorates, or if actual defaults are higher than our historical experience, or if other circumstances arise, our estimates of the recoverability of amounts due to us could be overstated, and additional allowances could be required, which could have an adverse impact on our revenue.

Cisco's allowance for uncollectible accounts increased slightly as a percentage of gross receivables from the prior year, from 4.0% to 4.4%. As the level of uncollectible accounts increases, the company recognizes more bad debts expense. The effect is to lower net income. Cisco alludes to the level of estimation required, and cautions the reader that additional allowances (provisions) could be required under certain circumstances, and that would adversely affect profit.

Cisco provides a footnote reconciliation of its allowance for uncollectible (doubtful) accounts for the past three years as shown in Exhibit 6.4.

EXHIBIT 6.4 Reconciliation of Cisco's Allowance for Uncollectible Accounts	
$ millions	**Allowance for Doubtful Accounts**
Allowances For Accounts Receivable	
Year ended July 29, 2006	
Balance at beginning of fiscal year.	$162
Provision.	24
Write-offs and other	(11)
Balance at end of fiscal year	$175
Year ended July 28, 2007	
Balance at beginning of fiscal year.	$175
Provision.	6
Write-offs and other	(15)
Balance at end of fiscal year	$166
Year ended July 26, 2008	
Balance at beginning of fiscal year.	$166
Provision.	34
Write-offs and other	(23)
Balance at end of fiscal year	$177

Reconciling Cisco's allowance account provides insight into the level of the provision (expense) each year relative to the actual write-offs. Cisco wrote off $11 million of accounts receivable in 2006, $15 million in 2007, and $23 million in 2008. Over the same period, Cisco reduced its allowance as a percentage of gross receivables from 5.0% ($175 million/$3,478 million) in 2006 to 4.0% ($166 million/$4,155 million) in 2007; then, increased it slightly to 4.4% ($177 million/$3,998 million) in 2008. Its allowance account as a percentage of gross accounts receivable as of 2008 is markedly less than the 10% level it reported five years earlier.

Analysis Implications

This section considers analysis of accounts receivable and the allowance for uncollectible accounts.

Adequacy of Allowance Account

A company makes two representations when reporting accounts receivable (net) in the current asset section of its balance sheet:

1. It expects to collect the amount reported on the balance sheet (remember, accounts receivable are reported net of allowance for uncollectible accounts).

2. It expects to collect the amount within the next year (implied by the classification of accounts receivable as a current asset).

From an analysis viewpoint, we scrutinize the adequacy of a company's provision for its uncollectible accounts. If the provision is inadequate, the cash ultimately collected will be less than the net receivables reported on the balance sheet.

How can an outsider assess the adequacy of the allowance account? One answer is to compare the allowance account to gross accounts receivable for the company and for its competitors. For Cisco, the 2008 percentage is 4.4% (see above), a 44% decline from the level it reported in 2003. What does such a decline signify? Perhaps the overall economic environment has improved, rendering write-offs less likely. Perhaps the company has improved its credit underwriting or receivables collection efforts. The MD&A section of the 10-K report is likely to discuss such new initiatives. Or perhaps the company's customer mix has changed and it is now selling to more creditworthy customers (or, it eliminated a risky class of customers).

The important point is that we must be comfortable with the percentage of uncollectible accounts reported by the company. We must remember that management controls the size of the allowance account—albeit with audit assurances.

Income Shifting

We noted that the financial statement effects of uncollectible accounts transpire when the allowance is increased for new bad debts expense and not when the allowance is decreased for the write-off of uncollectible accounts. It is also important to note that management controls the amount and timing of the bad debts expense. Although external auditors assess the reasonableness of the allowance for uncollectible accounts, they do not possess management's inside knowledge and experience. This puts the auditors at an information disadvantage, particularly if any dispute arises.

Studies show that many companies use the allowance for uncollectible accounts to shift income from one year into another. For example, a company can increase current-period income by deliberately under-estimating bad debts expense. However, in the future it will become apparent that the bad debts expense was too low when the company's write-offs exceed the balance in the allowance account. Then, the company will need to increase the allowance to make up for the earlier period's underestimate. As an example, consider a company that accurately estimates that it has $1,000 of uncollectible accounts at the end of 2008. Assume that the current balance in the allowance for uncollectible accounts is $200. But instead of recording bad debts expense of $800 as needed to have an adequate ($1,000) allowance, the company records only $100 of bad debts expense and reports an allowance of $300 at the end of 2008. Now if the company's original estimate was accurate, in 2009 it will write off accounts totaling $1,000. The write-offs ($1,000) are greater than the allowance balance ($300) and the company will need to increase the allowance by recording an additional $700 in 2009. The effect of this is that the company borrowed $700 of income from 2009 to report higher income in 2008. This is called "income shifting."

Why would a company want to shift income from a later period into the current period? Perhaps it is a lean year and the company is in danger of missing income targets. For example, internal targets influence manager bonuses and external targets set by the market influence stock prices. Or, perhaps the company is in danger of defaulting on loan agreements tied to income levels. The reality is that income pressures are great and these pressures can cause managers to bend (or even break) the rules.

Companies can just as easily shift income from the current period to one or more future periods by overestimating the current period bad debts expense and allowance for uncollectible accounts. Why would a company want to shift income to one or more future periods? Perhaps current times are good and the company wants to "bank" some of that income for future periods, sometimes called a *cookie jar reserve*. It can then draw on that reserve, if necessary, to boost income in one or more future lean years. Another reason for a company to shift income from the current period is that it does not wish to unduly inflate market expectations for future period income. Or perhaps the company is experiencing a very bad year and it feels that overestimating the provision will not drive income materially lower than it is. Thus, it decides to take a big bath (a large loss) and create a reserve that can be used in future periods. (Sears provides an interesting case as described in the Business Insight box).

BUSINESS INSIGHT   **Sears' Cookie Jar**

A column several years ago in *The Wall Street Journal* reported on an equity analyst that asserted Sears' earnings growth was aided by a balance sheet maneuver of three years earlier that softened the impact of soaring levels of bad credit card debt. Namely, despite soaring credit losses, Sears had reported an earnings *increase*. How so? The analyst explained that Sears had markedly increased its allowance for uncollectible accounts in that earlier year (to a level twice that of similar companies) and had reported the related bad debts expense in that year when its earnings were high. The resulting reserve was much higher than needed. Then, when earnings were low, Sears charged its credit losses to the allowance for uncollectible accounts. However, since the balance of the allowance for uncollectible accounts was so large, no increase in that account was necessary and little or no bad debts expense was reported. Why is this a concern? The overstated reserve allowed Sears to prop up its earnings at a time when losses in its credit card unit were soaring. The analyst concluded that the increase in Sears' year-to-date earnings has depended entirely on its over-reserved allowance.

Use of the allowance for uncollectible accounts to shift income is a source of concern. This is especially so for banks where the allowance for loan losses is a large component of banks' balance sheets and loan loss expense is a major component of reported income. Our analysis must scrutinize the allowance for uncollectible accounts to identify any changes from past practices or industry norms and, then, to justify those changes before accepting them as valid.

Accounts Receivable Turnover and Average Collection Period

The net operating asset turnover (NOAT) is sales divided by average net operating assets. An important component of this measure is the **accounts receivable turnover (ART)**, which is defined as:[3]

Accounts Receivable Turnover = Sales/Average Accounts Receivable, gross

Accounts receivable turnover reveals how many times receivables have turned (been collected) during the period. More turns indicate that receivables are being collected more quickly.

A companion measure to accounts receivable turnover is the **average collection period (ACP)** for accounts receivable, also called *days sales outstanding*, which is defined as:

Average Collection Period = Accounts Receivable, gross/Average Daily Sales

where average daily sales equals sales divided by 365 days. The average collection period indicates how long, on average, the receivables are outstanding before being collected.[4]

To illustrate, Cisco's 2008 total net sales (products and services) are $39,540 million, gross accounts receivable are $3,998 million at year-end, and $4,155 million at the prior year-end (average is $4,076.5 million). Thus, its accounts receivable turnover is 9.7, computed as $39,540/$4,076.5, and its average collection period (days sales outstanding) is 37 days, computed as $3,998/($39,540/365 days).

The accounts receivable turnover and the average collection period yield valuable insights on at least two dimensions:

1. *Receivables quality* Changes in receivable turnover (and collection period) speak to accounts receivable quality. If turnover slows (collection period lengthens), the reason could be deterioration in collectibility. However, there are at least three alternative explanations:

   a. *A seller can extend its credit terms.* If the seller is attempting to enter new markets or take market share from competitors, it may extend credit terms to attract buyers.

   b. *A seller can take on longer-paying customers.* For example, facing increased competition, automobile and other manufacturing companies began leasing their products, thus reducing customers' cash outlays and stimulating sales. Moving away from cash sales and toward leasing reduced receivables turnover and increased the collection period.

   c. *The seller can increase the allowance provision.* Receivables turnover is sometimes computed using net receivables (after the allowance for uncollectible accounts). In this case, overestimating the provision reduces net receivables and increases the turnover ratio. Accordingly, the apparent improvement in turnover could be incorrectly attributed to improved operating performance rather than a decline in the quality of the receivables.

---

[3] Technically, the numerator should be net credit sales because receivables arise from credit sales. Including cash sales in the numerator inflates the ratio. Typically, outsiders do not know the level of cash sales and, therefore, must use total sales to calculate the turnover ratio.

[4] The average collection period computation in this module uses *ending* accounts receivable. This focuses the analysis on the most current receivables. Cisco uses a variant of this approach, described in its MD&A section as follows: Accounts receivable/ Average annualized 4Q sales (or AR/[(4Q Sales × 4)/365]). Arguably, Cisco's variant focuses even more on the most recent collection period because ending accounts receivable relate more closely to 4Q sales than to reported annual sales. Most analysts use the reported annual sales instead of the annualized 4Q sales because the former are easily accessed in financial statement databases. As an alternative, we could also examine average daily sales in *average* accounts receivable (Average accounts receivable/Average daily sales). The approach we use in the text addresses the average collection period of *current* (ending) accounts receivable, and the latter approach examines the average collection period of *average* accounts receivable. The "correct" ratio depends on the issue we wish to investigate. It is important to choose the formula that best answers the question we are asking.

2. *Asset utilization* Asset turnover is an important financial performance measure used both by managers for internal performance goals, as well as by the market in evaluating companies. High-performing companies must be both effective (controlling margins and operating expenses) and efficient (getting the most out of their asset base). An increase in receivables ties up cash. As well, slower-turning receivables carry increased risk of loss. One of the first "low-hanging fruits" that companies pursue in efforts to improve overall asset utilization is efficiency in receivables collection.

The following chart shows the average collection period for accounts receivable of Cisco and three peer competitors that Cisco indentifies in its 10-K.

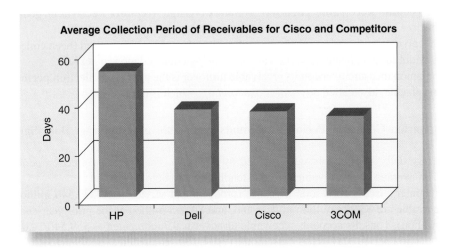

Cisco's average collection period of 37 days compares favorably with its primary competitors. HP's longer collection period is a result of its leasing activities.

To appreciate differences in average collection periods across industries, let's compare the average collection periods across a number of industries as follows:

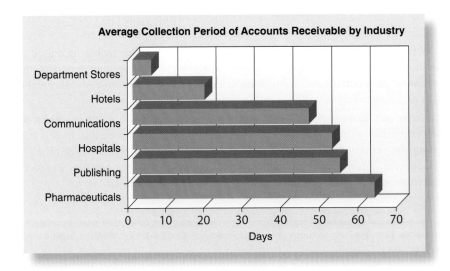

Department stores and hotels have the shortest collection periods. For those industries, receivables are minimal because sales are made mainly via cash, check or credit card. Most of the other industries in the table have collection periods ranging from 30 to 60 days. This corresponds with typical credit terms offered on commercial transactions. Pharmaceutical companies and hospitals have longer collection periods because they often require payment from third-party insurers and government agencies such as Medicare and the Veterans' Administration.

MANAGERIAL DECISION	You Are the Receivables Manager

You are analyzing your receivables turnover report for the period and you are concerned that the average collection period is lengthening. What specific actions can you take to reduce the average collection period? [Answer, p. 6-37]

MID-MODULE REVIEW 1

At December 31, 2009, assume that 3COM had a balance of $770,000 in its Accounts Receivable account and a balance of $7,000 in its Allowance for Uncollectible Accounts. The company then analyzed and aged its accounts receivable as shown below. Assume that 3COM experienced past losses as follows: 1% of current balances, 5% of balances 1-60 days past due, 15% of balances 61-180 days past due, and 40% of balances over 180 days past due. The company bases its provision for credit losses on the aging analysis.

Current	$468,000
1-60 days past due	244,000
61-180 days past due	38,000
Over 180 days past due	20,000
Total accounts receivable	$770,000

Required

1. What amount of uncollectible accounts (bad debts) expense will 3COM report in its 2009 income statement?
2. Show how Accounts Receivable and the Allowance for Uncollectible Accounts appear in its December 31, 2009, balance sheet.
3. Assume that 3COM's allowance for uncollectible accounts has maintained an historical average of 2% of gross accounts receivable. How do you interpret the current allowance percentage?

Solution

1. As of December 31, 2009:

Current	$468,000 ×	1% =	$ 4,680	
1-60 days past due	244,000 ×	5% =	12,200	
61-180 days past due	38,000 ×	15% =	5,700	
Over 180 days past due	20,000 ×	40% =	8,000	
Amount required			30,580	
Unused allowance balance			7,000	
Provision			$ 23,580	2009 bad debts expense

2. Current assets section of balance sheet:

Accounts receivable, net of $30,580 in allowances . . .	$739,420

3. The information here reveals that 3COM has markedly increased the percentage of the allowance for uncollectible accounts to gross accounts receivable; from the historical 2% to the current 4% ($30,580/$770,000). There are at least two possible interpretations:

   a. The quality of 3COM's receivables has declined. Possible causes include the following: (1) Sales have stagnated and the company is selling to lower-quality accounts to maintain sales volume; (2) It may have introduced new products for which average credit losses are higher; and (3) Its administration of accounts receivable has become lax.

   b. The company has intentionally increased its allowance account above the level needed for expected future losses so as to reduce current period income and "bank" that income for future periods (income shifting).

INVENTORY

LO2 Explain accounting for inventories and assess the effects on the balance sheet and income statement from different inventory costing methods.

The second major component of operating working capital is inventory. To help frame this discussion, we refer to the following graphic that highlights inventory, a major asset for manufacturers and merchandisers. The graphic also highlights cost of goods sold on the income statement, which reflects the matching of inventory costs to related sales. This section explains the accounting, reporting, and analysis of inventory and related items.

Income Statement	Balance Sheet	
Sales	Cash	Current liabilities
Cost of goods sold	Accounts receivable, net	Long-term liabilities
Selling, general & administrative	**Inventory**	
Income taxes	Property, plant, and equipment, net	Shareholders' equity
Net income	Investments	

Inventory is reported on the balance sheet at its purchase price or the cost to manufacture goods that are internally produced. Inventory costs vary over time with changes in market conditions. Consequently, the cost per unit of the goods available for sale varies from period to period—even if the quantity of goods available remains the same.

When inventory is purchased or produced, it is "capitalized." That is, it is carried on the balance sheet as an asset until it is sold, at which time its cost is transferred from the balance sheet to the income statement as an expense (cost of goods sold). The process by which costs are removed from the balance sheet is important. For example, if higher cost units are transferred from the balance sheet, then cost of goods sold is higher and gross profit (sales less cost of goods sold) is lower. Conversely, if lower cost units are transferred to cost of goods sold, gross profit is higher. The remainder of this section discusses the accounting for inventory including the mechanics, reporting, and analysis of inventory costing.

Capitalization of Inventory Cost

Capitalization means that a cost is recorded on the balance sheet and is not immediately expensed on the income statement. Once costs are capitalized, they remain on the balance sheet as assets until they are used up, at which time they are transferred from the balance sheet to the income statement as expense. If costs are capitalized rather than expensed, then assets, current income, and current equity are all higher.

For purchased inventories (such as merchandise), the amount of cost capitalized is the purchase price. For manufacturers, cost capitalization is more difficult, as **manufacturing costs** consist of three components: cost of direct materials used in the product, cost of direct labor to manufacture the product, and manufacturing overhead. Direct materials cost is relatively easy to compute. Design specifications list the components of each product, and their purchase costs are readily determined. The direct labor cost per unit of inventory is based on how long each unit takes to construct and the rates for each labor class working on that product. Overhead costs are also capitalized into inventory, and include the costs of plant asset depreciation, utilities, supervisory personnel, and other costs that contribute to manufacturing activities—that is, all costs of manufacturing other than direct materials and direct labor. (How these costs are assigned to individual units and across multiple products is a *managerial accounting* topic.)

When inventories are sold, their costs are transferred from the balance sheet to the income statement as cost of goods sold (COGS). COGS is then deducted from sales to yield **gross profit**:

$$\textbf{Gross Profit} = \textbf{Sales} - \textbf{Cost of Goods Sold}$$

The manner in which inventory costs are transferred from the balance sheet to the income statement affects both the level of inventories reported on the balance sheet and the amount of gross profit (and net income) reported on the income statement.

Inventory Costing Methods

Exhibit 6.5 shows the computation of cost of goods sold.

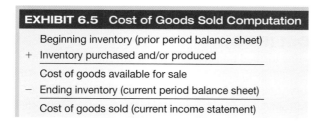

EXHIBIT 6.5   Cost of Goods Sold Computation

Beginning inventory (prior period balance sheet)
+ Inventory purchased and/or produced

Cost of goods available for sale
− Ending inventory (current period balance sheet)

Cost of goods sold (current income statement)

The cost of inventory available at the beginning of a period is a carryover from the ending inventory balance of the prior period. Current period inventory purchases (or costs of newly manufactured inventories) are added to the beginning inventory balance, yielding the total cost of goods (inventory) available for sale. Then, the goods available are either sold, and end up in cost of goods sold for the period (reported on the income statement), or the goods available remain unsold and are still in inventory at the end of the period (reported on the balance sheet). Exhibit 6.6 shows this cost flow graphically.

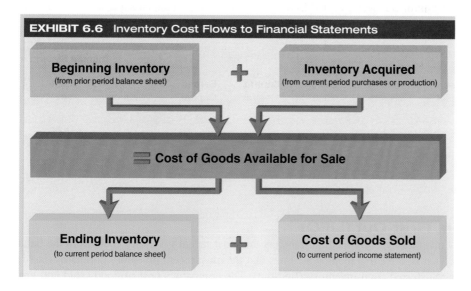

EXHIBIT 6.6   Inventory Cost Flows to Financial Statements

Beginning Inventory
(from prior period balance sheet)

Inventory Acquired
(from current period purchases or production)

Cost of Goods Available for Sale

Ending Inventory
(to current period balance sheet)

Cost of Goods Sold
(to current period income statement)

Understanding the flow of inventory costs is important. If all inventory purchased or manufactured during the period is sold, then COGS is equal to the cost of the goods purchased or manufactured. However, when inventory remains at the end of a period, companies must distinguish the cost of the inventories that were sold from the cost of the inventories that remain. GAAP allows for several options.

Exhibit 6.7 illustrates the partial inventory records of a company.

EXHIBIT 6.7   Summary Inventory Records

Inventory on January 1, 2009.	500 units	@ $100 per unit	$ 50,000
Inventory purchased in 2009	200 units	@ $150 per unit	30,000
Total cost of goods available for sale in 2009	700 units		$ 80,000
Inventory sold in 2009	450 units	@ $250 per unit	$112,500

This company began the period with 500 units of inventory that were purchased or manufactured for $50,000 ($100 each). During the period the company purchased and/or manufactured an additional 200 units costing $30,000. The total cost of goods available for sale for this period equals $80,000.

The company sold 450 units during 2009 for $250 per unit for total sales of $112,500. Accordingly, the company must remove the cost of the 450 units sold from the inventory account on the balance sheet and match this cost against the revenues generated from the sale. An important question is which costs should management remove from the balance sheet and report as cost of goods sold in the income statement? Three inventory costing methods (FIFO, LIFO and average cost) are common and all are acceptable under GAAP.

First-In, First-Out (FIFO)

The FIFO inventory costing method transfers costs from inventory in the order that they were initially recorded. That is, FIFO assumes that the first costs recorded in inventory (first-in) are the first costs transferred from inventory (first-out). Applying FIFO to the data in Exhibit 6.7 means that the costs of the 450 units sold comes from *beginning* inventory, which consists of 500 units costing $100 each. The company's cost of goods sold and gross profit, using FIFO, is computed as follows:

Sales.	$112,500
COGS (450 @ $100 each).	45,000
Gross profit.	$ 67,500

The cost remaining in inventory and reported on the 2009 year-end balance sheet is $35,000 ($80,000 goods available for sale less $45,000 COGS). The following financial statement effects template captures the transaction.

	Balance Sheet						Income Statement		
Transaction	**Cash Asset**	**+ Noncash Assets**	**= Liabil- ities**	**+ Contrib. Capital**	**+ Earned Capital**		**Rev- enues**	**– Expen- ses**	**= Net Income**
Sold 450 units using FIFO costing (450 @ $100 each)		−45,000 Inventory =			−45,000 Retained Earnings			+45,000 – Cost of Goods Sold	= −45,000

COGS 45,000
  INV   45,000

COGS
45,000 |
      INV
      | 45,000

Last-In, First-Out (LIFO)

The LIFO inventory costing method transfers the most recent inventory costs from the balance sheet to COGS. That is, the LIFO method assumes that the most recent inventory purchases (last-in) are the first costs transferred from inventory (first-out). The company's cost of goods sold and gross profit, using LIFO, is computed as follows:

Sales.		$112,500
COGS: 200 @ $150 per unit	$30,000	
250 @ $100 per unit	25,000	55,000
Gross profit.		$ 57,500

The cost remaining in inventory and reported on the company's 2009 balance sheet is $25,000 (computed as $80,000 − $55,000). This is reflected in our financial statements effects template as follows.

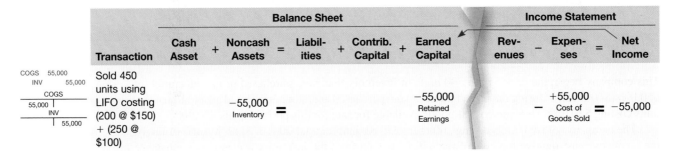

	Balance Sheet						Income Statement		
Transaction	**Cash Asset**	**+ Noncash Assets**	**= Liabil- ities**	**+ Contrib. Capital**	**+ Earned Capital**		**Rev- enues**	**– Expen- ses**	**= Net Income**
Sold 450 units using LIFO costing (200 @ $150) + (250 @ $100)		−55,000 Inventory =			−55,000 Retained Earnings			+55,000 – Cost of Goods Sold	= −55,000

COGS 55,000
  INV   55,000

COGS
55,000 |
      INV
      | 55,000

Average Cost (AC)

The average cost method computes the cost of goods sold as an average of the cost to purchase or manufacture all of the inventories that were available for sale during the period. To calculate the average cost of $114.286 per unit the company divides the total cost of goods available for sale by the number of units available for sale ($80,000/700 units). The company's sales, cost of sales, and gross profit follow.

Sales.	$112,500
COGS (450 @ $114.286 per unit)	51,429
Gross profit.	$ 61,071

The cost remaining in inventory and reported on the company's 2009 balance sheet is $28,571 ($80,000 − $51,429). This is reflected in our financial statements effects template as follows.

Transaction	Balance Sheet					Income Statement		
	Cash Asset	+ Noncash Assets	= Liabil- ities	+ Contrib. Capital	+ Earned Capital	Rev- enues	− Expen- ses	= Net Income
Sold 450 units using average cost method (450 @ $114.286)		−51,429 Inventory =			−51,429 Retained Earnings		+51,429 − Cost of Goods Sold =	−51,429

COGS 51,429
INV 51,429

COGS
51,429 |

INV
| 51,429

It is important to understand that the inventory costing method a company chooses is independent of the actual flow of inventory. The method choice determines COGS and ending inventory but not the actual physical inventory sold. For example, many grocery chains use LIFO inventory but certainly do not sell the freshest products first. (Companies do not frequently change inventory costing methods. Companies can adopt a new inventory costing method if doing so enhances the quality of the company's financial reports. Also, IRS regulations prohibit certain inventory costing method changes.)

Lower of Cost or Market

Companies must write down the carrying amount of inventories on the balance sheet *if* the reported cost (using FIFO, for example) exceeds market value (determined by current replacement cost). This process is called reporting inventories at the **lower of cost or market** and creates the following financial statement effects:

■ Inventory book value is written down to current market value (replacement cost), reducing inventory and total assets.

■ Inventory write-down is reflected as an expense (part of cost of goods sold) on the income statement, reducing current period gross profit, income, and equity.

To illustrate, assume that a company has inventory on its balance sheet at a cost of $27,000. Management learns that the inventory's replacement cost is $23,000 and writes inventories down to a balance of $23,000. The following financial statement effects template shows the adjustment.

Transaction	Balance Sheet					Income Statement		
	Cash Asset	+ Noncash Assets	= Liabil- ities	+ Contrib. Capital	+ Earned Capital	Rev- enues	− Expen- ses	= Net Income
Write down inventory from $27,000 to $23,000.		−4,000 Inventory =			−4,000 Retained Earnings		+4,000 − Cost of Goods Sold =	−4,000

COGS 4,000
INV 4,000

COGS
4,000 |

INV
| 4,000

The inventory write-down (a noncash expense) is reflected in cost of goods sold and reduces gross profit by $4,000. Inventory write-downs are included in cost of goods sold. They are *not* reported in selling, general, and administrative expenses, which is common for other asset write-downs. The most common occurrence of inventory write-downs is in connection with restructuring activities.

The write-down of inventories can potentially shift income from one period to another. If, for example, inventories were written down below current replacement cost, future gross profit would be increased via lower future cost of goods sold. GAAP anticipates this possibility by requiring that inventories not be written down below a floor that is equal to net realizable value less a normal markup. Although this still allows some discretion (and the ability to manage income), the auditors must assess net realizable value and markups.

IFRS INSIGHT   Inventory Measurement under IFRS

Like GAAP, IFRS measures inventories at the lower of cost or market. The cost of inventory generally is determined using the FIFO (first-in, first-out) or weighted average cost method; use of the LIFO (last-in, first-out) method is prohibited under IFRS.

Footnote Disclosures

Notes to financial statements describe the inventory accounting method a company uses. To illustrate, Cisco reports $1,235 million in inventory on its 2008 balance sheet as a current asset. Cisco includes a general footnote on inventory along with more specific disclosures in other footnotes. Following is an excerpt from Cisco's general footnote on inventories.

> **Inventories.** Inventories are stated at the lower of cost or market. Cost is computed using standard cost, which approximates actual cost, on a first-in, first-out basis. The Company provides inventory write-downs based on excess and obsolete inventories determined primarily by future demand forecasts. The write down is measured as the difference between the cost of the inventory and market based upon assumptions about future demand and charged to the provision for inventory, which is a component of cost of sales. At the point of the loss recognition, a new, lower-cost basis for that inventory is established, and subsequent changes in facts and circumstances do not result in the restoration or increase in that newly established cost basis.

This footnote includes at least two items of interest for our analysis of inventory:

1. Cisco uses the FIFO method of inventory costing.
2. Inventories are reported at the lower of cost or market (LCM). For example, if the current value of Cisco's inventories is less than its reported cost, Cisco would set up an "allowance" for inventories, similar to the allowance for uncollectible accounts. The inventory allowance reduces the reported inventory amount to the current (lower) market value.

Cisco also includes a more detailed inventory footnote as follows:

Inventories ($ millions)	July 26, 2008		July 28, 2007	
Raw materials.		$ 111		$ 173
Work in process		53		45
Finished goods.				
Distributor inventory and deferred cost of sales.	$ 452		$ 544	
Manufacturing finished goods	381		314	
Total finished goods		833		858
Service related spares		191		211
Demonstration systems		47		35
Total		$1,235		$1,322

This disclosure separately reports inventory costs by the following stages in the production cycle:

- *Raw materials and supplies* These are costs of direct materials and inputs into the production process including, for example, chemicals in raw state, plastic and steel for manufacturing, and incidental direct materials such as screws and lubricants.
- *Work in process* These are costs of partly finished products (also called work-in-progress).
- *Finished goods* These are the costs of products that are completed and awaiting sale.

Why do companies disclose such details about inventory? First, investment in inventory is typically large—markedly impacting both balance sheets and income statements. Second, risks of inventory losses are often high, due to technical obsolescence and consumer tastes. This is an important issue for a company such as Cisco that operates in a technology-sensitive industry. Indeed, Cisco reported a loss of over $2 billion in 2001 when the tech bubble burst, demand dried up, and the company had to write down unsalable inventories. Third, inventory details can provide insight into future performance—both good and bad. Fourth, high inventory levels result in substantial costs for the company, such as the following:

- Financing costs to hold inventories (when not purchased on credit or when held beyond credit period)
- Storage costs (such as warehousing and related facilities)
- Handling costs (including wages)
- Insurance costs

Consequently, companies seek to minimize inventory levels provided this does not exceed the cost of holding insufficient inventory, called stock-outs. Stock-outs result in lost sales and production delays if machines and employees must be reconfigured to fill order backlogs. Cisco's total inventories have remained at 2004 levels despite a $14.5 billion increase in sales.

Financial Statement Effects of Inventory Costing

This section describes the financial statement effects of different inventory costing methods.

Income Statement Effects

The three inventory costing methods yield differing levels of gross profit as Exhibit 6.8 shows.

EXHIBIT 6.8	Income Effects from Inventory Costing Methods		
	Sales	Cost of Goods Sold	Gross Profit
FIFO	$112,500	$45,000	$67,500
LIFO	112,500	55,000	57,500
Average cost	112,500	51,429	61,071

Recall that inventory costs rose during this period from $100 per unit to $150 per unit. The higher gross profit reported under FIFO arises because FIFO matches older, lower cost inventory against current selling prices. To generalize: in an inflationary environment, FIFO yields higher gross profit than do LIFO or average cost methods.

In recent years, the gross profit impact from using the FIFO method has been minimal for companies due to lower rates of inflation and increased management focus on reducing inventory quantities through improved manufacturing processes and better inventory controls. The FIFO gross profit effect can still arise, however, with companies subject to high inflation and slow inventory turnover.

Balance Sheet Effects

In our illustration above, the ending inventory using LIFO is less than that reported using FIFO. In periods of rising costs, LIFO inventories are markedly lower than under FIFO. As a result, balance sheets using LIFO do not accurately represent the cost that a company would incur to replace its current investment in inventories.

Caterpillar (CAT), for example, reports 2007 inventories under LIFO costing $7,204 million. As disclosed in the footnotes to its 10-K (see below), if CAT valued these inventories using FIFO, the reported amount would be $2,617 million greater, a 36% increase. This suggests that CAT's balance sheet omits over $2,617 million in inventories.

Cash Flow Effects

Unlike for most other accounting method choices, inventory costing methods affect taxable income and, thus, taxes paid. When a company adopts LIFO in its tax filings, the IRS requires it to also use LIFO for financial reporting purposes (in its 10-K). This requirement is known as the *LIFO conformity rule*. In an inflationary economy, using FIFO results in higher taxable income and, consequently, higher taxes payable. Conversely, using LIFO reduces the tax liability.

Caterpillar, Inc., discloses the following inventory information in its 2007 10-K:

> Inventories are stated at the lower of cost or market. Cost is principally determined using the last-in, first-out (LIFO) method. The value of inventories on the LIFO basis represented about 75% of total inventories at December 31, 2007 and 2006, and about 80% of total inventories at December 31, 2005.
> If the FIFO (first-in, first-out) method had been in use, inventories would have been $2,617 million, $2,403 million and $2,345 million higher than reported at December 31, 2007, 2006 and 2005, respectively.

CAT uses LIFO for most of its inventories.[5] The use of LIFO has reduced the carrying amount of 2007 inventories by $2,617 million. Had it used FIFO, its inventories would have been reported at $9,821 million ($7,204 million + $2,617 million) rather than the $7,204 million that is reported on its balance sheet as of 2007. This difference, referred to as the **LIFO reserve**, is the amount that must be added to LIFO inventories to adjust them to their FIFO value.

$$\textbf{FIFO Inventory = LIFO Inventory + LIFO Reserve}$$

This relation also impacts cost of goods sold (COGS) as follows:

$$\textbf{FIFO COGS = LIFO COGS − Increase in LIFO Reserve (or + Decrease)}$$

Use of LIFO reduced CAT's inventories by $2,617 million, resulting in a cumulative increase in cost of goods sold and a cumulative decrease in gross profit and pretax profit of that same amount.[6] Because CAT also uses LIFO for tax purposes, the decrease in pretax profits reduced CAT's cumulative tax bill by about $916 million ($2,617 million × 35% assumed corporate tax rate). This had real cash flow consequences: CAT's cumulative operating cash flow was $916 million higher because CAT used LIFO instead of FIFO. The increased cash flow from tax savings is often cited as a compelling reason for management to adopt LIFO.

Because companies use different inventory costing methods, their financial statements are often not comparable. The problem is most serious when companies hold large amounts of inventory and when prices markedly rise or fall. To compare companies using different inventory costing methods, say LIFO and FIFO, we need to adjust the LIFO numbers to their FIFO equivalents or vice versa. For example, one way to compare CAT with another company that uses FIFO, is to add CAT's LIFO reserve to its LIFO inventory. As explained above, this $2,617 million increase in 2007 inventories would have increased its cumulative pretax profits by $2,617 million and taxes by $916 million. Thus, to adjust the 2007 balance sheet we increase inventories by $2,617 million, tax liabilities by $916 million (the extra taxes CAT would have had to pay under FIFO), and equity by the difference of $1,701 million (computed as $2,617 − $916).

---

[5] Neither the IRS nor GAAP requires use of a single inventory costing method. That is, companies are allowed to, and frequently do, use different inventory costing methods for different types of inventory (such as spare parts versus finished goods).

[6] Recall: Cost of Goods Sold = Beginning Inventories + Purchases − Ending Inventories. Thus, as ending inventories decrease, cost of goods sold increases.

To adjust CAT's 2007 income statement from LIFO to FIFO, we use the change in LIFO reserve. For CAT, the LIFO reserve increased by $214 million during 2007, from $2,403 million in 2006 to $2,617 million in 2007. This means that had it been using FIFO, its COGS would have been $214 million lower, and 2007 gross profit and pretax income would have been $214 million higher. In 2007, CAT would have paid $75 million more in taxes had it used FIFO ($214 million × 35% assumed tax rate).

RESEARCH INSIGHT | **LIFO and Stock Prices**

The value-relevance of inventory disclosures depends at least partly on whether investors rely more on the income statement or the balance sheet to assess future cash flows. Under LIFO, cost of goods sold reflects current costs, whereas FIFO ending inventory reflects current costs. This implies that LIFO enhances the usefulness of the income statement to the detriment of the balance sheet. This trade-off partly motivates the required LIFO reserve disclosure (the adjustment necessary to restate LIFO ending inventory and cost of good sold to FIFO). Research suggests that LIFO-based income statements better reflect stock prices than do FIFO income statements that are restated using the LIFO reserve. Research also shows a negative relation between stock prices and LIFO reserve—meaning that higher magnitudes of LIFO reserve are associated with lower stock prices. This is consistent with the LIFO reserve being viewed as an inflation indicator (for either current or future inventory costs), which the market views as detrimental to company value.

Tools of Inventory Analysis

This section describes several useful tools for analysis of inventory and related accounts.

Gross Profit Analysis

The **gross profit margin (GPM)** is gross profit divided by sales. This important ratio is closely monitored by management and outsiders. Exhibit 6.9 shows the gross profit margin on Cisco's product sales for the past three years.

EXHIBIT 6.9 Gross Profit Margin for Cisco			
Fiscal Year	**2008**	**2007**	**2006**
Product sales	$33,099	$29,462	$23,917
Product cost of goods sold	11,631	10,548	8,114
Gross profit.	$21,468	$18,914	$15,803
Gross profit margin.	64.9%	64.2%	66.1%

The gross profit margin is commonly used instead of the dollar amount of gross profit as the GPM allows for comparisons across companies and over time. A decline in GPM is usually cause for concern since it indicates that the company has less ability to pass on increased product cost to customers or that the company is not effectively managing product costs. Some possible reasons for a GPM decline follow:

- *Product line is stale.* Perhaps products are out of fashion and the company must resort to markdowns to reduce overstocked inventories. Or, perhaps the product lines have lost their technological edge, yielding reduced demand.
- *New competitors enter the market.* Perhaps substitute products are now available from competitors, yielding increased pressure to reduce selling prices.
- *General decline in economic activity.* Perhaps an economic downturn reduces product demand.
- *Inventory is overstocked.* Perhaps the company overproduced goods and finds itself in an overstock position. This can require reduced selling prices to move inventory.
- *Manufacturing costs have increased.* This could be due to poor planning, production glitches, or unfavorable supply chain reconfiguration.
- *Changes in product mix.* Perhaps the company is selling a higher proportion of low margin goods.

Cisco's gross profit margin on product sales has declined by 1.2 percentage points over the past two years. Following is Cisco's discussion of its gross profit situation taken from its 2008 10-K:

Product Gross Margin The increase in product gross margin percentage during fiscal 2008 compared with fiscal 2007 was due to the following factors:

- Lower overall manufacturing costs related to lower component costs and value engineering, partially offset by other manufacturing-related costs, increased product gross margin percentage by 2.1%. Value engineering is the process by which production costs are reduced through component redesign, board configuration, test processes, and transformation processes.
- Higher shipment volume, net of certain variable costs, increased product gross margin percentage by 0.5%.
- Sales discounts, rebates, and product pricing decreased product gross margin percentage by 1.7%.
- Changes in the mix of products sold decreased product gross margin percentage by 0.1%.
- Net effects of amortization of purchased intangible assets and share-based compensation expense decreased product gross margin percentage by 0.1%.

Product gross margin may be adversely affected in the future by changes in the mix of products sold, including further periods of increased growth of some of our lower-margin products; introduction of new products, including products with price performance advantages; our ability to reduce production costs; entry into new markets, including markets with different pricing structures and cost structures, as a result of internal development or through acquisitions; changes in distribution channels; price competition, including competitors from Asia, especially from China; changes in geographic mix of our product sales; the timing of revenue recognition and revenue deferrals; sales discounts; increases in material or labor costs; excess inventory and obsolescence charges; warranty costs; changes in shipment volume; loss of cost savings due to changes in component pricing; effects of value engineering; inventory holding charges; and the extent to which we successfully execute on our strategy and operating plans.

Cisco's gross profit margin increased in 2008 because of lower manufacturing costs and higher shipment volume. This increase was partially offset by increased sales discounts and changes in its product mix to lower margin products. Cisco's report includes a general discussion of factors that can adversely affect gross profit margins: changes in product mix, introduction of new products at lower introductory prices to gain market share, increases in production costs, sales discounts, inventory obsolescence and warranty costs, and changes in production volume.

Competitive pressures mean that companies rarely have the opportunity to completely control gross profit with price increases. Improvements in gross profit on existing product lines typically arise from better management of supply chains, production processes, or distribution networks. Companies that succeed do so because of better performance on basic business processes. This is one of Cisco's primary objectives.

Inventory Turnover

Inventory turnover (INVT) reflects the management of inventory and is computed as follows:

$$\textbf{Inventory Turnover = Cost of Goods Sold/Average Inventory}$$

Cost of goods sold is in the numerator because inventory is reported at cost. Inventory turnover indicates how many times inventory turns (is sold) during a period. More turns indicate that inventory is being sold more quickly, which decreases the risk of obsolete inventory and increases liquidity.

Average inventory days outstanding (AIDO), also called *days inventory outstanding*, is a companion measure to inventory turnover and is computed as follows:

Average Inventory Days Outstanding = Inventory/Average Daily Cost of Goods Sold

where average daily cost of goods sold equals cost of goods sold divided by 365 days.[7]

For Cisco, cost of products sold, in 2008, is $11,631 million, inventory at year-end is $1,235 million, inventory at prior year-end was $1,322 million (average is $1,278.5 million). Thus, its inventory turnover is 9.1, computed as $11,631 million/$1,278.5 million, which implies that, in 2008, Cisco sold its average inventory 9.1 times. Its 2008 average inventory days outstanding is 39 days, computed as $1,235 million/($11,631 million/365 days), which implies that it takes Cisco 39 days to sell its year-end inventory.

Overall, analysis of inventory turnover and days outstanding is important for at least two reasons:

1. *Inventory quality.* Inventory turnover can be compared over time and across competitors. Higher turnover is viewed favorably, because it implies that products are salable, preferably without undue discounting (we would compare profit margins to assess discounting). Conversely, lower turnover implies that inventory is on the shelves for a longer period of time, perhaps from excessive purchases or production, missed fashion trends or technological advances, increased competition, and so forth. Our conclusions about higher or lower turnover must consider alternative explanations including the following:

   - Product mix can include more (or less) higher margin, slower turning inventories. This can occur from business acquisitions that consolidate different types of inventory.

   - A company can change its promotion policies. Increased, effective advertising is likely to increase inventory turnover. Advertising expense is in SG&A, not COGS. This means the additional advertising cost is in operating expenses, but the benefit is in gross profit and turnover. If the promotion campaign is successful, the positive effects in margin and turnover should more than offset the promotion cost in SG&A.

   - A company can realize improvements in manufacturing efficiency and lower investments in direct materials and work-in-process inventories. Such improvements reduce inventory and, consequently, increase inventory turnover. Although a good sign, it does not yield any information about the desirability of a company's product line.

2. *Asset utilization.* Companies strive to optimize their inventory investment. Carrying too much inventory is expensive, and too little inventory risks stock-outs and lost sales (current and future). Companies can make the following operational changes to reduce inventory.

   - Improved manufacturing processes can eliminate bottlenecks and the consequent buildup of work-in-process inventories.

   - Just-in-time (JIT) deliveries from suppliers, which provide raw materials to the production line when needed, can reduce the level of raw materials and associated holding costs.

   - Demand-pull production, in which raw materials are released into the production process when final goods are demanded by customers instead of producing for estimated demand, can reduce inventory levels. Dell Computer, for example, does not manufacture a computer until it receives the customer's order; thus, Dell produces for actual, rather than estimated, demand.

Reducing inventories reduces inventory carrying costs, thus improving profitability and increasing cash flows. The reduction in inventory is reflected as an operating cash inflow in the statement of cash flows.

[7] Similar to the average receivables collection period, this formula examines the average daily COGS in *ending* inventories to focus analysis on current inventories. One can also examine average daily COGS in *average* inventories (Average inventories/Average daily COGS). These two approaches address different issues: the first addresses the average days outstanding of *current ending* inventories, and the second examines the average days outstanding of *average* inventories. It is important that we first identify the issue under investigation and then choose the formula that best addresses that issue.

There is normal tension between the sales side of a company that argues for depth and breadth of inventory, and the finance side that monitors inventory carrying costs and seeks to maximize cash flow. Companies, therefore, seek to *optimize* inventory investment, not minimize it.

Following is a chart comparing Cisco's average inventory days outstanding with its peer companies.

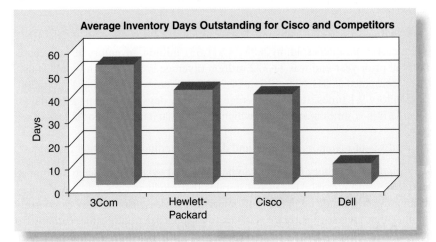

Cisco's average inventory days outstanding of 39 days compares favorably with its peers. Cisco's 2008 10-K provides the following comments regarding inventory management:

> Inventory and supply chain management remain areas of focus as we balance the need to maintain supply chain flexibility to help ensure competitive lead times with the risk of inventory obsolescence because of rapidly changing technology and customer requirements. We believe the amount of our inventory and purchase commitments is appropriate for our revenue levels.

Dell's average inventory days outstanding of 9 days is markedly lower than other companies shown in this graph. Dell has traditionally focused on excellence in this area, and views this as a competitive advantage. Dell's 2007 10-K reports the following:

> Our direct business model, as well as our manufacturing and supply chain efficiencies, give us the ability to operate with reduced levels of component and finished goods inventories. Our financial success is partly due to our supply chain management practices, including our ability to achieve rapid inventory turns. Because we maintain minimal levels of component inventory, a disruption in component availability could harm our financial performance and our ability to satisfy customer needs. Our direct business model allows us to maintain an efficient asset management system in comparison to our major competitors. We are capable of minimizing inventory risk while collecting amounts due from customers before paying vendors, thus allowing us to generate annual cash flows from operating activities that typically exceed net income. The following table presents the components of our cash conversion cycle for each of the past three fiscal years:
>
> | | February 2, 2007 | February 3, 2006 | January 28, 2005 |
> |---|---|---|---|
> | Days of sales outstanding . . . . | 31 | 29 | 27 |
> | Days of supply in inventory . . . . | 5 | 5 | 4 |
> | Days in accounts payable . . . . | (78) | (77) | (73) |
> | Cash conversion cycle . . . . | (42) | (43) | (42) |

In Dell's description above, it describes its cash conversion cycle, which measures the days from initial investment of cash in inventories to collection of the receivable arising from credit sales and repayment of amounts due to inventory suppliers. Normally, this is a positive number. Companies continually strive to reduce the cash conversion cycle to reduce the amount of investment in net operating assets (NOA), thereby improving the return on net operating assets (RNOA) and increasing cash flow. For Dell, its cash conversion cycle is negative because the company takes longer to pay its suppliers than the time invested in inventories and receivables. This is mainly the result of Dell's manufacturing process that effectively reduces raw materials, work-in-process, and finished goods inventories. Bottom line: Dell's operating efficiency is generating excess cash that can be invested in operating assets to further increase profitability.

Returning to the average inventory days outstanding, it is instructive to compare this measure across selected industries.

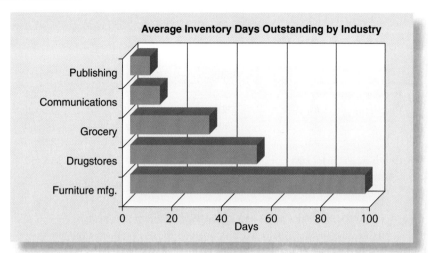

Publishing and communications companies carry only a few days' inventory at any point in time. Inventories are low in the publishing industry because newspapers are printed and sold daily, and communications companies do not carry large amounts of retail inventories (most of their assets are in PPE). On the other hand, grocery and drugstores must carry high levels of inventory to support customer demand, and manufacturers must carry raw materials, and work-in-process and finished goods inventories.

> **MANAGERIAL DECISION** **You Are the Plant Manager**
>
> You are analyzing your inventory turnover report for the month and are concerned that the average inventory days outstanding is lengthening. What actions can you take to reduce average inventory days outstanding? [Answer, p. 6-37]

LIFO Liquidations

When companies acquire inventory at different costs, they are required to account for each cost level as a separate inventory pool or layer (for example, there are the $100 and $150 units in our Exhibit 6.7 illustration). When companies reduce inventory levels, older inventory costs flow to the income statement. Because LIFO costs are older (by definition), they are often markedly different than current replacement costs. Given the usual inflationary environment, sales of older pools often yield a boost to gross profit as older, lower costs are matched against current selling prices on the income statement.

The increase in gross profit resulting from a reduction of inventory quantities in the presence of rising costs is called **LIFO liquidation.** The effect of LIFO liquidation is evident in the following footnote from Newell Rubbermaid's 2007 10-K:

> Inventory costs include direct materials, direct labor and manufacturing overhead, or when finished goods are sourced, the cost is the amount paid to the third-party. Cost of certain domestic inventories (approximately 59.2% and 59.6% of gross inventory costs at December 31, 2007 and 2006, respectively) was determined by the LIFO method; for the balance, cost was determined using the FIFO method. As of December 31, 2007 and 2006, LIFO reserves were $40.0 million and $38.1 million, respectively. The Company recognized a gain (loss) of $3.6 million, ($2.7) million, and $0.1 million in 2007, 2006 and 2005, respectively, related to the liquidation of LIFO based inventories.

Newell Rubbermaid reports that reductions in inventory quantities in 2007 led to the sale (at current selling prices) of products that carried lower costs from prior years. As a result of these inventory reductions, COGS were lower, which increased pretax income by $3.6 million. In the prior year, however, liquidation of LIFO inventory layers resulted in a $2.7 million loss because the cost of those layers was *higher* than current costs. We must be aware of potentially different income effects from LIFO liquidations when inventory costs fluctuate.

MID-MODULE REVIEW 2

At the beginning of the current period, assume that Hewlett-Packard (HP) holds 1,000 units of a certain product with a unit cost of $18. A summary of purchases during the current period follows:

		Units	Unit Cost	Cost
Beginning Inventory		1,000	$18.00	$18,000
Purchases:	#1	1,800	18.25	32,850
	#2	800	18.50	14,800
	#3	1,200	19.00	22,800
Goods available for sale		4,800		$88,450

During the current period, HP sells 2,800 units.

Required

1. Assume that HP uses the first-in, first-out (FIFO) method for this product. Compute the product's cost of goods sold for the current period and the ending inventory balance.
2. Assume that HP uses the last-in, first-out (LIFO) method for this product. Compute the product's cost of goods sold for the current period and the ending inventory balance.
3. Assume that HP uses the average cost (AC) method for this product. Compute the product's cost of goods sold for the current period and the ending inventory balance.
4. As manager, which of these three inventory costing methods would you choose:
   a. To reflect what is probably the physical flow of goods? Explain.
   b. To minimize income taxes for the period? Explain.
5. Assume that HP utilizes the LIFO method and delays purchasing lot #3 until the next period. Compute cost of goods sold under this scenario and discuss how the LIFO liquidation affects profit.

Solution

Preliminary computation: Units in ending inventory = 4,800 available − 2,800 sold = 2,000

1. First-in, first-out (FIFO)

Cost of goods sold computation:	Units		Cost		Total
	1,000	@	$18.00	=	$18,000
	1,800	@	$18.25	=	32,850
	2,800				$50,850

Cost of goods available for sale	$88,450
Less: Cost of goods sold	50,850
Ending inventory ($22,800 + $14,800)	$37,600

2. Last-in, first-out (LIFO)

Cost of goods sold computation:	Units		Cost		Total
	1,200	@	$19.00	=	$22,800
	800	@	$18.50	=	14,800
	800	@	$18.25	=	14,600
	2,800				$52,200

Cost of goods available for sale	$88,450
Less: Cost of goods sold	52,200
Ending inventory ($18,000 + [1,000 × $18.25])	$36,250

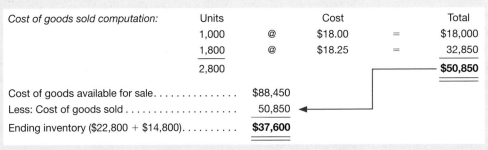

3. Average cost (AC)

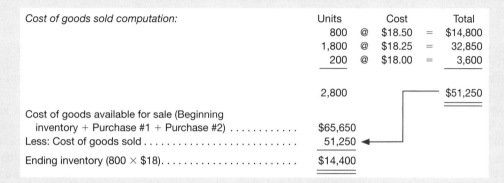

Average unit cost = $88,450/4,800 units = $18.427	
Cost of goods sold = 2,800 × $18.427 = $51,596	
Ending inventory = 2,000 × $18.427 = $36,854	

4. a. FIFO is normally the method that most closely reflects physical flow. For example, FIFO would apply to the physical flow of perishable units and to situations where the earlier units acquired are moved out first because of risk of deterioration or obsolescence.

   b. LIFO results in the highest cost of goods sold during periods of rising costs (as in the HP case); and, accordingly, LIFO yields the lowest net income and the lowest income taxes.

5. Last-in, first-out with LIFO liquidation

Cost of goods sold computation:	Units		Cost		Total
	800	@	$18.50	=	$14,800
	1,800	@	$18.25	=	32,850
	200	@	$18.00	=	3,600
	2,800				$51,250
Cost of goods available for sale (Beginning inventory + Purchase #1 + Purchase #2)	$65,650				
Less: Cost of goods sold	51,250				
Ending inventory (800 × $18).	$14,400				

The company's LIFO gross profit has increased by $950 ($52,200 − $51,250) because of the LIFO liquidation. The reduction of inventory quantities matched older (lower) cost layers against current selling prices. The company has, in effect, dipped into lower cost layers to boost current period profit—all from a simple delay of inventory purchases.

PROPERTY, PLANT AND EQUIPMENT (PPE)

Many companies' largest operating asset is property, plant, and equipment. To frame our PPE discussion, the following graphic highlights long-term operating assets on the balance sheet, and selling, general and administrative expenses on the income statement. The latter includes depreciation and asset write-downs that match the assets' cost against sales derived from the assets. (Depreciation on manufacturing facilities is included in cost of goods sold.) This section explains the accounting, reporting, and analysis of PPE and related items.

LO3 Describe accounting for property, plant and equipment and explain the impacts on profit and cash flows from depreciation methods, disposals and impairments.

Income Statement	Balance Sheet	
Sales	Cash	Current liabilities
Cost of goods sold	Accounts receivable, net	Long-term liabilities
Selling, general & administrative	Inventory	
Income taxes	**Property, plant, and equipment, net**	Shareholders' equity
Net income	Investments	

Capitalization of Asset Costs

Companies capitalize costs as an asset on the balance sheet only if that asset possesses both of the following characteristics:

1. The asset is owned or controlled by the company.

2. The asset provides future expected benefits.

Owning the asset means the company has title to the asset as provided in a purchase contract. (Assets acquired under leases are also capitalized if certain conditions are met—see Module 10.) Future expected benefits usually refer to future cash inflows. Companies capitalize the full cost to acquire the asset, including the purchase price, transportation, setup, and all other costs necessary to get the asset into service. This is called the asset's acquisition cost.

Companies can only capitalize asset costs that are *directly linked* to future cash inflows, and the costs capitalized as an asset can be no greater than the related expected future cash inflows. This means that if a company reports a $200 asset, we can reasonably expect that it will derive at least $200 in expected cash inflows from the use and ultimate disposal of the asset.

The *directly linked* condition for capitalization of asset cost is important. When a company acquires a machine, it capitalizes the cost because the company expects the machine's output to yield cash inflows from the sale of products associated with the machine and from the cash received when the company eventually disposes of the machine. On the other hand, when it comes to research and development (R&D) activities, it is more difficult to directly link expected cash inflows with the R&D expenditures because R&D activities are often unsuccessful. Further, companies cannot reliably estimate the future cash flows from successful R&D activities. Accordingly, GAAP requires that R&D expenditures be expensed when paid. Similar arguments are applied to advertising, promotion and wages to justify expensing of those costs. Each of these latter examples relates to items or activities that we generally think of as intangible assets. That is, we reasonably expect R&D efforts and advertising campaigns to produce results. If not, companies would not pursue them.

We also generally view employee activities as generating future benefits. Indeed, we often refer to the *human resources* (asset) of a company. However, the link between these items or activities and their outputs is not as direct as GAAP requires for capitalizing such costs. The nonrecognition of these assets is one reason why it is difficult to analyze and value knowledge-based companies and such companies are less suited to traditional ROE disaggregation analysis. Capitalization and non-capitalization of costs can markedly impact financial statements and our analysis inferences and assessment of a company as an investment prospect.

BUSINESS INSIGHT | **WorldCom and Improper Cost Capitalization**

WorldCom's CEO, Bernie Ebbers, and chief financial officer, Scott Sullivan, were convicted in 2005 of *cooking the books* so the company would not show a loss for 2001 and subsequent quarters. Specifically, WorldCom incurred large costs in anticipation of an increase in Internet-related business that did not materialize. Instead of expensing the costs as GAAP requires and reporting a loss in the WorldCom income statement, executives shifted the costs to the balance sheet. By capitalizing these costs (recording them on the balance sheet) as PPE, WorldCom was able to disguise these costs as assets, thereby inflating current profitability. Although the WorldCom case involved massive fraud, which is difficult for outsiders to detect, an astute analyst might have suspected something was amiss from analysis of WorldCom's long-term asset turnover (Sales/Average long-term assets) as shown below. The obvious decline in turnover reveals that WorldCom's assets constituted an ever-increasing percent of total sales during periods leading up to 2002. This finding does not, in itself, imply fraud. It does, however, raise serious questions that analysts should have posed to WorldCom executives in analyst meetings.

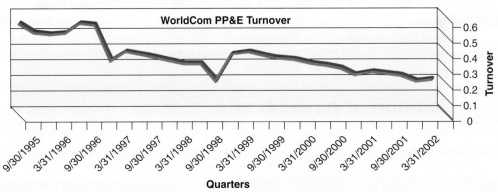

Depreciation

Once the cost of PPE is capitalized on the balance sheet as an asset, it must be systematically transferred from the balance sheet to the income statement as depreciation expense to match the asset's cost to the revenues it generates. The depreciation process requires the following estimates:

1. **Useful life.** Period of time over which the asset is expected to generate cash inflows or other measurable benefits
2. **Salvage value.** Expected disposal amount at the end of the asset's useful life
3. **Depreciation rate.** An estimate of how the asset will be used up over its useful life

Management must determine each of these factors when the asset is acquired. Depreciation commences immediately upon asset acquisition and use. Management also can revise estimates that determine depreciation during the asset's useful life.

The **depreciation base**, also called *nonrecoverable cost*, is the amount to be depreciated. The depreciation base is the acquisition cost less estimated salvage value. This means that at the end of the asset's useful life, only the salvage value remains on the balance sheet.

Depreciation method relates to the manner in which the asset is used up. Companies choose from three methods by determining which of the following assumptions best describes the asset's use:

1. Asset is used up by the same amount each period.
2. Asset is used up more in the early years of its useful life.
3. Asset is used up in proportion to its actual usage.

A company can depreciate different assets using different depreciation methods (and different useful lives). After a depreciation method is chosen, however, the company must generally stick with that method throughout the asset's useful life. This is not to say that companies cannot change depreciation methods, but changes must be justified as providing more useful financial reports.

The using up of an asset generally relates to physical or technological obsolescence. *Physical obsolescence* relates to an asset's diminished capacity to produce output. *Technological obsolescence* relates to an asset's diminished efficiency in producing output in a competitive manner.

All depreciation methods have the following general formula:

$$\text{Depreciation Expense} = \text{Depreciation Base} \times \text{Depreciation Rate}$$

Remembering this general formula helps us understand the depreciation process. Also, each depreciation method reports the same amount of depreciation expense *over the life of the asset*. The only difference is in the amount of depreciation expense reported *for a given period*. To illustrate, consider a machine with the following details: $100,000 cost, $10,000 salvage value, and a five-year useful life. We look at two of the most common methods of depreciation.

Straight-Line Method

Under the straight-line (SL) method, depreciation expense is recognized evenly over the estimated useful life of the asset as follows:

Depreciation Base	Depreciation Rate
Cost − Salvage value = $100,000 − $10,000 = $90,000	1/Estimated useful life = 1/5 years = 20%

Depreciation expense per year for this asset is $18,000, computed as $90,000 × 20%. For the asset's first full year of usage, $18,000 of depreciation expense is reported in the income statement. (If an asset is purchased midyear, it is typically depreciated only for the portion of the year it is used. For example, had the asset in this illustration been purchased on May 31, the company would report $10,500 of depreciation in the first year, computed as 7/12 × $18,000, assuming the company has a December 31 year-end.) This depreciation is reflected in the company's financial statements as follows:

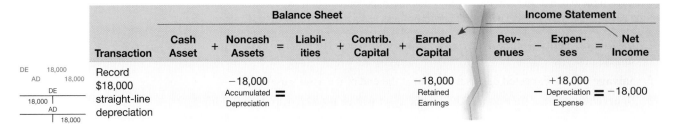

The accumulated depreciation (contra asset) account increases by $18,000, thus reducing net PPE by the same amount. Also, $18,000 of the asset cost is transferred from the balance sheet to the income statement as depreciation expense. At the end of the first year the asset is reported on the balance sheet as follows:

Machine, at cost.................	$100,000
Less accumulated depreciation......	18,000
Net book value → Machine, net (end of Year 1).........	$ 82,000

Accumulated depreciation is the sum of all depreciation expense that has been recorded to date. The asset **net book value (NBV)**, or *carrying value*, is cost less accumulated depreciation. Although the word value is used here, it does not refer to market value. Depreciation is a cost allocation concept (transfer of costs from the balance sheet to the income statement), not a valuation concept.

In the second year of usage, another $18,000 of depreciation expense is recorded in the income statement and the net book value of the asset on the balance sheet follows:

Machine, at cost.................	$100,000
Less accumulated depreciation......	36,000
Net book value → Machine, net (end of Year 2).........	$ 64,000

Accumulated depreciation of $36,000 now includes the sum of the first and second years' depreciation, and the net book value of the asset is now reduced to $64,000. After the fifth year, a total of $90,000 of accumulated depreciation will be recorded ($18,000 per year × 5 years), yielding a net book value for the machine of $10,000. The net book value at the end of the machine's useful life is exactly equal to the salvage value that management estimated when the asset was acquired.

Double-Declining-Balance Method

GAAP also allows *accelerated* methods of depreciation, the most common being the double-declining-balance method. This method records more depreciation in the early years of an asset's useful life (hence the term *accelerated*) and less depreciation in later years. At the end of the asset's useful life, the balance sheet will still report a net book value equal to the asset's salvage value. The difference between straight-line and accelerated depreciation methods is not in the total amount of depreciation, but in the rate at which costs are transferred from the balance sheet to the income statement.

For the double-declining-balance (DDB) method, the depreciation base is net book value, which declines over the life of the asset (this is why the method is called "declining balance"). The depreciation rate is twice the straight-line (SL) rate (which explains the word "double"). The depreciation base and rate for the asset in our illustrative example are computed as follows:

Depreciation Base	Depreciation Rate
Net Book Value = Cost − Accumulated Depreciation	2 × SL rate = 2 × 20% = 40%

The depreciation expense for the first year is $40,000, computed as $100,000 × 40%. This depreciation is reflected in the company's financial statements as follows:

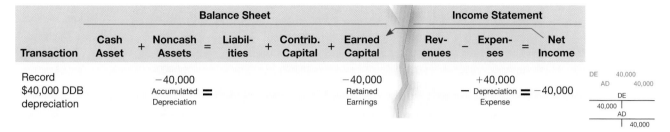

	Balance Sheet							Income Statement		
Transaction	Cash Asset	+	Noncash Assets	=	Liabil-ities	+	Contrib. Capital	+	Earned Capital	
Record $40,000 DDB depreciation			−40,000 Accumulated Depreciation	=					−40,000 Retained Earnings	

	Rev-enues	−	Expen-ses	=	Net Income
			+40,000 Depreciation Expense	=	−40,000

The accumulated depreciation (contra asset) account increases by $40,000 which reduces net PPE (compare this to the $18,000 depreciation under straight-line). This means that $40,000 of the asset cost is transferred from the balance sheet to the income statement as depreciation expense. At the end of the first year, the asset is reported on the balance sheet as follows:

Machine, at cost.	$100,000
Less accumulated depreciation	40,000
Net book value → Machine, net (end of Year 1).	$ 60,000

In the second year, the net book value of the asset is the new depreciable base, and the company records depreciation of $24,000 ($60,000 × 40%) in the income statement. At the end of the second year, the net book value of the asset on the balance sheet is:

Machine, at cost.	$100,000
Less accumulated depreciation	64,000
Net book value → Machine, net (end of Year 2).	$ 36,000

Under the double-declining-balance method, a company continues to record depreciation expense in this manner until the salvage value is reached, at which point the depreciation process is discontinued. This leaves a net book value equal to the salvage value, as with the straight-line method.[8] The DDB depreciation schedule for the life of this asset is in Exhibit 6.10.

EXHIBIT 6.10   Double-Declining-Balance Depreciation Schedule

Year	Book Value at Beginning of Year	Depreciation Expense	Book Value at End of Year
1	$100,000	$40,000	$60,000
2	60,000	24,000	36,000
3	36,000	14,400	21,600
4	21,600	8,640	12,960
5	12,960	2,960*	10,000

*The formula value of $5,184 ($12,960 × 40%) is *not* reported because it would depreciate the asset below salvage value; only the $2,960 needed to reach salvage value is reported.

Exhibit 6.11 shows the depreciation expense and net book value for both the SL and DDB methods. During the first two years, the DDB method yields a higher depreciation expense compared to the SL method. Beginning in the third year, this pattern reverses and the SL method produces higher depreciation expense. Over the asset's life, the same $90,000 of asset cost is transferred to the income statement as depreciation expense, leaving a salvage value of $10,000 on the balance sheet under both methods.

[8] A variant of DDB allows for a change from DDB to SL at the point when SL depreciation exceeds that for DDB.

EXHIBIT 6.11 Comparison of Straight-Line and Double-Declining-Balance Depreciation

	Straight-Line		Double-Declining-Balance	
Year	Depreciation Expense	Book Value at End of Year	Depreciation Expense	Book Value at End of Year
1	$18,000	$82,000	$40,000	$60,000
2	18,000	64,000	24,000	36,000
3	18,000	46,000	14,400	21,600
4	18,000	28,000	8,640	12,960
5	18,000	10,000	2,960	10,000
	$90,000		$90,000	

All depreciation methods yield the same salvage value

Total depreciation expense over asset life is identical for all methods

Companies typically use the SL method for financial reporting purposes and an accelerated depreciation method for tax returns.[9] The reason is that in early years the SL depreciation yields higher income on shareholder reports, whereas accelerated depreciation yields lower taxable income. Even though this relation reverses in later years, companies prefer to have the tax savings sooner rather than later so that the cash savings can be invested to produce earnings. Further, the reversal may never occur—if depreciable assets are growing at a fast enough rate, the additional first year's depreciation on newly acquired assets more than offsets the lower depreciation expense on older assets, yielding a "permanent" reduction in taxable income and taxes paid.[10]

Asset Sales and Impairments

This section discusses gains and losses from asset sales, and the computation and disclosure of asset impairments.

Gains and Losses on Asset Sales

The gain or loss on the sale (disposition) of a long-term asset is computed as follows.

Gain or Loss on Asset Sale = Proceeds from Sale − Net Book Value of Asset Sold

An asset's net book value is its acquisition cost less accumulated depreciation. When an asset is sold, its acquisition cost and related accumulated depreciation are both removed from the balance sheet and any gain or loss is reported in income from continuing operations.

Gains and losses on asset sales can be large, and analysts must be aware that these gains are usually *transitory operating* income components. Financial statements do not typically report gains and losses from asset sales because, if the gain or loss is small (immaterial), companies include the item in selling, general and administrative expenses. Footnotes can sometimes be informative. To illustrate, International Paper Company provides the following footnote disclosure to its 2006 10-K relating to the sale of its forestlands ($ millions):

> In the fourth quarter of 2006, the Company completed sales of 5.1 million acres of forestlands for $6.1 billion, including $1.4 billion in cash and $4.7 billion in installment notes, resulting in pre-tax gains totaling $4.4 billion.

International Paper sold forestlands, carried on its balance sheet at a net book value of $1.7 billion (computed as $6.1 billion sale less $4.4 billion gain), for $6.1 billion. The impacts on its financial statements follow:

---

[9] The IRS mandates the use of MACRS (Modified Accelerated Cost Recovery System) for tax purposes. This method fixes the useful life for various classes of assets, assumes no salvage value, and generally uses the double-declining-balance method.

[10] A third, common depreciation method is **units-of-production**, which depreciates assets according to use. Specifically, the depreciation base is cost less salvage value, and the depreciation rate is the units produced and sold during the year compared with the total expected units to be produced and sold. For example, if a truck is driven 10,000 miles out of a total expected 100,000 miles, 10% of its nonrecoverable cost is reflected as depreciation expense. This method is common for extractive industries like timber and coal.

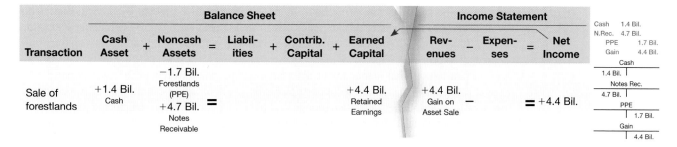

Transaction	Cash Asset	+	Noncash Assets	=	Liabil-ities	+	Contrib. Capital	+	Earned Capital		Rev-enues	−	Expen-ses	=	Net Income
Sale of forestlands	+1.4 Bil. Cash		−1.7 Bil. Forestlands (PPE) +4.7 Bil. Notes Receivable	=					+4.4 Bil. Retained Earnings		+4.4 Bil. Gain on Asset Sale	−		=	+4.4 Bil.

T-accounts (right margin):
Cash 1.4 Bil.
N.Rec. 4.7 Bil.
PPE 1.7 Bil.
Gain 4.4 Bil.

Cash
1.4 Bil.

Notes Rec.
4.7 Bil.

PPE
1.7 Bil.

Gain
4.4 Bil.

Asset Impairments

Property, plant, and equipment (PPE) assets are reported at their net book values (original cost less accumulated depreciation). This is the case even if the market values of these assets increase subsequent to acquisition. As a result, there can be unrecognized gains hidden within the balance sheet.

On the other hand, if market values of PPE assets subsequently decrease—and the asset value is deemed as permanently impaired—then companies must write off the impaired cost and recognize losses on those assets. **Impairment** of PPE assets is determined by comparing the asset's net book value to the sum of the asset's *expected* future (undiscounted) cash flows. If the sum of expected cash flow is greater than net book value, there is no impairment. However, if the sum of the expected cash flow is less than net book value, the asset is deemed impaired and it is written down to its current fair value (generally, the present value of those expected cash flows). Exhibit 6.12 depicts this impairment analysis.

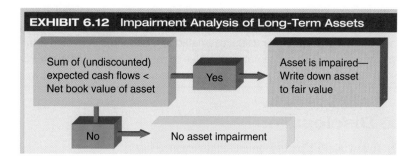

EXHIBIT 6.12 Impairment Analysis of Long-Term Assets

Sum of (undiscounted) expected cash flows < Net book value of asset → Yes → Asset is impaired— Write down asset to fair value

No → No asset impairment

When a company takes an impairment charge, assets are reduced by the amount of the write-down and the loss is recognized in the income statement. To illustrate, a footnote to the 2008 10-K of TJX Corporation, reports the following about asset impairments:

> TJX periodically reviews the value of its property and intangible assets in relation to the current and expected operating results of the related business segments in order to assess whether there has been an other than temporary impairment of their carrying values. An impairment exists when the undiscounted cash flow of an asset is less than the carrying cost of that asset . . . In the fourth quarter of fiscal 2008, TJX recorded a pre-tax impairment charge of $7.6 million ($5.0 million, after tax, or $.01 per share), related to Bob's Stores, which is reflected in Bob's Stores' segment results. The impairment charge relates to certain long-lived assets at Bob's Stores and represents the excess of recorded carrying values over the estimated fair value of these assets at fiscal 2008 year end.

TJX's pretax write-down of impaired assets affected its financial statements as follows:

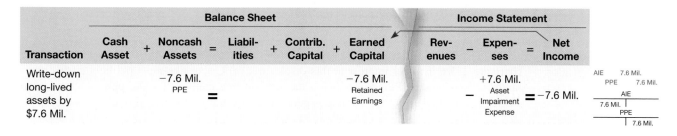

Transaction	Cash Asset	+	Noncash Assets	=	Liabil-ities	+	Contrib. Capital	+	Earned Capital		Rev-enues	−	Expen-ses	=	Net Income
Write-down long-lived assets by $7.6 Mil.			−7.6 Mil. PPE	=					−7.6 Mil. Retained Earnings			−	+7.6 Mil. Asset Impairment Expense	=	−7.6 Mil.

T-accounts (right margin):
AIE 7.6 Mil.
PPE 7.6 Mil.

AIE
7.6 Mil.

PPE
7.6 Mil.

TJX wrote down the carrying value (net book value) of its long-lived assets by $7.6 million. This write-down accelerated the transfer of the asset's cost from the balance sheet to the income statement. Consequently, TJX recognized a pretax expense of $7.6 million in the current year rather than over time via the depreciation process.

It is important to note that management determines if and when to recognize asset impairments. Thus, there is room for management to opportunistically over- or under-estimate asset impairments. Write-downs of long-term assets are often recognized in connection with a restructuring program.

Analysis of asset write-downs presents at least two potential challenges:

1. *Insufficient write-down.* Assets sometimes are impaired but an impairment charge is not recognized. This can arise if management is overly optimistic about future prospects or is reluctant to recognize the full impairment in income.

2. *Aggressive write-down.* This *big bath* scenario can arise if income is already very low in a given year. Management's view is that the market will not penalize the company's stock for an extra write-off when the year was already bad. Taking a larger impairment charge purges the balance sheet of costs that would otherwise hit future years' income.

GAAP does not condone either of these cases. Yet, because management must estimate future cash flows for the impairment test, it has some degree of control over the timing and amount of the asset write-off and can use that discretion to manage reported income.

IFRS INSIGHT   PPE Valuation under IFRS

Like GAAP, companies reporting under IFRS must periodically assess long-lived assets for possible impairment. Unlike the two-step GAAP approach, IFRS use a one-step approach: firms compare an asset's net book value to its current fair value (estimated as discounted expected future cash flows) to test for impairment and then reduce net book value to that fair value. Another IFRS difference is that PPE can be re-valued upwards to fair value if fair value can be measured reliably.

Footnote Disclosures

Cisco reports the following PPE asset amounts in its balance sheet:

($ millions)	July 26, 2008	July 28, 2007
Property, Plant and Equipment, net	$4,151	$3,893

In addition to its balance sheet disclosure, Cisco provides two footnotes that more fully describe its PPE assets:

1. *Summary of Significant Accounting Policies.* This footnote describes Cisco's accounting for PPE assets in general terms:

Depreciation and Amortization Property and equipment are stated at cost, less accumulated depreciation and amortization. Depreciation and amortization are computed using the straight-line method over the following periods.

Buildings.	25 years
Furniture and fixtures	5 years
Production, engineerng, and other equipment	Up to 5 years
Computer equipment and related software	30 to 36 months
Depreciation and amortization of leasehold improvements.	Shorter of remaining lease term or 5 years

There are a two items of interest in this disclosure: (a) Cisco, like most publicly traded companies, depreciates its PPE assets using the straight-line method (for tax purposes it uses an accelerated method). (b) Cisco provides general disclosures on the useful lives of its assets: 30

months to 25 years. We will discuss a method to more accurately estimate the useful lives in the next section.

2. *Supplemental balance sheet information.* This footnote provides a breakdown of Cisco's PPE assets by category as well as the balance in the accumulated depreciation account:

Property and equipment, net (millions)	
Land, buildings and leasehold improvements	$ 4,445
Computer equipment and related software	1,770
Production, engineering and other equipment.	4,839
Furniture and fixtures and other.	648
	11,702
Less accumulated depreciation and amortization	(7,551)
Total	$ 4,151

Analysis Implications

This section explains how to measure long-term asset utilization and asset age.

PPE Turnover

A crucial issue in analyzing PPE assets is determining their productivity (utilization). For example, what level of plant assets is necessary to generate a dollar of revenues? How capital intensive are the company and its competitors? To address these and similar questions, we use **PPE turnover**, defined as follows:

$$\text{PPE Turnover (PPET)} = \text{Sales/Average PPE Assets, net}$$

Cisco's 2008 PPE turnover is 9.8 ($39,540 million/[($4,151 million + $3,893 million)/2]). (We use net PPE in the computation above; arguments for using gross PPE are not as compelling as with receivables because managers have less latitude over accumulated depreciation vis-a-vis the allowance for uncollectibles.) This turnover places Cisco somewhat lower than its peers (see chart below). Dell's asset utilization is legendary and its PPE turnover of 24 is much higher than the other companies Cisco identifies as its peers.

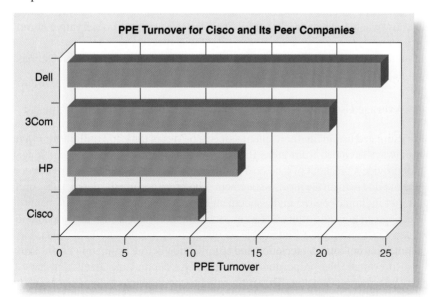

Higher PPE turnover is preferable to lower. A higher PPE turnover implies a lower capital investment for a given level of sales. Higher turnover, therefore, increases profitability because the company avoids asset carrying costs and because the freed-up assets can generate operating cash flow.

PPE turnover is lower for capital-intensive manufacturing companies than it is for companies in service or knowledge-based industries. To this point, consider the following chart of PPE turnover for selected industries.

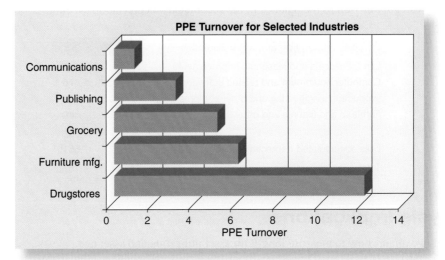

Communications and publishing companies are capital-intensive businesses. Their PPE turnover rates are, correspondingly, lower than for other industries. On the other hand, drug and grocery stores and furniture manufacturers require comparatively less capital investment. Their PPE turnover rates are much higher.

MANAGERIAL DECISION **You Are the Division Manager**

You are the manager for a main operating division of your company. You are concerned that a declining PPE turnover is adversely affecting your division's return on net operating assets. What specific actions can you take to increase PPE turnover? [Answer, p. 6-37]

Useful Life and Percent Used Up

Cisco reports that the useful lives of its depreciable assets range from 30 months for computer equipment to 25 years for buildings. The longer an asset's useful life, the lower the annual depreciation expense reported in the income statement and the higher the income each year. It might be of interest, therefore, to know whether a company's useful life estimates are more conservative or more aggressive than its competitors.

If we assume straight-line (SL) depreciation and zero salvage value, we can estimate the average useful life for depreciable assets as follows:

Average Useful Life = Depreciable Asset Cost/Depreciation Expense

For Cisco, the estimated useful life for its plant assets is 6.7 years ($11,702 million/$1,744 million). Land cost is nearly always excluded from gross PPE cost because land is a nondepreciable asset. However, Cisco does not provide a breakout of land cost in its footnotes and Cisco does not report depreciation expense as a separate line item on the income statement. Therefore, we use the depreciation and amortization expense of $1,744 million (reported in the statement of cash flows). (For many companies, amortization expense is like depreciation, and often relates, in part, to tangible assets such as leasehold improvements. However, if amortization relates to intangible assets such as patents and copyrights, the amortization should be subtracted from total depreciation and amortization before estimating useful life.)

We can also estimate the proportion of a company's depreciable assets that have already been transferred to the income statement. This ratio reflects the percent of depreciable assets that are no longer productive—as follows:

Percent Used Up = Accumulated Depreciation/Depreciable Asset Cost

Cisco's assets are 65% used up, computed as $7,551 million/$11,702 million. If a company replaced all of its assets evenly each year, the percent used up ratio would be 50%. Cisco's depreciable assets are slightly older than this benchmark. Knowing the degree to which a company's assets are used up is of interest in forecasting future cash flows. If, for example, depreciable assets are 80% used up, we might anticipate a higher level of capital expenditures in the near future. We also expect that older assets are less efficient and will incur higher maintenance costs.

MODULE-END REVIEW

On January 2, assume that Hewlett-Packard purchases equipment that fabricates a key-product part. The equipment costs $95,000, and its estimated useful life is five years, after which it is expected to be sold for $10,000.

Required
1. Compute depreciation expense for each year of the equipment's useful life for each of the following depreciation methods:
   a. Straight-line
   b. Double-declining-balance
2. Show how HP reports the equipment on its balance sheet at the end of the third year assuming straight-line depreciation.
3. Assume that this is the only depreciable asset the company owns and that it uses straight-line depreciation. Estimate the useful life and the percent used up for this asset at the end of the third year.
4. Assume that HP estimates that, at the end of the third year, the equipment will generate $40,000 in cash flow over its remaining life and that it has a current fair value of $36,000. Is the equipment impaired? If so, what is the effect on HP's financial statements?
5. Instead of the facts in part 4, assume that, at the end of the third year, HP sells the equipment for $50,000 cash. What amount of gain or loss does HP report from this sale?

Solution
1. *a.* Straight-line depreciation expense = ($95,000 − $10,000)/5 years = $17,000 per year

   b. Double-declining-balance (note: twice straight-line rate = 2 × [100%/5 years] = 40%)

Year	Net Book Value × Rate	Depreciation Expense	Accumulated Depreciation
1........	$95,000 × 0.40 =	$38,000	$38,000
2........	($95,000 − $38,000) × 0.40 =	22,800	60,800
3........	($95,000 − $60,800) × 0.40 =	13,680	74,480
4........	($95,000 − $74,480) × 0.40 =	8,208	82,688
5........	($95,000 − $82,688) × 0.40 =	2,312*	85,000

*The formula value of $4,925 is not reported for Year 5 because doing so would depreciate the asset below the estimated salvage value; only the $2,312 needed to reach salvage value is depreciated.

2. HP reports the equipment on its balance sheet at its net book value of $44,000.

Equipment, cost.....................................	$95,000
Less accumulated depreciation ($17,000 × 3)	51,000
Equipment, net (end of Year 3).......................	$44,000

3. The estimated useful life is computed as: Depreciable asset cost/Depreciation expense = $95,000/ $17,000 = 5.6 years. Because companies do not usually disclose salvage values (not required disclosure), the useful-life estimate is a bit high for this asset. This estimate is still informative because companies typically only provide a range of useful lives for depreciable assets in the footnotes.

   The percent used up is computed as: Accumulated depreciation/Depreciable asset cost = $51,000/ $95,000 = 53.7%. The equipment is more than one-half used up at the end of the third year. Again, the lack of knowledge of salvage value yields an underestimate of the percent used up. Still, this estimate is useful in that we know that the company's asset is over one-half used up and is likely to require replacement in about two years (estimated as less than one-half of its estimated useful life of 5.6 years). This replacement will require a cash outflow or financing and should be considered in our projections of future cash flows.

4. The equipment is impaired since the undiscounted expected cash flows ($40,000) are less than the net book value of the equipment ($44,000). HP must write down the equipment to its fair value of $36,000. The effect of this write-down is to reduce the net book value of the equipment by $8,000 ($44,000 − $36,000) and recognize a loss in the income statement.

5. HP must report a gain on this sale of $6,000, computed as proceeds of $50,000 less the net book value of the equipment of $44,000 (see part 2).

GUIDANCE ANSWERS

MANAGERIAL DECISION   You Are the Receivables Manager

First, we must realize that extending credit is an important tool in the marketing of your products, often as important as advertising and promotion. Given that receivables are necessary, there are certain ways to speed their collection. (1) We can better screen the customers to whom we extend credit. (2) We can negotiate advance or progress payments from customers. (3) We can use bank letters of credit or other automatic drafting procedures that obviate billing. (4) We can make sure products are sent as ordered to reduce disputes. (5) We can improve administration of past-due accounts to provide for more timely notices of delinquencies and better collection procedures.

MANAGERIAL DECISION   You Are the Plant Manager

Companies need inventories to avoid lost sales opportunities; however, there are several ways to minimize inventory needs. (1) We can reduce product costs by improving product design to eliminate costly features that customers don't value. (2) We can use more cost-efficient suppliers; possibly producing in lower wage-rate parts of the world. (3) We can reduce raw material inventories with just-in-time delivery from suppliers. (4) We can eliminate production bottlenecks that increase work-in-process inventories. (5) We can manufacture for orders rather than for estimated demand to reduce finished goods inventories. (6) We can improve warehousing and distribution to reduce duplicate inventories. (7) We can monitor product sales and adjust product mix as demand changes to reduce finished goods inventories.

MANAGERIAL DECISION   You Are the Division Manager

PPE is a difficult asset to reduce. Because companies need long-term operating assets, managers usually try to maximize throughput to reduce unit costs. Also, many companies form alliances to share administrative, production, logistics, customer service, IT, and other functions. These alliances take many forms (such as joint ventures) and are designed to spread ownership of assets among many users. The goal is to identify under-utilized assets and to increase capacity utilization. Another solution might be to reconfigure the value chain from raw material to end user. Examples include the sharing of IT, or manufacturing facilities, outsourcing of production or administration such as customer service centers, and the use of special purpose entities for asset securitization (see Module 10).

DISCUSSION QUESTIONS

Q6-1. Explain how management can shift income from one period into another by its estimation of uncollectible accounts.

Q6-2. Why do relatively stable inventory costs across periods reduce the importance of management's choice of an inventory costing method?

Q6-3. Explain why using the FIFO inventory costing method will increase gross profit during periods of rising inventory costs.

Q6-4. If inventory costs are rising, which inventory costing method—first-in, first-out; last-in, first-out; or average cost—yields the (a) lowest ending inventory? (b) lowest net income? (c) largest ending inventory? (d) largest net income? (e) greatest cash flow, assuming the same method is used for tax purposes?

Q6-5. Even though it may not reflect their physical flow of goods, why might companies adopt last-in, first-out inventory costing in periods when costs are consistently rising?

Q6-6. In a recent annual report, Kaiser Aluminum Corporation made the following statement in reference to its inventories: "The Company recorded pretax charges of approximately $19.4 million because of a reduction in the carrying values of its inventories caused principally by prevailing lower prices for alumina, primary aluminum, and fabricated products." What basic accounting principle caused Kaiser Aluminum to record this $19.4 million pretax charge? Briefly describe the rationale for this principle.

Kaiser Aluminum
Corporation (KALU)

Q6-7. Why is depreciation expense necessary to properly match revenues and expenses?

Q6-8. How might a company revise its depreciation expense computation due to a change in an asset's estimated useful life or salvage value?

Q6-9. When is a PPE asset considered to be impaired? How is an impairment loss computed?

Q6-10. What is the benefit of accelerated depreciation for income tax purposes when the total depreciation taken over the asset's life is identical under any method of depreciation?

Q6-11. What factors determine the gain or loss on the sale of a PPE asset?

**Assignments with the WebAssign. logo in the margin are available in WebAssign.
See the Preface of the book for details.**

MINI EXERCISES

M6-12. Estimating Uncollectible Accounts and Reporting Accounts Receivable (LO1)
Mohan Company estimates its uncollectible accounts by aging its accounts receivable and applying percentages to various aged categories of accounts. Mohan computes a total of $2,100 in estimated uncollectible accounts as of its current year-end. Its Accounts Receivable has a balance of $98,000, and its Allowance for Uncollectible Accounts has an unused balance of $500 before any year-end adjustments.

a. What amount of bad debts expense will Mohan report in its income statement for the current year?

b. Determine the net amount of accounts receivable reported in current assets at year-end.

M6-13. Interpreting the Allowance Method for Accounts Receivable (LO1)
At a recent board of directors meeting of Ascot, Inc., one of the directors expressed concern over the allowance for uncollectible accounts appearing in the company's balance sheet. "I don't understand this account," he said. "Why don't we just show accounts receivable at the amount owed to us and get rid of that allowance?" Respond to the director's question, include in your response (a) an explanation of why the company has an allowance account, (b) what the balance sheet presentation of accounts receivable is intended to show, and (c) how the matching principle relates to the presentation of accounts receivable.

M6-14. Analyzing the Allowance for Uncollectible Accounts (LO1)
Following is the current asset section from the Kraft Foods, Inc., balance sheet.

Kraft Foods, Inc. (KFT)

$ millions	2007	2006
Cash and cash equivalents	$ 567	$ 239
Receivables (less allowances of $94 in 2007 and $84 in 2006)	5,197	3,869
Inventories		
Raw materials	1,605	1,389
Finished product	2,491	2,117
Total inventories	4,096	3,506
Deferred income taxes	575	387
Other current assets	302	253
Total current assets	$10,737	$8,254

a. Compute the gross amount of accounts receivable for both 2007 and 2006. Compute the percentage of the allowance for uncollectible accounts relative to the gross amount of accounts receivable for each of those years.

b. How do you interpret the change in the percentage computed in part *a*?

Procter & Gamble
(PG)

Colgate-Palmolive
(CL)

M6-15. **Evaluating Accounts Receivable Turnover for Competitors   (LO1)**

Procter & Gamble (PG) and Colgate-Palmolive (CL) report the following sales and accounts receivable balances ($ millions) for two recent years.

$ millions	Procter & Gamble		Colgate-Palmolive	
	Sales	Accounts Receivable	Sales	Accounts Receivable
Prior year	$76,476	$6,629	$12,238	$1,523
Current year	83,503	6,761	13,790	1,681

 a.   Compute the current year's accounts receivable turnover for both companies.
 b.   Identify and discuss a potential explanation for the difference between these competitors' accounts receivable turnover.

M6-16. **Computing Cost of Goods Sold and Ending Inventory under FIFO, LIFO, and Average Cost   (LO2)**

Assume that Gode Company reports the following initial balance and subsequent purchase of inventory.

Beginning inventory, 2009	1,000 units @ $100 each	$100,000
Inventory purchased in 2009	2,000 units @ $150 each	300,000
Cost of goods available for sale in 2009	3,000 units	$400,000

Assume that 1,700 units are sold during 2009. Compute the cost of goods sold for 2009 and the ending inventory on the 2009 balance sheet under the following inventory costing methods:

 a.   FIFO
 b.   LIFO
 c.   Average Cost

M6-17. **Computing Cost of Goods Sold and Ending Inventory under FIFO, LIFO and Average Cost   (LO2)**

Bartov Corporation reports the following beginning inventory and inventory purchases.

Beginning inventory, 2009	400 units @ $10 each	$ 4,000
Inventory purchased in 2009	700 units @ $12 each	8,400
Cost of goods available for sale in 2009	1,100 units	$12,400

Bartov sells 600 of its inventory units. Compute the cost of goods sold for 2009 and the ending inventory on the 2009 balance sheet under the following inventory costing methods:

 a.   FIFO
 b.   LIFO
 c.   Average Cost

M6-18. **Computing and Evaluating Inventory Turnover for Two Companies   (LO2)**

Abercrombie & Fitch
(ANF)

TJX Companies (TJX)

Abercrombie & Fitch (ANF) and TJX Companies (TJX) report the following information in their respective January 2008 10-K reports.

$ millions	Abercrombie & Fitch			TJX Companies		
	Sales	Cost of Goods Sold	Inventories	Sales	Cost of Goods Sold	Inventories
2007	$3,318	$1,109	$427	$17,405	$13,214	$2,582
2008	3,750	1,238	333	18,647	14,082	2,737

 a.   Compute the 2008 inventory turnover for each of these two retailers.
 b.   Discuss any difference you observe in inventory turnover between these two companies. Does the difference confirm your expectations given their respective business models? Explain. (*Hint:* ANF is a higher-end retailer and TJX sells more value-priced clothing.)
 c.   Describe ways that a retailer can improve its inventory turnover.

M6-19. Computing Depreciation under Straight-Line and Double-Declining-Balance (LO3)

A delivery van costing $18,000 is expected to have a $1,500 salvage value at the end of its useful life of five years. Assume that the truck was purchased on January 1, 2009. Compute the depreciation expense for 2009 and 2010 (its second year) under the following depreciation methods:

a. Straight-line.
b. Double-declining-balance.

M6-20. Computing Depreciation under Straight-Line and Double-Declining-Balance for Partial Years (LO3)

A company with a calendar year-end, purchases a machine costing $145,800 on May 1, 2009. The machine is expected to be obsolete after three years (36 months) and, thereafter, no longer useful to the company. The estimated salvage value is $5,400. The company's depreciation policy is to record depreciation for the portion of the year that the asset is in service. Compute depreciation expense for both 2009 and 2010 under the following depreciation methods:

a. Straight-line.
b. Double-declining-balance.

M6-21. Computing and Comparing PPE Turnover for Two Companies (LO3)

Texas Instruments (TXN) and Intel Corporation (INTC) report the following information.

Texas Instruments (TXN)

Intel Corporation (INTC)

	Intel Corp		Texas Instruments	
$ millions	Sales	Plant, Property and Equipment, net	Sales	Plant, Property and Equipment, net
2006	$35,382	$17,602	$14,255	$3,950
2007	38,334	16,918	13,835	3,609

a. Compute the 2007 PPE turnover for both companies. Comment on any difference you observe.
b. Discuss ways in which high-tech manufacturing companies like these can increase their PPE turnover.

EXERCISES

E6-22. Estimating Uncollectible Accounts and Reporting Accounts Receivable (LO1)

WebAssign.

LaFond Company analyzes its accounts receivable at December 31, 2009, and arrives at the aged categories below along with the percentages that are estimated as uncollectible.

Age Group	Accounts Receivable	Estimated Loss %
0–30 days past due	$ 90,000	1%
31–60 days past due	20,000	2
61–120 days past due	11,000	5
121–180 days past due	6,000	10
Over 180 days past due	4,000	25
Total accounts receivable	$131,000	

The unused balance of the allowance for uncollectible accounts is $520 on December 31, 2009, before any adjustments.

a. What amount of bad debts expense will LaFond report in its income statement for 2009?
b. Use the financial statement effects template to record LaFond's bad debts expense for 2009.
c. What is the balance of accounts receivable on its December 31, 2009, balance sheet?

E6-23. Analyzing and Reporting Receivable Transactions and Uncollectible Accounts (using percentage of sales method) (LO1)

At the beginning of 2009, Penman Company had the following account balances.

Accounts Receivable	$122,000
Allowance for Uncollectible Accounts	7,900

During 2009, Penman's credit sales were $1,173,000 and collections on accounts receivable were $1,150,000. The following additional transactions occurred during the year.

Feb. 17   Wrote off Nissim's account, $3,600.

May 28   Wrote off Weiss's account, $2,400.

Dec. 15   Wrote off Ohlson's account, $900.

Dec. 31   Recorded the bad debts expense assuming that Penman's policy is to record bad debts expense as 0.8% of credit sales. (*Hint*: The allowance account is increased by 0.8% of credit sales regardless of write-offs.)

Compute the ending balances in accounts receivable and the allowance for uncollectible accounts. Show how Penman's December 31, 2009, balance sheet reports the two accounts.

E6-24. **Interpreting the Accounts Receivable Footnote**   **(LO1)**

Hewlett-Packard (HPQ)

Hewlett-Packard Company (HP) reports the following in its 2007 10-K report.

October 31 (In millions)	2007	2006
Accounts receivable, net of allowance for doubtful accounts of $226 and $220 as of 2007 and 2006, respectively	$13,420	$10,873

HP's footnotes to its 10-K provide the following additional information relating to its allowance for doubtful accounts.

For the fiscal years ended October 31 (In millions)	2007	2006	2005
Allowance for doubtful accounts—accounts receivable			
Balance, beginning of period	$220	$227	$286
Amount acquired through acquisition.	3	4	—
Addition of bad debts provision	32	37	17
Deductions, net of recoveries.	(29)	(48)	(76)
Balance, end of period	$226	$220	$227

a.   What is the gross amount of accounts receivables for HP in fiscal 2007 and 2006?

b.   What is the percentage of the allowance for doubtful accounts to gross accounts receivable for 2007 and 2006?

c.   What amount of bad debts expense did HP report each year 2005 through 2007? How does bad debts expense compare with the amounts of its accounts receivable actually written off? (Identify the amounts and explain.)

d.   Explain the changes in the allowance for doubtful accounts from 2005 through 2007. Does it appear that HP increased or decreased its allowance for doubtful accounts in any particular year beyond what seems reasonable?

E6-25. **Estimating Bad Debts Expense and Reporting Receivables**   **(LO1)**

At December 31, 2009, Sunil Company had a balance of $375,000 in its accounts receivable and an unused balance of $4,200 in its allowance for uncollectible accounts. The company then aged its accounts as follows:

Current	$304,000
1–60 days past due	44,000
61–180 days past due	18,000
Over 180 days past due.	9,000
Total accounts receivable.	$375,000

The company has experienced losses as follows: 1% of current balances, 5% of balances 1–60 days past due, 15% of balances 61–180 days past due, and 40% of balances over 180 days past due. The company continues to base its allowance for uncollectible accounts on this aging analysis and percentages.

a.   What amount of bad debts expense does Sunil report on its 2009 income statement?

b. Show how Sunil's December 31, 2009, balance sheet will report the accounts receivable and the allowance for uncollectible accounts.

E6-26. Estimating Uncollectible Accounts and Reporting Receivables over Multiple Periods (LO1)

Barth Company, which has been in business for three years, makes all of its sales on credit and does not offer cash discounts. Its credit sales, customer collections, and write-offs of uncollectible accounts for its first three years follow:

Year	Sales	Collections	Accounts Written Off
2007	$751,000	$733,000	$5,300
2008	876,000	864,000	5,800
2009	972,000	938,000	6,500

a. Barth recognizes bad debts expense as 1% of sales. (*Hint:* This means the allowance account is increased by 1% of credit sales regardless of any write-offs and unused balances.) What does Barth's 2009 balance sheet report for accounts receivable and the allowance for uncollectible accounts? What total amount of bad debts expense appears on Barth's income statement for each of the three years?

b. Comment on the appropriateness of the 1% rate used to provide for bad debts based on your analysis in part *a.*

E6-27. Applying and Analyzing Inventory Costing Methods (LO2)

At the beginning of the current period, Chen carried 1,000 units of its product with a unit cost of $20. A summary of purchases during the current period follows:

	Units	Unit Cost	Cost
Beginning Inventory	1,000	$20	$20,000
Purchases: #1.	1,800	22	39,600
#2.	800	26	20,800
#3.	1,200	29	34,800

During the current period, Chen sold 2,800 units.

a. Assume that Chen uses the first-in, first-out method. Compute both cost of goods sold for the current period and the ending inventory balance. Use the financial statement effects template to record cost of goods sold for the period.

b. Assume that Chen uses the last-in, first-out method. Compute both cost of goods sold for the current period and the ending inventory balance.

c. Assume that Chen uses the average cost method. Compute both cost of goods sold for the current period and the ending inventory balance.

d. Which of these three inventory costing methods would you choose to:
   1. Reflect what is probably the physical flow of goods? Explain.
   2. Minimize income taxes for the period? Explain.
   3. Report the largest amount of income for the period? Explain.

E6-28. Analyzing an Inventory Footnote Disclosure (LO2)

General Electric Company reports the following footnote in its 10-K report.

December 31 (In millions)	2007	2006
Raw materials and work in process	$ 7,893	$ 5,870
Finished goods.	5,025	4,263
Unbilled shipments.	539	409
	13,457	10,542
Less revaluation to LIFO.	(623)	(564)
	$12,834	$ 9,978

The company reports its inventories using the LIFO inventory costing method.

a. What is the balance in inventories reported on GE's 2007 balance sheet?

WebAssign.

WebAssign.

General Electric
Company (GE)

b. What would GE's 2007 balance sheet have reported for inventories had the company used FIFO inventory costing?

c. What *cumulative* effect has GE's choice of LIFO over FIFO had on its pretax income as of year-end 2007? Explain.

d. Assume GE has a 35% income tax rate. As of the 2007 year-end, how much has GE saved in taxes by choosing LIFO over FIFO method for costing inventory? Has the use of LIFO increased or decreased GE's cumulative taxes paid?

e. What effect has the use of LIFO inventory costing had on GE's pretax income and tax expense for 2007 only (assume a 35% income tax rate)?

WebAssign. **E6-29.** **Computing Cost of Sales and Ending Inventory** **(LO2)**

Stocken Company has the following financial records for the current period.

	Units	Unit Cost
Beginning inventory	100	$46
Purchases: #1.	650	42
#2.	550	38
#3.	200	36

Ending inventory is 350 units. Compute the ending inventory and the cost of goods sold for the current period using (a) first-in, first out, (b) average cost, and (c) last-in, first-out.

E6-30. **Analyzing an Inventory Footnote Disclosure** **(LO2)**

Deere & Co. (DE)

The inventory footnote from the Deere & Company's 2007 10-K follows.

Inventories Most inventories owned by Deere & Company and its United States equipment subsidiaries are valued at cost, on the "last-in, first-out" (LIFO) basis. Remaining inventories are generally valued at the lower of cost, on the "first-in, first-out" (FIFO) basis, or market. The value of gross inventories on the LIFO basis represented 58 percent and 60 percent of worldwide gross inventories at FIFO value on October 31, 2007 and 2006, respectively. If all inventories had been valued on a FIFO basis, estimated inventories by major classification at October 31 in millions of dollars would have been as follows:

($ millions)	2007	2006
Raw materials and supplies	$ 882	$ 712
Work-in-process.	425	372
Finished machines and parts	2,263	2,013
Total FIFO value	3,570	3,097
Less adjustment to LIFO value.	1,233	1,140
Inventories	$2,337	$1,957

This footnote reveals that not all of Deere's inventories are reported using the same inventory costing method (companies can use different inventory costing methods for different inventory pools).

a. What amount does Deere report for inventories on its 2007 balance sheet?

b. What would Deere have reported as inventories on its 2007 balance sheet had the company used FIFO inventory costing for all of its inventories?

c. What *cumulative* effect has the use of LIFO inventory costing had, as of year-end 2007, on Deere's pretax income compared with the pretax income it would have reported had it used FIFO inventory costing for all of its inventories? Explain.

d. Assuming a 35% income tax rate, by what *cumulative* dollar amount has Deere's tax expense been affected by use of LIFO inventory costing as of year-end 2007? Has the use of LIFO inventory costing increased or decreased Deere's cumulative tax expense?

e. What effect has the use of LIFO inventory costing had on Deere's pretax income and tax expense for 2007 only (assume a 35% income tax rate)?

WebAssign. **E6-31.** **Computing Straight-Line and Double-Declining-Balance Depreciation** **(LO3)**

On January 2, Haskins Company purchases a laser cutting machine for use in fabrication of a part for one of its key products. The machine cost $80,000, and its estimated useful life is five years, after which the expected salvage value is $5,000. For both parts *a* and *b* below: (1) Compute depreciation expense for *each year* of the machine's five-year useful life under that depreciation method. (2) Use the financial statements effects template to show the effect of depreciation for the first year only for that method.

    a.   Straight-line
    b.   Double-declining-balance

E6-32. **Computing Depreciation, Net Book Value, and Gain or Loss on Asset Sale** **(LO3)**

Sloan Company owns an executive plane that originally cost $800,000. It has recorded straight-line depreciation on the plane for six full years, calculated assuming an $80,000 expected salvage value at the end of its estimated 10-year useful life. Sloan disposes of the plane at the end of the sixth year.

    a.   At the disposal date, what is the (1) cumulative depreciation expense and (2) net book value of the plane?
    b.   How much gain or loss is reported at disposal if the sales price is:
        1. A cash amount equal to the plane's net book value.
        2. $195,000 cash.
        3. $600,000 cash.

E6-33. **Computing Straight-Line and Double-Declining-Balance Depreciation** **(LO3)**

On January 2, 2009, Dechow Company purchases a machine that manufactures a part for one of its key products. The machine cost $218,700 and is estimated to have a useful life of six years, with an expected salvage value of $23,400. Compute depreciation expense for 2009 and 2010 for each of the following depreciation methods.

    a.   Straight-line.
    b.   Double-declining-balance.

E6-34. **Computing Depreciation, Net Book Value, and Gain or Loss on Asset Sale** **(LO3)**

Palepu Company owns and operates a delivery van that originally cost $27,200. Palepu has recorded straight-line depreciation on the van for three years, calculated assuming a $2,000 expected salvage value at the end of its estimated six-year useful life. Depreciation was last recorded at the end of the third year, at which time Palepu disposes of this van.

    a.   Compute the net book value of the van on the disposal date.
    b.   Compute the gain or loss on sale of the van if the disposal proceeds are:
        1. A cash amount equal to the van's net book value.
        2. $15,000 cash.
        3. $12,000 cash.

E6-35. **Estimating Useful Life and Percent Used Up** **(LO3)**

The property and equipment footnote from the Deere & Company balance sheet follows.   Deere & Co. (DE)

Property and Depreciation   A summary of property and equipment at October 31 follows:

Equipment Operations ($ millions)	Average Useful Lives (Years)	2007	2006
Land		$ 83	$ 83
Buildings and building equipment	25	1,795	1,592
Machinery and equipment	10	3,355	3,088
Dies, patterns, tools, etc.	7	920	931
All other	5	594	591
Construction in progress		245	231
Total at cost		6,992	6,516
Less accumulated depreciation		4,271	4,102
Total		$2,721	$2,414

Total property and equipment additions in 2007, 2006 and 2005 for continuing operations were $1,064 million, $781 million and $523 million, and depreciation was $402 million, $379 million and $354 million, respectively.

a. Compute the estimated useful life of Deere's depreciable assets at year-end 2007. (*Hint:* Exclude land and construction in progress.) How does this estimate compare with the useful lives reported in Deere's footnote disclosure?

b. Estimate the percent used up of Deere's depreciable assets at year-end 2007. How do you interpret this figure?

E6-36. **Computing and Evaluating Receivables, Inventory and PPE Turnovers** **(LO1, 2, 3)**

Intel Corp. (INTC)

Intel Corporation reports the following financial statement amounts in its 2007 10-K report.

$ millions	Sales	Cost of Goods Sold	Receivables, net	Inventories	Plant, property and equipment, net
2005	38,826	15,777	3,914	3,126	17,111
2006	35,382	17,164	2,709	4,314	17,602
2007	38,334	18,430	2,576	3,370	16,918

a. Compute the receivables, inventory, and PPE turnover ratios for both 2006 and 2007.

b. What changes are evident in the turnover rates of Intel for these years? Discuss ways in which a company such as Intel can improve receivables, inventory, and PPE turnover ratios.

WebAssign

E6-37. **Computing and Assessing Plant Asset Impairment** **(LO3)**

On July 1, 2005, Zeibart Company purchases equipment for $225,000. The equipment has an estimated useful life of 10 years and expected salvage value of $25,000. The company uses straight-line depreciation. On July 1, 2009, economic factors cause the fair value of the equipment to decline to $90,000. On this date, Zeibart examines the equipment for impairment and estimates $125,000 in undiscounted expected cash inflows from this equipment.

a. Compute the annual depreciation of the equipment for fiscal years ending July 1, 2006 through July 1, 2009.

b. Compute the equipment's net book value at July 1, 2009.

c. Apply the test of impairment to this equipment as of July 1, 2009. Is the equipment impaired? Show supporting computations.

d. If the equipment is impaired at July 1, 2009, compute the impairment loss.

PROBLEMS

P6-38. **Evaluating Turnover Rates for Different Companies** **(LO1, 2, 3)**

Best Buy (BBY)
Carnival (CCL)
Caterpillar (CAT)
Harley-Davidson (HOG)
Microsoft (MSFT)
Oracle (ORCL)

Following are asset turnover rates (using year-end account values) for accounts receivable; inventory; and property, plant, and equipment (PPE) for Best Buy (retailer of consumer products), Carnival (vacation cruise line), Caterpillar (manufacturer of heavy equipment), Harley-Davidson (manufacturer of motorcycles), Microsoft (software company), and Oracle (software company).

Company Name	Receivables Turnover	Inventory Turnover	Plant, Property and Equipment Turnover
Best Buy Co	72.90	6.47	12.11
Carnival Corp	29.89	2.26	0.49
Caterpillar Inc	2.85	4.53	4.50
Harley-Davidson Inc.........	3.26	10.33	5.40
Microsoft Corp	4.45	11.77	9.68
Oracle Corp...............	3.87	n/a	13.29

Required

a. Interpret and explain differences in receivables turnover for the retailer (Best Buy) vis-à-vis that for the manufacturers (Caterpillar and Harley-Davidson).

b. Interpret and explain the difference in inventory turnover for Harley-Davidson versus Caterpillar. Why is Oracle's inventory turnover reported as n.a.?

c. Interpret and explain the difference in PPE turnover for Carnival versus Microsoft.

d. What are some general observations you might draw regarding the relative levels of these turnover rates across the different industries?

WebAssign

W.W. Grainger, Inc. (GWW)

P6-39. **Interpreting Accounts Receivable and Its Footnote Disclosure** **(LO1)**

Following is the current asset section from the W.W. Grainger, Inc., balance sheet.

As of December 31 ($ 000s)	2007	2006	2005
Cash and cash equivalents	$ 113,437	$ 348,471	$ 544,894
Marketable securities at cost, which approximates market value.	20,074	12,827	—
Accounts receivable (less allowances for doubtful accounts of $25,830, $18,801 and $18,401, respectively)	602,650	566,607	518,625
Inventories	946,327	827,254	791,212
Prepaid expenses and other assets	61,666	58,804	54,334
Deferred income taxes	56,663	48,123	76,474
Total current assets	$1,800,817	$1,862,086	$1,985,539

Grainger reports the following footnote relating to its receivables.

Allowance for Doubtful Accounts The following table shows the activity in the allowance for doubtful accounts.

For Years Ended December 31 ($ 000s)	2007	2006	2005
Balance at beginning of period	$18,801	$18,401	$23,375
Provision for uncollectible accounts	15,436	6,057	1,326
Write-off of uncollectible accounts, less recoveries	(8,755)	(5,660)	(6,380)
Foreign currency exchange impact	348	3	80
Balance at end of period	$25,830	$18,801	$18,401

Required

a. What amount do customers owe Grainger at each of the year-ends 2005 through 2007?
b. What percentage of its total accounts receivable does Grainger feel are uncollectible? (*Hint:* Percentage of uncollectible accounts = Allowance for uncollectible accounts/Gross accounts receivable)
c. What amount of bad debts expense did Grainger report in its income statement for each of the years 2005 through 2007?
d. Explain the change in the balance of the allowance for uncollectible accounts since 2005. Specifically, did the allowance increase or decrease as a percentage of gross accounts receivable, and why?
e. If Grainger had kept its 2007 allowance for uncollectible accounts at the same percentage of gross accounts receivable as it was in 2006, by what amount would its profit have changed (ignore taxes)? Explain.
f. Overall, what is your assessment of Grainger's allowance for uncollectible accounts and the related bad debts expense?

P6-40. **Analyzing and Interpreting Receivables and Related Ratios** (LO1)
Following is the current asset section from Intuit's balance sheet. Intuit, Inc. (INTU)

July 31 ($ 000s)	2008	2007
Cash and cash equivalents	$ 413,340	$ 255,201
Investments	414,493	1,048,470
Accounts receivable, net of allowance for doubtful accounts of $15,636 and $15,248, respectively	127,230	131,691
Income taxes receivable	60,564	54,178
Deferred income taxes	101,730	84,682
Prepaid expenses and other current assets	45,457	54,854
Current assets of discontinued operations	—	8,515
Current assets before funds held for customers	1,162,814	1,637,591
Funds held for customers	610,748	314,341
Total current assets	$1,773,562	$1,951,932

Total revenues were $3,071 million ($1,497 million in product sales and $1,574 million in service revenues and other) in 2008.

Required

a. What are Intuit's gross accounts receivable at the end of 2008 and 2007?

b. For both 2008 and 2007, compute the ratio of the allowance for uncollectible accounts to gross receivables. What trend do you observe?

c. Compute the receivables turnover ratio and the average collection period for 2008 based on gross receivables computed in part *a*. Does the collection period (days sales in receivables) appear reasonable given Intuit's lines of business (Intuit's products include QuickBooks, TurboTax and Quicken, which it sells to consumers and small businesses)? Explain.

d. Is the percentage of Intuit's allowance for uncollectible accounts to gross accounts receivable consistent with what you expect for Intuit's line of business? Explain.

e. Intuit discloses the following table related to its allowance for uncollectible accounts from its 10-K. Comment on the change in the allowance account during 2006 through 2008.

(In thousands)	Balance at Beginning of Period	Additions Charged to Expense	Deductions	Balance at End of Period
Year ended July 31, 2008				
Allowance for doubtful accounts	$15,248	$14,269	$(13,881)	$15,636
Year ended July 31, 2007				
Allowance for doubtful accounts	$11,532	$14,743	$(11,027)	$15,248
Year ended July 31, 2006				
Allowance for doubtful accounts	$14,967	$ 9,222	$(12,657)	$11,532

P6-41. **Analyzing and Interpreting Inventories and Related Ratios and Disclosures** (LO2)

Dow Chemical (DOW)

The current asset section from The Dow Chemical Company's 2007 annual report follows.

December 31 (In millions)	2007	2006
Cash and cash equivalents	$ 1,736	$ 2,757
Marketable securities and interest-bearing deposits......	1	153
Accounts and notes receivable		
Trade (net of allowance for doubtful receivables—2007: $118; 2006: $122)....	5,944	4,988
Other......	3,740	3,060
Inventories	6,885	6,058
Deferred income tax assets—current......	348	193
Total current assets	$18,654	$17,209

The Dow Chemical inventory footnote follows.

The following table provides a breakdown of inventories:

Inventories at December 31 (In millions)	2007	2006
Finished goods......	$4,085	$3,498
Work in process	1,595	1,319
Raw materials......	566	672
Supplies	639	569
Total inventories	$6,885	$6,058

The reserves reducing inventories from a FIFO basis to a LIFO basis amounted to $1,511 million at December 31, 2007 and $1,092 million at December 31, 2006. Inventories valued on a LIFO basis, principally hydrocarbon and U.S. chemicals and plastics product inventories, represented 34 percent of the total inventories at December 31, 2007 and 38 percent of total inventories at December 31, 2006.

Required

a. What inventory costing method does Dow Chemical use? As of 2007, what is the effect on cumulative pretax income and cash flow of using this inventory costing method? (Assume a 35% tax rate.) What is the effect on 2007 pretax income and cash flow of using this inventory costing method.

b. Compute inventory turnover and average inventory days outstanding for 2007 (2007 cost of goods sold is $46,400 million). Comment on the level of these two ratios. Is the level what you expect given Dow's industry? Explain.

c. Dow provides the following additional disclosure in its inventory footnote: "A reduction of certain inventories resulted in the liquidation of some of the Company's LIFO inventory layers, increasing pretax income $321 million in 2007, $97 million in 2006, and $110 million in 2005." Explain why a reduction of inventory quantities increased income in 2005, 2006 and 2007.

P6-42. Estimating Useful Life and Percent Used Up (LO3)

The property and equipment section of the Abbott Laboratories 2007 balance sheet follows.

Abbott Laboratories (ABT)

Property and equipment, at cost ($ thousands)	
Land	$ 494,021
Buildings	3,589,050
Equipment	10,393,402
Construction in progress	1,121,328
	15,597,801
Less: accumulated depreciation and amortization	8,079,652
Net property and equipment	$ 7,518,149

The company also provides the following disclosure relating to the useful lives of its depreciable assets.

Property and Equipment—Depreciation and amortization are provided on a straight-line basis over the estimated useful lives of the assets. The following table shows estimated useful lives of property and equipment.

Classification	Estimated Useful Lives
Buildings	10 to 50 years (average 27 years)
Equipment	3 to 20 years (average 11 years)

During 2007, the company reported $1,072,855 ($ 000s) for depreciation expense.

Required

a. Compute the estimated useful life of Abbott Laboratories' depreciable assets. How does this compare with its useful lives footnote disclosure above?

b. Compute the estimated percent used up of Abbott Laboratories' depreciable assets. How do you interpret this figure?

P6-43. Interpreting and Applying Disclosures on Property and Equipment (LO3)

Following are selected disclosures from the Rohm and Haas Company (a specialty chemical company) 2007 10-K.

Web**Assign**.

Rohm and Haas Company (ROH)

Land, Building and Equipment, Net

(in millions)	2007	2006
Land	$ 146	$ 142
Buildings and improvements	1,855	1,729
Machinery and equipment	6,155	5,721
Capitalized interest	352	340
Construction in progress	271	218
	8,779	8,150
Less: Accumulated depreciation	5,908	5,481
Total	$2,871	$2,669

continued

continued from prior page

The principal lives (in years) used in determining depreciation rates of various assets are: buildings and improvement (10–50); machinery and equipment (5–20); automobiles, trucks and tank cars (3–10); furniture and fixtures, laboratory equipment and other assets (5–10); capitalized software (5–7). The principal life used in determining the depreciation rate for leasehold improvements is the years remaining in the lease term or the useful life (in years) of the asset, whichever is shorter.

IMPAIRMENT OF LONG-LIVED ASSETS

Long-lived assets, other than investments, goodwill and indefinite-lived intangible assets, are depreciated over their estimated useful lives, and are reviewed for impairment whenever changes in circumstances indicate the carrying value of the asset may not be recoverable. Such circumstances would include items such as a significant decrease in the market price of a long-lived asset, a significant adverse change in the manner the asset is being used or planned to be used or in its physical condition or a history of operating or cash flow losses associated with the use of the asset . . . When such events or changes occur, we assess the recoverability of the asset by comparing the carrying value of the asset to the expected future cash flows associated with the asset's planned future use and eventual disposition of the asset, if applicable . . . We utilize marketplace assumptions to calculate the discounted cash flows used in determining the asset's fair value . . . For the year ended December 31, 2007, we recognized approximately $24 million of fixed asset impairment charges.

Required

a.   Compute the PPE (land, buildings and equipment) turnover for 2007 (Sales in 2007 are $8,897 million). Does the level of its PPE turnover suggest that Rohm and Haas is capital intensive? (*Hint:* The median PPE turnover for all publicly traded companies is approximately 5.03 in 2007.) Explain. Do you believe that Rohm and Haas' balance sheet reflects all of the company's operating assets? Explain.

b.   Rohm and Haas reported depreciation expense of $412 million in 2007. Estimate the useful life, on average, for its depreciable PPE assets.

c.   By what percentage are Rohm and Haas' assets "used up" at year-end 2007? What implication does the assets used up computation have for forecasting cash flows?

d.   Rohm and Haas reports an asset impairment charge in 2007. How do companies determine if assets are impaired? How do asset impairment charges affect Rohm and Haas' cash flows for 2007? How would we treat these charges for analysis purposes?

MANAGEMENT APPLICATIONS

MA6-44.   Managing Operating Asset Reduction   (LO1, 2, 3)

Return on net operating assets (RNOA = NOPAT/Average NOA, see Module 4) is commonly used to evaluate financial performance. If managers cannot increase NOPAT, they can still increase this return by reducing the amount of net operating assets (NOA). List specific ways that managers could reduce the following assets:

a.   Receivables

b.   Inventories

c.   Plant, property and equipment

MA6-45. **Ethics and Governance: Managing the Allowance for Uncollectible Accounts** **(LO1)**

Assume that you are the CEO of a publicly traded company. Your chief financial officer (CFO) informs you that your company will not be able to meet earnings per share targets for the current quarter. In that event, your stock price will likely decline. The CFO proposes reducing the quarterly provision for uncollectible accounts (bad debts expense) to increase your EPS to the level analysts expect. This will result in an allowance account that is less than it should be. The CFO explains that outsiders cannot easily detect a reduction in this allowance and that the allowance can be increased next quarter. The benefit is that your shareholders will not experience a decline in stock price.

a. Identify the parties that are likely to be affected by this proposed action.
b. How will reducing the provision for uncollectible accounts affect the income statement and the balance sheet?
c. How will reducing the provision for uncollectible accounts in the current period affect the income statement and the balance sheet in a future period?
d. What argument might the CFO use to convince the company's external auditors that this action is justified?
e. How might an analyst detect this earnings management activity?
f. How might this action affect the moral compass of your company? What repercussions might this action have?

Module Seven

Reporting and Analyzing Intercorporate Investments

LEARNING OBJECTIVES

LO1 Describe and illustrate accounting for passive investments. (p. 7-4)

LO2 Explain and illustrate accounting for equity method investments. (p. 7-11)

LO3 Describe and illustrate accounting for consolidations. (p. 7-17)

GOOGLE

How does Google make money? A recent *BusinessWeek* article explains: "everybody knows that Google Inc.'s innovations in search technology made it the No. 1 search engine. But Google didn't make money until it started auctioning ads that appear alongside the search results. Advertising today accounts for 99% of revenue." This seems to suggest that Google is a media company. Indeed, with a market capitalization of over $200 billion as of December, 2008, (four times that of Time Warner), Google is the world's largest media company and among America's top 30 most valuable companies. Since its IPO in 2004, Google's (GOOG) stock price has increased more than sevenfold as of early 2009 making Google one of the fastest growing companies on any stock exchange.

Google's operations generated nearly $5.7 billion of cash in 2007, over twice the cash generated two years before. During 2007, Google completed its second public offering, netting $4.3 billion. By fiscal year-end 2007, Google reported over $6 billion of cash and $8 billion of investments in marketable securities.

Google has considerable investments in government bonds. It holds these investments because it has excess cash awaiting deployment in other business activities. In the interim, the company expects to earn dividends and (potentially) capital gains from these securities. The accounting for these types of marketable securities differs markedly from the accounting for most other assets—Google's balance sheet reports these marketable securities at their current fair (or market) value instead of at their historical cost. As a result, the assets on Google's balance sheet fluctuate with the stock market. This causes stockholders' equity to fluctuate because, as we know from the accounting equation, assets equal liabilities plus equity.

We might wonder why Google would report these assets at fair value when nearly all other assets are reported at historical cost. As well, we might ask how these fluctuations in fair value affect Google's reported profit, if at all. This module answers both questions and explains the accounting for, and analysis of, such "passive" investments in marketable securities.

To expand its business activities beyond its current search-engine and advertising base, Google has strategically invested in the stock of other companies, which is a second category of investments. Through these strategic investments, Google can acquire substantial ownership of the companies such that Google can significantly influence their operations. The nature and purpose of these investments differs from Google's passive investment in marketable securities and, accordingly, the accounting reflects that difference. In particular, if Google owns enough voting stock to exert significant influence over another company, Google uses the *equity method* to account for those investments. Under the equity method, Google carries the investment on its balance sheet at an amount equal to its proportionate share of the investee company's equity. An equity method investment increases and decreases, not with changes in

the stock's market value, but with changes in the investee company's stockholders' equity.

An interesting by-product of the equity method is that Google's balance sheet does not reflect the investee company's individual assets and liabilities, but only its net assets (its stockholders' equity). This is important because Google could be using the investee's assets and be responsible, to some extent, for the investee's liabilities. Yet, those liabilities are not detailed on Google's balance sheet. This creates what is called *off-balance-sheet financing*, potentially of great concern to accountants, analysts, creditors, and others who rely on financial reports. This module describes the equity method of accounting for investments, including the implications of this type of off-balance-sheet financing.

When an investor company acquires a sufficiently large proportion of the voting stock of another company, it can effectively control the other company. At that point, the acquired company is *consolidated*. Most of the financial statements of public companies are titled "consolidated." Consolidation essentially adds together the financial statements of two or more companies. It is important that we understand what consolidated financial statements tell us and what they do not. This module covers consolidation along with a discussion of its implications for analysis.

There was much consternation among investors when Google's stock price passed $100, then $200, then $600. At each milestone, investors became increasingly con-cerned that Google's stock was overvalued. That concern still abounds. But, as Google continues to make strategic investments necessary to broaden its revenue base, its share price will likely increase. Google's management believes that investments are a crucial part of the company's strategic plan. Understanding the accounting for all three types of intercorporate investment is, thus, important to our understanding of Google's (and other companies') ongoing operations.

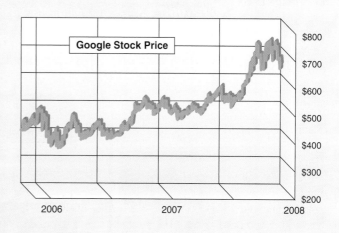

Sources: *Google Form 10-K*, 2007; *Google Annual Report*, 2007; *Business-Week*, 2006; and *Fortune*, 2006 and 2009.

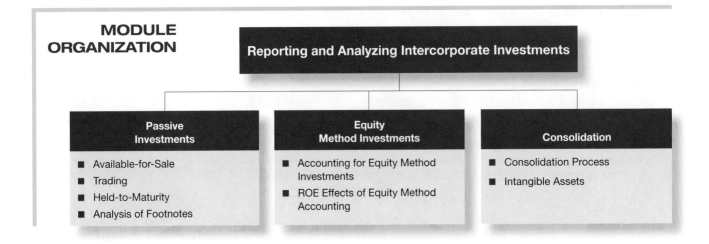

It is common for one company to purchase the voting stock of another. These purchases, called *inter-corporate investments,* have the following strategic aims:

■ **Short-term investment of excess cash.** Companies might invest excess cash to use during slow times of the year (after receivables are collected and before seasonal production begins) or to maintain liquidity (such as to counter strategic moves by competitors or to quickly respond to acquisition opportunities).

■ **Alliances for strategic purposes.** Companies might acquire an equity interest in other companies for strategic purposes, such as gaining access to their research and development activities, to their supply or distribution markets, or to their production and marketing expertise.

■ **Market penetration or expansion.** Companies might acquire control of other companies to achieve vertical or horizontal integration in existing markets or to penetrate new and growth markets.

Accounting for intercorporate investments follows one of three different methods, each of which affects the balance sheet and the income statement differently. These differences can be quite substantial. To help assimilate the materials in this module, Exhibit 7.1 graphically depicts the accounting for investments.

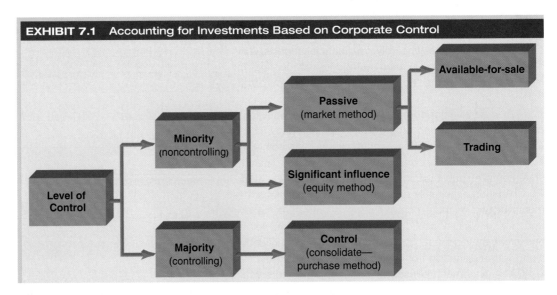

EXHIBIT 7.1   Accounting for Investments Based on Corporate Control

The degree of influence or control that the investor company (purchaser) can exert over the investee company (the company whose securities are being purchased) determines the accounting method. GAAP identifies three levels of influence/control.

1. **Passive.** A passive investment is one where the purchasing company has a relatively small invest-ment and cannot exert influence over the investee company. The investor's goal is to realize divi-dends and capital gains. Generally, the investment is considered passive if the investor company owns less than 20% of the outstanding voting stock of the investee company.

2. **Significant influence.** A company can sometimes exert significant influence over, but not con-trol, the activities of the investee company. Significant influence can result when the per-centage of voting stock owned is greater than a passive, short-term investment. However, an investment can also exhibit "significant influence" if there exist legal agreements between the investor and investee, such as a license to use technology, a formula, or a trade secret like production know-how. Absent other contractual arrangements such as those described above, significant influence is presumed at investment levels between 20% and 50%.

3. **Control.** When a company has control over another, it has the ability to elect a majority of the board of directors and, as a result, the ability to affect the investee company's strategic direction and the hiring of executive management. Control is generally presumed if the investor company owns more than 50% of the outstanding voting stock of the investee company; but can sometimes occur at less than 50% stock ownership by virtue of legal agreements, technology licensing, or other contractual means.

The level of influence/control determines the specific accounting method applied and its financial statement implications as outlined in Exhibit 7.2.

EXHIBIT 7.2	Investment Type, Accounting Treatment, and Financial Statement Effects			
	Accounting	**Balance Sheet Effects**	**Income Statement Effects**	**Cash Flow Effects**
Passive	Market method	Investment account is reported at fair value	Dividends and capital gains included in income Interim changes in fair value affect income if the investor actively trades the securities Sale of investment yields capital gain or loss	Dividends and sale proceeds are cash inflows from investing activities Purchases are cash outflows from investing activities
Significant influence	Equity method	Investment account equals percent owned of investee company's equity*	Dividends reduce investment account Investor reports income equal to percent owned of investee income Sale of investment yields capital gain or loss	Dividends and sale proceeds are cash inflows from investing activities Purchases are cash outflows from investing activities
Control	Consolidation	Balance sheets of investor and investee are combined	Income statements of investor and investee are combined Sale of investee yields capital gain or loss	Cash flows of investor and investee are combined and retain original classification (operating, investing, or financing) Sale and purchase of investee are investing cash flows

*Investments are often acquired at purchase prices in excess of book value (the market price of S&P 500 companies was 1.7 times their book value as of early 2008). In this case the investment account exceeds the proportionate ownership of the investee's equity.

There are two basic reporting issues with investments: (1) how investment income should be recognized in the income statement and (2) at what amount (cost or fair value) the investment should be reported on the balance sheet. We next discuss both of these issues as we consider the three investment types.

PASSIVE INVESTMENTS

Short-term investments of excess cash are typically passive investments. Passive investments can in-volve equity or debt securities. Equity securities involve an ownership interest such as common stock or preferred stock, whereas debt securities have no ownership interest. A voting stock investment is passive when the investor does not possess sufficient ownership to either influence or control the

LO1 Describe and illustrate accounting for passive investments.

investee company. The *fair-value method* is used to account for passive investments in both debt and equity securities.

Acquisition and Sale

When a company makes a passive investment, it records the shares acquired on the balance sheet at fair value, that is, the purchase price. This is the same as accounting for the acquisition of other assets such as inventories or plant assets. Subsequent to acquisition, passive investments are carried on the balance sheet as current or long-term assets, depending on management's expectations about their ultimate holding period.

When investments are sold, any recognized gain or loss on sale is equal to the difference between the proceeds received and the book (carrying) value of the investment on the balance sheet as follows:

Gain or Loss on Sale = Proceeds from Sale − Book Value of Investment Sold

To illustrate the acquisition and sale of a passive investment, assume that Microsoft purchases 1,000 shares of Yahoo! for $20 cash per share (this includes transaction costs such as brokerage fees). Microsoft, subsequently, sells 400 of the 1,000 shares for $23 cash per share. The following financial statement effects template shows how these transactions affect Microsoft.

		Balance Sheet					Income Statement		
Transaction	Cash Asset	+ Noncash Assets	= Liabil-ities	+ Contrib. Capital	+ Earned Capital		Rev-enues	− Expen-ses	= Net Income
1. Purchase 1,000 shares of Yahoo! common stock for $20 cash per share	−20,000 Cash	+20,000 Marketable Securities	=				−	=	
2. Sell 400 shares of Yahoo! common stock for $23 cash per share	+9,200 Cash	−8,000 Marketable Securities	=		+1,200 Retained Earnings		+1,200 Gain on Sale	−	= +1,200

MS   20,000
   Cash   20,000

MS
20,000 |
   Cash
        | 20,000

Cash   9,200
   MS   8,000
   GN   1,200

Cash
9,200 |
   MS
        | 8,000
   GN
        | 1,200

Income statements include the gain or loss on sale of marketable securities as a component of *other income*, which is typically reported separately from operating income and often aggregated with interest and dividend revenue. Accounting for the purchase and sale of passive investments is the same as for any other asset. Further, there is no difference in accounting for purchases and sales across the different types of passive investments discussed in this section. However, there are differences in accounting for different types of passive investments between their purchase and their sale. We next address this issue.

Fair-Value versus Cost

If a passive investment in securities has an active market with published prices, that investment is reported on the balance sheet at fair value. For marketable securities, **fair value** is the published price (as listed on a stock exchange) multiplied by the number of shares owned. This is one of few assets that are reported at fair value instead of historical cost.[1] For marketable securities, the current market value is almost always equal to the "fair" value and, thus, the two terms are often used interchangeably. If there exists no active market with published prices for the stock, the investment is reported at its historical cost.

---

[1] Other assets reported at fair value include (1) derivative securities (such as forward contracts, options, and futures) that are purchased to provide a hedge against price fluctuations or to eliminate other business risks (such as interest or exchange rate fluctuations), and (2) inventories and long-term assets that must be written down to market when their values permanently decline.

Why are passive investments recorded at current fair value on the balance sheet? The answer lies in understanding the trade-off between the *objectivity* of historical cost and the *relevance* of market value. All things equal, current fair values of assets are more relevant in determining the market value of the company as a whole. However, for most assets, market values cannot be reliably determined. Adding unreliable "market values" to the balance sheet would introduce undue subjectivity into financial reports.

In the case of marketable securities, market prices result from numerous transactions between willing buyers and sellers. Market prices in this case provide an unbiased (objective) estimate of fair value to report on balance sheets. This reliability is the main reason GAAP allows passive investments to be recorded at fair value instead of at historical cost.

This fair-value method of accounting for securities causes asset values (the marketable securities) to fluctuate, with a corresponding change in equity (liabilities are unaffected). This is reflected in the following accounting equation:

$$\text{Assets} \uparrow = \text{Liabilities} + \text{Equity} \uparrow \qquad \text{or} \qquad \text{Assets} \downarrow = \text{Liabilities} + \text{Equity} \downarrow$$

An important issue is whether such changes in equity should be reported as income (with a consequent change in retained earnings), or whether they should bypass the income statement and directly impact equity via *accumulated other comprehensive income (AOCI)*. The answer differs depending on the classification of securities, which we explain next.

Investments Marked to Market

For accounting purposes, marketable securities are classified into two types, both of which are reported on the balance sheet at fair value. Remember that for marketable securities, current market value is usually synonymous with fair value, thus we say that marketable securities are *marked to market*.

1. **Available-for-sale (AFS).** These are securities that management intends to hold for capital gains and dividend revenue; although, they might be sold if the price is right.
2. **Trading (T).** These are investments that management intends to actively buy and sell for trading profits as market prices fluctuate.

Management classifies securities depending on the degree of turnover (transaction volume) it expects in the investment portfolio, which reflects management's intent to actively trade the securities or not. Available-for-sale portfolios exhibit less turnover than trading portfolios. (GAAP permits companies to have multiple portfolios, each with a different classification, and management can change portfolio classification provided it adheres to strict disclosure and reporting requirements about its expectations of turnover change.) The classification as either available-for-sale or trading determines the accounting treatment, as Exhibit 7.3 summarizes.

EXHIBIT 7.3	Accounting Treatment for Available-for-Sale and for Trading Investments	
Investment Classification	Reporting of Fair-Value Changes	Reporting of Dividends Received and Gains and Losses on Sale
Available-for-Sale (AFS)	Fair-value changes bypass the income statement and are reported in accumulated other comprehensive income (AOCI) as part of equity	Reported as *other income* in income statement
Trading (T)	Fair-value changes are reported in the income statement and impact equity via retained earnings	Reported as *other income* in income statement

The difference between the accounting treatment of available-for-sale and trading investments relates to how fair-value changes affect equity. Changes in the fair value of available-for-sale securities have no income effect; changes in fair value of trading securities have an income effect. The impact on total stockholders' equity is identical for both classifications. The only difference is whether the change is reflected in retained earnings or in the accumulated other comprehensive income (AOCI) component of stockholders' equity. Dividends and any gains or losses on security sales are reported in the other income section of the income statement for both classifications. (GAAP gives companies an option to account for available-for-sale securities like trading securities and report all changes in fair value on the income statement.)

Fair-Value Adjustments

To illustrate the accounting for changes in fair value subsequent to purchase (and before sale), assume that Microsoft's investment in Yahoo! (600 remaining shares purchased for $20 per share) increases in value to $25 per share at year-end. The investment must be marked to market to reflect the $3,000 unrealized gain ($5 per share increase for 600 shares). The financial statement effects depend on whether the investment is classified as available-for-sale or as trading as follows:

		Balance Sheet						Income Statement		
Transaction	Cash Asset	+	Noncash Assets	=	Liabil- ities	+	Contrib. Capital	+	Earned Capital		Rev- enues	−	Expen- ses	=	Net Income

If classified as available-for-sale

| MS 3,000 | | | | | | | | | |
| AOCI 3,000 | | | | | | | | | |

$5 increase in fair value of Yahoo! investment — Noncash Assets: +3,000 Marketable Securities = ; Earned Capital: +3,000 AOCI ; Income Statement: − =

If classified as trading

| MS 3,000 | | | | | | | | | |
| UG 3,000 | | | | | | | | | |

$5 increase in fair value of Yahoo! investment — Noncash Assets: +3,000 Marketable Securities = ; Earned Capital: +3,000 Retained Earnings ; Revenues: +3,000 Unrealized Gain − = +3,000

Under both classifications, the investment account increases by $3,000 to reflect the increase in the stock's market value. If Microsoft classifies these securities as available-for-sale, the unrealized gain increases the accumulated other comprehensive income (AOCI) account (which analysts typically view as a component of earned capital). However, if Microsoft classifies the securities as trading, the unrealized gain is recorded as income, thus increasing both reported income and retained earnings for the period. (Our illustration uses a portfolio with only one security for simplicity. Portfolios usually consist of multiple securities, and the unrealized gain or loss is computed based on the total cost and total market value of the entire portfolio.)

These fair-value adjustments only apply if market prices are available, that is, for publicly traded securities. Thus, this mark-to-market accounting does not apply to investments in start-up companies or privately held corporations. Investments in nonpublicly traded companies are accounted for at cost as we discuss later in this section.

> **IFRS Alert**
> IFRS permits similar accounting for financial assets, including that for trading, available-for-sale, and held-to-maturity portfolios.

Financial Statement Disclosures

Companies are required to disclose cost and fair values of their investment portfolios in footnotes to financial statements. Google reports the accounting policies for its investments in the following footnote to its 10-K report:

> **Cash and Cash Equivalents and Marketable Securities** We invest our excess cash primarily in money market funds and in highly liquid debt instruments of U.S. municipalities, and the U.S. government and its agencies. All highly liquid investments with stated maturities of three months or less from date of purchase are classified as cash equivalents; all highly liquid investments with stated maturities of greater than three months are classified as marketable securities . . . Our marketable securities have been classified and accounted for as available-for-sale . . . These securities are carried at fair value, with the unrealized gains and losses, net of taxes, reported as a component of stockholders' equity, except for unrealized losses determined to be other than temporary which are recorded as interest income and other, net . . . Any realized gains or losses on the sale of marketable securities are determined on a specific identification method, and such gains and losses are reflected as a component of interest income and other, net.

Google accounts for its investments in marketable securities at fair value. Because Google classifies those investments as "available-for-sale," unrealized gains and losses flow to the accumulated other comprehensive income component of stockholders' equity. When Google sells the securities, it will record any *realized* gains or losses in income together with dividend and/or interest income.

Following is the current asset section of Google's 2007 balance sheet reflecting these investments.

December 31 ($ 000s)	2006	2007
Cash and cash equivalents	$ 3,544,671	$ 6,081,593
Marketable securities	7,699,243	8,137,020
Accounts receivable, net of allowances of $16,914 and $32,887	1,322,340	2,162,521
Deferred income taxes, net	29,713	68,538
Income taxes receivable	—	145,253
Prepaid revenue share, expenses and other assets	443,880	694,213
Total current assets	$13,039,847	$17,289,138

Google's investments in marketable securities that are expected to mature within 90 days of the balance sheet date are recorded together with cash as cash equivalents. Its remaining investments are reported as marketable securities.

Footnotes to the Google 10-K provide further information about the composition of its investment portfolio.

As of December 31 ($ 000s)	2006	2007
Cash and cash equivalents		
Cash	$ 1,579,702	$ 2,869,528
Cash equivalents		
U.S. government agencies	323,900	110,272
Time deposits	—	500,000
Municipal securities	216,529	232,278
Money market mutual funds	1,424,540	2,369,515
Total cash and cash equivalents	3,544,671	6,081,593
Marketable securities		
U.S. government notes	2,697,880	475,781
U.S. government agencies	2,839,430	2,120,972
Municipal securities	1,622,570	4,991,564
Time deposits	500,000	500,000
Auction rate preferred securities	39,363	48,703
Total marketable securities	7,699,243	8,137,020
Total cash, cash equivalents and marketable securities	$11,243,914	$14,218,613

The majority of Google's 2007 investments are in government debt securities such as bonds and T-bills, with a relatively small portion invested in equity securities. Google accounts for all of these investments as available-for-sale and reports them in the current asset section of the balance sheet because they mature within the coming year or can be readily sold, if necessary.

Google provides additional (required) disclosures on the costs, fair values, and unrealized gains and losses for its available-for-sale investments as follows:

December 31, 2007 ($ 000s)	Adjusted Cost	Gross Unrealized Gains	Gross Unrealized Losses	Fair Value
U.S. government notes	$ 472,040	$ 3,745	$ (4)	$ 475,781
U.S. government agencies	2,102,710	18,306	(44)	2,120,972
Municipal securities	4,975,587	16,308	(331)	4,991,564
Time deposits	500,000	—	—	500,000
Auction rate preferred securities	48,703	—	—	48,703
Total marketable securities	$8,099,040	$38,359	$(379)	$8,137,020

Google's net unrealized gain of $37,980 ($38,359 − $379) is reported net of tax in the accumulated other comprehensive income (AOCI) section of its stockholders' equity as follows ($ 000s):

December 31 ($ 000s)	2006	2007
Class A and Class B common stock	$ 309	$ 313
Additional paid-in capital	11,882,906	13,241,221
Accumulated other comprehensive income	23,311	113,373
Retained earnings	5,133,314	9,334,772
Total stockholders' equity	$17,039,840	$22,689,679

Google does not identify the components of its 2007 accumulated other comprehensive income of $113,373 except to report that the other component, beyond the unrealized gains on available-for-sale investments, is the cumulative translation adjustment relating to subsidiaries whose balance sheets are denominated in currencies other than $US. This lack of information can be confusing because the amount of unrealized gain (loss) reported in the investment footnote and the amount reported in accumulated other comprehensive income differ. Part of this difference relates to taxes: the net unrealized gain of $37,980 reported in the investment footnote is pretax while the amount reported in the accumulated other comprehensive income section of stockholders' equity is after-tax.

Investments Reported at Cost

Companies often purchase debt securities, including bonds issued by other companies or by the U.S. government. Such debt securities have maturity dates—dates when the security must be repaid by the borrower. If a company buys debt securities, and *management intends to hold the securities to maturity* (as opposed to selling them early), the securities are classified as **held-to-maturity** (HTM). The cost method applies to held-to-maturity securities. Exhibit 7.4 identifies the reporting of these securities.

EXHIBIT 7.4 Accounting Treatment for Held-to-Maturity Investments		
Investment Classification	Reporting of Fair-Value Changes	Reporting Interest Received and the Gains and Losses on Sale
Held-to-Maturity (HTM)	Fair-value changes are *not* reported in either the balance sheet or income statement	Reported as *other income* in income statement

Changes in fair value do not affect either the balance sheet or the income statement. The presumption is that these investments will indeed be held to maturity, at which time their market value will be exactly equal to their face value. Fluctuations in fair value, as a result, are less relevant for this investment classification. Finally, any interest received, and gains and losses on the sale of these investments, are recorded in current income. (GAAP gives companies an option to report held-to-maturity investments at fair value; if this fair value option is elected, the accounting for held-to-maturity securities is like that for trading securities.)

Sometimes companies acquire held-to-maturity debt securities for more or less than the security's face value. Because the value of debt securities fluctuates with the prevailing rate of interest, the market value of the security will be greater than its face value if current market interest rates are lower than what the security pays for interest. In that case, the acquirer will pay a premium for the security. Conversely, if current market interest rates exceed what the security pays in interest, the acquirer will purchase the security at a discount. (We cover premiums and discounts on debt securities in more detail in Module 8.) Either way, the company records the investment at its acquisition cost (like any other asset) and amortizes any discount or premium over the remaining life of the held-to-maturity investment. At any point in time, the acquirer's balance sheet carries the investment at "amortized cost," which is never adjusted for subsequent market value changes.

Companies can acquire equity interests in other companies that are not traded on an organized exchange. These might be start-ups that have never issued stock or established privately held companies. Because there is no market for such securities, they cannot be classified as marketable securities and are carried at historical cost on the balance sheet. Google references one such investment in its 2005 10-K.

> We have accounted for non-marketable equity security investments at historical cost because we do not have significant influence over the underlying investees. These investments are subject to a periodic impairment review. To the extent any impairment is considered other-than-temporary, the investment is written down to its fair value and the loss is recorded as interest income and other, net.

Google uses historical cost to account for investments in non-marketable securities (equity investments where Google cannot exert significant influence over the investee company). Google monitors the value of these investments and writes them down to market value if they suffer a permanent decline in value. If such an investee company ever goes public, Google will change its accounting method. If Google's ownership percentage does not allow it to exert significant influence or control, Google will account for this investment following the procedures described above for marketable securities. However, if Google can exert significant influence or control, it will apply different accounting methods that we explain in later sections of this module.

MID-MODULE REVIEW 1

Part 1: Available-for-sale securities

Using the financial statement effects template, enter the effects (amount and account) relating to the following four transactions involving investments in marketable securities classified as available-for-sale.

1. Purchased 1,000 shares of Netscape common stock for $15 cash per share.
2. Received cash dividend of $2.50 per share on Netscape common stock.
3. Year-end market price of Netscape common stock is $17 per share.
4. Sold all 1,000 shares of Netscape common stock for $17,000 cash in the next period.

Solution for Part 1

	Balance Sheet						Income Statement			
Transaction	Cash Asset	+	Noncash Assets	=	Liabil-ities	+	Contrib. Capital	+	Earned Capital	
1. Purchased 1,000 shares of Netscape common stock for $15 cash per share	−15,000 Cash		+15,000 Marketable Securities	=						
2. Received cash dividend of $2.50 per share on Netscape common stock	+2,500 Cash			=					+2,500 Retained Earnings	
3. Year-end market price of Netscape common stock is $17 per share			+2,000 Marketable Securities	=					+2,000 AOCI	
4. Sold 1,000 shares of Netscape common stock for $17,000 cash	+17,000 Cash		−17,000 Marketable Securities	=					−2,000 AOCI +2,000 Retained Earnings	

Rev-enues	−	Expen-ses	=	Net Income
	−		=	
+2,500 Dividend Income	−		=	+2,500
	−		=	
+2,000 Gain on Sale	−		=	+2,000

MS   15,000
  Cash   15,000
          MS
15,000 |
    Cash
      | 15,000

Cash   2,500
   DI   2,500
         Cash
2,500 |
      DI
      | 2,500

MS   2,000
   AOCI   2,000
          MS
2,000 |
      AOCI
      | 2,000

Cash 17,000
AOCI   2,000
    MS   17,000
    GN   2,000
        Cash
17,000 |
      AOCI
2,000 |
       MS
       | 17,000
       GN
       | 2,000

Part 2: Trading securities

Using the financial statement effects template and the transaction information 1 through 4 from part 1, enter the effects (amount and account) relating to these transactions assuming that the investments are classified as trading securities.

Solution for Part 2

	Balance Sheet						Income Statement		
Transaction	Cash Asset	+ Noncash Assets	= Liabil- ities	+ Contrib. Capital	+ Earned Capital		Rev- enues	− Expen- ses	= Net Income
1. Purchased 1,000 shares of Netscape common stock for $15 cash per share	−15,000 Cash	+15,000 Marketable Securities	=				−	=	
2. Received cash dividend of $2.50 per share on Netscape common stock	+2,500 Cash		=		+2,500 Retained Earnings		+2,500 Dividend Income	− =	+2,500
3. Year-end market price of Netscape common stock is $17 per share		+2,000 Marketable Securities	=		+2,000 Retained Earnings		+2,000 Unrealized Gain	− =	+2,000
4. Sold 1,000 shares of Netscape common stock for $17,000 cash	+17,000 Cash	−17,000 Marketable Securities	=				−	=	

Margin journal entries:
MS 15,000 / Cash 15,000
Cash 2,500 / DI 2,500
MS 2,000 / UG 2,000
Cash 17,000 / MS 17,000

Part 3: Footnote Disclosure

Yahoo! reports the following table in the footnotes to its 2007 10-K.

December 31, 2007 ($ millions)	Gross Amortized Costs	Gross Unrealized Gains	Gross Unrealized Losses	Estimated Fair Value
U.S. Government and agency securities	$219,681	$ 1,648	$ (239)	$221,090
Municipal bonds...........................	4,634	44	—	4,678
Corporate debt securities....................	623,212	2,133	(1,571)	623,774
Corporate equity securities	71,178	55,860	(1,125)	125,913
Total investments in available-for-sale securities...	$918,705	$59,685	$(2,935)	$975,455

Required

a. What amount does Yahoo! report as investments on its balance sheet? What does this balance represent?
b. How did the net unrealized gains affect reported income in 2007?

Solution for Part 3

a. Yahoo! reports an investment portfolio of $975,455. This represents the portfolio's current market value.
b. Yahoo! classifies these investments as available-for-sale. Consequently, the net unrealized gains of $56,750 million (computed as gross unrealized gains of $59,685 million less gross unrealized losses of $2,935 million), had no effect on Yahoo!'s reported income. Yahoo! will realize gains and losses only when it sells the investments. Then, Yahoo! will recognize the gains or losses in current-period income.

L02 Explain and illustrate accounting for equity method investments.

INVESTMENTS WITH SIGNIFICANT INFLUENCE

Many companies make equity investments that yield them significant influence over the investee companies. These intercorporate investments are usually made for strategic reasons such as the following:

■ **Prelude to acquisition.** Significant ownership can allow the investor company to gain a seat on the board of directors from which it can learn much about the investee company, its products, and its industry.

■ **Strategic alliance.** Strategic alliances permit the investor to gain trade secrets, technical know-how, or access to restricted markets. For example, a company might buy an equity share in a company that provides inputs for the investor's production process. This relationship is closer than the usual supplier-buyer relationship and will convey benefits to the investor company.

■ **Pursuit of research and development.** Many research activities in the pharmaceutical, software, and oil and gas industries are conducted jointly. The common motivation is to reduce the investor's risk or the amount of capital investment. The investment often carries an option to purchase additional shares, which the investor can exercise if the research activities are fruitful.

A crucial feature in each of these investments is that the investor company has a level of ownership that is sufficient for it to exert *significant influence* over the investee company. GAAP requires that such investments be accounted for using the *equity method*.

Significant influence is the ability of the investor to affect the financing, investing and operating policies of the investee. Ownership levels of 20% to 50% of the outstanding common stock of the investee typically convey significant influence. Significant influence can also exist when ownership is less than 20%. Evidence of such influence can be that the investor company is able to gain a seat on the board of directors of the investee by virtue of its equity investment, or the investor controls technical know-how or patents that are used by the investee, or the investor is able to exert significant influence by virtue of legal contracts with the investee. (There is growing pressure for determining significant influence by the facts and circumstances of the investment instead of a strict ownership percentage rule.)

Accounting for Investments with Significant Influence

GAAP requires that investors use the **equity method** when significant influence exists. The equity method reports the investment on the balance sheet at an amount equal to the percentage of the investee's equity owned by the investor; hence, the name equity method. (This assumes acquisition at book value. Acquisition at an amount greater than book value is covered later in this section.) Contrary to passive investments whose carrying amounts increase or decrease with the market value of the investee's stock, equity method investments increase (decrease) with increases (decreases) in the investee's stockholders' equity.

Equity method accounting is summarized as follows:

■ Investments are recorded at their purchase cost.

■ Dividends received are treated as a recovery of the investment and, thus, reduce the investment balance (dividends are not reported as income).

■ The investor reports income equal to its percentage share of the investee's reported net income; the investment account is increased by the percentage share of the investee's income or is decreased by the percentage share of any loss.

■ Changes in fair value do not affect the investment's carrying value. (GAAP gives companies an option to report equity method investments at fair value unless those investments relate to consolidated subsidiaries; we discuss consolidation later in the module.)

> **IFRS Alert**
> There is no fair value option for investments accounted for by the equity method under IFRS.

To illustrate the equity method, consider the following scenario: Assume that Google acquires a 30% interest in Mitel Networks, a company seeking to develop a new technology. This investment is a strategic alliance for Google. At the acquisition date, Mitel's balance sheet reports $1,000 of stockholders' equity, and Google purchases a 30% stake for $300, giving it the ability to exert significant influence over Mitel. At the first year-end, Mitel reports profits of $100 and pays $20 in cash dividends to its shareholders ($6 to Google). Following are the financial statement effects for Google from this investment using the equity method.

	Balance Sheet							Income Statement		
Transaction	Cash Asset	+	Noncash Assets	=	Liabil- ities	+	Contrib. Capital	+ Earned Capital	Rev- enues	− Expen- ses	= Net Income

1. Purchase 30% investment in Mitel for $300 cash	−300 Cash		+300 Investment in Mitel =							−	=
2. Mitel reports $100 income; Google's share is $30			+30 Investment in Mitel =					+30 Retained Earnings	+30 Investment Income	−	= +30
3. Mitel pays $20 cash dividends; $6 to Google	+6 Cash		−6 Investment in Mitel =							−	=
Ending balance of Google's investment account			324								

Margin journal entries:

```
EMI        300
   Cash        300
        EMI
  300 |
        Cash
              | 300

EMI         30
   EI          30
        EMI
   30 |
         EI
              | 30

Cash         6
   EMI          6
        Cash
    6 |
        EMI
              | 6
```

The investment is initially reported on Google's balance sheet at its purchase price of $300, representing a 30% interest in Mitel's total stockholders' equity of $1,000. During the year, Mitel's equity increases to $1,080 ($1,000 plus $100 income and less $20 dividends). Likewise, Google's investment increases by $30 to reflect its 30% share of Mitel's $100 income, and decreases by $6, relating to its share of Mitel's dividends. After these transactions, Google's investment in Mitel is reported on Google's balance sheet at 30% of $1,080, or $324.

Google's investment in Mitel is an asset, just like any other asset. As such, it must be tested annually for impairment. If the investment is found to be permanently impaired, Google must reduce the investment amount on the balance sheet and report a loss on the write down of the investment in its income statement. If and when Google sells Mitel, any gain or loss on the sale is reported in Google's income statement. The gain or loss is computed as the difference between the sales proceeds and the investment's carrying value on the balance sheet. For example, if Google sold Mitel for $500, Google would report a gain on sale of $176 ($500 proceeds − $324 balance sheet value).

Companies often pay more than book value when they make equity investments. For example, if Google paid $400 for its 30% stake in Mitel, Google would initially report its investment at its $400 purchase price. The $400 investment consists of two parts: the $300 equity investment described above and the $100 additional investment. Google is willing to pay the higher purchase price because it believes that Mitel's reported equity is below its current market value. Perhaps some of Mitel's assets are reported at costs that are below market values or Mitel has intangible assets like internally generated goodwill that are missing from the balance sheet. The $300 portion of the investment is accounted for as described above. Google's management must decide how to allocate the excess of the amount paid over the book value of the investee company's equity and accounts for the excess accordingly. For example, if management decides that the $100 relates to depreciable assets, the $100 is depreciated over the assets' estimated useful lives. Or, if it relates to identifiable intangible assets that have a determinable useful life (like patents), it is amortized over the useful lives of the intangible assets. If it relates to goodwill, however, it is not amortized and remains on the balance sheet at $100 unless and until it is deemed to be impaired. (See Appendix 7A for an expanded illustration.)

Two final points about equity method accounting: First, there can be a substantial difference between the book value of an equity method investment and its fair value. An increase in value is not recognized until the investment is sold. If the fair value of the investment has permanently declined, however, the investment is deemed impaired and it is written down to that lower fair value. Second, if the investee company reports income, the investor company reports its share. Recognition of equity income by the investor, however, does not mean that it has received that income in cash. Cash is only received if the investee pays a dividend. To highlight this, the investor's statement of cash flows will include a reconciling item (a deduction from net income in computing operating cash flow) for its percentage share of the investee's net income. This is typically reported net of any cash dividends received.

RESEARCH INSIGHT | **Equity Income and Stock Prices**

Under the equity method of accounting, the investor does not recognize as income any dividends received from the investee, nor any changes in the investee's fair value, until the investment is sold. However, research has found a positive relation between investors' and investees' stock prices at the time of investees' earnings and dividend announcements. This suggests that the market includes information regarding investees' earnings and dividends when assessing the stock prices of investor companies, and implies that the market looks beyond the book value of the investment account in determining stock prices of investor companies.

Equity Method Accounting and ROE Effects

The investor company reports equity method investments on the balance sheet at an amount equal to the percentage owned of the investee company's equity when that investment is acquired at book value. To illustrate, consider the case of Abbott Laboratories, Inc., which owns 50% of TAP Pharmaceutical Products Inc. (TAP is a joint venture with Takeda Pharmaceutical Company, Limited of Japan). TAP Pharmaceuticals (TAP) develops and markets pharmaceutical products mainly for the U.S. and Canada. Abbott accounts for its investment in TAP using the equity method as described in the following footnote to its 2007 10-K report:

> **Equity Method Investments ($ millions)** Abbott's 50 percent-owned joint venture, TAP Pharmaceutical Products Inc. (TAP), is accounted for under the equity method of accounting. The investment in TAP was $159, $162 and $167 at December 31, 2007, 2006 and 2005, respectively, and dividends received from TAP were $502, $487 and $343 in 2007, 2006 and 2005, respectively. Abbott performs certain administrative and manufacturing services for TAP at negotiated rates that approximate fair value.

At the end of 2007, the TAP joint venture reported stockholders' equity of $318 million and net income of $996 million. (TAP's financial statements are included in an exhibit to Abbott's 2007 10-K; not reproduced here.) In the footnote above, Abbott reports an investment balance at December 31, 2007, of $159 million (TAP equity of $318 million × 50%). In its income statement (not shown here), Abbott reports income of $498 million (TAP net income of $996 million × 50%). Provided the investment was originally acquired at book value these relations will always hold.

Let's look a bit closer at TAP. TAP's balance sheet reports assets of $1,354.2 million, liabilities of $1,036.7 million, and stockholders' equity of $317.5 million. TAP is a highly leveraged company with considerable assets. The $159 million investment balance on Abbott's balance sheet does not provide investors with any clue about the level of TAP's total assets nor about the substantial amount of TAP's financial obligations. It reflects only Abbott's share of TAP's net assets (assets less liabilities, or equity).

Further, Abbott makes the following additional disclosure in its footnotes relating to the cumulative payment of dividends by TAP:

> Undistributed earnings of investments accounted for under the equity method amounted to approximately $136 as of December 31, 2007.

Cumulatively, Abbott has recorded $136 million more of income than it has received in cash dividends from TAP. This shows that equity income does not necessarily equal cash inflow. This is particularly true for equity investments in growth-stage companies that do not pay dividends, or for foreign subsidiaries of U.S. nationals that might not pay dividends for tax reasons or other restrictions.

Another area of concern with equity method accounting relates to unreported liabilities. As described above, TAP reports total liabilities of $1,036.7 million as of 2007, none of which appear on Abbott's balance sheet (Abbott only reports its investment in TAP's equity as an asset).

Pharmaceutical companies face large potential liabilities arising from drug sales. (For example, TAP reported a loss of $150 million relating to litigation that it settled in 2004.) Although Abbott might have no direct legal obligation for TAP's liabilities, it might need to fund settlement costs via additional investment or advances to maintain TAP's viability if the company is important to Abbott's strategic plan. Further, companies that routinely fund R&D activities through equity investments in other companies, a common practice in the pharmaceutical and software industries, can find themselves supporting underperforming equity investments to assure continued capital market funding for these entities. One cannot always assume, therefore, that the investee's liabilities will not adversely affect the investor.

The concern with unreported liabilities becomes particularly problematic when the investee company reports losses that are substantial. In extreme cases, the investee company can become insolvent (when equity is negative) as the growing negative balance in Retained Earnings more than offsets paid-in capital. Once the equity of the investee company reaches zero, the investor must discontinue accounting for the investment by the equity method. Instead, it accounts for the investment at cost with a zero balance and no further recognition of its proportionate share of investee company losses. In this case, the investor's income statement no longer includes the losses of the investee company and its balance sheet no longer reports the troubled investee company. Unreported liabilities can be especially problematic in this case.

To summarize, under equity method accounting, only the net equity owned is reported on the balance sheet (not the underlying assets and liabilities), and only the net equity in earnings is reported in the income statement (not the investee's sales and expenses). From an analysis standpoint, because the assets and liabilities are left off the balance sheet, and because the sales and expenses are omitted from the income statement, the *components* of ROE are markedly affected as follows:

- **Net operating profit margin (NOPM = NOPAT/Sales).** Most analysts include equity income (sales less expenses) in NOPAT since it relates to operating investments. However, investee's sales are not included in the NOPM denominator. The reported NOPM is, thus, *overstated*.

- **Net operating asset turnover (NOAT = Sales/Average NOA).** Investee's sales are excluded from the NOAT numerator, and net operating assets in excess of the investment balance are excluded from the denominator. This means the impact on NOAT is *indeterminate*.

- **Financial leverage (FLEV = Net nonoperating obligations/Average equity).** Financial leverage is understated due to the absence of investee liabilities in the numerator.

Although ROE components are affected, ROE is unaffected by equity method accounting because the correct amount of investee net income and equity *is* included in the ROE numerator and denominator, respectively. Still, the evaluation of the quality of ROE is affected. Analysis using reported equity method accounting numbers would use an overstated NOPM and an understated FLEV because the numbers are based on net balance sheet and net income statement numbers. As we discuss in a later module, analysts frequently adjust reported financial statements for these types of items before conducting analysis. One such adjustment might be to consolidate (for analysis purposes) the equity method investee with the investor company.

IFRS INSIGHT   Equity Method Investments and IFRS

Like US GAAP, IFRS requires use of the equity method for investments in "associates" where the investor has significant influence. Unlike US GAAP, IFRS does not permit an investor that continues to have significant influence over an associate to cease applying the equity method when the associate is operating under severe long-term restrictions that impair its ability to transfer funds to the investor. Instead, significant influence must be lost before the equity method ceases to apply. US GAAP allows the equity method to cease once the investee's equity reaches zero.

MANAGERIAL DECISION   You Are the Chief Financial Officer

You are receiving capital expenditure requests for long-term operating asset purchases from various managers. You are concerned that capacity utilization is too low. What potential courses of action can you consider? Explain. [Answer, p. 7-32]

MID-MODULE REVIEW 2

Part 1: Using the financial statement effects template, enter the effects (amount and account) relating to the following five transactions involving investments in marketable securities accounted for using the equity method.

1. Purchased 5,000 shares of LookSmart common stock at $10 cash per share; these shares reflect 30% ownership of LookSmart.
2. Received a $2 per share cash dividend on LookSmart common stock.
3. Recorded an accounting adjustment to reflect $100,000 income reported by LookSmart.
4. Year-end market price of LookSmart has increased to $12 per common share.
5. Sold all 5,000 shares of LookSmart common stock for $90,000 cash in the next period.

Solution to Part 1

	Balance Sheet					Income Statement		
Transaction	Cash Asset	+ Noncash Assets	= Liabil- ities	+ Contrib. Capital	+ Earned Capital	Rev- enues	− Expen- ses	= Net Income
1. Purchased 5,000 shares of LookSmart common stock at $10 cash per share; these shares reflect 30% ownership	−50,000 Cash	+50,000 Investments =				−	=	
2. Received a $2 per share cash dividend on Look- Smart stock	10,000 Cash	−10,000 Investments =				−	=	
3. Made an adjustment to reflect $100,000 income reported by LookSmart		+30,000 Investments =			+30,000 Retained Earnings	+30,000 Equity Income	− =	+30,000
4. Market value has increased to $12 per share		NOTHING RECORDED						
5. Sold all 5,000 shares of LookSmart stock for $90,000	+90,000 Cash	−70,000 Investments =			+20,000 Retained Earnings	+20,000 Gain on Sale	− =	+20,000

EMI   50,000
　Cash   50,000

　　EMI
50,000 |
　Cash
　　| 50,000

Cash 10,000
　EMI   10,000

　　Cash
10,000 |
　　EMI
　　| 10,000

EMI   30,000
　EI   30,000

　　EMI
30,000 |
　　EI
　　| 30,000

Cash 90,000
　EMI   70,000
　GN   20,000

　　CASH
90,000 |
　　EMI
　　| 70,000
　　GN
　　| 20,000

Part 2: Yahoo! reports a $636 million equity investment in Yahoo! Japan related to its 34.0% ownership interest. Yahoo's footnotes reveal the following financial information about Yahoo! Japan ($ millions).

Twelve Months Ended September 30	2005	2006	2007
Operating data			
Revenues	$1,367	$1,671	$1,933
Gross profit.	1,252	1,584	1,836
Income from operations	656	807	984
Net income	382	451	508

September 30	2006	2007
Balance sheet data		
Current assets	$ 732	$1,131
Long-term assets	1,692	1,783
Current liabilities.	535	692
Long-term liabilities	509	348

Required

a. How much income does Yahoo! report in its 2007 income statement related to this equity investment?
b. Show the computations required to yield the $636 million balance in the equity investment account on Yahoo!'s balance sheet.

Solution to Part 2

a. Yahoo! reports $172 million ($508 million × 34.0%; $1 rounding difference) of equity income related to this investment in its 2007 income statement.

b. Yahoo! Japan's stockholders' equity is $1,874 million (computed as $1,131 + $1,783 − $692 − $348, in $ millions), and Yahoo!'s investment account equals $636 million, computed as $1,874 million × 34.0% ($1 difference due to rounding as Yahoo! reports in $ thousands).

INVESTMENTS WITH CONTROL

LO3 Describe and illustrate accounting for consolidations.

This section discusses accounting for investments where the investor company "controls" the investee company. For example, in its footnote describing its accounting policies, Google reports the following:

> **Basis of Consolidations** The consolidated financial statements include the accounts of Google and wholly-owned subsidiaries. All intercompany balances and transactions have been eliminated.

This means that Google's financial statements are an aggregation (an adding up) of those of the parent company, Google, and all its subsidiary companies, less any intercompany activities.

Accounting for Investments with Control

Accounting for business combinations (acquiring a controlling interest) goes one step beyond equity method accounting. Under the equity method, the investor's investment balance represents the proportion of the investee's equity owned by the investor, and the investor company's income statement includes its proportionate share of the investee's income. Once "control" over the investee company is achieved, GAAP requires consolidation for financial statements issued to the public (not for the internal financial records of the separate companies). Consolidation accounting includes 100% of the investee's assets and liabilities on the investor's balance sheet and 100% of the investee's sales and expenses on its income statement. Specifically, the consolidated balance sheet includes the gross assets and liabilities of the investee company, and the income statement includes the investee's gross sales and expenses rather than just the investor's share of the investee company's net assets or income. All intercompany sales and expenses are eliminated in the consolidation process to avoid double counting when, for example, goods are sold from the investee (called a subsidiary) to the investor (called the parent company) for resale to the parent's ultimate customers.

IFRS Alert
Consolidation accounting is generally similar with IFRS; differences exist in technical details, but not with presentation of consolidated financial statements.

Investments Purchased at Book Value: Subsidiary Wholly-Owned To illustrate, consider the following scenario. Penman Company acquires 100% of the common stock of Nissim Company by exchanging newly issued Penman shares for all of Nissim's common stock. The purchase price is equal to the $3,000 book value of Nissim's stockholders' equity (contributed capital of $2,000 and retained earnings of $1,000). On its balance sheet, Penman accounts for the investment in Nissim Co. using the equity method. This is important. Even if the investor (the parent) owns 100% of the investee, it records the investment on its (parent-company) balance sheet using the equity method described in the previous section. That is, Penman records an initial balance in the investment account of $3,000, equal to the purchase price. The balance sheets for Penman and Nissim immediately after the acquisition, together with the consolidated balance sheet, are shown in Exhibit 7.5.

Beginning on the date that Penman "controls" the activities of Nissim, GAAP requires consolidation of the two balance sheets, as well as the consolidation of the two income statements (not shown here). This process, shown in Exhibit 7.5, involves summing the individual lines for each balance sheet, after eliminating any intercompany transactions (such as investments and loans, and sales and purchases), within the consolidated group. The consolidated balances for accounts such as current assets, PPE, and liabilities are computed as the sum of those accounts from each balance sheet. The equity investment account, however, represents an intercompany transaction that Penman must eliminate during the consolidation process. This is accomplished by removing the equity investment of $3,000 (from Penman's balance sheet), and removing Nissim's stockholders' equity to which Penman's investment relates.

EXHIBIT 7.5 Mechanics of Consolidation Accounting
(Wholly-Owned Subsidiary, Purchased at Book Value)

	Penman Company	Nissim Company	Consolidating Adjustments	Consolidated
Current assets	$ 5,000	$1,000		$ 6,000
Investment in Nissim	3,000	0	(3,000)	0
PPE, net	10,000	4,000		14,000
Total assets.	$18,000	$5,000		$20,000
Liabilities.	$ 5,000	$2,000		$ 7,000
Contributed capital.	10,000	2,000	(2,000)	10,000
Retained earnings	3,000	1,000	(1,000)	3,000
Total liabilities and equity	$18,000	$5,000		$20,000

Exhibit 7.5 shows the consolidated balance sheet in the far right column. It shows total assets of $20,000, total liabilities of $7,000 and stockholders' equity of $13,000. Notice that consolidated equity equals the equity of the parent company—this is always the case. (Likewise, consolidated net income always equals the parent company's net income as the subsidiary's net income is already reflected in the parent's income statement as equity income from its investment.)

Investments Purchased at Book Value: Subsidiary _Not_ Wholly-Owned In the event that Penman acquires less than 100% of the stock of Nissim, consolidated equity must increase to maintain the accounting equation. This equity account is titled **minority interest** or **noncontrolling interest**. For example, assume that Penman acquires 80% of Nissim for $2,400 (80% of $3,000). The consolidating adjustments follow. The claim of noncontrolling shareholders is recognized in consolidated stockholders' equity, just like that of the majority shareholders. Exhibit 7.6 shows the consolidation adjustments and minority (noncontrolling) interest reported in the equity section of the consolidated balance sheet.

EXHIBIT 7.6 Mechanics of Consolidation Accounting
(Subsidiary Not Wholly-Owned, Purchased at Book Value)

	Penman Company	Nissim Company	Consolidating Adjustments	Consolidated
Current assets	$ 5,000	$1,000		$ 6,000
Investment in Nissim	2,400	0	(2,400)	0
PPE, net	10,000	4,000		14,000
Total assets.	$17,400	$5,000		$20,000
Liabilities.	$ 5,000	$2,000		$7,000
Contributed capital.	9,400	2,000	(2,000)	9,400
Retained earnings	3,000	1,000	(1,000)	3,000
Minority (noncontrolling) interest			600	600
Total liability and equity	$17,400	$5,000		$20,000

The consolidated income statement lists the consolidated revenues, consolidated expenses, and consolidated net income. When less than 100% of the subsidiary is own by the parent, the consolidated income statement allocates net income into that portion attributable to the parent's (controlling) shareholders and that which is attributable to the minority (noncontrolling) shareholders.

Investments Purchased above Book Value The illustrations above assume that the purchase price of the acquisition equals the book value of the investee company. It is more often the case, however, that the purchase price exceeds the book value. This might arise, for example, if an investor company believes it is acquiring something of value that is not reported on the investee's balance sheet—such as tangible assets whose market values have risen above book value, or unrecorded intangible assets, like patents or corporate synergies. When the acquisition price exceeds book value, all net assets acquired (both tangible and intangible) must be recognized on the consolidated balance sheet.

BUSINESS INSIGHT Accounting for Noncontrolling Interests

When a company acquires less than 100% of a subsidiary, it must account for the interests of the noncontrolling shareholders separately from those of its own shareholders. This has two implications for consolidated financial statements:

1. The noncontrolling interest must be separately valued on the acquisition date. Consequently, the subsidiary is initially reported on the consolidated balance sheet at 100% of its fair value on the acquisition date (the fair value of the consideration paid plus the fair value of the noncontrolling interest on the acquisition date).
2. Consolidated net income is first computed for the company as a whole as revenues less expenses. Then, it is allocated to the portion attributable to the parent's shareholders and the noncontrolling shareholders in proportion to their respective ownership interests.

The balance of the noncontrolling interests is reported on the balance sheet in the stockholders' equity section. It is increased each year by the net income allocated to noncontrolling interests and is decreased by any dividends paid to those noncontrolling shareholders. A final point: if the subsidiary is acquired in a series of purchases, then once enough shares are purchased to gain control, the subsidiary is valued on the date control is achieved and any previously acquired shares are revalued on that acquisition date; this revaluation can result in recognition of a gain on previously acquired shares.

To illustrate, assume that Penman Company acquires 100% of the voting stock of Nissim Company for $4,000. Also assume that in determining its purchase price, Penman paid the additional $1,000 because (1) Nissim's PPE is worth $300 more than its book value, and (2) Penman expects to realize $700 in additional value from corporate synergies (these "synergies" are an intangible asset with an unidentifiable useful life; they are classified as an asset called goodwill). The $4,000 investment account reflects two components: the book value acquired of $3,000 (as before) and an additional $1,000 of newly acquired assets. Exhibit 7.7 shows the post-acquisition balance sheets of the two companies, together with the consolidating adjustments and the consolidated balance sheet.

EXHIBIT 7.7 Mechanics of Consolidation Accounting (Purchase Price above Book Value)

	Penman Company	Nissim Company	Consolidating Adjustments	Consolidated
Current assets	$ 5,000	$1,000		$ 6,000
Investment in Nissim	4,000	0	(4,000)	0
PPE, net	10,000	4,000	300	14,300
Goodwill			700	700
Total assets.	$19,000	$5,000		$21,000
Liabilities.	$ 5,000	$2,000		$ 7,000
Contributed capital.	11,000	2,000	(2,000)	11,000
Retained earnings	3,000	1,000	(1,000)	3,000
Total liabilities and equity	$19,000	$5,000		$21,000

The consolidated current assets, PPE, and liabilities are the sum of those accounts on each company's balance sheet. The investment account, however, includes the $1,000 of additional newly acquired assets that must be reported on the consolidated balance sheet. The consolidation process in this case has two steps. First, the $3,000 equity of Nissim Company is eliminated against the investment account as before. Then, the remaining $1,000 of the investment account is eliminated and the newly acquired assets ($300 of PPE and $700 of goodwill not reported on Nissim's balance sheet) are added to the consolidated balance sheet. Thus, the consolidated balance sheet reflects the book value of Penman and the *fair market value* of Nissim (the book value plus the excess of Nissim's market value over its book value). For example, the consolidated PPE includes the book value of Penman's PPE ($10,000) along with the acquisition date fair value of Nissim's PPE ($4,300) for a total consolidated PPE of $14,300.

Consolidation is similar in successive periods. The excess purchase price assigned to depreciable assets, or identifiable intangible assets, must be amortized over the assets' useful lives. For example, if the additional $300 fair value of Nissim's PPE has an estimated life of 10 years with no salvage value, Penman would add $30 to depreciation expense on the consolidated income statement. This would reduce the consolidated PPE each year. And, as the excess of the purchase price over book value acquired is depreciated and/or amortized, the investment account on Penman's balance sheet gradually declines. Because goodwill is not amortized under GAAP, it remains at its carrying amount of $700 on the consolidated balance sheet unless it is impaired and written down (we discuss this below).

Consolidation Disclosures To illustrate consolidation mechanics with an actual case, consider the consolidated balance sheet (parent company, subsidiary, consolidating adjustments, and consolidated balance sheet) that Caterpillar Inc. (CAT) reports in a supplemental schedule to its 10-K report as shown in Exhibit 7.8. Caterpillar Inc. owns 100% of its financial products subsidiaries, principally Caterpillar Financial Services Corporation, whose stockholders' equity is $3,948 million as of 2007. The Investments in Financial Products subsidiaries account is also reported at $3,948 million on CAT's (parent company)

EXHIBIT 7.8 Caterpillar Inc.'s Consolidated Balance Sheet

At December 31, 2007 (In millions, except share amounts)	Machinery and Engines (Parent)	Financial Products (Subsidiary)	Consolidating Adjustments	Consolidated
Assets				
Cash and short-term investments	$ 862	$ 260	$ —	$ 1,122
Receivables—trade and other	4,715	525	3,009	8,249
Receivables—finance	—	10,961	(3,458)	7,503
Deferred and refundable income taxes	746	70	—	816
Prepaid expenses and other current assets	565	39	(21)	583
Inventories	7,204	—		7,204
Total current assets	14,092	11,855	(470)	25,477
Property, plant and equipment—net	6,782	3,215	—	9,997
Long-term receivables—trade and other	90	30	565	685
Long-term receivables—finance	—	14,057	(595)	13,462
Investments in unconsolidated affiliated companies	610	12	(24)	598
Investments in Financial Products subsidiaries	3,948	—	(3,948)	—
Noncurrent deferred and refundable income taxes	1,803	68	(318)	1,553
Intangible assets	471	4		475
Goodwill	1,963	—		1,963
Other assets	293	1,629	—	1,922
Total assets	$30,052	$30,870	$(4,790)	$56,132
Liabilities and Equity				
Short-term borrowings	$ 187	$ 5,556	$ (275)	$ 5,468
Accounts payable	4,518	373	(168)	4,723
Accrued expenses	1,932	1,273	(27)	3,178
Accrued wages, salaries and employee benefits	1,108	18	—	1,126
Customer advances	1,442	—	—	1,442
Dividends payable	225	—	—	225
Other current liabilities	867	105	(21)	951
Long-term debt due within one year	180	4,952	—	5,132
Total current liabilities	10,459	12,277	(491)	22,245
Long-term debt due after one year	3,669	14,190	(30)	17,829
Liability for postemployment benefits	5,058	1	—	5,059
Other liabilities	1,983	454	(321)	2,116
Total liabilities	21,169	26,922	(842)	47,249
Stockholders' equity				
Common stock	2,744	860	(860)	2,744
Treasury stock	(9,451)	—	—	(9,451)
Profit employed in the business	17,398	2,566	(2,566)	17,398
Accumulated other comprehensive income	(1,808)	522	(522)	(1,808)
Total stockholders' equity	8,883	3,948	(3,948)	8,883
Total liabilities and stockholders' equity	$30,052	$30,870	$(4,790)	$56,132

balance sheet. This investment account is subsequently removed (eliminated) in the consolidation process, together with the equity of the subsidiaries to which it relates. Following this elimination, *and the elimination of all other intercompany transactions*, the adjusted balance sheets of the two companies are summed to yield the consolidated balance sheet that is reported in CAT's 10-K.

In sum, the consolidated balance sheet lists the consolidated assets, consolidated liabilities, and consolidated equity. (In some cases it also reports *minority interest in equity of consolidated entities*, reflecting the ownership claim of the noncontrolling shareholders to the net assets of the subsidiary in which they are investors.)

Reporting of Acquired Intangible Assets

As previously discussed, acquisitions are routinely made at a purchase price in excess of the book value of the investee company's equity. The purchase price is first allocated to the fair values of tangible assets and liabilities. Then, the remainder is allocated to acquired intangible assets: first to identifiable intangible assets, then, any remainder is allocated to goodwill. As of the acquisition date, the purchasing company values the tangible assets acquired and liabilities assumed in the purchase and records them on the consolidated balance sheet at fair market value. A sampling of the types of intangible assets that are often recognized during acquisitions follows:

- Marketing-related assets like trademarks and Internet domain names
- Customer-related assets like customer lists and customer contracts
- Artistic-related assets like plays, books, and videos
- Contract-based assets like licensing, lease contracts, and franchise and royalty agreements
- Technology-based assets like patents, in-process research and development, software, databases, and trade secrets

To illustrate, Procter & Gamble (P&G) reported the following allocation of its $53.4 billion purchase price for Gillette in the footnotes to its 10-K report ($ millions).

Tangible assets	Current assets	$ 5,681
	Property, plant and equipment	3,655
	Other noncurrent assets	382
Acquired intangible assets	Goodwill	35,298
	Intangible assets	29,707
	Total assets acquired	74,723
Liabilities assumed	Current liabilities	5,346
	Noncurrent liabilities	15,951
	Total liabilities assumed	21,297
	Net assets acquired	53,426

Identifiable Intangible Assets (excluding goodwill) In its acquisition of Gillette, P&G allocated $29,707 million of its purchase price to identifiable intangible assets (other than goodwill), as described in the following footnote to P&G's 10-K ($ millions):

The purchase price allocation to the identifiable intangible assets included in these financial statements is as follows:

Intangible Assets with Determinable Lives		Average Life
Brands	$ 1,627	20
Patents and technology	2,716	17
Customer relationships	1,436	27
Brands with indefinite lives	23,928	Indefinite
Total intangible assets	29,707	

continued

continued from prior page

> The majority of the intangible asset valuation relates to brands. Our assessment as to brands that have an indefinite life and those that have a determinable life was based on a number of factors, including the competitive environment, market share, brand history, product life cycles, operating plan and macroeconomic environment of the countries in which the brands are sold. The indefinite-lived brands include Gillette, Venus, Duracell, Oral-B and Braun. The determinable lived brands include certain brand sub-names, such as Mach3 and Sensor in the blades and razors business, and other regional or local brands. The determinable-lived brands have asset lives ranging from 10 to 40 years. The patents and technology intangibles are concentrated in the blades and razors and oral care businesses and have asset lives ranging from 5 to 20 years. The customer relationship intangible asset useful lives ranging from 20 to 30 years reflect the very low historical and projected customer attrition rates among Gillette's major retailer and distributor customers.

P&G allocated a portion of the purchase price to the following identifiable intangible assets:

■ Brands
■ Patents and technology
■ Customer relationships

P&G deemed these identifiable intangible assets as amortizable assets, which are those having a finite useful life. P&G will subsequently amortize them over their useful lives (similar to depreciation).

| **BUSINESS INSIGHT** | **Restructuring Liabilities** |

Many acquisitions are accompanied by restructuring activities that are designed to maximize asset utilization. These restructuring activities typically involve relocation and retraining or termination of employees and the exiting of less profitable product lines resulting in costs from closure of manufacturing, retailing, and administrative facilities and the write-off of assets. Acquirers can recognize restructuring liabilities when they purchase a subsidiary *only* if that subsidiary has previously accrued those liabilities. It also requires the Board of Directors to approve a formal restructuring plan and to communicate that plan to affected employees. Restructuring activities beginning *after* acquisition must be accrued and the expense recognized in post-acquisition consolidated income statements.

> **IFRS Alert**
> Unlike U.S. GAAP, when a firm purchases in-process research and development in the course of an acquisition, those costs can be capitalized as an intangible asset under IFRS. U.S. GAAP requires such costs be immediately expensed, consistent with the GAAP prohibition of capitalizing R&D costs.

Goodwill Once the purchase price has been allocated to identifiable tangible and intangible assets (net of liabilities assumed), any remaining purchase price is allocated to goodwill. Goodwill, thus, represents the remainder of the purchase price that is not allocated to other assets. P&G allocated $35.3 billion (66%) of the Gillette purchase price to goodwill. The SEC is also scrutinizing companies that assign an excessive proportion of the purchase price to goodwill (companies might do this to avoid the future earnings drag from the amortization expense relating to identifiable intangible assets with useful lives).

| **BUSINESS INSIGHT** | **Valuation of Earn-Outs** |

Martha Stewart Living Omnimedia agreed to acquire some business units run by celebrity chef Emeril Lagasse for $50 million in cash and stock and a lucrative *earn-out* that could reach $20 million if Lagasse and company met specific profit goals by 2012. An earn-out is an incentive offered to key employees of a target company to entice them to remain with the company and increase value. Then, if the target company hits profit goals set by the buyer, the identified key employees earn a share of the profit. Under current GAAP, buyers must determine the estimated fair value of the future earn-out on the day of acquisition and record it as part of the purchase price. One impetus for an earn-out is when the buyer and seller cannot agree on a purchase price; in this way, the buyer is saying "I will pay if you make hay." Finally, any difference between the estimated fair value and the ultimate actual payout is recorded as an expense or gain.

Reporting of Goodwill

Goodwill is not amortized. Instead, GAAP requires companies to test the goodwill asset annually for impairment just like any other asset. The impairment test is a two-step process:

1. The fair value of the investee company is compared with the book value of the investor's equity investment account.[2]

2. If the fair value is less than the investment balance, the *investment* is deemed impaired. Next, one determines if the *goodwill* portion of the investment is impaired. The investor estimates the goodwill value as if the subsidiary were acquired at current fair value, and the imputed balance for goodwill becomes the balance in the goodwill account. If this imputed goodwill amount is less than its book value, the company writes goodwill down, resulting in an impairment loss on the consolidated income statement. (If not, no impairment of goodwill exists and no write-down is necessary; which, implies the impairment in this case relates to the investee's tangible assets, such as PPE, that must be tested separately for impairment.)

To illustrate the impairment computation, assume that an investment, currently reported at $1 million on the investor's balance sheet, has a current fair value of $900,000 (we know, therefore, that the investment is impaired); also assume the consolidated balance sheet reports goodwill at $300,000. Management's review reveals that the current fair value of the net assets of the investee company (absent goodwill) is $700,000. This indicates that the goodwill component of the investment account is impaired by $100,000, which is computed as follows:

Fair value of investee company	$ 900,000
Fair value of net assets (absent goodwill)	(700,000)
Implied goodwill	200,000
Current goodwill balance	(300,000)
Impairment loss	$(100,000)

This analysis implies that goodwill must be written down by $100,000. The impairment loss is reported in the consolidated income statement. The related footnote disclosure would describe the reasons for the write-down and the computations involved.

FedEx provides an example of a goodwill impairment disclosure in its 10-K report:

Our operating results for 2008 include a charge of approximately $891 million ($696 million, net of tax, or $2.23 per diluted share) recorded during the fourth quarter, predominantly related to noncash impairment charges associated with the decision to minimize the use of the Kinko's trade name and goodwill resulting from the Kinko's acquisition. The components of the charge include the following (in millions):

Trade name	$515
Goodwill	367
Other	9
	$891

During the fourth quarter we decided to change the name of FedEx Kinko's to FedEx Office. The impairment of the Kinko's trade name was due to the decision to minimize the use of the Kinko's trade name and rebrand our centers over the next several years. In accordance with SFAS 142, "Goodwill and Other Intangible Assets," a two-step impairment test is performed on goodwill. In the first step, we compared the estimated fair value of the reporting unit to its carrying value. The valuation methodology to estimate the fair value of the FedEx Office reporting unit was based primarily

continued

---

[2] GAAP allows firms to estimate fair value in three ways: using quoted market prices for identical assets, using quoted prices on similar assets, or using other valuation methods (such as the discounted cash flow model or residual operating income model—see Module 12). The FedEx footnote, which follows, provides an example of the third method of determining fair value: an income approach.

continued from prior page

on an income approach that considered market participant assumptions to estimate fair value. Key assumptions considered were the revenue and operating income forecast, the assessed growth rate in the periods beyond the detailed forecast period, and the discount rate. In the second step of the impairment test, we estimated the current fair values of all assets and liabilities to determine the amount of implied goodwill and consequently the amount of the goodwill impairment. Upon completion of the second step of the impairment test, we concluded that the recorded goodwill was impaired and recorded an impairment charge of $367 million during the fourth quarter of 2008.

FedEx determined that goodwill, reported on its balance sheet at $1,542 million, had a current (implied) market value $1,175 million. That is, FedEx's goodwill was impaired, resulting in a write-down of $367 million. In addition, FedEx recorded a $515 million charge to write off the Kinko's trade name that it had acquired four years earlier.

IFRS INSIGHT **Goodwill Impairment and Revaluation**

Similar to GAAP, all long-term assets, including goodwill, must be periodically evaluated for impairment. But, under IFRS, any previous impairment losses must be reversed if the asset subsequently increases in value. However, this does not apply to goodwill; once it is impaired under IFRS, it can not be revalued upwards. This is consistent with GAAP. Impairment losses are typically larger in magnitude under IFRS because IFRS computes the impairment loss as the excess of the carrying amount of the goodwill over its recoverable amount. Under GAAP, the impairment is relative to the implied fair value of the goodwill, which by definition is higher than the recoverable amount. Thus, for identical circumstances, goodwill impairments will be larger under IFRS.

Reporting Subsidiary Stock Issuances

After subsidiaries are acquired, they can, and often do, issue stock. If issued to outside investors, the result is an infusion of cash into the subsidiary and a reduction in the parent's percentage ownership. For example, Clear Channel Communications' (CCU) 10-K report discloses the following stock issuance by one of its subsidiaries.

Initial Public Offering ("IPO") of Clear Channel Outdoor Holdings ("CCO") The Company completed the IPO on November 11, 2005, which consisted of the sale of 35.0 million shares, for $18.00 per share, of Class A common stock of CCO, its indirect, wholly owned subsidiary prior to the IPO. After completion of the IPO, the Company owns all 315.0 million shares of CCO's outstanding Class B common stock, representing approximately 90% of the outstanding shares of CCO's common stock and approximately 99% of the total voting power of CCO's common stock. The net proceeds from the offering, after deducting underwriting discounts and offering expenses, were approximately $600.6 million. All of the net proceeds of the offering were used to repay a portion of the outstanding balances of intercompany notes owed to the Company by CCO. Under the guidance in SEC Staff Accounting Bulletin Topic 5H, *Accounting for Sales of Stock by a Subsidiary*, the Company has recorded approximately $120.9 million of minority interest and $479.7 million of additional paid in capital on its consolidated balance sheet at December 31, 2005 as a result of this transaction.

While this disclosure is complicated, the gist is that CCO, a Clear Channel Communications' subsidiary, issued stock to the public (an IPO). This increased the amount that Clear Channel reports on its balance sheet for this equity investment. To better understand this transaction, consider Parent Company that acquires 100% of Subsidiary Company at book value, and assume the latter has a book value for stockholders' equity of $500. The investment account on Parent's balance sheet, using the equity method, is $500. Next, Subsidiary issues shares to outsiders for $100, which reduces Parent's ownership to, say, 90%. Parent now owns 90% of Subsidiary whose book value of equity has increased to $600. The Parent's investment should therefore, have a balance sheet value of $540 (90% × $600). The value of Parent's equity method investment account rose by $40 ($540 vs. $500) because of the Subsidiary's stock sale.

Returning to Clear Channel's transaction, its equity method investment account increased by $600.6 million. This increase must be matched with a corresponding increase in Clear Channel's stockholders' equity. Clear Channel recognized a $600.6 million increase in stockholders' equity in two parts. First, Clear Channel added $479.7 million to additional paid-in capital. Second, it recorded minority interest for $120.9 million, which represents the book value of the CCO shares that were sold to the public. Minority interest is the part of CCO not owned by Clear Channel.

BUSINESS INSIGHT | **Pitfalls of Acquired Growth**

One of the greatest destructions of shareholder value occurred during the bull market between 1995 and 2001 when market exuberance fueled a tidal wave of corporate takeovers. Companies often overpaid as a result of overestimating the cost-cutting and synergies their planned takeovers would bring. Then, acquirers failed to quickly integrate operations. The result? Subsequent years' market returns of most acquirers fell below those of their peers and were often negative. Indeed, 61% of corporate buyers saw their shareholders' wealth *decrease* after the acquisition. Who won? The sellers; the target-company shareholders who sold their stock within the first week of the takeover and reaped enormous profits at the expense of the acquirers' shareholders.

Reporting the Sale of Subsidiary Companies

Discontinued operations refer to any separately identifiable business unit that the company sells or intends to sell. The income or loss of the discontinued operations (net of tax), and the after-tax gain or loss on sale of the unit, are reported in the income statement below income from continuing operations. The segregation of discontinued operations means that revenues and expenses of the discontinued business unit are *not* reported with revenues and expenses from continuing operations.

To illustrate, assume that Google's recent periods' results were generated by both continuing and discontinued operations as follows:

	Continuing Operations	Discontinued Operations	Total
Revenues	$10,000	$3,000	$13,000
Expenses	7,000	2,000	9,000
Pretax Income	3,000	1,000	4,000
Tax expense (40%).	1,200	400	1,600
Net Income.	$ 1,800	$ 600	$ 2,400

Google's reported income statement would appear as follows—notice the separate disclosure for discontinued operations (as highlighted).

Revenues	$10,000
Expenses	7,000
Pretax Income	3,000
Tax expense (40%).	1,200
Income from continuing operations	1,800
Income from discontinued operations, net	**600**
Net income.	$ 2,400

Revenues and expenses reflect those of the continuing operations only, and the (persistent) income from continuing operations is reported net of its related tax expense. Results from the (transitory) discontinued operations are collapsed into one line item and reported separately net of its own tax (this includes any gain or loss from sale of the discontinued unit's net assets). The net income figure is unchanged by this presentation.

Importantly, results of the discontinued operations are segregated from those of continuing operations. This presentation facilitates the prediction of results from the (persistent) continuing operations. Discontinued operations are segregated (reported on one line) in the current year and for the two prior years. To illustrate, Campbell Soup reports the following footnote to its 2008 10-K relating to the decision to divest its Godiva chocolate business ($ millions).

Discontinued Operations On March 18, 2008, the company completed the sale of its Godiva Chocolatier business for $850 million. The purchase price was subject to certain post-closing adjustments, which resulted in an additional $20 million of proceeds. The company has reflected the results of this business as discontinued operations in the consolidated statements of earnings for all years presented . . . Results of discontinued operations were as follows:

Godiva ($ millions)	2008
Net sales	$393
Earnings from operations before taxes	$ 49
Taxes on earnings—operations	(17)
Gain on sale	698
Deferred tax expense/after-tax costs associated with sale	—
Tax impact of gain on sale	(236)
Earnings from discontinued operations	$494

The 2008 results included a $462 million after-tax gain, or $1.21 per share, on the Godiva Chocolatier sale.

This footnote highlights two important items. First, in 2008 the Godiva operations had revenues of $393 million and net income of $32 million ($49 million before tax less tax of $17 million). Companies often discontinue profitable operations, selling them to recoup investments and/or to focus on other lines of business. Second, the sale of Godiva for $870 million generated a gain of $698 million before tax. The reported gain or loss on sale is equal to the proceeds received less the balance of the equity method investment reported on the parent's balance sheet at the sale date. (From the footnote, we can infer that Campbell's carrying value of the Godiva investment was $172 million.) Both of these two components—the net income or loss from operations during the year and any gain or loss on disposal of the discontinued operations—are reported, on one line, in Campbell's income statement. For comparative years (2006 and 2007) only the first component is included in the discontinued operations line item because Godiva was not sold until 2008.

Limitations of Consolidation Reporting

Consolidation of financial statements is meant to present a financial picture of the entire set of companies under the control of the parent. Since investors typically purchase stock in the parent company, and not in the subsidiaries, a consolidated view is more relevant than the parent company merely reporting subsidiaries as equity investments in its balance sheet. Still, we must be aware of certain limitations of consolidation:

1. Consolidated income does not imply that the parent company has received any or all of the subsidiaries' net income as cash. The parent can only receive cash from subsidiaries via dividend payments. Conversely, the consolidated cash is not automatically available to the individual subsidiaries. It is quite possible, therefore, for an individual subsidiary to experience cash flow problems even though the consolidated group has strong cash flows. Likewise, unguaranteed debts of a subsidiary are not obligations of the consolidated group. Thus, even if the consolidated balance sheet is strong, creditors of a failing subsidiary are often unable to sue the parent or other subsidiaries to recoup losses.

2. Consolidated balance sheets and income statements are a mix of the various subsidiaries, often from different industries. Comparisons across companies, even if in similar industries, are often complicated by the different mix of subsidiary companies.

3. Segment disclosures on individual subsidiaries are affected by intercorporate transfer pricing policies relating to purchases of products or services that can artificially inflate the profitability of one

segment at the expense of another. Companies also have considerable discretion in the allocation of corporate overhead to subsidiaries, which can markedly affect segment profitability.

BUSINESS INSIGHT   **Determining the Parent Company in an Acquisition**

Sensor, Inc., is acquiring Boston Instrument Company through an exchange of stock valued at $500 million. Sensor will survive as the continuing company, and the senior management of Boston Instrument will own 65% of the outstanding stock, reflecting a premium in the exchange ratios paid by Sensor to acquire Boston Instrument. Sensor's Chairman will remain as Chairman of the company, but the purchase agreement specifies that the board of directors will elect a new Chairman within six months of the deal's close. Boston Instrument's President and CFO will assume those same positions in the new entity. Following are the market values of the tangible and intangible net assets of both companies on the date of acquisition: Sensor, $400 million; and Boston Instrument, $200 million. Which of these two companies should be viewed as the acquiring firm (parent company) for purposes of consolidation, and how does this decision affect the amount of goodwill recorded on the consolidated balance sheet? Sensor is the larger firm, its name will survive, and its Chairman will serve in that capacity in the combined company. However, most accountants would likely conclude that Boston Instrument is the parent company for purposes of consolidation. This determination is based on the 65% ownership interest of the Boston Instrument shareholders who control the new entity. Further, these shareholders will be able to elect a new Chairman within six months. The amount of goodwill recorded following the acquisition is equal to the purchase price less the fair value of the net tangible and identifiable intangible assets acquired. If Sensor is the acquiring firm, $100 million ($500 million − $400 million) of goodwill will be recorded. If Boston Instrument is the acquiring firm, $300 million ($500 million − $200 million) of goodwill will be recorded. This decision will dramatically affect both the balance sheet (relative amounts of goodwill and other assets recorded) as well as the income statement (depreciation of tangible assets and amortization of identifiable intangible assets recognized vs. annual impairment testing for goodwill).

MODULE-END REVIEW

On January 1 of the current year, assume that Yahoo!, Inc., purchased all of the common shares of EarthLink for $600,000 cash—this is $200,000 more than the book value of EarthLink's stockholders' equity. Balance sheets of the two companies immediately after the acquisition follow:

	Yahoo! (Parent)	EarthLink (Subsidiary)	Consolidating Adjustments	Consolidated
Current assets	$1,000,000	$100,000		
Investment in EarthLink	600,000	—		
PPE, net	3,000,000	400,000		
Goodwill	—	—		_____
Total assets.	$4,600,000	$500,000		
Liabilities.	$1,000,000	$100,000		
Contributed capital.	2,000,000	200,000		
Retained earnings	1,600,000	200,000		_____
Total liabilities and equity	$4,600,000	$500,000		

During purchase negotiations, EarthLink's PPE was appraised at $500,000, and all of EarthLink's remaining assets and liabilities were appraised at values approximating their book values. Also, Yahoo! concluded that payment of an additional $100,000 was warranted because of anticipated corporate synergies. Prepare the consolidating adjustments and the consolidated balance sheet at acquisition.

Solution

	Yahoo! (Parent)	EarthLink (Subsidiary)	Consolidating Adjustments	Consolidated
Current assets	$1,000,000	$100,000		$1,100,000
Investment in EarthLink	600,000	—	$(600,000)	
PPE, net	3,000,000	400,000	100,000	3,500,000
Goodwill	—	—	100,000	100,000
Total assets.	$4,600,000	$500,000		$4,700,000
Liabilities.	$1,000,000	$100,000		$1,100,000
Contributed capital.	2,000,000	200,000	(200,000)	2,000,000
Retained earnings	1,600,000	200,000	(200,000)	1,600,000
Total liabilities and equity	$4,600,000	$500,000		$4,700,000

Explanation: The $600,000 investment account is eliminated together with the $400,000 book value of EarthLink's equity to which Yahoo's investment relates. The remaining $200,000 consists of the additional $100,000 in PPE assets and the $100,000 in goodwill from expected corporate synergies. Following these adjustments, the balance sheet items are summed to yield the consolidated balance sheet.

APPENDIX 7A: Accounting for Derivatives

Although there is some speculative use of derivatives by U.S. companies (both industrial and financial), most companies use derivatives to shelter their income statements and cash flows from fluctuations in the market prices of currencies, commodities, and financial instruments, as well as for market rates of interest. Companies routinely face risk exposures that can markedly affect their balance sheets, profitability, and cash flows. These exposures can be grouped into two general categories:[3]

1. Exposure to changes in the **fair value** of an asset (such as accounts receivable, inventory, marketable securities, or a firm contract to sell an asset) or of a liability (such as accounts payable, a firm commitment to purchase an asset, or a fixed-rate liability).

2. Exposure to variation in **cash flows** relating to a forecasted transaction (such as *planned* inventory purchases or anticipated foreign revenues) or cash flow exposure relating to a variable-rate debt obligation.

Both of these types of risks can be managed (hedged) with a variety of financial instruments, including futures, forward contracts, options, and swap contracts. For an example in the first category, consider a company with a fair-value exposure from a receivable denominated in a foreign currency. If the $US strengthens subsequently, the receivable declines in value and the company incurs a foreign currency loss. To avoid this situation, the company can hedge the receivable with a foreign-currency derivative. Ideally, when the $US strengthens, the derivative will increase in value by an amount that exactly offsets the decrease in the value of the receivable. As a result, the company's net asset position (receivable less derivative) remains unaffected and no gain or loss arises when the $US weakens or strengthens. For accounting purposes, this is called a **fair-value hedge**.

As an example for the second category, consider a company that routinely purchases a food commodity used in its manufacturing process. Any price increases during the coming year will flow to cost of goods sold and profit will decrease (unless the company can completely pass the price increase along to its customers, which is rarely the case). To avoid this situation, the company can hedge the inventory purchases with a commodity derivative contract that locks in a price today. When the price of the commodity increases, the derivative contract will shelter the company and, as a result, the company's cost of goods sold remains unaffected. For accounting purposes, this is called a **cash-flow hedge**.

Accounting for derivatives essentially boils down to this: all derivatives are reported at fair value on the balance sheet. For fair-value hedges, the asset or liability being hedged (the foreign receivable in the example above), is reported on the balance sheet at fair value. If the market value of the hedged asset or liability changes, the value of the derivative changes in the opposite direction if the hedge is effective and, thus, net assets and liabilities are unaffected. Likewise, the related gains and losses are largely offsetting, leaving income unaffected.

---

[3] Risks relating to changes in the fair value of a recognized asset or liability, or the variation in cash flows relating to a contractual obligation or a forecasted transaction, that results from fluctuations in the exchange value of the $US vis-à-vis other world currencies are particularly troublesome for companies. The use of derivatives to mitigate **foreign currency risk** can fall into either of the risk categories.

For cash-flow hedges, there is no hedged asset or liability on the books. In our example above, it is the anticipated commodity purchases that are being hedged. Thus, the company has no inventory yet and changes in the fair value of the derivative are not met with opposite changes in an asset or liability. For these cash-flow hedges, gains or losses from the fair value of the derivative are not reported on the income statement. Instead they are held in accumulated other comprehensive income (AOCI), as part of shareholders' equity. Later, when the hedged item impacts income (say, when the commodity cost is reflected in cost of goods sold), the derivative gain or loss is reclassified from AOCI to income. If the hedge was effective, the gain or loss on the hedged transaction is offset with the loss or gain on the derivative and income is unaffected.

For both fair-value and cash-flow hedges, income is impacted only to the extent that the hedging activities are ineffective. Naturally, if derivative use is for speculative activities, gains and losses are not offset and directly flow to income. It is this latter activity, in particular, that prompted regulators to formulate newer, tougher accounting standards for derivatives.

Disclosures for Derivatives

Companies must disclose both qualitative and quantitative information about derivatives in notes to their financial statements and elsewhere (in the Management's Discussion and Analysis section). The aim of these disclosures is to inform outsiders about potential risks associated with derivative use. We present footnotes relating to fair value hedges and cash flow hedges below as examples of common transactions relating to use of derivatives to mitigate risk. We discuss the accounting for each and how we should interpret these disclosures in our analysis of the company.

Fair Value Hedge

Fair value hedges are used to mitigate risks relating to the change in the fair values of existing assets and liabilities. These fair values can change, for example, with changes in commodity prices, interest rates, or foreign exchange rates. Following is an example from the Baker Hughes 2008 10-K.

> **FOREIGN CURRENCY AND FOREIGN CURRENCY FORWARD CONTRACTS** We conduct operations around the world in a number of different currencies . . . At December 31, 2008, we had entered into several foreign currency forward contracts with notional amounts aggregating $125 million to hedge exposure to currency fluctuations in various foreign currency denominated accounts payable and accounts receivable, including the British Pound Sterling, Norwegian Krone, Euro, and the Brazilian Real. These contracts are designated and qualify as fair value hedging instruments. Based on quoted market prices as of December 31, 2008, for contracts with similar terms and maturity dates, we recorded a loss of $0.5 million to adjust these foreign currency forward contracts to their fair market value. This loss offsets designated foreign currency exchange gains resulting from the underlying exposures and is included in marketing, general, and administrative expenses in the consolidated statement of operations.

To illustrate the accounting for the Baker Hughes fair value hedge, assume that the company sells goods for €3.7 million ($5 million equivalent) on account to a customer located in Ireland. The company is concerned about the potential effects of a strengthening or weakening of the $US and enters into a forward contract to hedge that foreign currency (FX) risk. Before the receivable is collected, the $US weakens vis-à-vis the Euro, and the Euros received (€3.7 million) is converted to $5.5 million. The transactions are accounted for as follows:

		Balance Sheet						Income Statement				
Transaction	**Cash Asset**	+	**Noncash Assets**	=	**Liabilities**	+	**Contrib. Capital**	+	**Earned Capital**	**Revenues**	− **Expenses**	= **Net Income**
1. Credit sale for €3.7 mil. ($5 mil. equivalent)			+5.0 mil. Accounts Receivable	=					+5.0 mil. Retained Earnings	+5.0 mil. Sales	−	= +5.0 mil.
2a. Receive €3.7 mil. ($5.5 mil. equivalent) per transaction 1	+5.5 mil. Cash		−5.0 mil. Accounts Receivable	=					+0.5 mil. Retained Earnings	+0.5 mil. Gain on Foreign Currency Transaction	−	= +0.5 mil.
2b. Record loss on settlement of foreign exchange contract	−0.5 mil. Cash			=					−0.5 mil. Retained Earnings		+0.5 mil. Loss on Foreign Exchange Derivative Contract −	= −0.5 mil.

AR   5.0M
Sales   5.0M

AR
5M
Sales
5M

Cash   5.5M
AR   5.0M
GN on FX 0.5M
Cash
5.5M
AR
5M
Gain on FX
0.5M

LS on Cont. 0.5M
Cash   0.5M
Loss on Contract
0.5M
Cash
0.5M

In this transaction, the company has hedged its foreign exchange exposure via a forward contract. As the $US weakens, the value of the accounts receivable increases by $0.5 million, resulting in a foreign exchange gain, and the fair value of the derivative contract decreases by $0.5 million, resulting in an offsetting loss. The net cash received is the $5.5 million from the receivable less the $0.5 million to settle the forward contract.

Why would the company want to enter into a contract such as this that resulted in a loss? After all, had the company not "hedged" the Euro receivable, the cash collected would have been $5.5 million and the company would have reported a gain. The answer is that a company does not know in advance which way currencies will move. As the Baker Hughes footnote indicates, sometimes the derivative suffers a loss, and at other times creates a gain. The purpose of the derivative is to lock in the operating profit on the sale and to shield the company from risk in the form of fluctuating foreign currency exchange rates.

Cash Flow Hedge

Following is Southwest Airlines' disclosures from its 2007 10-K report relating to its use of derivatives:

Financial Derivative Instruments Airline operators are inherently dependent upon energy to operate and, therefore, are impacted by changes in jet fuel prices. Jet fuel and oil consumed during 2007, 2006, and 2005 represented approximately 28.0 percent, 26.2 percent, and 19.6 percent of Southwest's operating expenses, respectively . . . The Company currently has a mixture of purchased call options, collar structures, and fixed price swap agreements in place to protect against over 70 percent of its 2008 total anticipated jet fuel requirements at average crude oil equivalent prices of approximately $51 per barrel, and has also added refinery margins on most of those positions. Based on current growth plans, the Company also has fuel derivative contracts in place for over 55 percent of its expected fuel consumption for 2009 at approximately $51 per barrel, nearly 30 percent for 2010 at approximately $63 per barrel, over 15 percent for 2011 at $64 per barrel, and over 15 percent in 2012 at $63 per barrel. Upon proper qualification, the Company endeavors to account for its fuel derivative instruments as cash flow hedges, as defined in Statement of Financial Accounting Standards No. 133, *Accounting for Derivative Instruments and Hedging Activities*, as amended (SFAS 133). Under SFAS 133, all derivatives designated as hedges that meet certain requirements are granted special hedge accounting treatment. Generally, utilizing the special hedge accounting, all periodic changes in fair value of the derivatives designated as hedges that are considered to be effective, as defined, are recorded in "Accumulated other comprehensive income" until the underlying jet fuel is consumed . . . The following table presents the location of pre-tax gains and/or losses on derivative instruments within the Consolidated Statement of Income:

(In millions)	2007	2006	2005
Fuel hedge (gains) included in Fuel and oil expense	$(686)	$(634)	$(892)
Mark-to-market impact from fuel contracts settling in future periods— included in Other (gains) losses, net	(219)	42	(77)
Ineffectiveness from fuel hedges settling in future periods— included in Other (gains) losses, net	(51)	39	(9)
Realized ineffectiveness and mark-to-market (gains) or losses— included in Other (gains) losses, net	(90)	20	(24)
Premium cost of fuel contracts included in Other (gains) losses, net	58	52	35

Southwest Airlines uses derivatives mainly to hedge fuel costs. Those hedges place a ceiling on fuel cost and are used for up to 70% of Southwest Airlines' fuel purchases.

These derivatives are cash flow hedges. Thus, unrealized gains and losses on these derivative contracts are added to the Accumulated Other Comprehensive Income (AOCI) (part of stockholders' equity) until the fuel is purchased. Once that fuel is purchased, any unrealized gains and losses are removed from AOCI and recognized in current-period income. The gain (loss) on the derivative contract offsets the increased (decreased) cost of fuel. In 2007, $686 million of hedging gains were used to offset fuel expense for Southwest Airlines. This use of fuel derivatives is the prime reason that soaring oil prices in that year did not affect Southwest Airlines as harshly as other large carriers.

Although the market value of derivatives and their related assets or liabilities can be large, the net effect on stockholders' equity is usually minor. This is because companies use derivatives mainly to hedge and not to speculate. The FASB enacted SFAS 133, "Accounting for derivative instruments and hedging activities," to respond to concerns that speculative activities were not adequately disclosed. However, subsequent to the passage of SFAS 133, the financial effects have been minimal. Either companies were not speculating to the extent suspected, or they have since reduced their level of speculation in response to increased scrutiny from better disclosures.

To illustrate the accounting for the Southwest Airlines cash flow hedge, assume that Southwest knows that it must purchase jet fuel over the coming year. The fuel would cost $1 billion at the current market prices but Southwest anticipates price increases. Simultaneously, Southwest purchases call options to lock in the $1 billion purchase price. (Southwest would pay an option premium which would be recorded as an asset and amortized over time; to keep the example simple, we ignore this premium.) Delivery of jet fuel takes place over the year and the market price of the combined jet fuel purchases is $1.686 billion. During the year, Southwest adjusts the option to fair-value, the combined mark-to-market adjustments are $0.686 billion. Those transactions are accounted for as follows:

Transaction	Balance Sheet					Income Statement		
	Cash Asset	+ Noncash Assets	= Liabil- ities	+ Contrib. Capital	+ Earned Capital	Rev- enues	− Expen- ses	= Net Income
1. Record unrealized fair-value gain on call option		+0.686 bil. Call Option =			+0.686 bil. AOCI		−	=
2a. Purchase and use jet fuel during the year	−1.686 bil. Cash	=			−1.686 bil. Retained Earnings		+1.686 bil. Fuel − Expense	−1.686 bil. =
2b. Exercise call option as Southwest purchases jet fuel	+0.686 bil. Cash	−0.686 bil. Call = Option					−	=
2c. Recognize unrealized fair-value gain as Southwest uses jet fuel		=			+0.686 bil. Retained Earnings −0.686 bil. AOCI		−0.686 bil. Fuel − Expense	+0.686 bil. =

Left-margin T-accounts:

1.
Call Op 0.686B
AOCI 0.686B
Call Option	
0.686B	
AOCI	
	0.686B

2a.
FE 1.686B
Cash 1.686B
Fuel Exp	
1.686B	
Cash	
	1.686B

2b.
Cash 0.686B
Call Op 0.686B
Cash	
0.686B	
Call Option	
	0.686B

2c.
AOCI 0.686B
FE 0.686B
AOCI	
0.686B	
Fuel Exp	
	0.686B

In this transaction, Southwest has hedged its jet fuel purchase via call options. As the price of jet fuel increases, so does the value of the call option. This unrealized gain on the option is reflected in AOCI until the jet fuel is consumed. At that time, the unrealized gain is removed from AOCI and expenses are reduced, thereby offsetting the increase in fuel resulting from the higher jet fuel cost. The net effect is that Southwest reports $1 billion for fuel expense. The net cash outlay for fuel is also $1 billion as a result of the cash inflow related to the call option. The purpose of Southwest Airlines' derivative program is to attempt to lock in the price of jet fuel. This is an operating activity and the gain on the derivative contract should be included in NOPAT to offset the increased cost of the jet fuel. Because Southwest hedged the fuel purchases, there is no net effect on income.

In both of our illustrations, the derivative contract is perfectly correlated with the asset or cash flow to which it relates. In practice, this is unlikely. Southwest Airlines, for example, cannot purchase call options on "jet fuel" because they do not exist. Instead, it uses a basket of financial instruments, some correlated with crude oil and some with home heating oil, that are positively correlated with jet fuel costs. As a result, the change in the fair value of the derivatives might not exactly offset the change in the cost of the jet fuel. Only the effective portion of the hedge is deferred in AOCI. The ineffective portion of the hedge affects current income. Bottom line, some of the risk will impact net income if the company cannot perfectly hedge the risk or chooses not to manage 100% of the risk (Southwest only hedges about a third of its jet fuel costs).

BUSINESS INSIGHT Counter-Party Risk

The purpose of derivative financial instruments is to transfer risk from one company to another. For example, a company might be concerned about the possible decline in the $US value of a foreign currency-denominated account receivable. In order to hedge that risk, the company might execute a forward contract to sell the foreign currency and receive $US. That forward contract only has value, however, if the party on the other side of the transaction (the counter-party) ultimately purchases the foreign currency for $US when the contract matures. If the counter-party fails to honor its part of the agreement, the forward contract is of no value. The risk that the other party might not live up to its part of the bargain is known as *counter-party risk*. The only justification for recognizing a gain in a forward contract to offset the loss in a foreign currency-denominated receivable is the expectation that the counter-party has the intention and ability to purchase the foreign currency in exchange for $US when the contract matures. Counter-party risk is very real. Many companies require counter-parties to back up their agreement with cash collateral or other acceptable forms of guarantees (like a bank letter of credit, for example). As a result, there is a hidden risk in companies' use of derivatives that is difficult to quantify.

Analysis of Derivatives

Derivatives relate to a specific balance sheet account or forecasted transaction. The fair value of the derivatives and their ultimate gains (losses) should be classified with the account to which they relate. For example, in the Baker Hughes example, the fair value of the foreign exchange contract is grouped with the accounts receivable to which it relates, and the gain (loss) on that derivative is considered an operating item (part of NOPAT). The derivative investments that Southwest Airlines uses are treated similarly. In this case, both the balance sheet accounts and income statement effects are treated as operating.

Companies also frequently use a variety of derivative instruments to hedge exposure to interest rates. Companies can, for example, use swap contracts to convert floating rate debt to fixed rate debt and vice-versa. In this case, the fair values of the derivatives and their ultimate income statement effects are nonoperating because they relate to interest-bearing debt.

In addition to proper classification of balance sheet and income statement accounts for computation of NOPAT and NOA, we are interested in understanding the extent to which the company is hedged. That is, are there still risks over which the company has no control and that are not hedged? Unfortunately, footnote disclosures do not provide a completely satisfactory answer. We are not privy to the internal risk analysis that the company performs. As a result, we do not know, for example, the precise extent to which the hedges are ineffective, to what degree the company has decided to hedge, and whether the company is facing risks for which a derivative instrument is not available. To gain further insight into these questions, we must often look to other sources of information such as analyst reports, the financial press, and communications from the company.

GUIDANCE ANSWERS

MANAGERIAL DECISION   You Are the Chief Financial Officer

Capacity utilization is important. If long-term operating assets are used inefficiently, cost per unit produced is too high. Cost per unit does not relate solely to manufacturing products, but also applies to the cost of providing services and many other operating activities. However, if we purchase assets with little productive slack, our costs of production at peak levels can be excessive. Further, the company may be unable to service peak demand and risks losing customers. In response, the company might explore strategic alliances. These take many forms. Some require a simple contract to use another company's manufacturing, service, or administrative capability for a fee (note: these executory contracts are not recorded under GAAP). Another type of alliance is that of a joint venture to share ownership of manufacturing or IT facilities. In this case, if demand can be coordinated with that of a partner, perhaps operating assets can be more effectively used. Finally, a special purpose entity (SPE) can be formed to acquire the asset for use by the company and its partner—explained in Module 10.

Superscript [A] denotes assignments based on Appendix 7A.

DISCUSSION QUESTIONS

Q7-1.   What measure (fair value or amortized cost) is on the balance sheet for (a) trading securities, (b) available-for-sale securities, and (c) held-to-maturity securities?

Q7-2.   What is an unrealized holding gain (loss)? Explain.

Q7-3.   Where are unrealized holding gains and losses related to trading securities reported in the financial statements? Where are unrealized holding gains and losses related to available-for-sale securities reported in the financial statements?

Q7-4.   What does *significant influence* imply regarding intercorporate investments? Describe the accounting procedures used for such investments.

Q7-5.   On January 1 of the current year, Yetman Company purchases 40% of the common stock of Livnat Company for $250,000 cash. This 40% ownership allows Yetman to exert significant influence over Livnat. During the year, Livnat reports $80,000 of net income and pays $60,000 in cash dividends. At year-end, what amount should appear in Yetman's balance sheet for its investment in Livnat?

Q7-6.   What accounting method is used when a stock investment represents more than 50% of the investee company's voting stock and allows the investor company to "control" the investee company? Explain.

Q7-7.   What is the underlying objective of consolidated financial statements?

Q7-8.   Finn Company purchases all of the common stock of Murray Company for $750,000 when Murray Company has $300,000 of common stock and $450,000 of retained earnings. If a consolidated balance sheet is prepared immediately after the acquisition, what amounts are eliminated in consolidation? Explain.

Q7-9. Bradshaw Company owns 100% of Dee Company. At year-end, Dee owes Bradshaw $75,000 arising from a loan made during the year. If a consolidated balance sheet is prepared at year-end, how is the $75,000 handled? Explain.

Q7-10. What are some limitations of consolidated financial statements?

Assignments with the WebAssign. logo in the margin are available in WebAssign.
See the Preface of the book for details.

MINI EXERCISES

M7-11. Interpreting Disclosures of Available-for-Sale Securities (LO1)

Pfizer Inc. (PFE)

Use the following year-end footnote disclosure from Pfizer's 10-K report to answer parts *a* and *b*.

(Millions of Dollars)	2007
Cost of available-for-sale equity securities	$202
Gross unrealized gains.	127
Gross unrealized losses	(13)
Fair value of available-for-sale equity securities	$316

a. What amount does Pfizer report on its balance sheet as available-for-sale equity securities? Explain.

b. How does Pfizer report the net unrealized gain of $114 million ($127 million − $13 million) in its financial statements?

M7-12. Accounting for Available-for-Sale and Trading Securities (LO1)

Assume that Wasley Company purchases 6,000 common shares of Pincus Company for $12 cash per share. During the year, Wasley receives a cash dividend of $1.10 per common share from Pincus, and the year-end market price of Pincus common stock is $13 per share. How much income does Wasley report relating to this investment for the year if it accounts for the investment as:

a. Available-for-sale investment

b. Trading investment

M7-13. Interpreting Disclosures of Investment Securities (LO1)

Abbott Laboratories (ABT)

Abbott Laboratories reports the following disclosure relating to its December 31 comprehensive income. (*a*) How is Abbott accounting for its investment in marketable equity securities? How do you know? (*b*) Explain how its 2007 financial statements are impacted by Abbott's investment in marketable equity securities.

Comprehensive Income, net of tax ($ 000s)	2007
Foreign currency gain (loss) translation adjustments.	$1,153,209
Net actuarial gains and prior service cost and credits and amortization of net actuarial losses and prior service cost and credits, net of taxes of $(225,500)	342,724
Unrealized gains (losses) on marketable equity securities, net of income taxes of $(31,100) in 2007 and $118,500 in 2006	53,844
Net adjustments for derivative instruments designated as cash flow hedges.	(39,614)
Other comprehensive income (loss).	1,510,163
Net earnings.	3,606,314
Comprehensive income	$5,116,477

M7-14. Analyzing and Interpreting Equity Method Investments (LO2)

Stober Company purchases an investment in Lang Company at a purchase price of $1 million cash, representing 30% of the book value of Lang. During the year, Lang reports net income of $100,000 and pays cash dividends of $40,000. At the end of the year, the market value of Stober's investment is $1.2 million.

a. What amount does Stober report on its balance sheet for its investment in Lang?

b. What amount of income from investments does Stober report? Explain.

continued

    c.   Stober's $200,000 unrealized gain in the market value of the Lang investment (choose one and explain):

        (1) Is not reflected on either its income statement or balance sheet.

        (2) Is reported in its current income.

        (3) Is reported on its balance sheet only.

        (4) Is reported in its accumulated other comprehensive income.

M7-15. Computing Income for Equity Method Investments   (LO2)

Kross Company purchases an equity investment in Penno Company at a purchase price of $5 million, representing 40% of the book value of Penno. During the current year, Penno reports net income of $600,000 and pays cash dividends of $200,000. At the end of the year, the fair value of Kross's investment is $5.3 million. What amount of income does Kross report relating to this investment in Penno for the year? Explain.

M7-16. Interpreting Disclosures on Investments in Affiliates   (LO2)

Merck's 10-K report included the following footnote disclosure:

    Merck & Co., Inc. (MRK)

> Investments in affiliates accounted for using the equity method . . . totaled $3.9 billion at December 31, 2007. These amounts are reported in Other assets.

    a.   At what amount are the equity method investments reported on Merck's balance sheet? Does this amount represent Merck's adjusted cost or fair value?

    b.   How does Merck account for the dividends received on these investments?

    c.   What sources of income does the company report for these investments?

M7-17. Computing Consolidating Adjustments and Minority Interest   (LO3)

Philipich Company purchases 80% of Hirst Company's common stock for $600,000 cash when Hirst Company has $300,000 of common stock and $450,000 of retained earnings. If a consolidated balance sheet is prepared immediately after the acquisition, what amounts are eliminated when preparing that statement? What amount of minority interest appears in the consolidated balance sheet?

M7-18. Computing Consolidated Net Income   (LO3)

Benartzi Company purchased a 90% interest in Liang Company on January 1 of the current year and the purchase price reflected 90% of Liang's book value of equity. Benartzi Company had $600,000 net income for the current year *before* recognizing its share of Liang Company's net income. If Liang Company had net income of $150,000 for the year, what is the consolidated net income for the year?

M7-19. Assigning Purchase Price in Acquisitions   (LO3)

Weaver Company acquired 80% of Koonce Company at the beginning of the current year. Weaver paid $50,000 more than the book value of Koonce's shareholders' equity and determined that this excess purchase price related to intangible assets. How does the $50,000 appear on the consolidated Weaver Company balance sheet if the intangible assets acquired related to (*a*) patents, or alternatively (*b*) goodwill? How would the consolidated income statement be affected under each scenario?

EXERCISES

E7-20. Assessing Financial Statement Effects of Trading and Available-for-Sale Securities   (LO1)

    Web**Assign**.

    a.   Use the financial statement effects template to record the following four transactions involving investments in marketable securities classified as trading.

        (1) Purchased 6,000 common shares of Liu, Inc., for $12 cash per share.

        (2) Received a cash dividend of $1.10 per common share from Liu.

        (3) Year-end market price of Liu common stock was $11.25 per share.

        (4) Sold all 6,000 common shares of Liu for $66,900.

    b.   Using the same transaction information as above, complete the financial statement effects template (with amounts and accounts) assuming the investments in marketable securities are classified as available-for-sale.

E7-21. Assessing Financial Statement Effects of Trading and Available-for-Sale Securities   (LO1)

Use the financial statement effects template to record the accounts and amounts for the following four transactions involving investments in marketable securities:

    (1) Ohlson Co. purchases 5,000 common shares of Freeman Co. at $16 cash per share.
    (2) Ohlson Co. receives a cash dividend of $1.25 per common share from Freeman.
    (3) Year-end market price of Freeman common stock is $17.50 per share.
    (4) Ohlson Co. sells all 5,000 common shares of Freeman for $86,400 cash.

a.   Assume the investments are classified as trading.

b.   Assume the investments are classified as available-for-sale.

E7-22.   **Interpreting Footnotes on Security Investments**   **(LO1)**

Berkshire Hathaway
(BRKA)

Berkshire Hathaway reports the following footnotes with its 10-K report.

Years Ended December 31 ($ millions)	2007	2006	2005
Accumulated Other Comprehensive Income			
Unrealized appreciation of investments.	$ 2,523	$ 9,278	$ 2,081
Applicable income taxes.	(872)	(3,246)	(728)
Reclassification adjustment of investment appreciation			
included in net earnings	(5,494)	(1,646)	(6,261)
Applicable income taxes.	1,923	576	2,191
Foreign currency translation adjustments	456	603	(359)
Applicable income taxes.	(26)	1	(26)
Prior service cost and actuarial gains (losses) of defined benefit plans	257	563	(62)
Applicable income taxes.	(102)	(196)	38
Other, including minority interests	(22)	(13)	51
Other comprehensive income	(1,357)	5,920	(3,075)
Adoption of SFAS 158	—	(303)	—
Accumulated other comprehensive income at beginning of year	22,977	17,360	20,435
Accumulated other comprehensive income at end of year	$21,620	$22,977	$17,360

Investments in equity securities are summarized below. Amounts are in millions.	2007	2006
Cost	$44,695	$28,353
Gross unrealized gains	31,289	33,217
Gross unrealized losses	(985)	(37)
Fair value	$74,999	$61,533

a.   At what amount does Berkshire Hathaway report its equity securities investment portfolio on its balance sheet? Does that amount include any unrealized gains or losses? Explain.

b.   How is Berkshire Hathaway accounting for its equity securities investment portfolio—as an available-for-sale or trading portfolio? How do you know?

c.   What does the number $2,523 represent in the Accumulated Other Comprehensive Income footnote? Is this number pretax or after-tax? Explain.

E7-23.   **Interpreting Footnote Disclosures for Investments**   **(LO1)**

WebAssign.

CNA Financial
Corporation (CNA)

CNA Financial Corporation provides the following footnote to its 2007 10-K report.

Valuation of investments CNA classifies its fixed maturity securities (bonds and redeemable preferred stocks) and its equity securities as either available-for-sale or trading, and as such, they are carried at fair value. Changes in fair value of trading securities are reported within net investment income. The amortized cost of fixed maturity securities classified as available-for-sale is adjusted for amortization of premiums and accretion of discounts to maturity, which are included in net investment income. Changes in fair value related to available-for-sale securities are reported as a component of other comprehensive income. Investments are written down to fair value and losses are recognized in Realized investment gains (losses) on the Consolidated Statements of Operations when a decline in value is determined to be other-than-temporary.

The following table provides a summary of fixed maturity and equity securities investments.

Summary of Fixed Maturity and Equity Securities					
	Cost or	Gross	Gross Unrealized Losses		Estimated
	Amortized	Unrealized	Less than	Greater than	Fair
December 31, 2007 (In millions)	Cost	Gains	12 Months	12 Months	Value
Fixed maturity securities available-for-sale					
U.S. Treasury securities and obligations					
of government agencies	$ 594	$ 93	$ —	$ —	$ 687
Asset-backed securities	11,776	39	223	183	11,409
States, municipalities and political					
subdivisions—tax-exempt securities	7,615	144	82	2	7,675
Corporate bonds.	8,867	246	149	12	8,952
Other debt securities	4,143	208	48	4	4,299
Redeemable preferred stock	1,216	2	160	—	1,058
Total fixed maturity securities					
available-for-sale.	34,211	732	662	201	34,080
Total fixed maturity securities trading	177	—	—	—	177
Equity securities available-for-sale					
Common stock	246	207	1	—	452
Preferred stock	120	7	11	—	116
Total equity securities available-for-sale. . . .	366	214	12	—	568
Total	$34,754	$946	$674	$201	$34,825

a. At what amount does CNA report its investment portfolio on its balance sheet? In your answer identify the portfolio's fair value, cost, and any unrealized gains and losses.

b. How do CNA's balance sheet and income statement reflect any unrealized gains and/or losses on the investment portfolio?

c. How do CNA's balance sheet and income statement reflect gains and losses realized from the sale of available-for-sale securities?

E7-24. **Assessing Financial Statement Effects of Equity Method Securities** (LO2)

Use the financial statement effects template (with amounts and accounts) to record the following transactions involving investments in marketable securities accounted for using the equity method:

a. Purchased 12,000 common shares of Barth Co. at $9 per share; the shares represent 30% ownership in Barth.

b. Received a cash dividend of $1.25 per common share from Barth.

c. Barth reported annual net income of $80,000.

d. Sold all 12,000 common shares of Barth for $120,500.

E7-25. **Assessing Financial Statement Effects of Equity Method Securities** (LO2)

Use the financial statement effects template (with amounts and accounts) to record the following transactions involving investments in marketable securities accounted for using the equity method:

a. Healy Co. purchases 15,000 common shares of Palepu Co. at $8 per share; the shares represent 25% ownership of Palepu.

b. Healy receives a cash dividend of $0.80 per common share from Palepu.

c. Palepu reports annual net income of $120,000.

d. Healy sells all 15,000 common shares of Palepu for $140,000.

E7-26. **Assessing Financial Statement Effects of Passive and Equity Method Investments** (LO1, 2)

On January 1, Ball Corporation purchased shares of Leftwich Company common stock.

a. Assume that the stock acquired by Ball represents 15% of Leftwich's voting stock and that Ball classifies the investment as available-for-sale. Use the financial statement effects template (with amounts and accounts) to record the following transactions:

(1) Ball purchased 10,000 common shares of Leftwich at $15 cash per share.

(2) Leftwich reported annual net income of $80,000.

(3) Ball received a cash dividend of $1.10 per common share from Leftwich.

(4) Year-end market price of Leftwich common stock is $19 per share.

b. Assume that the stock acquired by Ball represents 30% of Leftwich's voting stock and that Ball accounts for this investment using the equity method since it is able to exert significant influence. Use the financial statement effects template (with amounts and accounts) to record the following transactions:

WebAssign.

(1) Ball purchased 10,000 common shares of Leftwich at $15 cash per share.
(2) Leftwich reported annual net income of $80,000.
(3) Ball received a cash dividend of $1.10 per common share from Leftwich.
(4) Year-end market price of Leftwich common stock is $19 per share.

E7-27. Interpreting Equity Method Investment Footnotes (LO2)

DuPont (DD)

DuPont's 2007 10-K report includes information relating to the company's equity method investments ($ millions). The following footnote reports summary balance sheets for affiliated companies for which DuPont uses the equity method of accounting. The information below is shown on a 100 percent basis followed by the carrying value of DuPont's investment in these affiliates.

Financial Position at December 31 (in millions)	2007	2006
Current assets	$1,345	$1,367
Noncurrent assets	1,325	1,752
Total assets	$2,670	$3,119
Short-term borrowings	$ 420	$ 639
Other current liabilities	689	687
Long-term borrowings	82	238
Other long-term liabilities	118	112
Total liabilities	$1,309	$1,676
DuPont's investment in affiliates (includes advances of $27 and $58, respectively)	$ 818	$ 803

a. DuPont reports its investment in equity method affiliates on its balance sheet at $818 million. Does this reflect the adjusted cost or fair value of DuPont's interest in these companies?
b. What is the total stockholders' equity of the affiliates at the end of 2007? What is the carrying (book value) of DuPont's investment without the advances, at the end of 2007? Approximately what percentage does DuPont own, on average, of these affiliates? Explain.
c. DuPont reports equity income for 2007 of $(130) million, which includes an: "impairment charge of $165 million to write down the company's investment in a polyester films joint venture in the Performance Materials segment. As a result, at December 31, 2007, DuPont ceased using the equity method of accounting for three legal entities within the joint venture." Explain why DuPont ceased using the equity method to account for its investment. Why might this cessation be bothersome for our analysis and interpretation?

E7-28. Analyzing and Interpreting Disclosures on Equity Method Investments (LO2)

WebAssign.

Caterpillar, Inc. (CAT)

Shin Caterpillar
Mitsubishi, Ltd.

Caterpillar, Inc. (CAT) reports investments in affiliated companies, consisting mainly of its 50% ownership of Shin Caterpillar Mitsubishi, Ltd. Caterpillar reports those investments on its balance sheet at $582 million, and provides the following footnote in its 10-K report.

Investments in unconsolidated affiliated companies Our investments in affiliated companies accounted for by the equity method consist primarily of a 50% interest in Shin Caterpillar Mitsubishi Ltd. (SCM) located in Japan. Combined financial information of the unconsolidated affiliated companies accounted for by the equity method (generally on a three-month lag, e.g., SCM results reflect the periods ending September 30) was as follows:

Years Ended December 31 (Millions of Dollars)	2007	2006	2005
Results of operations:			
Sales	$4,007	$4,420	$4,140
Cost of sales	3,210	3,526	3,257
Gross profit	$ 797	$ 894	$ 883
Profit	$ 157	$ 187	$ 161
Caterpillar's profit	$ 73	$ 81	$ 73

Sales from SCM to Caterpillar of approximately $1.67 billion, $1.81 billion and $1.73 billion in 2007, 2006 and 2005 respectively, are included in the affiliated company sales. In addition, SCM purchased $268 million, $273 million and $282 million of products from Caterpillar in 2007, 2006 and 2005, respectively.

continued

continued from prior page

December 31 (Millions of Dollars)	2007	2006	2005
Financial position:			
Assets			
Current assets.............................	$2,062	$1,807	$1,714
Property, plant and equipment—net............	1,286	1,119	1,120
Other assets	173	176	194
	3,521	3,102	3,028
Liabilities			
Current liabilities	1,546	1,394	1,348
Long-term debt due after one year.............	269	309	318
Other liabilities...........................	393	145	188
	2,208	1,848	1,854
Ownership.................................	$1,313	$1,254	$1,174

Caterpillar's investment in unconsolidated affiliated companies, December 31 (Millions of Dollars)	2007	2006	2005
Investment in equity method companies............	$582	$542	$540
Plus: Investment in cost method companies.........	16	20	25
Investment in unconsolidated affiliated companies....	$598	$562	$565

a. What assets and liabilities of unconsolidated affiliates are omitted from CAT's balance sheet as a result of the equity method of accounting for those investments?

b. Do the liabilities of the unconsolidated affiliates affect CAT directly? Explain.

c. Compute CAT's reported profit from its investment in Shin as a percentage of Shin's reported profit. What percentage would we expect? Explain why the actual percentage is different from our expectation.

d. Both CAT and Shin include sales to each other in their respective income statements. Why are these intercompany sales not eliminated?

e. How does the equity method impact CAT's ROE and its RNOA components (net operating asset turnover and net operating profit margin)?

E7-29. Reporting and Interpreting Stock Investment Performance (LO1)

WebAssign.

Kasznik Company began operations on June 15 of the current calendar year and, by year-end (December 31), had made six stock investments. Year-end information on these stock investments follows.

December 31	Cost or Equity Basis (as appropriate)	Year-End Fair Value	Market Classification
Barth, Inc.	$ 68,000	$ 65,300	Trading
Foster, Inc.	162,500	160,000	Trading
McNichols, Inc.	197,000	192,000	Available-for-sale
Patell Company	157,000	154,700	Available-for-sale
Ertimur, Inc.	100,000	102,400	Equity method
Soliman, Inc.	136,000	133,200	Equity method

a. What does Kaznik's balance sheet report for trading stock investments at December 31?

b. What does Kaznik's balance sheet report for available-for-sale investments at December 31?

c. What does Kaznik's balance sheet report for equity method investments at December 31?

d. What total amount of unrealized holding gains or unrealized holding losses related to investments appear in Kasnik's income statement?

e. What total amount of unrealized holding gains or unrealized holding losses related to investments appear in the stockholders' equity section of Kasnik's December 31, balance sheet?

continued

f. What total amount of fair-value adjustment to investments appears in the December 31, balance sheet? Which category of investments does the fair-value adjustment relate to? Does the fair-value adjustment increase or decrease the carrying value of these investments?

E7-30. Interpreting Equity Method Investment Footnotes (LO2)

AT&T, Inc. (T)

AT&T reports the following footnote to its 2005 10-K report ($ millions).

Equity Method Investments We account for our nationwide wireless joint venture, Cingular, and our investments in equity affiliates under the equity method of accounting. The following table is a reconciliation of our investments in and advances to Cingular as presented on our Consolidated Balance Sheets.

($ millions)	2005	2004
Beginning of year	$33,687	$11,003
Contributions	—	21,688
Equity in net income	200	30
Other adjustments	(2,483)	966
End of year	$31,404	$33,687

Undistributed earnings from Cingular were $2,711 and $2,511 at December 31, 2005 and 2004. "Other adjustments" in 2005 included the net activity of $2,442 under our revolving credit agreement with Cingular, consisting of a reduction of $1,747 (reflecting Cingular's repayment of their shareholder loan during 2005) and a decrease of $695 (reflecting Cingular's net repayment of their revolving credit balance during 2005). During 2004, we made an equity contribution to Cingular in connection with its acquisition of AT&T Wireless. "Other adjustments" in 2004 included the net activity of $972 under our revolving credit agreement with Cingular, consisting of a reduction of $30 (reflecting Cingular's repayment of advances during 2004) and an increase of $1,002 (reflecting the December 31, 2004 balance of advances to Cingular under this revolving credit agreement).

We account for our 60% economic interest in Cingular under the equity method of accounting in our consolidated financial statements since we share control equally (i.e., 50/50) with our 40% economic partner in the joint venture. We have equal voting rights and representation on the Board of Directors that controls Cingular. The following table presents summarized financial information for Cingular at December 31, or for the year then ended.

Cingular ($ millions)	2005	2004	2003
Income Statements			
Operating revenues	$34,433	$19,565	$15,577
Operating income	1,824	1,528	2,254
Net income	333	201	977
Balance Sheets			
Current assets	$ 6,049	$ 5,570	
Noncurrent assets	73,270	76,668	
Current liabilities	10,008	7,983	
Noncurrent liabilities	24,333	29,719	

We have made a subordinated loan to Cingular that totaled $4,108 and $5,855 at December 31, 2005 and 2004, which matures in June 2008. This loan bears interest at an annual rate of 6.0%. During 2005, Cingular repaid $1,747 to reduce the balance of this loan in accordance with the terms of a revolving credit agreement. We earned interest income on this loan of $311 during 2005, $354 in 2004 and $397 in 2003. This interest income does not have a material impact on our net income as it is mostly offset when we record our share of equity income in Cingular.

a. At what amount is the equity investment in Cingular reported on AT&T's balance sheet? (*Hint:* the table in the footnote reports AT&T's investment plus its "advances" of $4,108 to Cingular plus

$311 of interest accrued on the advances.) Next, confirm (with computations) that this amount is equal to AT&T's proportionate share of Cingular's equity.

b. Did Cingular pay out any of its earnings as dividends in 2005? How do you know?

c. How much income did AT&T report in 2005 relating to this investment in Cingular?

d. Interpret the AT&T statement that "undistributed earnings from Cingular were $2,711 and $2,511 at December 31, 2005 and 2004."

e. How does use of the equity method impact AT&T's ROE and its RNOA components (net operating asset turnover and net operating profit margin)?

f. AT&T accounts for its investment in Cingular under the equity method, despite its 60% economic ownership position. Why?

g. In 2006, AT&T merged with Bell South, its joint venture partner in Cingular. What impact will this merger have on the way AT&T accounts for its investment in Cingular?

E7-31. Interpreting Equity Method Investment Footnotes (LO2)
On December 29, 2006, AT&T acquired Bell South. Prior to the acquisition, AT&T and Bell South jointly owned AT&T Mobility (formerly known as Cingular Wireless) and each accounted for its investment in AT&T Mobility under the equity method (see exercise E7-30). AT&T purchased Bell South for $66,834 million and reports the following allocation of the purchase price in its 2007 10-K:

AT&T (T)
Bell South

Bell South Purchase Price Allocation ($ millions)	As of 12/31/06	Adjustments	As of 12/29/07
Assets acquired			
Current assets.	$ 4,875	$ 6	$ 4,881
Property, plant and equipment	18,498	225	18,723
Intangible assets not subject to amortization			
Trademark/name	330	—	330
Licenses	214	100	314
Intangible assets subject to amortization			
Customer lists and relationships	9,230	(25)	9,205
Patents	100	—	100
Trademark/name	211	—	211
Investments in AT&T Mobility	32,759	2,039	34,798
Other investments.	2,446	(3)	2,443
Other assets	11,211	(168)	11,043
Goodwill	26,467	(1,554)	24,913
Total assets acquired	106,341	620	106,961
Liabilities assumed			
Current liabilities, excluding current portion of long-term debt	5,288	(427)	4,861
Long-term debt.	15,628	(4)	15,624
Deferred income taxes	10,318	(89)	10,229
Postemployment benefit obligation	7,086	163	7,249
Other noncurrent liabilities	1,223	941	2,164
Total liabilities assumed.	39,543	584	40,127
Net assets acquired	$ 66,798	$ 36	$ 66,834

a. Describe how AT&T accounts for its investment in AT&T Mobility (formerly Cingular Wireless) following its acquisition of Bell South.

b. AT&T had the following disclosure in its 2007 10-K regarding the reporting of its investment in AT&T Mobility: "We recorded the consolidation of AT&T Mobility as a step acquisition, retaining 60% of AT&T Mobility's prior book value and adjusting the remaining 40% to fair value." Why is AT&T only adjusting 40% of its investment in AT&T Mobility to fair value? How would its balance sheet and income statement differ had it adjusted 100% of its investment to fair value?

c. AT&T adjusted the purchase price allocation for Bell South subsequent to the acquisition. Most of the allocation relates to an increased value placed on Bell South's equity investment in AT&T Mobility due to "increased value of licenses and customer lists and relationships acquired." Why did the increase in the allocation of the purchase price to Bell South's investment in AT&T Mobility decrease the allocation to goodwill? How will this increase in allocation to the equity investment impact AT&T's income statement?

d.   One-third of the purchase price is allocated to goodwill. How is the fair value of customer lists and relationships estimated? How is the fair value of goodwill estimated? Why does it matter whether the allocation of the purchase price for intangible assets relates to "customer lists and relationships" or to goodwill?

WebAssign.   **E7-32.**   **Constructing the Consolidated Balance Sheet at Acquisition   (LO3)**
On January 1 of the current year, Healy Company purchased all of the common shares of Miller Company for $500,000 cash. Balance sheets of the two firms immediately after the acquisition follow:

	Healy Company	Miller Company	Consolidating Adjustments	Consolidated
Current assets	$1,700,000	$120,000		
Investment in Miller	500,000	—		
Plant assets, net.	3,000,000	410,000		
Goodwill	—	—		
Total assets.	$5,200,000	$530,000		
Liabilities.	$ 700,000	$ 90,000		
Contributed capital.	3,500,000	400,000		
Retained earnings	1,000,000	40,000		
Total liabilities and equity	$5,200,000	$530,000		

During purchase negotiations, Miller's plant assets were appraised at $425,000 and all of its remaining assets and liabilities were appraised at values approximating their book values. Healy also concluded that an additional $45,000 (for goodwill) demanded by Miller's shareholders was warranted because Miller's earning power was better than the industry average. Prepare the consolidating adjustments and the consolidated balance sheet at acquisition.

E7-33.   **Constructing the Consolidated Balance Sheet at Acquisition   (LO3)**
Rayburn Company purchased all of Kanodia Company's common stock for cash on January 1, at which time the separate balance sheets of the two corporations appeared as follows:

	Rayburn Company	Kanodia Company	Consolidating Adjustments	Consolidated
Investment in Kanodia	$ 600,000	—		
Other assets.	2,300,000	$700,000		
Goodwill	—	—		
Total assets.	$2,900,000	$700,000		
Liabilities.	$ 900,000	$160,000		
Contributed capital.	1,400,000	300,000		
Retained earnings	600,000	240,000		
Total liabilities and equity	$2,900,000	$700,000		

During purchase negotiations, Rayburn determined that the appraised value of Kanodia's Other Assets was $720,000; and, all of its remaining assets and liabilities were appraised at values approximating their book values. The remaining $40,000 of the purchase price was ascribed to goodwill. Prepare the consolidating adjustments and the consolidated balance sheet at acquisition.

E7-34.   **Assessing Financial Statement Effects from a Subsidiary Stock Issuance   (LO3)**
Ryan Company owns 80% of Lev Company. Information reported by Ryan Company and Lev Company as of the current year end follows:

Ryan Company

Shares owned of Lev	40,000
Book value of investment in Lev.	$320,000

Lev Company

Shares outstanding.	50,000
Book value of equity	$400,000
Book value per share	$8

Assume Lev Company issues 30,000 additional shares of previously authorized but unissued common stock solely to outside investors (none to Ryan Company) for $12 cash per share. Indicate the financial statement effects of this stock issuance on Ryan Company using the financial statement effects template.

Ryan Company's Financial Statements

	Balance Sheet							Income Statement		
Transaction	Cash Asset	+ Noncash Assets	= Liabil- ities	+ Contrib. Capital	+ Earned Capital			Rev- enues	− Expen- ses	= Net Income
Lev Co. issues 30,000 shares			=						−	=

E7-35. **Estimating Goodwill Impairment** (LO3)

On January 1 of the current year, Engel Company purchases 100% of Ball Company for $16.8 million. At the time of acquisition, the fair value of Ball's tangible net assets (excluding goodwill) is $16.2 million. Engel ascribes the excess of $600,000 to goodwill. Assume that the fair value of Ball declines to $12.5 million and that the fair value of Ball's tangible net assets is estimated at $12.3 million as of December 31.

a. Determine if the goodwill has become impaired and, if so, the amount of the impairment.
b. What impact does the impairment of goodwill have on Engel's financial statements?

E7-36. **Allocating Purchase Price Including In-Process R&D** (LO3)

Adobe Systems, Inc., reports the following footnote to its 10-K report.

WebAssign.

Adobe Systems
(ADBE)

During fiscal 2006, we completed the acquisition of Macromedia, a provider of software technologies that enables the development of a wide range of Internet and mobile application solutions... The total $3.5 billion purchase price is allocated to the acquired net assets of Macromedia based on their estimated fair values as of December 3, 2005 and the associated estimated useful lives at that date:

(in $000)	Amount	Estimated Useful Life
Net tangible assets.	$ 713,164	N/A
Identifiable intangible assets		
Acquired product rights	365,500	4 years
Customer contracts and relationships	183,800	6 years
Non-competition agreements.	500	2 years
Trademarks	130,700	5 years
Goodwill	1,993,898	N/A
Stock-based compensation.	150,951	2.18 years
Total purchase price.	$3,538,513	

a. Of the total assets acquired, what portion is allocated to tangible assets and what portion to intangible assets?
b. Are the assets (both tangible and intangible) of Macromedia reported on the consolidated balance sheet at the book value or at the fair value on the date of the acquisition? Explain.
c. How are the tangible and intangible assets accounted for subsequent to the acquisition?
d. Describe the accounting for goodwill. Why is an impairment test difficult to apply?

E7-37.   Constructing the Consolidated Balance Sheet at Acquisition   (LO3)

Easton Company acquires 100 percent of the outstanding voting shares of Harris Company. To obtain these shares, Easton pays $210,000 in cash and issues 5,000 of its $10 par value common stock. On this date, Easton's stock has a fair value of $36 per share, and Harris's book value of stockholders' equity is $280,000. Easton is willing to pay $390,000 for a company with a book value for equity of $280,000 because it believes that (1) Harris's buildings are undervalued by $40,000, and (2) Harris has an unrecorded patent that Easton values at $30,000. Easton considers the remaining balance sheet items to be fairly valued (no book-to-market difference). The remaining $40,000 of the purchase price is ascribed to corporate synergies and other general unidentifiable intangible assets (goodwill). The balance sheets at the acquisition date follow:

	Easton Company	Harris Company	Consolidating Adjustments	Consolidated
Cash...................	$ 84,000	$ 40,000		
Receivables	160,000	90,000		
Inventory...............	220,000	130,000		
Investment in Harris........	390,000	—		
Land...................	100,000	60,000		
Buildings, net.............	400,000	110,000		
Equipment, net...........	120,000	50,000		
Total assets..............	$1,474,000	$480,000		_____
Accounts payable..........	$ 160,000	$ 30,000		
Long-term liabilities	380,000	170,000		
Common stock...........	500,000	40,000		
Additional paid-in capital....	74,000	—		
Retained earnings	360,000	240,000		_____
Total liabilities & equity......	$1,474,000	$480,000		

a. Show the breakdown of the investment into the book value acquired, the excess of fair value over book value, and the portion of the investment representing goodwill.

b. Prepare the consolidating adjustments and the consolidated balance sheet on the date of acquisition.

c. How will the excess of the purchase price over book value acquired be treated in years subsequent to the acquisition?

WebAssign.
Hewlett-Packard
(HPQ)

E7-38.[A] **Reporting and Analyzing Derivatives   (LO1)**

Hewlett-Packard reports the following schedule of comprehensive income (net income plus other comprehensive income) in its 2007 10-K report ($ millions):

2007 Comprehensive income (millions)	
Net earnings..	$7,264
Net change in unrealized gains on available-for-sale securities ...	(12)
Net change in unrealized losses on cash flow hedges	(18)
Net change in cumulative translation adjustment	106
Net change in additional minimum pension liability.............	(3)
Comprehensive income	$7,337

a. Describe how firms like Hewlett-Packard typically use derivatives.

b. How does HP report its derivatives designated as fair-value hedges and the hedged assets (and/or liabilities) on its balance sheet?

c. By what amount have the unrealized losses of $(18) million on the cash flow hedges affected its current income? What are the analysis implications?

PROBLEMS

P7-39. **Analyzing and Interpreting Available-for-Sale Securities Disclosures** (LO1)

Following is a portion of the investments footnote from MetLife's 2007 10-K report. Investment earnings are a crucial component of the financial performance of insurance companies such as MetLife, and investments comprise a large part of MetLife's assets. MetLife accounts for its fixed maturity (debt security or bond) investments as available-for-sale securities.

WebAssign.

MetLife, Inc. (MET)

December 31, 2007 (in millions)	Cost or Amortized Cost	Gross Unrealized		Estimated Fair Value
		Gain	Loss	
U.S. corporate securities	$ 77,875	$1,725	$2,174	$ 77,426
Residential mortgaged-backed securities	56,267	611	389	56,489
Foreign corporate securities.	37,359	1,740	794	38,305
U.S. treasury/agency securities	19,771	1,487	13	21,245
Commercial mortgaged-backed securities . . .	17,676	251	199	17,728
Foreign government securities.	13,535	1,924	188	15,271
Asset-backed securities.	11,549	41	549	11,041
State and political subdivision securities	4,394	140	115	4,419
Other fixed maturity securities	335	13	30	318
Total fixed maturity securities	$238,761	$7,932	$4,451	$242,242
Common stock.	$ 2,488	$ 568	$ 108	$ 2,948
Non-redeemable preferred stock	3,403	61	362	3,102
Total equity securities	$ 5,891	$ 629	$ 470	$ 6,050

December 31, 2006 (in millions)	Cost or Amortized Cost	Gross Unrealized		Estimated Fair Value
		Gain	Loss	
U.S. corporate securities	$ 74,010	$ 2,047	$ 983	$ 75,074
Residential mortgaged-backed securities	51,602	385	321	51,666
Foreign corporate securities.	33,029	1,687	378	34,338
U.S. treasury/agency securities	29,897	984	248	30,633
Commercial mortgaged-backed securities . . .	16,467	193	138	16,522
Foreign government securities.	11,406	1,835	34	13,207
Asset-backed securities.	13,851	75	53	13,873
State and political subdivision securities	6,121	230	51	6,300
Other fixed maturity securities	385	7	77	315
Total fixed maturity securities	$236,768	$7,443	$2,283	$241,928
Common stock.	$ 1,798	$ 487	$ 16	$ 2,269
Non-redeemable preferred stock	2,751	103	29	2,825
Total equity securities	$ 4,549	$ 590	$ 45	$ 5,094

Required

a. At what amount does MetLife report its fixed maturity securities on its balance sheets for 2007 and 2006?

b. What are the net unrealized gains (losses) for 2007 and 2006 on its fixed maturity securities? How did these unrealized gains (losses) affect the company's reported income in 2007 and 2006?

c. What is the difference between *realized* and *unrealized* gains and losses? Are realized gains and losses treated differently in the income statement than unrealized gains and losses?

P7-40. **Analyzing and Interpreting Disclosures on Equity Method Investments** (LO2)

General Mills invests in a number of joint ventures to manufacture and distribute its food products as discussed in the following footnote to its fiscal year 2007 10-K report:

General Mills (GIS)

Investments in Joint Ventures We have a 50 percent equity interest in Cereal Partners Worldwide. We have a 50 percent equity interest in CPW that manufactures and markets ready-to-eat cereal products in more than 130 countries and republics outside the United States and Canada . . . We have 50 percent equity interests in Häagen-Dazs Japan, Inc. and Häagen-Dazs Korea Company Limited . . . These joint ventures manufacture, distribute and market *Häagen-Dazs* frozen ice cream products and novelties... We also have a 50 percent equity interest in Seretram, a joint venture for the production of Green Giant canned corn in France . . . We have a 50 percent equity interest in 8th Continent, LLC, a domestic joint venture to develop and market soy-based products . . .

Fiscal 2005 results of operations includes our share of the after-tax earnings of SVE through the date of its termination on February 28, 2005 . . . In February 2006, CPW announced a restructuring of its manufacturing plants in the United Kingdom. Our after-tax earnings from joint ventures were reduced by $8 million in each of fiscal 2007 and 2006 for our share of the restructuring costs, primarily accelerated depreciation and severance.

Our cumulative investment in these joint ventures was $295 million at the end of fiscal 2007 and $186 million at the end of fiscal 2006. Our investments in these joint ventures include aggregate advances of $158 million as of May 27, 2007 and $48 million as of May 28, 2006. Our sales to these joint ventures were $32 million in fiscal 2007, $35 million in fiscal 2006, and $47 million in fiscal 2005. We made net investments in the joint ventures of $103 million in fiscal 2007, $7 million in fiscal 2006, and $15 million in fiscal 2005. We received dividends from the joint ventures of $45 million in fiscal 2007, $77 million in fiscal 2006, and $83 million in fiscal 2005.

Summary combined financial information for the joint ventures (including income statement information for SVE through the date of its termination on February 28, 2005) on a 100 percent basis follows:

Combined Financial Information—Joint Ventures—100 Percent Basis

In Millions, Fiscal Year	2007	2006	2005
Net sales.	$2,016	$1,796	$2,652
Gross margin	835	770	1,184
Earnings before income taxes . . .	167	157	231
Earnings after income taxes.	132	120	184

In Millions, Fiscal Year Ended	May 27, 2007	May 28, 2006
Current assets	$ 815	$634
Noncurrent assets	898	578
Current liabilities.	1,228	756
Noncurrent liabilities.	82	6

Required

a. How does General Mills account for its investments in joint ventures? How are these investments reflected on General Mills' balance sheet, and how generally is income recognized on these investments?

b. General Mills reports the total of all of these investments on its May 27, 2007, balance sheet at $137 million net of advances. Approximately what percent of these joint ventures does General Mills own, on average?

c. Does the $137 million investment reported on General Mills' balance sheet sufficiently reflect the assets and liabilities required to conduct these operations? Explain.

d. Do you believe that the liabilities of these joint venture entities represent actual obligations of General Mills? Explain.

e. What potential problem(s) does equity method accounting present for analysis purposes?

P7-41. **Analyzing and Interpreting Disclosures on Consolidations** **(LO3)**

Caterpillar Inc. (CAT)

Caterpillar Inc. consists of two business units: the manufacturing company (parent corporation) and a wholly-owned finance subsidiary. These two units are consolidated in Caterpillar's 10-K report. Following is a supplemental disclosure that Caterpillar includes in its 10-K report that shows the separate balance sheets of the parent and the subsidiary, as well as consolidating adjustments and the consolidated balance sheet presented to shareholders. This supplemental disclosure is not mandated under GAAP, but is voluntarily reported by Caterpillar as useful information for investors and creditors. Using this disclosure, answer the following requirements:

Required

a. Do the parent and subsidiary companies each maintain their own financial statements? Explain. Why does GAAP require consolidation instead of separate financial statements of individual companies?

b. What is the balance of Investments in Financial Products subsidiaries as of December 31, 2007, on the parent's balance sheet? What is the equity balance of the financial products subsidiaries to which this relates as of December 31, 2007? Do you see a relation? Will this relation always exist?

c. Refer to your answer for part a. How does the equity method of accounting for the investment in the subsidiary companies obscure the actual financial condition of the parent company that is revealed in the consolidated financial statements?

d. Refer to the Consolidating Adjustments column reported—it is used to prepare the consolidated balance sheet. Generally, what do these adjustments accomplish?

e. Compare the consolidated balance of stockholders' equity with the stockholders' equity of the parent company (Machinery and Engines). Will the relation that is evident always hold? Explain.

f. Recall that the parent company uses the equity method of accounting for its investment in the subsidiaries, and that this account is eliminated in the consolidation process. What is the relation between consolidated net income and the net income of the parent company? Explain.

g. What is the implication for the consolidated balance sheet if the fair value of the Financial Products subsidiaries (subsequent to acquisition) is greater than the book value of its stockholders' equity?

| | Supplemental Consolidating Data | | | | | | | |
| | Machinery and Engines | | Financial Products | | Consolidating Adjustments | | Consolidated | |
December 31 (Millions of Dollars)	2007	2006	2007	2006	2007	2006	2007	2006
Assets								
Cash and short-term investments	$ 862	$ 319	$ 260	$ 211	—	—	$ 1,122	$ 530
Receivables—trade and other	4,715	3,924	525	368	3,009	4,315	8,249	8,607
Receivables—finance	—	—	10,961	11,379	(3,458)	(4,575)	7,503	6,804
Deferred and refundable income taxes	746	656	70	77	—	—	816	733
Prepaid expenses and other current assets	565	616	39	41	(21)	(19)	583	638
Inventories	7,204	6,351	—	—	—	—	7,204	6,351
Total current assets	14,092	11,866	11,855	12,076	(470)	(279)	25,477	23,663
Property, plant and equipment—net	6,782	6,046	3,215	2,805	—	—	9,997	8,851
Long-term receivables—trade and other	90	155	30	30	565	675	685	860
Long-term receivables—finance	—	—	14,057	12,236	(595)	(705)	13,462	11,531
Investments in unconsolidated affiliated companies	610	559	12	12	(24)	(9)	598	562
Investments in Financial Products subsidiaries	3,948	3,513	—	—	(3,948)	(3,513)	—	—
Noncurrent deferred and refundable income taxes	1,803	2,218	68	39	(318)	(308)	1,553	1,949
Intangible assets	471	382	4	5	—	—	475	387
Goodwill	1,963	1,904	—	—	—	—	1,963	1,904
Other assets	293	352	1,629	1,390	—	—	1,922	1,742
Total assets	$30,052	$26,995	$30,870	$28,593	$(4,790)	$(4,139)	$56,132	$51,449
Liabilities								
Short-term borrowings	$ 187	$ 165	$ 5,556	$ 5,077	$ (275)	$ (87)	$ 5,468	$ 5,155
Accounts payable	4,518	3,907	373	344	(168)	(166)	4,723	4,085
Accrued expenses	1,932	1,848	1,273	1,101	(27)	(26)	3,178	2,923
Accrued wages, salaries and employee benefits	1,108	922	18	16	—	—	1,126	938
Customer advances	1,442	921	—	—	—	—	1,442	921
Dividends payable	225	194	—	—	—	—	225	194
Other current liabilities	867	1,026	105	127	(21)	(8)	951	1,145
Long-term debt due within one year	180	418	4,952	4,043	—	—	5,132	4,461
Total current liabilities	10,459	9,401	12,277	10,708	(491)	(287)	22,245	19,822
Long-term debt due after one year	3,669	3,724	14,190	13,986	(30)	(30)	17,829	17,680
Liability for postemployment benefits	5,058	5,879	1	—	—	—	5,059	5,879
Other liabilities	1,983	1,132	454	386	(321)	(309)	2,116	1,209
Total liabilities	21,169	20,136	26,922	25,080	(842)	(626)	47,249	44,590
Stockholders' equity								
Common stock	$ 2,744	$ 2,465	$ 860	$ 862	$ (860)	$ (862)	$ 2,744	$ 2,465
Treasury stock	(9,451)	(7,352)	—	—	—	—	(9,451)	(7,352)
Profit employed in the business	17,398	14,593	2,566	2,325	(2,566)	(2,325)	17,398	14,593
Accumulated other comprehensive income	(1,808)	(2,847)	522	326	(522)	(326)	(1,808)	(2,847)
Total stockholders' equity	8,883	6,859	3,948	3,513	(3,948)	(3,513)	8,883	6,859
Total liabilities and stockholders' equity	$30,052	$26,995	$30,870	$28,593	$(4,790)	$(4,139)	$56,132	$51,449

MANAGEMENT APPLICATIONS

MA7-42. **Determining the Reporting of an Investment** **(LO1, 2, 3)**

Assume that your company acquires 20% of the outstanding common stock of APEX Software as an investment. You also have an option to purchase the remaining 80%. APEX is developing software (its only activity) that it hopes to eventually package and sell to customers. You do not intend to exercise your option unless its software product reaches commercial feasibility. APEX has employed your software engineers to assist in the development efforts and you are integrally involved in its software design. Your ownership interest is significant enough to give you influence over APEX' software design specifications.

Required

a. Describe the financial statement effects of the three possible methods to accounting for this investment (fair-value, equity, or consolidation).
b. What method of accounting is appropriate for this investment (fair-value, equity, or consolidation)? Explain.

MA7-43. **Ethics and Governance: Establishing Corporate Governance** **(LO2, 3)**

Effective corporate governance policies are a crucial component of contemporary corporate management.

Required

What provisions do you believe should be incorporated into such a policy? How do such policies impact financial accounting?

Module Eight

Reporting and Analyzing Nonowner Financing

LEARNING OBJECTIVES

LO1 Describe the accounting for current operating liabilities, including accounts payable and accrued liabilities. (p. 8-4)

LO2 Describe the accounting for current and long-term nonoperating liabilities. (p. 8-10)

LO3 Explain how credit ratings are determined and identify their effect on the cost of debt. (p. 8-21)

VERIZON COMMUNICATIONS

Verizon Communications, Inc., began doing business in 2000, when Bell Atlantic Corporation merged with GTE Corporation. Verizon is one of the world's leading providers of communications services. It is the largest provider of wireline and wireless communications in the U.S., and is the largest of the "Baby Bells" as of 2007 with over $93 billion in revenues and $186 billion in assets.

When Ivan Seidenberg became sole CEO of Verizon in mid-2002 (and its chairman in late 2003), the Internet frenzy had cooled and Verizon's stock price had plunged, falling from an all-time high of $70 in late 1999 to $27 in mid-2002. Since then, the stock has increased to the mid-$40s as of early 2008.

Verizon survived the Internet and telecom downturn. Now it faces a formidable new challenger: cable. Cable companies spent over $14 billion in the three years ended 2007 upgrading their infrastructure to offer customers discounted bundled packages of local voice, high-speed Internet connections, and video (Verizon spent nearly $50 billion during the same period). Market analysts estimate

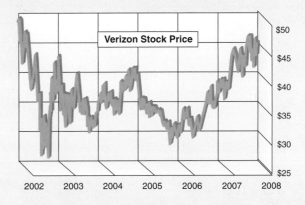

that cable companies could capture a quarter of the local voice market over the next decade as they deploy new voice over Internet protocol (VOIP) technology.

While Verizon and the other traditional phone companies see their market positions erode, they also struggle to retain their image as innovators. They face creative pressures from researchers and from companies (including Intel) who con-

Getty Images

tinue to develop new wireless technologies. *BusinessWeek* (2006) explains:

> AT&T and Verizon are rushing to build networks to deliver TV service and high-speed broadband access . . . Verizon is spending billions to roll out a next-generation phone, data, and video network called FiOS (as in "fiber optic") to give its customers faster Internet service and an alternative to cable. Indeed, over the past three years, Verizon has spent $40 billion on capital expenditures in addition to its 2006 acquisition of MCI. The demand for new capital spending is coming at an inopportune time for Verizon. Saddled with a debt load of over $36 billion as of 2005, a third of which matures over the next five years, Verizon must also pay over $4 billion in stock dividends annually plus nearly $20 billion in accumulated employee pensions and health-care costs. Verizon is concerned. Faced with a question from a stockholder about why Verizon isn't repurchasing its stock given its decline in value, Seidenberg said "our number-one priority for using free cash flow over the last two years has been reducing debt."

This module focuses on liabilities; that is, short-term and long-term obligations. Liabilities are one of two financing sources for a company. The other is shareholder financing. Bonds and notes are a major part of most companies' liabilities. In this module, we show how to price liabilities and how the issuance and subsequent payment of the principal and interest affect financial statements. We also discuss the required disclosures that enable us to effectively analyze a company's ability to pay its debts as they come due.

Verizon is now working harder than ever to transform itself in an era of fiber optics and wireless communication. The dilemma facing Seidenberg is how to allocate available cash flow between strategic investment and debt payments.

Sources: *BusinessWeek* 2009 and 2006; *TheStreet.Com* 2003; *Verizon* 2007 and 2008 10-Ks.

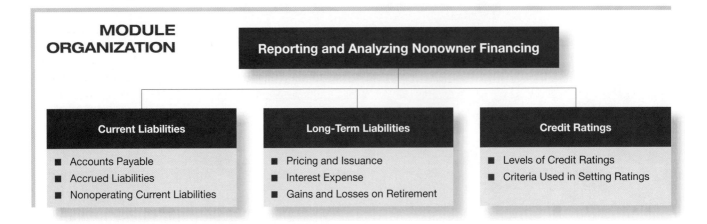

The accounting equation (Assets = Liabilities + Equity) is a useful tool in helping us think about how the balance sheet and income statement are constructed, the linkages among the financial statements, and the effects of transactions on financial statements. The accounting equation is also useful in helping us think about the statements from another perspective, namely, how the business is financed. Consider the following representation of the accounting equation:

$$\underbrace{\textbf{Assets}}_{\textbf{Uses}} \; = \; \underbrace{\textbf{Liabilities + Equity}}_{\textbf{Sources}}$$

Assets represent investments (uses of funds) that management has made. It includes current operating assets such as cash, accounts receivable, and inventories. It also includes long-term operating assets such as manufacturing and administrative facilities. Most companies also invest a portion of funds in nonoperating assets (marketable securities) that provide the liquidity a company needs to conduct transactions and to react to market opportunities and changes.

Just as asset disclosures provide us with information on where a company invests its funds, its liability and equity disclosures inform us as to how those assets are financed. These are the sources of funds. To be successful, a company must not only invest funds wisely, but must also be astute in the manner in which it raises funds. Companies strive to finance their assets at the lowest possible cost. Current liabilities (such as accounts payable and accrued liabilities) are generally non-interest-bearing. As a result, companies try to maximize the financing of their assets with these sources of funds.

Current liabilities, as the name implies, are short-term in nature, generally requiring payment within the coming year. As a result, they are not a suitable source of funding for long-term assets that generate cash flows over several years. Instead, companies often finance long-term assets with long-term liabilities that require payments over several years. Generally, companies try to link the pattern of the cash outflows of the financing source with the cash inflows of the related asset. As such, long-term financing is usually in the form of bonds, notes, and stock issuances.

When a company acquires assets, and finances them with liabilities, its financial leverage increases. Also, the required liability payments increase proportionally with the level of liabilities, and those larger payments imply a higher probability of default should a downturn in business occur. Greater levels of liabilities, then, make the company riskier to investors who, consequently, demand a higher return. Assessing the appropriate level of liabilities is part of liquidity and solvency analysis.

This module describes and analyzes *on-balance-sheet financing,* namely current and noncurrent liabilities that are reported on financial statements. If companies can find a way to purchase assets and have neither the asset, nor its related financing, appear on the balance sheet, they can report higher levels of asset turnover and appear less risky. This creates off-balance-sheet financing, which is the focus of Module 10.

CURRENT LIABILITIES

Current liabilities consist of both operating and nonoperating liabilities. Most *current operating liabilities* such as those related to inventory (accounts payable) or to utilities, wages, insurance, rent, and taxes (accrued liabilities), impact operating expenses such as cost of goods sold or selling, general and administrative expenses. *Current nonoperating liabilities* comprise short-term bank notes or the current portion of long-term debt. Verizon's balance sheet reports the following current liabilities:

LO1 Describe the accounting for current operating liabilities, including accounts payable and accrued liabilities.

At December 31 ($ millions)	2007	2006
Debt maturing within one year...................	$ 2,954	$ 7,715
Accounts payable and accrued liabilities............	14,462	14,320
Liabilities of discontinued operations...............	—	2,154
Other.......................................	7,325	8,091
Total current liabilities.........................	$24,741	$32,280

Verizon reports four categories of current liabilities: (1) long-term obligations that are scheduled for payment in the upcoming year, (2) accounts payable and accrued liabilities, (3) current liabilities from discontinued operations (these operations were sold in 2007, hence they are no longer reported on Verizon's current balance sheet), and (4) other current liabilities, which consist mainly of customer deposits, dividends payable, and miscellaneous obligations.

Analysis and interpretation of the return on net operating assets (RNOA) requires that we separate current liabilities into operating and nonoperating components. In general, these two components consist of the following:

1. **Current operating liabilities**

   ■ **Accounts payable** Obligations to others for amounts owed on purchases of goods and services; these are usually non-interest-bearing.

   ■ **Accrued liabilities** Obligations for which there is no related external transaction in the current period. These include, for example, accruals for employee wages earned but yet unpaid, accruals for taxes (usually quarterly) on payroll and current period profits, and accruals for other liabilities such as rent, utilities, and insurance. Companies make accruals to properly reflect the liabilities owed as of the financial statement date and the expenses incurred for the period.

   ■ **Unearned revenue** Obligations to provide goods or services in the coming year; these arise from customers' deposits, subscriptions, or prepayments.

2. **Current nonoperating liabilities**

   ■ **Short-term interest-bearing debt** Short-term bank borrowings and notes expected to mature in whole or in part during the upcoming year; this item can include any accrued interest payable.

   ■ **Current maturities of long-term debt** Long-term borrowings that are scheduled to mature in whole or in part during the upcoming year; this current portion of long-term debt includes maturing principal payments only. Any unpaid interest is usually included in the prior item.

The remainder of this section describes, analyzes and interprets current operating liabilities followed by a discussion of current nonoperating liabilities.

Accounts Payable

Accounts payable arise from the purchase of goods and services from others. Accounts payable are normally non-interest-bearing and are, thus, an inexpensive financing source. Verizon does not break out accounts payable on its balance sheet but, instead, reports them with other accruals. It reports $14,462 million in accounts payable and accrued liabilities in 2007, and $14,320 million in 2006. The footnotes reveal that accounts payable represent $4,491 million in 2007, and $4,392 million in 2006, or 31% of the total each year.

The following financial statement effects template shows the accounting for a typical purchase of goods on credit and the ultimate sale of those goods. A series of four connected transactions illustrate the revenue and cost cycle.

Transaction	Balance Sheet					Income Statement		
	Cash Asset	+ Noncash Assets =	Liabilities	+ Contrib. Capital	+ Earned Capital	Revenues	− Expenses	= Net Income
1. Purchase $100 inventory on credit		+100 Inventory =	+100 Accounts Payable				−	=
2a. Sell inventory on credit for $140		+140 Accounts Receivable =			+140 Retained Earnings	+140 Sales	−	= +140
2b. Record $100 cost of inventory sold in 2a		−100 Inventory =			−100 Retained Earnings		+100 Cost of − Goods Sold	= −100
3. Collect $140 on accounts receivable	+140 Cash	−140 Accounts Receivable =					−	=
4. Pay $100 cash for accounts payable	−100 Cash	=	−100 Accounts Payable				−	=

T-accounts shown in left margin:
- INV 100 / AP 100; INV 100 | / AP | 100
- AR 140 / Sales 140; AR 140 | / Sales | 140
- COGS 100 / INV 100; COGS 100 | / INV | 100
- Cash 140 / AR 140; Cash 140 | / AR | 140
- AP 100 / Cash 100; AP 100 | / Cash | 100

The financial statement effects template reveals several impacts related to the purchase of goods on credit and their ultimate sale.

1. Purchase of inventory is reflected on the balance sheet as an increase in inventory and an increase in accounts payable.

2a. Sale of inventory involves two components—revenue and expense. The revenue part reflects the increase in sales and the increase in accounts receivable (revenue is recognized when earned, even though cash is not yet received).

2b. The expense part of the sales transaction reflects the decrease in inventory and the increase in cost of goods sold (COGS). COGS is reported in the same income statement as the related sale (this expense is recognized because the inventory asset is sold, even though inventory-related payables may not yet be paid).

3. Collection of the receivable reduces accounts receivable and increases cash. It is solely a balance sheet transaction and does not impact the income statement.

4. Cash payment of accounts payable is solely a balance sheet transaction and does not impact income statement accounts (expense relating to inventories is recognized when the inventory is sold or used up, not when the liability is paid).

Accounts Payable Turnover (APT)

Inventories are financed, in large part, by accounts payable (also called *trade credit* or *trade payables*). Such payables usually represent interest-free financing and are, therefore, less expensive than using available cash or borrowed money to finance purchases or inventory production. Accordingly, companies use trade credit whenever possible. This is called *leaning on the trade*.

The **accounts payable turnover** reflects management's success in using trade credit to finance purchases of goods and services. It is computed as:

Accounts Payable Turnover (APT) = Cost of Goods Sold/Average Accounts Payable

Payables reflect the cost of inventory, not its retail value. Thus, to be consistent with the denominator, the ratio uses cost of goods sold (and not sales) in the numerator. Management desires to use trade credit to the greatest extent possible for financing. This means that a lower accounts payable turnover is preferable. Verizon's accounts payable turnover rate has decreased slightly from 8.63 times per year in 2005 to 8.45 times per year in 2007. (APT for 2007 is computed as $37,547 million/[($ 4,491 million + $4,392 million)/2].) This decrease in accounts payable turnover indicates that Verizon is paying its obligations more slowly, which is a positive development so long as supplier relations are not damaged and unless the prior year APT was excessively high.

A metric analogous to accounts payable turnover is the **accounts payable days outstanding**, which is defined as follows:

Accounts Payable Days Outstanding (APDO) = Accounts Payable/Average Daily Cost of Goods Sold

Because accounts payable are a source of low-cost financing, management desires to extend the accounts payable days outstanding as long as possible, provided that this action does not harm supply channel relations. Verizon's accounts payable remain unpaid for 43.66 days in 2007, up from 42.27 days in 2005. (Its 2007 APDO is computed as $4,491 million/[$37,547 million/365 days].) Verizon is, therefore, leaning on the trade slightly more than it has in the recent past. As with APT, this is generally a positive development so long as supplier relations are not damaged as a result of delaying payment for invoices.[1]

Accounts payable reflect a source of interest-free financing. Increased payables reduce the amount of net operating working capital as payables (along with other current operating liabilities) are deducted from current operating assets in the computation of net operating working capital. Also, increased payables mean increased cash flow (as increased liabilities increase net cash from operating activities) and increased profitability (as the level of interest-bearing debt that is required to finance operating assets declines). RNOA increases when companies make use of this low-cost financing source.[2] Yet, companies must be careful to avoid excessive "leaning on the trade" as short-term income gains can yield long-term costs such as damaged supply channels.

MID-MODULE REVIEW 1

Verizon's accounts payable turnover (Cost of goods sold/Average accounts payable) decreased from 8.63 in 2005 to 8.45 in 2007.

a. Does this change indicate that accounts payable have increased or decreased relative to cost of goods sold? Explain.

b. What effect does this change have on net cash flows from operating activities?

c. What management concerns, if any, might this change in accounts payable turnover pose?

Solution

a. We know that accounts payable turnover is computed as cost of goods sold divided by average accounts payable. Thus, a decrease in accounts payable turnover indicates that accounts payable have increased relative to cost of goods sold (all else equal).

---

[1] Excessive delays in payment of payables can result in suppliers charging a higher price for their goods or, ultimately, refusing to sell to certain buyers. Although a hidden "financing" cost is not interest, it is still a real cost.

[2] Accounts payable often carry credit terms such as 2/10, net 30. These terms give the buyer, for example, 2% off the invoice price of goods purchased if paid within 10 days. Otherwise the entire invoice is payable within 30 days. By failing to take a discount, the buyer is effectively paying 2% interest charge to keep its funds for an additional 20 days. Because there are approximately 18 such 20-day periods in a year (365/20), this equates to an annual rate of interest of about 36%. Thus, borrowing funds at less than 36% to pay this liability within the discount period would be cost effective.

b. An increase in accounts payable results in an increase in net cash flows from operating activities because Verizon is not using cash to pay bills more quickly.

c. Increased accounts payable decreases net operating working capital (all else equal), with a consequent increase in cash flow. While favorable to cash flow, the less timely payment of accounts payable can strain supplier relations. Analysts must be aware of the potentially damaging consequences of companies leaning on the trade too heavily.

Accrued Liabilities

Accrued liabilities reflect expenses that have been incurred during the period but not yet paid in cash. Accrued liabilities can also reflect unearned revenue as explained in Module 5. Verizon reports details of its accrued liabilities (along with accounts payable) in the following footnote to its 2007 10-K report.

At December 31 ($ in millions)	2007	2006
Accounts payable.	$ 4,491	$ 4,392
Accrued expenses	2,400	2,982
Accrued vacation, salaries and wages.	4,828	3,575
Interest payable	473	614
Accrued taxes	2,270	2,757
Total accounts payable and accrued liabilities.	$14,462	$14,320

(Accrued Liabilities brackets: Accrued expenses, Accrued vacation, salaries and wages, Interest payable, Accrued taxes)

Verizon reports one nonoperating accrual: interest payable. Its other accrued liabilities are operating accruals that include miscellaneous accrued expenses, accrued vacation pay, accrued salaries and wages, and accrued taxes. Verizon's accruals are typical. To record accruals, companies recognize a liability on the balance sheet and a corresponding expense on the income statement. This means that liabilities increase, current income decreases, and equity decreases. When an accrued liability is ultimately paid, both cash and the liability decrease (but no expense is recorded because it was recognized previously).

Accounting for Accrued Liabilities

Accounting for a typical accrued liability such as accrued wages, for two consecutive periods, follows:

	Balance Sheet						Income Statement			
Transaction	Cash Asset	+ Noncash Assets	= Liabil-ities	+ Contrib. Capital	+ Earned Capital		Rev-enues	− Expen-ses	=	Net Income
Period 1: Accrued $75 for employee wages earned at period-end			+75 Wages Payable		−75 Retained Earnings			+75 Wages Expense		−75
Period 2: Paid $75 for wages earned in prior period	−75 Cash		−75 Wages Payable							

WE 75
WP 75
WE
75 |
WP
| 75

WP 75
Cash 75
WP
75 |
Cash
| 75

The following financial statement effects result from this accrual of employee wages:

■ Employees have worked during a period and have not yet been paid. The effect of this accrual is to increase wages payable on the balance sheet and to recognize wages expense on the income statement. Failure to recognize this liability and associated expense would understate liabilities on the balance sheet and overstate income in the current period and understate income in the subsequent period.

■ When the company pays employees in the following period, cash and wages payable both decrease. This payment does not result in expense because the expense was recognized in the prior period when incurred.

The accrued wages illustration relates to events that are fairly certain. We know, for example, when wages are incurred but not paid. Other examples of accruals that are fairly certain are rental costs, insurance premiums, and taxes owed.

Contingent Accrued Liabilities Some accrued liabilities are less certain than others. Consider a company facing a lawsuit. Should it record the possible liability and related expense? The answer depends on the likelihood of occurrence and the ability to estimate the obligation. Specifically, if the obligation is *probable* and the amount *estimable* with reasonable certainty, then a company will recognize this obligation, called a **contingent liability**. If an obligation is only *reasonably possible* (or cannot be reliably estimated), the contingent liability is not reported on the balance sheet and is merely disclosed in the footnotes. All other contingent liabilities that are less than reasonably possible are not disclosed.

Management of Accrued Liabilities Managers have some latitude in determining the amount and timing of accruals. This latitude can lead to misreporting of income and liabilities (unintentional or otherwise). Here's how: If accruals are underestimated, then expenses are underestimated, income is overestimated, and retained earnings are overestimated. In subsequent periods when an understated accrued liability is settled (for more than the "under" estimate), reported income is lower than it should be; this is because prior period income was higher than it should have been. (The reverse holds for overestimated accruals.) The misreporting of accruals, therefore, shifts income from one period into another. We must be keenly aware of this potential for income shifting as we analyze the financial condition of a company.

Experience tells us that accrued liabilities related to restructuring programs (including severance accruals and accruals for asset write-downs), or to legal and environmental liabilities, or business acquisitions are somewhat problematic. These accruals too often represent early recognition of expenses. Sometimes companies aggressively overestimate one-time accruals and record an even larger expense. This is called taking a *big bath*. The effect of a big bath is to depress current period income, which relieves future periods of these expenses (thus, shifting income forward in time). Accordingly, we must monitor any change or unusual activity with accrued liabilities and view large one-time charges with skepticism.

IFRS INSIGHT   **Accruals and Contingencies under IFRS**

IFRS requires that a "provision" be recognized as a liability if a present obligation exists, if it is probable that an outflow of resources is required, and if the obligation can be reasonably estimated. These provisions are basically the same as accruals under GAAP. However, unlike GAAP, contingent liabilities are not recorded for IFRS. Contingencies do not meet the IFRS provisions definition because a present obligation does *not* exist as it may or may not be confirmed by uncertain future events. IFRS requires footnote disclosure of such contingent liabilities unless the eventual payment is remote in which no disclosure is required.

Estimating Accruals

Some accrued liabilities require more estimation than others. Warranty liabilities are an example of an accrual that requires managerial assumptions and estimates. Warranties are commitments that manufacturers make to their customers to repair or replace defective products within a specified period of time. The expected cost of this commitment can be reasonably estimated at the time of sale based on past experience. As a result, GAAP requires manufacturers to record the expected cost of warranties as a liability, and to record the related expected warranty expense in the income statement in the same period that the sales revenue is reported.

To illustrate, assume that a company estimates that its defective units amount to 1% of sales and that each unit costs $10 to replace. If sales during the period are $10,000, the estimated warranty expense is $1,000 ($10,000 × 1% × $10). The entries to accrue this liability and its ultimate payment follow.

		Balance Sheet					Income Statement		
Transaction	Cash Asset +	Noncash Assets =	Liabil- ities +	Contrib. Capital +	Earned Capital		Rev- enues −	Expen- ses =	Net Income
Period 1: Accrued $1,000 of expected warranty costs on units sold during the period		=	+1,000 Warranty Payable		−1,000 Retained Earnings		−	+1,000 Warranty Expense =	−1,000
Period 2: Delivered $1,000 in replacement products to cover warranty claims		−1,000 Inventory =	−1,000 Warranty Payable				−	=	

WRE 1,000
  WRP   1,000
       WRE
  1,000 |
        WRP
        | 1,000

WRP 1,000
  INV   1,000
       WRP
  1,000 |
        INV
        | 1,000

Accruing warranty liabilities has the same effect on financial statements as accruing wages expense in the previous section. That is, a liability is recorded on the balance sheet and an expense is reported in the income statement. When the defective product is later replaced (or repaired), the liability is reduced together with the cost of the inventory and/or the cash paid for other costs that were necessary to satisfy the claim. (Only a portion of the products estimated to fail does so in the current period; we expect other product failures in future periods. Management monitors this estimate and adjusts it if failure is higher or lower than expected.) As in the accrual of wages, the expense and the liability are reported when incurred and not when paid.

To illustrate, Harley-Davidson reports $70,523,000 of warranty liability on its 2007 balance sheet. Its footnotes reveal the following additional information:

Product Warranty and Safety Recall Campaigns The Company currently provides a standard two-year limited warranty on all new motorcycles sold worldwide, except for Japan, where the Company provides a standard three-year limited warranty on all new motorcycles sold. The warranty coverage for the retail customer includes parts and labor and begins when the motorcycle is sold to a retail customer. The Company maintains reserves for future warranty claims using an estimated cost per unit sold, which is based primarily on historical Company claim information. Additionally, the Company has from time to time initiated certain voluntary safety recall campaigns. The Company reserves for all estimated costs associated with safety recalls in the period that the safety recalls are announced. Changes in the Company's warranty and safety recall liability were as follows (in thousands):

Warranty and Safety Recall Liability (in thousands)	2007	2006
Balance, beginning of period	$66,385	$43,073
Warranties issued during the period	54,963	56,008
Settlements made during the period	(66,422)	(57,267)
Safety recalls and changes to pre-existing warranty liabilities	15,597	24,571
Balance, end of period	$70,523	$66,385

Of the $66,385,000 balance at the beginning of 2007, Harley incurred costs of $66,422,000 to replace or repair defective motorcycles during 2007. This reduced Harley's liability by that amount. These costs include cash paid to customers, or to employees as wages, and the cost of parts used for repairs. Harley accrued an additional $70,560,000 ($54,963,000 + $15,597,000) in new warranty liabilities in 2007. It is important to understand that only the increase in the liability resulting from additional accruals impacts the income statement, reducing income through additional warranty expense. Payments made to settle warranty claims do not affect current period income; they merely reduce the preexisting liability.

GAAP requires that the warranty liability reflects the estimated amount of cost that the company expects to incur as a result of warranty claims. This is often a difficult estimate to make and is prone to error. There is also the possibility that a company might underestimate its warranty liability to report higher current income, or overestimate it so as to depress current income and create an additional liability on the balance sheet (*cookie jar reserve*) that can be used to absorb future warranty costs and, thus, to reduce future expenses. The overestimation would shift income from the current period to one or more future periods. Warranty liabilities must, therefore, be examined closely and compared with sales levels. Any deviations from the historical relation of the warranty liability to sales, or from levels reported by competitors, should be scrutinized.

MID-MODULE REVIEW 2

Assume that Verizon's employees worked during the current month and earned $10,000 in wages that Verizon will not pay until the first of next month. Must Verizon recognize any wages liability and expense for the current month? Explain. Use the financial statement effects template to show the effect of this accrual.

Solution

Yes. Verizon must recognize liabilities and expenses when incurred, regardless of when payment is made. Accruing expenses as incurred will match the expenses to the revenues they helped generate. Failure to recognize the wages owed to employees for the period would understate liabilities and overstate income. Verizon must reflect the wages earned and the related expense in its financial statements as follows:

		Balance Sheet						Income Statement		
Transaction	Cash Asset	+ Noncash Assets	= Liabil-ities	+ Contrib. Capital	+ Earned Capital		Rev-enues	− Expen-ses	= Net Income	

Accrue $10,000 in wages expense			+10,000 **=** Wages Payable		−10,000 Retained Earnings			+10,000 **−** Wages Expense	**=** −10,000	WE 10,000
										  WP 10,000
										WE
										10,000 |
										  WP
										
											10,000

Current Nonoperating Liabilities

Current nonoperating liabilities include short-term bank loans, accrued interest on those loans, and the current maturities of long-term debt. Companies generally try to structure their financing so that debt service requirements (payments) coincide with the cash inflows from the assets financed. This means that current assets are usually financed with current liabilities, and that long-term assets are financed with long-term liabilities (and equity).

> **LO2** Describe the accounting for current and long-term nonoperating liabilities.

To illustrate, assume that a seasonal company's investment in current assets tends to fluctuate during the year as depicted in the graphic below:

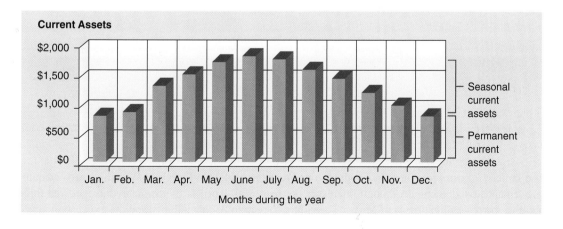

This company does most of its selling in the summer months. More inventory is purchased and manufactured in the early spring than at any other time of the year. High summer sales give rise to accounts receivable that are higher than normal during the fall. The company's working capital peaks at the height of the selling season and is lowest as the business slows in the off-season. There is a permanent level of working capital required for this business (about $750), and a seasonal component (maximum of about $1,000). Different businesses exhibit different patterns in their working capital requirements, but many have both permanent and seasonal components.

The existence of permanent and seasonal current operating assets often requires that financing sources also have permanent and seasonal components. Consider again the company depicted in the graphic above. A portion of the company's assets is in inventories that are financed, in part, with accounts payable and accruals. Thus, we expect that current operating liabilities also exhibit a seasonal component that fluctuates with the level of operations. These payables are generally non-interest-bearing and, thus, provide low-cost financing that should be used to the greatest extent possible. Additional financing needs are covered by short-term interest-bearing debt.

This section focuses on current nonoperating liabilities, which include short-term debt, current maturities of long-term liabilities, and accrued interest expenses.

Short-Term Interest-Bearing Debt

Seasonal swings in working capital are often financed with a bank line of credit (short-term debt). In this case the bank provides a commitment to lend up to a maximum amount with the understanding that the amounts borrowed will be repaid in full sometime during the year. An interest-bearing note evidences any such borrowing.

When the company borrows these short-term funds, it reports the cash received on the balance sheet together with an increase in liabilities (notes payable). The note is reported as a current liability because the company expects to repay it within a year. This borrowing has no effect on income or equity. The borrower incurs (and the lender earns) interest on the note as time passes. GAAP requires the borrower to accrue the interest liability and the related interest expense each time financial statements are issued.

To illustrate, assume that Verizon borrows $1,000 cash on January 1. The note bears interest at a 12% annual rate, and the interest (3% per quarter) is payable on the first of each subsequent quarter (April 1, July 1, October 1, January 1). Assuming that Verizon issues calendar-quarter financial statements, this borrowing results in the following financial statement effects for January 1 through April 1.

		Balance Sheet									Income Statement				
Transaction	Cash Asset	+	Noncash Assets	=	Liabilities	+	Contrib. Capital	+	Earned Capital		Revenues	−	Expenses	=	Net Income
Jan 1: Borrow $1,000 cash and issue note payable	+1,000 Cash			=	+1,000 Note Payable							−		=	
Mar 31: Accrue quarterly interest on 12%, $1,000 note payable				=	+30 Interest Payable				−30 Retained Earnings			−	+30 Interest Expense	=	−30
Apr 1: Pay $30 cash for interest due	−30 Cash			=	−30 Interest Payable							−		=	

Left-margin T-accounts:

Cash 1,000
NP 1,000
Cash | 1,000
1,000 |
NP
| 1,000

IE 30
IP 30
IE | 30
30 |
IP
| 30

IP 30
Cash 30
IP | 30
30 |
Cash
| 30

The January 1 borrowing increases both cash and notes payable. On March 31, Verizon issues its quarterly financial statements. Although interest is not paid until April 1, the company has incurred three months' interest obligation as of March 31. Failure to recognize this liability and the expense incurred would not fairly present the financial condition of the company. Accordingly, the quarterly accrued interest payable is computed as follows:

Interest Expense = Principal × Annual Rate × Portion of Year Outstanding
$$\$30 \quad = \quad \$1,000 \quad \times \quad 12\% \quad \times \quad 3/12$$

The subsequent interest payment on April 1 reduces both cash and the interest payable that Verizon accrued on March 31. There is no expense reported on April 1, as it was recorded the previous day (March 31) when Verizon prepared its financial statements. (For fixed-maturity borrowings specified in days, such as a 90-day note, we assume a 365-day year for interest accrual computations, see Mid-Module Review 3.)

Current Maturities of Long-Term Debt

Principal payments that must be made during the upcoming 12 months on long-term debt (such as for a mortgage), or on bonds and notes that mature within the next year, are reported as current liabilities called *current maturities of long-term debt*. All companies must provide a schedule of the maturities of their long-term debt in the footnotes to the financial statements. To illustrate, Verizon reports $2,954 million in long-term debt due within one year in the current liability section of the balance sheet shown earlier in the module.

MID-MODULE REVIEW 3

Assume that on January 15, Verizon borrowed $10,000 on a 90-day, 6% note payable. The bank accrues interest daily based on a 365-day year. Use the financial statement effects template to show the January 31 interest accrual.

Solution

	Balance Sheet								Income Statement			
Transaction	Cash Asset	+	Noncash Assets	=	Liabil- ities	+	Contrib. Capital	+	Earned Capital	Rev- enues	−	Expen- ses	=	Net Income
Jan 31: Accrue $26 interest expense*				=	+26 Interest Payable				−26 Retained Earnings		−	+26 Interest Expense	=	−26

*Accrued interest = $10,000 × 0.06 × 16/365 = $26.

LONG-TERM NONOPERATING LIABILITIES

Companies often include long-term nonoperating liabilities in their capital structure to fund long-term assets. Smaller amounts of long-term debt can be readily obtained from banks, private placements with insurance companies, and other credit sources. However, when a large amount of financing is required, the issuance of bonds (and notes) in capital markets is a cost-efficient way to raise funds. The following discussion uses bonds for illustration, but the concepts also apply to long-term notes.

Bonds are structured like any other borrowing. The borrower receives cash and agrees to pay it back with interest. Generally, the entire **face amount** (principal) of the bond is repaid at maturity (at the end of the bond's life) and interest payments are made in the interim (usually semiannually).

Companies that raise funds in the bond market normally work with an underwriter (like Merrill Lynch) to set the terms of the bond issue. The underwriter then sells individual bonds (usually in $1,000 denominations) from this general bond issue to its retail clients and professional portfolio managers (like The Vanguard Group), and receives a fee for underwriting the bond issue. These bonds are investments for individual investors, other companies, retirement plans and insurance companies.

After they are issued, the bonds can trade in the secondary market just like stocks. Market prices of bonds fluctuate daily despite the fact that the company's obligation for payment of principal and interest normally remains fixed throughout the life of the bond. Then, why do bond prices change? The answer is that the bond's fixed-rate of interest can be higher or lower than the interest rates offered on other securities of similar risk. Because bonds compete with other possible investments, bond prices are set relative to the prices of other investments. In a competitive investment market, a particular bond will become more or less desirable depending on the general level of interest rates offered by competing securities. Just as for any item, competitive pressures will cause bond prices to rise and fall.

This section analyzes and interprets the reporting for bonds. We also examine the mechanics of bond pricing and describe the accounting for, and reporting of, bonds.

Pricing of Debt

The following two different interest rates are crucial for pricing debt.

- **Coupon (contract or stated) rate** The coupon rate of interest is stated in the bond contract; it is used to compute the dollar amount of (semiannual) interest payments that are paid to bondholders during the life of the bond issue.
- **Market (yield or effective) rate** This is the interest rate that investors expect to earn on the investment in this debt security; this rate is used to price the bond.

The coupon (contract) rate is used to compute interest payments and the market (yield) rate is used to price the bond. The coupon rate and the market rate are nearly always different. This is because the coupon rate is fixed prior to issuance of the bond and normally remains fixed throughout its life. Market rates of interest, on the other hand, fluctuate continually with the supply and demand for bonds in the marketplace, general macroeconomic conditions, and the borrower's financial condition.

The bond price, both its initial sales price and the price it trades at in the secondary market subsequent to issuance, equals the present value of the expected cash flows to the bondholder. Specifically, bondholders normally expect to receive two different types of cash flows:

1. **Periodic interest payments** (usually semiannual) during the bond's life; these payments are called an *annuity* because they are equal in amount and made at regular intervals.
2. **Single payment** of the face (principal) amount of the bond at maturity; this is called a *lump-sum* because it occurs only once.

The bond price equals the present value of the periodic interest payments plus the present value of the single payment. If the present value of the two cash flows is equal to the bond's face value, the bond is sold at par. If the present value is less than or greater than the bond's face value, the bond sells at a discount or premium, respectively. We next illustrate the issuance of bonds at three different prices: at par, at a discount, and at a premium.

Bonds Issued at Par

To illustrate a bond issued (also said to be sold) at par, assume that a bond with a face amount of $10 million, has a 6% annual coupon rate payable semiannually (3% semiannual rate), and a maturity of 10 years. Semiannual interest payments are typical for bonds. This means that the issuer pays bondholders two interest payments per year. Each semiannual interest payment is equal to the bond's face value times the annual rate divided by two. Investors purchasing these bonds receive the following cash flows.

	Number of Payments	Dollars per Payment	Total Cash Flows
Semiannual interest payments.....	10 years × 2 = 20	$10,000,000 × 3% = $300,000	$ 6,000,000
Principal payment at maturity......	1	$10,000,000	10,000,000
			$16,000,000

Specifically, the bond agreement dictates that the borrower must make 20 semiannual payments of $300,000 each, computed as $10,000,000 × (6%/2). At maturity, the borrower must repay the $10,000,000 face amount. To price bonds, investors identify the *number* of interest payments and use that number when computing the present value of *both* the interest payments and the principal (face) payment at maturity.

The bond price is the present value of the periodic interest payments (the annuity) plus the present value of the principal payment (the lump sum). In our example, assuming that investors desire a 3% semiannual market rate (yield), the bond sells for $10,000,000, which is computed as follows:

	Payment	Present Value Factor[a]	Present Value
Interest	$ 300,000	14.87747[b]	$ 4,463,200[d]
Principal	$10,000,000	0.55368[c]	5,536,800
			$10,000,000

> Present value factors are from Appendix A

[a] Mechanics of using tables to compute present values are explained in Appendix 8A; present value factors come from Appendix A near the end of the book.

[b] Present value of an ordinary annuity for 20 periods discounted at 3% per period.

[c] Present value of a single payment in 20 periods discounted at 3% per period.

[d] Rounded.

Because the bond contract pays investors a 3% semiannual rate when investors demand a 3% semiannual market rate, given the borrower's credit rating and the time to maturity, the investors purchase those bonds at the **par (face) value** of $10 million.

Discount Bonds

As a second illustration, assume investors demand a 4% semiannual return for the 3% semiannual coupon bond, while all other details remain the same. The bond now sells for $8,640,999, computed as follows:

	Payment	Present Value Factor	Present Value
Interest	$ 300,000	13.59033[a]	$4,077,099
Principal	$10,000,000	0.45639[b]	4,563,900
			$8,640,999

[a] Present value of an ordinary annuity for 20 periods discounted at 4% per period.

[b] Present value of a single payment in 20 periods discounted at 4% per period.

Because the bond carries a coupon rate *lower* than what investors demand, the bond is less desirable and sells at a **discount**. More generally, bonds sell at a discount whenever the coupon rate is less than the market rate.

Premium Bonds

As a third illustration, assume that investors demand a 2% semiannual return for the 3% semiannual coupon bonds, while all other details remain the same. The bond now sells for $11,635,129, computed as follows:

	Payment	Present Value Factor	Present Value
Interest	$ 300,000	16.35143[a]	$ 4,905,429
Principal	$10,000,000	0.67297[b]	6,729,700
			$11,635,129

[a] Present value of an ordinary annuity for 20 periods discounted at 2% per period.

[b] Present value of a single payment in 20 periods discounted at 2% per period.

Because the bond carries a coupon rate *higher* than what investors demand, the bond is more desirable and sells at a **premium**. More generally, bonds sell at a premium whenever the coupon rate is greater than the market rate.[3] Exhibit 8.1 summarizes this relation for bond pricing.

---

[3] Bond prices are often stated in percent form. For example, a bond sold at par is said to be sold at 100 (that is, 100% of par). The bond sold at $8,640,999 is said to be sold at 86.41 (86.41% of par, computed as $8,640,999/$10,000,000). The bond sold for a premium is said to be sold at 116.35 (116.35% of the bond's face value).

EXHIBIT 8.1	Coupon Rate, Market Rate, and Bond Pricing	
Coupon rate > market rate	→	Bond sells at a **premium** (above face amount)
Coupon rate = market rate	→	Bond sells at **par** (at face amount)
Coupon rate < market rate	→	Bond sells at a **discount** (below face amount)

Exhibit 8.2 shows an announcement (called a *tombstone*) of a General Electric $5 billion debt issuance. It has a 5% coupon rate paying 2.5% semiannual interest, maturing in 2013, with an issue price of 99.626 (sold at a discount). GE's underwriters took 0.425% in fees (more than $21 million) for underwriting and selling this debt issue.[4]

EXHIBIT 8.2 Announcement (Tombstone) of Debt Offering to Public

General Electric Company

$5,000,000,000
5% Notes due 2013

Issue price: 99.626%

We will pay interest on the notes semiannually on February 1 and August 1 of each year, beginning August 1, 2003. The notes will mature on February 1, 2013. We may not redeem the notes prior to maturity.

The notes will be unsecured obligations and rank equally with our other unsecured debt securities that are not subordinated obligations. The notes will be issued in registered form in denominations of $1,000.

Neither the Securities and Exchange Commission nor any state securities commission has approved or disapproved of the notes or determined if this prospectus supplement or the accompanying prospectus is truthful or complete. Any representation to the contrary is a criminal offense.

	Per Note	Total
Public Offering Price(1)	99.626%	$4,981,300,000
Underwriting Discounts	.425%	$ 21,250,000
Proceeds to General Electric Company (before expenses)	99.201%	$4,960,050,000

(1) Plus accrued interest from January 28, 2003, if settlement occurs after that date.

The underwriters expect to deliver the notes in book-entry form only through the facilities of The Depository Trust Company, Clearstream, Luxembourg or the Euroclear System, as the case may be, on or about January 28, 2003.

Joint Bookrunners

Morgan Stanley   **Salomon Smith Barney**

Senior Co-Managers

Banc of America Securities LLC	**Credit Suisse First Boston**	**Deutsche Bank Securities**
Goldman. Sachs & Co.	**JPMorgan**	**Merrill Lynch & Co.**
	UBS Warburg	

Co-Managers

Banc One Capital Markets, Inc.	**Barclays Capital**	**Blaylock & Partners, L.P.**
BNP PARIBAN	**Dresdner Kleinwort Wasserstein**	**Guzman & Company**
HSBC	**Loop Capital Markets**	**Ormes Capital Markets, Inc.**
Utendahl Capital Partners, L.P.	**The Williams Capital Group, L.P.**	

---

[4] The tombstone makes clear that if we purchase any of these notes (in denominations of $1,000) after the semiannual interest date, we must pay accrued interest in addition to the purchase price. This interest is returned to us in the regular interest payment. (This procedure makes the bookkeeping easier for the issuer/underwriter because all interest payments are equal regardless of when GE actually sold the bond.)

Effective Cost of Debt

When a bond sells for par, the cost to the issuing company is the cash interest paid. In our first illustration above, the *effective cost* of the bond is the 6% interest paid by the issuer.

When a bond sells at a discount, the issuer must repay more (the face value when the bond matures) than the cash received at issuance (the discounted bond proceeds). This means that the effective cost of a discount bond is greater than if the bond had sold at par. A discount is a cost and, like any other cost, must eventually be transferred from the balance sheet to the income statement as an expense.

When a bond sells at a premium, the borrower received more cash at issuance than it must repay. The difference, the premium, is a benefit that must eventually find its way into the income statement as a *reduction* of interest expense. As a result of the premium, the effective cost of a premium bond is less than if the bond had sold at par.

Bonds are priced to yield the return (market rate) demanded by investors. Consequently, the effective rate of a bond *always* equals the yield (market) rate demanded by investors, regardless of the coupon rate of the bond. This means that companies cannot influence the effective cost of debt by raising or lowering the coupon rate. Doing so will only result in a bond premium or discount. We discuss the factors affecting the yield demanded by investors later in the module.

The effective cost of debt is reflected in the amount of interest expense reported in the issuer's income statement. Because of bond discounts and premiums, interest expense is usually different from the cash interest paid. The next section discusses how management reports, and how we interpret, bonds on the balance sheet and interest expense on the income statement.

REPORTING OF DEBT FINANCING

This section identifies and describes the financial statement effects of bond transactions.

Financial Statement Effects of Debt Issuance

Bonds Issued at Par

When a bond sells at par, the issuing company receives the cash proceeds and accepts an obligation to make payments per the bond contract. Specifically, cash is increased and a long-term liability (bonds payable) is increased by the same amount. There is no revenue or expense at bond issuance. Using the facts from our $10 million bond illustration above, the issuance of bonds at par has the following financial statement effects:

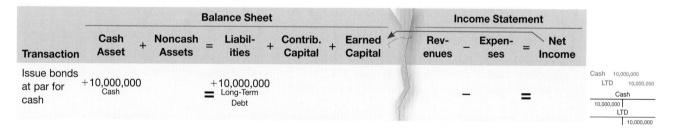

Discount Bonds

When a bond is sold at a discount, the cash proceeds and net bond liability are recorded at the amount of the proceeds received (not the face amount of the bond). Again, using the facts above from our bond discount illustration, the financial statement effects follow:

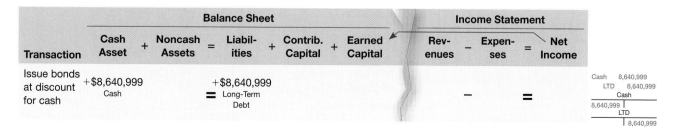

The net bond liability (long-term debt) reported on the balance sheet consists of two components as follows:

Bonds payable, face.	$10,000,000
Less bond discount	(1,359,001)
Bonds payable, net	$ 8,640,999

Bonds are reported on the balance sheet net of any discount. When the bond matures, however, the company is obligated to repay the face amount ($10 million). Accordingly, at maturity, the bonds payable account needs to read $10 million, the amount that is owed. This means that between the bond issuance and its maturity, the discount must decline to zero. This reduction of the discount over the life of the bond is called **amortization**. The next section shows how discount amortization results in additional interest expense in the income statement. This amortization causes the effective interest expense to be greater than the periodic cash interest payments.

BUSINESS INSIGHT Verizon's Zero Coupon Debt

Zero coupon bonds and notes, called *zeros,* do not carry a coupon rate. Pricing of these bonds and notes is done in the same manner as those with coupon rates—the exception is the absence of an interest annuity. This means that the price is the present value of the principal payment at maturity; hence the bond is sold at a *deep discount.* Verizon reported on its zero-coupon debt in its 2007 10-K:

> **Zero-Coupon Convertible Notes** The previously issued $5.4 billion zero-coupon convertible notes due 2021, which resulted in gross proceeds of approximately $3 billion, were redeemable at the option of the holders on May 15th in each of the years 2004, 2006, 2011, and 2016. On May 15, 2004, $3,292 million of principal amount of the notes ($1,984 million after unamortized discount) were redeemed. On May 15, 2006, we redeemed the remaining $1,375 million accreted principal of the remaining outstanding zero-coupon convertible principal. The total payment on the date of redemption was $1,377 million.

When Verizon issued its zero-coupon convertible notes in May 2001, they had a maturity value of $5.4 billion and were slated to mature in 2021. No interest is paid in the interim. The notes sold for $3 billion. The difference between the $3 billion sales proceeds and the $5.4 billion maturity value represents Verizon's interest costs, which is the return to the investor. The effective cost of the debt is the interest rate that equates the issue price and maturity value, or approximately 3%.

Premium Bonds

When a bond is sold at a premium, the cash proceeds and net bond liability are recorded at the amount of the proceeds received (not the face amount of the bond). Again, using the facts above from our premium bond illustration, the financial statement effects follow:

	Balance Sheet							Income Statement		
Transaction	Cash Asset	+	Noncash Assets	=	Liabil-ities	+	Contrib. Capital	+	Earned Capital	Rev-enues − Expen-ses = Net Income
Issue bonds at premium for cash	+$11,635,129 Cash			=	+$11,635,129 Long-Term Debt					− =

Cash 11,635,129
LTD 11,635,129

Cash
11,635,129 |
LTD
| 11,635,129

The bond liability reported on the balance sheet, again, consists of two parts:

Bonds payable, face.	$10,000,000
Add bond premium	1,635,129
Bonds payable, net	$11,635,129

The $10 million must be repaid at maturity, and the premium amortized to zero over the life of the bond. The premium represents a *benefit,* which *reduces* interest expense on the income statement.

Effects of Discount and Premium Amortization

For bonds issued at par, interest expense reported on the income statement equals the cash interest payment. However, for bonds issued at a discount or premium, interest expense reported on the income statement also includes any amortization of the bond discount or premium as follows:

	Cash interest paid			Cash interest paid
+	Amortization of discount	or	−	Amortization of premium
	Interest expense			Interest expense

Specifically, periodic amortization of a discount is added to the cash interest paid to get interest expense. Amortization of the discount reflects the additional cost the issuer incurs from issuing the bonds at a discount. Over the bond's life, the discount is transferred from the balance sheet to the income statement via amortization, as an increase to interest expense. For a premium bond, the premium is a benefit the issuer receives at issuance. Amortization of the premium reduces interest expense over the bond's life. In both cases, interest expense on the income statement represents the *effective cost* of debt (the *nominal cost* of debt is the cash interest paid).

Companies amortize discounts and premiums using the effective interest method. To illustrate, assume that Verizon issues bonds with a face amount of $600,000, a 3% annual coupon rate payable semiannually (1.5% semiannual rate), a maturity of three years (six semiannual payment periods), and a market (yield) rate of 4% annual (2% semiannual). These facts yield a bond issue price of $583,195.71, which we round to $583,196 for the bond discount amortization table of Exhibit 8.3.

EXHIBIT 8.3	**Bond Discount Amortization Table**				
Period	[A] ([E] × market%) Interest Expense	[B] (Face × coupon%) Cash Interest Paid	[C] ([A] − [B]) Discount Amortization	[D] (Prior bal − [C]) Discount Balance	[E] (Face − [D]) Bond Payable, Net
0				$16,804	$583,196
1	$11,664	$ 9,000	$2,664	14,140	585,860
2	11,717	9,000	2,717	11,423	588,577
3	11,772	9,000	2,772	8,651	591,349
4	11,827	9,000	2,827	5,824	594,176
5	11,884	9,000	2,884	2,940	597,060
6	11,940	9,000	2,940	0	600,000
	$70,804	$54,000	$16,804		

During the bond life, carrying value is adjusted to par and the discount to zero

Cash paid plus discount amortization equals interest expense

The interest period is denoted in the left-most column. Period 0 is the point at which the bond is issued, and period 1 and following are successive six-month periods (recall, interest is paid semiannually). Column [A] is interest expense, which is reported in the income statement. Interest expense is computed as the bond's net balance sheet value (the carrying amount of the bond) at the beginning of the period (column [E]) multiplied by the 2% semiannual rate used to compute the bond issue price. Column [B] is cash interest paid, which is a constant $9,000 per the bond contract (face amount × coupon rate). Column [C] is discount amortization, which is the difference between interest expense and cash interest paid. Column [D] is the discount balance, which is the previous balance of the discount less the discount amortization in column [C]. Column [E] is the net bond payable, which is the $600,000 face amount less the unamortized discount from column [D].

The table shows amounts for the six interest payment periods. The amortization process continues until period 6, at which time the discount balance is 0 and the net bond payable is $600,000 (the maturity value). Each semiannual period, interest expense is recorded at 2%, the market rate of interest at the bond's issuance. This rate does not change over the life of the bond, even if the prevailing market interest rates change. An amortization table reveals the financial statement effects of the bond for its duration.

Specifically, we see the income statement effects in column [A], the cash effects in column [B], and the balance sheet effects in columns [D] and [E].

To illustrate amortization of a premium bond, we assume that Verizon issues bonds with a $600,000 face value, a 3% annual coupon rate payable semiannually (1.5% semiannual rate), a maturity of three years (six semiannual interest payments), and a 2% annual (1% semiannual) market interest rate. These facts yield a bond issue price of $617,386.43, which we round to $617,386. Exhibit 8.4 shows the premium amortization table for this bond.

	[A] ([E] × market%) Interest	[B] (Face × coupon%) Cash	[C] ([B] − [A]) Premium	[D] (Prior bal − [C]) Premium	[E] (Face + [D]) Bond
Period	Expense	Interest Paid	Amortization	Balance	Payable, Net
0				$17,386	$617,386
1	$ 6,174	$ 9,000	$ 2,826	14,560	614,560
2	6,146	9,000	2,854	11,706	611,706
3	6,117	9,000	2,883	8,823	608,823
4	6,088	9,000	2,912	5,911	605,911
5	6,059	9,000	2,941	2,970	602,970
6	6,030	9,000	2,970	0	600,000
	$36,614	$54,000	$17,386		

EXHIBIT 8.4   Bond Premium Amortization Table

Cash paid less premium amortization equals interest expense

During the bond life, carrying value is adjusted to par and the premium to zero

Interest expense is computed using the same process that we used for discount bonds. The difference is that the yield rate is 1% semiannual in the premium case. Also, cash interest paid follows from the bond contract (face amount × coupon rate), and the other columns' computations reflect the premium amortization. After period 6, the premium is fully amortized (equals zero) and the net bond payable balance is $600,000, the amount owed at maturity. Again, an amortization table reveals the financial statement effects of the bond—the income statement effects in column [A], the cash effects in column [B], and the balance sheet effects in columns [D] and [E].

Financial Statement Effects of Bond Repurchase

Companies report bonds payable at *historical (adjusted) cost*. Specifically, net bonds payable amounts follow from the amortization table, as do the related cash flows and income statement numbers. All financial statement relations are set when the bond is issued; they do not subsequently change.

Once issued, however, bonds trade in secondary markets. The yield rate used to compute bond prices for these subsequent transactions is the market interest rate prevailing at the time. These rates change daily based on the level of interest rates in the economy and the perceived creditworthiness of the bond issuer.

Companies can and sometimes do repurchase (or *redeem* or *retire*) their bonds prior to maturity. The bond indenture (contract agreement) can include provisions giving the company the right to repurchase its bonds directly from the bond holders. Or, the company can repurchase bonds in the open market. To illustrate, Verizon's 2007 10-K includes the following footnote relating to its repurchase of MCI debt in connection with the MCI acquisition:

Redemption of Debt Assumed in Merger   On January 17, 2006, Verizon announced offers to purchase two series of MCI senior notes, MCI $1,983 million aggregate principal amount of 6.688% Senior Notes Due 2009 and MCI $1,699 million aggregate principal amount of 7.735% Senior Notes Due 2014, at 101% of their par value . . . In addition, on January 20, 2006, Verizon announced an offer to repurchase MCI $1,983 million aggregate principal amount of 5.908% Senior Notes Due 2007 at 101% of their par value . . . We recorded pretax charges of $26 million ($16 million after-tax) during the first quarter of 2006 resulting from the extinguishment of the debt assumed in connection with the completion of this merger.

When a bond repurchase occurs, a gain or loss usually results, and is computed as follows:

Gain or Loss on Bond Repurchase = Net Bonds Payable − Repurchase Payment

The net bonds payable, also referred to as the *book value,* is the net amount reported on the balance sheet. If the issuer pays more to retire the bonds than the amount carried on its balance sheet, it reports a loss on its income statement, usually called *loss on bond retirement.* The issuer reports a *gain on bond retirement* if the repurchase price is less than the net bonds payable.

GAAP prescribes that gains or losses on bond repurchases be reported as part of ordinary income unless the repurchase meets the criteria for treatment as an extraordinary item (unusual and infrequent, see Module 5). Relatively few debt retirements meet these criteria and, hence, most gains and losses on bond repurchases are reported as part of income from continuing operations.

How should we treat these gains and losses for analysis purposes? That is, do they carry economic effects? The answer is no—the gain or loss on repurchase is exactly offset by the present value of the future cash flow implications of the repurchase (Appendix 8B demonstrates this).

Another analysis issue involves assessing the fair value of bonds and other long-term liabilities. This information is relevant for some investors and creditors in revealing unrealized gains and losses (similar to that reported for marketable securities). GAAP requires companies to provide information about current fair values of their long-term liabilities in footnotes (see Verizon's fair value of debt disclosure in the next section). However, these fair values are *not* reported on the balance sheet and changes in these fair values are not reflected in net income. We must make our own adjustments to the balance sheet and income statement if we want to include changes in fair values of liabilities.

Financial Statement Footnotes

Companies are required to disclose details about their long-term liabilities, including the amounts borrowed under each debt issuance, the interest rates, maturity dates, and other key provisions. Following is Verizon's disclosure for its long-term debt.

Long-Term Debt Outstanding long-term obligations are as follows:

At December 31 ($ millions)	Interest Rates %	Maturities	2007	2006
Notes payable	4.00–8.23	2008–2037	$14,923	$14,805
Telephone subsidiaries—debentures	4.63–7.00	2008–2033	10,580	11,703
	7.15–7.63	2012–2032	850	1,275
	7.85–8.75	2010–2031	1,679	1,679
Other subsidiaries—debentures and other	6.46–8.75	2008–2028	2,450	2,977
Employee stock ownership plan loans:				
NYNEX debentures	9.55	2010	70	92
Capital lease obligations (average rate 6.8% and 8.0%)			312	360
Unamortized discount, net of premium			(97)	(106)
Total long-term debt, including current maturities			30,767	32,785
Less: debt maturing within one year			(2,564)	(4,139)
Total long-term debt			$28,203	$28,646

Verizon reports a net book value for long-term debt of $30,767 million at year-end 2007. Of this amount, $2,564 million matures in the next year and is classified as a current liability (current maturities of long-term debt). The remainder of $28,203 matures after 2008. Verizon also reports $97 million in unamortized discount (net of premium) on this debt.

In addition to long-term debt amounts, rates, and due dates, and as required under GAAP, Verizon reports aggregate maturities for the five years subsequent to the balance sheet date as follows:

Maturities of Long-Term Debt Maturities of long-term debt outstanding at December 31, 2007 are as follows:

Years	(dollars in millions)
2008	$ 2,564
2009	2,966
2010	2,908
2011	2,671
2012	4,291
Thereafter	15,367

This reveals that Verizon is required to make principal payments that total $15,400 million in the next five years and an additional $15,367 million in principal payments thereafter. Such maturities are important information as a company must either meet its required payments, negotiate a rescheduling of the indebtedness, or refinance the debt to avoid default. Failing to repay debts (defaulting) usually has severe consequences as debtholders have legal remedies available to them that can bankrupt the company.

Verizon's disclosure on the fair value of its total debt follows:

December 31, 2007 ($ millions)	Carrying Amount	Fair Value
Short- and long-term debt	$30,845	$32,380

As of 2007, indebtedness with a book value of $30,845 million had a fair value of $32,380 million, resulting in an unrecognized liability (which would be realized if Verizon redeemed the debt) of $1,535 million. The increase in fair value is due mainly to a decline in interest rates subsequent to the bonds' issuance (Verizon's credit ratings have not changed in recent years—see next section). The justification for not recognizing unrealized gains and losses on the balance sheet and income statement is that such amounts can reverse with future fluctuations in interest rates. Further, since only the face amount of debt is repaid at maturity, unrealized gains and losses that arise during intervening years are not necessarily relevant. This is the same logic for nonrecognition of gains and losses on held-to-maturity debt investments (see Module 7).

CREDIT RATINGS AND THE COST OF DEBT

LO3 Explain how credit ratings are determined and identify their effect on the cost of debt.

Earlier in the module we explained that the effective cost of debt to the issuing company is the market (yield) rate of interest used to price the bond, regardless of the bond coupon rate. The market rate of interest is usually defined as the yield on U.S. Government borrowings such as treasury bills, notes, and bonds, called the *risk-free rate,* plus a *risk premium* (also called a *spread*).

Yield Rate = Risk-Free Rate + Risk Premium

Both the treasury yield (the so-called risk-free rate) and the corporate yield vary over time as illustrated in the following graphic.

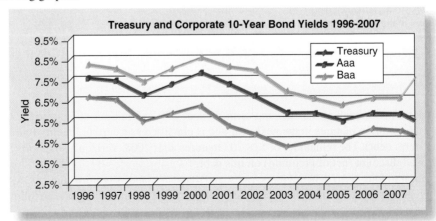

The rate of interest that investors expect for a particular bond is a function of the risk-free rate and the risk premium, where the latter depends on the creditworthiness of the issuing entity.

The yield increases (shifts upward) as debt quality moves from Treasury securities (generally considered to be risk free), which is the highest quality debt reflected in the lowest line in the graph, to the Aaa (highest) rated corporates and, finally, to the Baa (lower-rated) corporates shown in this graph. That is, higher credit-rated issuers warrant a lower rate than lower credit-rated issuers. This difference is substantial. For example, in 2007, the average 10-year treasury bond yield is 4.63%, while the Aaa corporate bond yield is 5.56% and the average Baa (the lowest investment grade corporate bond) yield is 6.48%.

RESEARCH INSIGHT | **Accounting Conservatism and Cost of Debt**

Research indicates that companies that use more conservative accounting policies incur a lower cost of debt. Research also suggests that while accounting conservatism can lead to lower-quality accounting income (because such income does not fully reflect economic reality), creditors are more confident in the numbers and view them as more credible. Evidence also implies that companies can lower the required return demanded by creditors (the risk premium) by issuing high-quality financial reports that include enhanced footnote disclosures and detailed supplemental reports.

What Are Credit Ratings?

A company's credit rating, also referred to as debt rating, credit quality, or creditworthiness, is related to default risk. **Default** refers to the nonpayment of interest and principal and/or the failure to adhere to the various terms and conditions (covenants) of the bond indenture. Companies that want to obtain bond financing from the capital markets, normally first seek a rating on their proposed debt issuance from one of several rating agencies such as Standard & Poor's, Moody's Investors Service, or Fitch Ratings. The aim of rating agencies is to rate debt so that its default risk is more accurately conveyed to, and priced by, the market. Each rating agency uses its own rating system, as Exhibit 8.5 shows. This exhibit includes the general description for each rating class—for example, AAA is assigned to debt of prime maximum safety (highest in creditworthiness).

EXHIBIT 8.5 Corporate Debt Ratings and Descriptions

Moody's	S&P	Fitch	Description
Aaa	AAA	AAA	Prime Maximum Safety
Aa1	AA+	AA+	High Grade, High Quality
Aa2	AA	AA	
Aa3	AA−	AA−	
A1	A+	A+	Upper-Medium Grade
A2	A	A	
A3	A−	A−	
Baa1	BBB+	BBB+	Lower-Medium Grade
Baa2	BBB	BBB	
Baa3	BBB−	BBB−	
Ba1	BB+	BB+	Non-Investment Grade
Ba2	BB	BB	Speculative
Ba3	BB−	BB−	
B1	B+	B+	Highly Speculative
B2	B	B	
B3	B−	B−	
Caa1	CCC+	CCC	Substantial Risk
Caa2	CCC		In Poor Standing
Caa3	CCC−		
Ca			Extremely Speculative
C			May be in Default
		DDD	Default
		DD	
	D	D	

MANAGERIAL DECISION   You Are the Vice President of Finance

Your company is currently rated B1/B+ by the Moody's and S&P credit rating agencies, respectively. You are considering restructuring to increase your company's credit rating. What types of restructurings might you consider? What benefits will your company receive from those restructurings? What costs will your company incur to implement such restructurings? [Answer, p. 8-32]

What Determines Credit Ratings?

Verizon bonds are rated A, A3, and A+ by Moody's, S&P, and Fitch, respectively, as of 2007. It is this rating, in conjunction with the maturity of Verizon's bonds, that establishes the market interest rate and the bonds' selling price. There are a number of considerations that affect the rating of a bond. Standard & Poor's lists the following factors, categorized by business risk and financial risk, among its credit rating criteria:

Business Risk	Financial Risk
Industry characteristics	Financial characteristics
Competitive position (marketing, technology, efficiency, regulation)	Financial policy
	Profitability
	Capital structure
Management	Cash flow protection
	Financial flexibility

Debt ratings convey information primarily to debt investors who are interested in assessing the probability that the borrower will make interest and principal payments on time. If a company defaults on its debt, debtholders seek legal remedies, including forcing the borrower to liquidate its assets to settle obligations. However, in forced liquidations, debtholders rarely realize the entire amounts owed to them.

It's important to bear in mind that debt ratings are opinions. Rating agencies use several financial ratios to assess default risk. A partial listing of ratios utilized by Moody's, together with median averages for various ratings, is in Exhibit 8.6. In examining the ratios, recall that debt is increasingly more risky as we move from the first row, Aaa, to the last, C.

EXHIBIT 8.6   Ratio Values for Different Risk Classes of Corporate Debt*

	EBITA/ Avg AT	EBITA/ Int Exp	EBITA Margin	Oper Margin	(FFO + Int Exp)/ Int Exp	FFO/ Debt	RCF/ Debt	Debt/ EBITDA	Debt/ Book Cap	CAPEX/ Dep
Aaa.....	20.9%	17.0	17.8%	16.0%	15.5	117.3%	96.3%	0.9	22.7%	1.4
Aa......	19.4%	13.4	19.0%	18.8%	12.3	66.7%	56.4%	1.2	36.8%	1.4
A.......	14.1%	8.1	18.1%	16.1%	9.2	43.9%	38.8%	1.7	39.5%	1.2
Baa.....	10.9%	5.6	13.9%	12.7%	6.9	33.4%	32.6%	2.2	43.6%	1.3
Ba......	10.0%	3.5	12.7%	11.6%	4.8	22.3%	20.3%	3.2	52.9%	1.1
B.......	7.3%	1.5	9.5%	8.6%	2.6	12.0%	11.2%	5.2	70.9%	1.0
C.......	2.0%	0.3	2.4%	1.6%	1.5	4.3%	4.6%	6.3	92.5%	0.9

* Table reports 2007 median values; from Moody's Financial Metrics™, Key Ratios by rating and industry for North American nonfinancial corporations: October 2007 (reproduced with permission).

Ratio	Definition
EBITA/Average Assets	EBITA/Average of Current and Previous Year Assets
EBITA/Interest Expense	EBITA/Interest Expense
EBITA Margin	EBITA/Net Revenue
Operating Margin	Operating Profit/Net Revenue
(FFO + Interest Exp)/Interest Exp	(Funds From Operations + Interest Expense)/Interest Expense
FFO/Debt	Funds From Operations/(Short-Term Debt + Long-Term Debt)
RCF/Debt	(FFO − Preferred Dividends − Common Dividends − Minority Dividends)/(Short-Term Debt + Long-Term Debt)
Debt/EBITDA	(Short-Term Debt + Long-Term Debt)/EBITDA
Debt/Book Capitalization	(Short-Term Debt + Long-Term Debt)/(Short-Term Debt + Long-Term Debt + Deferred Taxes + Minority Interest + Book Equity)
CAPEX/Depreciation Exp	Capital expenditures/Depreciation Expense

where: EBITA = Earnings from continuing operations before interest, taxes, and amortization
EBITDA = Earnings from continuing operations before interest and taxes, depreciation, and amortization
FFO = Net income from continuing operations plus depreciation, amortization, deferred income taxes, and other noncash items

A review of these ratios indicates that Moody's considers the following factors, grouped by area of emphasis, as relevant in evaluating a company's ability to meet its debt service requirements:

1. Profitability ratios (1, 2, 3, 4)
2. Cash flow ratios (5, 6, 7)
3. Solvency ratios (8, 9, 10)

Further, these ratios are variants of many of the ratios we describe in Module 4 and elsewhere in the book. Other relevant debt-rating factors include the following:

- **Collateral** Companies can provide security for debt by pledging certain assets against the bond. This is like mortgages on assets. To the extent debt is secured, the debtholder is in a preferred position vis-à-vis other creditors.

- **Covenants** Debt agreements (indentures) can restrict the behavior of the issuing company so as to protect debtholders. For example, covenants commonly prohibit excessive dividend payment, mergers and acquisitions, further borrowing, and commonly prescribe minimum levels for key liquidity and solvency ratios. These covenants provide debtholders an element of control over the issuer's operations because, unlike equity investors, debtholders have no voting rights.

- **Options** Options are sometimes written into debt contracts. Examples are options to convert debt into stock (so that debtholders have a stake in value creation) and options allowing the issuing company to repurchase its debt before maturity (usually at a premium).

> **IFRS Alert**
> Unlike GAAP, IFRS requires that companies treat the conversion feature like an option and revalue it each period using the appropriate market rate. The difference in value each period is recorded as nonoperating revenue or expense.

RESEARCH INSIGHT | **Valuation of Debt Options**

Debt instruments can include features such as conversion options, under which the debt can be converted to common stock. Such conversion features are not accounted for separately under GAAP. Instead, convertible debt is accounted for just like debt with no conversion features (unless the conversion option can be separately traded). However, option-pricing models can be used to estimate the value of such debt features even when no market for those features exists. Empirical results suggest that those debt features represent a substantial part of debt value. These findings contribute to the current debate regarding the separation of compound financial instruments into debt and equity portions for financial statement presentation and analysis.

Any Trends with Credit Ratings?

Companies strive to maintain an "investment-grade" credit rating. This allows them to sell their bonds to institutional investors such as pension, mutual and other investment funds. Many institutional investors will not invest in bonds that are rated below investment-grade rating of BBB. To achieve a higher credit rating, companies must have lower financial leverage and maintain greater liquidity. This is costly to shareholders. As a result, financial managers face a difficult task in finding the optimal capital structure that maximizes returns to shareholders while reducing the cost of debt capital.

Companies have become generally more financially leveraged over the past decade. While greater financial leverage can increase ROE (see Module 4), leverage adds risk. The severity of the economic downturn in 2008-2009 was due, in part, to the use of borrowed money to finance the purchase of risky assets, and the process of "de-leveraging" further worsened what was already a recession.

A second trend in financial markets is increased credit complexity. The increasing use of off-balance-sheet financing, hybrid securities, asset securitization, convertibles, debt in unconsolidated subsidiaries, and other techniques, has complicated the credit analysis process and has lessened the reliability of credit ratings. Bottom line: during the decade leading up to the recession of 2009, companies made increasing use of financial leverage and engineered more complex methods of disguising it.

What Financial Ratios Matter?

We cited a number of financial and nonfinancial factors that analysts consider when developing credit ratings. UBS (www.UBS.com), global investment banking and securities firm, measured the correlation between credit ratios, such as those described in this section, and bond ratings. The "t-statistics" from those correlations are in the following chart ("The New World of Credit Ratings," *UBS Investment Bank*, 2004):

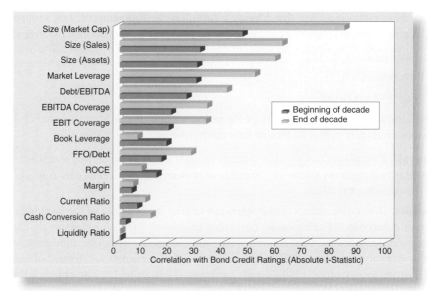

Measures relating to the size of the company, its financial leverage, and its cash flow in relation to its debt payment obligations, are most highly correlated with bond credit ratings (implying a higher "t-statistic"). These findings are consistent with the analysis and focus of this module.

Can Financial Ratios Predict Actual Credit Ratings?

UBS looked at the relation between actual and estimated credit ratings for a broad cross-section of U.S. companies. UBS used statistics to estimate each company's credit rating. Their analysis included ratios and measures like those in the graphic above. Then, UBS plotted the estimated ratings against companies' actual S&P ratings. The following graphic illustrates two interesting facts.

1. There is a relatively wide range of *estimated* credit ratings (reflected in the blue dots on the solid vertical line) for each credit rating. For example, the highest rated bonds (AAA) include companies with estimated credit ratings that range from AA+ to BB+; and, the most frequent bond rating (BBB) has estimated ratings that range from AA to BB−. If the estimated credit rating and the actual credit ratings are identical, the firm would fall on the black solid line. By comparing the number of observations (blue dots) above and below the black line, we see that, for the highest ratings (AAA to A−), more firms are overrated than underrated. The opposite is true for the lower rated firms as they seem to be underrated compared to expectations.

2. The *actual* credit ratings tend to be somewhat higher on average than the *estimated* ratings as measured by the dotted (regression) line. The companies that the model predicts will be rated BBB, for example, are actually rated BBB+, and those that the model predicts would carry the AA− rating are actually rated AAA.

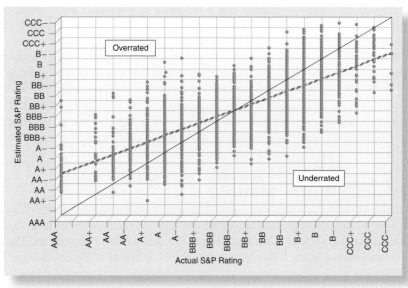

Does Industry Play a Role in Using Ratios for Credit Ratings?

Industries exhibit different levels of financial leverage as illustrated in the following graphic from UBS. As we know, lower levels of financial leverage result in higher credit ratings—this is evident in this graphic as we move from left (BB rating) to right (A rating). Interesting, within each credit rating, we see a fairly wide range of financial leverage for the companies from each industry that received that rating. For example, for companies rated BB, we see financial leverage ranging from under 3 to over 6. Of course, there are many factors that contribute to a company's credit rating and some of them, such as size and cash flow in relation to debt payments, can counter-balance the leverage effect. Still, as this graph highlights, we *cannot* generally infer that all companies within a particular credit rating carry about the same proportion of debt in their capital structures.

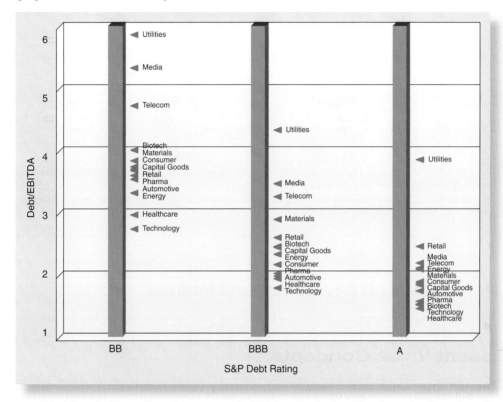

In summary, although the credit rating process is highly quantitative, the determination of credit ratings is far from mechanical. Again, credit ratings are an *opinion* of a company's creditworthiness. We must not rely exclusively upon credit ratings any more than we rely solely on "buy" or "sell" ratings by securities analysts.

MODULE-END REVIEW

On January 1, assume that Sprint Nextel Corporation issues $300,000 of 15-year, 10% bonds payable for $351,876, yielding an effective semiannual interest rate of 4%. Interest is payable semiannually on June 30 and December 31. (1) Show computations to confirm the issue price of $351,876, and (2) complete Sprint's financial statement effects template for (a) bond issuance, (b) semiannual interest payment and premium amortization on June 30 of the first year, and (c) semiannual interest payment and premium amortization on December 31 of the first year.

Solution

1.

Issue price for $300,000, 15-year bonds that pay 10% interest semiannually, discounted at 8%:	
Present value of principal payment ($300,000 × 0.30832)	$ 92,496
Present value of semiannual interest payments ($15,000 × 17.29203).	259,380
Issue price of bonds.	$351,876

2.

		Balance Sheet						Income Statement		
Transaction	Cash Asset	+	Noncash Assets	=	Liabil- ities	+	Contrib. Capital	+	Earned Capital	Rev- enues	−	Expen- ses	=	Net Income

Transaction	Cash Asset	Noncash Assets	Liabilities	Contrib. Capital	Earned Capital	Revenues	Expenses	Net Income
January 1: Issue 10% bonds	+351,876 Cash		+351,876 Long-Term Debt				–	=
June 30: Pay interest and amortize bond premium[1]	−15,000 Cash		−925 Long-Term Debt		−14,075 Retained Earnings		+14,075 Interest Expense	= −14,075
December 31: Pay interest and amortize bond premium[2]	−15,000 Cash		−962 Long-Term Debt		−14,038 Retained Earnings		+14,038 Interest Expense	= −14,038

Side T-accounts:
```
Cash      351,876
  LTD          351,876
Cash
351,876 |
  LTD
        | 351,876
IE      14,075
LTD        925
  Cash      15,000
     IE
14,075 |
  LTD
925 |
  Cash
     | 15,000
IE      14,038
LTD        962
  Cash      15,000
     IE
14,038 |
  LTD
962 |
  Cash
     | 15,000
```

[1] $300,000 × 0.10 × 6/12 = $15,000 cash payment; 0.04 × $351,876 = $14,075 interest expense; the difference of $925, is the bond premium amortization, which reduces the net bond carrying amount.

[2] 0.04 × ($351,876 − $925) = $14,038 interest expense. The difference between this amount and the $15,000 cash payment ($962) is the premium amortization, which reduces the net bond carrying amount.

APPENDIX 8A: Compound Interest

This appendix explains the concepts of present and future value, which are useful for our analysis purposes.

Present Value Concepts

Would you rather receive a dollar now or a dollar one year from now? Most people would answer, a dollar now. Intuition tells us that a dollar received now is more valuable than the same amount received sometime in the future. Sound reasons exist for choosing the dollar now, the most obvious of which concerns risk. Because the future is uncertain, any number of events can prevent us from receiving the dollar a year from now. To avoid this risk, we choose the earlier date. Another reason is that the dollar received now could be invested. That is, one year from now, we would have the dollar and the interest earned on that dollar.

Present Value of a Single Amount

Risk and interest factors yield the following generalizations: (1) the right to receive an amount of money now, its **present value,** is worth more than the right to receive the same amount later, its **future value;** (2) the longer we must wait to receive an amount, the less attractive the receipt is; (3) the greater the interest rate the greater the amount we will receive in the future. (Putting 2 and 3 together we see that difference between the present value of an amount and its future value is a function of both interest rate and time, that is, Principal × Interest Rate × Time); and (4) the more risk associated with any situation, the higher the interest rate.

To illustrate, let's compute the amount we would need to receive today (the present value) that would be equivalent to receiving $100 one year from now if money can be invested at 10%. We recognize intuitively that, with a 10% interest rate, the present value (the equivalent amount today) will be less than $100. The $100 received in the future must include 10% interest earned for the year. Thus, the $100 received in one year (the future value) must be 1.10 times the amount received today (the present value). Dividing $100/1.10, we obtain a present value of $90.91 (rounded). This means that we would do as well to accept $90.91 today as to wait one year and receive $100. To confirm the equality of the $90.91 receipt now to a $100 receipt one year later, we calculate the future value of $90.91 at 10% for one year as follows:

$$\$90.91 \times 1.10 \times 1 \text{ year} = \$100 \text{ (rounded)}$$

To generalize, we compute the present value of a future receipt by *discounting* the future receipt back to the present at an appropriate interest rate (also called the *discount rate*). We present this schematically below:

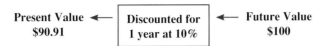

| Present Value ← | Discounted for | ← Future Value |
| $90.91 | 1 year at 10% | $100 |

If either the time period or the interest rate were increased, the resulting present value would decrease. If more than one time period is involved, our future receipts include interest on interest. This is called *compounding*.

Time Value of Money Tables

Appendix A near the end of the book includes time value of money tables. Table 1 is a present value table that we can use to compute the present value of future amounts. A present value table provides present value factors (multipliers) for many combinations of time periods and interest rates that determine the present value of $1.

Present value tables are used as follows. First, determine the number of interest compounding periods involved (three years compounded annually are 3 periods, and three years compounded semiannually are 6 periods). The extreme left-hand column indicates the number of periods. It is important to distinguish between years and compounding periods. The table is for compounding periods (years × number of compounding periods per year).

Next, determine the interest rate per compounding period. Interest rates are usually quoted on a *per year* (annual) basis. The rate per compounding period is the annual rate divided by the number of compounding periods per year. For example, an interest rate of 10% *per year* would be 10% per period if compounded annually, and 5% *per period* if compounded semiannually.

Finally, locate the present value factor, which is at the intersection of the row of the appropriate number of compounding periods and the column of the appropriate interest rate per compounding period. Multiply this factor by the dollars that will be paid or received in the future.

All values in Table 1 are less than 1.0 because the present value of $1 received in the future is always smaller than $1. As the interest rate increases (moving from left to right in the table) or the number of periods increases (moving from top to bottom), the present value factors decline. This illustrates two important facts: (1) present values decline as interest rates increase, and (2) present values decline as the time lengthens. Consider the following three cases:

Case 1. Compute the present value of $100 to be received one year from today, discounted at 10% compounded semiannually:

> Number of periods (one year, semiannually) = 2
> Rate per period (10%/2) = 5%
> Multiplier = 0.90703
> Present value = $100.00 × 0.90703 = $90.70 (rounded)

Case 2. Compute the present value of $100 to be received two years from today, discounted at 10% compounded semiannually:

> Number of periods (two years, semiannually) = 4
> Rate per period (10%/2) = 5%
> Multiplier = 0.82270
> Present value = $100 × 0.82270 = $82.27 (rounded)

Case 3. Compute the present value of $100 to be received two years from today, discounted at 12% compounded semiannually:

> Number of periods (two years, semiannually) = 4
> Rate per period (12%/2) = 6%
> Multiplier = 0.79209
> Present value = $100 = 0.79209 = $79.21 (rounded)

In Case 2, the present value of $82.27 is less than for Case 1 ($90.70) because the time increased from two to four compounding periods—the longer we must wait for money, the lower its value to us today. Then in Case 3, the present value of $79.21 was lower than in Case 2 because, while there were still four compounding periods, the interest rate per year was higher (12% annually instead of 10%)—the higher the interest rate the more interest that could have been earned on the money and therefore the lower the value today.

Present Value of an Annuity

In the examples above, we computed the present value of a single amount (also called a lump sum) made or received in the future. Often, future cash flows involve the same amount being paid or received each period. Examples include semiannual interest payments on bonds, quarterly dividend receipts, or monthly insurance premiums. If the payment or the receipt (the cash flow) is equally spaced over time and each cash flow is the same dollar amount, we have an *annuity*. One way to calculate the present value of the annuity would be to calculate the present value of each future cash flow separately. However, there is a more convenient method.

To illustrate, assume $100 is to be received at the end of each of the next three years as an annuity. When annuity amounts occur at the *end of each period*, the annuity is called an *ordinary annuity*. As shown below, the present value of this ordinary annuity can be computed from Table 1 by computing the present value of each of the three individual receipts and summing them (assume a 5% annual rate).

Future Receipts (ordinary annuity)			PV Multiplier (Table 1)		Present Value
Year 1	Year 2	Year 3			
$100			× 0.95238	=	$ 95.24
	$100		× 0.90703	=	90.70
		$100	× 0.86384	=	86.38
			2.72325		$272.32

Table 2 in Appendix A provides a single multiplier for computing the present value of an ordinary annuity. Referring to Table 2 in the row for three periods and the column for 5%, we see that the multiplier is 2.72325. When applied to the $100 annuity amount, the multiplier gives a present value of $272.33. As shown above, the same present value (with 1 cent rounding error) is derived by summing the three separate multipliers from Table 1. Considerable computations are avoided by using annuity tables.

Bond Valuation

Recall that a bond agreement specifies a pattern of future cash flows—usually a series of interest payments and a single payment of the face amount at maturity, and bonds are priced using the prevailing market rate on the day the bond is sold. This is the case for the original bond issuance and for subsequent open-market sales. The market rate on the date of the sale is the rate we use to determine the bond's market value (its price). That rate is the bond's *yield*. The selling price of a bond is determined as follows:

1. Use Table 1 to compute the present value of the future principal payment at the prevailing market rate.
2. Use Table 2 to compute the present value of the future series of interest payments (the annuity) at the prevailing market rate.
3. Add the present values from steps 1 and 2.

We illustrate in Exhibit 8A.1 the price of $100,000, 8%, 4-year bonds paying interest semiannually and sold when the prevailing market rate was (1) 8%, (2) 10% or (3) 6%. Note that the price of 8% bonds sold to yield 8% is the face (or par) value of the bonds. A bond issue price of $93,537 (discount bond) yields 10%. A bond issue price of $107,020 (premium bond) yields 6%.

Time Value of Money Computations Using a Calculator

We can use a financial calculator for time value of money computations. There are five important function keys for these calculations. If we know values for four of those five, the calculator will compute the fifth. Those function keys are:

N	Number of compounding (or discounting) periods
I/Yr	Interest (yield) rate per period—entered in % terms, for example, 12% is entered as 12 and not as 0.12. This key is labeled "interest per year" but it can handle any rate per different compounding periods; for example, if we have semiannual interest payments, our compounding periods are semiannual and the interest rate is the semiannual rate.
FV	Future value of the cash flows, this is a lump sum
PMT	Annuity (coupon) per discount period
PV	Present value of the cash flows, this is a lump sum

Calculator inputs follow for the three examples in Exhibit 8A.1. In these examples, the unknown value is the bond price, which is the present value (PV) of the bond's cash flows. (For additional instruction on entering inputs into a specific calculator, or how to do more complicated computations, review the calculator's user manual or review online calculator tutorials.)

Example (1), Exhibit 8A.1: Bond priced to yield 8%.

N	=	8 (4 years × 2 periods per year = 8 semiannual periods)
I/Yr	=	4 (8% annual yield ÷ 2 periods per year = 4% semiannually)
FV	=	100,000 (face value, which is the lump sum that must be repaid in the future)
PMT	=	4,000 ($100,000 × 4% semiannual coupon rate)

PV = 100,000 (output obtained from calculator)

Example (2), Exhibit 8A.1: Bond priced to yield 10%.

N = 8   I/Yr = 5   FV = 100,000   PMT = 4,000   PV = 93,537

Example (3), Exhibit 8A.1: Bond priced to yield 6%.

N = 8   I/Yr = 3   FV = 100,000   PMT = 4,000   PV = 107,020

EXHIBIT 8A.1 Calculation of Bond Price Using Present Value Tables

Future Cash Flows	Multiplier (Table 1)	Multiplier (Table 2)	Present Values at 4% Semiannually
(1) $100,000 of 8%, 4-year bonds with interest payable semiannually priced to yield 8%.			
Principal payment, $100,000 (a single amount received after 8 semiannual periods).............	0.73069		$ 73,069
Interest payments, $4,000 at end of each of 8 semiannual periods.........		6.73274	26,931
Present value (issue price) of bonds			$100,000

Future Cash Flows	Multiplier (Table 1)	Multiplier (Table 2)	Present Values at 5% Semiannually
(2) $100,000 of 8%, 4-year bonds with interest payable semiannually priced to yield 10%.			
Principal payment, $100,000 (a single amount received after 8 semiannual periods).............	0.67684		$ 67,684
Interest payments, $4,000 at end of each of 8 semiannual periods.........		6.46321	25,853
Present value (issue price) of bonds			$ 93,537

Future Cash Flows	Multiplier (Table 1)	Multiplier (Table 2)	Present Values at 3% Semiannually
(3) $100,000 of 8%, 4-year bonds with interest payable semiannually priced to yield 6%.			
Principal repayment, $100,000 (a single amount received after 8 semiannual periods).............	0.78941		$ 78,941
Interest payments, $4,000 at end of each of 8 semiannual periods.........		7.01969	28,079
Present value (issue price) of bonds			$107,020

Future Value Concepts

Future Value of a Single Amount

The **future value** of a single sum is the amount that a specific investment is worth at a future date if invested at a given rate of compound interest. To illustrate, suppose that we decide to invest $6,000 in a savings account that pays 6% annual interest and we intend to leave the principal and interest in the account for five years. We assume that interest is credited to the account at the end of each year. The balance in the account at the end of five years is determined using Table 3 in Appendix A, which gives the future value of a dollar, as follows:

Calculator
N = 5
I/Yr = 6
PMT = 0
PV = 6,000
FV = 8,029

Principal × Factor = Future Value
$6,000 × 1.33823 = $8,029

The factor 1.33823 is at the intersection of the row for five periods and the column for 6%.

Next, suppose that the interest is credited to the account semiannually rather than annually. In this situation, there are 10 compounding periods, and we use a 3% semiannual rate (one-half the annual rate because there are two compounding periods per year). The future value calculation follows:

$$\text{Principal} \times \text{Factor} = \text{Future Value}$$
$$\$6{,}000 \times 1.34392 = \$8{,}064$$

Future Value of an Annuity

If, instead of investing a single amount, we invest a specified amount *each period,* then we have an annuity. To illustrate, assume that we decide to invest $2,000 at the end of each year for five years at an 8% annual rate of return. To determine the accumulated amount of principal and interest at the end of five years, we refer to Table 4 in Appendix A, which furnishes the future value of a dollar invested at the end of each period. The factor 5.86660 is in the row for five periods and the column for 8%, and the calculation is as follows:

$$\text{Periodic Payment} \times \text{Factor} = \text{Future Value}$$
$$\$2{,}000 \times 5.86660 = \$11{,}733$$

If we decide to invest $1,000 at the end of each six months for five years at an 8% annual rate of return, we would use the factor for 10 periods at 4%, as follows:

$$\text{Periodic Payment} \times \text{Factor} = \text{Future Value}$$
$$\$1{,}000 \times 12.00611 = \$12{,}006$$

APPENDIX 8B: Economics of Gains and Losses on Bond Repurchases

Is a reported gain or loss on bond repurchases before maturity of economic substance? The short answer is no. To illustrate, assume that on January 1, a company issues $50 million face value bonds with an 8% annual coupon rate. The interest is to be paid semiannually (4% each semiannual period) for a term of five years (10 semiannual periods), at which time the principal will be repaid. If investors demand a 10% annual return (5% semiannually) on their investment, the bond price is computed as follows:

Present value of semiannual interest ($2,000,000 × 7.72173)	=	$15,443,460
Present value of principal ($50,000,000 × 0.61391)	=	30,695,500
Present value of bond	=	$46,138,960

This bond's amortization table follows:

EXHIBIT 8B.1 Bond Premium Amortization Table

Period	[A] ([E] × market%) Interest Expense	[B] (Face × coupon%) Cash Interest Paid	[C] ([A] − [B]) Discount Amortization	[D] (Prior bal − [C]) Discount Balance	[E] (Face − [D]) Bond Payable, Net
0				$3,861,040	$46,138,960
1	$2,306,948	$2,000,000	$306,948	3,554,092	46,445,908
2	2,322,295	2,000,000	322,295	3,231,797	46,768,203
3	2,338,410	2,000,000	338,410	2,893,387	47,106,613
4	2,355,331	2,000,000	355,331	2,538,056	47,461,944
5	2,373,097	2,000,000	373,097	2,164,959	47,835,041
6	2,391,752	2,000,000	391,752	1,773,207	48,226,793
7	2,411,340	2,000,000	411,340	1,361,867	48,638,133
8	2,431,907	2,000,000	431,907	929,960	49,070,040
9	2,453,502	2,000,000	453,502	476,458	49,523,542
10	2,476,458	2,000,000	476,458	0	50,000,000

Next, assume we are at period 6 (three years after issuance) and the market rate of interest for this bond has risen from 10% to 12%. The firm decides to retire (redeem) the outstanding bond issue and finances the retirement by issuing new bonds. That is, it issues bonds with a face amount equal to the market value of the old bonds and uses the proceeds to retire the existing (old) bonds. The new bond issue will have a term of two years (four semiannual periods), the remaining life of the existing bond issue.

At the end of the third year, there are four $2,000,000 semiannual interest payments remaining on the old bonds, plus the repayment of the face amount of the bond due at the end of the fourth semiannual period. The present value of this cash flow stream, discounted at the current 12% annual rate (6% semiannual rate) is:

Present value of semiannual interest ($2,000,000 × 3.46511)	=	$ 6,930,220
Present value of principal ($50,000,000 × 0.79209)	=	39,604,500
Present value of bond	=	$46,534,720

> **Calculator**
> N = 4
> I/Yr = 6
> PMT = 2,000,000
> FV = 50,000,000
>
> PV = 46,534,894*
> *rounding difference

This means the company pays $46,534,720 to redeem a bond that is on its books at a carrying amount of $48,226,793. The difference of $1,692,073 is reported as a gain on repurchase (also called *redemption*). GAAP requires this gain be reported in income from continuing operations unless it meets the tests for treatment as an extraordinary item (the item is both unusual and infrequent).

Although the company reports a gain in its income statement, has it actually realized an economic gain? Consider that this company issues new bonds that carry a coupon rate of 12% (6% semiannually) for $46,534,720. If we assume that those bonds are sold with a coupon rate equal to the market rate, they will sell at par (no discount or premium). The interest expense per six-month period, therefore, equals the interest paid in cash, or $2,792,083 ($46,534,720 × 6%). Total expense for the four-period life of the bond is $11,168,333 ($2,792,083 × 4). That amount, plus the $46,534,720 face amount of bonds due at maturity, results in total bond payments of $57,703,053. Had this company not redeemed the bonds, it would have paid four additional interest payments of $2,000,000 each plus the face amount of $50,000,000 at maturity, for total bond payments of $58,000,000. On the surface, it appears that the firm is able to save $296,947 by redeeming the bonds and, therefore, reports a gain. (Also, total interest expense on the new bond issue is $3,168,333 [$11,168,333 − $8,000,000] more than it would have recorded under the old issue; so, although it is recording a present gain, it also incurs future higher interest costs which are not recognized under GAAP.)

However, this gain is misleading. Specifically, this gain has two components. First, interest payments increase by $792,083 per year ($2,792,083 − $2,000,000). Second, the face amount of the bond that must be repaid in four years decreases by $3,465,280 ($50,000,000 − $46,534,720). To evaluate whether a real gain has been realized, we must consider the present value of these cash outflows and savings. The present value of the increased interest outflow, a four-period annuity of $792,083 discounted at 6% per period, is **$2,744,655** ($792,083 × 3.46511). The present value of the reduced maturity amount, $3,465,280 in four periods, is **$2,744,814** ($3,465,280 × 0.79209)—note: the two amounts differ by $159, which is due to rounding. The conclusion is that the two amounts are the same.

This analysis shows there is no real economic gain from early redemption of debt. The present value of the increased interest payments exactly offsets the present value of the decreased amount due at maturity. Why, then, does GAAP yield a gain? The answer lies in use of historical costing. Bonds are reported at amortized cost, that is, the face amount less any applicable discount or plus any premium. These amounts are a function of the bond issue price and its yield rate at issuance, which are both fixed for the life of the bond. Market prices for bonds, however, vary continually with changes in market interest rates. Companies do not adjust bond liabilities for these changes in market value. As a result, when companies redeem bonds, their carrying amount differs from market value and GAAP reports a gain or loss equal to this difference.

GUIDANCE ANSWERS

MANAGERIAL DECISION **You Are the Vice President of Finance**

You might consider the types of restructuring that would strengthen financial ratios typically used to assess liquidity and solvency by the rating agencies. Such restructuring includes generating cash by reducing inventory, reallocating cash outflows from investing activities (PPE) to debt reduction, and issuing stock for cash and using the proceeds to reduce debt (an equity for debt recapitalization). These actions increase liquidity or reduce financial leverage and, thus, should improve debt rating. An improved debt rating will attract more investors because your current debt rating is below investment grade and is not a suitable investment for many professionally managed portfolios. An improved debt rating will also lower the interest rate on your debt. Offsetting these benefits are costs such as the following: (1) potential loss of sales from inventory stock-outs; (2) potential future cash flow reductions and loss of market power from reduced PPE investments; and (3) costs of equity issuances (equity costs more than debt because investors demand a higher return to compensate for added risk and, unlike interest payments, dividends are not tax deductible for the company), which can yield a net increase in the total cost of capital. All cost and benefits must be assessed before you pursue any restructuring.

Superscript ^A(^B) denotes assignments based on Appendix 8A (8B).

DISCUSSION QUESTIONS

Q8-1. What does the term *current liabilities* mean? What assets are usually used to settle current liabilities?

Q8-2. What is an accrual? How do accruals impact the balance sheet and the income statement?

Q8-3. What is the difference between a bond's coupon rate and its market interest rate (yield)?

Q8-4. Why do companies report a gain or loss when they repurchase their bonds? Is this a real economic gain or loss.

Q8-5. How do credit (debt) ratings affect the cost of borrowing for a company?

Q8-6. How would you interpret a company's reported gain or loss on the repurchase of its bonds?

Assignments with the Web**Assign** logo in the margin are available in WebAssign.
See the Preface of the book for details.

MINI EXERCISES

M 8-7. **Interpreting a Contingent Liability Footnote** **(LO1)**

NCI Building Systems
(NCS)

NCI Building Systems, reports the following footnote to its 2007 10-K related to its manufacturing of metal coil coatings and metal building components.

> We have discovered the existence of trichloroethylene in the ground water at our Southlake, Texas facility. Horizontal delineation concentrations in excess of applicable residential assessment levels have not been fully identified. We have filed an application with the Texas Commission of Environmental Quality ("TCEQ") for entry into the voluntary cleanup program. We expect to perform further testing in the first quarter of fiscal 2008. The cost of required remediation, if any, will vary depending on the nature and extent of the contamination which is expected to be determined in the first or second quarter of fiscal 2008. As of October 28, 2007, we have accrued $0.1 million to complete site analysis and testing. At this time, we cannot estimate a loss for any potential remediation costs, but we do not believe there will be a material adverse effect on our Consolidated Financial Statements.

a. How has NCI reported this potential liability on its balance sheet?

b. Does the $0.1 million accrual "to complete site analysis and testing" relate to a contingent liability? Explain.

M8-8. **Analyzing and Computing Financial Statement Effects of Interest** **(LO1)**

DeFond Company signed a 90-day, 8% note payable for $7,200 on December 16. Use the financial statement effects template to illustrate the year-end December 31 accounting adjustment DeFond must make.

M8-9. **Analyzing and Determining Liability Amounts** **(LO1)**

For each of the following situations, indicate the liability amount, if any, that is reported on the balance sheet of Basu, Inc., at December 31, 2009.

a. Basu owes $110,000 at year-end 2009 for inventory purchases.

b. Basu agreed to purchase a $28,000 drill press in January 2010.

c. During November and December of 2009, Basu sold products to a customer and warranted them against product failure for 90 days. Estimated costs of honoring this 90-day warranty during 2010 are $2,200.

d. Basu provides a profit-sharing bonus for its executives equal to 5% of reported pretax annual income. The estimated pretax income for 2009 is $600,000. Bonuses are not paid until January of the following year.

M8-10. **Interpreting Relations among Bond Price, Coupon, Yield, and Credit Rating** **(LO2, 3)**

Boston Scientific
(BSX)

The following notice appeared in *The Wall Street Journal* regarding a bond issuance by Boston Scientific.

> **Boston Scientific Corp.—**$500 million of notes was priced with the following terms in two parts via joint lead managers Merrill Lynch & Co., UBS Securities and Wachovia:
> (1) Amount: $250 million; Maturity: Jan. 12, 2011; Coupon: 4.25%; Price: 99.476; Yield: 4.349%; Ratings: Baa1 (Moody's), A2 (S&P).
> (2) Amount: $250 million; Maturity: Jan. 12, 2017; Coupon: 5.125%; Price: 99.926; Yield: 5.134%; Ratings: Baa1 (Moody's), A2 (S&P).

    a.   Discuss the relation among the coupon rate, issuance price, and yield for the 2011 issuance.

    b.   Compare the yields on the two parts of the bond issuances. Why are the yields different when the credit ratings are the same?

M8-11. **Determining Gain or Loss on Bond Redemption** **(LO2)**

On April 30, one year before maturity, Nissim Company retired $200,000 of its 9% bonds payable at the current market price of 101 (101% of the bond face amount, or $200,000 × 1.01 = $202,000). The bond book value on April 30 is $197,600, reflecting an unamortized discount of $2,400. Bond interest is currently fully paid and recorded up to the date of retirement. What is the gain or loss on retirement of these bonds? Is this gain or loss a real economic gain or loss? Explain.

M8-12. **Interpreting Bond Footnote Disclosures** **(LO2)**

Amgen (AMGN) reports the following in the long-term debt footnote to its 2007 10-K.   Amgen (AMGN)

The aggregate contractual maturities of all long-term debt obligations due subsequent to December 31, 2007, are as follows (in millions):

Maturity Date	Amount
2008	$ 2,000
2009	1,000
2010	—
2011	2,500
2012	84
Thereafter	5,600
Total	$11,184

    a.   What does the $2,000 million in 2008 and $1,000 million in 2009 indicate about Amgen's future payment obligations?

    b.   What implications does this payment schedule have for our evaluation of Amgen's liquidity and solvency?

M8-13. **Classifying Liability-Related Accounts into Balance Sheet or Income Statement** **(LO2)**

Indicate the proper financial statement classification (balance sheet or income statement) for each of the following liability-related accounts.

    a.   Gain on Bond Retirement   *e.*   Bond Interest Expense

    b.   Discount on Bonds Payable   *f.*   Bond Interest Payable (due next period)

    c.   Mortgage Notes Payable   *g.*   Premium on Bonds Payable

    d.   Bonds Payable   *h.*   Loss on Bond Retirement

M8-14. **Interpreting Bond Footnote Disclosures** **(LO2)**

Comcast Corporation reports the following information from its Management Discussion and Analysis section of its 2007 10-K.   Comcast Corporation (CMCSA)

Debt Covenants We and our cable subsidiaries that have provided guarantees are subject to the covenants and restrictions set forth in the indentures governing our public debt securities and in the credit agreements governing our bank credit facilities. We and the guarantors are in compliance with the covenants, and we believe that neither the covenants nor the restrictions in our indentures or loan documents will limit our ability to operate our business or raise additional capital. Our credit facilities' covenants are tested on an ongoing basis. The only financial covenant in our $5.0 billion revolving credit facility and our amended and restated $7.0 billion revolving credit facility relates to leverage (ratio of debt to operating income before depreciation and amortization). As of December 31, 2007, we met our financial covenant in our $5 billion revolving credit facility by a sigificant margin. Our ability to comply with this financial covenant in the future does not depend on further debt reduction or on improved operating results.

    a.   The financial ratios to which Comcast refers are similar to those discussed in the section on credit ratings and the cost of debt. What effects might these ratios have on the degree of freedom that management has in running Comcast?

    b.   Violation of debt covenants can be a serious event that could trigger an "immediately due and payable" provision in the debt contract. What pressures might management face if the company's ratios are near covenant limits?

M8-15. Analyzing Financial Statement Effects of Bond Redemption (LO2)

Holthausen Corporation issued $400,000 of 11%, 20-year bonds at 108 on January 1, 2005. Interest is payable semiannually on June 30 and December 31. Through January 1, 2010, Holthausen amortized $5,000 of the bond premium. On January 1, 2010, Holthausen retired the bonds at 103. Use the financial statement effects template to illustrate the bond retirement at January 1, 2010.

M8-16. Analyzing Financial Statement Effects of Bond Redemption (LO2)

Dechow, Inc., issued $250,000 of 8%, 15-year bonds at 96 on July 1, 2005. Interest is payable semiannually on December 31 and June 30. Through June 30, 2010, Dechow amortized $3,000 of the bond discount. On July 1, 2010, Dechow retired the bonds at 101. Use the financial statement effects template to illustrate the bond retirement.

WebAssign

M8-17. Analyzing and Computing Accrued Interest on Notes (LO1)

Compute any interest accrued for each of the following notes payable owed by Penman, Inc., as of December 31, 2009 (assume a 365-day year).

Lender	Issuance Date	Principal	Coupon Rate (%)	Term
Nissim......	11/21/2009	$18,000	10%	120 days
Klein.......	12/13/2009	14,000	9	90 days
Bildersee....	12/19/2009	16,000	12	60 days

M8-18. Interpreting Credit Ratings (LO3)

Cummins (CMI)

Cummins reports the following information in the Management Discussion & Analysis section of its 2007 10-K report.

Financial Covenants and Credit Rating A number of our contractual obligations and financing agreements, such as our revolving credit facility and our equipment sale-leaseback agreements have restrictive covenants and/or pricing modifications that may be triggered in the event of downward revisions to our corporate credit rating. There have been no events in 2007 to impede our compliance with these covenants. On July 20, 2007, Fitch upgraded our senior unsecured debt ratings from "BBB-" to "BBB" and revised our outlook to stable citing the continued improvement in Cummins' balance sheet, increased sales diversification, an improved competitive profile and solid operating performance in North America in 2007 despite the downturn in the heavy truck cycle, among other factors. On August 16, 2007, Standard & Poor's (S&P) upgraded our outlook from stable to positive as S&P cited Cummins' prospects for continued good operating performance and its improved financial profile resulting from a steady reduction in financial leverage over the last several years. Our current ratings and outlook from each of the credit rating agencies are shown in the table below.

Credit Rating Agency	Senior L-T Debt Rating	S-T Debt Rating	Outlook
Moody's Investors Service, Inc......	Baa3	Non-Prime	Stable
Standard and Poor's.............	BBB−	NR	Positive
Fitch........................	BBB	BBB	Stable

a. Why does the reduction in financial leverage result in an increase in the credit ratings for Cummins' debt?

b. What effect will a higher credit rating have on Cummins' borrowing costs? Explain.

M8-19. Computing Bond Issue Price (LO2)

Bushman, Inc., issues $500,000 of 9% bonds that pay interest semiannually and mature in 10 years. Compute the bond issue price assuming that the prevailing market rate of interest is:

a. 8% per year compounded semiannually.

b. 10% per year compounded semiannually.

M8-20. Computing Issue Price for Zero Coupon Bonds (LO2)

Abarbanell, Inc., issues $500,000 of zero coupon bonds that mature in 10 years. Compute the bond issue price assuming that the bonds' market rate is:

a. 8% per year compounded semiannually.

b. 10% per year compounded semiannually.

M8-21. **Determining the Financial Statement Effects of Accounts Payable Transactions** **(LO1)**
Petroni Company had the following transactions relating to its accounts payable.

    a. Purchases $300 of inventory on credit.
    b. Sells inventory for $420 on credit.
    c. Records $300 cost of sales for transaction *b.*
    d. Receives $420 cash toward accounts receivable.
    e. Pays $300 cash to settle accounts payable.

Use the financial statement effects template to identify the effects (both amounts and accounts) for these transactions.

M8-22. **Computing Bond Issue Price and Preparing an Amortization Table in Excel** **(LO2)**
On January 1, 2009, Bushman, Inc., issues $500,000 of 9% bonds that pay interest semiannually and mature in 10 years (December 31, 2018).

    a. Using the Excel PRICE function, compute the issue price assuming that the bonds' market rate is 8% per year compounded semiannually. (Use 100 for the redemption value to get a price as a percentage of the face amount, and use 1 for the basis.)
    b. Prepare an amortization table in Excel to demonstrate the amortization of the book (carrying) value to the $500,000 maturity value at the end of the 20th semiannual period.

EXERCISES

E8-23. **Analyzing and Computing Accrued Warranty Liability and Expense** **(LO1)**
Waymire Company sells a motor that carries a 60-day unconditional warranty against product failure. From prior years' experience, Waymire estimates that 2% of units sold each period will require repair at an average cost of $100 per unit. During the current period, Waymire sold 69,000 units and repaired 1,000 units.

    a. How much warranty expense must Waymire report in its current period income statement?
    b. What warranty liability related to current period sales will Waymire report on its current period-end balance sheet? (*Hint:* Remember that some units were repaired in the current period.)
    c. What analysis issues must we consider with respect to reported warranty liabilities?

E8-24. **Analyzing Contingent and Other Liabilities** **(LO1)**
The following independent situations represent various types of liabilities. Analyze each situation and indicate which of the following is the proper accounting treatment for the company: (a) record a liability on the balance sheet, (b) disclose the liability in a financial statement footnote, or (c) neither record nor disclose any liability.

    1. A stockholder has filed a lawsuit against **Clinch Corporation**. Clinch's attorneys have reviewed the facts of the case. Their review revealed that similar lawsuits have never resulted in a cash award and it is highly unlikely that this lawsuit will either.
    2. **Foster Company** signed a 60-day, 10% note when it purchased items from another company.
    3. The Environmental Protection Agency notifies **Shevlin Company** that a state where it has a plant is filing a lawsuit for groundwater pollution against Shevlin and another company that has a plant adjacent to Shevlin's plant. Test results have not identified the exact source of the pollution. Shevlin's manufacturing process often produces by-products that can pollute ground water.
    4. **Sloan Company** manufactured and sold products to a retailer that later sold the products to consumers. The Sloan Company will replace the product if it is found to be defective within 90 days of the sale to the consumer. Historically, 1.2% of the products are returned for replacement.

E8-25. **Recording and Analyzing Warranty Accrual and Payment** **(LO1)**
Refer to the discussion of and excerpt from the Harley-Davidson warranty reserve on page 8-9 to answer the following questions.

    a. Using the financial statement effects template, record separately the accrual of warranty liability relating (1) to the "Warranties issued during the period" and (2) to the "Settlements made during the period."
    b. Does the level of Harley-Davidson's warranty accrual appear to be reasonable?

WebAssign.

WebAssign.

WebAssign.
Harley-Davidson
(HOG)

WebAssign.

E8-26.   **Analyzing and Computing Accrued Wages Liability and Expense   (LO1)**
Demski Company pays its employees on the 1st and 15th of each month. It is March 31 and Demski is preparing financial statements for this quarter. Its employees have earned $25,000 since the 15th of March and have not yet been paid. How will Demski's balance sheet and income statement reflect the accrual of wages on March 31? What balance sheet and income statement accounts would be incorrectly reported if Demski failed to make this accrual (for each account indicate whether it would be overstated or understated)?

E8-27.   **Analyzing and Reporting Financial Statement Effects of Bond Transactions   (LO2)**
On January 1, Hutton Corp. issued $300,000 of 15-year, 10% bonds payable for $351,876, yielding an effective interest rate of 8%. Interest is payable semiannually on June 30 and December 31. (a) Show computations to confirm the issue price of $351,876. (b) Indicate the financial statement effects using the template for (1) bond issuance, (2) semiannual interest payment and premium amortization on June 30 of the first year, and (3) semiannual interest payment and premium amortization on December 31 of the first year.

E8-28.   **Analyzing and Reporting Financial Statement Effects of Mortgages   (LO2)**
On January 1, Piotroski, Inc., borrowed $700,000 on a 12%, 15-year mortgage note payable. The note is to be repaid in equal semiannual installments of $50,854 (payable on June 30 and December 31). Each mortgage payment includes principal and interest. Interest is computed using the effective interest method. Indicate the financial statement effects using the template for (a) issuance of the mortgage note payable, (b) payment of the first installment on June 30, and (c) payment of the second installment on December 31.

E8-29.   **Assessing the Effects of Bond Credit Rating Changes   (LO3)**
Ford (F)
Ford reports the following information from its Management Discussion and Analysis section of its 2007 10-K report.

> **Ratings**   Our short- and long-term debt is rated by four credit rating agencies designated as nationally recognized statistical rating organizations ("NRSROs") by the Securities and Exchange Commission:
> - Dominion Bond Rating Service Limited ("DBRS");
> - Fitch, Inc. ("Fitch");
> - Moody's Investors Service, Inc. ("Moody's"); and
> - Standard & Poor's Rating Services, a division of The McGraw-Hill Companies ("S&P").
>
> Lower credit ratings generally result in higher borrowing costs and reduced access to capital markets. The NRSROs have indicated that our lower ratings are primarily a reflection of the rating agencies' concerns regarding our automotive cash flow and profitability, declining market share and product portfolio strength, excess industry capacity and industry pricing pressure. The following ratings actions were taken in the fourth quarter 2007:
>
> **Ford**
> - DBRS: In November 2007, DBRS changed Ford's trend to "Stable" from "Negative."
> - Fitch: No ratings actions taken in Q4 2007.
> - Moody's: In November 2007, Moody's changed Ford's outlook to "Stable" from "Negative."
> - S&P: In November 2007, S&P changed Ford's outlook to "Stable" from "Negative."
>
> **Ford Credit**
> - DBRS: In November 2007, DBRS changed Ford Credit's trend to "Stable" from "Negative."
> - Fitch: No ratings actions taken in Q4 2007.
> - Moody's: In November 2007, Moody's changed Ford Credit's outlook to "Stable" from "Negative."
> - S&P: In November 2007, S&P changed Ford Credit's outlook to "Stable" from "Negative."

a.   What financial ratios do credit rating companies such as the four NRSROs listed above, use to evaluate the relative riskiness of borrowers?
b.   Why might a reduction in credit ratings result in higher interest costs and restrict Ford's access to credit markets?
c.   What type of actions can Ford take to improve its credit ratings?

WebAssign.

E8-30.   **Analyzing and Reporting Financial Statement Effects of Bond Transactions   (LO2)**
Lundholm, Inc., reports financial statements each December 31 and issues $500,000, 9%, 15-year bonds dated May 1, 2009, with interest payments on October 31 and April 30. Assuming the bonds are sold at

par on May 1, 2009, complete the financial statement effects template to reflect the following events: (a) bond issuance, (b) the first semiannual interest payment, and (c) retirement of $300,000 of the bonds at 101 on November 1, 2009.

E8-31. **Analyzing and Reporting Financial Statement Effects of Bond Transactions** (LO2)

On January 1, 2009, McKeown, Inc., issued $250,000 of 8%, 9-year bonds for $220,776, which implies a market (yield) rate of 10%. Semiannual interest is payable on June 30 and December 31 of each year. (a) Show computations to confirm the bond issue price. (b) Indicate the financial statement effects using the template for (1) bond issuance, (2) semiannual interest payment and discount amortization on June 30, 2009, and (3) semiannual interest payment and discount amortization on December 31, 2009.

E8-32. **Analyzing and Reporting Financial Statement Effects of Bond Transactions** (LO2)

On January 1, 2009, Shields, Inc., issued $800,000 of 9%, 20-year bonds for $879,172, yielding a market (yield) rate of 8%. Semiannual interest is payable on June 30 and December 31 of each year. (a) Show computations to confirm the bond issue price. (b) Indicate the financial statement effects using the template for (1) bond issuance, (2) semiannual interest payment and premium amortization on June 30, 2009, and (3) semiannual interest payment and premium amortization on December 31, 2009.

E8-33. **Determining Bond Prices, Interest Rates, and Financial Statement Effects** (LO2)

Deere & Company's 2007 10-K reports the following footnote relating to long-term debt. Deere's borrowings include $300 million, 7.125% notes, due in 2031 (highlighted below).

WebAssign.
Deere & Co (DE)

Long-term borrowings at October 31 consisted of the following in millions of dollars:

Notes and Debentures	2007	2006
7.85% debentures due 2010	$ 306	$ 306
6.95% notes due 2014: ($700 principal)		
Swapped to variable interest rates		
of 6.1%—2007, 6.4%—2006	743	734
8.95% debentures due 2019	56	56
8-1/2% debentures due 2022	105	105
6.55% debentures due 2028	200	200
8.10% debentures due 2030	250	250
7.125% notes due 2031	300	300
Other notes.	13	18
Total	$1,973	$1,969

A recent price quote (from Yahoo! Finance Bond Center) on Deere's 7.125% notes follows.

Type	Issuer	Price	Coupon (%)	Maturity	YTM (%)	Current Yield (%)	Fitch Rating	Callable
Corp	Deere & CO	134.29	7.125	3-Mar-2031	4.638	5.306	A	No

This price quote indicates that Deere's 7.125% notes have a market price of 134.29 (134.29% of face value), resulting in a yield to maturity of 4.638%.

a.   Assuming that these notes were originally issued at par value, what does the market price reveal about interest rate changes since Deere issued its notes? (Assume that Deere's credit rating has remained the same.)

b.   Does the change in interest rates since the issuance of these notes affect the amount of interest expense that Deere reports in its income statement? Explain.

c.   How much cash would Deere have to pay to repurchase the 7.125% notes at the quoted market price of 134.29. (Assume no interest is owed when Deere repurchases the notes.) How would the repurchase affect Deere's current income?

d.   Assuming that the notes remain outstanding until their maturity, at what market price will the notes sell on their due date in 2031?

E8-34. **Computing Present Values of Single Amounts and Annuities** **(LO2)**
Refer to Tables 1 and 2 in Appendix A near the end of the book to compute the present value for each of the following amounts:
a. $90,000 received 10 years hence if the annual interest rate is:
   1. 8% compounded annually.
   2. 8% compounded semiannually.
b. $1,000 received at the end of each year for the next eight years discounted at 10% compounded annually.
c. $600 received at the end of each six months for the next 15 years if the interest rate is 8% per year compounded semiannually.
d. $500,000 received 10 years hence discounted at 10% per year compounded annually.

E8-35. **Analyzing and Reporting Financial Statement Effects of Bond Transactions** **(LO2)**
On January 1, 2009, Trueman Corporation issued $600,000 of 20-year, 11% bonds for $554,860, yielding a market (yield) rate of 12%. Interest is payable semiannually on June 30 and December 31. (a) Confirm the bond issue price. (b) Indicate the financial statement effects using the template for (1) bond issuance, (2) semiannual interest payment and discount amortization on June 30, 2009, and (3) semiannual interest payment and discount amortization on December 31, 2009.

E8-36. **Analyzing and Reporting Financial Statement Effects of Bond Transactions** **(LO2)**
On January 1, 2009, Verrecchia Company issued $400,000 of 5-year, 13% bonds for $446,329, yielding a market (yield) rate of 10%. Interest is payable semiannually on June 30 and December 31. (a) Confirm the bond issue price. (b) Indicate the financial statement effects using the template for (1) bond issuance, (2) semiannual interest payment and premium amortization on June 30, 2009, and (3) semiannual interest payment and premium amortization on December 31, 2009.

PROBLEMS

P8-37. **Interpreting Term Structures of Coupon Rates and Yield Rates** **(LO2)**

The Pepsi Bottling Group (PBG)

The Pepsi Bottling Group reports $4,788 million of long-term debt outstanding as of December 2007 in the following schedule to its 10-K report.

Short-term Borrowings and Long-term Debt

Short-Term Borrowings ($ millions)	2007	2006
Current maturities of long-term debt and capital leases	$ 7	$ 17
Other short-term borrowings	240	357
	$247	$374

Long-Term Debt ($ millions)	2007	2006
5.63% (6.4% effective rate) senior notes due 2009	$1,300	$1,300
4.63% (4.6% effective rate) senior notes due 2012	1,000	1,000
5.00% (5.2% effective rate) senior notes due 2013	400	400
4.13% (4.4% effective rate) senior notes due 2015	250	250
5.50% (5.4% effective rate) senior notes due 2016	800	800
7.00% (7.1% effective rate) senior notes due 2029	1,000	1,000
Capital lease obligations	9	33
Other (average rate 6.9%)	29	13
	4,788	4,796
SFAS 133 adjustment.	—	(13)
Unamortized discount, net.	(11)	(12)
Current maturities of long-term debt and capital leases	(7)	(17)
	$4,770	$4,754

continued

continued from prior page

Debt Covenants Certain of our senior notes have redemption features and non-financial covenants that will, among other things, limit our ability to create or assume liens, enter into sale and lease-back transactions, engage in mergers or consolidations and transfer or lease all or substantially all of our assets. Additionally, certain of our credit facilities and senior notes have financial covenants consisting of the following:

- Our debt to capitalization ratio should not be greater than .75 on the last day of a fiscal quarter when PepsiCo's ratings are A− by S&P and A3 by Moody's or higher. Debt is defined as total long-term and short-term debt plus accrued interest plus total standby letters of credit and other guarantees less cash and cash equivalents not in excess of $500 million. Capitalization is defined as debt plus shareholders' equity plus minority interest, excluding the impact of the cumulative translation adjustment.

- Our debt to EBITDA ratio should not be greater than five on the last day of a fiscal quarter when PepsiCo's ragings are less than A- by S&P or A3 by Moody's. EBITDA is defined as the last four quarters of earnings before depreciation, amortization, net interest expense, income taxes, minority interest, net other non-operating expenses and extraordinary items.

- New secured debt should not be greater than 15 percent of our net tangible assets. Net tangible assets are defined as total assets less current liabilities and net intangible assets.

As of December 29, 2007 we were in compliance with all debt covenants.

As of December 2008, the price of the $1,000 million 7% senior notes due 2029 follows (from Capital IQ):

Maturity Date	Issuer	Security Type	Seniority	Coupon	Offer Date	Amt. Outstanding ($mm)	Current Price	Current Yield
Mar-01-2029	Pepsi Bottling Group (NYSE: PBG)	Corporate Debentures	Senior Unsecured	7.000	Jul-01-1999	1,000.00	98.919	7.060

Required

a. PBG reports current maturities of long-term debt of $7 million as part of short-term debt. Why is this amount reported that way? PBG reports $1,300 million of long-term debt due in 2009. What does this mean? Is this amount important to our analysis of Pepsi Bottling Group? Explain.

b. The $1,000 million 7% senior notes maturing in 2029 are priced at 98.919 (98.919% of face value, or $989.19 million) as of December 2008, resulting in a yield to maturity of 7.06%. Assuming that the credit rating of PBG has not changed, what does the pricing of this 7% coupon bond imply about interest rate changes since PBG issued the bond?

c. PBG identifies a number of financial covenants relating to its long-term debt. Describe each of these covenants and how they affect our financial analysis.

d. PBG reports an unamortized discount of $11 million. How does a discount arise and what effect will its amortization have on reported interest expense?

P8-38. Interpreting Debt Footnotes on Interest Rates and Interest Expense (LO2)

CVS Corporation discloses the following as part of its long-term debt footnote in its 10-K.

CVS Corporation (CVS)

BORROWING AND CREDIT AGREEMENTS
Following is a summary of the Company's borrowings as of the respective balance sheet dates.

continued

continued from prior page

In millions	Dec. 29, 2007	Dec. 30, 2006
Commercial paper	$2,085.0	$1,842.7
3.875% senior notes due 2007	—	300.0
4.0% senior notes due 2009	650.0	650.0
Floating rate notes due 2010	1,750.0	—
5.75% senior notes due 2011	800.0	800.0
4.875% senior notes due 2014	550.0	550.0
6.125% senior notes due 2016	700.0	700.0
5.75% senior notes due 2017	1,750.0	—
6.25% senior notes due 2027	1,000.0	—
8.52% ESOP notes due 2008	44.5	82.1
6.302% Enhanced Capital Advantage Preferred Securities	1,000.0	—
Mortgage notes payable	7.3	11.7
Capital lease obligations	145.1	120.9
	10,481.9	5,057.4
Less: Short-term debt	(2,085.0)	(1,842.7)
Current portion of long-term debt	(47.2)	(344.3)
	$8,349.7	$2,870.4

CVS also discloses the following information.

Interest expense, net—Interest expense was $468.3 million, $231.7 million and $117.0 million, and interest income was $33.7 million, $15.9 million and $6.5 million in 2007, 2006 and 2005, respectively. Interest paid totaled $468.2 million in 2007, $228.1 million in 2006 and $135.9 million in 2005.

Maturities of long-term debt—The aggregate maturities of long-term debt for each of the five years subsequent to December 29, 2007 are $47.2 million in 2008, $653.0 million in 2009, $1.8 billion in 2010, $803.9 million in 2011 and $1.0 billion in 2012.

The price of the $1,750 million 5.75% senior notes due 2017 as of December 2008 follows (from Capital IQ):

Maturity Date	Issuer	Security Type	Seniority	Coupon	Offer Date	Amt. Outstanding ($mm)	Current Price	Current Yield
Jun-01-2017	CVS Caremark (NYSE: CVS)	Corporate Debentures	Senior Unsecured	5.750	May-22-2007	1,750.00	86.539	7.960

Required

a. What is the average coupon rate (interest paid) and the average effective rate (interest expense) on CVS' long-term debt? (*Hint:* Use the disclosure for interest expense.)

b. Does your computation of the coupon rate in part *a* seem reasonable given the footnote disclosure relating to specific bond issues? Explain.

c. Explain how the amount of interest paid can differ from the amount of interest expense recorded in the income statement.

d. On its 2007 balance sheet, CVS reports current maturities of long-term debt of $47.2 million as part of short-term debt. Why is this amount reported that way? CVS reports $1.8 billion of long-term debt maturing in 2010. What does this mean? Is this amount important to our analysis of CVS? Explain.

e. The $1,750 million 5.75% senior unsecured debentures maturing in 2017 are priced at 86.539 (86.539% of face value, or $1,514 million) as of December 2008, resulting in a yield to maturity of 7.96%. Assuming that the credit rating of CVS has not changed, what does the pricing of this 5.75% coupon bond imply about interest rate changes since CVS issued the bond?

P8-39.   Analyzing Debt Terms, Yields, Prices, and Credit Ratings   (LO2, 3)
Reproduced below is the long-term debt footnote from the 10-K report of Southwest Airlines.

Long-Term Debt (In millions)	2007	2006
7⅞% Notes due 2007	$ —	$ 100
French Credit Agreements due 2012	32	37
6½% Notes due 2012	386	369
5¼% Notes due 2014	352	336
5¾% Notes due 2016	300	300
5⅛% Notes due 2017	311	300
French Credit Agreements due 2017	94	100
Pass Through Certificates	480	—
7⅜% Debentures due 2027	103*	100
Capital leases	52	63
	2,110	1,705
Less current maturities	41	122
Less debt discount and issuance costs	19	16
	$2,050	$1,567

*The carrying value of these debentures is 103 while the face value is 100. The
company marks these debentures to market each period because the debentures
are hedged with interest-rate swaps. The swap and the debentures are both marked
to market, where any gains and losses offset each other.

As of December 31, 2007, aggregate annual principal maturities of debt and capital leases (not
including amounts associated with interest rate swap agreements and interest on capital leases)
for the five-year period ending December 31, 2012, were $40 million in 2008, $42 million in
2009, $50 million in 2010, $44 million in 2011, $418 million in 2012, and $1.5 billion thereafter.

Reproduced below is a summary of the market values of the Southwest Airlines' bonds maturing from
2012 to 2027 (from Capital IQ).

Maturity Date	Security Type	Coupon	Offer Date	Amt. Outstanding ($mm)	Current Price	Yield
Mar-01-2012	Corporate Debentures	6.500	Feb-26-2002	385.00	97.290	7.450
Oct-01-2014	Corporate Debentures	5.250	Sep-14-2004	350.00	83.164	9.024
Mar-01-2027	Corporate Debentures	7.375	Feb-25-1997	100.00	82.409	9.408

Required

a.   What is the amount of long-term debt reported on Southwest's 2007 balance sheet? What are the
scheduled maturities for this indebtedness? Why is information relating to a company's scheduled
maturities of debt useful in an analysis of its financial condition?

b.   Southwest reported $119 million in interest expense in its 2007 income statement. In the note to its
statement of cash flows, Southwest indicates that the cash portion of this expense is $63 million.
What could account for the difference between interest expense and interest paid? Explain.

c.   Southwest's long-term debt is rated "BBB+" by Fitch and similarly by other credit rating
agencies. What factors would be important to consider in attempting to quantify the relative
riskiness of Southwest compared with other borrowers? Explain.

d.   Southwest's $385 million 6.5% notes traded at 97.290, or 97.29% of par, as of December 2008.
What is the market value of these notes on that date? How is the difference between this market
value and the $385 million face value reflected in Southwest's financial statements? What effect
would the repurchase of this entire note issue have on Southwest's financial statements? What
does the 97.290 price tell you about the general trend in interest rates since Southwest sold this
bond issue? Explain.

e.   Examine the yields to maturity of the three bonds in the table above. What relation do we observe
between these yields and the maturities of the bonds? Also, explain why this relation applies in
general.

P8-40 **Analyzing Notes, Yields, Financial Ratios, and Credit Ratings** **(LO2, LO3)**

Comcast Corporation reports long-term senior notes totaling over $31 billion in its 2007 10-K. Following are selected ratios from Exhibit 8.6 computed for Comcast Corp. utilizing its 2007 data.

EBITA/Average assets	6.95%
EBITA/Interest expense	3.40
EBITA margin	41.70%
Operating margin	16.57%
(Funds from operations + Interest expense)/Interest expense	4.84
Funds from operations/Debt	28.07%
Debt/EBITDA	2.43
Debt/Book capitalization	31.39%

Required

This debt is rated "Baa" by Moody's, which is a lower medium grade. Examine the ratios provided above. *(Hint:* Compare Comcast's ratios to the ratio values reported in Exhibit 8.6.) What factors do you believe contribute to Comcast's credit rating being less than stellar?

MANAGEMENT APPLICATIONS

MA8-41. **Coupon Rate versus Effective Rate** **LO2**

Assume that you are the CFO of a company that intends to issue bonds to finance a new manufacturing facility. A subordinate suggests lowering the coupon rate on the bond to lower interest expense and to increase the profitability of your company. Is the rationale for this suggestion a good one? Explain.

MA8-42. **Ethics and Governance: Bond Covenants** **(LO2)**

Because lenders do not have voting rights like shareholders do, they often reduce their risk by invoking various bond covenants that restrict the company's operating, financing and investing activities. For example, debt covenants often restrict the amount of debt that the company can issue (in relation to its equity) and impose operating restrictions (such as the ability to acquire other companies or to pay dividends). Failure to abide by these restrictions can have serious consequences, including forcing the company into bankruptcy and potential liquidation. Assume that you are on the board of directors of a company that issues bonds with such restrictions. What safeguards can you identify to ensure compliance with those restrictions?

Module Nine

Reporting and Analyzing Owner Financing

LEARNING OBJECTIVES

LO1 Describe and illustrate accounting for contributed capital, including stock sales and repurchases, and equity-based compensation. (p. 9-4)

LO2 Explain and illustrate accounting for earned capital, including cash dividends, stock dividends, and comprehensive income. (p. 9-15)

LO3 Describe accounting for equity carve outs and convertible debt. (p. 9-24)

HEWITT ASSOCIATES

Hewitt Associates is a leading global provider of human resource benefits, outsourcing, and consulting services. It employs over 20,000 workers based in 33 countries. Hewitt helps its clients generate greater value from their employees by developing strategies to address human resource challenges, improve workforce performance, and streamline human resources operations. Hewett's business has evolved over the past six decades, and it continues to extend, expand and create new human resources services that focus on the clients' changing workforce-related needs and challenges.

Hewitt is organized into three business segments: Benefits Outsourcing, Human Resource Business Process Outsourcing (HR BPO), and Consulting. Each segment helps clients develop, implement and deliver strategies and programs for effective human resources design and administration. Each segment also aims to help clients manage the complex human elements necessary to acquire, develop, motivate and retain the talent required to meet business objectives. Hewitt currently has more than 300 benefits outsourcing clients, 32 large, multi-service clients, a number of smaller single-service clients in HR BPO, and over 3,000 consulting clients, many of which are *Global 1000* companies.

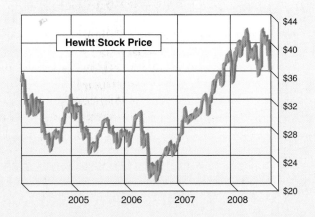

Hewitt's value lies not in plant assets, such as land and buildings, but in the knowledge capital of its employees, most of whom are Hewitt shareholders. This module considers how shareholders' investment is accounted for on a company's financial statements. We consider common stock features, stock options, share issuances, share repurchases, and dividend payments.

Hewitt has one class of stock. Of the 750 million shares that have been authorized for issuance, 130 million have been issued to date. It also has restricted stock and restricted stock units. This stock is awarded to employees as incentive compensation. As further incentive, it offers employee stock options. This module explains and assesses these various forms of equity-based compensation.

Hewitt has repurchased over 36 million shares of its stock at a purchase price of nearly $1.2 billion. Many companies routinely repurchase their common stock as it is the best use of excess cash when there exist no better outside investment opportunities. Some companies repurchase their stock to offset the dilutive effect of stock-based compensation programs. This module explains and analyzes stock repurchases. The module also discusses a variety of equity transactions under the general heading of equity carve outs and convertibles. These transactions include several methods by which companies seek to unlock hidden value for the benefit of their shareholders.

Source: Hewitt Associates, 2008 Form 10-K; *The Wall Street Journal*, January 2009.

A company finances its assets through operating cash flows or it taps one or both of the following sources: either it borrows funds or it sells stock to shareholders. On average, companies obtain about half of their external financing from borrowed sources and the other half from shareholders. This module describes the issues relating to stockholders' equity, including the accounting for stock transactions (sales and repurchases of stock, dividends, stock-based compensation, and convertible securities). We also discuss equity carve outs, a process by which companies can unlock substantial shareholder value via spin-offs and split-offs of business units into separate companies. Finally, we discuss the accumulated other comprehensive income component of stockholders' equity.

When a company issues stock to the public, it records the receipt of cash (or other assets) and an increase in stockholders' equity, representing the shareholders' investment in the company. The increase in cash and equity is equal to the market price of the stock on the issue date multiplied by the number of shares sold.

Like bonds, stockholders' equity is accounted for at *historical cost*. Consequently, the company's financial statements do not reflect fluctuations in the market price of the stock subsequent to its issuance. The company's stock price results from market transactions that involve outside parties and not the company. However, if the company repurchases and/or resells shares of its own stock, the balance sheet will be affected because those transactions involve the company.

There is an important difference between accounting for stockholders' equity and accounting for transactions involving assets and liabilities: *there is never any gain or loss reported on the purchase and sale of a company's own stock or the payment of dividends to its shareholders.* Instead, these "gains and losses" are reflected as increases and decreases in stockholders' equity.

The typical balance sheet has two broad categories of stockholders' equity:

1. **Contributed capital** These accounts report the proceeds received by the issuing company from original stock issuances. It often includes common stock, preferred stock, and additional paid-in capital. Netted against these contributed capital accounts is treasury stock, the amounts paid to repurchase shares of the issuer's stock from its investors, less the proceeds from the resale of such shares. Collectively, these accounts are referred to as contributed capital (or *paid-in capital*).

2. **Earned capital** This section consists of (a) retained earnings, which represent the cumulative income and losses of the company, less any dividends to shareholders, and (b) accumulated other comprehensive income (AOCI), which includes changes to equity that have not yet impacted income and are, therefore, not reflected in retained earnings.

Exhibit 9.1 illustrates the stockholders' equity section of Hewitt's balance sheet (both contributed capital and earned capital). Hewitt's balance sheet reports three equity accounts that make up contributed capital: common stock, additional paid-in capital, and treasury (repurchased) stock. Hewitt's balance sheet also reports two earned capital accounts: retained earnings and accumulated other comprehensive income (loss).

EXHIBIT 9.1 Stockholders' Equity from Hewitt's Balance Sheet		
Stockholders' Equity (In thousands except for share amounts)	September 30, 2008	September 30, 2007
Class A common stock, par value $0.01 per share, 750,000,000 shares authorized, 130,390,880 and 127,672,253 issued, 94,227,120 and 107,126,309 shares outstanding as of September 30, 2008 and 2007, respectively	$ 1,304	$ 1,277
Additional paid-in capital	1,579,077	1,472,409
Cost of common stock in treasury, 36,163,760 and 20,545,944 shares of Class A common stock as of September 30, 2008 and 2007, respectively	(1,183,427)	(597,200)
Retained earnings	206,558	38,144
Accumulated other comprehensive income, net	46,690	123,382
Total stockholders' equity	$ 650,202	$1,038,012

Contributed Capital and *Earned Capital* brackets are shown at left.

We discuss contributed capital and earned capital in turn. For each section, we provide a graphic that displays the part of stockholders' equity in the balance sheet impacted by the discussion of that section.

CONTRIBUTED CAPITAL

Contributed capital represents the cumulative cash inflow that the company has received from the sale of various classes of stock, less the net cash that it has paid out to repurchase its stock from the market. The contributed capital of Hewitt is highlighted in the following graphic.

Stockholders' Equity (In thousands except for share amounts)	September 30, 2008	September 30, 2007
Class A common stock, par value $0.01 per share, 750,000,000 shares authorized, 130,390,880 and 127,672,253 issued, 94,227,120 and 107,126,309 shares outstanding as of September 30, 2008 and 2007, respectively	$ 1,304	$ 1,277
Additional paid-in capital	1,579,077	1,472,409
Cost of common stock in treasury, 36,163,760 and 20,545,944 shares of Class A common stock as of September 30, 2008 and 2007, respectively	(1,183,427)	(597,200)
Retained earnings	206,558	38,144
Accumulated other comprehensive income, net	46,690	123,382
Total stockholders' equity	$ 650,202	$1,038,012

In 2008, Hewitt's contributed capital consists of par value and additional paid-in capital for the 130,390,880 shares of its common stock. Its contributed capital is reduced by the cost of treasury stock (36,163,760 repurchased shares).

Classes of Stock

There are two general classes of stock: preferred and common. The difference between the two lies in the legal rights conferred upon each class.

Preferred Stock

Preferred stock generally has preference, or priority, with respect to common stock. Two usual preferences are:

1. **Dividend preference** Preferred shareholders receive dividends on their shares before common shareholders do. If dividends are not paid in a given year, those dividends are normally forgone. However, some preferred stock contracts include a *cumulative provision* stipulating that any

LO1 Describe and illustrate accounting for contributed capital, including stock sales and repurchases.

forgone dividends (dividends in *arrears*) must first be paid to preferred shareholders, together with the current year's dividends, before any dividends are paid to common shareholders.

2. **Liquidation preference** If a company fails, its assets are sold (liquidated) and the proceeds are paid to the creditors and shareholders, in that order. Shareholders, therefore, have a greater risk of loss than creditors. Among shareholders, the preferred shareholders receive payment in full before common shareholders. This liquidation preference makes preferred shares less risky than common shares. Any liquidation payment to preferred shares is normally at par value, although sometimes the liquidation is specified in excess of par; called a *liquidating value*.

To illustrate the typical provisions contained in preferred stock agreements, consider the following footnote disclosure from Fortune Brands, Inc. (2008 10-K).

> **$2.67 Convertible Preferred Stock—Redeemable at Company's Option** We have 60 million authorized shares of Preferred stock. There were 178,504 and 187,347 shares of the $2.67 Convertible Preferred stock issued and outstanding at December 31, 2008 and 2007, respectively . . . The holders of $2.67 Convertible Preferred stock are entitled to cumulative dividends, three-tenths of a vote per share together with holders of common stock . . . [and] preference in liquidation over holders of common stock of $30.50 per share plus accrued dividends and to convert each share of Convertible Preferred stock into 6.601 shares of common stock . . . The Company may redeem the Convertible Preferred stock at a price of $30.50 per share, plus accrued dividends. The Company paid cash dividends of $2.67 per share in the aggregate amount of $0.5 million, $0.5 million and $0.6 million in each of the years ended December 31, 2008, 2007 and 2006.

Following are several important features of Fortune Brands' convertible preferred stock:

- Holders of convertible preferred are entitled to $2.67 dividends per share; during 2008, the company paid dividends on preferred shares amounting to $476,606, computed as 178,504 shares $\times$ $2.67, which Fortune Brands rounds off to $0.5 million.

- Each share of convertible preferred stock is entitled to 3/10 of a vote per share.

- Holders of convertible preferred have a preference in liquidation over common shareholders amounting to $30.50; this means that they receive $30.50 per share in liquidation before common shareholders receive a payment.

- Each share of convertible preferred is convertible into 6.601 shares of common stock. Upon conversion, the preferred shareholder tenders each share to the company and receives 6.601 shares of common. Subsequent to conversion, then, the shareholder loses preferences accorded to preferred shareholders (for example, in dividends and liquidation) as well as the $2.67 of dividends per share. Instead, the shareholder is now able to participate in the wealth creation of the company with unlimited upside potential both for dividends and share price appreciation.

- Fortune Brands has an option to redeem each share at a price of $30.50; upon redemption, the preferred shareholder will receive that cash amount and will surrender that share to the company.

Fortune Brands' convertible preferred shares carry a dividend $2.67 per share. This preferred dividend returns about 8.75% to the preferred shareholders ($2.67/$30.50 preferred stock price), which compares favorably with the $1.72 of dividends per share paid to its common shareholders in 2008 (which is a return of 4.22% based on year-end stock price of $40.75). Generally, preferred stock can be an attractive investment for shareholders seeking higher dividend yields, especially when tax laws wholly or partially exempt such dividends from taxation. (In comparison, interest payments received by debt holders are not tax exempt.)

In addition to the sorts of conversion features outlined above, preferred shares sometimes carry a *participation feature* that allows preferred shareholders to share ratably with common stockholders in dividends. The dividend preference over common shares can be a benefit when dividend payments are meager, but a fixed dividend yield limits upside potential if the company performs exceptionally well. A participation feature can overcome this limitation.

IFRS INSIGHT Preferred Stock under IFRS

Under IFRS, preferred stock (called *preference shares*) is classified according to its underlying characteristics. Preference shares are classified as equity if they are not redeemable, or redeemable at the option of the issuer. Preference shares are classified as liabilities if the company must redeem the shares (mandatorily redeemable) or if they are redeemable at the option of the shareholder. Accounting for payments to preference shareholders follows from the balance sheet classification: cash paid out is recorded as interest expense or dividends, when the shares are classified as liabilities or equity, respectively.

Common Stock

Hewitt has one class of common stock, Class A, which has the following important characteristics:

- Hewitt's Class A common stock has a par value of $0.01 per share. **Par value** is an arbitrary amount set by company organizers at the time of formation and has no relation to, or impact on, the stock's market value. Generally, par value has no substance from a financial reporting or financial statement analysis perspective (there are some legal implications, which are usually minor). Its main impact is in specifying the allocation of proceeds from stock issuances between the two contributed capital accounts on the balance sheet: common stock and additional paid-in capital, as we describe below.

- Hewitt has 750 million shares of stock that have been **authorized** for issuance. The company cannot issue (sell) more shares than have been authorized. So, if more shares are needed, say for an acquisition or for one of its various stock purchase programs, it must first get additional authorization by its shareholders.

- To date, Hewitt's management has **issued** (sold) 130,390,880 shares of stock. The number of issued shares is a cumulative amount. As of 2007, Hewitt had issued 127,672,253 shares of stock and it issued an additional 2,718,627 (130,390,880 − 127,672,253) shares in 2008.

- Hewitt has repurchased 36,163,760 shares from its shareholders. These shares are currently held in the company's treasury, hence the name treasury stock. These shares neither have voting rights nor do they receive dividends.

- The number of **outstanding** shares is equal to the issued shares less treasury shares. There were 94,227,120 (130,390,880 − 36,163,760) shares outstanding at the end of 2008.

Accounting for Stock Transactions

We analyze the accounting for stock transactions in this section, including the accounting for stock issuances and repurchases.

Stock Issuance

Companies issue stock to obtain cash and other assets for use in their business. Stock issuances increase assets (cash) by the issue proceeds: the number of shares sold multiplied by the price of the stock on the issue date. Equity increases by the same amount, which is reflected in contributed capital accounts. If the stock has a par value, the common stock account increases by the number of shares sold multiplied by its par value. The additional paid-in capital account increases for the remainder. Stock can also be issued as "no-par" or as "no-par with a stated value." For no-par stock, the common stock account is increased by the entire proceeds of the sale and no amount is assigned to additional paid-in capital. For no-par stock with a stated value, the stated value is treated just like par value, that is, common stock is increased by the number of shares multiplied by the stated value, and the remainder is assigned to the additional paid-in capital account.

To illustrate, assume that Hewitt issues 100,000 shares of its $0.01 par value common stock at a market price of $43 cash per share. This stock issuance has the following financial statement effects:

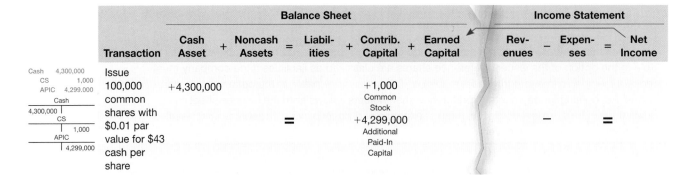

Cash 4,300,000
CS 1,000
APIC 4,299,000

	Cash	
4,300,000		

	CS	
		1,000

	APIC	
		4,299,000

Specifically, the stock issuance affects the financial statements as follows:

1. Cash increases by $4,300,000 (100,000 shares × $43 per share)
2. Common stock increases by the par value of shares sold (100,000 shares × $0.01 par value = $1,000)
3. Additional paid-in capital increases by the $4,299,000 difference between the issue proceeds and par value ($4,300,000 − $1,000)

Once shares are issued, they are traded in the open market among investors. The proceeds of those sales and their associated gains and losses, as well as fluctuations in the company's stock price subsequent to issuance, do not affect the issuing company and are not recorded in its accounting records.

Refer again to the following report of common stock on Hewitt's balance sheet:

IFRS Alert
Stock terminology commonly differs between IFRS and GAAP. Common stock is called *share capital* and additional paid-in capital (APIC) is called *share premium*. Accounting for these items is identical under both systems.

(In thousands except for share amounts)	September 30, 2008	September 30, 2007
Class A common stock, par value $0.01 per share, 750,000,000 shares authorized, 130,390,880 and 127,672,253 issued, 94,227,120 and 107,126,309 shares outstanding as of September 30, 2008 and 2007, respectively	$ 1,304	$ 1,277
Additional paid-in capital	1,579,077	1,472,409

Hewitt's Class A common stock, in the amount of $1,304 thousand, equals the number of shares issued multiplied by the common stock's par value: 130,390,880 × $0.01 = $1,303,908.80 (rounded to $1,304 thousand). Total proceeds from its stock issuances are $1,580,381,000, the sum of the par value and additional paid-in capital. This implies that Class A shares were sold, on average, for $12.12 per share ($1,580,381,000/130,390,880 shares).

RESEARCH INSIGHT **Stock Issuance and Stock Returns**

Research shows that, historically, companies issuing equity securities experience unusually low stock returns for several years following those offerings. Evidence suggests that this poor performance is partly due to overly optimistic estimates of long-term growth for these companies by equity analysts. That optimism causes offering prices to be too high. This over-optimism is most pronounced when the analyst is employed by the brokerage firm that underwrites the stock issue. There is also evidence that companies manage earnings upward prior to an equity offering. This means the observed decrease in returns following an issuance likely reflects the market's negative reaction, on average, to lower earnings, especially if the company fails to meet analysts' forecasts.

Stock Repurchase

Hewitt has repurchased over $1.1 billion of its common stock. One reason a company repurchases shares is because it believes that the market undervalues them. The logic is that the repurchase sends a favorable signal to the market about the company's financial condition that positively impacts its share price and, thus, allows it to resell those shares for a "gain." Any such gain on resale is *never* reflected in the income statement. Instead, any excess of the resale price over the repurchase price is added to additional paid-in capital. GAAP prohibits companies from reporting gains and losses from stock transactions with their own shareholders.

Another reason companies repurchase shares is to offset the dilutive effects of an employee stock option program. When an employee exercises stock options, the number of shares outstanding increases. These additional shares reduce earnings per share and are, therefore, viewed as *dilutive*. In response, many companies repurchase an equivalent number of shares in a desire to keep outstanding shares constant.

A stock repurchase reduces the size of the company (cash declines and, thus, total assets decline). A repurchase has the opposite financial statement effects from a stock issuance. That is, cash is reduced by the price of the shares repurchased (number of shares repurchased multiplied by the purchase price per share), and stockholders' equity is reduced by the same amount. The reduction in equity is achieved by increasing a contra equity (negative equity) account called **treasury stock,** which reduces stockholders' equity. Thus, when the treasury stock contra equity account increases, total equity decreases.

When the company subsequently reissues treasury stock there is no accounting gain or loss. Instead, the difference between the proceeds received and the original purchase price of the treasury stock is reflected as an increase or decrease to additional paid-in capital.

To illustrate, assume that 3,000 common shares of Hewitt previously issued for $43 are repurchased for $40. This repurchase has the following financial statement effects:

		Balance Sheet						Income Statement		
Transaction	Cash Asset	+ Noncash Assets	= Liabil- ities	+ Contrib. Capital	+ Earned Capital		Rev- enues	– Expen- ses	= Net Income	
Repurchase 3,000 com- mon shares for $40 cash per share	−120,000 Cash		=	−120,000 Treasury Stock				–	=	

TS 120,000
    Cash 120,000

TS
120,000 |
    Cash
    | 120,000

Assets (cash) and equity both decrease. Treasury stock (a contra equity account) increases by $120,000, which reduces stockholders' equity by that amount.

Assume that these 3,000 shares are subsequently resold for $42 cash per share. This resale of treasury stock has the following financial statement effects:

		Balance Sheet						Income Statement		
Transaction	Cash Asset	+ Noncash Assets	= Liabil- ities	+ Contrib. Capital	+ Earned Capital		Rev- enues	– Expen- ses	= Net Income	
Reissue 3,000 trea- sury (com- mon) shares for $42 cash per share	+126,000 Cash		=	+120,000 Treasury Stock +6,000 Additional Paid-In Capital				–	=	

Cash 126,000
    TS 120,000
    APIC 6,000

Cash
126,000 |
    TS
    | 120,000
    APIC
    | 6,000

Cash assets increase by $126,000 (3,000 shares × $42 per share), the treasury stock account is reduced by the $120,000 cost of the treasury shares issued, and the $6,000 excess (3,000 shares × $2 per share) is reported as an increase in additional paid-in capital. (If the reissue price is below the repurchase price, then additional paid-in capital is reduced until it reaches a zero balance, after which retained earnings are reduced.) Again, there is no effect on the income statement as companies are prohibited from reporting gains and losses from repurchases and reissuances of their own stock.

IFRS Alert
Accounting for stock repurchases under IFRS is similar to GAAP except that IFRS provides little guidance on how to allocate the treasury stock to equity accounts. Thus, repurchases can be recorded as an increase to treasury stock, or as a decrease to common stock and APIC (share capital and premium), retained earnings (reserves), or some combination.

The treasury stock section of Hewitt's balance sheet is reproduced below:

(In thousands except for share amounts)	2008	2007
Cost of common stock in treasury, 36,163,760 and 20,545,944 shares of Class A common stock as of September 30, 2008 and 2007, respectively....	$(1,183,427)	$(597,200)

Hewitt has repurchased a cumulative total of 36,163,760 shares of its common stock for $1,183,427, an average repurchase price of $32.72 per share. This compares with total contributed capital of $1,580,381 ($1,304 + $1,579,077), all $ in 000s, see Exhibit 9.1. Thus, Hewitt has repurchased about 75% of its original contributed capital in dollar terms, which represents 27.7% of contributed capital in terms of shares (36,163,760/130,390,880). Although some of Hewitt's treasury purchases were to meet stock option exercises, it appears that most of these purchases are motivated by a perceived low stock price by Hewitt management.

MANAGERIAL DECISION | **You Are the Chief Financial Officer**

As CFO, you believe that your company's stock price is lower than its real value. You are considering various alternatives to increase that price, including the repurchase of company stock in the market. What are some factors you should consider before making your decision? [Answer, p. 9-29]

Stock-Based Compensation

Common stock has been an important component of executive compensation for decades. The general idea follows: If the company executives own stock they will have an incentive to increase its value. This aligns the executives' interests with those of other shareholders. Although the strength of this alignment is the subject of much debate, its logic compels boards of directors of most American companies to use stock-based compensation.

Employee Stock Options

One popular incentive plan is to give an employee the right to purchase common stock at a pre-specified price for a given period of time. This is called a *stock option plan*. Options allow employees to purchase a predetermined number of shares at a fixed price (called the *exercise price* or *strike price*) for a specified period of time. Because there is a good chance of future stock price increases, options are valuable to employees when they receive them, even if the exercise price is exactly equal to the stock's market price the day the options are awarded. The intrinsic value of an option is the difference between the current stock price and the options' strike price. When an option is issued with a strike price equal to the current stock price, which is common practice among U.S. companies, the option has a $0 intrinsic value.

Companies use employee stock options (ESO) as a means to compensate employees and to better align the interests of employees and shareholders. The notion is that employees will work harder to increase their company's stock price when they can benefit directly from future price increases. Because an employee with stock options can purchase stock at a fixed price and resell it at the prevailing (expectedly higher) market price, the options create the possibility of a future gain. Unlike cash compensation, options give employees the same incentives as shareholders—to increase stock price.

Over the past 30 years, use of stock options has skyrocketed and options now make up the bulk of many executive compensation packages. Despite their popularity, stock options have a downside—they can create incentives for employees to increase stock price at any cost and by any means, including misstating earnings and engaging in transactions whose sole purpose is to inflate stock price. Options can also induce managerial myopia—managers want stock price to increase, at least till they can exercise their options and capture their gains.

Until recently, companies were not required to record the value of stock options as compensation expense. Previous GAAP rules (APB 25) held that options had value only to the extent that the predetermined purchase price (exercise price) was less than the market stock price on the date that the options were granted to the employee. If a company set the exercise price equal to the market price on the date of grant, the view was that nothing of value had been given to the employee. This meant that no compensation expense was ever reported on such options. This reduced the quality of reported earnings because companies sheltered their income statements merely by setting the exercise price equal to the market price of the stock on the date of grant. Analysts and investors have long expressed serious concerns about accounting for stock options and the amount of unrecorded compensation expense tied to options.

Under considerable pressure and controversy, the FASB issued a pronouncement (SFAS 123R) that applies to stock options granted after 2005. Under the pronouncement, companies must expense the fair value of options and recognize an equivalent increase in stockholders' equity (to the additional paid-in capital account).

To illustrate the accounting for stock options, assume that Hewitt grants an employee 100,000 stock options with a strike price of $26, which will vest over a four-year period. The vesting period is the time over which an employee gains ownership of the shares, commonly over three to seven years. Employees usually acquire ownership ratably over time, such as 1/4 each year over four years, or acquire full (100%) vesting after the vesting period ends, called *cliff vesting*. Under SFAS 123R, Hewitt recognizes the fair value of the stock options granted over the employees' service period (generally interpreted as the options' vesting period).

A first step, then, is to determine the "fair value" of the option. SFAS 123R does not specify the method companies must use to estimate fair value, but most companies use the *Black-Scholes model* to estimate the value of exchange-traded options. This model, developed by professors Fisher Black and Myron Scholes, has six inputs, two of which are observable (the company's current stock price and the option's strike price). Companies must estimate the other four model inputs: option life, risk-free interest rate, stock price volatility, and dividend payout rate. These six inputs yield an estimate of the option's fair value. It is important we recognize that management selects the model inputs and, thus, can exercise some discretion over the reported fair value. The option's value computed using Black-Scholes increases with the estimated option life, risk-free interest rate, and stock price volatility; it decreases with the estimated dividend payout. (Free online Black-Scholes option calculators abound, which simplifies fair value estimation.) For analysis purposes, we can partly assess the quality of the reported fair values by comparing a company's model inputs to industry standards and to historical measures (of stock price volatility, for example).

Some companies have recently switched from the common Black-Scholes model to a more complicated binomial valuation method (currently fewer than 1,000 of the 17,000 publicly-traded U.S. companies use the binomial method). The basic mathematics of the Black-Scholes and binomial methods are identical, but the binomial method allows companies to insert additional assumptions into Black-Scholes and some claim that this provides a more accurate fair value. It also generally provides a lower fair value estimate than the Black-Scholes model.

Returning to our Hewitt example, assume that the Black-Scholes fair value of the 100,000 options granted is $1,000,000. Thus, Hewitt records fair value compensation expense of $250,000 each year (fair value of $1,000,000 spread over the four-year vesting period) and its additional paid-in capital increases by $250,000 each year (or $1,000,000 over the four years). Two points are worth noting. First, Hewitt expenses the entire fair value of the options granted ($1,000,000) regardless of whether the employee actually exercises the options. Second, subsequent changes in the options' value are *not* recognized in financial statements. Thus, the stock option expense and the increase to additional paid-in capital reflect the ESO fair value measured at the grant date.

As with any expense, there are tax consequences to stock option expense. That is, net income is affected on an after-tax basis—each dollar of expense is offset by a reduction in tax expense. Granting stock options creates a book-tax timing difference because the expense is recognized in the income statement at the grant date but is deductible for income tax purposes at the exercise date (see Module 5 for more details about book-tax timing differences). The general approach is that a deferred tax asset is recorded at the statutory rate for this timing difference. This difference reverses when the options are exercised. (Most companies grant *nonqualified stock options* (NQSOs), which are taxed like other compensation but *not* until the options are exercised; when NQSOs are exercised, the options' intrinsic value is taxed as ordinary income to the employee and the employer takes a corresponding tax deduction for the intrinsic value.)

Continuing with our Hewitt example, the company reports a deferred tax asset to recognize the future tax deduction of the compensation payment. Specifically, Hewitt reports a deferred tax benefit of \$87,500 (\$250,000 × 0.35) in each of the four years of the vesting period to reflect the expected reduction in future tax liability when the options are exercised. Thus, the after-tax stock option compensation expense is \$162,500 (computed as \$250,000 − \$87,500). Each year, Hewitt increases the deferred tax asset account (on the balance sheet) by \$87,500. The balance grows until the fourth year when the deferred tax asset balance is \$350,000. When the employee exercises the options and Hewitt realizes the tax benefits, the company reduces taxes payable and reverses the deferred tax asset previously set up.[1] The financial statement effects template would record these transactions as follows in each of the four years of the vesting period.

		Balance Sheet				Income Statement		
Transaction	Cash Asset	+ Noncash Assets =	Liabil- ities	+ Contrib. Capital	+ Earned Capital	Rev- enues	− Expen- ses =	Net Income
Years 1,2,3,4: Grant 100,000 stock options with fair value of \$10 per share, vesting over 4 years		+87,500 Deferred Tax Asset =		+250,000 Additional Paid-In Capital	−162,500 Retained Earnings		+250,000 Wages Expense −87,500 Tax Expense =	−162,500 Net Income
At exercise: 100,000 stock options exer- cised at a \$26 exercise price	+2,600,000 Cash	=		+2,600,000 Additional Paid-In Capital			− =	
At exercise: Tax effect of the exercised stock options		−350,000 Deferred Tax Asset =	−350,000 Taxes Payable				− =	

Left-margin journal entries:

```
WE     250,000
DTA     87,500
  TE            87,500
  APIC         250,000
         WE
250,000 |
        DTA
 87,500 |
         TE
        |  87,500
        APIC
        |  250,000

Cash  2,600,000
  APIC        2,600,000
        Cash
2,600,000 |
        APIC
        |  2,600,000

TP     350,000
  DTA          350,000
         TP
350,000 |
        DTA
        |  350,000
```

Hewitt's following footnote discloses many details of its stock option activities. Hewitt reports that 772,620 options were granted in 2008 with an average strike price of \$37.53. These options had a fair value of \$12.81 per share. The company also reports how many of its options outstanding have already vested and could potentially be exercised. (Recall that outstanding options affect the company's diluted EPS calculation, see Module 5.)

Stock Options The Committee may grant both incentive stock options and nonqualified stock options to purchase shares of Class A common stock. Subject to the terms and provisions of the Plan, options may be granted to participants, as determined by the Committee, provided that incentive stock options may not be granted to non-employee directors. The option price is determined by the Committee, provided that for options issued to participants in the United States, the option price may not be less than 100% of the fair market value of the shares on the date the option is granted and no option may be exercisable later than the tenth anniversary of its grant. The nonqualified stock options generally vest in equal annual installments over a period of four years. The fair value used to determine compensation expense for the years ended September 30, 2008, 2007 and 2006 was estimated at the date of grant using a Black-Scholes option pricing model with the following weighted average assumptions:

---

[1] The tax benefit the company receives is based on the options' intrinsic value (current stock price less strike price) on the exercise date. Often, the exercise-date intrinsic value is greater than the grant-date fair value. Recall that deferred taxes are recorded based on grant-date fair value. Thus, the tax benefit received is often larger than the deferred tax asset on the company's balance sheet. In that case, any tax benefit in excess of the deferred tax asset is included in additional paid-in capital and not in net income. The excess tax benefit is classified as cash from financing activities on the statement of cash flows.

continued from prior page

	2008	2007	2006
Expected volatility	26.61%	28.15%	28.89%
Risk-free interest rate.	3.83	4.42	4.73
Expected life (in years)	6.03	6.23	5.68
Dividend yield.	0%	0%	0%

The Company used the "simplified method," as defined in SEC Staff Accounting Bulletin ("SAB") No. 107, to determine the expected life assumption for all of its options. The Company continues to use the "simplified method," as permitted by SAB N0. 110, as it does not believe that it has sufficient historical exercise data to provide a reasonable basis upon which to estimate expected life due to the limited time its equity shares have been publicly traded. The following table summarizes stock option activity during 2008, 2007 and 2006:

	2008		2007		2006	
	Options	Weighted Average Exercise Price	Options	Weighted Average Exercise Price	Options	Weighted Average Exercise Price
Outstanding at beginning of fiscal year	7,611,095	$24.12	9,664,292	$23.73	10,364,866	$23.75
Granted.	772,620	37.53	937,650	25.66	331,600	22.80
Exercised	(1,847,653)	23.61	(2,377,618)	22.78	(647,740)	22.44
Forfeited	(199,426)	29.65	(197,847)	24.95	(183,863)	24.23
Expired	(52,709)	23.69	(415,382)	25.79	(200,571)	26.49
Outstanding at end of fiscal year	6,283,927	25.75	7,611,095	24.12	9,664,292	23.73
Exercisable options at end of fiscal year	5,271,903	$24.53	6,758,976	$23.94	8,677,556	$23.66

The weighted average estimated fair value of employee stock options granted during 2008, 2007 and 2006 was $12.81, $9.74 and $8.49 per share, respectively. These stock options were granted at exercise prices equal to the current fair market value of the underlying stock on the grant date.

Option grants and option exercises both affect the statement of cash flows. At grant, there is no cash inflow or outflow. However, the noncash stock option compensation expense is added back as a reconciling item in the operating section of the statement of cash flows (indirect method). Hewitt reported an add-back on its 2008 statement of cash flows of $48,345,000.

An interesting, often underappreciated, fact is that stock option expense now pervades the income statement. Below is a footnote from Cisco System's 2008 10-K that details the allocation of its stock option expense to cost of sales, research and development, sales and marketing expenses, and general and administrative expenses.

Valuation and Expense Information Under SFAS 123 (R) Share-based compensation expense recognized under SFAS 123(R) consists primarily of expenses for stock options, stock purchase rights, restricted stock, and restricted stock units granted to employees. The following table summarizes employee share-based compensation expense (in millions):

Years Ended	July 26, 2008	July 28, 2007	July 29, 2006
Cost of sales—product	$ 40	$ 39	$ 50
Cost of sales—service	108	104	112
Employee share-based compensation expense in cost of sales.	148	143	162
Research and development	295	289	346
Sales and marketing.	434	392	427
General and administrative.	148	107	115
Employee share-based compensation expense in operating expenses	877	788	888
Total employee share-based compensation expense	$1,025	$931	$1,050

Restricted Stock and Restricted Stock Units

Many companies, including Hewitt, compensate employees with restricted stock instead of with stock options. Under a restricted stock plan, the company transfers shares to the employee, but the shares are restricted in that they cannot be sold until the end of a vesting period. Restricted stock units differ from restricted stock in two key ways: first, the company does not distribute shares of stock to employees until certain conditions are met; and second, the number of shares ultimately given to employees is typically a function of their performance relative to specified targets. Hewitt describes its restricted stock unit plan (called *performance share units*) as follows:

Performance share units (PSUs) are intended to provide an incentive for achieving specific performance objectives over a defined period. Performance share units represent an obligation of the Company to deliver at the end of the performance period, a number of shares ranging from zero to 200% of the initial number of units granted, depending on performance against objective, pre-established financial metrics. The Company assumes that such goals will be achieved for shares which vest upon meeting certain financial performance conditions, and these goals are evaluated quarterly. If such goals are not met or it is probable the goals will not be met, no compensation cost is recognized and any recognized compensation cost is reversed.

During fiscal 2008, 112,900 PSUs were granted to certain Hewitt leadership which is included in the restricted stock unit amount disclosed above. The financial metrics for these grants are based on Hewitt's corporate performance in fiscal 2008 and are calculated to be paid out at a rate of 195%. These grants are scheduled to vest in one-third increments on September 30, 2008, 2009 and 2010. During fiscal 2007, 137,000 PSUs were granted to certain Hewitt leadership which is included in the restricted stock unit amount disclosed above. The financial metrics for these grants were based on Hewitt's fiscal 2007 corporate performance and are to be paid out at a rate of 180%. The fiscal 2007 grants are scheduled to cliff vest on September 30, 2010. During fiscal year 2006, 186,111 performance-based restricted stock grants were awarded which is included in the restricted stock unit amount disclosed above. The Company evaluated the goals under the fiscal 2006 performance plan in fiscal 2006 and it was determined that it was probable that the goals would not be met. No compensation expense was recognized for these grants during fiscal 2006. The final measurement period for this plan is fiscal year 2008. The Company's final evaluation of the results confirm that no payout will be made on the fiscal 2006 grants.

The accounting for restricted stock and restricted stock units is similar to that which we describe for stock options. Specifically, compensation expense is recognized at an amount equal to the value of the shares given to employees as those shares are earned. The consequent decline in retained earnings is offset by an increase in paid-in capital. Stockholders' equity is, therefore, unaffected. Accounting for restricted stock is illustrated in the following template:

		Balance Sheet						Income Statement		
Transaction	Cash Asset	+ Noncash Assets	= Liabil- ities	+ Contrib. Capital	+ Earned Capital		Rev- enues	− Expen- ses	= Net Income
Year 1: Company issues 100 shares of $10 par restricted stock with a market value of $30 per share, vesting ratably over 6 years			=	+1,000 Common Stock +2,000 Additional Paid-In Capital −3,000 Deferred Compensation			−		=
Years 1,2,3,4,5,6: Record compensation expense for year			=	+500 Deferred Compensation	−500 Retained Earnings			− 500 Wage Expense	= −500

Margin notes:

DC   3,000
  CS   1,000
  APIC   2,000

DC	
3,000	
	CS
	1,000
	APIC
	2,000

WE   500
  DC   500

WE	
500	
	DC
	500

The company records the restricted stock grants as a share issuance exactly as if the shares were sold. That is, the common stock account increases by the par value of the shares and additional paid-in capital increases for the remainder of the share value. However, instead of cash received, the company records a deferred compensation (contra equity) account for the value of the shares that have not yet been issued. This reduces equity. Thus, granting restricted shares leaves the total dollar amount of equity unaffected.

Subsequently, the value of shares given to employees is treated as compensation expense and recorded over the vesting period. Each year, the deferred compensation account is reduced by the vested shares and wage expense is recorded, thus reducing retained earnings. Total equity is unaffected by this transaction as the reduction of the deferred compensation contra equity account (thereby increasing stockholders' equity) is exactly offset by the decrease in retained earnings. The remaining deferred compensation account decreases total stockholders' equity until the end of the vesting period when the total restricted stock grant has been recognized as wage expense. Equity is, therefore, never increased when restricted stock is issued.

MID-MODULE REVIEW 1

Part 1 Assume that BearingPoint (BGPTQ) reported the following transactions relating to its stock accounts in 2009.

Jan   15   Issued 10,000 shares of $5 par value common stock at $17 cash per share
Mar   31   Purchased 2,000 shares of its own common stock at $15 cash per share.
June 25   Reissued 1,000 shares of its treasury stock at $20 cash per share.

Use the financial statement effects template to identify the effects of these stock transactions.

Solution

Part 2 BearingPoint reports the following table in its 10-K, which is related to its stock compensation plan.

	Number of Options	Weighted Average Exercise Price	Weighted Average Remaining Contractual Life (Years)	Aggregate Intrinsic Value
Outstanding at December 31, 2006.	36,037,278	$11.10		
Granted.	30,000	$ 5.93		
Forfeited	(5,397,609)	$10.96		
Outstanding at December 31, 2007	30,669,669	$11.11		
Vested or expected to vest at December 31, 2007	30,624,891	$11.12	5.0	$ —
Exercisable at December 31, 2007	30,041,149	$11.17	4.9	$ —

As of December 31, 2007, there was $368 million of total unrecognized compensation cost, net of expected forfeitures, related to nonvested options. That cost is expected to be recognized over a weighted-average period of one year.

Required

a. Explain the terms "Granted," "Exercised," and "Lapsed." What is the meaning of "Weighted Average Exercise Price"?

b. Explain how the total unrecognized compensation cost of $368 is computed.

Solution

a. *Granted* relates to the number of shares under option that have been awarded to employees to the year. *Exercised* refers to the number of shares that employees have purchased that were previously under option. *Lapsed* relates to the number of shares under option that are no longer exercisable because the options were not exercised before they expired. The "Weighted Average Exercise Price" is the average price at which employees can purchase shares of stock that are under option, weighted by the number of shares at each exercise price.

b. Compensation cost is computed as the total value of employee stock options spread over the vesting period. For example, if BearingPoint grants employees stock options with an estimated value of $1 billion that vest over a four-year period, the expense that is recognized over the subsequent four years is $250 million per year. The "unrecognized compensation cost" is that portion of the total estimated value of the stock options that has not yet been recognized as expense in the income statement.

EARNED CAPITAL

LO2 Explain and illustrate accounting for earned capital, including cash dividends, stock dividends, and comprehensive income.

We now turn to the earned capital portion of stockholders' equity. Earned capital represents the cumulative profit that the company has retained. Recall that earned capital increases each period by income earned and decreases by any losses incurred. Earned capital also decreases by dividends paid to shareholders. Not all dividends are paid in the form of cash. Companies can pay dividends in many forms, including property (land, for example) or additional shares of stock. We cover both cash and stock dividends in this section. Earned capital also includes the positive or negative effects of accumulated other comprehensive income (AOCI). The earned capital of Hewitt is highlighted in the following graphic.

Stockholders' Equity (In thousands except for share amounts)	September 30, 2008	September 30, 2007
Class A common stock, par value $0.01 per share, 750,000,000 shares authorized, 130,390,880 and 127,672,253 issued, 94,227,120 and 107,126,309 shares outstanding as of September 30, 2008 and 2007, respectively	$ 1,304	$ 1,277
Additional paid-in capital	1,579,077	1,472,409
Cost of common stock in treasury, 36,163,760 and 20,545,944 shares of Class A common stock as of September 30, 2008 and 2007, respectively	(1,183,427)	(597,200)
Retained earnings	206,558	38,144
Accumulated other comprehensive income, net	46,690	123,382
Total stockholders' equity	$ 650,202	$1,038,012

Cash Dividends

Many companies, but not all, pay dividends. Their reasons for dividend payments are varied. Most dividends are paid in cash on a quarterly basis. The following is a description of Hewitt's dividend policy from its 10-K.

Outsiders closely monitor dividend payments. It is generally perceived that the level of dividend payments is related to the company's expected long-term recurring income. Accordingly, dividend increases are usually viewed as positive signals about future performance and are accompanied by stock price increases. By that logic, companies rarely reduce their dividends unless absolutely necessary because dividend reductions are often met with substantial stock price declines.

Financial Effects of Cash Dividends

Cash dividends reduce both cash and retained earnings by the amount of the cash dividends paid. To illustrate, assume that Hewitt declares and pays cash dividends in the amount of $10 million. The financial statement effects of this cash dividend payment are as follows:

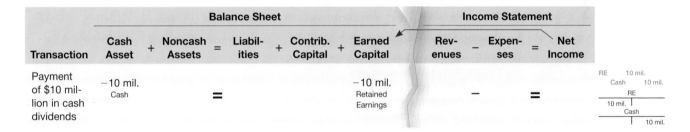

Dividend payments do not affect net income. They directly reduce retained earnings and bypass the income statement.

Dividends on preferred stock have priority over those on common stock, including unpaid prior years' preferred dividends (called *dividends in arrears*) when preferred stock is cumulative. To illustrate, assume that a company has 15,000 shares of $50 par value, 8% preferred stock outstanding; assume that the preferred stock is cumulative, which means that any unpaid dividends cumulate and must be paid before common dividends. The company also has 50,000 shares of $5 par value common stock outstanding. During its first three years in business, assume that the company declares $20,000 dividends in the first year, $260,000 of dividends in the second year, and $60,000 of dividends in the third year. Cash dividends paid to each class of stock in each of the three years follows:

	Preferred Stock	Common Stock
Year 1—$20,000 cash dividends paid		
Current year dividend (15,000 shares × $50 par × 8%; but only $20,000 paid, leaving $40,000 in arrears)	$20,000	
Balance to common		$ 0
Year 2—$260,000 cash dividends paid		
Dividends in arrears from Year 1 ([15,000 shares × $50 par × 8%] − $20,000)	40,000	
Current year dividend (15,000 shares × $50 par × 8%)	60,000	
Balance to common		160,000
Year 3—$60,000 cash dividends paid		
Current year dividend (15,000 shares × $50 par × 8%)	60,000	
Balance to common		0

MID-MODULE REVIEW 2

Assume that Accenture (ACN) has outstanding 10,000 shares of $100 par value, 5% preferred stock and 50,000 shares of $5 par value common stock. During its first three years in business, assume that Accenture declared no dividends in the first year, $300,000 of cash dividends in the second year, and $80,000 of cash dividends in the third year.

a. If preferred stock is cumulative, determine the dividends paid to each class of stock for each of the three years.
b. If preferred stock is noncumulative, determine the dividends paid to each class of stock for each of the three years.

Solution

a.

Cumulative Preferred Stock	Preferred Stock	Common Stock
Year 1—$0 cash dividends paid..........................	$ 0	$ 0
Year 2—$300,000 cash dividends paid		
Dividends in arrears from Year 1 ($1,000,000 × 5%)........	50,000	
Current year dividend ($1,000,000 × 5%)	50,000	
Balance to common		200,000
Year 3—$80,000 cash dividends paid		
Current year dividend ($1,000,000 × 5%)	50,000	
Balance to common		30,000

b.

Noncumulative Preferred Stock	Preferred Stock	Common Stock
Year 1—$0 cash dividends paid..........................	$ 0	$ 0
Year 2—$300,000 cash dividends paid		
Current year dividend ($1,000,000 × 5%)	50,000	
Balance to common		250,000
Year 3—$80,000 cash dividends paid		
Current year dividend ($1,000,000 × 5%)	50,000	
Balance to common		30,000

Stock Dividends and Splits

Dividends need not be paid in cash. Many companies pay dividends in the form of additional shares of stock. Companies can also distribute additional shares to their stockholders with a stock split. We cover both of these distributions in this section.

Stock Dividends

When dividends are paid in the form of the company's stock, retained earnings are reduced and contributed capital is increased. However, the amount by which retained earnings are reduced depends on the proportion of the outstanding shares distributed to the total outstanding shares on the dividend distribution date. Exhibit 9.2 illustrates two possibilities depending on whether stock dividends are classified as small stock dividends or large stock dividends. The break point between small and large is 20–25% of the outstanding shares. When the number of additional shares issued as a stock dividend is so great that it could materially reduce share price, the transaction is akin to a stock split. The 20–25% guideline is used as a rule of thumb to distinguish material stock price effects.

For *small stock dividends,* retained earnings are reduced by the *market* value of the shares distributed (dividend shares × market price per share), and par value and contributed capital together are increased by the same amount. For *large stock dividends,* retained earnings are reduced by the *par* value of the shares distributed (dividend shares × par value per share), and common stock is increased by the same amount (no change to additional paid-in capital).

EXHIBIT 9.2 Analysis of Stock Dividend Effects		
Percentage of Outstanding Shares Distributed	**Retained Earnings**	**Contributed Capital**
Less than 20-25% (*small stock dividend treated as a dividend*)	Reduce by **market value** of shares distributed	Common stock increased by: Dividend shares × Par value per share; Additional paid-in capital increased for the balance
More than 20-25% (*large stock dividend treated as a stock split*)	Reduce by **par value** of shares distributed	Common stock increased by: Dividend shares × Par value per share

To illustrate the financial statement effects of stock dividends, assume that BearingPoint has 1 million shares of $5 par common stock outstanding. It then declares a small stock dividend of 15% of the outstanding shares (1,000,000 shares × 15% = 150,000 shares) when the market price of the stock is $30 per share. This small stock dividend has the following financial statement effects:

	Balance Sheet						Income Statement		
Transaction	Cash Asset	+ Noncash Assets	= Liabil- ities	+ Contrib. Capital	+ Earned Capital		Rev- enues	− Expen- ses	= Net Income
Distribute 150,000 shares with a market value of $4.5 mil. as a *small* stock dividend			=	+750,000 Common Stock +$3,750,000 Additional Paid-In Capital	−$4,500,000 Retained Earnings			−	=

RE 4.5 mil.
   CS 0.75 mil.
   APIC 3.75 mil.

RE
4.5 mil. |
  CS
   | 0.75 mil.
  APIC
   | 3.75 mil.

The company reduces retained earnings by $4,500,000, which equals the market value of the small stock dividend (150,000 shares × $30 market price per share). The increase in contributed capital is split between the par value of $750,000 (150,000 shares × $5 par value) and additional paid-in capital ($3,750,000). Similar to cash dividend payments, stock dividends, whether large or small, never impact income.

Next, assume that instead, BearingPoint declares a large stock dividend of 70% of the 1 million outstanding common ($5 par) shares when the market price of the stock is $30 per share. This large stock dividend is treated like a stock split and has the following financial statement effects:

	Balance Sheet						Income Statement		
Transaction	Cash Asset	+ Noncash Assets	= Liabil- ities	+ Contrib. Capital	+ Earned Capital		Rev- enues	− Expen- ses	= Net Income
Distribute 700,000 shares as a *large* stock dividend			=	+$3,500,000 Common Stock	−$3,500,000 Retained Earnings			−	=

RE 3.5 mil.
   CS 3.5 mil.

RE
3.5 mil. |
  CS
   | 3.5 mil.

The company's retained earnings declines by $3,500,000, which equals the par value of the large stock dividend (700,000 shares × $5 par value per share). Common stock is increased by the par value of $3,500,000. There is no effect on additional paid-in capital since large stock dividends are reported at par value.

For both large and small stock dividends, companies are required to show comparable shares outstanding for all prior periods for which earnings per share (EPS) is reported in the statements. The reasoning is that a stock dividend has no effect on the ownership percentage of each common stockholder. As such, to show a dilution in reported EPS would erroneously suggest a decline in profitability when it is simply due to an increase in shares outstanding.

Stock Splits

A stock split is a proportionate distribution of shares and, as such, is similar in substance to a large stock dividend. A typical stock split is 2-for-1, which means that the company distributes one additional share for each share owned by a shareholder. Following the distribution, each investor owns twice as many shares, so that their percentage ownership in the company is unchanged.

A stock split is not a monetary transaction and, as such, there are no financial statement effects. However, companies must disclose the new number of shares outstanding for all periods presented in the financial statements. Further, many states require that the par value of shares be proportionately adjusted as well (for example, halved for a 2-for-1 split).

If state law requires that par value not be reduced for a stock dividend, this event should be described as a *stock split affected in the form of a dividend*. The following disclosure from John Deere's 2007 annual report provides such an example:

> **Stock Split in Form of Dividend** On November 14, 2007, a special meeting of stockholders was held authorizing a two-for-one stock split effected in the form of a 100 percent stock dividend to holders of record on November 26, 2007, distributed on December 3, 2007. All share and per share data (except par value) have been adjusted to reflect the effect of the stock split for all periods presented. The number of shares of common stock issuable upon exercise of outstanding stock options, vesting of other stock awards, and the number of shares reserved for issuance under various employee benefit plans were proportionately increased in accordance with terms of the respective plans.

MID-MODULE REVIEW 3

Assume that the stockholders' equity of Ceridian Corporation at December 31, 2009, follows.

5% preferred stock, $100 par value, 10,000 shares authorized; 4,000 shares issued and outstanding.........................	$ 400,000
Common stock, $5 par value, 200,000 shares authorized; 50,000 shares issued and outstanding.......................	250,000
Paid-in capital in excess of par value-Preferred stock..............	40,000
Paid-in capital in excess of par value-Common stock.............	300,000
Retained earnings	656,000
Total stockholders' equity	$1,646,000

Use the template to identify the financial statement effects for each of the following transactions that occurred during 2010:

Apr. 1   Declared and issued a 100% stock dividend on all outstanding shares of common stock when the market value of the stock was $11 per share.

Dec. 7   Declared and issued a 3% stock dividend on all outstanding shares of common stock when the market value of the stock was $7 per share.

Dec. 31   Declared and paid a cash dividend of $1.20 per share on all outstanding shares.

Solution

Transaction	Cash Asset	+	Noncash Assets	=	Liabil-ities	+	Contrib. Capital	+	Earned Capital		Rev-enues	−	Expen-ses	=	Net Income
Apr. 1: Declare and issue 100% stock dividend; stock is $11 per share				=			+250,000 Common Stock		−250,000[1] Retained Earnings			−		=	
Dec. 7: Declare and issue 3% stock dividend; stock is $7 per share				=			+15,000 Common Stock +6,000 Additional Paid-In Capital		−21,000[2] Retained Earnings			−		=	
Dec. 31: Declare and pay cash dividend of $1.20 per share	−123,600 Cash			=					−123,600[3] Retained Earnings			−		=	

RE 250,000
  CS 250,000

RE
250,000 |
  CS
  | 250,000

RE 21,000
  CS 15,000
  APIC 6,000

RE
21,000 |
  CS
  | 15,000
  APIC
  | 6,000

RE 123,600
  Cash 123,600

RE
123,600 |
  Cash
  | 123,600

[1] This large stock dividend reduces retained earnings at the par value of shares distributed (50,000 shares × 100% × $5 par value = $250,000). Contributed capital (common stock) increases by the same amount.

[2] This small stock dividend reduces retained earnings at the market value of shares distributed (3% × 100,000 shares × $7 per share = $21,000). Contributed capital increases by the same amount ($15,000 to common stock and $6,000 to paid-in capital). Note that the number of common shares outstanding on December 7 was 100,000—the large stock dividend on April 7 doubled the number of common stock outstanding.

[3] At the time of the cash dividend, there are 103,000 shares outstanding. The cash paid is, therefore, 103,000 shares × $1.20 per share = $123,600.

Accumulated Other Comprehensive Income

Comprehensive income is a more inclusive notion of company performance than net income. It includes all recognized changes in equity (assets less liabilities) that occur during a period except those resulting from contributions by and distributions to owners. It's important to note that comprehensive income includes both net income and other items.

Specifically, comprehensive income includes (and net income excludes) foreign currency translation adjustments, unrealized changes in market values of available-for-sale securities, pension liability adjustments, and changes in market values of certain derivative investments. Comprehensive income, therefore, includes the effects of economic events that are often outside of management's control. Accordingly, some assert that net income measures management's performance, while comprehensive income measures company performance. Each period, net income or loss is added to retained earnings so that the balance sheet maintains a running total of the company's cumulative net income and losses (less any dividends paid out). In the same way, each period, comprehensive income items that are not included in net income are added to a balance sheet account called Accumulated Other Comprehensive Income (or Accumulated Other Comprehensive Loss if the comprehensive items are losses). This account maintains a running balance of the cumulative differences between net income and comprehensive income.

Hewitt reports the following components of its accumulated other comprehensive income in its 10-K report:

IFRS Alert
IFRS does not use the term "other comprehensive income" but reports the same in a *statement of recognized income and expenses* (SoRIE). As with GAAP's other comprehensive income, SoRIE includes all changes to equity, absent transactions with owners.

($ thousands)	Foreign Currency Translation Adjustments	Minimum Pension Liability	Unrealized Gains (Losses) on Investments	Retirement Plans	Net Unrealized Losses on Hedging Transactions	Accumulated Other Comprehensive Income
As of September 30, 2005	$ 72,320	$(2,397)	$ (135)	$ —	$ —	$ 69,788
Other comprehensive income.	2,760	2,397	127	—	—	5,284
As of September 30, 2006	75,080	—	(8)	—	—	75,072
Other comprehensive income.	49,827	—	8	—	—	49,835
Adjustment to initially apply SFAS No. 158 (net of tax)	—	—	—	(1,525)	—	(1,525)
As of September 30, 2007	124,907	—	—	(1,525)	—	123,382
Other comprehensive loss	(42,173)	—	(4,273)	(23,834)	(6,412)	(76,692)
As of September 30, 2008	$ 82,734	$ —	$(4,273)	$(25,359)	$(6,412)	$ 46,690

Hewitt's accumulated other comprehensive income includes the four following items that affect stockholders' equity and are not reflected in net income:

1. **Foreign currency translation adjustment,** $82,734,000. This is the unrecognized gain on assets and liabilities denominated in foreign currencies. A gain implies that the $US has weakened relative to foreign currencies; such as when assets denominated in foreign currencies translate to more $US. We discuss the effects of foreign currency translation adjustments on accumulated other comprehensive income in more detail below.

2. **Unrealized gains (losses) on available-for-sale securities,** $(4,273,000). Unrealized gains and losses on available-for-sale securities are not reflected in net income. Instead, they are accumulated in a separate equity account, AOCI, until the securities are sold.

3. **Retirement Plans,** $(25,359,000). This amount primarily relates to unrealized losses on pension investments or can derive from changes in pension plans that increase the pension liability.

4. **Net Unrealized Losses on Hedging Transactions,** $(6,412,000). Hedging transactions relate to the company's use of financial instruments (derivatives) to hedge exposure to various risks such as fluctuations in foreign currency exchange rates, commodity prices, and interest rates.

We discuss accounting for available-for-sale securities and derivatives in Module 7, pensions in Module 10, and the income statement effects of foreign currency translation adjustments in Module 5. In the next section, we discuss the balance sheet effects of foreign currency translation adjustments, specifically their impact on accumulated other comprehensive income. During 2008, Hewitt reported other comprehensive loss of $76,692,000, which is the sum of the changes in each of the four components of AOCI, as shown on the second-last line on the statement above. This other comprehensive loss when added to Hewitt's net income of $188,142,000 yields comprehensive income for the year of $111,450,000, as we explain later for Exhibit 9.4.

Foreign Currency Translation Effects on Accumulated Other Comprehensive Income

Many companies have international transactions denominated in foreign currencies. They might purchase assets in foreign currencies, borrow money in foreign currencies, and transact business with their customers and suppliers in foreign currencies. Other companies might have subsidiaries whose entire balance sheets and income statements are stated in foreign currencies. Financial statements prepared according to U.S. GAAP must be reported in $US. This means that financial statements of foreign subsidiaries must be translated into $US before they are consolidated with those of the U.S. parent company. This translation process can markedly alter both the balance sheet and income statement. We discuss the income statement effects of foreign currency translation in Module 5 and the balance sheet effects in this section.

Consider a U.S. company with a foreign subsidiary that conducts its business in Euros. The subsidiary prepares its financial statements in Euros. Assume that the $US weakens vis-à-vis the Euro during the current period—that is, each Euro can now purchase more $US. When the balance sheet is translated into $US, the assets and liabilities are reported at higher $US than before the $US weakened. This result is shown in accounting equation format in Exhibit 9.3.[2]

EXHIBIT 9.3 Balance Sheet Effects of Changes in U.S. Dollar to Euro Exchange Rates

Currency	Assets	=	Liabilities	+	Equity
$US weakens.............	Increase	=	Increase	+	Increase
$US strengthens...........	Decrease	=	Decrease	+	Decrease

The amount necessary to balance the accounting equation is reported in equity and is called a **foreign currency translation adjustment**. The *cumulative* foreign currency translation adjustment is included in accumulated other comprehensive income (or loss) as illustrated above for Hewitt. Foreign currency translation adjustments are direct adjustments to stockholders' equity; they do not impact reported net income. Because assets are greater than liabilities for solvent companies, the cumulative translation adjustment is positive when the $US weakens and negative when the dollar strengthens.

Referring to Hewitt's accumulated other comprehensive income table on the previous page, the cumulative foreign currency translation is a gain of $124,907,000 at the beginning of 2008, which shrinks by $42,173,000 during the year to yield a cumulative year-end gain of $82,734,000. The $42,173,000 reduction in Hewitt's equity reflects a strengthening of the $US vis-à-vis the foreign currencies in which Hewitt transacted in 2008. That is, as the $US strengthened, Hewitt's foreign assets and liabilities translated into fewer $US at year-end. This decreased Hewitt's equity. In general, unrealized losses (or gains) remain in other accumulated comprehensive income as long as the company owns the foreign subsidiaries to which the losses relate. The translation adjustments fluctuate between positive and negative amounts as the value of the $US fluctuates. However, when a subsidiary is sold, any remaining foreign currency translation adjustment (positive or negative) is immediately recognized in current income along with other gains or losses arising from sale of the subsidiary.

Summary of Stockholders' Equity

The statement of shareholders' equity summarizes the transactions that affect stockholders' equity during the period. This statement reconciles the beginning and ending balances of important stockholders' equity accounts. Hewitt's statement of stockholders' equity is in Exhibit 9.4.

Hewitt's statement of shareholders' equity reveals the following key transactions for 2008:

- Line 2: Hewitt's retained earnings increased by $188,142,000 from net income (the company paid no dividends in 2008).

- Lines 3–6: Accumulated other comprehensive income began the year with a positive balance of $123,382,000. Other comprehensive income or loss recorded during the year included an unrealized loss on available-for-sale securities of $4,273,000, deferred losses on retirement plans of $23,834,000, unrealized losses on hedging (derivative) securities of $6,412,000, and a foreign currency translation adjustment loss of $42,173,000. Together, these four items decreased the accumulated other comprehensive income by $76,692,000 to a balance of $46,690,000 by year-end. We see that none of these items affected reported income for the year.

- Line 7: Hewitt reported $48,345,000 of compensation expense related to employee stock options and restricted stock plans during the year. This expense is included in net income and, therefore, reduces retained earnings. The fair-value of options granted or restricted shares issued increases additional paid-in capital. The effect of stock compensation plans is to reallocate capital from retained earnings to paid-in capital.

IFRS Alert
The IFRS counterpart to AOCI is the *General Reserve* and other reserve accounts. Reserves is the IFRS term for all equity accounts other than contributed capital. Retained earnings is typically the largest reserve. The components of AOCI are reported individually as additional reserve accounts rather than as one account.

[2] We assume that the company translates the subsidiary's financial statements using the more common **current rate method**, which is required for subsidiaries operating independently from the parent. Under the current rate method, most items in the balance sheet are translated using exchange rates in effect at the period-end consolidation date and the income statement is translated using the average exchange rate for the period. An alternative procedure is the *temporal method*, which is covered in advanced accounting courses.

EXHIBIT 9.4   Hewitt's Statement of Stockholders' Equity

(In thousands, except for shares)	Class A Common Shares Shares	Amount	Additional Paid-in Capital	Treasury Stock, at Cost Shares	Amount	Retained Earnings	Accumulated Other Comprehensive Income	Total
1 Balance at September 30, 2007	127,672,253	$1,277	$1,472,409	20,545,944	$ (597,200)	$ 38,144	$123,382	$1,038,012
Comprehensive income:								
2 Net income	—	—	—	—	—	188,142	—	188,142
Other comprehensive loss:								
3 Unrealized losses on investments, net of tax	—	—	—	—	—	—	(4,273)	(4,273)
4 Retirement plans, net of tax							(23,834)	(23,834)
5 Unrealized gains (losses) on hedging transactions, net of tax							(6,412)	(6,412)
6 Foreign currency translation adjustments, net of tax	—	—	—	—	—	—	(42,173)	(42,173)
Total other comprehensive loss.							(76,692)	(76,692)
Total comprehensive income								111,450
7 Share-based compensation expense	—	—	48,345	—	—	—	—	48,345
8 Excess tax benefits from stock plans.	—	—	14,744	—	—	—	—	14,744
9 Restricted stock unit vesting	938,872	9	(9)	—	—	—	—	—
10 Purchase of Class A shares for treasury	—	—	—	15,617,816	(586,227)	—	—	(586,227)
11 Issuance of Class A shares for employee stock options	1,847,653	18	43,588	—	—	—	—	43,606
12 Net forfeiture of restricted common stock . . .	(67,898)	—	—	—	—	—	—	—
13 Adoption of FIN 48	—	—	—	—	—	(7,036)	—	(7,036)
14 Adoption of EITF 06-02, net of tax.	—	—	—	—	—	(12,692)	—	(12,692)
15 Balance at September 30, 2008.	130,390,880	$1,304	$1,579,077	36,163,760	$(1,183,427)	$206,558	$ 46,690	$ 650,202

- Line 8: Tax benefits (in excess of the deferred tax asset previously recorded) arising from the exercise of employee stock options are recorded as an increase in additional paid-in capital (not as a reduction of tax expense).

- Line 9: As restricted stock vests, the par value of the shares is transferred from additional paid-in capital (its original account) to common stock. During 2008, a total of 938,872 shares vested, resulting in a transfer of $9,389 (938,872 × $0.01) to common stock. (Hewitt reports its balance sheet in $000s, hence the increase of $9 reported in its statement of stockholders' equity.)

- Line 10: Hewitt repurchased 15,617,816 shares of its common stock. Stockholders' equity decreased by the purchase price of $586,227,000 ($37.53 average price), and treasury stock increased by the same amount, which means a greater negative balance as treasury stock is a contra equity account.

- Line 11: Hewitt issued 1,847,653 shares to employees exercising stock options during 2008. The total proceeds of $43,606,000 ($18,000 + $43,588,000) reflects an average purchase price of $23.61 (we also see those numbers in Hewitt's table of stock option activity shown previously).

- Line 12: Employees forfeited 67,898 shares of restricted common stock. There is no dollar amount for this event as the shares were not yet vested. Hence, only the number of shares outstanding decreases.

- Lines 13–14: Hewitt's retained earnings decreased by $19,728,000 as a result of adopting new accounting standards (FIN 48 relates to accounting for uncertainty in tax estimates and EITF 06-02 relates to accounting for employee benefits).

One final point: the financial press sometimes refers to a measure called **book value per share**. This is the net book value of the company that is available to common shareholders, defined as: stockholders' equity less preferred stock (and preferred additional paid-in capital) divided by the number of common shares outstanding (issued common shares less treasury shares). Hewitt's book value per share of its Class A stock at the end of 2008 is computed as: $650,202,000/(130,390,880 shares − 36,163,760 shares) = $6.90 book value per share. In contrast, Hewitt's **market price per share** ranged from $34.40 to $42.22 in the 4th quarter of 2008.

EQUITY CARVE OUTS AND CONVERTIBLES

Corporate divestitures, or **equity carve outs**, are increasingly common as companies seek to augment shareholder value through partial or total divestiture of operating units. Generally, equity carve outs are motivated by the notion that consolidated financial statements often obscure the performance of individual business units, thus complicating their evaluation by outsiders. Corporate managers are concerned that this difficulty in assessing the performance of individual business units limits their ability to reach full valuation. Shareholder value is, therefore, not maximized. In response, conglomerates have divested subsidiaries so that the market can individually price them.

LO3 Describe accounting for equity carve outs and convertible debt.

Sell-Offs

Equity carve outs take many forms. The first and simplest form of divestiture is the outright sale of a business unit, called a **sell-off**. In this case, the company sells its equity interest to an unrelated party. The sale is accounted for just like the sale of any other asset. Specifically, any excess (deficit) of cash received over the book value of the business unit sold is recorded as a gain (loss) on the sale.

To illustrate, in 2008, Hewitt sold its Cyborg business for $42,420,000 cash and recorded a gain on sale of $35,667,000 as disclosed in the following excerpt from its 2008 annual report:

> **Sale of Cyborg** On January 31, 2008, the Company sold the net assets of its Cyborg business ("Cyborg"). Cyborg was acquired in 2003 and provides licensed, processed and hosted payroll software services. Its operations were included in the HR BPO segment. The divestiture is a part of the Company's continued efforts to streamline its HR outsourcing service offerings. The Company recorded a pre-tax gain of $35,667 during the quarter ended March 31, 2008 as a result of the sale.

The financial statement effects of this transaction follow:

- Hewitt received $42,420,000 cash; disclosed in Hewitt's cash flows from investing activities in its statement of cash flows.

- The Cyborg business was carried on Hewitt's balance sheet as an investment with a book value of $6,753,000 million (inferred from the proceeds less gain).

- Hewitt's gain on sale equaled the sale proceeds less the book value: $42,420,000 − 6,753,000 = $35,667,000 gain on sale.

- Hewitt reports the gain on sale in its 2008 income from continuing operations.

- Hewitt subtracts the $35,667,000 gain from net income in its statement of cash flows to compute net cash flows from operations since the transaction generated a noncash operating gain (the $42,420,000 cash inflow is reporting under investing activities).

Spin-Offs

A **spin-off** is a second form of divestiture. In this case, the parent company distributes the subsidiary shares that it owns as a dividend to its shareholders who, then, own shares in the subsidiary directly rather than through the parent company. In recording this dividend, the parent company reduces retained earnings by the book value of the equity method investment, thereby removing the investment in the subsidiary from the parent's balance sheet.

The spin-off of the Kraft Foods subsidiary by Altria is an example of this type of equity carve out. Altria describes its spin-off of Kraft as follows:

> **Kraft Spin-Off** On March 30, 2007 (the "Kraft Distribution Date"), Altria Group, Inc. distributed all of its remaining interest in Kraft on a pro-rata basis to Altria Group, Inc. stockholders of record as of the close of business on March 16, 2007 (the "Kraft Record Date") in a tax-free distribution. The distribution ratio was 0.692024 of a share of Kraft for each share of Altria Group, Inc. common stock outstanding. Altria Group, Inc. stockholders received cash in lieu of fractional shares of Kraft. Following the distribution, Altria Group, Inc. does not own any shares of Kraft.

Altria treats the distribution of its Kraft shares as a dividend, which Altria reports in the following excerpt from its 2007 statement of stockholders' equity.

| (In millions, except per share) | Common Stock | Additional Paid-in Capital | Earnings Reinvested in the Business | Accumulated Other Comprehensive Earnings (Losses) | | | Cost of Repurchased Stock | Total Stock-holders' Equity |
				Currency Translation Adjustments	Other	Total		
Balances, December 31, 2006.................	$935	$6,356	$59,879	$ (97)	$(3,711)	$(3,808)	$(23,743)	$39,619
Comprehensive earnings:								
Net earnings...............................			9,786					9,786
Other comprehensive earnings (losses), net of income taxes:								
Currency translation adjustments............				736		736		736
Change in net loss and prior service cost.......					744	744		744
Change in fair value of derivatrives accounted for as hedges............................					(18)	(18)		(18)
Total other comprehensive earnings............								1,462
Total comprehensive earnings..................								11,248
Adoption of FIN 48 and FAS 13-2			711					711
Exercise of stock options and issuance of other stock awards........................		528					289	817
Cash dividends declared ($3.05 per share).........			(6,430)					(6,430)
Spin-off of Kraft Foods Inc....................			(29,520)	89	2,020	2,109		(27,411)
Balances, December 31, 2007.................	$935	$6,884	$34,426	$728	$ (965)	$ (237)	$(23,454)	$18,554

The $29,520 million book value of the Kraft subsidiary (the amount at which this equity investment is reported on Altria's balance sheet) is removed from Altria's balance sheet when the shares are distributed to Altria's shareholders, and that amount is subtracted from Altria's retained earnings (titled "Earnings Reinvested in the Business"). Altria also removes all amounts relating to Kraft that impacted its Accumulated Other Comprehensive Earnings (a net of $2,109 million). In total, the Kraft spin-off reduced Altria's equity by $27,411 million.

Split-Offs

The **split-off** is a third form of equity carve out. In this case, the parent company buys back its own stock using the shares of the subsidiary company instead of cash. After completing this transaction, the subsidiary is an independent publicly traded company.

The parent treats the split-off like any other purchase of treasury stock. As such, the treasury stock account is increased and the equity method investment account is reduced, reflecting the distribution of that asset. The dollar amount recorded for this treasury stock depends on how the distribution is set up. There are two possibilities:

1. **Pro rata distribution.** Shares are distributed to stockholders on a pro rata basis. Namely, a shareholder owning 10% of the outstanding stock of the parent company receives 10% of the shares of the subsidiary. The treasury stock account is increased by the *book value* of the investment in the subsidiary. The accounting is similar to the purchase of treasury stock for cash, except that shares of the subsidiary are paid to shareholders instead of cash.

2. **Non pro rata distribution.** This case is like a tender offer where individual stockholders can accept or reject the distribution. The treasury stock account is recorded at the *market value* of the shares of the subsidiary distributed. Since the investment account can only be reduced by its book value, a gain or loss on distribution is recorded in the income statement for the difference. (The SEC allows companies to record the difference as an adjustment to additional paid-in capital; the usual practice, as might be expected, is for companies to report any gain as part of income.)

Halliburton's non pro rata split-off of its subsidiary, KBR, Inc., (KBR), provides an example. This transaction is described in the following excerpt from footnotes to Halliburton's 10-K:

KBR Separation In November 2006, KBR completed an initial public offering (IPO), in which it sold approximately 32 million shares of KBR common stock at $17.00 per share. Proceeds from the IPO were approximately $508 million, net of underwriting discounts and commissions and offering expenses. The increase in the carrying amount of our investment in KBR, resulting from the IPO, was recorded in "Paid-in capital in excess of par value" on our consolidated balance sheet at December 31, 2006. On April 5, 2007, we completed the separation of KBR from us by exchanging the 135.6 million shares of KBR common stock owned by us on that date for 85.3 million shares of our common stock. In the second quarter of 2007, we recorded a gain on the disposition of KBR of approximately $933 million, net of tax . . . which is included in income from discontinued operations on the consolidated statement of operations.

Halliburton reports on two key financial statement effects of this split-off transaction:

1. **KBR IPO** It's wholly-owned subsidiary (KBR) sold common stock to outside shareholders, thus increasing its stockholders' equity by the sale proceeds and reducing Halliburton's percentage ownership in that subsidiary. The investment in KBR account that Halliburton carried on its balance sheet increased with the increase in the stockholders' equity of its subsidiary (see Module 7 for a discussion of the equity method of accounting for intercorporate investments). That increase in Halliburton's assets was matched by a corresponding increase in its additional paid-in capital (Halliburton refers to this account as "Paid-in capital in excess of par value").

2. **Split-off of KBR** Halliburton exchanged with its shareholders 135.6 million shares of KBR common stock that it owned for 85.3 million shares of common stock of Halliburton that its shareholders owned. This exchange is treated like the purchase of treasury stock. Because the exchange was on a non-pro rata basis, Halliburton increased the carrying value of the KBR shares to their fair value on the date of exchange, resulting in an after-tax gain on this transaction of $933 million.

This split-off was affected by a tender offer with Halliburton shareholders. Consequently, it is a non-pro rata exchange and is, therefore, valued at market value with a resulting gain.

Analysis of Equity Carve Outs

Sell-offs, spin-offs, and split-offs all involve the divestiture of an operating segment. Although they are one-time occurrences, they can result in substantial gains that can markedly alter the income statement and balance sheet. Consequently, we need to interpret them carefully. This involves learning as many details about the carve out as possible from the annual report, the Management Discussion and Analysis, and other publicly available information.

Following an equity carve out, the parent company loses the cash flows (positive or negative) of the divested business unit. As such, the divestiture should be treated like any other discontinued operation. Any recognized gain or loss from divestiture is treated as a nonoperating activity. The sale price of the divested unit reflects the valuation of *future expected* cash flows by the purchaser and is best viewed as a nonoperating activity. Income (and cash flows) of the divested unit up to the date of sale, however, is part of operations, although discontinued operations are typically segregated.

MID-MODULE REVIEW 4

Assume that BearingPoint announced the split-off of its Canadian subsidiary. BearingPoint reported a gain from the split-off. (1) Describe the accounting for a split-off. (2) Why was BearingPoint able to report a gain on this transaction?

Solution

1. A split-off is like a treasury stock transaction, but instead of repurchasing stock with cash, shares of the parent company owned by the shareholders are exchanged for shares of the subsidiary owned by the parent. If the distribution is non pro rata, the parent can report a gain equal to the difference between the fair value of the subsidiary and its book value on the parent's balance sheet.

2. BearingPoint met the conditions for a split-off as described in part 1, which enabled it to report a gain.

Convertible Securities

Convertible securities are debt and equity securities that provide the holder with an option to convert those securities into other securities. In this section, we consider two specific types of convertibles: convertible debt securities, where debt is converted to common stock, and convertible preferred securities, where preferred stock is converted to common stock.

Convertible Debt Securities

Symantec Corporation had convertible debt transactions in 2003, as explained in the following excerpt from footnotes to its 10-K report:

> **Convertible Subordinated Notes** On October 24, 2001, we completed a private offering of $600 million of 3% convertible subordinated notes due November 1, 2006, the net proceeds of which were $585 million. The notes are convertible into shares of our common stock by the holders at any time before maturity at a conversion price of $17.07 per share, subject to certain adjustments. We had the right to redeem the remaining notes on or after November 5, 2004, at a redemption price of 100.75% of stated principal during the period November 5, 2004 through October 31, 2005. Interest was paid semiannually and we commenced making these payments on May 1, 2002. Debt issuance costs of $16 million related to the notes were being amortized on a straight-line basis through November 1, 2006. We had reserved 70.3 million shares of common stock for issuance upon conversion of the notes. On July 20, 2004, our Board of Directors approved the redemption of all of the outstanding convertible subordinated notes and in September 2004 we sent notice to registered holders that all notes would be redeemed November 5, 2004. As of November 4, 2004 (the day prior to the redemption date), substantially all of the outstanding convertible subordinated notes were converted into 70.3 million shares of our common stock. The remainder was redeemed for cash. Unamortized debt issuance costs of $6 million relative to the converted notes were charged to Capital in excess of par value on the Consolidated Balance Sheet during fiscal 2005.

To summarize, in 2001, Symantec issued $600 million of 3% convertible notes. The noteholders (Symantec's creditors) could convert the notes into 35,149,385 common shares at the initial conversion price of $17.07 ($600,000,000/$17.07 per share = 35,149,385 shares). At any time before October 2005, Symantec could redeem the notes (repay them before maturity and without conversion). In July 2004, Symantec announced that it would exercise its redemption option in November that year. In response, all of the noteholders converted their notes to Symantec common stock. Symantec's statement of stockholders' equity records the effects of the conversion as follows.

(In thousands)	Common Stock		Capital In Excess of Par Value	Accumulated Other Comprehensive Income (Loss)	Retained Earnings	Total Stockholders' Equity
	Shares	Amount				
Conversion of convertible debt . . .	35,142	$352	$593,182	—	—	$593,534

On the conversion date, Symantec's balance sheet carried the notes at $593,534,000. The notes were retired and Symantec issued 35,142,000 shares to the noteholders. The market price of Symantec common stock on November 4, 2005, (the date of conversion) was $18.63. The conversion at $17.07 per share, therefore, made economic sense for the noteholders.

When Symantec originally issued the convertible notes, the balance sheet reported their issue price without consideration of the conversion feature, because a conversion option is *not* valued on the balance sheet unless it is detachable from the security (and can be separately sold). Instead, the convertible debt was recorded just like debt that does not have a conversion feature. Accounting for the conversion of the Symantec bonds is illustrated in the following financial statement effects template.

	Balance Sheet						Income Statement		
Transaction	**Cash Asset**	**+ Noncash Assets**	**= Liabil- ities**	**+ Contrib. Capital**	**+ Earned Capital**		**Rev- enues**	**− Expen- ses**	**= Net Income**
Conversion of Symantec notes into common stock			− 593,534 = Long-Term Debt	+352 Common Stock +593,182 Additional Paid-In Capital			−	=	

LTD 593,534
   CS   352
   APIC 593,182

LTD
593,534 |
         CS
            | 352
          APIC
              | 593,182

Accounting for the Symantec conversion is straightforward and yields the following effects:

■ The debt's carrying amount is removed from the balance sheet because the debt is retired.

■ Symantec issues 35,142,000 shares of $0.01 par value common stock for an "issue" price of $593,534,000 (book value of bonds); common stock, therefore, increases by $352 million (35,142,000 × $0.01, rounded up), and capital in excess of par value (additional paid-in capital) increases by the amount of $593,182,000.

■ No gain or loss (or cash inflow or outflow) is recorded from the conversion.

Convertible Preferred Stock

Preferred stock can also contain a conversion privilege. Textron provides an example of the latter in its 2009 10-K report:

> **Capital Stock** We have authorization for 15 million shares of preferred stock with no par value and 500 million shares of $0.125 par value common stock. Each share of $2.08 Cumulative Convertible Preferred Stock, Series A ($23.63 approximate stated value) is convertible into 8.8 shares of common stock, and we can redeem it for $50 per share. At the end of 2008, 2007 and 2006, we had approximately 67,000, 72,000 and 147,000 shares, respectively, of $2.08 Cumulative Convertible Preferred Stock, Series A issued with approximately 67,000, 72,000 and 78,000 shares outstanding, respectively.

Accounting for the conversion of preferred stock is essentially the same as that for convertible debt that we describe above: the preferred stock account is removed from the balance sheet and common stock is issued for the dollar amount of the preferred.

Conversion privileges offer an additional benefit to the holder of a security. That is, debtholders and preferred stockholders carry senior positions as claimants in bankruptcy, and also carry a fixed interest payment or dividend yield. Thus, they are somewhat protected from losses and their annual return is guaranteed. With a conversion privilege, debtholders or preferred stockholders can enjoy the residual benefits of common shareholders should the company perform well.

A conversion option is valuable and yields a higher price for the securities than they would other-wise command. However, conversion privileges impose a cost on common shareholders. That is, the higher market price received for convertible securities is offset by the cost imposed on the subordinate (common) securities.

One final note, diluted earnings per share (EPS) takes into account the potentially dilutive effect of convertible securities. Specifically, the diluted EPS computation assumes conversion at the beginning of the year (or when the security is issued if during the year). The earnings available to common shares in the numerator are increased by any forgone after-tax interest expense or preferred dividends, and the additional shares that would have been issued in the conversion, increase the shares outstanding in the denominator (see Module 5).

IFRS INSIGHT Convertible Securities under IFRS

Unlike GAAP, convertible securities (called *compound financial instruments* under IFRS) are split into separate debt and equity components. The idea is that the conversion premium is akin to a call option on the company's stock. This embedded option has a value of its own even if it is not legally detachable. Thus, under IFRS, the proceeds from the issuance are allocated between the liability component (at fair value) and an equity component (the residual amount).

MODULE-END REVIEW

Assume that Express Scripts, Inc., has issued the following convertible debentures: each $1,000 bond is convertible into 200 shares of $1 par common. Assume that the bonds were sold at a discount, and that each bond has a current unamortized discount equal to $150. Using the financial statements effect template, illustrate the effects on the financial statements of the conversion of one of these convertible debentures.

Solution

	Balance Sheet						Income Statement		
Transaction	Cash Asset	+ Noncash Assets	= Liabil- ities	+ Contrib. Capital	+ Earned Capital		Rev- enues	− Expen- ses	= Net Income
Convert a bond with $850 book value into 200 common shares with $1 par value			= −850 Long-Term Debt	+200 Common Stock +650 Additional Paid-In Capital			−		=

LTD | 850
CS | | 200
APIC | | 650

LTD
850 |

CS
| 200

APIC
| 650

GUIDANCE ANSWERS

MANAGERIAL DECISION You Are the Chief Financial Officer

Several points must be considered. (1) Buying stock back reduces the number of shares outstanding, which can prop up earnings per share (EPS). However, foregone earnings from the cash used for repurchases can dampen earnings. The net effect is that EPS is likely to increase because of the reduced shares in the denominator. (2) Another motivation is that, if the shares are sufficiently undervalued (in management's opinion), the stock repurchase and subsequent resale can provide a better return than alternative investments. (3) Stock repurchases send a strong signal to the market that management feels its stock is undervalued. This is more credible than merely making that argument with analysts. On the other hand, company cash is diverted from other investments. This is bothersome if such investments are mutually exclusive either now or in the future.

DISCUSSION QUESTIONS

Q9-1. Define *par value stock*. What is the significance of a stock's par value from an accounting and analysis perspective?

Q9-2. What are the basic differences between preferred stock and common stock? What are the typical features of preferred stock?

Q9-3. What features make preferred stock similar to debt? Similar to common stock?

Q9-4. What is meant by preferred dividends in arrears? If dividends are two years in arrears on $500,000 of 6% preferred stock, and dividends are declared at the end of this year, what amount of total dividends must the company pay to preferred shareholders before paying any dividends to common shareholders?

Q9-5. Distinguish between authorized shares and issued shares. Why might the number of shares issued be more than the number of shares outstanding?

Q9-6. Describe the difference between contributed capital and earned capital. Specifically, how can earned capital be considered as an investment by the company's shareholders?

Q9-7. How does the account "additional paid-in capital" (APIC) arise? Does the amount of APIC reported on the balance sheet relative to the common stock amount provide any information about the financial condition of the company?

Q9-8. Define *stock split*. What are the major reasons for a stock split?

Q9-9. Define *treasury stock*. Why might a corporation acquire treasury stock? How is treasury stock reported in the balance sheet?

Q9-10. If a corporation purchases 600 shares of its own common stock at $10 per share and resells them at $14 per share, where would the $2,400 increase in capital be reported in the financial statements? Why is no gain reported?

Q9-11. A corporation has total stockholders' equity of $4,628,000 and one class of $2 par value common stock. The corporation has 500,000 shares authorized; 300,000 shares issued; and 40,000 shares as treasury stock. What is its book value per share?

Q9-12. What is a stock dividend? How does a common stock dividend distributed to common shareholders affect their respective ownership interests?

Q9-13. What is the difference between the accounting for a small stock dividend and the accounting for a large stock dividend?

Q9-14. Employee stock options potentially dilute earnings per share (EPS). What can companies do to offset these dilutive effects and how might this action affect the balance sheet?

Q9-15. What information is reported in a statement of stockholders' equity?

Q9-16. What items are typically reported under the stockholders' equity category of other comprehensive income (OCI)?

Q9-17. What is the difference between a spin-off and a split-off? Under what circumstances can either result in the recognition of a gain in the income statement?

Q9-18. Describe the accounting for a convertible bond. Can the conversion ever result in the recognition of a gain in the income statement?

Assignments with the WebAssign. logo in the margin are available in WebAssign.
See the Preface of the book for details.

MINI EXERCISES

M9-19. **Analyzing and Identifying Financial Statement Effects of Stock Issuances** **(LO1)**
During the current year, Beatty Company, (*a*) issues 8,000 shares of $50 par value preferred stock at $68 cash per share and (*b*) issues 12,000 shares of $1 par value common stock at $10 cash per share. Indicate the financial statement effects of these two issuances using the financial statement effects template.

M9-20. **Analyzing and Identifying Financial Statement Effects of Stock Issuances** **(LO1)**
During the current year, Magliolo, Inc., (*a*) issues 18,000 shares of $10 par value preferred stock at $48 cash per share and (*b*) issues 120,000 shares of $2 par value common stock at $37 cash per share. Indicate the financial statement effects of these two issuances using the financial statement effects template.

M9-21. **Distinguishing between Common Stock and Additional Paid-in Capital** **(LO1)**
Following is the 2008 stockholders' equity section from the Cisco Systems, Inc., balance sheet.

Cisco Systems, Inc. (CSCO)

Shareholders' Equity (in millions, except par value)	July 26, 2008
Preferred stock, no par value: 5 shares authorized; none issued and outstanding.......	$ —
Common stock and additional paid-in capital, $0.001 par value: 20,000 shares authorized; 5,893 shares issued and outstanding at July 26, 2008.................	33,505
Retained earnings	120
Accumulated other comprehensive income.....................................	728
Total shareholders' equity	$34,353

   a. For the $33,505 million reported as "common stock and additional paid-in capital," what portion is common stock and what portion is additional paid-in capital?

   b. Explain why Cisco does not report the two components described in part *a* separately.

M9-22. **Identifying Financial Statement Effects of Stock Issuance and Repurchase** **(LO1)**
On January 1, Bartov Company issues 5,000 shares of $100 par value preferred stock at $250 cash per share. On March 1, the company repurchases 5,000 shares of previously issued $1 par value common stock at $83 cash per share. Use the financial statement effects template to record these two transactions.

M9-23.   Assessing the Financial Statement Effects of a Stock Split   (LO2)

Cigna Corp. (CI)

Cigna Corporation discloses the following footnote to its 10-K report.

> On April 25, 2007, the Company's Board of Directors approved a three-for-one stock split (in the form of a stock dividend) of the Company's common shares. The stock split was effective on June 4, 2007, for shareholders of record as of the close of business on May 21, 2007. All weighted average shares, per share amounts and references to stock compensation data for all periods presented have been adjusted to reflect the effect of the stock split.

What restatements has Cigna made to its balance sheet as a result of the stock split?

WebAssign.

Abercrombie & Fitch
(ANF)

M9-24.   Reconciling Common Stock and Treasury Stock Balances   (LO1)

Following is the stockholders' equity section from the Abercrombie & Fitch balance sheet.

Shareholders' Equity ($ thousands)	February 2, 2008	February 3, 2007
Class A common stock—$.01 par value: 150,000,000 shares authorized and 103,300,000 shares issued at February 2, 2008, and February 3, 2007, respectively	$ 1,033	$ 1,033
Paid-in capital	319,451	289,732
Retained earnings	2,051,463	1,646,290
Accumulated other comprehensive income (loss), net of tax.	7,118	(994)
Treasury stock at average cost: 17,141,116 and 14,999,945 shares at February 2, 2008 and February 3, 2007, respectively	(760,752)	(530,764)
Total shareholders' equity	$1,618,313	$1,405,297

a.   Show the computation to yield the $1,033 balance reported for common stock.
b.   How many shares are outstanding at 2008 fiscal year-end?
c.   Use the common stock and paid-in capital accounts to determine the average price at which Abercrombie & Fitch issued its common stock.
d.   Use the treasury stock account to determine the average price Abercrombie & Fitch paid when it repurchased its common shares.

M9-25.   Identifying and Analyzing Financial Statement Effects of Cash Dividends   (LO2)

Freid Company has outstanding 6,000 shares of $50 par value, 6% preferred stock, and 40,000 shares of $1 par value common stock. The company has $328,000 of retained earnings. At year-end, the company declares and pays the regular $3 per share cash dividend on preferred stock and a $2.20 per share cash dividend on common stock. Use the financial statement effects template to indicate the effects of these two dividend payments.

M9-26.   Identifying and Analyzing Financial Statement Effects of Stock Dividends   (LO2)

Dutta Corp. has outstanding 70,000 shares of $5 par value common stock. At year-end, the company declares and issues a 4% common stock dividend when the market price of the stock is $21 per share. Use the financial statement effects template to indicate the effects of this stock dividend declaration and payment.

M9-27.   Identifying, Analyzing and Explaining the Effects of a Stock Split   (LO2)

On September 1, Weiss Company has 250,000 shares of $15 par value ($165 market value) common stock that are issued and outstanding. Its balance sheet on that date shows the following account balances relating to its common stock:

Common stock.	$3,750,000
Paid-in capital in excess of par value.	2,250,000

On September 2, Weiss splits its stock 3-for-2 and reduces the par value to $10 per share.

a.   How many shares of common stock are issued and outstanding immediately after the stock split?
b.   What is the dollar balance of the common stock account immediately after the stock split?
c.   What is the likely reason that Weiss Company split its stock?

M9-28. Determining Cash Dividends to Preferred and Common Shareholders (LO2)

Dechow Company has outstanding 20,000 shares of $50 par value, 6% cumulative preferred stock and 80,000 shares of $10 par value common stock. The company declares and pays cash dividends amounting to $160,000.

a. If there are no preferred dividends in arrears, how much in total dividends, and in dividends per share, does Dechow pay to each class of stock?

b. If there are one year's dividends in arrears on the preferred stock, how much in total dividends, and in dividends per share, does Dechow pay to each class of stock?

M9-29. Reconciling Retained Earnings (LO2)

Use the following data to reconcile the 2008 retained earnings for Bamber Company (that is, explain the change in retained earnings during the year).

Total retained earnings, December 31, 2007	$347,000
Stock dividends declared and paid in 2008	28,000
Cash dividends declared and paid in 2008	35,000
Net income for 2008	94,000

M9-30. Interpreting a Spin-Off Disclosure (LO3)

NCR Corporation discloses the following in notes to its 2007 10-K report.

NCR Corp. (NCR)

Spin-off of Teradata Data Warehousing Business On September 30, 2007, NCR completed the spin-off of its Teradata Data Warehousing business through the distribution of a tax-free dividend to its stockholders. NCR distributed one share of common stock of Teradata Corporation (Teradata) for each share of NCR common stock to NCR stockholders of record as of the close of business on September 14, 2007. Upon the distribution of Teradata, NCR stockholders received 100% (approximately 181 million shares) of the common stock of Teradata, which is now an independent public company trading under the symbol "TDC" on the New York Stock Exchange.

a. Describe the difference between a spin-off and a split-off.

b. What effects did NCR's spin-off of Teradata have on NCR's balance sheet and income statement?

M9-31. Interpreting a Proposed Split-Off Disclosure (LO3)

Viacom, Inc., reports the following footnote in its 2005 10-K.

Viacom, Inc. (VIA)

Discontinued Operations In 2004, Viacom completed the exchange offer for the split-off of Blockbuster Inc. ("Blockbuster") (NYSE: BBI and BBI.B). Under the terms of the offer, Viacom accepted 27,961,165 shares of Viacom common stock in exchange for the 144 million common shares of Blockbuster that Viacom owned. Each share of Viacom Class A or Class B common stock accepted for exchange by Viacom was exchanged for 5.15 shares of Blockbuster common stock, consisting of 2.575 shares of Blockbuster class A common stock and 2.575 shares of Blockbuster class B common stock.

a. Describe the accounting for a split-off.

b. How will the proposed split-off affect the number of Viacom shares outstanding?

c. Under what circumstances will Viacom be able to report a gain for this proposed split-off?

M9-32. Interpreting Disclosure Related to Split-Off (LO3)

IMS Health, Inc., reports the following footnote to its 2003 10-K.

IMS Health, Inc. (RX)

Split-Off of Cognizant Technology Solutions Corporation Segment ("CTS") Until February 6, 2003, we consolidated CTS, which provides custom Information Technology ("IT") design, development, integration and maintenance services. CTS is a publicly traded corporation on the NASDAQ national market system. We owned 55.3% of the common shares outstanding of CTS (92.5% of the outstanding voting power) as of December 31, 2002. On February 6, 2003, we divested CTS through a split-off transaction, and as a result, during 2003, we recorded a net gain from discontinued operations of $496,887,000. Our share of CTS' results are presented as discontinued operations for 2003 through the date of divestiture.

   a. Describe the accounting for a split-off.
   b. Describe the circumstances that allowed IMS to recognize a gain on this split-off.
   c. How should you interpret the gain from this split-off in your analysis of IMS for 2003?

M9-33. **Analyzing Financial Statement Effects of Convertible Securities** **(LO3)**

JetBlue Airways
Corporation (JBLU)

JetBlue Airways Corporation reports the following footnote to its 2005 10-K.

> In March 2005, we completed a public offering of $250 million aggregate principal amount of 3¾% convertible unsecured debentures due 2035, which are currently convertible into 14.6 million shares of our common stock at a price of approximately $17.10 per share.

   a. Describe the effects on JetBlue's balance sheet if the convertible bonds are converted.
   b. Would the conversion affect earnings? Explain.

EXERCISES

E9-34. **Identifying and Analyzing Financial Statement Effects of Stock Transactions** **(LO1)**

Lipe Company reports the following transactions relating to its stock accounts in the current year.

   Feb 20 Issued 10,000 shares of $1 par value common stock at $25 cash per share
   Feb 21 Issued 15,000 shares of $100 par value, 8% preferred stock at $275 cash per share.
   Jun 30 Purchased 2,000 shares of its own common stock at $15 cash per share.
   Sep 25 Sold 1,000 shares of its treasury stock at $21 cash per share.

Use the financial statement effects template to indicate the effects from each of these transactions.

E9-35. **Identifying and Analyzing Financial Statement Effects of Stock Transactions** **(LO1)**

McNichols Corp. reports the following transactions relating to its stock accounts in the current year.

   Jan 15   Issued 25,000 shares of $5 par value common stock at $17 cash per share
   Jan 20   Issued 6,000 shares of $50 par value, 8% preferred stock at $78 cash per share.
   Mar 31   Purchased 3,000 shares of its own common stock at $20 cash per share.
   June 25 Sold 2,000 shares of its treasury stock at $26 cash per share.
   July 15 Sold the remaining 1,000 shares of treasury stock at $19 cash per share.

Use the financial statement effects template to indicate the effects from each of these transactions.

WebAssign.

Campbell Soup (CPB)

E9-36. **Analyzing and Computing Average Issue Price and Treasury Stock Cost** **(LO1)**

Following is the stockholders' equity section from the Campbell Soup Company balance sheet.

Shareholders' Equity (millions, except per share amounts)	August 3, 2008	July 29, 2007
Preferred stock: authorized 40 shares; none issued	$ —	$ —
Capital stock, $.0375 par value; authorized 560 shares; issued 542 shares.	20	20
Additional paid-in capital	337	331
Earnings retained in the business	7,909	7,082
Capital stock in treasury, 186 shares in 2008 and 163 shares in 2007, at cost.	(6,812)	(6,015)
Accumulated other comprehensive loss	(136)	(123)
Total shareowners' equity.	$1,318	$1,295

Campbell Soup Company also reports the following statement of stockholders' equity.

(Millions, except per share amounts)	Capital Stock				Additional Paid-in Capital	Earnings Retained in the Business	Accumulated Other Comprehensive Income (Loss)	Total Share-owners' Equity
	Issued		In Treasury					
	Shares	Amount	Shares	Amount				
Balance at July 29, 2007	542	$20	(163)	$(6,015)	$331	$7,082	$(123)	$1,295
Comprehensive income (loss)								
Net earnings						1,165		1,165
Foreign currency translation								
adjustments, net of tax							112	112
Cash-flow hedges, net of tax							11	11
Pension and postretirement								
benefits, net of tax							(136)	(136)
Other comprehensive loss							(13)	(13)
Total comprehensive income								1,152
Impact on adoption of FIN 48								
(Note 10)						(6)		(6)
Dividends ($0.88 per share)						(332)		(332)
Treasury stock purchased			(26)	(903)				(903)
Treasury stock issued under								
management incentive and								
stock option plans.			3	106	6			112
Balance at August 3, 2008	542	$20	(186)	$(6,812)	$337	$7,909	$(136)	$1,318

a. Show the computation, using par value and share numbers, to arrive at the $20 million in the common stock account.

b. At what average price were the Campbell Soup shares issued?

c. Reconcile the beginning and ending balances of retained earnings.

d. Campbell Soup reports a $112 gain as part of Accumulated Other Comprehensive Income relating to foreign currency translation adjustments. Explain what foreign currency translation adjustments represent. What effect did foreign currency translation adjustments have on net earnings for the year?

e. Campbell Soup reports an increase in stockholders' equity relating to the exercise of stock options (titled "Treasury stock issued under management incentive and stock option plans"). This transaction involves the purchase of common stock by employees at a preset price. Describe how this set of transactions affects stockholders' equity.

f. Describe the transaction relating to the "Treasury stock purchased" line in the statement of stockholders' equity.

E9-37. **Analyzing Cash Dividends on Preferred and Common Stock** **(LO2)**

Moser Company began business on March 1, 2007. At that time, it issued 20,000 shares of $60 par value, 7% cumulative preferred stock and 100,000 shares of $5 par value common stock. Through the end of 2009, there has been no change in the number of preferred and common shares outstanding.

a. Assume that Moser declared and paid cash dividends of $0 in 2007, $183,000 in 2008, and $200,000 in 2009. Compute the total cash dividends and the dividends per share paid to each class of stock in 2007, 2008, and 2009.

b. Assume that Moser declared and paid cash dividends of $0 in 2007, $84,000 in 2008, and $150,000 in 2009. Compute the total cash dividends and the dividends per share paid to each class of stock in 2007, 2008, and 2009.

E9-38. **Analyzing Cash Dividends on Preferred and Common Stock** **(LO2)**

WebAssign.

Potter Company has outstanding 15,000 shares of $50 par value, 8% preferred stock and 50,000 shares of $5 par value common stock. During its first three years in business, it declared and paid no cash dividends in the first year, $280,000 in the second year, and $60,000 in the third year.

a. If the preferred stock is cumulative, determine the total amount of cash dividends paid to each class of stock in each of the three years.

b. If the preferred stock is noncumulative, determine the total amount of cash dividends paid to each class of stock in each of the three years.

E9-39.   **Analyzing and Computing Issue Price, Treasury Stock Cost, and Shares Outstanding**   **(LO1)**

Altria (MO)

Following is the stockholders' equity section from Altria's 2007 balance sheet.

December 31 ($ million)	2007
Common stock, par value $0.33\frac{1}{3}$ per share (2,805,961,317 shares issued)	$ 935
Additional paid-in capital	6,884
Earnings reinvested in the business.	34,426
Accumulated other comprehensive losses	(237)
Cost of repurchased stock (698,284,555 shares in 2007)	(23,454)
Total stockholders' equity	$18,554

a.   Show the computation to derive the $935 million for common stock.
b.   At what average price has Altria issued its common stock?
c.   How many shares of Altria common stock are outstanding as of December 31, 2007?
d.   At what average cost has Altria repurchased its treasury stock as of December 31, 2007?
e.   Why would a company such as Altria want to repurchase $23,454 million of its common stock?

E9-40.   **Analyzing Cash Dividends on Preferred and Common Stock**   **(LO2)**

Skinner Company began business on June 30, 2007. At that time, it issued 18,000 shares of $50 par value, 6% cumulative preferred stock and 90,000 shares of $10 par value common stock. Through the end of 2009, there has been no change in the number of preferred and common shares outstanding.

a.   Assume that Skinner declared and paid cash dividends of $63,000 in 2007, $0 in 2008, and $378,000 in 2009. Compute the total cash dividends and the dividends per share paid to each class of stock in 2007, 2008, and 2009.
b.   Assume that Skinner declared and paid cash dividends of $0 in 2007, $108,000 in 2008, and $189,000 in 2009. Compute the total cash dividends and the dividends per share paid to each class of stock in 2007, 2008, and 2009.

E9-41.   **Identifying and Analyzing Financial Statement Effects of Dividends**   **(LO2)**

Chaney Company has outstanding 25,000 shares of $10 par value common stock. It also has $405,000 of retained earnings. Near the current year-end, the company declares and pays a cash dividend of $1.90 per share and declares and issues a 4% stock dividend. The market price of the stock the day the dividends are declared is $35 per share. Use the financial statement effects template to indicate the effects of these two separate dividend transactions.

E9-42.   **Identifying and Analyzing Financial Statement Effects of Dividends**   **(LO2)**

The stockholders' equity of Pagach Company at December 31, 2008, appears below.

Common stock, $10 par value, 200,000 shares authorized; 80,000 shares issued and outstanding.	$800,000
Paid-in capital in excess of par value.	480,000
Retained earnings	305,000

During 2009, the following transactions occurred:

May 12   Declared and issued a 7% stock dividend; the common stock market value was $18 per share.

Dec. 31   Declared and paid a cash dividend of 75 cents per share.

a.   Use the financial statement effects template to indicate the effects of these transactions.
b.   Reconcile retained earnings for 2009 assuming that the company reports 2009 net income of $283,000.

Module 9 | Reporting and Analyzing Owner Financing 9-36

E9-43. **Identifying and Analyzing Financial Statement Effects of Dividends** (LO2)
The stockholders' equity of Kinney Company at December 31, 2008, is shown below.

WebAssign.

5% preferred stock, $100 par value, 10,000 shares authorized; 4,000 shares issued and outstanding.	$ 400,000
Common stock, $5 par value, 200,000 shares authorized; 50,000 shares issued and outstanding.	250,000
Paid-in capital in excess of par value—preferred stock.	40,000
Paid-in capital in excess of par value—common stock.	300,000
Retained earnings	656,000
Total stockholders' equity	$1,646,000

The following transactions, among others, occurred during 2009:

Apr. 1 Declared and issued a 100% stock dividend on all outstanding shares of common stock. The market value of the stock was $11 per share.

Dec. 7 Declared and issued a 3% stock dividend on all outstanding shares of common stock. The market value of the stock was $14 per share.

Dec. 20 Declared and paid (1) the annual cash dividend on the preferred stock and (2) a cash dividend of 80 cents per common share.

a. Use the financial statement effects template to indicate the effects of these separate transactions.
b. Compute retained earnings for 2009 assuming that the company reports 2009 net income of $253,000.

E9-44. **Identifying, Analyzing and Explaining the Effects of a Stock Split** (LO2)
On March 1 of the current year, Zhang Company has 400,000 shares of $20 par value common stock that are issued and outstanding. Its balance sheet shows the following account balances relating to common stock.

Common stock.	$8,000,000
Paid-in capital in excess of par value.	3,400,000

On March 2, Zhang Company splits its common stock 2-for-1 and reduces the par value to $10 per share.
a. How many shares of common stock are issued and outstanding immediately after the stock split?
b. What is the dollar balance in the common stock account immediately after the stock split?
c. What is the dollar balance in the paid-in capital in excess of par value account immediately after the stock split?

E9-45. **Analyzing and Computing Issue Price, Treasury Stock Cost, and Shares Outstanding** (LO1)
Following is the stockholders' equity section of the 2007 Caterpillar, Inc., balance sheet.

Caterpillar, Inc. (CAT)

Stockholders' Equity ($ millions)	2007	2006	2005
Common stock of $1.00 par; Authorized shares: 900,000,000; Issued shares (2007, 2006 and 2005—814,894,624) at paid-in amount	$2,744	$2,465	$1,859
Treasury stock (2007—190,908,490 shares; 2006—169,086,448 shares; 2005—144,027,405 shares) at cost	(9,451)	(7,352)	(4,637)
Profit employed in the business.	17,398	14,593	11,808
Accumulated other comprehensive income.	(1,808)	(2,847)	(598)
Total stockholders' equity	$8,883	$6,859	$8,432

a. How many shares of Caterpillar common stock are outstanding at year-end 2007?
b. What does the phrase "at paid-in amount" in the stockholders' equity section mean?
c. At what average cost has Caterpillar repurchased its stock as of year-end 2007?
d. Why would a company such as Caterpillar want to repurchase its common stock?
e. Explain how CAT's "issued shares" remains constant over the three-year period while the dollar amount of its common stock account increases.

E9-46. **Analyzing Equity Changes from Convertible Preferred Stock and Employee Stock Options** **(LO3)**

Corning, Inc. (GLW)

Corning, Inc., reports the following stockholders' equity information in its 10-K report.

Shareholders' Equity (In millions, except share and per share amounts)	December 31	
	2005	2004
Preferred stock—Par value $100.00 per share; Shares authorized: 10 million Series C mandatory convertible preferred stock—Shares issued: 5.75 million; Shares outstanding: 0 and 637 thousand	$ —	$ 64
Common stock—Par value $0.50 per share; Shares authorized: 3.8 billion Shares issued: 1,552 million and 1,424 million.	776	712
Additional paid-in capital	11,548	10,363
Accumulated deficit	(6,847)	(7,432)
Treasury stock, at cost; Shares held: 16 million	(168)	(162)
Accumulated other comprehensive income	178	156
Total shareholders' equity	$ 5,487	$ 3,701

(In millions)	Series C Preferred Stock	Common Stock	Additional Paid-in Capital	Unearned Compensation	Accumulated Deficit	Treasury Stock	Accumulated Other Comprehensive Income (Loss)	Total Shareholders' Equity
Balance, December 31, 2004	$64	$712	$10,409	$(46)	$(7,432)	$(162)	$156	$3,701
Net income					585			585
Foreign currency translation adjustment							(171)	(171)
Reversal of foreign currency translation adjustment							(84)	(84)
Minimum pension liability adjustment							246	246
Net unrealized loss on investments							(13)	(13)
Unrealized derivative gain on cash flow hedges							23	23
Reclassification adjustments on cash flow hedges							21	21
Total comprehensive income								607
Series C preferred stock conversions	(64)	16	48					
Shares issued in equity offerings		10	313					323
Shares issued to benefit plans and for option exercises		20	493	(37)		1		477
Shares issued in debt retirements		18	370					388
Other, net			(2)			(7)		(9)
Balance, December 31, 2005	$ 0	$776	$11,631	$(83)	$(6,847)	$(168)	$178	$5,487

In 2002, Corning issued 5.75 million shares of 7.00% Series C Mandatory Convertible Preferred Stock. On the mandatory conversion date of August 15, 2005, the remaining outstanding shares were converted into Corning common stock at a conversion rate of 50,813 shares of common stock for each preferred share. Upon conversion of the preferred shares, we issued 31 million shares of Corning common stock resulting in an increase to equity of $62 million. The Series C Mandatory Convertible Preferred Stock had a liquidation preference of $100 per share, plus accrued and unpaid dividends.

The following table summarizes the activities related to our debt retirements:

(in millions)	Book Value of Debentures Retired	Cash Paid	Shares Issued	Gain (Loss)
2005 Activities				
Convertible debentures, 3.5%, due 2008	$297	$ 2	31	
Euro notes, 5.625%, due 2005	189	189		
Oak 4 7/8% Subordinated notes, due 2008	96		6	
Debentures, 7% due 2007	88	100		$(12)
Zero coupon convertible debentures, 2%, due 2015	277	277		(4)
Other loans payable	11	11		
Total 2005 activity	$958	$579	37	$(16)

Required

a.   At December 31, 2004, Corning reports $64 million of 7.00% Series C Mandatory Convertible Preferred stock. What is the dollar amount of dividends that Corning must pay on this stock? Some have argued that securities such as this are more like debt than equity. What is the basis for such an argument?

b.   Describe the effects of conversion of the Series C Mandatory Convertible Preferred stock on Corning's balance sheet and its income statement.

c.   Describe the effects on Corning's balance sheet and its income statement of the conversion of the Convertible debentures and of the Oak Subordinated notes.

d.   What is the benefit, if any, to Corning of issuing debt and equity securities with a conversion feature? How are these securities treated in the computation of earnings per share (EPS)?

e.   How do you interpret Corning's "Accumulated deficit"?

E9-47.   Analyzing and Computing Issue Price, Treasury Stock Cost, and Shares Outstanding   (LO1)

Following is the stockholders' equity and minority interest sections of the 2007 Merck & Co., Inc., balance sheet.

Merck & Co., Inc. (MRK)

Stockholders' Equity ($ millions)	2007
Common stock, one cent par value; Authorized—5,400,000,000 shares; Issued—2,983,508,675 shares—2007; 2,976,223,337 shares—2006	$ 29.8
Other paid-in capital.	8,014.9
Retained earnings	39,140.8
Accumulated other comprehensive loss	(826.1)
	46,359.4
Less treasury stock, at cost; 811,005,791 shares—2007 808,437,892 shares—2006.	28,174.7
Total stockholders' equity	$18,184.7

a.   Show the computation of the $29.8 million in the common stock account.

b.   At what average price were the Merck common shares issued?

c.   At what average cost was the Merck treasury stock purchased?

d.   How many common shares are outstanding as of December 31, 2007?

PROBLEMS

P9-48.   Identifying and Analyzing Financial Statement Effects of Stock Transactions   (LO1)

The stockholders' equity section of Gupta Company at December 31, 2008, follows:

8% preferred stock, $25 par value, 50,000 shares authorized; 6,800 shares issued and outstanding.	$170,000
Common stock, $10 par value, 200,000 shares authorized; 50,000 shares issued and outstanding.	500,000
Paid-in capital in excess of par value—preferred stock.	68,000
Paid-in capital in excess of par value—common stock.	200,000
Retained earnings	270,000

During 2009, the following transactions occurred:

Jan.   10   Issued 28,000 shares of common stock for $17 cash per share.

Jan.   23   Repurchased 8,000 shares of common stock at $19 cash per share.

Mar.   14   Sold one-half of the treasury shares acquired January 23 for $21 cash per share.

July   15   Issued 3,200 shares of preferred stock for $128,000 cash.

Nov.   15   Sold 1,000 of the treasury shares acquired January 23 for $24 cash per share.

Required

a.   Use the financial statement effects template to indicate the effects from each of these transactions.

b.   Prepare the December 31, 2009, stockholders' equity section of the balance sheet assuming the company reports 2009 net income of $59,000.

P9-49. **Identifying and Analyzing Financial Statement Effects of Stock Transactions** **(LO1)**
The stockholders' equity of Sougiannis Company at December 31, 2008, follows:

7% Preferred stock, $100 par value, 20,000 shares authorized; 5,000 shares issued and outstanding.	$ 500,000
Common stock, $15 par value, 100,000 shares authorized; 40,000 shares issued and outstanding.	600,000
Paid-in capital in excess of par value—preferred stock.	24,000
Paid-in capital in excess of par value—common stock.	360,000
Retained earnings	325,000
Total stockholders' equity	$1,809,000

The following transactions, among others, occurred during the following year:

Jan. 12 Announced a 3-for-1 common stock split, reducing the par value of the common stock to $5 per share. The authorized shares were increased to 300,000 shares.
Sept. 1 Repurchased 10,000 shares of common stock at $10 cash per share.
Oct. 12 Sold 1,500 treasury shares acquired September 1 at $12 cash per share.
Nov. 21 Issued 5,000 shares of common stock at $21 cash per share.
Dec. 28 Sold 1,200 treasury shares acquired September 1 at $9 cash per share.

Required
a. Use the financial statement effects template to indicate the effects from each of these transactions.
b. Prepare the December 31, 2009, stockholders' equity section of the balance sheet assuming that the company reports 2009 net income of $83,000.

WebAssign. **P9-50.** **Identifying and Analyzing Financial Statement Effects of Stock Transactions** **(LO1)**
The stockholders' equity of Verrecchia Company at December 31, 2008, follows:

Common stock, $5 par value, 350,000 shares authorized; 150,000 shares issued and outstanding.	$750,000
Paid-in capital in excess of par value.	600,000
Retained earnings	346,000

During 2009, the following transactions occurred:

Jan. 5 Issued 10,000 shares of common stock for $12 cash per share.
Jan. 18 Repurchased 4,000 shares of common stock at $14 cash per share.
Mar 12 Sold one-fourth of the treasury shares acquired January 18 for $17 cash per share.
July 17 Sold 500 shares of treasury stock for $13 cash per share.
Oct. 1 Issued 5,000 shares of 8%, $25 par value preferred stock for $35 cash per share. This is the first issuance of preferred shares from the 50,000 authorized preferred shares.

Required
a. Use the financial statement effects template to indicate the effects of each transaction.
b. Prepare the December 31, 2009, stockholders' equity section of the balance sheet assuming that the company reports net income of $72,500 for the year.

P9-51. **Identifying and Analyzing Financial Statement Effects of Stock Transactions** **(LO1)**
Following is the stockholders' equity of Dennis Corporation at December 31, 2008:

8% preferred stock, $50 par value, 10,000 shares authorized; 7,000 shares issued and outstanding.	$ 350,000
Common stock, $20 par value, 50,000 shares authorized; 25,000 shares issued and outstanding.	500,000
Paid-in capital in excess of par value—preferred stock.	70,000
Paid-in capital in excess of par value—common stock.	385,000
Retained earnings	238,000
Total stockholders' equity	$1,543,000

The following transactions, among others, occurred during 2009:

Jan. 15 Issued 1,000 shares of preferred stock for $62 cash per share.

Jan. 20 Issued 4,000 shares of common stock at $36 cash per share.

May 18 Announced a 2-for-1 common stock split, reducing the par value of the common stock to $10 per share. The number of shares authorized was increased to 100,000 shares.

June 1 Issued 2,000 shares of common stock for $60,000 cash.

Sept. 1 Repurchased 2,500 shares of common stock at $18 cash per share.

Oct. 12 Sold 900 treasury shares at $21 cash per share.

Dec. 22 Issued 500 shares of preferred stock for $59 cash per share.

Required

Use the financial statement effects template to indicate the effects of each transaction.

P9-52. **Analyzing and Interpreting Equity Accounts and Comprehensive Income** **(LO2)**
Following is the shareholders' equity section of the 2008 balance sheet for Procter & Gamble Company and its statement of shareholders' equity.

WebAssign.

Procter & Gamble
Company (PG)

June 30 (In millions, except per share amounts)	2008	2007
Shareholders' Equity		
Convertible Class A preferred stock, stated value $1 per share (600 shares authorized)	$ 1,366	$ 1,406
Non-Voting Class B preferred stock, stated value $1 per share (200 shares authorized)	—	—
Common stock, stated value $1 per share (10,000 shares authorized; shares issued: 2008—4,001.8, 2007—3,989.7)	4,002	3,990
Additional paid-in capital	60,307	59,030
Reserve for ESOP debt retirement	(1,325)	(1,308)
Accumulated other comprehensive income	3,746	617
Treasury stock, at cost (shares held: 2008—969.1, 2007—857.8)	(47,588)	(38,772)
Retained earnings	48,986	41,797
Total shareholders' equity	$69,494	$66,760

Consolidated Statement of Shareholders' Equity

Dollars in millions; Shares in thousands	Common Shares Outstanding	Common Stock	Preferred Stock	Additional Paid-in Capital	Reserve for ESOP Debt Retirement	Accumulated Other Comprehensive Income	Treasury Stock	Retained Earnings	Total
Balance June 30, 2007	3,131,946	$3,990	$1,406	$59,030	$(1,308)	$617	$(38,772)	$41,797	$66,760
Net earnings								12,075	12,075
Other comprehensive income:									
Financial statement translation						6,543			6,543
Net investment hedges, net of $1,719 tax						(2,951)			(2,951)
Other, net of tax benefits						(463)			(463)
Total comprehensive income									15,204
Cumulative impact for adoption of FIN 48								(232)	(232)
Dividends to shareholders:									
Common								(4,479)	(4,479)
Preferred, net of tax benefits								(176)	(176)
Treasury stock purchases	(148,121)						(10,047)		(10,047)
Employee plan issuances	43,910	12		1,272			1,196		2,480
Preferred stock conversions	4,982		(40)	5			35		—
ESOP debt impacts					(17)			1	(16)
Balance June 30, 2008	3,032,717	$4,002	$1,366	$60,307	$(1,325)	$3,746	$(47,588)	$48,986	$69,494

Required

a. What does the term *convertible* (in reference to the company's Class A preferred stock) mean?

continued

b. How many shares of common stock did Procter & Gamble issue when convertible Class A preferred stock was converted during fiscal 2008?

c. Assuming that the convertible Class A preferred stock was sold at par value, at what average price were the common shares issued as of year-end 2008?

d. What is the accumulated other comprehensive income account? Explain.

e. What cash dividends did Procter & Gamble pay in 2008 for each class of stock?

P9-53. **Analyzing and Interpreting Equity Accounts and Accumulated Other Comprehensive Income   (LO2)**

Fortune Brands (FO)

Following is the stockholders' equity section of Fortune Brands balance sheet and its statement of stockholders' equity.

December 31 (In millions, except per share amounts)	2007	2006
Stockholders' Equity		
$2.67 convertible preferred stock	$ 5.7	$ 6.3
Common stock, par value $3.125 per share, 234.9 shares issued	734.0	734.0
Paid-in capital	684.3	615.7
Accumulated other comprehensive income	349.1	37.9
Retained earnings	6,999.3	6,496.3
Treasury stock, at cost	(3,086.9)	(3,162.2)
Total stockholders' equity	$5,685.5	$4,728.0

(In millions, except per share amounts)	$2.67 Convertible Preferred Stock	Common Stock	Paid-in Capital	Accumulated Other Comprehensive Income (Loss)	Retained Earnings	Treasury Stock At Cost	Total
Balance at December 31, 2006	$6.3	$734.0	$615.7	$ 37.9	$6,496.3	$(3,162.2)	$4,728.0
Comprehensive income							
Net income	—	—	—	—	762.6	—	762.6
Foreign exchange adjustments, net of effect of hedging activities	—	—	—	258.1	—	—	258.1
Pension and postretirement benefit adjustments, net of tax	—	—	—	53.1	—	—	53.1
Total comprehensive Income	—	—	—	311.2	762.6	—	1,073.8
Adjustment to initially apply FASB Interpretation No. 48	—	—	—	—	(3.6)	—	(3.6)
Dividends ($1.62 per Common share and $2.67 per Preferred share)	—	—	—	—	(248.6)	—	(248.6)
Stock-based compensation	—	—	46.5	—	(7.4)	70.8	109.9
Tax benefit on exercise of stock options	—	—	26.0	—	—	—	26.0
Conversion of preferred stock (0.1 shares)	(0.6)	—	(3.9)	—	—	4.5	—
Balance at December 31, 2007	$ 5.7	$734.0	$684.3	$349.1	$6,999.3	$(3,086.9)	$5,685.5

Required

a. Explain the "$2.67" component of the convertible preferred stock account title.

b. Show (confirm) the computation that yields the $734.0 million common stock at year-end 2007.

c. Assuming that the convertible preferred stock was sold at par value, at what average price were Fortune Brands' common shares issued as of year-end 2007?

d. What is included in Fortune Brands' other comprehensive income for 2007? What other accounts are typically included in other comprehensive income?

e. Explain the $26 million tax benefit on exercise of stock options, reported in the statement of stockholders' equity.

P9-54. **Interpreting Footnote Disclosure on Convertible Debentures   (LO3)**

Alloy, Inc. (ALOY)

Alloy, Inc., reports the following footnote related to its convertible debentures in its 2007 10-K ($ thousands).

In August 2003, Alloy completed the issuance of $69,300 of 20-Year 5.375% Senior Convertible Debentures due August 1, 2023. If converted, bondholders would currently receive 29.851 shares of Alloy common for each $1,000 face amount bond. Alloy continues to be responsible for repaying the Convertible Debentures in full if they are not converted into shares of Alloy common stock. If not previously converted to common stock, Alloy may redeem the Convertible

continued

continued from prior page

Debentures after August 1, 2008 at 103% of their face amount from August 1, 2008 through December 31, 2008 and at declining prices to 100% in January 2011 and thereafter, with accrued interest. From August 30, 2006 through December 7, 2006, holders converted approximately $67,903 face amount of their Debentures, in accordance with their terms, into approximately 2,026,000 shares of Alloy common stock. During fiscal 2006, the Company's additional paid-in capital increased by $67,883 as a result of the conversions. At January 31, 2007, the Company had $1,397 in principal amount of outstanding Convertible Debentures. At January 31, 2007, the fair value of the Convertible Debentures was approximately $1,504, which is estimated based on quoted market prices.

Required

a. How did Alloy initially account for the issuance of the 5.375% debentures, assuming that the conversion option cannot be detached and sold separately?

b. Consider the conversion terms reported in the footnote. At what minimum stock price would it make economic sense for debenture holders to convert to Alloy common stock?

c. Use the financial statement effects template to show how Alloy accounted for the conversion of the 5.375% debentures in 2006. The par value of the company's stock is $0.01.

d. Assume that the conversion feature is valued by investors and, therefore, results in a higher initial issuance price for the bonds. What effect will the conversion feature have on the amount of interest expense and net income that Alloy reports?

e. How are the convertible debentures treated in the computation of basic and diluted earnings per share (EPS)?

P9-55. Interpreting Disclosure on Convertible Preferred Securities (LO3)

The 2008 annual report of Northrop Grumman Corporation includes the following disclosure in its shareholders' equity footnote:

Northrop Grumman Corp. (NOC)

Conversion of Preferred Stock On February 20, 2008, the company's board of directors approved the redemption of all of the 3.5 million shares of mandatorily redeemable convertible preferred stock on April 4, 2008. Prior to the redemption date, substantially all of the preferred shares were converted into common stock at the election of shareholders. All remaining unconverted preferred shares were redeemed by the company on the redemption date. As a result of the conversion and redemption, the company issued approximately 6.4 million shares of common stock.

Required

a. Explain what is meant by "mandatorily redeemable" and "convertible" preferred stock.

b. The company's balance sheet reports preferred stock of $350 million at December 31, 2007 (and $0 at December 31, 2008). As is typical, Northrop Grumman originally sold these preferred at par. Confirm that the par value of the preferred stock is $100 per share.

c. Northrop's footnotes report that the fair value of the preferred shares was $146 per share at December 31, 2008. What would explain this large increase in its preferred stock's market price?

d. Use the financial statement effects template to record the conversion of the preferred stock on April 4, 2008. Assume that all 3.5 million shares were converted. The par value of the company's common stock is $1 per share.

P9-56. Identifying and Analyzing Financial Statement Effects of Share-Based Compensation (LO1)

WebAssign.

Weaver Industries implements a new share-based compensation plan in 2009. Under the plan, the company's CEO and CFO each will receive non-qualified stock options to purchase 100,000, no par shares. The options vest ratably (1/3 of the options each year) over three years, expire in 10 years, and have an exercise (strike) price of $22 per share. Weaver uses the Black-Scholes model to estimate a fair-value per option of $15. The company's tax rate is 40%.

Required

a. Use the financial statement effects template to record the compensation expense related to these options for each year 2009 through 2011. Include the effects of any anticipated deferred tax benefits.

continued

b.   In 2012, the company's stock price is $19. If you were the Weaver Industries CEO, would you exercise your options? Explain.

c.   In 2014, the company's stock price is $40 and the CEO exercises all of her options. Use the financial statement effects template to record the exercise.

d.   What tax benefit will Weaver Industries receive related to the CEO's exercise in part *c*? What will be the tax consequences to the CEO?

WebAssign.

Intel Corporation
(INTC)

P9-57.   Interpreting Disclosure on Employee Stock Options   (LO1)

Intel Corporation reported the following in its 2008 10-K report.

Share-Based Compensation   Effective January 1, 2006, we adopted the provisions of SFAS No. 123(R) . . . Share-based compensation recognized in 2008 was $851 million ($952 million in 2007 and $1,375 million in 2006). We use the Black-Scholes option pricing model to estimate the fair value of options granted under our equity incentive plans and rights to acquire common stock granted under our stock purchase plan. We based the weighted average estimated values of employee stock option grants and rights granted under the stock purchase plan, as well as the weighted average assumptions used in calculating these values, on estimates at the date of grant, as follows:

Stock Options	2008	2007	2006
Estimated fair values	$5.74	$5.79	$5.21
Expected life (in years)	5.0	5.0	4.9
Risk-free interest rate	3.0%	4.5%	4.9%
Volatility	37%	26%	27%
Dividend yield	2.7%	2.0%	2.0%

Additional information with respect to stock option activity is as follows:

(In Millions, Except Per Share Amounts)	Number of Shares	Weighted Average Exercise Price
December 31, 2005	**899.9**	**$26.71**
Grants	52.3	$20.04
Exercises	(47.3)	$12.83
Cancellations and forfeitures	(65.4)	$28.07
December 30, 2006	**839.5**	**$26.98**
Grants	24.6	$22.63
Exercises	(132.8)	$19.78
Cancellations and forfeitures	(65.4)	$31.97
December 29, 2007	**665.9**	**$27.76**
Grants	24.9	$20.81
Exercises	(33.6)	$19.42
Cancellations and forfeitures	(42.8)	$31.14
Expirations	(2.4)	$22.84
December 27, 2008	**612.0**	**$27.70**

Required

a.   What did Intel expense for share-based compensation for 2008? How many options did Intel grant in 2008? Compute the fair value of all options granted during 2008. Why do the fair value of the option grants and the expense differ?

b.   Intel used the Black-Scholes formula to estimate fair value of the options granted each year. How did the change in volatility from 2007 to 2008 affect share-based compensation in 2008? What about the change in risk-free rate?

c.   How many options were exercised during 2008? Estimate the cash that Intel received from its employees when these options were exercised.

d.   What was the intrinsic value per share of the options exercised in 2008? If employees who exercised options in 2008 immediately sold them, what "profit" did they make from the shares? (*Hint:* Assume that Intel grants options at-the-money.)

continued

e. The tax benefit that Intel will receive on the options exercised is computed based on the intrinsic value of the options exercised. Estimate Intel's tax benefit from the 2008 option exercises assuming a tax rate of 34.7%.

f. What was the average exercise price of the options that expired in 2008? Explain why employees might have let these options expire without exercising them. (*Hint:* Assume that Intel grants options at-the-money.)

P9-58. **Interpreting Disclosure on Share-Based Compensation** **(LO1)**

Host Hotels & Resorts, Inc., reported the following information in its 2008 10-K related to its restricted stock plan.

Host Hotels & Resorts, Inc. (HST)

> **Restricted Stock** During 2008, 2007 and 2006, we recorded compensation expense of approximately $2 million, $3 million and $32 million respectively, related to the restricted stock awards to senior executives. The majority of these awards vested on December 31, 2008. The following table is a summary of the status of our senior executive plans for the three years ended December 31, 2008.

	2008		2007		2006	
	Shares (in millions)	Fair Value (per share)	Shares (in millions)	Fair Value (per share)	Shares (in millions)	Fair Value (per share)
Balance, at beginning of year	1.5	$ 7	2.4	$19	—	$—
Granted	0.2	18	—	—	3.5	16
Vested.	(0.3)	10	(0.2)	24	(1.1)	24
Forfeited/expired	(1.3)	—	(0.7)	8	—	—
Balance, at year-end	0.1	7	1.5	7	2.4	19
Issued in calendar year . . .	0.1	15	0.6	25	0.7	19

Required

a. How do restricted stock and stock options differ? In what respects are they the same?

b. Why do companies impose vesting periods on restricted stock grants?

c. Use the financial statement effects template to record the restricted stock granted to senior executives during 2008. The common stock has a par value of $0.01 per share.

d. Use the financial statement effects template to record the 2008 compensation expense related to Host Hotels' restricted stock awards.

MANAGEMENT APPLICATIONS

MA9-59. **Management Application: Convertible Debt** **(LO3)**

When convertible debt is issued, the conversion option is not separately recorded on the balance sheet, unless it can be detached and sold separately from the debt security. Since many conversion options cannot be separately sold, convertible debt is priced like any other debt (see Module 8). Explain why issuing convertible debt with nondetachable options can reduce interest expense.

MA9-60. **Ethics and Governance: Equity Carve Outs** **(LO3)**

Many companies use split-offs as a means to unlock shareholder value. The split-off effectively splits the company into two pieces, each of which can then be valued separately by the stock market. If managers are compensated based on reported profit, how might they strategically structure the split-off? What corporate governance issues does this present?

Module Ten

Reporting and Analyzing Off-Balance-Sheet Financing

LEARNING OBJECTIVES

LO1 Describe and illustrate the accounting for capitalized leases. (p. 10-4)

LO2 Describe and illustrate the accounting for pensions. (p. 10-12)

LO3 Explain the accounting for special purpose entities (SPEs). (p. 10-24)

AMERICAN AIRLINES

American Airlines (AMR) is solvent and profitable, but confronts competing demands for its available cash flow as a result of a heavy debt load that includes borrowed money, aircraft leases, and pension and other post-employment obligations. The magnitude of obligations arising from aircraft leases often surprises those outside the industry. Many airlines do not own the planes that they fly. To a large extent, those planes are owned by commercial leasing companies like General Electric Commercial Credit (GE's financial subsidiary), and are leased by the airlines.

If structured in a specific way, neither the leased planes (the assets) nor the lease obligation (the liability) would be on American Airlines' balance sheet. That nondisclosure can alter investors' perceptions of the capital investment American Airlines needs to operate its business as well as the level of debt it carries. In this module, we describe an analytical procedure that provides an alternative view of the company's investing and financing activities.

The analytical adjustment increases the liability on American Airlines' balance sheet: lease payment obligations on aircrafts total $5.3 billion in 2007, which is a staggering amount when compared to the company's net operating assets of $9.4 billion. This module discusses the accounting for leases and explains this analytical adjustment and how to apply it.

Pensions and long-term health care plans are another large obligation for many large companies, including American Airlines. Until recently, information about these pension and health care obligations was only in footnotes. Recent accounting rule changes now require companies to report that information on the balance sheet. In particular, the balance sheet now reports the net pension and health care liabilities (the total liability less related investments that fund the liabilities).

American Airlines' 2007 net pension and health care liability exceeds pension assets by $3.8 billion. That amount represents 13% of American's total liabilities and equity. This module explains the accounting for both pensions and health care obligations and examines footnote disclosures that convey a wealth of information relating to assumptions underlying estimates of these obligations.

Methods that companies apply to avoid reporting potential liabilities (and expenses), are commonly referred to as *off-balance-sheet financing*. Although companies have long practiced off-balance-sheet financing, more recent techniques have become increasingly complex and require careful analysis. We explain one such off-balance-sheet technique, special purpose entities (SPEs), in Appendix 10B.

Sources: American Airlines 2007 Form 10-K; *The Wall Street Journal*, January 2009.

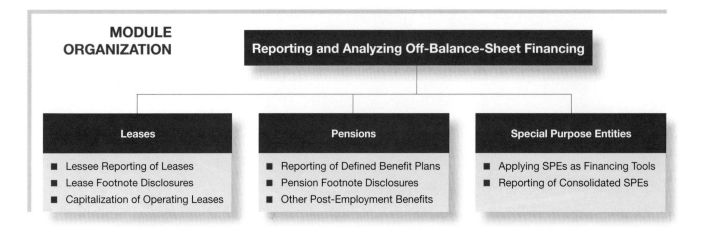

Company stakeholders pay attention to the composition of the balance sheet and its relation to the income statement. This attention extends to their analysis and valuation of both equity and debt securities. Of particular importance in this valuation process is the analysis of return on equity (ROE) and its components: return on net operating assets (RNOA)—including net operating profit margin (NOPM) and net operating asset turnover (NOAT)—and the degree of financial leverage (FLEV). Module 4 and its appendix explain these measures.

To value debt securities such as bonds and notes, one must consider a company's financial leverage (claims against assets) and the level of debt service (interest and principal payments), and compare them with expected cash flows. If analysis reveals that profitability (as measured by ROE and RNOA) and cash flows are inadequate, companies' credit ratings could decline. The resulting higher cost of debt capital could limit the number of investment projects that yield a return greater than their financing cost. This restricts the company's growth and profitability.

Financial managers are aware of the importance of how financial markets perceive their companies. They also recognize the market attention directed at the quality of their balance sheets and income statements. This reality can pressure managers to *window dress* financial statements to present the company's financial condition and performance in the best possible light. To increase reported solvency and decrease the risk metrics, companies generally wish to present a balance sheet with low levels of debt. Companies that are more liquid and less financially leveraged are viewed as less likely to go bankrupt. As a result, the risk of default on their debt is less, resulting in a better credit rating and a lower interest rate.

Companies also generally wish to present a balance sheet with fewer assets. This is driven by return considerations. ROE has two components: operating return and nonoperating return. The latter is a function of the company's effective use of debt. Investors generally prefer a company's ROE to be derived from operations (RNOA) rather than from its use of debt. So, if a company can maintain a given level of profitability with fewer assets, the related increase in ROE is perceived to be driven by higher RNOA (asset turnover), and not by increased financial leverage.

Off-balance-sheet financing means that assets or liabilities, or both, are not reported on the balance sheet. Even though GAAP requires detailed footnote disclosures, managers generally believe that keeping such assets and liabilities off the balance sheet improves market perception of their operating performance and financial condition. This belief presumes that the market is somewhat inefficient, a notion that persists despite empirical evidence suggesting that analysts adjust balance sheets to include assets and liabilities that managers exclude.

This module explains and illustrates several types of off-balance-sheet financing. Major topics we discuss are leases, pensions, health care liabilities, and special purpose entities (SPEs). This is not an exhaustive list of the techniques that managers employ to achieve off-balance-sheet financing, but it includes the most common methods. We must keep one point in mind: the relevant information to assess off-balance-sheet financing is mainly in footnotes. While GAAP footnote disclosures on such financing are fairly good, we must have the analytic tools to interpret them and to understand the nature and the magnitude of assets and liabilities that managers have moved off of the balance sheet. This module provides those tools.

LEASES

We begin the discussion of off-balance-sheet financing with leases. The following graphic shows that leasing impacts both sides of the balance sheet (liabilities and assets) and the income statement (leasing expenses are often reported in selling, general and administrative expenses).

LO1 Describe and illustrate the accounting for capitalized leases.

Income Statement	Balance Sheet	
Sales	Cash	Current liabilities
Cost of goods sold	Accounts receivable	**Long-term liabilities**
Selling, general and administrative expenses	Inventory	
Income taxes	**Long-term operating assets**	Shareholders' equity
Net income	Investments	

A lease is a contract between the owner of an asset (the **lessor**) and the party desiring to use that asset (the **lessee**). Since this is a private contract between two willing parties, it is governed only by applicable commercial law, and can include whatever provisions the parties negotiate.

Leases generally provide for the following terms:

■ Lessor allows the lessee the unrestricted right to use the asset during the lease term.

■ Lessee agrees to make periodic payments to the lessor and to maintain the asset.

■ Title to the asset remains with the lessor, who usually takes physical possession of the asset at lease-end unless the lessee negotiates the right to purchase the asset at its market value or other predetermined price.

From the lessor's standpoint, lease payments are set at an amount that yields an acceptable return on investment, commensurate with the lessee's credit rating. The lessor has an investment in the lease asset, and the lessee gains use of the asset.

The lease serves as a financing vehicle, similar to a secured bank loan. However, there are several advantages to leasing over bank financing:

■ Leases often require less equity investment by the lessee (borrower) compared with bank financing. Leases usually require the first lease payment be made at the inception of the lease. For a 60-month lease, this amounts to a 1/60 (1.7%) investment by the lessee, compared with a typical bank loan of 70-80% of the asset cost (thus requiring 20-30% equity investment by the borrower).

■ Because leases are contracts between two parties, their terms can be structured to meet both parties' needs. For example, a lease can allow variable payments to match the lessee's seasonal cash inflows or have graduated payments for start-up companies.

■ If the lease is properly structured, neither the lease asset nor the lease liability is reported on the balance sheet. Accordingly, leasing can be a form of off-balance-sheet financing.

Lessee Reporting of Leases

GAAP identifies two different approaches for the reporting of leases by the lessee:

■ **Capital lease method.** This method requires that both the lease asset and the lease liability be reported on the balance sheet. The lease asset is depreciated like any other long-term asset. The lease liability is amortized like debt, where lease payments are separated into interest expense and principal repayment.

■ **Operating lease method.** Under this method, neither the lease asset nor the lease liability is reported on the balance sheet. Lease payments are recorded as rent expense by the lessee when paid.

The financial statement effects for the lessee of these methods are summarized in Exhibit 10.1

EXHIBIT 10.1	Financial Statement Effects of Lease Type for the Lessee			
Lease Type	Assets	Liabilities	Expenses	Cash Flows
Capital	Lease asset reported	Lease liability reported	Depreciation and interest expense	Payments per lease contract
Operating	Lease asset **not** reported	Lease liability **not** reported	Rent expense	Payments per lease contract

GAAP defines criteria to determine whether a lease is capital or operating.[1] Managers seeking off-balance-sheet financing structure their leases around the GAAP rules so as to fail the "capitalization tests."

Under the operating method, lease assets and lease liabilities are *not* recorded on the balance sheet. The company merely discloses key details of the transaction in the lease footnote. The income statement reports the lease payment as rent expense. And, the cash outflows (payments to lessor) per the lease contract are included in the operating section of the statement of cash flows.

For capital leases, both the lease asset and lease liability are reported on the balance sheet. In the income statement, depreciation and interest expense are reported instead of rent expense. (Because only depreciation is an operating expense, NOPAT is higher when a lease is classified as a capital lease.) Further, although the cash payments to the lessor are identical whether or not the lease is capitalized on the balance sheet, the cash flows are classified differently for capital leases—that is, each payment is part interest (operating cash flow) and part principal (financing cash flow). Operating cash flows are, therefore, greater when a lease is classified as a capital lease.

Classifying leases as "operating" has four financial reporting consequences for the lessee:

1. The lease asset is not reported on the balance sheet. This means that net operating asset turnover (NOAT) is higher because reported operating assets are lower and revenues are unaffected.

2. The lease liability is not reported on the balance sheet. This means that balance sheet measures of financial leverage (like the total liabilities-to-equity ratio) are improved; many managers believe the reduced financial leverage will result in a better credit rating and, consequently, a lower interest rate on borrowed funds.

3. Without analytical adjustments (see later section on capitalization of operating leases), the portion of ROE derived from operating activities (RNOA) appears higher, which improves the perceived quality of the company's ROE.

4. During the early years of the lease term, rent expense reported for an operating lease is less than the depreciation and interest expense reported for a capital lease.[2] This means that net income is higher in those early years with an operating lease.[3] Further, if the company is growing and continually adding operating lease assets, the level of profits will continue to remain higher during the growth period.

The benefits of applying the operating method for leases are obvious to managers, thus leading some to avoid lease capitalization. Furthermore, the lease accounting standard includes rigid requirements relating to capitalization. Whenever accounting standards are rigidly defined, managers can structure transactions to meet the letter of the standard to achieve a desired accounting result when the essence of the transaction would suggest a different accounting treatment. This is *form over substance*.

---

[1] Leases must be capitalized when one or more of the following four criteria are met: (1) The lease automatically transfers ownership of the lease asset from the lessor to the lessee at termination of the lease. (2) The lease provides that the lessee can purchase the lease asset for a nominal amount (a bargain purchase) at termination of the lease. (3) The lease term is at least 75% of the economic useful life of the lease asset. (4) The present value of the lease payments is at least 90% of the fair market value of the lease asset at inception of the lease.

[2] This is true even if the company employs straight-line depreciation for the lease asset since interest expense accrues on the outstanding balance of the lease liability, which is higher in the early years of the lease life. Total expense is the same *over the life of the lease,* regardless of whether the lease is capitalized or not. That is: Total rent expense (from operating lease) = Total depreciation expense (from capital lease) + Total interest expense (from capital lease).

[3] However, NOPAT is *lower* for an operating lease because rent expense is an operating expense whereas only depreciation expense (and not interest expense) is an operating expense for a capital lease.

IFRS INSIGHT Lease Accounting under IFRS

U.S. GAAP and IFRS both require that leases be capitalized if the lease asset's risks and rewards are transferred to the lessee. The main difference between the two reporting systems is that IFRS are more principles based and GAAP is more rules based (as an example, see footnote 1). Given the broader application of principles, IFRS classify more leases as *finance leases* (termed "capital leases" under GAAP). Other small differences exist in the accounting for leases but these will not lead to materially different reporting outcomes in most cases.

Footnote Disclosure of Leases

Disclosures of expected payments for leases are required under both operating and capital lease methods. American Airlines provides a typical disclosure from its 2007 annual report:

Leases AMR's subsidiaries lease various types of equipment and property, primarily aircraft and airport facilities. The future minimum lease payments required under capital leases, together with the present value of such payments, and future minimum lease payments required under operating leases that have initial or remaining noncancelable lease terms in excess of one year as of December 31, 2007, were (in millions):

Year Ending December 31	Capital Leases	Operating Leases
2008	$ 243	$ 1,037
2009	180	932
2010	144	866
2011	146	859
2012	97	676
2013 and thereafter	559	5,798
	$1,369	$10,168
Less amount representing interest.	523	
Present value of net minimum lease payments	$ 846	

At December 31, 2007, the Company was operating 184 jet aircraft and 2 turboprop aircraft under operating leases and 84 jet aircraft under capital leases. The aircraft leases can generally be renewed at rates based on fair market value at the end of the lease term for one to five years. Some aircraft leases have purchase options at or near the end of the lease term at fair market value, but generally not to exceed a stated percentage of the defined lessor's cost of the aircraft or a predetermined fixed amount. Rent expense, excluding landing fees, was $1.4 billion, $1.4 billion and $1.3 billion in 2007, 2006 and 2005, respectively.

Lease disclosures such as this provide information concerning current and future payment obligations. These contractual obligations are similar to debt payments and must be factored into our evaluation of the company's financial condition.

American Airlines' footnote disclosure reports minimum (base) contractual lease payment obligations for each of the next five years and the total lease payment obligations that come due in year six and beyond. This is similar to disclosures of future maturities for long-term debt. The company also must provide separate disclosures for operating leases and capital leases (American Airlines has both operating and capital leases outstanding).

MANAGERIAL DECISION You Are the Division President

You are the president of an operating division. Your CFO recommends operating lease treatment for asset acquisitions to reduce reported assets and liabilities on your balance sheet. To achieve this classification, you must negotiate leases with shorter base terms and lease renewal options that you feel are not advantageous to your company. What is your response? [Answer, p. 10-29]

Capitalization of Operating Leases

Although not recognized on-balance-sheet, leased properties represent assets (and create liabilities) as defined under GAAP. That is, the company controls the assets and will profit from their future benefits. Also, lease liabilities represent real contractual obligations. Although the financial statements are prepared in conformity with GAAP, the failure to capitalize operating lease assets and lease liabilities for analysis purposes distorts ROE analysis—specifically:

- Net operating profit margin (NOPM) is understated with operating leases that should have been capitalized. Over the life of the lease, rent expense under operating leases equals depreciation plus interest expense under capital leases; however, only depreciation expense is included in net operating profit (NOPAT) as interest is a nonoperating expense. Operating expense is, therefore, overstated, and NOPM is understated. While cash payments are the same whether the lease is classified as operating or capital, *operating cash flow* is higher with capital leases since depreciation is an add-back, and the reduction of the capital lease obligation is classified as a *financing* outflow. Operating cash flows are, therefore, lower with operating leases than with capital leases.

- Net operating asset turnover (NOAT) is overstated with operating leases due to nonreporting of lease assets.

- Financial leverage (FLEV) is understated by the omitted lease liabilities—recall that lease liabilities are nonoperating.

Although aggregate ROE is relatively unaffected (assuming that the leases are at their midpoint on average so that rent expense is approximately equal to depreciation plus interest) failure to capitalize an operating lease results in a balance sheet that, arguably, neither reflects all of the assets that are used in the business, nor the nonoperating obligations for which the company is liable. Such noncapitalization of leases makes ROE appear to be of higher quality because it derives from higher RNOA (due to higher NOA turnover) and not from higher financial leverage. This is, of course, the main reason why some managers want to exclude leases from the balance sheet.

Lease disclosures that are required under GAAP allow us to capitalize operating leases for analysis purposes. This capitalization process involves three steps (this is the same basic process that managers would have used if all leases had been classified as capital leases):

1. Determine the discount rate.

2. Compute the present value of future operating lease payments.

3. Adjust statements to include the present value from step 2 as both a lease asset and a lease liability.

Step 1. There are at least two approaches to determine the appropriate discount rate for our analysis: (1) If the company discloses capital leases, we can impute (infer) an implicit rate of return: a rate that yields the present value computed by the company given the future capital leases payments (see Business Insight box later in this section). (2) Use the rate that corresponds to the company's credit rating or the rate from any recent borrowings involving intermediate-term secured obligations. Companies typically disclose these details in their long-term debt footnote. To illustrate the capitalization of operating leases, we use the American Airline lease footnote reproduced above. Step 1 estimates the implicit rate for American's capital leases to be 11.5% (see the following Business Insight box on computing the imputed discount rate for leases).

Step 2. Compute the present value of future operating lease payments using the 11.5% discount rate that we estimated in Step 1, see Exhibit 10.2. We demonstrate this computation using a spreadsheet (without rounding of numbers); we show those same computations using both a financial calculator and present value tables in Appendix 10C. The spreadsheet (and calculator) method is more exact, but may or may not yield a material difference to the number obtained when using present value tables. Given the widespread use of spreadsheets such as Excel, we use the spreadsheet method hereafter.

BUSINESS INSIGHT Imputed Discount Rate Computation for Leases

When companies report both operating and capital leases, the average rate used to discount capital leases can be imputed from disclosures in the leasing footnote. American Airlines reports total undiscounted minimum capital lease payments of $1,369 million and a discounted value for those lease payments of $846 million. Using Excel, we estimate the discount rate that American used for its capital lease computations with the IRR function (=**IRR(values**,guess)) as shown in the following spreadsheet. The entries in cells B2 through G2 are taken from American's reported schedule of lease maturities in the footnote shown earlier in this section, and those in cells H2 through M2 assume a continuation of the $97 million in capital lease payments in Year 5 until the $559 million of estimated payments after Year 5 is accounted for. The spreadsheet method yields an estimate of 11.5% for the discount rate that American implicitly used for capitalization of its capital leases in its 2007 balance sheet.

	A	B	C	D	E	F	G	H	I	J	K	L	M
1	N	0	1	2	3	4	5	6	7	8	9	10	11
2	Amount	-846	243	180	144	146	97	97	97	97	97	97	74
3	IRR	11.5% *									= 559		
4													
5	*Formula for cell B3 is =IRR(B2:M2,7%)												

EXHIBIT 10.2 Present Value of Operating Lease Payments ($ millions)

Year	Operating Lease Payment	Discount Factor ($i = 0.115$)	Present Value
1...................	$1,037	0.89686	$ 930
2...................	932	0.80436	750
3...................	866	0.72140	625
4...................	859	0.64699	556
5...................	676	0.58026	392
>5.................	5,798	5.27723 × 0.58026	2,070
			$5,323
Remaining life........	$5,798/$676 = 8.577 years		

Spreadsheet Method. The present value of the operating lease payments equals the sum of the present values for each of the five-year lease payments and the present value of the lease payments after Year 5. This two-step computation follows:

1. *Present values for years 1 through 5.* The present value of each forecasted lease payment for Years 1 through 5 is computed as the product of (a) the lease payment for that year and (b) the present value factor for that year using the following formula: $\frac{1}{(1+i)^t}$ where i is the discount factor and t is the year (1, 2, 3, 4 and 5). To illustrate using American Airlines, we enter the discount rate of 11.5% and the year 1, 2, 3, 4 and 5 separately for each year to obtain a present value factor for each year. For example, for Year 1 the present value factor is 0.89686, computed as $\frac{1}{(1.115)^1}$; and, for Year 2 the present value factor is 0.80436, computed as $\frac{1}{(1.115)^2}$; and so forth. Thus, the present value ($ in millions) of the Year 1 lease payment equals $930, computed from: $1,037 × $\left[\frac{1}{(1.115)^1}\right]$; the present value of the Year 2 lease payment equals $750, computed from: $932 × $\left[\frac{1}{(1.115)^2}\right]$; and so forth. In Excel, for Year 2, the present value factor is entered as: 1/1.115^2. The present values for Year 1 through Year 5 are in the far right column of Exhibit 10.2.

2. *Present value for Year 6 and thereafter.* To compute the present value of the lease payments remaining after Year 5, we make an assumption that the company continues to make lease payments at the Year 5 level for the remainder of the lease term. The remaining lease term is,

therefore, estimated as: (Total payments for Year 6 and thereafter)/(Year 5 lease payment). This means the remaining payments are an annuity for the remainder of the lease term, the present value of which equals the product of (a) the lease payment level for Year 5 and (b) the present value factor for that remaining annuity using the following formula: $\frac{1 - [1/(1 + i)^n]}{i} \times \frac{1}{(1 + i)^5}$, where i is the discount factor and n is the remainder of the lease term. To illustrate using American, we enter the 11.5% discount rate and the 8.577 years estimate of the remaining lease term (computed from $5,798/$676). The present value of the remaining lease payments equals $2,070, computed from:

$$\$676 \text{ million} \times \frac{1 - [1/(1.115)^{8.577}]}{0.115} \times \frac{1}{(1.115)^5}$$

The first term is the assumed payment level after Year 5; the second term is the present value factor for the remaining annuity after Year 5; and the third term discounts the second term to the present. In Excel, the second and third terms are entered as $((1-(1/(1.115)^8.577)) / 0.115) * (1/1.115^5)$. The present value of the lease payments for Year 6 and thereafter is in the sixth row of the far right column of Exhibit 10.2.

We sum the present values from parts 1 and 2 above to obtain the present value of future operating lease payments; for American, this totals $5,323 ($ millions), computed as $930 + $750 + $625 + $556 + $392 + $2,070.

Step 3. Use the computed present value of future operating lease payments to adjust the balance sheet, income statement, and financial ratios as we illustrate below.

Balance Sheet Effects   To adjust the balance sheet, add the present value from Step 2 to both operating assets (PPE) and nonoperating liabilities (long-term debt). Exhibit 10.3 shows the adjustments for American Airlines at year-end 2007. The capitalization of operating leases has a marked impact on American Airline's balance sheet. For the airline and retailing industries, in particular, lease assets (airplanes and real estate) comprise a large portion of net operating assets, which are typically accounted for using the operating lease method. Thus, companies in these industries usually have sizeable off-balance-sheet assets and liabilities.

EXHIBIT 10.3 Adjustments to Balance Sheet from Capitalization of Operating Leases				
American Airlines ($ millions)	**Reported Figures**	**Adjustments**	**Adjusted Figures**	**Percent Increase**
Net operating assets	$9,412	$5,323	$14,735	56.6%
Net nonoperating obligations. . .	6,755	5,323	12,078	78.8%
Equity	2,657	—	2,657	0.0%

Income Statement Effects   Capitalizing operating leases affects the income statement via depreciation of the leased equipment and interest on the lease liability. Operating lease payments are reported as rent expense, typically included in selling, general and administrative expenses. The income statement adjustments relating to the capitalization of operating leases involve two steps:[4]

1. Remove "rent expense" of $1,037 million from operating expense.
2. Add depreciation expense from the lease assets to operating expense and add interest expense from the lease obligation as a nonoperating expense. Lease assets are estimated at $5,323 million (see Exhibit 10.3). GAAP requires companies to depreciate capital lease assets over their useful lives or the lease terms, whichever is less. For this example, we assume that the remaining lease term is 13.577 years (five years reported in the lease schedule plus 8.577 years after the fifth year). Using this term and zero salvage value results in estimated straight-line depreciation for lease assets of

---

[4] This approach uses the operating lease payments from Year 1 of the projected payments to approximate the rent expense for operating leases. This approach also uses the computed present value of future lease payments (from Step 2) to compute the depreciation and interest expense for capital leases. An alternative approach is to use *actual* rent expense for the current year (disclosed in the leasing footnote) together with depreciation and interest computed based on capitalization of the *prior* year's future lease payments. Although, arguably more exact, most analysts use the simplified approach illustrated here given the extent of other estimates involved (such as discount rates, depreciation lives, and salvage values).

$392 million ($5,323 million/13.577 years). Interest expense on the $5,323 million lease liability at the 11.5% capitalization rate is $612 million ($5,323 million × 11.5%) for the first year.

American Airlines reports NOPAT of $1,061 million (AMR pays no taxes due to large tax loss carryforwards), nonoperating expense of $557 million, and net income of $504 million. The net adjustment to NOPAT is $645 million, computed as $1,037 million of rent expense less $392 million of depreciation, see Exhibit 10.4. The increase in nonoperating expense is $612 million, which is the additional interest expense on the capitalized lease obligation. Exhibit 10.4 summarizes those adjustments to American's profitability measures.

EXHIBIT 10.4 Adjustments to Income Statement from Capitalization of Operating Leases

American Airlines ($ millions)	Reported Figures	Adjustments	Adjusted Figures	Percent Increase
NOPAT	$1,061	$645	$1,706	60.8%
Nonoperating expense	557	612	1,169	109.8%
Net income	$ 504	$ 33*	$ 537	6.5%

*The $33 is the difference between $1,037 and the sum of ($392 + $612).

ROE and Disaggregation Effects Adjustments to capitalize operating leases can alter our assessment of ROE components. Using the adjustments we describe in Exhibits 10.3 and 10.4, the impact for ROE and its components (defined in Module 4), is summarized in Exhibit 10.5 for American Airlines.

EXHIBIT 10.5 Ratio Effects of Adjustments from Capitalization of Operating Leases

American Airlines ($ millions)	Reported	Adjusted	Computations for Adjusted Numbers
NOPM	4.6%	7.4%	$1,706/$22,935
NOAT	2.44	1.55	$22,935/($14,735 + $33*)
RNOA	11.3%	11.6%	$1,706/($14,735 + $33*)
Financial leverage (FLEV = NNO/Equity)	2.54	4.49	$12,078/($2,657 + $33*)
ROE	19.0%	20.0%	$537/($2,657 + $33*)
Nonoperating return	7.7%	8.4%	ROE − RNOA

* The $33 is the adjustment to net income per Exhibit 10.4 that affects both NOA and equity; for simplicity, we use year-end values for the denominator in lieu of average values.

Using *year-end* (reported and adjusted) data, and American Airlines' total revenues of $22,935 million, adjusted RNOA is 11.6% (up from 11.3% reported). RNOA increased because net operating profit margin increased (from 4.6% to 7.4%), but this was offset by a lower net operating asset turnover (from 2.44 to 1.55). After capitalization of its operating leases, American Airlines is more profitable and more capital intensive than we would infer from a review of its unadjusted income statement and balance sheet.

Although American's ROE increases by only 1% (from 19% to 20%), the analysis reveals that 42% (8.4%/20.0%) of its ROE results from nonoperating activities, up from 40% (7.7%/19.0%) using reported figures. The adjusted figures reveal greater financial leverage from capitalized lease obligations that is not apparent prior to capitalization. Specifically, financial leverage is 4.49 times equity using adjusted figures versus 2.54 times using reported figures. Financial leverage is, therefore, revealed to play a greater role in ROE.

Adjusted assets and liabilities arguably present a more realistic picture of the invested capital required to operate American Airlines and of the amount of leverage represented by its leases. Similarly, operating profitability is revealed to be higher than reported, since a portion of American's rent payments represent repayment of the lease liability (a nonoperating cash outflow) rather than operating expense.

Adjustments Assuming Income Taxes (Usual Situation) The adjustments made to American's income statement in Exhibit 10.4 *do not* reflect the usual tax situation. This is because American currently pays no income taxes due to loss carryforwards (see Module 5 for a discussion of tax loss carryforwards). However, it is important to know how to adjust for tax effects, which are common. To do so, *we assume that American's tax rate is 37.5%* (a common tax rate on operating income) rather than the 0% tax rate

IFRS Alert Both the FASB and IASB recognize limitations in accounting for leases and have convened a task force to consider revisions.

American currently reports. Using this assumed tax rate, American's NOPAT, nonoperating expense, and net income would equal the numbers in the first column ("Assumed Figures") of the following table, all of which are reduced by the assumed 37.5% rate.

($ millions)	Assumed Figures*	Adjustments	Adjusted Figures
NOPAT	$663	$403	$1,066
Nonoperating expense.	348	383	731
Net income.	$315	$ 20	$ 335

*Assumed figures = Reported figures × (1 − Tax rate).

The NOPAT adjustment, reflecting the elimination of rent expense and the addition of depreciation expense, is $403 million, computed as ($1,037 million − $392 million) × (1 − 37.5%), resulting in an adjusted NOPAT of $1,066 million. Next, the after-tax increase in nonoperating expense is $383 million, computed as $612 million × (1 − 37.5%), resulting in an adjusted after-tax nonoperating expense of $731 million. Finally, the net income adjustment is $20 million, increasing income from an assumed $315 million to an adjusted $335 million. The analysis that we explained for Exhibit 10.5 would proceed as illustrated, *but using these after-tax amounts.*

MID-MODULE REVIEW 1

Following is the leasing footnote disclosure from United Airlines' 2007 10-K report.

At December 31, 2007, the Company's leased aircraft, scheduled future minimum lease payments under capital leases (substantially all of which are for aircraft) and operating leases having initial or remaining noncancelable lease terms of more than one year were as follows:

	Operating Leases			
(In millions)	Mainline Aircraft	United Express Aircraft	Non-aircraft	Capital Leases
Number of aircraft				
United	162	251	—	72
UAL.	161	251	—	72
Payable during				
2008	$ 346	$ 410	$ 558	$ 341
2009	323	435	535	180
2010	307	433	516	465
2011	307	417	461	168
2012	297	372	422	119
After 2012.	936	1,380	3,284	592
UAL minimum lease payments.	$2,516	$3,447	$5,776	1,865
Imputed interest (at rates of 1.0% to 8.9%).				(509)
Present value of minimum lease payments				1,356
Current portion.				(250)
Long-term obligations under capital leases.				$1,106

Required

1. Impute the discount rate that United uses, on average, to compute the present value of its capital leases.
2. What adjustments would we make to United Airlines' balance sheet to capitalize the operating leases at the end of 2007? (*Hint:* The implicit rate on its capital leases is approximately 8.2%.)
3. Assuming the same facts as in part 2, what income statement adjustments might we consider?

Solution

1. The interest rate that United Airlines uses in the computation of its capital lease balance is imputed to be 8.2%; this rate is determined as follows (using a spreadsheet).

	A	B	C	D	E	F	G	H	I	J	K	L
1	N	0	1	2	3	4	5	6	7	8	9	10
2	Amount	-1356	341	180	465	168	119	119	119	119	119	116
3	IRR	8.2%										

2. Using the 8.2% discount rate, the present value of United Airline's operating leases follows ($ millions):

Year	Operating Lease Payment	Discount Factor (i = 8.2%)	Present Value
1	$ 1,314	0.92421	$1,214
2	1,293	0.85417	1,104
3	1,256	0.78944	992
4	1,185	0.72961	865
5	1,091	0.67432	736
>5	5,600	4.05750* × 0.67432	2,985**
			$7,896

Remaining life. . . . . . $5,600/$1,091 = 5.133 years

*The annuity factor for 5.133 years at 8.2% is 4.05750.

**$1,091 × 4.05750 × 0.67432 = $2,985.

UAL's operating leases represent $7,896 million in both unreported operating assets and unreported non-operating liabilities. These amounts should be added to the balance sheet for analysis purposes.

3. Income statement adjustments relating to capitalization of operating leases involve two steps:
   a. Remove rent expense of $1,314 million from operating expense.
   b. Add depreciation expense from lease assets to operating expense and also reflect interest expense on the lease obligation as a nonoperating expense. We assume that the remaining lease term is 10.133 years (five years reported in the lease schedule plus 5.133 years after Year 5). Using this term and zero salvage value, we get an estimated straight-line depreciation for lease assets of $779 million ($7,896 million/10.133 years). Interest expense on the $7,896 million lease liability at the 8.2% capitalization rate is $647 million ($7,896 million × 8.2%). The net adjustment to NOPAT, reflecting the elimination of rent expense and the addition of depreciation expense, is computed as: ($1,314 million rent expense − $779 million depreciation) × (1 − Tax rate on operating profit). The after-tax increase in nonoperating expense is computed as: $647 million × (1 − Federal and state statutory tax rate).

PENSIONS

Companies frequently offer pension plans as a benefit for their employees. There are two general types of pension plans:

LO2 Describe and illustrate the accounting for pensions.

1. **Defined contribution plan.** This plan requires the company make periodic contributions to an employee's account (usually with a third-party trustee like a bank), and many plans require an employee matching contribution. Following retirement, the employee makes periodic withdrawals from that account. A tax-advantaged 401(k) account is a typical example. Under a 401(k) plan, the employee makes contributions that are exempt from federal taxes until they are withdrawn after retirement.

2. **Defined benefit plan.** This plan also requires the company make periodic payments to a third party, which then makes payments to an employee after retirement. Payments are usually based on years of service and the employee's salary. The company may or may not set aside sufficient funds to cover these obligations (federal law does set minimum funding requirements). As a result, defined benefit plans can be overfunded or underfunded. All pension investments are retained by the third party until paid to the employee. In the event of bankruptcy, employees have the standing of a general creditor, but usually have additional protection in the form of government pension benefit insurance.

For a defined contribution plan, the company contribution is recorded as an expense in the income statement when the cash is paid or the liability accrued. For a defined benefit plan, it is not so simple.

This is because while the company contributes cash or securities to the pension investment account, the pension obligation is not satisfied until the employee receives pension benefits, which may be many years into the future. This section focuses on how a defined benefit plan impacts financial statements, and how we assess company performance and financial condition when such a plan exists.

Reporting of Defined Benefit Pension Plans

There are two accounting issues concerning the reporting of defined benefit pension plans.

1. How are pension plans (assets and liabilities) reported in the balance sheet (if at all)?
2. How is the expense relating to pension plans reported in the income statement?

The following graphic shows where pensions appear on the balance sheet (liabilities and assets) and the income statement (pension expense is usually reported in SG&A).

Income Statement	Balance Sheet	
Sales	Cash	Current liabilities
Cost of goods sold	Accounts receivable	**Long-term liabilities**
Selling, general and administrative expenses	Inventory	
Income taxes	**Long-term operating assets**	Shareholders' equity
Net income	Investments	

Balance Sheet Effects

Pension plan assets are primarily investments in stocks and bonds (mostly of other companies, but it is not uncommon for companies to invest pension funds in their own stock). Pension liabilities (called the **projected benefit obligation** or **PBO**) are the company's obligations to pay current and former employees. The difference between the market value of the pension plan assets and the projected benefit obligation is called the **funded status** of the pension plan. If the PBO exceeds the pension plan assets, the pension is **underfunded**. Conversely, if pension plan assets exceed the PBO, the pension plan is **overfunded**. Under current GAAP, companies are required to record only the funded status on their balance sheets (namely, the *net* amount, not the pension plan assets and PBO separately), either as an asset if the plan is overfunded, or as a liability if it is underfunded.

Pension plan assets consist of stocks and bonds whose value changes each period in three ways. First, the value of the investments increases or decreases as a result of interest, dividends, and gains or losses on the stocks and bonds held. Second, the pension plan assets increase when the company contributes additional cash or stock to the investment account. Third, the pension plan assets decrease by the amount of benefits paid to retirees during the period. These three changes in the pension plan assets are articulated below.

Pension Plan Assets
Pension plan assets, beginning balance
+ Actual returns on investments (interest, dividends, gains and losses)
+ Company contributions to pension plan
− Benefits paid to retirees
= Pension plan assets, ending balance

The pension liability, or PBO (projected benefit obligation), is computed as the present value of the expected future benefit payments to employees. The present value of these future payments depends on the number of years the employee is expected to work (years of service) and the employee's salary level at retirement. Consequently, companies must estimate future wage increases, as well as the number of employees expected to reach retirement age with the company and how long they are likely to receive pension benefits following retirement. Once the future retiree pool is determined, the expected future payments under the plan are discounted to arrive at the present value of the pension obligation. This is the PBO. A reconciliation of the PBO from beginning balance to year-end balance follows.

Pension Obligation	
	Projected benefit obligation, beginning balance
+	Service cost
+	Interest cost
+/−	Actuarial losses (gains)
−	Benefits paid to retirees
=	Projected benefit obligation, ending balance

As this reconciliation shows, the balance in the PBO changes during the period for four reasons.

■ First, as employees continue to work for the company, their pension benefits increase. The annual **service cost** represents the additional (future) pension benefits earned by employees during the current year.

■ Second, **interest cost** accrues on the outstanding pension liability, just as it would with any other long-term liability (see the accounting for bond liabilities in Module 8). Because there are no scheduled interest payments on the PBO, the interest cost accrues each year, that is, interest is added to the existing liability.

■ Third, the PBO can increase (or decrease) due to **actuarial losses (and gains)**, which arise when companies make changes in their pension plans or make *changes in actuarial assumptions* (such as the rate of wage inflation, termination and mortality rates, and the discount rate used to compute the present value of future obligations). For example, if a company increases the discount rate used to compute the present value of future pension plan payments from, say, 8% to 9%, the present value of future benefit payments declines (just like bond prices). Conversely, if the discount rate is reduced to 7%, the present value of the PBO increases. Other actuarial assumptions used to estimate the pension liability (such as the expected wage inflation rate or the expected life span of current and former employees) can also create similar actuarial losses or gains.

■ Fourth, pension benefit payments to retirees reduce the PBO (just as the payments reduce the pension plan assets).

Finally, companies are permitted to net the pension plan assets and the PBO and then report this net amount on the balance sheet. This net amount is called the **funded status** and is reported as an asset if pension assets exceed the PBO, and as a liability if the PBO exceeds pension assets.

Net Pension Asset (or Liability)	
	Pension plan assets (at market value)
−	Projected benefit obligation (PBO)
	Funded status

If the funded status is positive (assets exceed liabilities such that the plan is overfunded), the overfunded pension plan is reported on the balance sheet as an asset, typically called prepaid pension cost. If the funded status is negative (liabilities exceed assets and the plan is underfunded), it is reported as a liability.[5] During the late 2000s, long-term interest rates declined drastically and many companies lowered their discount rate for computing the present value of future pension payments. Lower discount rates meant higher PBO values. This period also witnessed a bear market and pension plan assets declined in value. The combined effect of the increase in PBO and the decrease in asset values caused many pension funds to become severely underfunded. Of the 2,123 publicly traded companies reporting pension plans in 2007, a total of 1,516 (71%) were underfunded. (American Airlines, for example, reports an underfunded pension plan of $1.35 billion in 2007.)

---

[5] Companies typically maintain many pension plans. Some are overfunded and others are underfunded. Current GAAP requires companies to separately group all of the overfunded and all of the underfunded plans, and to present a net asset for the overfunded plans and a net liability for the underfunded plans.

IFRS INSIGHT **Reporting of Pension Funded Status under IFRS**

Like U.S. GAAP, IFRS requires companies to report the funded status of their defined benefit pension plans on the balance sheet. The IFRS calculation of the unfunded status is slightly different than under GAAP. The IFRS unfunded status is calculated as projected benefit obligation minus the fair value of plan assets; but, unlike GAAP, any actuarial gains are added (losses are subtracted). There are other differences in detailed computations, which means that for pension assets and liabilities it is difficult to reliably compare GAAP and IFRS reports.

Income Statement Effects

A company's net pension expense is computed as follows.

Net Pension Expense
Service cost
+ Interest cost
− *Expected* return on pension plan assets
± Amortization of deferred amounts
Net pension expense

The net pension expense is rarely reported separately on the income statement. Instead, it is included with other forms of compensation expense in selling, general and administrative (SG&A) expenses. However, pension expense is disclosed separately in footnotes.

The net pension expense has four components. The previous PBO section described the first two components: service costs and interest costs. The third component of pension expense relates to the return on pension plan assets, which *reduces* total pension expense. To compute this component, companies use the long-term *expected* rate of return on the pension plan assets, rather than the *actual* return, and multiply that expected rate by the prior year's balance in pension plan assets account (usually the average balance in the prior year). Use of the expected return rather than actual return is an important distinction. Company CEOs and CFOs dislike income variability because they believe that stockholders react negatively to it, and so company executives intensely (and successfully) lobbied the FASB to use the more stable expected long-term investment return, rather than the actual return, in computing pension expense. Thus, the pension plan assets' expected return is deducted to compute net pension expense.[6]

Any difference between the expected and the actual return is accumulated, together with other deferred amounts, off-balance-sheet and reported in the footnotes. (Other deferred amounts include changes in PBO resulting from changes in estimates used to compute the PBO and from amendments to the pension plans made by the company.) However, if the deferred amount exceeds certain limits, the excess is recognized on-balance-sheet with a corresponding amount recognized (as amortization of deferred amounts) in the income statement.[7] This amortization is the fourth component of pension expense and can be either a positive or negative amount depending on the sign of the difference between expected and actual return on plan assets. (We discuss the amortization component of pension expense further in Appendix 10A.)

A final point to consider is the operating or nonoperating nature of the components of pension expense. Most analysts consider the service cost portion of pension expense to be an operating expense, similar to salaries and other benefits. However, the interest cost component is generally viewed as a nonoperating (financing) cost. Similarly, the expected return on plan assets is considered nonoperating.

---

[6] The FASB has issued an exposure draft containing a proposal to further amend the pension accounting standard to eliminate the use of the expected return. If passed, this amendment will result in increased earnings volatility as changes in the market value of the pension investments will impact net pension expense (and operating profits before tax) directly.

[7] To avoid amortization, the deferred amounts must be less than 10% of the PBO or pension investments, whichever is less. The excess, if any, is amortized until no further excess remains. When the excess is eliminated (by investment returns or company contributions, for example), the amortization ceases.

Footnote Disclosures—Components of Plan Assets and PBO

GAAP requires extensive footnote disclosures for pensions (and other post-employment benefits which we discuss later). These notes provide details relating to the net pension liability reported in the balance sheet and for the components of pension expense on the income statement.

American Airlines' pension footnote below indicates that the funded status of its pension plan is $(1,352) million on December 31, 2007. This means American's plan is underfunded. Following are the disclosures American Airlines makes in its pension footnote, $ millions.

Pension obligation at January 1, 2007	$11,048
Service cost	370
Interest cost	672
Actuarial loss (gain)	(1,021)
Benefit payments	(618)
Obligation at December 31, 2007	$10,451
Fair value of plan assets at January 1, 2007	$ 8,565
Actual return on plan assets	766
Employer contributions	386
Benefit payments	(618)
Fair value of plan assets at December 31, 2007	$ 9,099
Funded status at December 31, 2007	$ (1,352)

American Airlines' PBO began the year with a balance of $11,048 million. It increased by the accrual of $370 million in service cost and $672 million in interest cost. During the year, American also realized an actuarial gain of $1,021 million, which decreased the pension liability.[8] Finally, the PBO decreased as a result of $618 million in benefits paid to retirees, leaving a balance of $10,451 million at year-end.

Pension plan assets began the year with a fair market value of $8,565 million, which increased by $766 million from investment returns and by $386 million from company contributions. The company drew down its investments to make pension payments of $618 million to retirees. The $618 million payment reduced the PBO by the same amount, as discussed above, leaving the pension plan assets with a year-end balance of $9,099 million. The funded status of American Airlines' pension plan at year-end is $(1,352) million, computed as $10,451 million − $9,099 million. The negative balance indicates that its pension plan is underfunded. Most analysts *treat the funded status as an operating item* (either asset or liability).

American Airlines incurred $336 million of pension expense in 2007 and an additional $166 million of expense relating to defined contribution plans (companies typically maintain different types of retirement plans). The combined expense of $502 million is not broken out separately in the income statement. Instead, it is included in SG&A expense. Details of this expense are found in its 2007 pension footnote, which follows ($ millions):

Components of net periodic benefit cost	
Defined benefit plans:	
Service cost	$370
Interest cost	672
Expected return on assets	(747)
Amortization of:	
Prior service cost	16
Unrecognized net loss	25
Net periodic benefit cost for defined benefit plans	336
Defined contribution plans	166
	$502

---

[8] This actuarial gain results from two components. First, in 2007, federal law was changed, raising the mandatory retirement age for commercial pilots from 60 to 65; this change reduced the retirement period and, consequently, the company's pension liability. Second, American increased its discount rate from 6% to 6.5%; this change also reduced the pension liability.

The service and interest cost components of pension expense relate to the increase in the PBO of employees working another year for the company (expected benefits typically increase with longevity and salary, and the PBO increases because it is discounted for one less year). This expense is offset by the *expected* return on pension assets. Notice the use of expected returns rather than actual returns. Expected returns do not fluctuate as much as actual returns, and this yields a less volatile year-on-year pension expense and, consequently, less volatility in net income. The use of expected returns is in conformity with GAAP and companies lobbied for its use because of the reduced volatility for pension expense. Finally, because we cannot separate the operating and nonoperating components of a company's funded status and, hence, treat it entirely as operating, we do the same for pension expense and treat it entirely as operating. (We do this for consistency purposes even though we know that expense components related to interest cost, expected returns on plan assets, and many amortizations are nonoperating.)

RESEARCH INSIGHT | **Valuation of Pension Footnote Disclosures**

The FASB requires footnote disclosure of the major components of pension cost presumably because it is useful for investors. Pension-related research has examined whether investors assign different valuation multiples to the components of pension cost when assessing company market value. Research finds that the market does, indeed, attach different interpretation to pension components, reflecting differences in information about perceived permanence in earnings.

Footnote Disclosures and Future Cash Flows

Companies use their pension plan assets to pay pension benefits to retirees. When markets are booming, as during the 1990s, pension plan assets can grow rapidly. However, when markets reverse, as in the bear market of the late 2000s, the value of pension plan assets can decline. The company's annual pension plan contribution is an investment decision that is influenced, in part, by market conditions and minimum required contributions specified by law.[9] Companies' cash contributions come from borrowed funds or operating cash flows.

RESEARCH INSIGHT | **Why Do Companies Offer Pensions?**

Research examines why companies choose to offer pension benefits. It finds that deferred compensation plans and pensions help align the long-term interests of owners and employees. Research also examines the composition of pension investments. It finds that a large portion of pension fund assets are invested in fixed-income securities, which are of lower risk than other investment securities. This implies that pension assets are less risky than nonpension assets. The FASB has mandated new pension disclosures that will require firms (after 2009) to provide more detail about the types of assets held in pension plans. These disclosures will presumably help investors better assess the riskiness of pension assets.

American Airlines paid $618 million in pension benefits to retirees in 2007, yet it contributed only $386 million to pension assets that year. The remaining amount was paid out of available funds in the investment account. Cash contributions to the pension plan assets are the relevant amounts for an analysis of projected cash flows. Benefits paid in relation to the pension liability balance can provide a clue about the need for *future* cash contributions. Companies are required to disclose the expected benefit payments for five years after the statement date and the remaining obligations thereafter. Following is American Airlines' benefit disclosure statement:

---

[9] The Pension Protection Act of 2006 mandates that companies fully fund pension obligations by 2013. The bipartisan act also shields taxpayers from assuming airline pension plan obligations, tightens funding requirements so employers make greater cash contributions to pension funds, closes loopholes that allow companies with underfunded plans to skip cash pension payments, prohibits employers and union leaders from promising extra benefits if pension plans are markedly underfunded, and strengthens disclosure rules to give workers and retirees more information about the status of their pension plan.

The following benefit payments, which reflect expected future service as appropriate, are expected to be paid:

($ millions)	Pension
2008	$ 472
2009	514
2010	550
2011	594
2012	635
2013–2017	3,999

As of 2007, American Airlines pension plan assets account reports a balance of $9,099 million, as discussed above, and during the year, the plan assets generated actual returns of $766 million. The pension plan asset account is currently generating investment returns sufficient to cover the $500 million to $600 million in projected benefit payments outlined in the schedule above. Were investment returns not sufficient, the company would have to use operating cash flow or borrow money to fund the deficit.

One application of the pension footnote is to assess the likelihood that the company will be required to increase its cash contributions to the pension plan. This estimate is made by examining the funded status of the pension plan and the projected payments to retirees. For severely underfunded plans, the projected payments to retirees might not be covered by existing pension assets and projected investment returns. In this case, the company might need to divert operating cash flow from other prospective projects to cover its pension plan. Alternatively, if operating cash flows are not available, it might need to borrow to fund those payments. This can be especially troublesome as the debt service payments include interest, which increase the required pension contribution. General Motors' illustrates the problems associated with underfunded plans, as shown in the following Business Insight.

BUSINESS INSIGHT   Why GM's Bonds Were Rated Junk

Analysts have long been concerned with General Motors' mounting obligations to its employees stemming from generous pension and health care packages. The following graphic tracks the funded status of GM's pension and health care obligations since 1997. The unfunded obligation has exceeded $40 billion in nine out of eleven years, reaching a peak of over $70 billion in 2002. GM's underfunded status declined in 2006 and 2007 as the market value of its pension assets increased; those gains were wiped out in the market decline in 2008.

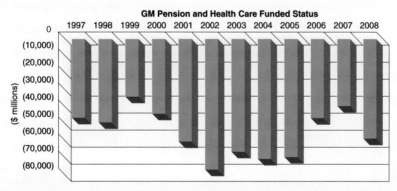

GM Pension and Health Care Funded Status

Companies can only look to two sources of funds to pay pension and health care liabilities. Either plan investments must increase in value or the company must make additional cash contributions to the plan. The latter, of course, uses operating cash flows or borrowed money, potentially at the expense of needed capital investment, R&D, or employee wages, resulting in long-term damage to the company's market position. The bond markets also became increasingly concerned about GM's ability to generate sufficient cash flow to pay its bonds when they mature and to make the payments promised to employees. That is one reason why GM's bonds were eventually downgraded to junk status.

Footnote Disclosures and Profit Implications

Recall the following earlier breakdown for pension expense:

Net Pension Expense
Service cost
+ Interest cost
− *Expected* return on pension plan assets
± Amortization of deferred amounts
Net pension expense

Interest cost is the product of the PBO and the discount rate. This discount rate is set by the company. The expected dollar return on pension assets is the product of the pension plan asset balance and the expected long-run rate of return on the investment portfolio. This rate is also set by the company. Further, PBO is affected by the expected rate of wage inflation, termination and mortality rates, all of which are estimated by the company.

GAAP requires disclosure of several rates used by the company in its estimation of PBO and the related pension expense. American Airlines discloses the following table in its pension footnote:

Pension Benefits	2007	2006
Weighted-average assumptions used to determine net periodic benefit cost for the years ended December 31		
Discount rate	6.00%	5.75%
Salary scale (ultimate).	3.78	3.78
Expected return on plan assets	8.75	8.75

During 2007, American Airlines increased its discount rate (used to compute the present value of its pension obligations, or PBO) by 0.25%, while leaving unchanged its estimates of the rate of wage inflation and the expected return on plan assets.

Changes in these assumptions have the following general effects on pension expense and, thus, profitability. This table summarizes the effects of increases in the various rates. Decreases have the exact opposite effects.[10]

Assumption	Estimate change	Probable effect on pension expense	Reason for effect
Discount rate	↑	↑	While the higher discount rate reduces the PBO, the lower PBO is multiplied by a higher rate when the company computes the interest component of pension expense. The rate effect is larger than the discount effect, resulting in increased pension expense.
Investment return . . .	↑	↓	The dollar amount of expected return on plan assets is the product of the plan assets balance and the expected long-term rate of return. Increasing the return increases the expected return on plan assets, thus reducing pension expense.
Wage inflation.	↑	↑	The expected rate of wage inflation affects future wage levels that determine expected pension payments. An increase, thus, increases PBO, which increases both the service and interest cost components of pension expense.

---

[10] The effect on the PBO and interest cost is seen in the following tables using the present values from an annuity of $1 for 10 and 40 years, respectively (dollar amounts are the present value factors from Appendix A; present value of an ordinary annuity, rounded to 2 decimal places).

	Discount rate	10 Years	40 Years
PBO	5%	$7.72	$17.16
	8%	6.71	11.92

As the discount rate increases, the PBO decreases. This is the discount effect. Second, the interest cost component of pension expense is computed as the PBO × Discount rate. For the four PBO amounts and related discount rates above, interest cost follows:

	Discount rate	10 Years	40 Years
Interest cost	5%	$0.39	$0.86
	8%	0.54	0.95

Interest cost increases with increases in the discount rate, regardless of the length of the liability. This is the rate effect.

In the case of American Airlines, the increase in the discount rate, coupled with no change in the expected rate of wage inflation and return on investments, served to increase pension costs and reduce profitability in that year. It is often the case that companies reduce the expected investment returns with a lag, but increase them without a lag, to favorably impact profitability. We must be aware of the impact of these changes in assumptions in our evaluation of company profitability.

Analysis Implications

There are two important analysis issues relating to pensions:

1. To what extent will the company's pension plans compete with investing and financing needs for the available cash flows?

2. In what ways has the company's choice of estimates affected its profitability?

Regarding the first issue, pension plan assets are the source of funds to pay benefits to retirees, and federal law mandates full pension funding by 2013. Consequently, if investment returns are insufficient, companies must make up the shortfall with additional contributions. Any such additional contributions compete for available operating cash flows with other investing and financing activities. This can be especially severe in a business downturn when operating cash flows are depressed. As debt payments are contractual, companies can be forced to postpone needed capital investment to make the contributions necessary to ensure funding of their pension plans as required by law or labor agreements. Analysts must be aware of these additional funding requirements when projecting future cash flows.

Regarding the second issue, accounting for pensions requires several assumptions, including the expected return on pension investments, the expected rate of wage inflation, the discount rate used to compute the PBO, and other actuarial assumptions that are not reported in footnotes (mortality rates, for example). Each of these assumptions affects reported profit as already explained. Analysts must be aware of changes in these assumptions and their effects on profitability. An increase in reported profit that is due to an increase in the expected return on pension investments, for example, is not related to core operating activities and, further, might not be sustainable. Such changes in estimates must be considered in our evaluation of reported profitability.

BUSINESS INSIGHT   **How Pensions Confound Income Analysis**

Overfunded pension plans and boom markets can inflate income. Specifically, when the stock market is booming, pension investments realize large gains that flow to income (via reduced pension expense). Although pension plan assets do not belong to shareholders (as they are the legal entitlement of current and future retirees), the gains and losses from those plan assets are reported in income. The following graph plots the funded status of General Electric's pension plans together with pension expense (revenue) that GE reported from 1998 through 2008.

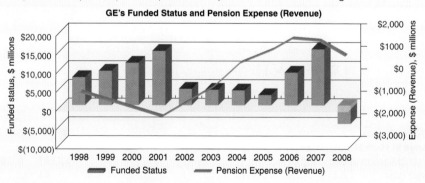

GE's Funded Status and Pension Expense (Revenue)

GE's funded status has consistently been positive (indicating an overfunded plan) until the market decline of 2008. The degree of overfunding peaked in 2001 at the height of the stock market, and began to decline during the bear market of the early 2000s. GE reported pension *revenue* (not expense) during this period. In 2001, GE's reported pension *revenue* was $2,095 million (10.6% of its pretax income). Because of the plan's overfunded status, the expected return and amortization of deferred gains components of pension expense amounted to $5,288 million, far in excess of the service and interest costs of $3,193 million. In the mid to late 2000s, GE recorded pension expense (rather than revenue) as the pension plan's overfunding and expected long-term rates of return declined.

Other Post-Employment Benefits

In addition to pension benefits, many companies provide health care and insurance benefits to retired employees. These benefits are referred to as **other post-employment benefits (OPEB)**. These benefits present reporting challenges similar to pension accounting. However, companies most often provide these benefits on a "pay-as-you-go" basis and it is rare for companies to make contributions in advance for OPEB. As a result, this liability, known as the **accumulated post-employment benefit obligation (APBO)**, is largely, if not totally, unfunded. GAAP requires that the unfunded APBO liability, net of any unrecognized amounts, be reported in the balance sheet and the annual service costs and interest costs be accrued as expenses each year. This requirement is controversial for two reasons. First, future health care costs are especially difficult to estimate, so the value of the resulting APBO (the present value of the future benefits) is fraught with error. Second, these benefits are provided at the discretion of the employer and can be altered or terminated at any time. Consequently, employers argue that without a legal obligation to pay these benefits, the liability should not be reported in the balance sheet.

These other post-employment benefits can produce large liabilities. For example, American Airlines' footnotes report a funded status for the company's health care obligation of $2,448 million, consisting of an APBO liability of $2,672 million less health care plan investments with a market value of $224 million. General Motors provides an extreme OPEB example (as described previously in the Business Insight box). Our analysis of cash flows related to pension obligations can be extended to other post-employment benefit obligations. For example, in addition to its pension payments, American Airlines discloses that it is obligated to make health care payments to retirees totaling nearly $200 million per year. Because health care obligations are rarely funded until payment is required (federal minimum funding standards do not apply to OPEB and there is no tax benefit to pre-funding), there are no investment returns to fund the payments. Our analysis of projected cash flows must consider this potential cash outflow.

RESEARCH INSIGHT | **Valuation of Nonpension Post-Employment Benefits**

The FASB requires employers to accrue the costs of all nonpension post-employment benefits; known as *accumulated post-employment benefit obligation* (APBO). These benefits consist primarily of health care and insurance. This requirement is controversial due to concerns about the reliability of the liability estimate. Research finds that the APBO (alone) is associated with company value. However, when other pension-related variables are included in the research, the APBO liability is no longer useful in explaining company value. Research concludes that the pension-related variables do a better job at conveying value-relevant information than the APBO number alone, which implies that the APBO number is less reliable.

MODULE-END REVIEW

Following is the pension disclosure footnote from Continental Airlines' 10-K report.

(In millions)	2007	2006
Change in Benefit Obligation		
Benefit obligation at beginning of year.	**$2,697**	$ 2,630
Service cost	**61**	59
Interest cost	**158**	146
Actuarial (gains) losses.	**(347)**	163
Benefits paid	**(59)**	(90)
Settlements	**(157)**	(211)
Benefit obligation at end of year	**$2,353**	$ 2,697

continued

continued from prior page

(In millions)	2007	2006
Change in Plan Assets		
Fair value of plan assets at beginning of year	$1,545	$ 1,421
Actual gain on plan assets	150	180
Employer contributions, including benefits paid under unfunded plans	338	249
Benefits paid	(59)	(90)
Lump sum settlements	(157)	(215)
Fair value of plan assets at end of year	$1,817	$ 1,545
Funded status at end of year	$ (536)	$(1,152)

Following is Continental Airlines' footnote for its pension cost as reported in its income statement.

Components of Net Periodic Benefit Expense (in millions)	2007	2006
Service cost	$ 61	$ 59
Interest cost	158	146
Expected return on plan assets	(137)	(122)
Amortization of unrecognized net actuarial loss	68	68
Amortization of prior service cost	10	9
Net periodic benefit expense	160	160
Settlement charges (included in special charges)	31	59
Net benefit expense	$191	$219

Required

1. In general, what factors impact a company's pension benefit obligation during a period?
2. In general, what factors impact a company's pension plan investments during a period?
3. What amount is reported on the balance sheet relating to the Continental Airlines pension plan?
4. How does the expected return on plan assets affect pension cost?
5. How does Continental Airlines' expected return on plan assets compare with its actual return (in $s) for 2007?
6. How much net pension expense is reflected in Continental Airlines' 2007 income statement?
7. Assess Continental Airlines' ability to meet payment obligations to retirees.

Solution

1. A pension benefit obligation increases primarily by service cost, interest cost, and actuarial losses (which are increases in the pension liability as a result of changes in actuarial assumptions). It is decreased by the payment of benefits to retirees and by any actuarial gains.
2. Pension investments increase by positive investment returns for the period and cash contributions made by the company. Investments decrease by benefits paid to retirees and by investment losses.
3. Continental Airlines' funded status is $(536) million ($2,353 million PBO − $1,817 million Pension Assets) as of 2007. The negative amount indicates that the plan is underfunded. Consequently, this amount is reflected as a liability on Continental's balance sheet.
4. Expected return on plan assets acts as an offset to service cost and interest cost in computing net pension cost. As the expected return increases, net pension cost decreases.
5. Continental Airlines' expected return of $137 million is less than its actual return of $150 million in 2007.
6. Continental Airlines reports a net pension expense of $191 million in its 2007 income statement.
7. Continental Airlines' funded status is negative, indicating an underfunded plan. In 2007, the company contributed $338 million to the pension plan, up from $249 million in the prior year. It is likely that the company will need to increase its future funding levels to cover the plan's requirements. This might have negative repercussions for its ability to fund other operating needs, and could eventually damage its competitive position.

APPENDIX 10A: Amortization Component of Pension Expense

One of the more difficult aspects of pension accounting relates to the issue of what is recognized on-balance-sheet and what is disclosed in the footnotes off-balance-sheet. This is an important distinction, and the FASB is moving toward more on-balance-sheet recognition and less off-balance-sheet disclosure. The FASB is considering whether to eliminate deferred gains and losses, and to require recognition in the income statement of *all* changes to pension assets and liabilities. Until this standard is enacted, deferred gains and losses will only impact reported pension expense via their amortization (the fourth component of pension expense described earlier in this module).

There are three sources of *unrecognized gains and losses*:

1. The difference between actual and expected return on pension investments.
2. Changes in actuarial assumptions such as expected wage inflation, termination and mortality rates, and the discount rate used to compute the present value of the projected benefit obligation.
3. Amendments to the pension plan to provide employees with additional benefits (called **prior service costs**).

Accounting for gains and losses resulting from these three sources is the same; specifically:

■ Balance sheets report the net pension asset (overfunded status) or liability (underfunded status) irrespective of the magnitude of deferred gains and losses; that is, based solely on the relative balances of the pension assets and PBO accounts.

■ Cumulative unrecognized gains and losses from all sources are recorded in one account, called deferred gains and losses, which is only disclosed in the footnotes, not on-balance-sheet.

■ When the balance in the deferred gains and losses account exceeds prescribed levels, companies transfer a portion of the deferred gain or loss onto the balance sheet, with a matching expense on the income statement. This is the amortization process described in the text.

Recall that a company reports the *estimated* return on pension investments as a component (reduction) of pension expense. The pension assets, however, increase (decrease) by the *actual* return (loss). The difference between the two returns is referred to as a deferred (unrecognized) gain or loss. To illustrate, let's assume that the pension plan is underfunded at the beginning of the year by $200, with pension assets of $800, a PBO of $1,000, and no deferred gains or losses. Now, let's assume that actual returns for the year of $100 exceed the long-term expected return of $70. We can illustrate the accounting for the deferred gain as follows:

	On Financial Statements				Footnotes	
Year 1	Funded Status (Liabilities)	Earned Capital	Accumulated Other Comprehensive Income (AOCI)	Income Statement	Pension Assets	PBO
Balance, Jan. 1.......	$200		$ 0	$ 0	$800	$1,000
Return.............	(100)	$70 (Retained Earnings) 30 (AOCI)	30	70	100	
Balance, Dec. 31	$100	$70 (Retained Earnings) 30 (AOCI)	$30	$70	$900	$1,000

The balance sheet at the beginning of the year reports the funded status of the pension plan as a $200 liability, reflecting the underfunded status of the pension plan. Neither the $800 pension asset account, nor the $1,000 PBO appear on-balance-sheet. Instead, their balances are only disclosed in a pension footnote.

During the year, pension assets (off-balance-sheet) increase by the actual return of $100 with no change in the PBO, thus decreasing the pension liability (negative funded status) by $100. The pension expense on the income statement, however, only reflects the expected return of $70, and retained earnings increase by that amount. The remaining $30 is recognized in accumulated other comprehensive income (AOCI), a component of earned capital.

These deferred gains and losses do not affect reported profit until they exceed prescribed limits, after which the excess is gradually recognized in income.[11] For example, assume that in the following year, $5 of the $30 deferred gain is amortized (recognized on the income statement as expense, which flows to retained earnings on the balance sheet). This amortization would result in the following effects:

[11] The upper (lower) bound on the deferred gains (losses) account is 10% of the PBO or Plan Asset account balance, whichever is greater, at the beginning of the year. Once this limit is exceeded, the excess is amortized until the account balance is below that threshold, irrespective of whether such reduction results from amortization, or changes in the PBO or Pension Asset accounts (from changes in actuarial assumptions, company contributions, or positive investment returns).

Year 2	Funded Status (Liabilities)	On Financial Statements			Footnotes	
		Earned Capital	Accumulated Other Comprehensive Income (AOCI)	Income Statement	Pension Assets	PBO
Balance, Jan. 1.......	$100	$70 (Retained Earnings) 30 (AOCI)	$30	$ 0	$900	$1,000
Amortization.........		$ 5 (Retained Earnings)	(5)	5		
Balance, Dec. 31	$100	$75 (Retained Earnings) 25 (AOCI)	$25	$ 5	$900	$1,000

The deferred gain is reduced by $5 and is now recognized in reported income as a reduction of pension expense. (This amortization is the fourth item in the Net Pension Expense computation table from earlier in this module.) This is the only change, as the pension assets still report a balance of $900 and the PBO reports a balance of $1,000, for a funded status of $(100) that is reported as a liability on the balance sheet.

In addition to the difference between actual and expected gains (losses) on pension assets, the deferred gains (losses) account includes increases or decreases in the PBO balance that result from changes in assumptions used to compute it, namely, the expected rate of wage inflation, termination and mortality rates for employees, and changes in the discount rate used to compute the present value of the pension obligations. Some of these can be offsetting, and all accumulate in the same deferred gains (losses) account. Justification for off-balance-sheet treatment of these items was the expectation that their offsetting nature would combine to keep the magnitude of deferred gains (losses) small. It is only in relatively extreme circumstances that this account becomes large enough to warrant amortization and, consequently, on-balance-sheet recognition. Further, the amortization portion of reported pension expense is usually small.

APPENDIX 10B: Special Purpose Entities (SPEs)

Special purpose entities (SPEs) allow companies to structure projects or transactions with a number of financial advantages. SPEs have long been used and are an integral part of corporate finance. The SPE concept is illustrated by the following graphic that summarizes information taken from Ford's 2007 10-K relating to the SPE structure it uses to securitize the receivables of Ford Credit (its financing sibsidiary):

LO3 Explain the accounting for special purpose entities (SPEs).

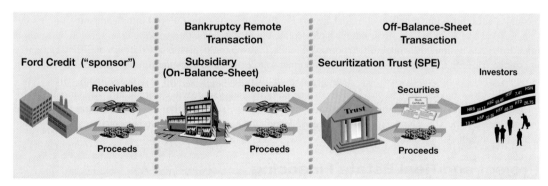

This graphic is typical of many SPEs and has the following characteristics of all SPEs:

■ A sponsoring company (here, Ford Credit) forms a subsidiary that is capitalized entirely with equity; this creates a *bankruptcy remote* structure. This means that even if Ford Credit becomes bankrupt, neither it nor its creditors will be able to access the subsidiary's assets; this reduces the risk for subsequent investors.

■ The subsidiary purchases assets from the sponsoring company and sells them to a securitization (off-balance-sheet) trust (the SPE), which purchases the assets using borrowed funds (here, the SPE purchases receivables from Ford Credit's subsidiary using cash from investors).

■ Cash flows from the acquired assets are used by the SPE to repay its debt (here, the SPE collects receivables and uses the funds to repay any borrowings).

The sponsoring company benefits in two ways. First, SPEs create direct economic benefits by speeding up receipt of the company's operating cash flows and by mitigating certain types of risk. Second, SPEs create indirect economic benefits by providing financial reporting benefits and alternatives. These indirect benefits derive from having assets, and their related debt, moved off-balance-sheet. Also, the SPE owns the sponsoring company's former assets. Thus, the sponsoring company enjoys an improved asset turnover ratio (assets are typically less in the denominator of the turnover ratio) and an improved financial leverage ratio (liabilities are less in the numerator of the liabilities-to-equity ratio).

Applying SPEs as Financing Tools

This section describes two common means of using SPEs as financing tools.

Asset Securitization

Consumer finance companies, retailers, and financial subsidiaries of manufacturing companies commonly use SPEs to securitize (sell) their financial assets. Ford Credit, the finance subsidiary of Ford Motor Company, provides a common example as illustrated in the footnotes to Ford's 2007 10-K report.

> **Securitization** Ford Credit securitizes finance receivables and net investment in operating leases through a variety of programs. . . . Most of Ford Credit's securitizations do not satisfy the requirements for accounting sale treatment, and the securitized assets and associated debt remain on Ford Credit's balance sheet. Some of Ford Credit's securitizations, however, do satisfy accounting sale treatment and are not reflected on its balance sheet in the same way as debt funding. Both on- and off-balance-sheet securitizations have an effect on its financial condition, operating results and liquidity.
>
> In a securitization transaction, the securitized assets are generally held by a bankruptcy-remote special purpose entity ("SPE") in order to isolate the securitized assets from the claims of Ford Credit's other creditors and to insure that the cash flows on the securitized assets are available for the benefit of securitization investors. As a result, payments to securitization investors are based on the creditworthiness of the securitized assets and any enhancements, and not on Ford Credit's creditworthiness. Senior asset-backed securities issued by the SPEs generally receive the highest short-term credit ratings and among the highest long-term credit ratings from the rating agencies that rate them. Ford Credit plans to meet a significant portion of its 2008 funding requirements through securitizations, and to continue to diversify its asset-backed funding by asset class and region.

Ford Credit's use of SPEs is typical. As Ford Credit provides financing to customers who purchase autos from Ford Motor Company, it accumulates the receivables on its balance sheet. Periodically, through a subsidiary, it packages certain receivables and sells them to its SPE, which funds the purchase by selling certificates entitling the holder to a portion of the cash receipts from eventual collection of receivables. Ford Credit does not provide any other form of protection to the outside certificate holders (its footnote indicates that the receivables are sold "without recourse," meaning without collection rights against Ford Credit or its parent, Ford Motor Company).

Ford Motor Company's credit ratings have declined in recent years, thus making its unsecured borrowings more costly and limiting its availability to borrowed funds. In response, it has increased its use of SPEs as a financing source. This funding mechanism is now an important source of liquidity for the company, as Ford Credit's cost of debt capital is substantially less, and exhibits less volatility, than that for Ford Motor Company. Thus, Ford's use of SPEs as a funding source provides necessary liquidity and also provides capital at a substantially lower interest rate. Due to the SPE's limited scope of operations, and its isolation from the general business risk of the parent company, the SPE's lenders face lower risk of default and can, therefore, charge a comparatively lower rate of interest on money they lend to the SPE.

Project and Real Estate Financing

Another common use of SPEs is to finance construction projects. For example, a sponsoring company desires to construct a manufacturing plant. It establishes an SPE and executes a contract with the SPE to build the plant and to later purchase output from the plant. The SPE uses the contract, and the newly constructed manufacturing plant assets, to collateralize debt that it issues to finance the plant's construction. The sponsoring company obtains the benefits of the plant, but does not recognize either the PPE asset or the related liability on its balance sheet. The sponsoring company has commitments with the SPE, labeled executory contracts, but GAAP currently does not require such contracts be recognized in the balance sheet, nor does it even require footnote disclosure of these contracts.

Clothing retailers such as Gap and Abercrombie & Fitch use these types of executory contracts involving outside manufacturers. The manufacturing assets, and related liabilities, are reported on the balance sheet of the SPE and not of the company itself.

A slight variation is to add leasing to this transaction. To illustrate, assume a company desires to construct an office building. It establishes an SPE to construct and finance the building and then leases the building back from the

SPE under an operating lease. As we explained earlier in this module, if the lease is structured as an operating lease, neither the lease asset nor the lease obligation is reported on the company's balance sheet. Thus, the company obtains the use and benefit of the building without recording either the building or the related debt on its balance sheet.

Reporting of SPEs

There is a concern that nonconsolidation of SPEs permits assets and liabilities related to the business to be reported off-balance-sheet. Accordingly, the reporting of SPEs is a current and controversial topic. Some put at least some of the blame for the economic meltdown of 2008 and 2009 on the off-balance-sheet treatment of SPEs by banks and industrial firms alike. Countless billions of dollars of assets such as home mortgages and car loans (like Ford's) were securitized and sold, and the balance sheets of sponsoring companies did not report the attendant risks of these securitized assets. To better understand, let's return to Ford and see that it discusses the following two ways of reporting for asset securitizations in its 10-K:

1. **Treatment of the securitization as a sale.** If the securitization is treated as a sale, the securitized assets (receivables in this case) are removed from the balance sheet and the difference between the sale proceeds and the carrying amount of the assets sold is recognized as a gain or loss on the sale. The important feature of this accounting is that neither the securitized assets nor the liabilities that are incurred to fund the purchase are reported on the seller's balance sheet. The seller, therefore, receives the cash without a requirement of recognizing the liability. This is called off-balance-sheet financing.
2. **Consolidation of the SPE.** The alternative method of accounting for the securitization is to consolidate the SPE just like any other sponsoring company's subsidiaries. The funding process proceeds as described above. However, instead of off-balance-sheet financing, the SPE is consolidated with the sponsoring company using the process we explain in Module 7. The effect of consolidation is, basically, to add the assets and liabilities of the SPE to those of the sponsoring company as though the assets had not been sold and the cash had been received by borrowing against the receivables.

The SEC and the FASB are concerned about any proliferation of off-balance-sheet financing, including through SPEs, and have proposed an amendment to accounting standards that, if enacted, requires consolidation of most, if not all, SPEs. As of the printing of this book, the standard has not yet been enacted, but its enactment is expected.

IFRS INSIGHT   Consolidation of SPEs under IFRS

Under both U.S. GAAP and IFRS, SPEs are consolidated based on the transfer of risks and rewards. But unlike GAAP's more rules-based orientation, IFRS requires a more conceptual analysis of risks and rewards. This leads to consolidation of more special purpose entities under IFRS as compared to GAAP. The FASB and the IASB are working toward convergence on this standard.

Analysis Implications of SPEs

Regardless of the consolidation (reporting) issue, the securitization process continues to provide a lower cost financing source to companies by reducing credit risk for the lenders. Accordingly, SPEs will continue to be part of the business landscape. As such, there are at least two analysis implications related to SPEs:

- **Cost of capital.** As discussed, SPEs reduce business risk and bankruptcy risk for their lenders. Consequently, the sponsoring company is able to obtain capital at a lower cost. Ford Motor Company (a manufacturer), for example, has witnessed a reduction in its credit ratings and a consequent increase in its cost of borrowed funds. Ordinarily, its negative credit rating would be ascribed to its subsidiaries as well, including its finance subsidiary. Using SPEs, however, the finance subsidiary, Ford Credit, is able to obtain financing at lower interest rates, which allows it to pass along that lower cost in the form of lower interest rates on auto and other loans to its customers. Without that financing source, Ford Credit would be less competitive in the marketplace vis-à-vis other, financially stronger, financial institutions.

- **Liquidity.** Financial institutions, and finance subsidiaries of manufacturing companies, rely on a business model of generating a high volume of loans, each of which carries a relatively small profit (spread of the interest rate over the cost of the funds). If they were forced to hold all of those loans on their own balance sheets, they would eventually need to raise costly equity capital to balance the increase in debt financing. That would also serve to reduce their competitiveness in the marketplace. These companies must, therefore, be able to package loans for sale, a crucial source of liquidity.

Given the importance of the cash flows contributed by its Ford Credit financing subsidiary to Ford Motor Company, analysts would be concerned about the welfare of the overall entity were there indications that its SPE financing sources would no longer be available (say, if further accounting standards limited Ford's ability to remove these loans from its consolidated balance sheet and record their transfer to the SPE as a sale). Analysts would also be concerned if the credit markets no longer favored this SPE structure as a financing mechanism (say, if the presumed bankruptcy protection of the SPEs was ultimately proven to be false following the bankruptcy of the sponsoring company and the consequent bankruptcy of an SPE that it sponsored). Neither of these events has occurred, and lenders rely on legal opinions that SPEs are "bankruptcy remote." Analysts must always assess these risks when assessing the financial strength of companies that rely on the SPE financial structure.

APPENDIX 10C: Lease Capitalization Using a Calculator and Present Value Tables

This Appendix identifies the keystrokes to compute both the present value of projected operating lease payments and the imputed discount rate using two popular financial calculators: **Hewlett-Packard 10bII** and **Texas Instruments BA II Plus**. It also computes the present value of projected lease payments using present value tables.

Hewlett-Packard 10bII: Present value of projected operating lease payments

Following are the keystrokes to compute the present value of the American Airlines projected lease payments. This approach utilizes the same computational steps as our illustrations.

Enter #	Key[a]	
1	P/YR	Enter the number of periods per year
0	CF$_i$	Enter the cash flow in year 0 (current year)
1037	CF$_i$	Enter the cash flow in year 1
932	CF$_i$	Enter the cash flow in year 2
866	CF$_i$	Enter the cash flow in year 3
859	CF$_i$	Enter the cash flow in year 4
676	CF$_i$	Enter the cash flow in year 5 (and assumed thereafter)
9	N$_i$	Enter the number of years the year 5 cash flow is repeated
390	CF$_i$	Enter the cash flow in final partial year (676×0.577 years)
11.5	I/YR	Enter the annual discount rate
	NPV	Pressing **NPV** button to get present value ($5,321)
0	DISP	Enter the number of decimal places desired

[a] To enter a number, type the number and then press the corresponding key; for example, to enter P/YR, type "1" and then press **P/YR**.

Hewlett-Packard 10bII: Imputed discount rate

This example computes the imputed discount rate given the capitalized lease disclosures in the lease footnote; we again use American Airlines.

Enter #	Key[a]	
1	P/YR	Enter the number of periods per year
−846[a]	CF$_i$	Enter the cash flow in year 0 (current year)
243	CF$_i$	Enter the cash flow in year 1
180	CF$_i$	Enter the cash flow in year 2
144	CF$_i$	Enter the cash flow in year 3
146	CF$_i$	Enter the cash flow in year 4
97	CF$_i$	Enter the cash flow in year 5 (and assumed thereafter)
6	N$_i$	Enter the number of years the year 5 cash flow is repeated
74	CF$_i$	Enter the cash flow in final partial year (97×0.763 years)
	IRR	Pressing **IRR** button to get implicit discount rate (11.471%)

[a] To enter a negative number, type in the absolute value of that number and then press +/− button; for example, to enter the initial cash flow in year 0, enter "846", press +/−, and then press **CF$_i$**.

Texas Instruments BA II Plus: Present value of projected operating lease payments

Following are the keystrokes to compute the present value of the American Airlines projected lease payments. This approach utilizes the same computational steps as our illustrations.

Key	Enter # [a]	
FORMAT	0	Press the **FORMAT** button and enter decimal places desired
CF	0	Enter the cash flow in year 0 (**CF$_O$**)
↓	1037	Enter the cash flow in year 1 (**CO1**)
↓		Frequency (**FO1**) should be pre-set at "1", so nothing need be entered
↓	932	Enter the cash flow in year 2 (**CO2**)
↓		Frequency (**FO2**) should be pre-set at "1"
↓	866	Enter the cash flow in year 3 (**CO3**)
↓		Frequency (**FO3**) should be pre-set at "1"
↓	859	Enter the cash flow in year 4 (**CO4**)
↓		Frequency (**FO4**) should be pre-set at "1"
↓	676	Enter the cash flow in year 5 (**CO5**) and assumed thereafter
↓	9	Enter the number of years the year 5 cash flow is repeated (**FO5**)
↓	390	Enter the cash flow in final partial year (676 × 0.577 years) (**CO6**)
↓		Frequency (**FO6**) should be pre-set at "1"
NPV	11.5	Press **NPV** button, the pre-set discount rate should say "0"; enter "11.5" the discount rate
↓, CPT	5,323	Press ↓ button and then press **CPT** to get present value

[a] After entering in a number from this column, press **ENTER**.

Texas Instruments BA II Plus: Imputed discount rate

Following are the keystrokes to compute the present value of the American Airlines projected lease payments. This approach utilizes the same computational steps as our illustrations.

Key	Enter [a]	
CF	−846[b]	Enter the cash flow in year 0 (**CF$_O$**)
↓	243	Enter the cash flow in year 1 (CO1)
↓		Frequency (FO1) should be pre-set at "1"
↓	180	Enter the cash flow in year 2 (CO2)
↓		Frequency (FO2) should be pre-set at "1"
↓	144	Enter the cash flow in year 3 (CO3)
↓		Frequency (FO3) should be pre-set at "1"
↓	146	Enter the cash flow in year 4 (CO4)
↓		Frequency (FO4) should be pre-set at "1"
↓	97	Enter the cash flow in year 5 and assumed thereafter (CO5)
↓	6	Enter the number of years the year 5 cash flow is repeated (FO5)
↓	74	Enter the cash flow in final partial year (CO6)
↓		Frequency (FO6) should be pre-set at "1"
IRR		Press **IRR** button, the pre-set IRR should say "0"
↓, CPT		Press ↓ button and then press **CPT** to get implicit discount rate

[a] After typing in a number from this column, press **ENTER**.

[b] To enter a negative number, type in the absolute value of that number and then press +/− button; for example, to enter the initial cash flow in year 0, press **CF**, enter "51", press +/−, and then press **ENTER**.

Lease Capitalization Using Present Value Tables

Present value tables list the factors for selected interest rates and discount periods (often in whole numbers). To compute the present value of the operating lease payments using those tables (see Appendix A near the end of this book), we must first round the remaining lease term (8.577 for American) to the nearest whole year (9), and round the discount rate (11.5% for American) to its nearest whole interest rate (12%). After that, computation of the present value of future operating lease payments is identical to the spreadsheet method and is shown below. We see that the present value of each projected lease payment for Years 1 through 5 is computed using the present value factor for that particular year (taken from Appendix A, Table 1, "Present Value of Single Amount") using a discount rate of 12%. To compute the present value of the lease payments remaining after Year 5, we again assume that lease payments continue at the Year 5 amount for the remainder of the lease term. Those payments represent an annuity, $676 million for 9 years (8.577 rounded to 9), that is discounted at 12% (taken from Appendix A, Table 2, "Present Value of Ordinary Annuity"), which is then discounted back five more years to the present.

Year ($ millions)	Operating Lease Payment	Discount Factor ($i = 0.12$)	Present Value
1.	$1,037	0.89286	$ 926
2.	932	0.79719	743
3.	866	0.71178	616
4.	859	0.63552	546
5.	676	0.56743	384
>5.	5,798 [$676 for ~9 years]	5.32825 × 0.56743	2,044
			$5,259
Remaining life.	$5,798/$676 = 8.577 years, rounded to 9 years		

Regardless of the method used, the computed amount is the present value of future operating lease payments. That value is $5,323 million using the spreadsheet method, $5,321 million using a calculator, and $5,259 million using present value tables.

GUIDANCE ANSWERS

MANAGERIAL DECISION **You Are the Division President**

Lease terms that are not advantageous to your company but are structured merely to achieve off-balance-sheet financing can destroy shareholder value. Long-term shareholder value is created by managing your operation well, including negotiating leases with acceptable terms. Lease footnote disclosures also provide sufficient information for skilled analysts to undo the operating lease treatment. This means that you can end up with de facto capitalization of a lease with lease terms that are not in the best interests of your company and with few benefits from off-balance-sheet financing. There is also the potential for lost credibility with stakeholders.

Superscript [A (B, C)] denotes assignments based on Appendix 10A (B, C).

DISCUSSION QUESTIONS

Q10-1. What are the financial reporting differences between an operating lease and a capital lease? Explain.

Q10-2. Are footnote disclosures sufficient to overcome nonrecognition on the balance sheet of assets and related liabilities for operating leases? Explain.

Q10-3. Is the expense of a lease over its entire life the same whether or not it is capitalized? Explain.

Q10-4. What are the economic and accounting differences between a defined contribution plan and a defined benefit plan?

Q10-5. Under what circumstances will a company report a net pension asset? A net pension liability?

Q10-6. What are the components of pension expense that are reported in the income statement?

Q10-7. What effect does the use of expected returns on pension investments and the deferral of unexpected gains and losses on those investments have on income?

Q10-8. What is a special purpose entity (SPE)? Provide an example of the use of an SPE as a financing vehicle.

Q10-9. What effect would consolidating SPEs have on both accounting for SPEs and the balance sheets of companies that sponsor them?

Assignments with the Web**Assign**. logo in the margin are available in WebAssign.
See the Preface of the book for details.

MINI EXERCISES

M10-10. Analyzing and Interpreting Lease Footnote Disclosures   (LO1)

The GAP, Inc., discloses the following schedule to its 2008 10-K report relating to its leasing activities.

The GAP, Inc. (GPS)

The aggregate minimum non-cancelable annual lease payments under leases in effect on February 2, 2008, are as follows:

Fiscal Year ($ millions)	
2008	$1,098
2009	1,006
2010	853
2011	642
2012	449
Thereafter	1,430
Total minimum lease commitments	$5,478

a. Compute the present value of GAP's operating leases using a 6% discount rate.
b. What types of adjustments might we consider to GAP's balance sheet and income statement for analysis purposes?

M10-11. Analyzing and Capitalizing Operating Lease Payments Disclosed in Footnotes   (LO1)

Costco Wholesale Corporation discloses the following in footnotes to its 10-K report relating to its leasing activities.

WebAssign.
Costco Corp. (COST)

Future minimum payments during the next five fiscal years and thereafter under non-cancelable leases with terms of at least one year, at August 31, 2008, were as follows ($ millions):

2009	$ 140
2010	142
2011	136
2012	124
2013	123
Thereafter	1,438
Total minimum payments	$2,103

Operating leases are not reflected on-balance-sheet. In our analysis of a company, we often desire to capitalize these operating leases, that is, add the present value of the future operating lease payments to both the reported assets and liabilities. (*a*) Compute the present value of Costco's operating lease payments assuming a 6% discount rate. (*b*) What effect does capitalization of operating leases have on Costco's total liabilities and total assets (it reported total liabilities and total assets of $11,408 million and $20,682 million, respectively)?

M10-12. Analyzing and Interpreting Pension Disclosures—Expenses and Returns   (LO2)

Black & Decker discloses the following pension footnote in its 10-K report.

Black & Decker (BDK)

($ millions)	2007
Service cost	$ 26.0
Interest cost	62.5
Expected return on plan assets	(75.6)
Amortization of prior service cost	2.1
Amortization of net actuarial loss	26.3
Net periodic cost	$ 41.3

a. How much pension expense does Black & Decker report in its 2007 income statement?
b. Explain, in general, how expected return on plan assets affects reported pension expense. How did expected return affect Black & Decker's 2007 pension expense?
c. Explain use of the word "expected" as it relates to pension plan assets.

M10-13. Analyzing and Interpreting Pension Disclosures—PBO and Funded Status **(LO2)**

YUM! Brands, Inc.
(YUM)

YUM! Brands, Inc., discloses the following pension footnote in its 10-K report.

Pension Benefit Obligation ($ millions)	2007	2006
Change in benefit obligation		
Benefit obligation at beginning of year	$864	$815
Service cost	33	34
Interest cost	50	46
Plan amendments	4	(3)
Curtailment gain	(4)	(1)
Benefits and expenses paid	(34)	(29)
Actuarial (gain) loss	(71)	2
Benefit obligation at end of year	$842	$864

a. Explain the terms "service cost" and "interest cost."
b. How do actuarial losses arise?
c. The fair market value of YUM!'s plan assets is $732 million as of 2007. What is the funded status of the plan, and how will this be reflected on YUM!'s balance sheet?

M10-14. Analyzing and Interpreting Pension Disclosures—Plan Assets and Cash Flow **(LO2)**

YUM! Brands, Inc.
(YUM)

YUM! Brands, Inc., discloses the following pension footnote in its 10-K report.

Pension Plan Assets ($ millions)	2007	2006
Fair value of plan assets at beginning of year	$673	$610
Actual return on plan assets	93	60
Employer contributions	2	35
Benefits paid	(33)	(29)
Administrative expenses	(3)	(3)
Fair value of plan assets at end of year	$732	$673

a. How does the "actual return on plan assets" of $93 million affect YUM!'s reported profits for 2007?
b. What are the cash flow implications of the pension plan for YUM! in 2007?
c. YUM!'s pension plan paid out $33 million in benefits during 2007. Where else is this payment reflected?

M10-15. Analyzing and Interpreting Retirement Benefit Footnote **(LO2)**

Abercrombie & Fitch
(ANF)

Abercrombie & Fitch discloses the following footnote relating to its retirement plans in its 2008 10-K report.

RETIREMENT BENEFITS The Company maintains the Abercrombie & Fitch Co. Savings & Retirement Plan, a qualified plan. All U.S. associates are eligible to participate in this plan if they are at least 21 years of age and have completed a year of employment with 1,000 or more hours of service. In addition, the Company maintains the Abercrombie & Fitch Nonqualified Savings and Supplemental Retirement Plan. Participation in this plan is based on service and compensation. The Company's contributions are based on a percentage of associates' eligible annual compensation. The cost of these plans was $21.0 million in Fiscal 2007, $15.0 million in Fiscal 2006 and $10.5 million in Fiscal 2005.

a. Does Abercrombie have a defined contribution or defined benefit pension plan? Explain.
b. How does Abercrombie account for its contributions to its retirement plan?
c. How does Abercrombie report its obligation for its retirement plan on the balance sheet?

M10-16. Analyzing and Interpreting Lease Disclosure (LO3)

Dow Chemical Company provided the following footnote in its 2007 10-K report relating to operating leases.

Dow Chemical
Company (DOW)

> **Leased Property** The Company routinely leases premises for use as sales and adminis-
> trative offices, warehouses and tanks for product storage, motor vehicles, railcars, com-
> puters, office machines, and equipment under operating leases. In addition, the Company
> leases a gas turbine and aircraft in the United States, and ethylene plants in Canada and
> The Netherlands. At the termination of the leases, the Company has the option to purchase
> these plants and certain other leased equipment and buildings based on a fair market value
> determination. Rental expenses under operating leases, net of sublease rental income,
> were $445 million in 2007, $441 million in 2006 and $451 million in 2005. Future minimum
> rental payments under operating leases with remaining non-cancelable terms in excess of
> one year are as follows:

Minimum Operating Lease Commitments (in millions)	December 31, 2007
2008	$ 231
2009	200
2010	171
2011	117
2012	93
2013 and thereafter	441
Total	$1,253

Required

a. Dow describes all of its leases as "operating." What is the significance of this designation?

b. How might we treat these operating leases in our analysis of the company?

M10-17. Analyzing and Interpreting Disclosure on Contract Manufacturers (LO3)

Nike reports the following information relating to its manufacturing activities in footnotes to its fiscal 2008 10-K report.

WebAssign.

Nike, Inc. (NKE)

> **Manufacturing** Virtually all of our footwear is produced outside of the United States. In
> fiscal 2008, contract suppliers in China, Vietnam, Indonesia and Thailand manufactured 36
> percent, 33 percent, 21 percent and 9 percent of total NIKE brand footwear, respectively. We
> also have manufacturing agreements with independent factories in Argentina, Brazil, India, Italy
> and South Africa to manufacture footwear for sale primarily within those countries. Our largest
> single footwear factory accounted for approximately 6 percent of total fiscal 2008 footwear
> production.

a. What effect does the use of contract manufacturers have on Nike's balance sheet?

b. How does Nike's use of contract manufacturers affect Nike's return on net operating assets
(RNOA) and its components, net operating profit margin (NOPM) and net operating asset
turnover (NOAT)? Explain.

c. Nike executes agreements with its contract manufacturers to purchase their output. How are such
"executory contracts" reported under GAAP? Does your answer suggest a possible motivation
for the use of contract manufacturing?

M10-18. Analyzing and Interpreting Pension Plan Benefit Footnotes (LO2)

Lockheed Martin Corporation discloses the following funded status for its defined benefit pension plans in its 10-K report.

Lockheed Martin
Corp. (LMT)

Defined Benefit Pension Plans (In millions)	2007	2006
Unfunded status of the plans.	$(879)	$(2,790)

Lockheed contributed $335 million to its pension plan assets in 2007, down from $693 million in the prior year. The company also reports that it is obligated for the following expected payments to retirees in the next five years.

(In millions)	Pension Benefits
2008	$ 1,560
2009	1,560
2010	1,610
2011	1,680
2012	1,750
Years 2013–2017	10,030

a.   How is this funded status reported in Lockheed's balance sheet under current GAAP?
b.   How should we interpret this funded status in our analysis of the company?
c.   Lockheed projects payments to retirees of over $1.5 billion per year. How is the company able to contribute only $335 million to its pension plan?
d.   What likely effect would a substantial decline in the financial markets have on Lockheed's contribution to its pension plans? Explain.

EXERCISES

E10-19.   Analyzing and Interpreting Leasing Footnote   (LO1)

Lowe's Companies
(LOW)

Lowe's Companies, Inc., reports the following footnote relating to its leased facilities in its 2007 10-K report.

The future minimum rental payments required under capital and operating leases having initial or remaining non-cancelable lease terms in excess of one year are summarized as follows:

(In millions)	Operating Leases
2008	$ 362
2009	359
2010	359
2011	358
2012	355
Later years	4,131
Total minimum lease payments . . .	$5,924

a.   Assuming that this is the only information available about its leasing activities, does Lowe's have any capital leases in 2007? Explain.
b.   What effect has its lease classification had on Lowe's balance sheet? Over the life of the lease, what effect does this classification have on net income?
c.   Compute the present value of these operating leases using a discount rate of 6%. How might we use this information in our analysis of the company?

WebAssign.

Verizon
Communications, Inc.
(VZ)

E10-20.   Analyzing and Interpreting Footnote on Operating and Capital Leases   (LO1)

Verizon Communications, Inc., provides the following footnote relating to its leasing activities in its 10-K report.

The aggregate minimum rental commitments under noncancelable leases for the periods shown at December 31, 2007, are as follows:

Years (dollars in millions)	Capital Leases	Operating Leases
2008	$ 75	$1,489
2009	63	1,276
2010	59	1,016
2011	55	756
2012	38	497
Thereafter	132	1,967
Total minimum rental commitments	422	$7,001
Less interest and executory costs	(110)	
Present value of minimum lease payments	312	
Less current installments	(46)	
Long-term obligation at December 31, 2007	$266	

a. Assuming that this is the only available information relating to its leasing activities, what amount does Verizon report on its balance sheet for its lease obligations? Does this amount represent its total obligation to lessors? How do you know?

b. What effect has its lease classification had on Verizon's balance sheet? Over the life of its leases, what effect does this lease classification have on net income?

c. Compute the present value of Verizon's operating leases, assuming an 8.02% discount rate. Confirm that the implicit discount rate for Verizon's capital leases is 8.02%. How might we use this additional information in our analysis of the company?

E10-21. **Analyzing, Interpreting and Capitalizing Operating Leases   (LO1)**

Staples, Inc., reports the following footnote relating to its capital and operating leases in its 2007 10-K report ($ thousands).   Staples, Inc. (SPLS)

Future minimum lease commitments due for retail and support facilities (including lease commitments for 127 retail stores not yet opened at February 2, 2008) and equipment leases under non-cancelable operating leases are as follows (in thousands):

Year	Total
2008	$ 756,963
2009	746,244
2010	700,751
2011	647,771
2012	586,167
Thereafter	2,787,403
	$6,225,299

a. What dollar adjustment(s) might we consider to Staples' balance sheet and income statement given this information and assuming that Staples intermediate-term borrowing rate is 8%? Explain.

b. Would the adjustment from part a make a substantial difference to Staples' total liabilities? (Staples reported total assets of $9 billion and total liabilities of $3.3 billion for 2008.)

E10-22. **Analyzing, Interpreting and Capitalizing Operating Leases** **(LO1)**

YUM! Brands, Inc., reports the following footnote relating to its capital and operating leases in its 2007 10-K report ($ millions).

Future minimum commitments under non-cancelable leases are set forth below. At December 29, 2007, and December 30, 2006, the present value of minimum payments under capital leases was $282 million and $228 million, respectively.

Commitments ($ millions)	Capital	Operating
2008	$ 24	$ 462
2009	24	417
2010	62	381
2011	20	340
2012	20	300
Thereafter	240	1,986
	$390	$3,886

a. Confirm that the implicit rate on YUM!'s capital leases is 4.31%. Using a 4.31% discount rate, compute the present value of YUM!'s operating leases. Describe the adjustments we might consider to YUM!'s balance sheet and income statement using that information.

b. YUM! reported total liabilities of $6,103 million for 2007. Would the adjustment from part a make a substantial difference to YUM!'s total liabilities? Explain.

E10-23. **Analyzing, Interpreting and Capitalizing Operating Leases** **(LO1)**

TJX Companies (TJX)

TJX Companies reports the following footnote relating to its capital and operating leases in its 2008 10-K report.

Following is a schedule of future minimum lease payments for continuing operations as of January 26, 2008:

Year ($ 000s)	Capital Leases	Operating Leases
2009	$ 3,726	$ 943,174
2010	3,726	898,667
2011	3,726	809,288
2012	3,897	708,300
2013	3,912	586,948
Later years	11,084	1,715,321
Total future minimum lease payments	30,071	$5,661,698
Less amount representing interest	(7,689)	
Net present value of minimum capital lease payments . .	$22,382	

Required

a. Confirm that the implicit rate on TJX's capital leases is 7.1%. Using the 7.1% discount rate, compute the present value of TJX's operating leases. Explain the adjustments we might consider to its balance sheet and income statement using that information.

b. TJX reported total liabilities of $4.5 billion for 2008. Would the adjustment from part a make a substantial difference to the company's total liabilities? Explain.

E10-24. **Analyzing and Interpreting Pension Disclosures** **(LO2)**

Web**Assign**.

General Mills (GIS)

General Mills reports the following pension footnote in its 10-K report.

Defined Benefit Pension Plans (In millions)	2008	2007
Change in Plan Assets		
Fair value at beginning of year	$4,097.8	$3,620.3
Actual return on assets.	181.1	625.9
Employer contributions.	14.2	10.6
Plan participant contributions.	3.6	2.8
Divestitures/acquisitions.	—	2.4
Benefit payments	(168.0)	(164.2)
Fair value at end of year.	$4,128.7	$4,097.8
Change in Projected Benefit Obligation		
Benefit obligation at beginning of year.	$3,257.5	$2,916.4
Service cost	80.1	73.1
Interest cost	196.7	185.6
Plan amendment.	1.9	0.2
Curtailment/other	(0.6)	(0.4)
Plan participant contributions.	3.6	2.8
Actuarial loss (gain).	(147.1)	244.0
Benefits payments	(168.0)	(164.2)
Projected benefit obligation at end of year	$3,224.1	$3,257.5

Estimated benefit payments, which reflect expected future service, as appropriate, are expected to be paid from fiscal 2009–2018 as follows:

(in millions)	Defined Benefit Pension Plans
2009	$ 176.3
2010	182.5
2011	189.8
2012	197.5
2013	206.6
2014–2018	1,187.3

a. Describe what is meant by *service cost* and *interest cost.*

b. What is the total amount paid to retirees during fiscal 2008? What is the source of funds to make these payments to retirees?

c. Compute the 2008 funded status for the company's pension plan.

d. What are actuarial gains and losses? What are the plan amendment adjustments, and how do they differ from the actuarial gains and losses?

e. General Mills projects payments to retirees of over $175 million per year. How is the company able to contribute only $14.2 million to its pension plan?

f. What effect would a substantial decline in the financial markets have on General Mills' contribution to its pension plans?

E10-25. **Analyzing and Interpreting Pension and Health Care Footnote** **(LO2)**

Web**Assign**.

Xerox Corporation (XRX)

Xerox reports the following pension and retiree health care ("Other") footnote as part of its 10-K report.

(in millions)	Pension Benefits		Retiree Health	
	2007	2006	2007	2006
Change in Benefit Obligation				
Benefit obligation, January 1	$10,467	$10,302	$ 1,592	$ 1,653
Service cost	237	244	17	19
Interest cost	578	732	87	92
Plan participants' contributions	12	13	20	19
Plan amendments	11	(234)	—	31
Actuarial gain	(508)	(85)	(114)	(105)
Currency exchange rate changes	331	564	21	—
Curtailments	(1)	(2)	—	—
Benefits paid/settlements	(669)	(1,067)	(122)	(117)
Benefit obligation, December 31	$10,458	$10,467	$ 1,501	$ 1,592
Change in Plan Assets				
Fair value of plan assets, January 1	$ 9,217	$ 8,444	$ —	$ —
Actual return on plan assets	667	959	—	—
Employer contribution	298	355	102	98
Plan participants' contributions	12	13	20	19
Currency exchange rate changes	280	513	—	—
Benefits paid/settlements	(669)	(1,067)	(122)	(117)
Fair value of plan assets, December 31	$ 9,805	$ 9,217	$ —	$ —
Net funded status (including under-funded and non-funded plans) at December 31	$ (653)	$ (1,250)	$(1,501)	$(1,592)

(in millions)	Pension Benefits			Retiree Health		
	2007	2006	2005	2007	2006	2005
Components of Net Periodic Benefit Cost						
Defined benefit plans						
Service cost	$ 237	$244	$234	$ 17	$ 19	$ 20
Interest cost	578	732	581	87	92	90
Expected return on plan assets	(668)	(802)	(622)	—	—	—
Recognized net actuarial loss	75	104	98	10	19	31
Amortization of prior service credit	(20)	(18)	(3)	(12)	(13)	(24)
Recognized net transition obligation (asset)	—	2	1	—	—	—
Recognized curtailment/settlement loss	33	93	54	—	—	—
Net periodic benefit cost	235	355	343	102	117	117
Defined contribution plans	80	70	71	—	—	—
Total	$ 315	$425	$414	$ 102	$117	$117
Other Changes in Plan Assets and Benefit Obligations Recognized in Other Comprehensive Income						
Net actuarial loss (gain)	(499)			(114)		
Prior service cost (credit)	5			—		
Amortization of net actuarial (loss) gain	(108)			(10)		
Amortization of prior service (cost) credit	20			12		
Total recognized in other comprehensive income	(582)			(112)		
Total Recognized in Net Periodic Benefit Cost and Other Comprehensive Income	$(267)			$ (10)		

a. Describe what is meant by *service cost* and *interest cost* (the service and interest costs appear both in the reconciliation of the PBO and in the computation of pension expense).

b. What is the actual return on the pension and the health care ("Other") plan investments in 2007? Was Xerox's profitability impacted by this amount?

c. Provide an example under which an "actuarial gain," such as the $508 million gain in 2007 that Xerox reports, might arise.

d. What is the source of funds to make payments to retirees?

continued

e. How much cash did Xerox contribute to its pension and health care plans in 2007?
f. How much cash did retirees receive in 2007 from the pension plan and the health care plan? How much cash did Xerox pay these retirees in 2007?
g. Show the computation of the 2007 funded status for the pension and health care plans.
h. The company reports $108 million "amortization of net actuarial (loss) gain" in the table relating to Other Comprehensive Income and $75 million "Recognized net actuarial loss" and $33 million "Recognized curtailment/settlement loss" in the net periodic benefit cost table. (Note that $75 million + $33 million = $108 million.) The company also reports a $20 million "Amortization of prior service (cost) credit" and a corresponding amount in the net periodic benefit cost table. Describe the process by which these amounts are transferred from Other Comprehensive Income to pension expense in the income statement.

E10-26. Analyzing and Interpreting Pension and Health Care Disclosures (LO2)
Verizon reports the following pension and health care benefits footnote as part of its 10-K report. Verizon (VZ)

At December 31 (dollars in millions)	Pension 2007	Pension 2006	Health Care and Life 2007	Health Care and Life 2006
Change in Benefit Obligation				
Beginning of year	$34,159	$35,540	$ 27,330	$ 26,783
Service cost	442	581	354	356
Interest cost	1,975	1,995	1,592	1,499
Plan amendments	—	—	—	50
Actuarial (gain) loss, net	123	(282)	(409)	152
Benefits paid	(4,204)	(2,762)	(1,561)	(1,564)
Termination benefits	—	47	—	14
Acquisitions and divestitures, net	—	477	—	40
Settlements	—	(1,437)	—	—
End of year	$32,495	$34,159	$ 27,306	$ 27,330
Change in Plan Assets				
Beginning of year	$41,509	$39,227	$ 4,303	$ 4,275
Actual return on plan assets	4,591	5,536	352	493
Company contributions	737	568	1,048	1,099
Benefits paid	(4,204)	(2,762)	(1,561)	(1,564)
Settlements	—	(1,437)	—	—
Acquisitions and divestitures, net	26	377	—	—
End of year	$42,659	$41,509	$ 4,142	$ 4,303
Funded Status				
End of year	$10,164	$ 7,350	$(23,164)	$(23,027)

Net Periodic Cost Years Ended December 31 (dollars in millions)	Pension 2007	Pension 2006	Pension 2005	Health Care and Life 2007	Health Care and Life 2006	Health Care and Life 2005
Service cost	$ 442	$ 581	$ 675	$ 354	$ 356	$ 358
Interest cost	1,975	1,995	1,959	1,592	1,499	1,467
Expected return on plan assets	(3,175)	(3,173)	(3,231)	(317)	(328)	(349)
Amortization of prior service cost	43	44	42	392	360	290
Actuarial loss, net	98	182	124	316	290	258
Net periodic benefit (income) cost	$ (617)	$ (371)	$ (431)	$2,337	$2,177	$2,024

a. Describe what is meant by *service cost* and *interest cost.*
b. What payments did retirees receive during fiscal 2007 from the pension and health care plans? What is the source of funds to make payments to retirees?
c. Show the computation of Verizon's 2007 funded status for both the pension and health care plans.
d. What expense does Verizon's income statement report for both its pension and health care plans?

E10-27.[B] **Analyzing and Interpreting Disclosure on Off-Balance-Sheet Financing** (LO3)

Harley-Davidson provides the following footnote in its 10-K report relating to the securitization of receivables by its finance subsidiary, Harley-Davidson Financial Services (HDFS).

> **OFF-BALANCE-SHEET ARRANGEMENTS** As part of its securitization program, HDFS transfers retail motorcycle loans to a special purpose bankruptcy-remote wholly-owned subsidiary. The subsidiary sells the retail loans to a securitization trust in exchange for the proceeds from asset-backed securities issued by the securitization trust. The asset-backed securities, usually notes with various maturities and interest rates, are secured by future collections of the purchased retail installment loans. Activities of the securitization trust are limited to acquiring retail loans, issuing asset-backed securities and making payments on securities to investors. Due to the nature of the assets held by the securitization trust and the limited nature of its activities . . . assets and liabilities of the [trust] are not consolidated in the financial statements of the Company.

a. Describe in your own words, the securitization process employed by HDFS.

b. What benefits does Harley derive by securitizing receivables in this manner?

c. The FASB has proposed an amendment to an existing standard that, if passed, could require consolidation of the trust. What effect will this have on Harley? Will there still be a benefit to securitization? Explain.

PROBLEMS

P10-28. **Analyzing, Interpreting and Capitalizing Operating Leases** (LO1)

The Abercrombie & Fitch 10-K report contains the following footnote relating to its leasing activities. This is the only information it discloses relating to its leasing activity.

> At February 2, 2008, the Company was committed to non-cancelable leases with remaining terms of one to 20 years. A summary of operating lease commitments under non-cancelable leases follows (thousands):
>
> | | |
> |---|---|
> | 2008 | $254,456 |
> | 2009 | 263,179 |
> | 2010 | 252,749 |
> | 2011 | 235,080 |
> | 2012 | 214,914 |
> | Thereafter | 953,417 |

Required

a. What lease assets and lease liabilities does Abercrombie report on its balance sheet? How do we know?

b. What effect does the lease classification have on A&F's balance sheet? Over the life of the lease, what effect does this classification have on the company's net income?

c. Using a 6% discount rate, estimate the assets and liabilities that A&F fails to report as a result of its off-balance-sheet lease financing.

d. What adjustments would we consider to A&F's income statement corresponding to the adjustments we would make to its balance sheet in part *c*.

e. Indicate the direction (increase or decrease) of the effect that capitalizing these leases would have on the following financial items and ratios for A&F: return on equity (ROE), net operating profit after tax (NOPAT), net operating assets (NOA), net operating profit margin (NOPM), net operating asset turnover (NOAT), and measures of financial leverage.

P10-29. **Analyzing, Interpreting and Capitalizing Operating Leases** (LO1)

The Best Buy 10-K report has the following footnote related to its leasing activities.

The future minimum lease payments under our capital and operating leases by fiscal year (not including contingent rentals) at March 1, 2008, are as follows ($ millions):

Fiscal Year	Capital Leases	Operating Leases
2009	$16	$ 772
2010	16	761
2011	8	716
2012	2	666
2013	2	635
Thereafter	19	3,282
Subtotal	63	$6,832
Less: imputed interest	(12)	
Present value of lease obligations	$51	

Required

a. What is the balance of the lease liabilities reported on Best Buy's balance sheet?
b. What effect has the operating lease classification had on its balance sheet? Over the life of the lease, what effect does this classification have on the company's net income?
c. Confirm that the implicit discount rate used by Best Buy for its capital leases is 5.27%. Use this discount rate to estimate the assets and liabilities that Best Buy fails to report as a result of its off-balance-sheet lease financing.
d. What adjustments would we make to Best Buy's income statement corresponding to the adjustments we made to its balance sheet in part c?
e. Indicate the direction (increase or decrease) of the effect that capitalizing the operating leases would have on the following financial items and ratios for Best Buy: return on equity (ROE), net operating profit after tax (NOPAT), net operating assets (NOA), net operating profit margin (NOPM), net operating asset turnover (NOAT), and measures of financial leverage.

P10-30. **Analyzing, Interpreting and Capitalizing Operating Leases** **(LO1)**

FedEx reports total assets of $25,633 and total liabilities of $11,107 for 2008 ($ millions). Its 10-K report has the following footnote related to its leasing activities.   FedEx (FDX)

A summary of future minimum lease payments under capital leases and noncancelable operating leases with an initial or remaining term in excess of one year at May 31, 2008, is as follows (in millions):

		Operating Leases		
	Capital Leases	Aircraft and Related Equipment	Facilities and Other	Total Operating Leases
2009	$ 13	$ 555	$ 1,248	$ 1,803
2010	97	544	1,103	1,647
2011	8	526	956	1,482
2012	8	504	828	1,332
2013	119	499	709	1,208
Thereafter	18	2,931	5,407	8,338
Total	263	$5,559	$10,251	$15,810
Less amount representing interest	43			
Present value of net minimum lease payments	$220			

Required

a. What is the balance of lease assets and lease liabilities as reported on FedEx's balance sheet? Explain.

b. Confirm that the implicit rate that FedEx uses to discount its capital leases is 5.07%. Use this discount rate to estimate the amount of assets and liabilities that FedEx fails to report as a result of its off-balance-sheet lease financing.

c. What adjustments would we make to FedEx's income statement corresponding to the adjustments we make to its balance sheet in part b?

d. Indicate the direction (increase or decrease) of the effect that capitalizing the operating leases would have on the following financial items and ratios for FedEx: return on equity (ROE), net operating profit after tax (NOPAT), net operating assets (NOA), net operating profit margin (NOPM), net operating asset turnover (NOAT), and measures of financial leverage.

e. What portion of total lease liabilities did FedEx report on-balance-sheet and what portion is off-balance-sheet?

f. Based on your analysis, do you believe that FedEx's balance sheet adequately reports its aircraft and facilities assets and related obligations? Explain.

DuPont (DD)

P10-31. Analyzing and Interpreting Pension Disclosures (LO2)

DuPont's 10-K report has the following disclosures related to its retirement plans ($ millions).

($ millions)	Pension Benefits	
	2007	2006
Change in benefit obligation		
Benefit obligation at beginning of year.	$22,849	$22,935
Service cost	383	388
Interest cost	1,228	1,192
Plan participants' contributions	13	9
Actuarial loss (gain)	(728)	(244)
Benefits paid	(1,544)	(1,506)
Amendments	—	(1)
Net effects of acquisitions/divestitures	5	76
Benefit obligation at end of year	$22,206	$22,849
Change in plan assets		
Fair value of plan assets at beginning of year	$21,909	$19,792
Actual gain on plan assets	1,963	3,306
Employer contributions	277	280
Plan participants' contributions	13	9
Benefits paid	(1,544)	(1,506)
Net effects of acquisitions/divestitures	—	28
Fair value of plan assets at end of year	$22,618	$21,909
Funded status		
U.S. plans with plan assets	$ 2,061	$ 892
Non-U.S. plans with plan assets	(90)	(317)
All other plans.	(1,559)	(1,515)
Total	$ 412	$ (940)

Components of net periodic benefit cost (credit) and amounts recognized in other comprehensive income	Pension Benefits (In millions)		
	2007	2006	2005
Net periodic benefit cost			
Service cost	$ 383	$ 388	$ 349
Interest cost	1,228	1,192	1,160
Expected return on plan assets	(1,800)	(1,648)	(1,416)
Amortization of loss	117	227	303
Amortization of prior service cost	18	29	37
Curtailment/settlement (gain) loss	—	3	(1)
Net periodic benefit cost	$ (54)	$ 191	$ 432

continued

continued from prior page

Components of net periodic benefit cost (credit) and amounts recognized in other comprehensive income	Pension Benefits (In millions)		
	2007	2006	2005
Changes in plan assets and benefit obligations recognized in other comprehensive income			
Net gain	(893)	—	—
Amortization of loss	(117)	—	—
Amortization of prior service cost	(18)	—	—
Total recognized in other comprehensive income . .	$(1,028)	$ —	$ —
Total recognized in net periodic benefit cost and other comprehensive income	$(1,082)	$ 191	$ 432

Weighted-average assumptions used to determine net periodic benefit cost for years ended December 31	Pension Benefits	
	2007	2006
Discount rate	5.56%	5.43%
Expected return on plan assets	8.74%	8.74%
Rate of compensation increase	4.32%	4.31%

The following benefit payments, which reflect future service, as appropriate, are expected to be paid:

($ millions)	Pension Benefits
2008	$1,525
2009	1,507
2010	1,493
2011	1,500
2012	1,500
Years 2013–2017	7,690

Required

a. How much pension expense (revenue) does DuPont report in its 2007 income statement?

b. DuPont reports a $1,800 million expected return on pension plan assets as an offset to 2007 pension expense. Approximately, how is this amount computed (estimate from the numbers reported)? What is DuPont's actual gain or loss realized on its 2007 pension plan assets? What is the purpose of using this expected return instead of the actual gain or loss?

c. What main factors (and dollar amounts) affected DuPont's pension liability during 2007? What main factors (and dollar amounts) affected its pension plan assets during 2007?

d. What does the term *funded status* mean? What is the funded status of the 2007 DuPont pension plans?

e. DuPont increased its discount rate from 5.43% to 5.56% in 2007. What effect(s) does this increase have on its balance sheet and its income statement?

f. How did DuPont's pension plan affect the company's cash flow in 2007? (Identify any inflows and outflows, including amounts.)

g. In 2007, DuPont contributed $277 million to its pension plan. Explain how the returns on pension assets affect the amount of cash that DuPont must contribute to fund the pension plan.

P10-32. **Analyzing and Interpreting Pension Disclosures** **(LO2)**

Johnson & Johnson provides the following footnote disclosures in its 10-K report relating to its defined benefit pension plans and its other post-retirement benefits.

Johnson & Johnson (JNJ)

($ in millions)	Retirement Plans		Other Benefit Plans	
	2007	2006	2007	2006
Change in Benefit Obligation				
Projected benefit obligation—beginning of year	$11,660	10,171	$ 2,668	$ 2,325
Service cost	597	552	140	122
Interest cost	656	570	149	136
Plan participant contributions	62	47	—	—
Amendments	14	7	—	—
Actuarial (gains) losses.	(876)	(99)	(1)	130
Divestitures & acquisitions	79	443	8	101
Curtailments & settlements	(46)	(7)	—	—
Benefits paid from plan	(481)	(402)	(255)	(147)
Effect of exchange rates.	337	378	12	1
Projected benefit obligation—end of year	$12,002	11,660	$ 2,721	$ 2,668
Change in Plan Assets				
Plan assets at fair value—beginning of year	$ 9,538	$ 8,108	$ 30	$ 34
Actual return on plan assets.	743	966	4	2
Company contributions	317	259	250	141
Plan participant contributions	62	47	—	—
Settlements	(38)	(7)	—	—
Divestitures & acquisitions	55	300	—	—
Benefits paid from plan assets.	(481)	(402)	(255)	(147)
Effect of exchange rates.	273	267	—	—
Plan assets at fair value—end of year	$10,469	$ 9,538	$ 29	$ 30
Funded status—end of year.	$ (1,533)	$ (2,122)	$(2,692)	$(2,638)

($ in millions)	Retirement Plans			Other Benefit Plans		
	2007	2006	2005	2007	2006	2005
Service cost	$597	$552	$462	$140	$122	$ 56
Interest cost	656	570	488	149	136	87
Expected return on plan assets	(809)	(701)	(579)	(2)	(3)	(3)
Amortization of prior service cost	10	10	12	(7)	(7)	(7)
Amortization of net transition asset . . .	1	(1)	(2)	—	—	—
Recognized actuarial losses.	186	251	219	66	74	25
Curtailments and settlements	5	4	2	—	—	—
Net periodic benefit cost	$646	$685	$602	$346	$322	$158

($ in millions)	Retirement Plans			Other Benefit Plans		
	2007	2006	2005	2007	2006	2005
U.S. Benefit Plans						
Discount rate	6.50%	6.00%	5.75%	6.50%	6.00%	5.75%
Expected long-term rate of return on plan assets.	9.00	9.00	9.00	9.00	9.00	9.00
Rate of increase in compensation levels.	4.50	4.50	4.50	4.50	4.50	4.50

Required

a. How much pension expense does Johnson & Johnson report in its 2007 income statement?

b. The company reports a $809 million expected return on pension plan assets as an offset to 2007 pension expense. Approximately, how is this amount computed? What is the actual gain or loss realized on its 2007 pension plan assets? What is the purpose of using this expected return instead of the actual gain or loss?

c. What factors affected the company's pension liability during 2007? What factors affected the pension plan assets during 2007?

continued

d.   What does the term *funded status* mean? What is the funded status of the 2007 pension plans and postretirement benefit plans?

e.   The company increased its discount rate from 6% to 6.5% in 2007. What effect(s) does this increase have on its balance sheet and its income statement?

f.   How did Johnson & Johnson's pension plan affect the company's cash flow in 2007?

MANAGEMENT APPLICATIONS

MA10-33. Management Ethics: Structuring Leases   (L01)

You are the CEO of a company. Your CFO is concerned about certain covenants in your debt agreement that specify a maximum ratio of liabilities to stockholders' equity. He proposes to structure your leases as "operating" so as to avoid capitalization. In order to do so, he proposes to structure the lease with an initial term of five years, and with three five-year renewal options instead of a flat 20-year lease. That way, the lease term will not exceed 75% of the useful life of the leased assets, and the present value of the lease payments will not exceed 90% of the fair market value of the leased assets. The CFO explains that these two requirements usually trigger lease capitalization. He asks for your input into this decision.

a.   What are the management issues that you feel are relevant for this decision? That is, how might this lease structure impact your company?

b.   What are the ethical issues that are raised by the CFO's proposal? Explain.

Forecasting Financial Statements

LEARNING OBJECTIVES

LO1 Explain the process of forecasting financial statements. (p. 11-3)

LO2 Forecast revenues and the income statement. (p. 11-7)

LO3 Forecast the balance sheet. (p. 11-17)

LO4 Forecast the statement of cash flows. (p. 11-25)

LO5 Prepare multiyear forecasts of financial statements. (p. 11-27)

LO6 Implement a parsimonious method for multiyear forecasting of net operating profit and net operating assets. (p. 11-35)

PROCTER & GAMBLE

Procter & Gamble (P&G) has successfully reinvented itself . . . again. It has shed its image as the "lumbering giant" of its industry with new products and directed marketing. Its annual sales now exceed $83 billion. P&G has focused on its higher-margin products such as those in beauty care. This has improved its profit margin and provided much needed dollars for marketing activities. Its advertising budget is over 10% of sales, which is nearly double the budget of its key competitors. P&G also spends over $2 billion per year (2.7% of sales) on R&D. *BusinessWeek* reported that P&G created "'technology entrepreneurs," or TEs, who act as scouts, searching for the latest breakthroughs. P&G's goal is for 50% of its new products to come from outside of the company.

P&G's financial performance has been impressive. In 2008, it generated over $15 billion of operating cash flow, and the company has only begun to fully exploit the resources acquired in the Gillette acquisition. Its abundant cash flow allows it to fund the level of advertising and R&D necessary to remain a dominant force in the consumer products industry as well as to pay over $4.6 billion in dividends to shareholders. *BusinessWeek* asserts that P&G is the undisputed leader in household products and enjoys the best management team among its peers.

P&G's product list is impressive. It consists of numerous well-recognized household brands. Total sales of Procter & Gamble products are distributed across its three business segments as illustrated in the chart to the side. A partial listing of its billion-dollar brands follows:

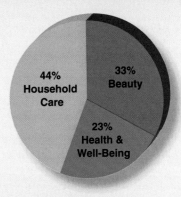

- **Beauty.** Head & Shoulders, Olay, Pantene, Wella, Braun, Fusion, Gillette, Mach3
- **Health and Well-Being.** Actonel, Always, Crest, Oral-B, Folgers, Iams, Pringles
- **Household Care.** Ariel, Dawn, Downy, Duracell, Gain, Tide, Bounty, Charmin, Pampers

P&G's recent successes have coincided with strong leadership. CEO A.G. Lafley's innovations and market savvy have consistently propelled P&G. *BusinessWeek* explains that from its Swiffer mop to battery-powered Crest SpinBrush toothbrushes and Whitestrip tooth whit-

eners, P&G has outshined its peers. Since assuming the CEO job, Lafley has guided P&G to successive increases in sales, income, and cash flows. Such increases have driven impressive gains in stock price as evident from the graph below:

Still, we know that *forecasts* of financial performance drive stock price. Historical financial statements are relevant to the extent that they provide information useful to forecast financial performance. Accordingly, considerable emphasis is placed on generating reliable forecasts.

This module explains the forecasting process, including the forecasting of the income statement, the balance sheet, and the statement of cash flows. From all accounts, the steady increase in P&G's stock price reflects continued optimism about its future financial performance and condition.

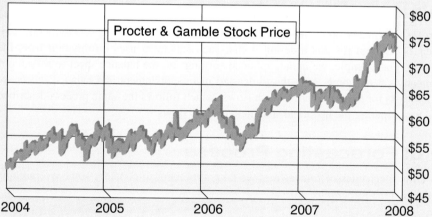

Procter & Gamble Stock Price

| 2004 | 2005 | 2006 | 2007 | 2008 |

$80
$75
$70
$65
$60
$55
$50
$45

Sources: *Procter & Gamble* 2005–2008 10-K and Annual Reports; *BusinessWeek,* April 2006; *Barron's,* November 2006; *The Wall Street Journal,* May 2009.

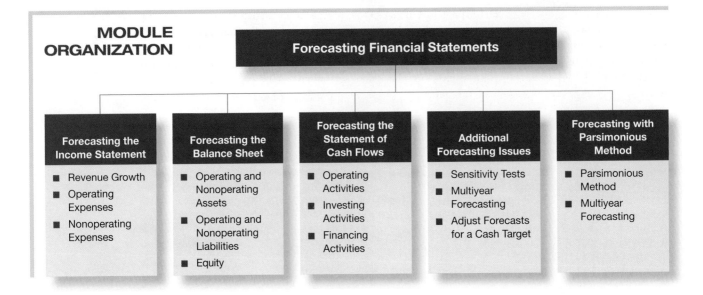

Forecasting financial performance is integral to a variety of business decisions ranging from investing to managing a company effectively. We might, for example, wish to value a company's common stock before purchasing its shares. To that end, we might use one of the valuation models we discuss in Module 12 that rely on financial statement forecasts as a crucial input. Or, we might be interested in evaluating the creditworthiness of a prospective borrower. In that case, we forecast the borrower's cash flows to estimate its ability to repay its obligations. We might also be interested in evaluating alternative strategic investment decisions. In this case, we can use our forecasts to evaluate the shareholder value that the strategic investment alternatives will create. All of these decisions require accurate financial forecasts. In this module, we illustrate the most common method to forecast the income statement, balance sheet, and statement of cash flows.

FORECASTING PROCESS

LO1 Explain the process of forecasting financial statements.

The forecasting process estimates future income statements, balance sheets, and statements of cash flows, in that order. The reason for this ordering is that each statement uses information from the preceding statement(s). For example, we update retained earnings on the balance sheet to reflect our forecast of the company's net income. And, the forecasted income statement and balance sheets are used in preparing forecasts for the statement of cash flows, which follows the same process described in Modules 2 and 3 for preparing the historical statement of cash flows.

Overview of Forecasting Process

Before we focus on the mechanics of forecasting, we take a moment to consider some overarching principles that guide us in the forecasting process.

Reformulated (Adjusted) Financial Statements

The forecasting process begins with a retrospective analysis. That is, we analyze current and prior years' statements to be sure that they accurately reflect the company's financial condition and performance. If we believe that they do not, we adjust those statements to reflect the company's net operating assets and the operating income that we expect to persist into the future. Once we've adjusted the historical results, we are ready to forecast future results. Why would we need to adjust historical results? The answer resides in the fact that financial statements prepared in conformity with GAAP do not always accurately reflect the "true" financial condition and performance of the company. This *adjusting process*, also referred to as recasting or reformulating (or *scrubbing the numbers*), is not "black and white." It requires judgment and estimation. Repeatedly in Modules 5 through 10, we have explained estimation, accounting choice, deliberate managerial intervention in reporting, and transitory versus persistent items. These concepts are integral to adjustments we make to financial statements. It is important to distinguish between the purposes of GAAP-based financial statements and the adjusting process for purposes of forecasting. Specifically, GAAP-based statements provide more than just information for forecasting. For example, financial statements are key inputs into contracts among business parties. This means that historical results, including any transitory activities, must be reported to meet management's fiduciary responsibilities. On the other hand, to forecast future performance, we need to create a set of financial statements that focus on those items that we expect to persist, with a special emphasis on persistent operating activities.

Garbage-In, Garbage-Out

All forecasts are based on a set of forecasting assumptions. For example, to forecast the income statement, we must make assumptions about revenue growth and other assumptions about how expenses will change in relation to changes in revenues. Then, to forecast the balance sheet, we make assumptions about the relation between balance sheet accounts and changes in revenues. Consequently, before we make business decisions based on forecasted financial statements, we must understand and agree with the underlying assumptions used to produce them. The old adage, "garbage-in, garbage-out," is apt. That is, the quality of our decision is only as good as the quality of the information on which it is based. We must be sure that our forecasting assumptions are consistent with our beliefs and predictions for future growth and key financial relations.

Optimism vs Conservatism

Many people believe that it is appropriate to be overly conservative in their financial forecasts so as to minimize the likelihood of making a bad decision. "Let's be conservative in our forecasts so that we are certain our forecast will be met" is a frequent prelude to the forecasting process. Although this approach might help us avoid costly mistakes, being too conservative can result in missed valuable opportunities that, in the end, can also be very costly. Instead, our objective is not to be overly optimistic or overly conservative. The objective for forecasting is accuracy.

Level of Precision

Computing forecasts out to the "nth decimal place" is easy using spreadsheets. This increased precision makes the resulting forecasts appear more "professional," but not necessarily more accurate. As we discuss in this module, our financial statement forecasts are highly dependent on our revenues forecast. Whether revenues are expected to grow by 4% or 5% can markedly impact profitability and other forecasts. Estimating cost of goods sold and other items to the nth decimal place is meaningless if we have imprecise revenue forecasts. Consequently, borderline decisions that depend on a high level of forecasting precision are probably ill-advised.

Smell Test

At the end of the forecasting process, we must step back and make sure that the numbers we predict pass the *smell test*. That is, we need to assess whether our forecasts are reasonable—do they make economic sense, do they fit with the underlying relations that drive financial forecasts? For example, if our forecasts are dependent on increasing selling prices, it is wise to explore the likely consequences of a price increase. Companies cannot raise prices without a consequent loss of demand unless the product in question is protected in some way from competitive attacks. Our forecasts must appear reasonable and consistent with basic business economics.

Internal Consistency

The forecasted income statement, balance sheet, and statement of cash flows are linked in the same way that historical financial statements are. That is, they must articulate (link together within and across time) as we explain in Module 2. Preparing a forecasted statement of cash flows, although tedious, is often a useful way to uncover miscalculations in forecasting. If the forecasted cash balance on the balance sheet agrees with that on the statement of cash flows, it is likely that our income statement and balance sheet articulate properly. We also must ensure that our forecast assumptions are internally consistent. It is nonsense to forecast an increased gross profit margin during an economic recession unless we can make compelling arguments based on economics.

Crucial Forecasting Assumptions

Analysts commonly perform sensitivity analyses of their forecasts. This entails increasing and decreasing the forecast assumptions to identify those assumptions that have the greatest impact. By "impact," we mean large enough to alter business decisions. Assumptions that are identified as crucial to a decision must be investigated thoroughly to ensure that forecast assumptions are as accurate as possible.

Summary of Forecasting Process

Some professionals assert that forecasting is more art than science. Whatever it is, it must begin with a business analysis, including an assessment of general economic activity and the competitive forces within the broader business environment that we discuss in Module 1. Ideally, forecasts should be developed at an individual-product level and consider competitive advantage, trends in manufacturing costs, logistical requirements, necessary marketing support, after-sale customer service, and so forth. The narrower the focus, the more we can focus on the business environment in which the company operates and the more informed our forecasts are. Unfortunately, as external users of financial statements, we only have access to general-purpose financial statements, which we adjust as we see fit, given publicly available information and our own assessments. Then, we formulate forecast assumptions that are reasonable and consistent with the economic realities defining that company.

All-Important Revenues Forecast

The revenues (sales) forecast is, arguably, the most crucial and difficult estimate in the forecasting process. It is a crucial estimate because other income statement and balance sheet accounts derive from, among other factors, the revenues forecast. As a result, both the income statement and balance sheet grow with increases in revenues. The income statement reflects this growth concurrently. However, different balance sheet accounts reflect revenue growth in different ways. Some balance sheet accounts anticipate (or lead) revenue growth (inventories are one example). Some accounts reflect this growth concurrently (accounts receivable). And some accounts reflect revenue growth with a lag (for example, companies usually expand plant assets only after growth is deemed sustainable). Conversely, when revenues decline, so does the income statement and balance sheet, as the company shrinks to cope with adversity. Such actions include reduction of overhead costs and divestiture of excess assets. Figure 11.1 highlights crucial relations that are impacted by the revenues forecast for both the income statement and the balance sheet.

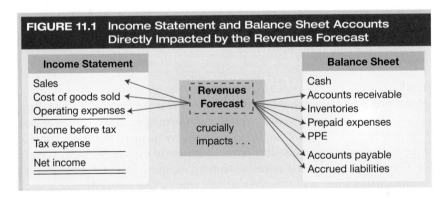

FIGURE 11.1 Income Statement and Balance Sheet Accounts Directly Impacted by the Revenues Forecast

Dynamics of Income Statement Growth

The following accounts are impacted directly, and with a relatively short lead or lag time, by the revenues forecast (for convenience, *our discussion assumes an increase in revenues*):

■ **Cost of goods sold** are impacted via increased inventory purchases in anticipation of increased demand, added manufacturing personnel, and greater depreciation from new manufacturing PPE.

■ **Operating expenses** increase concurrently with, or in anticipation of, increased revenues; these expenses include increased costs for buyers, higher advertising costs, payments to sales personnel, costs of after-sale customer support, logistics costs, and administrative costs.

- **Accounts receivable** increase directly with increases in revenues as more products and services are sold on credit.

- **Inventories** normally increase in anticipation of higher sales volume to ensure a sufficient stock of inventory available for sale.

- **Prepaid expenses** increase with increases in advertising and other expenditures made in anticipation of higher sales.

- **PPE** assets are usually acquired once the revenues increase is deemed sustainable and the capacity constraint is reached; thus, PPE assets increase with increased revenue, but with a lag.

- **Accounts payable** increase as inventories are purchased on credit.

- **Accrued liabilities** increase concurrent with increases in revenue-driven operating expenses.

Dynamics of Balance Sheet Growth

To understand the dynamics of growth in the balance sheet, it is useful to view it in three sections as depicted in Figure 11.2. Each of these sections experiences growth at different rates. As evident from Figure 11.1, most net operating assets grow roughly concurrently with increases in revenues. As net operating assets are normally positive, the asset side of the balance sheet grows faster than the liability side. This creates an imbalance that must be managed by the company's finance and treasury divisions.

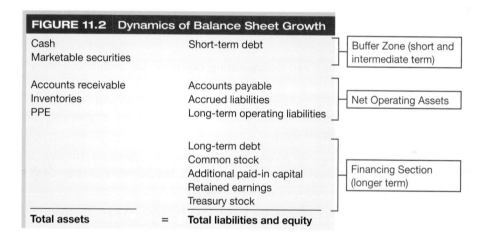

The "buffer zone" represents that section of the balance sheet that responds to short and intermediate-term imbalances. Cash declines as other operating assets increase, and companies typically finance that cash decline with short-term borrowings such as a seasonal line of credit from a bank. Conversely, companies typically invest excess cash in marketable securities to provide liquidity to meet future operating needs, investment opportunities, and similar near-term demands. Companies manage the "financing section" of the balance sheet on a long-term basis to provide funding for relatively permanent increases in net assets, such as the acquisition of PPE or even other companies. Further, income is reinvested in the business, long-term debt is borrowed, and equity securities are sold in proportions that are necessary to maintain the desired financial leverage for the company. Although the cash reinvestment decision is made continually, increases in long-term debt and equity occur relatively infrequently to meet longer-term funding needs. If the store of liquidity in the buffer zone is not needed for the foreseeable future, it can be used to retire long-term debt or to repurchase the company's outstanding shares.

Dynamics of Statement of Cash Flows Growth

The dynamics of the statement of cash flows mimic the dynamics of the income statement and balance sheet. This is because the statement of cash flows is prepared using both the income statement and balance sheet. Specifically, once we have forecasts of the income statement and balance sheet, we can compute the forecasted statement of cash flows just as we would its historical counterpart.

RESEARCH INSIGHT | Earnings Quality and Accounting Conservatism

Accounting researchers commonly measure *earnings quality* in terms of sustainability, meaning that the income items persist in future periods. Sustainability is important because persistent income items are better indicators of future earnings than are transitory items. One factor that affects earnings quality is accounting conservatism. Research finds that conservative accounting leads to transitory earnings changes when the levels of investment within the firm change. Researchers have constructed a conservatism index to study the effect conservatism and growth have on earnings changes. The index is defined as the level of estimated reserves created by conservative accounting (such as LIFO versus FIFO, and expensing of R&D and advertising) divided by the level of net operating assets. Earnings quality is then a function of changes in the conservatism index for each firm, and it is a function of the difference between the firm-specific and industry-specific conservatism index. Poor earnings quality occurs when the firm's accounting accruals grow more quickly or more slowly than net operating assets. A firm-specific conservatism index that substantially differs from industry benchmarks is one sign of poor earnings quality. This is because a firm's profitability reverts toward the industry mean. While the conservatism index appears to indicate whether or not a firm's earnings are sustainable, market participants do not appear to fully consider the information contained in this index when determining stock prices.

Identifying the Forecasting Steps

We apply the forecasting process in a three-step sequence:

1. **Forecast revenues.**
2. **Forecast operating and nonoperating expenses.** We assume a relation between revenue and each specific expense account.
3. **Forecast operating and nonoperating assets, liabilities and equity.** We assume a relation between revenue and each specific balance sheet account. We set cash equal to the amount necessary to balance the balance sheet.

Step 4 (optional) adjusts the balance sheet, and related statements, for any excess or deficit for the target cash balance. We view this step as important, but identify it as optional as it can be complex and can interfere with learning the forecasting basics.

4. **Adjust the balance sheet to the target cash balance.** We assume that excess cash is used to purchase marketable securities, reduce debt, or repurchase shares; whereas a cash deficit is financed with short-term debt. Then, we recompute net nonoperating expense to reflect any adjustments we make to nonoperating asset and liability account balances.

We illustrate the forecasting process using Procter & Gamble. As always, we begin by forecasting the income statement. P&G's income statement is reproduced in Exhibit 11.1 as a reference point.

STEP 1: FORECASTING REVENUES

LO2 Forecast revenues and the income statement.

Forecasting revenues is the most difficult and crucial step in the forecasting process. Further, much of the remaining income statement and the balance sheet are forecasted based on an assumed relation with forecasted revenues. We typically utilize both financial and nonfinancial information in developing forecasts. Each account must be separately analyzed using all relevant financial and nonfinancial information, including the insights gained from the first ten modules of this book.

To forecast revenues, then, we want to use all available, relevant information. But deciding what information is relevant and determining how to use the information varies across forecasters. As well, the level of information itself can vary across forecasters. For example, if we have access to inside information and we are developing forecasts as part of the strategic budgeting process for a company, we might have access to data regarding the competitive landscape, consumer trends and disposable income, new product introductions, production and marketing plans, and many other types of inside information. In this case, we can build our revenues forecast from the bottom up with unit sales and unit prices for each product or service sold. However, if we are a company outsider, we have much less information. In this

EXHIBIT 11.1 Procter & Gamble Income Statement			
Year ended June 30, amounts in millions except per share amounts	2008	2007	2006
Net sales.	$83,503	$76,476	$68,222
Cost of products sold.	40,695	36,686	33,125
Selling, general and administrative expense	25,725	24,340	21,848
Operating income.	17,083	15,450	13,249
Interest expense.	1,467	1,304	1,119
Other nonoperating income, net	462	564	283
Earnings before income taxes	16,078	14,710	12,413
Income taxes	4,003	4,370	3,729
Net earnings.	$12,075	$10,340	$ 8,684
Basic net earnings per common share.	$ 3.86	$ 3.22	$ 2.79
Diluted net earnings per common share	$ 3.64	$ 3.04	$ 2.64
Dividends per common share	$ 1.45	$ 1.28	$ 1.15

case, we must rely on public statements by company management in conference calls and meetings in addition to the information disclosed in the management discussion and analysis (MD&A) section of the 10-K and the growth of individual product lines from segment disclosures. We also use publicly available information from competitors, suppliers, and customers for additional insight into broader trends that can impact future revenues. Companies often provide "guidance" to outsiders to help refine forecasts, which is usually valuable as companies have a vested interest in correct forecasts so that their securities are accurately priced. Generally, the revenues forecast is obtained from the following formula:

$$\textbf{Forecasted revenues} = \textbf{Actual revenues} \times (\textbf{1 + Revenue growth rate})$$

The revenue growth rate can be either positive or negative depending on numerous company and economic factors, described above. The remainder of this section identifies and explains key factors that impact revenue growth and illustrates their application to Procter & Gamble.

Factors Impacting Revenue Growth

Forecasts are made within the broader context of the general economic environment and the competitive landscape in which the company operates. There are a number of specific factors that impact a company's ability to achieve revenue growth.

Impact of Acquisitions When one company acquires another, the revenues and expenses of the acquired company are consolidated but only from the date of acquisition onward (we discuss consolidation in Module 7). Acquisitions can greatly impact the acquirer's income statement, especially if the acquisition occurs toward the beginning of the acquirer's fiscal year. Procter & Gamble's acquisition of Gillette in October 2005 provides an example. In its June 30, 2006, fiscal year-end income statement (ending eight months following the acquisition), P&G reported the following for sales:

Amounts in millions except per share amounts; Years ended June 30	2006	2005	2004
Net sales.	$68,222	$56,741	$51,407

These net sales amounts include Gillette product sales only from October 2005 onward (for fiscal 2006), and none of Gillette's sales are reported in fiscal 2005 or fiscal 2004. Its 2006 sales growth of 20.2% ([$68,222/$56,741] −1) is not representative of P&G's organic growth, and we would be remiss in forecasting a 20.2% increase for fiscal 2007.

Importantly, until all of the three comparative income statements in the 10-K include the acquired company, the acquirer is required to disclose what revenue and net income would have been had the acquired company been consolidated for all three years reported in the current income statement. This "what if" disclosure is called *pro forma* disclosure. Procter & Gamble's pro forma disclosure in 2006 includes the following discussion and table:

The following table provides pro forma results of operations for the years ended June 30, 2006, 2005, and 2004, as if Gillette had been acquired as of the beginning of each fiscal year presented.

Pro forma results; Years ended June 30	2006	2005	2004
Net sales (in millions)	$71,005	$67,920	$61,112
Net earnings (in millions)	8,871	8,522	7,504
Diluted net earnings per common share	2.51	2.29	1.98

We use those pro forma results to compute a more accurate historical revenue growth rate for fiscal 2006, which equals 4.5% ([$71,005/$67,920] −1). This disclosure provides useful information in our forecasting of future performance. P&G is careful to point out, however, that the pro forma earnings estimate must be viewed with caution:

Pro forma results do not include any anticipated cost savings or other effects of the planned integration of Gillette. Accordingly, such amounts are not necessarily indicative of the results if the acquisition had occurred on the dates indicated or that may result in the future.

We must incorporate other public statements by P&G's management to better forecast the impact of Gillette on P&G profitability as a result of cost savings following the integration of Gillette. Nevertheless, the pro forma disclosure provides useful information on the impact of this acquisition.

Impact of Divestitures Companies are required to exclude sales and expenses of discontinued operations from the continuing operations portion of their income statements, and to present the net income and gain (loss) on sale of the divested entity, net of tax, below income from continuing operations (we discuss accounting for divestitures in Module 5). Owens-Illinois Group provides an example in its income statement.

Year ended December 31 ($ millions)	2007
Revenues	$7,679.2
Costs and expenses	7,057.6
Earnings from continuing operations before items below	621.6
Provision for income taxes	147.8
Minority share owners' interests in earnings of subsidiaries	59.5
Earnings from continuing operations	414.3
Net earnings of discontinued operations	2.8
Gain on sale of discontinued operations	1,038.5
Net earnings	$1,455.6

The following footnote to Owens-Illinois' 10-K provides information about the discontinued operations:

The consolidated financial statements of Owens-Illinois Group, Inc. ("Company") include the accounts of its subsidiaries. Newly acquired subsidiaries have been included in the consolidated financial statements from dates of acquisition. Results of operations for the plastics packaging business sold during 2007 have been presented as a discontinued operation . . . On June 11, 2007, the Company announced that it had concluded the strategic review process of its plastics portfolio and entered into a definitive agreement with Rexam PLC to sell its plastics packaging business. On July 31, 2007, the Company completed the sale for approximately $1.825 billion in cash . . . The following summarizes the revenues and expenses of the discontinued operations as reported in the consolidated results of operations for the periods indicated:

continued

continued from prior page

	2007
Net sales.	$ 455.0
Other revenue (expense), net	(0.1)
Total revenues	454.9
Cost and expenses:	
Manufacturing, shipping and delivery	343.5
Research, development and engineering	8.3
Selling and administrative	20.7
Interest	80.6
Other	1.2
	454.3
Earnings before items below	0.6
Provision (credit) for income taxes	(2.4)
Minority share owners' interests in earnings of subsidiaries	0.2
Gain on sale of discontinued operations	1,038.5
Net earnings from discontinued operations	$1,041.3

The revenues, expenses, and earnings for Owens-Illinois exclude the revenues, expenses, and earnings from its discontinued operations. The income statement above, prepared for the discontinued plastics packaging division, reports this division's excluded revenues, expenses, and earnings. The disclosure also reports the gain on sale of the division. This allows us to better evaluate revenue growth because the Owens-Illinois income statement reports only revenue from continuing operations. We would be remiss if we included revenue from the plastics packaging in our forecast.

Impact of Existing vs New Store Growth Retailers typically derive revenue growth from two sources: (1) from *existing* stores (organic growth), and (2) from *new* stores. We are interested in the breakdown between these two growth sources as the latter is obtained at considerably more cost. Target Corporation provides the following footnote disclosure to its 10-K report.

Comparable-store sales are sales from our online business and sales from general merchandise and SuperTarget stores open longer than one year:

Revenue Growth	2007	2006	2005
Comparable-store sales	3.0%	4.8%	5.6%
Sales (a)	6.2%	12.9%	12.2%
Credit card revenues (a)	17.6%	19.5%	16.5%
Total revenues (a)	6.5%	13.1%	12.3%

(a) 2006 consisted of 53 weeks.

In 2007, a 52-week year following a 53-week year, total revenues were $63,367 million compared with $59,490 in 2006, an increase of 6.5 percent. Total revenue growth was attributable to the opening of new stores, a comparable store sales increase of 3.0 percent and a 17.6 percent increase in credit card revenues. These factors were partially offset by the impact of an extra week in 2006 . . . In 2008, we expect to invest $4.5 billion to $4.7 billion in capital expenditures, including investments in approximately 116 new stores, adding about 95 new locations, net of relocations and closings, and two distribution centers that will open in 2008.

At least three points in Target's footnote disclosure are noteworthy for forecasting purposes.

1. Retailers typically operate on a 52/53 week year, closing their books on a particular day of the week rather than constant date. Target has the following fiscal year-end policy:

Our fiscal year ends on the Saturday nearest January 31. Unless otherwise stated, references to years in this report relate to fiscal years, rather than to calendar years. Fiscal year 2007 ended February 2, 2008, and consisted of 52 weeks. Fiscal year 2006 ended February 3, 2007, and consisted of 53 weeks.

Because Target's fiscal 2006 included an extra week, sales are growing at a higher rate in fiscal 2007 than it would first appear from the percent increase in sales for 2007. To accurately forecast revenue growth, we must use numbers and rates that reflect a consistent 52-week period each year. To do this, we assume that sales are recorded evenly each week and adjust revenues for the 53-week year (multiply by 52/53). Then, we use the 52-week pro forma sales figures to recompute growth rates. For Target, we adjust 2006 sales amounts. This decreases 2006 sales which has the effect of decreasing the 2006 growth rates and increasing the 2007 growth rates as follows (there is no change in 2005 growth rates):

	2007	2006	2005
Comparable-store sales.........	3.9%	4.0%	5.6%
Sales......................	8.3%	10.8%	12.2%
Credit card revenues	19.9%	17.2%	16.5%
Total revenues	8.6%	10.9%	12.3%

These pro forma numbers more accurately portray revenue trends. While the all important comparable-sales growth rate has slowed since 2005, it has stayed relatively constant from 2006 to 2007 (3.9%, down from 4.0%). This is counter to the trend depicted with the inflated 2006 sales figures. The adjusted rates also show that credit card revenue growth has increased in 2007 whereas the unadjusted numbers lead us to the opposite conclusion. This highlights the critical importance of adjusting numbers before we begin the forecasting process.

2. More than half (4.4% out of 8.3%, using our adjusted numbers) of Target's sales growth is attributable to new store openings.

3. The average per store planned capital expenditure is about $40 million (~$4.6 billion/116 stores). Although acquired growth provides the organic growth of the future, it comes at considerable cost per store.

Impact of Unit Sales and Price Disclosures Forecasts that are built from anticipated unit sales and current prices are generally more informative, and accurate, than those derived from historical dollar sales. Most companies, however, do not provide unit sales data in their 10-Ks. Apple, Inc., is an exception, and the following footnote disclosure from its 10-K provides useful information (see that, like Target, Apple operates on a 52/53 week fiscal year):

Net Sales Fiscal years 2008 and 2007 spanned 52 weeks while fiscal year 2006 spanned 53 weeks. An additional week is included in the first fiscal quarter approximately every six years to realign fiscal quarters with calendar quarters. The following table summarizes net sales and Mac unit sales by operating segment and net sales and unit sales by product during the three fiscal years ended September 27, 2008 (in millions, except unit sales in thousands and per unit amounts):

	2008	Change	2007	Change	2006
Net sales by product					
Desktops............................	$ 5,603	39%	$ 4,020	21%	$ 3,319
Portables...........................	8,673	38%	6,294	55%	4,056
Total Mac net sales....................	14,276	38%	10,314	40%	7,375
iPod	9,153	10%	8,305	8%	7,676
Other music related products and services	3,340	34%	2,496	32%	1,885
iPhone and related products and services.....	1,844	NM	123	NM	—
Peripherals and other hardware.............	1,659	32%	1,260	15%	1,100
Software, service, and other sales...........	2,207	46%	1,508	18%	1,279
Total net sales........................	$32,479	35%	$24,006	24%	$19,315

continued

continued from prior page

	2008	Change	2007	Change	2006
Unit sales by product					
Desktops................................	3,712	37%	2,714	12%	2,434
Portables................................	6,003	38%	4,337	51%	2,869
Total Mac unit sales	9,715	38%	7,051	33%	5,303
Net sales per Mac unit sold	$ 1,469	0%	$ 1,463	5%	$ 1,391
iPod unit sales	54,828	6%	51,630	31%	39,409
Net sales per iPod unit sold	$ 167	4%	$ 161	(17)%	$ 195
iPhone unit sales	11,627	NM	1,389	NM	—

From Apple's disclosure we can derive several useful insights for forecasting purposes.

1. On average, a Mac sells for $1,469 and the per unit selling price has not changed markedly for the past three years; unit sales, however, have increased by 33% to 38% per year for the past two years. (Adjusting numbers for the 53-week period in 2006 makes only a small difference in Apple's case.)

2. The rate of increase in iPod unit sales is slowing considerably, from a 31% unit sales increase in 2007 to a 6% unit sales increase in 2008, probably reflecting increased competition from other MP3 players and market saturation.

3. The average sales price of iPods in 2008 is much lower than the $195 unit price Apple received in 2006.

4. iPhone unit sales are 11,627,000 in 2008 and were nonexistent in 2006.

5. iPhone dollar sales are $1,844 million ($159 per unit); this per unit sales figure is deceiving, however, as other footnotes report that Apple recognizes revenues of iPhones ratably over the two-year service contract with AT&T. In addition to the iPhone market price, analysts estimate that AT&T is paying Apple $12 to $18 per month for each iPhone subscriber, or $288–$432 per phone over the course of a two-year contract (iPod sales do not contain such a subscriber subsidy payment).

Detailed disclosures such as Apple's allow us to prepare more informed forecasts that consider both unit sales and selling prices.

Forecasting Revenue Growth

To illustrate the forecasting process, we forecast revenue growth for P&G. Our information includes public disclosures by management in meetings and conference calls with analysts and the company's published financial reports including the management discussion and analysis (MD&A) section of the 10-K. We discuss the information in each of these sources.

Public Disclosures via Meetings and Calls P&G held meetings with analysts on September 16, 2008, and on December 11, 2008. Those are its most recent meetings prior to the publication of this book and both follow the issuance of P&G's annual report dated June 30, 2008. Its presentation, publicly available on the "Investor" section of P&G's Website, provides guidance in several areas that impact our forecasts. For example, to underscore the importance of organic growth, P&G provides the following table and presentation slide for analysis of its operations.

Procter & Gamble	2001–2008	2004–2008
Average annual reported net sales growth.............................	10%	14%
Less: Average annual foreign exchange and acquisition/divestiture impact	−5%	−7%
Average annual organic sales growth	5%	7%

P&G's organic growth has ranged from 5% to 7% in recent years. In 2008, the economy was in a recession, and it was widely expected that consumers would cut back on spending, including consumer staples. Consequently, P&G's forecast of its revenue growth through fiscal year 2010 was in the range of 4% to 6%. Company expectations are an important input to our forecasts of revenue growth.

Published Reports: Segment Disclosures and MD&A Companies are required to disclose summary financial results for each of their operating segments along with a discussion and analysis of each. (An operating segment is defined under GAAP as a component of the company for which financial information is available and disclosed to senior management.) P&G is organized into six operating segments as discussed in the following excerpt from its 2008 MD&A:

Our organizational structure is comprised of three Global Business Units (GBUs) and a Global Operations group . . . Our three GBUs are Beauty, Health and Well-Being, and Household Care . . . Under U.S. GAAP, the business units comprising the GBUs are aggregated into six reportable segments: Beauty; Grooming; Health Care; Snacks, Coffee and Pet Care; Fabric Care and Home Care; and Baby Care and Family Care. The following provides additional detail on our GBUs and reportable segments and the key product and brand composition within each.

GBU	Reportable Segment	% of Net Sales	% of Net Earnings	Key Products	Billion-Dollar Brands
Beauty	Beauty	23%	22%	Cosmetics, Deodorants, Hair Care, Personal Cleansing, Prestige Fragrances, Skin Care	Head & Shoulders, Olay, Pantene, Wella
	Grooming	10%	13%	Blades and Razors, Electric Hair Removal Devices, Face and Shave Products, Home Appliances	Braun, Fusion, Gillette, Mach3
Health and well-being	Health Care	17%	20%	Feminine Care, Oral Care, Personal Health Care, Pharmaceuticals	Actonel, Always, Crest, Oral-B
	Snacks, Coffee and Pet Care	6%	4%	Coffee, Pet Food, Snacks	Folgers, Iams, Pringles
Household care	Fabric Care and Home Care	28%	27%	Air Care, Batteries, Dish Care, Fabric Care, Surface Care	Ariel, Dawn, Downy, Duracell, Gain, Tide
	Baby Care and Family Care	16%	14%	Baby Wipes, Bath Tissue, Diapers, Facial Tissue, Paper Towels	Bounty, Charmin, Pampers

P&G also reports a revenue history for each segment and its MD&A provides additional information relating to the breakdown of revenue increases for the current year into the portion relating to increases in unit volume sales, increases in prices, effects of foreign currency translation, and changes in product mix. That disclosure and related discussion allow us to compile the following table:

Operating Segment	Year	Sales ($ millions)	% Change	Unit Effect	Foreign Exchange Effect	Price Effect	Mix Effect
Beauty	2008	$19,515	9.1%	2%	6%	0%	1%
	2007	17,889	7.2%				
	2006	16,687					
Grooming	2008	8,254	11.0%	5%	7%	2%	(3)%
	2007	7,437	45.4%				
	2006	5,114					
Health Care.	2008	14,578	8.9%	4%	5%	1%	(1)%
	2007	13,381	13.1%				
	2006	11,831					
Snacks, Coffee and Pet Care	2008	4,852	6.9%	2%	3%	3%	(1)%
	2007	4,537	3.5%				
	2006	4,383					
Fabric Care and Home Care.	2008	23,831	11.0%	6%	5%	1%	(1)%
	2007	21,469	13.5%				
	2006	18,918					
Baby Care and Family Care	2008	13,898	9.2%	4%	4%	1%	0%
	2007	12,726	6.3%				
	2006	11,972					
Corporate	2008	(1,425)					
	2007	(963)					
	2006	(683)					
Total Company	2008	83,503	9.2%	4%	5%	1%	
	2007	76,476	12.1%				
	2006	68,222					

P&G's total revenues increased by 9.2% in 2008, of which 5 percentage points relates to the effects of fluctuations in foreign exchange rates (see Module 5). During 2008, the $US weakened vis-à-vis other major world currencies. Thus, sales denominated in foreign currencies, including P&G's, increased when translated into $US, resulting in an increase in revenue growth.

Similar reasoning applies to the portion of revenue growth resulting from acquisitions. Although acquisition of brands is a normal component of P&G's operating activities, acquisitions are one-time occurrences and come at a price. We are, therefore, interested in the portion of revenue growth that has not been acquired. Organic sales growth provides us the best indicator of core operating revenue growth. P&G defines organic sales growth as follows:

Organic Sales Growth Organic sales growth measures sales growth excluding the impacts of foreign exchange, acquisitions and divestitures from year-over-year comparisons. The Company believes this provides investors with a more complete understanding of underlying results and trends by providing sales on a consistent basis.

Determining the Revenue Growth Forecast

Drawing on the segment disclosures from our table above, and using the percentage growth in units plus the percentage growth in prices as a proxy for organic growth, our initial forecast of P&G's 2009 sales follows.

Segment ($ millions)	2008 Account	2009 Est.	Computation
Beauty	$19,515	$19,905	$19,915 × 1.02
Grooming	8,254	8,832	$ 8,254 × 1.07
Health Care.	14,578	15,307	$14,578 × 1.05
Snacks, Coffee and Pet Care	4,852	5,095	$ 4,852 × 1.05
Fabric Care and Home Care.	23,831	25,499	$23,831 × 1.07
Baby Care and Family Care	13,898	14,593	$13,898 × 1.05
Corporate	(1,425)	(2,109)	$(1,425) × 1.48
Total Company	$83,503	$87,122	
Percent Change		4.33%	

To complete our forecast of revenue growth, we draw on P&G's estimate that the $US will strengthen about 5% vis-à-vis other world currencies in 2009 as revealed in the following P&G slide from its presentation to analysts.

Our final revenues forecast projects a *decline* in reported sales for 2009 of 0.67%, computed as 4.33% organic growth minus 5.00% currency effect. This yields a final P&G revenues forecast of $82,944 million, computed as $83,503 × (1 − 0.67%).

STEP 2: FORECASTING EXPENSES

The next step in the forecasting process is to predict expenses; for our purposes this includes operating expenses and nonoperating revenues and expenses.

Forecasting Operating Expenses

Generally, we use the following formula to forecast individual operating expenses:

Forecasted operating expense = Forecasted revenues × (Forecasted operating expense margin)

The forecasted operating expense margin is the expense expressed as a percent of sales (the common-sized expense). We normally start with the prior year's margin and then adjust it based on our business analysis. One exception to this general formula is for income taxes where we apply the following:

Forecasted income taxes = Forecasted income before taxes × (Forecasted effective tax rate)

The forecasted effective tax rate normally begins with the prior year's rate and then adjusts it for any predicted changes in government tax policies, predicted income levels, and company tax strategies.

Forecasting Nonoperating Expenses

Generally, forecasts of individual line items of nonoperating expenses are obtained from the following "no change" forecast model:

Forecasted nonoperating expense = Nonoperating expense for prior period

This assumes no change in nonoperating expenses, with an exception of a "zero forecast" for items related to discontinued operations. If we make balance sheet financing or investment adjustments in the optional Step 4, we must adjust one or more nonoperating expenses.

Forecasting Expenses for P&G

To illustrate the forecasting of operating and nonoperating expenses we turn to Procter & Gamble. Despite P&G's management forecast of a decline in revenue growth, its management forecasts an increase in operating profit and cash flow through 2010 as apparent from the following slide taken from the company's 2008 presentation to analysts.

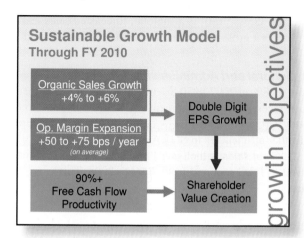

In addition to the ~5% revenue growth, P&G's report to analysts forecasts an improved operating profit margin of 50–75 basis points (bps refers to *basis points*, which is 1/100 of a percent) per year through 2010.

Drawing on all available information, we formulate assumptions regarding forecasted operating and nonoperating expenses (revenues) for P&G. Exhibit 11.2 shows Procter & Gamble's 2008 actual income statement numbers along with our forecasted numbers for 2009. The remainder of this section explains the details and logic behind our forecasts.

EXHIBIT 11.2 Forecasted Income Statement for P&G					
($ millions)	2008		Forecast Assumptions	2009 Est.	
Net sales.	$83,503	100.0%	$83,503 × 0.9933	$82,944	100.0%
Cost of products sold.	40,695	48.7%	$82,944 × 49.7%	41,223	49.7%
Gross profit.	42,808	51.3%	subtotal	41,721	50.3%
Selling, general and administrative expense	25,725	30.8%	$82,944 × 29.8%	24,717	29.8%
Operating income.	17,083	20.5%	subtotal	17,004	20.5%
Interest expense.	1,467	1.8%	no change	1,467	1.8%
Other nonoperating income, net	462	0.6%	no change	462	0.6%
Earnings before income taxes	16,078	19.3%	subtotal	15,999	19.3%
Income taxes	4,003	4.8%	$15,999 × 24.9%	3,984	4.8%
Net earnings.	$12,075	14.5%	subtotal	$12,015	14.5%

Operating Expenses for P&G

This section describes the process of forecasting operating expenses.

Forecasting Net Sales We forecast net sales to decline by 0.67%, which is the forecasted outcome from a predicted 4.33% increase in organic sales that is offset by a 5% decline reflecting the anticipated strengthening of the $US vis-à-vis other world currencies—details were described earlier.

Forecasting Cost of Products Sold Cost of products sold as a percent of sales increased from 48% in 2007 to 48.7% in 2008. Given the projected slowdown in consumer spending as a result of the recession of 2008–2009, further deterioration of the gross profit margin is likely. Our projection is for cost of goods sold to increase to 49.7% of sales, a 1.0 percentage point increase from the 48.7% for the prior year and a slightly higher increase in percentage points than P&G experienced in the prior year (0.7 percentage point from 48.0%). Our increase reflects the expected negative impact on selling prices during the 2008–2009 recession coupled with an expected increase in energy costs. Both of these factors were highlighted by P&G in its meetings with analysts.

Subtotaling Gross Profit Gross profit is a subtotal, forecasted sales less forecasted cost of goods sold. (In some cases we forecast gross profit; in that case, cost of goods sold is the "plug" figure.)

Forecasting Selling, General and Administrative Expense P&G has reduced SG&A expenses as a percent of sales from 31.8% in 2007 to 30.8% in 2008 and it cited further improvement during the meetings with analysts. A recessionary environment will encourage P&G to focus on overhead reduction, which, coupled with P&G's continued focus on manufacturing and supply chain improvements, supports a forecast of further efficiencies in SG&A expenses as a percent of sales. Our forecast is for SG&A expenses to be 29.8% of sales, which is a 1 percentage point improvement over 2008 and the same rate of improvement as P&G reported from 2007 to 2008. This is a trend that P&G highlighted in its meetings with analysts.

Subtotaling Operating Income Operating income is a subtotal, but we still check its reasonableness. Our forecasts imply a 20.5% operating income margin, which would be identical to the previous year. Further, it is reasonable to expect a flat operating income margin as improvements are less likely in the 2008–2009 economic environment.

Forecasting Income Taxes Our general method to forecast income taxes is to predict "no change" in a company's effective tax rate, assuming it is within reasonable limits. Accordingly, we forecast a continuation of P&G's 24.9% effective tax rate for 2008.

Nonoperating Expenses for P&G

This section describes the process of forecasting nonoperating expenses.

Forecasting Interest Expense and "Other" Nonoperating expenses for P&G consist of interest expense on debt and income from marketable securities. Our general approach to forecasting nonoperating expenses is to predict "no change" for the initial forecast. Although the level of interest rates might be expected to decline as a result of the 2008–2009 recessionary environment, the nearly $1 trillion government spending package in the 2008 stimulus bill is expected to put upward pressure on interest rates. Consequently, we forecast no change in interest expense and nonoperating income. However, we will revisit these forecasts after we obtain our cash forecast in the balance sheet to see if any adjustments are necessary.

The no-change forecasts for nonoperating expenses yield income before taxes of $15,999 million, which is 19.3% of sales ($15,999/$82,944) and identical to the 2008 percentage. Thus, applying P&G's 24.9% effective tax rate, we obtain net earnings of $12,015 million ($15,999 million × [1 − 24.9%]).

STEP 3: FORECASTING ASSETS, LIABILITIES AND EQUITY

LO3 Forecast the balance sheet.

Step 3 is to forecast balance sheet items, which consist of assets, liabilities, and equity. Special emphasis is on forecasts of operating assets and liabilities. We generally assume no change in nonoperating assets, liabilities, and equity (we discuss exceptions to this rule in this section and further adjustments to those accounts in Step 4). Step 3 proceeds with five steps as shown in Figure 11.3.

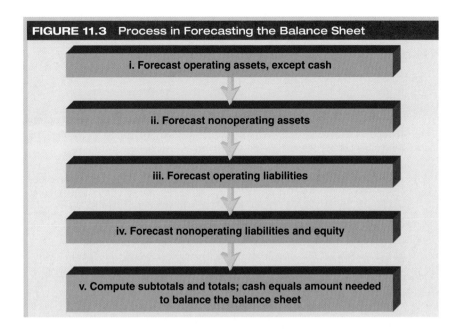

FIGURE 11.3 Process in Forecasting the Balance Sheet

i. Forecast operating assets, except cash

ii. Forecast nonoperating assets

iii. Forecast operating liabilities

iv. Forecast nonoperating liabilities and equity

v. Compute subtotals and totals; cash equals amount needed to balance the balance sheet

As a starting point, we begin with Procter & Gamble's balance sheet for 2008 in Exhibit 11.3. We will refer to these statements throughout this section.

Process of Forecasting Balance Sheet Items

We normally make one of three general assumptions when forecasting assets, liabilities, and equity.

1. **Forecast amounts with no change.** We can use a no-change forecast, which is common for nonoperating assets (investments in securities, discontinued operations, and other nonoperating investments). After we have generated forecasts of the balance sheet, we must reexamine the no-change forecasts to see if they are reasonable or if they require adjustment.

2. **Forecast contractual or specified amounts.** We can use contractual or other specified payment tables to forecast selected balance sheet items. For example, footnote disclosures contain scheduled maturities for long-term debt, capital leases, and mandatory redeemable preferred stock for a five-year period subsequent to the financial statement date. We can use those schedules and assume that the required payments are made as projected.

3. **Forecast amounts in relation to revenues.** We can use an item's relation to revenues to forecast that item. The underlying assumption is that, as revenues change, so does that item in some predictable manner. For example, in the case of operating assets, it is reasonable to assume that the required investment in receivables, inventories, and PPE is related, in some manner, to the level of revenues. Similarly, in the case of operating liabilities, it is reasonable to expect that accounts payable will grow with COGS (which grows with revenues), and accrued liabilities will grow with increases in payroll, utilities, advertising, and other expenses (which all grow with revenue).

When forecasting amounts in relation to revenues, the third forecasting assumption above, there are three common methods: (1) forecasts using the percent of revenues, (2) forecasts using turnover rates, and (3) forecasts using days outstanding ratios.

Forecasts Using Percent of Revenues Forecasts that use the percent of revenues build on the relation between revenues and the account being forecasted; this relation follows:

$$\text{Forecasted account balance} = \text{Forecasted revenues} \times \left(\frac{\text{Actual account balance}}{\text{Actual revenues}}\right)$$

For example, if the relation between the actual account balance to revenues is 10%, and forecasted revenues equal $100, then the forecasted account is $10, computed as $100 × 10%.

EXHIBIT 11.3 Procter & Gamble Balance Sheet		
June 30, amounts in millions	**2008**	**2007**
Assets*		
Cash and cash equivalents	$ 3,313	$ 5,354
Investment securities	228	202
Accounts receivable	6,761	6,629
Inventories	8,416	6,819
Deferred income taxes	2,012	1,727
Prepaid expenses and other current assets	3,785	3,300
Total current assets	24,515	24,031
Total property, plant and equipment	38,086	34,721
Accumulated depreciation	(17,446)	(15,181)
Net property, plant and equipment	20,640	19,540
Net goodwill and other intangible assets	94,000	90,178
Other noncurrent assets	4,837	4,265
Total assets	$143,992	$138,014
Liabilities and shareholders' equity		
Accounts payable	$ 6,775	$ 5,710
Accrued and other liabilities	10,154	9,586
Taxes payable	945	3,382
Debt due within one year	13,084	12,039
Total current liabilities	30,958	30,717
Long-term debt	23,581	23,375
Deferred income taxes	11,805	12,015
Other noncurrent liabilities	8,154	5,147
Total liabilities	74,498	71,254
Shareholders' equity		
Convertible Class A preferred stock, stated value $1 per share (600 shares authorized)	1,366	1,406
Non-voting Class B preferred stock, stated value $1 per share (200 shares authorized)	—	—
Common stock, stated value $1 per share (10,000 shares authorized; shares issued: 2008—4,001.8, 2007—3,989.7)	4,002	3,990
Additional paid-in capital	60,307	59,030
Reserve for ESOP debt retirement	(1,325)	(1,308)
Accumulated other comprehensive income	3,746	617
Treasury stock, at cost (shares held: 2008—969.1, 2007—857.8)	(47,588)	(38,772)
Retained earnings	48,986	41,797
Total shareholders' equity	69,494	66,760
Total liabilities and shareholders' equity	$143,992	$138,014

*The balance sheet combines the following accounts: (1) Materials and Supplies, Work in Process, and Finished Goods Inventories into total "Inventories," (2) Goodwill, Trademarks, and Other Intangible Assets into "Net goodwill and Other Intangible Assets," and (3) Buildings, Machinery and Equipment, and Land into "Total Property, Plant and Equipment."

Forecasts Using Turnover Rates Turnover rates have the following general form: Turnover rate = Revenues (or COGS)/Average account balance. Using algebra to rearrange terms, we obtain: Average account balance = Revenues (or COGS)/Turnover rate. Substituting forecasted values we get:

Forecasted account balance = Forecasted revenues (or COGS)/Turnover rate

Consequently, if we have forecasted revenues (or COGS) and a forecasted turnover rate, we can forecast the account balance. However, there is a problem with this method if we use turnover rates as traditionally defined using average account balances; in this case the method would forecast the *average account balance*. Balance sheets report *ending account balances*. This issue is resolved in one of two ways:

1. Compute the turnover rate using ending balances rather than average balances; then, our forecast is for the ending account balance.
2. Multiply the forecasted average account balance by 2 and then subtract the beginning account balance; this yields the forecast for the ending account balance.

Forecasts Using Days Outstanding Days outstanding ratios have the following general form: Days outstanding = Account balance/Average daily revenues (or COGS), where Average daily revenues (or COGS) = Revenues (or COGS)/365. We can forecast the account balance by rearranging terms as follows:

Forecasted account balance = Days outstanding × [Forecasted revenues (or COGS)/365]

If days outstanding is computed using the ending balance of the account, the resulting forecast is for the ending balance of that account. However, some analysts prefer a shortcut method to compute days outstanding as 365/Turnover rate. Their justification is based on the mathematical equality where [365/Turnover rate] = [365/(Revenues/Account balance)] = [(Account balance × 365)/Revenues] = [Account balance/(Revenues/365)]. Importantly, however, if this turnover rate is computed in the conventional way using the *average* account balance, we would forecast the average account balance rather than the ending account balance. In this case, we must make one of the two adjustments explained in the previous section.

Equivalence of the Three Forecasting Methods If we compute the turnover rate and the days outstanding using ending account balances (meaning that we are properly forecasting the ending account balance), it does not matter which of these three forecasting methods we use. To illustrate, consider a company with current period revenues of $1,000 and a forecasted revenue growth of 4% (or $1,040, computed as $1,000 × 1.04). Assume that the current accounts receivable ending balance is $200 and that we want to forecast accounts receivable for next year. Using each of the three methods above, our forecasted accounts receivable is $208 and is computed as follows:

Forecast Method	Forecast	Forecast Computation
Percent of revenues	$208	$1,040 × ($200/$1,000)
Turnover rate	$208	$1,040/($1,000/$200)
Days outstanding	$208	{[($200 × 365)/$1,000] × $1,040}/365

Each of these forecasting methods yields the same result. Analysts commonly use either percent of sales or days outstanding. The choice between percent of sales and days outstanding depends on the audience. Percent of sales is simple and intuitive. Days outstanding is well suited for analyses that are used in discussions with operating managers, as most managers are familiar with days outstanding ratios and can identify with projected changes (for example, what is the effect of collecting our receivables two days earlier?). The choice is a matter of personal preference as all three methods yield the same result. *We use the percent of sales in our forecasts of balance sheet accounts because (1) it appears to be the most commonly used method, (2) it is the method that P&G management uses in its meetings with analysts, and (3) it is the method used by* Oppenheimer *in the real-world analysis illustration we provide in Appendix 11A.*

Forecasting Balance Sheet Items

We illustrate the forecasting of balance sheet items for Procter & Gamble.

Forecasting Operating Assets

This section describes the process of forecasting operating assets using the percent of revenues method in most cases.

Forecasting Accounts Receivable Proctor & Gamble reports accounts receivable as a percentage of sales of 8.1% and 8.7% at year-end 2008 and 2007, respectively. In the MD&A section of its 10-K, P&G management ascribes the improved percentage to "the harmonization of Gillette trade terms, which historically carried longer payment terms than P&G." Gillette was acquired on October 1, 2005, and there have been no major acquisitions since Gillette. Thus, we are unlikely to see further improvement from any harmonization. Further, we are preparing forecasts during a recession and it is reasonable to expect a decline in the financial condition of P&G customers—some P&G customers are likely to pay more slowly, if at all. This will increase accounts receivable relative to sales. Accordingly, we forecast an increase in P&G's ratio of accounts receivables to sales from 8.1% to 8.4%, where 8.4% is the average for the past two years. This increase of 0.3% represents an increase of 1.1 days (0.003 ×

365 days) in the average collection period, from 29.6 days in 2008 to a forecasted 30.7 days in 2009. Applying our percent of revenues forecasting method, P&G's forecasted accounts receivable is $6,967, computed as $82,944 × 8.4%.

Forecasting Inventories P&G's inventories increased in 2008 from 8.9% of sales to 10.1% of sales. In the MD&A section of its 10-K, P&G's management attributes the increase to "higher material values," mainly relating to higher energy costs in 2008. Given the recessionary environment for 2009, it is unlikely that energy or commodity costs will increase markedly. That expectation argues for a reduction in the inventory-to-sales relation. Alternatively, customer purchases are expected to slow and inventories will increase unless managed carefully. We might argue that P&G is a well managed company that will not allow inventories to exceeded reasonable levels. This would support a lower inventories-to-sales forecast due to the projected decline in energy and commodity costs. Provided with these two conflicting expectations and no convincing evidence for either, we expect P&G's inventories-to-sales ratio to remain at the 2008 level. Applying the percent of revenues forecasting method we get forecasted inventories of $8,377, computed as $82,944 × 10.1%.

Forecasting Deferred Income Tax Assets We apply the no-change forecasting method to deferred income taxes. Rationale for this method is provided when we explain the forecasting of deferred income tax liabilities below.

Forecasting Prepaid Expenses and Other P&G ratio of prepaid expenses and other current assets to sales increased slightly from 4.3% in 2007 to 4.5% in 2008. P&G does not provide a breakdown of this account in its footnotes and does not discuss this line item in its MD&A. Given the lack of insight into the composition of this account, we forecast its balance at the 2008 level of 4.5% of sales. Applying the percent of revenues forecasting method we get forecasted prepaid expenses and other of $3,732, computed as $82,944 × 4.5%.

Forecasting Capital Expenditures, PPE, and Accumulated Depreciation Capital expenditures (CAPEX) are often a large cash outflow and a major component of free cash flow, which is the focus of cash-flow-based equity valuation models. (Free cash flow is defined in Module 12 as [NOPAT − Increase in NOA] and is also defined in finance literature as [Net cash flow from operating activities − CAPEX].) CAPEX is used in forecasting PPE (gross), where Forecasted PPE (gross) = Actual PPE (gross) + Forecasted CAPEX. (We typically do not forecast dispositions of PPE unless they are specifically identified by management in the MD&A section of the 10-K or other source.) P&G provided the following graph of its CAPEX as a percent of sales for several recent years in its meeting with analysts:

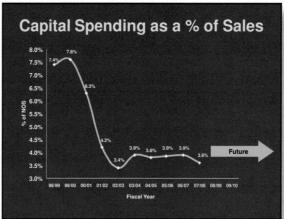

Its CAPEX, as a percent of sales, peaked in the late 1990s and early 2000s, but has settled into a range of 3.4% to 4.2% of sales since, declining slightly in 2008. P&G management forecasts a continuation of CAPEX at roughly the same percentage it has reported in the past seven years. Thus, we forecast CAPEX at 3.9% of sales (or $3,235), which is the rate for 2004–2007 (our forecast views the dip in 2008 CAPEX as an aberration). Our forecasted PPE (gross) for 2009 is $41,321, computed as $38,086 + ($82,944 × 3.9%).

To get net PPE we need the forecasted accumulated depreciation, which requires forecasted depreciation expense. We forecast depreciation as a percent of the actual PPE (gross). As is typical of companies, P&G does not report depreciation expense as a separate item on the income statement.

Instead, depreciation is part of SG&A expense. Thus, the forecasted depreciation expense impacts only accumulated depreciation on the balance sheet and the add-backs on the statement of cash flows. P&G's statement of cash flows reports $3,166 million for both depreciation and amortization expense in 2008 ($3,130 million and $2,627 million for 2007 and 2006, respectively). In footnotes to its 10-K, P&G states ($ millions):

> The amortization of intangible assets for the years ended June 30, 2008, 2007 and 2006 was $649, $640 and $587, respectively.

This disclosure allows us to compute depreciation expense separately as $2,517 million ($3,166 million − $649 million) for 2008. We assume that companies record depreciation on beginning-period PPE and not on any CAPEX for the period. The beginning-year PPE for 2008 was $34,721 million. We can, then, compute depreciation expense as a percentage of the actual *beginning* PPE (gross) balance of 7.2%, computed as $2,517/$34,721. Thus, our forecasted depreciation expense for 2009 is $2,742, computed as $38,086 × 7.2%. [An alternative computation for the depreciation rate is to divide by the average PPE (gross) for the period; for P&G, this would yield 6.9%, computed as $2,517/($34,721 + $38,086). For the forecasted depreciation, one could use the depreciation rate to add forecasted depreciation expense on one-half of forecasted CAPEX assuming that CAPEX is acquired evenly throughout the year.]

Forecasting Goodwill and Other Intangible Assets and Amortization Goodwill and other intangible assets arise mainly in connection with acquisitions of other companies. Unless an acquisition is pending at year-end, and we have sufficient information about its financial impact, we assume a no-change forecast for goodwill and other intangibles. Our only adjustment is to forecast amortization (reduction) of intangible assets (excluding goodwill, which is not amortized). P&G discloses amortization expense of $649 million for 2008 and a 2008 beginning balance for goodwill and other intangibles of $90,178 million. This yields an amortization rate of 0.7% of the actual *beginning* balance of goodwill and other intangible assets (computed as $649/$90,178). Applying that percentage to the 2008 ending balance of $94,000 million yields amortization expense of $658 million. Our forecast for goodwill and other intangible assets is $93,342 million, computed as $94,000 million − $658 million.

Forecasting Other Noncurrent Assets Other noncurrent assets are assumed part of operating assets unless information suggests otherwise. For P&G, the following excerpt from its 10-K footnotes suggests that other noncurrent assets are nonoperating. Further, we apply the no-change forecast model to this item, which means we forecast its 2009 balance at the 2008 level of $4,837.

> Auction rate securities are classified as other noncurrent assets with unrealized losses charged to shareholders' equity unless an impairment is judged to be other than temporary, in which case it is charged to earnings.

Forecasting Nonoperating Assets

This section forecasts nonoperating assets for P&G. Generally, we use the no-change forecast model for nonoperating assets. If we adjust the balance sheet for financing or investment reasons in the optional Step 4, we then adjust one or more nonoperating assets.

Forecasting Investment Securities For P&G, nonoperating assets include investment securities of $228 million in the current asset section. These are nonoperating assets as the footnote below makes clear. We forecast the same amount of investments for 2009.

> Investment securities consist of readily marketable debt and equity securities. Unrealized gains or losses are charged to earnings for investments classified as trading and to shareholders' equity for investments classified as available-for-sale.

Summary of Asset Forecasts To this point, we have forecasted all of P&G's operating and nonoperating assets other than cash. Following the forecast of liabilities and equity in the next section, we equate total assets with total liabilities and equity and then solve for cash. This balance reveals whether

P&G is expected to generate or use cash in 2009. We can then make a decision about the investment of excess cash or the way in which we expect to fund any cash shortfall. We explain this in Step 4.

Forecasting Operating Liabilities

This section describes the process of forecasting operating liabilities for P&G.

Forecasting Accounts Payable Accounts payable as a percent of sales increased from 7.5% in 2007 to 8.1% in 2008. P&G explains this increase:

> Accounts payable days were up 4 days due to higher material values and increased capital expenditures in the fourth quarter.

Although some reduction in the percentage might be justified due to the increased capital expenditures in the last quarter, we do not know the level of those expenditures. Thus, we forecast accounts payable at 8.1% of sales. Applying our percent of revenues forecasting method, P&G's forecasted accounts payable is $6,718, computed as $82,944 × 8.1%.

Forecasting Accrued and Other Liabilities Accruals as a percent of sales have remained fairly constant for P&G, decreasing from 12.5% in 2007 to 12.2% in 2008. P&G does not provide information relating to the composition of this account. Given the lack of information, we forecast accruals at the 2008 percentage of 12.2%. Applying the percent-of-revenues forecast method, we obtain forecasted accrued and other liabilities of $10,119, computed as $82,944 × 12.2%.

Forecasting Taxes Payable Companies typically make quarterly tax payments. Hence, some analysts forecast taxes payable using taxes payable as a percent of sales. However, because taxes payable relate directly to tax expense, we express taxes payable as a percentage of tax expense for forecasting purposes. In 2008, P&G's short-term taxes payable is 23.6% of its annual tax expense, computed as $945/$4,003. Thus, keeping the percentage constant at 23.6%, we forecast taxes payable as forecasted income taxes × 23.6%, which is $940, computed as $3,984 (from Exhibit 11.2) × 23.6%.

Forecasting Deferred Income Tax Liabilities P&G discloses the following footnote on deferred tax assets and liabilities in its 10-K.

June 30, in millions	2008	2007
Deferred tax assets		
Stock-based compensation	$ 1,082	$ 1,132
Unrealized loss on financial and foreign exchange transactions	1,274	723
Pension and postretirement benefits	633	560
Loss and other carryforwards	482	439
Advance payments	302	183
Goodwill and other intangible assets	267	249
Accrued marketing and promotion expense	125	161
Accrued interest and taxes	123	—
Inventory	114	95
Fixed assets	100	85
Other	1,048	1,119
Valuation allowances	(173)	(190)
Total	$ 5,377	$ 4,556
Deferred tax liabilities		
Goodwill and other intangible assets	$12,371	$12,102
Fixed assets	1,847	1,884
Other	151	132
Total	$14,369	$14,118

For deferred tax liabilities, there are no marked changes in either the total amount, or in the component accounts. Absent evidence of changes, either permanent or transitory, we apply the no-change forecast method for deferred tax liabilities. For deferred tax assets, there are no marked changes with the exception of the $551 million increase from an "unrealized loss on financial and foreign exchange transactions." Part of this increase might relate to derivative financial instruments (see Appendix 7A for a discussion) or to the effects of currency fluctuations. Neither of these is predictable with any confidence. Consequently, we apply the no-change method and forecast that deferred tax assets remain at the 2008 level. (Amounts of specific deferred tax components disclosed in footnotes rarely are reported on the balance sheet. Instead, companies aggregate certain amounts, and net others. For example, P&G reports a current deferred tax asset of $2,012 million and a long-term deferred tax liability of $11,805 million. Thus, we use the "no-change" method for both items for our 2009 forecast.)

Forecasting Other Noncurrent Liabilities P&G discloses the following other noncurrent liabilities in footnotes to its 10-K.

June 30, in millions	2008	2007
Other noncurrent liabilities		
Pension benefits..	$3,146	$2,898
Other postretirement benefits	512	503
Noncurrent FIN 48 liability	3,075	—
Other...	1,421	1,746
Total	$8,154	$5,147

The total includes two large components—pension benefits and a FIN 48 liability. The pension benefits are a function of the market value of pension investments, the estimated PBO, and P&G's cash contributions; further, the pension obligation cannot be predicted with any confidence. The FIN 48 liability relates to uncertain tax positions; the ultimate payment of this liability is uncertain as it relates to potential tax disputes. Due to the uncertainty of both of these major components of other noncurrent liabilities, we apply the no-change forecast for these liabilities.

Forecasting Nonoperating Liabilities and Equity

This section forecasts nonoperating liabilities and equity for P&G.

Forecasting Debt Due Within One Year P&G discloses the following table for its debt maturing within one year.

June 30, in millions	2008	2007
Short-term debt		
Current portion of long-term debt	$ 1,746	$ 2,544
Commercial paper	9,748	9,410
Floating rate note due February 2009	1,500	—
Other...	90	85
Total	$13,084	$12,039

Of the $13,084 million total debt maturing within one year, $1,746 million represents contractual maturities of long-term debt and the $11,338 remainder represents other short-term borrowings. We assume that all contractual maturities of long-term debt will be repaid. Thus, we forecast the $1,746 million to be repaid. For the remaining short-term debt we assume no-change (Step 4 revisits this). Commercial paper represents short-term unsecured borrowings that are typically refinanced by newly issued commercial paper and are not repaid at maturity unless refinanced into longer-term debt or equity. Similarly, we assume that the floating rate note will be refinanced when it comes due in February. Thus, we forecast the $11,338 as short-term debt before any current portion of long-term debt (see below).

Forecasting Long-Term Debt P&G's balance sheet reports long-term debt of $23,581. We use the no-change method to forecast long-term debt (and potentially modify this with optional Step 4). Companies are required to disclose the maturities of long-term debt for each of the five years subsequent to the statement date. Following is the disclosure by P&G in its long-term debt footnote:

> Long-term debt maturities during the next five years are as follows: 2009—$1,746; 2010—$5,508; 2011—$43; 2012—$1,643; and 2013—$2,240.

In our forecast for 2009, we classify the amount due in 2010, $5,508, as current portion of long-term debt, and the remaining balance of $18,073 is forecasted as long-term debt. The forecasted balance sheet will combine the current portion of long-term debt, $5,508, with the $11,338 of short-term debt, from above, for a total of $16,846.

Forecasting Equity Accounts Prior to Step 4, we forecast 2009 equity items with no change. The exception is retained earnings, which are increased by forecasted net income and are reduced by forecasted dividends. The dividend payout for 2008 is 38.6% ($4,655 million in dividends/$12,075 of net income). We forecast the same 38.6% dividend payout rate to obtain $4,638 million in forecasted dividends, computed as forecasted net income of $12,015 million × 38.6%. Thus, we forecast $56,363 million for ending retained earnings, computed as follows:

> $48,986 million beginning retained earnings
> \+ 12,015 million forecasted net income
> \- 4,638 million forecasted dividends
> ────────────────────────────
> $56,363 million ending retained earnings

Forecasting Cash—"Final Account" We now have forecasts for all asset, liability, and equity accounts other than cash. To forecast cash, we total the forecasts for liability and equity accounts ($149,526 million) and subtract from it the total of forecasts for all noncash asset accounts; those forecasts are in Exhibit 11.4. Essentially, forecasted cash of $8,898 is the "plug" figure to make the forecasted assets equal the forecasted liabilities plus equity, which is computed as follows:

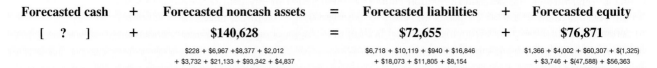

Forecasted cash	**+**	**Forecasted noncash assets**	**=**	**Forecasted liabilities**	**+**	**Forecasted equity**
[?]	+	$140,628	=	$72,655	+	$76,871
		$228 + $6,967 + $8,377 + $2,012 + $3,732 + $21,133 + $93,342 + $4,837		$6,718 + $10,119 + $940 + $16,846 + $18,073 + $11,805 + $8,154		$1,366 + $4,002 + $60,307 + $(1,325) + $3,746 + $(47,588) + $56,363

Forecasted Balance Sheet The forecasted balance sheet for Procter & Gamble is in Exhibit 11.4. We show the 2008 balance for each account, the computation used to obtain each forecast and the forecasted 2009 balance. Our forecasting process predicts that P&G generates considerable cash in 2009, increasing the cash balance from $3,313 million to $8,898 million. In the next section we illustrate the preparation of the forecasted statement of cash flows, which provides us insight into the cash increase. Then, we explain Step 4, which provides us several options for investment of the forecasted excess cash.

Forecasting Statement of Cash Flows

LO4 Forecast the statement of cash flows.

We forecast the statement of cash flows using the forecasted income statement and forecasted balance sheet. We refer to the historical statement of cash flows mainly to check the reasonableness of our forecasts. We draw on the mechanics behind the preparation of the statement of cash flows, which we discuss in Modules 2 and 3 and Appendix B. Specifically, once we have forecasts of the balance sheet and income statement, we can compute the forecasted statement of cash flows just as we would its historical counterpart.

Process of Forecasting the Statement of Cash Flows

To illustrate the forecasting of the statement of cash flows we again turn to Procter & Gamble. Given its forecasted income statement in Exhibit 11.2 and its forecasted balance sheet in Exhibit 11.4, we prepare its forecasted statement of cash flows using the procedures for preparing the statement of cash flows explained in Modules 2 and 3 and Appendix B. Our forecasted statement of cash flows is in Exhibit 11.5.

Forecasting Operating Activities We begin with the operating section and the forecasted net earnings of $12,015 million, from Exhibit 11.2. We, then, adjust net earnings for operating expenses and revenues that do not impact cash, and for changes in current assets and liabilities. For the first category we have depreciation and amortization, which are in SG&A expense and are added back in the statement of cash flows because they do not use cash. (Computations for these expenses are explained in our discussion of forecasting capital expenditures and PPE, and forecasting goodwill and other intangibles.) For the second category we have three current assets and three current liabilities whose cash-flow effects we must consider. For example, the forecasted increase in accounts receivable reduces the available cash. We apply this logic to each of the other current assets and liabilities. Thus, net cash flow from operating activities is forecasted at $15,204 million for 2009.

EXHIBIT 11.4	Forecasted Balance Sheet for P&G		
($ millions)	2008	Forecast Assumptions	2009 Est.
Assets			
Cash and cash equivalents	$ 3,313	computed to balance	$ 8,898
Investment securities	228	no change	228
Accounts receivable	6,761	$82,944 × 8.4%	6,967
Inventories	8,416	$82,944 × 10.1%	8,377
Deferred income taxes	2,012	no change	2,012
Prepaid expenses and other current assets	3,785	$82,944 × 4.5%	3,732
Total current assets	24,515	subtotal	30,214
Total property, plant and equipment	38,086	$38,086 + ($82,944 × 3.9%)	41,321
Accumulated depreciation	(17,446)	$17,446 + ($38,086 × 7.2%)	(20,188)
Net property, plant and equipment	20,640	subtotal	21,133
Goodwill and other intangible assets	94,000	$94,000 − ($94,000 × 0.7%)	93,342
Other noncurrent assets	4,837	no change	4,837
Total assets	$143,992	subtotal	$149,526
Liabilities and Equity			
Accounts payable	$ 6,775	$82,944 × 8.1%	$ 6,718
Accrued and other liabilities	10,154	$82,944 × 12.2%	10,119
Taxes payable	945	$ 3,984 × 23.6%	940
Debt due within one year	13,084	$5,508 + $11,338 (via footnote)	16,846
Total current liabilities	30,958	subtotal	34,623
Long-term debt	23,581	$23,581 − $5,508	18,073
Deferred income taxes	11,805	no change	11,805
Other noncurrent liabilities	8,154	no change	8,154
Total liabilities	74,498	subtotal	72,655
Shareholders' equity			
Preferred stock	1,366	no change	1,366
Common stock	4,002	no change	4,002
Additional paid-in capital	60,307	no change	60,307
Reserve for ESOP debt retirement	(1,325)	no change	(1,325)
Accumulated other comprehensive income	3,746	no change	3,746
Treasury stock	(47,588)	no change	(47,588)
Retained earnings	48,986	$48,986 + $12,015 − $4,638	56,363
Total shareholders' equity	69,494	subtotal	76,871
Total liabilities and shareholders' equity	$143,992	subtotal	$149,526

Forecasting Investing Activities The forecasted investing section reports cash expenditures for short- and long-term investments as well as the purchase and sale of long-term operating assets. The only item for P&G is the forecasted $3,235 million outflow for capital expenditures (CAPEX). We discuss the computation of this amount in the section on forecasting capital expenditures and PPE, above. The remaining long-term assets are intangible and other nonoperating assets and we assumed no changes in those assets except for amortization of intangibles. Had we forecasted other changes in those assets, we would include the cash flow effects in the investing section.

Forecasting Financing Activities The forecasted financing section reports items expected to impact long-term nonoperating liabilities and equity. We forecast a reduction of long-term debt in the amount of $1,746 million relating to its contractual maturities. Those maturities are reported as part of debt due within one year on the 2008 balance sheet and we assume that all contractual obligations are paid as agreed. The next item assumes continuation of the dividend payout percentage of 38.6% of net income, which yields forecasted dividends of $4,638 million for 2009 based on net income of $12,015 million.

In sum, we forecast an increase in cash of $5,585 million for 2009. This increase is due mainly to net cash generated from operating activities, which is more than sufficient to cover capital expenditures, repayment of long-term debt, and payment of dividends. (Our optional Step 4 considers alternatives for investment of this excess cash.)

This concludes our initial forecasts of the financial statements for Procter & Gamble. Appendix 11A reproduces an actual analyst forecast of P&G's financial statements from Oppenheimer & Co., which applies the percent of revenues approach that we describe above. (Module 12 estimates the value

EXHIBIT 11.5	Forecasted Statement of Cash Flows for P&G	
($ millions)	Forecast Assumptions	2009 Est.
Operating activities		
Net earnings...	via forecasted income stmt.	$12,015
Depreciation..	$38,086 × 7.2%	2,742
Amortization..	$94,000 × 0.7%	658
Accounts receivable increase............................	$6,761 − $6,967	(206)
Inventories decrease....................................	$8,416 − $8,377	39
Prepaid expenses and other current assets decrease.........	$3,785 − $3,732	53
Accounts payable decrease..............................	$6,718 − $6,775	(57)
Accrued and other liabilities decrease....................	$10,119 − $10,154	(35)
Taxes payable decrease................................	$940 − $945	(5)
Net cash flow from operating activities....................	subtotal	15,204
Investing activities		
Capital expenditures....................................	$82,944 × 3.9%	(3,235)
Net cash flow from investing activities....................	subtotal	(3,235)
Financing activities		
Changes in short- and long-term debt....................	current maturities via footnote	(1,746)
Dividends to shareholders...............................	$12,015 × 38.6%	(4,638)
Net cash flow from financing activities....................	subtotal	(6,384)
Change in cash and cash equivalents.....................	subtotal	5,585
Cash and cash equivalents, beginning of year..............	from balance sheet	3,313
Cash and cash equivalents, end of year...................	subtotal	$ 8,898

of P&G's stock using our forecasts and compares our estimate with that which Oppenheimer develops from its forecasts and valuation model.)

ADDITIONAL FORECASTING ISSUES

Reassessing Financial Statement Forecasts

After preparing the forecasted financial statements, it is useful to reassess whether they are reasonable in light of current economic and company conditions. This task is subjective and benefits from the forecaster's knowledge of company, industry, and economic factors. Many analysts and managers prepare "what-if" forecasted financial statements. Specifically, they change key assumptions, such as the forecasted sales growth or key cost ratios and then recompute the forecasted financial statements. These alternative forecasting scenarios indicate the sensitivity of a set of predicted outcomes to different assumptions about future economic conditions. Such sensitivity estimates can be useful for setting contingency plans and in identifying areas of vulnerability for company performance and condition.

Multiyear Forecasting of Financial Statements

LO5 Prepare multiyear forecasts of financial statements.

Many business decisions require forecasted financial statements for more than one year ahead. For example, managerial and capital budgeting, security valuation, and strategic analyses all benefit from reliable multiyear forecasts. Module 12 uses multiyear forecasts of financial results to estimate stock price for investment decisions.

Although there are different methods to achieve multiyear forecasts, we forecast two years ahead using the assumptions for our one-year-ahead forecasts and adjust those assumptions as necessary. To illustrate, we forecast P&G's 2010 sales as $86,535 million, computed as $82,944 million × 1.0433, the historical growth rate in the absence of the foreign currency effects we projected for 2009; we do not project the same currency effects in 2010 as exchange rates are unpredictable (P&G only provides one-year-ahead currency rate predictions in its communications with analysts). The remainder of the income statement is forecasted from this sales level using the methodology we describe earlier for one-year-ahead forecasts. Exhibit 11.6 illustrates a two-year-ahead (2010) forecast for P&G's income statement; the 2009 forecasts are shown in the first column for reference.

EXHIBIT 11.6   Forecasted Two-Year-Ahead Financial Statements for P&G

Income Statement ($ millions)	2009 Est.	Forecast Assumptions	2010 Est.
Net sales.	$82,944	$82,944 × 1.0433	$86,535
Cost of products sold.	41,223	$86,535 × 49.7%	43,008
Gross profit.	41,721	subtotal	43,527
Selling, general and administrative expense	24,717	$86,535 × 29.8%	25,787
Operating income.	17,004	subtotal	17,740
Interest expense.	1,467	no change	1,467
Other nonoperating income, net	462	no change	462
Earnings before income taxes	15,999	subtotal	16,735
Income taxes	3,984	$16,735 × 24.9%	4,167
Net earnings.	$12,015	subtotal	$12,568

Balance Sheet ($ millions)	2009 Est.	Forecast Assumptions	2010 Est.
Assets			
Cash and cash equivalents	$ 8,898	computed to balance	$ 11,305
Investment securities	228	no change	228
Accounts receivable.	6,967	$86,535 × 8.4%	7,269
Inventories	8,377	$86,535 × 10.1%	8,740
Deferred income taxes	2,012	no change	2,012
Prepaid expenses and other current assets.	3,732	$86,535 × 4.5%	3,894
Total current assets	30,214	subtotal	33,448
Total property, plant and equipment.	41,321	$41,321 + ($86,535 × 3.9%)	44,696
Accumulated depreciation	(20,188)	$20,188 + ($41,321 × 7.2%)	(23,163)
Net property, plant and equipment.	21,133	subtotal	21,533
Goodwill and other intangible assets	93,342	$93,342 − ($93,342 × 0.7%)	92,689
Other noncurrent assets.	4,837	no change	4,837
Total assets.	$149,526	subtotal	$152,507
Liabilities and Equity			
Accounts payable.	$ 6,718	$86,535 × 8.1%	$ 7,009
Accrued and other liabilities.	10,119	$86,535 × 12.2%	10,557
Taxes payable.	940	$4,167 × 23.6%	983
Debt due within one year	16,846	$43 via footnote + $11,338	11,381
Total current liabilities.	34,623	subtotal	29,930
Long-term debt	18,073	$18,073 − $43	18,030
Deferred income taxes	11,805	no change	11,805
Other noncurrent liabilities	8,154	no change	8,154
Total liabilities.	72,655	subtotal	67,919
Shareholders' equity			
Preferred stock.	1,366	no change	1,366
Common stock.	4,002	no change	4,002
Additional paid-in capital	60,307	no change	60,307
Reserve for ESOP debt retirement.	(1,325)	no change	(1,325)
Accumulated other comprehensive income.	3,746	no change	3,746
Treasury stock	(47,588)	no change	(47,588)
Retained earnings	56,363	$56,363 + $12,568 − $4,851	64,080
Total shareholders' equity	76,871	subtotal	84,588
Total liabilities and shareholders' equity.	$149,526	subtotal	$152,507

continued

continued from prior page

EXHIBIT 11.6	Forecasted Two-Year-Ahead Financial Statements for P&G		
Statement of Cash Flows ($ millions)	**2009 Est.**	**Forecast Assumptions**	**2010 Est.**
Operating activities			
Net earnings	$12,015	via forecasted income stmt.	$12,568
Depreciation	2,742	$41,321 × 7.2%	2,975
Amortization	658	$93,342 × 0.7%	653
Accounts receivable	(206)	$6,967 − $7,269	(302)
Inventories	39	$8,377 − $8,740	(363)
Prepaid expenses and other current assets	53	$3,732 − $3,894	(162)
Accounts payable	(57)	$7,009 − $6,718	291
Accrued and other liabilities	(35)	$10,557 − $10,119	438
Taxes payable	(5)	$983 − $940	43
Net cash flow from operating activities	15,204	subtotal	16,141
Investing activities			
Capital expenditures	(3,235)	$86,535 × 3.9%	(3,375)
Net cash flow from investing activities	(3,235)	subtotal	(3,375)
Financing activities			
Changes in short- and long-term debt	(1,746)	current maturities via footnote	(5,508)
Dividends to shareholders	(4,638)	$12,568 × 38.6%	(4,851)
Net cash flow from financing activities	(6,384)	subtotal	(10,359)
Change in cash and cash equivalents	5,585	subtotal	2,407
Cash and cash equivalents, beginning of year	3,313	from balance sheet	8,898
Cash and cash equivalents, end of year	$ 8,898	subtotal	$11,305

Assuming a continuation of the percent-of-revenues relation for current assets and liabilities, we can forecast current assets and liabilities applying the same methodology used for one-year-ahead forecasts (see Exhibit 11.4). For example, 2010 accounts receivable are forecasted as $7,269 million, computed as $86,535 million × 8.4%. Exhibit 11.6 illustrates two-year-ahead (2010) forecast for P&G's balance sheet; again, 2009 forecasts are shown in the first column.

Exhibit 11.6 also reports the two-year-ahead forecasted statement of cash flows. The forecasted change in cash for 2010 of $2,407 million is much lower than the forecasted change in cash of $5,585 million for 2009. The reason is that P&G reports that it will retire $5,508 million in contractual maturities of long-term debt in 2010. For forecasting purposes we assume that all scheduled debt payments are made.

To simplify exposition and to focus on the forecasting mechanics, we altered only one assumption for the 2010 forecast—revenue growth would be 4.33%. We did not alter any of the other forecast assumptions for our two-year-ahead forecasts in Exhibit 11.6. Any forecast assumptions (such as percent of revenues relation, depreciation rates, or dividend payouts) can be changed in future years as necessary. For example, we might reduce expected sales growth if we feel that the market is becoming saturated or we might increase the accounts receivable to sales percent if we expect the economy to slow. Further, we can replicate the process for any desired forecast horizon.

STEP 4 (OPTIONAL): ADJUST FORECASTED FINANCIAL STATEMENTS FOR CASH TARGET

Our forecasted (initial) balance sheet, see Exhibit 11.4, yields a cash amount of $8,898 million, which is 6.0% (rounded to one-tenth of a percent) of forecasted total assets of $149,526 million. P&G's cash as a percentage of total assets is 2.3% in 2008 (3.9% in 2007)—both rounded to one-tenth of a percent. Assuming that the 2.3% level is P&G's targeted level of cash, our 2009 forecasts imply there is excess cash of $5,532 million ([6.0% − 2.3%] × $149,526 million). In this case we must decide how to invest the excess cash. There are several possible investments for excess cash:

1. **Invest excess cash in marketable securities.** Many high-tech companies accumulate substantial balances of cash to provide financial flexibility to quickly take advantage of opportunities or to respond to strategic shifts by competitors. They hold this cash in liquid, marketable securities.

2. **Use excess cash to retire short-term debt.** If a company has substantial short-term debt (especially if the debt level is above industry benchmarks) and reveals a preference for debt reduction in its MD&A or other public disclosures, we can use excess cash to retire that debt.

3. **Use excess cash to acquire treasury stock.** Some companies, including P&G, operate an ongoing program of share repurchases; in this case, we can use excess cash for share repurchases.

When adjusting the balance sheet to reflect a target-cash level, we must take care to not inadvertently change the company's financial leverage. Recall that companies balance levels of debt and equity to achieve a desired credit rating for their debt. Thus, we must maintain the past debt-to-equity relation when adjusting to a desired cash amount. For example, if our decision is to retire debt or to repurchase common stock, we should do it so that the historical debt-to-equity relation is maintained. Determining whether the resulting cash balance is too high or too low is a judgment call. We choose to use the historical cash balance as a percentage of total assets as a benchmark. Alternatively, one could use an industry average for this benchmark.

Forecasting One Year Ahead with a Cash Target

Our forecasts suggest P&G generates excess cash in 2009. During the prior three years, P&G repurchased common stock for a cumulative total of about $30 billion or an average of $10 billion per year. Further, P&G disclosed its intention to repurchase an additional $8 to $10 billion per year in 2009 and in 2010 as revealed in the following slide from its 2008 presentation to analysts.

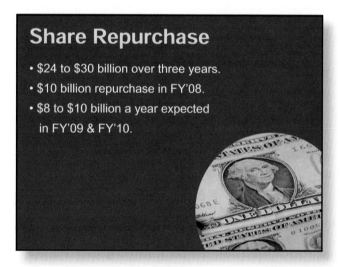

It is reasonable to assume, therefore, that P&G will invest its excess cash, at least in part, for repurchase of treasury shares. Were P&G to reduce its cash balance by $5,532 million and invest it in the repurchase of treasury shares, the cash balance would fall to $3,366 million, which is 2.3% of total assets and in line with the prior year's balance. The resulting liabilities-to-equity ratio would end the year at 1.02, somewhat less than the 1.07 liabilities-to-equity ratio in 2008 (and 1.05 in 2007). It seems reasonable, therefore, to apply the forecasted excess cash for that purpose. Exhibit 11.7 reflects the adjustment to use excess cash to repurchase common stock in 2009. (A more complete, but more complex, adjustment process for resolving excess cash is explained in Appendix 11B.)

Forecasting Two Years Ahead with a Cash Target

As with the one-year-ahead forecast, we can adjust the final cash balance when forecasting two years ahead. Similar to 2009, P&G again generates excess forecasted cash for the 2010 fiscal year. Its forecasted cash of $5,773 million (computations are not reported for brevity) represents 3.9% of total assets whereas the historical relation (from 2008) is 2.3%. To return the cash balance to 2.3% of total assets,

EXHIBIT 11.7	Forecasted Balance Sheet for P&G with Adjustment for *Excess* Cash		
($ millions)	**2009 Est.**	**Adjustment**	**Adjusted 2009 Est.**
Assets			
Cash and cash equivalents	$ 8,898	$5,532 less	$ 3,366
Investment securities	228		228
Accounts receivable.	6,967		6,967
Inventories	8,377		8,377
Deferred income taxes.	2,012		2,012
Prepaid expenses and other current assets.	3,732		3,732
Total current assets	30,214	subtotal	24,682
Total property, plant and equipment.	41,321		41,321
Accumulated depreciation	(20,188)		(20,188)
Net property, plant and equipment.	21,133		21,133
Goodwill and other intangible assets.	93,342		93,342
Other noncurrent assets.	4,837		4,837
Total assets.	$149,526	subtotal	$143,994
Liabilities and Equity			
Accounts payable.	$ 6,718		$ 6,718
Accrued and other liabilities.	10,119		10,119
Taxes payable.	940		940
Debt due within one year	16,846		16,846
Total current liabilities.	34,623		34,623
Long-term debt	18,073		18,073
Deferred income taxes.	11,805		11,805
Other noncurrent liabilities	8,154		8,154
Total liabilities.	72,655		72,655
Shareholders' equity			
Preferred stock.	1,366		1,366
Common stock.	4,002		4,002
Additional paid-in capital	60,307		60,307
Reserve for ESOP debt retirement.	(1,325)		(1,325)
Accumulated other comprehensive income.	3,746		3,746
Treasury stock	(47,588)	$(5,532) more	(53,120)
Retained earnings	56,363		56,363
Total shareholders' equity	76,871	subtotal	71,339
Total liabilities and shareholders' equity.	$149,526	subtotal	$143,994

we reduce cash by $2,352 million ([3.9% − 2.3%] × $146,975 million) to $3,421 million, and use that cash to repurchase common stock as summarized in the following table.

($ millions)	**2010 Est.**	**Adjustment**	**Adjusted 2010 Est.**
Total assets.	$146,975	$(2,352)	$144,623
Total liabilities	67,919	—	67,919
Shareholders' equity	79,056	(2,352)	76,704

As a result of this adjustment, the liabilities-to-equity ratio for 2009 increases from 0.95 ($72,655/$76,871) to 1.02 ($72,655/$71,339), which is still below the 1.07 level of 2008 (the current year). The reason that we cannot achieve the same financial leverage as in 2008 is due to the required long-term debt payment of $5,508 million in 2010 that we discuss above. In 2011, however, the current maturity of long-term debt is only $43 million. Given the level of P&G's forecasted operating cash flows, additional treasury stock purchases in that year will return the liabilities-to-equity ratio to historical levels. In sum, using excess cash to simply repurchase shares appears to be a sensible solution for P&G as it yields financial leverage that is only slightly lower than in the past.

This approach to multiyear forecasting is admittedly quite simple. However, many argue that this simple approach is sufficient because forecasting is, by definition, filled with many estimates and assumptions. Appendix 11B expands our discussion to consider some alternative adjustments that impact the balance sheet and forecasts of the income statement and the statement of cash flows.

MID-MODULE REVIEW

Following is financial statement information from Colgate-Palmolive Company.

Income Statement For year ended December 31 ($ millions)	2007	2006
Net sales.	$13,789.7	$12,237.7
Cost of sales.	6,042.3	5,536.1
Gross profit.	7,747.4	6,701.6
Selling, general and administrative expenses	4,973.0	4,355.2
Other (income) expense, net	121.3	185.9
Operating profit	2,653.1	2,160.5
Interest expense, net	156.6	158.7
Income before income taxes	2,496.5	2,001.8
Provision for income taxes	759.1	648.4
Net income	$ 1,737.4	$ 1,353.4

Balance Sheet As of December 31 ($ millions)	2007	2006
Assets		
Cash and cash equivalents.	$ 428.7	$ 489.5
Receivables (net of allowances of $50.6 and $46.4, respectively)	1,680.7	1,523.2
Inventories	1,171.0	1,008.4
Other current assets	338.1	279.9
Total current assets.	3,618.5	3,301.0
Property, plant, and equipment, net.	3,015.2	2,696.1
Goodwill and other intangible assets, net	3,116.8	2,912.9
Other assets	361.5	228.0
Total assets.	$10,112.0	$9,138.0
Liabilities and Shareholders' Equity		
Notes and loans payable	$ 155.9	$ 174.1
Current portion of long-term debt	138.1	776.7
Accounts payable.	1,066.8	1,039.7
Accrued income taxes	262.7	161.5
Other accruals	1,539.2	1,317.1
Total current liabilities	3,162.7	3,469.1
Long-term debt	3,221.9	2,720.4
Deferred income taxes	264.1	309.9
Other liabilities	1,177.1	1,227.7
Total liabilities	7,825.8	7,727.1
Shareholders' equity		
Preference stock.	197.5	222.7
Common stock, $1 par value (1,000,000,000 shares authorized, 732,853,180 shares issued)	732.9	732.9
Additional paid-in capital	1,517.7	1,218.1
Retained earnings.	10,627.5	9,643.7
Accumulated other comprehensive income	(1,666.8)	(2,081.2)
	11,408.8	9,736.2
Unearned compensation	(218.9)	(251.4)
Treasury stock, at cost	(8,903.7)	(8,073.9)
Total shareholders' equity	2,286.2	1,410.9
Total liabilities and shareholders' equity	$10,112.0	$9,138.0

Forecast the Colgate-Palmolive balance sheet, income statement, and statement of cash flows for 2008 using the following additional information; assume no change for all other accounts not listed below. All percentages, other than sales growth, are based on percent of revenues; assume all capital expenditures are purchases of PPE, and that depreciation and amortization are included as part of selling, general and administrative expenses.

Key Financial Relations and Measures ($ millions)	2007
Net sales growth.	12.7%
Gross profit margin.	56.2%
Selling, general and administrative expenses	36.1%
Depreciation/Prior year property, plant and equipment, gross	6.0%
Amortization/Prior year goodwill and other intangible assets, net.	0.6%
Provision for income taxes/Income before income taxes	30.4%
Receivables, net/Net sales	12.2%
Inventories/Net sales	8.5%
Capital expenditures	$583.1
Capital expenditures/Net sales	4.2%
Property, plant and equipment, gross	$6,138.1
Depreciation expense.	$315.7
Amortization expense.	$18.2
Accounts payable/Net sales.	7.7%
Accrued income taxes/Provision for income taxes	34.6%
Other accruals/Net sales	11.2%
Dividends/Net income	43.1%
Long-term debt due in 2008 (via footnote).	$100.8

Solution

Forecasted 2008 financial statements for Colgate-Palmolive follow.

Forecasted Income Statement			
For year ended December 31 ($ millions)	2007	Forecast Assumptions	2008 Est.
Net sales	$13,789.7	$13,789.7 × 1.127	$15,541.0
Cost of sales.	6,042.3	$15,541.0 × 43.8%	6,807.0
Gross profit.	7,747.4	subtotal	8,734.0
Selling, general, administrative, and other expenses. . .	4,973.0	$15,541.0 × 36.1%	5,610.3
Other (income) expense, net	121.3	no change	121.3
Operating profit	2,653.1	subtotal	3,002.4
Interest expense, net	156.6	no change	156.6
Income before income taxes	2,496.5	subtotal	2,845.8
Provision for income taxes.	759.1	$2,845.8 × 30.4%	865.1
Net income.	$ 1,737.4	subtotal	$ 1,980.7

Forecasted Balance Sheet			
As of December 31 ($ millions)	2007	Forecast Assumptions	2008 Est.
Assets			
Cash and cash equivalents (total forecasted liabilities and equity less all noncash assets)	$ 428.7	computed	$ 1,154.5
Receivables	1,680.7	$15,541.0 × 12.2%	1,896.0
Inventories	1,171.0	$15,541.0 × 8.5%	1,321.0
Other current assets.	338.1	no change	338.1
Total current assets	3,618.5	subtotal	4,709.6
PPE, gross	6,138.1	$6,138.1 + ($15,541.0 × 4.2%)	6,790.8
Accumulated depreciation.	(3,122.9)	$3,122.9 + ($6,138.1 × 6.0%)	(3,491.2)
Property, plant and equipment, net	3,015.2	subtotal	3,299.6
Goodwill and other intangible assets, net	3,116.8	$3,116.8 − ($3,116.8 × 0.6%)	3,098.1
Other assets (no change).	361.5	no change	361.5
Total assets (total).	$10,112.0	subtotal	$11,468.8

continued

continued from prior page

As of December 31 ($ millions)	2007	Forecast Assumptions	2008 Est.
Liabilities and Shareholders' Equity			
Notes and loans payable	$ 155.9	no change	$ 155.9
Current portion of long-term debt	138.1	footnote disclosure	100.8
Accounts payable.	1,066.8	$15,541.0 × 7.7%	1,196.7
Accrued income taxes	262.7	$865.1 × 34.6%	299.3
Other accruals	1,539.2	$15,541.0 × 11.2%	1,740.6
Total current liabilities.	3,162.7	subtotal	3,493.3
Long-term debt	3,221.9	less current portion	3,121.1
Deferred income taxes.	264.1	no change	264.1
Other liabilities	1,177.1	no change	1,177.1
Total liabilities.	7,825.8	subtotal	8,055.6
Shareholders' equity			
Preference stock	197.5	no change	197.5
Common stock.	732.9	no change	732.9
Additional paid-in capital	1,517.7	no change	1,517.7
Retained earnings	10,627.5	computed	11,754.5
Accumulated other comprehensive income.	(1,666.8)	no change	(1,666.8)
Unearned compensation	(218.9)	no change	(218.9)
Treasury stock	(8,903.7)	no change	(8,903.7)
Total shareholders' equity	2,286.2	subtotal	3,413.2
Total liabilities and shareholders' equity.	$10,112.0	subtotal	$11,468.8

Total assets $11,468.8 − Noncash assets $10,314.3 = Cash $1,154.5

Beginning retained earnings $10,627.5 + Net income $1,980.7 − Dividends $853.7 = Ending retained earnings $11,754.5

Forecasted Statement of Cash Flows		
($ millions)	Forecast Assumptions	2008 Est.
Net income.	via forecast income stmt.	$1,980.7
Depreciation.	$6,138.1 × 6.0%	368.3
Amortization.	$3,116.8 × 0.6%	18.7
Receivables.	$1,680.7 − $1,894	(215.3)
Inventories.	$1,171.0 − $1,321	(150.0)
Accounts payable	$1,196.7 − $1,066.8	129.9
Accrued income taxes.	$299.3 − $262.7	36.6
Other accruals	$1,740.6 − $1,539.2	201.4
Net cash flow from operating activities	subtotal	2,370.3
Capital expenditures	$15,541.0 × 4.2%	(652.7)
Net cash flow from investing activities.	subtotal	(652.7)
Long-term debt	prior year current portion	(138.1)
Dividends	$1,980.7 × 43.1%	(853.7)
Net cash flows from financing activities.	subtotal	(991.8)
Net change in cash and cash equivalents	subtotal	725.8
Cash and cash equivalents, beginning year.	via prior bal. sheet	428.7
Cash and cash equivalents, ending year	subtotal	$1,154.5

Our forecasts indicate that Colgate will generate $725.8 million of cash in 2008. The resulting cash balance of $1,154.5 million represents 10.1% of total assets, compared with 4.24% in the prior year. The excess cash can either be accumulated to serve as an additional store of liquidity for the future, or Colgate can retire some of its debt and/or equity. We did not adjust our forecast for this apparent excess cash.

PARSIMONIOUS MULTIYEAR FORECASTING

LO6 Implement a parsimonious method for multiyear forecasting of net operating profit and net operating assets.

The forecasting process described above uses a considerable amount of available information to derive accurate forecasts. We can, however, simplify the process by using less information without sometimes seriously impairing accuracy. Stock valuation models commonly use more parsimonious methods to compute multiyear forecasts for an initial screening of prospective securities. For example, in Module 12 we introduce two stock valuation models that use parsimonious forecasting methods. One model utilizes forecasted free cash flows and the other uses forecasted net operating profits after tax (NOPAT) and net operating assets (NOA); see Module 4 for descriptions of these variables. Because free cash flows are equal to net operating profits after tax (NOPAT) less the change in net operating assets (NOA), we can accommodate both stock valuation models with forecasts of NOPAT and NOA.

Parsimonious Method for Forecasting

Our parsimonious approach to forecast NOPAT and NOA requires three crucial inputs:

1. Sales growth
2. Net operating profit margin (NOPM); defined in Module 4 as NOPAT divided by sales
3. Net operating asset turnover (NOAT); defined in Module 4 as sales divided by average NOA. For forecasting purposes, we define NOAT as sales divided by *year-end* NOA instead of average NOA because we want to forecast year-end values.

Multiyear Forecasting with Parsimonious Method

The remainder of this module describes and illustrates this parsimonious approach. To illustrate, we use Procter & Gamble's 2008 income statement, from Exhibit 11.1, and its 2008 balance sheet, from Exhibit 11.3, to determine the following measures. We assume that P&G's statutory tax rate is 37.5% on nonoperating revenues and expenses.

($ millions)	2008
Sales.	$83,503
Net operating profit after tax ($17,083 − {$4,003 + [($1,467 − $462) × 37.5%]})	$12,703
NOA ($143,992 − $228 − $4,837) − ($6,775 + $10,154 + $945 + $11,805 + $8,154)*	$101,094
NOPM ($12,703/$83,503).	15.2%
NOAT ($83,503/$101,094)**	0.826

*Footnotes to the 10-K reveal that Other Noncurrent Assets consist of marketable securities and are, thus, treated as nonoperating.

**We use ending balance sheet amounts rather than average amounts because we forecast *ending* balance sheet amounts.

Using these inputs, we forecast P&G's sales, NOPAT, and NOA. Each year's forecasted sales is the prior year sales multiplied successively by (1+ Growth rate) and then rounded to whole digits. Consistent with our prior revenue growth rate assumptions for P&G, we define "1 + Growth rate" as 0.9933 for 2009 and as 1.0433 for 2010 onward. NOPAT is computed using forecasted (and rounded) sales each year times the 2008 NOPM of 15.2%; and NOA is computed using forecasted (and rounded) sales divided by the 2008 NOAT of 0.826. Forecasted numbers for 2009 through 2012 are in Exhibit 11.8; supporting computations are in parentheses.

This forecasting process can be continued for any desired forecast horizon. Also, the forecast assumptions such as sales growth, NOPM, and NOAT can be varied by year, if desired. This alternative, parsimonious method is much simpler than the primary method illustrated in this module. However, its simplicity does forgo information that can impact forecast accuracy.

EXHIBIT 11.8 Procter & Gamble Multiyear Forecasts of Sales, NOPAT and NOA

($ millions)	Current 2008	Forecast 2009 Est.	2010 Est.	2011 Est.	2012 Est.
Net sales growth.		−0.67%	4.33%	4.33%	4.33%
Net sales (unrounded) . .	$83,503	**$82,943.53** ($83,503 × 0.9933)	**$86,535.48** ($82,943.53 × 1.0433)	**$90,281.97** ($86,535.48 × 1.0433)	**$94,191.21** ($90,281.97 × 1.0433)
Net sales (rounded)		**$82,944**	**$86,535**	**$90,282**	**$94,191**
NOPAT[1].	$12,703	**$12,607** ($82,944 × 0.152)	**$13,153** ($86,535 × 0.152)	**$13,723** ($90,282 × 0.152)	**$14,317** ($94,191 × 0.152)
NOA[2].	$101,094	**$100,416** ($82,944/0.826)	**$104,764** (86,535/0.826)	**$109,300** ($90,282/0.826)	**$114,033** ($94,191/0.826)

[1] Forecasted NOPAT = Forecasted net sales (rounded) × 2008 NOPM

[2] Forecasted NOA = Forecasted net sales (rounded)/2008 NOAT

MODULE-END REVIEW

Johnson & Johnson (J&J) reports 2007 sales of $61,095 million, net operating profit after tax (NOPAT) of $10,478 million, and net operating assets (NOA) of $51,309 million. J&J's NOPM is computed as 17% ($10,478 million/$61,095 million) and its NOAT is computed as 1.2 ($61,095/$51,309).

Required
Use the parsimonious forecast model to project J&J's sales, NOPAT, and NOA for 2008 through 2011 assuming a sales growth rate of 6%.

Solution

	2007	2008	2009	2010	2011
Sales (unrounded)	$61,095	**$64,760.70** ($61,095 × 1.06)	**$68,646.34** ($64,760.70 × 1.06)	**$72,765.12** ($68,646.34 × 1.06)	**$77,131.03** ($72,765.12 × 1.06)
Sales (rounded)	$61,095	**$64,761**	**$68,646**	**$72,765**	**$77,131**
NOPAT	$10,478 (given)	**$11,009** ($64,761 × 0.17)	**$11,670** ($68,646 × 0.17)	**$12,370** ($72,765 × 0.17)	**$13,112** ($77,131 × 0.17)
NOA	$51,309 (given)	**$53,968** ($64,761/1.2)	**$57,205** ($68,646/1.2)	**$60,638** ($72,765/1.2)	$64,276 ($77,131/1.2)

APPENDIX 11A Oppenheimer's Forecast Report on Procter & Gamble

Oppenheimer analysts developed their forecasts of P&G shortly after attending the analyst meetings held by P&G management. We completed our analysis and developed our forecasts at about the same time. Thus, we have an opportunity to compare the analysis in this module with the Oppenheimer analyst report. Following are excerpts from that report dated December 11, 2008 (used with permission).

> The issues impacting the company's organic sales growth in fiscal 2Q appear to be fairly straight-forward, and can be broken down into three primary buckets. First, consumption appears to have slowed at least somewhat in some of the company's categories, due largely to the deteriorating global economy, while consumers are also increasingly utilizing pantry inventory rather than purchasing more products at retail. Second, retailers are responding to slowing consumer consumption by reducing inventory levels and repurchase orders. Finally, some third-party distributors are finding it increasingly difficult to obtain credit, which is impacting their ability to place even routine purchase orders. Interestingly, the top-line weakness seems to be broad-based, as it is impacting both developing and developed markets to roughly the same relative degree.

continued from prior page

. . . Although It's Not All Bad News

While the company did lower its organic sales target for fiscal 2Q, we believe it is important to keep the negative data point in some perspective. In fact, there were a number of data points that came out of Thursday's meeting which indicate that P&G's underlying fundamentals are still healthy. For example, while below 4%, organic sales growth is still expected to be up in the quarter, which is not exactly a given in the current operating environment. Also, P&G's markets are growing at around a 3% clip overall, and down just 1%–2% from pre-credit crisis levels. Further, while private label has gained some market share in the company's categories (perhaps 1/2 point, to a little over 10% on average), P&G's market shares are holding steady and if anything are actually up very slightly. While management did acknowledge that there has been some trade-down in its categories, in many instances the trade-down is from one P&G brand to another (Tide to Gain in fabric care, Pampers to Luvs in diapers, Bounty/Charmin to Bounty/Charmin Basics in towel/tissue, to name a few examples). To underscore this point, management noted that Luvs and Gain sales are up 14% and 12%, respectively, over the past year. The company also spent some time on Thursday discussing the positive impact it is starting to see from the recent pullback in commodity and energy costs. Recall that coming into fiscal 2009, P&G envisioned incremental commodity costs of roughly $3 billion from fiscal 2008 levels. This was subsequently lowered to $2.7 billion during the company's fiscal 1Q conference call in late October, and on Thursday management said it expects cost inflation will be "just" $2 billion. This $700 million reduction from the prior guidance equates to a boost to EPS of roughly $0.17 per share, although we roughly estimate that perhaps as much as two-thirds of this is being offset by the impact of the strong dollar. Also, P&G is not getting any significant pressure from retailers to roll back price increases taken throughout fiscal 2008 to combat higher commodity costs, for a handful of reasons. First, the pullback in commodities has been rather rapid, and management pointed out that its current cost basis reflected in its P&L does not incorporate current low spot levels yet. In addition, with the U.S. dollar strengthening substantially against most major currencies, in some instances the cost of commodities that are denominated in dollars is actually rising in overseas markets when measured in local currencies.

Consumer Spending Is the Wildcard, But Other Headwinds Remain

As we look at the three primary causes of the lower than expected top line for the December quarter, we are confident that two—retailer inventory reductions and distributor credit issues—will prove to be rather temporary. In the case of retailer inventories, we expect they will eventually need to increase the pace of their repurchase orders or risk losing sales due to stockouts, while distributors should benefit as the general credit crisis eases (hopefully) over the coming weeks and months. That said, we are less sanguine about the consumer, which we view as the major wildcard for fiscal 2009 (no surprise there). This relates not only to overall spending levels in P&G's more discretionary categories (such as Beauty Care), but also to trade-down in the company's more commodity categories (such as towel/tissue). Thus, we will continue to monitor these trends closely in the coming quarters. In the case of the distributors obtaining credit, we expect this will eventually fix itself as the credit markets begin to stabilize.

Lowering Estimates, Maintaining Bullish Stance

In light of the company's reduced fiscal 2Q top-line guidance, we are lowering our sales and EPS estimates, as we now feel more comfortable being at the lower end of guidance range. With this in mind, we are reducing our fiscal 2009 GAAP EPS estimate to $4.28 from $4.33 prior. Recall that this includes a $0.63 per share gain from the Folgers transaction (which is likely to be adjusted in the coming weeks) and $0.12 per share in related restructuring. We are also lowering our fiscal 2Q GAAP EPS estimate to $1.58 from $1.60 prior, as we believe this is more appropriate given the number of moving parts that are expected to impact this quarter's results. Importantly, this is now based on 3% organic sales growth in fiscal 2Q, which is down from 5% prior, while our full-year estimate drops to 4%, also from 5% prior. In addition, we are lowering our fiscal 2010 EPS estimate to $4.10 from $4.20 previously, while our DCF-derived target price falls to $70 from $73. Despite our revised estimates and target price, we are maintaining our Outperform rating on the shares. We have as much confidence in P&G's ability to execute in the current challenging environment as in any company in our coverage universe, while its balanced, diversified and staples-oriented product portfolio should prove adequately defensive in a period of slowing consumer spending. Finally, we continue to view the shares as attractive from a valuation perspective, at 15.8× our adjusted fiscal 2009 EPS estimate of $3.77 (excluding the impact of the Folgers sale and restructuring).

PG Income Statement (In U.S. millions, except per share data)	F2008A	Sep08A	Dec08E	Mar09E	Jun09E	F2009E	Sep09E	Dec09E	Mar10E	Jun10E	F2010E
Beauty	19,515	5,128	4,983	4,364	4,633	19,108	5,231	5,232	4,582	4,865	19,909
Y/Y Change (%)	9%	12%	−3%	−8%	−8%	−2%	2%	5%	5%	5%	4%
Grooming	8,254	2,142	2,010	1,760	1,933	7,844	2,185	2,110	1,848	2,030	8,172
Y/Y Change (%)	11%	6%	−7%	−11%	−8%	−5%	2%	5%	5%	5%	4%
Health Care	14,578	3,700	3,583	3,249	3,308	13,841	3,737	3,798	3,412	3,474	14,421
Y/Y Change (%)	9%	4%	−5%	−11%	−8%	−5%	1%	6%	5%	5%	4%
Snacks, Coffee & Pet Care	4,852	1,229	1,068	676	671	3,644	762	854	696	691	3,003
Y/Y Change (%)	7%	9%	−18%	−44%	−45%	−25%	−38%	−20%	3%	3%	−18%
Fabric Care & Home Care	23,831	6,510	6,074	5,586	5,911	24,081	6,575	6,378	5,866	6,207	25,025
Y/Y Change (%)	11%	10%	0%	−3%	−3%	1%	1%	5%	5%	5%	4%
Baby Care & Family Care	13,898	3,772	3,441	3,390	3,466	14,069	3,810	3,614	3,559	3,639	14,622
Y/Y Change (%)	9%	10%	2%	−4%	−3%	1%	1%	5%	5%	5%	4%
Segment Net Sales	84,928	22,481	21,159	19,024	19,922	82,587	22,299	21,986	19,962	20,905	85,152
Corporate	(1,425)	(455)	(250)	(400)	(350)	(1,455)	(455)	(250)	(400)	(350)	(1,455)
Net Sales	**83,503**	**22,026**	**20,909**	**18,624**	**19,572**	**81,132**	**21,844**	**21,736**	**19,562**	**20,555**	**83,697**
Y/Y Change (%)	9%	9%	−3%	−9%	−8%	−3%	−1%	4%	5%	5%	3%
Organic (ex. F/X, Acq/Div)	5%	5%	3%	4%	5%	4%	5%	5%	5%	5%	5%
Cost of Goods Sold	40,695	10,905	10,309	8,957	9,723	39,894	10,489	10,417	9,323	10,077	40,305
Gross profit	**42,808**	**11,121**	**10,600**	**9,668**	**9,849**	**41,238**	**11,356**	**11,319**	**10,239**	**10,478**	**43,392**
Margin	51.3%	50.5%	50.7%	51.9%	50.3%	50.8%	52.0%	52.1%	52.3%	51.0%	51.8%
Y/Y Change (bps)	(70)	(240)	(110)	60	110	(50)	150	140	40	70	100
SG&A	25,725	6,436	6,064	5,587	5,872	23,959	6,226	6,195	5,771	6,064	24,255
% of sales	30.8%	29.2%	29.0%	30.0%	30.0%	29.5%	28.5%	28.5%	29.5%	29.5%	29.0%
Operating Income—Reported	17,083	4,685	4,537	4,080	3,977	17,279	5,130	5,124	4,468	4,414	19,137
Margin	20.5%	21.3%	21.7%	21.9%	20.3%	21.3%	23.5%	23.6%	22.8%	21.5%	22.9%
Y/Y Change (bps)	30	(60)	(10)	180	220	80	220	190	90	120	160
Y/Y Change (%)	11%	6%	−4%	−1%	4%	1%	10%	13%	10%	11%	11%
Operating Income—Adjusted	**17,083**	**4,776**	**4,670**	**4,213**	**4,154**	**17,812**	**5,130**	**5,124**	**4,468**	**4,414**	**19,137**
Margin	20.5%	21.7%	22.3%	22.6%	21.2%	22.0%	23.5%	23.6%	22.8%	21.5%	22.9%
Y/Y Change (bps)	30	(20)	50	250	310	150	180	130	20	30	90
Y/Y Change (%)	11%	8%	−1%	2%	8%	4%	7%	10%	6%	6%	7%
Interest Expense	1,467	339	349	363	350	1,402	347	370	362	364	1,443
Implied Interest Rate, Annualized		4.1%	4.0%	4.0%	4.0%		4.0%	4.0%	4.0%	4.0%	
Other Non-Operating Income	462	337	2,798	10	10	3,155	10	10	10	10	40
Pre-Tax Income, Reported	16,078	4,683	6,985	3,727	3,637	19,032	4,793	4,764	4,116	4,060	17,734
Plus: Incremental Restructuring in SG&A	—	91	133	132	176	532	—	—	—	—	—
Less: Gain on Folgers Spin/Merge	—	—	(2,788)	—	—	(2,788)	—	—	—	—	—
Pre-Tax Income—Adjusted	**16,078**	**4,774**	**4,330**	**3,859**	**3,814**	**16,777**	**4,793**	**4,764**	**4,116**	**4,060**	**17,734**
Income Taxes—Reported	4,003	1,335	1,956	1,044	1,018	5,353	1,342	1,334	1,153	1,137	4,966
Plus: Tax on Incremental Restructuring	—	26	37	37	49	149	—	—	—	—	—
Less: Tax on Gain on Folgers Spin/Merge	—	—	(781)	—	—	(781)	—	—	—	—	—
Income Taxes—Adjusted	**4,462**	**1,361**	**1,212**	**1,081**	**1,068**	**4,722**	**1,342**	**1,334**	**1,153**	**1,137**	**4,966**
Effective Tax Rate—Reported	24.9%	28.5%	28.0%	28.0%	28.0%	28.1%	28.0%	28.0%	28.0%	28.0%	28.0%
Impact of Tax Benefits	2.9%	0.0%	0.0%	0.0%	0.0%	0.0%	0.0%	0.0%	0.0%	0.0%	0.0%
Effective Tax Rate—Adjusted	**27.8%**	**28.5%**	**28.0%**	**28.0%**	**28.0%**	**28.1%**	**28.0%**	**28.0%**	**28.0%**	**28.0%**	**28.0%**
Net Income—Reported	12,075	3,348	5,029	2,683	2,619	13,679	3,451	3,430	2,964	2,923	12,768
Plus: Incremental Restructuring	—	65	96	95	127	383	—	—	—	—	—
Less: Gain on Folgers Spin/Merge	—	—	(2,007)	—	—	(2,007)	—	—	—	—	—
Less: One-Time Tax Benefits	(459)	—	—	—	—	—	—	—	—	—	—
Net Income—Adjusted	**11,616**	**3,413**	**3,118**	**2,779**	**2,746**	**12,055**	**3,451**	**3,430**	**2,964**	**2,923**	**12,768**
Avg. Diluted Shares Outstanding	3,317	3,240	3,186	3,180	3,174	3,195	3,151	3,128	3,106	3,084	3,117
Avg. Basic Shares Outstanding	3,080	3,012	2,962	2,957	2,952	2,971	2,930	2,908	2,888	2,868	2,899
EPS—Reported	$3.64	$1.03	$1.58	$0.84	$0.83	$4.28	$1.10	$1.10	$0.95	$0.95	$4.10
Plus: Incremental Restructuring	$0.00	$0.02	$0.03	$0.03	$0.04	$0.12	$0.00	$0.00	$0.00	$0.00	$0.00
Less: Gain on Folgers Divestitures	$0.00	$0.00	($0.63)	$0.00	$0.00	($0.63)	$0.00	$0.00	$0.00	$0.00	$0.00
Less: One-Time Tax Benefits	($0.14)	$0.00	$0.00	$0.00	$0.00	$0.00	$0.00	$0.00	$0.00	$0.00	$0.00
EPS—Adjusted	**$3.50**	**$1.05**	**$0.98**	**$0.87**	**$0.87**	**$3.77**	**$1.10**	**$1.10**	**$0.95**	**$0.95**	**$4.10**
Y/Y Change (%)	15%	17%	0%	6%	9%	8%	5%	12%	9%	9%	9%
EBITDA—Adjusted	**20,249**	**5,586**	**5,496**	**4,964**	**4,934**	**20,979**	**5,979**	**5,970**	**5,244**	**5,222**	**22,414**
Y/Y Change (%)	9%	8%	1%	2%	4%	4%	7%	9%	6%	6%	7%

Sources: Company financial statements and Oppenheimer & Co. Inc. estimates

PG Segment Analysis (In U.S. millions, except per share data)	F2008A	Sep08A	Dec08E	Mar09E	Jun09E	F2009E	Sep09E	Dec09E	Mar10E	Jun10E	F2010E
Beauty											
Volume (Reported)	2%	4%	0%	1%	2%	2%	3%	5%	5%	5%	4%
Volume (Organic)	3%	4%	0%	1%	2%	2%	3%	5%	5%	5%	4%
FX	6%	6%	−6%	−12%	−12%	−6%	−3%	0%	0%	0%	−1%
Price	0%	2%	3%	3%	2%	2%	2%	0%	0%	0%	1%
Mix/Other	1%	0%	0%	0%	0%	0%	0%	0%	0%	0%	0%
Net Sales	**19,515**	**5,128**	**4,983**	**4,364**	**4,633**	**19,108**	**5,231**	**5,232**	**4,582**	**4,865**	**19,909**
Y/Y Change	*9%*	*12%*	*−3%*	*−8%*	*−8%*	*−2%*	*2%*	*5%*	*5%*	*5%*	*4%*
Organic (ex. F/X, Acq/Div)	*4%*	*6%*	*3%*	*4%*	*4%*	*4%*	*5%*	*5%*	*5%*	*5%*	*5%*
Earnings Before Income Taxes	**3,528**	**983**	**1,096**	**785**	**764**	**3,629**	**1,072**	**1,203**	**871**	**851**	**3,997**
Margin	18.1%	19.2%	22.0%	18.0%	16.5%	19.0%	20.5%	23.0%	19.0%	17.5%	20.1%
Y/Y Change (%)	*3%*	*11%*	*−2%*	*0%*	*3%*	*3%*	*9%*	*10%*	*11%*	*11%*	*10%*
Net Earnings	**2,730**	**754**									
Margin	14.0%	14.7%									
Effective Tax Rate	22.6%	23.3%									
Grooming											
Volume (Reported)	5%	−1%	−4%	0%	3%	−1%	4%	5%	5%	5%	5%
Volume (Organic)	6%	−1%	−4%	0%	3%	−1%	4%	5%	5%	5%	5%
FX	7%	6%	−6%	−12%	−12%	−6%	−3%	0%	0%	0%	−1%
Price	2%	3%	4%	2%	2%	3%	2%	0%	0%	0%	1%
Mix/Other	−3%	−2%	−1%	−1%	−1%	−1%	−1%	0%	0%	0%	0%
Net Sales	**8,254**	**2,142**	**2,010**	**1,760**	**1,933**	**7,844**	**2,185**	**2,110**	**1,848**	**2,030**	**8,172**
Y/Y Change	*11%*	*6%*	*−7%*	*−11%*	*−8%*	*−5%*	*2%*	*5%*	*5%*	*5%*	*4%*
Organic (ex. F/X, Acq/Div)	*5%*	*0%*	*−1%*	*1%*	*4%*	*1%*	*5%*	*5%*	*5%*	*5%*	*5%*
Earnings Before Income Taxes	**2,299**	**645**	**553**	**510**	**532**	**2,239**	**666**	**591**	**545**	**568**	**2,371**
Margin	27.9%	30.1%	27.5%	29.0%	27.5%	28.5%	30.5%	28.0%	29.5%	28.0%	29.0%
Y/Y Change (%)	*21%*	*5%*	*−7%*	*−7%*	*−1%*	*−3%*	*3%*	*7%*	*7%*	*7%*	*6%*
Net Earnings	**1,679**	**478**									
Margin	20.3%	22.3%									
Effective Tax Rate	27.0%	25.9%									
Health Care											
Volume (Reported)	4%	0%	−1%	−1%	2%	0%	3%	6%	5%	5%	5%
Volume (Organic)	4%	1%	−2%	0%	2%	0%	4%	6%	5%	5%	5%
FX	5%	5%	−5%	−11%	−11%	−5%	−3%	0%	0%	0%	−1%
Price	1%	2%	3%	3%	3%	3%	2%	0%	0%	0%	1%
Mix/Other	−1%	−3%	−2%	−2%	−2%	−2%	−1%	0%	0%	0%	0%
Net Sales	**14,578**	**3,700**	**3,583**	**3,249**	**3,308**	**13,841**	**3,737**	**3,798**	**3,412**	**3,474**	**14,421**
Y/Y Change	*9%*	*4%*	*−5%*	*−11%*	*−8%*	*−5%*	*1%*	*6%*	*5%*	*5%*	*4%*
Organic (ex. F/X, Acq/Div)	*4%*	*0%*	*−1%*	*1%*	*4%*	*1%*	*5%*	*6%*	*5%*	*5%*	*5%*
Earnings Before Income Taxes	**3,746**	**990**	**1,003**	**877**	**761**	**3,632**	**1,065**	**1,121**	**955**	**834**	**3,975**
Margin	25.7%	26.8%	28.0%	27.0%	23.0%	26.2%	28.5%	29.5%	28.0%	24.0%	27.6%
Y/Y Change (%)	*11%*	*1%*	*−5%*	*−7%*	*−1%*	*−3%*	*8%*	*12%*	*9%*	*10%*	*9%*
Net Earnings	**2,506**	**658**									
Margin	17.2%	17.8%									
Effective Tax Rate	33.1%	33.5%									
Snacks, Coffee & Pet Care											
Volume (Reported)	2%	2%	−20%	−40%	−40%	−20%	−35%	−20%	3%	3%	−13%
Volume (Organic)	2%	2%	0%	0%	2%	1%	3%	3%	3%	3%	3%
FX	3%	2%	−2%	−8%	−8%	−3%	−3%	0%	0%	0%	−1%
Price	3%	7%	6%	5%	3%	6%	0%	0%	0%	0%	0%
Mix/Other	−1%	−2%	−2%	−1%	0%	−1%	0%	0%	0%	0%	0%
Net Sales	**4,852**	**1,229**	**1,068**	**676**	**671**	**3,644**	**762**	**854**	**696**	**691**	**3,003**
Y/Y Change	*7%*	*9%*	*−18%*	*−44%*	*−45%*	*−25%*	*−38%*	*−20%*	*3%*	*3%*	*−18%*
Organic (ex. F/X, Acq/Div)	*4%*	*7%*	*4%*	*4%*	*5%*	*5%*	*3%*	*3%*	*3%*	*3%*	*3%*
Earnings Before Income Taxes	**762**	**194**	**160**	**81**	**94**	**529**	**118**	**141**	**87**	**100**	**446**
Margin	15.7%	15.8%	15.0%	12.0%	14.0%	14.5%	15.5%	16.5%	12.5%	14.5%	14.9%
Y/Y Change (%)	*0%*	*5%*	*−20%*	*−53%*	*−54%*	*−31%*	*−39%*	*−12%*	*7%*	*7%*	*−18%*
Net Earnings	**477**	**120**									
Margin	9.8%	9.8%									
Effective Tax Rate	37.4%	38.1%									
Fabric Care & Home Care											
Volume (Reported)	6%	2%	−1%	1%	3%	1%	4%	5%	5%	5%	5%
Volume (Organic)	6%	2%	−1%	1%	3%	1%	4%	5%	5%	5%	5%
FX	5%	4%	−4%	−10%	−10%	−5%	−5%	0%	0%	0%	−1%
Price	1%	4%	6%	6%	4%	5%	2%	0%	0%	0%	1%
Mix/Other	−1%	0%	−1%	0%	0%	0%	0%	0%	0%	0%	0%
Net Sales	**23,831**	**6,510**	**6,074**	**5,586**	**5,911**	**24,081**	**6,575**	**6,378**	**5,866**	**6,207**	**25,025**
Y/Y Change	*11%*	*10%*	*0%*	*−3%*	*−3%*	*1%*	*1%*	*5%*	*5%*	*5%*	*4%*
Organic (ex. F/X, Acq/Div)	*6%*	*6%*	*4%*	*7%*	*7%*	*8%*	*6%*	*5%*	*5%*	*5%*	*5%*
Earnings Before Income Taxes	**5,078**	**1,268**	**1,184**	**1,229**	**1,360**	**5,041**	**1,545**	**1,467**	**1,349**	**1,490**	**5,851**
Margin	21.3%	19.5%	19.5%	22.0%	23.0%	20.9%	23.5%	23.0%	23.0%	24.0%	23.4%
Y/Y Change (%)	*9%*	*−6%*	*−9%*	*5%*	*9%*	*−1%*	*22%*	*24%*	*10%*	*10%*	*18%*
Net Earnings	**3,422**	**831**									
Margin	14.4%	12.8%									
Effective Tax Rate	32.6%	34.5%									

continued

continued from prior page

PG Segment Analysis (In U.S. millions, except per share data)	F2008A	Sep08A	Dec08E	Mar09E	Jun09E	F2009E	Sep09E	Dec09E	Mar10E	Jun10E	F2010E
Baby Care & Family Care											
Volume (Reported)	4%	1%	0%	2%	3%	1%	4%	5%	5%	5%	5%
Volume (Organic)	8%	7%	2%	2%	3%	4%	4%	5%	5%	5%	5%
FX	4%	4%	−4%	−10%	−10%	−5%	−5%	0%	0%	0%	−1%
Price	1%	5%	7%	5%	4%	5%	2%	0%	0%	0%	1%
Mix/Other	0%	0%	−1%	−1%	0%	0%	0%	0%	0%	0%	0%
Net Sales	13,898	3,772	3,441	3,390	3,466	14,069	3,810	3,614	3,559	3,639	14,622
Y/Y Change	9%	10%	2%	−4%	−3%	1%	1%	5%	5%	5%	4%
Organic (ex. F/X, Acq/Div)	9%	12%	9%	9%	7%	9%	8%	5%	5%	5%	5%
Earnings Before Income Taxes	2,700	807	723	780	693	3,003	838	777	836	746	3,197
Margin	19.4%	21.4%	21.0%	23.0%	20.0%	21.3%	22.0%	21.5%	23.5%	20.5%	21.9%
Y/Y Change (%)	18%	19%	11%	5%	10%	11%	4%	8%	7%	8%	8%
Net Earnings	1,728	514									
Margin	12.4%	13.6%									
Effective Tax Rate	36.0%	36.3%									
Consolidated											
Volume (Reported)	4%	2%	−2%	−1%	1%	0%	2%	4%	5%	5%	4%
Volume (Organic)	5%	3%	−1%	1%	3%	2%	4%	5%	5%	5%	5%
FX	5%	5%	−5%	−11%	−11%	−5%	−4%	0%	0%	0%	−1%
Price	1%	3%	5%	4%	3%	4%	2%	0%	0%	0%	1%
Mix/Other	−1%	−1%	−1%	−1%	0%	−1%	0%	0%	0%	0%	0%
Net Sales—Segments	84,928	22,481	21,159	19,024	19,922	82,587	22,299	21,986	19,962	20,905	85,152
Corporate	(1,425)	(455)	(250)	(400)	(350)	(1,455)	(455)	(250)	(400)	(350)	(1,455)
Net Sales	83,503	22,026	20,909	18,624	19,572	81,132	21,844	21,736	19,562	20,555	83,697
Y/Y Change	9%	9%	−3%	−9%	−8%	−3%	−1%	4%	5%	5%	3%
Organic (ex. F/X, Acq/Div)	5%	5%	3%	4%	5%	4%	5%	5%	5%	5%	5%
Earnings Before Income Taxes—Segments	18,113	4,887	4,720	4,263	4,204	18,073	5,305	5,299	4,643	4,589	19,837
Interest Expense, Net	(1,467)	(339)	(349)	(363)	(350)	(1,402)	(347)	(370)	(362)	(364)	(1,443)
Other Non-Operating Income	462	337	2,798	10	10	3,155	10	10	10	10	40
Other Corporate	(1,030)	(202)	(183)	(182)	(226)	(794)	(175)	(175)	(175)	(175)	(700)
Corporate	(2,035)	(204)	2,265	(536)	(566)	959	(512)	(535)	(527)	(529)	(2,103)
Earnings Before Income Taxes	16,078	4,683	6,985	3,727	3,637	19,032	4,793	4,764	4,116	4,060	17,734
Margin	19.3%	21.3%	33.4%	20.0%	18.6%	23.5%	21.9%	21.9%	21.0%	19.8%	21.2%
Y/Y Change (%)	9%	10%	55%	−1%	2%	19%	2%	−32%	10%	12%	−7%
Net Earnings—Segments	12,542	3,355									
Corporate	(467)	(7)									
Net Earnings	12,075	3,348									
Margin	14.5%	15.2%									
Effective Tax Rate	24.9%	28.5%									

Sources: Company financial statements and Oppenheimer & Co. Inc. estimates

PG Cash Flow Statement (In U.S. millions, except per share data)	F2008A	Sep08A	Dec08E	Mar09E	Jun09E	F2009E	Sep09E	Dec09E	Mar10E	Jun10E	F2010E
Net Earnings	12,075	3,348	5,029	2,683	2,619	13,679	3,451	3,430	2,964	2,923	12,768
Depreciation & Amortization	3,166	910	926	751	780	3,167	849	845	776	808	3,277
Share-Based Compensation Expense	555	126	150	150	150	576	150	150	150	150	600
Deferred Income Taxes	1,214	247	—	—	—	247	—	—	—	—	—
Non-Cash Adjustments to Net Income	4,935	1,183	976	901	930	3,990	999	995	926	958	3,877
Accounts Receivable	432	(725)	(509)	580	550	(105)	(390)	(479)	329	335	(205)
Inventories	(1,050)	(833)	381	(230)	583	(99)	(387)	322	(507)	315	(257)
Accounts Payable/Accrued/Other Liabilities	134	398	1,274	46	(347)	1,371	(1,252)	975	601	201	526
Other Operating Assets & Liabilities	(1,239)	265	(497)	460	34	262	4	(17)	(19)	(20)	(51)
Change in Assets & Liabilities	(1,723)	(895)	649	856	820	1,430	(2,025)	801	404	832	13
Other	527	(385)	—	—	—	(385)					
Operating Cash Flow	15,814	3,251	6,654	4,440	4,369	18,714	2,425	5,227	4,294	4,713	16,659
Capital Expenditures	(3,046)	(699)	(627)	(652)	(1,076)	(3,055)	(655)	(652)	(685)	(1,131)	(3,123)
% of Net Sales	3.6%	3.2%	3.0%	3.5%	5.5%	3.8%	3.0%	3.0%	3.5%	5.5%	3.7%
Free Cash Flow	12,768	2,552	6,027	3,788	3,292	15,660	1,770	4,575	3,609	3,583	13,536
Y/Y Change	22%	−5%	72%	3%	13%	23%	−31%	−24%	−5%	9%	−14%
Free Cash Flow Productivity (FCF/NI)	106%	76%	120%	141%	126%	114%	51%	133%	122%	123%	106%

PG Balance Sheet	F2008A	Sep08A	Dec08E	Mar09E	Jun09E	F2009E	Sep09E	Dec09E	Mar10E	Jun10E	F2010E
Cash & Cash Equivalents	3,313	4,502	5,080	4,970	4,868	4,868	4,857	4,907	4,963	5,022	5,022
% of Net Sales (LTM)	4.0%	5.3%	6.0%	6.0%	6.0%	6.0%	6.0%	6.0%	6.0%	6.0%	6.0%
Investment Securities	228	—	—	—	—	—	—	—	—	—	—
Accounts Receivable	6,761	7,111	7,620	7,040	6,491	6,491	6,881	7,360	7,031	6,696	6,696
% of Net Sales (LTM)	8.1%	8.3%	9.0%	8.5%	8.0%	8.0%	8.5%	9.0%	8.5%	8.0%	8.0%
Y/Y Change (%)	2%	−4%	−1%	2%	−4%	−4%	−3%	−3%	0%	3%	3%
Inventories	8,416	8,847	8,466	8,697	8,113	8,113	8,500	8,178	8,685	8,370	8,370
% of Net Sales (LTM)	10.1%	10.4%	10.0%	10.5%	10.0%	10.0%	10.5%	10.0%	10.5%	10.0%	10.0%
Y/Y Change (%)	23%	15%	10%	3%	−4%	−4%	−4%	−3%	0%	3%	3%

continued

continued from prior page

PG Balance Sheet	F2008A	Sep08A	Dec08E	Mar09E	Jun09E	F2009E	Sep09E	Dec09E	Mar10E	Jun10E	F2010E
Deferred Income Taxes..................	2,012	1,547	1,547	1,547	1,547	1,547	1,547	1,547	1,547	1,547	1,547
Other Current Assets	3,785	3,062	3,810	3,313	3,245	3,245	3,238	3,271	3,309	3,348	3,348
% of Net Sales (LTM)	4.5%	3.6%	4.5%	4.0%	4.0%	4.0%	4.0%	4.0%	4.0%	4.0%	4.0%
Current Assets	24,515	25,069	26,523	25,566	24,264	24,264	25,023	25,262	25,534	24,982	24,982
Property, Plant & Equipment, Net.........	20,640	19,724	19,682	19,738	20,188	20,188	20,145	20,101	20,160	20,633	20,633
Goodwill & Intangible Assets, Net	94,000	91,238	91,081	90,926	90,772	90,772	90,622	90,473	90,323	90,173	90,173
Other Non-Current Assets	4,837	4,648	4,233	4,141	4,462	4,462	4,048	4,089	4,136	4,603	4,603
% of Net Sales (LTM)	5.8%	5.4%	5.0%	5.0%	5.5%	5.5%	5.0%	5.0%	5.0%	5.5%	5.5%
Total Assets.........................	**143,992**	**140,679**	**141,519**	**140,372**	**139,686**	**139,686**	**139,837**	**139,925**	**140,152**	**140,391**	**140,391**
Accounts Payable.....................	6,775	6,006	5,503	5,798	6,896	6,896	5,667	5,316	5,790	7,114	7,114
% of Net Sales (LTM)	8.1%	7.0%	6.5%	7.0%	8.5%	8.5%	7.0%	6.5%	7.0%	8.5%	8.5%
Y/Y Change (%).......................	19%	15%	14%	5%	2%	2%	−6%	−3%	0%	3%	3%
Accrued & Other Liabilities	10,154	9,653	11,430	11,181	9,736	9,736	9,714	11,040	11,166	10,044	10,044
% of Net Sales (LTM)	12.2%	11.3%	13.5%	13.5%	12.0%	12.0%	12.0%	13.5%	13.5%	12.0%	12.0%
Taxes Payable.......................	945	1,442	1,693	1,657	1,623	1,623	1,619	1,636	1,654	1,674	1,674
% of Net Sales (LTM)	1.1%	1.7%	2.0%	2.0%	2.0%	2.0%	2.0%	2.0%	2.0%	2.0%	2.0%
Non-Interest Bearing Current Liabilities.......	17,874	17,101	18,626	18,636	18,255	18,255	17,000	17,991	18,611	18,832	18,832
Total Debt	36,665	39,447	41,422	39,971	39,553	39,553	41,884	41,131	41,340	42,110	42,110
Deferred Income Taxes.................	11,805	11,736	11,736	11,736	11,736	11,736	11,736	11,736	11,736	11,736	11,736
Other Non-Current Liabilities	8,154	7,833	5,419	5,301	5,192	5,192	4,452	4,498	4,549	4,603	4,603
% of Net Sales (LTM)	9.8%	9.2%	6.4%	6.4%	6.4%	6.4%	5.5%	5.5%	5.5%	5.5%	5.5%
Shareholders' Equity..................	69,494	64,562	64,317	64,728	64,950	64,950	64,765	64,569	63,917	63,110	63,110
Total Liabilities & Equity.................	**143,992**	**140,679**	**141,519**	**140,372**	**139,686**	**139,686**	**139,837**	**139,925**	**140,152**	**140,391**	**140,391**

Sources: Company financial statements and Oppenheimer & Co. Inc. estimates

APPENDIX 11B Forecasting Financial Statements with Cash-Target Adjustments

Earlier in the module, the Procter & Gamble forecasted financial statements predict excess cash that we applied toward the repurchase of common stock. This approach implicitly assumes no impact on the income statement. However, under different circumstances, we might apply excess cash to reduce debt, equity, or some combination. Further, we might forecast a cash deficit, which would necessitate additional borrowing or liquidation of investments to increase cash. In these cases, the adjustments to cash will impact the income statement in addition to the balance sheet and statement of cash flows. This appendix introduces the mechanics to deal with these cases.

Adjustments for Excess Cash

To illustrate, we return to the P&G forecasted statements from this module. For its 2009 forecasts, instead of assuming that all excess cash is used to repurchase common stock, let's assume that the excess cash of $5,532 million is used to repurchase common stock and to pay down its debt in equal amounts of $2,766. First, with a $2,766 repayment of short-term debt, total interest-bearing debt is now forecasted as follows:

($ millions)	2008	Adjustment	2009 Est.
Debt due within one year	$13,084	$16,846 (forecasted) − $2,766	$14,080
Long-term debt	23,581	from forecasted balance sheet	18,073
Total interest-bearing debt	$36,665	subtotal	$32,153

After this repayment, the average interest-bearing debt forecasted for 2009 is $34,409, computed as ($36,665 + $32,153)/2, which assumes repayment is made evenly over the year. The debt repayment reduces interest-bearing debt by 6.2%, computed as ($34,409/$36,665) − 1. Accordingly, we expect that interest expense will also fall by 6.2%, from $1,467 million to $1,376 million (computed as $1,467 × [1 − 0.062]), which yields a $91 million increase in pretax income, from $15,999 million to $16,090 million. Assuming an estimated income tax rate of 24.9% (that we used for P&G forecasts), income tax expense is estimated at $4,006 million ($16,090 × 24.9%). The end result is to increase net income from $12,015 million to $12,084 million, with a consequent increase in dividends paid of $26 million (computed as $4,664 million in dividends [$12,084 million × 38.6% payout rate] less $4,638 million in dividends [$12,015 million × 38.6% payout rate]). And, on the balance sheet, debt due within one year decreases and treasury stock increases, each by $2,766 million. Because tax expense changes, taxes payable also changes by $5 million, computed as ($4,006 updated tax expense − $3,984) × 23.6%.

Exhibit 11B.1 shows the "adjusted" forecasted income statement, forecasted balance sheet, and forecasted statement of cash flows, which reflect the target-cash adjustment and the resulting impact of that adjustment on the income statement and statement of cash flows.

EXHIBIT 11.B1 Adjusted Forecasts of Income Statement, Balance Sheet and Statement of Cash Flows

Income Statement ($ millions)	2008		Forecast Assumptions	2009 Est.	Adjustment	Adjusted 2009 Est.
Net sales.	$83,503	100.0%	$83,503 × 0.993	$82,944		$82,944
Cost of products sold.	40,695	48.7%	$82,944 × 49.7%	41,223		41,223
Gross profit.	42,808	51.3%	subtotal	41,721		41,721
Selling, general and admin. expense	25,725	30.8%	$82,944 × 29.8%	24,717		24,717
Operating income.	17,083	20.5%	subtotal	17,004		17,004
Interest expense.	1,467	1.8%	no change	1,467	$91 less	1,376
Other nonoperating income, net	462	0.6%	no change	462		462
Earnings before income taxes	16,078	19.3%	subtotal	15,999		16,090
Income taxes	4,003	4.8%	$15,999 × 24.9%	3,984	$22 more	4,006
Net earnings.	$12,075	14.5%	subtotal	$12,015	$69 more	$12,084

Balance Sheet ($ millions)	2008	Forecast Assumptions	2009 Est.	Adjustment	Adjusted 2009 Est.
Assets					
Cash and cash equivalents	$ 3,313	computed to balance	$ 8,898	via stmt of c.f.	$ 3,414
Investment securities	228	no change	228		228
Accounts receivable.	6,761	$82,944 × 8.4%	6,967		6,967
Inventories	8,416	$82,944 × 10.1%	8,377		8,377
Deferred income taxes	2,012	no change	2,012		2,012
Prepaid expenses and other current assets.	3,785	$82,944 × 4.5%	3,732		3,732
Total current assets	24,515	subtotal	30,214		24,730
Total property, plant and equipment.	38,086	$38,086 + ($82,944 × 3.9%)	41,321		41,321
Accumulated depreciation	(17,446)	$17,446 + ($38,086 × 7.2%)	(20,188)		(20,188)
Net property, plant and equipment.	20,640	subtotal	21,133		21,133
Goodwill and other intangible assets.	94,000	$94,000 − ($94,000 × 0.7%)	93,342		93,342
Other noncurrent assets.	4,837	no change	4,837		4,837
Total assets.	$143,992	subtotal	$149,526		$144,042
Liabilities and Equity					
Accounts payable.	$ 6,775	$82,944 × 8.1%	$ 6,718		$ 6,718
Accrued and other liabilities.	10,154	$82,944 × 12.2%	10,119		10,119
Taxes payable.	945	$3,984 × 23.6%	940	($4,006 − $3,984) × 23.6%	945
Debt due within one year	13,084	$5,508 + $11,338 (via footnotes)	16,846	$2,766 less	14,080
Total current liabilities.	30,958	subtotal	34,623		31,862
Long-term debt	23,581	$23,581 − $5,508	18,073		18,073
Deferred income taxes.	11,805	no change	11,805		11,805
Other noncurrent liabilities.	8,154	no change	8,154		8,154
Total liabilities.	74,498	subtotal	72,655	$2,761 less	69,894
Shareholders' equity					
Preferred stock.	1,366	no change	1,366		1,366
Common stock.	4,002	no change	4,002		4,002
Additional paid-in capital	60,307	no change	60,307		60,307
Reserve for ESOP debt retirement.	(1,325)	no change	(1,325)		(1,325)
Accumulated other comprehensive income.	3,746	no change	3,746		3,746
Treasury stock	(47,588)	no change	(47,588)	$(2,766) TS	(50,354)
Retained earnings	48,986	$48,986 + $12,015 − $4,638	56,363	$69 more NI − $26 more DIV	56,406
Total shareholders' equity	69,494	subtotal	76,871		74,148
Total liabilities and shareholders' equity.	$143,992	subtotal	$149,526		$144,042

continued

continued from prior page

EXHIBIT 11.B1	Adjusted Forecasts of Income Statement, Balance Sheet and Statement of Cash Flows			
Statement of Cash Flows ($ millions)	**Forecast Assumptions**	**2009 Est.**	**Adjustment**	**Adjusted 2009 Est.**
Operating activities				
Net earnings..................................	via forecasted income stmt.	$12,015	$69 inflow	$12,084
Depreciation...........................	$38,086 × 7.2%	2,742		2,742
Amortization...........................	$94,000 × 0.7%	658		658
Accounts receivable...................	$6,761 − $6,967	(206)		(206)
Inventories............................	$8,416 − $8,377	39		39
Prepaid expenses and other current assets	$3,785 − $3,732	53		53
Accounts payable	$6,718 − $6,775	(57)		(57)
Accrued and other liabilities	$10,119 − $10,154	(35)		(35)
Taxes payable	$940 − $945	(5)	$5 inflow	(0)
Net cash flow from operating activities	subtotal	15,204		15,278
Investing activities				
Capital expenditures	$82,944 × 3.9%	(3,235)		(3,235)
Net cash flow from investing activities...............	subtotal	(3,235)		(3,235)
Financing activities				
Changes in short- and long-term debt...............	$1,746 via footnote	(1,746)	$2,766 outflow	(4,512)
Repurchases of common stock....................		0	$2,766 outflow	(2,766)
Dividends to shareholders	$12,015 × 38.6%	(4,638)	$12,084 × 38.6%	(4,664)
Net cash flow from financing activities...............	subtotal	(6,384)		(11,942)
Change in cash and cash equivalents	subtotal	5,585		101
Cash and equivalents, beginning of year..............	from balance sheet	3,313		3,313
Cash and equivalents, end of year...................	subtotal	$ 8,898		$ 3,414

Adjustments for Cash Deficit

This section explains the adjustments required when the initial forecast reveals a negative balance for cash. This can occur for poorly performing companies that are generating insufficient cash to meet operating and financing needs. It can also occur for profitable companies that are growing rapidly and require substantial expenditures for working capital and long-term assets. A forecasted negative cash balance implies that additional cash must be acquired. This is commonly accomplished through any or all of the following means:

1. Selling marketable securities.
2. Borrowing money.
3. Issuing common stock.

The first two options increase the cash balance in the same amount as investments are reduced and/or debt is increased. Each of these financing options also impacts the income statement by reducing investment income and/or increasing interest expense. The third option increases cash through stock issuance, which does not impact the income statement. To illustrate, assume that we forecast the following simplified balance sheet and income statement.

Forecasted Balance Sheet			
Assets		**Liabilities and Equity**	
Cash.........................	$ (300)	Liabilities (at 5% interest rate)	$1,000
Other operating assets...........	1,300		
Investments (earning 5% return)	1,000	Equity	1,000
Total assets....................	$2,000	Total liabilities and equity	$2,000

Forecasted Income Statement	
Net operating profit after tax (NOPAT)	$200
Net nonoperating expenses (NNE)........	0
Net income........................	$200

These forecasts imply a negative cash balance of $(300). Assume that the historical cash to total assets relation is 8%. Options 1 and 2 will have income statement impacts. To illustrate these impacts, we also assume that the investment return and borrowing rate both equal 5%, and that the tax rate is 35%.

If we implement Option 1 we must liquidate sufficient marketable securities to get to the 8% cash target. Option 1 will not change total assets, thus, we need a cash balance of $160 ($2,000 × 0.08) and must liquidate $460 of marketable securities. The income statement will report a higher net nonoperating expense (recall that nonoperating income earned on investments decreases NNE). Interest earned on $460 is $14.95 after tax, computed as $460 × 5% × (1 − 35%). The forecasted income statement follows:

Adjusted Forecast of Income Statement	
Net operating profit after tax (NOPAT)	$200.00
Net nonoperating expenses (NNE).	(14.95)
Net income	$185.05

If we implement Option 2, total assets will change. Given our 8% cash target, we need to borrow $500. After the borrowing, total assets will be $2,500 and the cash balance will be $200 ($2,500 × 0.08). The income statement will report a higher net nonoperating expense because interest expense will be $16.25 higher after tax, computed as $500 × 5% × (1 − 35%). The forecasted income statement follows:

Adjusted Forecast of Income Statement	
Net operating profit after tax (NOPAT)	$200.00
Net nonoperating expenses (NNE).	(16.25)
Net income	$183.75

The lower net income can also result in a reduction of dividends paid as we discuss in the prior section. A final point is that we must be careful that any increase in borrowed money does not markedly increase our forecasted financial leverage from historical norms. If it does, we must consider raising a portion of the required funds via issuance of common stock.

DISCUSSION QUESTIONS

Q11-1. Identify at least two applications that use forecasted financial statements.

Q11-2. Forecasts of the income statement typically require estimates of cost of goods sold (gross profit) and operating and nonoperating expenses (revenues) as a percentage of revenues. Identify at least three financial statement adjustments that we discuss in previous modules that might affect our forecasts for gross profit margin and operating expense percentages.

Q11-3. Forecasts of the balance sheet commonly require estimates of the relative percentage of balance sheet accounts to revenues. Identify at least three financial statement adjustments to reported balance sheet items that can impact that item's relation to revenues. These can include adjustments to recognize assets and/or liabilities that are not recognized under GAAP.

Q11-4. What does the concept of financial statement articulation mean in the forecasting process?

Q11-5. Net operating assets typically move proportionately with revenues. How do the "buffer zone" and "financing" sections of the balance sheet offset some of these changes in net operating assets?

Q11-6. Identify and describe the four major steps in forecasting financial statements.

Q11-7. In addition to recent revenues trends, what other types and sources of information can we use to help us forecast revenues?

Q11-8. Describe the rationale for use of year-end balances in the computation of turnover rates (and other percentages) that are used to forecast selected balance sheet accounts.

Q11-9. What are "comparable store sales" for retailers and why are they important?

Q11-10. Capital expenditures are usually an important cash outflow for a company, and they figure prominently into forecasts of net operating assets. What are the sources of information about capital expenditures that we can draw upon?

Assignments with the WebAssign logo in the margin are available in WebAssign.
See the Preface of the book for details.

MINI EXERCISES

M11-11. Forecasting an Income Statement (LO2)

Abercrombie & Fitch reports the following income statements.

WebAssign.

Abercrombie & Fitch
(ANF)

Income Statement, For Fiscal Years Ended ($ thousands)	2008	2007
Net sales..	$3,749,847	$3,318,158
Cost of goods sold.......................................	1,238,480	1,109,152
Gross profit..	2,511,367	2,209,006
Stores and distribution expense..........................	1,386,846	1,187,071
Marketing, general and administrative expense.............	395,758	373,828
Other operating (income), net............................	(11,734)	(9,983)
Operating income..	740,497	658,090
Interest income, net	(18,828)	(13,896)
Income before income taxes	759,325	671,986
Provision for income taxes...............................	283,628	249,800
Net Income...	$ 475,697	$ 422,186

Forecast Abercrombie & Fitch's 2009 income statement assuming the following income statement relations. Assume no change for all other accounts not listed below. All percentages, other than sales growth and provision for income taxes, are based on percent of net sales.

Net sales growth.......................................	13.0%
Gross profit margin....................................	67.0%
Stores and distribution expense/Net sales	37.0%
Marketing, general and administrative expense/Net sales	10.6%
Other operating (income), net/Net sales	−0.3%
Provision for income taxes/Income before income taxes	37.4%

M11-12. Forecasting an Income Statement (LO2)

Best Buy (BBY)

Best Buy reports the following income statements.

Income Statement, Fiscal Years Ended ($ millions)	2008	2007
Revenue	$40,023	$35,934
Cost of goods sold......................................	30,477	27,165
Gross profit..	9,546	8,769
Selling, general and administrative expenses	7,385	6,770
Operating income.......................................	2,161	1,999
Other income*	61	130
Earnings before income tax expense......................	2,222	2,129
Income tax expense.....................................	815	752
Net earnings...	$ 1,407	$ 1,377

* Other income combines investment income, interest expense, minority interest in earnings, and equity in loss of affiliates.

Forecast Best Buy's 2009 income statement assuming the following income statement relations; assume no change for all other accounts not listed below. All percentages, other than revenue growth and income tax expense, are based on percent of revenue.

Revenue growth	11.4%
Gross profit margin..	23.9%
Selling, general and administrative expenses/Revenue........................	18.5%
Income tax expense/Earnings before income tax expense......................	36.7%

M11-13. Forecasting an Income Statement (LO2)

General Mills (GIS)

General Mills reports the following fiscal year income statements (amounts rounded to whole millions).

Income Statement, Fiscal Years Ended (in millions)	2008	2007
Net sales.	$13,652	$12,442
Cost of sales.	8,778	7,955
Selling, general and administrative expenses	2,625	2,389
Restructuring, impairment, and other exit costs	21	39
Interest, net	422	427
Earnings before income taxes and after-tax earnings from joint ventures. . . .	1,806	1,631*
Income taxes	622	560
After-tax earnings from joint ventures	111	73
Net earnings.	$ 1,295	$ 1,144

* $1 rounding error in subtotal.

Forecast General Mills' fiscal year 2009 income statement assuming the following income statement relations (assume no change for Interest, net). All percentages, other than for net sales growth and income taxes, are based on percent of sales.

Net sales growth.	9.7%
Cost of sales/Net sales	64.3%
Selling, general and administrative expenses/Net sales	19.2%
Restructuring, impairment, and other exit costs/Net sales	0.2%
After-tax earnings from joint ventures/Net sales	0.8%
Income taxes/Earnings before income taxes and after-tax earnings from joint ventures	34.4%

M11-14. Analyzing, Forecasting, and Interpreting Working Capital Using Turnover Rates (LO2)

Harley-Davidson reports 2007 net operating working capital of $4,513 million and 2007 long-term operating assets of $1,518 million.

Harley-Davidson (HOG)

a. Forecast Harley-Davidson's 2008 net operating working capital and 2008 long-term operating assets. Assume forecasted 2008 net revenue of $6,150 million, net operating working capital turnover of 1.32 times, and long-term operating asset turnover of 3.93 times. (Both turnover rates are computed here using year-end balances. Finance receivables and related debt are considered operating under the assumption that they are an integral part of Harley's operating activities.)

b. Most of Harley's receivables arise from its financing activities relating to purchases of motorcycles by consumers and dealers. What effect will these receivables have on Harley's operating working capital turnover rate?

M11-15. Analyzing, Forecasting, and Interpreting Working Capital Using Turnover Rates (LO2)

Nike reports 2008 net operating working capital of $5,060 million and 2008 long-term operating assets of $2,139 million.

Nike (NKE)

a. Forecast Nike's 2009 net operating working capital assuming forecasted sales of $19,372 million, net operating working capital turnover of 3.68 times, and long-term operating asset turnover of 8.71 times. (Both turnover rates are computed here using year-end balances.)

b. Does it seem reasonable that Nike's operating working capital turnover is less than its long-term operating asset turnover? Explain.

M11-16. Interpreting and Adjusting Balance Sheet Forecasts for a Negative Cash Balance (LO3)

Assume that your initial forecast of a balance sheet yields a negative cash balance.

a. What does a forecasted negative cash balance imply?

b. Given a negative cash balance, what would be your next step in forecasting the balance sheet? Explain.

M11-17. Forecasting the Balance Sheet and Operating Cash Flows Using Turnover Rates (LO2, 3)

Refer to the General Mills information in M11-13. Assume the following forecasts of 2009 net sales and cost of sales ($ millions): $14,976 and $9,630, respectively. Use the following financial statement relations to forecast General Mills' receivables, inventories, and accounts payable as of the end of May 2009.

General Mills (GIS)

Year-end turnover rates	2008
Net sales/Year-end receivables	12.62
Cost of sales/Year-end inventories.	6.42
Cost of sales/Year-end accounts payable	9.37

M11-18. Adjusting the Income Statement **(LO2)**

Campbell Soup (CPB)

Campbell Soup Company reports the following footnote to its 2008 10-K.

> **Discontinued Operations** On March 18, 2008, the company completed the sale of its Godiva Chocolatier business for $850 million . . . The company has reflected the results of this business as discontinued operations in the consolidated statements of earnings for all years presented . . . The company recognized a pretax gain of $698 million ($462 million after tax or $1.21 per share) on the sale. The company used $600 million of the net proceeds from the sale to purchase company stock.

What adjustment(s) might we consider before we forecast Campbell Soup's income for 2009? How would we treat the cash proceeds that Campbell Soup realized on such a sale?

EXERCISES

E11-19. Analyzing, Forecasting, and Interpreting Income Statement and Balance Sheet **(LO2, 3)**

Abercrombie & Fitch (ANF)

Following are the income statements and balance sheets of Abercrombie & Fitch.

Consolidated Statements of Net Income			
For Fiscal Years Ended (Thousands)	2008	2007	2006
Net sales.	$3,749,847	$3,318,158	$2,784,711
Cost of goods sold.	1,238,480	1,109,152	933,295
Gross profit.	2,511,367	2,209,006	1,851,416
Stores and distribution expense.	1,386,846	1,187,071	1,000,755
Marketing, general and administrative expense.	395,758	373,828	313,457
Other operating income, net	(11,734)	(9,983)	(5,534)
Operating income.	740,497	658,090	542,738
Interest income, net	(18,828)	(13,896)	(6,674)
Income before income taxes	759,325	671,986	549,412
Provision for income taxes.	283,628	249,800	215,426
Net income.	$ 475,697	$ 422,186	$ 333,986

Consolidated Balance Sheets		
(Thousands, except share amounts)	February 2, 2008	February 3, 2007
Assets		
Cash and equivalents.	$ 118,044	$ 81,959
Marketable securities.	530,486	447,793
Receivables	53,801	43,240
Inventories	333,153	427,447
Deferred income taxes.	36,128	33,170
Other current assets.	68,643	58,469
Total current assets	1,140,255	1,092,078
Property and equipment, net	1,318,291	1,092,282
Other assets.	109,052	63,707
Total assets.	$2,567,598	$2,248,067

continued

continued from prior page

(Thousands, except share amounts)	February 2, 2008	February 3, 2007
Liabilities and shareholders' equity		
Accounts payable.	$ 108,437	$ 100,919
Outstanding checks	43,361	27,391
Accrued expenses	280,910	260,219
Deferred lease credits	37,925	35,423
Income taxes payable	72,480	86,675
Total current liabilities.	543,113	510,627
Deferred income taxes	22,491	30,394
Deferred lease credits	213,739	203,943
Other liabilities	169,942	97,806
Total long-term liabilities.	406,172	332,143
Shareholders' equity:		
Class A common stock—$.01 par value: 150,000,000 shares authorized and 103,300,000 shares issued at February 2, 2008 and February 3, 2007, respectively.	1,033	1,033
Paid-in capital	319,451	289,732
Retained earnings	2,051,463	1,646,290
Accumulated other comprehensive income (loss), net of tax	7,118	(994)
Treasury stock, at average cost 17,141,116 and 14,999,945 shares at February 2, 2008, and February 3, 2007, respectively	(760,752)	(530,764)
Total shareholders' equity	1,618,313	1,405,297
Total liabilities and shareholders' equity.	$2,567,598	$2,248,067

a. Forecast Abercrombie & Fitch's 2009 income statement and balance sheet using the following relations; assume no change for all other accounts not listed here. Assume all capital expenditures are purchases of property and equipment.

Net sales growth.	13.0%
Gross profit margin.	67.0%
Stores and distribution expense/Net sales	37.0%
Marketing, general and administrative expense/Net sales	10.6%
Other operating income, net/Net sales	−0.3%
Provision for income taxes/Income before income taxes	37.4%
Receivables/Net sales	1.4%
Inventories/Net sales	8.9%
Accounts payable/Net sales.	2.9%
Capital expenditures/Net sales	10.8%
Accrued expenses/Net sales	7.5%
Income taxes payable/Provision for income taxes.	25.6%
Dividends/Net income	11.0%
Property and equipment, gross (February 2, 2008)	$2,054,275
Depreciation expense/Prior year property and equipment, gross	11%

b. What does the forecasted cash balance from part *a* reveal to us about the forecasted financing needs of the company? Explain.

E11-20. **Forecasting the Statement of Cash Flows** **(LO4)**

Refer to the Abercrombie & Fitch financial information in Exercise 11-19. Prepare a forecast of 2009 statement of cash flows.

Abercrombie & Fitch (ANF)

E11-21. **Analyzing, Forecasting, and Interpreting Both Income Statement and Balance Sheet** **(LO2, 3)**

Following are the income statements and balance sheets of Best Buy Co., Inc.

Web**Assign**.

Best Buy Co., Inc. (BBY)

Balance Sheet ($ millions, except share amounts)	March 1, 2008	March 3, 2007
Assets		
Cash and cash equivalents	$ 1,438	$ 1,205
Short-term investments	64	2,588
Receivables	549	548
Merchandise inventories	4,708	4,028
Other current assets	583	712
Total current assets	7,342	9,081
Property and equipment*	5,608	4,904
Less accumulated depreciation	2,302	1,966
Net property and equipment	3,306	2,938
Other assets**	2,110	1,551
Total assets	$12,758	$13,570
Liabilities and shareholders' equity		
Accounts payable	$ 4,297	$ 3,934
Unredeemed gift card liabilities	531	496
Accrued liabilities, accrued compensation and related expenses†	1,348	1,322
Accrued income taxes	404	489
Short-term debt	156	41
Current portion of long-term debt	33	19
Total current liabilities	6,769	6,301
Long-term liabilities	838	443
Long-term debt	627	590
Minority interests	40	35
Shareholders' equity		
Preferred stock, $1.00 par value: Authorized—400,000 shares; Issued and outstanding—none	—	—
Common stock, $0.10 par value: Authorized—1.0 billion shares; Issued and outstanding—410,578,000 and 480,655,000 shares, respectively	41	48
Additional paid-in capital	8	430
Retained earnings	3,933	5,507
Accumulated other comprehensive income	502	216
Total shareholders' equity	4,484	6,201
Total liabilities and shareholders' equity	$12,758	$13,570

* Land, buildings, fixtures, equipment, leasehold improvements, and property under capital leases are combined.

** Goodwill, tradenames, equity and other investments, and other noncurrent assets are combined.

† Accrued liabilities and accrued compensation and related expenses are combined.

Income Statement, Fiscal Years Ended ($ millions)	2008	2007
Revenue	$40,023	$35,934
Cost of goods sold	30,477	27,165
Gross profit	9,546	8,769
Selling, general and administrative expenses	7,385	6,770
Operating income	2,161	1,999
Other income*	61	130
Earnings before income tax expense	2,222	2,129
Income tax expense	815	752
Net earnings	$ 1,407	$ 1,377

* Other income combines investment income, interest expense, minority interest in earnings, and equity in loss of affiliates.

a. Forecast Best Buy's 2009 income statement and balance sheet using the following relations; assume no change for all other accounts not listed below. Assume that all capital expenditures are purchases of property and equipment, and that depreciation is included as part of selling, general and administrative expenses ($ millions).

Revenue growth	11.4%
Gross profit margin.	23.9%
Selling, general and administrative expenses/Revenue.	18.5%
Income tax expense/Earnings before income tax expense	36.7%
Receivables/Revenue.	1.4%
Merchandise inventories/Revenue	11.8%
Depreciation expense/Prior year property and equipment, gross	11.8%
Accounts payable/Revenue	10.7%
Capital expenditures/Revenue	2.0%
Accrued liabilities, accrued compensation and related expenses/Revenue	3.4%
Accrued income taxes/Income tax expense	49.6%
Portion of long-term debt due in 2010	$16
Portion of long-term debt due in 2010	$16
Dividends/Net earnings	14.5%

 b.   What does the forecasted cash balance from part *a* reveal to us about the forecasted financing needs of the company? Explain.

E11-22. **Forecasting the Statement of Cash Flows** **(LO4)**

Refer to the Best Buy Co., Inc., financial information from Exercise 11-21. Prepare a forecast of its fiscal year 2009 statement of cash flows.

E11-23. **Analyzing, Forecasting, and Interpreting Income Statement and Balance Sheet** **(LO2, 3)**

Following are the income statements and balance sheets of General Mills, Inc.

WebAssign.
Best Buy Co., Inc.
(BBY)

WebAssign.
General Mills, Inc.
(GIS)

Income Statement, Fiscal Years Ended (in millions)	2008	2007
Net sales.	$13,652.1	$12,441.5
Cost of sales.	8,778.3	7,955.1
Selling, general and administrative expenses	2,625.0	2,389.3
Restructuring, impairment, and other exit costs	21.0	39.3
Interest, net	421.7	426.5
Earnings before income taxes and after-tax earnings from joint ventures. . . .	1,806.1	1,631.3
Income taxes	622.2	560.1
After-tax earnings from joint ventures	(110.8)	(72.7)
Net earnings.	$ 1,294.7	$ 1,143.9

Balance Sheet (In millions)	May 25, 2008	May 27, 2007
Assets		
Cash and cash equivalents	$ 661.0	$ 417.1
Receivables	1,081.6	952.9
Inventories	1,366.8	1,173.4
Prepaid expenses and other current assets.	510.6	443.1
Deferred income taxes	0.0	67.2
Total current assets.	3,620.0	3,053.7
Land, buildings and equipment	6,471.3	6,095.7
Accumulated depreciation	(3,363.2)	(3,081.8)
Land, buildings and equipment, net.	3,108.1	3,013.9
Goodwill, other intangibles, and other assets*.	12,313.5	12,116.1
Total assets.	$19,041.6	$18,183.7

continued

continued from prior page

(In millions)	May 25, 2008	May 27, 2007
Liabilities and equity		
Accounts payable..	$ 937.3	$ 777.9
Current portion of long-term debt	442.0	1,734.0
Notes payable	2,208.8	1,254.4
Deferred income taxes and other current liabilities**	1,268.2	2,078.8
Total current liabilities......................................	4,856.3	5,845.1
Long-term debt	4,348.7	3,217.7
Deferred income taxes.....................................	1,454.6	1,433.1
Other liabilities..	1,923.9	1,229.9
Total liabilities..	12,583.5	11,725.8
Minority interests	242.3	1,138.8
Stockholders' equity		
Common stock, 377.3 and 502.3 shares issued, $0.10 par value ...	37.7	50.2
Additional paid-in capital	1,149.1	5,841.3
Retained earnings.......................................	6,510.7	5,745.3
Common stock in treasury, at cost, shares of 39.8 and 161.7......	(1,658.4)	(6,198.0)
Accumulated other comprehensive income (loss)	176.7	(119.7)
Total stockholders' equity.................................	6,215.8	5,319.1
Total liabilities and equity...................................	$19,041.6	$18,183.7

* Goodwill, other intangible assets, and other assets are combined.

** Deferred income taxes and other current liabilities are combined.

a. Forecast General Mills' 2009 income statement and balance sheet using the following relations (assume no change for all other accounts not listed below). Assume all capital expenditures are purchases of land, buildings and equipment, net, and that depreciation and amortization are included as part of selling, general and administrative expense ($ millions).

Net sales growth..	9.7%
Cost of sales/Net sales	64.3%
Selling, general and administrative expenses/Net sales	19.2%
Restructuring, impairment, and other exit costs/Net sales	0.2%
Income taxes/Earnings before income taxes and after-tax earnings from joint ventures ...	34.4%
After-tax earnings from joint ventures/Net sales	0.8%
Receivables/Net sales	7.9%
Inventories/Net sales	10.0%
Capital expenditures/Net sales	3.8%
Depreciation expense/Prior year land, buildings and equipment, gross	7.4%
Amortization expense/Prior year goodwill, other intangibles, and other assets	0.04%
Accounts payable/Net sales....................................	6.9%
Portion of long-term debt due in 2010..	$509.0
Dividends/Net earnings	40.9%

b. What does the forecasted cash balance from part *a* reveal to us about the forecasted financing needs of the company? Explain.

E11-24. **Forecasting the Statement of Cash Flows** (LO4)

General Mills, Inc.
(GIS)

Refer to the General Mills, Inc., financial information from Exercise 11-23. Forecast General Mills' 2009 statement of cash flows.

E11-25. **Adjusting the Balance Sheet for Operating Leases** (LO1, 2, 3)

Southwest Airlines
(LUV)

Southwest Airlines reports total net operating assets of $8,466 million, nonoperating liabilities of $1,525 million, and equity of $6,941 in its 2007 10-K. Footnotes reveal the existence of operating leases that have a present value of $1,795 million (see Module 10 for computations).

a. What balance sheet adjustment(s) might we consider relating to the leases before we forecast financial statements for Southwest Airlines? (*Hint:* Consider the distinction between operating and nonoperating assets and liabilities.)

b. What income statement adjustment(s) might we consider? (*Hint:* Reflect on the operating and nonoperating distinction for lease-related expenses.)

E11-26. Adjusting the Balance Sheet for Equity Method Investments (LO3)

Abbott Laboratories, Inc., reports its 50% joint venture investment in TAP Pharmaceutical Products Inc. using the equity method of accounting. The Abbott balance sheet reports an investment balance of $159 million. TAP has total assets of $1,354.2 million, liabilities of $1,036.7 million, and equity of $317.5 million. Abbott's investment balance is, thus, equal to its 50% interest in TAP's equity ($317.5 million × 50% = $158.75 million, rounded to $159 million). What adjustment(s) might we consider to Abbott's balance sheet before we forecast its financial statements? (*Hint:* Consider the distinction between operating and nonoperating assets and liabilities.) What risks might Abbott Laboratories face that are not revealed on the face of its balance sheet?

Abbott Laboratories, Inc. (ABT)

TAP Pharmaceutical Products Inc.

E11-27. Analyzing, Forecasting, and Interpreting Income Statement and Balance Sheet (LO2, 3)

Following are the income statement and balance sheet of Whole Foods Market, Inc.

WebAssign.

Whole Foods Market, Inc. (WFMI)

Income Statement, For Years Ended (in $ 000s)	2008	2007	2006
Sales	$7,953,912	$6,591,773	$5,607,376
Cost of goods sold and occupancy costs	5,247,207	4,295,170	3,647,734
Gross profit	2,706,705	2,296,603	1,959,642
Direct store expenses	2,107,940	1,711,229	1,421,968
General and administrative expenses	270,428	217,743	181,244
Pre-opening expenses	55,554	59,319	32,058
Relocation, store closures and lease termination costs	36,545	10,861	5,363
Operating income	236,238	297,451	319,009
Interest expense	(36,416)	(4,208)	(32)
Investment and other income	6,697	11,324	20,736
Income before income taxes	206,519	304,567	339,713
Provision for income taxes	91,995	121,827	135,885
Net income	$ 114,524	$ 182,740	$ 203,828

Balance Sheet (in $000s)*	2008	2007
Assets		
Cash and cash equivalents	$ 30,534	$ —
Restricted cash	617	2,310
Accounts receivable	115,424	105,209
Proceeds receivable for divestiture	—	165,054
Merchandise inventories	327,452	288,112
Prepaid expenses and other current assets	68,150	40,402
Deferred income taxes	80,429	66,899
Total current assets	622,606	667,986
Property and equipment	2,894,329	2,483,350
Accumulated depreciation	(994,212)	(816,791)
Property and equipment, net	1,900,117	1,666,559
Goodwill and intangible assets, net	738,058	766,533
Deferred income taxes	109,002	104,877
Other assets	10,953	7,173
Total assets	$3,380,736	$3,213,128

continued

continued from prior page

(in $000s)*	2008	2007
Liabilities and shareholders' equity		
Current installments of long-term debt and capital lease obligations	$ 380	$ 24,781
Accounts payable.	183,134	225,728
Accrued payroll, bonus and other benefits due team members	196,233	181,290
Dividends payable	—	25,060
Other current liabilities	286,430	315,491
Total current liabilities	666,177	772,350
Long-term debt and capital lease obligations, less current installments.	928,790	736,087
Deferred lease liabilities and other long-term liabilities	279,745	245,887
Total liabilities.	1,874,712	1,754,324
Shareholders' equity		
Common stock, no par value, 300,000 shares authorized, 140,286 and 143,787 shares issued, 140,286 and 139,240 shares outstanding in 2008 and 2007, respectively.	1,066,180	1,232,845
Common stock in treasury, at cost	—	(199,961)
Accumulated other comprehensive income.	422	15,722
Retained earnings	439,422	410,198
Total shareholders' equity	1,506,024	1,458,804
Total liabilities and shareholders' equity.	$3,380,736	$3,213,128

* Gross property and equipment and its accumulated depreciation are inserted in the balance sheet; both are taken from footnotes to financial statements. Goodwill and other intangible assets are combined, as are deferred lease liabilities and other long-term liabilities.

a. Forecast Whole Foods Market's 2009 income statement and balance sheet using the following relations; assume no change for all other accounts not listed below ($ 000s).

Sales growth.	20.7%
Gross profit margin.	34.0%
Direct store expenses/Sales.	26.5%
General and administrative expenses/Sales	3.4%
Pre-opening expenses/Sales	0.7%
Relocation, store closures and lease termination costs/Sales.	0.5%
Provision for income taxes/Income before income taxes	41.0%
Accounts receivable/Sales.	1.5%
Merchandise inventories/Sales	4.1%
Capital expenditures/Sales	6.6%
Depreciation/Prior year property and equipment, gross	9.8%
Amortization/Prior year goodwill and intangible assets.	0.8%
Accounts payable/Sales.	2.3%
Accrued payroll, bonus and other benefits due team members/Sales	2.5%
Dividends	$109,072
Installments of long-term debt and capital lease obligations, due in 2009 and 2010 . . .	$0

b. What does the forecasted cash balance from part *a* reveal to us about the forecasted financing needs of the company? Whole Foods reported that its long-term debt was downgraded in 2008. What insight do your forecasts provide for reasons for this downgrade?

E11-28 **Forecasting the Statement of Cash Flows** **(LO4)**

Whole Foods Market, Inc. (WFMI)

Refer to the Whole Foods Market, Inc., financial information from Exercise 11-27. Prepare a forecast of its fiscal year 2009 statement of cash flows.

E11-29. **Projecting NOPAT and NOA Using Parsimonious Forecasting Method** **(LO6)**

Intel (INTC)

Following are Intel's sales, net operating profit after tax (NOPAT), and net operating assets (NOA) for its year ended December 31, 2007 ($ millions).

Sales.	$38,334
Net operating profit after tax (NOPAT)	6,364
Net operating assets (NOA)	31,443

Forecast Intel's sales, NOPAT and NOA for years 2008 through 2011 using the following assumptions:

Sales growth per year.	8.3%
Net operating profit margin (NOPM).	16.6%
Net operating asset turnover (NOAT), based on NOA at December 31, 2007.	1.22

E11-30. Projecting NOPAT and NOA Using Parsimonious Forecasting Method (LO6)

Following are 3M's sales, net operating profit after tax (NOPAT), and net operating assets (NOA) for its fiscal year ended 2007 ($ millions).

Web**Assign**.

3M Co. (MMM)

Sales.	$24,462
Net operating profit after tax (NOPAT)	4,201
Net operating assets (NOA)	15,310

Forecast 3M's sales, NOPAT and NOA for fiscal years 2008 through 2011 using the following assumptions:

Sales growth per year.	6.7%
Net operating profit margin (NOPM).	17.2%
Net operating asset turnover (NOAT), based on NOA at 2007 fiscal year-end.	1.60

PROBLEMS

P11-31. Forecasting the Income Statement, Balance Sheet, and Statement of Cash Flows (LO2, 3, 4)

Following are fiscal year financial statements of Oracle Corporation.

Oracle Corporation (ORCL)

Consolidated Balance Sheets		
May 31 (in millions, except per share data)*	2008	2007
Assets		
Cash and cash equivalents	$ 8,262	$ 6,218
Marketable securities	2,781	802
Trade and other receivables, net	5,799	4,589
Deferred tax assets	853	968
Prepaid expenses and other current assets.	408	306
Total current assets.	18,103	12,883
Property	3,640	3,459
Accumulated depreciation	(1,952)	(1,856)
Property, net	1,688	1,603
Goodwill, intangible assets, and other assets, net.	27,477	20,086
Total noncurrent assets.	29,165	21,689
Total assets.	$47,268	$34,572
Liabilities and Stockholders' Equity		
Notes payable, current and other current borrowings	$ 1,001	$ 1,358
Accounts payable.	383	315
Income taxes payable	390	1,237
Accrued compensation and related benefits	1,770	1,349
Accrued restructuring.	308	201
Deferred revenues	4,492	3,492
Other current liabilities.	1,685	1,435
Total current liabilities.	10,029	9,387

continued

continued from prior page

May 31 (in millions, except per share data)*	2008	2007
Noncurrent liabilities		
Notes payable and other noncurrent borrowings...............	10,235	6,235
Deferred tax liabilities and income taxes payable	2,784	1,121
Accrued restructuring.......................................	260	258
Deferred revenues	262	93
Other long-term liabilities...................................	673	559
Total noncurrent liabilities................................	14,214	8,266
Stockholders' equity		
Preferred stock, $0.01 par value—authorized: 1.0 shares; outstanding: none.......................................	—	—
Common stock, $0.01 par value and additional paid in capital—authorized: 11,000 shares; outstanding: 5,150 shares and 5,107 shares as of May 31, 2008 and 2007	12,446	10,293
Retained earnings	9,961	6,223
Accumulated other comprehensive income....................	618	403
Total stockholders' equity.................................	23,025	16,919
Total liabilities and stockholders' equity......................	$47,268	$34,572

* Gross property and its accumulated depreciation are inserted in the balance sheet; both are taken from footnotes to financial statements. The balance sheet combines the following line items from the 10-K filing for brevity:

- Trade receivables with Other receivables
- Intangible assets with Software support agreements, Intangible assets, net, Goodwill, and Other assets
- Deferred tax liabilities with Income taxes payable

Consolidated Statements of Operations			
Year ended May 31 (in millions)	2008	2007	2006
Total revenues*.................................	$22,430	$17,996	$14,380
Operating expenses			
Sales and marketing..........................	4,679	3,907	3,177
Software license updates and product support	997	842	719
Cost of services	3,984	3,349	2,516
Research and development	2,741	2,195	1,872
General and administrative.....................	808	692	555
Amortization of intangible assets	1,212	878	583
Acquisition related and other	124	140	137
Restructuring	41	19	85
Total operating expenses.........................	14,586	12,022	9,644
Operating income...............................	7,844	5,974	4,736
Interest expense...............................	(394)	(343)	(169)
Nonoperating income, net	384	355	243
Income before provision for income taxes...........	7,834	5,986	4,810
Provision for income taxes.......................	2,313	1,712	1,429
Net income....................................	$ 5,521	$ 4,274	$ 3,381

* Total revenues is a combination of New software licenses revenues, Software license updates and product support revenues, and Software revenues.

Year Ended May 31 ($ millions)	2008	2007	2006
Cash Flows From Operating Activities			
Net income	$5,521	$4,274	$3,381
Adjustments to reconcile net income to net cash provided by operating activities:			
Depreciation	268	249	223
Amortization of intangible assets	1,212	878	583
Provision for trade receivable allowances	164	244	241
Deferred income taxes	(135)	(56)	(40)
Minority interests in income	60	71	41
Stock-based compensation	369	207	49
Tax benefits on the exercise of stock awards	588	338	162
Excess tax benefits from stock-based compensation	(454)	(259)	—
In-process research and development	24	151	78
Other gains, net	(66)	(22)	(39)
Changes in assets and liabilities, net of effects from acquisitions:			
Increase in trade receivables	(825)	(723)	(355)
(Increase) decrease in prepaid expenses and other assets	(191)	(153)	14
Increase (decrease) in accounts payable and other liabilities	(153)	(345)	23
Increase (decrease) in income taxes payable	368	279	(98)
Increase in deferred revenues	652	387	278
Net cash provided by operating activities	7,402	5,520	4,541
Cash Flows From Investing Activities			
Purchases of marketable securities and other investments	(5,624)	(5,405)	(2,986)
Proceeds from maturities and sales of marketable securities and other investments	4,281	5,756	3,676
Acquisitions, net of cash acquired	(7,643)	(5,005)	(3,953)
Capital expenditures	(243)	(319)	(236)
Proceeds from sale of property	153	2	140
Net cash used for investing activities	(9,076)	(4,971)	(3,359)
Cash Flows From Financing Activities			
Payments for repurchases of common stock	(2,023)	(3,937)	(2,067)
Proceeds from issuances of common stock	1,288	924	632
Proceeds from borrowings, net of issuance costs	6,171	4,079	12,636
Repayments of borrowings	(2,560)	(2,418)	(9,635)
Excess tax benefits from stock-based compensation	454	259	—
Distributions to minority interests	(49)	(46)	(39)
Net cash provided by (used for) financing activities	3,281	(1,139)	1,527
Effect of exchange rate changes on cash and cash equivalents	437	149	56
Net increase (decrease) in cash and cash equivalents	2,044	(441)	2,765
Cash and cash equivalents at beginning of period	6,218	6,659	3,894
Cash and cash equivalents at end of period	$8,262	$6,218	$6,659

Required

Forecast Oracle's 2009 income statement, balance sheet, and statement of cash flows; round forecasts to $ millions. (*Note*: Oracle's long-term debt footnote reports that current maturities of long-term debt are $1.0 billion for May 2009; Oracle includes the current maturities with "Notes payable, current and other current borrowings" on its balance sheet. Oracle reports it has "not paid cash dividends and does not anticipate declaring cash dividends on common stock.") Identify all financial statement relations estimated and assumptions made; estimate forecasted income statement relations to 1 decimal (assume no change for: interest expense, nonoperating income, marketable securities, deferred tax assets and liabilities, prepaid expenses, accrued restructuring noncurrent liability, deferred revenues noncurrent liability, other long-term liabilities, common stock, additional paid-in capital, and accumulated other comprehensive income). What do the forecasts imply about the financing needs of Oracle?

P11-32. Forecasting the Income Statement, Balance Sheet, and Statement of Cash Flows (LO2, 3, 4)
Following are the financial statements of Nike, Inc.

Web**Assign**

Nike, Inc. (NKE)

Consolidated Statements of Income			
Year ended May 31 (in millions)	2008	2007	2006
Revenues	$18,627.0	$16,325.9	$14,954.9
Cost of sales.	10,239.6	9,165.4	8,367.9
Gross margin	8,387.4	7,160.5	6,587.0
Selling and administrative expense	5,953.7	5,028.7	4,477.8
Interest income, net	77.1	67.2	36.8
Other (expense) income, net	(7.9)	0.9	(4.4)
Income before income taxes	2,502.9	2,199.9	2,141.6
Income taxes	619.5	708.4	749.6
Net Income.	$ 1,883.4	$ 1,491.5	$ 1,392.0

Consolidated Balance Sheets		
May 31 (in millions, except share data)*	2008	2007
Assets		
Cash and equivalents.	$ 2,133.9	$ 1,856.7
Short-term investments	642.2	990.3
Accounts receivable, net	2,795.3	2,494.7
Inventories	2,438.4	2,121.9
Deferred income taxes	227.2	219.7
Prepaid expenses and other current assets.	602.3	393.2
Total current assets.	8,839.3	8,076.5
Property, plant and equipment.	4,103.0	3,619.1
Accumulated depreciation	(2,211.9)	(1,940.8)
Property, plant and equipment, net	1,891.1	1,678.3
Goodwill and identifiable intangible assets (net)	1,191.9	540.7
Deferred income taxes and other assets	520.4	392.8
Total assets.	$12,442.7	$10,688.3
Liabilities and Shareholders' Equity		
Current portion of long-term debt	$ 6.3	$ 30.5
Notes payable	177.7	100.8
Accounts payable.	1,287.6	1,040.3
Accrued liabilities	1,761.9	1,303.4
Income taxes payable	88.0	109.0
Total current liabilities	3,321.5	2,584.0
Long-term debt	441.1	409.9
Deferred income taxes and other liabilities	854.5	668.7
Redeemable preferred stock	0.3	0.3
Shareholders' equity:		
Common stock at stated value, Class A and Class B	2.8	2.8
Capital in excess of stated value	2,497.8	1,960.0
Accumulated other comprehensive income.	251.4	177.4
Retained earnings	5,073.3	4,885.2
Total shareholders' equity.	7,825.3	7,025.4
Total liabilities and shareholders' equity.	$12,442.7	$10,688.3

* Gross property and its accumulated depreciation are inserted in the balance sheet; both are taken from footnotes to financial statements. Goodwill and identifiable intangible assets are combined, as are Class A and Class B common stock.

Required

Forecast Nike's fiscal year 2009 income statement, balance sheet, and statement of cash flows; round forecasts to one-tenth $ millions. Identify all financial statement relations estimated and assumptions made; estimate forecasted income statement relations to 1 decimal (assume no change for: interest income, other expense or income, short-term investments, notes payable, redeemable preferred stock, common stock, capital in excess of stated value, and accumulated other comprehensive income). For 2008, capital expenditures are $449.2 million, depreciation expense is $303.6 million, amortization is $17.9 million, and dividends are $412.9 million. Footnotes reveal that the current portion on long-term debt due in 2010 is $31.3 million. What do the forecasts imply about Nike's financing needs for the upcoming year?

P11-33. Two-Year-Ahead Forecasting of Financial Statements (LO5)

Following are the financial statements of Cisco Systems, Inc.

Cisco Systems, Inc. (CSCO)

Consolidated Balance Sheets		
($ millions)*	July 26, 2008	July 28, 2007
Assets		
Cash and cash equivalents	$ 5,191	$ 3,728
Investments	21,044	18,538
Accounts receivable, net of allowance for doubtful accounts of $177 at July 26, 2008, and $166 at July 28, 2007	3,821	3,989
Inventories	1,235	1,322
Deferred tax assets, prepaid expenses and other current assets	4,408	3,997
Total current assets	35,699	31,574
Property and equipment	11,702	10,466
Accumulated depreciation	(7,551)	(6,573)
Property and equipment, net	4,151	3,893
Goodwill and purchased intangible assets (net)	14,481	14,661
Other assets	4,403	3,212
Total assets	$58,734	$53,340
Liabilities and Shareholders' Equity		
Current portion of long-term debt	$ 500	$ —
Accounts payable	869	786
Income taxes payable	107	1,740
Accrued compensation	2,428	2,019
Deferred revenue	6,197	5,391
Other current liabilities	3,757	3,422
Total current liabilities	13,858	13,358
Long-term debt	6,393	6,408
Deferred revenue	2,663	1,646
Income taxes payable and other long-term liabilities	1,418	438
Total liabilities	24,332	21,850
Minority interest	49	10
Shareholders' equity		
Preferred stock, no par value: 5 shares authorized; none issued and outstanding	—	—
Common stock and additional paid-in capital, $0.001 par value: 20,000 shares authorized: 5,893 and 6,100 shares issued and outstanding at July 26, 2008, and July 28, 2007, respectively	33,505	30,687
Retained earnings	120	231
Accumulated other comprehensive income	728	562
Total shareholders' equity	34,353	31,480
Total liabilities and shareholders' equity	$58,734	$53,340

* Gross property and its accumulated depreciation are inserted in the balance sheet; both are taken from footnotes to financial statements. The balance sheet combines the following line items from the 10-K filing for brevity:
• Deferred tax assets with Prepaid expenses and other current assets
• Goodwill with Purchased intangible assets, net
• Noncurrent taxes payable with Other long-term liabilities

Consolidated Statements of Operations

Year ended ($ millions)*	July 26, 2008	July 28, 2007	July 29, 2006
Total net sales.	$39,540	$34,922	$28,484
Total cost of sales.	14,056	12,586	9,737
Gross margin	25,484	22,336	18,747
Operating expenses			
Research and development	5,153	4,499	4,067
Sales and marketing	8,380	7,215	6,031
General and administrative.	2,007	1,513	1,169
Amortization of purchased intangible assets, and in-process research and development	502	488	484
Total operating expenses	16,042	13,715	11,751
Operating income.	9,442	8,621	6,996
Interest income and other income, net.	813	840	637
Income before provision for income taxes.	10,255	9,461	7,633
Provision for income taxes.	2,203	2,128	2,053
Net income.	$ 8,052	$ 7,333	$ 5,580

* The statement here combines the following line items from the 10-K filing for brevity:
- Product sales with Service sales
- Cost of sales: products with Cost of sales: services
- Amortization of purchased intangible assets with In-process research and development
- Interest income, net, with Other income (loss), net

Consolidated Statements of Cash Flows

Year ended ($ millions)	July 26, 2008	July 28, 2007	July 29, 2006
Cash flows from operating activities			
Net income	$ 8,052	$ 7,333	$ 5,580
Adjustments to reconcile net income to net cash provided by operating activities:			
Depreciation and amortization	1,744	1,413	1,293
Employee share-based compensation expense.	1,025	931	1,050
Share-based compensation expense related to acquisitions and investments	87	34	87
Provision for doubtful accounts	34	6	24
Deferred income taxes	(772)	(622)	(343)
Excess tax benefits from share-based compensation	(413)	(918)	(432)
In-process research and development	3	81	91
Net gains and impairment charges on investments	(103)	(210)	(124)
Other	—	—	31
Change in operating assets and liabilities, net of effects of acquisitions:			
Accounts receivable	171	(597)	(913)
Inventories	104	61	121
Lease receivables, net.	(488)	(156)	(171)
Accounts payable	62	(107)	(43)
Income taxes payable and receivable.	178	1,104	743
Accrued compensation	351	479	150
Deferred revenue.	1,812	1,293	575
Other assets	(361)	(452)	(300)
Other liabilities.	603	431	480
Net cash provided by operating activities	12,089	10,104	7,899
Cash flows from investing activities			
Purchases of investments.	(22,399)	(20,532)	(21,732)
Proceeds from sales and maturities of investments.	19,990	17,368	18,480
Acquisition of property and equipment.	(1,268)	(1,251)	(772)
Acquisition of businesses, net of cash and cash equivalents acquired	(398)	(3,684)	(5,399)
Change in investments in privately held companies.	(101)	(92)	(186)
Purchase of minority interest of Cisco Systems, K.K. (Japan)	—	—	(25)
Other.	(17)	(151)	(10)
Net cash used in investing activities	(4,193)	(8,342)	(9,644)

continued

continued from prior page

Year ended ($ millions)	July 26, 2008	July 28, 2007	July 29, 2006
Cash flows from financing activities			
Issuance of common stock....................................	3,117	5,306	1,682
Repurchase of common stock	(10,441)	(7,681)	(8,295)
Issuance of debt...	—	—	6,481
Proceeds from the termination of interest rate swaps	432	—	—
Excess tax benefits from share-based compensation	413	918	432
Other...	46	126	—
Net cash (used in) provided by financing activities	(6,433)	(1,331)	300
Net increase (decrease) in cash and cash equivalents	1,463	431	(1,445)
Cash and cash equivalents, beginning of fiscal year........................	3,728	3,297	4,742
Cash and cash equivalents, end of fiscal year.....................	$ 5,191	$ 3,728	$ 3,297

The following is a breakdown of its depreciation and amortization expense.

($ millions)	2008	2007
Depreciation[1]	$1,012	$850
Amortization[2]	732	563

[1] Depreciation is included in various operating expense accounts including Cost of sales and Research and development.

[2] Amortization expense is recorded, in part, on the income statement as a separate line item, and the remainder is included in other operating expenses.

Cisco provides the following footnote disclosures relating to its stock purchase program.

Stock Repurchase Program In September 2001, our Board of Directors authorized a stock repurchase program. As of July 26, 2008, our Board of Directors had authorized an aggregate repurchase of up to $62 billion of common stock under this program and the remaining authorized repurchase amount was $8.4 billion with no termination date. The stock repurchase activity under the stock repurchase program in fiscal 2007 and 2008 is summarized as follows (in millions, except per-share amounts):

	Shares Repurchased	Weighted-Average Price per Share	Amount Repurchased
Cumulative balance at July 29, 2006.....	1,931	$18.36	$35,448
Repurchase of common stock [(1)]	297	26.12	7,781
Cumulative balance at July 28, 2007 ...	2,228	$19.40	$43,229
Repurchase of common stock [(1)]	372	27.80	10,350
Cumulative balance at July 26, 2008 ...	2,600	$20.60	$53,579

(1) Includes stock repurchases that were pending settlement as of period end.

The purchase price for the shares of our common stock repurchased is reflected as a reduction to shareholders' equity. In accordance with Accounting Principles Board Opinion No. 6, "Status of Accounting Research Bulletins," we are required to allocate the purchase price of the repurchased shares as (i) a reduction to retained earnings until retained earnings are zero and then as an increase to accumulated deficit and (ii) a reduction of common stock and additional paid-in capital. Issuance of common stock and the tax benefit related to employee stock incentive plans are recorded as an increase to common stock and additional paid-in capital. As a result of future repurchases, we may report an accumulated deficit as a component in shareholders' equity.

Required

Forecast Cisco's 2009 *and* 2010 income statements, balance sheets, and statements of cash flows; round forecasts to $ millions. Using the same forecasting assumptions for both years; estimate forecasted income statement relations to 1 decimal (assume no change for: deferred tax and prepaid assets, other assets, other current liabilities, long-term debt, deferred revenue, long-term debt, long-term income taxes payable and other long-term liabilities, minority interest, common stock and additional paid-in capital, and accumulated other comprehensive income). Cisco's long-term debt footnote indicates no maturities of long-term debt until 2011. Forecast an increase in interest income from investment of any excess cash, whether included in cash and cash equivalents or in marketable securities, under the assumption that any excess cash is invested whether or not separately classified as investments on the balance sheet. What investment or financing assumptions are required for forecasting purposes? (*Hint:* Consider Cisco's stock repurchase footnote.) What is our assessment of Cisco's financial condition over the next two years?

WebAssign.

Staples, Inc. (SPLS)

P11-34   Two-Year-Ahead Forecasting of Financial Statements   (LO5)

Following are the financial statements of Staples, Inc.

Consolidated Balance Sheets		
($ thousands)	February 2, 2008	February 3, 2007
Assets*		
Cash and cash equivalents	$1,245,448	$1,017,671
Short-term investments	27,016	457,759
Receivables, net	822,254	720,797
Merchandise inventories, net	2,053,163	1,919,714
Deferred income tax asset, prepaid expenses, and other current assets	407,501	315,422
Total current assets	4,555,382	4,431,363
Property and equipment		
Land and buildings	859,751	791,264
Leasehold improvements	1,135,132	996,434
Equipment	1,819,381	1,539,617
Furniture and fixtures	871,361	757,408
Total property and equipment	4,685,625	4,084,723
Less accumulated depreciation and amortization	2,524,486	2,110,602
Net property and equipment	2,161,139	1,974,121
Goodwill and other intangible assets, net	1,996,238	1,687,496
Other assets and lease acquisition costs, net	323,585	304,285
Total assets	$9,036,344	$8,397,265
Liabilities and Stockholders' Equity		
Accounts payable	$1,560,728	$1,486,188
Accrued expenses and other current liabilities	1,025,364	1,087,030
Debt maturing within one year	23,806	215,165
Total current liabilities	2,609,898	2,788,383
Long-term debt	342,169	316,465
Other long-term obligations	356,043	261,643
Stockholders' Equity		
Preferred stock, $0.01 par value, 5,000,000 shares authorized; no shares issued	—	—
Common stock, $0.0006 par value, 2,100,000,000 shares authorized; issued 867,366,103 shares at February 2, 2008, and 849,338,568 shares at February 3, 2007	520	510
Additional paid-in capital	3,720,319	3,338,412
Cumulative foreign currency translation adjustments and other	486,626	198,224
Retained earnings	4,793,542	4,005,424
Less: treasury stock at cost, 162,728,588 shares at February 2, 2008, and 130,605,591 shares at February 3, 2007	(3,272,773)	(2,511,796)
Total stockholders' equity	5,728,234	5,030,774
Total liabilities and stockholders' equity	$9,036,344	$8,397,265

* The balance sheet combines the following line items from the 10-K filing for brevity:
  • Deferred income tax asset with Prepaid expenses and other current assets
  • Goodwill with Intangible assets, net of accumulated amortization
  • Lease acquisition costs, net of accumulated amortization with Other assets (noncurrent)
  • Cumulative foreign currency translation adjustments with Minority interest

Consolidated Statements of Income

Fiscal Year Ended ($ thousands)	February 2, 2008	February 3, 2007	January 28, 2006
Sales.	$19,372,682	$18,160,789	$16,078,852
Cost of goods sold and occupancy costs	13,822,011	12,966,788	11,496,234
Gross profit	5,550,671	5,194,001	4,582,618
Operating and other expenses			
Operating and selling	3,131,774	2,946,249	2,647,567
General and administrative	854,984	770,268	687,962
Amortization of intangibles	15,664	14,415	13,008
Total operating expenses	4,002,422	3,730,932	3,348,537
Operating income	1,548,249	1,463,069	1,234,081
Other income (expense)*	7,035	8,580	920
Income before income taxes	1,555,284	1,471,649	1,235,001
Income tax expense	559,614	497,972	450,884
Net income	$ 995,670	$ 973,677	$ 784,117

* This line item combines the following line items from the 10-K filing for brevity: Interest income and Interest expense with Miscellaneous expense and with Minority interests.

Consolidated Statements of Cash Flows

Fiscal Year Ended ($ thousands)	February 2, 2008	February 3, 2007	January 28, 2006
Operating activities			
Net income	$ 995,670	$ 973,677	$ 784,117
Adjustments to reconcile net income to net cash provided by operating activities:			
Depreciation and amortization	388,895	339,299	303,900
Stock-based compensation	173,343	168,736	129,806
Deferred income tax benefit	(8,788)	(65,401)	(96,189)
Excess tax benefits from stock-based compensation arrangements	(18,557)	(36,069)	(36,748)
Other	4,831	(365)	(6,513)
Change in assets and liabilities, net of companies acquired:			
Increase in receivables	(64,293)	(128,010)	(80,166)
Increase in merchandise inventories	(30,175)	(191,957)	(97,538)
Increase in prepaid expenses and other assets	(89,558)	(44,298)	(15,646)
Increase in accounts payable	295	34,379	187,402
(Decrease) increase in accrued expenses and other current liabilities	(90,054)	79,187	105,274
Increase in other long-term obligations	99,407	21,823	20,922
Net cash provided by operating activities	1,361,016	1,151,001	1,198,621
Investing activities			
Acquisition of property and equipment	(470,377)	(528,475)	(456,103)
Acquisition of businesses and investments in joint ventures, net of cash acquired	(178,077)	(31,750)	(57,196)
Proceeds from the sale of short-term investments	4,579,460	8,358,384	8,097,199
Purchase of short-term investments	(4,148,716)	(8,223,063)	(8,218,049)
Net cash used in investing activities	(217,710)	(424,904)	(634,149)

continued

continued from prior page

Fiscal Year Ended ($ thousands)	February 2, 2008	February 3, 2007	January 28, 2006
Financing activities			
Proceeds from the exercise of stock options and the sale of stock under employee stock purchase plans	178,504	195,263	181,997
Proceeds from borrowings	11,796	13,988	535
Payments on borrowings	(206,515)	(5,191)	(16,735)
Cash dividends paid	(207,552)	(160,883)	(123,402)
Excess tax benefits from stock-based compensation arrangements	18,557	36,069	36,748
Purchase of treasury stock, net	(760,977)	(775,822)	(663,145)
Net cash used in financing activities	(966,187)	(696,576)	(584,002)
Effect of exchange rate changes on cash	50,658	10,328	42
Net increase (decrease) in cash and cash equivalents	227,777	39,849	(19,488)
Cash and cash equivalents at beginning of period	1,017,671	977,822	997,310
Cash and cash equivalents at end of period	$1,245,448	$1,017,671	$ 977,822

The following is a breakdown of 2008 depreciation and amortization expense ($ thousands).

Depreciation	$373,595
Amortization	15,300

Staples provides the following footnote disclosures relating to its stock purchase program.

Stockholders' Equity In fiscal 2007, the Company repurchased 31.6 million shares of the Company's common stock for a total purchase price (including commissions) of $750.0 million under the Company's 2005 and 2007 share repurchase programs. The 2007 share repurchase program replaced the 2005 $1.5 billion share repurchase program (the "2005 Share Repurchase Program") and went into effect during the second quarter of 2007. The 2007 share repurchase program allows for the repurchase of $1.5 billion of Staples common stock and has no expiration date. In 2006, the Company repurchased 30.3 million shares of the Company's common stock for a total purchase price (including commissions) of $749.9 million. In 2005, the Company repurchased 30.1 million shares of the Company's common stock for a total purchase price (including commissions) of $649.6 million.

Required

Forecast Staples' 2009 *and* 2010 income statements, balance sheets, and statements of cash flow; round forecasts to $ thousands. Use the same forecasting assumptions for both years; estimate forecasted income statement relations to 1 decimal (assume no change for: other assets, other long-term obligations, common stock, additional paid-in capital, and accumulated other comprehensive income). Staples' long-term debt footnote indicates maturities of $4,023 thousand in 2010, and maturities of $2,601 thousand in 2011. Forecast an increase in interest income from investment of any excess cash, whether included in cash and cash equivalents or in marketable securities, under the assumption that any excess cash is invested whether or not separately classified as investments on the balance sheet. What investment or financing assumptions are required for forecasting purposes? (*Hint:* Consider Staples' stock repurchase footnote.) What is our assessment of Staples' financial condition over the next two years?

MANAGEMENT APPLICATIONS

MA11-35. Adjusting the Income Statement Prior to Forecasting **(LO1, 2)**

CBS Corporation (CBS)

Following is the income statement of CBS Corporation, along with an excerpt from its MD&A section.

Income Statement

Year ended December 31 ($ millions)	2005	2004	2003
Revenues	$14,536.4	$14,547.3	$13,554.5
Expenses			
Operating	8,671.8	8,643.6	8,165.4
Selling, general and administrative	2,699.4	2,552.5	2,376.1
Impairment charges	9,484.4	17,997.1	—
Depreciation and amortization	498.7	508.6	501.7
Total expenses	21,354.3	29,701.8	11,043.2
Operating income (loss)	$ (6,817.9)	$(15,154.5)	$ 2,511.3

Operating Expenses: Table below presents consolidated operating expenses by type

Operating expenses by type Year ended December 31	2005	2004	Increase (Decrease) 2005 vs. 2004		2003	Increase (Decrease) 2004 vs. 2003	
Programming	$3,453.2	$3,441.8	$ 11.4	—%	$3,080.3	$361.5	12%
Production	2,453.5	2,584.7	(131.2)	(5)	2,661.9	(77.2)	(3)
Outdoor operations	1,134.2	1,102.7	31.5	3	1,012.6	90.1	9
Publishing operations	525.0	517.6	7.4	1	486.3	31.3	6
Parks operations	243.8	232.7	11.1	5	212.2	20.5	10
Other	862.1	764.1	98.0	13	712.1	52.0	7
Total operating expenses	$8,671.8	$8,643.6	$ 28.2	—%	$8,165.4	$478.2	6%

For 2005, operating expenses of $8.67 billion increased slightly over $8.64 billion in 2004. For 2004, operating expenses of $8.64 billion increased 6% over $8.17 billion in 2003. The major components and changes in operating expenses were as follows:

- Programming expenses represented approximately 40% of total operating expenses in 2005 and 2004 and 38% in 2003, and reflect the amortization of acquired rights of programs exhibited on the broadcast and cable networks, and television and radio stations. Programming expenses increased slightly to $3.45 billion in 2005 from $3.44 billion in 2004 principally reflecting higher costs for Showtime Networks theatrical titles. Programming expenses increased 12% to $3.44 billion in 2004 from $3.08 billion in 2003 reflecting higher program rights expenses for sports events and primetime series at the broadcast networks.
- Production expenses represented approximately 28% of total operating expenses in 2005, 30% in 2004, and 33% in 2003, and reflect the cost and amortization of internally developed television programs, including direct production costs, residuals and participation expenses, and production overhead, as well as television and radio costs including on-air talent and other production costs. Production expenses decreased 5% to $2.45 billion in 2005 from $2.58 billion in 2004 principally reflecting lower network costs due to the absence of *Frasier* partially offset by increased costs for new network series. Production expenses decreased 3% to $2.58 billion in 2004 from $2.66 billion in 2003 reflecting fewer network series produced in 2004 partially offset by higher news costs for political campaign coverage.
- Outdoor operations costs represented approximately 13% of total operating expenses in 2005 and 2004, and 12% in 2003, and reflect transit and billboard lease, maintenance, posting and rotation expenses. Outdoor operations expenses increased 3% to $1.13 billion in 2005 from $1.10 billion in 2004 principally reflecting higher billboard lease costs and maintenance costs associated with the impact of hurricanes in 2005. Outdoor operations costs increased 9% to $1.10 billion in 2004 from $1.01 billion in 2003 primarily reflecting higher transit and billboard lease costs.
- Publishing operations costs, which represented approximately 6% of total operating expenses in each of the years 2005, 2004 and 2003, reflect cost of book sales, royalties and other costs incurred with respect to publishing operations. Publishing operations expenses

continued

continued from prior page

for 2005 increased 1% to $525.0 million and increased 6% to $517.6 million in 2004 from $486.3 million in 2003 primarily due to higher revenues.

- Parks operations costs, which represented approximately 3% of total operating expenses in each of the years 2005, 2004 and 2003, increased 5% to $243.8 million in 2005 from $232.7 million in 2004 principally reflecting the cost of fourth quarter 2005 winter events held at the parks and the impact of foreign currency translation. In 2004, Parks operations costs increased 10% to $232.7 million from $212.2 million in 2003 primarily from the impact of foreign currency translation.

- Other operating expenses, which represented approximately 10% of total operating expenses in 2005 and 9% in 2004 and 2003, primarily include distribution costs incurred with respect to television product, costs associated with digital media and compensation. Other operating expenses increased 13% to $862.1 million in 2005 from $764.1 million in 2004 primarily reflecting a 10% increase in distribution costs due to the DVD release of *Charmed* and increased costs associated with digital media from the inclusion of SportsLine.com, Inc. ("SportsLine.com") since its acquisition in December 2004. Other operating expenses for 2004 increased 7% to $764.1 million in 2004 from $712.1 million in 2003 principally reflecting 15% higher distribution costs due to additional volume of DVD releases of the *Star Trek* series and higher compensation.

Impairment Charges   SFAS 142 requires the Company to perform an annual fair value-based impairment test of goodwill. The Company performed its annual impairment test as of October 31, 2005, concurrently with its annual budgeting process which begins in the fourth quarter each year. The first step of the test examines whether or not the book value of each of the Company's reporting units exceeds its fair value. If the book value for a reporting unit exceeds its fair value, the second step of the test is required to compare the implied fair value of that reporting unit's goodwill with the book value of the goodwill. The Company's reporting units are generally consistent with or one level below the operating segments underlying the reportable segments. As a result of the 2005 annual impairment test, the Company recorded an impairment charge of $9.48 billion in the fourth quarter of 2005. The $9.48 billion reflects charges to reduce the carrying value of goodwill at the CBS Television reporting unit of $6.44 billion and the Radio reporting unit of $3.05 billion. As a result of the annual impairment test performed for 2004, the Company recorded an impairment charge of $18.0 billion in the fourth quarter of 2004. The $18.0 billion reflects charges to reduce the carrying value of goodwill at the Radio reporting unit of $10.94 billion and the Outdoor reporting unit of $7.06 billion as well as the reduction of the carrying value of intangible assets of $27.8 million related to the FCC licenses at the Radio segment. Several factors led to a reduction in forecasted cash flows and long-term growth rates for both the Radio and Outdoor reporting units. Radio and Outdoor both fell short of budgeted revenue and operating income growth targets in 2004. Competition from other advertising media, including Internet advertising and cable and broadcast television reduced Radio and Outdoor growth rates. Also, the emergence of new competitors and technologies necessitated a shift in management's strategy for the Radio and Outdoor businesses, including changes in composition of the sales force and operating management as well as increased levels of investment in marketing and promotion.

Required

Identify and explain any income statement line items over the past three years that you believe should be considered for potential adjustment in preparation for forecasting the income statement of CBS.

Module Twelve

Analyzing and Valuing Equity Securities

LEARNING OBJECTIVES

LO1 Identify equity valuation models and explain the information required to value equity securities. (p. 12-3)

LO2 Describe and apply the discounted free cash flow model to value equity securities. (p. 12-4)

LO3 Describe and apply the residual operating income model to value equity securities. (p. 12-8)

LO4 Explain how equity valuation models can aid managerial decisions. (p. 12-11)

JOHNSON & JOHNSON

Pharmaceutical companies have long been the growth stocks of choice for many investors. Their cash flows were steady and climbing, their stocks grew in value, and their growth appeared limitless as the population aged. Stockholders pushed growth by encouraging pharmaceuticals to acquire competitors, and they further promoted the marketing of existing drugs and the pursuit of new products. All looked rosy, and high profit margins fueled further expansion.

Meanwhile, many of these pharmaceutical companies sold off their lower-growth business segments such as those manufacturing and distributing medical instruments

and devices. For example, Pfizer sold off segments that manufactured surgical devices, heart valves, and orthopedic implants, while Eli Lilly sold off many of its medical device segments, including Guidant.

A few pharmaceutical companies bucked the trend to reorganize and consolidate. One of those was Johnson & Johnson (J&J). In contrast with the operating strategies of other pharmaceutical companies, J&J seemed to anticipate the gradual decline in pharmaceutical operating profits and steadily increased its investment in medical devices and instruments. The following graphics, using data from J&J's 10-K report, reflect these trends.

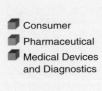

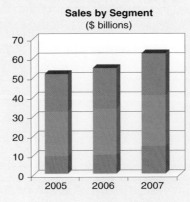

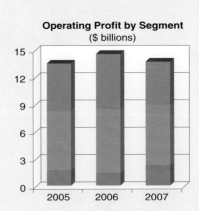

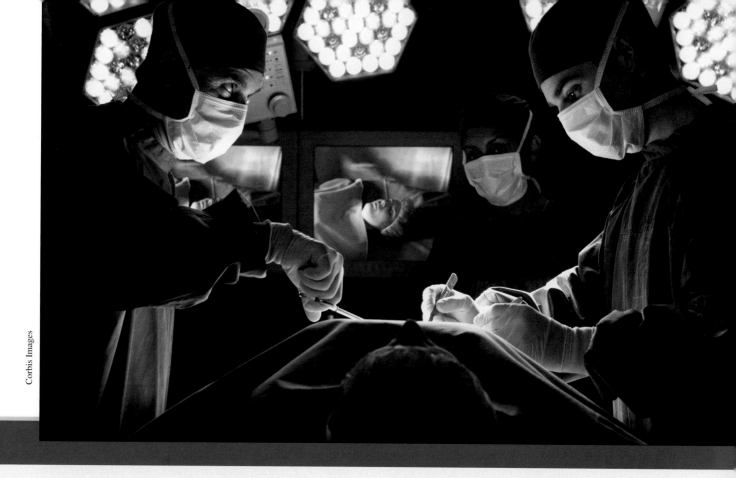

J&J's performance is holding steady while many other pharmaceutical companies are struggling. A drug-industry consultant asserts that J&J is ". . . casting a broader net for innovation, it's not just blockbuster drugs. They've held their value or grown, and the pure pharma plays that everyone thought could grow forever are the companies that have lost their luster."

Supported by its more diversified operations and fueled by a steady increase in operating profits, J&J's stock price has climbed since 2004, as shown here.

This raises several questions. What factors drive the J&J stock price? Why do analysts expect its price to continue to rise? How do accounting measures of performance and financial condition impact stock price? This module provides insights and answers to these questions. It explains how we can use forecasts of operating profits and cash flows to price equity securities such as J&J's stock.

Sources: *Johnson & Johnson* 2003-2007 10-K and Annual Reports; *The Wall Street Journal*, December 2004; *Fortune*, April 2009.

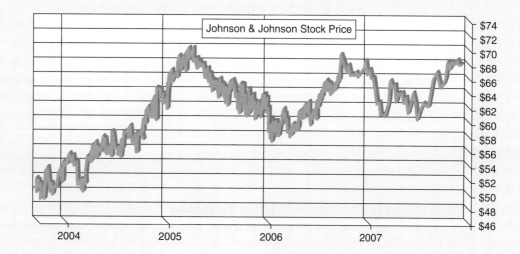

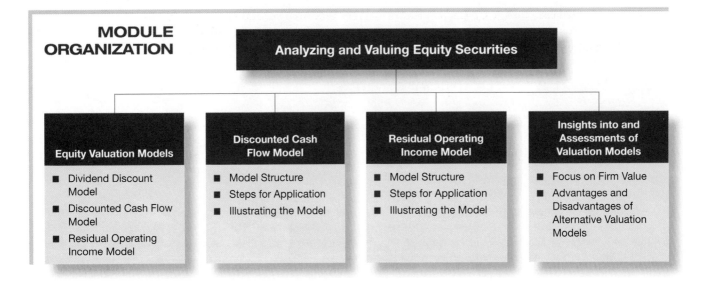

This module focuses on valuing equity securities (we explain the valuation of debt securities in Module 8). Specifically, we describe two approaches: the discounted free cash flow model (DCF) and residual operating income model (ROPI). We then conclude by discussing the management implications from an increased understanding of the factors that impact values of equity securities. It is important that we understand the determinants of equity value to make informed decisions. Employees at all levels of an organization, whether public or private, should understand the factors that create shareholder value so that they can work effectively toward that objective. For many senior managers, stock value serves as a scorecard. Successful managers are those who better understand the factors affecting that scorecard.

EQUITY VALUATION MODELS

LO1 Identify equity valuation models and explain the information required to value equity securities.

Module 8 explains that the value of a debt security is the present value of the interest and principal payments that the investor *expects* to receive in the future. The valuation of equity securities is similar in that it is also based on expectations. The difference lies in the increased uncertainty surrounding the timing and amount of payments from equity securities.

Dividend Discount Model

There are many equity valuation models in use today. Each of them defines the value of an equity security in terms of the present value of forecasted amounts. They differ primarily in terms of what is forecasted.

The basis of equity valuation is the premise that the value of an equity security is determined by the payments that the investor can expect to receive. Equity investments involve two types of payoffs: (1) dividends received during the holding period and (2) capital gains when the security is sold.[1] The value of an equity security is, then, based on the present value of expected dividends plus the present value of the security at the end of the forecasted holding period. This **dividend discount model** is appealing in its simplicity and its intuitive focus on dividend distribution. As a practical matter, however, the model is not always useful because many companies that have a positive stock price have never paid a dividend, and are not expected to pay a dividend in the foreseeable future.

Discounted Cash Flow Model

A more practical approach to valuing equity securities focuses on the company's operating and investing activities; that is, on the *generation* of cash rather than the *distribution* of cash. This approach is

---

[1] The future stock price is, itself, also assumed to be related to the expected dividends that the new investor expects to receive; as a result, the expected receipt of dividends is the sole driver of stock price under this type of valuation model.

called the **discounted cash flow (DCF)** model. The focus of the forecasting process for the DCF model is the company's expected *free cash flows to the firm*, which are defined as operating cash flows net of the expected new investments in net operating assets that are required to support the business.

Residual Operating Income Model

A second approach to equity valuation also focuses on operating and investing activities. It is known as the **residual operating income (ROPI)** model. This model uses both net operating profits after tax (NOPAT) and the net operating assets (NOA) to determine equity value; see Module 4 for complete descriptions of the NOPAT and NOA measures. This approach highlights the importance of return on net operating assets (RNOA), and the disaggregation of RNOA into net operating profit margin and NOA turnover. We discuss the implications of this insight for managers later in this module.

DISCOUNTED CASH FLOW (DCF) MODEL

The discounted cash flow (DCF) model defines firm value as follows:

Firm Value = Present Value of Expected Free Cash Flows to Firm

LO2 Describe and apply the discounted free cash flow model to value equity securities.

The expected free cash flows to the firm include cash flows arising from the operating side of the business; that is, cash generated from the firm's operating activities (but not from nonoperating activities such as interest paid on debt or dividends received on investments), and they do not include the cash flows from financing activities.

DCF Model Structure

Free cash flows to the firm (FCFF) equal net operating profit after tax that is not used to grow net operating assets. Using the terminology of Module 4 we can define FCFF as follows (see Business Insight box on next page for a more traditional definition):

FCFF = NOPAT − Increase in NOA

where

> **NOPAT = Net operating profit after tax**
> **NOA = Net operating assets**

Net operating profit after tax is normally positive and the net cash flows from increases in net operating assets are normally negative assuming that net operating assets increase each period. The sum of the two (positive or negative) represents the net cash flows available to creditors and shareholders. Positive FCFF imply that there are funds available for distribution to creditors and shareholders, either in the form of debt repayments, dividends, or stock repurchases (treasury stock). Negative FCFF imply that the firm requires additional funds from creditors and/or shareholders, in the form of new loans or equity investments, to support its business activities.

The DCF valuation model requires forecasts of *all* future free cash flows; that is, free cash flows for the remainder of the company's life. Generating an infinite stream of forecasts is not realistic. Consequently, analysts typically estimate FCFF over a horizon period, often 4 to 10 years, and then make simplifying assumptions about the FCFF subsequent to that horizon period.

MANAGERIAL DECISION | **You Are the Chief Financial Officer**

Assume that you are the CFO of a company that has a large investment in plant assets and sells its products on credit. Identify steps you can take to increase your company's cash flow and, hence, your company's firm value. [Answer p. 12-18]

BUSINESS INSIGHT Definitions of Free Cash Flow

We often see free cash flows to the firm (unlevered free cash flow) defined as follows:

FCFF = Net cash flow from operating activities − Capital expenditures

Although similar to the definition in this book, NOPAT − Increase in NOA, there are important differences:

■ Net cash flow from operating activities uses net income as the starting point; net income, of course, comingles both operating and nonoperating components (such as selling expense and interest expense). Analysts sometimes correct for this by adding back items such as after-tax net interest expense, which is the approach used by the Oppenheimer analysts in Appendix 12B.

■ Income tax expense (in net income) includes the effect of the interest tax shield (see Module 4); the usual NOPAT definition includes only the tax on operating income.

■ Net cash flow from operating activities also includes nonoperating items in working capital, such as changes in interest payable and dividends payable, as well as inflows from securitization of receivables (see Module 10); NOA focuses only on operating activities.

■ The FCFF definition in this box consists of net income, changes in working capital accounts, and capital expenditures; the usual NOA consists of changes in operating working capital accounts, capital expenditures, *and* changes in long-term operating liabilities.

We must be attentive to differences in definitions for free cash flow so that we understand the analytical choices we make and their implications to equity valuation. It also aids us in drawing proper inferences from analyst research reports that might apply different definitions of free cash flow.

Steps in Applying the DCF Model

Application of the DCF model to equity valuation involves five steps:

1. Forecast and discount FCFF for the **horizon period**.[2]
2. Forecast and discount FCFF for the post-horizon period, called **terminal period**.[3]
3. Sum the present values of the horizon and terminal periods to yield firm (enterprise) value.
4. Subtract net nonoperating obligations (NNO) from firm value to yield firm equity value. If NNO is positive, the usual case, we subtract it in step 4; if NNO is negative, we add it. (For most companies, NNO is positive because nonoperating liabilities exceed nonoperating assets.)
5. Divide firm equity value by the number of shares outstanding to yield stock value per share.

Illustrating the DCF Model

To illustrate, we apply the DCF model to Johnson & Johnson. J&J's recent financial statements are reproduced in Appendix 12A. Forecasted financials for J&J (forecast horizon of 2008–2011 and terminal period of 2012) are in Exhibit 12.1.[4] The forecasts (in bold) are for sales, NOPAT, and NOA. These forecasts assume an annual 6.0% sales growth during the horizon period, a terminal period sales

---

[2] When discounting FCFF, the appropriate discount rate (r_w) is the **weighted average cost of capital (WACC)**, where the weights are the relative percentages of debt (d) and equity (e) in the capital structure applied to the expected returns on debt (r_d) and equity (r_e), respectively: WACC $= r_w = (r_d \times \%$ of debt$) + (r_e \times \%$ of equity$)$.

[3] For an assumed growth, g, the terminal period (T) present value of FCFF in perpetuity (beyond the horizon period) is given by, $\frac{FCFF_T}{r_w - g}$, where $FCFF_T$ is the free cash flow to the firm for the terminal period, r_w is WACC, and g is the assumed long-term growth rate of those cash flows. The resulting amount is then discounted back to the present using the horizon-end-period discount factor.

[4] We use a four-period horizon in the text and assignments to simplify the exposition and to reduce the computational burden. In practice, analysts use spreadsheets to forecast future cash flows and value the equity security, and typically have a forecast horizon of seven to ten periods.

growth of 1%, net operating profit margin (NOPM) of 17%, and a year-end net operating asset turnover (NOAT) of 1.2 (which is the 2007 turnover rate based on year-end NOA; year-end amounts are used because we are forecasting year-end account balances, not average balances).[5,6]

EXHIBIT 12.1 Application of Discounted Cash Flow Model

(In millions, except per share values and discount factors)	2007	Horizon Period				Terminal Period
		2008	2009	2010	2011	
Sales (unrounded)	$ 61,095	**$64,760.70** (61,095 × 1.06)	**$68,646.34** (64,760.70 × 1.06)	**$72,765.12** (68,646.34 × 1.06)	**$77,131.03** (72,765.12 × 1.06)	**$77,902.34** (77,131.03 × 1.01)
Sales (rounded)	61,095	**64,761**	**68,646**	**72,765**	**77,131**	77,902
NOPAT*	10,478	**11,009**	**11,670**	**12,370**	**13,112**	13,243
NOA**	51,309	**53,968**	**57,205**	**60,638**	**64,276**	64,918
Increase in NOA		2,659	3,237	3,433	3,638	642
FCFF (NOPAT − Increase in NOA)		8,350	8,433	8,937	9,474	12,601
Discount factor [1/(1 + r_w)^t]‡		0.94340	0.89000	0.83962	0.79209	
Present value of horizon FCFF		7,877	7,505	7,504	7,504	
Cum present value of horizon FCFF	$ 30,390					
Present value of terminal FCFF	199,623					
Total firm value	230,013					
Less (plus) NNO†	7,990					
Firm equity value	$222,023					
Shares outstanding	2,840.2					
Stock value per share	$ 78.17					

*Given J&J's combined federal and state statutory tax rate of 37.1%, NOPAT for 2007 is computed as follows ($ millions): ($61,095 − $17,751 − $20,451 − $7,680 − $807 − $745 − $534) − ($2,707 − {0.371 × [$452 − $296]}) = $10,478. A note on rounding: To forecast sales, we multiply prior year's unrounded sales by (1 + Growth rate); this is done for the horizon and terminal periods. Then, we round each year's forecasted sales to whole units and use rounded sales to compute NOPAT and NOA, where both are rounded to whole units. At each successive step, we round the number to whole units before proceeding to the next step.

**NOA computations for 2007 follow ($ millions): ($80,954 − $1,545 − $2) − ($6,909 + $6,412 + $2,318 + $1,512 + $223 + $1,493 + $5,402 + $3,829) = $51,309.

†NNO is the difference between NOA and total shareholders' equity; in this case NNO ($ millions) = $51,309 − $43,319 = $7,990.

‡For simplification, present value computations use discount factors rounded to 5 decimal places.

The bottom line of Exhibit 12.1 is the estimated J&J equity value of $222,023 million, or a per share stock value of $78.17 (computed as $222,023/2,840.2 shares). The present value computations use a 6% WACC(r_w) as the discount rate.[7] Specifically, we obtain this stock valuation as follows:

1. **Compute present value of horizon period FCFF.** We compute the forecasted 2008 FCFF of $8,350 million from the forecasted 2008 NOPAT less the forecasted increase in 2008 NOA. The

---

[5] **NOPAT** equals revenues less operating expenses such as cost of goods sold, selling, general, and administrative expenses, and taxes. NOPAT excludes any interest revenue and interest expense and any gains or losses from financial investments. NOPAT reflects the operating side of the firm as opposed to nonoperating activities such as borrowing and security investment activities. **NOA** equals operating assets less operating liabilities. (See Module 4.)

[6] NOPAT and NOA are typically forecasted using the detailed forecasting procedures discussed in Module 11. In this module we use the parsimonious method to multiyear forecasting (see Module 11) to focus attention on the valuation process.

[7] The weighted average cost of capital (WACC) for J&J is computed using the following three-step process:

1. The cost of equity capital is given by the capital asset pricing model (CAPM): $r_e = r_f + \beta (r_m - r_f)$, where β is the beta of the stock (an estimate of stock price variability that is reported by several services such as Standard and Poors), r_f is the risk-free rate (commonly assumed as the 10-year treasury bond rate), and r_m is the expected return to the entire market. The expression $(r_m - r_f)$ is the "spread" of equities over the risk-free rate, often assumed to be around 5%. For J&J, given its beta of 0.54 and a 10-year treasury bond rate of 3.86% (r_f) as of February 26, 2008, r_e is estimated as 6.56%, computed as 3.86% + (0.54 × 5%).

2. Two alternative computations for pretax cost debt capital are: (1) Interest expense/Average interest-bearing debt, and (2) Weighted-average effective interest rate on debt. For the latter, J&J reports its 5.47% rate in footnote 6 to its 10-K, which we use. To obtain J&J's after-tax cost of debt capital, we multiply 5.47% by 1 − 0.371, where 37.1% is the federal and state statutory tax rate from its tax footnote, yielding 3.44% (J&J's after-tax cost of debt).

3. WACC is the weighted average of the cost of equity capital and the cost of debt capital. J&J capital structure is 82% equity and 18% debt. Thus, J&J's weighted average cost of capital is (82% × 6.56%) + (18% × 3.44%) = 6.0%.

present value of this $8,350 million as of 2007 is $7,877 million, computed as $8,350 million $\times$ 0.94340 (the present value factor for one year at 6%). Similarly, the present value of 2009 FCFF (two years from the current date) is $7,505 million, computed as $8,433 million $\times$ 0.89000, and so on through 2011. The sum of these present values (*cumulative present value*) is $30,390 million.

2. **Compute present value of terminal period FCFF.** The present value of the terminal period FCFF is $199,623 million, computed as $\dfrac{\left(\dfrac{\$12,601 \text{ million}}{0.06 - 0.01}\right)}{(1.06)^4}$, or ($12,601/0.05) $\times$ 0.79209.

3. **Compute firm equity value.** Sum present values from the horizon and terminal period FCFF to get firm (enterprise) value of $230,013 million. Subtract the value of J&J's net nonoperating obligations of $7,990 million to get firm equity value of $222,023. Dividing firm equity value by the 2,840.2 (computed as 3,119.8 − 279.6) million shares outstanding yields the estimated per share valuation of $78.17.

We perform this valuation as of February 26, 2008, which is the SEC filing date for J&J's 10-K. J&J's stock closed at $63.72 on February 26, 2008. Our valuation estimate of $78.17 indicates that the stock is undervalued as of that date. J&J's stock price peaked in September of 2008 at $72.22; by early 2009 its stock was trading at roughly $60. Although this represents a large stock price decline, it was far less severe than many other companies suffered during this recessionary period (analysts continued to recommend it as a BUY stock).

BUSINESS INSIGHT | **Analysts' Forecasts**

Estimates of earnings and cash flows are key to security valuation. Following are earnings estimates as of January 11, 2009, for Johnson & Johnson by Thomson First Call analysts' reports, a division of Thomson Financial™. The mean (consensus) EPS estimate for 2008 (current year) is $4.53 per share, with a high of $4.55 and a low of $4.50. For 2009 (slightly more than one year ahead), the mean (consensus) EPS estimate is $4.66, with a high of $4.76 and a low of $4.60. The estimated long-term growth rate for EPS (similar to our horizon period growth rate) is 9%, and the mean buy rating is 2.1, a BUY.

Period	Ending	Mean EPS Est.	High EPS Est.	Low EPS Est.	PE Est.
Fiscal Year	Dec. 2008	$4.53	$4.55	$4.50	$13.0
Fiscal Year	Dec. 2009	$4.66	$4.76	$4.60	$12.7

5-year growth rate: 9.0%
Mean recommendation: 2.1 (1 = Strong Buy, 3 = Hold, 5 = Strong Sell)

MID-MODULE REVIEW

Following are forecasts of Procter & Gamble's sales, net operating profit after tax (NOPAT), and net operating assets (NOA). These are taken from our forecasting process in Module 11 and now include a terminal period forecast that reflects a long-term growth rate of 1% (Recall that "Other noncurrent assets" are excluded from P&G's NOA because it reports that auction rate securities are included in those "other" assets.)

(In millions)	2008	Horizon Period				Terminal Period
		2009	2010	2011	2012	
Sales growth.		−0.67%	4.33%	4.33%	4.33%	1.00%
Net sales (unrounded) . . .	$ 83,503	$ 82,943.53	$ 86,535.48	$ 90,281.97	$ 94,191.21	$ 95,133.12
		($83,503 × 0.9933)	($82,943.53 × 1.0433)	($86,535.48 × 1.0433)	($90,281.97 × 1.0433)	($94,191.21 × 1.01)
Net sales (rounded)	$ 83,503	$ 82,944	$ 86,535	$ 90,282	$ 94,191	$ 95,133
NOPAT	12,703	12,607	13,153	13,723	14,317	14,460
NOA	101,094	100,416	104,764	109,300	114,033	115,173

Use the forecasts above to compute P&G's free cash flows to the firm (FCFF) and an estimate of its stock value using the DCF model. Make the following assumptions: discount rate (WACC) of 6%, shares outstanding of 3,032.7 million, and net nonoperating obligations (NNO) of $31,600 million.

Solution

The following DCF results yield a P&G stock value estimate of $70.92 as of July 31, 2008. P&G's stock closed at $65.48 on that date. This estimate suggests that P&G's stock is marginally undervalued on that date.

(In millions, except per share values and discount factors)	2008	Horizon Period				Terminal Period
		2009	2010	2011	2012	
Increase in NOA[a]		$ (678)	$ 4,348	$ 4,536	$ 4,733	$ 1,140
FCFF (NOPAT − Increase in NOA)		13,285	8,805	9,187	9,584	13,320
Discount factor [$1/(1 + r_w)^t$]		0.94340	0.89000	0.83962	0.79209	
Present value of horizon FCFF		12,533	7,836	7,714	7,591	
Cum present value of horizon FCFF. . . .	$ 35,674					
Present value of terminal FCFF	211,013[b]					
Total firm value	246,687					
Less NNO	31,600					
Firm equity value	$215,087					
Shares outstanding	3,032.7					
Stock value per share	$ 70.92					

[a] NOA increases are viewed as a cash outflow.

[b] Computed as $\dfrac{\frac{\$13,320 \text{ million}}{0.06 - 0.01}}{(1.06)^4}$, or ($13,320/0.05) × 0.79209, where 6% is WACC and 1% is the long-term (terminal period) growth rate.

RESIDUAL OPERATING INCOME (ROPI) MODEL

The residual operating income (ROPI) model focuses on net operating profit after tax (NOPAT) and net operating assets (NOA). This means it uses key measures from both the income statement and balance sheet in determining firm value.

LO3 Describe and apply the residual operating income model to value equity securities.

ROPI Model Structure

The ROPI model defines firm value as the sum of two components:

Firm Value = NOA + Present Value of Expected ROPI

where

NOA = Net operating assets

ROPI = Residual operating income

Net operating assets (NOA) are the foundation of firm value under the ROPI model. This is potentially problematic because we measure NOA using the balance sheet, which is unlikely to fully and contemporaneously capture the true (or intrinsic) value of all of a firm's operating assets.[8] How-

---

[8] If the assets earn more than expected, it could be because NOA does not capture all of the firms' assets. For example, R&D and advertising are not fully and contemporaneously reflected on the balance sheet as assets though they likely produce future cash inflows. Likewise, internally generated goodwill is not fully reflected on the balance sheet as an asset. Similarly, assets are generally not written up to reflect unrealized gains. Conversely, sometimes the balance sheet overstates the true value of NOA. For example, companies can delay the write-down of impaired assets and, thus, overstate their book values. These examples, and a host of others, can yield reported values of NOA that differ from the fair value of operating assets.

ever, the ROPI model adds an adjustment that corrects for the undervaluation or overvaluation of NOA. This adjustment is the present value of expected residual operating income, and is defined as follows:

$$\textbf{ROPI} = \textbf{NOPAT} - \underbrace{(\textbf{NOA}_{\textbf{Beg}} \times r_w)}_{\textbf{Expected NOPAT}}$$

where

$$\textbf{NOA}_{\textbf{Beg}} = \textbf{Net operating assets at beginning (\textit{Beg}) of period}$$
$$r_w = \textbf{Weighted average cost of capital (WACC)}$$

Residual operating income (ROPI) is the net operating profit a firm earns over and above the return that the operating assets are expected to earn given the firm's WACC. Shareholders expect the company to use NOA to generate, at least, a "hurdle" profit to cover the cost of capital (WACC). Companies that earn profits over and above that hurdle, create value for shareholders. This is the concept of residual income: that is, income earned over and above the minimum amount of return required by investors.

Understanding the ROPI model helps us reap the benefits from the disaggregation of return on net operating assets (RNOA) in Module 4. In addition, the ROPI model is the foundation for many internal and external performance evaluation and compensation systems marketed by management consulting and accounting services firms.[9]

Steps in Applying the ROPI Model

Application of the ROPI model to equity valuation involves five steps:

1. Forecast and discount ROPI for the horizon period.[10]
2. Forecast and discount ROPI for the terminal period.[11]
3. Sum the present values from both the horizon and terminal periods; then add this sum to current NOA to get firm (enterprise) value.
4. Subtract net nonoperating obligations (NNO) from firm value to yield firm equity value.
5. Divide firm equity value by the number of shares outstanding to yield stock value per share.

Illustrating the ROPI Model

To illustrate application of the ROPI model, we again use Johnson & Johnson. Forecasted financials for J&J (forecast horizon of 2008–2011 and terminal period of 2012) are in Exhibit 12.2. The forecasts (in bold) are for sales, NOPAT, and NOA (the same forecasts from illustration of the DCF model). These forecasts assume an annual 6.0% sales growth for the horizon period, a terminal period sales growth of 1%, net operating profit margin (NOPM) of 17%, and a year-end net operating asset turnover (NOAT) of 1.20 (which is the 2007 turnover rate based on year-end NOA; year-end amounts are used because we are forecasting year-end account balances, not average balances).

The bottom line of Exhibit 12.2 is the estimated J&J equity value of $222,021 million, or a per share stock value of $78.17. The present value computations use a 6% WACC as the discount rate. Specifically, we obtain this stock valuation as follows:

1. **Compute present value of horizon period ROPI.** The forecasted 2008 ROPI of $7,930 million is computed from the forecasted 2008 NOPAT ($11,009) less the product of beginning

---

[9] Examples are economic value added (EVA™) from Stern Stewart & Company, the economic profit model from McKinsey & Co., the cash flow return on investment (CFROI™) from Holt Value Associates, the economic value management from KPMG, and the value builder from PricewaterhouseCoopers (PwC).

[10] The present value of expected ROPI uses the weighted average cost of capital (WACC) as its discount rate; same as with the DCF model.

[11] For an assumed growth, g, the present value of the perpetuity of ROPI beyond the horizon period is given by $\frac{\text{ROPI}_T}{r_w - g}$, where ROPI_T is the residual operating income for the terminal period, r_w is WACC for the firm, and g is the assumed growth rate of ROPI_T following the horizon period. The resulting amount is then discounted back to the present using the WACC, computed over the length of the horizon period.

EXHIBIT 12.2 Application of Residual Operating Income Model

(In millions, except per share values and discount factors)	2007	Horizon Period				Terminal Period
		2008	2009	2010	2011	
Sales (unrounded)	$ 61,095	**$64,760.70** (61,095 × 1.06)	**$68,646.34** (64,760.70 × 1.06)	**$72,765.12** (68,646.34 × 1.06)	**$77,131.03** (72,765.12 × 1.06)	**$77,902.34** (77,131.03 × 1.01)
Sales (rounded)	61,095	**64,761**	**68,646**	**72,765**	**77,131**	**77,902**
NOPAT*	10,478	**11,009**	**11,670**	**12,370**	**13,112**	**13,243**
NOA**	51,309	**53,968**	**57,205**	**60,638**	**64,276**	**64,918**
ROPI (NOPAT − [NOA$_{Beg}$ × r_w])		7,930	8,432	8,938	9,474	9,386
Discount factor [1/(1 + r_w)^t]‡		0.94340	0.89000	0.83962	0.79209	
Present value of horizon ROPI		7,481	7,504	7,505	7,504	
Cum present value of horizon ROPI . . .	$ 29,994					
Present value of terminal ROPI	148,691					
NOA	51,309					
Total firm value	229,994					
Less NNO†	7,990					
Firm equity value	$222,004					
Shares outstanding	2,840.2					
Stock value per share	$ 78.17					

*Given J&J's combined federal and state statutory tax rate of 37.1%, NOPAT for 2007 is computed as follows ($ millions): ($61,095 − $17,751 − $20,451 − $7,680 − $807 − $745 − $534) − ($2,707 − {0.371 × [$452 − $296]}) = $10,478. A note on rounding: To forecast sales, we multiply prior year's unrounded sales by (1 + Growth rate); this is done for the horizon and terminal periods. Then, we round each year's forecasted sales to whole units and use rounded sales to compute NOPAT and NOA, where both are rounded to whole units. At each successive step, we round the number to whole units before proceeding to the next step.

**NOA computations for 2007 follow ($ millions): ($80,954 − $1,545 − $2) − ($6,909 + $6,412 + $2,318 + $1,512 + $223 + $1,493 + $5,402 + $3,829) = $51,309.

†NNO is the difference between NOA and total shareholders' equity; in this case NNO ($ millions) = $51,309 − $43,319 = $7,990.

‡For simplification, present value computations use discount factors rounded to 5 decimal places.

period NOA ($51,309) and WACC (0.06). The present value of this ROPI as of 2007 is $7,481 million, computed as $7,930 million × 0.94340 (the present value one year hence discounted at 6%). Similarly, the present value of 2009 ROPI (two years hence) is $7,504 million, computed as $8,432 million × 0.89000, and so on through 2011. The sum of these present values (*cumulative present value*) is $29,994 million.

2. **Compute present value of terminal period ROPI.** The present value of the terminal period ROPI is $148,691 million, computed as $\dfrac{\left(\dfrac{\$9,386\ \text{million}}{0.06 - 0.01}\right)}{(1.06)^4}$, or ($9,386/0.05) × 0.79209.

3. **Compute firm equity value.** We must sum the present values from the horizon period ($29,995 million) and terminal period ($148,691 million), plus NOA ($51,309 million), to get firm (enterprise) value of $229,994 million. We then subtract the value of net nonoperating obligations of $7,990 million to get firm equity value of $222,004. Dividing firm equity value by the 2,840.2 million shares outstanding yields the estimated per share valuation of $78.17.

We perform this valuation as of February 26, 2008, which is the SEC filing date for J&J's 10-K. J&J's stock closed at $63.72 on February 26, 2008. Our valuation estimate of $78.17 indicates that the company's stock is undervalued as of that date. J&J's stock price peaked in September of 2008 at $72.22; by early 2009 its stock was trading at roughly $60. Although this represents a large stock price decline, it was far less severe than many other companies suffered during this recessionary period (analysts continued to recommend it as a BUY stock).

The ROPI model estimate is equal to that computed using the DCF model illustrated earlier in this module. This is the case so long as the firm is in a steady state, that is, NOPAT and NOA are growing at the same rate (for example, when RNOA is constant). When the steady-state condition is not met, for example, when a company has variable growth rates over time or when profit margins are changing from year to year, the two models yield different valuations. Analysts typically compute values from several models and use qualitative analysis to determine a final price estimate.

RESEARCH INSIGHT Power of NOPAT Forecasts

Discounted cash flow (DCF) and residual operating income (ROPI) models yield identical estimates when the expected payoffs are forecasted for an infinite horizon. For practical reasons, we must use horizon period forecasts and a terminal period forecast. This truncation of the forecast horizon is a main cause of any difference in value estimates for these models. Importantly, if we can forecast (GAAP-based) NOPAT and NOA more accurately than forecasts of cash inflows and outflows, we will obtain more accurate estimates of firm value given a finite horizon.

MANAGERIAL INSIGHTS FROM THE ROPI MODEL

LO4 Explain how equity valuation models can aid managerial decisions.

The ROPI model defines firm value as the sum of NOA and the present value of expected residual operating income as follows:

$$\textbf{Firm Value} = \textbf{NOA} + \textbf{Present Value of } \underbrace{[\textbf{NOPAT} - (\textbf{NOA}_{Beg} \times r_w)]}_{\textbf{ROPI}}$$

Increasing ROPI, therefore, increases firm value. Managers can increase ROPI in two ways:

1. Decrease the NOA required to generate a given level of NOPAT (improve efficiency)
2. Increase NOPAT with the same level of NOA investment (improve profitability)

These are two very important observations. It means that achieving better performance requires effective management of *both* the balance sheet and the income statement. Most operating managers are accustomed to working with income statements. Further, they are often evaluated on profitability measures, such as achieving desired levels of sales and gross profit or efficiently managing operating expenses. The ROPI model focuses management attention on the balance sheet as well.

The two points above highlight two paths to increase ROPI and, accordingly, firm value. First, let's consider how management can reduce the level of NOA while maintaining a given level of NOPAT. Many managers begin by implementing procedures that reduce net operating working capital, such as:

- Reducing receivables through:
  - Better assessment of customers' credit quality
  - Better controls to identify delinquencies and automated payment notices
  - More accurate and timely invoicing
- Reducing inventories through:
  - Use of less costly components (of equal quality) and production with lower wage rates
  - Elimination of product features not valued by customers
  - Outsourcing to reduce product cost
  - Just-in-time deliveries of raw materials
  - Elimination of manufacturing bottlenecks to reduce work-in-process inventories
  - Producing to order rather than to estimated demand
- Increasing payables through:
  - Extending the payment of low or no-cost payables (so long as the supplier relationships are unharmed)

Management would next look at its long-term operating assets for opportunities to reduce unnecessary operating assets, such as the:

- Sale of unnecessary property, plant or equipment
- Acquisition of production and administrative assets in partnership with other entities for greater throughput
- Acquisition of finished or semifinished goods from suppliers to reduce manufacturing assets

The second path to increase ROPI and, accordingly, firm value is to increase NOPAT with the same level of NOA investment. Management would look to strategies that maximize NOPAT, such as:

- Increasing gross profit dollars through:
  - Better pricing and mix of products sold
  - Reduction of raw material and labor cost without sacrificing product quality, perhaps by outsourcing, better design, or more efficient manufacturing
  - Increase of throughput to minimize overhead costs per unit (provided inventory does not build up)
- Reducing selling, general, and administrative expenses through:
  - Better management of personnel
  - Reduction of overhead
  - Use of derivatives to hedge commodity and interest costs
  - Minimization of tax expense

Before undertaking any of these actions, managers must consider both short- and long-run implications for the company. The ROPI model helps managers assess company performance (income statement) relative to the net operating assets committed (balance sheet).

> **MANAGERIAL DECISION** **You Are the Chief Financial Officer**
>
> The residual operating income (ROPI) model highlights the importance of increasing NOPAT and reducing net operating assets, which are the two major components of the return on net operating assets (RNOA). What specific steps can you take to improve RNOA through improvement of its components: net operating profit margin and net operating asset turnover? [Answer, p. 12-19]

ASSESSMENT OF VALUATION MODELS

Exhibit 12.3 provides a brief summary of the advantages and disadvantages of the DCF and ROPI models. Neither model dominates the other, and both are theoretically equivalent. Instead, professionals must choose the model that performs best under practical circumstances.

EXHIBIT 12.3	Advantages and Disadvantages of DCF and ROPI Valuation Models		
Model	**Advantages**	**Disadvantages**	**Performs Best**

DCF	• Popular and widely accepted model
	• Cash flows are unaffected by accrual accounting
	• FCFF is intuitive
		• Cash investments in plant assets are treated as cash outflows, even though they create shareholder value
		• Value not recognized unless evidenced by cash flows
		• Computing FCFF can be difficult as operating cash flows are affected by
		  – Cutbacks on investments (receivables, inventories, plant assets); can yield short-run benefits at long-run cost
		  – Securitization, which GAAP treats as an operating cash flow when many view it as a financing activity
			• When the firm reports positive FCFF
			• When FCFF grows at a relatively constant rate

ROPI	• Focuses on value drivers such as profit margins and asset turnovers • Uses both balance sheet and income statement, including accrual accounting information • Reduces weight placed on terminal period value	• Financial statements do not reflect all company assets, especially for knowledge-based industries (for example, R&D assets and goodwill) • Requires some knowledge of accrual accounting	• When financial statements reflect all assets and liabilities; including those items often reported off-balance-sheet

There are numerous other equity valuation models in practice. Many require forecasting, but several others do not. A quick review of selected models follows:

The **method of comparables** (often called *multiples*) **model** predicts equity valuation or stock value using price multiples. Price multiples are defined as stock price divided by some key financial statement number. That financial number varies across investors but is usually one of the following: net income, net sales, book value of equity, total assets, or cash flow. The method then compares companies' multiples to those of their competitors to assign value.

The **net asset valuation model** draws on the financial reporting system to assign value. That is, equity is valued as reported assets less reported liabilities. Some investors adjust reported assets and liabilities for several perceived shortcomings in GAAP prior to computing net asset value. This method is commonly applied when valuing privately held companies.

The **dividend discount model** predicts that equity valuation or stock values equal the present value of expected cash dividends. This model is founded on the dividend discount formula and depends on the reliability of forecasted cash dividends.

There are additional models applied in practice that involve dividends, cash flows, research and development outlays, accounting rates of return, cash recovery rates, and real option models. Further, some practitioners, called *chartists* and *technicians,* chart price behavior over time and use it to predict equity value.

RESEARCH INSIGHT | **Using Models to Identify Mispriced Stocks**

Implementation of the ROPI model can include parameters to capture differences in growth opportunities, persistence of ROPI, and the conservatism in accounting measures. Research finds differences in how such factors, across firms and over time, affect ROPI and changes in NOA. This research also hints that investors do not entirely understand the properties underlying these factors and, consequently, individual stocks can be mispriced for short periods of time. Other research contends that the apparent mispricing is due to an omitted valuation variable related to riskiness of the firm.

MODULE-END REVIEW

Following are forecasts of Procter & Gamble's sales, net operating profit after tax (NOPAT), and net operating assets (NOA). These are taken from our forecasting process in Module 11 and now include a terminal period forecast that reflects a long-term growth rate of 1%. (Recall that "Other noncurrent assets" are excluded from P&G's NOA because it reports that auction rate securities are included in those "other" assets.)

(In millions)	2008	Horizon Period				Terminal Period
		2009	2010	2011	2012	
Sales growth.		−0.67%	4.33%	4.33%	4.33%	1.00%
Net sales (unrounded) . . .	$ 83,503	$ 82,943.53	$ 86,535.48	$ 90,281.97	$ 94,191.21	$ 95,133.12
		($83,503 × 0.9933)	($82,943.53 × 1.0433)	($86,535.48 × 1.0433)	($90,281.97 × 1.0433)	($94,191.21 × 1.01)
Net sales (rounded)	$ 83,503	$ 82,944	$ 86,535	$ 90,282	$ 94,191	$ 95,133
NOPAT	12,703	12,607	13,153	13,723	14,317	14,460
NOA	101,094	100,416	104,764	109,300	114,033	115,173

Drawing on these forecasts, compute P&G's residual operating income (ROPI) and an estimate of its stock value using the ROPI model. Assume the following: discount rate (WACC) of 6%, shares outstanding of 3,032.7 million, and net nonoperating obligations (NNO) of $31,600 million.

Solution

Results from the ROPI model below yield a P&G stock value estimate of $70.92 as of July 31, 2008. P&G's stock closed at $65.48 on that date. This estimate suggests that P&G's stock is marginally undervalued as of that date.

(In millions, except per share values and discount factors)	2008	Horizon Period 2009	2010	2011	2012	Terminal Period
ROPI (NOPAT − [NOA$_{Beg}$ × r_w])		$6,541	$7,128	$7,437	$7,759	$7,618
Discount factor [1/(1 + r_w)^t]		0.94340	0.89000	0.83962	0.79209	
Present value of horizon ROPI		6,171	6,344	6,244	6,146	
Cum present value of horizon ROPI	$ 24,905					
Present value of terminal ROPI	120,683[a]					
NOA	101,094					
Total firm value	246,682					
Less NNO	31,600					
Firm equity value	$215,082					
Shares outstanding	3,032.7					
Stock value per share	$ 70.92					

[a] Computed as $\frac{\left[\frac{\$7,618\ million}{0.06 - 0.01}\right]}{(1.06^4)}$, or ($7,618/0.05) × 0.79209.

The P&G stock price chart, extending from 2004 through 2008, follows.

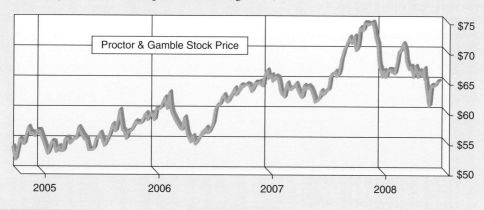

APPENDIX 12A: Johnson & Johnson Financial Statements

JOHNSON & JOHNSON Balance Sheet		
At Fiscal Year End ($ millions, except shares and per share)	2007	2006
Assets		
Cash and cash equivalents	$ 7,770	$ 4,083
Marketable securities	1,545	1
Accounts receivable trade, net of allowances for doubtful accounts $193 (2006, $160)	9,444	8,712
Inventories	5,110	4,889
Deferred taxes on income	2,609	2,094
Prepaid expenses and other receivables	3,467	3,196
Total current assets	$29,945	$22,975
Marketable securities, noncurrent	$ 2	$ 16
Property, plant and equipment, net	14,185	13,044
Intangible assets, net	14,640	15,348
Goodwill, net	14,123	13,340
Deferred taxes on income	4,889	3,210
Other assets	3,170	2,623
Total assets	$80,954	$70,556

continued

continued from prior page

At Fiscal Year End ($ millions, except shares and per share)	2007	2006
Liabilities and Shareholders' Equity		
Loans and notes payable	$ 2,463	$ 4,579
Accounts payable	6,909	5,691
Accrued liabilities	6,412	4,587
Accrued rebates, returns and promotions	2,318	2,189
Accrued salaries, wages and commissions	1,512	1,391
Accrued taxes on income	223	724
Total current liabilities	19,837	19,161
Long-term debt	7,074	2,014
Deferred taxes on income	1,493	1,319
Employee related obligations	5,402	5,584
Other liabilities	3,829	3,160
Total liabilities	37,635	31,238
Shareholders' equity		
Preferred stock—without par value (authorized and unissued 2,000,000 share)	—	—
Common stock—par value $1.00 per share (authorized 4,320,000,000 shares; issued 3,119,843,000 shares)	3,120	3,120
Accumulated other comprehensive income	(693)	(2,118)
Retained earnings	55,280	49,290
	57,707	50,292
Less: common stock held in treasury, at cost (279,620,000 shares and 226,612,000 shares)	14,388	10,974
Total shareholders' equity	43,319	39,318
Total liabilities and shareholders' equity	$80,954	$70,556

JOHNSON & JOHNSON
Income Statement

For Fiscal Year Ended ($ millions)	2007	2006	2005
Sales to customers	$61,095	$53,324	$50,514
Cost of products sold	17,751	15,057	14,010
Gross profit	43,344	38,267	36,504
Selling, marketing and administrative expenses	20,451	17,433	17,211
Research expense	7,680	7,125	6,462
Purchased in-process research and development	807	559	362
Restructuring	745	—	—
Interest income	(452)	(829)	(487)
Interest expense, net of portion capitalized	296	63	54
Other (income) expense, net	534	(671)	(214)
	30,061	23,680	23,388
Earnings before provision for taxes on income	13,283	14,587	13,116
Provision for taxes on income	2,707	3,534	3,056
Net earnings	$10,576	$11,053	$10,060

JOHNSON & JOHNSON Statement of Cash Flows			
For Fiscal Year Ended ($ millions)	**2007**	**2006**	**2005**
Cash flows from operating activities			
Net earnings.	$10,576	$11,053	$10,060
Adjustments to reconcile net earnings to cash flows:			
Depreciation and amortization of property and intangibles	2,777	2,177	2,093
Stock based compensation	698	659	540
Purchased in-process research and development.	807	559	362
Intangible asset write-down	678	—	—
Deferred tax provision.	(1,762)	(1,168)	(235)
Accounts receivable allowances.	22	(14)	(31)
Changes in assets and liabilities, net of effects from acquisitions:			
Increase in accounts receivable	(416)	(699)	(568)
Decrease/(increase) in inventories	14	(210)	(396)
Increase/(decrease) in accounts payable and accrued liabilities	2,642	1,750	(911)
(Increase)/decrease in other current and noncurrent assets	(1,351)	(269)	542
Increase in other current and noncurrent liabilities.	564	410	343
Net cash flows from operating activities	15,249	14,248	11,799
Cash flows from investing activities			
Addition to property, plant and equipment.	(2,942)	(2,666)	(2,632)
Proceeds from the disposal of assets	230	511	154
Acquisitions, net of cash acquired.	(1,388)	(18,023)	(987)
Purchases of investments	(9,659)	(467)	(5,660)
Sales of investments	7,988	426	9,187
Other (primarily intangibles)	(368)	(72)	(341)
Net cash used by investing activities.	(6,139)	(20,291)	(279)
Cash flows from financing activities			
Dividends to shareholders	(4,670)	(4,267)	(3,793)
Repurchase of common stock.	(5,607)	(6,722)	(1,717)
Proceeds from short-term debt	19,626	6,385	1,215
Retirement of short-term debt	(21,691)	(2,633)	(732)
Proceeds from long-term debt.	5,100	6	6
Retirement of long-term debt.	(18)	(13)	(196)
Proceeds from the exercise of stock options/excess tax benefits	1,562	1,135	774
Net cash used by financing activities.	(5,698)	(6,109)	(4,443)
Effect of exchange rate changes on cash and cash equivalents.	275	180	(225)
(Decrease)/increase in cash and cash equivalents	3,687	(11,972)	6,852
Cash and cash equivalents, beginning of year	4,083	16,055	9,203
Cash and cash equivalents, end of year	$ 7,770	$ 4,083	$16,055

APPENDIX 12B: Oppenheimer Valuation of Procter & Gamble

We explain the forecasting process in Module 11 and reproduce an analyst report on forecasted financial statements for Procter & Gamble in Appendix 11A. In this appendix, we extend that report and reproduce an analyst forecasted stock price for P&G. We include below, two excerpts from the Oppenheimer valuation. The first excerpt provides a qualitative and quantitative analysis from Oppenheimer's report as of December 11, 2008 (*reproduced with permission*):

> **Maintaining our Outperform rating** We have as much confidence in P&G's ability to execute in the current challenging environment as in any company we cover, while its balanced, diversified and staples-oriented product portfolio should prove adequately defensive in a period of slowing consumer spending.

continued

continued from prior page

Lowering Estimates, Maintaining Bullish Stance In light of the company's reduced fiscal 2Q top-line guidance, we are lowering our sales and EPS estimates, as we now feel more comfortable being at the lower end of guidance range. With this in mind, we are reducing our fiscal 2009 GAAP EPS estimate to $4.28 from $4.33 prior. Recall that this includes a $0.63 per share gain from the Folgers transaction (which is likely to be adjusted in the coming weeks) and $0.12 per share in related restructuring. We are also lowering our fiscal 2Q GAAP EPS estimate to $1.58 from $1.60 prior, as we believe this is more appropriate given the number of moving parts that are expected to impact this quarter's results. Importantly, this is now based on 3% organic sales growth in fiscal 2Q, which is down from 5% prior, while our full-year estimate drops to 4%, also from 5% prior. In addition, we are lowering our fiscal 2010 EPS estimate to $4.10 from $4.20 previously, while our DCF-derived target price falls to $70 from $73. Despite our revised estimates and target price, we are maintaining our Outperform rating on the shares. We have as much confidence in P&G's ability to execute in the current challenging environment as in any company in our coverage universe, while its balanced, diversified and staples-oriented product portfolio should prove adequately defensive in a period of slowing consumer spending. Finally, we continue to view the shares as attractive from a valuation perspective, at 15.8× our adjusted fiscal 2009 EPS estimate of $3.77 (excluding the impact of the Folgers sale and restructuring).

Price Target Calculation Our 12–18 month target price for P&G of $70 per share is derived from our five-year discounted cash flow analysis, using a weighted average cost of capital of 8.9%, a terminal (fiscal 2013) unlevered free cash flow estimate of $17 billion and a residual free cash flow growth rate into perpetuity of 2.50%.

Key Risks to Price Target Risks to the shares achieving our price target include, but are not limited to, management's ability to continue to deliver growth above market averages, achieve its targeted top- and bottom-line synergies from the Gillette acquisition, and weather intense competition through product innovation and marketing.

Our second excerpt is a set of assumptions and computations developed by Oppenheimer analysts to forecast P&G's target stock price reported as of late 2008 (*reproduced with permission*).

(In U.S. $ millions, except per share data)

Procter & Gamble DCF Model	F2009E	F2010E	F2011E	F2012E	F2013E
Net Income	13,679	12,768	13,556	14,426	15,372
Plus: Interest Expense (After-Tax)	1,008	1,039	1,090	1,126	1,151
Plus: Depreciation & Amortization	3,167	3,277	3,320	3,385	3,473
Less: Capital Expenditures	(3,055)	(3,123)	(3,240)	(3,368)	(3,505)
Plus/Less: Changes in W/C & Other	1,868	614	613	614	617
Unlevered Free Cash Flow	**16,667**	**14,575**	**15,341**	**16,186**	**17,109**
PV of Unlevered Free Cash Flow	**15,303**	**12,286**	**11,873**	**11,502**	**11,162**

PV of Free Cash Flow	62,128
Plus: PV of Residual Value	178,314
Enterprise Value	240,440
Less: Total Debt/Preferred	(40,799)
Equity Value	199,641
Mid-Year Adjustment Factor	1.04
Equity Value (Adjusted)	208,352
Shares Outstanding	2,986
Value Per Share	**$70**

Assumptions:	
Risk-free Rate	5.00%
Beta	0.75
Market Risk Premium	6.00%
Cost of Equity	9.50%
Tax Rate (Statutory)	35.00%
Cost of Debt (Pre-Tax)	5.50%
Cost of Debt (After-Tax)	3.58%
Cost of Preferred	5.00%
Shares Outstanding	2,986
Price	$59
Market Cap	174,903
Total Debt	39,447
Preferred	1,352
Total Capitalization	215,702

Capitalization		Current	Target
Equity		81%	90%
Debt		18%	9%
Preferred		1%	1%
WACC			8.9%
Residual FCF Growth Rate			2.50%

Terminal Free Cash Flow Growth Rate

WACC	1.5%	2.0%	2.5%	3.0%	3.5%
7.9%	$73	$78	$85	$94	$104
8.4%	$66	$71	$77	$84	$92
8.9%	$61	$65	**$70**	$75	$82
9.4%	$56	$60	$64	$68	$74
9.9%	$52	$55	$58	$62	$67

Sources: Company financial statements and Oppenheimer & Co. Inc. estimates.

We make four observations regarding this analyst report regarding P&G's target stock price.

1. The analyst report defines unlevered (before debt) free cash flow as follows. Earlier in this module we described differences in this type of FCFF computation from our FCFF definition.

	Net income
+	Interest expense
+	Depreciation and amortization expense
−	Capital expenditures
−	Increases in working capital
=	Unlevered free cash flow

2. This analyst report uses the same DCF computation we describe in this module. The analyst highlights the importance of the terminal year computation with a matrix that quantifies the impact on stock price of (1) growth rates subsequent to the forecasting horizon and (2) WACC. This type of sensitivity analysis is a useful way to identify crucial assumptions. We see that a 1 percentage point change in WACC results in a roughly 20% change in stock price estimate. Further, a 1 percentage point change in the terminal growth rate results in a 13% to 17% change in stock price estimate.

3. The cost of equity capital is estimated using the capital asset pricing model (CAPM) as we describe in the module.

4. Bottom line: We see that this analyst's $70 stock price target is nearly identical to the $70.92 stock price estimate that we independently determined in this module.

APPENDIX 12C: Derivation of Free Cash Flow Formula

Derivation of the free cash flow formula follows; our thanks to Professor Jim Boatsman for this exposition:

$$\textbf{Assets} = \textbf{Liabilities} + \textbf{Stockholders' Equity (SE)}$$
$$\textbf{NOA} = \textbf{NNO} + \textbf{SE}$$
$$\Delta\textbf{NOA} = \Delta\textbf{NNO} + \Delta\textbf{SE} \quad \text{[in change form, where } \Delta \text{ refers to change]}$$
$$\Delta\textbf{NOA} = \Delta\textbf{NNO} + \Delta\textbf{Contributed Capital (CC)} + \textbf{Net Income} - \textbf{Dividends (DIV)} \quad \text{[substituting for SE]}$$
$$\Delta\textbf{NOA} = \Delta\textbf{NNO} + \Delta\textbf{CC} + (\textbf{NOPAT} - \textbf{NNE}) - \textbf{DIV} \quad \text{[substituting for NI]}$$
$$-\textbf{NOPAT} + \Delta\textbf{NOA} = \Delta\textbf{NNO} + \Delta\textbf{CC} - \textbf{NNE} - \textbf{DIV} \quad \text{[rearranging terms]}$$
$$\textbf{NOPAT} - \Delta\textbf{NOA} = \textbf{NNE} - \Delta\textbf{NNO} - \Delta\textbf{CC} + \textbf{DIV} \quad \text{[multiplying by } -1\text{]}$$

Free cash flows to the firm (FCFF)	Net payments to holders of net nonoperating obligations and stock

GUIDANCE ANSWERS

MANAGERIAL DECISION   **You Are the Chief Financial Officer**

Cash flow can be increased by reducing assets. For example, receivables can be reduced by the following:

- Encouraging up-front payments or progress billings on long-term contracts
- Increasing credit standards to avoid slow-paying accounts before sales are made
- Monitoring account age and sending reminders to past-due customers
- Selling accounts receivable to a financial institution or special purpose entity

As another example of asset reduction, plant assets can be reduced by the following:

- Selling unused or excess plant assets
- Forming alliances with other companies to share specialized plant assets
- Owning assets in a special purpose entity with other companies
- Selling production facilities to a contract manufacturer and purchasing the output

---

MANAGERIAL DECISION **You Are the Chief Financial Officer**

RNOA can be disaggregated into its two key drivers: net operating profit margin and net operating asset turnover. Net operating profit margin can be increased by improving gross profit margins (better product pricing, lower cost manufacturing, etc.) and closely monitoring and controlling operating expenses. Net operating asset turnover can be increased by reducing net operating working capital (better monitoring of receivables, better management of inventories, carefully extending payables, etc.) and making more effective use of plant assets (disposing of unused assets, forming corporate alliances to increase plant asset capacity, selling productive assets to contract producers and purchasing the output, etc.). The ROPI model effectively focuses managers on the balance sheet *and* income statement.

Superscript $^{A\,(B,\,C)}$ denotes assignments based on Appendix 12A (B, C).

DISCUSSION QUESTIONS

Q12-1. Explain how information contained in financial statements is useful in pricing securities. Are there some components of earnings that are more useful than others in this regard? What nonfinancial information might also be useful?

Q12-2. In general, what role do expectations play in pricing equity securities? What is the relation between security prices and expected returns (the discount rate, or WACC, in this case)?

Q12-3. What are free cash flows to the firm (FCFF) and how are they used in the pricing of equity securities?

Q12-4. Define the weighted average cost of capital (WACC).

Q12-5. Define net operating profit after tax (NOPAT).

Q12-6. Define net operating assets (NOA).

Q12-7. Define the concept of residual operating income. How is residual operating income used in pricing equity securities?

Q12-8. What insight does disaggregation of RNOA into net operating profit margin and net operating asset turnover provide for managing a company?

Assignments with the WebAssign logo in the margin are available in WebAssign.
See the Preface of the book for details.

MINI EXERCISES

M12-9. Interpreting Earnings Announcement Effects on Stock Prices (LO1, 2)

Starbucks (SBUX)

In a recent quarterly earnings announcement, Starbucks announced that its earnings had markedly increased (up 7 cents per share over the prior year) and were 1 cent higher than analysts' expectations. Starbucks' stock "edged higher," according to *The Wall Street Journal*, but did not markedly increase. Why do you believe that Starbucks' stock price did not markedly increase given the good news?

M12-10. Computing Residual Operating Income (ROPI) (LO3)

3M Company (MMM)

3M Company reports net operating profit after tax (NOPAT) of $4,201 million in 2007. Its net operating assets at the beginning of 2007 are $12,561 million. Assuming a 6% weighted average cost of capital (WACC), what is 3M's residual operating income for 2007? Show computations.

M12-11. Computing Free Cash Flows to the Firm (FCFF) (LO2)

3M Company (MMM)

3M Company reports net operating profit after tax (NOPAT) of $4,201 million in 2007. Its net operating assets at the beginning of 2007 are $12,561 million and are $15,310 million at the end of 2007. What are 3M's free cash flows to the firm (FCFF) for 2007? Show computations.

M12-12. Computing, Analyzing and Interpreting Residual Operating Income (ROPI) (LO3)

PepsiCo (PEP)

In its 2007 fiscal year annual report, PepsiCo reports net operating income after tax (NOPAT) of $5,721 million. As of the beginning of fiscal year 2007 it reports net operating assets of $17,021 million.

a. Did PepsiCo earn positive residual operating income (ROPI) in 2007 if its weighted average cost of capital (WACC) is 6%? Explain.

b. At what level of WACC would PepsiCo not report positive residual operating income for 2007? Explain.

M12-13. Estimating Share Value Using the DCF Model (LO1, 2)

Following are forecasts of Target Corporation's sales, net operating profit after tax (NOPAT), and net operating assets (NOA) as of January 31, 2008.

Target Corporation (TGT)

(In millions)	Reported 2008	Horizon Period 2009	2010	2011	2012	Terminal Period
Sales............	$61,471	$65,282	$69,330	$73,628	$78,193	$78,975
NOPAT	3,244	3,445	3,658	3,885	4,126	4,167
NOA	32,397	34,406	36,539	38,804	41,210	41,622

Answer the following requirements assuming a terminal period growth rate of 1%, discount rate (WACC) of 5.8%, shares outstanding of 818.7 million, and net nonoperating obligations (NNO) of $17,090 million.

a. Estimate the value of a share of Target common stock using the discounted cash flow (DCF) model as of January 31, 2008.

b. Target Corporation (TGT) stock closed at $50.68 on March 31, 2008. How does your valuation estimate compare with this closing price? What do you believe are some reasons for the difference?

M12-14. Estimating Share Value Using the ROPI Model (LO3)

Refer to the information in M12-13 to answer the following requirements.

Target Corporation (TGT)

a. Estimate the value of a share of Target common stock using the residual operating income (ROPI) model as of January 31, 2008.

b. Target Corporation (TGT) stock closed at $50.68 on March 31, 2008. How does your valuation estimate compare with this closing price? What do you believe are some reasons for the difference?

EXERCISES

E12-15. Estimating Share Value Using the DCF Model (LO1, 2)

Following are forecasts of Abercrombie & Fitch's sales, net operating profit after tax (NOPAT), and net operating assets (NOA) as of January 31, 2008.

Web**Assign**.

Abercrombie & Fitch (ANF)

(In millions)	Reported 2008	Horizon Period 2009	2010	2011	2012	Terminal Period
Sales............	$3,750	$4,500	$5,400	$6,480	$7,776	$7,853
NOPAT	464	557	668	802	962	972
NOA	1,339	1,607	1,928	2,314	2,777	2,804

Answer the following requirements assuming a discount rate (WACC) of 13.3%, a terminal period growth rate of 1%, common shares outstanding of 86.2 million, and net nonoperating obligations (NNO) of $(279) million (negative NNO reflects net nonoperating assets such as investments rather than net obligations).

a. Estimate the value of a share of Abercrombie & Fitch common stock using the discounted cash flow (DCF) model as of January 31, 2008.

b. Abercrombie & Fitch (ANF) stock closed at $77.56 on March 2, 2008. How does your valuation estimate compare with this closing price? What do you believe are some reasons for the difference?

E12-16. Estimating Share Value Using the ROPI Model (LO3)

Refer to the information in E12-15 to answer the following requirements.

Web**Assign**.

Abercrombie & Fitch (ANF)

a. Estimate the value of a share of Abercrombie & Fitch common stock using the residual operating income (ROPI) model as of January 31, 2008.

b. Abercrombie & Fitch stock closed at $77.56 on March 2, 2008. How does your valuation estimate compare with this closing price? What do you believe are some reasons for the difference?

E12-17. **Estimating Share Value Using the DCF Model** (LO1, 2)

Following are forecasts of sales, net operating profit after tax (NOPAT), and net operating assets (NOA) as of March 1, 2008, for Best Buy, Inc.

	Reported	Horizon Period				Terminal
(In millions)	2008	2009	2010	2011	2012	Period
Sales............	$40,023	$44,577	$49,650	$55,300	$61,592	$62,208
NOPAT	1,448	1,613	1,797	2,001	2,229	2,251
NOA	5,276	5,876	6,545	7,290	8,119	8,201

Answer the following requirements assuming a discount rate (WACC) of 11%, a terminal period growth rate of 1%, common shares outstanding of 410.5 million, and net nonoperating obligations (NNO) of $792 million.

a. Estimate the value of a share of Best Buy's common stock using the discounted cash flow (DCF) model as of March 1, 2008.

b. Best Buy (BBY) stock closed at $43.47 on April 1, 2008. How does your valuation estimate compare with this closing price? What do you believe are some reasons for the difference?

E12-18. **Estimating Share Value Using the ROPI Model** (LO3)

Refer to the information in E12-17 to answer the following requirements.

a. Estimate the value of a share of Best Buy common stock using the residual operating income (ROPI) model as of March 1, 2008.

b. Best Buy (BBY) stock closed at $43.47 on April 1, 2008. How does your valuation estimate compare with this closing price? What do you believe are some reasons for the difference?

E12-19. **Identifying and Computing Net Operating Assets (NOA) and Net Nonoperating Obligations (NNO)** (LO1, 2)

3M Company (MMM)

Following is the balance sheet for 3M Company.

3M COMPANY Balance Sheet		
(Dollars in millions, except per share amount)	2007	2006
Assets		
Cash and cash equivalents..................................	$ 1,896	$ 1,447
Marketable securities—current............................	579	471
Accounts receivable—net of allowances of $75 and $71.........	3,362	3,102
Inventories		
Finished goods	1,349	1,235
Work in process.....................................	880	795
Raw materials and supplies	623	571
Total inventories	2,852	2,601
Other current assets.....................................	1,149	1,325
Total current assets.....................................	9,838	8,946
Marketable securities.....................................	480	166
Investments	298	314
Property, plant and equipment.............................	18,390	17,017
Less: Accumulated depreciation	(11,808)	(11,110)
Property, plant and equipment—net	6,582	5,907
Goodwill..	4,589	4,082
Intangible assets—net	801	708
Prepaid pension and postretirement benefits	1,378	395
Other assets..	728	776
Total assets..	$24,694	$21,294

continued

continued from prior page

(Dollars in millions, except per share amount)	2007	2006
Liabilities and Stockholders' Equity		
Short-term borrowings and current portion of long-term debt.....	$ 901	$ 2,506
Accounts payable......................................	1,505	1,402
Accrued payroll.......................................	580	520
Accrued income taxes	543	1,134
Other current liabilities	1,833	1,761
Total current liabilities................................	5,362	7,323
Long-term debt	4,019	1,047
Other liabilities	3,566	2,965
Total liabilities......................................	12,947	11,335
Stockholders' equity		
Common stock, par value $.01 per share:		
Shares outstanding—2007: 709,156,031		
Shares outstanding—2006: 734,362,802	9	9
Additional paid-in capital	2,785	2,484
Retained earnings.....................................	20,316	17,933
Treasury stock.......................................	(10,520)	(8,456)
Unearned compensation	(96)	(138)
Accumulated other comprehensive income (loss)	(747)	(1,873)
Stockholders' equity—net	11,747	9,959
Total liabilities and stockholders' equity......................	$24,694	$21,294

a. Compute net operating assets (NOA) and net nonoperating obligations (NNO) for 2007.

b. For 2007, show that: NOA = NNO + Stockholders' equity.

E12-20. Identifying and Computing Net Operating Profit after Tax (NOPAT) and Net Nonoperating Expense (NNE) (LO1, 2)

Following is the income statement for 3M Company.   3M Company (MMM)

3M COMPANY Income Statement			
Year Ended December 31 (millions)	2007	2006	2005
Net sales.......................................	$24,462	$22,923	$21,167
Operating expenses			
Cost of sales....................................	12,735	11,713	10,408
Selling, general and administrative expenses	5,015	5,066	4,631
Research, development and related expenses	1,368	1,522	1,274
Gain on sale of businesses........................	(849)	(1,074)	—
Total..	18,269	17,227	16,313
Operating income.................................	6,193	5,696	4,854
Interest expense and income			
Interest expense.................................	210	122	82
Interest income..................................	(132)	(51)	(56)
Total..	78	71	26
Income before income taxes, minority interest and cumulative effect of accounting change	6,115	5,625	4,828
Provision for income taxes.........................	1,964	1,723	1,627
Minority interest	55	51	55
Income before cumulative effect of accounting change	4,096	3,851	3,146
Cumulative effect of accounting change	—	—	(35)
Net income.....................................	$ 4,096	$ 3,851	$ 3,111

Compute net operating profit after tax (NOPAT) for 2007, assuming a federal and state statutory tax rate of 35.9%.

3M Company (MMM)

E12-21. **Estimating Share Value Using the DCF Model** **(LO1, 2)**

Following are forecasts of 3M Company's sales, net operating profit after tax (NOPAT), and net operating assets (NOA) as of December 31, 2007.

| (In millions) | Reported 2007 | Horizon Period | | | | Terminal Period |
		2008	2009	2010	2011	
Sales.............	$24,462	$25,318	$26,204	$27,121	$28,071	$28,351
NOPAT	4,201	3,545	3,669	3,797	3,930	3,969
NOA	15,310	16,879	17,469	18,081	18,714	18,901

Answer the following requirements assuming a discount rate (WACC) of 6%, a terminal period growth rate of 1%, common shares outstanding of 709.1 million, and net nonoperating obligations (NNO) of $3,563 million.

a. Estimate the value of a share of 3M's common stock using the discounted cash flow (DCF) model as of January 31, 2008.

b. 3M (MMM) stock closed at $79.15 on January 31, 2008. How does your valuation estimate compare with this closing price? What do you believe are some reasons for the difference?

E12-22. **Estimating Share Value Using the ROPI Model** **(LO3)**

3M Company (MMM)

Refer to the information in E12-21 to answer the following requirements.

a. Estimate the value of a share of 3M Company common stock using the residual operating income (ROPI) model as of January 31, 2008.

b. 3M Company stock closed at $79.15 on January 31, 2008. How does your valuation estimate compare with this closing price? What do you believe are some reasons for the difference?

E12-23. **Explaining the Equivalence of Valuation Models and the Relevance of Earnings** **(LO1, 2, 3)**

This module focused on two different valuation models: the discounted cash flow (DCF) model and the residual operating income (ROPI) model. The models focus on free cash flows to the firm and on residual operating income, respectively. We stressed that these two models are theoretically equivalent.

a. What is the *intuition* for why these models are equivalent?

b. Some analysts focus on cash flows as they believe that companies manage earnings, which presumably makes earnings less relevant. Are earnings relevant? Explain.

E12-24. **Applying and Interpreting Value Driver Components of RNOA** **(LO3)**

The net operating profit margin and the net operating asset turnover components of net operating assets are often termed *value drivers,* which refers to their positive influence on stock value by virtue of their role as components of return on net operating assets (RNOA).

a. How do profit margins and asset turnover ratios influence stock values?

b. Assuming that profit margins and asset turnover ratios are value drivers, what insight does this give us about managing companies if the goal is to create shareholder value?

PROBLEMS

WebAssign.

Intel Corporation
(INTC)

P12-25. **Forecasting and Estimating Share Value Using the DCF Model** **(LO1, 2)**

Following are the income statement and balance sheet for Intel Corporation.

INTEL CORPORATION Income Statement			
Year Ended (In millions)	**December 29, 2007**	**December 30, 2006**	**December 31, 2005**
Net revenue	$38,334	$35,382	$38,826
Cost of sales.	18,430	17,164	15,777
Gross margin	19,904	18,218	23,049
Research and development	5,755	5,873	5,145
Marketing, general and administrative.	5,401	6,096	5,688
Restructuring and asset impairment charges . . .	516	555	—
Amortization of acquisition-related intangibles and costs	16	42	126
Operating expenses.	11,688	12,566	10,959
Operating income.	8,216	5,652	12,090
Gains (losses) on equity securities, net	157	214	(45)
Interest and other, net	793	1,202	565
Income before taxes.	9,166	7,068	12,610
Provision for taxes	2,190	2,024	3,946
Net income.	$ 6,976	$ 5,044	$ 8,664

INTEL CORPORATION Balance Sheet		
As of Year-Ended (In millions, except par value)	**December 29, 2007**	**December 30, 2006**
Assets		
Cash and cash equivalents.	$ 7,307	$ 6,598
Short-term investments	5,490	2,270
Trading assets.	2,566	1,134
Accounts receivable, net of allowance for doubtful accounts of $27 ($32 in 2006).	2,576	2,709
Inventories	3,370	4,314
Deferred tax assets.	1,186	997
Other current assets	1,390	258
Total current assets.	23,885	18,280
Property, plant and equipment, net	16,918	17,602
Marketable equity securities	987	398
Other long-term investments	4,398	4,023
Goodwill	3,916	3,861
Other long-term assets	5,547	4,204
Total assets.	$55,651	$48,368
Liabilities and stockholders' equity		
Short-term debt	$ 142	$ 180
Accounts payable.	2,361	2,256
Accrued compensation and benefits	2,417	1,644
Accrued advertising	749	846
Deferred income on shipments to distributors.	625	599
Other accrued liabilities	1,938	1,192
Income taxes payable.	339	1,797
Total current liabilities	8,571	8,514

continued

continued from prior page

As of Year-Ended (In Millions, Except Par Value)	December 29, 2007	December 30, 2006
Long-term income taxes payable.	785	—
Deferred tax liabilities.	411	265
Long-term debt	1,980	1,848
Other long-term liabilities.	1,142	989
Stockholders' equity		
Preferred stock, $0.001 par value, 50 shares authorized;		
none issued.	—	—
Common stock, $0.001 par value, 10,000 shares authorized;		
5,818 issued and outstanding (5,766 in 2006) and capital		
in excess of par value	11,653	7,825
Accumulated other comprehensive income.	261	(57)
Retained earnings.	30,848	28,984
Total stockholders' equity	42,762	36,752
Total liabilities and stockholders' equity.	$55,651	$48,368

Required

a. Compute Intel's net operating assets (NOA) for year-end 2007.

b. Compute net operating profit after tax (NOPAT) for 2007, assuming a federal and state statutory tax rate of 35.6%.

c. Forecast Intel's sales, NOPAT, and NOA for years 2008 through 2011 using the following assumptions:

Sales growth.	8.00%
Net operating profit margin (NOPM).	16.50%
Net operating asset turnover (NOAT) at year-end	1.20

Forecast the terminal period value assuming a 1% terminal period growth and using the NOPM and NOAT assumptions above.

d. Estimate the value of a share of Intel common stock using the discounted cash flow (DCF) model as of December 29, 2007; assume a discount rate (WACC) of 10%, common shares outstanding of 5,818 million, and net nonoperating obligations (NNO) of $(11,319) million (NNO is negative which means that Intel has net nonoperating investments).

e. Intel (INTC) stock closed at $21.10 on January 31, 2008. How does your valuation estimate compare with this closing price? What do you believe are some reasons for the difference? What investment position is suggested from your results?

WebAssign.

Intel Corporation
(INTC)

P12-26. **Estimating Share Value Using the ROPI Model** **(LO3)**

Refer to the information in P12-25 to answer the following requirements.

Required

a. Estimate the value of a share of Intel common stock using the residual operating income (ROPI) model as of December 29, 2007.

b. Intel stock closed at $21.10 on January 31, 2008. How does your valuation estimate compare with this closing price? What do you believe are some reasons for the difference? What investment position is suggested from your results?

WebAssign.

TJX Companies, Inc.
(TJX)

P12-27. **Forecasting and Estimating Share Value Using the DCF Model** **(LO1, 2)**

Following are the income statement and balance sheet for TJX Companies.

TJX COMPANIES Balance Sheet		
Year Ended (In thousands)	**January 26, 2008**	**January 27, 2007**
Assets		
Cash and cash equivalents.	$ 732,612	$ 856,669
Accounts receivable, net	143,289	115,245
Merchandise inventories.	2,737,378	2,581,969
Prepaid expenses and other current assets.	215,550	159,105
Current deferred income taxes, net	163,465	35,825
Total current assets.	3,992,294	3,748,813
Property at cost:		
Land and buildings	277,988	268,056
Leasehold costs and improvements.	1,785,429	1,628,867
Furniture, fixtures and equipment.	2,675,009	2,373,117
Total property at cost.	4,738,426	4,270,040
Less accumulated depreciation and amortization	2,520,973	2,251,579
Net property at cost	2,217,453	2,018,461
Property under capital lease, net of accumulated amortization of $14,890 and $12,657, respectively.	17,682	19,915
Other assets	190,981	115,613
Goodwill and tradename, net of amortization	181,524	182,898
Total assets.	$6,599,934	$6,085,700
Liabilities		
Obligation under capital lease due within one year	$ 2,008	$ 1,854
Accounts payable.	1,516,754	1,372,352
Accrued expenses and other liabilities.	1,213,987	1,008,774
Federal, foreign and state income taxes payable.	28,244	—
Total current liabilities	2,760,993	2,382,980
Other long-term liabilities	811,333	583,047
Non-current deferred income taxes, net.	42,903	21,525
Obligation under capital lease, less portion due within one year.	20,374	22,382
Long-term debt, exclusive of current installments	833,086	785,645
Shareholders' equity		
Common stock, authorized 1,200,000,000 shares, par value $1, issued and outstanding 427,949,533 and 453,649,813, respectively.	427,950	453,650
Additional paid-in capital	—	—
Accumulated other comprehensive income (loss)	(28,685)	(33,989)
Retained earnings.	1,731,980	1,870,460
Total shareholders' equity	2,131,245	2,290,121
Total liabilities and shareholders' equity.	$6,599,934	$6,085,700

TJX COMPANIES Income Statement			
Fiscal Year Ended (In thousands)	January 26, 2008	January 27, 2007	January 28, 2006
Net sales.	$18,647,126	$17,404,637	$15,955,943
Cost of sales, including buying and occupancy costs.	14,082,448	13,213,703	12,214,671
Selling, general and administrative expenses	3,126,565	2,923,560	2,703,271
Provision for Computer Intrusion related costs	197,022	4,960	—
Interest (income) expense, net	(1,598)	15,566	29,632
Income from continuing operations before provision for income taxes	1,242,689	1,246,848	1,008,369
Provision for income taxes.	470,939	470,092	318,535
Income from continuing operations	771,750	776,756	689,834
Discontinued operations:			
Loss on disposal of discontinued operations, net of income taxes. . .	—	(38,110)	—
Income (loss) of discontinued operations, net of income taxes.	—	(607)	589
Net income.	$ 771,750	$ 738,039	$ 690,423

Required

a. Compute net operating assets (NOA) as of January 26, 2008.

b. Compute net operating profit after tax (NOPAT) for fiscal year ended January 26, 2008, assuming a federal and state statutory tax rate of 39.1%.

c. Forecast TJX's sales, NOPAT, and NOA for 2009 through 2012 using the following assumptions:

Sales growth.	7.10%
Net operating profit margin (NOPM).	4.10%
Net operating asset turnover (NOAT) at fiscal year-end. . . .	6.20

Forecast the terminal period value assuming a 1% terminal period growth and using the NOPM and NOAT assumptions above.

d. Estimate the value of a share of TJX common stock using the discounted cash flow (DCF) model as of January 26, 2008; assume a discount rate (WACC) of 7%, common shares outstanding of 427.9 million, and net nonoperating obligations (NNO) of $856 million.

e. TJX Companies' (TJX) stock closed at $33.31 on February 26, 2008. How does your valuation estimate compare with this closing price? What do you believe are some reasons for the difference?

WebAssign.

TJX Companies, Inc. (TJX)

P12-28. **Estimating Share Value Using the ROPI Model** **(LO3)**

Refer to the information in P12-27 to answer the following requirements.

Required

a. Estimate the value of a share of TJX common stock using the residual operating income (ROPI) model as of January 26, 2008.

b. TJX stock closed at $33.31 on February 26, 2008. How does your valuation estimate compare with this closing price? What do you believe are some reasons for the difference? What investment position is suggested from your results?

Abbott Laboratories (ABT)

P12-29. **Forecasting and Estimating Share Value Using the DCF Model** **(LO1, 2)**

Following are the income statement and balance sheet for Abbott Laboratories (ABT).

ABBOTT LABORATORIES Income Statement			
Year Ended December 31 ($ 000)	2007	2006	2005
Net sales.	$25,914,238	$22,476,322	$22,337,808
Cost of products sold.	11,422,046	9,815,147	10,641,111
Research and development	2,505,649	2,255,271	1,821,175
Acquired in-process and collaborations research and development.	—	2,014,000	17,131
Selling, general and administrative	7,407,998	6,349,685	5,496,123
Total operating cost and expenses	21,335,693	20,434,103	17,975,540
Operating earnings.	4,578,545	2,042,219	4,362,268
Interest expense.	593,142	416,172	241,355
Interest revenue	(136,752)	(123,825)	(87,693)
(Income) from TAP Pharmaceutical Products joint venture	(498,016)	(475,811)	(441,388)
Net foreign exchange (gain) loss	14,997	28,441	21,804
Other (income) expense, net	135,526	(79,128)	8,270
Earnings before taxes.	4,469,648	2,276,370	4,619,920
Taxes on earnings.	863,334	559,615	1,247,855
Net earnings.	$ 3,606,314	$ 1,716,755	$ 3,372,065

ABBOTT LABORATORIES Balance Sheet			
December 31 ($ 000)	2007	2006	2005
Assets			
Cash and cash equivalents	$ 2,456,384	$ 521,192	$ 2,893,687
Investment, including $307,500 of investments measured at fair value at December 31, 2007.	364,443	852,243	62,406
Trade receivables, less allowances of—2007: $258,288; 2006: $215,443; 2005: $203,683	4,946,876	4,231,142	3,576,794
Inventories			
Finished products.	1,677,083	1,338,349	1,203,557
Work in process	681,634	686,425	630,267
Materials.	592,725	781,647	708,155
Total inventories	2,951,442	2,806,421	2,541,979
Deferred income taxes	2,109,872	1,716,916	1,248,569
Other prepaid expenses and receivables.	1,213,716	1,153,969	1,062,593
Total current assets	14,042,733	11,281,883	11,386,028
Investments	1,125,262	1,229,873	134,013
Property and equipment, at cost:			
Land.	494,021	488,342	370,949
Buildings.	3,589,050	3,228,485	2,655,356
Equipment	10,393,402	9,947,503	8,813,517
Construction in progress	1,121,328	737,609	920,599
	15,597,801	14,401,939	12,760,421
Less: accumulated depreciation and amortization	8,079,652	7,455,504	6,757,280
Net property and equipment	7,518,149	6,946,435	6,003,141
Intangible assets, net of amortization	5,720,478	6,403,619	4,741,647
Goodwill.	10,128,841	9,449,281	5,219,247
Deferred income taxes and other assets	1,178,461	867,081	1,657,127
Total assets.	$39,713,924	$36,178,172	$29,141,203

continued

continued from prior page

December 31 ($ 000)	2007	2006	2005
Liabilities and Shareholders' Investment			
Short-term borrowings.	$1,827,361	$5,305,985	$ 212,447
Trade accounts payable	1,219,529	1,175,590	1,032,516
Salaries, wages and commissions	859,784	807,283	625,254
Other accrued liabilities	3,713,104	3,850,723	2,783,473
Dividends payable	504,540	453,994	423,335
Income taxes payable	80,406	262,344	488,926
Current portion of long-term debt	898,554	95,276	1,849,563
Total current liabilities.	9,103,278	11,951,195	7,415,514
Long-term debt	9,487,789	7,009,664	4,571,504
Post-employment obligations and other long-term liabilities.	3,344,317	3,163,127	2,155,837
Deferred income taxes	—	—	583,077
Shareholders' investment			
Preferred shares, one dollar par value			
Authorized—1,000,000 shares, none issued	—	—	—
Common shares, without par value,			
Authorized—2,400,000,000 shares			
Issued at stated capital amount—			
Shares: 2007: 1,580,854,677; 2006: 1,550,590,438;			
2005: 1,553,769,958.	6,104,102	4,290,929	3,477,460
Common shares held in treasury, at cost—			
Shares: 2007: 30,944,537; 2006: 13,347,272;			
2005: 14,534,979	(1,213,134)	(195,237)	(212,255)
Earnings employed in the business	10,805,809	9,568,728	10,404,568
Accumulated other comprehensive income (loss)	2,081,763	389,766	745,498
Total shareholders' investment.	17,778,540	14,054,186	14,415,271
Total liabilities and shareholders' investment.	$39,713,924	$36,178,172	$29,141,203

Required

a. Compute net operating assets (NOA) for year end 2007.

b. Compute net operating profit after tax (NOPAT) for 2007 assuming a federal and state statutory tax rate of 35.4%.

c. Forecast Abbott Laboratories' sales, NOPAT, and NOA for 2008 through 2011 using the following assumptions:

Sales growth.	8.00%
Net operating profit margin (NOPM).	15.00%
Net operating asset turnover (NOAT), year-end	0.90

Forecast the terminal period value assuming a 1% terminal period growth and using the NOPM and NOAT assumptions above.

d. Estimate the value of a share of Abbott Laboratories' common stock using the discounted cash flow (DCF) model as of December 31, 2008; assume a discount rate (WACC) of 5%, common shares outstanding of 1,549.2 million, and net nonoperating obligations (NNO) of $11,228 million.

e. Abbott Laboratories (ABT) stock closed at $56.18 on January 31, 2008. How does your valuation estimate compare with this closing price? What do you believe are some reasons for the difference? What investment position is suggested from your results?

P12-30. **Estimating Share Value Using the ROPI Model** **(LO3)**

Abbott Laboratories (ABT)

Refer to the information in P12-29 to answer the following requirements.

Required

a. Estimate the value of a share of Abbott Laboratories common stock using the residual operating income (ROPI) model as of December 31, 2007.

b. Abbott Laboratories stock closed at $56.18 on January 31, 2008. How does your valuation estimate compare with this closing price? What do you believe are some reasons for the difference? What investment position is suggested from your results?

P12-31. Forecasting and Estimating Share Value Using the DCF Model **(LO1, 2)**

Following are the income statement and balance sheet for Kellogg Company.

Kellogg Co. (K)

KELLOGG COMPANY Income Statement			
For Year Ended (in millions)	December 29, 2007	December 30, 2006	December 31, 2005
Net sales.	$11,776	$10,907	$10,177
Cost of goods sold.	6,597	6,082	5,612
Selling, general, and administrative expense. . .	3,311	3,059	2,815
Operating profit	1,868	1,766	1,750
Interest expense.	319	307	300
Other income (expense), net	(2)	13	(25)
Earnings before income taxes	1,547	1,472	1,425
Income taxes	444	467	445
Earnings (loss) from joint ventures	—	(1)	—
Net earnings.	$ 1,103	$ 1,004	$ 980

KELLOGG COMPANY Balance Sheet		
(In millions, except share amounts)	December 29, 2007	December 30, 2006
Assets		
Cash and cash equivalents	$ 524	$ 411
Accounts receivable, net	1,026	945
Inventories	924	824
Other current assets.	243	247
Total current assets.	2,717	2,427
Property, net.	2,990	2,816
Goodwill	3,515	3,448
Other intangibles, net.	1,450	1,420
Other assets.	725	603
Total assets.	$11,397	$10,714
Liabilities and Shareholders' Equity		
Current maturities of long-term debt	$ 466	$ 723
Notes payable	1,489	1,268
Accounts payable.	1,081	910
Other current liabilities	1,008	1,119
Total current liabilities	4,044	4,020
Long-term debt	3,270	3,053
Other liabilities	1,557	1,572
Shareholders' equity		
Common stock, $.25 par value, 1,000,000,000 shares authorized issued: 418,669,193 in 2007 and 418,515,339 in 2006	105	105
Capital in excess of par value	388	292
Retained earnings	4,217	3,630
Treasury stock at cost:		
28,618,052 shares in 2007 and 20,817,930 shares in 2006. . . .	(1,357)	(912)
Accumulated other comprehensive income (loss)	(827)	(1,046)
Total shareholders' equity	2,526	2,069
Total liabilities and shareholders' equity.	$11,397	$10,714

Required

a. Compute net operating assets (NOA) as of year-end 2007.

b. Compute net operating profit after tax (NOPAT) for 2007, assuming a federal and state statutory tax rate of 36.1%.

continued

    c. Forecast Kellogg's sales, NOPAT, and NOA for 2008 through 2011 using the following assumptions:

Sales growth	6.00%
Net operating profit margin (NOPM)	11.00%
Net operating asset turnover (NOAT), year-end	1.50

Forecast the terminal period value assuming a 1% terminal period growth and using the NOPM and NOAT assumptions above.

    d. Estimate the value of a share of Kellogg common stock using the discounted cash flow (DCF) model; assume a discount rate (WACC) of 6%, common shares outstanding of 390.1 million, and net nonoperating obligations (NNO) of $5,225 million.

    e. Kellogg's stock closed at $47.80 on January 31, 2008. How does your valuation estimate compare with this closing price? What do you believe are some reasons for the difference?

P12-32. **Estimating Share Value Using the ROPI Model** **(LO3)**

Kellogg Co. (K)

Refer to the information in P12-31 to answer the following requirements.

Required

    a. Estimate the value of a share of Kellogg common stock using the residual operating income (ROPI) model.

    b. Kellogg stock closed at $47.80 on January 31, 2008. How does your valuation estimate compare with this closing price? What do you believe are some reasons for the difference? What investment position is suggested from your results?

MANAGEMENT APPLICATIONS

MA12-33. **Management Application: Operating Improvement versus Financial Engineering** **(LO4)**

Assume that you are the CEO of a small publicly traded company. The operating performance of your company has fallen below market expectations, which is reflected in a depressed stock price. At your direction, your CFO provides you with the following recommendations that are designed to increase your company's return on net operating assets (RNOA) and your operating cash flows, both of which will, presumably, result in improved financial performance and an increased stock price.

1. To improve net cash flow from operating activities, the CFO recommends that your company reduce inventories (raw material, work-in-progress, and finished goods) and receivables (through selective credit granting and increased emphasis on collection of past due accounts).

2. The CFO recommends that your company sell and lease back its office building. The lease will be structured so as to be classified as an operating lease under GAAP. The assets will, therefore, not be included in the computation of net operating assets (NOA), thus increasing RNOA.

3. The CFO recommends that your company lengthen the time taken to pay accounts payable (lean on the trade) to increase net cash flows from operating activities.

4. Because your company's operating performance is already depressed, the CFO recommends that you take a "big bath;" that is, write off all assets deemed to be impaired and accrue excessive liabilities for future contingencies. The higher current period expense will, then, result in higher future period income as the assets written off will not be depreciated and your company will have a liability account available to absorb future cash payments rather than recording them as expenses.

5. The CFO recommends that your company increase its estimate of expected return on pension investments. This will reduce pension expense and increase operating profit, a component of net operating profit after tax (NOPAT) and, thus, of RNOA.

6. The CFO recommends that your company share ownership of its outbound logistics (trucking division) with another company in a joint venture. This would have the effect of increasing throughput, thus spreading overhead over a larger volume base, and would remove the assets from your company's balance sheet since the joint venture would be accounted for as an equity method investment.

Evaluate each of the CFO's recommendations. In your evaluation, consider whether each recommendation will positively impact the operating performance of your company or whether it is cosmetic in nature.

Compound Interest Tables

TABLE 1 Present Value of Single Amount $p = 1/(1 + i)^t$

| | Interest Rate | | | | | | | | | | | |
Period	0.01	0.02	0.03	0.04	0.05	0.06	0.07	0.08	0.09	0.10	0.11	0.12
1	0.99010	0.98039	0.97087	0.96154	0.95238	0.94340	0.93458	0.92593	0.91743	0.90909	0.90090	0.89286
2	0.98030	0.96117	0.94260	0.92456	0.90703	0.89000	0.87344	0.85734	0.84168	0.82645	0.81162	0.79719
3	0.97059	0.94232	0.91514	0.88900	0.86384	0.83962	0.81630	0.79383	0.77218	0.75131	0.73119	0.71178
4	0.96098	0.92385	0.88849	0.85480	0.82270	0.79209	0.76290	0.73503	0.70843	0.68301	0.65873	0.63552
5	0.95147	0.90573	0.86261	0.82193	0.78353	0.74726	0.71299	0.68058	0.64993	0.62092	0.59345	0.56743
6	0.94205	0.88797	0.83748	0.79031	0.74622	0.70496	0.66634	0.63017	0.59627	0.56447	0.53464	0.50663
7	0.93272	0.87056	0.81309	0.75992	0.71068	0.66506	0.62275	0.58349	0.54703	0.51316	0.48166	0.45235
8	0.92348	0.85349	0.78941	0.73069	0.67684	0.62741	0.58201	0.54027	0.50187	0.46651	0.43393	0.40388
9	0.91434	0.83676	0.76642	0.70259	0.64461	0.59190	0.54393	0.50025	0.46043	0.42410	0.39092	0.36061
10	0.90529	0.82035	0.74409	0.67556	0.61391	0.55839	0.50835	0.46319	0.42241	0.38554	0.35218	0.32197
11	0.89632	0.80426	0.72242	0.64958	0.58468	0.52679	0.47509	0.42888	0.38753	0.35049	0.31728	0.28748
12	0.88745	0.78849	0.70138	0.62460	0.55684	0.49697	0.44401	0.39711	0.35553	0.31863	0.28584	0.25668
13	0.87866	0.77303	0.68095	0.60057	0.53032	0.46884	0.41496	0.36770	0.32618	0.28966	0.25751	0.22917
14	0.86996	0.75788	0.66112	0.57748	0.50507	0.44230	0.38782	0.34046	0.29925	0.26333	0.23199	0.20462
15	0.86135	0.74301	0.64186	0.55526	0.48102	0.41727	0.36245	0.31524	0.27454	0.23939	0.20900	0.18270
16	0.85282	0.72845	0.62317	0.53391	0.45811	0.39365	0.33873	0.29189	0.25187	0.21763	0.18829	0.16312
17	0.84438	0.71416	0.60502	0.51337	0.43630	0.37136	0.31657	0.27027	0.23107	0.19784	0.16963	0.14564
18	0.83602	0.70016	0.58739	0.49363	0.41552	0.35034	0.29586	0.25025	0.21199	0.17986	0.15282	0.13004
19	0.82774	0.68643	0.57029	0.47464	0.39573	0.33051	0.27651	0.23171	0.19449	0.16351	0.13768	0.11611
20	0.81954	0.67297	0.55368	0.45639	0.37689	0.31180	0.25842	0.21455	0.17843	0.14864	0.12403	0.10367
21	0.81143	0.65978	0.53755	0.43883	0.35894	0.29416	0.24151	0.19866	0.16370	0.13513	0.11174	0.09256
22	0.80340	0.64684	0.52189	0.42196	0.34185	0.27751	0.22571	0.18394	0.15018	0.12285	0.10067	0.08264
23	0.79544	0.63416	0.50669	0.40573	0.32557	0.26180	0.21095	0.17032	0.13778	0.11168	0.09069	0.07379
24	0.78757	0.62172	0.49193	0.39012	0.31007	0.24698	0.19715	0.15770	0.12640	0.10153	0.08170	0.06588
25	0.77977	0.60953	0.47761	0.37512	0.29530	0.23300	0.18425	0.14602	0.11597	0.09230	0.07361	0.05882
30	0.74192	0.55207	0.41199	0.30832	0.23138	0.17411	0.13137	0.09938	0.07537	0.05731	0.04368	0.03338
35	0.70591	0.50003	0.35538	0.25342	0.18129	0.13011	0.09366	0.06763	0.04899	0.03558	0.02592	0.01894
40	0.67165	0.45289	0.30656	0.20829	0.14205	0.09722	0.06678	0.04603	0.03184	0.02209	0.01538	0.01075

TABLE 2 Present Value of Ordinary Annuity $p = \{1 - [1/(1 + i)^t]\}/i$

| | Interest Rate | | | | | | | | | | | |
Period	0.01	0.02	0.03	0.04	0.05	0.06	0.07	0.08	0.09	0.10	0.11	0.12
1	0.99010	0.98039	0.97087	0.96154	0.95238	0.94340	0.93458	0.92593	0.91743	0.90909	0.90090	0.89286
2	1.97040	1.94156	1.91347	1.88609	1.85941	1.83339	1.80802	1.78326	1.75911	1.73554	1.71252	1.69005
3	2.94099	2.88388	2.82861	2.77509	2.72325	2.67301	2.62432	2.57710	2.53129	2.48685	2.44371	2.40183
4	3.90197	3.80773	3.71710	3.62990	3.54595	3.46511	3.38721	3.31213	3.23972	3.16987	3.10245	3.03735
5	4.85343	4.71346	4.57971	4.45182	4.32948	4.21236	4.10020	3.99271	3.88965	3.79079	3.69590	3.60478
6	5.79548	5.60143	5.41719	5.24214	5.07569	4.91732	4.76654	4.62288	4.48592	4.35526	4.23054	4.11141
7	6.72819	6.47199	6.23028	6.00205	5.78637	5.58238	5.38929	5.20637	5.03295	4.86842	4.71220	4.56376
8	7.65168	7.32548	7.01969	6.73274	6.46321	6.20979	5.97130	5.74664	5.53482	5.33493	5.14612	4.96764
9	8.56602	8.16224	7.78611	7.43533	7.10782	6.80169	6.51523	6.24689	5.99525	5.75902	5.53705	5.32825
10	9.47130	8.98259	8.53020	8.11090	7.72173	7.36009	7.02358	6.71008	6.41766	6.14457	5.88923	5.65022
11	10.36763	9.78685	9.25262	8.76048	8.30641	7.88687	7.49867	7.13896	6.80519	6.49506	6.20652	5.93770
12	11.25508	10.57534	9.95400	9.38507	8.86325	8.38384	7.94269	7.53608	7.16073	6.81369	6.49236	6.19437
13	12.13374	11.34837	10.63496	9.98565	9.39357	8.85268	8.35765	7.90378	7.48690	7.10336	6.74987	6.42355
14	13.00370	12.10625	11.29607	10.56312	9.89864	9.29498	8.74547	8.24424	7.78615	7.36669	6.98187	6.62817
15	13.86505	12.84926	11.93794	11.11839	10.37966	9.71225	9.10791	8.55948	8.06069	7.60608	7.19087	6.81086
16	14.71787	13.57771	12.56110	11.65230	10.83777	10.10590	9.44665	8.85137	8.31256	7.82371	7.37916	6.97399
17	15.56225	14.29187	13.16612	12.16567	11.27407	10.47726	9.76322	9.12164	8.54363	8.02155	7.54879	7.11963
18	16.39827	14.99203	13.75351	12.65930	11.68959	10.82760	10.05909	9.37189	8.75563	8.20141	7.70162	7.24967
19	17.22601	15.67846	14.32380	13.13394	12.08532	11.15812	10.33560	9.60360	8.95011	8.36492	7.83929	7.36578
20	18.04555	16.35143	14.87747	13.59033	12.46221	11.46992	10.59401	9.81815	9.12855	8.51356	7.96333	7.46944
21	18.85698	17.01121	15.41502	14.02916	12.82115	11.76408	10.83553	10.01680	9.29224	8.64869	8.07507	7.56200
22	19.66038	17.65805	15.93692	14.45112	13.16300	12.04158	11.06124	10.20074	9.44243	8.77154	8.17574	7.64465
23	20.45582	18.29220	16.44361	14.85684	13.48857	12.30338	11.27219	10.37106	9.58021	8.88322	8.26643	7.71843
24	21.24339	18.91393	16.93554	15.24696	13.79864	12.55036	11.46933	10.52876	9.70661	8.98474	8.34814	7.78432
25	22.02316	19.52346	17.41315	15.62208	14.09394	12.78336	11.65358	10.67478	9.82258	9.07704	8.42174	7.84314
30	25.80771	22.39646	19.60044	17.29203	15.37245	13.76483	12.40904	11.25778	10.27365	9.42691	8.69379	8.05518
35	29.40858	24.99862	21.48722	18.66461	16.37419	14.49825	12.94767	11.65457	10.56682	9.64416	8.85524	8.17550
40	32.83469	27.35548	23.11477	19.79277	17.15909	15.04630	13.33171	11.92461	10.75736	9.77905	8.95105	8.24378

TABLE 3 Future Value of Single Amount $f = (1 + i)^t$

Interest Rate

Period	0.01	0.02	0.03	0.04	0.05	0.06	0.07	0.08	0.09	0.10	0.11	0.12
1	1.01000	1.02000	1.03000	1.04000	1.05000	1.06000	1.07000	1.08000	1.09000	1.10000	1.11000	1.12000
2	1.02010	1.04040	1.06090	1.08160	1.10250	1.12360	1.14490	1.16640	1.18810	1.21000	1.23210	1.25440
3	1.03030	1.06121	1.09273	1.12486	1.15763	1.19102	1.22504	1.25971	1.29503	1.33100	1.36763	1.40493
4	1.04060	1.08243	1.12551	1.16986	1.21551	1.26248	1.31080	1.36049	1.41158	1.46410	1.51807	1.57352
5	1.05101	1.10408	1.15927	1.21665	1.27628	1.33823	1.40255	1.46933	1.53862	1.61051	1.68506	1.76234
6	1.06152	1.12616	1.19405	1.26532	1.34010	1.41852	1.50073	1.58687	1.67710	1.77156	1.87041	1.97382
7	1.07214	1.14869	1.22987	1.31593	1.40710	1.50363	1.60578	1.71382	1.82804	1.94872	2.07616	2.21068
8	1.08286	1.17166	1.26677	1.36857	1.47746	1.59385	1.71819	1.85093	1.99256	2.14359	2.30454	2.47596
9	1.09369	1.19509	1.30477	1.42331	1.55133	1.68948	1.83846	1.99900	2.17189	2.35795	2.55804	2.77308
10	1.10462	1.21899	1.34392	1.48024	1.62889	1.79085	1.96715	2.15892	2.36736	2.59374	2.83942	3.10585
11	1.11567	1.24337	1.38423	1.53945	1.71034	1.89830	2.10485	2.33164	2.58043	2.85312	3.15176	3.47855
12	1.12683	1.26824	1.42576	1.60103	1.79586	2.01220	2.25219	2.51817	2.81266	3.13843	3.49845	3.89598
13	1.13809	1.29361	1.46853	1.66507	1.88565	2.13293	2.40985	2.71962	3.06580	3.45227	3.88328	4.36349
14	1.14947	1.31948	1.51259	1.73168	1.97993	2.26090	2.57853	2.93719	3.34173	3.79750	4.31044	4.88711
15	1.16097	1.34587	1.55797	1.80094	2.07893	2.39656	2.75903	3.17217	3.64248	4.17725	4.78459	5.47357
16	1.17258	1.37279	1.60471	1.87298	2.18287	2.54035	2.95216	3.42594	3.97031	4.59497	5.31089	6.13039
17	1.18430	1.40024	1.65285	1.94790	2.29202	2.69277	3.15882	3.70002	4.32763	5.05447	5.89509	6.86604
18	1.19615	1.42825	1.70243	2.02582	2.40662	2.85434	3.37993	3.99602	4.71712	5.55992	6.54355	7.68997
19	1.20811	1.45681	1.75351	2.10685	2.52695	3.02560	3.61653	4.31570	5.14166	6.11591	7.26334	8.61276
20	1.22019	1.48595	1.80611	2.19112	2.65330	3.20714	3.86968	4.66096	5.60441	6.72750	8.06231	9.64629
21	1.23239	1.51567	1.86029	2.27877	2.78596	3.39956	4.14056	5.03383	6.10881	7.40025	8.94917	10.80385
22	1.24472	1.54598	1.91610	2.36992	2.92526	3.60354	4.43040	5.43654	6.65860	8.14027	9.93357	12.10031
23	1.25716	1.57690	1.97359	2.46472	3.07152	3.81975	4.74053	5.87146	7.25787	8.95430	11.02627	13.55235
24	1.26973	1.60844	2.03279	2.56330	3.22510	4.04893	5.07237	6.34118	7.91108	9.84973	12.23916	15.17863
25	1.28243	1.64061	2.09378	2.66584	3.38635	4.29187	5.42743	6.84848	8.62308	10.83471	13.58546	17.00006
30	1.34785	1.81136	2.42726	3.24340	4.32194	5.74349	7.61226	10.06266	13.26768	17.44940	22.89230	29.95992
35	1.41660	1.99989	2.81386	3.94609	5.51602	7.68609	10.67658	14.78534	20.41397	28.10244	38.57485	52.79962
40	1.48886	2.20804	3.26204	4.80102	7.03999	10.28572	14.97446	21.72452	31.40942	45.25926	65.00087	93.05097

TABLE 4 Future Value of an Ordinary Annuity $f = [(1 + i)^t - 1]/i$

Interest Rate

Period	0.01	0.02	0.03	0.04	0.05	0.06	0.07	0.08	0.09	0.10	0.11	0.12
1	1.00000	1.00000	1.00000	1.00000	1.00000	1.00000	1.00000	1.00000	1.00000	1.00000	1.00000	1.00000
2	2.01000	2.02000	2.03000	2.04000	2.05000	2.06000	2.07000	2.08000	2.09000	2.10000	2.11000	2.12000
3	3.03010	3.06040	3.09090	3.12160	3.15250	3.18360	3.21490	3.24640	3.27810	3.31000	3.34210	3.37440
4	4.06040	4.12161	4.18363	4.24646	4.31013	4.37462	4.43994	4.50611	4.57313	4.64100	4.70973	4.77933
5	5.10101	5.20404	5.30914	5.41632	5.52563	5.63709	5.75074	5.86660	5.98471	6.10510	6.22780	6.35285
6	6.15202	6.30812	6.46841	6.63298	6.80191	6.97532	7.15329	7.33593	7.52333	7.71561	7.91286	8.11519
7	7.21354	7.43428	7.66246	7.89829	8.14201	8.39384	8.65402	8.92280	9.20043	9.48717	9.78327	10.08901
8	8.28567	8.58297	8.89234	9.21423	9.54911	9.89747	10.25980	10.63663	11.02847	11.43589	11.85943	12.29969
9	9.36853	9.75463	10.15911	10.58280	11.02656	11.49132	11.97799	12.48756	13.02104	13.57948	14.16397	14.77566
10	10.46221	10.94972	11.46388	12.00611	12.57789	13.18079	13.81645	14.48656	15.19293	15.93742	16.72201	17.54874
11	11.56683	12.16872	12.80780	13.48635	14.20679	14.97164	15.78360	16.64549	17.56029	18.53117	19.56143	20.65458
12	12.68250	13.41209	14.19203	15.02581	15.91713	16.86994	17.88845	18.97713	20.14072	21.38428	22.71319	24.13313
13	13.80933	14.68033	15.61779	16.62684	17.71298	18.88214	20.14064	21.49530	22.95338	24.52271	26.21164	28.02911
14	14.94742	15.97394	17.08632	18.29191	19.59863	21.01507	22.55049	24.21492	26.01919	27.97498	30.09492	32.39260
15	16.09690	17.29342	18.59891	20.02359	21.57856	23.27597	25.12902	27.15211	29.36092	31.77248	34.40536	37.27971
16	17.25786	18.63929	20.15688	21.82453	23.65749	25.67253	27.88805	30.32428	33.00340	35.94973	39.18995	42.75328
17	18.43044	20.01207	21.76159	23.69751	25.84037	28.21288	30.84022	33.75023	36.97370	40.54470	44.50084	48.88367
18	19.61475	21.41231	23.41444	25.64541	28.13238	30.90565	33.99903	37.45024	41.30134	45.59917	50.39594	55.74971
19	20.81090	22.84056	25.11687	27.67123	30.53900	33.75999	37.37896	41.44626	46.01846	51.15909	56.93949	63.43968
20	22.01900	24.29737	26.87037	29.77808	33.06595	36.78559	40.99549	45.76196	51.16012	57.27500	64.20283	72.05244
21	23.23919	25.78332	28.67649	31.96920	35.71925	39.99273	44.86518	50.42292	56.76453	64.00250	72.26514	81.69874
22	24.47159	27.29898	30.53678	34.24797	38.50521	43.39229	49.00574	55.45676	62.87334	71.40275	81.21431	92.50258
23	25.71630	28.84496	32.45288	36.61789	41.43048	46.99583	53.43614	60.89330	69.53194	79.54302	91.14788	104.60289
24	26.97346	30.42186	34.42647	39.08260	44.50200	50.81558	58.17667	66.76476	76.78981	88.49733	102.17415	118.15524
25	28.24320	32.03030	36.45926	41.64591	47.72710	54.86451	63.24904	73.10594	84.70090	98.34706	114.41331	133.33387
30	34.78489	40.56808	47.57542	56.08494	66.43885	79.05819	94.46079	113.28321	136.30754	164.49402	199.02088	241.33268
35	41.66028	49.99448	60.46208	73.65222	90.32031	111.43478	138.23688	172.31680	215.71075	271.02437	341.58955	431.66350
40	48.88637	60.40198	75.40126	95.02552	120.79977	154.76197	199.63511	259.05652	337.88245	442.59256	581.82607	767.09142

Appendix B

Constructing the Statement of Cash Flows

LEARNING OBJECTIVES

LO1 Define and describe the framework for the statement of cash flows. (p. B-3)

LO2 Define and explain net cash flows from operating activities. (p. B-6)

LO3 Define and explain net cash flows from investing activities. (p. B-11)

LO4 Define and explain net cash flows from financing activities. (p. B-12)

LO5 Describe and apply ratios based on operating cash flows. (p. B-16)

STARBUCKS

Starbucks Corporation is the leading retailer, roaster, and brander of specialty coffee. It has more than 9,200 company-owned retail locations throughout the world. Starbucks' recent fiscal year yielded $10.4 billion in total net revenues and $316 million in net income, a decrease of 53% from the prior year after $267 million of restructuring charges. Indeed, all is not well in latte land. Starbucks, which had cultivated an upscale image, has met stiff competition from Dunkin' Donuts and McDonald's that poke fun at the names that Starbucks' uses for drink sizes and its yuppie image, which plays well in recessionary times. *Barron's* reports that "Starbucks sparked a premium-coffee revolution, which now threatens to devour the world's largest coffee-house chain. With Dunkin' Donuts, McDonald's, the local deli and even Target getting in on the act—and that's just a partial list—Seattle-based Starbucks has found itself saddled with rising costs, declining revenue, a sinking stock price and customer fatigue." And, as Starbucks' profits have waned, so has its stock price as the following chart graphically illustrates:

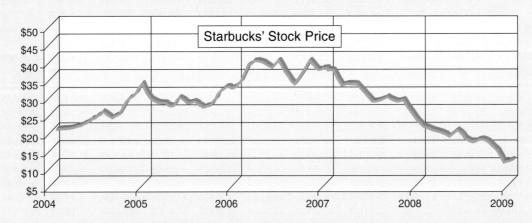

Although Starbucks' profits declined by 53% in 2008, operating cash flow declined by only 5%. Over the 2004 through 2007 period, Starbucks generated twice the level of cash flow as it reported in net income; see the following graphic. What is behind this relation? What does it mean? This appendix helps answer these and other questions.

It begins by describing the process of constructing the statement of cash flows. Next, it explains how we use and interpret the statement of cash flows to aid both internal and external business decisions.

Sources: Starbucks 2008 10-K and Annual Report; *Barron's*, 2008.

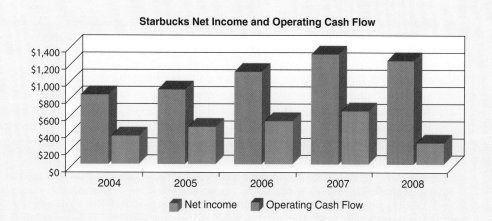

Starbucks Net Income and Operating Cash Flow

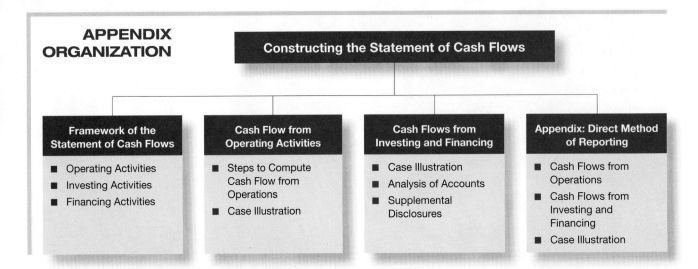

The **statement of cash flows** is a financial statement that summarizes information about the flow of cash into and out of a company. In this appendix, we discuss the preparation, analysis, and interpretation of the statement of cash flows. The statement of cash flows complements the balance sheet and the income statement. The balance sheet reports the company's financial position at a point in time (the end of each period) whereas the statement of cash flows explains the change in one of its components—cash—from one balance sheet date to the next. The income statement reveals the results of the company's operating activities for the period, and these operating activities are a major contributor to the change in cash as reported in the statement of cash flows.

FRAMEWORK FOR STATEMENT OF CASH FLOWS

LO1 Define and describe the framework for the statement of cash flows.

The statement of cash flows classifies cash receipts and cash payments into one of three categories:

- **Operating activities**   Operating activities measure the net cash inflows and outflows as a result of the company's transactions with its customers. We generally prefer operating cash flows to be positive, although companies can report net cash outflows for operating activities in the short run during periods of growth (as outflows to increase working capital accounts outstrip inflows from profits).

- **Investing activities**   Investing activities relate to net cash flows generally relating to long-term assets. Outflows occur when a company purchases long-term assets and inflows occur when long-term assets are sold.

- **Financing activities**   Financing activities relate to long-term debt and stockholders' equity. Cash inflows result from borrowing money and issuing stock to investors. Outflows occur when a company repays debt, repurchases stock, or pays dividends to shareholders.

Classifying cash flows into these categories readily identifies the effects on cash from each of these three major activities of a company. The combined effects on cash of all three categories explain the net change in cash for that period.[1]

Preparation of the statement of cash flows draws mainly on information from the income statement and the balance sheet. Specifically, the three sections draw generally on the following information:

---

[1] The statement of cash flows explains the change in a firm's cash *and* cash equivalents. **Cash equivalents** are short-term, highly liquid investments that are (1) easily convertible into a known cash amount and (2) close enough to maturity so that their market value is not sensitive to interest rate changes (generally, investments with initial maturities of three months or less). Treasury bills, commercial paper (short-term notes issued by corporations), and money market funds are typical examples of cash equivalents.

When preparing a statement of cash flows, the cash and cash equivalents are added together and treated as a single sum. This is done because the purchase and sale of investments in cash equivalents are considered to be part of a firm's overall management of cash rather than a source or use of cash. As statement users evaluate and project cash flows, for example, it should not matter whether the cash is readily available, deposited in a bank account, or invested in cash equivalents. Transfers back and forth between a firm's cash account and its investments in cash equivalents, therefore, are not treated as cash inflows and cash outflows in its statement of cash flows. When discussing the statement of cash flows, managers generally use the word *cash* rather than the term *cash and cash equivalents*. We follow the same practice in this appendix.

- **Net cash flows from operating activities** draws on the current asset and current liabilities sections of the balance sheet.
- **Net cash flows from investing activities** draws on the long-term assets section of the balance sheet.
- **Net cash flows from financing activities** draws on the long-term liabilities and stockholders' equity sections of the balance sheet.

These relations do not hold exactly, but they provide us a useful way to visualize the construction of the statement of cash flows.

Exhibit B.1 reproduces Starbucks' statement of cash flows ($ millions). During 2008, Starbucks reported net income of $315.5 million and generated $1,258.7 million of cash from operating activities. The

EXHIBIT B.1   Statement of Cash Flows for Starbucks

Consolidated Statements of Cash Flows Fiscal Year Ended ($ millions)	Sept. 28, 2008	Sept. 30, 2007	Oct. 1, 2006
Operating activities			
Net earnings	$ 315.5	$ 672.6	$ 564.3
Adjustments to reconcile net earnings to net cash provided by operating activities:			
Cumulative effect of accounting change for FIN 47, net of taxes	—	—	17.2
Depreciation and amortization	604.5	491.2	412.6
Provision for impairments and asset disposals	325.0	26.0	19.6
Deferred income taxes, net	(117.1)	(37.3)	(84.3)
Equity in income of investees	(61.3)	(65.7)	(60.6)
Distributions of income from equity investees	52.6	65.9	49.2
Stock-based compensation	75.0	103.9	105.7
Tax benefit from exercise of stock options	3.8	7.7	1.3
Excess tax benefit from exercise of stock options	(14.7)	(93.1)	(117.4)
Other	(0.1)	0.7	2.0
Cash provided (used) by changes in operating assets and liabilities:			
Inventories	(0.6)	(48.6)	(85.5)
Accounts payable	(63.9)	36.1	105.0
Accrued taxes	7.3	86.4	132.7
Deferred revenue	72.4	63.2	56.6
Other operating assets and liabilities	60.3	22.2	13.2
Net cash provided by operating activities	1,258.7	1,331.2	1,131.6
Investing activities			
Purchase of available-for-sale securities	(71.8)	(237.4)	(639.2)
Maturity of available-for-sale securities	20.0	178.2	269.1
Sale of available-for-sale securities	75.9	47.5	431.2
Acquisitions, net of cash acquired	(74.2)	(53.3)	(91.7)
Net purchases of equity, other investments and other assets	(52.0)	(56.6)	(39.2)
Net additions to property, plant, and equipment	(984.5)	(1,080.3)	(771.2)
Net cash used by investing activities	(1,086.6)	(1,201.9)	(841.0)
Financing activities			
Repayments of commercial paper	(66,068.0)	(16,600.9)	—
Proceeds from issuance of commercial paper	65,770.8	17,311.1	—
Repayments of short-term borrowings	(228.8)	(1,470.0)	(993.1)
Proceeds from short-term borrowings	528.2	770.0	1,416.1
Proceeds from issuance of common stock	112.3	176.9	159.2
Excess tax benefit from exercise of stock options	14.7	93.1	117.4
Principal payments on long-term debt	(0.6)	(0.8)	(0.9)
Proceeds from issuance of long-term debt	—	549.0	—
Repurchase of common stock	(311.4)	(996.8)	(854.0)
Other	(1.7)	(3.5)	—
Net cash used by financing activities	(184.5)	(171.9)	(155.3)
Effect of exchange rate changes on cash and cash equivalents	0.9	11.3	3.5
Net increase (decrease) in cash and cash equivalents	(11.5)	(31.3)	138.8
Cash and cash equivalents:			
Beginning of period	281.3	312.6	173.8
End of period	$ 269.8	$ 281.3	$ 312.6

company used $1,086.6 million of cash for investing activities and $184.5 million of cash for financing activities. In sum, Starbucks decreased its cash reserves by $11.5 million (including foreign exchange effects), from $281.3 million at the beginning of fiscal 2008 to $269.8 million at the end of fiscal 2008.

Operating Activities

A company's income statement reflects primarily the transactions and events that constitute its operating activities. Generally, the cash effects of these operating transactions and events determine the net cash flow from operating activities. The usual focus of a firm's **operating activities** is on selling goods or rendering services, but the activities are defined broadly enough to include any cash receipts or payments that are not classified as investing or financing activities. For example, cash received from collection of receivables and cash payments to purchase inventories are treated as cash flows from operating activities. The following are examples of cash inflows and outflows relating to operating activities.

Operating Activities

Cash Inflows ↑
- Receipts from customers for sales made or services rendered.
- Receipts of interest and dividends.
- Other receipts that are not related to investing or financing activities, such as lawsuit settlements and refunds received from suppliers.

Cash Outflows ↓
- Payments to employees or suppliers.
- Payments to purchase inventories.
- Payments of interest to creditors.
- Payments of taxes to government.
- Other payments that are not related to investing or financing activities, such as contributions to charity.

Investing Activities

A firm's transactions involving (1) the acquisition and disposal of property, plant, and equipment (PPE) assets and intangible assets, (2) the purchase and sale of stocks, bonds, and other securities (that are not cash equivalents), and (3) the lending and subsequent collection of money constitute the basic components of its **investing activities**. The related cash receipts and payments appear in the investing activities section of the statement of cash flows. Examples of these cash flows follow.

Investing Activities

Cash Inflows ↑
- Receipts from sales of property, plant, and equipment (PPE) assets and intangible assets.
- Receipts from sales of investments in stocks, bonds, and other securities (other than cash equivalents).
- Receipts from repayments of loans by borrowers.

Cash Outflows ↓
- Payments to purchase property, plant, and equipment (PPE) assets and intangible assets.
- Payments to purchase stocks, bonds, and other securities (other than cash equivalents).
- Payments made to lend money to borrowers.

Financing Activities

A firm engages in **financing activities** when it obtains resources from owners, returns resources to owners, borrows resources from creditors, and repays amounts borrowed. Cash flows related to these transactions are reported in the financing activities section of the statement of cash flows. Examples of these cash flows follow.

Financing Activities

Cash Inflows

- Receipts from issuances of common stock and preferred stock and from sales of treasury stock.
- Receipts from issuances of bonds payable, mortgage notes payable, and other notes payable.

Cash Outflows

- Payments to acquire treasury stock.
- Payments of dividends.
- Payments to settle outstanding bonds payable, mortgage notes payable, and other notes payable.

CASH FLOW FROM OPERATING ACTIVITIES

The first section of a statement of cash flows presents a firm's net cash flow from operating activities. Two alternative formats are used to report the net cash flow from operating activities: the *indirect method* and the *direct method. Both methods report the same amount of net cash flow from operating activities.* (Net cash flows from investing and financing activities are prepared in the same manner under both the indirect and direct methods; only the format for cash flows from operating activities differs.)

LO2 Define and explain net cash flows from operating activities.

The *indirect method* starts with net income and applies a series of adjustments to net income to convert it to a cash-basis income number, which is the net cash flow from operating activities. Accountants estimate that *more than 98% of companies preparing the statement of cash flows use the indirect method.* The indirect method is popular because (1) it is easier and less expensive to prepare than the direct method and (2) the direct method requires a supplemental disclosure showing the indirect method (thus, essentially reporting both methods).

The remainder of this appendix discusses the preparation of the statement of cash flows. The indirect method is presented in this section, and the direct method is presented in Appendix B1. (These discussions are independent of each other; both provide complete coverage of the preparation of the statement of cash flows.)

To prepare a statement of cash flows, we need a firm's income statement, comparative balance sheets, and some additional data taken from the accounting records. Exhibit B.2 presents this information for Java

---

EXHIBIT B.2 Financial Data of Java House

JAVA HOUSE
Income Statement
For Year Ended December 31, 2009

Sales.		$250,000
Cost of goods sold. . . .	$148,000	
Wages expense	52,000	
Insurance expense	5,000	
Depreciation expense. .	10,000	
Income tax expense. . .	11,000	
Gain on sale of land . . .	(8,000)	218,000
Net income.		$ 32,000

Additional Data for 2009

1. Purchased the entirety of long-term stock investments for cash at year-end.
2. Sold land costing $20,000 for $28,000 cash.
3. Acquired $60,000 patent at year-end by issuing common stock at par.
4. All accounts payable relate to merchandise purchases.
5. Issued common stock at par for $10,000 cash.
6. Declared and paid cash dividends of $13,000.

JAVA HOUSE
Balance Sheet

	Dec. 31, 2009	Dec. 31, 2008
Assets		
Cash	$ 35,000	$ 10,000
Accounts receivable.	39,000	34,000
Inventory.	54,000	60,000
Prepaid insurance.	17,000	4,000
Long-term investments	15,000	—
PPE assets	180,000	200,000
Accumulated depreciation . . .	(50,000)	(40,000)
Patent.	60,000	—
Total assets.	$350,000	$268,000
Liabilities and Equity		
Accounts payable.	$ 10,000	$ 19,000
Income tax payable	5,000	3,000
Common stock.	260,000	190,000
Retained earnings	75,000	56,000
Total liabilities and equity	$350,000	$268,000

House. We use these data to prepare Java's 2009 statement of cash flows using the indirect method. Java's statement of cash flows explains the $25,000 increase in cash that occurred during 2009 (from $10,000 to $35,000) by classifying the firm's cash flows into operating, investing, and financing categories.

Steps to Compute Net Cash Flow from Operating Activities

The following four steps are applied to construct the net cash flows from operating activities section of the statement of cash flows:

1. **Begin with net income** The first line of the operating section of the statement of cash flows is net income, which is the bottom line from the income statement. This amount is recorded as a positive amount for net income and as a negative amount for a net loss.

2. **Adjust net income (loss) for *noncash* revenues, expenses, gains and losses**
   a. **Noncash revenues and expenses** The income statement often includes noncash expenses such as depreciation and amortization. These expenses are allocations of asset costs over their useful lives to match the revenues generated from those assets. The cash outflow normally occurs when the asset is acquired, which is reported in the *investing* section. Depreciation and amortization expenses do not have cash outflows. Hence, we must eliminate them from the statement of cash flows by adding them back (to "zero them out" because they are negative amounts in the net income computation).
   b. **Gains and losses** Gains and losses on sales of assets are part of investing activities, not operating activities (unless the company is in the business of buying and selling assets). Thus, we must zero them out in the operating section and record the net cash inflows or outflows in the investing section; namely, gains on sales are subtracted from income and losses on sales are added to income.

3. **Adjust net income (loss) for changes in current assets and current liabilities** Net income must be adjusted for changes in current assets and current liabilities (the operating section of the balance sheet). A decrease (from prior year to current year) in a noncash current asset is identified as a cash inflow and an increase is identified as a cash outflow. Conversely, an increase in a current liability is identified as a cash inflow and a decrease as a cash outflow. To make this computation, we use the following guide:

Balance Sheet Account	Cash flow increases from	Cash flow decreases from
Current assets (excluding cash)...	**Account decreases**	**Account increases**
Current liabilities..............	**Account increases**	**Account decreases**

4. **Sum the amounts from steps 1, 2 and 3 to get net cash flows from operating activities.**

   Exhibit B.3 summarizes the adjustments to net income in determining operating cash flows. These are the adjustments applied under the indirect method of computing cash flow from operations.

EXHIBIT B.3 Converting Net Income to Net Cash Flow from Operating Activities	Add (+) or Subtract (−) from Net Income
Net income	$ #
Add depreciation and amortization..	+
Add (subtract): Losses (gains) on asset and liability dispositions	±
Adjust for changes in noncash current assets	
Subtract increases in noncash current assets	−
Add decreases in noncash current assets	+
Adjust for changes in current liabilities	
Add increases in current liabilities..	+
Subtract decreases in current liabilities	−
Net cash flow from operating activities	$ #

Adjustments for noncash revenues, expenses, gains & losses

Adjustments for changes in noncash current assets and current liabilities

To better understand the adjustments for current assets and liabilities, the following table provides brief explanations of adjustments for receivables, inventories, payables and accruals.

	Change in account balance . . .	Means that . . .	Which requires this adjustment to net income to yield cash profit . . .
Receivables	Increase	Sales and net income increase, but cash is not yet received	Deduct increase in receivables from net income
	Decrease	More cash is received than is reported in sales and net income	Add decrease in receivables to net income
Inventories	Increase	Cash is paid for inventories that are not yet reflected in cost of goods sold	Deduct increase in inventories from net income
	Decrease	Cost of goods sold includes inventory costs that were paid for in a prior period	Add decrease in inventories to net income
Payables and accruals	Increase	More goods and services are acquired on credit, delaying cash payment	Add increase in payables and accruals to net income
	Decrease	More cash is paid than that reflected in cost of goods sold or operating expenses	Deduct decrease in payables and accruals from net income

Java House Case Illustration

We next explain and illustrate these adjustments with Java House's data from Exhibit B.2.

Depreciation and Amortization Expenses

Depreciation and amortization expenses represent write-offs of previously recorded assets; so-called noncash expenses. Because depreciation and amortization expenses are subtracted in computing net income, we add these expenses to net income as we convert it to a related net operating cash flow. Adding these expenses to net income eliminates them from the income statement and is a necessary adjustment to obtain cash income. Java House had $10,000 of 2009 depreciation expense, so this amount is added to Java's net income of $32,000.

Net income	$32,000
Add: Depreciation	**10,000**

Gains and Losses Related to Investing or Financing Activities

The income statement can contain gains and losses that relate to investing or financing activities. Gains and losses from the sale of investments, PPE assets, or intangible assets illustrate gains and losses from investing (not operating) activities. A gain or loss from the retirement of bonds payable is an example of a financing gain or loss. The full cash flow effect from these types of events is reported in the investing or financing sections of the statement of cash flows. Therefore, the related gains or losses must be eliminated as we convert net income to net cash flow from operating activities. To eliminate their impact on net income, gains are subtracted and losses are added to net income. Java House had an $8,000 gain from the sale of land in 2009. This gain relates to an investing activity, so it is subtracted from Java's net income.

Net income	$32,000
Add: Depreciation	10,000
Deduct: Gain on sale of land	**(8,000)**

Accounts Receivable Change

Credit sales increase accounts receivable; cash collections on account decrease accounts receivable. If, overall, accounts receivable decrease during a year, then cash collections from customers exceed credit sales revenue by the amount of the decrease. Because sales are added in computing net income, the decrease in accounts receivable is added to net income. In essence, this adjustment replaces the sales amount with the larger amount of cash collections from customers. If accounts receivable increase during a year, then sales revenue exceeds the cash collections from customers by the amount of the increase. Because sales are added in computing net income, the increase in accounts receivable is subtracted from net income as we convert it to a net cash flow from operating activities. In essence, this adjustment replaces the sales amount with the smaller amount of cash collections from customers. Java's accounts receivable increased $5,000 during 2009, so this increase is subtracted from net income under the indirect method.

Net income..	$32,000
Add: Depreciation.....................................	10,000
Deduct: Gain on sale of land	(8,000)
Deduct: Accounts receivable increase.................	**(5,000)**

Inventory Change

The adjustment for an inventory change is one of two adjustments to net income that together cause the cost of goods sold expense to be replaced by an amount representing the cash paid during the period for merchandise purchased. The second adjustment, which we examine shortly, is for the change in accounts payable. The effect of the inventory adjustment alone is to adjust net income for the difference between the cost of goods sold and the cost of merchandise purchased during the period. The cost of merchandise purchased increases inventory; the cost of goods sold decreases inventory. An overall decrease in inventory during a period must mean, therefore, that the cost of merchandise purchased was less than the cost of goods sold by the amount of the decrease. Because cost of goods sold was subtracted in computing net income, the inventory decrease is added to net income. After this adjustment, the effect of the cost of goods sold on net income has been replaced by the smaller cost of merchandise purchased. Similarly, if inventory increased during a period, the cost of merchandise purchased is larger than the cost of goods sold by the amount of the increase. To replace the cost of goods sold with the cost of merchandise purchased, the inventory increase is subtracted from net income. Java's inventory decreased $6,000 during 2009, so this decrease is added to net income.

Net income..	$32,000
Add: Depreciation.....................................	10,000
Deduct: Gain on sale of land	(8,000)
Deduct: Accounts receivable increase....................	(5,000)
Add: Inventory decrease	**6,000**

Prepaid Expenses Change

Cash prepayments of various expenses increase a firm's prepaid expenses. When the related expenses for the period are subsequently recorded, the prepaid expenses decrease. An overall decrease in prepaid expenses for a period means that the cash prepayments were less than the related expenses. Because the expenses were subtracted in determining net income, the indirect method adds the decrease in prepaid expenses to net income as it is converted to a cash flow amount. The effect of the addition is to replace the expense amount with the smaller cash payment amount. Similarly, an increase in prepaid expenses is subtracted from net income because an increase means that the cash prepayments during the year were more than the related expenses. Java's prepaid insurance increased $13,000 during 2009, so this increase is deducted from net income.

Net income..	$32,000
Add: Depreciation.....................................	10,000
Deduct: Gain on sale of land	(8,000)
Deduct: Accounts receivable increase....................	(5,000)
Add: Inventory decrease	6,000
Deduct: Prepaid insurance increase...................	**(13,000)**

Accounts Payable Change

When merchandise is purchased on account, accounts payable increase by the amount of the goods' cost. Accounts payable decrease when cash payments are made to settle the accounts. An overall decrease in accounts payable during a year means that cash payments for purchases were more than the cost of the purchases. An accounts payable decrease, therefore, is subtracted from net income under the indirect method. The deduction, in effect, replaces the cost of merchandise purchased with the larger cash payments for merchandise purchased. (Recall that the earlier inventory adjustment replaced the cost of goods sold with the cost of merchandise purchased.) In contrast, an increase in accounts payable means that cash payments for purchases were less than the cost of purchases for the period. Thus, an accounts payable increase is added to net income as it is converted to a cash flow amount. Java House shows a $9,000 decrease in accounts payable during 2009. This decrease is subtracted from net income.

Net income.	$32,000
Add: Depreciation.	10,000
Deduct: Gain on sale of land	(8,000)
Deduct: Accounts receivable increase.	(5,000)
Add: Inventory decrease	6,000
Deduct: Prepaid insurance increase	(13,000)
Deduct: Accounts payable decrease	**(9,000)**

Accrued Liabilities Change

Changes in accrued liabilities are interpreted the same way as changes in accounts payable. A decrease means that cash payments exceeded the related expense amounts; an increase means that cash payments were less than the related expenses. Decreases are subtracted from net income; increases are added to net income. Java has one accrued liability, income tax payable, and it increased by $2,000 during 2009. The $2,000 increase is added to net income.

Net income.	$32,000
Add: Depreciation.	10,000
Deduct: Gain on sale of land	(8,000)
Deduct: Accounts receivable increase.	(5,000)
Add: Inventory decrease	6,000
Deduct: Prepaid insurance increase	(13,000)
Deduct: Accounts payable decrease.	(9,000)
Add: Income tax payable increase	**2,000**

We have now identified the adjustments to convert Java's net income to its net cash flow from operating activities. The operating activities section of the statement of cash flows appears as follows under the indirect method:

Net income.	$32,000
Add (deduct) items to convert net income to cash basis:	
Depreciation	10,000
Gain on sale of land	(8,000)
Accounts receivable increase.	(5,000)
Inventory decrease	6,000
Prepaid insurance increase.	(13,000)
Accounts payable decrease	(9,000)
Income tax payable increase	2,000
Net cash provided by operating activities	**$15,000**

To summarize, net cash flows from operating activities begins with net income (loss) and eliminates noncash expenses (such as depreciation) and any gains and losses that are properly reported in the investing and financing sections. Next, cash inflows (outflows) relating to changes in the level of current operating assets and liabilities are added (subtracted) to yield net cash flows from operating activities. During the period, Java earned cash operating profits of $34,000 ($32,000 + $10,000 − $8,000), but used $19,000 of cash (−$5,000 + $6,000 − $13,000 − $9,000 + $2,000) to increase net working capital. Cash outflows relating to the increase in net working capital are a common occurrence for growing companies, and this net asset increase must be financed just like the increase in PPE assets.

BUSINESS INSIGHT   **Starbucks' Add-Backs for Operating Cash Flow**

Starbucks reports $315.5 million of net income for 2008 and $1,258.7 million of operating cash inflows. The difference between these numbers is mainly due to $604.5 million of depreciation and amortization expense that is included in net income. Depreciation is a noncash charge; an expense not requiring cash payment. It is added back to income in computing operating cash flows. Starbucks also reports a $325.0 million asset impairment (write-down). This, too, is a noncash charge and is an addback in computing operating cash flows. Starbucks subtracts $117.1 million for deferred taxes, indicating that cash payments of taxes are greater than tax expense reported in income. It also adds $52.6 million for equity in income of investees, meaning that it received more in dividends from affiliated companies than it reported in equity income (see Module 7). Starbucks also adds back its $75.0 million of stock option expense since that compensation is paid in stock, not in cash, and reclassifies the $14.7 million of tax benefits it receives for the exercise of these options from operating activities to financing activities as required under current GAAP.

MANAGERIAL DECISION   **You Are the Securities Analyst**

You are analyzing a company's statement of cash flows. The company has two items relating to its accounts receivable. First, the company finances the sale of its products to some customers; the increase to notes receivable is classified as an investing activity. Second, the company sells its accounts receivable to a separate entity, such as a trust. As a result, sale of receivables is reported as an asset sale; this reduces receivables and yields a gain or loss on sale (in this case, the company is not required to consolidate the trust as a Primary Beneficiary of a Variable Interest Entity). This action increases its operating cash flows. How should you interpret this cash flow increase?

[Answer, p. B-25]

CASH FLOWS FROM INVESTING ACTIVITIES

Analyze Remaining Noncash Assets

LO3 Define and explain net cash flows from investing activities.

Investing activities cause changes in asset accounts. Usually the accounts affected (other than cash) are noncurrent asset accounts such as property, plant and equipment assets and long-term investments, although short-term investment accounts can also be affected. To determine the cash flows from investing activities, *we analyze changes in all noncash asset accounts not used in computing net cash flow from operating activities.* Our objective is to identify any investing cash flows related to these changes.

As before, changes in long-term assets accounts (and investment accounts) are classified as cash inflows and cash outflows according to the following decision rule:

Balance Sheet Account	Cash flow increases from	Cash flow decreases from
Noncurrent assets	Account decreases	Account increases

Increases in long-term assets and investment accounts are identified as cash outflows. Decreases are identified as cash inflows.

Java House Case Illustration

Analyze Change in Long-Term Investments

Java's comparative balance sheets show that long-term investments increased $15,000 during 2009. The increase means that investments must have been purchased, and the additional data reported indicates that cash was spent to purchase long-term stock investments. Purchasing stock is an investing activity. Thus, a $15,000 purchase of stock investments is reported as a cash outflow from investing activities in the statement of cash flows.

Analyze Change in Property, Plant and Equipment Assets

Java's PPE assets decreased $20,000 during 2009. PPE assets decrease as the result of disposals, and the additional data for Java House indicate that land was sold for cash in 2009. Selling land is an investing activity. Thus, the sale of land for $28,000 is reported as a cash inflow from investing activities in the statement of cash flows. (Recall that the $8,000 gain on sale of land was deducted as a reconciling item in the operating section; see above.)

Analyze Change in Accumulated Depreciation

Java's accumulated depreciation increased $10,000 during 2009. Accumulated depreciation increases when depreciation expense is recorded. Java's 2009 depreciation expense was $10,000, so the total change in accumulated depreciation is the result of the recording of depreciation expense. As previously discussed, there is no cash flow related to the recording of depreciation expense, and we have previously adjusted for this expense in our computation of net cash flows from operating activities.

Analyze Change in Patent

We see from the comparative balance sheets that Java had an increase of $60,000 in a patent. The increase means that a patent was acquired, and the additional data indicate that common stock was issued to obtain a patent. This event is a noncash investing (acquiring a patent) and financing (issuing common stock) transaction that must be disclosed as supplementary information to the statement of cash flows.

BUSINESS INSIGHT   **Starbucks' Investing Activities**

Starbucks used $1,086.6 million cash for investing activities in 2008. Of this, $24.1 million [($71.8) million + $20.0 million + $75.9 million] is related to the purchase of securities. Starbucks also spent $74.2 million on acquisitions of other companies; which is the cash portion of the acquisition cost. It might also have issued debt and stock to finance this acquisition, which would be excluded from this statement and would be identified as noncash financing and investing activities in a footnote. Starbucks invested $984.5 million in property, plant, and equipment (PPE). These expenditures might have been for owned property or for leasehold improvements on leased property. It also spent $52.0 million on other investments. Investing activities on the statement of cash flows can involve investments in operating assets (such as purchases of PPE or acquisitions of other companies) or investments in nonoperating assets (such as purchases and sales of marketable securities and other investments).

CASH FLOWS FROM FINANCING ACTIVITIES
Analyze Remaining Liabilities and Equity

Financing activities cause changes in liability and stockholders' equity accounts. Usually the accounts affected are noncurrent accounts such as bonds payable and common stock, although a current liability such as short-term notes payable can also be affected. To determine the cash flows from financing activities, *we analyze changes in all liability and stockholders' equity accounts that were not used in computing net cash flow from operating activities.* Our objective is to identify any financing cash flows related to these changes.

LO4 Define and explain net cash flows from financing activities.

As before, changes in long-term liability and equity accounts are classified as cash inflows and cash outflows according to the following decision rule:

Balance Sheet Account	Cash flow increases from	Cash flow decreases from
Noncurrent liabilities and equity....	Account increases	Account decreases

Increases in long-term liabilities and equity accounts are identified as cash inflows. Decreases are identified as cash outflows.

Java House Case Illustration

Analyze Change in Common Stock

Java's common stock increased $70,000 during 2009. Common stock increases when shares of stock are issued. As noted in discussing the patent increase, common stock with a $60,000 par value was issued in exchange for a patent. This event is disclosed as a noncash investing and financing transaction. The other $10,000 increase in common stock, as noted in the additional data, resulted from an issuance of stock for cash. Issuing common stock is a financing activity, so a $10,000 cash inflow from a stock issuance appears as a financing activity in the statement of cash flows.

Analyze Change in Retained Earnings

Retained earnings grew from $56,000 to $75,000 during 2009—a $19,000 increase. This increase is the net result of Java's $32,000 of net income (which increased retained earnings) and a $13,000 cash dividend (which decreased retained earnings). Because every item in Java's income statement was considered in computing the net cash provided by operating activities, only the cash dividend remains to be considered. Paying a cash dividend is a financing activity. Thus, a $13,000 cash dividend appears as a cash outflow from financing activities in the statement of cash flows. We have now completed the analysis of all of Java's noncash balance sheet accounts and can prepare the 2009 statement of cash flows. Exhibit B.4 shows this statement.

If there are cash inflows and outflows from similar types of investing and financing activities, the inflows and outflows are reported separately (rather than reporting only the net difference). For example, proceeds from the sale of plant assets are reported separately from outlays made to acquire plant assets. Similarly, funds borrowed are reported separately from debt repayments, and proceeds from issuing stock are reported separately from outlays to acquire treasury stock.

BUSINESS INSIGHT **Starbucks' Financing Activities**

Starbucks realized cash *outflows* of $199.1 million ($112.3 million − $311.4 million) from issuance of common stock, net of repurchases. Only stock issued for cash is reflected in the statement of cash flows. Stock issued in connection with acquisitions is not reflected because it does not involve cash. Issuance of stock is often related to the exercise of employee stock options, and companies frequently repurchase stock to offset the dilutive effect of granting the options and to have stock to sell to employees when they exercise their options. Starbucks also reports a cash inflow of $298.8 million ($528.2 million − $228.8 million − $0.6 million) from borrowings during the year. Starbucks also realized a net cash outflow for commercial-paper activities of $297.2 million ($66,068.0 million − $65,770.8 million). The net effect is a decrease in cash of $184.5 million from financing activities.

SUMMARY OF NET CASH FLOW REPORTING

Income statement accounts are all identified within the operating section of the statement of cash flows. Balance sheet items are classified as follows:

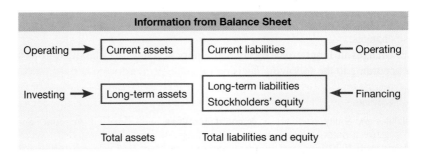

More specifically, and drawing on the Java House illustration, we can summarize the cash flow effects of the income statement and balance sheet information and categorize them into the operating, investing and financing classifications in the following table:

Account	Change	Source or Use	Cash flow effect	Classification on SCF
Current assets				
Accounts receivable	+5,000	Use	−5,000	Operating
Inventories	−6,000	Source	+6,000	Operating
Prepaid insurance.	+13,000	Use	−13,000	Operating
Noncurrent assets				
PPE related.				Investing
Accumulated depreciation . . .	+10,000	Neither	+10,000	Operating
Sale of land				
Proceeds	+28,000	Source	+28,000	Investing
Gain	−8,000	Neither	−8,000	Operating
Investments	+15,000	Use	−15,000	Investing
Current liabilities				
Accounts payable.	−9,000	Use	−9,000	Operating
Income tax payable	+2,000	Source	+2,000	Operating
Long-term liabilities				Financing
Stockholders' equity				
Common stock	+10,000	Source	+10,000	Financing
Retained earnings.				
Net income	+32,000	Source	+32,000	Operating
Dividends	+13,000	Use	−13,000	Financing
Total (net cash flow)			+25,000	

The current year's cash balance increases by $25,000, from $10,000 to $35,000. Formal preparation of the statement of cash flows can proceed once we have addressed one final issue: required supplemental disclosures. We discuss that topic in the next section.

Supplemental Disclosures for Indirect Method

When the indirect method is used in the statement of cash flows, three separate disclosures are required: (1) two specific operating cash outflows—cash paid for interest and cash paid for income taxes, (2) a schedule or description of all noncash investing and financing transactions, and (3) the firm's policy for determining which highly liquid, short-term investments are treated as cash equivalents. Noncash investing and financing activities include the issuance of stocks, bonds, or leases in exchange for property, plant, and equipment (PPE) assets or intangible assets; the exchange of long-term assets for other long-term assets; and the conversion of long-term debt into common stock.

Java House Case Illustration

Java House incurred no interest cost during 2009. It did pay income taxes. Our discussion of the $2,000 change in income tax payable during 2009 revealed that the increase meant that cash tax payments were less than income tax expense by the amount of the increase. Income tax expense was $11,000, so the cash paid for income taxes was $2,000 less than $11,000, or $9,000.

Java House did have one noncash investing and financing event during 2009: the issuance of common stock to acquire a patent. This event, as well as the cash paid for income taxes, is disclosed as supplemental information to the statement of cash flows in Exhibit B.4.

EXHIBIT B.4   Statement of Cash Flows for Indirect Method with Supplemental Disclosures

JAVA HOUSE
Statement of Cash Flows
For Year Ended December 31, 2009

Net cash flow from operating activities		
Net income	$32,000	
Add (deduct) items to convert net income to cash basis		
Depreciation	10,000	
Gain on sale of land	(8,000)	
Accounts receivable increase	(5,000)	
Inventory decrease	6,000	
Prepaid insurance increase	(13,000)	
Accounts payable decrease	(9,000)	
Income tax payable increase	2,000	
Net cash provided by operating activities		$15,000
Cash flows from investing activities		
Purchase of stock investments	(15,000)	
Sale of land	28,000	
Net cash provided by investing activities		13,000
Cash flows from financing activities		
Issuance of common stock	10,000	
Payment of dividends	(13,000)	
Net cash used by financing activities		(3,000)
Net increase in cash		25,000
Cash at beginning of year		10,000
Cash at end of year		$35,000
Supplemental cash flow disclosures		
Cash paid for income taxes	$ 9,000	
Schedule of noncash investing and financing activities		
Issuance of common stock to acquire patent	$60,000	

APPLICATIONS OF CASH FLOW INFORMATION

Usefulness of Classifications

The classification of cash flows into three categories of activities helps financial statement users interpret cash flow data. To illustrate, assume that companies D, E, and F are similar companies operating in the same industry. Each company reports a $100,000 cash increase during the current year. Information from their statements of cash flows is summarized below.

	Company D	Company E	Company F
Net cash provided by operating activities	$100,000	$ 0	$ 0
Cash flows from investing activities			
Sale of property, plant, and equipment (PPE)	0	100,000	0
Cash flows from financing activities			
Issuance of notes payable	0	0	100,000
Net increase in cash	$100,000	$100,000	$100,000

Although each company's net cash increase was the same, the source of the increase varied by company. This variation affects the analysis of the cash flow data, particularly for potential short-term creditors who must evaluate the likelihood of obtaining repayment in the future for any funds loaned to the company. Based only on these cash flow data, a potential creditor would feel more comfortable lending money to D than to either E or F. This is because D's cash increase came from its operating activities, whereas both E and F could only break even on their cash flows from operations. Also, E's cash increase came from the sale of property, plant, and equipment (PPE) assets, a source that is not likely to recur regularly. F's cash increase came entirely from borrowed funds. This means F faces additional cash burdens in the future when the interest and principal payments on the note payable become due.

| BUSINESS INSIGHT | Objectivity of Cash |

Usefulness of financial statements is enhanced when the underlying data are objective and verifiable. Measuring cash and the changes in cash are among the most objective measurements that accountants make. Thus, the statement of cash flows is arguably the most objective financial statement. This characteristic of the statement of cash flows is welcomed by those investors and creditors interested in evaluating the quality of a firm's income.

Usefulness of the Statement of Cash Flows

A statement of cash flows shows the periodic cash effects of a firm's operating, investing, and financing activities. Distinguishing among these different categories of cash flows helps users compare, evaluate, and predict cash flows. With cash flow information, creditors and investors are better able to assess a firm's ability to settle its liabilities and pay its dividends. A firm's need for outside financing is also better evaluated when using cash flow data. Over time, the statement of cash flows permits users to observe and access management's investing and financing policies.

A statement of cash flows also provides information useful in evaluating a firm's financial flexibility. *Financial flexibility* is a firm's ability to generate sufficient amounts of cash to respond to unanticipated needs and opportunities. Information about past cash flows, particularly cash flows from operations, helps in assessing financial flexibility. An evaluation of a firm's ability to survive an unexpected drop in demand, for example, should include a review of its past cash flows from operations. The larger these cash flows, the greater is the firm's ability to withstand adverse changes in economic conditions. Other financial statements, particularly the balance sheet and its notes, also contain information useful for judging financial flexibility.

Some investors and creditors find the statement of cash flows useful in evaluating the quality of a firm's income. As we know, determining income under accrual accounting procedures requires many accruals, deferrals, allocations, and valuations. These adjustment and measurement procedures introduce more subjectivity into income determination than some financial statement users prefer. These users relate a more objective performance measure—cash flow from operations—to net income. To these users, the higher this ratio is, the higher is the quality of income.

In analyzing the statement of cash flows, we must not necessarily conclude that the company is better off if cash increases and worse off if cash decreases. It is not the cash change that is most important, but the sources of that change. For example, what are the sources of cash inflows? Are these sources transitory? Are these sources mainly from operating activities? We must also review the uses of cash. Has the company invested its cash in operating areas to strengthen its competitive position? Is it able to comfortably meet its debt obligations? Has it diverted cash to creditors or investors at the expense of the other? Such questions and answers are key to properly interpreting the statement of cash flows for business decisions.

Ratio Analyses of Cash Flows

Data from the statement of cash flows enter into various financial ratios. Two such ratios are the operating cash flow to current liabilities ratio and the operating cash flow to capital expenditures ratio.

LO5 Describe and apply ratios based on operating cash flows.

Operating Cash Flow to Current Liabilities Ratio

Two measures previously introduced—the current ratio and the quick ratio—emphasize the relation of current assets to current liabilities in an attempt to measure the ability of the firm to liquidate current liabilities when they become due. The **operating cash flow to current liabilities ratio** is another measure of the ability to liquidate current liabilities and is calculated as follows:

Operating Cash Flow to Current Liabilities = Cash Flow from Operating Activities/Average Current Liabilities

Net cash flow from operating activities is obtained from the statement of cash flows; it represents the excess amount of cash derived from operations during the year after deducting working capital needs and payments required on current liabilities. The denominator is the average of the beginning and ending current liabilities for the year.

To illustrate, the following amounts are taken from the 2008 financial statements for Cisco Systems, Inc.

Net cash flow from operating activities	$12,089 million
Current liabilities at beginning of the year	13,358 million
Current liabilities at end of the year	13,858 million

Its operating cash flow to current liabilities ratio of 0.89 is computed as follows:

$$\text{\$12,089 million}/[(\text{\$13,358 million} + \text{\$13,858 million})/2] = 0.89$$

The higher this ratio, the stronger is a firm's ability to settle current liabilities as they come due. A ratio of 0.5 is considered a good ratio, so, Cisco's ratio of 0.89 is above average.

Operating Cash Flow to Capital Expenditures Ratio

To remain competitive, an entity must be able to replace, and expand when appropriate, its property, plant, and equipment. A ratio that helps assess a firm's ability to do this from internally generated cash flow is the **operating cash flow to capital expenditures ratio**, which is computed as follows:

Operating Cash Flow to Capital Expenditures = Cash Flow from Operating Activities/Annual Capital Expenditures

The numerator in this ratio comes from the first section of the statement of cash flows—the section reporting the net cash flow from operating activities. Information for the denominator can be found in one or more places in the financial statements and related disclosures. Data on capital expenditures are part of the required industry segment disclosures in notes to the financial statements. Capital expenditures are often also shown in the investing activities section of the statement of cash flows. Also, capital expenditures often appear in the comparative selected financial data presented as supplementary information to the financial statements. Finally, management's discussion and analysis of the statements commonly identify the annual capital expenditures.

A ratio in excess of 1.0 means that the firm's current operating activities are providing cash in excess of the amount needed to provide the desired level of plant capacity and would normally be considered a sign of financial strength. This ratio is also viewed as an indicator of long-term solvency—a ratio exceeding 1.0 means that there is operating cash flow in excess of capital needs that can then be used to repay outstanding long-term debt.

The interpretation of this ratio for a firm is influenced by its trend in recent years, the ratio size being achieved by other firms in the same industry, and the stage of the firm's life cycle. A firm in the early stages of its life cycle, when periods of rapid expansion occur, is expected to experience a lower ratio than a firm in the mature stage of its life cycle, when maintenance of plant capacity is more likely than expansion of capacity.

To illustrate the ratio's computation, Cicso Systems reported capital expenditures in 2008 of $1,268 million. Cisco's operating cash flow to capital expenditures ratio for that same year is 9.53, computed as $12,089 million/$1,268 million. Following are recent operating cash flow to capital expenditures ratios for several companies:

Colgate-Palmolive (consumer grocery products).	3.78
Lockheed Martin (aerospace).	4.51
Verizon Communications (telecommunications)	1.47
Harley-Davidson (motorcycle manufacturer)	3.30
Home Depot (home products).	1.61

APPENDIX-END REVIEW

Part A

1. Which of the following is not disclosed in a statement of cash flows?
   a. A transfer of cash to a cash equivalent investment
   b. The amount of cash at year-end
   c. Cash outflows from investing activities during the period
   d. Cash inflows from financing activities during the period
2. Which of the following events appears in the cash flows from investing activities section of the statement of cash flows?
   a. Cash received as interest
   b. Cash received from issuance of common stock
   c. Cash purchase of equipment
   d. Cash payment of dividends
3. Which of the following events appears in the cash flows from financing activities section of the statement of cash flows?
   a. Cash purchase of equipment
   b. Cash purchase of bonds issued by another company
   c. Cash received as repayment for funds loaned
   d. Cash purchase of treasury stock
4. Tyler Company has a net income of $49,000 and the following related items:

Depreciation expense.	$ 5,000
Accounts receivable increase.	2,000
Inventory decrease.	10,000
Accounts payable decrease.	4,000

   Using the indirect method, what is Tyler's net cash flow from operations?
   a. $42,000   b. $46,000   c. $58,000   d. $38,000

Solution

   1. *a*   2. *c*   3. *d*   4. *c*

Part B

Expresso Royale's income statement and comparative balance sheets follow:

EXPRESSO ROYALE Income Statement For Year Ended December 31, 2009		
Sales.		$385,000
Dividend income.		5,000
		390,000
Cost of goods sold.	$233,000	
Wages expense	82,000	
Advertising expense.	10,000	
Depreciation expense.	11,000	
Income tax expense.	17,000	
Loss on sale of investments.	2,000	355,000
Net income.		$ 35,000

EXPRESSO ROYALE Balance Sheets	Dec. 31, 2009	Dec. 31, 2008
Assets		
Cash..	$ 8,000	$ 12,000
Accounts receivable............................	22,000	28,000
Inventory.......................................	94,000	66,000
Prepaid advertising.............................	12,000	9,000
Long-term investments—Available-for-sale........	30,000	41,000
Fair value adjustment to investments.............	—	(1,000)
Plant assets	178,000	130,000
Accumulated depreciation......................	(72,000)	(61,000)
Total assets...................................	$272,000	$224,000
Liabilities and Equity		
Accounts payable..............................	$ 27,000	$ 14,000
Wages payable................................	6,000	2,500
Income tax payable	3,000	4,500
Common stock.................................	139,000	125,000
Retained earnings	97,000	79,000
Unrealized loss on investments	—	(1,000)
Total liabilities and equity......................	$272,000	$224,000

Cash dividends of $17,000 were declared and paid during 2009. Plant assets were purchased for cash in 2009, and, later in the year, additional common stock was issued for cash. Investments costing $11,000 were sold for cash at a $2,000 loss in 2009; an unrealized loss of $1,000 on these investments had been recorded in 2008 (at December 31, 2009, the cost and fair value of unsold investments are equal).

Required
a. Compute the change in cash that occurred during 2009.
b. Prepare a 2009 statement of cash flows using the indirect method.

Solution
a. $8,000 ending balance − $12,000 beginning balance = $4,000 decrease in cash
b. (1) Use the indirect method to determine the net cash flow from operating activities.
   - Adjustments to convert Expresso Royale's net income of $35,000 to a net cash provided by operating activities of $38,000 are shown in the following statement of cash flows.
   (2) Analyze changes in remaining noncash asset (and contra asset) accounts to determine cash flows from investing activities.
   - Long-Term Investments: $11,000 decrease resulted from sale of investments for cash at a $2,000 loss. Cash received from sale of investments = $9,000 ($11,000 cost − $2,000 loss).
   - Fair Value Adjustment to Investments: $1,000 decrease resulted from the elimination of this account balance (and the Unrealized Loss on Investments) at the end of 2009. No cash flow effect.
   - Plant Assets: $48,000 increase resulted from purchase of plant assets for cash. Cash paid to purchase plant assets = $48,000.
   - Accumulated Depreciation: $11,000 increase resulted from the recording of 2009 depreciation. No cash flow effect.
   (3) Analyze changes in remaining liability and stockholders' equity accounts to determine cash flows from financing activities.
   - Common Stock: $14,000 increase resulted from the issuance of stock for cash. Cash received from issuance of common stock = $14,000.
   - Retained Earnings: $18,000 increase resulted from net income of $35,000 and dividend declaration of $17,000. Cash dividends paid = $17,000.

- Unrealized Loss on Investments: $1,000 decrease resulted from the elimination of this account balance (and the Fair Value Adjustment to Investments) at the end of 2009. No cash flow effect.

The statement of cash flows follows:

EXPRESSO ROYALE Statement of Cash Flows For Year Ended December 31, 2009		
Net cash flow from operating activities		
Net income.	$35,000	
Add (deduct) items to convert net income to cash basis		
Depreciation	11,000	
Loss on sale of investments	2,000	
Accounts receivable decrease	6,000	
Inventory increase.	(28,000)	
Prepaid advertising increase.	(3,000)	
Accounts payable increase.	13,000	
Wages payable increase.	3,500	
Income tax payable decrease.	(1,500)	
Net cash provided by operating activities		$38,000
Cash flows from investing activities		
Sale of investments	9,000	
Purchase of plant assets	(48,000)	
Net cash used by investing activities.		(39,000)
Cash flows from financing activities		
Issuance of common stock.	14,000	
Payment of dividends	(17,000)	
Net cash used by financing activities.		(3,000)
Net decrease in cash		(4,000)
Cash at beginning of year		12,000
Cash at end of year		$ 8,000

APPENDIX B1: Direct Method Reporting for the Statement of Cash Flows

To prepare a statement of cash flows, we need a firm's income statement, comparative balance sheets, and some additional data taken from the accounting records. Exhibit B.2 presents this information for Java House. We use these data to prepare Java's 2009 statement of cash flows using the direct method. Java's statement of cash flows explains the $25,000 increase in cash that occurred during 2009 (from $10,000 to $35,000) by classifying the firm's cash flows into operating, investing, and financing categories. To get the information to construct the statement, we do the following:

1. **Use the direct method to determine individual cash flows from operating activities.** We use changes that occurred during 2009 in various current asset and current liability accounts.
2. **Determine cash flows from investing activities.** We do this by analyzing changes in noncurrent asset accounts.
3. **Determine cash flows from financing activities.** We do this by analyzing changes in liability and stockholders' equity accounts.

The net cash flows from investing and financing are identical to those prepared using the indirect method. Only the format of the net cash flows from operating activities differs between the two methods, not the total amount of cash generated from operating activities.

Cash Flows from Operating Activities

The **direct method** presents net cash flow from operating activities by showing the major categories of operating cash receipts and payments. The operating cash receipts and payments are usually determined by converting the accrual revenues and expenses to corresponding cash amounts. It is efficient to do it this way because the accrual revenues and expenses are readily available in the income statement.

Converting Revenues and Expenses to Cash Flows

Exhibit B.5 summarizes the procedures for converting individual income statement items to corresponding cash flows from operating activities.

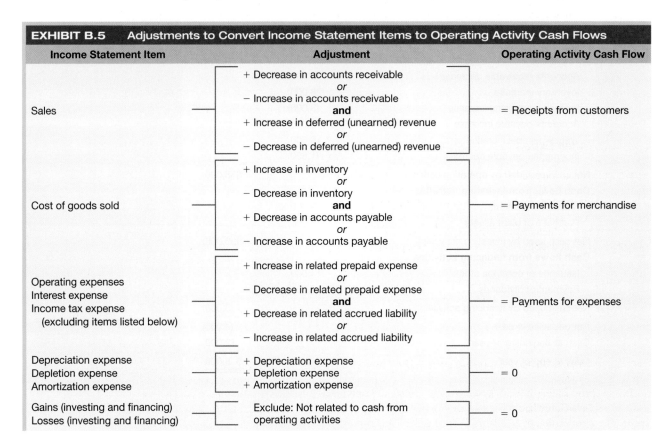

EXHIBIT B.5   Adjustments to Convert Income Statement Items to Operating Activity Cash Flows

Income Statement Item	Adjustment	Operating Activity Cash Flow
Sales	+ Decrease in accounts receivable or − Increase in accounts receivable **and** + Increase in deferred (unearned) revenue or − Decrease in deferred (unearned) revenue	= Receipts from customers
Cost of goods sold	+ Increase in inventory or − Decrease in inventory **and** + Decrease in accounts payable or − Increase in accounts payable	= Payments for merchandise
Operating expenses Interest expense Income tax expense (excluding items listed below)	+ Increase in related prepaid expense or − Decrease in related prepaid expense **and** + Decrease in related accrued liability or − Increase in related accrued liability	= Payments for expenses
Depreciation expense Depletion expense Amortization expense	+ Depreciation expense + Depletion expense + Amortization expense	= 0
Gains (investing and financing) Losses (investing and financing)	Exclude: Not related to cash from operating activities	= 0

Java House Case Illustration

We next explain and illustrate the process of converting Java House's 2009 revenues and expenses to corresponding cash flows from operating activities under the direct method.

Convert Sales to Cash Received from Customers

During 2009, accounts receivable increased $5,000. This increase means that during 2009, cash collections on account (which decrease accounts receivable) were less than credit sales (which increase accounts receivable). We compute cash received from customers as follows (this computation assumes that no accounts were written off as uncollectible during the period):

Sales	$250,000
− Increase in accounts receivable	(5,000)
= Cash received from customers	$245,000

Convert Cost of Goods Sold to Cash Paid for Merchandise Purchased

The conversion of cost of goods sold to cash paid for merchandise purchased is a two-step process. First, cost of goods sold is adjusted for the change in inventory to determine the amount of purchases during the year. Then the purchases amount is adjusted for the change in accounts payable to derive the cash paid for merchandise purchased. Inventory decreased from $60,000 to $54,000 during 2009. This $6,000 decrease indicates that the cost of goods sold exceeded the cost of goods purchased during the year. The year's purchases amount is computed as follows:

Cost of goods sold	. . . .	$148,000
− Decrease in inventory	. . . .	(6,000)
= Purchases	. . . .	$142,000

During 2009, accounts payable decreased $9,000. This decrease reflects the fact that cash payments for merchandise purchased on account (which decrease accounts payable) exceeded purchases on account (which increase accounts payable). The cash paid for merchandise purchased, therefore, is computed as follows:

Purchases	. . . .	$142,000
+ Decrease in accounts payable	. . . .	9,000
= Cash paid for merchandise purchased	. . . .	$151,000

Convert Wages Expense to Cash Paid to Employees

No adjustment to wages expense is needed. The absence of any beginning or ending accrued liability for wages payable means that wages expense and cash paid to employees as wages are the same amount: $52,000.

Convert Insurance Expense to Cash Paid for Insurance

Prepaid insurance increased $13,000 during 2009. The $13,000 increase reflects the excess of cash paid for insurance during 2009 (which increases prepaid insurance) over the year's insurance expense (which decreases prepaid insurance). Starting with insurance expense the cash paid for insurance is computed as follows:

Insurance expense	. . . .	$ 5,000
+ Increase in prepaid insurance	. . . .	13,000
= Cash paid for insurance	. . . .	$18,000

Eliminate Depreciation Expense and Other Noncash Operating Expenses

Depreciation expense is a noncash expense. Because it does not represent a cash payment, depreciation expense is eliminated (by adding it back) as we convert accrual expense amounts to the corresponding amounts of cash payments. If Java House had any amortization expense or depletion expense, it would eliminate them for the same reason. The amortization of an intangible asset and the depletion of a natural resource are noncash expenses.

Convert Income Tax Expense to Cash Paid for Income Taxes

The increase in income tax payable from $3,000 at December 31, 2008, to $5,000 at December 31, 2009, means that 2009's income tax expense (which increases income tax payable) was $2,000 more than 2009's tax payments (which decrease income tax payable). If we start with income tax expense, then we calculate cash paid for income taxes as follows:

Income tax expense	. . . .	$11,000
− Increase in income tax payable	. . . .	(2,000)
= Cash paid for income taxes	. . . .	$ 9,000

Omit Gains and Losses Related to Investing and Financing Activities

The income statement may contain gains and losses related to investing or financing activities. Examples include gains and losses from the sale of plant assets and gains and losses from the retirement of bonds payable. Because these gains and losses are not related to operating activities, we omit them as we convert income statement items to various cash flows from operating activities. The cash flows relating to these gains and losses are reported in the investing activities or financing activities sections of the statement of cash flows. Java House had an $8,000 gain from the sale of land in 2009. This gain is excluded; no related cash flow appears within the operating activities category.

We have now applied the adjustments to convert each accrual revenue and expense to the corresponding operating cash flow. We use these individual cash flows to prepare the operating activities section of the statement of cash flows; see Exhibit B.6

EXHIBIT B.6   Direct Method Operating Section of Statement of Cash Flows

Cash received from customers		$245,000
Cash paid for merchandise purchased	$151,000	
Cash paid to employees.	52,000	
Cash paid for insurance	18,000	
Cash paid for income taxes	9,000	230,000
Net cash provided by operating activities		$ 15,000

Cash Flows from Investing and Financing

The reporting of investing and financing activities in the statement of cash flows is identical under the indirect and direct methods. Thus, we simply refer to the previous sections in Appendix B for explanations.

Supplemental Disclosures

When the direct method is used for the statement of cash flows, three separate disclosures are required: (1) a reconciliation of net income to the net cash flow from operating activities, (2) a schedule or description of all noncash investing and financing transactions, and (3) the firm's policy for determining which highly liquid, short-term investments are treated as cash equivalents. The firm's policy regarding cash equivalents is placed in the financial statement notes. The other two separate disclosures are reported either in the notes or at the bottom of the statement of cash flows.

The required reconciliation is essentially the indirect method of computing cash flow from operating activities. *Thus, when the direct method is used in the statement of cash flows, the indirect method is a required separate disclosure.* We discussed the indirect method earlier in this appendix.

Java House did have one noncash investing and financing event during 2009: the issuance of common stock to acquire a patent. This event is disclosed as supplemental information to the statement of cash flows in Exhibit B.4.

APPENDIX-END REVIEW

Expresso Royale's income statement and comparative balance sheets follow:

EXPRESSO ROYALE Income Statement For Year Ended December 31, 2009		
Sales.		$385,000
Dividend income.		5,000
		390,000
Cost of goods sold.	$233,000	
Wages expense	82,000	
Advertising expense.	10,000	
Depreciation expense.	11,000	
Income tax expense.	17,000	
Loss on sale of investments.	2,000	355,000
Net income.		$ 35,000

EXPRESSO ROYALE Balance Sheets	Dec. 31, 2009	Dec. 31, 2008
Assets		
Cash.	$ 8,000	$ 12,000
Accounts receivable.	22,000	28,000
Inventory.	94,000	66,000
Prepaid advertising.	12,000	9,000
Long-term investments—Available-for-sale.	30,000	41,000
Fair value adjustment to investments.	—	(1,000)
Plant assets	178,000	130,000
Accumulated depreciation	(72,000)	(61,000)
Total assets.	$272,000	$224,000
Liabilities and Equity		
Accounts payable.	$ 27,000	$ 14,000
Wages payable.	6,000	2,500
Income tax payable	3,000	4,500
Common stock.	139,000	125,000
Retained earnings	97,000	79,000
Unrealized loss on investments	—	(1,000)
Total liabilities and equity	$272,000	$224,000

Cash dividends of $17,000 were declared and paid during 2009. Plant assets were purchased for cash in 2009, and later in the year, additional common stock was issued for cash. Investments costing $11,000 were sold for cash at a $2,000 loss in 2009; an unrealized loss of $1,000 on these investments had been recorded in 2008 (at December 31, 2009, the cost and fair value of unsold investments are equal).

Required

a. Compute the change in cash that occurred during 2009.
b. Prepare a 2009 statement of cash flows using the direct method.

Solution

a. $8,000 ending balance − $12,000 beginning balance = $4,000 decrease in cash
b. (1) Use the direct method to determine the individual cash flows from operating activities.
   • $385,000 sales + $6,000 accounts receivable decrease = $391,000 cash received from customers
   • $5,000 dividend income = $5,000 cash received as dividends
   • $233,000 cost of goods sold + $28,000 inventory increase − $13,000 accounts payable increase = $248,000 cash paid for merchandise purchased
   • $82,000 wages expense − $3,500 wages payable increase = $78,500 cash paid to employees
   • $10,000 advertising expense + $3,000 prepaid advertising increase = $13,000 cash paid for advertising
   • $17,000 income tax expense + $1,500 income tax payable decrease = $18,500 cash paid for income taxes
   (2) Analyze changes in remaining noncash asset (and contra asset) accounts to determine cash flows from investing activities.
   • Long-term investments: $11,000 decrease resulted from sale of investments for cash at a $2,000 loss. Cash received from sale of investments = $9,000 ($11,000 cost − $2,000 loss).
   • Fair value adjustment to investments: $1,000 decrease resulted from the elimination of this account balance (and the unrealized loss on investments) at the end of 2009. No cash flow effect.
   • Plant assets: $48,000 increase resulted from purchase of plant assets for cash. Cash paid to purchase plant assets = $48,000.
   • Accumulated depreciation: $11,000 increase resulted from the recording of 2009 depreciation. No cash flow effect.

(3) Analyze changes in remaining liability and stockholders' equity accounts to determine cash flows from financing activities.
- Common stock: $14,000 increase resulted from the issuance of stock for cash. Cash received from issuance of common stock = $14,000.
- Retained earnings: $18,000 increase resulted from net income of $35,000 and dividend declaration of $17,000. Cash dividends paid = $17,000.
- Unrealized loss on investments: $1,000 decrease resulted from the elimination of this account balance (and the fair value adjustment to investments) at the end of 2009. No cash flow effect.

The statement of cash flows under the direct method follows:

EXPRESSO ROYALE Statement of Cash Flows For Year Ended December 31, 2009		
Cash flows from operating activities		
Cash received from customers.	$391,000	
Cash received as dividends	5,000	
Cash paid for merchandise purchased.	(248,000)	
Cash paid to employees.	(78,500)	
Cash paid for advertising	(13,000)	
Cash paid for income taxes	(18,500)	
Net cash provided by operating activities		$ 38,000
Cash flows from investing activities		
Sale of investments	9,000	
Purchase of plant assets	(48,000)	
Net cash used by investing activities		(39,000)
Cash flows from financing activities		
Issuance of common stock.	14,000	
Payment of dividends.	(17,000)	
Net cash used by financing activities		(3,000)
Net decrease in cash		(4,000)
Cash at beginning of year		12,000
Cash at end of year		$ 8,000

GUIDANCE ANSWERS

MANAGERIAL DECISION You Are the Securities Analyst

Many companies, but not all, treat customers' notes receivable as an investing activity. In 2005, the SEC became concerned with this practice and issued letters to a number of companies objecting to this accounting classification. "Presenting cash receipts from receivables generated by the sale of inventory as investing activities in the company's consolidated statements of cash flows is not in accordance with GAAP," wrote the chief accountant for the SEC's division of corporation finance, in her letter to the companies ("Little Campus Lab Shakes Big Firms—Georgia Tech Crew's Report Spurs Change in Accounting for Operating Cash Flow," March 1, 2005, *The Wall Street Journal*). The SEC's position is that these notes receivable are an operating activity and analysts are certainly justified in treating them likewise. Concerning the sale of receivables, so long as the separate entity (a trust in this case) is properly structured, the transaction can be treated as a sale (rather than require consolidation) with a consequent reduction in receivables and a gain or loss on the sale recorded in the income statement. Many analysts treat this as a financing activity and argue that the cash inflow should not be regarded as an increase in operating cash flows. Bottom line: many argue that operating cash flows do not increase as a result of these two transactions and analysts should adjust the statement of cash flows to properly classify the financing of receivables as an operating activity and the sale of receivables as a financing activity.

Superscript ^{B1} denotes assignments based on Appendix B1.

DISCUSSION QUESTIONS

Q B-1. What is the definition of *cash equivalents?* Give three examples of cash equivalents.

Q B-2. Why are cash equivalents included with cash in a statement of cash flows?

Q B-3. What are the three major types of activities classified on a statement of cash flows? Give an example of a cash inflow and a cash outflow in each classification.

Q B-4. In which of the three activity categories of a statement of cash flows would each of the following items appear? Indicate for each item whether it represents a cash inflow or a cash outflow:
  a. Cash purchase of equipment.
  b. Cash collection on loans.
  c. Cash dividends paid.
  d. Cash dividends received.
  e. Cash proceeds from issuing stock.
  f. Cash receipts from customers.
  g. Cash interest paid.
  h. Cash interest received.

Q B-5. Traverse Company acquired a $3,000,000 building by issuing $3,000,000 worth of bonds payable. In terms of cash flow reporting, what type of transaction is this? What special disclosure requirements apply to a transaction of this type?

Q B-6. Why are noncash investing and financing transactions disclosed as supplemental information to a statement of cash flows?

Q B-7. Why is a statement of cash flows a useful financial statement?

Q B-8. What is the difference between the direct method and the indirect method of presenting net cash flow from operating activities?

Q B-9. In determining net cash flow from operating activities using the indirect method, why must we add depreciation back to net income? Give an example of another item that is added back to net income under the indirect method.

Q B-10. Vista Company sold for $98,000 cash land originally costing $70,000. The company recorded a gain on the sale of $28,000. How is this event reported in a statement of cash flows using the indirect method?

Q B-11. A firm uses the indirect method. Using the following information, what is its net cash flow from operating activities?

Net income................................	$88,000
Accounts receivable decrease.............	13,000
Inventory increase	9,000
Accounts payable decrease................	3,500
Income tax payable increase	1,500
Depreciation expense.....................	6,000

Q B-12. What separate disclosures are required for a company that reports a statement of cash flows using the indirect method?

Q B-13. If a business had a net loss for the year, under what circumstances would the statement of cash flows show a positive net cash flow from operating activities?

Q B-14.^{B1} A firm is converting its accrual revenues to corresponding cash amounts using the direct method. Sales on the income statement are $925,000. Beginning and ending accounts receivable on the balance sheet are $58,000 and $44,000, respectively. What is the amount of cash received from customers?

Q B-15.^{B1} A firm reports $86,000 wages expense in its income statement. If beginning and ending wages payable are $3,900 and $2,800, respectively, what is the amount of cash paid to employees?

Q B-16.^{B1} A firm reports $43,000 advertising expense in its income statement. If beginning and ending prepaid advertising are $6,000 and $7,600, respectively, what is the amount of cash paid for advertising?

Q B-17.^{B1} Rusk Company sold equipment for $5,100 cash that had cost $35,000 and had $29,000 of accumulated depreciation. How is this event reported in a statement of cash flows using the direct method?

Q B-18.^{B1} What separate disclosures are required for a company that reports a statement of cash flows using the direct method?

Q B-19.   How is the operating cash flow to current liabilities ratio calculated? Explain its use.

Q B-20.   How is the operating cash flow to capital expenditures ratio calculated? Explain its use.

Q B-21.   The statement of cash flows provides information that may be useful in predicting future cash flows, evaluating financial flexibility, assessing liquidity, and identifying financing needs. It is not, however, the best financial statement for learning about a firm's financial performance during a period; information about periodic financial performance is provided by the income statement. Two basic principles—the revenue recognition principle and the matching concept—work to distinguish the income statement from the statement of cash flows. (a) Define the revenue recognition principle and the matching concept. (b) Briefly explain how these two principles work to make the income statement a better report on periodic financial performance than the statement of cash flows.

**Assignments with the WebAssign. logo in the margin are available in WebAssign.
See the Preface of the book for details.**

MINI EXERCISES

M B-22.   Classification of Cash Flows   (LO1)
For each of the items below, indicate whether the cash flow relates to an operating activity, an investing activity, or a financing activity.
   a.   Cash receipts from customers for services rendered.
   b.   Sale of long-term investments for cash.
   c.   Acquisition of plant assets for cash.
   d.   Payment of income taxes.
   e.   Bonds payable issued for cash.
   f.   Payment of cash dividends declared in previous year.
   g.   Purchase of short-term investments (not cash equivalents) for cash.

M B-23.   Classification of Cash Flows   (LO1)
For each of the items below, indicate whether it is (1) a cash flow from an operating activity, (2) a cash flow from an investing activity, (3) a cash flow from a financing activity, (4) a noncash investing and financing activity, or (5) none of the above.
   a.   Paid cash to retire bonds payable at a loss.
   b.   Received cash as settlement of a lawsuit.
   c.   Acquired a patent in exchange for common stock.
   d.   Received advance payments from customers on orders for custom-made goods.
   e.   Gave large cash contribution to local university.
   f.   Invested cash in 60-day commercial paper (a cash equivalent).

M B-24.   Net Cash Flow from Operating Activities (Indirect Method)   (LO2)
The following information was obtained from Galena Company's comparative balance sheets. Assume that Galena Company's 2009 income statement showed depreciation expense of $8,000, a gain on sale of investments of $9,000, and a net income of $45,000. Calculate the net cash flow from operating activities using the indirect method.

	Dec. 31, 2009	Dec. 31, 2008
Cash.........................	$ 19,000	$ 9,000
Accounts receivable.................	44,000	35,000
Inventory........................	55,000	49,000
Prepaid rent	6,000	8,000
Long-term investments	21,000	34,000
Plant assets	150,000	106,000
Accumulated depreciation	40,000	32,000
Accounts payable..................	24,000	20,000
Income tax payable	4,000	6,000
Common stock....................	121,000	92,000
Retained earnings	106,000	91,000

M B-25.   Net Cash Flow from Operating Activities (Indirect Method)   (LO2)
Cairo Company had a $21,000 net loss from operations for 2009. Depreciation expense for 2009 was $8,600 and a 2009 cash dividend of $6,000 was declared and paid. Balances of the current asset and

current liability accounts at the beginning and end of 2009 follow. Did Cairo Company's 2009 operating activities provide or use cash? Use the indirect method to determine your answer.

	Ending	Beginning
Cash.	$ 3,500	$ 7,000
Accounts receivable.	16,000	25,000
Inventory.	50,000	53,000
Prepaid expenses.	6,000	9,000
Accounts payable.	12,000	8,000
Accrued liabilities	5,000	7,600

M B-26.[B1] **Operating Cash Flows (Direct Method)** **(LO2)**

Calculate the cash flow for each of the following cases.

a.   Cash paid for rent:

Rent expense	$60,000
Prepaid rent, beginning year	10,000
Prepaid rent, end of year	8,000

b.   Cash received as interest:

Interest income.	$16,000
Interest receivable, beginning year. . . .	3,000
Interest receivable, end of year	3,700

c.   Cash paid for merchandise purchased:

Cost of goods sold.	$98,000
Inventory, beginning year	19,000
Inventory, end of year.	22,000
Accounts payable, beginning year. . . .	11,000
Accounts payable, end of year.	7,000

M B-27.[B1] **Operating Cash Flows (Direct Method)** **(LO2)**

Howell Company's current year income statement reports the following:

Sales.	$825,000
Cost of goods sold.	550,000
Gross profit.	$275,000

Howell's comparative balance sheets show the following (accounts payable relate to merchandise purchases):

	End of Year	Beginning of Year
Accounts receivable.	$ 71,000	$60,000
Inventory.	109,000	96,000
Prepaid expenses.	3,000	8,000
Accounts payable.	31,000	37,000

Compute Howell's current-year cash received from customers and cash paid for merchandise purchased.

EXERCISES

E B-28.   **Net Cash Flow from Operating Activities (Indirect Method)** **(LO2)**

Lincoln Company owns no plant assets and reported the following income statement for the current year:

WebAssign.

Sales.		$750,000
Cost of goods sold.	$470,000	
Wages expense	110,000	
Rent expense	42,000	
Insurance expense.	15,000	637,000
Net income.		$113,000

Additional balance sheet information about the company follows:

	End of Year	Beginning of Year
Accounts receivable.	$54,000	$49,000
Inventory.	60,000	66,000
Prepaid insurance.	8,000	7,000
Accounts payable.	22,000	18,000
Wages payable.	9,000	11,000

Use the information to calculate the net cash flow from operating activities under the indirect method.

E B-29. **Statement of Cash Flows (Indirect Method)** **(LO2, 3, 4)**

Use the following information about Lund Corporation for 2009 to prepare a statement of cash flows under the indirect method.

Accounts payable increase	$ 9,000
Accounts receivable increase.	4,000
Accrued liabilities decrease	3,000
Amortization expense.	6,000
Cash balance, beginning of 2009.	22,000
Cash balance, end of 2009	15,000
Cash paid as dividends	29,000
Cash paid to purchase land	90,000
Cash paid to retire bonds payable at par.	60,000
Cash received from issuance of common stock	35,000
Cash received from sale of equipment.	17,000
Depreciation expense.	29,000
Gain on sale of equipment	4,000
Inventory decrease.	13,000
Net income.	76,000
Prepaid expenses increase	2,000

WebAssign.

Nike, Inc. (NKE)

E B-30. **Operating Section of Statement of Cash Flows (Indirect Method)** **(LO2)**

Following are the income statement and balance sheet for Nike for the year ended May 31, 2008, and a forecasted income statement and balance sheet for 2009.

Income Statement		
($ millions)	2008 Actual	2009 Est.
Revenues	$18,627.0	$21,253.0
Cost of sales.	10,239.6	11,689.0
Gross margin	8,387.4	9,564.0
Selling and administrative expense	5,953.7	6,801.0
Operating profit	2,433.7	2,763.0
Interest income, net	77.1	77.1
Other (expense) income, net	(7.9)	(7.9)
Income before income taxes	2,502.9	2,832.2
Income taxes	619.5	702.0
Net income.	$ 1,883.4	$ 2,130.2

Balance Sheet		
($ millions)	2008 Actual	2009 Est.
Assets		
Cash and equivalents.	$ 2,133.9	$ 3,311.4
Short-term investments	642.2	642.2
Accounts receivable, net	2,795.3	3,188.0
Inventories	2,438.4	2,784.0
Deferred income taxes	227.2	259.0
Prepaid expenses and other current assets.	602.3	680.0
Total current assets	8,839.3	10,864.6
Property, plant and equipment*	4,103.0	4,613.0
Accumulated depreciation	(2,211.9)	(2,556.9)
Property, plant and equipment, net	1,891.1	2,056.1
Goodwill and other current assets	1,191.9	1,152.9
Deferred income taxes and other noncurrent assets	520.4	594.0
Total assets.	$12,442.7	$14,667.6
Liabilities and Equity		
Current portion of long-term debt	$ 6.3	$ 31.3
Notes payable	177.7	177.7
Accounts payable.	1,287.6	1,466.0
Accrued liabilities	1,761.9	2,019.0
Income taxes payable	88.0	100.0
Total current liabilities.	3,321.5	3,794.0
Long-term debt	441.1	409.8
Deferred income taxes and other liabilities	854.5	975.0
Total liabilities.	4,617.1	5,178.8
Redeemable preferred stock	0.3	0.3
Common stock.	2.8	2.8
Capital in excess of stated value	2,497.8	2,497.8
Accumulated other comprehensive income.	251.4	251.4
Retained earnings	5,073.3	6,736.5
Stockholders' equity	7,825.6	9,488.8
Total liabilities and equity	$12,442.7	$14,667.6

* Gross property, plant and equipment and accumulated depreciation are inserted in the balance sheet; both are taken from footnotes to the financial statements.

Prepare the net cash flows from operating activities section of a forecasted statement of cash flows for 2009 using the indirect method. Treat current and noncurrent deferred tax assets and liabilities as operating. Operating expenses (such as Cost of sales and Selling and administrative expense) for 2009 include estimated depreciation expense of $345 million and amortization expense of $39 million. Estimated 2009 retained earnings includes dividends of $467 million.

E B-31 **Operating Section of Statement of Cash Flows (Indirect Method)** **(LO2)**

Following are the income statement and balance sheet for General Mills for the year ended May 25, 2008, and a forecasted income statement and balance sheet for 2009.

General Mills, Inc.
(GIS)

Income Statement		
($ millions)	2008 Actual	2009 Est.
Net sales	$13,652	$14,976
Cost of sales.	8,778	9,630
Gross profit.	4,874	5,346
Selling, general & administrative expenses	2,625	2,875
Restructuring, impairment, and other exit costs	21	30
Operating profit	2,228	2,441
Interest, net	422	422
Income before taxes and before earnings from joint ventures.	1,806	2,019
Income taxes	622	695
After-tax earnings from joint ventures	(111)	(120)
Net earnings.	$1,295	$1,444

Balance Sheet		
($ millions)	2008 Actual	2009 Est.
Cash and cash equivalents	$ 661	$ 850
Receivables	1,082	1,183
Inventories	1,367	1,498
Prepaid expenses and other current assets	511	511
Total current assets	3,621	4,042
Land, buildings and equipment*	6,471	7,040
Accumulated depreciation	(3,363)	(3,842)
Land, buildings and equipment, net	3,108	3,198
Goodwill, other intangible assets, and other assets	12,314	12,309
Total assets	$19,043	$19,549
Liabilities and Equity		
Accounts payable	$ 937	$ 1,033
Current portion of long-term debt	442	509
Notes payable	2,209	2,209
Other current liabilities	1,268	1,268
Total current liabilities	4,856	5,019
Long-term debt	4,349	3,840
Deferred income taxes	1,455	1,455
Other liabilities	1,924	1,924
Total liabilities	12,584	12,238
Minority interests	242	242
Common stock	38	38
Additional paid-in capital	1,149	1,149
Retained earnings	6,511	7,363
Common stock in treasury	(1,658)	(1,658)
Accumulated other comprehensive income	177	177
Total stockholders' equity	6,217	7,069
Total liabilities and equity	$19,043	$19,549

*Gross property, plant and equipment and accumulated depreciation are inserted in the balance sheet; both are taken from footnotes to the financial statements.

Prepare the net cash flows from operating activities section of a forecasted statement of cash flows for 2009 using the indirect method. Operating expenses (such as Cost of sales and Selling, general and administrative expenses) for 2009 include estimated depreciation expense of $479 million and amortization expense of $5 million. Estimated 2009 retained earnings includes dividends of $592 million.

E B-32.[B1] **Operating Cash Flows (Direct Method)   (LO2)**

Calculate the cash flow for each of the following cases.

a.   Cash paid for advertising:

Advertising expense	$62,000
Prepaid advertising, beginning of year	11,000
Prepaid advertising, end of year	15,000

b.   Cash paid for income taxes:

Income tax expense	$29,000
Income tax payable, beginning of year	7,100
Income tax payable, end of year	4,900

c.   Cash paid for merchandise purchased:

Cost of goods sold	$180,000
Inventory, beginning of year	30,000
Inventory, end of year	25,000
Accounts payable, beginning of year	10,000
Accounts payable, end of year	12,000

E B-33.[B1] **Statement of Cash Flows (Direct Method)** (LO2, 3, 4)

Use the following information about the 2009 cash flows of Mason Corporation to prepare a statement of cash flows under the direct method.

Cash balance, end of 2009	$ 12,000
Cash paid to employees and suppliers	148,000
Cash received from sale of land.	40,000
Cash paid to acquire treasury stock	10,000
Cash balance, beginning of 2009.	16,000
Cash received as interest.	6,000
Cash paid as income taxes	11,000
Cash paid to purchase equipment.	89,000
Cash received from customers	194,000
Cash received from issuing bonds payable. .	30,000
Cash paid as dividends	16,000

E B-34.[B1] **Operating Cash Flows (Direct Method)** (LO2)

Refer to the information in Exercise B-28. Calculate the net cash flow from operating activities using the direct method. Show a related cash flow for each revenue and expense.

E B-35. **Investing and Financing Cash Flows** (LO3, 4)

During 2009, Paxon Corporation's long-term investments account (at cost) increased $15,000, which was the net result of purchasing stocks costing $80,000 and selling stocks costing $65,000 at a $6,000 loss. Also, its bonds payable account decreased $40,000, the net result of issuing $100,000 of bonds at $103,000 and retiring bonds with a face value (and book value) of $140,000 at a $9,000 gain. What items and amounts appear in the (a) cash flows from investing activities and (b) cash flows from financing activities sections of its 2009 statement of cash flows?

PROBLEMS

P B-36. **Statement of Cash Flows (Indirect Method)** (LO2, 3, 4)

Wolff Company's income statement and comparative balance sheets follow.

WOLFF COMPANY		
Income Statement		
For Year Ended December 31, 2009		
Sales.		$635,000
Cost of goods sold.	$430,000	
Wages expense	86,000	
Insurance expense.	8,000	
Depreciation expense.	17,000	
Interest expense.	9,000	
Income tax expense.	29,000	579,000
Net income.		$ 56,000

WOLFF COMPANY		
Balance Sheets		
	Dec. 31, 2009	**Dec. 31, 2008**
Assets		
Cash.	$ 11,000	$ 5,000
Accounts receivable.	41,000	32,000
Inventory.	90,000	60,000
Prepaid insurance.	5,000	7,000
Plant assets	250,000	195,000
Accumulated depreciation	(68,000)	(51,000)
Total assets.	$329,000	$248,000

continued

continued from prior page

	Dec. 31, 2009	Dec. 31, 2008
Liabilities and Stockholders' Equity		
Accounts payable.................	$ 7,000	$ 10,000
Wages payable....................	9,000	6,000
Income tax payable	7,000	8,000
Bonds payable....................	130,000	75,000
Common stock....................	90,000	90,000
Retained earnings	86,000	59,000
Total liabilities and equity	$329,000	$248,000

Cash dividends of $29,000 were declared and paid during 2009. Also in 2009, plant assets were purchased for cash, and bonds payable were issued for cash. Bond interest is paid semiannually on June 30 and December 31. Accounts payable relate to merchandise purchases.

Required

a. Compute the change in cash that occurred during 2009.

b. Prepare a 2009 statement of cash flows using the indirect method.

P B-37. **Statement of Cash Flows (Indirect Method)** **(LO2, 3, 4)**

Best Buy (BBY)

Following are the income statement and balance sheet for Best Buy for the year ended March 1, 2008, and a forecasted income statement and balance sheet for 2009.

Balance Sheet		
($ millions)	2008 Actual	2009 Est.
Assets		
Cash and cash equivalents	$ 1,438	$ 1,884
Short-term investments	64	64
Receivables	549	612
Merchandise inventories	4,708	5,245
Other current assets................................	583	583
Total current assets	7,342	8,388
Property and equipment*............................	5,608	6,496
Accumulated depreciation	(2,302)	(2,400)
Property and equipment, net	3,306	4,096
Other assets......................................	2,110	2,110
Total assets......................................	$12,758	$14,594
Liabilities and Equity		
Accounts payable..................................	$ 4,297	$ 4,787
Unredeemed gift card liabilities	531	531
Accrued expenses and liabilities	1,348	1,502
Accrued income taxes	404	449
Short-term and current portion of long-term debt...........	189	16
Total current liabilities..............................	6,769	7,285
Long-term liabilities	838	838
Long-term debt	627	611
Total liabilities....................................	8,234	8,734
Minority interests	40	40
Common stock....................................	41	41
Additional paid-in capital	8	8
Retained earnings	3,933	5,269
Accumulated other comprehensive income.................	502	502
Total shareholders' equity	4,524	5,860
Total liabilities and equity	$12,758	$14,594

* Gross property and equipment and its accumulated depreciation are inserted in the balance sheet; both are taken from footnotes to financial statements.

Income Statement		
($ millions)	2008 Actual	2009 Est.
Revenue	$40,023	$44,586
Cost of goods sold.	30,477	33,930
Gross profit.	9,546	10,656
Selling, general & administrative expenses	7,385	8,248
Operating income.	2,161	2,408
Other nonoperating income, net	61	61
Income before tax	2,222	2,469
Income tax expense.	815	906
Net earnings.	$ 1,407	$ 1,563

Required

Prepare a forecasted statement of cash flows for 2009 using the indirect method. Operating expenses for 2009 (such as Cost of goods sold and Selling, general and administrative expenses) include estimated depreciation expense of $98 million; and estimated retained earnings assume the payment of $227 million in dividends.

P B-38. **Statement of Cash Flows (Indirect Method)** **(LO2, 3, 4)**

Arctic Company's income statement and comparative balance sheets follow.

ARCTIC COMPANY Income Statement For Year Ended December 31, 2009		
Sales.		$ 728,000
Cost of goods sold.	$534,000	
Wages expense	190,000	
Advertising expense.	31,000	
Depreciation expense.	22,000	
Interest expense.	18,000	
Gain on sale of land	(25,000)	770,000
Net loss		$(42,000)

ARCTIC COMPANY Balance Sheets		
	Dec. 31, 2009	Dec. 31, 2008
Assets		
Cash.	$ 49,000	$ 28,000
Accounts receivable.	42,000	50,000
Inventory.	107,000	113,000
Prepaid advertising.	10,000	13,000
Plant assets	360,000	222,000
Accumulated depreciation	(78,000)	(56,000)
Total assets.	$490,000	$370,000
Liabilities and Stockholders' Equity		
Accounts payable.	$ 17,000	$ 31,000
Interest payable	6,000	—
Bonds payable	200,000	—
Common stock.	245,000	245,000
Retained earnings	52,000	94,000
Treasury stock	(30,000)	—
Total liabilities and equity	$490,000	$370,000

During 2009, Arctic sold land for $70,000 cash that had originally cost $45,000. Arctic also purchased equipment for cash, acquired treasury stock for cash, and issued bonds payable for cash in 2009. Accounts payable relate to merchandise purchases.

Required

a.   Compute the change in cash that occurred during 2009.

b.   Prepare a 2009 statement of cash flows using the indirect method.

WebAssign.   **P B-39.**   **Statement of Cash Flows (Indirect Method)**   **(LO2, 3, 4)**

Dair Company's income statement and comparative balance sheets follow.

DAIR COMPANY Income Statement For Year Ended December 31, 2009		
Sales.		$700,000
Cost of goods sold.	$440,000	
Wages and other operating expenses	95,000	
Depreciation expense.	22,000	
Amortization expense.	7,000	
Interest expense.	10,000	
Income tax expense.	36,000	
Loss on bond retirement	5,000	615,000
Net income.		$ 85,000

DAIR COMPANY Balance Sheets	Dec. 31, 2009	Dec. 31, 2008
Assets		
Cash.	$ 27,000	$ 18,000
Accounts receivable.	53,000	48,000
Inventory.	103,000	109,000
Prepaid expenses.	12,000	10,000
Plant assets	360,000	336,000
Accumulated depreciation	(87,000)	(84,000)
Intangible assets	43,000	50,000
Total assets.	$511,000	$487,000
Liabilities and Stockholders' Equity		
Accounts payable.	$ 32,000	$ 26,000
Interest payable	4,000	7,000
Income tax payable	6,000	8,000
Bonds payable	60,000	120,000
Common stock.	252,000	228,000
Retained earnings	157,000	98,000
Total liabilities and equity	$511,000	$487,000

During 2009, the company sold for $17,000 cash old equipment that had cost $36,000 and had $19,000 accumulated depreciation. Also in 2009, new equipment worth $60,000 was acquired in exchange for $60,000 of bonds payable, and bonds payable of $120,000 were retired for cash at a loss. A $26,000 cash dividend was declared and paid in 2009. Any stock issuances were for cash.

Required

a.   Compute the change in cash that occurred in 2009.

b.   Prepare a 2009 statement of cash flows using the indirect method.

c.   Prepare separate schedules showing (1) cash paid for interest and for income taxes and (2) noncash investing and financing transactions.

P B-40. **Statement of Cash Flows (Indirect Method)** **(LO2, 3, 4)**

Following are the income statement and balance sheet for Cisco Systems, Inc., for the year ended July 26, 2008, and a forecasted income statement and balance sheet for 2009.

Cisco Systems, Inc. (CSCO)

Balance Sheet		
($ millions)	2008 Actual	2009 Est.
Assets		
Cash and cash equivalents	$ 5,191	$15,579
Investments	21,044	21,044
Accounts receivable	3,821	4,325
Inventories	1,235	1,398
Prepaid expenses and other	4,408	4,408
Total current assets	35,699	46,754
Property and equipment	11,702	13,137
Accumulated depreciation	(7,551)	(9,505)
Property and equipment, net	4,151	3,632
Goodwill and other intangible assets	14,481	13,749
Other assets	4,403	4,403
Total assets	$58,734	$68,538
Liabilities and Equity		
Current portion of long-term debt	$ 500	$ 0
Accounts payable	869	984
Income taxes payable	107	121
Accrued compensation	2,428	2,748
Deferred revenue	6,197	7,015
Other accrued liabilities	3,757	3,757
Total current liabilities	13,858	14,625
Long-term debt	6,393	6,393
Deferred revenue	2,663	2,663
Other long-term liabilities	1,418	1,418
Total liabilities	24,332	25,099
Minority interest	49	49
Common stock and additional paid-in capital	33,505	33,505
Retained earnings	120	9,157
Accumulated other comprehensive income	728	728
Total stockholders' equity	34,402	43,439
Total liabilities and equity	$58,734	$68,538

Income Statement		
($ millions)	2008 Actual	2009 Est.
Net sales	$39,540	$44,759
Cost of sales	14,056	15,889
Gross margin	25,484	28,870
Research and development	5,153	5,819
Sales and marketing	8,380	9,489
General and administrative	2,007	2,283
Other	502	582
Operating income	9,442	10,697
Other income	813	813
Income before provision for income taxes	10,255	11,510
Provision for income taxes	2,203	2,473
Net income	$ 8,052	$ 9,037

Required

Prepare a forecasted statement of cash flows for 2009 using the indirect method. Assume the following:

- Operating expenses for 2009 (such as General and administrative) include depreciation expense of $1,954 million and amortization expense of $732 million.
- The company did not dispose of or write-down any long-term assets during 2009.
- The company did not pay any dividends during 2009.

P B-41. **Statement of Cash Flows (Indirect Method)** **(LO2, 3, 4)**

Rainbow Company's income statement and comparative balance sheets follow.

RAINBOW COMPANY Income Statement For Year Ended December 31, 2009		
Sales.		$750,000
Dividend income.		15,000
		765,000
Cost of goods sold.	$440,000	
Wages and other operating expenses	130,000	
Depreciation expense.	39,000	
Patent amortization expense	7,000	
Interest expense.	13,000	
Income tax expense.	44,000	
Loss on sale of equipment.	5,000	
Gain on sale of investments.	(10,000)	668,000
Net income.		$ 97,000

RAINBOW COMPANY Balance Sheets		
	Dec. 31, 2009	Dec. 31, 2008
Assets		
Cash and cash equivalents	$ 19,000	$ 25,000
Accounts receivable.	40,000	30,000
Inventory.	103,000	77,000
Prepaid expenses.	10,000	6,000
Long-term investments—Available-for-sale.	—	50,000
Fair value adjustment to investments.	—	7,000
Land.	190,000	100,000
Buildings.	445,000	350,000
Accumulated depreciation—Buildings.	(91,000)	(75,000)
Equipment	179,000	225,000
Accumulated depreciation—Equipment	(42,000)	(46,000)
Patents.	50,000	32,000
Total assets.	$903,000	$781,000
Liabilities and Stockholders' Equity		
Accounts payable.	$ 20,000	$ 16,000
Interest payable	6,000	5,000
Income tax payable	8,000	10,000
Bonds payable.	155,000	125,000
Preferred stock ($100 par value)	100,000	75,000
Common stock ($5 par value)	379,000	364,000
Paid-in capital in excess of par value—Common	133,000	124,000
Retained earnings	102,000	55,000
Unrealized gain on investments.	—	7,000
Total liabilities and equity.	$903,000	$781,000

During 2009, the following transactions and events occurred in addition to the company's usual business activities:

1. Sold long-term investments costing $50,000 for $60,000 cash. Unrealized gains totaling $7,000 related to these investments had been recorded in earlier years. At year-end, the fair value adjustment and unrealized gain account balances were eliminated.
2. Purchased land for cash.
3. Capitalized an expenditure made to improve the building.
4. Sold equipment for $14,000 cash that originally cost $46,000 and had $27,000 accumulated depreciation.
5. Issued bonds payable at face value for cash.
6. Acquired a patent with a fair value of $25,000 by issuing 250 shares of preferred stock at par value.
7. Declared and paid a $50,000 cash dividend.
8. Issued 3,000 shares of common stock for cash at $8 per share.
9. Recorded depreciation of $16,000 on buildings and $23,000 on equipment.

Required
a. Compute the change in cash and cash equivalents that occurred during 2009.
b. Prepare a 2009 statement of cash flows using the indirect method.
c. Prepare separate schedules showing (1) cash paid for interest and for income taxes and (2) noncash investing and financing transactions.

P B-42.[B1] **Statement of Cash Flows (Direct Method) (LO2, 3, 4)**
Refer to the data for Wolff Company in Problem B-36.

Required
a. Compute the change in cash that occurred during 2009.
b. Prepare a 2009 statement of cash flows using the direct method.

P B-43.[B1] **Statement of Cash Flows (Direct Method) (LO2, 3, 4)**
Refer to the data for Arctic Company in Problem B-38.

Required
a. Compute the change in cash that occurred during 2009.
b. Prepare a 2009 statement of cash flows using the direct method.

P B-44.[B1] **Statement of Cash Flows (Direct Method) (LO2, 3, 4)**
Refer to the data for Dair Company in Problem B-39.

WebAssign.

Required
a. Compute the change in cash that occurred in 2009.
b. Prepare a 2009 statement of cash flows using the direct method. Use one cash outflow for "cash paid for wages and other operating expenses." Accounts payable relate to inventory purchases only.
c. Prepare separate schedules showing (1) a reconciliation of net income to net cash flow from operating activities (see Exhibit B.3) and (2) noncash investing and financing transactions.

P B-45.[B1] **Statement of Cash Flows (Direct Method) (LO2, 3, 4)**
Refer to the data for Rainbow Company in Problem B-41.

Required
a. Compute the change in cash that occurred in 2009.
b. Prepare a 2009 statement of cash flows using the direct method. Use one cash outflow for "cash paid for wages and other operating expenses." Accounts payable relate to inventory purchases only.
c. Prepare separate schedules showing (1) a reconciliation of net income to net cash flow from operating activities (see Exhibit B.3) and (2) noncash investing and financing transactions.

Amgen, Inc. (AMGN)

P B-46. Interpreting the Statement of Cash Flows (LO1, 5)
Following is the statement of cash flows of Amgen, Inc.

Year Ended December 31 (In millions)	2007	2006	2005
Cash flows from operating activities:			
Net income	$3,166	$2,950	$3,674
Depreciation and amortization	1,202	963	841
Write-off of acquired in-process research and development	590	1,231	—
Stock-based compensation expense.	263	403	106
Tax benefits related to employee stock-based compensation.	—	—	315
Deferred income taxes	136	(540)	(95)
Property, plant and equipment impairments	404	—	—
Other items, net	81	(81)	60
Cash provided by (used in) changes in operating assets and liabilities, net of acquisitions:			
Trade receivables, net	38	(355)	(308)
Inventories.	(109)	(561)	(370)
Other current assets	(119)	(6)	(47)
Accounts payable	(181)	(24)	72
Accrued income taxes	(810)	581	81
Other accrued liabilities.	740	828	582
Net cash provided by operating activities.	5,401	5,389	4,911
Cash flows from investing activities:			
Cash paid for acquisitions, net of cash acquired	(697)	(2,167)	—
Purchases of property, plant and equipment	(1,267)	(1,218)	(867)
Purchases of marketable securities	(5,579)	(5,386)	(9,597)
Proceeds from sales of marketable securities	5,073	3,065	9,835
Proceeds from maturities of marketable securities	454	785	603
Other.	24	(210)	(33)
Net cash used in investing activities	(1,992)	(5,131)	(59)
Cash flows from financing activities:			
Repurchases of common stock	(5,100)	(2,000)	(4,430)
Repayment of debt.	(1,840)	(653)	(1,175)
Proceeds from issuance of debt.	3,982	—	—
Proceeds from issuance of convertible notes and related transactions, net	—	439	—
Proceeds from issuance of warrants	—	774	—
Net proceeds from issuance of common stock in connection with the Company's equity award programs	277	528	1,087
Other.	13	97	(20)
Net cash used in financing activities.	(2,668)	(815)	(4,538)
Increase (decrease) in cash and cash equivalents.	741	(557)	314
Cash and cash equivalents at beginning of year	1,283	1,840	1,526
Cash and cash equivalents at end of year.	$2,024	$1,283	$1,840

Required

a. Amgen reports that it generated $5,401 million in net cash from operating activities in 2007. Yet, its net income for the year amounted to only $3,166 million. Much of this difference is the result of depreciation. Why is Amgen adding depreciation to net income in the computation of operating cash flows?

b. In determining cash provided by operating activities, Amgen adds $263 million relating to stock-based compensation expense in 2007. What is the purpose of this addition?

c. Amgen reports $315 million as a positive amount in the operating section for 2005 involving the tax benefits relating to employee stock-based compensation, but no amounts are included for 2006 and 2007. What does the amount for 2005 represent? How should we consider tax benefits from stock option exercises for analysis purposes; how predictable are cash inflows relating to these benefits?

d. Amgen reports $38 million relating to trade receivables. What does the sign (positive or negative) on this amount signify about the change in receivables during the year compared with the signs on the amounts for 2006 and 2005?

e. Amgen reports $404 relating to property, plant and equipment impairments. Explain why this amount is on the statement of cash flows.

f. Does the composition of Amgen's cash flow present a "healthy" picture for 2007? Explain.

P B-47. Interpreting the Statement of Cash Flows (LO1, 5)

Following is the statement of cash flows of Staples, Inc.

For Year Ended, In thousands	February 2, 2008
Operating activities	
Net income.	$ 995,670
Adjustments to reconcile net income to net cash provided by operating activities:	
Depreciation and amortization	388,895
Stock-based compensation	173,343
Deferred income tax benefit	(8,788)
Excess tax benefits from stock-based compensation arrangements	(18,557)
Other.	4,831
Change in assets and liabilities, net of companies acquired:	
Increase in receivables	(64,293)
Increase in merchandise inventories.	(30,175)
Increase in prepaid expenses and other assets	(89,558)
Increase in accounts payable	295
(Decrease) increase in accrued expenses and other current liabilities	(90,054)
Increase in other long-term obligations	99,407
Net cash provided by operating activities	1,361,016
Investing activities	
Acquisition of property and equipment	(470,377)
Acquisition of businesses and investments in joint ventures,	
net of cash acquired	(178,077)
Proceeds from the sale of short-term investments	4,579,460
Purchase of short-term investments	(4,148,716)
Net cash used in investing activities.	(217,710)
Financing activities	
Proceeds from the exercise of stock options and the sale of	
stock under employee stock purchase plans	178,504
Proceeds from borrowings	11,796
Payments on borrowings	(206,515)
Cash dividends paid.	(207,552)
Excess tax benefits from stock-based compensation arrangements	18,557
Purchase of treasury stock, net	(760,977)
Net cash used in financing activities	(966,187)
Effect of exchange rate changes on cash	50,658
Net increase (decrease) in cash and cash equivalents	227,777
Cash and cash equivalents at beginning of period	1,017,671
Cash and cash equivalents at end of period	$1,245,448

Required

a. Staples reports net income of $995,670 thousand and net cash inflows from operating activities of $1,361,016 thousand. Part of the difference relates to depreciation and amortization of $388,895 thousand. Why does Staples add this amount in the computation of operating cash flows?

b. Staples reports a positive amount of $173,343 thousand relating to stock-based compensation. What does this positive amount signify?

c. Staples reports a cash outflow of $470,377 thousand relating to the acquisition of property, plant and equipment. Is this cash outflow a cause for concern? Explain.

d. Staples' net cash flows from financing activities is $(966,187) thousand. For what purposes is Staples using this cash?

e. Staples' cash balance increased by $227,777 thousand during the year. Does Staples present a "healthy" cash flow picture for the year? Explain.

Chart of Accounts with Acronyms

Assets

Cash	Cash
MS	Marketable securities
EMI	Equity method investments
AR	Accounts receivable
AU	Allowance for uncollectible accounts
INV	Inventory (or Inventories)
SUP	Supplies
PPD	Prepaid expenses
PPDA	Prepaid advertising
PPRNT	Prepaid rent
PPI	Prepaid insurance
PPE	Property, plant and equipment (PPE)
AD	Accumulated depreciation
INT	Intangible assets
DTA	Deferred tax assets
OA	Other assets

Liabilities

NP	Notes payable
AP	Accounts payable
ACC	Accrued expenses
WP	Wages payable
RNTP	Rent payable
RSL	Restructuring liability
UP	Utilities payable
TP	Taxes payable
WRP	Warranty payable
IP	Interest payable
CMLTD	Current maturities of long-term debt
UR	Unearned (or deferred) revenues
LTD	Long-term debt
CLO	Capital lease obligations
DTL	Deferred tax liabilities

Equity

EC	Earned capital
CS	Common stock
APIC	Additional paid-in capital
RE	Retained earnings
DIV	Dividends
TS	Treasury stock
AOCI	Accumulated other comprehensive income
DC	Deferred compensation expense

Revenues and Expenses

Sales	Sales
REV	Revenues
COGS	Cost of goods sold (or Cost of sales)
OE	Operating expenses
WE	Wages expense
AE	Advertising expense
BDE	Bad debts expense
UTE	Utilities expense
DE	Depreciation expense
RDE	Research and development expense
RNTE	Rent expense
RSE	Restructuring expense
WRE	Warranty expense
AIE	Asset impairment expense
INSE	Insurance expense
SUPE	Supplies expense
GN (LS)	Gain (loss)–operating
TE	Tax expense
ONI (E)	Other nonoperating income (expense)
IE	Interest expense
UG (UL)	Unrealized gain (loss)
DI	Dividend income (or revenue)
EI	Equity income (or revenue)
GN (LS)	Gain (loss)–nonoperating

Closing Account

IS	Income summary

Appendix D

Expanded Coverage of International Financial Reporting Standards

This appendix provides a comparison of IFRS and U.S. GAAP for many of the accounting topics that we cover in this textbook. We have summarized and simplified many of the pronouncements. For more complete treatment of these topics (and other omitted topics) we refer students to the IASB and FASB Websites.

MODULE 2 Components of Financial Statements

IAS 1	FASB Concepts Statement No. 6
Summary: Elements of financial statements are largely equivalent with some differences in terminology.	
An asset is a resource controlled by the entity as a result of past events and from which future economic benefits are expected to flow to the entity (from IAS).	Assets are probable future economic benefits obtained or controlled by the company as a result of past events or transactions.
A liability is defined as a present obligation of the entity arising from past events, the settlement of which is expected to result in an outflow from the entity of resources embodying economic benefits (from IAS).	Liabilities are probable future economic sacrifices arising from present obligations to transfer assets or provide services to another entity as a result of past events or transactions.
Equity is the residual interest in the assets of the entity after deducting all its liabilities (from IAS).	Owners' equity is the residual interest in the company—the difference between assets and liabilities.
Income is increases in economic benefit during the accounting period in the form of inflows or enhancements of assets or decreases of liabilities that result in increases in equity, other than those relating to contributions from equity participants (from IAS).	Revenues are increases in assets or decreases in liabilities due to the firm performing activities (delivering goods or performing services) that are considered central to the firm's operations. Revenues are found on the income statement. At Weis, they are referred to as Net sales.
Expenses are decreases in economic benefits during the accounting period in the form of outflows or depletions of assets or incurrences of liabilities that result in decreases in equity, other than those relating to distributions to equity participants (from IAS).	Expenses are decreases in assets or increases in liabilities that result from the performing activities (delivering goods or performing services) that are considered central to the firm's operations.

MODULE 2 Balance Sheet

IAS 1	U.S. GAAP—SEC Reg. S-X
Summary: Balance sheet (called Statement of Financial Position) components are the same but presentation differs.	
Must present current period and one comparative period.	Must present current period and one comparative period.
No requirement about order of items presented. However, non-current assets are typically presented before current assets; and equity and non-current liabilities are presented before current liabilities.	May choose to present classified or unclassified balance sheet. Either way, items presented in order of liquidity.
Offsetting of assets and liabilities not permitted unless specifically allowed under a standard.	Offsetting permitted when there is an intention to offset the items, the amount is determinable, and offsetting is enforceable by law.
Noncontrolling (minority) interest is presented in equity section.	Noncontrolling (minority) interest is presented between liabilities and equity sections.

MODULE 2   Income Statement

IAS 1	U.S. GAAP
Summary: Presentation is much the same under both standards. Measurement issues will arise for certain items.	
Must present current period and one comparative period.	Must present current period and two comparative periods.
Must present the following six elements: Revenue, Finance costs, Profit or loss from equity method investments, Tax expense, Discontinued operations, and Profit or loss.	No formal guidance on elements to be included.
Income (i.e. revenue) and expenses presented either: (i) In a single statement of comprehensive income, or (ii) In two statements: an income statement (profit or loss) and a second statement beginning with profit or loss and displaying components of other comprehensive income.	No formal guidance on formatting. Firms use one of two formats to report income from continuing operations: (i) single-step (group all revenues and gains together and all expenses and losses together) or (ii) multi-step (includes intermediate subtotals before arriving at income from continuing operations)
Expenses may be presented by nature (depreciation, purchases, employee benefits, advertising, etc.) or by function (cost of sales, selling and administrative, research and development, etc.).	Expenses to be presented by function (cost of sales, selling and administrative, research and development, etc.).
No exceptional or extraordinary items.	Extraordinary items displayed separately (below the line).
The income statement must display: (i) Profit or loss attributable to noncontrolling interest, and (ii) Profit or loss attributable to equity holders of the parent.	Beginning in 2009 with SFAS 160 presentation of noncontrolling interest will be equivalent to IFRS.

MODULE 2   Cash Flow Statement

IAS 7	U.S. GAAP
Summary: More classification choices under IFRS.	
Must present current period and one comparative period.	Must present current period and two comparative periods.
Permits both direct and indirect methods.	Permits both direct and indirect methods.
Cash and equivalents include bank overdrafts.	Cash and equivalents do not include bank overdrafts, they are included as current liabilities.
The separate components of a single transaction are each classified as operating, investing, or financing.	Cash receipts and payments are classified based on the predominant source of the cash flow unless the underlying transaction is accounted for as having different components, like a loan repayment that comprises both principal and interest.
Income taxes are classified as operating activities, unless it is practical to identify them with, and therefore classify them as, financing or investing activities.	All income tax cash flows are classified as operating activities (except excess tax benefits related to share-based payments, which are classified as financing activities).
The classification of interest and dividends received and paid is not specified and is a policy decision. Thus, may classify interest and dividends received as operating or investing activities. May classify interest and dividends paid as operating or financing activities. Once the classification choice is made, entity must apply it consistently.	Interest and dividends received are classified as operating activities. Interest paid is classified as operating activity. Dividends paid are classified as financing activity.

MODULE 4   Discontinued Operations

IFRS 5	SFAS 144
Summary: Definition of discontinued operations is more restrictive under IFRS, fewer disposals will qualify as discontinued operations.	
Discontinued operations are limited to a component of an entity that either has been disposed of or is classified as held for sale and: ■ represents a separate major line of business or geographical area of operations; ■ is part of a coordinated plan to dispose of a separate major line of business or geographical area of operations; ■ is a subsidiary acquired exclusively to be resold.	Discontinued operations are limited to a component of an entity that either has been disposed of or is classified as held for sale and: ■ the operations and cash flows of the component have been (or will be) eliminated from the ongoing operations of the entity and ■ the entity will not have any significant continuing involvement in the operations of the component after the disposal.
Change from a controlling to a non-controlling interest would qualify as discontinued operations.	Change from a controlling to a noncontrolling interest would not qualify as discontinued operations due to continuing involvement.

MODULE 5   Revenue Recognition

IAS 11, IAS 18, IFRIC 13, IFRIC 15, SIC 31	FTB 90-1, SOP 81-1, SOP 97-2, EITF 99-17, EITF 01-09, EITF 00-21, CON 5, SAB 104
Summary: GAAP is more restrictive and will typically recognize revenue later than under IFRS.	
Revenue is termed "income."	
There is no specific guidance for identifying and accounting for multiple-element arrangements. Identification of elements is based on economic substance of the transaction.	Much guidance has been provided (mostly industry specific) for identifying and accounting for multiple-element arrangements.
Income is measured at the fair value of the consideration received. When sale involves multiple, identifiable components, total revenue is allocated to the components based on their relative fair values. Revenue can be recognized on delivery of each element if delivery of remaining elements is probable.	Revenue is measured at the transaction amount. When sale involves multiple, identifiable components, total revenue is allocated to the components based on their relative fair values. But the amount recognized for any component is restricted to the amount that is not contingent on the delivery of additional items or other specified performance conditions.
A written or formal evidence of an arrangement is not required.	Formal evidence of a contractual arrangement is required.
Vendor specific objective evidence concept does not exist.	Vendor specific objective evidence of fair value is required before revenue can be recognized.
When a specific act in a service contract is much more significant than any other acts, revenue is recognized only after the significant act is performed.	Revenue recognition often delayed until all acts are performed.
Completed contract method is not permitted for construction contracts.	Completed contract method permitted in certain circumstances for construction contracts.
The percentage of completion method is used for service contracts.	The percentage of completion method is not permitted for service contracts, must use proportional-performance or completed-performance method.
Amendments to contract revenue are recognized when they are probable and reliably measured.	Amendments to contract revenue are recognized when they are earned.

MODULE 5   Research and Development Costs

IAS 38	SFAS 2
Summary: Definition of R&D is the same under IFRS and U.S.-GAAP. IFRS requires capitalization of certain development costs.	
Development costs must be capitalized (as an intangible asset) if all of the following criteria can be demonstrated: 1. The technical feasibility of completing the intangible asset; 2. The intention to complete the intangible asset and use or sell it; 3. The ability to use or sell the intangible asset; 4. How the intangible asset will generate probable future economic benefits; 5. The availability of adequate technical, financial and other resources to complete the development and to use or sell the intangible assets; 6. The ability to measure reliably the expenditures attributable to the intangible asset during its development. The following expenditures must be capitalized: ■ Materials and services used or consumed; ■ Direct personnel costs; ■ Directly attributable costs such as legal fees to register rights; ■ Overhead that can be allocated on a reasonable and consistent basis including depreciation on equipment and amortization on licences or patents needed to generate the intangible asset. Expenditures for administrative expenses, staff training, selling (e.g. for market research, advertising, and promotion), and other general overhead expenditure cannot be capitalized. Amortization begins when the intangible asset is first available for use. The capitalized development costs should be tested annually for impairment.	Capitalization of development costs is not allowed, all R&D costs must be expensed as incurred.

MODULE 5   Restructuring Expenses

IAS 20, IAS 37	FAS 5, FAS 116, FAS 143, FAS 146, SOP 96-1
Summary: Requirements for recognizing restructuring liabilities are more restrictive and detailed under U.S.-GAAP. Restructuring provisions are usually higher under IFRS and recognized earlier.	
A provision for restructuring is recognized when there is a binding contract or a plan for the restructuring and if the affected employees expect that the plan will be implemented. The plan needs to include certain specifications such as the location of restructuring, the time of implementation, and the *approximate* number of employees affected.	A provision for restructuring is recognized when management approves of a plan with certain specifications such as the location and the *exact* number of employees affected. This plan may not exceed a time period of one year.
Compensation for employees who will be terminated, is recognized when employees are deemed redundant.	Compensation for employees who will be terminated, is recognized when employees are told they are redundant.
A provision for restructuring is recorded at its best estimate. This is usually the expected value or, in case of a single obligation the best estimate may be the most-likely outcome. If there is a range of possible outcomes that are equally likely, the provision is recorded as the midpoint of the range.	A provision for restructuring is recorded at its estimated fair value. This is usually the most-likely outcome. If there is a range of possible outcomes that are equally likely, the provision is recorded as the minimum amount of the range.
Liabilities related to offers for voluntary terminations are measured based on the number of employees expected to accept the offer.	Liabilities related to offers for voluntary terminations are recognized when (1) employees accept offers and (2) the amounts can be estimated.

MODULE 5 Income Tax Expense (and Deferred Taxes)	
IAS 1, IAS 12, IFRS 3, IFRS 3 (Revised)	**FAS 109, FAS 123(R), FAS 141, FAS 141(R), FIN 48, APB 23**
Summary: Substantively the same, some differences in financial statement presentation and detailed applications such as asset revaluation.	
Deferred tax liabilities are recognized for all timing differences.	Deferred tax liabilities are recognized for all timing differences.
Deferred tax assets should only be recognized for timing differences and unused tax losses to the extent that it is probable (probability > 50%) that future taxable profit will be available. No valuation allowance is permitted.	Deferred tax assets are recognized for timing differences and unused tax losses. A valuation allowance is recognized if it is more likely than not (probability > 50%) that some portion of the deferred tax assets will not be utilized.
Deferred tax is measured based on rates and laws enacted or substantively enacted at the reporting date.	Deferred tax is measured based on rates and laws enacted at the reporting date. Cannot use dates from substantively enacted laws.
All deferred taxes are classified as non-current. Must disclose amounts expected to be realized within coming year.	Deferred taxes are classified as either current or non-current according to the classification of the related assets or liability giving rise to the temporary difference. The valuation allowance is allocated against current and non-current deferred tax assets on a pro-rata basis.
Deferred taxes on revalued assets flow directly to equity (not via income statement).	Asset revaluations are not permitted, therefore there are no deferred tax consequences.
Deferred taxes on employee stock options are calculated based on options' intrinsic value at each reporting date. This results in partial mark-to-market accounting for the deferred tax asset.	Deferred taxes on employee stock options are calculated based on options' fair value at grant date.

MODULE 5 Earnings per Share	
IAS 33	**SFAS 128**
Summary: Substantively the same but more disclosure required under U.S. GAAP.	
Must present basic and diluted EPS on face of income statement.	Must present basic and diluted EPS on face of income statement.
No additional disclosure required.	Must present per share amounts for discontinued operations, extraordinary income/loss, and the cumulative effect of a change in accounting policy.

MODULE 6 Accounts Receivable	
IAS 1, IAS 39, IFRS 7	**U.S. GAAP**
Summary: Substantively the same, some minor measurement differences.	
AR is reduced by an allowance account to provide for uncollectible debt.	AR is reduced by an allowance account to provide for uncollectible debt.
Short-term receivables are considered financial assets and must be discounted if the effect of discounting is material. Accounts receivables are measured subsequently at amortised cost using the effective interest method.	Short-term accounts receivable are not discounted.

MODULE 6 Inventories	
IAS 2, IAS 16, IAS 41	**ARB 43**
Summary: Accounting for inventories is substantively the same under IFRS and U.S. GAAP.	
Inventories are recognized at the lower of cost or net realizable value, which is the estimated selling price less any costs of completion and disposal.	Inventories are recognized at the lower of cost or market, which is the current replacement cost, whether by purchase or by reproduction.
Write-downs on inventories must be reversed, if the net realizable value has increased, but the reversal is limited to the amount of the original write-down.	Inventory write-downs may not be reversed.
LIFO method of inventory costing is prohibited.	LIFO is permitted.
The same cost formula must be applied to all inventories with a similar nature and use to the entity.	No restrictions on how cost formulas can be applied.

MODULE 6   Property Plant and Equipment

IAS 16, IAS 23, IAS 36	SFAS 144
Summary: U.S. GAAP is more restrictive and will likely yield lower PPE values. Impairment charges will occur sooner under IFRS. More disclosure of PPE activity required under IFRS.	
Total expenditure for an asset is allocated to its component parts and each component is accounted for separately. Components that are replaced or renewed (e.g. major inspections or overhauls) are accounted for as a separate asset. The cost of this "new" asset replaces the previously identified cost of that component and is systematically amortized.	U.S. GAAP does not currently address or permit component accounting.
Testing PPE for impairment is a one-step-approach: an asset is impaired when its carrying amount exceeds its recoverable amount, which is the higher of an asset's fair value less costs to sell, and its value in use. The value in use is the discounted value of estimated future cash flows expected to arise from the continuing use of an asset.	Testing PPE for impairment is a two-step-approach: 1. An asset is impaired when its carrying amount exceeds the undiscounted cash flows expected to result from the use and eventual disposition of the asset. 2. An impairment loss is measured as the amount by which the carrying amount exceeds its fair value (that is, the asset's quoted market price if available, or the discounted value of estimated future cash flows expected to arise from the continuing use of an asset).
Previous impairment losses must be reversed if the asset subsequently increases in value (this does not apply to goodwill). The procedure for the reversal is the same as the procedure for identifying the impairment. The increased carrying amount cannot exceed what the depreciated historical cost would have been if the impairment had not been recognized. Depreciation is adjusted going forward.	Impairment losses may not be reversed in later periods.
PPE may be re-valued upwards to fair value if fair value can be measured reliably. All items in the same class must be re-valued and revaluations must be kept up to date (no selective revaluations). Revaluations are included in comprehensive income.	Revaluations are not permitted.
The PPE carrying amount at the beginning and the end of the period must be reconciled. For this reconciliation no comparative information is required.	Only comparative end-of-period balances must be displayed.

MODULE 7   Investments in Marketable Securities and Other Financial Instruments

IAS 32, IAS 39, IFRS 7	SFAS 115, SFAS 133, SFAS 157
Summary: More items considered financial instruments and more disclosure required under IFRS.	
Four specific types financial instruments defined: 1. Financial assets at fair value through profit or loss 2. Held to maturity investments 3. Loans and receivables 4. Available for sale financial assets	Three specific types financial instruments defined: 1. Trading accounts 2. Held to maturity investments 3. Available for sale financial assets Loans and receivables are not accounted for as financial instruments.
Any financial instrument may be accounted for at fair value (type 1, above)	Firms may elect to use full fair-value accounting on certain financial instruments, including loans and receivables.
Can classify loans and receivables as available for sale and record fair values on the balance sheet.	Cannot classify loans and receivables as available for sale.
Transfers of instruments in and out of fair-value (trading) category not permitted.	Transfers of instruments in and out of trading category permitted, recorded at fair value.
Offsetting not permitted.	Offsetting (for example of trading assets and liabilities) permitted in some cases.
Review annually for impairment, may reverse impairment losses if financial instruments subsequently regain value.	Review annually for impairment, may not reverse impairment losses.

MODULE 7 Equity Investments	
IAS 28	**FAS 144, FAS 160, FIN 35, APB 18**
Summary: Substantively the same, some terminology and disclosure differences.	
Investment called, "Investments in Associates."	Investment called, "Equity-method investments."
Investor and associate must have same accounting policies.	No requirement that investor and associate have same accounting policies.
Share of investee's profit must be disclosed on income statement.	No requirement for separate disclosure.
Investor and associate must adjust accounts for any significant intervening transactions.	Investor must disclose significant intervening transactions.
May elect to account for investment at fair value.	Must use equity-method to account for investment.
May use proportionate consolidation for joint ventures (include share of assets and liabilities, revenues and expenses).	Must use equity-method to account for joint-ventures.

MODULE 7 Consolidations	
IFRS 3, IAS 27, SIC 12	**SFAS 94, SFAS 140, SFAS 141, SFAS 142, AFAS 144, FIN 46R**
Summary: IFRS leads to increased consolidation. Minority share is typically larger under IFRS.	
Decision to consolidate depends on power acquirer has to govern operating, investing, and financing decisions of acquire.	Decision to consolidate depends on control of acquiree. Many exceptions permit companies to avoid consolidation.*
Share warrants, share call options, and convertible debt or equity instruments are considered when evaluating control (percentage of voting rights).	Potential voting rights not considered when evaluating control.
Buyer-specific view is not permitted	Buyer-specific view taken for business combinations.
Deal price includes contingent consideration.	Deal price includes contingent consideration as of FAS 141R.
Equity instruments are measured at acquisition date.	Equity instruments are measured at agreement date.
Goodwill allocated between the controlling and noncontrolling interests.	same as IFRS
Negative goodwill is immediately recognized in profit or loss after the measurement of the acquired assets, liabilities, and contingent liabilities.	same as IFRS
Contingent liabilities of the acquiree are recognized if they can be measured reliably.	same as IFRS
Acquired research costs acquired must be capitalised as an intangible asset.	same as IFRS
Special purpose entities must be consolidated if the SPE is controlled. There is no exception for qualifying SPEs.	Qualifying special purpose entities need not be consolidated. Variable interest entities should be consolidated if the reporting company is the primary beneficiary.*
A subsidiary is not consolidated if it is acquired and held exclusively for disposal for twelve months or less and management is actively seeking a buyer. These subsidiaries are classified as trading securities and accounted for at their fair value.	Subsidiaries are consolidated even if control is intended to be temporary.

*At the time this book was written, the FASB was deliberating changes that would converge GAAP and IFRS for these items.

MODULE 7 Goodwill (and Other Asset) Impairment Charges	
IAS 36	**SFAS 142**
Summary: Substantively the same but calculation methods differ which could yield higher impairment charges under IFRS.	
Impairment calculation performed at the Cash-Generating Unit (CGU) level, which is the smallest identifiable group of assets that generates cash inflows that are largely independent of the cash inflows of other groups of assets.	Impairment calculation is performed at the Reporting-Unit (RU) level, which is an operating segment, or one-step below an operating segment, for which management regularly reviews financial information.
One step approach: Impairment loss identified at the CGU level is first applied against goodwill. Once goodwill has been eliminated, any remaining impairment is allocated to the other assets of the CGU based on their carrying amounts.	Two-step approach: Impairment loss is identified at the RU level as a residual. First determine the fair value of the RU and the fair value of all other assets and liabilities of the reporting unit. Then, impairment loss is calculated for each asset and goodwill impairment is the residual loss.
The reversal of an impairment loss is required with the exception of an impairment loss for goodwill.	Subsequent reversal of a previously recognized impairment loss is prohibited.

MODULE 8 Current Liabilities and Accruals and Contingent Liabilities	
IAS 20, IAS 37	**SFAS 5, SFAS 10, SFAS 13, ARB 43, SFAS 116, SFAS 143, SFAS 146, SOP 96-1**
Summary: IFRS records liabilities earlier and at higher amounts, more disclosure required under IFRS.	
Provisions must be recognized if a present obligation exists, it is probable that outflow of resources is required, and the amount of the obligation can be reasonably estimated.	Liabilities must be recognized for similar conditions as IFRS.
Probable defined as more likely than not—will occur with a probability of more than 50%.	Probable defined as likely—will occur with a probability of more than 70%–80%.
Provisions must be recognized for a constructive obligation (at the unavoidable cost). A constructive obligation can arise, for example, from established business practice or from a public announcement in which the company commits itself to a certain obligation.	No liability is recognized for a constructive obligation; only recognized in case of a legal or contractual obligation.
Contingent obligations are not recorded because a present obligation does not exist—one may or may not be confirmed by uncertain future events. Footnote disclosure of contingent liabilities required unless the eventual payment is remote.	Contingent liabilities are recognized if the outcome is probable and the amount can be estimated, otherwise, only disclosure required.
Provisions must be discounted if the effect is material. A change in discounting is recognized as part of interest expense.	Liabilities and accruals are generally not discounted. If they are discounted in rare cases, a change in discounting is recognized as part of operating income.
A provision is recorded at its best estimate. This is usually the expected value. If there is a range of possible outcomes that are equally likely, the midpoint is recorded.	A liability is recorded at its estimated fair value. This is usually the most-likely outcome. If there is a range of possible outcomes that are equally likely, the minimum amount is recorded.
For each class of provision a brief description of its nature and the expected timing payment.	Disclosure required for specific commitments such as the disclosure of lease commitments and firm purchase commitments.
Must provide a reconciliation for each class of provision including: ■ The carrying amount at the beginning and end of the period ■ Additional provisions made and amounts used ■ Unused amounts reversed during the period	Must provide a reconciliation for restructuring liabilities only.

MODULE 8 Long-Term Liabilities	
IAS 32, IAS 39	**ARB 43, SFAS 133, SFAS 150, EITF 00-19, EITF 00-29, EITF D-98, FAS 150-3, ASR 268, CON 6**
Summary: Substantively the same, but more items will be classified as liabilities under IFRS.	
Convertible debt securities, called compound financial instruments, are split into separate debt and equity components. The proceeds from the issuance are allocated between the liability component (at fair value) and an equity component (the residual amount).	Convertible debt securities are classified as debt unless the conversion option is detachable, in which case, the option's fair value is included in equity.

MODULE 9 Contributed Capital	
IAS 1, IAS 32	**ARB 43, SFAS 133, SFAS 150, EITF 00-19, EITF 00-29, EITF D-98, FAS 150-3, ASR 268, CON 6**
Summary: Fewer items will be classified as equity under IFRS.	
Preferred stock (preference shares) classified according to underlying characteristics. Classified as equity if shares are not redeemable, or redeemable at the option of the issuer. Classified as liabilities if the company must redeem the shares (mandatorily redeemable) or if they are redeemable at the option of the shareholder.	Preferred stock classified as equity. Must classify as liability only if instrument is mandatorily redeemable, redeemable at the option of the shareholder, or contingently redeemable based on future events outside of the control of either party.
Payments to preference shareholders are consistent with the balance sheet classification—cash paid out is recorded as interest expense or dividends, when the shares are classified as liabilities or equity, respectively.	Preferred stock dividends classified as financing cash flow.
Common stock called share capital. Additional paid-in capital called share premium.	
No specific guidance as to how to classify repurchases. May record repurchase as an increase to treasury stock, or as a decrease to common stock and APIC (share capital and premium), retained earnings (reserves), or some combination of these accounts.	Repurchases of stock recorded at cost, carried in Treasury stock, a contra-equity account.

MODULE 9 Earned Capital (Retained Earnings)	
IAS 1, IAS 32	**U.S. GAAP**
Summary: Substantive the same, terminology and presentation differences.	
Retained earnings called "Reserve." Reserves is the term used for all equity accounts other than contributed capital.	Word "Reserve," is generally not used.
Firms provide "Statement of Recognized Income and Expenses" (SoRIE), which includes all changes to owner's equity (assets less liabilities) that are not transactions with owners.	Firms may report other comprehensive income with income statement, or statement of shareholders' equity, or as stand-alone statement.
Firms provide General reserve and other reserve accounts. Retained earnings is typically the largest reserve. The components of AOCI are reported as individual reserve accounts rather than as one account.	Components of AOCI generally reported as one account on balance sheet. Statement of shareholders' equity provides activity in, and balances for, individual components of AOCI.

MODULE 9 Employee Stock Options	
IFRS 2, IFRIC 8	**SFAS 123R, SOP 93-6, EITF 96-18, EITF D-98, ASR 268**
Summary: Substantive the same except for tax benefit. IFRS requires more disclosure.	
Share-based transactions (including compensation) recorded at fair value, determined by any option pricing model.	Share-based transactions (including compensation) recorded at fair value, determined by a particular option pricing model such as a lattice model or the Black-Scholes model.
Expected volatility should be estimated by the annualized standard deviation based on the continuously compounded rates of return of the share over a period of time.	No method is specified for estimating expected volatility. The method used might depend on the valuation method. The Black-Scholes method uses standard deviation.
There are two kinds of vesting conditions: market conditions and non-market conditions. Both are considered in determining vesting period.	Only service and performance conditions are considered as vesting conditions. Market conditions are not considered.
Deferred taxes on employee stock options are calculated based on options' intrinsic value at each reporting date. This results in partial mark-to-market accounting for the deferred tax asset.	Deferred taxes on employee stock options are calculated based on options' fair value at grant date.
Additional disclosure required, including: ■ Description of how the fair value was determined ■ All inputs to the options pricing model including weighted average share price and the exercise price ■ How company determined expected volatility (historical or other)	Disclosures required for activity during year, fair values, exercise prices, and four inputs to fair-value estimation model (volatility, riskfree rate, dividend yield, and option life).

MODULE 10 Leases

IAS 16, IAS 17, IAS 38	SFAS 13, SFAS 28
Summary: Main difference between the two standards is that IFRS are more principle based; IFRS will classify more leases as finance (capital) leases.	
Lease accounting applies to all assets, including intangible assets.	Lease accounting applies to property, plant, and equipment.
Leases to be carried on balance sheet, as finance leases, if five criteria met: 1. The lessee acquires ownership of the leased asset at the conclusion of the lease. 2. The lessee has a bargain purchase option. 3. The term of the lease covers the majority of the leased asset's economic life (no specific percentage). 4. The present value of minimum lease payments is equivalent to nearly all of the leased asset's fair value (no specific percentage). 5. Leased assets are of a specialized nature and are only usable by the lessee unless major modifications are made to the asset. Focus is on the substance of a lease—based on notion of risk and rewards.	Leases to be carried on balance sheet, as capital leases, if four criteria are met: 1. The lessee acquires ownership of the leased asset at the conclusion of the lease. 2. The lessee has a bargain purchase option. 3. The term of the lease covers the majority of the leased asset's economic life (75% or more). 4. The present value of minimum lease payments is equivalent to nearly all of the leased asset's fair value (90% or more). Focus is on the application of certain criteria.
Three additional criteria could lead to finance lease treatment: 1. The lessee is responsible for the lessor's losses if the lease is terminated early. 2. Lessee accepts responsibility for any gains and losses due to the fluctuation in the fair value. 3. The lessee has the option to continue the lease for a secondary period for a below market rate.	No additional criteria lead to capital lease treatment.
Present value of lease payments calculated using the interest rate implicit in the lease. The lessee's incremental borrowing rate may be used if the implicit rate is unknown.	Present value of lease payments calculated using the lessee's incremental borrowing unless the implicit rate of the lease can be calculated and is lower than the incremental borrowing rate.
A lease of land is classified as an operating lease unless title transfers at the end of the lease. A joint lease of land and building is treated as two separate leases if the land is material to the leased property. The two leases may be classified differently.	A lease of land is classified as an operating lease unless title transfers at the end of the lease. A joint lease of land and building is treated as two separate leases if the land is material to the leased property. However, the land is considered material only if its fair value is at least 25% of the fair value of the leased property as a whole.
Leased assets accounted for as PPE, revaluation possible.	No revaluation is permitted.
No additional disclosures are required.	Disclosure required for leased assets and lease liability, lease payments for next five years and in total.

MODULE 10 Pensions and Other Post-Employment Obligations

IAS 19, IFRIC 14	APB 12, SFAS 43, SFAS 87, SFAS 88, SFAS 106, SFAS 112, SFAS 146, SFAS 158, FSP FAS 146-1, FSP FAS 158-1, EITF 88-1, EITF 05-5, EITF 06-2
Summary: Several significant differences, IFRS requires more disclosure, classification differs for some items.	
All benefits provided after the cessation of employment, i.e., both before and during retirement, are accounted for as one obligation called post-employment benefits.	Post-employment benefits are divided into postretirement benefits (provided during retirement) and other post-employment benefits (provided after the cessation of employment but before retirement). The two are accounted for separately, accounting for post-employment benefits depends on the type of benefit provided.
The post-employment benefit obligation's funded status is recognized on the balance sheet, calculated as the projected benefit obligation minus the fair value of plan assets plus (minus) actuarial gains (losses). This places a cap on the assets that are recognized.	The pension's funded status is recognized on the balance sheet, calculated as the projected benefit obligation minus the fair value of plan assets.
No requirement for classification of pension liability.	The pension liability needs to be classified as current and non-current.
Actuarial gains/losses are not recognized when they initially occur. In subsequent years they are amortized to net income. (Recycling is not permitted.)	Actuarial gains/losses are recognized directly in equity. In subsequent years they are amortized to net income. (This is called recycling.)
Curtailment gains and curtailment losses both need to be recognized when the curtailment occurs.	Curtailment losses recognized as soon as they are probable, whereas curtailment gains not recognized until the curtailment occurs.
Prior service costs are recognized as a component of net periodic benefit cost over the related vesting period.	Prior service costs are recorded in other comprehensive income during the period of the amendment and amortized as a component of periodic benefit cost over the remaining service period of active participants.
Interest costs may be recognized as part of interest expense.	Interest costs recognized as part of pension expense.
Additional disclosure (over and above GAAP) ■ The reconciliation of the benefit obligation needs to also include the fair value of any reimbursement right ■ Plan assets: each category of an entity's own stock, percentages of major categories of plan assets ■ The accounting policy for recognising actuarial gains and losses ■ The amount not recognized as an asset (in case of a negative benefit obligation), due to the asset ceiling ■ No interim disclosure requirements	Disclosure to include: ■ Reconciliation of the benefit obligation ■ Reconciliation of the fair value/market-related value of plan assets; percentages of major categories of plan assets; estimated contributions to plan assets expected to be paid during the next year ■ Description of investment policies and of how the long-term rate of return was determined; benefits expected to be paid in each of the next five years and in the aggregate five years thereafter. ■ Expected return on plan assets for the next year ■ Amounts recognized in net income separated into prior service cost and actuarial gains/losses ■ Interim disclosure requirements: amount of pension costs and contributions to plan assets

MODULE 10 Special Purpose Entities

IAS 27, SIC–12	ARB 51, SFAS 94, SFAS 140, FIN 46R, SOP 78-9, SOP 93-6, EITF 85-12, EITF 95-6, EITF 96-16, EITF 97-2, EITF 00-4, EITF 04-5, EITF 06-9, SAB Topic 5-H
Summary: IFRS requires a more conceptual analysis of risks and rewards which leads to consolidation of more entities.	
A special purpose entity (SPE) is an entity created to accomplish a narrow and well-defined objective.	Narrow and well-defined objective not necessary for SPE designation.
All SPEs are consolidated based on control. Risks and rewards determine control. No concept of QSPE.	Qualifying SPEs (QSPEs) are not consolidated.*
There is no concept of variable interest entities (VIEs).	VIE is any entity in which the equity at risk either (1) is insufficient to finance its own operations without additional subordinated financial support; or (2) lacks certain characteristics of a controlling financial interest. A VIE is consolidated by the primary beneficiary (the party that realizes any residual loss or profit).

*At the time this book was written, the FASB was deliberating changes that would converge GAAP and IFRS for these items.

Glossary

A

accelerated cost recovery system (ACRS, MACRS) A system of accelerated depreciation for tax purposes introduced in 1981 (ACRS) and modified starting in 1987 (MACRS); it prescribes depreciation rates by asset classification for assets acquired after 1980

accelerated depreciation method Any depreciation method under which the amounts of depreciation expense taken in the early years of an asset's life are larger than the amounts expensed in the later years; includes the double-declining balance method

access control matrix A computerized file that lists the type of access that each computer user is entitled to have to each file and program in the computer system

account A record of the additions, deductions, and balances of individual assets, liabilities, equity, revenues, and expenses

accounting adjustments (adjusting entries) Entries made at the end of an accounting period under accrual accounting to ensure the proper recording of expenses incurred and revenues earned for the period

accounting cycle A series of basic steps followed to process accounting information during a fiscal year

accounting entity An economic unit that has identifiable boundaries and that is the focus for the accumulation and reporting of financial information

accounting equation An expression of the equivalency of the economic resources and the claims upon those resources of a specific entity; often stated as Assets = Liabilities + Owners' Equity

accounting period The time period, typically one year (or quarter), for which periodic accounting reports are prepared

accounting system The structured collection of policies, procedures, equipment, files, and records that a company uses to collect, record, classify, process, store, report, and interpret financial data

accounting The process of measuring the economic activity of an entity in money terms and communicating the results to interested parties; the purpose is to provide financial information that is useful in making economic decisions

accounts payable turnover The ratio obtained by dividing cost of goods sold by average accounts payable

accounts receivable A current asset that is created by a sale on a credit basis; it represents the amount owed the company by the customer

accounts receivable aging method A procedure that uses an aging schedule to determine the year-end balance needed in the allowance for uncollectible accounts account

accounts receivable turnover Annual net sales divided by average accounts receivable (net)

accrual accounting Accounting procedures whereby revenues are recorded when they are earned and realized and expenses are recorded in the period in which they help to generate revenues

accruals Adjustments that reflect revenues earned but not received or recorded and expenses incurred but not paid or recorded

accrued expense An expense incurred but not yet paid; recognized with an accounting adjustment

accrued revenue Revenue earned but not yet billed or received; recognized with an accounting adjustment

accumulated depreciation The sum of all depreciation expense recorded to date; it is subtracted from the cost of the asset in order to derive the asset's net book value

accumulated other comprehensive income (AOCI) current accumulation of all prior periods' other comprehensive income; *see* definition for *other comprehensive income*

adjusted trial balance A list of general ledger accounts and their balances taken after accounting adjustments have been made

adjusting The process of adjusting the historical financial statements prior to the projection of future results; also called recasting and reformulating

aging schedule An analysis that shows how long customers' accounts receivable balances have remained unpaid

allowance for uncollectible accounts A contra asset account with a normal credit balance shown on the balance sheet as a deduction from accounts receivable to reflect the expected realizable amount of accounts receivable

allowance method An accounting procedure whereby the amount of uncollectible accounts expense is estimated and recorded in the period in which the related credit sales occur

Altman's Z-score A predictor of potential bankruptcy based on multiple ratios

amortization The periodic writing off of an account balance to expense; similar to depreciation and usually refers to the periodic writing off of an intangible asset

annuity A pattern of cash flows in which equal amounts are spaced equally over a number of periods

articles of incorporation A document prepared by persons organizing a corporation in the United States that sets forth the structure and purpose of the corporation and specifics regarding the stock to be issued

articulation The linkage of financial statements within and across time

asset turnover Net income divided by average total assets

asset write-downs Adjustment of carrying value of assets down to their current fair value

assets The economic resources of an entity that are owned or controlled will provide future benefits and can be reliably measured

audit An examination of a company's financial statements by a firm of independent certified public accountants

audit report A report issued by independent auditors that includes the final version of the financial statements, accompanying notes, and the auditor's opinion on the financial statements

authorized stock The maximum number of shares in a class of stock that a corporation may issue

available-for-sale securities Investments in securities that management intends to hold for capital gains and dividend income; although it may sell them if the price is right

average cash conversion cycle Average collection period + average inventory days outstanding − average payable days outstanding

average collection period Determined by dividing accounts receivable by average daily sales, sometimes referred to as days sales outstanding or DSO

average inventory days outstanding (AIDO) An indication of how long, on average, inventories are on the shelves, computed as inventory divided by average daily cost of goods sold

B

balance sheet A financial statement showing an entity's assets, liabilities, and owners' equity at a specific date; sometimes called a statement of financial position

bearer One of the terms that may be used to designate the payee on a promissory note; means whoever holds the note

bond A long-term debt instrument that promises to pay interest periodically and a principal amount at maturity, usually issued by the borrower to a group of lenders; bonds may incorporate a wide variety of provisions relating to security for the debt involved, methods of paying the periodic interest, retirement provisions, and conversion options

book value per share The dollar amount of net assets represented by one share of stock; computed by dividing the amount of stockholders' equity associated with a class of stock by the outstanding shares of that class of stock

book value The dollar amount carried in the accounts for a particular item; the book value of a depreciable asset is cost less accumulated depreciation; the book value of an entity is assets less liabilities

borrows at a discount When the face amount of the note is reduced by a calculated cash discount to determine the cash proceeds

C

calendar year A fiscal year that ends on December 31

call provision A bond feature that allows the borrower to retire (call in) the bonds after a stated date

capital expenditures Expenditures that increase the book value of long-term assets; sometimes abbreviated as CAPEX

capital lease A lease that transfers to the lessee substantially all of the benefits and risks related to ownership of the property; the lessee records the leased property as an asset and establishes a liability for the lease obligation

capital markets Financing sources, which are formalized when companies issue securities that are traded on organized exchanges; they are informal when companies are funded by private sources

capitalization The recording of a cost as an asset on the balance sheet rather than as an expense on the income statement; these costs are transferred to expense as the asset is used up

capitalization of interest A process that adds interest to an asset's initial cost if a period of time is required to prepare the asset for use

cash An asset category representing the amount of a firm's available cash and funds on deposit at a bank in checking accounts and savings accounts

cash and cash equivalents The sum of cash plus short-term, highly liquid investments such as treasury bills and money market funds; includes marketable securities maturing within 90 days of the financial statement date

cash discount An amount that a purchaser of merchandise may deduct from the purchase price for paying within the discount period

cash-basis accounting Accounting procedures whereby revenues are recorded when cash is received and expenses are recorded when cash payments are made

cash (operating) conversion cycle The period of time from when cash is invested in inventories until inventory is sold and receivables are collected

certificate of deposit (CD) An investment security available at financial institutions generally offering a fixed rate of return for a specified period of time

change in accounting estimate Modification to a previous estimate of an uncertain future event, such as the useful life of a depreciable asset, uncollectible accounts receivable, and warranty expenses; applied currently and prospectively only

changes in accounting principles Modification of accounting methods (such as depreciation or inventory costing methods)

chart of accounts A list of all the general ledger account titles and their numerical code

clean surplus accounting Income that explains successive equity balances

closing procedures A step in the accounting cycle in which the balances of all temporary accounts are transferred to the retained earnings account, leaving the temporary accounts with zero balances

commitments A contractual arrangement by which both parties to the contract still have acts to perform

common stock The basic ownership class of corporate capital stock, carrying the rights to vote, share in earnings, participate in future stock issues, and share in any liquidation proceeds after prior claims have been settled

common-size financial statement A financial statement in which each item is presented as a percentage of a key figure such as sales or total assets

comparative financial statements A form of horizontal analysis involving comparison of two or more periods' financial statements showing dollar and/or percentage changes

compensating balance A minimum amount that a financial institution requires a firm to maintain in its account as part of a borrowing arrangement complex capital structure

comprehensive income The total change in stockholders' equity other than those arising from capital (stock) transactions; computed as net income plus other comprehensive income (OCI); typical components are unrealized gains (losses) on available-for-sale securities and derivatives, minimum pension liability adjustment, and foreign currency translation adjustments; also referred to as *other comprehensive income* (OCI)

conceptual framework A cohesive set of interrelated objectives and fundamentals for external financial reporting developed by the FASB

conservatism An accounting principle stating that judgmental determinations should tend toward understatement rather than overstatement of net assets and income

consistency An accounting principle stating that, unless otherwise disclosed, accounting reports should be prepared on a basis consistent with the preceding period

consolidated financial statements Financial statements reflecting a parent company and one or more subsidiary companies and/or a variable interest entity (VIE) and its primary beneficiary

contingent liabilities A potential obligation, the eventual occurrence of which usually depends on some future event beyond the control of the firm; contingent liabilities may originate with such events as lawsuits, credit guarantees, and environmental damages

contra account An account related to, and deducted from, another account when financial statements are prepared or when book values are computed

contract rate The rate of interest stated on a bond certificate

contributed capital The net funding that a company receives from issuing and acquiring its equity shares

convertible bond A bond incorporating the holder's right to convert the bond to capital stock under prescribed terms

convertible securities Debt and equity securities that provide the holder with an option to convert those securities into other securities

copyright An exclusive right that protects an owner against the unauthorized reproduction of a specific written work or artwork

core income A company's income from its usual business activities that is expected to continue (persist) into the future

corporation A legal entity created by the granting of a charter from an appropriate governmental authority and owned by stockholders who have limited liability for corporate debt

cost of goods sold percentage The ratio of cost of goods sold divided by net sales

cost of goods sold The total cost of merchandise sold to customers during the accounting period

cost method An investment is reported at its historical cost, and any cash dividends and interest received are recognized in current income

cost principle An accounting principle stating that asset measures are based on the prices paid to acquire the assets

coupon bond A bond with coupons for interest payable to bearer attached to the bond for each interest period; whenever interest is due, the bondholder detaches a coupon and deposits it with his or her bank for collection

coupon (contract or stated) rate The coupon rate of interest is stated in the bond contract; it is used to compute the dollar amount of (semiannual) interest payments that are paid to bondholder during the life of the bond issue

covenants Contractual requirements put into loan or bond agreements by lenders

credit (entry) An entry on the right side (or in the credit column) of any account

credit card fee A fee charged retailers for credit card services provided by financial institutions; the fee is usually stated as a percentage of credit card sales

credit guarantee A guarantee of another company's debt by cosigning a note payable; a guarantor's contingent liability that is usually disclosed in a balance sheet footnote

credit memo A document prepared by a seller to inform the purchaser that the seller has reduced the amount owed by the purchaser due to a return or an allowance

credit period The maximum amount of time, usually stated in days, that the purchaser of merchandise has to pay the seller

credit terms The prescribed payment period for purchases on credit with discount specified for early payment

cumulative (preferred stock) A feature associated with preferred stock whereby any dividends in arrears must be paid before dividends may be paid on common stock

cumulative effect of a change in principle The cumulative effect on net income to the date of change in accounting principle

cumulative translation adjustment The amount recorded in the equity section as necessary to balance the accounting equation when assets and liabilities of foreign subsidiaries are translated into $US at the rate of exchange prevailing at the statement date

current assets Cash and other assets that will be converted to cash or used up during the normal operating cycle of the business or one year, whichever is longer

current liabilities Obligations that will require within the coming year or operating cycle, whichever is longer, (1) the use of existing current assets or (2) the creation of other current liabilities

current rate method Method of translating foreign currency transactions under which balance sheet amounts are translated using exchange rates in effect at the period-end consolidation date and income statement amounts using the average exchange rate for the period

current ratio A firm's current assets divided by its current liabilities

D

days' sales in inventory Inventories divided by average cost of goods sold

debenture bond A bond that has no specific property pledged as security for the repayment of funds borrowed

debit (entry) An entry on the left side (or in the debit column) of any account

debt-to-equity ratio A firm's total liabilities divided by its total owners' equity

declining-balance method An accelerated depreciation method that allocates depreciation expense to each year by applying a constant percentage to the declining book value of the asset

default The nonpayment of interest and principal and/or the failure to adhere to the various terms and conditions of the bond indenture

deferrals Adjustments that allocate various assets and revenues received in advance to the proper accounting periods as expenses and revenues

deferred revenue A liability representing revenues received in advance; also called unearned revenue

deferred tax liability A liability representing the estimated future income taxes payable resulting from an existing temporary difference between an asset's book value and its tax basis

deferred tax valuation allowance Reduction in a reported deferred tax asset to adjust for the amount that is not likely to be realized

defined benefit plan A type of retirement plan under which the company promises to make periodic payments to the employee after retirement

defined contribution plan A retirement plan under which the company makes cash contribution into an employee's account (usually with a third-party trustee like a bank) either solely or as a matching contribution

depletion The allocation of the cost of natural resources to the units extracted and sold or, in the case of timberland, the board feet of timber cut

depreciation The decline in economic potential (using up) of plant assets originating from wear, deterioration, and obsolescence

depreciation accounting The process of allocating the cost of equipment, vehicles, and buildings (not land) to expense over the time period benefiting from their use

depreciation base The acquisition cost of an asset less estimated salvage value

depreciation rate An estimate of how the asset will be used up over its useful life-evenly over its useful life, more heavily in the early years, or in proportion to its actual usage

derivatives Financial instruments such as futures, options, and swaps that are commonly used to hedge (mitigate) some external risk, such as commodity price risk, interest rate risk, or risks relating to foreign currency fluctuations

diluted earnings per share The earnings per share computation taking into consideration the effects of dilutive securities

dilutive securities Securities that can be exchanged for shares of common stock and, thereby, increase the number of common shares outstanding

discontinued operations Net income or loss from business segments that are up for sale or have been sold in the current period

discount bond A bond that is sold for less than its par (face) value

discount on notes payable A contra account that is subtracted from the Notes Payable amount on the balance sheet; as the life of the note elapses, the discount is reduced and charged to interest expense

discount period The maximum amount of time, usually stated in days, that the purchaser of merchandise has to pay the seller if the purchaser wants to claim the cash discount

discounting The exchanging of notes receivable for cash at a financial institution at an amount that is less than the face value of the notes

discounted cash flow (DCF) model The value of a security is equal to the present value of the expected free cash flows to the firm, discounted at the weighted average cost of capital (WACC)

dividends account A temporary equity account used to accumulate owner dividends from the business

dividend discount model The value of a security today is equal to the present value of that security's expected dividends, discounted at the weighted average cost of capital

dividend payout ratio Annual dividends per share divided by the earnings per share or by net income

dividend yield Annual dividends per share divided by the market price per share

double-entry accounting system A method of accounting that recognizes the duality of a transaction such that the analysis results in a recording of equal amounts of debits and credits

E

earned When referring to revenue, the seller's execution of its duties under the terms of the agreement, with the resultant passing of title to the buyer with no right of return or other contingencies

earned capital The cumulative net income (losses) retained by the company (not paid out to shareholders as dividends)

earnings per share (EPS) Net income less preferred stock dividends divided by the weighted average common shares outstanding for the period

earnings quality The degree to which reported earnings represent how well the firm has performed from an economic standpoint

earnings smoothing Earnings management with a goal to provide an earnings stream with less variability

economic profit The number of inventory units sold multiplied by the difference between the sales price and the replacement cost of the inventories (approximated by the cost of the most recently purchased inventories)

economic value added (EVA) Net operating profits after tax less a charge for the use of capital equal to beginning capital utilized in the business multiplied by the weighted average cost of capital ($EVA = NOPAT - [r_w \times \text{Net operating assets}]$)

effective interest method A method of amortizing bond premium or discount that results in a constant rate of interest each period and varying amounts of premium or discount amortized each period

effective interest rate The rate determined by dividing the total discount amount by the cash proceeds on a note payable when the borrower borrowed at a discount

effective rate The current rate of interest in the market for a bond or other debt instrument; when issued, a bond is priced to yield the market (effective) rate of interest at the date of issuance

efficient markets hypothesis Capital markets are said to be efficient if at any given time, current equity (stock) prices reflect all relevant information that determines those equity prices

employee severance costs Accrued (estimated) costs for termination of employees as part of a restructuring program

employee stock options A form of compensation that grants a select group of employees the right to purchase a fixed number of company shares at a fixed price for a predetermined time period

equity carve out A corporate divestiture of operating units

equity method The prescribed method of accounting for investments in which the investor company has a significant influence over the investee company (usually taken to be ownership between 20-50% of the outstanding common stock of the investee company)

ethics An area of inquiry dealing with the values, rules, and justifications that governs one's way of life

executory contract A contract where a party has a material unperformed obligation that, if not performed, will result in a breach of contract

expenses Decreases in owners' equity incurred by a firm in the process of earning revenues

extraordinary items Revenues and expenses that are both unusual and infrequent and are, therefore, excluded from income from continuing operations

F

face amount The principal amount of a bond or note to be repaid at maturity

factoring Selling an account receivable to another company, typically a finance company or a financial institution, for less than its face value

fair value Value that an asset could be sold for (or an obligation discharged) in an orderly market, between willing buyers and sellers; often, but not always, is current market value

fair value method Method of accounting that records on the balance sheet, the asset or liabilities fair value, and records on the income statement, changes in the fair value

financial accounting The area of accounting activities dealing with the preparation of financial statements showing an entity's results of operations, financial position, and cash flows

Financial Accounting Standards Board (FASB) The organization currently responsible for setting accounting standards for reporting financial information by U.S. entitites

financial assets Normally consist of excess resources held for future expansion or unexpected needs; they are usually invested in the form of other companies' stock, corporate or government bonds, and real estate

financial leverage The proportionate use of borrowed funds in the capital structure, computed as net nonoperating obligations (NNO) divided by average equity

financial reporting objectives A component of the conceptual framework that specifies that financial statements should provide information (1) useful for investment and credit decisions, (2) helpful in assessing an entity's ability to generate future cash flows, and (3) about an entity's resources, claims to those resources, and the effects of events causing changes in these items

financial statement elements A part of the conceptual framework that identifies the significant components-such as assets, liabilities, owners' equity, revenues, and expenses-used to put financial statements together

financing activities Methods that companies use to raise the funds to pay for resources such as land, buildings, and equipment

finished goods inventory The dollar amount of inventory that has completed the production process and is awaiting sale

first-in, first-out (FIFO) method One of the prescribed methods of inventory costing; FIFO assumes that the first costs incurred for the purchase or production of inventory are the first costs relieved from inventory when goods are sold

fiscal year The annual accounting period used by a business firm

five forces of competitive intensity Industry competition, bargaining power of buyers, bargaining power of suppliers, threat of substitution, threat of entry

fixed assets An alternate label for long-term assets; may also be called property, plant, and equipment (PPE)

fixed costs Costs that do not change with changes in sales volume (over a reasonable range)

forecast The projection of financial results over the forecast horizon and terminal periods

foreign currency transaction The $US equivalent of an asset or liability denominated in a foreign currency

foreign exchange gain or loss The gain (loss) recognized in the income statement relating to the change in the $US equivalent of an asset or liability denominated in a foreign currency

forward earnings earnings expected to be reported in the next period.

franchise Generally, an exclusive right to operate or sell a specific brand of products in a given geographic area

free cash flow This excess cash flow (above that required to manage its growth and development) from which dividends can be paid; computed as NOPAT − Increase in NOA

full disclosure principle An accounting principle stipulating the disclosure of all facts necessary to make financial statements useful to readers

fully diluted earnings per share *See* diluted earnings per share

functional currency The currency representing the primary currency in which a business unit conducts its operations

fundamental analysis Uses financial information to predict future valuation and, hence, buy-sell stock strategies

funded status The difference between the pension obligation and the fair value of the pension investments

future value The amount a specified investment (or series of investments) will be worth at a future date if invested at a given rate of compound interest

G

general journal A journal with enough flexibility so that any type of business transaction can be recorded in it

general ledger A grouping of all of an entity's accounts that are used to prepare the basic financial statements

generally accepted accounting principles (GAAP) A set of standards and procedures that guide the preparation of financial statements

going concern concept An accounting principle that assumes that, in the absence of evidence to the contrary, a business entity will have an indefinite life

goodwill The value that derives from a firm's ability to earn more than a normal rate of return on the fair market value of its specific, identifiable net assets; computed as the residual of the purchase price less the fair market value of the net tangible and intangible assets acquired

gross margin The difference between net sales and cost of goods sold: also called gross profit

gross profit on sales The difference between net sales and cost of goods sold; also called gross margin

gross profit margin (GPM) (percentage) The ratio of gross profit on sales divided by net sales

H

held-to-maturity securities The designation given to a portfolio of bond investments that are expected to be held until they mature

historical cost Original acquisition or issuance costs

holding company The parent company of a subsidiary

holding gain The increase in replacement cost since the inventories were acquired, which equals the number of units sold multiplied by the difference between the current replacement cost and the original acquisition cost

horizon period The forecast period for which detailed estimates are made, typically 5-10 years

horizontal analysis Analysis of a firm's financial statements that covers two or more years

I

IFRS International Financial Reporting Standards, a body of accounting standards developed by the International Accounting Standards Board and used for financial reports across much of the world

impairment A reduction in value from that presently recorded

impairment loss A loss recognized on an impaired asset equal to the difference between its book value and current fair value

income statement A financial statement reporting an entity's revenues and expenses for a period of time

indirect method A presentation format for the statement of cash flows that refers to the operating section only; that section begins with net income and converts it to cash flows from operations

intangible assets A term applied to a group of long-term assets, including patents, copyrights, franchises, trademarks, and goodwill, that benefit an entity but do not have physical substance

interest cost (pensions) The increase in the pension obligation due to the accrual of an additional year of interest

internal auditing A company function that provides independent appraisals of the company's financial statements, its internal controls, and its operations

internal controls The measures undertaken by a company to ensure the reliability of its accounting data, protect its assets from theft or unauthorized use, make sure that employees are following the company's policies and procedures, and evaluate the performance of employees, departments, divisions, and the company as a whole

inventory carrying costs Costs of holding inventories, including warehousing, logistics, insurance, financing, and the risk of loss due to theft, damage, or technological or fashion change

inventory shrinkage The cost associated with an inventory shortage; the amount by which the perpetual inventory exceeds the physical inventory

inventory turnover Cost of goods sold divided by average inventory

investing activities The acquiring and disposing of resources (assets) that a company uses to acquire and sell its products and services

investing creditors Those who primarily finance investing activities

investment returns The increase in pension investments resulting from interest, dividends, and capital gains on the investment portfolio

invoice A document that the seller sends to the purchaser to request payment for items that the seller shipped to the purchaser

invoice price The price that a seller charges the purchaser for merchandise

IOU A slang term for a receivable

IRS Internal Revenue Service, the U.S. taxing authority

issued stock Shares of stock that have been sold and issued to stockholders; issued stock may be either outstanding or in the treasury

J

journal A tabular record in which business transactions are analyzed in debit and credit terms and recorded in chronological order

just-in-time (JIT) inventory Receive inventory from suppliers into the production process just at the point it is needed

L

land improvements Improvements with limited lives made to land sites, such as paved parking lots and driveways

last-in, first-out (LIFO) method One of the prescribed methods of inventory costing; LIFO assumes that the last costs incurred for the purchase or production of inventory are the first costs relieved form inventory when goods are sold

lease A contract between a lessor (owner) and lessee (tenant) for the rental of property

leasehold improvements Expenditures made by a lessee to alter or improve leased property

leasehold The rights transferred from the lessor to the lessee by a lease

lessee The party acquiring the right to the use of property by a lease

lessor The owner of property who transfers the right to use the property to another party by a lease

leveraging The use of borrowed funds in the capital structure of a firm; the expectation is that the funds will earn a return higher than the rate of interest on the borrowed funds

liabilities The obligations, or debts, that an entity must pay in money or services at some time in the future because of past transactions or events

LIFO conformity rule IRS requirement to cost inventories using LIFO for tax purposes if they are costed using LIFO for financial reporting purposes

LIFO liquidation The reduction in inventory quantities when LIFO costing is used; LIFO liquidation yields an increase in gross profit and income when prices are rising

LIFO reserve The difference between the cost of inventories using FIFO and the cost using LIFO

liquidation value per share The amount that would be received by a holder of a share of stock if the corporation liquidated

liquidity How much cash the company has, how much is expected, and how much can be raised on short notice

list price The suggested price or reference price of merchandise in a catalog or price list

long-term liabilities Debt obligations not due to be settled within the normal operating cycle or one year, whichever is longer

lower of cost or market (LCM) GAAP requirement to write down the carrying amount of inventories on the balance sheet if the reported cost (using FIFO, for example) exceeds market value (determined by current replacement cost)

M

maker The signer of a promissory note

management discussion and anaysis (MD&A) The section of the 10-K report in which a company provides a detailed discussion of its business activities

managerial accounting The accounting activities carried out by a firm's accounting staff primarily to furnish management with accounting data for decisions related to the firm's operations

manufacturers Companies that convert raw materials and components into finished products through the application of skilled labor and machine operations

manufacturing costs The costs of direct materials, direct labor, and manufacturing overhead incurred in the manufacture of a product

market cap Market capitalization of the firm, or value as perceived by investors; computed as market value per share multiplied by shares outstanding

market (yield) rate This is the interest rate that investors expect to earn on the investment in this debt security; this rate is used to price the bond issue

market value The published price (as listed on a stock exchange)

market value per share The current price at which shares of stock may be bought or sold

matching principle An accounting guideline that states that income is determined by relating expenses, to the extent feasible, with revenues that have been recorded

materiality An accounting guideline that states that transactions so insignificant that they would not affect a user's actions or perception of the company may be recorded in the most expedient manner

materials inventory The physical component of inventory; the other components of manufactured inventory are labor costs and overhead costs

maturity date The date on which a note or bond matures

measuring unit concept An accounting guideline noting that the accounting unit of measure is the basic unit of money

merchandise inventory A stock of products that a company buys from another company and makes available for sale to its customers

merchandising firm A company that buys finished products, stores the products for varying periods of time, and then resells the products

method of comparables model Equity valuation or stock values are predicted using price multiples, which are defined as stock price divided by some key financial statement number such as net income, net sales, book value of equity, total assets, or cash flow; companies are then compared with their competitors

minority interest The equity claim of a shareholder owning less than a majority or controlling interest in the company

modified accelerated cost recovery system (MACRS) *See* accelerated cost recovery system

N

natural resources Assets occurring in a natural state, such as timber, petroleum, natural gas, coal, and other mineral deposits

net assets The difference between an entity's assets and liabilities; net assets are equal to owners' equity

net asset based valuation model Equity is valued as reported assets less reported liabilities

net book value (NBV) The cost of the asset less accumulated depreciation; also called carrying value

net income The excess of a firm's revenues over its expenses

net loss The excess of a firm's expenses over its revenues

net nonoperating expense (NNE) Nonoperating expenses and losses less nonoperating revenues and gains

net nonoperating expense percentage (NNEP) Net nonoperating expense divided by net nonoperating obligations (NNO)

net nonoperating obligations (NNO) All nonoperating obligations less nonoperating assets

net operating assets (NOA) Current and long-term operating assets less current and long-term operating liabilities; or net operating working capital plus long-term net operating assets

net operating asset turnover (NOAT) Ratio obtained by dividing sales by net operating assets

net operating profit after tax (NOPAT) Operating revenues less operating expenses (including taxes)

net operating profit margin (NOPM) ratio obtained by dividing net operating profit after tax (NOPAT) by sales

net realizable value The value at which an asset can be sold, net of any costs of disposition

net sales The total revenue generated by a company through merchandise sales less the revenue given up through sales returns and allowances and sales discounts

net working capital Current assets less current liabilities

nominal rate The rate of interest stated on a bond certificate or other debt instrument

noncash investing and financing activities Significant business activities during the period that do not impact cash inflows or cash outflows

noncurrent liabilities Obligations not due to be paid within one year or the operating cycle, whichever is longer

nonoperating expenses Expenses that relate to the company's financing activities and include interest income and interest expense, gains and losses on sales of securities, and income or loss on discontinued operations

no-par stock Stock that does not have a par value

NOPAT Net operating profit after tax

normal operating cycle For a particular business, the average period of time between the use of cash in its typical operating activity and the subsequent collection of cash from customers

note receivable A promissory note held by the note's payee

notes to financial statements Footnotes in which companies discuss their accounting policies and estimates used in preparing the statements

not-sufficient-funds check A check from an individual or company that had an insufficient cash balance in the bank when the holder of the check presented it to the bank for payment

O

objectivity principle An accounting principle requiring that, whenever possible, accounting entries are based on objectively determined evidence

off-balance-sheet financing The structuring of a financing arrangement so that no liability shows on the borrower's balance sheet

operating activities Using resources to research, develop, produce, purchase, market, and distribute company products and services

operating cash flow to capital expenditures ratio A firm's net cash flow from operating activities divided by its annual capital expenditures

operating cash flow to current liabilities ratio A firm's net cash flow from operating activities divided by its average current liabilities

operating creditors Those who primarily finance operating activities

operating cycle The time between paying cash for goods or employee services and receiving cash from customers

operating expense margin (OEM) The ratio obtained by dividing any operating expense category by sales

operating expenses The usual and customary costs that a company incurs to support its main business activities; these include cost of goods sold, selling expenses, depreciation expense, amortization expense, research and development expense, and taxes on operating profits

operating lease A lease by which the lessor retains the usual risks and rewards of owning the property

operating profit margin The ratio obtained by dividing NOPAT by sales

operational audit An evaluation of activities, systems, and internal controls within a company to determine their efficiency, effectiveness, and economy

organization costs Expenditures incurred in launching a business (usually a corporation), including attorney's fees and various fees paid to the state

outstanding checks Checks issued by a firm that have not yet been presented to its bank for payment

outstanding stock Shares of stock that are currently owned by stockholders (excludes treasury stock)

owners' equity The interest of owners in the assets of an entity; equal to the difference between the entity's assets and liabilities

P

packing list A document that lists the items of merchandise contained in a carton and the quantity of each item; the packing list is usually attached to the outside of the carton

paid-in capital The amount of capital contributed to a corporation by various transactions; the primary source of paid-in capital is from the issuance of shares of stock

par (bonds) Face value of the bond

par value (stock) An amount specified in the corporate charter for each share of stock and imprinted on the face of each stock certificate, often determines the legal capital of the corporation

parent company A company owning one or more subsidiary companies

parsimonious method to multiyear forecasting Forecasting multiple years using only sales growth, net operating profit margin (NOPM), and the turnover of net operating assets (NOAT)

partnership A voluntary association of two or more persons for the purpose of conducting a business

password A string of characters that a computer user enters into a computer terminal to prove to the computer that the person using the computer is truly the person named in the user identification code

patent An exclusive privilege granted for 20 years to an inventor that gives the patent holder the right to exclude others from making, using, or selling the invention

payee The company or individual to whom a promissory note is made payable

payment approval form A document that authorizes the payment of an invoice

pension plan A plan to pay benefits to employees after they retire from the company; the plan may be a defined contribution plan or a defined benefit plan

percentage-of-completion method Recognition of revenue by determining the costs incurred per the contract as compared to its total expected costs

percentage of net sales method A procedure that determines the uncollectible accounts expense for the year by multiplying net credit sales by the estimated uncollectible percentage

period statement A financial statement accumulating information for a specific period of time; examples are the income statement, the statement of owners' equity, and the statement of cash flows

permanent account An account used to prepare the balance sheet; that is, asset, liability, and equity capital (capital stock and retained earnings) accounts; any balance in a permanent account at the end of an accounting period is carried forward to the next period

physical inventory A year-end procedure that involves counting the quantity of each inventory item, determining the unit cost of each item, multiplying the unit cost times quantity, and summing the costs of all the items to determine the total inventory at cost

plant assets Land, buildings, equipment, vehicles, furniture, and fixtures that a firm uses in its operations; sometimes referred to by the acronym PPE

pooling of interests method A method of accounting for business combinations under which the acquired company is recorded on the acquirer's balance sheet at its book value, rather than market value; this method is no longer acceptable under GAAP for acquisitions occurring after 2001

position statement A financial statement, such as the balance sheet, that presents information as of a particular date

post-closing trial balance A list of general ledger accounts and their balances after closing entries have been recorded and posted

postdated check A check from another person or company with a date that is later than the current date; a postdated check does not become cash until the date of the check

preemptive right The right of a stockholder to maintain his or her proportionate interest in a corporation by having the right to purchase an appropriate share of any new stock issue

preferred stock A class of corporate capital stock typically receiving priority over common stock in dividend payments and distribution of assets should the corporation be liquidated

premium bond A bond that is sold for more than its par (face) value

present value The current worth of amounts to be paid (or received) in the future; computed by discounting the future payments (or receipts) at a specified interest rate

price-earnings ratio Current market price per common share divided by earnings per share

pro forma income A computation of income that begins with the GAAP income from continuing operations (that excludes discontinued operations, extraordinary items and changes in accounting principle), but then excludes other transitory items (most notably, restructuring charges), and some additional items such as expenses arising from acquisitions (goodwill amortization and other acquisition costs), compensation expense in the form of stock options, and research and development expenditures; pro forma income is not GAAP

promissory note A written promise to pay a certain sum of money on demand or at a determinable future time

purchase method The prescribed method of accounting for business combinations; under the purchase method, assets and liabilities of the acquired company are recorded at fair market value, together with identifiable intangible assets; the balance is ascribed to goodwill

purchase order A document that formally requests a supplier to sell and deliver specific quantities of particular items of merchandise at specified prices

purchase requisition An internal document that requests that the purchasing department order particular items of merchandise

Q

qualitative characteristics of accounting information The characteristics of accounting information that contribute to decision usefulness; the primary qualities are relevance and reliability

quarterly data Selected quarterly financial information that is reported in annual reports to stockholders

quick ratio Quick assets (that is, cash and cash equivalents, short-term investments, and current receivables) divided by current liabilities

R

realized (or **realizable**) When referring to revenue, the receipt of an asset or satisfaction of a liability as a result of a transaction or event

recognition criteria The criteria that must be met before a financial statement element may be recorded in the accounts; essentially, the item must meet the definition of an element and must be measurable

registered bond A bond for which the issuer (or the trustee) maintains a record of owners and, at the appropriate times, mails out interest payments

relevance A qualitative characteristic of accounting information; relevant information contributes to the predictive and evaluative decisions made by financial statement users

reliability A qualitative characteristic of accounting information; reliable information contains no bias or error and faithfully portrays what it intends to represent

remeasurement The computation of gain or loss in the translation of subsidiaries denominated in a foreign currency into $US when the temporal method is used

residual operating income Net operating profits after tax (NOPAT) less the product of net operating assets (NOA) at the beginning of the period multiplied by the weighted average cost of capital (WACC)

residual operating income (ROPI) model An equity valuation approach that equates the firm's value to the sum of its net operating assets (NOA) and the present value of its residual operating income (ROPI)

retailers Companies that buy products from wholesale distributors and sell the products to individual customers, the general public

retained earnings Earned capital, the cumulative net income and loss, of the company (from its inception) that has not been paid to shareholders as dividends

retained earnings reconciliation The reconciliation of retained earnings from the beginning to the end of the year; the change in retained earnings includes, at a minimum, the net income (loss) for the period and dividends paid, if any, but may include other components as well; also called statement of retained earnings

return The amount earned on an investment; also called yield

return on assets (ROA) A financial ratio computed as net income divided by average total assets

return on common stockholders' equity (ROCE) A financial ratio computed as net income less preferred stock dividends divided by average common stockholders' equity

return on equity (ROE) The ultimate measure of performance from the shareholders' perspective; computed as net income divided by average equity

return on investment The ratio obtained by dividing income by average investment; sometimes referred to by the acronym ROI

return on net operating assets (RNOA) The ratio obtained by dividing NOPAT by average net operating assets

return on sales (ROS) The ratio obtained by dividing net income by net sales

revenue recognition principle An accounting principle requiring that revenue be recognized when earned and realized (or realizable)

revenues Increases in owners' equity a firm earns by providing goods or services for its customers

S

sale on account A sale of merchandise made on a credit basis

salvage value The expected net recovery when a plant asset is sold or removed from service; also called residual value

secured bond A bond that pledges specific property as security for meeting the terms of the bond agreement

Securities and Exchange Commission (SEC) The commission, created by the 1934 Securities Act, that has broad powers to regulate the issuance and trading of securities, and the financial reporting of companies issuing securities to the public

segments Subdivisions of a firm for which supplemental financial information is disclosed

serial bond A bond issue that staggers the bond maturity dates over a series of years

service cost (pensions) The increase in the pension obligation due to employees working another year for the employer

share-based payment Payment for a good or service using the entity's equity securities; an example is restricted stock used to compensate employees

significant influence The ability of the investor to affect the financing or operating policies of the investee

sinking fund provision A bond feature that requires the borrower to retire a portion of the bonds each year or, in some cases, to make payments each year to a trustee who is responsible for managing the resources needed to retire the bonds at maturity

solvency The ability to meet obligations, especially to creditors

source document Any written document or computer record evidencing an accounting transaction, such as a bank check or deposit slip, sales invoice, or cash register tape

special purpose entity (*See* variable interest entity)

spin-off A form of equity carve out in which divestiture is accomplished by distribution of a company's shares in a subsidiary to the company's shareholders who then own the shares in the subsidiary directly rather than through the parent company

split-off A form of equity carve out in which divestiture is accomplished by the parent company's exchange of stock in the subsidiary in return for shares in the parent owned by its shareholders

spread The difference between the return on net operating activities (RNOA) and the net nonoperating expense percentage (NNEP)

stated value A nominal amount that may be assigned to each share of no-par stock and accounted for much as if it were a par value

statement of cash flows A financial statement showing a firm's cash inflows and outflows for a specific period, classified into operating, investing, and financing categories

statement of equity *See* statement of stockholders' equity

statement of financial position A financial statement showing a firm's assets, liabilities, and owners' equity at a specific date; also called a balance sheet

statement of owners' equity A financial statement presenting information on the events causing a change in owners' equity during a period; the statement presents the beginning balance, additions to, deductions from, and the ending balance of owners' equity for the period

statement of retained earnings *See* retained earnings reconciliation

statement of stockholders' equity The financial statement that reconciles all of the components of stockholders' equity

stock dividends The payment of dividends in shares of stock

stock split Additional shares of its own stock issued by a corporation to its current stockholders in proportion to their current ownership interests without changing the balances in the related stockholders' equity accounts; a formal stock split increases the number of shares outstanding and reduces proportionately the stock's per share par value

straight-line depreciation A depreciation procedure that allocates uniform amounts of depreciation expense to each full period of a depreciable asset's useful life

subsequent events Events occurring shortly after a fiscal year-end that will be reported as supplemental information to the financial statements of the year just ended

subsidiaries Companies that are owned by the parent company

subsidiary ledger A set of accounts or records that contains detailed information about the items included in the balance of one general ledger account

summary of significant accounting policies A financial statement disclosure, usually the initial note to the statements, which identifies the major accounting policies and procedures used by the firm

sum-of-the-years'-digits method An accelerated depreciation method that allocates depreciation expense to each year in a fractional proportion, the denominator of which is the sum of the years' digits in the useful life of the asset and the numerator of which is the remaining useful life of the asset at the beginning of the current depreciation period

T

T account An abbreviated form of the formal account in the shape of a T; use is usually limited to illustrations of accounting techniques and analysis

temporary account An account used to gather information for an accounting period; at the end of the period, the balance is transferred to a permanent owners' equity account; revenue, expense, and dividends accounts are temporary accounts

term loan A long-term borrowing, evidenced by a note payable, which is contracted with a single lender

terminal period The forecast period following the horizon period

times interest earned ratio Income before interest expense and income taxes divided by interest expense

total compensation cost The sum of gross pay, payroll taxes, and fringe benefits paid by the employer

trade credit Inventories purchased on credit from other companies

trade discount An amount, usually based on quantity of merchandise purchased, that the seller subtracts from the list price of merchandise to determine the invoice price

trade name An exclusive and continuing right to use a certain term or name to identify a brand or family of products

trademark An exclusive and continuing right to use a certain symbol to identify a brand or family of products

trading on the equity The use of borrowed funds in the capital structure of a firm; the expectation is that the funds will earn a return higher than the rate of interest on the borrowed funds

trading securities Investments in securities that management intends to actively trade (buy and sell) for trading profits as market prices fluctuate

trailing earnings Earnings reported in the prior period

transitory items Transactions or events that are not likely to recur

translation adjustment The change in the value of the net assets of a subsidiary whose assets and liabilities are denominated in a foreign currency

treasury stock Shares of outstanding stock that have been acquired (and not retired) by the issuing corporation; treasury stock is recorded at cost and deducted from stockholders' equity in the balance sheet

trend percentages A comparison of the same financial item over two or more years stated as a percentage of a base-year amount

trial balance A list of the account titles in the general ledger, their respective debit or credit balances, and the totals of the debit and credit amounts

U

unadjusted trial balance A list of general ledger accounts and their balances taken before accounting adjustments have been made

uncollectible accounts expense The expense stemming from the inability of a business to collect an amount previously recorded as a receivable; sometimes called bad debts expense; normally classified as a selling or administrative expense

unearned revenue A liability representing revenues received in advance; also called deferred revenue

units-of-production method A depreciation method that allocates depreciation expense to each operating period in proportion to the amount of the asset's expected total production capacity used each period

useful life The period of time an asset is used by an entity in its operating activities, running from date of acquisition to date of disposal (or removal from service)

V

variable costs Those costs that change in proportion to changes in sales volume

variable interest entity (VIE) Any form of business organization (such as corporation, partnership, trust) that is established by a sponsoring company and provides benefits to that company in the form of asset securitization or project financing; VIEs were formerly known as special purpose entities (SPEs)

vertical analysis Analysis of a firm's financial statements that focuses on the statements of a single year

voucher Another name for the payment approval form

W

warranties Guarantees against product defects for a designated period of time after sale

wasting assets Another name for natural resources; *see* natural resources

weighted average cost of capital (WACC) The discount rate where the weights are the relative percentages of debt and equity in the capital structure and are applied to the expected returns on debt and equity respectively

work in process inventory The cost of inventories that are in the manufacturing process and have not yet reached completion

working capital The difference between current assets and current liabilities

Z

z-score The outcome of the Altman Z-score bankruptcy prediction model

zero coupon bond A bond that offers no periodic interest payments but that is issued at a substantial discount from its face value

Q

R

	Focus Company	Managerial Applications
MODULE 1 Financial Accounting for MBAs	Berkshire Hathaway	**Managerial Decision:** You are the Product Manager **Managerial Decision:** You are the Chief Financial Officer **Research Insight:** Are Earnings Important?
MODULE 2 Introducing Financial Statements and Transaction Analysis	Apple	**Managerial Decision:** You are the Securities Analyst **Managerial Decision:** You are the Operations Manager **Research Insight:** Market-to-Book Ratio
MODULE 3 Accounting Adjustments and Constructing Financial Statements	Apple	**Managerial Decision:** You are the Chief Financial Officer **Research Insight:** Accruals: Good or Bad?
MODULE 4 Analyzing and Interpreting Financial Statements	General Mills	**Managerial Decision:** You are the CEO **Research Insight:** Ratio Behavior Over Time **Research Insight:** NOPM and NOAT Explain Stock Prices
MODULE 5 Reporting and Analyzing Operating Income	Pfizer	**Managerial Decision:** You are the Financial Analyst **Research Insight:** Restructuring Costs and Managerial Incentives **Research Insight:** "Pro Forma" Income
MODULE 6 Reporting and Analyzing Operating Assets	Cisco	**Managerial Decision:** You are the Receivables Manager **Managerial Decision:** You are the Plant Manager **Managerial Decision:** You are the Division Manager **Research Insight:** LIFO and Stock Prices
MODULE 7 Reporting and Analyzing Intercorporate Investments	Google	**Managerial Decision:** You are the Chief Financial Officer **Research Insight:** Equity Income and Stock Prices
MODULE 8 Reporting and Analyzing Nonowner Financing	Verizon	**Managerial Decision:** You are the Vice President of Finance **Research Insight:** Accounting Conservatism and Cost of Debt **Research Insight:** Valuation of Debt Options
MODULE 9 Reporting and Analyzing Owner Financing	Hewitt Associates	**Managerial Decision:** You are the Chief Financial Officer **Research Insight:** Stock Issuance and Stock Returns
MODULE 10 Reporting and Analyzing Off-Balance-Sheet Financing	American Airlines	**Managerial Decision:** You are the Division President **Research Insight:** Valuation of Nonpension Post-Employment Benefits **Research Insight:** Why Do Companies Offer Pensions? **Research Insight:** Valuation of Pension Footnote Disclosures
MODULE 11 Forecasting Financial Statements	Procter & Gamble	**Managerial Decision:** You are the Corporate Analyst **Research Insight:** Earnings Quality and Accounting Conservatism
MODULE 12 Analyzing and Valuing Equity Securities	Johnson & Johnson	**Managerial Decision:** You are the Chief Financial Officer **Managerial Decision:** You are the Chief Financial Officer **Research Insight:** Power of NOPAT Forecasts **Research Insight:** Using Models to Identify Mispriced Stocks